The Routledge Handbook of Linguistics

The Routledge Handbook of Linguistics offers a comprehensive introduction and reference point to the discipline of linguistics. This wide-ranging survey of the field brings together a range of perspectives, covering all the key areas of linguistics and drawing on interdisciplinary research in subjects such as anthropology, psychology and sociology.

The 36 chapters, written by specialists from around the world, provide:

- an overview of each topic;
- an introduction to current hypotheses and issues;
- future trajectories;
- suggestions for further reading.

With extensive coverage of both theoretical and applied linguistic topics, *The Routledge Handbook of Linguistics* is an indispensable resource for students and researchers working in this area.

Keith Allan is Emeritus Professor of Linguistics at Monash University and Honorary Associate Professor at the University of Queensland.

Routledge Handbooks in Linguistics

Routledge Handbooks in Linguistics provide overviews of a whole subject area or sub-discipline in linguistics, and survey the state of the discipline including emerging and cutting edge areas. Edited by leading scholars, these volumes include contributions from key academics from around the world and are essential reading for both advanced undergraduate and postgraduate students.

The Routledge Handbook of Syntax
Edited by Andrew Carnie, Yosuke Sato and Daniel Siddiqi

The Routledge Handbook of Historical Linguistics
Edited by Claire Bowern and Bethwyn Evans

The Routledge Handbook of Language and Culture
Edited by Farzad Sharifan

The Routledge Handbook of Semantics
Edited by Nick Riemer

The Routledge Handbook of Morphology
Edited by Francis Katamba

The Routledge Handbook of Linguistics
Edited by Keith Allan

The Routledge Handbook of the English Writing System
Edited by Vivian Cook and Des Ryan

The Routledge Handbook of Language and Media
Edited by Daniel Perrin and Colleen Cotter

The Routledge Handbook of Phonological Theory
Edited by S.J. Hannahs and Anna Bosch

The Routledge Handbook of Language and Politics
Edited by Ruth Wodak and Bernhard Forchtner

The Routledge Handbook of Theoretical and Experimental Sign Language Research
Edited by Annika Hermann, Roland Pfau and Josep Quer

The Routledge Handbook of Linguistics

Edited by Keith Allan

LONDON AND NEW YORK

First published 2016 by Routledge

2 Park Square, Milton Park, Abingdon, Oxfordshire OX14 4RN
52 Vanderbilt Avenue, New York, NY 10017

Routledge is an imprint of the Taylor & Francis Group, an informa business

First issued in paperback 2019

Copyright © 2016 selection and editorial matter, Keith Allan; individual chapters, the contributors

The right of the editor to be identified as the author of the editorial material, and of the authors for their individual chapters, has been asserted in accordance with sections 77 and 78 of the Copyright, Designs and Patents Act 1988.

All rights reserved. No part of this book may be reprinted or reproduced or utilised in any form or by any electronic, mechanical, or other means, now known or hereafter invented, including photocopying and recording, or in any information storage or retrieval system, without permission in writing from the publishers.

Notice:
Product or corporate names may be trademarks or registered trademarks, and are used only for identification and explanation without intent to infringe.

British Library Cataloguing-in-Publication Data
A catalogue record for this book is available from the British Library

Library of Congress Cataloging-in-Publication Data
The Routledge handbook of linguistics / Edited by Keith Allan.
pages cm. -- (Routledge Handbooks in Linguistics)
Includes bibliographical references and index.
1. Linguistics--Handbooks, manuals, etc. I. Allan, Keith, 1943- editor.
PE1072.R68 2015
410--dc23
2014040885

ISBN: 978-0-415-83257-1 (hbk)
ISBN: 978-0-367-86807-9 (pbk)

Typeset in Times
by Saxon Graphics Ltd, Derby

Contents

List of figures		*viii*
List of tables		*ix*
Contributors		*x*
1	What is linguistics? Keith Allan	1
2	Evolutionary linguistics: how Language and languages got to be the way they are James R. Hurford	17
3	Gesture and sign: utterance uses of visible bodily action Adam Kendon	33
4	Writing systems: methods for recording language Geoffrey Sampson	47
5	Phonetics: the sounds humans make when speaking Andrew Butcher	62
6	Phonology Harry van der Hulst	83
7	Morphology: the structure of words Geert Booij	104
8	Syntax: putting words together Kersti Börjars	118
9	Syntax as the dynamics of language understanding Ruth Kempson	135

10	Semantics: the meaning of words and sentences *John Saeed*	153
11	Lexical semantics today *Nicholas Asher, Tim Van de Cruys and Márta Abrusán*	169
12	Lexicography: the construction of dictionaries and thesauruses *Pam Peters*	187
13	Pragmatics: language use in context *Yan Huang*	205
14	The linguistics of politeness and social relations *Marina Terkourafi*	221
15	Narrative and narrative structure *Michael Toolan*	236
16	Anthropological linguistics and field linguistics *William A. Foley*	250
17	Sociolinguistics: language in social environments *Maya Ravindranath and Suzanne Evans Wagner*	264
18	Psycholinguistics: language and cognition *Matthew J. Traxler*	281
19	Neurolinguistics: mind, brain, and language *David Kemmerer*	296
20	First language acquisition *Eve V. Clark and Marisa Casillas*	311
21	Second language acquisition and applied linguistics *Susan M. Gass*	329
22	Historical linguistics and relationships among languages *Kate Burridge*	344
23	Linguistic change in grammar *Walter Bisang*	366
24	Language endangerment *Simon Musgrave*	385

25	Linguistic typology and language universals *Jae Jung Song*	401
26	Translating between languages *Anthony Pym*	417
27	Structural linguistics *John E. Joseph*	431
28	Biolinguistics *Cedric Boeckx*	447
29	Cognitive linguistics *John R. Taylor*	455
30	Functional linguistics *J. Lachlan Mackenzie*	470
31	Computational linguistics *Ann Copestake*	485
32	Corpus linguistics *Andrew Hardie*	502
33	Linguistics and philosophy *Kasia M. Jaszczolt*	516
34	Linguistics and the law *Kate Haworth*	532
35	Linguistics and politics *George Lakoff*	546
36	Linguistics and social media *Ana Deumert*	561

Index   *574*

Figures

1.1	An oversimplified tree structure	3
4.1	*I want to go to the cinema* in Blissymbols	49
4.2	The word *Gaelach* ('Irish') in Irish script	57
4.3	Arabic words distinguished by dots	58
5.1	Schematic sagittal cross-section of the human vocal tract, showing places of articulation	67
5.2	Traditional vowel quadrilateral, showing symbols for the cardinal vowels and key words from Australian English	70
5.3	A waveform and time-aligned spectrogram of the word *scanty* as pronounced by the author	75
5.4	The pressure wave produced by the vibrating larynx	76
5.5	A formant chart	78
5.6	Perceptual equivalence: schematic spectrograms of synthesised speech demonstrating context sensitivity in speech perception	79
9.1	Action for reflexive anaphora	145
9.2	Parsing *Mary, John upset*	146
9.3	Mary/Bob context	150
10.1	Path schema	164
10.2	An image schema for *over*	165
11.1	A graphical representation of a word vector space	182
14.1	Strategies for doing FTAs	223
15.1	Oral narrative extract	240
16.1	Four cardinal directions in Guugu-Yimidhirr	254
16.2	Cognitive consequences of spatial reckoning systems	255
19.1	Gyral–sulcal and cytoarchitectonic organization of the left hemisphere of the human brain	298
19.2	Illustration of the major functional-anatomical correspondences discussed in the text	300
22.1	Tenth-century remedy for abdominal pain	345
22.2	Cognates for 'milk'	357
22.3	Family tree of Germanic languages	358
23.1	Reanalysis and analogy	371
23.2	S-curve	376

Tables

11.1	A word-by-word-context matrix	182
22.1	Comparison of English, Dutch and German	354
22.2	Comparison of early English and early Dutch	355
22.3	Comparison of Latvian and Hungarian	355
22.4	Word comparisons	356
23.1	Parameters of grammaticalization	369
24.1	Indicators used by McConvell and Thieberger	389
24.2	Factors used by UNESCO in assessing language vitality	389
24.3	Fishman's GIDS	390
24.4	Expanded Graded Intergenerational Disruption Scale	390
25.1	Four types of universal statements	413
31.1	Sample context set	497
36.1	Mobile phone access, Internet access and Facebook users, 2012	564

Contributors

Márta Abrusán is a CNRS Research Scientist at the Institut de Recherche en Informatique de Toulouse at the Université Paul Sabatier. After her PhD in linguistics at MIT she was a postdoctoral Fellow at the Collegium Budapest, the Institut Jean-Nicod in Paris and the universities of Oxford and Göttingen. Her published work includes papers in *Linguistics and Philosophy*, *Natural Language Semantics*, *Semantics and Pragmatics* and the *Journal of Semantics*.

Keith Allan MLitt, PhD (Edinburgh), FAHA, is Emeritus Professor of Linguistics at Monash University and Honorary Associate Professor at the University of Queensland. His research interests focus mainly on aspects of meaning in language, with a secondary interest in the history and philosophy of linguistics. He has authored and/or edited a dozen books and made scores of contributions to scholarly books and journals. Homepage: http://profiles.arts.monash.edu.au/keith-allan.

Nicholas Asher is currently Director of Research at the Centre Nationale de Recherche Scientifique and is a member of the Institut de Recherche en Informatique de Toulouse. Prior to that, he was Professor of Philosophy and of Linguistics at the University of Texas at Austin. He specializes in formal semantics and pragmatics and also has interests in computational semantics and NLP. He has recently authored a book on lexical semantics, *Lexical Meaning in Context* (Cambridge University Press, 2011). He has also written two books on SDRT, a theory of discourse structure and interpretation – *Reference to Abstract Objects in Discourse* (Kluwer Academic Publishers, 1993) – and *Logics of Conversation* (Cambridge University Press, 2003). He has written over 190 papers for journals, learned conferences and book chapters.

Walter Bisang Dr. phil. I (Zürich) has been Professor of General and Comparative Linguistics at the University of Mainz (Germany) since 1992. He was the Director of a Collaborative Research Center on Cultural and Linguistic Contact from 1999 to 2008 in Mainz. His research interests focus on linguistic typology, grammaticalization, language contact/areal typology and the comparison of different theoretical approaches to language. His languages of interest are East and mainland south-east Asian languages, Caucasian languages (Georgian and others), Austronesian languages (Bahasa Indonesia, Tagalog, Yabêm, Paiwan), and Yoruba (together with Remi Sonaiya). Homepage: www.linguistik.fb05.uni-mainz.de/mitarbeiter/walter-bisang/.

Contributors

Cedric Boeckx is Research Professor at ICREA (The Catalan Institute for Advanced Studies) and a member of the Department of Linguistics at the University of Barcelona. He also directs the Biolinguistics Initiative Barcelona, a research group dedicated to uncovering the biological basis of the language faculty. Homepage: http://biolinguistics-bcn.info.

Geert Booij was Professor of Linguistics in Amsterdam (1971–2005), and in Leiden (2005–2012). He is now Emeritus Professor. He is founder and editor of the book series *Yearbook of Morphology* and its successor, the journal *Morphology*, the author of a number of books, among which *Construction Morphology* (2010), and *The Grammar of Words* (2005, thirrd edition 2012), and of articles on phonology and morphology, with special focus on Dutch, in a wide range of books and journals. Homepage: http://geertbooij.wordpress.com.

Kersti Börjars is Professor of Linguistics at the University of Manchester and she has academic qualifications from the universities of Uppsala and Leiden. Her interests are in the areas of syntax and morphology, including general theoretical issues as well as how languages change over time. She has had funded projects on Pennsylvania German and on the possessive in Germanic. Homepage: http://staffprofiles.humanities.manchester.ac.uk/Profile.aspx?Id=kersti.borjars.

Kate Burridge is Professor of Linguistics at Monash University and a Fellow of the Australian Academy of the Humanities. Her main areas of research are: language change, the notion of linguistic taboo and the structure and history of English. Recent books include *Forbidden Words: Taboo and the Censoring of Language* (with Keith Allan, 2006), *Introducing English Grammar* (with Kersti Börjars, 2010), *Gift of the Gob: Morsels of English Language History* (2010) and *Wrestling with Words and Meanings: Essays in Honour of Keith Allan* (with Réka Benczes, 2014).

Andrew Butcher is Emeritus Professor of Communication Disorders at Flinders University, Adelaide. He has degrees in Linguistics and Phonetics from the universities of Edinburgh and London and a PhD in phonetics from the University of Kiel. His main areas of research involve the instrumental measurement of articulatory parameters such as tongue–palate contact, oral and nasal air flow and pressure, vocal fold activity and the acoustic analysis of voice and speech. His particular interest is in the phonetics of Australian Aboriginal languages, which he has been researching for over twenty years. His most recent project studies the relationship between speech production, speech perception and hearing impairment in Aboriginal children. Homepage: www.flinders.edu.au/people/andy.butcher.

Marisa Casillas, MA, PhD (Stanford), is a postdoctoral researcher in the Language and Cognition department at the Max Planck Institute for Psycholinguistics. Her work primarily examines the relationship between conversational turn-taking and linguistic processing in children and adults with a more general emphasis on the co-development of linguistic and pragmatic interactional skills. Homepage: www.mpi.nl/people/casillas-marisa.

Eve V. Clark, MA Hons, PhD (Edinburgh), KNAW, is the Richard Lyman Professor in the Humanities at Stanford University. Her research focuses on children's acquisition of meaning, the conceptual and social sources they draw on, how adult speech helps shape early meanings, and the pragmatics of adult and child communicative interaction. She has published several books on language acquisition, including two major texts in psycholinguistics, and a large number of journal articles and book chapters in the field. Homepage: http://web.stanford.edu/~eclark.

Ann Copestake (DPhil, Sussex) is Professor of Computational Linguistics at the Computer Laboratory, University of Cambridge. She is involved in the interdisciplinary Cambridge Language Sciences Initiative and previously worked at the Center for the Study of Language and Information, Stanford University. Her current research mainly concerns the development of models of compositional and lexical semantics which are compatible with broad-coverage computational processing. In conjunction with DELPH-IN, an informal international research consortium, she has produced widely-used grammar development software. Homepage: www.cl.cam.ac.uk/~aac10.

Ana Deumert is Associate Professor at the University of Cape Town. Her research programme is located within the broad field of African sociolinguistics and has a strong interdisciplinary focus (with particular attention to anthropology, sociology and economics). She has worked on the history of Afrikaans (*The Dynamics of Cape Dutch*, 2004) and co-authored *Introducing Sociolinguistics* (2009, with Rajend Mesthrie, Joan Swann and William Leap) and the *Dictionary of Sociolinguistics* (2004, with Joan Swann, Rajend Mesthrie and Theresa Lillis). Her latest book looks at mobile communication from a global perspective (*Sociolinguistics and Mobile Communication*, 2014). She is editor of *IMPACT – Studies in Language and Society* (Amsterdam/New York: John Benjamins) and co-editor of *Cambridge Approaches to Language Contact* (with Salikoko Mufwene). She is also an NRF-rated scientist.

William A. Foley MA, PhD (Berkeley) is Professor of Linguistics at the University of Sydney. His research interests focus on: one, the descriptive and historical linguistics of the languages of insular south-east Asia and Melanesia, especially the Papuan languages of New Guinea; two, morphosyntactic theory and typology and in particular bringing data from the languages of his fieldwork to bear on questions in this field; and three, anthropological linguistics. He has written four books and many journal articles and chapters of edited volumes. Web page: http://sydney.edu.au/arts/linguistics/staff/profiles/william.foley.php.

Susan M. Gass, PhD (Indiana University) is University Distinguished Professor and Chair of the Department of Linguistics and Germanic, Slavic, Asian and African Languages at Michigan State University, where she also directs the English Language Center, the Second Language Studies Program, the Center for Language Education and Research and co-directs the Center for Language Teaching Advancement. She is the recipient of numerous awards and has published widely in the field of second language acquisition (www.msu.edu/~gass/).

Andrew Hardie BA, PhD (Lancaster) is a Senior Lecturer in Linguistics at Lancaster University. His main research interests are the theory and methodology of corpus linguistics; corpus-based descriptive and theoretical grammatical analysis; the languages of Asia; and applications of corpus methods in the humanities and social sciences. He is also a lead developer of the *Corpus Workbench* analysis software, and the author of its online interface, *CQPweb*.

Kate Haworth MSt (Oxford), PhD (Nottingham) is a Lecturer in Applied Linguistics at the Centre for Forensic Linguistics, School of Languages and Social Sciences, Aston University, UK. She was previously a practising barrister. Her research interests include all aspects of language and communication in legal contexts, especially spoken interaction and the use of language data as evidence. Her research and publications to date have focused on the discourse of police investigative interviews. Homepage: www.aston.ac.uk/lss/staff-directory/kate-haworth.

Yan Huang (PhD Cambridge, DPhil Oxford) is Professor of Linguistics at the University of Auckland. He has previously taught Linguistics at the universities of Cambridge, Oxford and Reading, where he was Professor of Theoretical Linguistics. His main research interests are in pragmatics, especially the pragmatics–semantics interface and pragmatics–syntax interface including anaphora. His books include *The Syntax and Pragmatics of Anaphora* (Cambridge University Press, 1994, reissued in 2007), *Anaphora: A Cross-Linguistic Study* (Oxford University Press, 2000), *The Oxford Dictionary of Pragmatics* (Oxford University Press, 2012) and *Pragmatics* (Oxford University Press, first edition 2007, second edition 2014).

Harry van der Hulst (PhD 1984, University of Leiden) specializes in phonology. He has published four books, two textbooks and over 160 articles; he has edited twenty-four books and six journal theme issues in the above-mentioned areas. He has been Editor-in-Chief of the international linguistic journal *The Linguistic Review* since 1990 and he is co-editor of the series 'Studies in Generative Grammar'. He is currently (since 2000) Professor of Linguistics at the University of Connecticut. Homepage: http://homepage.uconn.edu/~hdv02001/vanderhulst.html.

James R. Hurford is Emeritus Professor of General Linguistics at the University of Edinburgh. Over the past twenty-five years, he has developed and promoted interdisciplinary research into the origins and evolution of language and languages. The main vehicles for these developments are EVOLANG, the series of International Conferences on the Evolution of Language, the Language Evolution and Computation Research Unit at the University of Edinburgh, and the Oxford University Press series on language evolution, all of which he co-founded.

Kasia M. Jaszczolt is Professor of Linguistics and Philosophy of Language at the University of Cambridge and Professorial Fellow of Newnham College, Cambridge. She published extensively on various topics in semantics, pragmatics and philosophy of language, including propositional attitude ascription, representation of time, semantics–pragmatics interface, her theory of Default Semantics, and ambiguity and underspecification. One of her current projects concerns attitudes *de se* and first-person reference, the other is a theory of *Interactive Semantics* (in progress, Oxford University Press). Her authored books include *Representing Time* (2009, Oxford University Press), *Default Semantics* (2005, Oxford University Press), *Semantics and Pragmatics* (2002, Longman) and *Discourse, Beliefs and Intentions* (1999, Elsevier). She is General Editor of a book series 'Oxford Studies of Time in Language and Thought' and serves on numerous editorial boards. She authored over eighty research articles and edited eleven volumes including *The Cambridge Handbook of Pragmatics* (2012, Cambridge University Press). In 2012 she was elected member of Academia Europaea. See also http://people.pwf.cam.ac.uk/kmj21.

John E. Joseph (BA, MA, PhD Michigan) is Professor of Applied Linguistics at the University of Edinburgh. He is co-editor of the journals *Language & Communication* and *Historiographia Linguistica*, and works in the areas of language and identity, language and politics and the history of linguistics. His books include *Eloquence and Power* (1988), *Limiting the Arbitrary* (2000), *From Whitney to Chomsky* (2002), *Language and Identity* (2004), *Language and Politics* (2006) and *Saussure* (2012).

David Kemmerer is a Professor at Purdue University with a 50:50 joint appointment in the Department of Speech, Language, and Hearing Sciences and the Department of Psychological Sciences. His research focuses on how different kinds of linguistic meaning are mediated by different neural systems, drawing on behavioural and lesion data from brain-damaged patients as well as behavioural and functional neuroimaging data from normal subjects. He is the author of over forty-five articles and chapters and recently published a textbook called *Cognitive Neuroscience of Language*.

Ruth Kempson FBA is Emeritus Professor of Linguistics at King's College London and Honorary Research Associate with the Cognitive Science research unit of Queen Mary University of London and with the School of Oriental and African Studies. She is the lead developer of the Dynamic Syntax framework, and has a long-term research interest in the interface of syntax and pragmatics. Homepage for the Dynamic Syntax group: www.kcl. ac.uk/innovation/groups/ds/index.aspx.

Adam Kendon, MA (Cambridge), DPhil (Oxford), has published *Sign Languages of Aboriginal Australia* (Cambridge, 1988); *Conducting Interaction* (Cambridge, 1990); *Gesture: Visible Action as Utterance* (Cambridge, 2004); and *Gesture in Naples and Gesture in Classical Antiquity* (Indiana, 2000), a translation of Andrea de Jorio's 1832 treatise on Neapolitan gesture. He is editor of the journal *Gesture* and an Honorary Professor at University College, London.

George Lakoff is Distinguished Professor of Cognitive Science and Linguistics at UC, Berkeley. He founded the field of Generative Semantics in 1963, integrating formal logic and pragmatics into generative grammar. With the 1975 discovery of embodied cognition, Lakoff, together with Ronald Langacker, Leonard Talmy and Gilles Fauconnier founded Cognitive Linguistics, uniting Cognitive Science with Linguistics. In 1978, he discovered the basic mechanism of embodied metaphorical thought as frame-to-frame mappings, and with Mark Johnson offered details of the system of metaphorical thought in *Metaphors We Live By* (1980), *Philosophy in the Flesh* (1999) and *Where Mathematics Comes From* (2000) with Rafael Núñez. In 1987, integrating Cognitive Semantics with grammar in the first paper on Construction Grammar (Case Study 3) in *Women, Fire, and Dangerous Things*. In 1988, with Jerome Feldman he founded the Neural Theory of Language Group at UC Berkeley. In 1996, he published *Moral Politics*, the first major application of Neurally Embodied Cognitive Linguistics to Politics, and has since published as major theoretical works *Whose Freedom?* (2006), *The Political Mind* (2008), *Don't Think of an Elephant!* (2004), *Thinking Points* (2006), *The Little Blue Book* with Elisabeth Wehling (2012), and most recently the updated and expanded *ALL NEW Don't Think of an Elephant!* (2014). He is now completing *How Brains Think*, with Srini Narayanan, an account of how thought and language arise from neural circuitry.

J. Lachlan Mackenzie MA, PhD (Edinburgh) is Professor of Functional Linguistics at VU University Amsterdam. Lachlan's research focuses mainly on the development of Functional Discourse Grammar but also on the valorization of linguistics and pragmatics in facilitating advanced language learning. He is editor of the journal *Functions of Language* and is author or editor of various books and numerous articles in books and journals. Homepage: www.lachlanmackenzie.info.

Simon Musgrave is a Lecturer in the Linguistics Program at Monash University. His research interests include Austronesian languages, especially languages of the Maluku region of Indonesia, endangered languages, communication in medical settings and linguistics as a part of the digital humanities. His publications include edited volumes on voice in Austronesian languages and on databases in linguistic research, as well as papers in *Language*, *Oceanic Linguistics*, the *International Journal of the Sociology of Language* and the *Australian Journal of Linguistics*.

Pam Peters is a Fellow of the Australian Academy of the Humanities, and an Emeritus Professor of Macquarie University. She previously held a Personal Chair in Linguistics, and was Director of the University's Dictionary Research Centre from 2001 to 2007. She was a member of the Editorial Committee of *Macquarie Dictionary* from 1986 to 2006, and authored the *Cambridge Guide to English Usage* (Cambridge University Press, 2004). She continues to conduct research in lexicography, terminography, and Australian and international English.

Anthony Pym, PhD (Paris), is Professor of Translation and Intercultural Studies at the Rovira i Virgili University in Spain, Visiting Professor at the Middlebury Institute of International Studies at Monterey in the United States, Professor Extraordinary at Stellenbosch University in South Africa, and President of the European Society for Translation Studies. His research interests focus on sociological aspects of translation. He has authored and/or edited two dozen books and more than 170 articles. Homepage: http://usuaris.tinet.cat/apym.

Maya Ravindranath, PhD (University of Pennsylvania), is Assistant Professor of Linguistics at the University of New Hampshire. Her research focuses broadly on the study of language variation and change, with a special interest in situations of language contact, language maintenance and language shift. She is currently working on three projects around the world, examining language shift in Indonesia, dialect change in New Hampshire and language contact in Belize.

John Saeed, PhD (SOAS, London), is a Fellow of Trinity College Dublin where he is Professor of Linguistics. His research interests are in the relations between grammar and pragmatics, with a particular focus on information structure. He has written monographs on Somali and Irish Sign Language. Homepage: https://www.tcd.ie/slscs/staff/jsaeed.php.

Geoffrey Sampson MA, PhD (Cambridge), FBCS, Professor Emeritus, is a Research Fellow in Linguistics at the University of South Africa, having retired from the Sussex University School of Informatics in 2009. His books and articles have contributed to most areas of linguistics, and also include works on statistics, computer science, political thought and ancient Chinese poetry. His most recent book is *Grammar Without Grammaticality* (with Anna Babarczy; de Gruyter, 2014). Homepage: www.grsampson.net.

Jae Jung Song is Professor of Linguistics at the University of Otago, New Zealand. His research interests include linguistic typology, Korean linguistics, Oceanic linguistics and language policy. He is the author of *Causatives and Causation* (1996), *Linguistic Typology: Morphology and Syntax* (2001), *The Korean Language: Structure, Use and Context* (2005) and *Word Order* (2012), and the editor of *Case, Typology and Grammar* (with Anna Siewierska, 1998) and *Oxford Handbook of Linguistic Typology* (2011).

John R. Taylor is Visiting Professor at Yanshan University, China. He is the author of *Possessives in English* (1996), *Cognitive Grammar* (2002), *Linguistic Categorization* (third edition 2003), and *The Mental Corpus* (2012), all published by Oxford University Press, and co-editor of the *Bloomsbury Companion to Cognitive Linguistics* (2014). He is a managing editor for the series 'Cognitive Linguistics Research' (Mouton de Gruyter) and an Associate Editor of the journal *Cognitive Linguistics*.

Marina Terkourafi (PhD, Cambridge) is Associate Professor of Linguistics at the University of Illinois at Urbana-Champaign. She has undertaken extensive fieldwork in Cyprus, which formed the basis for her formulation of the frame-based approach to politeness, the topic of her forthcoming book with Cambridge University Press. She has authored numerous articles on the topic of politeness, impoliteness, indirectness and face, and has secondary interests in experimental pragmatics, pragmatic variation, construction grammar and the history and use of Cypriot Greek. Homepage: http://faculty.las.illinois.edu/mt217.

Michael Toolan (MA Edinburgh, DPhil Oxford) is Professor of English Language at the University of Birmingham where he chiefly teaches courses in Stylistics and Narrative Analysis, convenes the MA programme in Literary Linguistics, and supervises research students working in those areas. Since 2002 he has been editor of the *Journal of Literary Semantics* (de Gruyter). He has published extensively, and has a book forthcoming entitled *Making Sense of Narrative Text* (Routledge). Homepage: http://professormichaeltoolan.wordpress.com.

Matthew J. Traxler is a Professor of Psychology and Interim Associate Vice Provost for Undergraduate Education at UC, Davis. His research focuses on reading and sentence processing in normal adults, deaf readers and patients with schizophrenia.

Tim Van de Cruys received his MA in Germanic Languages from the University of Leuven in 2004, his MSc in Artificial Intelligence from the University of Leuven in 2005, and his PhD in Arts from the University of Groningen in 2010. In 2010 he worked as a postdoctoral Researcher at the ALPAGE group of INRIA and Université Paris 7 in Paris. In 2011 he joined the Department of Theoretical and Applied Linguistics of the University of Cambridge as a Research Associate. Since October 2012, he has worked as a CNRS Researcher at IRIT, the Toulouse Institute of Computer Science Research at Université Paul Sabatier. His research focuses on the unsupervised extraction of semantics from text, with a particular interest in factorization methods and tensor algebra.

Suzanne Evans Wagner, PhD (University of Pennsylvania) is Assistant Professor of Linguistics at Michigan State University. Her research interests include the sociolinguistics of adolescence and young adulthood, and their intersection with gender, ethnicity and social class. At present she is pursuing the question of why some individuals significantly change their linguistic repertoires post-adolescence, via projects that encompass corpus, experimental and field methods. Homepage: www.msu.edu/~wagnersu.

1
What is linguistics?

Keith Allan

1.1 Linguistics studies language and languages

Linguistics is the study of the human ability to produce and interpret language in speaking, writing and signing (for the deaf). All languages and all varieties of every language constitute potential data for linguistic research, as do the relationships between them and the relations and structures of their components. A linguist is someone who studies and describes the structure and composition of language and/or languages in a methodical and rigorous manner.

1.1.1 Human language

Linguistics inquires into the properties of the human body and mind which enable us to produce and interpret language (see Chapter 19). Human infants unquestionably have an innate ability to learn language as a means of social interaction (see Chapters 2, 13, 14, 17 and 20). Most likely it is the motivation to communicate with other members of the species that explains the development of language in hominins. It follows that linguists study language as an expression of and vehicle for social interaction. They also research the origins of human language (see Chapter 2), though there is controversy over when language first became possible among hominins. Neanderthals (*Homo sapiens neanderthalensis*, *c.*300,000 to 30,000 years BP) almost certainly came to have the mental and physical capacity to use language naturally. No extant non-human animal has a communication system on a par with human language. Some creatures learn to respond to and even reproduce fragments of human language, but they never achieve what a human being is capable of. The so-called 'language' used within some animal communities may have a few identifiable meaningful forms and structures, but animal languages lack the depth and comprehensiveness of human language.

Human language is the most sophisticated means of communication among earthly life forms. It is a kind of interaction with our environment; and it is intentionally communicative. Inorganic matter interacts with its environment without intention, e.g. moving water reshapes land. Plants interact with their environment as individuals, e.g. many plants turn towards a light source and some insectivorous plants actively trap their prey, but this interaction does not result from intention. Non-human creatures often do intentionally communicate with each other, for instance when mating or seeking food, but only in very limited ways. Humans interact with their environment in many ways, of which human communication using language is the most sophisticated and results from intentional behaviour.

1.1.2 Some general characteristics of language(s)

Language has physical forms to be studied. You can hear speech, see writing and signing, and feel Braille. The forms can be decomposed into structured components: sentences, phrases, words, letters, sounds. These language constituents are expressed and combined in conventional ways that are largely (if not completely) rule-governed.

Chapter 3 examines gesture and sign as used in place of and along with spoken language. Gestures of various kinds accompany most spoken language (even when the speaker is on the telephone). Sign languages of the deaf vary from nation to nation, though each national sign language is also a complete language largely independent of the language spoken in the signer's community.

Speech precedes writing both phylogenetically and ontogenetically. The creation of a writing system around 5,000 years BP (see Chapter 4) is the earliest evidence we have of linguistic analysis: all writing systems require the creator to analyse spoken language into chunks that correspond to words, syllables, phonemes or other phonic data in order to render them in a visual medium. Although writing systems usually begin with a pictographic representation, this very quickly becomes abstract as representations of sounds, syllables, and/or elements of meaning come to replace pictographs. Thus did writing become more symbolic than iconic.

Chapter 5 discusses the phonetic inventory of sounds that can occur in human languages and reviews the character of human speech mechanisms. Phoneticians research the physical production, acoustic properties, and the auditory perception of the sounds of speech.

Less than a quarter of the sounds humans have the ability to make are systematically used within any one language and Chapter 6 focuses on properties of the various phonological systems to be found in the world's languages. Phonologists study the way that sounds function within a given language and across languages to give form to spoken language. For instance the English colloquialism *pa* 'father' in most dialects is pronounced with initial aspiration as [pʰaa] but in a few dialects without aspiration as [paa], which does not change the meaning.[1] In Thai, however, the word [pʰaa] means 'split' whereas the word [paa] means 'forest', so the difference between [pʰ] and [p] makes a meaningful difference in Thai, but not in English. This is just one instance of different phonological systems at work and there is, of course, much more.

Morphology (see Chapter 7) deals with the systematic correspondence between the phonological form and meaning in subword constructions called 'morphemes'. A morpheme is the smallest unit of grammatical analysis with semantic specification. A word may consist of one or more morphemes: for example, the morpheme *–able* may be suffixed to the verb root *desire* to create the adjective *desirable*. This adjective may take a negative prefix *un–* to form *undesirable* which can, in turn, be converted into the noun *undesirable* by a process sometimes called 'zero-derivation' because there is no overt marker of the nominalization. This noun may then be inflected with the abstract morpheme PLURAL which in this instance has the form of the suffix *–s* yielding the plural noun *undesirables*. Morphology deals with the creation of new word forms through inflections that add a secondary grammatical category to an existing lexical item (word) but do not create a new one. As we have seen, morphology is also concerned with the creation of new lexical items by derivational processes such as affixation, compounding (*chairwoman*), truncation (*math(s)* from *mathematics*), and stress change (*perVERT* [verb] vs *PERvert* [noun] – where upper case indicates the stressed syllable).

Syntax studies the manner in which morphemes and lexical items combine into larger taxonomic structures such as phrases, sentences and longer texts (see Chapters 8 and 9). Some languages incorporate many morphemes into a single word that requires a sentence to translate it into English. Relationships between sentence constituents can be signalled (1) by inflection, in which case word order can be comparatively free (as in Latin), or (2) by the sequence of items – making word order relatively rigid (as in English). Latin *dominus servos vituperabat, vituperabat dominus servos, servos dominus vituperabat* are all translated by the English sentence *the master* [dominus] *cursed* [vituperabat] *the slaves* [servos]. Although there are many ways of depicting syntactic structure, rooted labelled trees have become the norm in modern linguistics, e.g. the oversimplified tree in Figure 1.1. Chapter 9 argues that syntax should reflect the dynamics of language processing allowing for structural underspecification and update such that the patterns of dialogue can be shown to follow directly from the integrated account of context-dependent phenomena.

Language is metaphysical in that it has content; i.e. language expressions have meaning. Semantics investigates the meanings of sentences and their constituents and, also, the meaning relationships among language expressions. Linguistic semantics is informed by insights from philosophy, psychology, sociology and computer science. Notions of truth and compositionality are crucial in determining meaning (see Chapters 33 and 9). But so too are the cognitive processes of language users (see Chapters 29 and 35). There is a question of how lexical content corresponds with conceptual content and the structure of concepts. There is controversy over the place within lexical and discourse semantics of encyclopaedic knowledge about referents (things spoken of) and the domain within which a language expression occurs. There is also controversy about the optimal means of representing meaning in theoretical semantics. All these matters are reviewed in Chapters 10 and 11.

Every language comes with a lexicon – loosely equivalent to the vocabulary of that language. A lexicon (see Chapter 12) can be thought of as the mental counterpart to (and original model for) a dictionary such as the *Oxford English Dictionary*. Lexical items are stored as combinations of form and meaning, together with morphological and syntactic (morphosyntactic) information about the grammatical properties of the item and links to

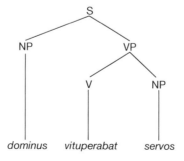

Figure 1.1 An oversimplified tree structure [S = sentence, NP = noun phrase, VP = verb phrase, V = verb]

encyclopaedic information about the item – such as its history and information about things it may be used to refer to. Typically, a lexical item cannot be further analysed into meaningful chunks whose combination permits its meaning to be computed. For instance, the lexical items *a*, *the*, *dog*, *sheep*, *kill* and morphemes like *–s* (PLURAL), *–ed* (PAST) can combine together under certain conditions, but none of these is subject to morphosyntactic analysis into smaller constituents.

The lexicon of a language bundles meaning with form in versatile chunks that speakers combine into phrases, sentences, and longer texts whose meanings are computable from their constituents. The lexical items and morphemes listed above can combine into the sentence in (1), the meaning of which is composed from not only the words and morphemes but also the syntactic relations between them.

(1) The dogs killed a sheep.

(1) has much the same meaning as (2) and a very different meaning from (3).

(2) A sheep was killed by the dogs.
(3) A sheep killed the dogs.

In (1) and (2) the dogs do the killing and the sheep ends up dead, whereas in (3) the sheep does the killing and it is the dogs which end up dead. Notice that the meanings of *dogs* and *killed* can be computed from their component morphemes: DOG+PLURAL and KILL+PAST; similarly for the phrases *the dogs* and *a sheep* and the whole of the sentences (1), (2) and (3).

If you find (1) and (2) more believable than (3), that is because you are applying your knowledge of the world to what is said. These judgements arise from pragmatic assessments of the semantics of (1), (2) and (3).

As said earlier, semantics is concerned with the meanings of, and the meaning relationships among, language expressions. For example, there is a semantic relationship between *kill* and *die* such that (4) is true.

(4) If X kills Y, then Y dies.

In (4) X has the role of actor and Y the undergoer. There are many other kinds of relationship, too. In order to die, Y has to have been living. If Y is a sheep, then Y is also an animal. In English, dogs and sheep are countable objects, i.e. they can be spoken of as singulars, like *a sheep* in (1)–(3), or as plural entities like *the dogs* in (1)–(3). Words referring to meat (such as *mutton*, *lamb*, *pork*) do not normally occur in countable noun phrases; the same is true of liquids like *beer* and granulated substances like *sugar*, *coffee* or *rice*. However, these nouns are used countably on some occasions to identify individual amounts or varieties, as in (5)–(7).

(5) Two sugars for me. [Two spoons of sugar]
(6) Three beers, please. [Three glasses or cans of beer]
(7) Two coffees are widely marketed in Europe. [Two species or varieties of coffee]

What this shows is that the grammatical properties of linguistic items can be, and regularly are, exploited to generate communicatively useful meaning differences.

When speakers employ language they add additional aspects of meaning. Although this is not obvious from (1), it is observable from the interchange between X and Y in (8).

(8) X: I don't understand why you are so upset.
    Y: The dogs killed a sheep.

Pragmatics (see Chapters 13 and 14) studies the meanings of utterances (an utterance is a sentence or sentence fragment used by a particular speaker on some particular occasion) with attention to the context in which the utterances are made. In (8) the reference of 'I' and 'you' is determined from context, as is the relevant time at which the addressee is judged upset and also the estimated degree of relevance of Y's response to X's statement. Language interchange is one form of social interactive behaviour and it is governed by sets of conventions that encourage cooperativeness in order that social relations be as harmonious as possible. There are competing notions of what constitutes cooperativeness, whether it exists independently of particular interlocutors or whether it is negotiated anew in every encounter, but, nonetheless, cooperative behaviour seems to be the default against which uncooperative behaviour such as insult and offensive language must be judged (see Chapter 14). What this amounts to is that interlocutors are socialized into having certain expectations of and from each other. These expectations are learned in childhood as one aspect of competent language usage; they are part of one's induction into being a member of a social group. Typically they constitute a part of common ground between interlocutors that enables them to understand one another. Looking again at (8) we observe that Y's response to X's question is apparently relevant, because we know that many people get upset when dogs kill a sheep. Y has assumed this knowledge is part of the common ground with X, enabling X to take Y's response as an appropriate one. This appropriateness is independent of whether or not Y is speaking truly. The default assumption for almost all language interchange is that speakers will be honest, which is the reason why lying is castigated in Anglo communities (and many others).

We see from (8) that spoken discourses have structures and constraints that render them coherent so as to be lucid and comprehensible to others. Were that not the case, the discourse in (9) between a therapist and a schizophrenic patient would not seem abnormal.

(9) THERAPIST: A stitch in time saves nine. What does that mean?
    SCHIZOPHRENIC: Oh! That's because all women have a little bit of magic in them. I found that out. And it's called, it's sort of good magic. And nine is a sort of magic number. Like, I've got nine colours here you will notice. I've got yellow, green, blue, grey, orange, blue and navy. And I've got black. And I've got a sort of clear white. The nine colours, to me they are the whole universe; and they symbolize every man, woman, and child in the world.
    (Rochester and Martin 1979: 94f)

Chapter 15 discusses the structures of spoken and written texts and narratives. What linguistics looks at in a text is not its literary or aesthetic quality, but the language used in order to give structure to the text so that hearers and readers can readily follow the speaker's or writer's intended meaning. Linguists identify what enables the hearer/reader to recognize the topic of discourse and to correctly distinguish the (animate and inanimate) participants in the narrative/conversation and what happens to each of them as the narrative/conversation unfolds.

1.1.3 The intersection of linguistics with other disciplines

Language is used within all human communities, many of which have no regular written form for their language, or did not until the twentieth century. Although it is now fairly common for linguists to enter a pre-literate community and attempt to describe their language, for most of the twentieth century it was anthropologists who undertook field work in such communities with the primary aim of describing their social structures and customs (see Chapter 16); to accomplish those goals most effectively, they needed to learn the people's language. Field linguistics applies the methods of data elicitation and data collection in order to document, describe and analyse languages and language practices in their natural habitat – within the community of native speakers under investigation. The primary mission of anthropological linguistics is to tie forms of language to the social structures and customs of a people.

There is a slight overlap here with the work of sociolinguists (see Chapter 17). A principal difference is that sociolinguistics focuses on the varieties of language used among different groups within a particular language community. Sociolinguists also investigate language change through time by plotting the spreading adoption of new forms and the decay of old ones, which is often accelerated during periods of social stress and change. Concepts of politeness and offensiveness (see Chapter 14) differ among different social groups, and such social conventions and their correlation with social relations are also topics relevant to sociolinguistics.

Psycholinguistics (Chapter 18) draws from linguistics, psychology, cognitive science and the study of language pathology. Psycholinguists research cognitive and psychological aspects of the perception of categorical similarities and differences among phenomena. They investigate language production on the one hand and language processing and comprehension on the other. Developmental psycholinguistics examines first language acquisition (Chapter 20) and psycholinguists also study the acquisition of second languages (Chapter 21). Knowing what is normal for human language use enables dysfunction to be recognized and potentially treated. Because linguistic dysfunction usually correlates with other mental dysfunction, language offers a path into (ab)normal cognitive behaviour.

Whereas psycholinguistics focuses on the human mind, neurolinguistics, the topic of Chapter 19, focuses on the allied physiological matter of the human brain: the organ that enables the cognitive abilities we associate with the mind. Since the mid-nineteenth century it has been known that trauma to certain parts of the brain causes fairly predictable linguistic deficiencies. Since the development of neural imaging techniques, knowledge of brain function has blossomed; as a result there has been progressive refinement in mapping the functions of different areas of the brain which has revealed the great extent to which different areas of the brain operate together to, among other things, facilitate language use.

1.1.4 Acquiring language

All normal human beings acquire language, even if they have a very low IQ. There is no doubt that human beings have an innate disposition to learn language, but they need exposure to the society of other humans in order to do so. Furthermore, many children are raised in multilingual situations and acquire two or more languages concurrently and they very quickly learn not to mix them. During the first year of life a child learns to discriminate the significant sounds of their care-givers' language(s) and they learn how to interact appropriately with people around them (see Chapter 20): it is the beginning of encultured socialization. By about one year old, a child supplements gesture and non-linguistic vocalization with words and later combines words into syntactic structures. The impetus is always to communicate with others.

Many people are taught a second or foreign language after they have already acquired native ability in their first language (see Chapter 21). The requirements for the process of second language learning apply insights from linguistics, and the primary focus of 'applied linguistics' is on language teaching. This means developing sound pedagogy that is responsive to research in linguistics. The instruction of phonology, morphology, vocabulary, semantics and syntax is important but so too is pragmatics, because it is not enough to know the grammar of a language: learners also have to know how to use the expressions from within the new language appropriately under any circumstances and in any context.

1.1.5 Languages through time

Every language has developed over time and most languages are related to some other languages; this is grist to the mill of historical (diachronic) linguistics (Chapter 22). All languages change over time and distinct varieties of a language may develop in the different regions where it is spoken. In recent times there has been overlap with sociolinguistics in that historical linguists have researched language variation and the social factors that generate language change at various points in time (synchronic change). Historical linguistics was launched in the nineteenth century by comparing and correlating sound changes in Indo-European languages as a way of identifying which languages belong to that family. Very quickly interest expanded to the cataloguing of lexical, morphological, syntactic and semantic change in Indo-European and other language families. Comparative studies of language contact and genetic relationship have led to well-accepted descriptions of relations among different languages and their grouping into families.

There is some commonality between Chapter 22 and Chapter 23 on linguistic change. All living languages change constantly, but how predictable are the results of the change? Internal changes are driven by variation due to children using language a little differently from their parents and from mutations in discourse conventions. Some changes arise through the grammaticalization of metaphorical extensions or the regularizing and standardization of pragmatic inferences: some of what begin as spontaneous novel meaning extensions achieve popularity and lose their novelty to become conventionalized. External influences include a need to create novel expressions for new phenomena, including cultural and social changes. Innovations begin within the dialect of one social group (sociolect) but must spread to the whole community to count as language change. Change that may seem to have been motivated by human cognition because it is so widespread may in fact result from contact between different sociolects, dialects or languages. Predicting the direction of language change seems to be almost impossible.

Chapter 24 takes up the topic of language endangerment. Languages are fast becoming extinct with the growth of urbanization and the dominance of linguae francae leading to the abandonment of languages that are spoken by only a small handful of people. Such people usually need to use a more dominant language to communicate with the wider community and their children will typically be schooled in the dominant language. Language documentation has the aim of recording for posterity not only the phonology, grammar and vocabulary of dying languages but their stories, songs, and the social and cultural contexts in which the language is or was used. The documentation requires audio and video recording and techniques of archiving samples of language interchange and language performance that can be readily updated as technology advances. One strand of this work is to mobilize communities whose language is dying into language management that encourages language maintenance and revitalization.

1.1.6 Looking across languages

Cross-linguistic research is the *sine qua non* of linguistic typology, discussed in Chapter 25. Languages fall into different types. For instance, there are tone languages like Chinese, Thai, Maa (Nilotic, East Africa), and Yoruba (Niger-Congo, West Africa), stressed timed languages like English, and syllable timed languages like French. More important, however, are the differences in morphological and syntactic properties: a language like Latin has many inflections that indicate syntactic and sometimes semantic relations between the constituents of a sentence; in English and Chinese, word order does a similar job. In an agglutinating language such as Turkish, morphemes adjoin to form very complex words such as *ceplerimizdekilerdenmiş* = pocket + plural + our + in + relativizer + plural + from + dubitative '[it] was supposedly from among those that are/were in our pockets'. An incorporating or polysynthetic language, like Chinook, has words like *ania'lot* = present tense [*a*] + him [*ni*] + her [*a*] + I to [*'l*]+from [*o*] + give [*t*] 'I gave it/him to her' where the constituents do not form morphemes that can regularly stand alone in other constructions. Linguistic typologists look for what is more probable versus less probable in a human language. There are implicational universals because if a given type of language has one kind of structure it will usually have another: for instance, verb-initial languages (like Maa) almost all have prepositions and not postpositions. So, one result of typological studies is the identification of language universals to throw light on the nature of human language.

Traditionally, translation has not been of much concern within linguistics, perhaps because linguistics has been predominantly theoretical whereas translation has been primarily practical. The typical analysis of a sentence in a linguistics textbook will be of very little value at all to the practical translator because it is simply too fragmentary and simplistic – not least because semantic analysis is its weakest aspect. As we see in Chapter 26, although we tend to think of translation as rendering a sentence of the source language into a semantically equivalent sentence in the target language, this grossly oversimplifies the notion of equivalence. In fact what needs to happen is that the sentence in the source language has to be understood with all its cultural nuances and then recast into what a native speaker of the target language would have said if s/he had spontaneously wanted to utter the 'same' thing. For instance, because Hungarian nouns and pronouns are not marked for gender, *He said yes and she said no* cannot be straightforwardly translated; on the other hand, the subtleties of the Hungarian levels of address will often be lost on translating a Hungarian novel into English. Recasting to take account of such intercultural differences forefronts the translator's interpretation of the source utterance which is obviously likely to deviate from it subjectively and therefore is open to criticism on grounds of accuracy.

1.1.7 Approaches to linguistics

It is sometimes said that modern linguistics began with the posthumous publication of Ferdinand de Saussure's *Cours de Linguistique Générale* in 1916 (see Chapter 27). Certainly that work inspired structuralist linguistics in Europe, although Leonard Bloomfield's *Language* of 1933 was a greater influence on American structuralist linguistics. The structuralist doctrine is based on relationships of contrast among elements in a language and, more widely, in a conceptual system. The structure is elicited from the taxonomic distribution of elements within the language system. The structuralist emphasis on contrast led to the development of phonemic theories (see Chapter 6). In Europe contrasts of function (Chapter 30) were as significant as contrasts of form, but American structuralism focused on contrasts of form to the near exclusion of function and meaning until late in the twentieth century – a position that persisted through Chomskyan linguistics (see Chapter 28). Saussure's dogma on the arbitrariness of the sign has had to be modified since the rise of cognitive linguistics (see Chapter 29).

The Chomskyan 'revolution' began with the publication of *Syntactic Structures* in 1957. Where structuralism induced language structures bottom-up from the constituent analysis of stretches of language, Chomsky's theory of syntax was rather a hypothetico-deductive model that proposed top-down analysis of a phrase marker generated from an initial symbol S (sentence) into its constituent phrases and their constituents such that the terminal constituents were morphemes entered from the lexicon.[2] These terminal strings were then phonetically interpreted. In later Chomskyan models the phrase markers were also semantically interpreted. Related structures such as active/passive and declarative/interrogative were related by transformational rules. In the early 1960s Chomsky favoured the 'mentalistic' cognitive basis for language as a guiding principle for his grammars (though it is questionable whether he ever sought confirmation of his postulates from psycholinguistic experimentation – which was not forthcoming). Since the 1980s Chomsky has been championing biolinguistics (see Chapter 28) which seeks to uncover the neurological origins that underpin the universal human capacity to acquire language. Nonetheless Chomskyan grammars still postulate an autonomous syntax at the core of grammar such that phonological and semantic components of grammar are interpretative of syntax.

Cognitive linguistics (Chapter 29) developed as an alternative vision to Chomsky's notions that syntax is autonomous and that the human language faculty is independent of other cognitive behaviour. For cognitivists, linguistic abilities are embedded in perception, attention, memory, categorization, abstraction, creativity and symbolic thought. Language is acquired from exposure to contextually dependent utterances on the basis of meaning, so corpora provide the most important source for data. Cognitivists focus on analogy and on the functional significance of metaphor and metonymy in language. In direct contrast with Chomskyan linguists, cognitive linguists argue that syntactic constructions are semantically and pragmatically motivated.

Functionalist linguistics (Chapter 30) has a lot in common with cognitive linguistics. Functionalism looks to the functions of language within society as the motivation for language structure and the motivation for the meaningfulness of linguistic elements. In other words, functional linguistics holds that linguistic structures can only be understood and explained with reference to the communicative functions of language, and it is a given that the primary function of language is to be a vehicle for social interaction among human beings. Thus communication influences, but does not necessarily determine, the forms that language takes. Functionalists assume that cognitive and socio-cultural factors explain linguistic phenomena. Syntax is semantically and pragmatically motivated: it exists for people to combine elements of meaning in a variety of dissimilar ways to capture different nuances of meaning. Corpora (see Chapter 32) and discourse (Chapter 15) are more relevant to functionalist theorizing than are the decontextualized sentences of Chomsky-style linguistics.

Computational linguistics applies machines to model human behaviour by generating, analysing and interpreting language texts. Computers implement parsers to analyse linguistic structures and computers are also used to generate texts. Ideally these machines would simulate human abilities to produce and interpret language by running procedures that, once set in motion, are devoid of human input yet whose output can be matched against natural language utterances for accuracy – thereby enabling the procedures to be evaluated as modelling human behaviour. In reality such a goal is a long way from being fully realized. Chapter 31 illustrates computational linguistics applying some parsing techniques, undertaking some computational semantics, and demonstrating the machine learning of a process to add linguistic tags that annotate a corpus.

Corpus linguistics (Chapter 32) collates corpora of texts. Corpora have become important data sources of language expressions that are actually used by speakers rather than what is intuitively believed to be used; they serve to check the grammaticality/acceptability judgements of native speakers. A corpus may comprise spoken and/or written texts, texts that date from different times, and/or texts that sample many genres and varieties of language or be restricted to just one or two. To aid researchers, a corpus designer may add to the source text metadata, markup and annotation. Researchers then use computer-aided quantitative and qualitative methods to investigate data from corpora, in order to accomplish such things as establishing the frequency of language items and structures, their collocations and concordances.

Since the time of the pre-Socratic philosophers in Ancient Greece, developments in linguistic semantics and pragmatics have been boosted by influence from philosophers writing about language (see Chapter 33). Judgements of truth in the way that language represents things spoken of has exercised philosophers since Plato (428–348 BCE), Aristotle (384–322 BCE), and the Stoics (from c.300 BCE), and there have been echoes ever since among researchers of language. Language philosophy has really flourished since Gottlob Frege's discussion of sense and reference in the late nineteenth century and Bertrand Russell's theory of definite descriptions in the early twentieth century. These sparked interest beyond classical truth conditional semantics to investigations of presupposition, intensional contexts, possible worlds and dynamic semantics (see also Chapter 11). After the middle of the twentieth century, ordinary language philosophers developed theories of speech acts and conversational implicature that have been welcomed by linguists as crucial to understanding meaning in language (see Chapter 13).

1.1.8 Linguistics in the community

The language in which laws are written represents an area of potential miscommunication between legislators, lawyers and the lay public; consequently linguistics and the law raises an important topic for any community (Chapter 34). The language of the law-makers and courts is significant within the community because the rights and freedoms of citizens are at stake. Police interviews and legal cross-examination are fraught with potential for misunderstanding in the language used by the different parties – even when they are all native speakers of the same dialect, the more so otherwise. It has become common for linguists to be called by both prosecution and defence as expert witnesses to comment on such things as the likelihood that a suspect in fact uttered a certain spoken or written text which is evidence in a prosecution; or, when a signed witness statement has linguistic anomalies that suggest the witness has been 'verballed' by an overzealous police officer.

Chapter 35 is on political language in the United States, but the hypothesis presented would seem to apply to other nations. The language of politics has in common with the language of advertising that its function is primarily persuasive. Most people are persuaded not by rational argument and reasoned evidence but by their emotional attachment to ideas. The way a topic is framed (presented) affects its acceptability: for example, on one frame taxation is a deprivation of the fruits of one's labours, on another it is the fee for membership to a community. Repetitive, comforting, emotionally attractive and morally appealing narratives, metaphors, mottos and mantras are most likely to gain traction with an audience; hence, politicians constantly repeat an emotive phrase such as *the war on terror* to strengthen neural connections in audience minds that enable them to gain ready community acceptance for curtailment of freedoms and privacy. Hearing those words again and again ordinary people get brainwashed into thinking in a way that suits the politician. So, typically, political language (re)configures neural pathways through repetitive populism rather than persuading us through reasoned argument.

For many people today communication is dominated by social media such as texting on phones, instant messaging on other platforms, and communication via Facebook, YouTube, and the like (see Chapter 36). The way these media are used challenges the notion that speech is primary because texters employ language expressions that are close to spoken forms and they frequently include performance phenomena (e.g. *lol* 'laughing out loud') and emoticons (:D 'laughing') which comment on the writer's supposed acts and actions in order to add those behavioural nuances that are typically present in face-to-face interaction but absent from formal written genres of communication.

1.2 A short history of linguistics

Ferdinand de Saussure has been described as the 'father' of modern linguistics through his influential *Cours de Linguistique Générale* (1916). There are three reasons for a belief that linguistics is of very recent origin: (1) Linguistics is a human science, and along with anthropology, psychology and sociology, it developed rapidly during the late nineteenth century and mushroomed in the twentieth century. (2) Towards the end of the nineteenth century technological developments allowed for the recording and reproduction of spoken language so that linguists could at last not only recognize the priority of the spoken over the written medium but study constant, non-ephemeral, data from the spoken medium. (3) The first university chairs in something like 'linguistics' were Franz Bopp's Chair in Oriental Literature and General Language-lore ('allgemeine Sprachkunde') at the University of Berlin in 1825 and Thomas Hewitt Key's Chair of Comparative Grammar at University College London in 1842. The *International Journal of American Linguistics* dates from 1917; the Linguistic Society of America from 1924, and its journal *Language* from 1925. Linguistics only became an independent university discipline several decades into the twentieth century: most university programmes in linguistics were established in the second half of the twentieth century; high school programmes in linguistics only started in the third millennium and they barely exist today.

If linguistics is a science it is because a linguist studies and describes the structure and composition of language and/or languages in a methodical and rigorous manner. However, prehistoric thought about the structure and composition of language set a pathway towards linguistics proper. As already mentioned, the earliest evidence of linguistic analysis is the development of writing to record events, transactions, agreements and observations more permanently than is possible in oral transmission. The oldest example known dates from fifth millennium BCE China. Bilingual Semitic word lists existed in the third millennium BCE and tabled equivalences between Sumerian and Akkadian phrases in the eighteenth century BCE. Such events count as early steps in linguistic analysis.

The first writing systems were logographic: the symbol represents a morpheme or word and its referent. Today, ♂ is a logograph for 'male', *4* is a logograph for 'four'. Often, logographs extend to homophones of the original word symbolized, as in a *4 Sale* sign that uses *4* in place of *for* because they sound the same. Once a logographic symbol is associated with phonetic form there is scope for its development into either a syllabary symbolizing the syllables of the language or into an alphabet symbolizing its phonemes. Because they segment the spoken language in order to give it visual and more permanent representation, syllabaries and alphabets exemplify prehistoric phonological analyses of language.

Although not known in the West until fairly recently, linguistic analysis in Ancient India developed to preserve the oral language of the Vedic hymns composed 1900–1100 BCE. From the sixth century BCE, there were systematic analyses of phonetics, phonology, and prosody. In the early fourth century BCE, Pāṇini composed a precise and fairly complete description of late Vedic Sanskrit consisting of lists of lexical and phonological units accompanied by phonetic, morphological, syntactic and semantic rules and conditions, and metarules for rule-ordering, and so on. The topics and methods used in these Ancient Indian works were far closer to practices in modern linguistics than to anything found in the Western Classical Tradition before the nineteenth or even twentieth century.

In Ancient Greece, language study grew out of philosophy on the basis that language enables truth-bearing presentations of the internal and external world and is also a vehicle of persuasion and education. Both Plato and Aristotle believed that language reflects speakers' experiences of the world and the relationships and structures they find in it. Their interest was aroused because we say such things as *X is the cause of Y*, and *B follows from A*, and they were concerned about the relation between what is said and what actually holds true in the world. To precisely account for the meaning of statements requires a prior account of their structure; and because statements are expressed through sentences, the Ancient Greek philosophers looked into the construction of sentences to establish what constitutes a statement. Thus began a long association between philosophy and language analysis, which revived in the Middle Ages and flowered in the second half of the twentieth century, leading to significant advances in linguistic semantics and pragmatics. In *Poetics* and *Rhetoric* Aristotle discusses language structures which are relevant to the success of poetic and rhetorical effect. In addition to talking about the functions of various parts of speech, he described some phonological aspects of Greek, because in his day, and for centuries after, literature was rarely read silently, but declaimed by actors or poets from the stage, and by pupils in the schoolroom. In *Rhetoric* he advocated something comparable with Grice's maxims of manner, quality and perhaps quantity (Grice 1975, and see Chapter 13), though his purpose was different from that of Grice.

In the Western Classical Tradition (see Allan 2010), the work of the early Greek philosophers and grammarians was adapted with little alteration to the grammar of Latin, the language that dominated scholarship in the West until the twentieth century. The basics for the parts of speech can be found in Plato and Aristotle, but it was the Stoics who noted regularities and irregularities indicating underlying rules of grammar and norms of behaviour governing the use of language. The Stoics recognized illocutionary types and under their influence, Apollonius Dyscolus (*c.*80–160 CE) identified the link between clause-type, mood, and illocutionary force that was not revived until the late twentieth century. In the second century BCE Aristarchus of Samothrace refers to all eight traditional parts of speech and to some of their subcategories (Smith n.d.); these were propagated in the *Tekhnē Grammatikē* (The Art of Grammar attributed to Dionysius Thrax, *c.*160–85 BCE; see Dionysius 1987) which was a model for the pedagogical *Ars grammatica* (The Art of Grammar) of Aelius Donatus (*c.*315–385 CE) – a cornerstone of Latin instruction throughout the Middle Ages. The Stoics were a major influence on Varro, Apollonius and Herodian, and – indirectly – their disciple Priscian (*c.*490–560 CE), whose *Institutiones grammaticae* (Grammatical Doctrine) is the foundational work on Latin grammar and remained the principal pedagogical source for Latin grammars until modern times.

The Alexandrian grammarians, Dionysius Thrax and Apollonius Dyscolus, were pedagogical grammarians and not philosophers. Their principal motivation was a perceived need to teach the correct meaning, forms, and pronunciation of Homeric and Attic Greek so that classical literature could be properly read, performed and understood. This is analogous to the motivation for the grammars of Ancient India. Donatus described the parts of speech to be found in classical Latin literature, although Vulgar (i.e. colloquial contemporary) Latin was in daily use about him. Priscian adopted the view that language reflects the way the world is and he explained a number of syntactic constructions on these grounds. For example, he said that because one cannot imagine an action without presupposing an actor the subject of a sentence always precedes the verb – i.e. all languages are either S(O)V or SV(O).[3] Many such assumptions are justified by the grammars of Latin and Greek, but turn out to be wrong when applied universally; for instance, Maa (Nilotic, East Africa) is VS(O), Malagasy (Austronesian, Madagascar) V(O)S, and Tohono O'odham (Uto-Aztecan, Arizona) arguably (O)VS. Priscian's classical Latin grammar, *Institutiones Grammaticae*, was based directly upon the classical Greek grammar of Apollonius Dyscolus. Dionysius, Apollonius, Donatus and Priscian were not philosophers but precursors to applied linguists within the Western Classical Tradition.

Some 600 years after Priscian, from about 1150 to 1350, grammar became once more wedded to philosophy. But all along, from the early Middle Ages to the present day, running on a more or less parallel track to philosophical grammar, there continued to be a pedagogic strain manifest in prescriptive grammars for the classroom. For several hundred years, education in Europe was education in Latin, access to which was through grammars of Latin; hence *grammar* as a school subject meant the 'grammar of Latin'. Except during the Middle Ages, when the fourth century Latin of the Vulgate Bible displaced the pagan Latin of antiquity, the best authors were said to be the classical authors; it was classical Latin and, to a certain extent, classical Greek that came to be regarded as the ideal model for grammatical construction. English and other so-called 'modern languages' were (mistakenly, we would now say) regarded as debased and corrupt compared with classical Latin and Greek; so teachers insisted that the best way to write a 'modern language' was to follow the rules of Latin grammar so far as possible. In other words, pedagogues believed that the grammar of classical Latin provides appropriate rules for the grammars of European vernaculars. Such a view was properly condemned by linguists in the first sixty years of the twentieth century; unfortunately, most of those critics rejected not only the excesses of traditional grammar but its successes too.

For several centuries the works of Aristotle were lost to scholars in Europe. But in the twelfth century they once more became available and there was renewed interest in Aristotelian philosophy. In the twelfth and thirteenth centuries in Western Europe, scholars had Priscian's rules for Latin syntax which, because of the focus on pedagogy, sought no explanation for why the rules operate as they do. Scholastic grammarians adopted the Aristotelian dictum that the world is the same for everyone, believing that language is like a *speculum* 'mirror, image' that reflects the world; so their grammars are described as 'speculative'. The speculative grammarians also followed Aristotle in believing that everyone has the same experience whatever their language; consequently mental experiences are the same for everyone. It led them to claim that what is signified is universal, but the means by which it is signified, the *modi significandi*, differ from language to language. Because of their interest in *modi significandi*, these medieval scholastics were also known as *modistae*. During the thirteenth century, the speculative grammarians began to establish the notion of a 'general' or 'universal' grammar common to all languages.

In the late seventeenth and throughout the eighteenth century, language was the province of rationalist grammarians, whom Noam Chomsky – undoubtedly the most prominent theoretician in the second half of the twentieth century – claimed for his intellectual forebears. Like the *modistae*, the rationalist grammarians were inspired by Aristotle; the essential difference between the two schools is that the *modistae* viewed human beings as all having similar experiences because of the nature of the world around them, whereas the rationalists believed that people have similar experiences because of the nature of the human mind. The rationalists were post-Renaissance scholars living in an age of exploration which had given rise to grammars of several exotic languages. Scholars in the seventeenth and eighteenth centuries knew that experience of the world differed greatly among different communities of human beings but that all of us possess minds through which to perceive, categorize and assimilate information about the world. On the rationalist view, the nature of the mind is to think; and because almost everyone is capable of being rational, they adapted the medieval notion that there must be an underlying 'general' or 'universal' grammar to locate it in the human mind. This idea is also found in the late twentieth century grammar of Chomsky. It follows that languages differ from one another only because the common underlying structure of human thought is expressed through different forms – in Chomskyan terms, different 'parameters' are switched on.

The traditional view that the structure of the world informs the structure of language is inverted by the 'linguistic relativity hypothesis' that arose in the Romantic movement which spread from Étienne Bonnot de Condillac (1715–1780) and Jean-Jacques Rousseau (1712–1778) in France to Johann Gottfried von Herder (1744–1803) and Wilhelm von Humboldt (1767–1835) in Germany, to re-emerge with Franz Boas (1858–1942) in America and be instilled into Edward Sapir (1884–1939) and Benjamin Lee Whorf (1897–1941). Known today as the 'Sapir–Whorf hypothesis' or, simply, 'Whorfian hypothesis', it postulates that the structure of language informs the structure of the world as conceived by speakers of a particular language when they are speaking it. However, it does not impose a mental straitjacket: the human mind can and does go anywhere.

The eighteenth to nineteenth centuries saw the development of comparative philology arising from the discovery and gradual identification of the Indo-European language family. The early cross-language comparisons used terminology directly derived from ancient Greek statements on phonology. For the most part, however, nineteenth century comparative philology took the Western Classical Tradition in a new direction by focusing on phonological systems. Twentieth century developments in phonetics and phonology and the whole paradigm of Saussurean structuralist and Bloomfieldian mechanistic linguistics were a new direction in, and sometimes a revolt against, the Western Classical Tradition. Nonetheless, linguistics in the nineteenth and early twentieth centuries was a crucial foundation for the post-structuralist linguistics that is the consequence of the so-called 'Chomsky revolution'. Chomsky's predecessors had rejected traditional grammar along with linguistic universals, rationalist theory and semantics. All of these are back in vogue. If modern linguistics began with a hiccup in the Western Classical Tradition, it is now back within the comfortable framework of two and a half millennia of linguistic description.

Modern linguistics developed from the investigations of the neo-grammarians into the origins and interrelations of Indo-European languages, which eventually merged with a mushrooming interest in the non-Indo-European languages of Native Americans and the peoples of Africa, Asia and Australasia. This interest was partly motivated by a fascination with exotic cultures and languages, and partly by ideas for generating literacy and education in indigenous languages. The development of linguistics was spurred on by technological advances during the nineteenth to the twenty-first centuries that have facilitated detailed study of the spoken medium and of the processes of language interaction.

Acknowledgement

I am very grateful to Jae Song, Kasia Jaszczolt, Mike Balint and Simon Musgrave for comments on an earlier version of this chapter. They are in no way to blame for such infelicities as appear in this version.

Notes

1. I am ignoring possible variations in vowel quality.
2. In truth all grammars combine insights from both bottom-up and top-down analysis but differently emphasize one or the other.
3. S = subject, O = object, V = verb.

Further reading

Akmajian *et al.* (2010); Aronoff and Rees-Miller (2001); Auroux *et al.* (2000–2006); Brown (2006); Everett (2012); Koerner and Asher (1995); O'Grady *et al.* (2011); Pinker (1994).

References

Akmajian, A., R.A. Demers, A.K. Farmer and R.M. Harnish (2010) *Linguistics: An Introduction to Language and Communication*, 6th edition. Cambridge, MA: MIT Press.
Allan, K. (2010 [2007]) *The Western Classical Tradition in Linguistics*, 2nd expanded edition. London: Equinox.
Apollonius Dyscolus (1981) *The Syntax of Apollonius Dyscolus*. Transl. Fred W. Householder. Amsterdam: John Benjamins.
Aronoff, M. and J. Rees-Miller (eds) (2001) *The Handbook of Linguistics*. Oxford and Malden, MA: Blackwell.
Auroux, S., E.F.K. Koerner, H.-J. Niederehe and K. Versteegh (eds) (2000–2006) *History of the Language Sciences*. 3 vols. Berlin: Walter de Gruyter.
Bloomfield, L. (1933) *Language*. New York: Holt, Rinehart and Winston.
Brown, E.K. (General editor) (2006) *Encyclopedia of Languages and Linguistics*, 2nd edition. 14 vols. Oxford: Elsevier.
Chomsky, N. (1957) *Syntactic Structures*. The Hague: Mouton.
Dionysius (1987) The *Tekhnē Grammatikē* of Dionysius Thrax translated into English [by Alan Kemp]. In D.J. Taylor (ed.) *The History of Linguistics in the Classical Period*, pp. 169–89. Amsterdam: John Benjamins.
Donatus, A. (1961) De partibus orationis: Ars minor & ars grammatica. In H. Keil (ed.) *Grammatici Latini*, Vol. 4, pp. 355–66 and pp. 367–402. Hildesheim: Georg Olms.

Everett, D.L. (2012) *Language: The Cultural Tool*. London: Profile.

Grice, H.P. (1975) Logic and conversation. In P. Cole and J.L. Morgan (eds) *Syntax and Semantics 3: Speech Acts*, pp. 41–58. New York: Academic Press. Reprinted in H.P. Grice, *Studies in the Way of Words*, pp. 22–40. Cambridge, MA: Harvard University Press, 1989.

Koerner, E.F.K. and R.E. Asher (eds) (1995) *Concise History of the Language Sciences: From the Sumerians to the Cognitivists*. Oxford: Pergamon.

O'Grady, W., J. Archibald and F. Katamba (eds) (2011) *Contemporary Linguistics: An Introduction*. Harlow: Longman.

Pinker, S. (1994) *The Language Instinct: The New Science of Language and Mind*. London: Allen Lane.

Priscian (1961) Institutiones grammaticae. In H. Keil (ed.) *Grammatici Latini* Vol. 2, pp. 2: 1–597 and Vol. 3, pp. 1–377. Hildesheim: Georg Olms.

Rochester, S. and J.R. Martin (1979) *Crazy Talk: A Study of the Discourse of Schizophrenic Speakers*. New York: Plenum Press.

Saussure, F. de (1916) *Cours de Linguistique Générale* [Publié par Charles Bally et Albert Sechehaye; avec la collaboration de Albert Riedlinger]. Paris: Payot.

Smith, W. (ed.) (n.d.) Aristarchus. In *A Dictionary of Greek and Roman Biography and Mythology*. www.perseus.tufts.edu/hopper/text?doc=Perseus%3Atext%3A1999.04.0104%3Aalphabetic+letter%3DA%3Aentry+group%3D40%3Aentry%3Daristarchus-bio-8.

2
Evolutionary linguistics
How Language and languages got to be the way they are

James R. Hurford

2.1 Introduction

'Nothing in biology makes sense except in the light of evolution' is a famous dictum of the biologist Theodosius Dobzhansky. To 'make sense' of a phenomenon is to (begin to) explain it. A high goal of linguistics has traditionally been to explain language (an ambiguous term, as we will see immediately), rather than merely to describe it. Given this high goal, it is vital to be clear about the thing or things to be explained, the explanandum or explananda of our subject. So linguists must distinguish between two senses of 'language'. One is the biologically given human faculty of language. This faculty is what constitutes the language-readiness of a normal newborn infant, prepared to absorb the torrent of experience assailing it from the buzz of conversation around it, and the associated activities, and after a few years to become a competent participant in this buzz and these activities. In this chapter, I will refer to this biologically given language faculty with a capitalized mass noun, 'Language'. The other sense of 'language' is any of the entities that historico-cultural processes have delivered to the world, that is, particular individual languages, such as Albanian, Dyirbal, Hmong, Navaho and Zulu. I will refer to them generically using a count noun, as in 'many languages' or 'this language'. Each language is a body of complex conventional behaviour (highly articulated spoken and written buzz and associated activities) in a more or less clearly defined community. The conventionality of the behaviour implies that each participant has mentally internalized a collection of normal patterns much like that also learned by his fellows in the community.

Clearly, different kinds of explanation are needed for the biological faculty, Language, and the historico-cultural entities, languages. Just as clearly, the thumb-nail definitions of them I have started with make some tricky presuppositions and need further amplification. And to complicate things further, it turns out that the biological and historico-cultural processes are to a degree intertwined, in processes of gene-culture co-evolution. The necessary amplifications and added complexities will be touched on as we proceed.

As this chapter is largely targeted at linguists, it will be useful to carve linguistics near to its commonly understood natural joints, so without too much revision of the usually assumed boundaries, it will be possible to deal with, for example, evolutionary semantics, evolutionary pragmatics and evolutionary phonetics. Equally, but calling on different explanatory mechanisms, and discussed in less detail here, one may distinguish evolutionary phonology and evolutionary morphosyntax. Any revision of boundaries is motivated by the distinction between different modes of explanation, biological and historico-cultural. I will take as biologically given to each normal newborn human the semantic, pragmatic and phonetic prerequisites of the Language faculty. Filling that out a bit, and still roughly speaking, the semantic prerequisites for Language include a faculty for concept formation, mental representation of propositions about the world, and computation of inference, the pragmatic prerequisites include a disposition to cooperative engagement with others and an ability to guess their intentions rather accurately, and the phonetic prerequisites include coordination of the acoustic patterns of speech with the motor control necessary for producing and decoding articulate sounds. All this, and more, has to be in place in a baby if it is to become a fluent speaker of its group's language. And all this had to be in place, at least in some rudimentary form, in the earliest hominin ancestors of *Homo sapiens*, otherwise Language as we know it would not have evolved. We will see small evolutionary seeds of these prerequisites for Language in the behaviour of non-human animals, more or less directly genetically related to humans.

By contrast, the complex morphosyntactic and phonological structures of individual languages are the products of centuries, in most cases many millennia, of culturally transmitted, and culturally enhanced, patterns of behaviour. A child experiences the behaviour of older people already regularly using and productively combining established words and constructions, and begins to use and productively combine the same words and constructions, perhaps with some tiny idiosyncratic innovations, which may or may not survive to be passed on in future generations. This conceives of evolutionary morphosyntax and evolutionary phonology as largely matters of cultural evolution, successive waves of learning and cumulating small innovations. There can be no doubt that, in the long view of prehistory at least back to the emergence of our species, the syntactic and phonological complexities that we see in languages today emerged out of something simpler. At the end of this chapter, I will very briefly argue that we can speculate rather confidently about what such simpler proto-forms of languages were like.

In this introductory delineation of the different mechanisms called on to explain Language and languages, we immediately see an instance of the phenomena studied by linguistics beginning to make sense in the light of evolution, as they would not if evolution were not considered. The rest of this chapter will discuss each of the branches of linguistics in suitable, biological or cultural, evolutionary terms.

Niko Tinbergen suggested four questions that need to be answered in seeking explanations for any biological phenomenon. These questions can be posed of the human faculty of Language, in the following ways.

2.1.1 Mechanism

How does the organism work? What are its parts and how do they interact with each other? Specifying the mechanism of languages is an interdisciplinary enterprise, in which linguists, psycholinguists and neuroscientists must collaborate. Linguists describe languages in terms specially developed, often over many centuries, for the specific task of describing languages, terms such as 'noun', 'verb', 'clause', 'passive', etc. Such terms are not part of the vocabulary of psychology, neuroscience or biology. Linguists' descriptions, quite abstracted from neural mechanisms, are nevertheless intended to be 'psychologically real' in the sense that neural correlates will presumably eventually be found for the parts of the linguist's descriptions. Some subtlety and skill will no doubt be involved in mapping the linguist's abstractions onto neural processes. Certainly, naive localization of 'addresses' in the brain where, for example, nouns 'can be found', is to be avoided. The more plausibly a neurological interpretation of the linguist's descriptions can be defined, the greater the psychological justification of the linguist's original descriptive apparatus. It is assumed that the mechanisms underlying all individual languages are significantly similar. When a person uses a language, mechanisms of both storage and computation are involved. Words and constructions are summoned up from memory, and in production combined by the brain into more or less complex structures. In language recognition, the same memory store is used, and the brain analyses received complex input, mapping it onto understandings of what was said, or even of what the speaker intended. All such specifically linguistic mechanisms collaborate in the brain with more language-peripheral processes, such as understanding and management of the social and physical context.

2.1.2 Function

What does the organism do? In the case of languages, they serve both for public communication between people and to some extent for the facilitation of private thought. It needs to be shown how the mechanism, the parts of a language and their workings, are applied to carry out these functions. The study of how precisely language facilitates private thought, relying on some independent characterization of what thought itself consists of, is challenging, and as yet little developed. It is the domain of linguists, psycholinguists and neuroscientists, with the possibility of some useful input from philosophers. The study of how languages serve communication is rather less challenging, just because communication is public. Philosophy, linguistics and even folk theories converge on ideas relevant to the communicative functions of language, ideas such as reference to objects and events, speech acts, and information structure. Parts of language (e.g. common nouns, verbs and adjectives) denote classes of objects and events, other parts (e.g. proper nouns and definite descriptions) pick out specific individuals, other parts (e.g. function words) serve as traffic signals to a hearer helping the parsing of an utterance, other parts (e.g. interrogative markers) signal what speech act is being carried out.

2.1.3 Ontogeny

How does the organism develop in an individual? In biology, this is the province of embryology, charting the route from a single cell to an adult organism. Developmental linguistics, studying children's acquisition of languages, can hardly start so far back. There is no linguistic analogue of the single cell. Instead, developmental linguistics has to make do with the first behavioural signs of language in newborns. Even in neonates, there is evidence of the influence of experience in the womb, with babies apparently sensitive to the different types of rhythm found in languages. The different subsystems of languages, their phonology, syntax and lexicon, have different sensitive periods for their development. Accurate native-like pronunciation is extremely difficult to achieve after about ten years of age, much syntax can be acquired after that age, though with more effort than earlier, and the acquisition of new vocabulary can continue into late life. In all cases, complex developments are built upon simpler foundations. Children start with one-word utterances, proceed to two-word utterances, and then move on quite fast. Likewise with syllable structure, with consonant–vowel (CV) syllables being the basis upon which other more complex syllables are built. The progression from simple units to more complex ones is a necessity of the learning process. Complex cases cannot be learned without the prior learning of simpler building blocks.

2.1.4 Phylogeny

How has the organism evolved in its species? This, obviously, is the domain of any putative evolutionary linguistics. Evolutionary linguistics is less well developed than other aspects of the subject, partly for the very good reason that solid evidence about the evolution of the Language faculty is hard to come by. Language leaves no fossils, in the sense of remnants of behaviour that can be dug up. Tinbergen was not concerned with any phylogeny other than the biological kind, the evolution of a species, as he was a biologist not concerned with human culture. Cultural transmission of behaviour in a group is far, far more developed in humans than in any other species. And human languages, in particular, are unique in life on Earth as complex culturally evolved artefacts. It seems reasonable to stretch Tinbergen's heading of Phylogeny to include the cultural evolution of languages as well as the biological evolution of the Language faculty. In speculating about the early evolution of syntactic and phonological systems, it is reasonable to give some attention to Haeckel's maxim that 'ontogeny recapitulates phylogeny'. That is, what is seen early in child language development is also likely to have occurred early in the emergence of the first languages in our species, probably around 150,000 years ago. There is no logical necessity for ontogeny to recapitulate phylogeny, and sometimes it does not. But the principle of simpler beginnings being the foundation for more complex structures also applies in phylogeny. In the case of language, modern children have the advantage of learning an existing system. For the phylogenetic story we wish to tell, the focus is necessarily on innovations not drawn from any existing system. Cases where modern children naturally come up with expressions that are not found in the ambient adult language are likely to be especially valuable as clues to the innovative possibilities that have driven the cultural evolution of languages.

2.2 Evolutionary semantics

Semantics deals with what Halliday (1973) usefully called 'ideational' meaning. Among other things, this concerns the denotations of predicating words, the referents of referring expressions, the combinations of these into meaningful propositions, and relations of valid inference among propositions. The evolutionary question is: where did this stuff come from? Naturally assuming that these are not metaphysical or Platonic entities, we take a mentalist approach to the question. That is, we suppose that relations between words in a language and things in the external world are mediated by mental representations in the heads of language users. A mentalist approach to predicates, reference and propositions is outlined in more detail just below.

Predicate words, like *person, red, run, hit, give* and *above* are linked to entrenched concepts in users' minds, and these concepts in turn relate to entities, properties and relations in the outside world. In describing something as red, for example, a speaker judges that the referent matches a certain range of the colour spectrum categorically defined in his mind, and distinguished there from other regions of the spectrum, denoted by other colour terms. Likewise, one carries a mental distinction between what counts as a person and, say, a rock or a tree. To a large extent, such mental categories are formed and kept distinct by nonlinguistic, perceptual experience of the world, although what words are appropriate to label them is, of course, a matter of linguistic experience. Imagine you are watching birds out of your window. You see various different repeating types, and perhaps note their different habits. You can do this without knowing what the different bird types are called. Likewise with flowers, trees, spicy tastes, smells, various sounds of nature, many of which you can recognize and keep distinct, without knowing their names. Thus, we assume that there exist mental acts of categorical judgement independent of any sentences in a language that might express predication. It is reasonable to call such judgements acts of 'nonlinguistic predication'. The qualification should be enough to satisfy any who insist on keeping predication pure and simple as a solely linguistic phenomenon. Mentally categorizing individual objects with their properties is relatively simple. Judging relationships between objects is more complex, obviously, because it involves more objects. Judging two objects to be of the same, or different, category involves first making individual judgements about each separate object, then mentally comparing the judgements arrived at. Another more abstract predication is that expressed, for example, by *Red is a colour*. This is more abstract because redness is a first-order property (predicate) of objects, such as ripe cherries and cricket balls, and being a colour is a second-order property (predicate) applicable to redness, along with blueness, greenness, etc. It is not clear whether this latter type of abstract predication is available to us independently of language. But, given language, it certainly is.

The most basic referring expressions, deictic terms such as *this* and *that*, in typical uses, are the linguistic expressions of mental indices provided by the attention system. These indices are temporarily linked to whatever object or event in the world an individual happens to be attending to at the time of use. The attention mentioned can be effected through any of the senses, but typically through vision and audition, which provide the possibility of joint attention by different individuals. Thus, if I say 'What's that?', I have some visual or auditory stimulus temporarily in mind, an uncategorized sight or a sound, referred to by the pronoun *that*, and I assume that my interlocutor can figure out from her own ongoing experience of the world which sight or sound I am asking about. The next time someone asks 'What's that?', it will almost certainly be about a different sight or sound, to which the speaker has attached a temporary mental index, again expressed in use as *that*. In the terms adopted here, acts of paying attention to things are mental acts of reference. Attention to something need not be accompanied by any linguistic act.

Less basic, non-deictic referring expressions, such as *The vicar's cat* or *Kevin* pick out individuals in the world by virtue of the user having a mental representation of the individual concerned as unique in its context of use. Each time someone uses *the vicar's cat* they may well be talking of a different animal or even a different vicar. But if communication is successful, the mental representations that users have of these referents are clear and well separated in their minds from other kinds of things, such as dogs and kangaroos. My mental representation of a particular animal, whom you or I might choose on some occasion to call *the vicar's cat*, and on another occasion *Kevin*, is distinct in my mind from my representation of other entities, whom people might call *the professor's dog* or *Amelia*. A person knows a whole lot of entities, their properties and behaviour, and this knowledge is largely, though not entirely, independent on language.

In logic, propositions are composed from two types of term, a predicating term and one or more referring terms. (A seldom discussed exception is the simplest type of proposition, with no referring terms, such as propositions about the weather, as expressed, for example, in *It's raining*.) Thus, for instance, *That is a cat* and *Kevin is furry* both express propositions. Propositions are sometimes identified as facts about a world, existing somehow independent of knowers and language. Taking a mentalistic view, a proposition is a mental combination of a category and a mental index. The index is the mental referent, the category the mental predicate. We can know propositions, without ever having expressed them in language, even subvocally. For instance, I know that a certain sort of grey caterpillar habitually munches a certain kind of plant in my garden, but I do not know the names of either caterpillar or plant. Oops, now I have just expressed that proposition linguistically, albeit with circumlocution, but before I did, I knew the proposition independently of language, an observed fact about those caterpillars and those plants. There surely are some facts (propositions) about the world that are either unobservable or ineffable, or both. We will never know everything, let alone be able to say it. Obviously, from the point of view of language, we are only interested in such propositions as can in principle be expressed in language.

Not only do we hold propositions in our heads, we can also manipulate them in chains of inference. If you know that Kevin is a cat, you know he is a quadrupedal mammal. More complexly, if you know Kevin is tougher than Amelia, my cat, and that Amelia is tougher than Sherman, my creampuff dog, then you also know that Kevin is tougher than Sherman. This shows that you can do transitive inference, among many other kinds of inferential calculations involving propositions.

Now, to repeat the evolutionary question: where did this stuff come from? Having taken a mentalist viewpoint, we cannot shrug the question off by assuming that, ever since the Big Bang, referents, predicates and propositions always existed, timelessly, even though there were not always brains adequate to entertain them. Their mental correlates have only existed for as long as there have been brains powerful enough to house and process the corresponding neural representations. At least, the existence of brains, or central nervous systems of some kind, is a convenient starting point here, though it is debatable. We cannot yet push our evolutionary question further back than the emergence of brains, say to protozoa. And even the emergence of brains does not necessarily immediately give rise to the type of fully-fledged semantic mental representations that are a basis for language.

The availability of mental indices for variable and versatile attachment to objects of attention is a prerequisite for dealing practically with the world, in any somewhat advanced animal. An animal manipulating, say, a stick, to fish termites out of a mound is attending to the stick and the hole in the mound. At other times, say when grooming another ape, the attentional indices may be linked to particular patches of skin and lice therein. A chimp spotting a louse in its friend's fur makes a judgement about the thing it has seen – not a freckle, not a hair, but a louse, worth catching. Such instances are fleeting, but are the basis for more permanent mental representations. A social animal that recognizes particular fellow troop members and behaves differentially and systematically toward them, e.g. by bullying them, or avoiding them, or grooming them, has formed somewhat permanent mental indices of particular individuals. In truth as well as proverb, elephants never forget. What this means, at the least, is that elephants can preserve, over many years, representations of particular individuals, who have behaved either well or badly toward them, be they humans or other elephants. Long-term memory for individual objects, linked to their significant properties, is uncontroversial among mammals and birds. Non-human animals (apart from honey-bees) do not communicate to each other about things distant in space and time, but they do clearly have memories about things distant in space and time. Starting to communicate about what they remember and know is another matter.

A more complex type of memory than memory for objects and their properties, a memory for specific events involving several individuals, is more debatable. This is known as episodic memory, and was once claimed to be unique to humans. It is the kind of memory impaired in some amnesics. Clearly, humans have a far greater capacity than other animals for remembering and recalling events from the past. Experiments with a wide range of animals, including apes, and some birds (scrub jays in particular) have shown that they have the ability to remember for a short time events they have observed or in which they have participated. A chimpanzee called Panzee was able to signal to a trainer the location of a kiwi fruit that another trainer had hidden the day before. Scrub jays have been shown to remember where they cached perishable food, and only to retrieve it if not too much time has elapsed since it was cached. By contrast they remember where non-perishable food was cached and go back to it after longer periods. As the researchers put it, the scrub jays remember the what (perishable/non-perishable food), the where (the caching spots), and the when (how long ago) of the caching events. Of course, human capacity for remembering events is much more far-reaching, in time, space and the kind of events recalled. But the existence of some kind of episodic memory in other animals, however simple, shows that this aspect of the mental representation of facts about the world is quite ancient, possibly dating from the emergence of birds and mammals, or possibly having evolved separately several times since.

Many non-human animals clearly engage in some degree of advance planning of their actions. This can involve representation of places, movements, objects and possibly planned complex events. Animals do not confuse planning of future actions with memories of past actions, although the actions themselves may be of the same type. Thus, an implicit understanding of the difference between past and future is attributable to non-human animals. Surely, this should be no surprise.

As for somewhat complex predications, those involving sameness or difference, a very wide range of animals has been shown to be capable of making same/different judgements. Some animals, for example one California sea lion, remembered a same/different task it had been trained on ten years earlier. Among symbol-trained animals, Alex the African grey parrot was capable of the kind of abstract judgement involved in *Red is a colour*. This is clear because experimenters would show Alex an object, and ask *What colour is this?* and he would reply, as appropriate, *red* or *blue*, etc. Note that the question was not the first-order question *Is this red?*, but relied on Alex making the mental connection between the perceived redness of some object, and the higher-level 'fact' that red is a colour. Now, Alex had been taught a set of language-like symbols, spoken words in his case. It has not yet been shown that any non-human animal is capable of this kind of second-order predication independent of having learned some overt symbols for the first-order predicates, e.g. *red*, *blue*.

Non-human animals are capable of a degree of computation involving the propositions they know. Social monkeys, such as baboons, know the pecking order of their troop in detail. They know, for any given pair of animals, which is dominant to which. It is likely that this knowledge is partly learned by direct experience of acts of aggression and submission, but also partly by transitive inference. The baboon thinks something like 'X submitted to Y, and Y submitted to Z, so X would submit to Z', even though it has not observed any interaction between X and Z. This capacity has been attributed to chickens as well.

An interesting experimental task involves reversal learning. An animal is first taught specific connections between two stimuli and two responses. Of course, many animals can be trained in such tasks, though their speed of learning differs considerably. Then the connection between stimuli and responses is deliberately reversed. So whereas previously it was correct to press bar X in response to stimulus A, and bar Y for stimulus B, now the new required connections are X for B and Y for A. Animals adapt to this reversal with differing degrees of aplomb. There is a significant difference between apes and (most) monkeys. For monkeys, the better they have learned the first set of connections, the more trouble they have in unlearning it and picking up the new connections. For apes, by contrast, the better they have learned the first set of connections, the quicker they adapt to the new task. A plausible explanation is that the apes, but not the monkeys, have formed a mental rule, and are able to apply an oppositeness operator to what they had first learned. Informally, 'Ah, I see, it's the opposite of what I was taught before'. Apes are genetically closer to humans than monkeys, and this difference in their learning abilities probably reflects an evolutionary development in our lineage toward more abstract mental computation.

In sum, much of the basis of human semantics is already present, though to a simpler degree in non-human animals. Non-human animals have somewhat rich mental representations of the world. They just do not communicate these to others. Communication with others is a matter for pragmatics, not evolutionary semantics, as here defined. The first steps in the evolution of our semantic abilities, taken long before the emergence of our own species, involved developing the mental capacity to store and compute with simple propositions, even somewhat abstract ones.

Of course, semantics to linguists is defined as the study of meaning in languages. So the linguist may feel cheated at this point in that I have traced the origins of semantics to a stage before language. I have identified meanings that get conveyed by words and sentences as private mental entities pre-existing the public application of labels to them for purposes of communication. The process of developing a communal shared vocabulary to describe communally shared types of experience is straightforward, and has been simulated in many computer models. This social process requires, of course, the prior existence of individuals with the apparatus for representing meanings, as outlined above, plus some cooperative disposition to communicate meanings.

In a significant minority of cases, meanings of words are the product of, not the precondition for, the social naming process. These include cases of technically defined words, such as *dodecahedron*, *hundred* and *thousand*. The exact concept of a hundred is not accessible without language, specific words with simpler meanings, such as *two*, *hands* and *ten*. We are explicitly taught that a hundred is ten tens. Once the concept of a hundred is established, a further linguistic definition of *thousand* is possible. So the evolution of some aspects of the meaning in languages is a matter of cultural evolution, far less ancient than the biological evolution of the basic capacities I have discussed above, and postdates the emergence of some language.

2.3 Evolutionary pragmatics

Halliday (1973) distinguished ideational meaning from interpersonal meaning and rhetorical meaning. The latter two belong in what is now gathered together under pragmatics, whose central topics include the theories of speech acts, implicature and information structure. Speech act theory, starting from J.L. Austin's work (1975 [1962]), emphasizes that when we speak we not only describe aspects of the world, but we also attempt to do things to the hearer, to influence her mind or his behaviour in some way. The theory of implicature, due originally to Paul Grice (1975), explains how apparently illogical assertions can nevertheless usefully convey meaning, because hearers are able to infer conclusions based on a premise of cooperativeness. The working out of implicatures, like the interpretation of indirect speech acts, involves a degree of mind-reading by interlocutors, the making of assumptions about what each party is likely to know and to want to know. Information structure is the way propositional information is presented. The same proposition can be expressed in a great variety of different ways, tuned to the assumed shared knowledge and conversational goals of the hearer. How ancient are our abilities to handle and interpret speech acts, to manipulate and interpret implicatures, and to structure the way information is presented? As in the case of semantics, the seeds of the necessary human abilities in two of these areas, speech acts and implicature, are not unique to us, but are present in many non-human animals, especially those closely related to us. Thus the evolution of much of pragmatics has ancient roots, pre-dating the emergence of *Homo sapiens*. The development of information structure is more recent, co-evolving with the rise of somewhat complex syntax in languages.

Many animals communicate, even those very distantly related to us, such as insects. With a tiny number of exceptions, all such communication is dyadic, in the sense of only involving two parties, the sender and the receiver of the communication. Most animal communication is not triadic, in the sense of involving some third entity in the outside world being communicated about. Vervet monkey alarm calls, along with the alarm calls of other monkeys and many species of bird, are triadic, in that they are triggered by entities outside the sender and receiver(s), namely the predator in question. Some primates also give food calls, indicating the presence of various types of food. None of these triadic calls are, as far as we know at present, learned. Rather, they are almost entirely innate, in the sense of being made by the animals without any prior learning experience. The slight reservation here is due to the fact that vervet babies do refine the category of predator to which they give alarm calls during their early life. The honey-bee waggle dance, also triadic, in indicating the whereabouts of food, is entirely innate, too. Humans are the only (non-captive) species who learn triadic signals. And we learn tens of thousands of them. Captive animals, from chimpanzees and dogs to parrots, can learn small vocabularies of referring words, but this ability is never exploited in the wild. Part of the story of the evolution of Language is the emergence of this impressive human learning ability.

In dyadic communication, an animal does something to another, be it threatening, submitting, expressing solidarity, keeping in touch with the group or inviting mating, for example. These acts do not describe or refer to anything outside the sender or receiver. Thus they are analogous to bare illocutionary expressions in human languages, such as *Hello, Whoa!, Ugh!* and *Bye*. All languages have expressions of this bare illocutionary dyadic kind. Indeed, in any language, all utterances addressed to a hearer are made with the intention, on the part of the speaker, to affect the hearer in some way, be it to warn him, to congratulate her, to advise him, to cheer her up, or to insult him. Why else would anyone speak to another, if not to achieve some effect? (Occasional solipsistic use of language, as when one mutters to oneself, clearly does not deliberately affect another person, but such uses are plausibly derivative of public utterances.) This pervasive doing-things-to-each-other aspect of using a language builds upon similar communicative acts by our remote non-human ancestors. Since human communication took on its mainly triadic function, with the vast majority of utterances involving reference to one or more entities outside the speaker and hearer, a greater range of illocutionary acts have become possible. Only with complex language, for example, can one make a promise, apologize explicitly for a misdeed, formally name a ship, or perform a legal marriage.

The direct illocution of an utterance is coded in its syntactic structure. Thus, English sentences in interrogative form, with inverted subject and auxiliary, have as their direct illocution the posing of a question, soliciting information. Often, however, the indirect illocution in uttering such a sentence may be other, such as to request an action (e.g. *Can you pass the salt?*) or point out the obviousness of some fact (e.g. *Is the Pope Catholic?*), and

How are you?, merely used as a routine greeting, and so forth. Some such cases are conventional and idiomatic, but others require some mind-reading on the part of the hearer. More generally, human language users are capable of drawing indirect conclusions from what is said, where these conclusions are not explicitly coded in what was said. This is implicature. If a mother asks her child *Have you done your homework and tidied your room?* and the child answers only *Well, I've done my homework*, the mother can reasonably conclude that the child has not tidied his room. Coming to this conclusion involves some rather complex reasoning, including making assumptions about what the child might have said if he had indeed tidied his room. The mother, like other language users, depends on knowing what is in the mind of another speaker, a kind of (non-telepathic) mind-reading.

Non-human animals can to some degree read the minds of others. 'Mind-reading' is not to be taken in any mystical sense. It involves being able to assess the intentions of others and predict their likely behaviour. In well-controlled experiments, chimpanzees have been shown to judge accurately where a dominant competitor is likely to go. In other experiments, chimps have been shown able to distinguish between when a human interactor is teasing them or merely fumbling, when the two actions are minimally distinct visually. Mind-reading in this sense involves a certain kind of self-knowledge. Thus chimpanzees are able to infer behaviour in others just where their own behaviour would be similar. For instance, chimpanzees are generally competitive and less cooperative than humans, and chimps are much better at reading another's competitive intentions than they are at anticipating a cooperative action. None of this, of course, involves language of any kind, but such mind-reading is at the heart of any account of how humans interpret the utterances of others, whether through calculating implicatures or getting to the indirect illocutions of speech acts. Human capacities in these domains has built upon pre-existing capacities in pre-human ancestors. Doubtless, we are better and subtler at it than our ancestors were, let alone our chimpanzee cousins.

Humans are naturally more disposed to cooperate with fellow members of their group than other species. Unless cruelly repressed, children show an instinctive drive to join in communicative exchanges. At first, not having learned the complex wherewithal, i.e. the necessary vocabulary and grammar, they resort to pointing. A remarkable difference between human infants and chimpanzees is that human toddlers spontaneously point to things merely, apparently, to share joint attention – 'Look!' In the wild, chimpanzees never point at things, and in captivity, they only point for the purpose of begging something from a human: even in captivity, chimpanzees do not point for fellow chimpanzees. This human characteristic has been labelled 'shared intentionality'.

The rhetorical manipulation of information in languages is manifested in the availability of a wide range of sentence structures, intonation patterns and lexical choices. There are literally dozens of different ways of presenting the proposition that a lorry crushed a car, depending on what has just been said in the conversation and where a speaker wants the conversation to go next. The syntactic devices used in English include passivization, topicalization, *What*-cleft sentences, *It*-cleft sentences, and combinations of all these. Examples are *It was the lorry that crushed the car, As for the car, it was what was crushed by the lorry*. Some such combinations are cumbersome, but English makes them available, and one can think of conversational contexts in which they would be appropriate. Children learn to control such complex cases late, pidgin languages lack such grammatical complexity, and it is reasonable to suppose that the growth of such devices was at least somewhat gradual, with the earliest languages of our species having few or none of them.

2.4 Evolutionary phonetics

Without concepts to express, and without the social motivation to express them, Language would not have got started. The speech medium is not absolutely crucial for the expression of complex meanings, as well-developed sign languages exist, with a similar expressive range to spoken languages. It is likely that the very earliest external forms of human language incorporated manual gestures, and the move to almost total dominance of speech followed over the millennia. Chimpanzees have great manual dexterity, under voluntary cortical control, and have nothing of the delicate vocal articulatory control that humans show in speech. The brain areas, predominantly left hemisphere, involved in complex language are close to the areas managing gestures with the dominant right hand. Gestures can be much more easily used in iconic, easily interpretable, ways to communicate actions and the shapes of objects, whereas the iconicity of speech is limited to a few natural sounds, mainly a small range of animal calls, e.g. *miau*, *moo*. Thus if modern languages were universally signed, rather than spoken, there would be little to explain about the medium itself. Given concepts to express, and the will to express them, manually gestured communication would emerge quite naturally from the dexterity of our primate ancestors, and their facility in deliberately using them. The primate visual system needs no special adaptation to perceive manual gestures.

Of course, speech has its advantages too. It can be used in the dark, with one's back to an interlocutor, and around corners. Another important advantage of speech is its apparent uselessness for any other purpose. A waving gesture might be interpreted as not carrying any meaning, but just waving insects away. A touch of the fingers to the cheek could be fixing an itch. Rubbing the hands together could be for generating some warmth. For a full sign language to emerge, a division must be established between practical non-communicative movements and conventionally meaningful ones. This can happen, as the emergence of natural sign languages shows. But speech, being pretty much useless for any practical non-communicative purpose, is likely to be taken as expressing meaning from the start, given suitable expectation that the actor could well be trying to say something meaningful. Speech rather naturally signals its own signalhood.

The evolution of articulate speech from primate vocalizations is a much greater step than the evolution of manual gestures. Our nearest primate relatives can manage essentially nothing in the speech domain. But some brain basis for the later evolution of meaningful speech is found in the fact that monkeys and apes generally process the meaningful calls of conspecifics in their left hemispheres, rather than bilaterally, as with other sounds. Over the roughly six million years since humans diverged from chimpanzees, the human vocal tract, and our complex control over it has evolved significantly. The main changes identified in the literature are: (1) lowering of the larynx in humans; (2) development of breath control; and (3) development of fine articulatory control. In addition, there are some small differences between human and chimpanzee hearing that reflect a likely adaptation to the range of vocal sounds that humans began to make. We will briefly deal with each of these.

The human larynx, almost but not quite uniquely among mammals, is low down in the vocal tract, relatively far from the junction of the oral and nasal passages. Thus in most mammals, any vibration initiated by the larynx only has the mouth chamber, or less importantly the nasal passages, to resonate through. With the human larynx far down in the neck, vibrations are channelled through a more complex L-shaped tube, first the pharynx, in the throat behind the tongue, and then outward through the mouth. It is this double resonator tract that makes it possible to produce different vowel qualities. A high front [i] vowel is produced with a widened pharynx and a narrowed mouth chamber, as the tongue body is pushed upward and forward. Contrastingly, a low back [a] vowel is produced with a narrowed pharynx and a widened oral cavity, the tongue being drawn downward and backward. In between these two extreme vowels, a range of other vowel qualities are available by different intermediate positions of the tongue and lower jaw. Rather prehensile lips also help to increase the acoustic variety that the human vocal tract is capable of; chimpanzees share prehensile lips with us, but the range of vowel-like qualities producible with only alteration of lip protrusion is limited. Over the last six million years the position of the adult human larynx has lowered from that typical of our closest relatives.

Although, as mentioned earlier, ontogeny does not necessarily recapitulate phylogeny, in the case of the position of the larynx, it does. The larynxes of human newborns are high up just behind the velum, where the oral and nasal passages meet, as in most adult mammals. This position allows the baby to breathe and suckle at the same time. In the first six months of life, the baby's larynx descends to nearer its eventual adult position, in this case recapitulating phylogeny. The timing during human evolution of the larynx's descent is hard to pin down, as soft tissue does not fossilize. But indirect evidence from the hyoid bones of Neanderthals suggests that this descent was in place in the common ancestor of humans and Neanderthals, dated tentatively to half a million years ago, and perhaps as much as a million years ago. The hyoid bone sits in the throat above the larynx, which it partially supports.

Breathing during speech is heavily imbalanced between in-breaths and out-breaths. While speaking, we breathe out in a highly controlled manner for about 90 per cent of the time, with quick pauses for inhalation. Fine control of breathing is mediated by the chest and stomach muscles. It is likely that this degree of control was made possible by bipedalism, which frees the upper torso from dependence on bracing the chest to take the impact of moving on the front limbs. Chimpanzee 'laughter' is a rhythmic see-sawing in-and-out breathing vocalization, with as much time on the in-breath as the out-breath. But human laughter, like human speech, is all on an out-breath, even though it has a similar rhythm to chimp 'laughter'. The Australopithecines of four million years ago walked bipedally, so this facilitating relaxation of constraints paving the way for an aspect of speech was in place very early in our evolution. Studies of the diameter of the vertebral canal, through which the nerves to the chest muscles pass, in modern specimens and in fossils, confirm that Neanderthals could have had similar breath control to modern humans, in contrast to *Homo erectus* and Australopithecines. Human operation of the vocal articulators, the tongue, jaw and velum, in coordination with well-controlled vibration of the vocal cords, is very delicate. Some speculative studies have attempted to relate this to the size of the hypoglossal canals, the little holes in the base of the skull through which nerves serving the tongue and jaw pass. Here, it has not been possible to identify any significant differences between modern humans, hominin ancestors and related primates. The era when fine control of the vocal articulators emerged has yet to be determined.

Human hearing is in most respects very similar to chimpanzee hearing, but there are small differences, relevant for sensing nuances of vowel quality. The most salient difference is that in the region of about 34000 Hz, chimpanzee auditory acuity is significantly poorer than human acuity. This acoustic region is important for the recognition of high front vowels such as [i] and [e], whose second formants are typically near this frequency. At some point since the chimp–human split, we developed acuity in this frequency range, and this could well be an adaptation to the range of vowels the human vocal tract, with its lowered larynx, is capable of.

2.5 Evolutionary morphosyntax and phonology

The previous sections have dealt exclusively with factors delivered by biological evolution, facilitating the subsequent cultural evolution of complex languages. In this final section, I will deal, more briefly, with the cultural evolution of the complex grammatical and phonological patterns that occupy descriptive linguists.

For the cultural evolution of languages to begin and continue, certain biological capacities had to be in place and to grow. The complex syntax of any language requires that individual speakers have a powerful storage capacity for the large vocabulary of basic items it combines. And individual speakers also need the computing power to recursively combine words and constructions up to quite impressive (though of course not infinite) levels of embedding. These capacities for vast storage and complex computation, aspects of Language, are not learned but encoded somehow in the DNA determining the growth patterns of the modern species. It is likely that during the cultural evolution of complex languages from simple beginnings over the past 150,000 years, these biologically given capacities also expanded somewhat, under pressure from the growing practices of the groups using the languages concerned. Co-evolution of genes and culture is well attested in cases outside L/language, and in fact it can happen very fast. The evolution of lactose tolerance in pastoral groups over at most 20,000 years is a case in point. Over many centuries, languages grew more complex grammars, and correspondingly, due to the great practical advantages of language, facility for managing such complexity grew in human brains.

Languages are not all equally complex in their grammar. This is now widely accepted, contrary to a long-standing dogma in linguistics. Simpler grammar does not necessarily entail poorer powers of expression. Some complexities of grammar contribute little or nothing to actual expressive power, as telegraphic language (e.g. newspaper headlines) testifies. And there is always a flexible negotiation between how much information is carried explicitly in the coded norms of a language and how much can safely be left to pragmatic inference from context.

Complex grammar arises by grammaticalization. This much is a tautology. Grammaticalization is simply the historical process by which grammar grows. Here, we can break grammaticalization down into two separate but closely related processes. By one process, a distinction emerges between function words and content words, and the set of function words expands, with concomitant increase in the range of different grammatical constructions signalled by these function words. By another process, free words get shortened and phonologically bound to content words, giving rise to the phenomenon of inflection. Rich inflectional systems have traditionally been the hallmark of complex grammar. I will give a few examples.

The growth of new function words can be seen nowadays in the emergence of creoles from pidgins. As pidgins and creoles borrow from a superstrate language, the origins of novel function words can be seen quite transparently. For example, in Tok Pisin, the English-based creole of Papua New Guinea, the form *bilong* functions roughly like the English prepositions *of* and *for*, linking nominal expressions as in *nambawan pikinini bilong misis kwin* 'first child of Mrs Queen'. The English source word *belong* is a content word, a main verb, not a function word. Tok Pisin, being a relatively new language, in fact only has two function words, in some analyses, the other one being *long*, also grammaticalized from an English content word, an adjective as it happens. With fewer function words than, for example, English, it is fair to say that in this respect Tok Pisin has less grammar. It is not so far along the cultural evolutionary scale that leads to languages with greater numbers of function words. As function words are closely associated with their own peculiar constructions, a language with fewer function words also has fewer distinct grammatical constructions. It seems an inevitable conclusion that the trajectory of complexification of languages has followed a similar path from the earliest beginnings of languages.

The other grammaticalization process that I have identified, namely the rise of inflections from independent words, can also be conveniently illustrated from Tok Pisin. Adjectives, numerals and demonstratives are marked in Tok Pisin by a suffix *pela*, as in *bigpela* 'big', *tupela* 'two' and *dispela* 'this'. This suffix derives from the independent English word *fellow*. Among non-creole languages, in Romance languages a suffix marking an adverb derived from an adjective, as in French *heureusement*, is historically derived from the Latin free form *mente* 'mind'.

Over the past two millennia, the complexity of inflectional morphology has significantly declined in many languages. Well-known examples are modern English, which has lost most of the inflections of Old English, and the Romance languages, which have lost most of the inflectional complexity of Latin. This might seem to be a case of 'anti-grammaticalization', but the mechanisms of growth and loss of inflections are different. The rise of inflection is mediated by phonological erosion of frequently used forms, with the eroded forms being learned as new norms by children acquiring a language. A priority for young children is to conform to the communicative practices of their community, and children quickly learn to mimic adult inflected forms. A different learning situation exists when adults are thrown into strange language communities. Here the first priority is to communicate messages without necessarily conforming to the complex local rules, which are usually too difficult for an adult to master. A Turkish immigrant to Germany needing to buy milk, and knowing the basic content words, can easily get her message across with the incorrect *Wo Milch kaufen?*, omitting the function words and inflections which would be present in an equivalent request from a native speaker.

To historical linguists of the nineteenth century, the loss of inflections in classical languages was a matter of decline, or loss of perfection. As such, it was a puzzle, unless one were of the pessimistic persuasion that all human behaviour was losing an earlier perfection. There was something of a Garden of Eden myth surrounding the complexities of the classical languages. The puzzle dissolves once one takes a broad view of the course of human history over the past ten millennia. During that recent era, the globe has become much more crowded with humans, who now have to rub up against each other in ways unprecedented during the previous age of isolated hunter-gatherer communities. Long-distance trade and warfare, and the rise of empires and cities inevitably bring adults with different native languages together, and the result is practical forms of communication adopted by adults whose priority is more to get messages across than to conform to the same niceties as their interlocutors. Language contact induces simplification of grammar. Pidgins are the classic and obvious example. Of course, the growth of complexity is not totally stifled, as children still grow up with parents speaking the same somewhat standardized language. But with increasing stirring of the mix of languages in a population, the languages themselves tend to lose the complexity that had been built up over millennia in which society was more stable and less prone to contact with foreigners.

A contrary effect of civilization on language complexity has occurred with the advent of writing, at least in literate people. Writing allows a reader more time to ponder the structure and meaning of a sentence. Hence the quantitative properties of language in use can be tolerably greater in writing than in speech. Sentences and phrases can be longer and there can be more degrees of embedding of subordinate clauses. Educated people start to use forms in speech that originally would have been characteristic of written language. It is socially impressive to talk like a book.

As in morphosyntax, a cline of complexity can also be seen in phonology. Where pidgins have few or no function words or inflections, they tend likewise to have simple CV syllable structure, and small phoneme inventories avoiding phonetic segments that are typically acquired later in normal acquisition. As with syntax and morphology, complexity of phonology grows over many generations in a stable population not influenced by the simplifying efforts of foreigners.

Summarizing this section, the complexity found in the grammar and phonology of extant languages has evolved by repeated cultural transmission of linguistic norms over many generations, with some reinterpretation by acquirers, leading to a ratcheting effect, so long as the language community is relatively stable. Bringing this whole chapter together, these recent evolutionary developments in complexity of grammar and phonology are built on a much more ancient foundation of cognitive and social evolution, allowing grasp of complex concepts (evolutionary semantics) and negotiation of cooperative social arrangements (evolutionary pragmatics).

Further reading

Over the last twenty-five years, increasingly nuanced views of the origins and evolution of language have developed. This is reflected both in the successive works of individual authors, and in differences between later authors and earlier ones. There is typically now more recognition of the complex interaction and co-evolution of language-related genes and the cultural emergence of complex languages. Inevitably, due to the dominance of the generative paradigm in syntax in the late twentieth century, much writing on language evolution has pivoted around features of Chomsky's ideas, such as the centrality of syntactic competence, attributed to a genetically determined Universal Grammar (UG), not motivated by function and natural selection. Some authors have consistently argued against such ideas, e.g. Philip Lieberman, who stresses function and phonetic performance. Others have moved over the years from an essentially pro-generative idea that the human syntactic faculty results from catastrophic accidental changes in human DNA to a claim that syntactic ability, and advanced cognition in general, are the inevitable expected outcome of long-term evolution on any planet; this is Derek Bickerton's intellectual trajectory over more than thirty years, always pursued with great rhetorical vigour. Other authors, especially those writing in the present century, have tended to steer a careful course between the influences of nature and nurture; here I include, in their separate ways, Tecumseh Fitch, Sverker Johansson and myself, James R. Hurford. It is fair to say that writers from within psychology, broadly interpreted, have tended to be strongly opposed to nativist non-functionalist ideas emanating from the dominant paradigm in linguistics; among such psychologists, I include Michael Tomasello, Morten Christiansen and Michael Arbib.

A very useful regular and up-to-date service on recent developments in language evolution is provided by Martin Edwardes at his website named Evolutionary Anthropology Online Research Cluster (EAORC), at http://martinedwardes.webplus.net/eaorc.html. Some of the most salient recent books on language evolution are listed below.

Bibliography

Arbib, M. (2012) *How the Brain Got Language: The Mirror System Hypothesis*. New York: Oxford University Press.
Austin, J.L. (1975 [1962]) *How To Do Things With Words*, 2nd edition, ed. J.O. Urmson and M. Sbisà. Oxford: Oxford University Press.
Bickerton, D. (1981) *Roots of Language*. Ann Arbor: Karoma Press.

Bickerton, D. (1990) *Language and Species*. Chicago: University of Chicago Press.
Bickerton, D. (1996) *Language and Human Behavior*. Seattle: University of Washington Press.
Bickerton, D. (2009) *Bastard Tongues*. New York: Hill and Wang.
Bickerton, D. (2014) *More than Nature Needs*. Cambridge, MA: Harvard University Press.
Christiansen, M. and S. Kirby (eds) (2003) *Language Evolution*. Oxford: Oxford University Press.
Deacon, T. (1997) *The Symbolic Species: The Coevolution of Language and the Brain*. New York: W.W. Norton and Company.
Fitch, W.T. (2010) *The Evolution of Language*. Cambridge: Cambridge University Press.
Givón, T. (2002) *Bio-Linguistics: The Santa Barbara Lectures*. Amsterdam: John Benjamins.
Givón, T. (2009) *The Genesis of Syntactic Complexity*. Amsterdam: John Benjamins.
Grice, H.P. (1975) Logic and conversation. In P. Cole and J.L. Morgan (eds) *Syntax and Semantics 3: Speech Acts*, pp. 41–58. New York: Academic Press. Reprinted in H.P. Grice, *Studies in the Way of Words*. Cambridge: Harvard University Press. 1989, pp. 22–40.
Halliday, M.A.K. (1973) *Explorations in the Functions of Language*. London: Edward Arnold.
Heine, B. and T. Kuteva (2007) *The Genesis of Grammar: A Reconstruction*. Oxford: Oxford University Press.
Hurford, J.R. (2007) *The Origins of Meaning: Language in the Light of Evolution*. Oxford: Oxford University Press.
Hurford, J.R. (2012) *The Origins of Grammar: Language in the Light of Evolution*. Oxford: Oxford University Press.
Hurford, J.R. (2014) *The Origins of Language: A Slim Guide*. Oxford: Oxford University Press.
Johansson, S. (2005) *Origins of Language: Constraints on Hypotheses*. Amsterdam: John Benjamins.
Lieberman, P. (1975) *On the Origins of Language*. New York: Macmillan.
Lieberman, P. (1984) *The Biology and Evolution of Language*. Cambridge, MA: Harvard University Press.
Lieberman, P. (2000) *Human Language and Our Reptilian Brain*. Cambridge, MA: Harvard University Press.
Lieberman, P. (2006) *Toward an Evolutionary Biology of Language*. Cambridge, MA: Harvard University Press.
Tallerman, M. and K.R. Gibson (eds) (2012) *The Oxford Handbook of Language Evolution*. Oxford: Oxford University Press.
Tomasello, Michael (1999) *The Cultural Origins of Human Cognition*. Cambridge, MA: Harvard University Press.
Tomasello, Michael (2008) *Origins of Human Communication*. Cambridge, MA: MIT Press.

3

Gesture and sign

Utterance uses of visible bodily action

Adam Kendon

3.1 Introduction

When engaging in an utterance, humans move various parts of the body in many different ways. When we are dealing with utterances involving speech, speaking is usually conjoined with a diverse range of body movements: the head pivots, nods, shakes, sustains itself in one pose or another; the eyebrows may move up and down, they may be drawn together and lowered; the brow may wrinkle or become smooth; the eyelids may widen or narrow; the eyes may move in various directions; there are mouth and cheek movements overlaying those used for speaking; the hands may be lifted and moved in a variety of ways, engaging in many different sorts of actions; the speaker may shift bodily orientation, or re-arrange posture. Such movements, coordinated in several different ways and at several different levels with the flow of speech, tend to be seen as patterned with the rhythm of speaking and, as well, are deemed to have expressive significances that are usually regarded as somehow coherent in meaning with concurrent spoken expression. When used in collaboration with speech, as explained below, there is always a degree of semantic interaction with spoken expressions: kinesics and speech taken together provide a richer interpretation of the utterance's meaning than is possible when either modality is considered on its own.

In circumstances of co-presence when speech cannot be used – whether for environmental reasons (e.g. high noise level, people too far apart to speak or when speaking might be disturbing in some way), for ritual reasons (as in some European monastic communities or in some Australian aboriginal societies) or for physiological reasons (as in deafness) – humans will readily resort to using bodily actions to express themselves. In the right circumstances, given enough time and enough complexity in social interaction, shared communication systems using visible bodily actions become established. When these reach a certain level of complexity and generality of use, they may be referred to as *sign languages*. As this comes about, the actions employed may show structural and semiotic features not found in the speaker kinesics. For example, whereas a speaker may employ a certain pattern of action which shows that a question is being asked, if speech is not available kinesics must also take over the task of expressing what the question is about. That is, the actions used must take on the functions of content words. Vocabularies of kinesic actions develop, accordingly, which have content-word properties. Further, these enter into patterns of syntactic use and relationship not seen in speaker kinesics.

With regard to sign languages, especially those arising among deaf persons (*primary* sign languages, as they may be called, to distinguish them from the *alternate* sign languages developed in some speaker communities – see §3.5) work since the 1960s has shown that structurally, functionally and semiotically, they are comparable to spoken languages. Comparing the semiotics of kinesics in speakers with that of established sign languages can throw light on what distinguishes a system regarded as 'language' from one that is not. Furthermore, through comparative studies of kinesic communication systems, from simple signalling systems, such as those developed in specific situations, as between underwater divers, traders on the floor of a stock exchange, or factory workers who must coordinate work operations at a distance, and the more complex systems observed when speech is unusable on all occasions (either for ritual or physiological reasons), light may be thrown on the social interaction conditions within which kinesic systems develop and converge functionally with spoken language. There are established systems such as British Sign Language or American Sign Language which have recognition and documentation (such as dictionaries) similar to spoken languages. There are also systems that are local in their development, in some cases even confined to a single family. There have been a few cases where it has been possible to compare a shared kinesic communication system from one period of time to the next, as it is developing, and thus to observe how such a system comes into being and how its features change as it does so. Thus we are allowed to observe a process of language formation. This is of great interest in relation to questions about the origin and evolution of languages.

3.2 Kinesics in partnership with speech

As already said, when speakers speak, they may also move their head, face, eyes, shift posture and mobilise their hands in various actions. In modern work on speaker kinesics, overwhelmingly, attention has been paid to the hand actions. This is not very surprising. As the Spanish-Roman rhetorician Quintilian observed about two thousand years ago, 'the movements of the other portions of the body merely help the speaker, whereas the hands may almost be said to speak' (Quintilian 1922: Book XI, III: 85–7). In this way he expressed the common observation that it is the motions of the hands that seem to produce expressions most closely related in meaning to what is expressed in speech. Movement in the face, head and trunk are also a part of utterance action, but these contribute more to showing to whom an utterance is addressed, the display of feelings, emotions and attitudes, or to emphasis or to the parsing of speech in various ways. These non-manual aspects of speaker kinesics (also important in signing) have been much less studied. Here we deal mostly with the hand actions.

Speakers employ their hands when speaking in many different ways. However, there are three main kinds of usage: *pragmatic, deictic (pointing)* and *representational*. *Pragmatic* actions show the kind of 'speech act' or 'move' that a speaker is engaging in. Here we find negation, refusal or denial; affirmation, presenting, questioning, requesting; marking discourse focus, contrasting topic from comment; differentiating parts of a discourse as contrastive, continuative, repetitive; showing what is being said is hypothetical, imagined. Kinesic actions with these functions account for much of what speakers do with their hands when speaking. It was these functions that were of greatest interest to Quintilian, and to those who came after him, who dealt in detail with manual actions in speaking as part of the art of rhetoric. Many of the forms with these functions are widely shared and, indeed, even if they differ from one community or group to the next by local convention, they often show similar features. For example, lifting the shoulders together with an outward display of open hands, palms up, is widespread as an expression of doubt, unwillingness to commit; lifting the open hand with palm oriented away from the speaker is widespread as a form of negation; holding an open hand forward, palm up, slightly cupped, is commonly used when the speaker is offering or asking for an example; rotating the forearm outward to bring the hand to a palm-up orientation, despite many variations, is widespread as an expression in questioning.

Deictic (pointing) actions direct another's attention to something, refer to some object, feature or location by a movement that is directed toward it. Such directed movements can be done with almost any part of the body. When the hand is used, an extended index finger is often employed, but other hand shapes or digits (for example the thumb) may also be used, and this may have consequences for how the deictic reference is to be understood. However, pointing may be done with a directed movement of the head, by protruding the lips, by a directed movement of the elbow, by combining a wrinkling of the nose with a directed head or gaze orientation, and so on. There are cultural differences in which of these forms may be common. Lip pointing is used among Australian aborigines, in South-East Asia and among the Kuna of Panama, the 'nose-wrinkle' in pointing is reported from New Guinea. Pointing may be directed toward objects, persons, features or locations in the currently shared environment, but also to such objectives in an imagined environment, to locations in a notional space: for instance, a speaker may establish locations in a temporary space for characters in a story or contrasting positions in an argument, and point to these as a way of referring to them (Kendon 2004 Ch. 11; Sherzer 1972; Enfield 2001; Cooperrider and Núñez 2012).

Representational actions are when the speaker uses hands to evoke or to display features of objects, actions, qualities of motion, spatial relationships between objects and movements between locations, among other things, whether these are literal or metaphorical. Actions of this sort (referred to variously as 'iconic gestures', 'lexical gestures', 'imagistic gestures' – among other terms) are part of how a speaker represents the referential content of an utterance. There is much individual variation, however they tend to follow certain principles. For example, objects are commonly represented by the way the hand might grasp it, either as in using it or in holding it up for display. Shapes of objects are shown by sketching, outlining or sculpting movements. Trajectories in space may be done with tracing movements, with the extended index finger used as if it is a pencil or marker.

There are many different ways in which representational actions may be conjoined with words. For example, they can reveal the manner of action of a verb, which may otherwise be specified verbally; they can help to set limits on how an adjective is to be interpreted; they can refer to visual features of a scene, such as how different persons or objects in it are disposed spatially; they can be used to suggest the sizes, shapes or orientations of objects referred to. The coordinate employment of representational actions allows speakers to produce constructions simultaneously in spatial and temporal dimensions. The study of the way speakers do this is thought to throw light upon how thoughts to be expressed are represented mentally. This has consequences for theories about the conceptual foundations of language and the processes of utterance production. These themes have been a major focus in the study of gesture in relation to speech in recent decades (see Kendon 2004 Chs 9–10; McNeill 1992).

It should be understood that the three-way division of how speakers use their hands in discourse is not categorial. An action that has a directional component may at once point and represent. Speakers quite often, as they direct their hand toward something to refer to it, also move the hand to characterise its features. For example, a speaker pointing out a window of architectural interest, moves his extended index finger as he does so to describe its distinctive shape. Representational actions can be rhythmically organised in relation to speech so that they also serve emphasis functions. Manual kinesic expressions should thus be thought of as operating in a multidimensional functional space: a given expression is not categorised; rather, it is assessed in terms of how it may be positioned within this functional space (see Kendon 2004 Ch. 6 for a discussion).

3.3 Conventionalisation in speaker manual kinesics

The manual actions just discussed, especially those deemed representational, have often been regarded as spontaneous, idiosyncratic, improvised productions. Viewed in this manner they have been looked upon as if they might be direct 'read-outs' of mental images and have been studied for the light they might throw upon an individual's internal representations. However, as mentioned above, although there is a good deal of individual variation, it seems clear that, comparing the way in which different speakers use their hands in object or action depiction, there are practices which are shared in common. For example, using extended index fingers as if they are pencils to outline a shape, managing the hands as if they are holding or manipulating an object of a certain shape and dimension, using the hand as if it is a blade and moving it as if chopping or cutting, or practices in which the hands act as if they are holding, manipulating, using or outlining the shape of objects, or as if they themselves are an object (as the hand is shaped and moved as if it is a blade of a knife) are widely employed. It happens that such actions may come to be done in so routine a manner and are used to refer to objects that are of such common use, that they may come to be part of a shared vocabulary of kinesic expressions. For example, holding both hands forward, palms down, moving spread fingers rapidly up and down, for many people is an established way of referring to typing or to a computer; holding a fisted hand with little finger and thumb extended toward the ear is a way of referring to 'telephone' and the various activities involving its use; lifting up both hands formed as fists as if holding something, and moving them alternately up and down, is a way of referring to driving a car. These are well-known forms, widely used, and could be included in any list of such actions that are so conventionalised that they can be quoted upon request. Expressions of this sort have been called 'quotable gestures' or 'emblems'.

Observations also suggest that, in respect to such features as amplitude of action and manner, complexity and consistency of articulation, there may be broad differences between different cultural or language groupings. This is the conclusion suggested by a famous study by David Efron (1972). He observed gestural practices among immigrants in Manhattan, who were still using their original languages. He compared the gesturing of Yiddish-speaking East European Jews with those of Italian (mostly southern Italian) speakers and found marked differences. The gesturings of the Americanised descendants of these groups, however, did not show such differences. This confirmed that kinesic practices are culturally patterned. Furthermore, comparative studies of manual kinesic action in children suggest that older children are less idiosyncratic and more coherent than are younger children. As children mature they come to use their hands in gesturing in similar ways. Evidently employing the hands in utterance involves learning how to do this in ways that are appropriate for that use. Very little is known about this learning process, however.

As just mentioned, within any population, widely shared kinesic expressions (like the 'keyboard', 'telephone', 'car-driving' described) may be found. It is a common observation that cultures may differ among themselves in the frequency of use of such forms and the sizes of the repertoires available. Further, when expressions with similar meanings from one culture to the next are compared, they often show differences. There are many publications describing such repertoires for several different cultures or language groups. These include France, Italy and the Hispanic countries (both in Iberia and in the Americas), Arabic countries, a few countries in sub-Saharan Africa and also Russia. Note that repertoires like this for English and other north-west European cultures are scarce. This may reflect the commonly accepted north-west European view (current since the fifteenth century, by the way) that it is among the peoples of the Mediterranean, notably in southern Italy, that kinesic expressivity, especially by way of manual action, is particularly well developed and in widespread use.

Despite the many publications (popular or semi-popular) describing the repertoires of conventional manual expressions (and the meanings attributed to them) for different language groups or cultures, there are few studies of their contexts of use, and their communicative and interactional functions. In consequence, we really understand little about them. To illustrate this issue, I refer to observations made among Neapolitans, who have long been famous for their richness of gestural expression. Among Neapolitans there are a number of widely shared expressions that are often identified as being equivalent to a single noun, verb, or adjective (for example gestures glossed as 'money', 'thief', 'drink', 'eat', 'little', 'delicious'). It is not uncommon to observe a speaker using kinesic expressions of this sort at the same time as they pronounce the words used to gloss them. For example, a shopkeeper complaining about undesirable customers entering her shop, when asked to give examples, replies '*ladri, truffatori* [thieves, swindlers]'. As she uttered each of these words, she also, with both hands, enacted the conventional expression usually glossed as 'thief'. She used a kinesic expression and a spoken expression simultaneously for the same notion (Kendon 2004: 278). This conjoining of a spoken word with a kinesic expression that matches it in meaning is quite common. However, speakers may often refer to thieves, or many other things, without a corresponding kinesic expression. However, at this time we can only speculate about when and why such word–gesture conjunctions are used. Since there are no context of use studies of this phenomenon, we can say little about why such usages develop. Is there something about everyday encounters in Naples that might encourage the emergence and use of gestures of this sort?

Various possibilities can be suggested. Perhaps if a notion is expressed kinesically at the same time as it is expressed verbally, this permits the recipient a different experience of the utterance of which it is a part. For example, it has been pointed out that many so-called performative verbs (for example, 'swear', 'promise', 'bless', 'congratulate', 'deny') have equivalent kinesic expressions which seem to count as an actual performance of the act, the verbal expression at times being not quite enough. Sometimes a manual expression can serve as means of making a concept physically present. Because the manual expression can be sustained for the course of a verbal utterance, a concept central to the discourse can be kept present for the recipient for its duration. Further, in circumstances where there are features that interfere with the transmission of speech, such as high ambient noise or physical distance, if repertoires of conventionalised kinesic expressions are available these may well be used as a way of ensuring the transmission of key parts of what is being said. On the other hand, a kinesic expression for a concept may be employed, instead of speaking it, when what is being referred to is somehow shameful or too shocking or too sacred to be uttered in words. At a time in black communities in South Africa when AIDS was becoming established, for many it was deemed shameful to mention it. A gesture for referring to it became established instead (Brookes 2011). Other circumstances which can encourage the employment of kinesic expressions may arise because it is silent, so it may be useful for discrete exchanges where speech would otherwise attract attention. Furthermore, spoken exchanges often require participants to orient to one another in specific ways so that, from a distance, it can be seen that two or more people are 'talking together'. Kinesic forms of expression do not seem to require this, at least not in the same way, so they can be used when participants wish to engage in exchanges that will be unnoticed by others who may be co-present at the time.

Considerations of this sort allow us to note that kinesic expressions are useful in many different ways and in many different circumstances. The approach sketched here tries to evaluate the relative roles of different expressive modalities within what (following Dell Hymes) may be called the 'communication economy'. This may help in understanding the complex of factors that encourage or discourage how different modalities of interaction are used and so help understand why there are cultural differences in gesture use and why different vocabularies of conventionalised forms become established.

A review of studies which have taken interaction ecology into account suggests some of the conditions which might encourage a more elaborate development of the use of kinesic expressions. For example, small communities in which there is a high degree of mutual acquaintance, where people see each other often, where there is much overlap of behaviour settings (as in Naples, spaces for domestic, social and commercial activities often overlap), where inconspicuous communication is useful, where ecological conditions make possible visual contact over large spaces, or where high voice volumes (shouting) can be intrusive, all may be circumstances in which we may expect an elaboration of kinesic action, including the development of large repertoires of shared or conventionalised forms (see Ekman and Friesen 1969; Morris *et al.* 1979; Kendon 1981, 1984; Kendon 2004: 349–54; Kendon 1989 Ch. 14; De Jorio 2000).

3.4 The emergence of systems for kinesic discourse – sign languages

So far, we have discussed the use of kinesic expression – mainly manual expression – in circumstances where speech is also in use. We have examined how speakers may employ manual expressions in partnership with speaking and we have seen how, in various circumstances, kinesic expression may become conventionalised and serve as a supplement and sometimes as an alternative to spoken utterance. However, circumstances also arise in which kinesic expression replaces speech entirely, it comes to be used as a mode of discourse on its own. Where this happens as a matter of routine, socially shared systems enabling kinesic discourse become established. The more complex of these, for the most part found in communities of deaf persons, develop to a point where they can be regarded, functionally, as fully the equivalent of spoken language. Such systems also display structural features that are analogous to those of spoken languages and they are regarded as being, in some fundamental sense, no different from them.

The study of such sign languages has flourished very greatly in the decades following 1980. An important reason for this has been that showing that a system that is fully functional as a language can develop in the kinesic medium, largely or even wholly without the influence of existing spoken languages, forces a modification of our concept of 'language' (as a human faculty) which, hitherto, had been so intimately bound up with *speaking*, that this was regarded as an essential part of it. Now it can be confidently maintained that 'language' is not dependent upon any particular modality of expression. Nevertheless, it may be that a language developed in the kinesic modality will have features that are different from those developed in the modality of speech. It becomes a matter of great interest to investigate what these features may be and to see what the consequences are, if any, for how users of sign language may develop different conceptual structures and manifest different cognitive processes from users of spoken languages. This could bear usefully on the question of the relationship between language and thought. The phenomena of kinesic discourse systems, including those deemed sign languages, also raise very interesting questions about our notions of 'language', both as a faculty and as a semiotic system. These, in turn, have relevance for questions about how language emerges. From the mid-1990s onwards, cases have come to notice in which it is possible to observe sign languages in the process of formation. Investigations into these cases are especially relevant to the question as to whether a 'language' is the consequence of a pre-existing faculty of the human brain, or whether it is something that gets built up through processes of social interaction.

3.5 Kinesic discourse systems in speaker communities – alternate sign languages

As we have already seen, among speakers, in all sorts of moments in everyday interaction, circumstances can occur that promote the separate use of manual expressions, even if only momentarily. It is clear that people are often ready to fill in such moments with appropriate kinesic expressions. When occasions in which it is useful to use kinesics rather than speech occur often and in routine ways (as, for instance, in the ancient centres of Naples with crowded urban city quarters with a high degree of mutual acquaintanceship), repertoires of conventional forms tend to be established.

Not surprisingly, therefore, where utterance-mediated interaction is necessary on a routine basis but where speech cannot be used, kinesics can elaborate into a system which makes discourse possible. There are numerous examples on record where speakers have developed such kinesic discourse systems, although complex systems in this modality allowing for extended discourse and serving as a medium for general everyday interaction are much rarer. Specialised kinesic codes have been described for a variety of work situations where speech cannot be used, including scuba diving, in broadcast studios, in floor-trading situations, in high-end restaurants, and the like. Occasionally such specialised codes may elaborate to permit various kinds of conversational exchanges. One of the best described of these was from a sawmill in the north-west of North America (Meissner and Philpott 1975). Here, the workers were in fixed locations, and though visible to each other, were too far away for vocal communication, and there was too much noise. They coordinated the flow of work using a set of pre-established manual actions, but over time these were elaborated and expanded into a vocabulary of more than 250 signs, which allowed for the exchange of gossip, news and joking interactions. Similar kinds of sawmill sign languages have been reported from elsewhere in north-west America, and there is even some suggestion that they are related to one another (Johnson 1978).

These systems remained quite specialised, however, and were only used by the workers when in the sawmill. Other examples of specialised systems elaborating in a similar fashion would include the various sign languages developed in monasteries where the use of speech is highly restricted for ritual reasons. Monastic orders that restrict the use of speech date from medieval times and the sign languages that have developed in these circumstances can be very old. Ritual restrictions on the use of speech are also well known among the indigenous peoples of Australia. Fairly complex kinesic sign systems were (and indeed still are) in common use among many of the peoples of Australia, especially among those dwelling in the more central areas of the continent, northern coastal areas, and in Queensland. These sign systems were used in all sorts of situations, in hunting, communicating with acquaintances at a distance, as a useful silent alternative to talking. However, in some parts of Australia, notably among central desert dwelling peoples such as the Warlpiri or the Warumungu, it was (and is) the custom for bereaved women, as a mourning ritual, to forgo the use of speech for very long periods. Notwithstanding, women observing this speech ban participated in everyday life. In consequence the sign system became highly elaborated, permitting every kind of conversational interaction, elaborating, thus, into highly complex *alternate* sign languages (each language group had a different version of this sign language) which, though fully kinesic, nevertheless were found to display interesting interrelations with the spoken language, developing as if it were, in large part, a kinesic representation of the lexical semantic units of the spoken language.

These central desert Australian sign languages are the most complex kinds of alternate sign languages to have been described. Similarly complex sign languages were also known to have been developed and to have been widely used among the Plains Indians of North America where, at least from the late eighteenth century and into the nineteenth century, they appear to have served as a *lingua franca,* allowing tribes using very different languages to converse with one another. The origins of these languages are not well understood, but they certainly pre-date the presence of Europeans in the Americas. The development of versions that could be used between tribes and the spread of the use of these languages through the Plains of North America, however, may well have been encouraged as part of a response to the European invasions of these areas, when a ready means of intertribal communication which these sign languages may have afforded would have been very useful.

How are alternate sign languages related to the spoken language or languages of the communities in which they develop? Among the central Australians, expert signers use a system that tends toward being one in which the meaning units of the spoken language's semantic morphemes are the meaning units rendered kinesically. Discourse in these sign languages follows the word order patterns of the spoken language. Studies of North American Plains Indian sign languages, on the other hand, suggest that these alternate sign languages are much less shaped by spoken languages. This may be because Warlpiri and other Pama-Nyungan languages in Australia are highly agglutinative, which means that it is quite easy to match signs to spoken language morphemes. Native American languages, on the other hand, have quite a different morphology, sometimes highly fusional, so that matching signs to morphemes as the Warlpiri do would not be possible.

It is also necessary to consider whether the sign language develops in situations where it will be used by speakers of different languages in the same community. In the Plains Indian case, the sign language most fully studied (West 1960) appears to have been used as an inter-language. If this is so, it would not be surprising if the sign language was not structured by any specific spoken language. Similarly, recent work on sign language among peoples in Arnhem Land in Australia suggests that it may not be patterned after a spoken language. The communities in Arnhem Land where this work is being done are multilingual, which is not the case among Warlpiri communities.

How an alternate sign language may or may not be related to the spoken language or languages of the communities in which they develop, may depend not only upon the morphology of the spoken language, but also upon whether the sign language is used between speakers of different languages or not (see Kendon 1988). Other factors may also be important, such as whether or not the communities in question use writing.

3.6 Kinesic discourse systems among the deaf – primary sign languages

It has been known since ancient times that persons deprived of hearing may often develop, among themselves or in relation to those with whom they are closely associated (such as family members), systems of communication using visible bodily actions. Socrates, in Plato's *Cratylus*, draws this to the attention of Hermogenes as part of his argument that there is a natural relationship between the form of an expression and its meaning. In Europe, at least since the sixteenth century, the communication systems of the deaf have attracted the interest of both philosophers and educators. From a philosophical point of view, kinesic communication systems used by the deaf (whether regarded as a 'language' or not), have been of great interest because of the issues they raise about the relationship between language and thought and because they have been supposed to be universal and could form the basis of a universal language. If we had a 'gesture language' understood by everyone, it was supposed, the divisions among peoples promoted by the diversity of spoken languages could be transcended.

Work undertaken to investigate kinesic communication systems using the approaches of scientific linguistics began in the late 1950s. William Stokoe's pioneering study of the system used by students at Gallaudet College in Washington DC (a college established for higher education for deaf students, now Gallaudet University), established that the kinesic communication system these students used, had structure and organisation much like a spoken language (Stokoe 1960). The system studied, which was prevalent in schools for the deaf and other centres which served them in much of North America, stemmed originally from a system that came into being from 1812 onwards at Hartford, Connecticut where a school for the deaf had been established. Here, sign was used as a medium of instruction and the method used was that first developed by Abbé L'Epée in an institution for the deaf in Paris. Laurent Clerc, a deaf Parisian who was a pupil of Sicard, L'Epée's successor, was brought to Hartford to promote the use of L'Epée's method, although he also used his own French sign language, from which L'Epée's method was partly derived. The deaf persons who came to the Hartford Asylum, however, already were using systems that had been developed in their home communities. The consequence was that the sign system that became established was an amalgam of the system Clerc had introduced, Clerc's own French sign language, and various sign systems the students themselves brought with them. A signing system common to the whole institution became established, which then spread to other schools for the deaf. In this way, a form of sign language developed that, eventually, became widespread in much of North America (for a history of ASL see Tabak 2006). This was the system that Stokoe had studied. Subsequent work confirmed the validity of Stokoe's approach and by 1970 the linguistic status of sign language was widely accepted and, as it came to be so, it came to be known not as 'sign language' but as 'American Sign Language'. By calling this system *American* Sign Language, recognition was given to the fact that sign languages in other nations were not the same. It soon came to be understood that deaf groups and deaf communities in other nations used different sign languages. Thus it was that British Sign Language, French Sign Language, Italian Sign Language, and so on, all came to be recognised as different languages.

Like American Sign Language, many of these other sign languages given national names had their origins in systems developed within one or more institutions for deaf education. Their use as a medium of instruction in such settings contributed in an important way to their elaboration and to their documentation. However, in many parts of the world locally developed sign languages have been reported, nowadays often referred to as 'village sign languages'. These have developed in small communities where there is a high proportion of deaf persons and in most of these cases the use of the sign language is shared between deaf and hearing persons (consequently sometimes termed 'shared sign languages').

Comparative studies of the history and development of these sign languages are valuable for the insight provided into the kinds of sociality that promote the emergence of shared systems. In a very few cases it has been possible to observe a community in which a sign language has developed over a period of time, and so see how its features change. In Nicaragua, the best known example (Kegl *et al.* 1999), where no schools for the deaf existed before 1979, it was possible to observe the process by which successive cohorts of children, over a period of several years, established a school-wide shared signing system which was repeatedly refashioned as new cohorts of children entered the school. As this happened, expressions became more categorial, less holistic, showing a tendency for stable meaning units to emerge from which more complex meaning units could be built, according to syntactic-like rules allowing for hierarchically organised expressions. Characteristics considered hallmarks of language were thus observed to emerge in the course of a developmental process over several successive cohorts of students. Whether this is evidence for an innate language faculty shaping the system, or whether it is evidence of a more general process, consequent upon the development, through social interaction, of a shared communication system, remains a point of controversy.

3.7 Some general features of primary sign languages

Comparative studies of primary sign languages reveal many differences, both in lexical signs, and in the ordering of elements in phrases and other grammatical features. Sign languages from different parts of the world are mutually unintelligible, just as different spoken languages are. The idea that there is one universal sign language, although with local dialects, as was once supposed in the nineteenth and early twentieth centuries, is no longer supported. At the same time, it has long been apparent that, in certain respects, even unrelated sign languages are much more similar to one another than spoken languages are. This may be because, in the kinesic modality, the representation of actions, of spatial relations between items, of movement in space and the use of the hands to represent the forms of entities, as well as the use of certain kinds of expressions for negation, interrogation, offering, refusal and other pragmatic operations, follow common principles, much as we noted this to be the case in speaker kinesics. Signers using different sign languages who encounter one another at gatherings such as international conferences, are able, quite quickly, to develop shared ways of communicating, something which does not happen when users of different spoken languages meet. Strategies of expression in the kinesic medium which all sign languages draw upon (which can be drawn upon by all humans) can be exploited by all signers, and this enables them to arrive at mutually intelligible modes of signing fairly quickly.

In all sign languages so far investigated, the contrastive features that make up manual signs (handshape, hand orientation, location and pattern of movement) occur, effectively all at once and not in temporal succession as do the sound segments of spoken words. Iconicity is also found to be a very common feature of individual lexical signs. It should be clear, however, that just because a sign for something is formed by representing some aspect of that thing, this does not mean this is always done in the same way. Different signs for the same thing in different sign languages can be very different, even though they may be regarded as 'iconic'. For example, a sign used to mean 'woman' may, in one sign language be derived from depicting long hair, in another breasts, in another the string of a bonnet, or earrings, among other features. A sign for 'cat' in American and British Sign Language chooses to represent whiskers, but each does so in a different way. In Auslan (Australian Sign Language) 'cat' is referred by an action derived from stroking a cat. The iconic derivation of a sign is often obscure, however. Signs must be adapted in form to contrast effectively with other signs in the vocabulary, and, also, a sign is always modified through economy of effort. For many signs the iconic origins can only be appreciated if the history of its development is known.

Signers do not only use their hands. Much use is made of eyebrow actions, mouth movements, head positions and the direction of gaze. Some lexical signs conjoin hand action with facial action. However extra-manual components more typically play a role as operators in relation to the lexical component of the discourse. For example they frame what is expressed as an interrogative, bracketing sequences of manual signs as being subordinate clauses, making successive segments of the discourse distinct, and the like.

Another feature found in most sign languages is the use that is made of the capacity to move the hands about in space to express grammatical relationships. For example, a sign for 'see' in American Sign Language is to extend the index and middle finger in a V-like arrangement. The hand so arranged may be pointed in different directions or moved from one orientation or position to another as it is used to express phrase such as 'she saw him', 'he kept looking at her', 'you can see me', and the like. Here the location of the signer serves as First Person, another location can be established for Second Person and other locations can be established for one or more Third Persons. Orienting the fingers so they point to the appropriate location or moving in its direction, is sufficient. Pronouns do not have to be signed separately. Likewise, as another example, the sign for 'give' may be moved from one location to another to express 'I give you' or 'You give me', and so on. The handshape in these phrases may also be modified to signify the object that is given. Thus the arguments of a verb need not be signed separately, but 'incorporated' into a single action. Not all sign languages make use of these strategies, but it is common, and found in sign languages not related to one another.

Because various segments of the body can be employed in signing at the same time, complex expressions can be accomplished within a single presentation. To give a specific example, in an episode in a story about a horse and a bird, the horse jumps a fence, injures its leg, and is helped by the bird (see Sallandre 2007). In telling this, the signer (who uses French Sign Language) gives an expression which, if expressed in English, might be 'The bird sees that the horse is getting ready to jump the fence'. In sign, the horse's gaze and its desire to jump is represented in the signer's facial expression and her direction of gaze, the fence (using a conventional handshape) is represented with one hand, the bird watching the horse with the other (using another conventional handshape). The spatial dispositions and orientations of the hands map the relative spatial positions of the bird and its orientation toward the horse, and the fence, situated, as it is, in front of the horse.

Finally, many sign languages make use of what are called 'classifiers' (this term is controversial). These are handshapes or patterns of action that stand for certain classes of entities and they may be used to show the behaviour of that entity or its position in space in relation to other entities (in the horse and bird example the hand designating 'fence' and the hand designating 'bird' are classifier handshapes). Another example in American Sign Language is the so-called 'vehicle classifier'. Here the hand in a particular configuration can stand for any sort of wheeled vehicle, for example a car. It then may be moved about freely allowing the signer to depict the path of the car in space, in relation to terrain, its speed and so on. As in the horse and bird example, classifiers readily allow complex presentations about the behaviour of entities.

Classifiers are an example of where, in a sign language, a categorial morphosyntactic approach to analysis does not easily apply. Using classifiers means using gradient or analogue expressions. In consequence, it is evident that a sign language cannot be completely described in terms of a spoken language linguistic model. It is semiotically mixed. The same can be said of spoken language, of course. Changes in voice tone and pitch, variations in speed of pronunciation, make important contributions to spoken expression. These analogue vocal devices are as integral to spoken expression as their kinesic counterparts are in signing. These considerations open discussion about where to draw the boundaries of what is 'linguistic'.

This point can also be raised in relation to speakers' use of manual actions. A look at how these enter into utterance construction shows that speakers, like signers, often have recourse to forms of expression that are deemed to lie outside what is commonly regarded as 'linguistic'. Yet these manual actions are often integral to the speaker's expression. Are they, then, part of 'language'? It is not only the study of sign languages that raises issues central to how we are to think of what counts as language, but the study of speaker kinesics as well.

3.8 Conclusion: the semiotic diversity of human kinesics

In this chapter I have surveyed the main ways in which visible bodily action is used as a part of utterance, necessarily in rather general terms. Much of the discussion has focused on the utterance roles of hand actions, since these have been studied most. In speakers we described how manual actions partner with speech in different ways, but we also saw that it may develop to function meaningfully in independence from speech. Some circumstances of everyday social interaction may favour the use of kinesic expressions separately from speech and we outlined what some of these may be. However, when speech cannot be used as a matter of routine, whether for environmental, ritual or physiological reasons, visible bodily action can develop in such a way as to become the equivalent of speaking. That is, shared communication systems may develop which use only the kinesic modality, and these can be structurally and functionally the equivalent of spoken languages. In the approach we have followed here, kinesics, or utterance dedicated visible bodily action, is viewed as a resource which is used by all humans. Structurally, functionally and semiotically it can develop in many different ways. The challenge its study presents is to describe these different forms and functions and give an account of how different circumstances associated with them contribute to their shaping. To understand this in detail should make an important contribution to our understanding of the faculty of language and how systems with linguistic properties may differentiate and develop.

Further reading

General: Kendon (2004); McNeill (1992); Streeck (2009); Calbris (2011).

Sign languages of the deaf: Klima and Bellugi (1979); Brennan (1993); Sutton-Spence and Woll (1999); Brentari (2010); Zeshan and de Vos (2012).
Sign languages in speaking communities: Kendon (2013); Davis (2010); Umiker-Sebeok and Sebeok (1987).
Cognitive functions of speaker gestures: Hostetter (2012); Goldin-Meadow (2003); Cienki and Muller (2008); Stam and Ishino (2011); McNeill (2000).
Kinesics and early language development: Capone and McGregor (2004); Volterra *et al.* (2005); Goldin-Meadow (2002); Liszkowski and Tomasello (2011).
Kinesics, language and the brain: Healey and Braun (2013); Andric and Small (2012); MacSweeney *et al.* (2008).

References

Andric, M. and S.L. Small (2012) Gesture's neural language. *Frontiers in Psychology* 3: 1–11.
Brennan, M. (1993) The visual world of BSL [British Sign Language]: An introduction. In *Dictionary of British Sign Language*, pp. 1–134. London: Faber and Faber.
Brentari, D. (ed.) (2010) *Sign Language.* Cambridge: Cambridge University Press.
Brookes, H. (2011) Amagama amthathu 'The Three Letters': The emergence of a quotable gesture (emblem). *Gesture* 11: 194–218.
Calbris, G. (2011) *Elements of Meaning in Gesture.* Amsterdam/Philadelphia: John Benjamins.
Capone, N.C. and K.K. McGregor (2004) Gesture development: A review for clinical and research practices. *Journal of Speech, Language and Hearing Research* 47: 173–86.
Cienki, A. and C. Muller (eds) (2008) *Metaphor and Gesture.* Amsterdam/Philadelphia: John Benjamins.
Cooperrider, K. and R. Núñez (2012) Nose pointing: Notes on a facial gesture of Papua New Guinea. *Gesture* 12: 103–29.
Davis, J.E. (2010) *Hand Talk: Sign Language Among American Indian Nations.* Cambridge: Cambridge University Press.
De Jorio, A. (2000) *Gesture in Naples and Gesture in Classical Antiquity.* Transl. Adam Kendon. Bloomington: Indiana University Press.
Efron, D. (1972) *Gesture, Race and Culture.* Berlin: Mouton de Gruyter.
Ekman, P. and W. Friesen (1969) The repertoire of nonverbal behavior: Origins usage and coding. *Semiotica* 1: 49–98.
Enfield, N.J. (2001) 'Lip pointing': With a discussion of form and function with reference to data from Laos. *Gesture* 1: 185–212.
Goldin-Meadow, S. (2002) Constructing communication by hand. *Cognitive Development* 17: 1385–405.
Goldin-Meadow, S. (2003) *Hearing Gesture: How Our Hands Help Us Think.* Cambridge: Harvard University Press.
Healey, M.L. and A.R. Braun (2013) Shared neural correlates for speech and gesture. In F. Signorelli and D. Chirchiglia (eds) *Functional Brain Mapping and the Endeavor to Understand the Working Brain* (InTech, DOI: 10.5772/56493).
Hostetter, A. (2012) When do gestures communicate? A meta-analysis. *Psychological Bulletin* 137: 297–315.
Johnson, R.E. (1978) A comparison of the phonological structure of two northwest sawmill languages. *Communication and Cognition* 11: 105–32.
Kegl, J., A. Senghas and M. Coppola (1999) Creation through contact: Sign language emergence and sign language change in Nicaragua. In M. Degraff (ed.) *Language Creation and Language Change. Creolization, Diachrony and Development*, pp. 179–237. Cambridge: MIT Press.
Kendon, A. (1981) Geography of gesture. *Semiotica* 37: 129–63.

Kendon, A. (1984) Did gesture have the happiness to escape the curse at the confusion of Babel? In A. Wolfgang (ed.) *Nonverbal Behavior: Perspectives, Applications, Intercultural Insights*, pp. 75–114. Toronto: C.J. Hogrefe.

Kendon, A. (1988) *Sign Languages of Aboriginal Australia: Cultural, Semiotic, and Communicative Perspectives.* Cambridge: Cambridge University Press.

Kendon, A. (2004) *Gesture: Visible Action as Utterance.* Cambridge: Cambridge University Press.

Kendon, A. (2013) *Sign Languages of Aboriginal Australia: Cultural, Semiotic, and Communicative Perspectives*, 1st paperback edition. Cambridge: Cambridge University Press.

Klima, E. and U. Bellugi (1979) *The Signs of Language.* Cambridge, MA: Harvard University Press.

Liszkowski, U. and M. Tomasello (2011) Individual difference in social, cognitive and morphological aspects of infant pointing. *Cognitive Development* 26: 16–29.

MacSweeney, M., C.M. Capek, R. Campbell and B. Woll (2008) The signing brain: the neurobiology of sign language. *Trends in Cognitive Sciences* 12: 432–40.

McNeill, D. (1992) *Hand and Mind: What Gestures Reveal About Thought.* Chicago: Chicago University Press.

McNeill, D. (ed.) (2000) *Language and Gesture.* Cambridge: Cambridge University Press.

Meissner, M. and S.B. Philpott (1975) The sign language of sawmill workers in British Columbia. *Sign Language Studies* 9: 291–308.

Morris, D., P. Collett, P. Marsh and M. O'Shaughnessy (1979) *Gestures: Their Origins and Distribution.* London: Jonathan Cape.

Quintilian, M.F. (1922) *The Institutio Oratoria of Quintilian.* Transl. H.E. Butler. Loeb Classical Library. London: G.P. Putnam.

Sallandre, M.-A. (2007) Simultaneity in French Sign Language. In M. Vermeerbergen, L. Leeson and O.A. Crasborn (eds) *Simultaneity in Signed Languages: Form and Function*, pp. 102–25. Amsterdam: John Benjamins.

Sherzer, J. (1972) Verbal and nonverbal deixis: the pointed lip gesture among the San Blas Cuna. *Language in Society* 2: 117–31.

Stam, G. and M. Ishino (eds) (2011) *Integrating Gestures.* Amsterdam: John Benjamins.

Stokoe, W.C. (1960) *Sign Language Structure: An Outline of the Visual Communication Systems of the American Deaf.* Buffalo: Department of Anthropology and Linguistics, University of Buffalo.

Streeck, J. (2009) *Gesturecraft: The Manu-facture of Meaning.* Amsterdam: John Benjamins.

Sutton-Spence, R. and B. Woll (1999) *The Linguistics of British Sign Language.* Cambridge: Cambridge University Press.

Tabak, J. (2006) *Significant Gestures: A History of American Sign Language.* Westport: Praeger.

Umiker-Sebeok, D.J. and T.A. Sebeok (eds) (1987) *Monastic Sign Languages.* Berlin: Mouton de Gruyter.

Volterra, V., M.C. Caselli, O. Capirci and E. Pizzuto (2005) Gesture and the emergence and development of language. In M. Tomasello and D. Slobin (eds) *Beyond Nature-Nurture: Essays in Honor of Elizabeth Bates*, pp. 3–40. Hillsdale: Lawrence Erlbaum.

West, L.M. Jr (1960) The sign language: An analysis. 2 vols. PhD dissertation, Indiana University.

Zeshan, U. and C. de Vos (eds) (2012) *Sign Languages in Village Communities.* Berlin: De Gruyter Mouton.

4
Writing systems
Methods for recording language

Geoffrey Sampson

4.1 The study of writing systems as a branch of linguistics

Until recently, the study of writing systems was something of a Cinderella subject within the discipline of linguistics. For a long time there was only one standard monograph, I.J. Gelb's 1952 book *A Study of Writing*, which was valuable but was little influenced by the insights of modern structural linguistics. Many linguists saw human language as a window onto biologically-determined structures and processes of cognition; writing, as a technology evolved only within the past few thousand years and hence clearly a cultural rather than biological endowment, seemed accordingly less interesting than spoken language.

Large misunderstandings of the nature of non-European scripts were rife. As recently as 1963 the distinguished anthropologist Jack Goody claimed that the non-alphabetic Chinese script (the vehicle of one of the world's greatest civilizations for three thousand years) was a limited system, which was incapable of expressing a complete range of ideas and hindered the adoption of standards of logic usual in 'literate' societies (by which Goody meant societies using an alphabet) (Goody and Watt 1963). The Maya script of Central America has been recognized since its decipherment as the clearest case anywhere of a writing system which developed entirely independently of the ultimate Middle Eastern ancestors of European writing; until his death in 1975 the influential Mayanist Eric Thompson continued to insist against the decipherers that the system was not writing at all, but consisted only of stylized illustrations of Maya mythology (Thompson 1960).

Happily, in recent decades things have changed. The study of writing is acknowledged now as a valid branch of linguistics alongside its other branches. Globalization has led Westerners to be less credulous about absurd misrepresentations of alien systems. The claim that different human languages all reflect an innate universal grammar looks less plausible to linguists today than it once did, and if languages are products of culture rather than biology then there is no reason to ignore written languages merely because they are newer cultural developments than their spoken counterparts. Writing may be a relatively recent form of language, but in the circumstances of modern life it is a very important one.

The main difficulty in placing the study of writing systems on a scientific footing, arguably, is not nowadays lack of good information about non-European scripts, but the fewness of independent examples. There are thousands of spoken languages in the world, falling into dozens, perhaps hundreds, of apparently unrelated families, but writing appears to have been independently invented only a few times in world history. Very many of the quite different-looking scripts used for various languages of the Old World all ultimately trace their ancestry to the second millennium BCE Phoenician alphabet from which our own Roman alphabet descends, and it is likely that the forerunners of the Phoenician alphabet were themselves influenced in their creation by some of the older non-alphabetic scripts of the Middle East. Probably Chinese script was a purely indigenous creation (as Maya script certainly must have been), but there is little extant evidence for the earliest stages of Chinese writing and some have argued for cultural links with Middle Eastern writing through Central Asia. It can be difficult to arrive at reliable generalizations, in a field where there are limited possibilities of checking them against independent evidence.

4.2 Types of script

The most straightforward way to bring order into the diversity of present-day and past scripts is to classify them by type. (The term *script* will be used for a set of written marks together with conventions for using them to record a particular language; thus e.g. English and Finnish use the same alphabet, but their 'scripts' are rather different – English spelling being highly irregular and Finnish extremely regular.) As in the case of typology of spoken languages, in classifying scripts it is necessary to define a range of ideal types, and to bear in mind that real examples rarely or never perfectly exemplify the type under which they are categorized.

In the first place, we can ask of a script whether it represents a spoken language at all. We usually think of 'writing' as a means of visually recording spoken utterances, even if the utterances are only potentially spoken (probably most twenty-first-century written documents are never read aloud, and there are cases like Latin where a written language continues to be used for some purposes but the colloquial spoken language it originally represented is long dead). In principle, though, there is no reason why a system of communication by visible marks could not be developed independently of any spoken language. Within certain limited domains, such systems have become widespread over the past century: two examples are the international system of road signs, and the symbols for garment care. These symbols form conventional systems that have to be learned (one could not guess without instruction that, say, a triangle crossed by parallel diagonals means 'use non-chlorine bleach', or that a red-bordered white disc means 'closed to vehicles'). But at the same time they do not represent particular sequences of words of English or any other language – they are international, and the road sign mentioned could equally well be translated into English as 'no wheeled traffic allowed', or as 'vehicular access forbidden'.

These two systems are very limited in their spheres of application. Many aboriginal cultures, for instance in the Americas and in Siberia, have used conventional systems of graphic marks to indicate ideas independently of words, but those systems too have been quite limited relative to any spoken language – often they seem to have served more as mnemonics to remind users of details of a message or story, rather than as devices to communicate information to people having no prior knowledge of it. But more comprehensive systems of speech-independent graphic communication have been created. Probably the most fully worked out system is *Blissymbolics*, developed by Charles Bliss, a chemical engineer who escaped Nazi Europe for Australia, which is intended to be comparable in expressive power with spoken languages, containing thousands of symbols. (An example is shown in Figure 4.1.) Blissymbolics is claimed to be particularly helpful to people with

Figure 4.1 I want to go to the cinema in Blissymbols

cerebral palsy and other disabilities which interfere with reading and speaking, and has been used with disabled children particularly in Canada and Sweden.

Systems such as these are called *semasiographic*, as opposed to *glottographic* writing systems which express ideas by representing the elements of a spoken language. Many scholars prefer to reserve the term 'writing' for glottographic systems (so that for them Blissymbolics would not count as writing, however complete its communicative resources). That is clearly an issue about definitions only, rather than a disagreement about substance. However, the remainder of this chapter will focus exclusively on glottographic systems of various kinds.

A striking property of all spoken languages is what André Martinet called 'double articulation'. That is, any particular language chops reality up into discrete categories in some particular way – so, for instance, English divides the inherently continuous rainbow spectrum into *red*, *orange*, *yellow* and so on, while other languages may divide the same spectrum into fewer colours, or more; and at the same time a language divides speech sound into discrete units – some languages divide the physically-continuous range of front vowel sounds into three contrasting phonemes, /i e a/, while other languages recognize only two front-vowel phonemes, and others again recognize four or more. A language works by making these two articulations, and linking units of the first articulation (words, or morphemes such as *re–*, *–ceive*, *–ing*) with groups of units of the second, phonetic articulation.[1]

Among glottographic writing systems, then, the next question is what type of spoken-language units are represented by individual units of the script. A script whose elements stand for elements of the first articulation, such as words, is *logographic*; a script in which they stand for elements of the phonetic articulation is *phonographic*.

Phonographic scripts can be further classified in terms of the size of phonetic units represented by the script elements. In the West, laymen tend to think of division of the continuous speech stream into consonants and vowels as the 'natural', 'obvious' form of segmentation. But it only seems so because the tradition of alphabetic writing has trained us to divide speech that way. (Chinese philologers, whose script was not phonographic, did not analyse speech-sounds into linear sequences of consonants and vowels before China's encounter with the West.) A more natural unit than the phoneme is the syllable. And an individual consonant or vowel can be analysed into a set of phonetic features: for instance the English phoneme /m/ may be treated as a name for the combination of bilabial closure, voice, and nasality.

Different phonographic scripts can be based on any of these levels of phonetic unit: a phonographic script can be *syllabic*, *alphabetic* or *featural*. The term 'alphabetic' is used here in preference to 'phonemic' or 'segmental', because the latter terms carry irrelevant theoretical baggage. The word 'phoneme' is commonly used in connection with the fact that related but distinct sounds may 'count as the same' within a particular language, as the distinct first and last consonants of the word *lull* count as the same in English – they are 'allophones' of one 'phoneme'. This issue has little significance in the study of writing systems. In practice, whether a phonographic script writes allophones alike or differently usually has little to do with linguistic theory, and much more to do with the prior values associated with the script symbols when they were first adapted to write the language in question.

We see this if we look at how romanization systems have been devised in our own time for languages that were previously unwritten or written with other kinds of script. For instance, Chinese has a single mid vowel phoneme with three allophones: in neutral environments it is back spread [ɤ], but adjacent to labials or rounded vowels it is [o], and adjacent to front vowels it is [e]. In the now-standard *pinyin* romanization system for Chinese, [o] is spelled as *o*, but [ɤ] and [e] are both spelled *e*; it would not occur to anyone (other than an academic linguist!) that the three sounds 'ought' all to be written the same way, or 'ought' to be assigned three different spellings. What mattered in practice was that the Roman alphabet offered two and only two letters customarily standing for mid vowels, and had no letters standardly used for back spread vowels.

That is typical of the processes by which alphabetic scripts were evolved long ago for European languages which have never been written any other way. Sometimes novel sounds do force script devisers to innovate; when in the ninth century St Cyril adapted his Greek alphabet to write Slavonic languages, the latter contained so many sounds unknown to Greek that, for instance, Cyril borrowed the Hebrew letter ש *shin* to write the [ʃ] sound (ш in modern Russian printing), and even added an arbitrary hook to write the complex sound [çc] as щ. But cases like this are exceptions rather than the rule. In the main, tradition outweighs linguistic theory in shaping writing systems.

As for 'segmental': linguists use the term 'segment' specifically for consonant- or vowel-sized sound units, but to the layman a 'segment' of speech sounds as though it could be of any length, so that a whole syllable might be a segment. To avoid misunderstandings, it is best to call the European type of script 'alphabetic'.

These typological distinctions will be made clearer by discussing examples.

4.3 Logographic script exemplified

Taking the logographic category first, the obvious example to cite is Chinese script. To explain how Chinese writing works, we need to look at its historical development.

The beginnings of the script are unknown. By the time of the oldest extant inscriptions, from the late second millennium BCE, the script was already so elaborate that it must have emerged from a period of development that is lost to the record. But those oldest examples allow us to see how the script evolved. Chinese, and particularly the Old Chinese of that period, was an 'isolating' language in which each word was a single invariant morpheme (there was no inflexion), and was pronounced as a single syllable. To write the language adequately, what was needed was a recognizable graphic shape for each word. We shall use the term *graph* for the symbol used to write a Chinese word ('character' is used synonymously).

Initially, rather more than a thousand words were equipped with graphs by drawing pictures representing their meanings. The pictures were highly stylized (for instance, animals would commonly be shown with an eye representing their entire head), and sometimes we cannot now tell what the original form of a graph was intended to depict, but many early graph forms are recognizable as pictures today. (This transparency did not last. Changes in writing materials caused the shapes to change, with curved lines replaced by straight lines and angles; by about 200 BCE the elements of Chinese script had become arbitrary shapes with no pictorial value.) Two methods were adopted to create writings for more words. First, a graph created for one word would be used also for other words pronounced the same or similarly. Then, the ambiguities thus created were resolved by adding, to a graph chosen for its phonetic value, a subsidiary graph indicating the broad semantic category into which the target word fell. In Chinese script as it exists today, most graphs have this bipartite structure, combining a *phonetic* with a *signific* element.

Take, as an example, the graph 昔. The original shape of this graph appears to have depicted strips of meat and the sun, making it a suitable writing for the word /sjak/ 'dried meat'. (Reconstructed Old Chinese pronunciations follow the system proposed by William Baxter.) 'Dried meat' had a homophone meaning 'formerly', and the same graph was borrowed to represent that word also. Then, 扌 'hand' was added to form a graph for 措 /tsʰaks/ 'to place'; the addition of 足 'foot' gave 踖 /tsʰjak/ 'walk reverently'; 口 'mouth' gave a graph 唶 for /tsjaks/ 'sigh', and 亻 'human being' gave 借 for its homophone /tsjaks/ 'borrow'; and so on. Also, 'dried meat' came to be written with the addition of the 'flesh' graph, 腊, leaving the simple graph 昔 to be used only for 'formerly'. ('Dried meat' was the word corresponding to the original picture, but 'formerly' was the concept that was difficult to indicate via a signific element.)

The Old Chinese pronunciations of these words were not identical, but they were close enough to make the logic of the system apparent. If nothing had changed, one might be inclined to see Chinese script as fundamentally a syllabic phonographic system, though with a logographic aspect in terms of the significs, and with considerable imprecision in the relationship between syllables and graphs. (Not only are the words sharing a phonetic element, not perfect homophones, but other words pronounced similarly are written with different simple graphs – a word 'slipper, sole' was pronounced /sjak/ like 'dried meat' but was written with an unrelated graph, which in turn was used as phonetic in further phonetic/signific combinations.) Some scholars who maintain, as a linguistic universal, that all writing systems are based on sound have described Chinese script in that way.

However, over the more than three thousand years that have followed the creation of the graphs, Chinese pronunciation has changed hugely, and one consequence is that the phonetic elements of graphs offer far less reliable indications of pronunciation than they once did. 'Formerly', Old Chinese /sjak/, is pronounced in modern Mandarin *xī* (*x* represents a sound between English *s* and *sh*); and the other words listed as written with 昔 as phonetic are now: *cuò* 'to place'; *qì* 'walk reverently'; *zhà* 'sigh'; *jiè* 'borrow'. These spoken forms no longer share much family resemblance. With respect to the present-day language, one must describe Chinese script as a fundamentally logographic system, though one in which the graph for a word will often contain vague hints at its pronunciation and its meaning.

It may have been essentially a chance matter that Chinese script originally achieved precision by incorporating logographic elements, rather than finding ways to make its phonetic indications more exact. But as the spoken language has developed, logography has come to suit it very well. One consequence of the sound changes which led to modern Mandarin has been a vast increase in the incidence of homophony. Although the word for 'dried meat' is now pretty well obsolete, there are twenty or so morphemes of the modern spoken language which were pronounced differently from 'formerly' in the Old Chinese period but have now fallen together with that word as *xī*. Most other Mandarin syllables are similarly overloaded with alternative meanings. In the modern spoken language the resulting ambiguities have been mitigated through innovations in vocabulary structure, and in any case ambiguity can be negotiated away in face-to-face speech by people who share a common frame of reference. But for public writing, where far less shared knowledge can be assumed, a phonographic script for Mandarin Chinese would scarcely be usable.

And since, over about the past 1,400 years, the Chinese language has fissioned into a number of regional dialects that are not mutually comprehensible, the script has the further large advantage of preserving the unity of the language. The dialects differ greatly in pronunciation but little in vocabulary or grammar, so written Chinese can be understood by speakers of any dialect.

4.4 Phonographic script-types exemplified

Turning to phonographic systems: readers of this book will not need an explanation of alphabetic writing, but we shall look at examples of syllabic and of featural scripts.

One modern language using a *syllabic* script is Japanese. The Japanese writing system is exceptionally complex, which is a consequence of the fact that the Japanese borrowed the notion of writing from China, but the Japanese language is quite different in type from Chinese (the two languages are not genetically related). Unlike Chinese, Japanese has an extensive system of grammatical inflexion. Roots of inflected words are written using Chinese logographs (we shall look at that aspect of Japanese script later), but the inflexional affixes, together with 'grammar words' comparable to English *the*, *of*, are written syllabically.

The phonology of Japanese is simple, with almost all syllables consisting just of one consonant followed by one vowel, and the numbers of distinct consonants and vowels are not large by world standards. Consequently a system of forty-nine basic symbols, together with two diacritics marking consonant variations, is enough to write any Japanese syllable.[2] (If a language like English, with syllables like *grand*, *squeeze*, were written syllabically, far more symbols would be needed.)

The crucial point making this aspect of Japanese script truly 'syllabic' rather than segmental is that the signs for various syllables sharing the same consonant, or sharing the same vowel, are not graphically related in any way. Thus, the syllables /na ne ni no nu/ are written な ね に の ぬ; /a ha ka ma na ra sa ta wa ya/ are written あ は か ま な ら さ た わ や. Any partial visual similarities that might appear to exist in these respective series would be purely coincidental.

At the other phonographic extreme, a *featural* script is one in which the various phonetic features which jointly go to make up a speech-sound are separately indicated in the script. Japanese syllabic writing in fact has minor elements of this. Japanese has a voiced/voiceless contrast in stop consonants; rather than providing separate symbols for syllables with the two kinds of stop, the script writes a voiced-consonant syllable by adding a small double tick to the corresponding voiceless-consonant syllable: /ta da/ た だ, /ki gi/ き ぎ. And, historically, the /h/ phoneme originated as a fricative counterpart to the stop /p/; syllables in /p-/ are written by adding a small circle to the symbols for syllables in /h-/: /he pe/ へ ぺ.

It is possible, though, for a script to be more thoroughly feature-based than this. A particularly clear case is Pitman's shorthand, devised in the nineteenth century by the teacher and educational publisher Isaac Pitman, which became the most widely-used shorthand system in Britain. In this system, consonants are written as extended lines, vowels as small marks adjacent to them. Among consonants, the voiced/voiceless contrast is represented by thick versus thin lines. Stops versus fricatives correspond to straight versus curved lines. Long vowels and diphthongs are distinguished from short vowels as heavy versus light vowel marks; and so on.

Probably no script used as the standard writing system for any language takes the featural principle this far. But the Korean 'alphabet' comes close. Korea, for many centuries, used Chinese as its written language, as mediaeval Europe used Latin, but in the fifteenth century a phonographic system was devised to enable Koreans to write their own language – Hangeul. This is now the normal script of North and South Korea.

Korean has a three-way 'manner' contrast in stop consonants, between lax, tense and aspirated stops. For a given place of articulation, a simple graphic form represents a continuant made at that place, and stops are written by adding one horizontal and two horizontals for the lax and aspirated stops, respectively, and by doubling the lax symbol for the tense counterpart. Thus (marking tense stops with asterisks): /n t th t*/ are respectively ㄴ ㄷ ㅌ ㄸ; /s ts tsh ts*/ are ㅅ ㅈ ㅊ ㅉ. (The precise realization of the sibilants varies and would not always be transcribed narrowly with the [s] symbol, but the script ignores subphonemic detail.) Among the vowels, front vowels are written by combining the corresponding back vowel symbol with the symbol for /i/.

Admittedly, the scheme is not carried through with total consistency. Thus, /m/ is a square, ㅁ, but /p/ is written as ㅂ rather than with a horizontal above the square. On the other hand, in another respect one might see Korean script as *more* featural than Pitman's shorthand. The basic place-of-articulation shapes were originally chosen to depict the corresponding gestures of the vocal organs. Thus, ㄴ for the apical series shows the tongue-tip of a (left-facing) speaker raised to the hard palate; and the original shape for the sibilant series, thought of by Koreans as 'tooth sounds', was a simple inverted V representing a tooth.

A cautionary remark is in order in connection with featural scripts, though. We have seen that it takes training to learn to break syllables down into smaller phonetic elements, and the smaller the elements the less self-evident they are likely to be. There is a question about how real, for users of a featural script, the implicit analysis into phonetic features is. Surely, many British shorthand typists have become skilled users of Pitman's system without being consciously aware of concepts like voice, stop versus fricative, etc. One could simply learn that e.g. a thick straight vertical means /d/ without any awareness of the underlying rationale, and perhaps most Pitman's users have learned it that way. Likewise, a Korean might learn that ㅌ spells /tʰ/ without breaking this down into apical+aspiration. For a script to be 'featural' may be a fact relating more to the process of its invention than to its use as an established system.

4.5 Completeness of representation

Apart from the type of units represented, another principle by which one can categorize scripts is *completeness*. A script may omit some meaningful components of speech, or record them in an ambiguous fashion which does not uniquely determine the spoken form intended. For instance, many languages written with the Roman alphabet have a contrast between long and short vowels, and some languages mark that contrast in their spelling: Finnish *kaatua* 'to fall' is different from *katua* 'to regret', Czech *chůdy* 'stilts' contrasts with *chudý* 'poor'. But the language for which the Roman alphabet was first used, Latin, never marked its own length contrast; e.g. *mălus* 'bad' and *mālus* 'apple tree' were written identically (the lunette and macron used to show the difference here are a modern scholarly convention). Some scripts are much less complete than this.

As an example of incomplete logographic writing, consider the Japanese use of Chinese writing. We have seen that the grammatical words and the inflexions of Japanese are written in a phonographic script, but the roots of the content words are written with Chinese graphs. In the Chinese language, most words are represented unambiguously with a unique graph (there are occasional cases analogous to English *lead*, which can represent either /lid/

'conduct' or /lɛd/ as 'metal', but this type of ambiguity is not very salient). In Japanese the situation is different. Although the Japanese language is genetically unrelated to Chinese, for historical reasons it has borrowed a vast quantity of vocabulary from Chinese, and the borrowings occurred at different periods between which Chinese pronunciations changed considerably. A native Japanese root is written with the graph for some Chinese word with the same or similar meaning; but that Chinese word is likely itself to have been borrowed into Japanese, perhaps in different phonetic forms at different periods, and those borrowings are also written with the same Chinese graph.

As an extreme case, the Chinese word 行, meaning 'move, practise' and pronounced in Middle Chinese /hæŋ/, is used for the native Japanese root *ik–* 'to go', but it also has three different pronunciations as a Chinese loan: *gyō* in e.g. *shugyō* 'training'; *kō* in e.g. *ginkō* 'bank' (in the financial sense); and *an* in e.g. *angya* 'walking tour'. These pronunciations may look rather different, but each of them (other than *ik–*) developed historically by various routes from Chinese /hæŋ/. However, nothing in the writing of a particular instance of 行 in a Japanese text tells the reader whether to pronounce it *ik–*, *gyō*, *kō* or *an*. That has to be inferred from context and knowledge of the language.

To offer an analogy: if English were written with a Japanese-style script, we would find a particular symbol standing either for a word of the native Germanic vocabulary, or alternatively for a root with the same meaning borrowed from Latin or from its descendant language Norman French. Writing *X* for such a symbol, if a reader were faced with examples like (1)–(3) only knowledge of English, not the symbol itself, would tell him that *X* is to be read in (a) as native *cow*, in (b) as the Latin root *bov–*, and in (c) as *beef*, the Anglicized form of French *bœuf*.

(1) The Xs have escaped into the lane.
(2) He has a Xine temperament.
(3) We need to X up security.

(And comparable ambiguities would also arise in the writings of *escape*, *lane*, *temperament*, etc.)

Incidentally, the use of Chinese graphs to write the roots of the native layer of Japanese vocabulary represents an unanswerable objection to those writers who urge that all scripts of the world are in some fundamental sense phonographic. The phonetic element of a Chinese compound graph was originally selected for its sound, but the graph used to write a native Japanese root is chosen for its *semantic* similarity to the Chinese word originally written with that graph, and, since Chinese and Japanese belong to separate language families, there will be no relationship at all between Chinese and Japanese pronunciations. (The Japanese root *ik–* does not sound anything like /hæŋ/, and there is no reason to expect them to sound similar.) Hence the native Japanese pronunciations associated with a set of graphs sharing the same 'phonetic' element will differ quite randomly.

In the case of phonographic scripts, there are many cases where significant elements of speech are omitted altogether. Arguably, this is true for all scripts with respect to intonation. English and other European languages have rich systems of contrasting intonation patterns that add considerably to the sense of an utterance, but no alphabetic or other script offers a serious attempt to represent these graphically. Intonation is a difficult case, though, since there is little agreement even among linguists about how to analyse it. For a clearer case, let us look at the treatment of vowels in Semitic languages.[3]

The Phoenician alphabet originally used to write Semitic languages was a purely consonantal alphabet. When it was eventually adapted to write Greek and later other European languages, letters for consonants which do not occur in Greek were turned into vowel letters (e.g. the letter O originally stood for a pharyngeal approximant, /ʕ/, but Greek, like English, has no pharyngeal consonants). Semitic speakers, though, continued to use the letters with their original values. At an early period, vowels were entirely ignored in Semitic writing. Later, some of the consonant letters were assigned a secondary role to indicate related vowels, for instance in Hebrew <w> could be used for long /ō/ or /ū/: /ʔārōn/, 'chest, Ark', originally written <ʔrn>, came to be written <ʔrwn>. But this system never came close to providing full information about vowels. All short vowels continued to be ignored, long /ā/ was ignored unless word-final, <w> was ambiguous between /ō/, /ū/, and its original consonantal value, and so forth.

The nature of spoken Semitic languages is such that inadequate recording of vowels is less troublesome to readers than it would be in a European language. Much of the vocabulary consists of verbs or words derived from verbs, and verbal roots comprise consonants only, with the vowels of a form contributing to the inflexion or derivation rather than determining the root. In Hebrew the root 'guard' is /ʃ-m-r/: /ʃāmar/ is 'he guarded', /ʃōmēr/ is 'guarding', /ʔeʃmōr/ is 'I shall guard', /məʃummār/ is 'guardroom', and so on. Context, together with the clues provided by affix consonants (such as the /ʔ-/ of 'I shall guard') and consonant letters used as vowels ('guarding' would commonly be spelled <ʃwmr>) are often enough for a skilled reader to know what all the vowels must be. Israelis feel no need for more. By the tenth century of the common era, in order to preserve the language of the scriptures uncorrupted, Jewish scholars had devised a very complete and precise notation for specifying vowels and other pronunciation details by means of small dots and lines adjacent to the consonant letters; but although this notation is used in editions of the Bible and in language textbooks, everyday Israeli publications such as newspapers or novels make scarcely any use of it. Nevertheless, while vowel information is evidently less crucial for readers of a Semitic language than for readers of European languages, it remains true that Semitic scripts are relatively incomplete, and ambiguities arise. Hebrew <jwn> can be /jōn/ 'dove' (where <w> represents the vowel), or it can be /jāwēn/ 'mud' or /jāwān/ 'Greece' (where <w> has its consonantal value).

Semitic scripts are probably the most incomplete phonographic scripts in common use today. In the past, there have been scripts which were less complete than they are. Linear B, the script used in the second millennium BCE by the Mycenaeans, was a syllabic script which ignored not just vowel length but manner of articulation of most stops (Greek contrasted aspirated, unaspirated and voiced stops, but a single Linear B symbol stood for each of e.g. the syllables /kʰa ka ga/), and it omitted syllable-final consonants altogether.

4.6 Shallow versus deep spelling

Another respect in which phonographic scripts differ from one another is in terms of the 'depth' at which they reflect the phonology of the language in question. Many languages have *morphophonemic variation*: that is, the same root is pronounced differently in different circumstances, as in English the root *house* has a final /s/ in isolation but /z/ in e.g. *housing*, or the root *metr–*, from the Greek for 'measure', has the vowel /ɛ/ in *metric*, /i/ in *metre*, and /ə/ in *geometry*. In a 'shallow' phonographic script, spellings vary to reflect varying pronunciations. In a 'deeper' script, roots tend to retain a fixed graphic shape (as the above examples do in English spelling), at least when the phonetic variation is regular and predictable.

Regular morphophonemic variation in a language commonly results from the operation of historical sound changes that happen to affect a particular sound in one environment but not in another. Consequently deep spelling can easily be taken to reflect conservatism: forms which were written alike because originally they were pronounced alike have not adapted their spelling to keep up with changes in speech. Conservatism certainly is one significant factor in the evolution of writing systems. But there are cases where we can observe scripts developing from shallow to deep in circumstances where this represents innovation rather than stasis.

Consider, for instance, the case of Korean script, already described above. Korean as a spoken language has a rich system of regular morphophonemic alternation. The alternations are largely the outcome of historical sound changes; but most of the sound changes had already occurred by the fifteenth century, when the script was invented. When the Korean script was fairly new, it was used in a shallow way, but more recently it has been turned into a deep orthography. Thus, the name of the Yalu River (which divides Korea from China) derives, in both modern languages, from Middle Chinese /ʔæp ljok^w kæŋ^w/ 'duck green river', but is pronounced in Korean /ʔamnok*aŋ/. By successive sound laws, /l/ became /n/ where not 'protected' by a preceding vowel (so /p l/ > /p n/); oral stops became nasal before another nasal (/p n/ > /m n/); and (simplifying somewhat) pairs of lax stops coalesced to form single tense stops (/k^w k/ > /k*/). In the early use of the Korean script, /ʔamnok*aŋ/ would have been written as it is pronounced. Nowadays it is spelled <qap lok kaq> (using <q> to represent a Korean letter that stands for both of the sounds /ʔ/ and /ŋ/, which are in complementary distribution). In this spelling, 'green' begins with an /l/ (as it does in speech, after a vowel); 'duck' ends in an oral stop (as it does in speech when not followed by a nasal); and the single tense /k*/ sound is resolved into the separate lax stops from which it derives. Rather than the consistent relationship between letters and sounds which obtained earlier, what we now find is a consistent relationship between spellings and vocabulary items.

We see something akin to this (though less clearly) in the history of European punctuation. When first introduced, the hierarchy of punctuation marks seems to have been thought of as representing pauses of different lengths, that is as reflecting purely phonetic facts. Later the marks came to be used as they are today, to display the logical structure of a passage, independently of how it might be read aloud. M.B. Parkes compares the punctuation of an eighth-century and an eleventh-century copy of a text by Bede: in the latter, punctuation 'is no longer merely a guide to the oral performance of the written word but has already become an essential component of the written medium, which contributes directly to the reader's comprehension of the message of the text' (Parkes 1992: 69).

The common feature in both cases seems to be that when phonographic writing is novel for a society, script users feel a need to hug the phonetic ground closely, as children learning to read and write do today. Later, when literacy is well-established and widespread, people read for meaning rather than sound: they need the meaningful units of the language to be readily recognizable, and they are less concerned with superficial issues of pronunciation. The fact that English orthography largely ignores morphophonemic alternations may be an index less of conservatism than of the fact that England has had a high level of literacy for a long time.

In this light, the issue of spelling reform (which has enthused numerous English-speakers, George Bernard Shaw being the most famous) looks like a movement to privilege the interests of literacy-learners over those of experienced readers. Since greater life expectancy means that the proportion of an average lifetime spent mastering the system has shrunk, it is not clear why this would be a rational direction for our societies to move in.

4.7 Scripts as badges of identify

Equipping a spoken language with a script might seem to be a purely technical issue, to be solved in terms of efficiency and economy. The nature of the shapes used as letterforms in a particular script tends to be largely determined by the physical materials available for writing. Sometimes these influences are less than obvious. The runic script used by pre-Christian Germanic peoples was formed from straight lines that were never horizontal, so that F, H, T took the forms ᛃ, ᚻ, ↑. This angularity doubtless contributes to the aura of magic and witchcraft which runes possess for present-day romantics, but the real reason was more prosaic. In a paperless society, runes were commonly carved on wooden staves. Horizontal cuts, that is cuts along the grain, would be hard to see against the grain and would risk splitting the wood.

However, few aspects of human culture are determined solely by pragmatic considerations. Anything that can be invested with emotional or political associations probably will be, and writing systems are no exception.

Consider, as a case study, the distinctive script used for Irish Gaelic until recent decades (see Figure 4.2). Before the Norman Conquest of England, these letterforms were common to Britain and Ireland and are known to epigraphists accordingly as 'insular hand'; but they were originally developed in Dark Age Ireland, and after roman script became usual for writing English they were perceived as distinctively Irish. One of the strategies through which Elizabeth I of England attempted to win her Irish Catholic subjects over to her reformed church was to make the scriptures newly translated into their vernacular more acceptable to them by commissioning a fount of Irish type. The first book printed anywhere in the literary Gaelic common to Ireland and Scotland had been John Knox's prayer-book, published in Edinburgh in 1567 in roman type. As Mathew Staunton sees it, for Elizabeth this publication posed a threat of fostering allegiance among the Irish to what was then a foreign country and its more radical Presbyterian religion; using Irish script for Gaelic printing in Ireland was intended to ensure that Elizabeth's were the documents for which the Irish felt affinity.

Once Elizabeth had begun using Irish script to promote Anglicanism, exiled Irish priests on the Continent adopted it for literature aiming to keep the Irish loyal to Catholicism. The distinctive script became an important icon of Irish nationalism, a visible token of the separateness of Irish culture. The population grew hostile to the idea of printing Irish in roman script, despite the severe practical difficulties of providing special founts of type for a small market, and of teaching children two scripts. One early nineteenth-century prison governor reported that if he presented his charges with an Irish Bible printed in roman, he had to promise to swap it for one in Irish type when available.

As pressure for independence from Britain grew in the late nineteenth century, nationalists 'used the language and the letterforms to justify their claims for independence ... it can be argued that ... Irish nationalism was very much a conspiracy of printers' (quoting Staunton 2005: 91). Irish script started popping up in unexpected places like the side of delivery vans; '[s]cript became a form of resistance to British rule' (Staunton and Decottignies 2010: 58). Only a few twentieth-century Irish people could master the Irish language, but all could recognize the distinctive script.

ᵹaelaċ

Figure 4.2 The word *Gaelach* ('Irish') in Irish script

Yet, once the Republic of Ireland was established in 1949, the heat went out of the issue. There were scarcely any objections when, in the early 1960s, the Irish government switched the language over to roman script.

4.8 Writers' versus readers' convenience

It is understandable that political considerations may sometimes outweigh simple efficiency in deciding what form of writing a society uses. One might suppose, though, that where politics does not impinge, functional considerations would constrain the ways in which a script could evolve. Functionally speaking, the only important quality in an alphabetic letter is to look clearly different from all the other letters, so while letterforms might evolve over the centuries (particularly before printing technology was available to 'freeze' them) one might expect such evolution not to compromise their distinctiveness too much.

Perhaps surprisingly, this is not so. Visual distinctiveness is desirable for readers, but a writer wants to economize effort. These considerations can pull in different directions, and the outcome does not seem to be predictable. Consider the divergent developments of the ancestral Phoenician alphabet, as used for later Semitic languages, and as used for European languages (the Greek and Roman alphabets). The Phoenician letters were distinctive in shape; some of the outlines were simplified in their Greek and Roman descendants (e.g. the letter ancestral to H had three crossbars rather than one), but they retained their distinctiveness. In cursive handwriting letters may of course be carelessly distorted, but Europeans never lost sight of the careful forms, and scribes used them in formal writing. For speakers of Semitic languages, on the other hand, hasty cursive forms became the only forms. The Greek and Roman letter O continues to be written as a circle, like the Phoenician letter <ʕ> from which it descends. In Hebrew and Aramaic writing the circle was formed as two semicircles touching at top and bottom, but the strokes were allowed to splay apart at the top and meet imprecisely at the bottom: by the time of Christ, <ʕ> was written as in modern Hebrew, ע. Because of this cursive simplification, visual contrasts between Hebrew letters are often minimal: compare for instance the letters ג נ כ ב (reading from right to left) with their Roman cognates B K N C, or ד ר ו with D R F.

With Arabic script this process went further. Arabic words are always written continuously (there is no concept of 'block capitals'), and various sets of letters were reduced so far that they became indistinguishable. In subsequent Arabic writing they have been made different again by adding dots in various patterns. For instance, word-internally the cognates of Roman B I N T are each written as an identical upward kink in the horizontal stroke joining them to the preceding and following letters, but with the addition respectively of one dot below, two dots below, one dot above, and two, or three, dots above. Consider Figure 4.3: the basic outline is the same for each word, but with the first (that is, rightmost) letter one versus two dots marks the difference between <f> and <q>, and with the middle letter (as we have seen) two dots above versus one below marks the difference between <t> and <b>. (The vowels are ignored.) But these dots do not derive from any features of the original Phoenician alphabet. They were added, after 700 CE, purely in order to rescue the script from ambiguity.

It is rather mysterious why the tension between economy of scribal effort, and readers' need for clarity, should have been resolved so differently in different societies.

فتل   قتل   قبل

qabila *qatala* *fatala*   'he accepted he killed he plaited'

Figure 4.3 Arabic words distinguished by dots

4.9 The psychology of reading

Over the past forty years there has been a great deal of research by psychologists seeking to discover how the reading process works. Apart from being a scientifically interesting topic, this research area has received impetus through its links with issues of broader public significance. There was widespread interest in a claim published in Makita 1968 that in Japan, with its complex but largely logographic script, the phenomenon of dyslexia is rare. And much of the psychological research appears to offer evidence potentially relevant to debates (which in Britain have become a national political issue) between alternative methods of teaching children to read.

For users of an alphabetic script, the most obvious question (perhaps at first sight the only question) is: how, exactly, does a reader move from a particular sequence of letters to identification of the meaningful word represented by those letters? For instance, how far in practice is it important that the word as a whole consists of a set of letter units arranged in linear sequence? Very different hypotheses are available. At one extreme, it could be that an experienced reader recognizes a word as a single distinctive shape, with the fact that the shape is formed from separate letter units having little practical relevance to the psychological process by which meaning is retrieved from graphic form. (That is, a phonographic script might be read as if it were a logographic script. An idea like this seems to underlie the 'look and say' approach to the teaching of reading, which was fashionable at one time though currently out of favour.) At the other extreme, it might be that the process of reading a word reflects in reverse the process by which words are spoken: that is, letters would be identified one after another in sequence, and once the entire sequence has been identified the corresponding word with its meaning is somehow retrieved from memory.

By now, the experimental data have shown rather clearly that the truth lies between these extremes. Reading a word does involve identifying its component letters, but (at least for short words) the letters are processed simultaneously, rather than sequentially as the sounds of a word are pronounced. (With longer words, successive groups of letters are each processed in parallel.)

Furthermore, while it is clear that the process of reading a word always includes identifying its pronunciation (even if a skilled reader is not consciously aware of the sounds during silent reading), there are alternative hypotheses about how that happens. One possibility (called *addressed phonology*) would be that a letter-sequence acts as an arbitrary code leading to a particular storage location in long-term memory, and that location holds the pronunciation as well as the meaning of the relevant word. Alternatively (*assembled phonology*) letter-to-sound correspondences are used to construct a pronunciation from the letter-string, and the pronunciation is used as a key to identify the word with its meaning. The evidence suggests that neither of these mechanisms has a monopoly: even in the case of languages with much more regular spelling than English, readers appear to use both types of process, with addressed phonology perhaps playing a greater role for common words, and assembled phonology being more important for less common words.

The experiments which have yielded these conclusions involve doing things like measuring the speed and accuracy with which readers carry out tasks such as recognizing words whose spelling has been distorted in different ways. In case it may appear from what was said so far that the upshot of this experimentation is merely a set of rather bland, middle-of-the-road conclusions, it is worth pointing out that some of the findings are by no means intuitive. Thus, although we know that the consonants of a word are more important than the vowels in helping a reader to identify it (which is unsurprising, since there is a larger range of consonants, i.e. they carry more information), when readers try to identify words in which all letters are present but some are misplaced, swapping a pair of vowels creates greater difficulty than swapping a pair of consonants.

Furthermore, it also turns out, contrary to many people's first assumption, that identifying individual words is only one part of the total mental activity comprised in the reading process, and (for skilled readers) not the most demanding part of the total process. For instance, words, once identified, have to be fitted together into a meaningful grammatical structure (sequences of words must be *parsed*), and psychological experiments are shedding light on how that is achieved. But to date there is too little consensus about these higher-level reading processes to discuss them here, and in some respects they fall outside the purview of this chapter. (Parsing is not specifically a written-language phenomenon; spoken utterances must be parsed too, though their grammar tends to be simpler and more predictable.)

4.10 Conclusion

After Ferdinand de Saussure (1916) promulgated the notion of 'synchronic linguistics' early in the twentieth century, there was a surprising delay before linguists began to recognize that written language is worthy of consideration within the discipline. In 1976 Jacques Derrida characterized writing as 'the wandering outcast of linguistics' (p. 44). But we have come a long way in the past thirty to forty years. By now, we can say that the outcast has definitively been welcomed back into the fold.

Notes

1. In this chapter, /solidi/ and [square brackets] will be used to enclose 'broad' and 'narrow' phonetic transcriptions, as is standard in linguistics; <angle brackets> will enclose romanizations of letters of non-Roman scripts, thus 'the Hebrew letter <d>' will refer to the letter of the Hebrew alphabet which is pronounced as /d/ (and whose shape is ד).
2. For completeness it should be mentioned that Japanese in fact uses two different syllabaries: any given syllable can be written in two ways, depending on the linguistic context. The examples shown below represent the 'hiragana' syllabary.
3. I thank Prof. Gideon Goldenberg, of the Hebrew University of Jerusalem, for advice on Semitic languages.

Further reading

Daniels, P.T. and W. Bright (eds) (1996) *The World's Writing Systems*. Oxford: Oxford University Press.
Gelb, I.J. (1952) *A Study of Writing*. Chicago: University of Chicago Press.
Hooker, J.T. (ed.) (1990) *Reading the Past: Ancient Writing from Cuneiform to the Alphabet*. London: British Museum Publications.
Houston, S. (ed.) (2004) *The First Writing: Script Invention as History and Process*. Cambridge: Cambridge University Press.
Man, J. (2009) *Alpha Beta: How Our Alphabet Shaped the Western World*. London: Bantam Books.
Parkes, M.B. (1992) *Pause and Effect: Punctuation in the West*. Aldershot: Scolar Press.
Rayner, K., A. Pollatsek, J. Ashby and C. Clifton (2012) *Psychology of Reading*, 2nd edition. New York: Psychology Press.
Robinson, A. (2007) *The Story of Writing: Alphabets, Hieroglyphs and Pictograms*, 2nd edition. London: Thames & Hudson.

Rogers, H. (2005) *Writing Systems: A Linguistic Approach.* Oxford: Blackwell.
Sampson, G.R. (2015) *Writing Systems*, 2nd edition. Sheffield: Equinox.

References

Derrida, J. (1976) *Of Grammatology.* Transl. G.C. Spivak. Baltimore: Johns Hopkins University.
Gelb, I.J. (1952) *A Study of Writing.* Chicago: University of Chicago Press.
Goody, J. and I.P. Watt (1963) The consequences of literacy. *Comparative Studies in Society and History* 5: 304–45.
Makita, K. (1968) The rarity of reading disability in Japanese children. *American Journal of Orthopsychiatry* 38: 599–613.
Parkes, M.B. (1992) *Pause and Effect: Punctuation in the West.* Aldershot: Scolar Press.
Saussure, Ferdinand de (1916) *Cours de Linguistique Générale.* [Publié par Charles Bally et Albert Sechehaye; avec la collaboration de Albert Riedlinger.] Paris: Payot.
Staunton, M.D. (2005) Trojan horses and friendly faces: Irish Gaelic typography as propaganda. *Revue LISA/LISA* e-journal 3: 85–98.
Staunton, M.D. and Decottignies, O. (2010) Letters from Ankara: Scriptural change in Turkey and Ireland in 1928. In C. Gillissen (ed.) *Ireland: Looking East*, pp. 51–74. Brussels: Peter Lang.
Thompson, E.S. (1960) *Maya Hieroglyphic Writing: An Introduction.* Norman: University of Oklahoma Press.

5

Phonetics

The sounds humans make when speaking

Andrew Butcher

5.1 Introduction

Phonetics is traditionally defined as the scientific study of speech sounds, their articulation, transmission and reception. It deals with *substance* – with physical events which take place in time. Phonology, on the other hand, is the study of how speech sounds are used in language. It deals with *form* – with mental targets and symbolic representations. I use the term phonology in the same way as Hulst (see Chapter 6) uses the term 'phonemics'. Unlike Hulst, I regard phonetics and phonology as separate disciplines and thus I have no overarching term to encompass the two. But there can be no doubt that they are inextricably linked, and a central question for phonetic research (sometimes known as 'the invariance question') concerns the nature of the phonetics/phonology interface: how are the discrete, static, context-free mental targets (phonemes) translated by the speaker into a continuous, dynamic, context-sensitive stream of sound and how does the listener retrieve those same mental targets from the continuous stream? Traditional descriptive phonetics relies on the fact that human beings are capable of doing this, and that literate speakers of languages with alphabetic writing systems in particular become aware of phonemes at an early age. The objects of our description are thus chunks of the speech stream which we perceive as corresponding to phonemes. That this is not as straightforward as it seems becomes apparent if one attempts to discover such chunks in a language one does not speak.

Phonetics is probably the oldest of the linguistic sciences, with a tradition that goes back at least to the India of the fifth century BCE and the work of Pāṇini on the sounds of Sanskrit. Interest in systems of notation continued in Europe in the eighteenth and nineteenth centuries, often with a prescriptive goal. Modern experimental phonetics began towards the end of the nineteenth century with the invention of the phonograph. The discipline is often divided into the subfields of articulatory phonetics – concerning itself principally with the physiology of speech production; acoustic phonetics – concentrating on the transmission of the speech signal through the air; and auditory phonetics – investigating the perception of speech by human listeners. But this is somewhat misleading: no serious researcher in either speech production or speech perception would work without knowledge of or reference to acoustic phonetics. Similarly the study of acoustic phonetics for its own sake would seem to be a somewhat esoteric exercise.

5.2 The basics

Traditional descriptive phonetics is based on how speech sounds are produced in physiological terms, rather than on their measurable acoustic qualities. An assumption is made that we can identify stable and repeatable patterns of simultaneous gestures within an utterance which correspond to single phonemes in the speaker's brain. We distinguish between these sound *segments* and the *prosodies* – mainly variations in pitch, loudness and duration – which can extend over longer stretches of speech. In acoustic phonetics the same assumptions are made regarding patterns in a wave form or spectrogram and we now have algorithms which will automatically segment large corpora of speech signals on this basis. Much speech perception research is similarly focused on investigating how we perceive individual sounds. Ironically a great deal of research is also devoted to 'connected speech processes' – i.e. what happens when we put the putative sound units back together in a natural utterance. As a general rule, the description of any speech sound comprises three components (although not all will be explicitly stated): the airstream mechanism, the state of the vocal folds and the position of the articulators within the *vocal tract* – the pharynx and oral and nasal cavities.

5.2.1 Airstream mechanisms – the powerhouse of speech

In order to produce audible speech a power source is needed and this comes in the form of a moving stream of air. This is sometimes known as *initiation*. All the languages of the world use a system of initiation which relies on the movement of air outwards from the lungs – the *egressive pulmonic* airstream mechanism. A vanishingly small number of languages (perhaps two) have been claimed to use an ingressive pulmonic mechanism to realise linguistically contrastive sounds, although individual speakers in many cultures may produce isolated syllables on an intake of breath. About a quarter of the world's languages, however, require the use of additional, *non-pulmonic* mechanisms to intersperse linguistically contrastive consonant sounds within the basic pulmonic egressive stream. One such mechanism involves a vertical movement of the closed larynx, either down, to draw air in, or up, to push air out. This is the *glottalic* airstream mechanism. *Ingressive* sounds produced in this way are known as *implosives* and occur in about 10 per cent of the world's languages, mainly in equatorial Africa and in south-east Asia. Glottalic egressive sounds are called *ejectives*; these are found in another 18 per cent or so of the world's languages. They are particularly common in the Americas and also in the languages of the Caucasus. A third mechanism achieves inward air flow by using the tongue as a suction pad. This is traditionally known as the *velaric ingressive* airstream mechanism, but the term velaric is increasingly being replaced by the more appropriate term *lingual*. It is a mechanism commonly used paralinguistically in many cultures (English *tut-tut* – expression of disapproval), but used to signal linguistic contrasts in only about 2 per cent of the world's languages – all of them in southern and eastern Africa. Sounds made in this way are commonly called *clicks*. There are thus four airstream mechanisms in common use linguistically.

But the universal basic powerhouse for human speech is the respiratory system. This system, consisting of the lungs, ribcage, diaphragm and abdominal muscles, has the primary function of keeping the body alive by replenishing the oxygen in the bloodstream and removing carbon dioxide. The lungs themselves are two spongy masses without any muscles. Expanding and contracting them in order to move air in and out is thus dependent on there being a vacuum between the outside of the lung wall and the inside of the ribcage and diaphragm; when the latter move, the lungs must move with them. Breathing in is an active process, requiring the contraction of various muscles to increase the volume of the chest cavity. There are two main mechanisms for achieving this: we can contract and thereby flatten the diaphragm, which is dome shaped when at rest, or we can raise the ribcage relative to the backbone by using the external intercostal muscles (it is easy to learn to control these two mechanisms separately). When the volume of the lungs increases, the pressure within becomes lower than the prevailing atmospheric pressure and air flows into the lungs until the pressures are equalised. The average total lung capacity of human adults is about 6 litres in men and about 4.5 litres in women; the *vital capacity*, which is the amount of air which can be moved in and out of the lungs, is about 1.5 litres less than this in each case. During tidal (relaxed) breathing, we utilise only a fraction of this capacity – about half a litre – breathing in until our lungs are about 45 per cent full and breathing out again until they are about one-third full – our resting expiratory level. When speaking, we commonly breathe in about twice as much air as this and we tend to do so much more quickly. The times spent breathing in and out – the *inspiratory* and *expiratory fractions* – in tidal breathing are approximately equal (in 40–50 per cent, out 50–60 per cent); the corresponding fractions in conversational speech are extremely variable, but average out to about 15 per cent of the time spent breathing in and about 85 per cent of the time speaking. These two facts about the timing of breathing (greatly increased variability and greatly increased expiratory fraction in speech) indicate that the respiratory mechanism becomes very much subject to the requirements of the task of speaking. In tidal breathing, expiration is achieved through relaxation pressure – largely driven by the elastic recoil of the soft tissues with some help from gravity. In speech the descent of the ribcage may be braked by the action of the external intercostal muscles and the diaphragm held in the relaxed convex position by the action of the major abdominal muscles (external obliques, transverse abdominis, rectus abdominis) compressing the internal organs below it. The outward flow of air from the lungs is thus very precisely controlled by a delicate balance of (active) muscular pressure and (passive) relaxation pressure. The imperative for this precise control is to maintain a constant overpressure beneath the vocal folds. The vibration of the vocal folds is known as *phonation* and this is the main generator of the sound waves which carry speech. In order for phonation to begin the pressure below the folds (subglottal pressure) must be between 200 and 1,000 Pascals (Pa) greater than the pressure above (depending on the desired pitch). A somewhat lower pressure differential is required to maintain phonation once it has been initiated. Increased loudness is achieved through increasing the volume velocity of air from the lungs. Normally this will also result in an increase in pitch (frequency of vibration). However, fine control of this parameter is performed by the intrinsic muscles of the larynx. We return to this in the following section.

The production of a consonant using the glottalic airstream mechanism involves three stages:

1. the enclosure of a part of the vocal tract by tightly closing three valves – the vocal folds, the soft palate against the pharyngeal wall and an articulatory closure forward of this, involving the tongue or lips;
2. raising or lowering the larynx in order to decrease or increase the volume of this enclosed cavity; and

3. the release of the articulatory closure, allowing air to flow from the area of high pressure to the area of low pressure.

Ejective sounds involve raising the tightly closed larynx by some 5–10 mm. The resulting pressure within the oral cavity varies from language to language and from speaker to speaker, with the more posterior articulations resulting in smaller cavities and higher pressures. Bilabial articulations can have pressures as low as 500 Pa, while pressures as high as 900 Pa have been measured in uvular articulations. It will be obvious that this mechanism is incompatible with vocal fold vibration (voicing). Implosive sounds, however, are commonly voiced, as lowering the larynx, as well as decreasing the pressure in the mouth, also increases the pressure in the trachea, causing air to leak through the glottis and set the vocal folds in motion, if the latter are not tightly closed. This means that the intraoral pressure decrease is usually minimal and often non-existent, with no air flow in or out, leading to the conclusion that voiced implosives are perhaps distinguished from their pulmonic counterparts by 'lack of explosion' rather than by ingressive air flow.

The velaric airstream mechanism also involves the enclosure of a small space within the vocal tract, with subsequent volume change and articulatory release. In this case the posterior boundary of the space is a closure between the tongue dorsum and the soft palate or *velum* – hence the traditional term for the mechanism. In a very few languages there is a contrast between clicks made with a closure at the front part of the velum and those made with a closure further back, at the uvula. The anterior boundary is formed by the front part of the tongue, which is positioned anywhere between the front of the hard palate and the back of the teeth, with a complete seal between both lateral edges of the tongue and the upper teeth and gums. In fact at the start of the process there is typically no space at all between the tongue and the roof of the mouth. A cavity is then formed by lowering the centre of the tongue whilst leaving the seals intact. Within this tiny cavity there is very high degree of negative pressure (−1,500 to −2,000 Pa), so that the subsequent release of the articulators results in an inrush of air and a relatively loud click sound. Since the main initiator of the air flow for these sounds is the tongue, it seems more logical to refer to this as the lingual airstream mechanism, but if we do so, we must acknowledge that bilabial clicks are made in a different way, using the cheeks rather than the tongue as the initiator, making this a *buccal* airstream mechanism. To change the volume of the cavity the cheeks may be sucked in (an 'air kiss') or blown out (French *pouah* – the so-called 'audible shrug') before the release of the lip closure. The small size and anterior location of the cavity means that the remainder of the vocal tract is free to produce a variety of accompaniments, including various types of phonation and nasality.

5.2.2 Phonation – the sound source of speech

The larynx has a far more important and widely occurring function in speech than acting as an airstream initiator. It is the means by which the audible tone is generated that is the main carrier of acoustic information for the listener. Phonation occurs when the air flow generated by the pulmonic egressive airstream mechanism passes through the glottis – the space between the vocal folds, which are situated within the larynx. The larynx is a cartilaginous structure, suspended from the hyoid bone, which is anchored by a number of muscles within the neck. Its primary functions are to prevent foreign objects from entering the lungs and to provide abdominal fixation in muscular exertion, such as required for lifting heavy objects and for childbirth. The suprahyoid muscles contract to move the larynx upwards for glottalic egressive sounds and the infrahyoid muscles (the so-called 'strap' muscles) pull the larynx down for glottalic ingressive sounds. It consists of nine cartilages in all, but in describing phonation we need only refer to four: the ring-shaped cricoid cartilage, positioned at the top of the trachea, the shield-shaped thyroid cartilage which sits 'astride' the cricoid, and the paired arytenoid cartilages which are positioned within the larynx on the posterior rim of the cricoid. The vocal folds are symmetrical folds of mucous membrane, about 1.25–2.50 cm in length, running from front to back across the larynx, attaching posteriorly to the vocal processes of the arytenoid cartilages and anteriorly to the inner surface of the thyroid. If they are held lightly together, the egressive pulmonic airstream will raise the subglottal pressure until they are forced apart. As the air passes between the vocal folds they are drawn together again by a combination of tissue elasticity and reduced air pressure until they are once again touching. At this point the pressure begins to increase again and the whole cycle repeats itself.

The rate and the mode of vibration is controlled by the intrinsic laryngeal muscles. In order to increase the rate of vibration, the folds must be stiffened. This is achieved in two ways: the muscles running within the folds – known as the *vocalis* muscles – can be tensed, thereby stiffening the 'body' of the fold itself, or the muscles running between the cricoid and thyroid cartilages at the front of the larynx (the *cricothyroid* muscles) can be contracted. This has the effect of pulling the two major cartilages together anteriorly, pivoting at the cricothyroid joint, thereby stretching the mucous membrane 'cover' of the folds. Normal or *modal* voice requires relatively high tension in the body and less tension in the cover of the vocal folds. We perceive the rate of vibration of the vocal folds as the *pitch* of the voice. Languages use pitch variation in two main ways: in all languages pitch variation is used to signal differences in meaning at the level of the phrase or sentence, such as differences between statements and questions, differences in focus on words within the sentence and differences in syntactic structure. In addition to this function, about half the world's languages – mainly concentrated in sub-Saharan Africa, south-east Asia and parts of the Americas – use pitch variation to signal lexical or grammatical differences between words (so-called 'tone languages'). If the vocalis muscles are relaxed and a high degree of longitudinal tension is applied to the vocal fold covers by the cricothyroid muscles alone, the folds will no longer vibrate in the usual modal register, but will move into falsetto register, with the stretched edges vibrating like strings, rather than closing fully at each cycle. This is used in singing, but rarely in speech and never contrastively in language.

Other modes of vibration – producing different voice qualities or *phonation types* – are controlled by muscles at the back and sides of the larynx. In particular, the interarytenoid muscles pull the arytenoid cartilages together along the rim of the cricoid, applying adductive tension to the folds; the lateral cricoarytenoid muscles swivel the arytenoids on the cricoid rim, bringing the vocal processes together, applying medial compression to the folds. The only muscles which abduct (open) the vocal folds are the posterior cricoarytenoids, which pull the arytenoids apart along the cricoid rim. Full abduction is required for voiceless consonants, especially if aspirated; about two-thirds of the world's languages make a contrast between consonants made with modal voice and consonants made with abduction of the vocal folds (*voiced* and *voiceless* respectively). Partial abduction with little longitudinal tension may also be used during phonation to create a breathy voice quality (also known as murmur). This is used to contrast with modal voice in some languages in vowels and nasals and, more rarely, in the release of stops. A high degree of adductive tension coupled with high medial compression produces a phonation type known as *creak* (also laryngealisation or vocal fry). With the arytenoids tightly together, only the front, ligamental portion of the

Phonetics

vocal folds can vibrate, and only then when the longitudinal tension is very low – leading to a lower frequency of vibration. A number of languages contrast creaky voice with modal voice in vowels and sonorants. A few languages make a three-way contrast between, breathy, creaky and modal voiced vowels. Very high adductive tension and medial compression will result in complete glottal closure – a *glottal stop*. As with other glottal 'articulations' (see §5.2.3) this may be analysed as a segment in some languages and as a prosody in others.

5.2.3 Articulation – the shaping of sounds

Once a flow of air has been generated – and in the majority of cases modulated by the vibration of the vocal folds – it will be modified by its passage through the vocal tract. The nature of this modification allows us to define two major categories of sound in languages: *consonants* and *vowels*. Consonants are defined as sounds made by forming an identifiable constriction somewhere in the vocal tract. We can describe or label such sounds in terms of where the constriction is made – the *place of articulation* – and how it is made – the *manner of articulation* – as well as specifying the accompanying state of the glottis – most often simply voiced or voiceless. A consonant can be articulated anywhere between the glottis and the lips and its place of articulation is generally identified in relation to a nearby relatively stable landmark in the vocal tract, as shown in Figure 5.1. In some cases it is necessary to refer to the part of the tongue involved in the articulation or even its overall shape. Sounds made with a constriction between both lips (1 in Figure 5.1) – as both consonants in the English word *map* – are known as *bilabial*; sounds made with the tongue tip against the upper incisors (2) – as in *thigh* – are known as *dental* and sounds made by

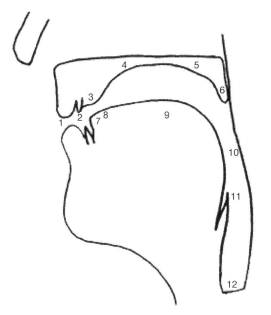

(1) Lips – bilabial sounds
(2) Upper incisors – dental sounds
(3) Alveolar ridge – alveolar sounds
(4) Hard palate – palatal sounds
(5) Soft palate (velum) – velar sounds
(6) Uvula – uvular sounds
(7) Tongue tip (apex) – apical sounds
(8) Tongue blade (lamina) – laminal sounds
(9) Tongue body (dorsum) – dorsal sounds
(10) Upper pharynx – pharyngeal sounds
(11) Epiglottis – epiglottal sounds
(12) Vocal folds – glottal sounds

Figure 5.1 Schematic sagittal cross-section of the human vocal tract, showing places of articulation

pressing the lower lip against the upper teeth (as both consonants in *five*) are known as *labiodental*. The bony ridge in which the teeth sit is known as the alveolar ridge and sounds which are made with the tongue tip articulating against the part of this ridge just behind the upper incisors (3) are called *alveolar* sounds; there are a quite a few of these in English, including all of the consonants in the words *nose*, *tide* and *loose*. Sounds made articulating the body of the tongue against the bony part of the roof of the mouth – the hard palate (4) – are called *palatal* sounds. The only true palatal sound in English is the initial consonant of the word *yes*, but other palatal sounds occur in European languages – such as in French (*agneau*), Italian (*gli*) and German (*ich*). However, English does have consonants which are made at the very front of the palate, just behind the alveolar ridge; these sounds are known as *palato-alveolar* and are found in words such as *ash* and *edge*. Another type of sound is also made in this area, but involves the tip of the tongue (or even the underside) bent back to the front of the palate; these sounds are known as *retroflex* and are not found in British or Australian English. They occur in many Indian languages (Hindi, Tamil), including Indian English, which pronounces *t*, *d*, *n* and *l* in this way. The soft posterior portion of the palate is known as the velum (5); sounds which are articulated here are called *velars* (both consonants in English *gang*). Further back still, the back of the tongue can be articulated against the end of the soft palate (6) to form *uvular* consonants. These sounds are not found in English, but the *r* sounds in standard French and German are both pronounced at this place of articulation (French *rue*, German *roh*). If further differentiation is needed, the tip and blade of the tongue can be distinguished from the tongue body (the blade is the part of the tongue extending about 15–20 mm back from the tip, and normally lying beneath the alveolar ridge when the tongue is at rest). Sounds made with the tongue tip (7) are *apical*; sounds made with the blade (8) are *laminal*; and sounds made with the tongue body (9) are *dorsal*. A limited range of sounds can be articulated by narrowing the upper pharynx (10) or articulating the epiglottis (11) against the rear wall of the pharynx. These *pharyngeal* and *epiglottal* sounds are not found in English; they sound very similar and are not in contrast with one another in any language. They occur in Hebrew and Arabic (the word for the Arabic lute, *'ud*, begins with a pharyngeal sound). As mentioned above, the vocal folds (12) are sometimes regarded as an articulator, as in the production of *h* (air blown through an open vocal tract), the voiced version of this sound (breathy voice in an open vocal tract), and the glottal stop.

At each place of articulation, a number of different types of constriction can be made. To begin with, there are three degrees of narrowness which can be employed. These are definable in aerodynamic terms. A *stop* is made with complete closure of the articulators, completely interrupting the flow of air from the mouth. Air pressure builds up behind the closure and is audibly released when the articulators are parted. A *plosive* is a pulmonic egressive oral stop, but the two terms are often used interchangeably (all the consonants in *bide*, *pike* and *gate*). A *fricative* requires 'close approximation' of the articulators, which means that they must be close enough together for the prevailing airstream to become turbulent – i.e. produce audible friction – at the point of constriction (all the consonants in *five*, *size*, *thigh* and *shy*). If the airstream is slightly reduced or the constriction is slightly wider, such that no friction is produced, this is said to be 'open approximation' and the result is an *approximant* (all the consonants in *yell*, *row* and *war*). However, manner of articulation is not just a question of degree of constriction; there are a number of other variables which cut across these categories to produce further sound distinctions. Chief among these is the oral/nasal distinction – which in theory can be applied to all articulations from lips to uvula, but in languages is found chiefly amongst stops and, in some cases, vowels. The velum can be raised to close off the nasal cavity from the mouth or it can be lowered to allow air from the lungs to pass through the nose. Oral sounds are made with a raised velum; nasal sounds are made with a lowered velum. Nasal stops are commonly referred to simply as *nasals*; there are three such sounds in English (*sum*, *sun* and *sung*). A second major distinction, applying only to lingual articulations, is between sounds where the airstream is channelled centrally along the tongue and those where the air is channelled over one or both sides of the tongue. The latter are known as *laterals* and can be produced as fricatives or approximants (there is only one in English, an alveolar approximant, as in *lull*, but Welsh has a voiceless lateral fricative, as in *llan*). At a few places in the vocal tract the articulators are sufficiently flexible to be set in vibration by the airstream in exactly the same way as the vocal folds are set in motion for phonation. These sounds are known as *trills*, and can be produced at the lips (paralinguistic *brr* – expression of cold), at the tongue tip (stereotypical Scottish English *r*) and at the uvula (standard French and German *r*). The tongue tip can also be struck against the alveolar ridge to produce a *tap* (casual pronunciation of *ought to* or *order*, which may sound the same in Australian English). An *affricate* consists of a short stop articulation followed by a short fricative (both consonants in *charge*). Whether or not such sequences are regarded as single segments is largely a phonological question. For example the final sounds in English *plaits* are regarded as constituting two segments, whereas the final consonants of German *Platz* are regarded as one. This is not because of any phonetic differences, but because German *ts* behaves like a single consonant (appearing initially in words such as *Zeit*, for example), whereas English *ts* behaves as a sequence of stop+fricative, which cannot occur word-initially.

The above descriptive framework is not commonly used for vowels. By definition, these sounds involve a more open configuration of the vocal tract (what would be the manner of articulation?), they involve the whole of the body of the tongue (where would be the place of articulation?) and they are almost always voiced (this part of the description would be redundant). Fortunately the contour of the tongue when articulating vowels is almost always convex; traditionally, therefore, we describe vowels in terms of the notional position of the highest point of the tongue horizontally – whether at the *back*, *front* or *centre* of the mouth – and vertically – whether it is *close*, *half-close*, *half-open* or *open* in relation to the roof of the mouth. In addition to this we need to state whether the lips are *rounded* or *unrounded*. In British and Australian English the vowels of *beat*, *be* and *bat* are front unrounded vowels; *put* and *port* have back rounded vowels and *bird* has an (unrounded) central vowel. *Beat* and *boot* are close, *pet* and *port* are half-close; *pot* is half-open, and *putt* and *part* have open vowels. Although this framework appears to be based on articulation, it is probably more accurate to say that it is auditorily based; there are also, as we shall see, some fairly close acoustic correlates.

The cardinal vowel system is a system of reference vowels which define the periphery of the available 'space' for the articulation of vowels. With considerable practice, the vowels of any language can be described by a skilled listener according to their position within this (two-dimensional) space, with reference to the cardinal vowels. The space is traditionally represented as a quadrilateral as in Figure 5.2, with the edges of the quadrilateral representing the limits of tongue movement. Two anchor points are established aerodynamically – the closest and most front vowel that can be articulated without producing (palatal) friction [i] and the most open and furthest back vowel that can be produced without (pharyngeal) friction [ɑ]. The remaining vowels along the front and back edges of the space are positioned at intervals which are, supposedly, auditorily equidistant from one another. Of the eight primary cardinal vowels, the first five (on the front and bottom edges) are unrounded; the four on the back edge of the space are said to have increased lip rounding from open to

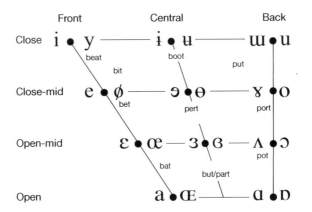

Figure 5.2 Traditional vowel quadrilateral, showing symbols for the cardinal vowels and key words from Australian English. Each symbol pair represents a pair of vowels with the same tongue position; the left symbol represents a vowel with spread lips and the right symbol a vowel with rounded lips

close. The eight secondary cardinal vowels have the same tongue positions but the opposite lip rounding from their primary counterparts. Three pairs of central vowels also feature on later versions of the chart.

Vowels may vary in other ways than tongue position. One of these is duration; many languages have vowels which contrast in length, either with or without an accompanying variation in tongue position. The vowels in the English words *beat, boot, bought* and *barred* are long; those in *bit, put, pot* and *butt* are short. Another common contrast among vowels is between those made with a single target tongue position – so-called 'pure vowels' or *monophthongs* – and those which are made with a tongue movement between a starting target and an end target – known as *diphthongs*. The vowels of *bead, barred, bed* and *bud* are monophthongs; those of *bide, paid, buoyed* and *bode* are diphthongs. As mentioned above, vowels can also contrast in terms of whether the velum is closed or open during their articulation. This contrast is not found in English but it occurs in French and Portuguese. The French words *veau, vais, vas* all contain oral vowels; the words *vont, vin, vent* contain nasal vowels with the same three tongue positions.

5.3 Speech production

5.3.1 Goals of speech production research

In real speech the sets of gestures required for neighbouring consonants and vowels are rarely produced strictly sequentially. For example, the English word *fence* consists of four phonemes – three consonants and a vowel. But in many people's pronunciation the velum will open during the articulation of the vowel, rather than at the same moment that the tongue tip reaches the alveolar ridge for the articulation of [n], so the vowel will be nasalised. This is easier to explain if we regard the tongue tip raising gesture and the velum lowering gesture as produced in parallel by two of the subsystems we have outlined above and therefore not necessarily precisely synchronised. We have identified three major vocal tract subsystems: the laryngeal, the velic and the oral. At the boundary between the final two consonants in *fence* a change is required in all three: in passing from [n] to [s] we need to change from voiced to voiceless in the laryngeal subsystem, from nasal to oral in the velic subsystem and from stop to fricative in the oral subsystem. Most people pronounce this sequence as [nts] (to rhyme with *vents*), because they make the first and second changes together, but the final change is delayed. They change from voiced to voiceless and from nasal to oral, but because they delay the change from stop to fricative, the result is a voiceless oral stop [t] separating the other two consonants. We can further divide the oral subsystem into three 'sub-subsystems': the lips, the tongue tip and blade, and the tongue body. The concept of coarticulation – of overlapping gestures being produced in parallel by separate subsystems – is a more transparent way of describing what happens in connected speech than the linear sequential approach. The latter was perpetuated by the dominance of *generative phonology* and its offshoots (including 'natural' phonology) which required phonetics to explain how individual speech sounds are 'glued' back together again by means of such 'processes' as assimilation, elision, epenthesis and vowel reduction. In the last thirty years nonlinear approaches, especially articulatory phonology and feature geometry, have found a rather more comfortable alignment with a parametric approach to phonetics. A major goal of speech production research remains, however, the explication of the invariance question from the encoding end: how discrete, static, context-free mental targets are transformed by the speaker into continuous, dynamic, context-sensitive gestures. This can be broken down into a number of sub-questions:

1. What are the units of speech production: are they equivalent in size to phonological features, phonemes, syllables, words – or something else entirely? Is there a single unit or do we invoke different-sized units at different stages of the process?
2. How is serial ordering achieved? The ordering of units is crucial to how the utterance will be perceived: how does the system ensure that the units emerge in the right order?
3. How does the system cope with the enormous number of degrees of freedom? Each occurrence of the 'same' sound requires a different set of muscle movements: how are the various vocal tract subsystems coordinated in order to produce the appropriate gesture (motor equivalence)?
4. (related to the above) How does the system take into account context sensitivity? Starting points, endpoints and trajectories of gestures will differ according to segmental and prosodic context.

A 'coproduction' approach to speech production assumes that gestures have their own temporal structure and can overlap with each other in time, the degree of overlap being controlled at the plan stage, rather than being an incidental outcome of the execution of the plan. Thus gestures are not 'modified' or 'influenced' by other gestures, they simply overlap with one another – they are 'coproduced' – and the degree of overlap depends on the extent to which different or identical subsystems are involved.

5.3.2 Techniques in speech production research

Since speech is a dynamic and multisystem process, phonetic research must employ a variety of dynamic instrumental techniques to capture it. Most of these techniques are based around a multichannel speech data acquisition system, and large amounts of data can be processed using specially developed software for semi-automatic segmentation, labelling and statistical processing of the parallel signals.

Volume velocity of the air flow during speech is normally registered by means of a device known as a pneumotachograph. Oral and nasal air flow are best recorded via separate airtight masks in order to eliminate the risk of leakage between the two channels. As the air exits the mask, the pressure drop across a nylon gauze screen is registered by a variable reluctance differential pressure transducer. Intraoral pressure can also be measured by inserting a catheter through the nose and into the pharynx. Aerodynamic data are particularly useful for investigating obstruent voicing contrasts, for verifying the direction of air flow (egressive or ingressive), and for determining the degree and timing of nasalisation.

The most commonly used and least invasive technique for observing the laryngeal subsystem is electroglottography (EGG), also known as (electro)laryngography, which records the degree of vocal fold contact over time. A pair of electrodes placed externally either side of the larynx measures the variations in impedance to a very small electrical current passed between them. As well as producing an excellent 'clean' signal for deriving a pitch contour, the technique is useful for investigating subtle differences in the timing of vocal fold vibration and distinguishing phonation types such as breathiness and glottalisation, although waveforms must always be interpreted with care. EGG is also a useful way of looking at glottal stops and glottalised consonants, which are commonly accompanied by a single sharp rise in the signal.

Techniques for recording gestures of the oral subsystems are usually more invasive, or at least more uncomfortable. Electropalatography (EPG) is a method of registering the contact between the tongue and the roof of the mouth, using an electropalate – a denture-like acrylic plate (minus teeth), which is individually moulded to fit the palate of each speaker and is held in place by stainless steel clasps around the teeth. Mounted on the underside of this plate are a number of electrodes (>60), each of which is connected to a thin copper wire. The wires are collected into two bundles which emerge at the corners of the mouth and are connected to a control unit, and thence to the computer. During recording the speaker holds a hand electrode connected to the control unit, which supplies a small AC signal to the body; this signal is conducted from the tongue to the palate electrodes whenever contact is made. The changing patterns of linguo-palatal contact can be displayed in real time on the computer screen, usually together with a simultaneously recorded acoustic signal, and stored for subsequent analysis. A range of data reduction procedures can then be performed to extract a number of quantitative measures of contact patterns in the form of single numerical values. EPG is a useful tool for the study of the tongue tip/blade and tongue body subsystems, but can give no information on articulations further back than the front edge of the velum, no information on labial articulations and no information where there is no actual contact between the articulators (e.g. vowels).

Electromagnetic mid-sagittal articulography (EMA) is in many ways complementary to EPG. This is what is known as a flesh-point tracking technique, which tracks the movement of the tongue, lips and jaw and velum in the two dimensions of the mid-sagittal plane. Small sensors are stuck on to the surface of the articulators of interest and speakers wear a helmet that contains a number of transmitter coils which produce alternating low strength magnetic fields. These in turn generate currents in the sensors as they move through the fields enabling them to be tracked by computer. More recently 3D systems have been developed, allowing for calculation of the XYZ coordinates of the sensors, giving more complete and accurate tongue visualisation than 2D models. These systems use external fixed transmitters, thus doing away with the need for a helmet. They provide high quality information on the spatio-temporal coordination of the supralaryngeal subsystems, including labial and velar/uvular articulations, as well as movements of the velum and the jaw. Since they do not rely on actual contact between articulators for the registration of a signal, they can also provide accurate information on vowel gestures.

A technique which is less invasive, but still provides 3D information on the oral subsystems even without articulatory contact, is ultrasound. It relies on hundreds of piezoelectric crystals, which each in turn emit and receive ultra-high-frequency sound waves. Given that different media have different sound transmission properties, these waves are reflected back at different delays and with different amplitudes. Specifically, the ultrasound wave is reflected back very strongly at the intersection between the soft tissue of the tongue and the air layer above. Since muscle tissue and air have very different sound transmitting properties, the edge of the tongue can be seen as a bright white line on a good ultrasound image. The currently used real-time B-scan arrays have sample rates up to 124 Hertz (Hz, i.e. each crystal is sampled 124 times a second). As well as tracking the time course of overall tongue shape, ultrasound enables the observation of parts of the vocal tract other techniques cannot reach, especially tongue root and pharynx wall, as well as non-sagittal lingual measures such as lateral release and tongue grooving. If data are obtained in both planes, 3D images of the tongue can be constructed.

Other techniques used in the study of speech production include electromyography (EMG), which measures electrical activity in the muscles of the articulators. There are also various endoscopy-based techniques. A fibre-optic nasendoscope, for example, introduced through the nostril, with a light source and camera can be used to record the movements of the velic subsystem and, if inserted further through the velo-pharyngeal port, can be positioned over the vocal folds to study the laryngeal subsystem. In videofluoroscopy a speaker is placed between an X-ray source and an image intensifier coupled to a video camera, allowing the images to be recorded and played on a monitor. This technique is used more commonly in research into swallowing and velopharyngeal function. Magnetic resonance imaging (MRI) relies on detecting a radio-frequency signal emitted by excited hydrogen atoms in the body, using energy from an oscillating magnetic field applied at the appropriate resonant frequency. Until recently this has been anything but a 'dynamic' technique, as the speaker must maintain the vocal tract shape of the target sound for several seconds while the image is produced. The last few years has seen the advent of real-time MRI, which allows the continuous monitoring of moving tissues in real time, offering interesting possibilities for future use in speech research.

5.4 Speech acoustics

5.4.1 Goals of acoustic phonetic research

The overall goal of acoustic phonetics is to understand the relation of vocal tract shape and vocal tract subsystem gestures to the sounds that result. We seek to describe speech acoustically in sufficient detail to be able to characterise the nature of the crucial distinctions in speech: first and foremost, what distinguishes one sound from another in normal speakers of any language; but also what distinguishes a pathological speaker from the normal population (and possibly one pathology from another), what distinguishes one individual speaker from others, and what is the range of 'accidental' variation. Unlike speech production techniques, acoustic recording is totally non-invasive and can indeed take place without the knowledge of the speaker. As well as its use in linguistic description and the development of linguistic theory, acoustic phonetics has a number of practical applications, including clinical speech pathology (assessment, diagnosis and treatment), speech technology (telephony, speech synthesis and automatic speech recognition) and in forensic science (especially speaker comparison).

5.4.2 Basic principles: pressure waves

Sound consists of a series of pressure waves that produce a sensation in the human ear; these pressure waves are produced by the oscillation of air molecules. In the case of speech the source of the sound is the vibration of the vocal folds, which modulates ('chops up') the flow of air from the lungs. This produces tiny variations of between 20 μPa (= 20 millionths of a Pascal) and 20 Pa around an average atmospheric pressure of just over 100,000 Pa. These variations repeat themselves on average 110 times a second in adult men and at about twice that rate in women. The rate of repetition is known as the *fundamental frequency*, and is measured in Hertz (cycles per second). This corresponds to what we hear as the pitch of a sound. The volume of sound (what we hear as loudness) is measured in two ways: one is the *sound pressure level* (SPL), which is the force necessary to displace the air molecules per unit area (measured in Pascals) and *intensity*, which is the power transmitted per unit area (and is measured in Watts per square centimetre). Both of these ways of measuring produce inconveniently large ranges of numbers when applied to human hearing – in the case of SPL from 0.00002 Pa to 200 Pa and in the case of intensity from 10^{-16} W/cm^2 to 10^{-2} W/cm^2 (which means that the intensity of sound that causes pain is one hundred trillion times the intensity of the quietest sound we can hear). It is much more convenient (and much closer to the way our hearing works) to use a ratio scale, with a unit called the deciBel (dB). On this scale a sound that is ten times the intensity of the threshold of hearing is 10 dB, but a sound that is one million times threshold level is only 60 dB – the level of typical conversation. Waves that repeat the same pattern of pressure variation for a number of cycles are known as *periodic* waves. Since this is the type of wave produced by the vibrating vocal folds, such wave patterns (waveforms) are characteristic of voiced sounds. Waves that show random pressure variation are known as *aperiodic* waves. These are characteristic of fricatives and some stop releases. Silent intervals, mainly the result of complete closure of the articulators, are also an important part of the speech signal. Periodic waves, aperiodic waves, and silent intervals are each visible in the upper part of Figure 5.3.

5.4.3 Basic principles: harmonics and formants

The simplest kind of periodic waveform is known as a *sine* wave. It describes the kind of motion exhibited by a perfect pendulum or spring – known as simple harmonic motion – where the object in question is moved away from its point of rest (thereby storing up potential energy) and then released. It moves with constant acceleration until it reaches its maximum velocity as it passes its point of rest, thence moving with constant deceleration until it reaches a point opposite its point of release, where it moves once more with constant acceleration back to its point of rest, whereupon the next cycle begins. We can describe any sine wave in terms of just two numbers: the amplitude of vibration and the frequency of vibration. This is how air molecules behave when a sound is transmitted, but only sounds of a certain type – so-called pure tones – produce simple harmonic motion. The periodic vibrations produced by the laryngeal subsystem are much more complex. Nevertheless, like any complex periodic wave, they can be analysed in terms of a finite number of sine waves and thus described as a finite series of pairs of numbers, corresponding to the frequency and amplitude of each sine wave component or *harmonic*. In speech, the first harmonic is the

Phonetics

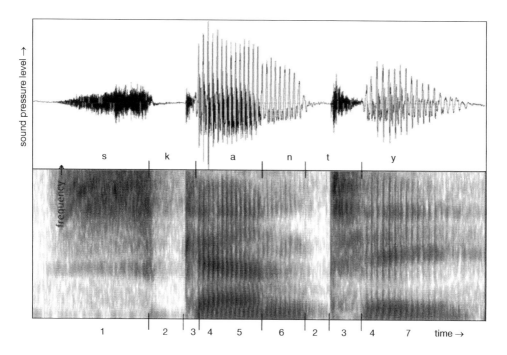

Figure 5.3 A waveform (top) and time-aligned spectrogram (bottom) of the word *scanty* as pronounced by the author (made with Praat software). (1) high-frequency aperiodic vibration (fricative); (2) silent stop closures; (3) aperiodic vibration (aspiration); (4) formant transitions from stop into vowel; (5) high amplitude periodic vibration with high first formant and mid-range second formant (open front vowel); (6) lower amplitude periodic vibration (nasal); (7) high amplitude periodic vibration with low first formant and high second formant (close front vowel)

fundamental frequency and the others (around thirty in the adult male voice) are all at whole multiples of the fundamental frequency. This means that we can represent a complex periodic waveform at any moment in time by a graph of intensity versus frequency: this is called a sound *spectrum*. The spectrum shows all of the harmonics and their intensity as generated at the larynx (see the bottom of Figure 5.4). When the fundamental frequency decreases, the first harmonic will move down the frequency axis and, as they are whole multiples of it, all the higher harmonics will move closer together. When the fundamental increases, the opposite occurs; thus the harmonics of a woman's voice are roughly twice as far apart as those of a man's. Different voice qualities will result in different relative amplitudes among the harmonics. Modal voice usually produces a spectrum which falls in amplitude from the first harmonic at a rate of roughly −12 dB per octave. The first and second harmonics (H1 and H2) will be roughly equal in amplitude, although H1 is likely to be somewhat lower. In creaky voice the spectral tilt is much shallower and the amplitude of H1 will be considerably lower than that of H2. In breathy voice the spectral tilt is much steeper than in modal voice and the amplitude of H2 is lower than that of H1.

If we want to show changes in the spectrum over time, we have to introduce a third dimension. The way this is usually done is to plot time along the horizontal axis and frequency on the vertical axis, with intensity shown by the darkness of the shading. Areas of

A. Butcher

intense energy are shown as black; less intense energy appears in a corresponding shade of grey. This is called a sound *spectrogram* – an example of one is shown in the lower half of Figure 5.3. According to the acoustic theory of speech production, the picture we see here is the product of a source and a filter: the source, as we have already seen, is the complex periodic sound made by the vocal folds, consisting of a series of harmonics. The filter is formed by the oral and nasal subsystems. Figure 5.4, consisting of component sine waves or

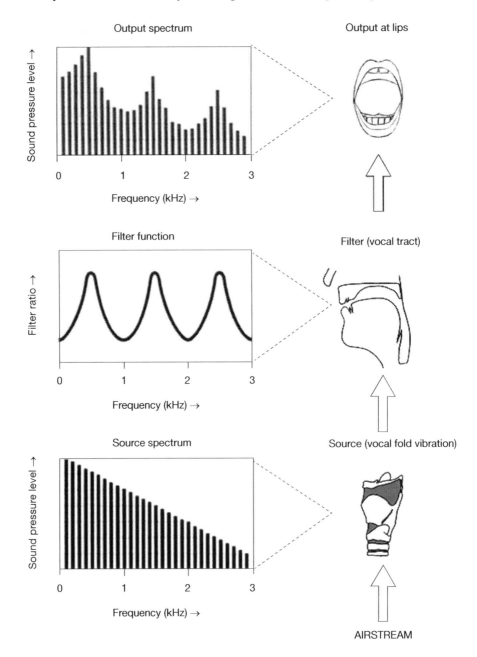

Figure 5.4 The pressure wave produced by the vibrating larynx

harmonics, shows the pressure wave produced by the vibrating larynx which is the source of the speech signal. From bottom to top, it passes through the vocal tract which acts as a filter, with a set of resonant frequencies. Harmonics in the source wave which correspond to these frequencies pass through unmodified; those in between these frequencies have their amplitude reduced. The result is the output wave emerging from the lips. A filter is a mechanism which, because of its shape, will attenuate (reduce the energy of) sounds at certain frequencies and let through sounds at other frequencies – the latter are the resonances of the filter (which can also be called a resonator). Using the same dimensions as for a spectrum (frequency on the horizontal axis, intensity on the vertical axis), we can draw a resonance curve to describe the effect that any filter will have on a source sound (see the middle of Figure 5.4). The peaks show the frequencies of the resonances and the troughs show the frequencies at which sound will be attenuated. The combination of source and filter produces a spectrum in which the harmonics vary in amplitude according to the vocal tract resonances (see top of Figure 5.4). The peaks are called *formants* and their frequency and amplitude will vary as the shape of the vocal tract changes over time during speech. They can be seen as three or four broad bands of energy on the spectrogram in Figure 5.3 (5) and (7). It is important to realise that the source component (from the laryngeal subsystem) and the filter component (from the vocal tract subsystems) vary independently of one another – i.e. the fundamental frequency goes up and down independently of whether the formants are going up or down. One of the crucial measurement tasks in acoustic phonetics is to separate out the contribution of these two components in the output signal.

There is an approximate correlation between the frequency of the lowest two formants (F1 and F2) and the position of the tongue in the mouth. Broadly speaking tongue height is inversely correlated with first formant frequency: high vowels have low F1 and low vowels have a high F1. Tongue position on the front–back dimension is correlated with second formant frequency: front vowels have high F2 and back vowels have low F2. Lip rounding lowers second formant frequency. In high front vowels (such as in *pea*) the tongue forms a narrow front cavity and a wide back cavity, resulting in a low F1 and a high F2 (see Figure 5.3 (7)). Open back vowels (such as in *pod*) have a wide front cavity and a narrow back cavity, which gives a high first formant and a low(ish) second formant. Close back rounded vowels (such as in *pool*) have two cavities of similar shape and volume, producing a low F1 and a low F2. Plotting vowels on a chart with F1 as the horizontal axis and F2 as the vertical axis shows an acoustic relationship between vowels which is remarkably similar to the traditional cardinal vowel chart (especially if the axes are flipped, so that the origins are at the top right), as can be seen in Figure 5.5.

5.4.4 Basic principles: formant transitions, noise and anti-formants

Formants also play a role in distinguishing between consonants. The rapid changes in vocal tract shape which occur when the articulators move from a consonant to a vowel or vice versa give rise to correspondingly rapid movements of the formants. These movements are known as *formant transitions*; they can easily be identified on a spectrogram, and they help differentiate between various manners of articulation. Broadly speaking, approximants have rather slow transitions, whereas stops have much faster transitions. Going from a consonant into a vowel, voiceless stops have a much abbreviated F1 transition (see Figure 5.3 (4)), laterals show an abrupt increase in F1, and nasals show jumps up in both F1 and F2. These characteristics are shown in mirror image as the articulators move from a vowel to a consonant. But it is in distinguishing places of articulation that second formant transitions

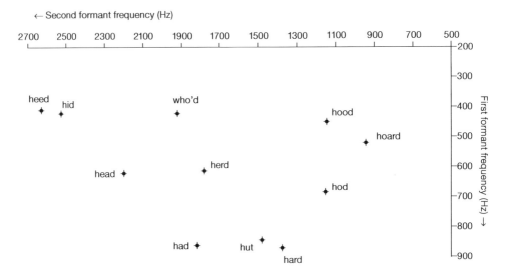

Figure 5.5 A formant chart: plotting the first formant frequency against the second formant frequency of a set of vowels produces a configuration very similar to that of the traditional vowel quadrilateral (cf. Figure 5.2)

play their most important role. Every combination of consonant place of articulation and adjacent vowel will result in a different F2 slope; the initial consonant–vowel transition in English *deep*, for example, will be slightly rising, while that of *dart* will be falling (see Figure 5.6b). This is an example of the context sensitivity issue discussed above. It can be shown, however, that if all the F2 transitions for a given place of articulation are extrapolated in time towards the consonant, they all converge at about the same frequency. This is known as the *locus* frequency and it appears to be one of the major perceptual cues to place of articulation. In general, bilabial sounds have a low-frequency locus (approximately 750 Hz in English), alveolar sounds have a mid-frequency locus (around 1,800 Hz in English) and allophones of velars before front vowels (*key*, *care*) have a high-frequency locus (around 3,000 Hz in English). Back allophones of velars (*cot*, *cook*) have a low- to mid-frequency locus (around 1,200 Hz in English). The third formant frequency is not immensely important for the differentiation of most speech sounds – with one exception: retroflex sounds have an extremely low F3 and this helps to distinguish them from their neighbours, especially the alveolars. The F3 transition at the beginning of the vowel in English *raft*, for example is extremely steep – rising from below 1,500 Hz to the 2,500 Hz target for the vowel within a few milliseconds.

There is one other major source of sound in speech other than the vibration of the vocal folds. When flowing in a wide, unconstricted space, the molecules of a liquid or gas flow smoothly in straight lines, like the water in a broad flat river bed. There are two ways to speed up the motion of the fluid and cause its flow to become turbulent. We can create channel turbulence by forming a constriction in part of the vocal tract (like a narrow river gorge) or we can create wake turbulence by introducing an obstacle into the stream, such as the upper incisors (like a rock in the river). This will cause aperiodic vibration or *noise* (like white water). All fricatives have channel turbulence, as do the voiceless stops of English at their release (see Figure 5.3 (3)); the so-called strident fricatives (such as in *see* and *she*) also

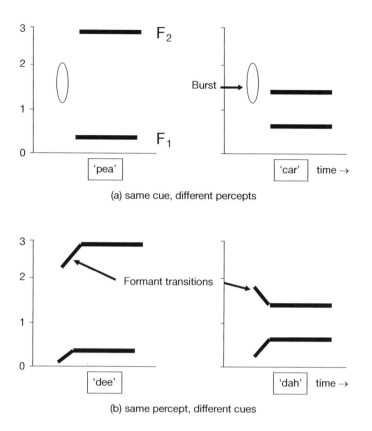

Figure 5.6 Perceptual equivalence: schematic spectrograms of synthesised speech demonstrating context sensitivity in speech perception. (a) The same burst of noise, centred at 1,500 Hz, is perceived as the release of a 'p' when followed by a high front vowel but as a 't' when followed by an open central vowel. (b) In order for listeners to hear a 'd' a completely different F2 transition is required before a high front vowel than before a low central vowel

have wake turbulence also (see Figure 5.3 (1)). The acoustic theory of speech production holds for these sounds too: the source sound generated by the turbulence is filtered by the resonances of the cavities in front of it. Meanwhile the cavities behind it, with no opening to the outside and no sound source of their own, behave as 'side branch resonators', which actually absorb energy from the source, forming valleys in the spectrum called anti-formants or *zeroes*.

All nasal stops have the pharynx plus the nasal cavity as the main resonator. They thus have a so-called nasal formant (N1) at a very low frequency (below 400 Hz) and higher nasal formants at odd multiples of this. In these sounds it is the oral cavity which is the side branch resonator. In laterals the supra-lingual space is the side branch resonator. In nasalised vowels, the pharynx and oral cavity form the main resonator just as in oral vowels, but the nasal cavities form a side branch resonator, giving these sounds great spectral complexity, which makes them more difficult to distinguish from one another than oral vowels.

5.5 Speech perception

5.5.1 Goals of speech perception research

Speech perception research is ultimately seeking answers to the invariance question from the decoding end: how continuous, dynamic, context-sensitive gestures are transformed by the listener into discrete, static, context-free mental targets. Again this can be broken down into sub-questions which mirror those of speech production research.

1. What are the units of speech perception: are they equivalent in size to phonological features, phonemes, syllables, words – or something else entirely? Is there a single unit or do we invoke different-sized units at different stages of the process?
2. How do we remember the order of phonemes that make up a word: how is the serial structure of speech represented neurally? Perceptual processing of one unit may depend on information from a preceding unit. The ordering of units is crucial to how the utterance will be perceived.
3. How does the system take into account context sensitivity? Starting points, endpoints and trajectories of gestures will differ according to segmental and prosodic context. There will be multiple cues to the same percept and the same cue may signal more than one percept (perceptual equivalence) (see Figure 5.6).
4. How does the perceptual process cope with the enormous number of degrees of freedom? How do we recognise a sound from one speaker as being perceptually equivalent to a sound from another speaker, despite differences in gender, dialect and vocal tract size?

Up until fairly recently there have been basically two ways to approach the invariance question: either look harder for invariant units in the speech signal or ignore the signal and look for invariant units 'higher up' in the central nervous system. Theories of speech perception which take the first approach are sometimes referred to as *passive* theories as they invoke the sensory pathways only. The premise is that the production and perception of speech may well share a common set of units, but that production need not be referred to for perception. The invariant units are in our perception: we learn to produce them. One such model is the exemplar-based approach which claims that particular instances of speech sounds are stored in the memory of a listener. Incoming speech signals are compared with these exemplars in the simultaneous and interactive processes of speech perception and speaker recognition.

Theories that take the second approach are often called *active* theories of speech perception, as they involve the motor neural pathways in a conversion of acoustic–phonetic information to a speech representation via articulatory knowledge. This type of theory takes the view that, since production and perception share a common set of units, therefore they must be linked. The invariant units are in our production: we learn to hear them – an idea apparently supported by the recent discovery of mirror neurones. The best known of these theories is probably the motor theory of speech perception. Theories of this type usually invoke the idea of 'duplex' perception – that listening to speech switches on a specialised module for perceiving speech. There is no doubt that there are some apparently special aspects to speech perception. For example, the sequential order of natural-sounding speech sounds is accurately reported, whereas that of non-speech sounds is not. Furthermore, highly encoded stimuli, such as initial voiced stops, appear to be perceived categorically (i.e. discriminated better at phoneme boundaries than within them), whereas less encoded stimuli, such as vowels, appear to be perceived continuously (i.e. discriminated equally well across the phonetic continuum). The preferred version of this theory nowadays is that, rather than a specific speech mode, there may be a specialised mode of listening for any acoustic signal that requires complex auditory processing.

There is, however, another approach to the invariance question, which does not look at variability in speech as a problem, but sees perception as 'exploiting' it. This is the approach taken by parallel distributed processing (PDP) theories. In contrast to the 'bottom-up' processing approach taken by passive theories and modularist active theories alike, PDP models of speech perception recognise the importance of 'top-down' processing, using multiple sources of information including acoustic cues, phonological context, syntactic/semantic context and the overlapping of information in time (right and left context effects). Listeners are said to make use of the so-called 'lawful' (i.e. rule-based) variability in speech: the invariant units are in our heads and we utilise all available information in perceiving the speech signal in terms of them. Furthermore, it is now well recognised that speech perception also integrates information from the visual modality when this is available.

Most researchers agree that there are two initial stages in the speech perception process prior to categorisation in terms of linguistic units. These are known by various names (1 sensory memory, echoic memory, sensory register, primary auditory analysis; 2 auditory short-term memory, working memory, pre-categorical acoustic storage, articulatory loop). Results from a number of different experimental paradigms point to a decay time for post-stimulatory sound traces in sensory memory of $200(\pm 50)$ ms. This figure may have a physiological explanation in terms of the short-term adaptation time in single auditory nerve fibres. Auditory attributes of sounds (such as duration, pitch, loudness and spectral form) are stored in a short-term auditory memory. Results from serial recall experiments suggest a survival time in short-term memory of one to two seconds, during which active rehearsal of items takes place (the so-called 'articulatory loop'). Research suggests that the survival time of sounds in this loop depends on the quality of information. As suggested above, there are no qualitative differences between vowels and consonants in this respect, but there are differences according to the ease of discrimination of items (and vowels typically tend to be more easily discriminable than consonants).

As to the question of units of speech perception, it would appear that the syllable may be the minimal unit of perception (needed for prosodic information and some consonantal cues). Signal chopping and alternating speech between ears is most disruptive to recognition at an interval equivalent to the duration of the syllable. This is not to say that the syllable is necessarily the basic unit of perception; in fact there may not be a single unit of perception, but rather a series or network of processing levels. Any one of these levels can be the focus of the listener's attention, but listeners normally focus on the highest level – the meaning of the message.

5.5.2 Techniques in speech perception research

Until recently one of the main barriers to understanding speech perception has been our inability to observe the process directly. Researchers were limited to the behavioural paradigm commonly used in psychology, whereby subjects are presented with stimuli and asked to respond to them in one of a number of standard ways: identifying them (yes/no, forced choice labelling), discriminating between them, rating their similarity, etc. Stimuli may be natural or synthesised, presented under ideal conditions or in noise or subjected to attenuation, filtering, or gating (shortening), presented in one or both ears or alternating between the two. We may present other sounds or images first in order to test the 'priming' effect on the subject's perception. The data may be derived by measuring the accuracy of the responses or the reaction times of the subjects. Special paradigms have been developed to test speech perception in infants and prelingual children, who respond to a presentation by e.g. increasing their sucking rate or turning their head towards a visual stimulus. In recent years eye-tracking methodology has been used, as a more accurate way of measuring reaction times and also to follow the scan path of the subject in choosing between items on a screen.

The development of neurophysiological techniques has enabled researchers to observe the brain's responses to speech stimuli unmediated by the overt behaviour of the listener (see Chapter 19). Using traditional presentation paradigms the responses of the brain can be measured employing a number of non-invasive methodologies. These show that responses at this level can be more sensitive and subtle than those measured via behavioural paradigms. For example, brain responses may reveal a sensitivity to the difference between two speech sounds which the subject may not show sensitivity to in a discrimination test. Methods used to measure neural responses to speech include electroencephalography (EEG), which measures electrical signals in biological tissue by means of a sensor net on the scalp, and magnetoencephalography (MEG), which records the magnetic signals corresponding to those electric currents by means of magnetometers. Both methods can be used to record event-related potentials (ERPs) in the brain. Such studies can indicate the timing, the degree of engagement (amplitude) and the functional equivalence of underlying processes (distribution across the scalp). Near-infrared spectroscopy (NIRS) is an optical imaging technique that estimates changes in neuronal activity through detecting regional changes in total haemoglobin concentration and oxygenation by measuring the transmission of near-infrared light through the tissue, thus yielding an index of local activation on the surface of the brain. These techniques are particularly useful in the study of infant (and even *in utero*) speech perception, and can be used to map the very early development of brain structures, and their interaction in speech perception.

Further reading

Catford, J.C. (1977) *Fundamental Problems in Phonetics*. Edinburgh: Edinburgh University Press.
Gick, B., I. Wilson and D. Derrick (2013) *Articulatory Phonetics*. Hoboken: Wiley-Blackwell.
Harrington, J.M. (2010) *Phonetic Analysis of Speech Corpora*. Oxford: Blackwell.
Harrington, J.M. and M. Tabain (eds) (2006) *Speech Production: Models, Phonetic Processes and Techniques*. New York: Psychology Press.
Ingram, J.C.L. (2007) *Neurolinguistics: An Introduction to Spoken Language Processing and its Disorders*. Part II. Cambridge: Cambridge University Press.
Johnson, K. (2011) *Acoustic and Auditory Phonetics*, 3rd edition. Hoboken: Wiley-Blackwell.
Jones, M.J. and R.-A. Knight (eds) (2013) *The Bloomsbury Companion to Phonetics*. London: Bloomsbury.
Ladefoged, P. and K. Johnson (2014) *A Course in Phonetics*, 7th edition. Boston: Wadsworth, Cengage Learning.
Ladefoged, P. and I. Maddieson (1996) *The Sounds of the World's Languages*. Oxford: Blackwell.
Laver, J. (1994) *Principles of Phonetics*. Cambridge: Cambridge University Press.
Massaro, D.W. (1987) *Speech Perception by Ear and Eye: A Paradigm for Psychological Inquiry*. Hillsdale: Lawrence Erlbaum.

6
Phonology

Harry van der Hulst

6.1 Introduction

In this chapter I present a 'conservative' view of phonology, i.e. a view that recognizes the phoneme/allophone distinction and a distinction between three rule types (morpho-lexical rules, phonemic rules and allophonic rules). The model attributes a central role to constraints (both at the phonemic and the phonetic level), not as the sole agents in phonology (as in Optimality Theory[1]), but rather as driving the application of (repair) rules (again at both levels). A model of this sort captures what in my view are unavoidable distinctions, although many models have tried to eliminate aspects of it. Along the way, I will indicate how various models deviate from this conservative model. §§6.2, 6.3 and 6.4 address some general, preliminary issues, paving the way for §6.5 which discuss the notions *levels* and *rules*. §6.6 offers some concluding remarks which make brief reference to several important topics that could not be covered in this chapter.

6.2 Is phonology necessary?

I take it to be self-evident that language, as a collection of utterances, is dependent on a grammar, which is a property of human brains. This mental grammar is a system of basic units and constraints on their combinations which generates (or recognizes) an infinite set of linguistic expressions that have a meaning and a form. A perhaps surprising recent debate among linguists is whether the form side of linguistic expressions includes information about perceptible events (e.g. events that can be heard or seen when linguistic expressions are realized as utterances). In the current view of Noam Chomsky, linguistic expressions are purely mind-internal (mental states), their function being 'to organize thought.' In this view, the mental grammar is primarily a syntactic module that generates these expressions in terms of a syntactic structure which groups basic units (packages of a conceptual structure and a syntactic labeling) into labeled constituents. In this view, the 'form' of basic units and expressions *is* the syntactic labeling and the syntactic structure with labeled terminal and non-terminal nodes (the syntactic form). This syntactic module, with the infinite set of expressions that it characterizes, is called I(nternal)-language. I-language, in Chomsky's view, does not contain a module that deals with the perceptible utterances which, for him, fall in the domain of E(xternal)-language. There must thus be an externalization module which relates the internal expressions to external perceptible events. This externalization is brought about by linking the concept/label packages referred to above to a third type of information which specifies the perceptible events (as psycho-acoustic templates and as articulatory plans). This information is also usually called 'form,' in this case meaning perceptible form. Here I define phonology as the module that achieves the externalization of linguistic expressions. It seems to me that this module is just as internal as Chomsky's notion of I-language in the sense of being a mental system. The claim that the externalization system does not belong to the so-called 'narrow language faculty' is a purely terminological matter, especially since it is far from obvious that the syntactic module comprises mechanisms that are unique to language any more or less than the externalization module.

For our purposes it is noteworthy that Chomsky's conception of the mental grammar delegates one aspect of utterances that is traditionally seen as the domain of syntactic form to phonological form, namely the linear order in which the minimal concept-label packages occur once they have been externalized in perceptible form. The need for linear order is, as the argument goes, entirely caused by the external perceptible properties which, given their nature, must mostly be produced (and perceived) one after the other.[2] Thus, Chomsky's syntactic structures are like mobiles and it is the task of 'phonology' to serialize the terminal elements of this structure. In this chapter I will not deal with this kind of external 'syntactic phonology,' which I happily will leave to the syntacticians. Clearly, even though the *necessity* for linearization can be attributed to the nature of the externalization system (and the perceptual systems that process utterances back to linguistic expressions), the principles or conventions that govern the specific linearizations that languages display are mostly non-phonological.

6.3 Phonology = phonemics and phonetics

To both lay people and many linguists it is not clear why there are two disciplines that deal with the perceptible form of linguistic expressions. Traditionally, both phonology and phonetics seem to refer to the study of sound. We must first note that the use of the morpheme 'phon' is a historical accident, due to the fact that linguists did not until recently include sign languages in their studies. This leads to the often heard equation 'language = speech,' which in addition to conflating internal and external language, implies that the external side always uses the auditory channel. If we include sign languages, the 'phon' part of these terms is an anachronism.[3] For this reason, I will consistently speak of the perceptible form of language, rather than the audible or visible form. Any humanly perceptible form would in principle qualify as the potential form side of language. But why two disciplines? While phonology and phonetics are different (according to some, completely non-overlapping) fields, in the tradition of American Structuralism, phonology is a term that includes phonetics and, in addition, phonemics. In this view, phonetics studies the complete array of physical aspects of language form (in terms of acoustic, auditory and articulatory properties), while phonemics focuses on properties of the signal that are distinctive (or contrastive), i.e. that distinguish one morpheme from another. Thus, phonetics covers both distinctive and predictable properties (which are not treated differently at this level), in practice (but not in principle) abstracting away from properties that are due to paralinguistic factors, i.e. physical and psychological properties of the speaker. Phonemics, on the other hand, studies the way in which morphemes and words are stored in the mental lexicon, on the assumption that at this *level* only distinctive properties are specified. In practice (but not in principle) non-distinctive properties are then assumed to be un(der)specified in the lexical representations.

Attention for the phonemic angle became prevalent toward the end of the nineteenth century when the development of increasingly sophisticated phonetic equipment brought to light the apparent infinite variability of the speech signal and of the 'speech sounds' in it. To explain the obvious fact that language users neglect most of that variability when they 'home in' on the linguistic expression, it was proposed that the perceptible form of this expression must be represented in terms of units that lie beneath all this 'irrelevant' variability.[4] This step can be identified as the reason for distinguishing between phonemes (relevant, i.e. distinctive properties) and 'speech sounds' (or allophones; 'all' properties) and thus between phonemics and phonetics.[5] In mostly European schools, the term 'phonology' came to be used for 'phonemics.' Here we follow the American Structuralists and use the term phonology in the general sense of covering both phonemics and phonetics.

6.4. The general form of a phonological theory

As shown in Anderson (1985), phonological theorizing (like many other human systems of thought) seems to follow a dialectic pattern such that the attention and creativity of scholars shift back and forth between what are the two major aspects of any phonological system: representations (involving the identification of units and their combinations at various levels) and derivations (dealing with relations between levels). In a general sense, then, all phonological theories agree that phonology is an input–output mapping system:

(1) F (Input): output

The function F forms the derivational aspect of the theory, whereas both inputs and outputs form the representational aspect. The derivational aspect deals with the issue of how many levels are distinguished and how these levels are related. The representational aspect concerns the structure of each level in terms of its basic units, their grouping and the constraints that capture their combinations. As shown in (2), it is possible that the phonological module contains more than one F function, such as an allophonic function (F1) and an implementation function (F2).

(2) Phonology
  F1 (phonemic representation): allophonic/phonetic representation
  F2 (phonetic representation): phonetic event

It is generally assumed that representations have a discrete compositional structure, which means that there are basic units (primes), which are either deemed universal and innate or language-specific and learned (or a combination of these), that are combined in accordance with universal and language-specific constraints. A major development in phonology in the 1940s, due to the work of Roman Jakobson, has been that the original primes, i.e. the *sequential* phonemes (taken thus far to be indivisible, holistic units), were 'decomposed' into smaller *simultaneous* units, called (distinctive) features (Jakobson *et al.* 1952). Motivation for such smaller sub-phonemic units was that rules often refer to what appear to be non-arbitrary (i.e. recurrent) groupings of phonemes. We see this, for example, in the English aspiration rule which accounts for the aspirated allophones of the *group* /p, t, k/ in the onset of stressed syllables. This grouping can be found in other rules or constraints in English or other languages. Assuming that the members of this group share a property, or set of properties, which are represented in terms of features, the aspiration rule can make reference to these features rather than to a (random) list of phonemes. In addition, with features, the change from /p/ to [pʰ] does not involve the substitution of one 'whole segment' by another, but rather can be stated as the change or addition of specific property.[6]

In the remainder of this chapter we focus on derivational issues. For reasons of space, there is no review of representational issues.

6.5 Derivational issues: levels and rules

6.5.1 Three levels

The recognition of phonemes as distinct from allophones implies that we recognize at least two levels of representation: the phonemic level and the phonetic (or allophonic) level. The phonemic representation can be identified as the manner in which the phonological form of linguistic expressions is represented in the mental lexicon. However, the phonetic representation, although closer to the actual perceptible event, is usually not identified with it. Most phonologists take both the phonemic and the phonetic level to be mental and symbolic. At the phonetic level, the symbols (i.e. features) refer to phonetic events (articulatory plans or actions and psycho-acoustic 'images' or actual acoustic properties). We could regard the phonetic level as an articulatory plan: 'The result of phonological encoding [of the lexical form] is a *phonetic* or *articulatory plan*. It is not yet overt speech; it is an internal representation of how the planned utterance should be articulated – a program for articulation' (Levelt 1989: 12). Whether the features at the phonological level also refer to phonetic events has remained a matter of dispute and in some approaches, phonemic symbols are taken to be substance-free, their only role being 'to be different' so that they can differentiate morphemes (see Hjemslev 1953). A more common view is to regard phonological features (taken to characterize units at *both* the phonemic and phonetic level) as mental concepts of phonetic events. (Below I discuss the view that the phonetic level requires additional phonetic features or distinctions.)

That the phonetic representation is symbolic is suggested by the use of IPA symbols for units at this level, which imply a discreteness that is not present in the physical (articulatory or acoustic) event. Indeed, the term 'speech sound,' as a 'slice' of the speech signal, refers to an abstract unit. Therefore, if one refers to IPA symbols at the phonetic level as 'speech sounds,' this is misleading since the term refers to symbolic units which, as such, are not present in the speech signal. This means that there is yet a third 'level' which a phonological model must recognize, which is the output of a system of phonetic implementation, i.e. a set of rules that count as instructions to a device (such as the human vocalization system) that will deliver a physical event that is based on the articulatory plan (i.e. the phonetic representation). We thus end up with the following phonological model shown in (3).

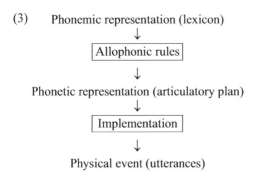

Most phonologists would assume that not only the implementation system but also the allophonic system apply 'on line,' i.e. in the actual externalization of a linguistic expression. In this chapter, I will not discuss phonetic implementation explicitly.

Allophonic properties can depend on the position of phonemes with respect to the edge of constituents (such as syllable, foot or the word). The allophonic rules that account for them are 'habits of articulation' (Hockett 1955) that characterize the speech characteristics of a specific language. These rules are not universal (not all languages aspirate stops), although they are phonetically 'natural' or phonetically 'motivated,' i.e. grounded in phonetic 'tendencies.' These rules are often said to be automatic in that they apply wherever the appropriate context is met. In this sense, such rules cannot have arbitrary exceptions.[7]

The rather simple diagram in (3) raises a host of questions, answers to which lead to different phonological theories. Theories differ in terms of how many levels are taken to be necessary to connect the representation that language users store in their mental lexicon (i.e. the phonemic representation) to physical events as well as in the way that 'comparable levels' are defined. Additionally, if rules are ordered (e.g. within the allophonic function), there will be so-called intermediate levels. However, even though there are several different views on the nature of these levels and about procedural methods to derive phonemes from phonetic transcriptions, it would seem that a distinction between a phonemic and a phonetic/allophonic level has been foundational to the development of phonology.[8]

At the level of language description, however, the phoneme/allophone distinction is 'universally' accepted. It is taught to all students who take linguistic courses and forms the basis of all language description. In practical terms, Pike (1947) refers to phonemics as a technique to reduce speech to writing, since writing systems predominantly provide symbols for distinctive units, and indeed, most often use alphabetic units that symbolize phonemes.[9] In this context it is important to see, however, that the 'emic/etic' distinction is not committed to slicing the speech signal into the kinds of units that are represented in alphabetic writing systems. If one were to hold the view that the basic distinctive units are bigger (e.g. syllable-sized) or smaller (features), the same distinction can be applied. Correspondingly, writing systems can be based on such larger or smaller units (see Rogers 2005 and Chapter 4, this volume).

6.5.2 The phonetic level

An important (and unresolved) question is what kind of variation is taken to fall within the realm of allophony (as opposed to what is referred to as the implementation system). Even when one excludes variation due to paralinguistic factors and restricts oneself to phonetic properties that are due to the linguistic environment (i.e. surrounding phonemes, stress and word edges) language descriptions (i.e. IPA transcriptions) often ignore 'very minute' variation, which is then referred to as resulting from co-articulation when the variation is due to the influence of neighboring phonemes, but even positionally determined properties may be relegated to another 'lower' level of analysis (i.e. implementation). For example, in phonological works on English, the slight difference in place of articulation for the phoneme /k/ in words like *cool* and *keel* is taken for granted. Implicitly or explicitly, this minute variation is relegated to phonetic implementation, implying that 'proper allophony' is part of the phonology. In practice, we see that allophonic rules are mostly proposed for predictable properties that could have been distinctive, as witnessed by the fact in some other language they are distinctive. For example, aspiration is distinctive in Thai where minimal pairs can be found (as in 4a) that contrast only in this difference, which leads the phonological analyses in (4b) for English and Thai, respectively:[10]

(4) a. [pɔ:n] to wish   [pʰɔ:n] also
    [tɔp] to support   [tʰɔp] be suffocate
    [kat] to cut   [khat] to polish
    b. English   Thai

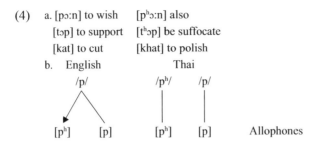

Allophones

Knowing what kinds of properties could be distinctive, but not yet knowing that they actually are distinctive in the language at issue, prompts the linguist to take note of them in the IPA transcription. However, limiting allophonic variation to variation that could be distinctive is *not* an official rule of phonological analysis. Actual descriptive practices differ and many descriptions will also write allophonic rules for phonetic properties that have not been found to be ever distinctive. In fact, IPA, with its rich set of diacritics allows for a narrow transcription which captures minute co-articulatory or positional effects (although up to the limit that is allowed by the diacritics).[11] Arguably, a broad transcription could be defined as one that aims at registering potentially distinctive properties. But this practice is not always followed. For example, many analyses of English propose an allophonic rule that derives an unreleased variant of stops in English (e.g. [p˺]) in syllable final position. However, a difference between released and unreleased stops has never been shown to be distinctive in any language and there is therefore no generally recognized distinctive feature that allows us to express this difference. An additional issue is that one cannot always be sure whether a case of phonetic variation should be expressed in terms of a distinctive feature because it is not clear how to value a phonetic distinction as falling within the scope of a given distinctive feature. Distinctive features do not necessarily correlate with the exact same phonetic property (or set of properties) cross-linguistically.

The view of a phonetic representation as encoding predictable properties that are, at least potentially, distinctive is thus not the only view, although that view is necessary if one adopts the strategy that the phonemic and the allophonic level are stated in terms of one set of features. However, another view of what ought to be expressed at the phonetic level is that this level should encode everything that is under the 'control' of the speaker which means that it regards phonetic effects that are characteristic of a specific language and thus not universally present in all languages as a matter of phonetic necessity. In this view everything that goes above and beyond the call of what is universally necessary (given the nature and working of articulatory organs) belongs to the phonetic level (see Anderson and Lightfoot 2002 for a defense of this view). This view implies that the vocabulary of the phonetic level is different from that of the phonemic level. It requires a special set of phonetic features in addition to the distinctive features. In addition, Anderson and Lightfoot (2002 Ch. 6) argue that what must be expressed at the phonetic level is not just what can be stated in positive properties, it can also regard negative properties when a language displays a suppression of some phonetic tendency, e.g. the suppression of phonetic pitch raising after voiceless consonants in languages that use pitch distinctively. The difference between the two views that we have discussed is dependent on whether non-universal phonetic processes must be attributed to the phonetic level (keeping implementation universal) or not; in the latter case we allow phonetic implementation to include language-specific properties (see Pierrehumbert 1990).

One possible conclusion (which gives credit to both views) is that it may be necessary to recognize that specific cases of phonetic variation are ambiguous, i.e. analyzable as allophonic or as implementational, given that the implementational system is not limited to universal effects only. This, I would argue, is not a bad result, because ambiguity of this kind will allow phonological processes to migrate from one submodule (implementation) to the next (allophony), and from there on to the phonemic level (see Chapter 7).

6.5.3 The phonemic level: redundant properties

Allophonic rules specify contextually (i.e. syntagmatically) predictable properties of phones at the phonetic level. In this section, we discuss the idea that phonemes as such have predictable properties as well. We must try to establish whether these predictable properties are truly different from those that have been called allophonic.

For example, one commonly finds the claim that in a typical five vowel system (/i/, /u/, /e/, /o/, /a/), the value for the feature [±round] is fully predictable in terms of the rules in (5), where the value of α is either + or −.

(5) a.   [+low] → [−round]
    b. [−low, αback] → [αround]

In Chomsky and Halle (1968) (henceforth: *SPE*, for *The Sound Pattern of English*) rules of this sort are called segment structure rules (or conditions). Predictable specifications of this kind are often called redundant and for this reason rules like (5) are also called redundancy rules.

However, the context-free segment structure rules are not the only rules that characterize redundancy in phonemic representations. Let us consider an example of a context-sensitive redundancy. In English we can find words that start with three consonants (*splash, strap, squash*). In such cases the initial consonant is always /s/, the second is always a stop and the third is always an approximant. This means that the phonemic string /spl/, /str/ or /skw/ can be represented with minimal specification, leaving out many feature specifications of /s/, /p/ or /t/ and /l/, /r/ or /w/. In fact the first consonant need not be featurally specified at all. All of its properties are predictable. For the second and third consonant we only need to know that it is a labial and an approximant, respectively (6).

(6) /s/   /p/   /l/
    -      [−continuant] [+approximant]
         [+labial]

It would seem that, just as there are paradigmatic constraints on the combination of features within a phoneme (as expressed in segment structure rules or conditions), there are also syntagmatic constraints on feature specifications. These constraints are often called phonotactic constraints (which in some uses also include the segment structure rules). In the case of (6) many feature specifications are dependent on the mere presence of other consonants in the word-initial cluster. While these, then, are predictable, they do not fall within the scope of allophony since there is no complementary distribution of two phonetic entities. The 's' phone in (6) is not in complementary distribution with any other phonetically similar phone. Rather, we are dealing here with specific statements about the defective distribution of phonemes. In the spot before 'pl' no other consonant than /s/ can appear. To put it differently: in this position all consonantal distinctions are neutralized and the product of this neutralization is /s/. We see a similar distributional fact in languages that limit the number of consonants that can occur in the syllabic coda position (Itô 1986). The fact is that there are constraints regarding the distribution of phonemes and such constraints entail predictabilities regarding the feature specification of consonants that occupy positions that are excluded for other consonants. These predictabilities hold at the phonemic level and are thus different in nature from the syntagmatic predictabilities that hold at the phonetic level and which are captured in allophonic rules.

Whether redundancies that follow from the context-free, paradigmatic constraints should be stated at the phonemic level or can be included in the set of allophonic rules is not so easy to decide. It could be argued that the predictable (redundant) roundness of back vowels falls within the same realm as the predictable (allophonic) aspiration of voiceless obstruents in English. In both cases, one might argue that the predictable properties have the function of enhancing the phonetic identity of phonemes and that, in some other language, these properties could be distinctive. For example in Turkish the roundness value of /u/ is not predictable because this language has a back unrounded vowel at the same vowel height. We can then say that phonemes can have predictable properties which occur in all their occurrences or in occurrences in certain positions and there is no obvious reason why we would not capture both in allophonic rules. However, if one would have empirical or theoretical reasons to claim that there has to be a level with fully specified phonemic units (stripped only of contextual predictabilities), it would have to follow that paradigmatic constraints must be met at the phonemic level in which they cannot be collapsed with contextual allophonic rules.

Concluding then that fully specified phonemes contain redundant properties (at the very least those that are syntagmatically conditioned), it has been assumed in several models that redundant properties at the phonemic level remain unspecified in the lexical representation. This requires redundancy statements to function as rules that fill in redundant values at some point in the derivation, presumably before phonetic implementation and perhaps even before the application of allophonic rules. *SPE* decided against such underspecification on technical grounds. Redundancies would still be captured in rules or conditions that function as indications of the 'low cost' of redundant specifications. An early argument in favor of underspecification based on 'saving memory space' is no longer deemed convincing given the vast storage capacity of the human mind. How could we decide between the full-specification theory and the impoverished theory? A possible window on how the human brain represents the form of words lexically comes from research that uses neuro-imaging techniques (see Lahiri and Reetz 2010). At present, what this kind of work is going to show is still in dispute.[12]

We have thus far assumed that in case of contrast, where both values of a feature are non-redundant, both values of a feature must be lexically specified. This is called contrastive specification. In Archangeli (1984) and Kiparsky (1982) it is proposed that even in case of contrast one of the values can be left unspecified. This increases the degree of underspecification since now, in addition to leaving out truly redundant values, we also leave out one value for each distinctive feature. This is called radical underspecification. In this approach, we get an additional set of 'fill-in' rules (often called default rules) which specify for each feature the complement value of the lexically specified value. For example, in a language having a contrast between stops and fricatives we could specify only the latter as [+continuant], which requires a default fill-in rule:

(7) [∅continuant] → [+continuant]

A decision on which value is left unspecified would have to be based on the 'activity' of this value in the sense of playing an active part in the phonology. The default value could be universally fixed or what is default could be language-specific. Archangeli (1984) suggests that there is a universal bias for the default, but allows that languages may overturn this bias. The default value is also often called the unmarked value, which seems fitting, because it is literally unmarked. This would make the lexically specified value the marked value.

Unary features (also called privative, single-valued) embody a radicalization of radical underspecification in the sense that it is now claimed that for each distinctive dimension only one 'value' plays a role in the phonology. This 'value' then is equal to the feature label itself, [round], [nasal], [low], etc. Anderson and Ewen's (1987) Dependency Phonology model presents the most explicit defense of unary features. Government Phonology (Kaye *et al.* 1985) claims that the unary features all have stand-alone potential, i.e. each of them by themselves represents a possible phoneme. There can still be redundancy in a model of this kind in the sense that for any given phoneme system certain unary features may be predictable on the basis of others. For example, a feature [ATR] (Advanced Tongue Root) would be redundant for high vowels if there is no ATR-distinction at this height, and assuming that the high vowels would be phonetically [ATR]. It is even possible to conceive of radical underspecification, if a system of this sort would make use of the null-option. For example, a three vowel system (/i/, /u/, /a/) could be represented as in (8).

(8) /i/ /u/ /a/
    -   U   A   (Default element: I)

For extensive discussion of binary and unary feature theories, see Ewen and Hulst (2000).

In conclusion, we have two understandings of the phonemic level, one impoverished, being stripped of redundant values and one fully specified. Dresher (2009) offers a recent defense of the minimal, i.e. impoverished view, on the grounds that this approach explains why redundant value would appear to play no active role in phonological rules that apply at the phonemic level (i.e. the rules we discuss in §6.5.5).

6.5.4 Phonemic overlap and the morphophonemic level

Returning to the allophonic rule of English that creates aspirated variants for voiceless stops (see (4)) we note that in this case the phonemes /p/, /t/ and /k/ each have two allophones that uniquely belong to each phoneme. Voiceless stops occur in aspirated and unaspirated variants which are in complementary distribution (which means that they occur in non-overlapping sets of contexts). The standard analysis has been to analyze aspiration as contextually conditioned, occurring before a stressed vowel (unless preceded by /s/), with unaspirated stops occurring elsewhere. This then leads to postulating the phonemes /p/, /t/ and /k/ (where the symbol choice reflects that the unaspirated stop is seen as 'the basic variant') and an aspiration rule (see (4b)) which accounts for the predictable property of aspiration, creating aspirated allophones [pʰ], [tʰ] and [kʰ] in addition to the allophones [p], [t] and [k] (which reflect the 'direct realization' of the phoneme). However, it may also occur that an allophone counts as the manifestation of two different phonemes such as the flap [ɾ] in American English which is an allophone of the /t/ and the /d/ when these two phonemes occur intervocalically with stress on the preceding vowel, as in [ɹaɪɾɔɹ], which is the phonetic form for 'writer' and 'rider.'[13] This is known as phonemic overlap (9).

(9) 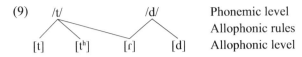 Phonemic level
Allophonic rules
Allophonic level

(There may of course be additional allophones for both phonemes; the bold allophones are taken to be the 'basic' ones.)

Rules that create phonemic overlap are called neutralizing rules. Neutralization occurs when in a given context the contrast between two phonemes of language L is neutralized.[14] In the case of flapping the product of neutralizing the contrast between /t/ and /d/ is a shared phone that is unique to that context. In other cases, the phone can be identical to another allophone of one of the phonemes. A famous example of this occurs in Dutch where in syllable final position there is no contrast between voiced and voiceless obstruents. The product of neutralization is a voiceless obstruent. Consider the pairs of words in (10).

(10)   [hɔnt]   'dog' SG   [hɔndən]   'dog' PL
       [wɑnt]   'wall' SG [wɑndən]   'wall' PL

The suffix –ən indicates plurality. Observe that the final [t] corresponds to [d] when the plural suffix is present. This means that [t] alternates with [d]. We can analyze this by postulating that the morphemes in question end in /d/ in their lexical representation (as witnessed by the plural) and that this /d/ gets 'realized' as [t] when it occurs word finally. The observed alternation thus provides evidence for the allophonic rule of final devoicing which responds to the phonetic constraint in (11a).[15]

(11)   a.   * [–son, +voice])$_\sigma$
       b.   [d] → [t] / _)$_\sigma$

The effect of this rule is that it causes phonemic overlap (12).

(12)   /t/   /d/
         /\   /\
       [t] [t] ← [d]
            11(b)

Thus, flapping and final devoicing neutralize a contrast that exists in the language under analysis. I take both rules to be allophonic rules because they are fully automatic. There are no lexical exceptions to either rule.

We should note that final devoicing, just like flapping and aspiration, creates what I will call phonetic allomorphy, i.e. allomorphy due to an allophonic rule (13).

(13)   Aspiration: for 'invite ~ invit-ee': [ɪnvaɪt] ~ [ɪnvaɪtʰ]
       Flapping: for 'write ~ writ-er': [raɪt] ~ [raɪɾɚ]; for 'ride' ~ 'rid-er': [raɪd] ~ [raɪɾ]
       Final devoicing: for 'hond ~ hond-en': [hɔnt] ~ [hɔnd]

The analysis of flapping and final devoicing as allophonic rules departs from the American Structuralist school which adopted a principle (called biuniqueness in Chomsky and Halle 1965) stating that each phone could only be an allophone of one phoneme. In the Dutch devoicing case this implies that since [t] is clearly an allophone of /t/ (in all non-final positions as well as in final position where there is no 'd~t' alternation), it must be an allophone of /t/ in all final positions, even where it alternates with [d].

The biuniqueness principle disallowed American Structuralists from analyzing the final devoicing alternation as a rule that mediates between the phonemic and the allophonic level and, as a result, this alternation could not be captured at all. To this end they postulated an extra phonemic level, called the morphophonemic level (where the units, called morphophonemes, are placed between double slant lines) and a rule like final devoicing (now called a morphophonemic rule) would relate these two levels:

(14) //b// //d// //g// //v// //z// //ɣ//   morphophonemic level
      ↓   ↓   ↓   ↓   ↓   ↓   final devoicing as a morphophonemic rule
     /p/   /t/   /d/   /f/   /s/   /χ/   phonemic level
      | | | | | | (allophonic rules)
     [p]   [t]   [d]   [f]   [s]   [x]   phonetic level

The morphophonemic level represents all morphemes in an invariant form (i.e. /hɔnd/ for the two allomorphs), but American Structuralists did not attribute a specific (psychologically realistic) value to this level. They saw it as a convenient way to capture alternations between what they regarded as independent phonemes.

Generative phonologists rejected the distinction between the morphophonemic and the phonemic level, following Halle (1959) who argued that this approach leads to undesirable consequences because sometimes what looks like a single process can have non-neutralizing effects in some cases and neutralizing effects in others. Consider the following case in Dutch. Voiceless stops become voiced before voiced stops (15).

(15)   o[p] + [d]oen   >   o[bd]oen   'up+do: to put up'
       ui[t]+rengen   >   ui[db]rengen   'out+bring: to bring out'
       za[k] + [d]oek   >   za[gd]oek   'pocket+cloth: handkerchief'

In the first two cases we get neutralization because /b/ and /d/ are independent phonemes, distinct from /p/ and /t/. Hence changing /p/ in to 'b' and /t/ into 'd' is neutralizing. Therefore, in the morphophonemic approach the process changes //p// and //t// into /b/ and /d/. However in the third case the rule is non-neutralizing because Dutch does not have a phoneme /g/. So, now we have to describe this as an allophonic rule which 'realizes' /k/ as [g]. It follows that we have to state what seems to be the same process twice, once as a morphophonemic rule and once as an allophonic rule (16).

(16)   //p// //t// //k//   morphophonemic level
        ↓   ↓ | morphophonemic rule
       /b/   /d/   /k/   phonemic level
        | | ↓   allophonic rule
       [b]   [d]   [g]   phonetic level

Clearly, this is not a desirable result. If one has to state the same process twice, it feels like one misses a generalization. Halle (1959) argued that we therefore need to abandon the phonemic level and go directly from the morphophonemic level (taken to be the lexical or underlying level) to the phonetic (surface) level. This claim went into history as implying that the phoneme was no longer needed. This, of course, is not the correct conclusion.

Rather, what cases of this sort show is that we must allow allophonic process to be neutralizing (as I in fact assumed thus far), so that we can state all three changes as an allophonic rule. This implies a rejection of biuniqueness. Now the phonemic and morphophonemic level can be collapsed into one level, which we should call the phonemic level (whether impoverished or fully specified) because it represents the distinctive units that are stripped of their allophonic properties.

6.5.5 Allomorphy

6.5.5.1 Morpho-lexical rules

Allophonic rules, as we have seen, create allophonic variation. In doing so they can also create what I called phonetic allomorphy, i.e. form variation of morphemes at the systematic phonetic level, such as [invaɪt^h] in *invitee* and [invaɪt] in *invite*. We concluded that phonetic allomorphy results from rules that apply at the phonetic level, called allophony rules. We now turn to another kind of rule that applies at the phonemic level and that changes the phonemic make-up of morphemes, depending on the occurrence of these morphemes in combination with other morphemes. There are in fact two major kinds of phonemic rules, namely morpho-lexical rules and phonotactically-motivated rules. In this section I discuss the former class. The second class forms the subject of §6.5.5.2.

The morpho-lexical rules form a somewhat heterogeneous group and finer distinctions have been made. Different theories and text books use these or other terms sometimes with differences in definition. *SPE* refers to a (not clearly defined) category of 'adjustment rules.' These are rules that 'express properties of lexical formatives in restricted syntactic contexts and they modify syntactically generated structures in a variety of ways' (*SPE*: 236). In other words, readjustment rules bridge the morphosyntactically generated structure and the phonological component for the purpose of phonological rules that apply word-internally and across word boundaries. Those that perform segmental changes fail to qualify as 'phonological rules proper' because they are restricted to specific morphemes and/or triggered by specific morphemes. Here I will include adjustment rules within the class of morpho-lexical rules which in addition contains rules that *SPE* would treat as proper phonological rules because they appear to be largely phonologically conditioned, although often in addition being dependent on idiosyncratic non-phonological information such as lexical marking (for triggering or undergoing the rule) up to reference to specific morphemes and perhaps also word class. For example, in *SPE* a rule is proposed (called *velar softening*) that replaces the /k/ by /s/ in words like *electric* ~ *electricity*. There could be doubt, however, that this substitution is conditioned by phonemic context and it has been argued that the trigger here is a specific suffix, or rather a set of suffixes (see Strauss 1982).

Morpho-lexical rules create allomorphy that is clearly not due to allophonic processes. However, they share with neutralizing allophonic rules the fact that they have phonemes as outputs, which makes them structure-preserving (Kiparsky 1982). In the American Structuralist approach these rules, if stated at all, are included in the class of morphophonemic rules, together with the neutralizing allophonic rules (see §6.5.3), since the biuniqueness principle forces all rules that seem to have phonemes as outputs in that category. In doing so this approach collapsed into the morphophonemic set two very different kinds of rules, namely neutralizing allophonic rules and morpho-lexical rules. *SPE*, on the other hand, recognizes only two levels and thus only one set of rules that also lumps together two very different kinds of rules, namely morpho-lexical rules and all allophonic rules. This aspect of standard Generative Phonology was an important reason for having to acknowledge extrinsic rule ordering since, as one might expect, morpho-lexical rules (applying *at* the phonemic level) tend to precede allophonic rules (applying at the phonetic level).

On a very large scale the phonological research community responded to *SPE* by re-establishing the distinction between morpho-lexical rules and allophonic rules in one form or another (although the rejection of biuniqueness was not disputed), leading to models in which morpho-lexical rules apply in a separate component, after or in conjunction with the morphology, and before all the allophonic rules.

Models differ with regard to the characterization of morpho-lexical rules. In some models, such as Natural Generative Phonology (Hooper 1986), allomorphy rules are not considered to be rules at all. Rather it is assumed that allomorphy is dealt with by listing the allomorphs in the lexicon (adopting a proposal by Hudson 1974). This could be done in a maximally economic way (17).

(17)   /ilɛktrɪ{k/s}/

This requires a distribution rule which states that /s/ occurs before a specified set of suffixes. Alternatively, one could list allomorphs separately with insertion frames:

(18)   /ilɛktrɪs/ [_ ity, ...]
        /ilɛktrɪk/ (elsewhere)

Hudson's proposal narrows the gap between phonological allomorphy and suppletion. Full suppletion would occur when the two allomorphs do not share a phonemic substring and thus must be listed as completely independent forms (such as /go/ and /wen/). In other proposals morpho-lexical rules are recognized as string-altering rules, but denied phonological status and treated as adjuncts of morphological rules.

In the lexical phonology model of Kiparsky (1982), the difference between morpho-lexical rules and allophonic rules was acknowledged by relegating these classes of rules to different components of the grammar, leading to the model in (19):

(19)   Lexical representations
            |
        Class I morphology   ↔ level 1 phonology
            | lexical phonology
        Class II morphology   ↔ level 2 phonology   (phonemic)
            |
        Syntax > prosodic structure ↔ phonology (post-lexical: allophonic)

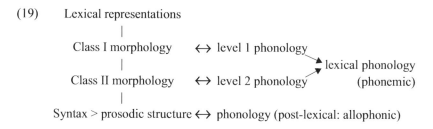

Post-lexical rules are not sensitive to morphological structure or morpheme identity; they can only see phonological information. In fact, they cannot see the syntactic structure either, but rather refer to the prosodic organization that is derived from it (Nespor and Vogel 1986). By separating affixes over two levels, all rules that apply at level 1 can be formulated without much specific reference to morpheme identity and rule features so that they appear as purely phonological rules. While this is true to a large extent for a subclass of level 1 rules (namely the phonotactically-motivated rules that we focus on in the next section), many instances of level 1 rule lack full generality and therefore squarely fall within the morpho-lexical rule class. Rather than 'indexing' every rule individually for those affixations that trigger them, level 1 rules are thus indexes as a group. Clearly, level ordering is a mechanism that avoids having to limit a certain rule to a subclass of affixed, which gives such rules the appearance of rules that are morphology-insensitive. The lexical model has been criticized on various grounds; see Strauss (1982) and Harris (1987).

6.5.5.2 Phonotactically-motivated phonemic rules

There is a class of rules that the American Structuralists included in their class of morphophonemic rules that is much less dependent on morphological information than morpho-lexical rules. Recall that, following the principle of biuniqueness, *all* rules that output phonemes had to be included in this class. However, apart from neutralizing allophonic rules, there are two different kinds of non-allophonic rules that output phonemes. On the one hand there are the morpho-lexical rules that were discussed in the previous section, while on the other hand there are rules that would appear to be driven by phonotactic constraints that hold of the phonemic level. There are constraints on the combination of phonemes that refer to such domains as the syllable, the foot or the word. These constraints capture regularities in the composition of words that need to be stated. Such constraints, called phonotactic constraints in §6.5.3, effectively account for the distribution of phonemes, which is always defective, implying that no phoneme can occur in combinations (following or preceding) with all other phonemes.[16]

It is not so obvious that the /k/~/s/ rule is motivated by a phonemic phonotactic constraint that is valid for English words (20).

(20)   * kɪ (unstressed)

If one were to pronounce *electricity* with a /k/ instead of /s/, this does not seem violate a phonotactic constraint on phoneme combinations. In other cases, such as the rule that changes the nature of vowels in *serene ~ serenity* (called 'trisyllabic laxing') we actually find exceptions such as *obese ~ obesity, nice ~ nicety* which can be taken as an indication that this change is not driven by a phonotactic constraint that holds of the word domain at the phonemic level.

Another case of allomorphy that might more plausibly be said to be enforced by a phonotactic constraint involves the negative prefix in English. Consider the word pairs in (21).

(21)   edible   i/n/-edible
       possible   i/m/-possible
       credible   i/ŋ/-credible
       legal   i/l/-legal
       regular   i/r/-regular

We note that the prefix form varies in its consonant: it ends in /n/, /m/, /ŋ/, /l/ or /r/. One of the constraints on phoneme sequences within simplex words in English forbids sequences like /np/ and /nk/. I will state these constraints simply, as in (22).

(22)   * /np/, */nk/

To support the validity of these constraints, we can point to the fact that there are no monomorphemic words that display sequences of this sort. We have /pump/, but not /punp/, /iŋk/ but not /ink/. It turns out that the constraints that are valid for monomorphemic words are also valid for a subclass of polymorphic words, i.e. domains that are simplex as far as the phonology is concerned, even though they may have morphological structure. This means that when we combine the morphemes 'in' and 'possible' or 'credible,' the grammar produces a unit that is ill-formed in terms of its phonemic form (23).

(23)   i/n-p/ossible
        i/n-k/redible

The idea here is that when the morphology has produced a new form, this form needs to be checked by the phonology against the list of phonotactic constraints at the phonemic level. At this point it could have been that these derivations are simply blocked, deemed to be ungrammatical. The grammar tells you: find some other way to say that something is not possible, or think it, but do not try to say it all! But this is not what happens in this case. Rather, the phonology makes available a rule to 'repair' the ill-formed product which in this case is done by replacing /n/ by either /m/ or /ŋ/ (24).

(24)   /n/   →   /m/
        /n/   →   /ŋ/

We then assume that a repair rule will only come into action when a constraint violation is detected and also that there is a general way of guaranteeing that the correct repair is applied; see Calabrese (2005) for an extensive discussion of the constraint-and-repair approach. Clearly, the repair rules are not random. Before a /p/, a so-called nasal consonant can only be /m/ and before /k/ it can only be /ŋ/. Thus, given that the basic form has a nasal consonant to begin with, the repair rules make a minimal adjustment to ensure that the complex word no longer violates the constraints that 'flag' it as ill-formed. The motivation for taking the form with /n/ as basic is that this is the consonant that occurs when the base starts with a vowel.[17]

Note that the change in *illegal* and *irregular* does not follow from the constraints in (23) but it is likely that English has a phonotactic constraint that forbids /nl/ and /nr/, since a search in this chapter *only* delivers the example 'only.' We can thus posit two other repair rules, as in (25).

(25)   /n/   →   /l/
        /n/   →   /r/

While it could be argued that morpho-lexical rules, if they apply actively, replace whole phonemes by other phonemes, phonotactically-motivated rules lend themselves more readily to formulations that refer to features.

Many phonotactically-motivated rules directly serve syllable structure constraints. For example, when a language prohibits hiatus, and morphology creates a sequence /...v+v.../, repair rules must be applied. It is possible that either a consonant is inserted or a vowel is deleted. The famous case of Yawelmani, analyzed in Kisseberth (1970), who drew attention to the central role of constraints, provides a good example of insertion and vowel shortening rules that conspire to prevent syllable rhymes that consist of three phonemes (either VCC, which trigger epenthesis, or VVC which triggers vowel shortening).

Concluding, we end up with the model given in (26).

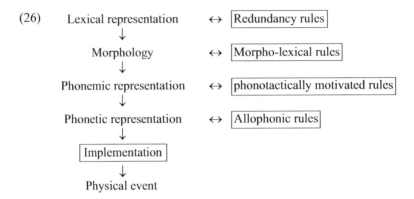

In a model of this kind, there is very little if any need for extrinsic rule ordering, since it imposes an extrinsic ordering on phonological generalizations of different kinds. Anderson (1975), while admitting that this ordering scheme obtains in general, presents some cases in which allophonic rules seem to precede rules lower in the ranking, especially when the lower-ranking rules are reduplicative operations. Many rules are not so easy to classify. Also, given that phonotactically-motivated rules can have exceptions there is a continuum to morpho-lexical rules once exceptions accumulate.

As mentioned in §6.1, models differ greatly with respect to the issue of levels. In some models, no sharp distinction is made between allophonic rules and the implementation module (Liberman and Pierrehumbert 1984). This is also essentially the model that is proposed in Linell (1979) who offers a very detailed and still very relevant discussion of many aspect of phonological theory. In such models, one could still recognize rules that apply at the phonemic level. However, some single-level, so-called monostratal models do not differentiate between phonemic rules and allophonic rules, such as Declarative Phonology (Scobbie 1997) and Government Phonology (Kaye *et al.* 1985, 1990). A rather extreme monostratal view (called exemplar-based phonology, Bybee 2001; Pierrehumbert 2001) is that lexical representations are phonetic in nature, i.e. episodic 'recordings' of actual speech events. Still other models, instead of having fewer levels, distinguish additional levels, such as for example stratificational theory, versions of which postulate a multitude of levels (Lamb 1966). Goldsmith (1993) proposes a model with three levels (morpheme level, word level and phonetic level) with rules applying at these levels and rules relating levels. Koskenniemi (1983) develops a two-level model with rules that state simultaneous correspondences between units at two levels (one lexical, the other 'surface'; this model, like *SPE*, does also not differentiate between phonemic and allophonic relations). Optimality Theory (Prince and Smolensky 1993; McCarthy 2001) was originally claimed to be a non-derivational theory. What this means is that its derivational aspect relates the lexical level to a (phonemic or phonetic) 'surface level' without the 'intermediate levels' that *SPE* creates due to the fact that its rules applied in an ordered fashion. By rejecting rule ordering, OT could not account for opacity, i.e. the situation in which an apparent phonological rule is contradicted by the output data and yet deemed valid because the contradicting data are the result of a later rule. Earlier critics of *SPE* had rejected rule ordering as a valid mechanism and thus concluded that most opaque rules are actually morpho-lexical rules. Proponents of OT, however, remained faithful to *SPE* and thus proposed numerous ways to have their cake and eat it (reject ordering and yet account for opacity). In recent influential versions, extrinsic ordering (of blocks of constraints) has been brought back, so that OT no longer can do with just two levels (see Kiparsky's 2000 Stratal OT and the model proposed in McCarthy 2007).

6.5.5.3 Back to neutralization

We now need to make explicit that allophonic rules that are neutralizing can in principle be analyzed as applying either at the phonetic or the phonemic level, precisely because neutralizing rules output phonemes (or, as in the case of flapping can be stated as outputting phonemes which then undergo an allophonic rule). If we require that phonetic rules have no exceptions we could not relegate morpho-lexical rules or phonotactically-motivated phonemic rules that have exceptions to the phonetic level, but, unless we require that phonemic rules must have exceptions, we cannot ban automatic rules from the phonemic level, precisely because they can be analyzed as producing phonemes as outputs.

Turning back to final devoicing in Dutch one thus can explore two possible analyses, which I will discuss here. In §6.5.4, I assumed that final devoicing (FD) follows from a phonetic constraint (27).

(27)   * [−son, +voice])$_{\sigma op}$

If we analyze final devoicing at the phonetic level we must specify alternating obstruents as lexically [+voice]. When occurring without an affix such forms violate the phonetic constraint in (27) which triggers a repair rule that changes [+voice] to [−voice]. Since non-alternating voiceless stops can be specified as [∅voice], the final devoicing rule can fill in [−voice], while this same rule is allowed to change [+voice] to [−voice] in a 'derived environment' (where 'derived' here means that the obstruent in question is followed by a word boundary). This requires the formulation in (28) (i.e. one that does not require either [∅voice] or [+voice] in the input).

(28)   [−son] → [−voice] / _)$_\sigma$

I stress that if final devoicing is seen as serving a phonetic constraint, there is no phonemic illformedness in ending in a voiced obstruent.

However, since final devoicing is neutralizing, we could also analyze the alternation in terms of a phonemic repair rule, in which case we regard constraint (28) to refer to the phonemic level. Everything else can be the same as in the phonetic analysis.

Apparently we have to accept that rules that output phonemes and that are not dependent on morphological information *can* be analyzed in two ways, i.e. that they are ambiguous. This ambiguity does not have to be regarded as a theoretical flaw. Rather it provides a channel for neutralizing allophonic rules to become phonemic rules and then, subsequently, become tolerant to exceptions.

However, in this case, it is unlikely that the final devoicing case is a phonemic rule. Recently, it has been argued in a variety of cases that alleged neutralizing rules are, in fact, not neutralizing at all. For example, it has been argued for various languages that have final devoicing that devoicing is not complete (see Brockhaus 1995). Whether alleged neutralizing rules are truly ambiguous or not must be decided on a case-by-case basis.

6.6 Concluding remarks

In this chapter I have been unable to provide a complete overview of phonology and several important subjects have not been touched upon. In the domain of allophonic rules, I have not considered the issue of stylistic rules, also called fast speech rules, casual speech rules or allegro rules. We could also include in this class, the variable rules proposed by Labov (1966). Where in the phonological model do we account for such differences? There are two ways to go. If we assume that all registers share phonological properties up to the phonetic level, we could assume an additional 'stylistic' module which produces a set of stylistic phonetic representations, based on a set of variables that determine these registers, which then all connect to the implementation module, or we could build these variables directly into the phonetic implementation module. The fact that word forms are subject to stylistic rules raises the further question of which pronunciation is taken to be the basis for the lexical representation. I refer to Linell (1979) for arguments that the so-called careful pronunciation serves as the basis for lexical representations, which, in fact, is an implicit practice observed by almost every linguist.

This leads us to further questions regarding the nature of lexical entries. I have presented a model in which lexical representations are phonemic representations that abstract away from allophonic properties. The issue remains whether such representations are impoverished (in that redundant specifications are left out). A further question is whether lexical representations are actual word forms or can be more abstract, including morphemes such as /hɔnd/. If, as Linell (1979) argues, lexical representations must be word forms, the lexical form of words that alternate in final voicing cannot be the form ending in a voiced obstruent since this form never occurs as an actual word form which enforces a representation such as /hɔn{t/d}/ (cf. (17)), where 't/d' means that the 't' alternates with a 'd' in related word forms. This strikes me as undesirable.

It was stated in §6.3 that all phonological theories deal with derivations and representations. In this chapter I have focused on derivational issues. I have assumed that representations are discretely compositional with features organized in segmental units at the phonemic and phonetic level. I have mentioned constraints that govern wellformed combinations of such segments (at both levels) that refer to hierarchical units such as syllables and feet. I refer to Ewen and Hulst (2000) for an overview of representational aspect up to the word level and to Nespor and Vogel (1986) for higher level organization.

Notes

1. See Prince and Smolensky (1993); McCarthy (2001).
2. In support of accounting for linear order in the phonology, we note that sign languages allow a higher degree of parallelism of the basic packages because the visual system can compute independent articulatory actions of the hands, the face and the body simultaneously. Parallelism also occurs in spoken language, for example with reference to the parallelism of intonation and segmental properties of words, or in the case of so-called (e.g. tonal) suprafixes.
3. See Lillo-Martin and Sandler (2006) for a broad overview of the linguistic study of sign language.
4. The development of the International Phonetic Alphabet (IPA), despite its use of the term 'phonetic,' was in fact meant to have a set of symbols for these units that were stripped of their 'irrelevant' properties. The justification for calling this system 'phonetic' is that in the initial stage of analysis, the linguist wants to keep his or her options open as to which phonetic properties are going to be 'relevant' or not.
5. The 'reduction' from variable perceptual inputs to abstract mental 'concepts' is an essential cognitive instrument for dealing with the infinite variability of percepts, not just in processing

language utterances, but in processing all information. From this perspective, phonemic representations are 'conceptual structures' for parts of speech events and phonemes are 'central concepts' (although features would be the basic concept); see Taylor (2003) for a cognitive view on phonology that emphasizes the role of categorization.

6 In this case the IPA practice to represent aspiration in terms of a superscripted diacritic symbol anticipated a feature analysis. In general, IPA diacritics can be set to be 'featural.' But apart from that IPA treats phonemes as holistic. Bell's visible speech transcription system was almost entirely feature-based (Bell 1867).

7 Here we must reckon with the fact that allophonic processes may constitute an innovation in the language and as such be subject to lexical diffusion, i.e. gradual integration in the lexicon, targeting certain classes of words (e.g. the more frequent ones) before others. The end point of lexical diffusion can leave some lexemes unaffected, which, then, are technically exceptions. New allophonic processes can also lead to variability. Harris (1987) has shown that allophonic rules can sometimes display sensitivity to morphological structure.

8 See Hulst (2013) for historical overviews and references.

9 It forms the basis for the earliest phonographic writing systems. One of the earliest works on the development of an alphabetic writing system by the First Grammarian embodies an explicit account of the phoneme–allophone distinction. This shows that this distinction was recognized long before the dawn of phonology in linguistics.

10 As usual, slant lines and square brackets are used for segments at the phonemic and phonetic level, respectively.

11 See Pullum and Ladusaw (1986) for a comprehensive survey of commonly used phonetic symbols. In the study of phonological acquisition by children or of phonological disorders it may be crucial to record very fine phonetic detail, irrespective of the issue of potential distinctiveness and we see that for that purpose special IPA versions with many additional diacritics have been developed.

12 Even in a full-specification approach it is not the case that each segment must be specified for every feature. We need to know which features are applicable to different types of phonemes. It can be argued that features like [continuant], [lateral], [anterior] etc. are not ever needed for vowels. Likewise there are features that we need for vowels, but never for consonants.

13 I ignore here the possibility of a difference in the length of the vowel, due to the difference between a following /d/ and /t/ at the phonemic level.

14 Neutralization of contrast can be the result of rules, such as the flapping rule, or result from defective distribution of phonemes as discussed in §6.5.3. See Silverman (2012) for a broad overview of the notion neutralization.

15 In (4b) I informally depicted allophony as resulting from a rule that converts a phoneme into an allophone. In (11) I switch to the explicit perspective that the allophonic rules apply at the phonetic level, responding to a phonotactic constraint at this level.

16 The reader should bear in mind that the term phonotactic constraint is relevant both with respect to the phonemic level and the phonetic level. There are phonotactic constraints that, simply put, account for wellformedness at any given level.

17 There is more to this example, however, since in the word *infantile*, we replace the /n/ by a sound that does not occur as a phoneme of English, namely [ɱ]. I take this to be the result of an allophonic or implementation rule.

References

Anderson, J.M. and C.J. Ewen (1987) *Principles of Dependency Phonology*. Cambridge: Cambridge University Press.

Anderson, S.R. (1975) On the interaction of phonological rules of various types. *Journal of Linguistics* 11: 39–62.

Anderson, S.R. (1985) *Phonology in the Twentieth Century: Theories of Rules and Theories of Representations*. Chicago: University of Chicago Press.

Anderson, S.R. and D. Lightfoot (2002) *The Language Organ: Linguistics as Cognitive Physiology*. Cambridge: Cambridge University Press.

Archangeli, D. (1984) *Underspecification in Yawelmani Phonology and Morphology*. PhD dissertation, MIT. Published 1988, New York: Garland.
Bell, A.M. (1867) *Visible Speech: The Science of Universal Alphabetics*. London: Simplin, Marshall and Co.
Brockhaus, W. (1995) *Final Devoicing in the Phonology of German*. Tübingen: Max Niemeyer Verlag.
Bybee, J. (2001) *Phonology and Language Use*. Cambridge: Cambridge University Press.
Calabrese, A. (2005) *Markedness and Economy in a Derivational Model of Phonology*. Berlin/New York: Mouton de Gruyter.
Chomsky, N. and M. Halle (1965) Some controversial questions in phonological theory. *Journal of Linguistics* 1: 97–138.
Chomsky, N. and M. Halle (1968) *The Sound Pattern of English*. New York: Harper and Row.
Dresher, B.E. (2009) *The Contrastive Hierarchy in Phonology*. Cambridge: Cambridge University Press.
Ewen, C. and H. van der Hulst (2000) *The Phonological Structure of Words: An Introduction*. Cambridge: Cambridge University Press.
Goldsmith, J. (1993) Harmonic phonology. In J. Goldsmith (ed.) *The Last Phonological Rule*, pp. 21–60. Chicago/London: University of Chicago Press.
Halle, M. (1959) *The Sound Pattern of Russian: A Linguistic and Acoustical Investigation*. The Hague: Mouton.
Harris, J. (1987) Non-structure preserving rules in lexical phonology. *Lingua* 72: 255–92.
Hjemslev, L. (1953 [1943]) *Prolegomena to a Theory of Language*. Transl. by Francis Whitfield. Madison: University of Wisconsin Press.
Hockett, C. (1955) *A Manual of Phonology*. Bloomington: Indiana University Press.
Hooper, J. (1986) *An Introduction to Natural Generative Phonology*. New York: Academic Press.
Hudson, G. (1974) The representation of non-productive alternations. In J. Anderson and C. Jones (eds.) *The First International Conference on Historical Linguistics*, Volume II, pp. 203–29. Amsterdam: North Holland.
Hulst, H. van der (2013) The discoverers of the phoneme. In K. Allan (ed.) *Oxford Handbook of the History of Linguistics*, pp. 167–91. Oxford: Oxford University Press.
Itô, J. (1986) *Syllable Theory in Prosodic Phonology*. Doctoral dissertation, University of Massachusetts, Amherst. [Published 1988, Outstanding Dissertations in Linguistics series. New York: Garland.]
Jakobson, R., C.G.M. Fant and M. Halle (1952) *Preliminaries to Speech Analysis: The Distinctive Features and Their Correlates*, 2nd edition. Cambridge: MIT Press.
Kaye, J., J. Lowenstamm and J.-R. Vergnaud (1985) The internal structure of phonological elements: A theory of charm and government. In C. Ewen and J. Anderson (eds) *Phonology Yearbook 2*, pp. 305–28. Cambridge: Cambridge University Press.
Kaye, J., J. Lowenstamm and J.-R. Vergnaud (1990) Constituent structure and government in phonology. *Phonology* 7: 193–232.
Kiparsky, P. (1982) From cyclic phonology to lexical phonology. In H. van der Hulst and N. Smith (eds.) *The Structure of Phonological Representations*, pp. 131–77. Dordrecht: Foris.
Kiparsky, P. (2000) Opacity and cyclicity. *The Linguistic Review* 17: 351–67.
Kisseberth, C. (1970) On the functional unity of phonological rules. *Linguistic Inquiry* 1: 291–306.
Koskenniemi, K.M. (1983) Two-level morphology: A general computational model for word-form recognition and production. Doctoral dissertation, University of Helsinki.
Labov, W. (1966) *The Social Stratification of English in New York City*. Washington, DC: Center for Applied Linguistics.
Lahiri, A. and H. Reetz (2010) Distinctive features: Phonological underspecification in representation and processing. *Journal of Phonetics* 38: 44–59.
Lamb, S. (1966) Prolegomena to a theory of phonology. *Language* 42: 536–73.
Levelt, W.J.M. (1989) *Speaking: From Intention to Articulation*. Cambridge: MIT Press.

Liberman, M. and J. Pierrehumbert (1984) Intonational invariance under changes in pitch range and length. In M. Aronoff and R.T. Oehrle (eds.) *Language and Sound Structure*, pp. 157–233. Cambridge: MIT Press.

Lillo-Martin, D. and W. Sandler (2006) *Sign Language and Linguistic Universals*. Cambridge: Cambridge University Press.

Linell, P. (1979) *Psychological Reality in Phonology*. Cambridge: Cambridge University Press.

McCarthy, J.J. (2001) *A Thematic Guide to Optimality Theory*. Cambridge: Cambridge University Press.

McCarthy, J.J. (2007) *Hidden Generalizations: Phonological Opacity in Optimality Theory*. London: Equinox.

Nespor, M. and I. Vogel (1986) *Prosodic Phonology*. Dordrecht: Foris Publications.

Pierrehumbert, J. (1990) Phonological and phonetic representation. *Journal of Phonetics* 18: 375–94.

Pierrehumbert, J. (2001) Exemplar dynamics: Word frequency, lenition and contrast. In J. Bybee and P. Hopper (eds.) *Frequency and the Emergence of Linguistic Structure*, pp. 137–57. Amsterdam/Philadelphia: John Benjamins.

Pike, K.L. (1947) *Phonemics: A Technique for Reducing Languages to Writing*. Ann Arbor: University of Michigan.

Prince, A. and P. Smolensky (1993) Optimality theory: Constraint interaction in generative grammar. *Technical Report #2 of the Rutgers Center for Cognitive Science*. Piscataway: Rutgers University. [Published 2004, Malden/Oxford: Blackwell.]

Pullum, G. and W. Ladusaw (1986) *Phonetic Symbol Guide*. Chicago: University of Chicago Press.

Rogers, H. (2005) *Writing Systems. A Linguistic Approach*. Oxford: Blackwell Publishing.

Scobbie, J. (1997) *Autosegmental Representation in a Declarative Constraint-Based Framework*. New York/London: Garland Press. [Original dissertation: Attribute Value Phonology. Edinburgh, 1991.]

Silverman, D. (2012) *Neutralization*. Cambridge: Cambridge University Press.

Strauss, S. (1982) *Lexicalist Phonology of English and German*. Dordrecht: Foris Publications.

Taylor, J. (2003) *Linguistic Categorization*. Oxford: Oxford University Press.

7
Morphology
The structure of words

Geert Booij

7.1 Introduction

Words are the basic building blocks of sentences.[1] Most words are a pairing of sound and meaning, and the meaning of a sentence is computed on the basis of the meanings of the constituent words, and the way in which they are combined. The relation between sound and meaning may be arbitrary. The meaning of the verb *sing*, for instance, cannot be read off its sound form, and the relation between sound and meaning in this word is therefore arbitrary. However, the relation between sound and meaning of a word may be (partially or completely) non-arbitrary, or motivated. This is the case for complex words, words with an internal structure. For instance, the English word *singer* can be divided into two constituents, *sing* and *–er*. Both constituents contribute to the meaning of the word as a whole. These constituents are referred to as morphemes, usually defined as 'the minimal meaning-bearing units of a language.' The word *singer* is therefore a complex word, as opposed to the word *sing*, which has no internal morphological structure and is therefore a simplex word. The morpheme *sing* is classified as a lexical morpheme, as it can occur as a word of its own, whereas the morpheme *–er*, which serves to evoke the meaning 'agent of the action' when combined with verbs, is a bound morpheme of a particular type, a suffix, that is attached at the right edge of a base word.

How do we know that *singer* is a complex word, whereas other words that also end in *–er* are not considered complex, such as *border*, *father* and *order*? The reason is that for a word to be considered complex we expect a systematic correspondence between its form and meaning. The internal structure of the noun *singer* is determined on the basis of a comparison of sets of words such as in (1).

(1) | VERB | AGENT NOUN |
    | bake | baker |
    | speak | speaker |
    | dance | dancer |
    | use | user |

The two sets of words stand in a systematic form-meaning relationship, and on the basis of this relationship we can assign an internal morphological structure to nouns in *–er* with a verbal subconstituent: [V–er]$_N$. We call these nouns deverbal, as they are derived from base words that are verbs. In the case of *border*, *father* and *order* there is no base word to be found, and there is no agentive meaning either, and hence we consider these words as simplex. This also makes it clear why we want to assign internal morphological structure to words like *singer*: the meaning of this word is not completely arbitrary, but motivated, namely, by its constituents and their arrangement.

However, the distinction between simplex and complex word is not always that straightforward. In a word like *solips-ism*, we recognize a suffix *–ism*, even though there is no base word *solips* in English. The reason is that the suffix *–ism* is used systematically in English to coin, among others, nouns denoting philosophical theories such as *Marxism*.

Another example is the series of English verbs that contain the Latin root *–duce*, as in *deduce, induce, produce* and *seduce*. There is no word *duce*, yet, these verbs are similar in that the presence of *–duce* implies that their nominalization always ends in *–duction*: *deduction, induction, production, seduction*. These latter roots, without a clear meaning, are referred to as submorphemic units. A similar observation can be made for Dutch verbs such as *begin* 'to begin' and *vergeet* 'to forget.' These verbs behave as if they begin with a prefix *be–* and *ver–* respectively, even though there are no verbs *gin* and *geet*. Dutch past participles normally have a prefix *ge–*, but this prefix has to be absent if the verbal stem begins with a prefix. Hence, the past participle of the verb *be-treur* 'to deplore' derived from the base verb *treur* 'be sad' is *betreurd*, not **gebetreurd*. Similarly, the past participles of *begin* and *vergeet* are *begonnen* and *vergeten*, without the prefix *ge–*.

One might also assume a certain internal complexity for words with phonaesthemes, (sequences of) sounds such as the initial consonants of *glass, gleam, glow, glare* and *glimpse* that all express the idea of 'light, shine' (Marchand 1969: 411). It is not possible to divide a word like *glow* into two meaningful morphemes, *gl–* and *–ow*, yet language users are able to observe a certain systematicity here.

A second example of complex words are the following plural nouns in English: *apples, books, pages*, which all end in the plural morpheme *–s* (a morpheme with different phonetic realizations: [z], [s], [ɪz]). These words are also complex since they show a systematic form-meaning correspondence with the words *apple, book* and *page*. The difference with the agent nouns is that this is not a case of word formation, but of inflection. Whereas *sing* and *singer* are two different words, with their own entry in a dictionary, this is not the case for *apples*, which is an inflectional form of the lexeme APPLE, as is the singular form *apple*. A lexeme is the abstract unit that stands for the set of inflectional forms of a word, and is usually represented with small capitals.

The two basic functions of morphological operations that create complex words are (a) word formation and (b) inflection. Word formation processes create new words, and hence expand the lexicon of a language. Once the speaker of English has discovered the pattern exemplified in (1), (s)he may hit on a word formation schema which we can characterize, informally, as follows:

(2) [[x]$_V$ er]$_N$ 'Agent of action V'

This schema states that nouns may consist of a verbal base of whatever phonological composition, followed by the suffix *–er*. The meaning correlation of this structure is a compositional function of the meaning of the base verb, and the agent interpretation is a property of this morphological configuration as a whole (the affix *–er* does not have a meaning by itself in isolation). The speaker may then use this schema to create new words with the appropriate form and meaning, such as *skyper*, derived from the verb *(to) skype*, or *texter*, derived from the verb *(to) text*. The new words may not only have the meaning predicted by the schema, but also additional idiosyncratic properties. For instance, the *Urban Dictionary*[2] defines a *texter* not just as someone who texts, but as 'a person who prefers to send text messages instead of picking up the phone.'

Instead of agent nouns, deverbal nouns in *–er* might also denote instruments, as in *cooker*, *fastener* and *vacuum cleaner*, and other meanings such as location (as in *diner*, an American type of restaurant (Booij and Lieber 2004)). This is a case of polysemy of word formation patterns, a pervasive phenomenon in the languages of the world. It has to do with semantic extension mechanisms: language users can easily jump from one semantic concept to a related one. In this case, instruments can be seen as a kind of impersonal agents (Jurafsky 1996).

Inflection is the subsystem of the grammar of natural languages that deals with the proper form of words, often in relation to specific syntactic contexts. In Dutch, for instance, the verb *werk* 'to work' has five different finite forms. The selection of a present or past form depends on which kind of information the speaker wants to convey, and this is called inherent inflection. The choice of a particular present or past form, on the other hand, depends on the number and person of the subject of the clause in which the verb occurs, and is therefore a case of contextual inflection (3) (Booij 1996).

(3) werk present first person singular
werk-t present second/third person singular
werk-en present first/second/third person plural
werk-te past first/second/third person singular
werk-te-n past first/second/third person plural

We consider these five forms as forms of the same word, and this more abstract notion of word is usually referred to as 'lexeme.' Thus, Dutch has a lexeme WERK. The stem form of this lexeme is *werk*, and the different inflectional affixes are added to this stem. The Dutch word *werker* 'worker' is a different lexeme than the word *werk* 'to work' (so Dutch has the lexemes WERK and WERKER). The plural form of this noun *werkers* 'workers' has the morphological structure seen in (4).

(4) werk-er-s
work-agent-plural
'workers'

This is a simple example of the morphological analysis of a complex word, and presented in a form that follows the conventions of interlinear morphemic glossing. The first line presents the internal constituency of the complex word. The second line provides a morpheme by morpheme glossing, and the third line gives a paraphrase of the meaning of the linguistic expression. The rules for glossing are codified as the Leipzig glossing rules.[3]

Morphology is a subdiscipline of linguistics with its own textbooks, reference works and journals. Two recent textbooks are Haspelmath and Sims (2010) and Booij (2012). Reference works are Spencer and Zwicky (1998) and Booij *et al.* (2000, 2004). A recent reference work for English morphology is Bauer *et al.* (2013). Two journals devoted to morphology are *Morphology* (1988–, published by Springer), and *Word Structure* (2008–, published by Edinburgh University Press).

7.2 Types of morphological operation

Cross-linguistically, the most common form of word formation is compounding, the combination of two or more lexemes into a complex word, such as the English word *songbook* composed of the nouns *song* and *book*. Many languages also make use of derivation, the process in which bound morphemes (affixes) such as *–er* are attached to a base word. These two mechanisms are instances of concatenative morphology, in which complex words are created by means of the concatenation, or stringing together, of affixes and words. In addition, languages may also allow for deriving new words from existing ones by only changing the syntactic category of a word. This is referred to as conversion. Examples are the English verbs *to skype* and *to text* mentioned above which are verbs derived from the nouns *skype* and *text* respectively, without this derivational relationship being marked overtly by means of an affix. In English, the conversion of nouns to verbs is a very productive process. Conversely, nouns may be derived from verbs in this way, as is illustrated by nouns such as *fall* and *help*.

Word formation by means of affixation means that an affix is added to a base form. The affix can appear before the base word (prefixation), after the base word (suffixation), or, far more rarely, within the base word. Examples of English prefixes are *un–* and *re–*. The negative prefix *un–* can attach to verbs (*un-do*), adjectives (*un-kind*) and nouns (*un-belief*). The suffix *re–* attaches to verbs (and may also appear in nouns and adjectives derived from such verbs), as in *re-do* and *re-use*. An example of suffixation is the addition of the suffix *–able* to a verb for making adjectives, as in *do-able* and *re-us-able*. An example of infixation is the use of *fucking* and *goddamn* as pejorative infixes in words like *un-fucking-believable* and *in-goddamn-consistent*.

Compounding is an intensively studied word formation process, as can be seen from a recent handbook on compounding (Lieber and Stekauer 2009). Its defining property is that two or more words (in the sense of lexemes) are concatenated. The form of the lexeme used is often the stem form. In English there is no phonological difference between a concrete word and its stem: a word like *dog* is both a concrete word and a stem, as in *dog food*. However, in many languages stems do not occur as words by themselves, and must be supplemented by an overt inflectional ending for their use of concrete words in a sentence. For example, in Modern Greek the compound for 'deer hunter' is *elaf-o-kinig-os*. The first constituent is the stem form of *elafi* 'deer,' without its inflectional ending *–i*. This stem is followed by a linking element *–o–*, a meaningless constituent, and is then followed by the head constituent *kinig-os*. The inflectional ending on the second stem *kinig–*, *–os* is the inflectional ending for the whole compound.

A major division of the class of compounds is that between endocentric compounds and exocentric compounds. In endocentric compounds one of the constituent words is the semantic and syntactic head. In English and other Germanic languages the rightmost constituent is the head. For instance, a post office is a particular type of office, and not a particular kind of post. In languages with gender, such as Dutch, the gender of the compound is also determined by the gender of the right constituent (also referred to as the head). The Dutch gloss for *post office* is *post-kantoor*. Its head *kantoor* is of neuter gender, and hence, the word *postkantoor* is also neuter, as can be seen from the selection of the neuter definite singular determiner *het* (*het kantoor*, *het postkantoor*), whereas *post* is non-neuter, and selects the definite singular determiner *de* as in *de kantoorpost* 'the office mail.'

The position of the head in compounds is language-specific. For instance, in Indonesian compounds, the head is on the left. Hence, the Indonesian word for 'post office' is the compound *kantoor-pos* (with *kantoor* and *pos* being loans from Dutch), with the reverse order of the two words.

In the case of exocentric compounds there is no constituent that functions as the head. An example is English *pick-pocket*, where the semantic head is the agent who picks pockets, and neither *pick* nor *pocket* is the head. A famous example of such exocentric compounds are the verb-noun compounds in Romance languages like Italian. The compound *lava-piatti* 'lit. wash-dishes, dish washer' denotes a person or a machine who washes the dishes, but this semantic component is not expressed by one of its building blocks. Another example comes from the class of coordinated compounds in Chuvash, a Turkic language spoken in Russia. The compound *erex-săra* 'lit. vodka-beer' denotes all alcoholic beverages. Hence the compound is semantically a hypernym of the meaning of its constituents (Wälchli 2005: 141).

However, derivation, conversion and compounding are not the only means of making complex words. In the morphological process of reduplication, a complete or partial copy of a word is added to that base word. Total reduplication may be seen as a specific form of compounding with two identical constituents, whereas in the case of partial reduplication only part of a word is copied and affixed to the base word. In (5) are some examples of both types of reduplication from Papua Malay (Angela Kluge, pers. comm.).

(5) TOTAL REDUPLICATION
    ada 'sibling'   ada-ada 'siblings'
    lari 'run'   lari-lari 'keep running'
    PARTIAL REDUPLICATION
    anak 'child'   an-anak 'children'

In this case of partial reduplication, a copy of the first part of the base word forms a prefix attached to that base word.

The meaning of reduplication patterns is often that of increase: increase in number in the case of nouns, increase in intensity or repetition in the case of verbs, and increase in quality in the case of adjectives. Therefore, reduplication is often qualified as being a case of iconicity, a parallelism between form and meaning because an increase of the size of a word correlates here with an increase in meaning. However, this parallelism does not always obtain.

Other, non-concatenative, morphological operations are the use of specific vowel and/or consonantal patterns (as in creating English past tense form and past participles: *sing–sang–sung, bring–brought*), and tonal patterns (used a lot in the languages of Africa, for instance). The use of vowel alternations for morphological purposes is a characteristic of Indo-European languages such as English. The Semitic languages are well known for their system of creating related verbal lexemes by combining a consonantal root with a specific pattern of C and V positions, and a vowel melody. This type of morphology is called root-and-pattern morphology. A set of verbal lexemes with the same morphological pattern is called a *binyan* ('building,' plural *binyanim*). The root *qtl* 'to kill' as used in Biblical Hebrew has the following five binyan forms with active meaning (Aronoff 1994: 124), of which the 3SG. MASC.PERF forms are illustrated in (6).[4]

(6) BINYAN   3sg.m.pf   CV-pattern   V-pattern   GLOSS
    Qal   qâtal   CVCVC   â-a   to kill
    Nifʻal   ni-qtal   ni-CCVC   a   to kill oneself
    Piʻel   qittel   CVC$_i$C$_i$VC   i-e   to massacre
    Hifʻil   hi-qtil   hi-CCVC   i   to cause to kill
    Hitpaʻel hit-qattel hit-CVC$_i$C$_i$VC a-e   to kill oneself

In addition to these five binyanim, there are two binyanim with a passive meaning, the Puʻal as a passive variant of the Piʻel, and the Hofʻal as the passive of the Hifʻil. In addition, affixes may be used in Semitic languages.

The use of a tone pattern as a morphological marker can be found in tone languages. Here, in (7), is an example from Ngiti, a central-Sudanic language of Congo (Kutsch Lojenga 1994: 135).

(7) SINGULAR   PLURAL
    màlimò   màlímó   teacher(s)
    màlàyikà   màlàyíká   angel(s)
    kamà   kámá   chief(s)

In the plural forms, the tones of the last two syllables (Mid–Low) of the singular forms are replaced by High tones (High tones are indicated by an acute accent on the vowel letter, e.g. á, Low tone by a grave accent, e.g. à, and Mid tone by absence of an accent). Thus, plurality is systematically marked by a specific tone pattern.

Word formation can also take place by what is called back formation: a word is reinterpreted as a complex word, and its base word is then created afterwards. A classic example is the verb *to babysit*, back formed from the compound noun *babysitter*. Another example is the formation of the verb *to buttle* 'to do what a butler does,' from the noun *butler*, by interpreting its ending *–er* as a suffix *–er*.

Finally, there are operations like blending (*smog* < *smoke* + *fog*), the formation of acronyms (NATO, spoken as [neɪtəʊ] < North Atlantic Treaty Organization), clippings (*mike* < *microphone*), and truncations (*commie* < *communist*, *Becky* < *Rebecca*) in which only parts of words appear in the derived word.

In the domain of concatenative morphology, the structure of a complex word can be represented by means of labeled bracketing of a concatenation of morphemes and complex words. For instance, the English compound *songbook*, the derived word *singer*, and the plural noun *books* can be represented as in (8).

(8) [[song]$_N$ [book]$_N$]$_N$
    [[sing]$_V$ er]$_N$
    [[book]$_N$ s]$_N$

Since compounding can be reapplied to a complex word, we can get recursive compounds, with complex structures, as exemplified by the compound [[[[*song book*] *shop*] *assistant*] *salary*].

In the case of non-concatenative morphology it is not possible to represent the structure of a word in terms of a sequence of morphemes. For instance, the structure of *smog* can be represented linearly as *smog*, but these two constituents are not morphemes. The same applies to *brunch*, the combination of the first part of *breakfast* and the second part of *lunch*.

7.3 The place of morphology in grammar

The position of morphology in the architecture of the grammar of natural languages has been debated for decades in the linguistic literature, and it is impossible to summarize this debate in detail in this chapter.

In a syntactic approach, morphology is defined as the 'syntax of morphemes' and the way in which morphemes are combined is accounted for by the same syntax that accounts for the construction of sentences from words. The most recent form of this approach is the theoretical framework of Distributed Morphology (Harley and Noyer 1999; Marantz 2013).

In the lexicalist approach to word formation, on the other hand, there is a separate morphological component in the grammar that accounts for word formation, and precedes the syntactic component that serves to combine words into grammatical sentences. This component enriches the lexicon of a language which provides the words that can be used in the construction of sentences. The inflectional forms of a word may be generated pre-syntactically, or post-syntactically. In the first option, the proper inflectional form of a word in a particular syntactic context is selected by syntactic rules such as agreement rules; in the second option, the stem of words is selected for lexical insertion into syntactic structure, and this stem is then operated upon by the post-syntactic rules of inflection. For instance, the verb form *sings* in *My father sings wonderfully* is either selected as the proper form (third person singular present tense) by the rule of Subject–Verb agreement, or this rule assigns the features [third person singular] to the present tense stem *sing*, and this configuration is then spelled out as *sings*.

The view of inflectional rules as spelling out the phonological form of a word with a specific array of morphosyntactic features is referred to as realizational morphology (Stump 2001). An alternative model of inflection is the Word-and-Paradigm model in which inflectional forms are computed on the basis of other forms in the paradigm of the same word (Matthews 1974 [2nd edition 1991]; Blevins 2006; Ackerman *et al.* 2009; Blevins 2012).

In recent theories of the architecture of grammar, the distinction between lexicon and morphological rules or schemas has been relativized. The lexicon is considered to contain both the set of existing (simplex and complex) words of a language, and the abstract schemas of the type (2) that motivate existing complex words and define how new words can be coined (Booij 2010). Moreover, it cannot be the case that word formation always precedes syntax, since syntactic phrases can form part of complex words, as illustrated in (9) for English.

(9) a one-of-a-kind vacation
    a run-of-the-mill blockbuster
    all-you-can-eat buffet
    a get-it-done attitude

These facts imply that syntax may define the wellformedness of parts of words, and hence can stand in a feeding relationship to morphology.

The lexicon of a language does not only contain its simplex and (established) complex words, but also larger lexical units that are used to denote concepts or entities. For example, the English phrase *yellow fever* (with main stress on its second constituent) functions as a lexical unit, and denotes a particular disease. In other words, all words are lexical units, but not all lexical units are words.

The demarcation of syntactic units and morphological units (=complex words) follows from the principle of Lexical Integrity: complex words are islands for syntactic rules. The Modern Greek phrase *psichros polemos* 'cold war,' for instance, is considered a phrase, even though it is a lexical unit, as the adjective *psichros* agrees in number and gender with the noun *polemos*. Other examples of phrasal lexical units are the particle verbs of Germanic languages, such as English *to look up* and the Dutch particle verb *aan-vallen* 'lit. at-fall, to attack.' The particle verb *aanvallen* is clearly a lexically stored unit, with an unpredictable meaning. Yet, it is phrasal in nature, as its constituents *aan* and *vallen* are split in main clauses:

(10) De insecten vallen ons aan
 The insects fall us at
 'The insects attack us'

The coinage of new particle verbs can be characterized by schemas similar to those for affixation as given in (2) (Los *et al.* 2012).

7.4 Interfaces

The term 'interface' means that different levels of representation in the grammar (phonological form, morphosyntactic form, meaning) are related in a systematic fashion. Morphological word structure plays a role in phonology since the proper phonetic realization of morpheme sequences may depend, directly or indirectly, on their morphological structure. For instance, in many English compounds, the main stress of the word is located on its first constituent, as in *kite runner*, where the monosyllabic constituent [kajt] carries the main stress of the compound word. In phrases, the main stress is always on the right constituents. Hence, the proper application of phonological rules of stress assignment to words requires access to their morphological structure.

Another example of the morphology–phonology interface is that morphological constituents may form domains of phonological rules. This can be illustrated by means of Hungarian. Hungarian is well known for having vowel harmony, the requirement that within a word all vowels are either front vowels or back vowels. This is why Hungarian suffixes may have more than one phonetic form, depending on the vowels of the stem to which they are attached. For instance, we find *Buda-nál* 'in Buda' versus *Pest-nél* 'in Pest' because *Buda* contains back vowels and hence selects an allomorph of the adhesive suffix 'at, in,' with a back vowel, *–nál*, whereas *Pest* contains a front vowel, and hence selects an allomorph with a front vowel, *–nél*. The name of these two cities combined is the compound *Budapest*, a city which is indeed composed of two cities, *Buda* on the right bank of the river Danube, and *Pest* on the left bank. This compound does not violate the constraint of vowel harmony, even though it has both back vowels and front vowels, because the domain of this constraint is the phonological word rather than the morphological word. In many languages, including Hungarian, each word component of a compound forms a phonological word of its own, and therefore, *Budapest* consists of two phonological words.

Morphological structure is also revealed by the phonotactics of a word. For instance, if a Dutch word contains the sequence /fp/, you know for certain that there must be a morphological boundary between /f/ and /p/, as this consonant cluster never occurs within one and the same phonological word; hence, this cluster must have been created by a morphological operation, the concatenation of two words, as in the compound *straf-pleiter* 'criminal lawyer.'

Morphological structure may also determine the syntactic properties of a complex word, in particular its word class and its syntactic valence. Many affixes determine the syntactic category of a word. For instance, English words with the adjective *–less* are adjectives. Syntactic valence is the term for the combinatorial properties of a word in sentences. Verbs may be either intransitive or transitive. In the first case, they do not select a direct object, in the second case they do. Examples are *to die* and *to kill* respectively. An example of morphology affecting syntactic valence is that the addition of the suffix *–ize* turns the noun *alphabet* into the transitive verb *alphabetize*. Hence, there may be a systematic correlation between the morphological structure of a word, and its morphosyntactic properties. This also applies to gender properties: as we saw above, the gender of a Dutch compound is identical to the gender of its head.

The semantic interpretation of compounds provides a simple illustration of the interface between morphological structure and meaning: the formal head of a compound in Germanic languages is also the semantic head. That is why a song book is a kind of book, and not a kind of song. A morphological operation may also be motivated by pragmatic meaning. A famous case is the use of diminutive forms of nouns for the expression of endearment. The Dutch diminutive word *mann-etje* 'man-diminutive' derived from the noun *man* 'man' is not only used for referring to men of small size but also to express one's affection for a boy or a man, without a small size of the person being implied.

7.5 Morphological classification

Languages may be classified according to the role and nature of their morphology (Comrie 1981; Haspelmath 2009).[5] A first dimension is the index of synthesis: languages that do not make use of morphology are called analytic or isolating, languages with a lot of morphology are called synthetic. Hence, languages may be ranked on an index of synthesis. Traditionally, Chinese is referred to as an analytic or isolating language because it has almost no inflection. Yet, there is no doubt that word formation, in particular compounding, is very productive in this language (Packard 2000). Hence, Chinese is not analytic in an absolute sense.

The second index on which languages can be ranked is that of polysynthesis: some languages allow the incorporation of lexical morphemes, leading to relatively complex words, as illustrated by the following one-word sentence of Central Alaskan Yup'ik in which the lexical morpheme *tuntu* 'moose' is incorporated in the verb *te* 'to catch' (Mithun 2000: 923):

(11) tuntu-te-u-q = gguq
moose-catch-indicative.intransitive-3singular = hearsay
'He got a moose'

In this example, the complex word is followed by a clitic morpheme of evidentiality that indicates the nature of the information source. (A clitic is a word that is phonologically dependent on an adjacent host word, '=' is the symbol for the link between a host word and a clitic.)

The third dimension of morphological classification of languages is the index of fusion. In fusional languages, one morpheme may express more than one grammatical feature. Dutch is an example of such a language. For instance, in (3), the inflectional suffix *–te* expresses both 'past tense' and 'singular number.' Fusional languages differ from agglutinating languages in which each bound morpheme corresponds with one grammatical feature. Turkish is the textbook example of an agglutinating language. For instance, case and number in Turkish are expressed by different suffixes:

(12)   çocuk-lar-ın
       child-plural-genitive
       'of the children'

These three indices of morphological complexity are useful in giving a global characterization of the morphology of a language. One should be aware, however, that languages are not homogeneous with respect to these indices. For instance, many Indo-European languages are fusional in their inflectional system, but agglutinating in their derivational morphology. Chinese also illustrates this point since it is synthetic as far as word formation is concerned, but analytic as far as inflection is concerned, as it has no inflection.

7.6 Storage and computation

Morphology plays an important role in linguistic research of language processing. An important empirical question is the division of labor between storage and computation. To what extent are complex words retrieved ready-made from lexical memory, and to what extent are complex words coined during the process of language production? In the domain of word formation it is quite clear that lots of complex words are memorized and retrieved from memory. This can be concluded from frequency effects. Words with a higher frequency use will have a higher level of activation, and hence more easily recognized as correct words in lexical decision tasks. In the domain of inflection this may be different, as a word may have quite a number of different forms, in particular in languages with rich inflectional systems. On the other hand, there is solid evidence that the plural forms of nouns in Dutch and Italian are often memorized when they have a sufficiently high frequency, even though they could have been computed on line quite easily (Baayen *et al.* 1997, 2003). These findings go against the hypothesis defended in Pinker (1999) that regular inflectional forms are computed on line, and only irregular forms such as past tense forms of English verbs with vowel alternation of the type *sing–sang* are retrieved directly from memory.

It remains true, however, that there is a strong correlation between frequency and exceptionality. The English irregular verbs that create past tense and past participle forms by means of vowel alternation such as *to sing* appear to belong to the top frequency class of English verbs. High frequency means a high degree of entrenchment, and thus these verbs do not easily regularize, as their vowel alternation patterns are so well entrenched (Bauer *et al.* 2013: 67).

7.7 Acquisition of morphology

How are morphological schemas or rules for word formation and inflection acquired by children who are in the process of acquiring their native language? First, they will acquire a small set of complex words that instantiate a particular word formation schema. After sufficient exposure (stage 1) they will be able to recognize an abstract schema as in (2) that summarizes their knowledge of a subset of complex words (stage 2). Thus, they will be able to coin new complex words themselves. In coining new words, they might not be hampered by knowledge of exceptions and lexical conventions. Hence, they might overgeneralize, and create the regular plural form *foots* instead of *feet*, or the compound *war man* for soldier. At stage 3, they will also have learned exceptions like *feet*, and thus command the whole system, both the rules and the exceptions (Berko 1958/2004).

The number of compounds is very high in Germanic languages like Dutch and English and, hence, children acquire the competence to coin new compounds at an early age, in particular the class of noun–noun compounds. Hence these children make a lot of new compounds, also because they are not hampered by the conventions of the language community to which they are going to belong (Clark 2003 [2009, 2nd edition]). For example, one of my daughters made the compound *oorlog-s-man* 'war man' to denote soldiers. The conventional Dutch word for 'soldier' is *soldaat* but this word was not yet known to her. These newly coined compounds will normally not survive, because children will learn the conventional word for a certain concept in due course.

7.8 Morphological change

The morphology of language has interesting historical dimensions. A first question is how the morphological system of a language may have arisen in the course of time, and second, we may ask how such a system can change. Change does not only occur on the level of the language system, but also at the level of the individual complex word: complex words, once formed, may lose their transparency through a number of factors. In this section, more will be said about these different aspects of morphological change.

Let us first focus on the rise of morphology. A classical idea is that 'today's morphology is yesterday's syntax' (Givón 1971: 413). For example, phrase structures may develop into compounds. An example is the change of noun phrases of the type [$N_{Genitive}$ N], with a first noun case-marked as genitive preceding the head noun of the phrase, into a NN compound, in which the old genitive case marker is reinterpreted as a linking morpheme. For instance, the Middle Dutch noun phrase *coninc-s sone* 'king's son' was reinterpreted as the compound [N-s-N], with the *s* as a linking element. Hence, in present day Dutch we finds lots of NN compounds with the semantically empty linking element *–s*.

A famous example from Romance languages is the development of the adverbial suffix *mente* from the Latin word *mens* 'mind,' embedded in phrases with ablative case such as *clara mente* 'with a clear mind.' This phrase was reinterpreted as one word, with *mente* being reinterpreted as a suffix that denotes the manner of an action. The English suffix *–ment* as in *government* is a reflex of this historical development, as English borrowed the French form of *–mente, ment*.

This change of a phrase into a word is called univerbation. Many words, some still felt as complex, arose this way. For instance, the preposition *beside* derives from the Old English phrase *be sidan* 'by side,' and the reflexive pronoun *himself* derives from the phrase *him self*. This shows that the source of a complex word is not always a morphological process, it may also have originated as an effect of univerbation (Brinton and Traugott 2005).

Parts of compounds may develop into derivational affixes. This is exemplified by the English suffixes *–dom*, *–hood* and *–ship* as in *kingdom, brotherhood, friendship*, that were once words and appeared as the right part of compounds (Trips 2009). For instance, *–hood* derived from the Old English word *had* 'state, rank, order.' These words became very productive as suffixes, witness the recent coinings *gurudom, guruhood* and *guruship*. Such words acquired more general meanings when used as parts of compounds, and ended up as derivational affixes. In some cases, the lexical origin is still visible, as in words beginning with *great* such as *great-grandfather* and *great-grandchild*. The adjective *great* has acquired a specialized use for denoting family relationships, which is only available when this word forms part of a complex word. Similarly, a number of English words turned into prefixes with a more specific meaning than the corresponding preposition, as *out* in *out-perform*, *over* in *over-do*, and *under* in *under-line* (Booij and Hüning 2014).

A second dimension of morphological change is that complex words, once formed, may lose their semantic transparency, and might even become simplex words. An example of semantic opacity is the compound *breakfast*, with the original meaning of breaking the overnight fasting. For most English speakers, this word will no longer be perceived as a compound word. This may also affect the pronunciation. In a compound such as *postman*, the second part is experienced as a kind of affix for 'agent,' and hence, the vowel of *man* is usually realized as [ə]. Similarly, the vowel of the second syllable in *breakfast* is also pronounced as [ə], and not with the original full vowel of *fast*.

Morphological systems may also change through language contact. This is clearly visible in English that has a lot of non-native suffixes due to its contact with French, Greek and Latin. For instance, besides the suffix *–ness* (of Germanic origin) we have *–ity* as a suffix for nouns, as in *obesity* and *opacity*. Most of these non-native suffixes prefer to be attached to a non-native base word. For the adjective *good*, the noun *goodness* is chosen, and *goodity* is odd, whereas both *denseness* and *density* are grammatical, since native suffixes can usually be attached to both native and non-native base words. There are also lots of non-native prefixes such as *super–* and *re–*. These non-native prefixes are often less choosy about their base words, and also attach to native words, witness *super-man* and *re-send*.

One may wonder how affixes, that is, bound morphemes, can be borrowed from another language, as they are not independent entities. The answer is that in borrowing, a number of words of a certain morphological type may be borrowed, for instance a number of words in *–ity* (the English adaptation of French *–ité*), and on the basis of such a set of morphologically similar words, the language user may discover a pattern, for instance [A-*ity*]$_N$. Hence, there will be English words in *–ity* without a correspondent word in *–ité* in French, for example *oddity*.

Even one borrowed word with sufficient impact may lead to the borrowing of an affix. This is the case for the prefix *über*, which was borrowed in English from German on the basis of the philosophical notion of *Über-mensch* from Nietzsche's philosophical work. Nowadays, we find lots of English words with this prefix, as in *über-burger*, *über-guru*, *über-diva*, *über-style* and *über-station wagon*. In all these cases the meaning of über is something like 'exhibiting the characteristic properties to an extreme extent.'

Languages may also lose parts of their morphological system. A well-known example is the loss of case morphology in almost all Germanic languages, and most Romance languages. The function of case markers has been taken over, at least partially, by other formal means such as word order, or the use of prepositions and postpositions. Remnants of the old case system may still be seen in lexicalized expressions (as in Dutch *te-gelijk-er-tijd* 'at the same time, simultaneously,' with the case ending *–er* on the adjective *gelijk* 'same'), and in the recycled form of the genitive case marker of English, now a possessor marker (as in *John's book* and *the king of England's hat*).

Notes

1 The text of this section and of §7.2 is partially based on the text of §1 of Booij (2015).
2 See www.urbandictionary.com.
3 See www.eva.mpg.de/lingua/resources/glossing-rules.php.

4   The apostrophe ' indicates a glottal stop, and the symbol â stands for an open /o/; CiCi stands for two identical consonants.
5   The text of this section is partially based on the text of §2 of Booij (2015).

References

Ackerman, F., J.P. Blevins and R. Malouf (2009) Parts and wholes: Implicative patterns in inflectional paradigms. In J.P. Blevins and J. Blevins (eds) *Analogy in Grammar*, pp. 54–82. Oxford: Oxford University Press.

Aronoff, M. (1994) *Morphology by Itself: Stems and Inflectional Classes*. Cambridge: MIT Press.

Baayen, R.H., C. Burani and R. Schreuder (1997) Effects of semantic markedness in the processing of regular nominal singulars and plurals in Italian. In G. Booij and J. van Marle (eds) *Yearbook of Morphology 1996*, pp. 13–34. Dordrecht: Kluwer.

Baayen, R.H., J.M. McQueen, T. Dijkstra and R. Schreuder (2003) Frequency effects in regular inflectional morphology: Revisiting Dutch plurals. In R.H. Baayen and R. Schreuder (eds) *Morphological Structure in Language Processing*, pp. 355–90. Berlin: Mouton de Gruyter.

Bauer, L., R. Lieber and I. Plag (2013) *The Oxford Reference Guide to English Morphology*. Oxford: Oxford University Press.

Berko, J.G. (1958/2004) The child's learning of English morphology. In B. Lust and C. Foley (eds) *First Language Acquisition: The Essential Readings*, pp. 253–73. Malden: Blackwell.

Blevins, J.P. (2006) Word-based morphology. *Journal of Linguistics* 42: 531–73.

Blevins, J.P. (2012) Word-based morphology from Aristotle to modern WP. In K. Allan (ed.) *The Oxford Handbook of the History of Linguistics*, pp. 397–417. Oxford: Oxford University Press.

Booij, G. (1996) Inherent versus contextual inflection and the split morphology hypothesis. In G. Booij and J. van Marle (eds) *Yearbook of Morphology 1995*, pp. 1–16. Dordrecht/Boston: Kluwer.

Booij, G. (2010) *Construction Morphology*. Oxford: Oxford University Press.

Booij, G. (2012) *The Grammar of Words: An Introduction to Morphology*, 3rd edition. Oxford: Oxford University Press.

Booij, G. (2015) The structure of words. In J. Taylor (ed.) *The Oxford Handbook of the Word*, Ch. 11. Oxford: Oxford University Press.

Booij, G. and M. Hüning (2014) Affixoids and constructional idioms. In R. Boogaart, T. Colleman and G. Rutten (eds) *Extending the Scope of Construction-Based Grammar*, pp. 77–105. Berlin: De Gruyter Mouton.

Booij, G. and R. Lieber (2004) On the paradigmatic nature of affixal semantics in English. *Linguistics* 42: 327–57.

Booij, G., C. Lehmann and J. Mugdan (eds) (2000) *Morphologie/Morphology. Ein internationales Handbuch zur Flexion und Wortbildung/An International Handbook on Inflection and Word Formation (in Colloboration with Wolfgang Kesselheim and Stavros Skopeteas)*, vol. 1. Handbücher zur Sprachwissenschaft. Berlin: De Gruyter.

Booij, G., C. Lehmann, J. Mugdan and S. Skopeteas (eds) (2004) *Morphologie/Morphology: Ein internationales Handbuch zur Flexion und Wortbildung/An International Handbook on Inflection and Word Formation (in colloboration with Wolfgang Kesselheim)*, vol. 2. Handbücher zur Sprachwissenschaft. Berlin: De Gruyter.

Brinton, L.J. and E.C. Traugott (2005) *Lexicalization and Language Change*. Cambridge: Cambridge University Press.

Clark, E. (2003) *First Language Acquisition* [2nd edition 2009]. Cambridge: Cambridge University Press.

Comrie, B. (1981) *Language Universals and Linguistic Typology*. Oxford: Blackwell.

Givón, T. (1971) Historical syntax and synchronic morphology: an archeologist's field trip. *Chicago Linguistics Society* 7: 394–415.

Harley, H. and R. Noyer (1999) Distributed morphology. *Glot International* 4(4): 3–9.

Haspelmath, M. (2009) An empirical test of the agglutination hypothesis. In E. Magni, S. Scalise and A. Bisetto (eds) *Universals of Language Today*, pp. 13–29. Dordrecht: Springer.

Haspelmath, M. and A.D. Sims (2010) *Understanding Morphology*. London: Hodder Education.

Jurafsky, D. (1996) Universal tendencies in the semantics of the diminutive. *Language* 72: 533–78.

Kutsch Lojenga, C. (1994) *Ngiti, A Central-Sudanic language of Zaire*. Köln: Rüdiger Köppe Verlag.

Lieber, R. and P. Stekauer (2009) *The Oxford Handbook of Compounding*. Oxford: Oxford University Press.

Los, B., C. Blom, G. Booij, M. Elenbaas and A. van Kemenade (2012) *Morphosyntactic Change: A Comparative Study of Particles and Prefixes*. Cambridge: Cambridge University Press.

Marantz, A. (2013) No escape from morphemes in morphological processing. *Language and Cognitive Processes* 28: 905–16.

Marchand, H. (1969) *The Categories and Types of Present-Day English Word Formation*. München: Beck.

Matthews, P.H. (1974) *Morphology* [2nd edition 1991]. Cambridge: Cambridge University Press.

Mithun, M. (2000) Incorporation. In G. Booij, J. Mugdan and C. Lehmann (eds) *Morphologie/ Morphology. Ein internationales Handbuch zur Flexion und Wortbildung/An International Handbook on Inflection and Word Formation (in collaboration with Wolfgang Kesselheim and Stavros Skopeteas)*, pp. 916–28. Berlin: De Gruyter.

Packard, J. (2000) *The Morphology of Chinese: A Linguistic and Cognitive Approach*. Cambridge: Cambridge University Press.

Pinker, S. (1999) *Words and Rules: The Ingredients of Language*. New York: Basic Books.

Spencer, A. and A.M. Zwicky (1998) Introduction. In A. Spencer and A.M. Zwicky (eds) *The Handbook of Morphology*, pp. 1–10. Oxford: Oxford University Press.

Stump, G.T. (2001) *Inflectional Morphology: A Theory of Paradigm Structure*. Cambridge: Cambridge University Press.

Trips, C. (2009) *Lexical Semantics and Diachronic Morphology: The Development of the Derivational Suffixes hood, dom, and ship in the History of English*. Tübingen: Niemeyer.

Wälchli, B. (2005) *Co-compounds and Natural Coordination*. Oxford: Oxford University Press.

8
Syntax
Putting words together

Kersti Börjars

8.1 Introduction

Syntax is the subdiscipline of linguistics that analyses *structure*; how words and phrases are put together. In this chapter, we will look at *categories* – the smallest building blocks of syntax – how these are combined to form *constituents*, and at some of the *functions* that these constituents can have. To start with, I will use examples from English only, but in §8.5 I will show that there is a fair amount of structural variation between languages. In §8.6, I will consider the representation of structure and in §8.7, I will examine the role that structure plays in theoretical approaches to language.

8.2 Categories

The smallest unit of analysis in syntax is the word. In written language, it is relatively easy to establish where a word begins and ends. For instance, there is general agreement that this sentence consists of thirteen words. However, even for English there are some difficult issues; if I had used *there's* instead of *there is* in the third sentence of this paragraph, would there only have been twelve words? For a language that does not have a written form, it is generally even more difficult to establish what the smallest unit of the syntactic analysis should be. However, this is an issue that is dealt with within *morphology* (Chapter 7), and in this chapter I will assume that you know what a word is.

Words can be divided into classes or syntactic categories on the basis of their behaviour. It is not uncommon to start defining these categories in terms of meaning: nouns are words that refer to a 'person, place or thing' and verbs refer to 'actions'. There are approaches to syntax in which semantic criteria play an important role (for instance the Cognitive Grammar of Langacker 1990), but generally, categories are defined on the basis of form instead. Linguists use categories in order to capture groups of words that behave in a similar way as far as the syntax goes, and this does not always depend on meaning. If we take the example in (1), we see that *mother*, *handbag*, *anger* and *existence* appear to be able to do the same thing as far as the syntax is concerned, but whereas the first two fall under the semantic definition of a noun, *anger* and *existence* would not normally be considered a 'person, place or thing'.

(1) His {mother/handbag/anger/existence} has always struck me as interesting.

A similar point can be made for a semantic definition of other categories. For this reason we use *formal criteria*, this means that the criteria used to define categories are based on the form and the syntactic behaviour of the words.

Four major categories are generally recognised: NOUNS, VERBS, ADJECTIVES and PREPOSITIONS. In English, nouns can combine with *the* to form a full phrase, many nouns can also take a plural marker, generally *–s*, and combine with *a(n)*. In other languages the criteria may be different, there may for instance not be a word similar to *the* or there may be things like case markers that can attach only to nouns. Verbs can take a third person singular *–s* in English – and can occur in past tense. Adjectives modify nouns and can occur with a comparative form *–er* (or *more*) and a superlative form *–est* (or *most*). Prepositions are the most difficult to define structurally, largely because they do not take any inflection. They can be recognised structurally because they combine with a noun phrase to form a full phrase (see §8.3 for phrasal categories).

You may wonder what happened to ADVERBS: do they not form a major category? In many descriptions of English it is indeed included as a fifth category. They are the words which modify verbs, adjectives or other adverbs and they frequently end in *–ly*. An alternative to recognising adverbs as a separate category is to put them together with adjectives and define them as modifying words that surface in their adjective form when they modify nouns and in their adverb form when they modify any other category. This merger of the two categories may be especially tempting when considering American varieties of English such as the title of Jim Leonard Jr's 1986 play, given in (2).

(2) And they dance real slow in Jackson.

Here *slow* modifies the verb *dance* and hence would be an adverb, *real* modifies *slow* and would therefore also be an adverb, but still they have the same form they would have if they modified a noun and hence were adjectives: *a real fairy* or *a slow dance*. In British English, it would generally have been expressed as *really slowly*. Tempting though it may be to consider adjectives and adverbs as belonging to the same category, there are also reasons to keep them separate, though this is not the place to go into the details of the arguments (see Payne *et al.* (2010)).

For almost all the criteria mentioned here, there are exceptions. Not all things that would normally be classified as nouns can take a plural form – they are non-count nouns – and not all adjectives can occur in a comparative or superlative form – they are not gradable. When we come across words that do not have the characteristics we have established for the categories, we can use similarity in distribution to argue for category membership. Take *dead* for instance; if your life depended on assigning it to a category, you would probably say 'adjective'. Still, it does not have any of the formal properties: **deader/*deadest*, even *?more dead* and *?most dead* sound distinctly odd. We can create a sentence with a more well-behaved adjective such as *happy* (*happier/happiest*) and test whether *dead* could replace *happy* in this sentence. If it can, we can take this as evidence that it is an adjective, this is using *distributional criteria* to establish category membership. Using this approach, we can indeed argue that *dead* is an adjective: *The customer said that it was a happy/dead parrot*.

The categories we have looked at so far are often referred to as the *lexical categories*. These categories have a large membership, and the words that belong to them tend to have lexical content, they have full semantics. In addition, there are a number of *functional categories* which are closed in the sense that there is a limited membership and their members serve a grammatical function and have a less full meaning. They tend also not to accept modification. Examples of such categories are DETERMINERS such as *the* and *this*, SUBORDINATING CONJUNCTIONS such as *whether* and *because* and COORDINATING CONJUNCTIONS such as *and* and *but*. You may object here that prepositions also form a relatively small closed class with little lexical meaning and little opportunity for modification. A particularly striking example is *of*, which alternates with the grammatical marker *'s* in pairs such as *the oldest man's car*/*the car of the oldest man*. Though prepositions are generally considered a lexical category, they share some characteristics with functional categories and in some descriptions are classed as such. As you will see in the next section, the term lexical category is also used in another sense, but it is generally clear which meaning is intended.

For the lexical categories, I will use the labels N(oun), V(erb), A(djective), Adv(erb) and P(reposition). I will return to the functional categories in §8.7. Now we have sorted out the basic building blocks of syntax, we can move on and start building phrases.

8.3 Constituents

A sentence is not just a string of words, but words combine together to form bigger units, called *constituents*. These constituents in turn combine to form bigger constituents, to give a hierarchical structure. In order to establish the constituent structure of a language, tests can be applied that aim at exploring the extent to which a string of words behaves like a unit. Since we are aiming to explore the formal structure, rather than the semantics, these tests should ideally not make reference to meaning, but on the assumption that there is frequently a close correlation between form and meaning, sometimes semantics slips into our constituency tests. However, given that native speakers have intuitions about structure also in nonsensical sentences, it is best to focus on tests that do not refer to meaning. For instance a sentence like *An outrageous beach admired the screaming abstraction* does not make sense, but native speakers would probably agree that *outrageous beach* forms a unit, but *beach admired* does not.

I will exemplify with four tests here that all aim to assess the extent to which a string of words behaves as an independent unit within a particular sentence. It is important that we test constituents within their contexts since a particular string may form a constituent in one sentence but not in another. For instance, a native speaker of English who heard the two sentences *Mitch was drinking the milk* and *While Mitch was drinking the milk fell off the table* would probably have an intuition that *drinking the milk* is a constituent of the first but not of the second. Indeed, many writers would add a comma between *drinking* and *milk* in the second sentence.

Four commonly assumed constituency tests are:

- *substitution*: if a string of words can be replaced by one word, this can generally be taken as evidence that it forms a constituent
- *coordination*: if a string can be coordinated with another string, it is likely to form a constituent
- *sentence fragment*: if a string can stand on its own it is likely to be a constituent
- *movement*: if a string can be moved as a whole to a different position within the sentence then it is usually a constituent.

Syntax

These tests are phrased with caution, words such as *generally*, *likely* and *usually* are used. This is because none of the tests is absolutely sound. The tests also do not state what happens if they do not go through, for instance, if you cannot move a string of words within a sentence, this may be because the strict word order of English does not allow it, particular if a string is deeply embedded within the structure.

Let's apply the four tests to the two example sentences about *Mitch* to test whether *drinking the milk* is a constituent. The asterisk indicates that the example is ungrammatical and the hash symbol that the example is odd or does not have the required meaning.

(3) Mitch was drinking the milk.
    Substitution: Mitch was yawning.
    Coordination: Mitch was [drinking the milk] and [eating the food].
    Sentence fragment: – What was Mitch doing?
        – Drinking the milk.
    Movement: Drinking the milk is what Mitch was doing.

(4) While Mitch was drinking the milk fell off the table.
    Substitution: *Mitch was yawning fell off the table.
    Coordination: *While Mitch was [drinking the milk] and [eating the food] fell off the table.
    Sentence fragment: – #What was Mitch doing when fell off the table? / #What fell off the table when Mitch was?
        – #Drinking the milk.
    Movement: *Drinking the milk is what Mitch was doing fell off the table.

For the sentence fragment test, I have added a question. What we are exploring here is whether the string *drinking the milk* is a constituent **of this sentence**, and in order to make sure that we test the constituent in the right environment, I have made it the answer to a question based on the original sentence.

When you test a string of words that is not a constituent, these tests will generally yield an ungrammatical sentence. Since we are all trying to use only grammatical sentences when we write or speak, it can be difficult to make the ungrammatical sentences. Take the coordination test in (4), we are testing *drinking the milk* and all we do is to try to coordinate that with a string of words that looks similar, *eating the food*. The movement test is more difficult to apply, because there are many different ways of trying to move a constituent. In both (3) and (4), I have used the 'SOMETHING *is what* SOMEONE *was doing*' test, where the initial 'something' is the string moved out of the sentence, which is replaced within the sentence by *was doing*, but everything else in the original sentence stays the same. Even though some of the examples are complicated, the application of the tests in (3) and (4) should convince you that *drinking the milk* is a constituent in (3) but not in (4).

Let's now try a string that is more deeply embedded.

(5) Mitch ate the really big sandwich.
    Substitution: Mitch ate the tasty sandwich.
    Coordination: Mitch ate the [really big] and [very tasty] sandwich.
    Sentence fragment: – #How / #What was Mitch eating the sandwich?
        – #Really big.
    Movement: *It was really big that Mitch ate the sandwich.

Here the results are clearly a little harder to interpret. Movement and sentence fragment do not work as well as they did in (3). When this happens, we can adopt an alternative strategy: if *big* does not form a constituent with *really*, it would have to form one with *sandwich*. So we can test that constituent instead and then compare the results with (5).

(6) Mitch ate the really big sandwich.
  Substitution: *Mitch ate the really pie. / *Mitch ate the really horrible.
  Coordination: ?Mitch ate the really [big sandwich] and [tasty pie].
  Sentence fragment: – #What was Mitch eating the really?
                       – #Big sandwich.
  Movement: *It was big sandwich that Mitch ate the really.

The only test that might possibly be deemed to give an acceptable result here is coordination. However, since we are coordinating only *big sandwich* and *tasty pie*, *really* would modify both constituents, so that it should mean *really big sandwich and really tasty pie*. It is not clear that this is the case in this example. The results in (6) are clearly worse than those in (5), and we can conclude that *really big* is a constituent of the sentence, but that *big sandwich* is not. The reason the tests do not work quite as nicely in (5) as they did in (3) is that *really big* is deeply embedded within the sentence. When I come to represent structure in a later section, I will be able to make this visually clear.

In §8.2, I showed how individual words can be assigned to categories such as nouns and verbs on the basis of their behaviour. The same categories can be used to describe the constituents formed by words. Generally, when two constituents form a new larger constituent, one of the component constituents is more central than the other. This constituent is called the *head*, and its category will be used also for the larger constituent (I will return to discuss constituents that do not have a head in §8.7). However, a distinction needs to be made between the categories of words and the categories of larger units. This is where the second use of the term *lexical category* that I mentioned in §8.2 comes in; a word belongs to a lexical category whereas a larger unit belongs to a *phrasal category*. In one sense 'lexical' contrasts with 'functional' and in another with 'phrasal'.

In order to establish what the phrasal category of a constituent is, we need to know which element is the head. As a first guideline, we can use a 'kind of' criterion: in a phrase like *tasty pie*, *pie* is the head because a *tasty pie* is a kind of *pie*. In a similar spirit, the head can be defined as the element that can represent the whole and that is obligatory, though non-heads can also be obligatory. The head is also where features crucial to the phrase are marked. The phrase *the child's toy duck with orange feet* is singular as witness the fact that it combines with *is* rather than *are* as the appropriate form of the verb in (7a), whereas *the child's toy ducks with orange feet* is plural, as illustrated by (7b). We could change the number of any other noun in the sentence, but it would not make any difference to the verb as illustrated in (7c).

(7) a. The child's toy **duck** with orange feet **is** not in the bathtub.
    b. The child's toy **ducks** with orange feet **are** not in the bathtub.
    c. The children's toy **duck** with an orange beak **is** not in the bathtub.

This is then used to argue that *duck* is the head of *the child's toy duck with orange feet*.

A number of other criteria for head status have been proposed, but many of these rely on theoretical assumptions made about syntax. In fact, even the general criteria I have mentioned here do not always yield an unambiguous result. In *the duck*, *duck* is the head by both the 'kind of' criterion and the morphological marking criteria: *the duck – the ducks*. However, if we take an example like *that duck*, we get a different outcome. If we make it plural, both elements need to be marked for number: *those ducks*. There are even phrases in which *that/those* is the only element that marks number: *that sheep/those sheep*. Still, we would not want to say that *duck* is the head of *the duck*, but *that* is the head of *that duck*.

Determining what is the head within a phrase is not an absolutely straightforward matter. As you will see in a later section, this has meant that there is some disagreement in the literature as to what the category of some phrases are. At this point, I will follow tradition and assume that *duck* is the head of *the duck* and *that duck* as indeed it is of *the child's toy duck with orange feet*. Since the head is a noun, the phrase is a NOUN PHRASE (NP). In (8)–(11), I provide sentences exemplifying the other major categories, with the phrasal category in bold and the head word underlined.

(8) Verb Phrases (VPs)
  a. Mitch **devoured the fish**.
  b. Mitch **gave the referee the ball**.
  c. Mitch **smiled**.

(9) Adjective Phrases (APs)
  a. The children are **responsible for the dreadful mess in the fridge**.
  b. The children are **terribly curious**.
  c. The children are **tired**.

(10) Adverb Phrases (AdvPs)
  a. The lawyer works **independently of the commission**.
  b. The lawyer works **ridiculously slowly**.
  c. The lawyer works **tirelessly**.

(11) Preposition Phrases (PPs)
  a. The protesters walked **right into the council meeting**.
  b. The protesters appeared **from behind the wall**.
  c. The protesters jumped **down**.

A number of comments are in order here. In (11b), *behind the wall* is a PP, which means that the PP *from behind the wall* contains another PP. In fact all phrasal categories can contain elements of the same phrasal category, another example is (10b), where an AdvP *ridiculously* appears inside an AdvP.

In all the (c) examples above, the phrase consists of just one word. The question then arises why this word is deemed to be of the phrasal category, rather than of the lexical category; why is *smiled* in (8c) a VP, and not a V? The answer is that it is both a V and a VP. Every word belongs to a lexical category and *smiled* is a V. However, since *smiled* has the same distribution as the other VPs in (8), we can assume that it is also a VP. Similar arguments can be made for the other (c) examples. In each category, there are words which do not require any additional elements and therefore can act as a phrasal category on their own.

Devoured in (8a) is different from *smiled* in that it cannot occur without a phrase like *the fish* accompanying it. These phrases that are required by an element are referred to as

COMPLEMENTS; *the fish* is the complement of the head *devour*. A complement does not have to be obligatory, but it will have a close relationship with the head. Compare the behaviour of *eat* with that of *devour* in (8a); though *Mitch ate the fish* seems identical in structure to (8a), *Mitch ate* is also a grammatical sentence on its own and hence *the fish* is not obligatory here. However, because of the similarity in behaviour, *the fish* is still referred to as the complement of *ate*.

Verbs and Prepositions generally occur with complements; all examples a, b and c in (8) to (11) include complements. In (9a) and (10a), there is an adjective and an adverb, respectively, taking a complement, but such examples are rarer.

The notion of complement may become a little clearer when we contrast it with another type of element that heads can combine with. Consider the examples in (12).

(12) a. Mitch ate the fish.
b. Mitch ate yesterday.
c. Mitch ate the fish yesterday.
d. ?Mitch ate yesterday the fish.

Even though *ate* combines with something in both (12a) and (12b), it does so in different ways. *Yesterday*, which I will refer to as a MODIFIER, does not have the close relationship with the verb in (12b) that *the fish* does in (12a). For one thing, as (12c) and (12d) show, under normal circumstances, the complement occurs closer to the head than the modifier does. The verb also determines how many complements it can have: *smile* takes no complement, *eat* takes one and *give* takes two, as in (8b). However, all these verbs can occur with any number of modifiers; we can add a string of modifiers like *yesterday in the kitchen before he left* to any of the verb phrases *smile*, *devour the fish* or *give the referee the ball*. A VP can then consist not just of the verb and its complement as in (8), but can also include modifiers, so that *ate the fish yesterday* is a VP in (12c). I will return to the internal structure of this phrase in §8.6.

The distinction between complement and modifier can be made with respect to all the categories discussed in this chapter. I will turn now to another structural relation and illustrate it with respect to NPs. In (13), there is a phrase with a noun as a head, it contains a complement *of rare birds* and a modifier *with many great illustrations*.

(13) study of rare birds with many great illustrations

It should be clear why *study* is the head here. There are a number of reasons to consider *of rare birds* a complement; it is closely connected to *study*, there can only be one such phrase and it has to occur close to *study*. The phrase *study of rare birds* can also be compared with the VP *study rare birds*, where *rare birds* is the complement of the verb. *With many great illustrations* in (13), on the other hand, is not unique – we could add another similar phrase to make *study of rare birds with great illustrations on the top shelf*. However, the phrase in (13) is not quite complete; it could not be inserted in a sentence as it stands, as the ungrammaticality of (14a) shows. What is required to make it a complete noun phrase is a determiner, as in (14b).

(14) a. *Study of rare birds with many great illustrations is expensive.
b. A/The/This study of rare birds with many great illustrations is expensive.

These elements that can be said to complete phrases are called SPECIFIERS. Like complements, they are there because the head word requires them, but they are not as closely related to the head as complements.

A phrasal category can then consist of just the head, or it can include a complement (if the head selects for one), a specifier and any number (in principle) of modifiers. However, not all of the phrase types are equally liberal when it comes to complements, modifiers and specifiers. Prepositions usually require a complement, but are quite limited in what modifiers they can occur with. Adjectives tend to occur without either complements or modifiers, and adverbs even more so. It can be argued that adjectives, adverbs and prepositions do not have specifiers. Though the different phrasal categories show some variation, there is a system which incorporates specifiers, modifiers and complements and that assumes the different categories have a parallel structure. This system is called X-bar syntax and I shall return to it in §8.6.

In the discussion of phrasal categories, I have said nothing about sentences. This is because they do not play a central role in the system of lexical and phrasal categories. There is not really any better way of defining 'sentence' than 'that which occurs between two major punctuation marks'. For our purposes it is also not a terribly interesting notion. A CLAUSE, on the other hand, is of interest. A clause consists of a verb, everything required by the verb and any modifiers of the verb. In the examples in (8) and (12), I included only the verb, its complements and modifiers in the VP. However, having now introduced specifiers as that which makes a phrase complete, we might want to reconsider this. A verb phrase like *devoured the fish* or *ate the fish yesterday* is not really complete until you add *Mitch*. *Mitch devoured the fish* and *Mitch ate the fish yesterday* are both clauses (in (8) and (12) they are also sentences, but that is not so interesting to us here), but we could also refer to them as VPs. As I will show in §8.7, in syntactic theories, there is some variation with respect to the category assigned to clauses.

8.4 Functions

We have established above that *the toy duck* is a noun phrase (though I did point out that it can also be argued that the determiner has some head-like qualities, a fact that I will return to in §8.7). However, this is not all we need to know about the phrase in order to be able to talk about its role in the syntax of a sentence. Compare the sentences in (15).

(15) a. The toy duck was floating in the bath tub.
b. The dog chewed the toy duck.
c. The child fed the toy duck some soap.

In all examples, *the toy duck* forms a constituent, but it has a different *function* or *grammatical relation* in each sentence. In (15a), it is a SUBJECT, recognisable as such in English for instance because it can invert with the following verb to make a question: *Was the toy duck floating in the bath tub?* Not all verbs allow this, but once you have a verb that can do it, it is the subject it inverts with. In (15b) and (15c), it functions as an OBJECT. A common test for object status is whether the phrase can become the subject of a corresponding passive sentence: *The toy duck was chewed by the dog* and *The toy duck was fed some soap by the child*. Though *the toy duck* passes the test for object status in both (15b) and (15c), the two instances are different. In examples like (15c), there is always a parallel example where the same phrase occurs with *to* and follows the other phrase: *The child fed some soap to the toy duck*. An object that can occur with *to* instead is called an INDIRECT OBJECT and the other object is the DIRECT OBJECT. Note that once you have turned the indirect object into a *to*-phrase, you can make a passive sentence with *some soap* as the subject: *Some soap was fed to the toy duck by the child*. Hence *some soap* is also an object in (15c), since it cannot be replaced by a *to*-phrase, it is a direct object.

What functions are possible depends on the verb: *chew* can take only one object, whereas *feed* may combine with two. In §8.3, I used the term *complement* for those elements that are selected by the head. The difference between the two terms is that complement is a general term indicating a structural relationship with a head, whereas object describes a function a phrase may have within the clause. An object is then a function that the complement of a verb may have, but there are also a number of other functions that the complements of verbs may have (see for instance Börjars and Burridge 2010: Ch. 4).

The functions we have looked at here are all selected by a verb, and terms such as subject and object tend to be used mainly at this level, though it can also be used with other categories. The centrality of the functions to verbs is indicated by the fact that verbs are subcategorised according to which functions they permit. A verb that takes no object is classed as INTRANSITIVE, one that takes one object is described as MONO-TRANSITIVE and those that take two objects as DI-TRANSITIVE. The functions we have considered here are not the only functions that can be distinguished. For a more complete list, see Börjars and Burridge (2010: Ch. 4).

8.5 Cross-linguistic syntactic variation

Languages vary greatly as to the role that syntax plays in their organisation. There are some languages where syntax can be said to play a smaller role than it does in English, these are called *polysynthetic* languages, and they rely heavily on morphology (see Chapter 7). These languages may use one word to express that which English expresses through a sentence. Mithun (1999: 38) gives the example *kaipiallrulliniuk* from Yup'ik, an Eskimo-Aleut language, which can be shown to be one word even though in meaning it equates to the English sentence *The two of them were apparently really hungry*. At the other extreme are languages that make little or no use of morphology, so that syntax becomes more important. One such language is Vietnamese, where even the plural marker is a separate word, so that the word for 'I' is *tôi* and 'we' is *chúng tôi*.[1] Such languages are referred to as *analytic* or *isolating*.

Languages also vary with respect to what categories can be distinguished. It is generally assumed that nouns and verbs can be distinguished in most languages, though not quite all. Samoan and Tagalog are languages for which it has been argued that no meaningful distinction can be made between these two word classes (see for instance Rijkhoff 2003). The word class adjective is more generally assumed not to be universal. When we say that a language lacks a certain word class, we do not mean that it is impossible to talk about the kinds of concepts that these word classes tend to express in English. A language that lacks a distinction between verbs and nouns does have words to refer to both actions and things, it is just that there is no morphosyntactic criterion that can be used to divide them into two categories. If we take the distinction between verbs and adjectives in English, a set of criteria can be established to distinguish the two. The most obvious one is maybe that verbs can be marked for present or past tense, but adjectives cannot. So, if you want to talk about an event of walking having taken place in the past, we add *–ed* and use *walked*. If, however, you want to talk about a house that was red in the past, we cannot add *–ed* to *red*. Instead we have to use a verb in the past tense: *was red*. In many languages, the words that express the same things as adjectives in English behave just like intransitive verbs, so that you can add a past tense marker to the word for 'red' and get the same meaning as the English *was red*. In the Malayo-Polynesian language Kambera, for instance, the sentences *The mango was ripe* and *The mango fell* would be structurally identically; there would be one word for FALL+PAST and a word with a similar structure RIPE+PAST (Klamer 1998: 115–18).

I used constituency tests in §8.3 to establish that English sentences have internal structure. In (3) above, I showed that *drinking the milk* is a constituent of *Mitch was drinking the milk*. The verb and its object form a structural unit in English, and since the verb is the head of this unit, *drinking the milk* is a VP in this sentence. Languages that have structure in this way are described as *configurational*. There are languages, where it can be argued that the object does not form a closer unit with the verb than the subject does. One such language is Irish, where the standard word order is verb-subject-object, so that the object is not adjacent to the verb, and there is also further evidence that the verb and the object do not form a constituent (see Carnie 2005). It is common to refer to languages with no evidence of a VP as *non-configurational*. Whereas it can be argued that there is no evidence of a VP in Irish, the component parts of noun phrases do stick together and occur in a specific order, hence the language is assumed to have NPs. There are, however, languages which are more thoroughly non-configurational than this, for instance in that noun phrases can be discontinuous. In (16), there is an example from Wambaya where the determiner and the noun of the subject noun phrase (in bold) are separated (Nordlinger 1998: 31).[2]

(16) **Nganki** *ngiy-a*   *lurrgbanyi*   **wardangarringa-ni**
this.SG.II.ERG 3SG.F.A.PST grab   moon.II-ERG
alaji   *gulug-barda*
child.II(ACC)   sleep-INF
'The moon grabbed her sleeping child.'

One characteristic feature of Wambaya is that there is an element representing features such as past tense and subject agreement features (see Chapter 7) that has to occur in second position, here this is *ngiya*. This element can be compared with *does* in *He does eat* in the sense that it has little meaning beyond the features. Apart from this second-position element, the word order is very free. In (16) the first element is a determiner, equivalent to something like *the* or *this* in English. It is marked as singular and the II indicates feminine gender and ERG is a case marker showing that it will be part of the subject of the clause. You can see that the word for moon has the same marking and this is how the hearer knows that the determiner forms a unit with the word for moon and not with the word for child. The equivalent of *the moon* forms a semantic unit, even though the two words are not adjacent and hence do not form a constituent in the usual sense (though I will return to different theoretical approaches to constituency in §8.7).

From a typological perspective, English is a language with quite rigid structure. If you were to study syntax using only English data, you would get a simpler picture than if you include a broad range of typological data. In this section, I have provided examples of how both categories and constituency can play quite a different role in languages. It will not surprise you that there is also some variation with respect to functions. In §8.7 we will return to the issue of how to capture this variation.

8.6 Representing syntactic structure

In §8.3 I introduced X-bar syntax and the notions of head, complement, modifier and specifier. A head may combine with a complement; whether it does or not is determined by the head. This unit may then combine with any number of modifiers: this is not determined by the head, but is a matter of speaker choice. Finally, the phrase may contain a specifier, which is unique and which is again determined by the head. I introduced the notion of a lexical versus a phrasal category; nouns can combine with complements, modifiers and specifiers to form noun phrases; we get NPs headed by Ns. In (14), I gave an example of a phrase built around an N which was not a full NP, so that a category between N and NP is required. This category is referred to as N', pronounced N-bar. Within this notation, NP is also sometimes referred to as N" or N-double-bar, but that is getting less common.

In §8.3 I pointed out that the categories I identified there – N, V, A, Adv and P – all behave a little differently with respect to complements, modifiers and specifiers. Within X-bar syntax they are, however, assumed to have the same basic structure so that if we use X as a variable over any category, we have the categories X, X' and XP (or X"), hence the name X-bar syntax.

Having identified names for the different types of constituent, I turn now to different ways of representing the constituent structure. It used to be common to mark constituency boundaries with square brackets and to label the brackets with the category of that constituent. If we take the noun phrase *a teacher of early music with false teeth*, where *of early music* is a complement, *with false teeth* is a modifier, and *a* is the specifier, we would get the representation in (17).

(17)   [[a]$_D$ [[[teacher]$_N$ [of early music]$_{PP}$]$_{N'}$ [with false teeth]$_{PP}$]$_{N'}$]$_{NP}$

This does not provide a good visual representation of the structure and now that word-processing systems allow us to use graphics more easily, constituent structure is almost exclusively represented by trees. This gives the tree in (18) instead of (17).

(18)
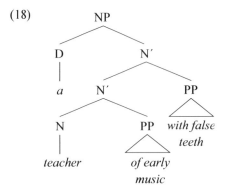

In a phrase structure tree such as (18), each node represents a constituent. The category of the constituent is indicated by the label on the node. A string of words is a constituent if there is a node that dominates that string and nothing else, where a node dominates another node if it is above it in the tree and there is a direct line of branches between them. Hence *with false teeth* is a constituent because there is a node which dominates just that string and it is of category PP as indicated by the label on the node. The triangle notation below both

PPs indicates that we are not interested in the internal structure of these phrases here. The string *a teacher*, on the other hand, is not a constituent here because the only node that dominates both *a* and *teacher* dominates other words too, in fact it is the node which dominates the whole of the noun phrase.

Phrase structure trees can be said to be generated, or licensed, by phrase structure rules. The rules required to generate the tree in (18) are provided in (19).

(19) a. NP → Det N′   introduces a specifier
      b. N′ → N′ PP   introduces a modifier
      c. N′ → N PP   introduces a complement

This does not represent the full range of noun-phrase structure of course, but these rules will serve to illustrate a couple of issues in relation to X-bar syntax. The relationships between nodes tend to be described using female family terminology: the NP node in (18) is the mother of D and the highest N′, the N and the lowest PP are sisters. The rule in (19a) states that a tree may contain a subtree which has an NP as its mother and has two daughters: a D and an N′. The bottom part of the tree in (18) is licensed by the rule in (19c), which allows a tree which has an N′ mother and two daughters: N and PP. The rule in (19b) is particularly interesting since it has an N′ on both the left and the right of the arrow. This means that the rule can apply to its own output. If we apply (19b) once we get the tree in (20a). Since this has an N′ daughter, we can apply the rule again and get (20b) and in principle we could repeat this an infinite number of times. This is called *recursion* and is appropriate for a rule introducing modifiers since these can be repeated: *a teacher of early music with false teeth*, *a teacher of early music from Birmingham with false teeth* until it becomes too difficult to process for the hearer.

(20) a.

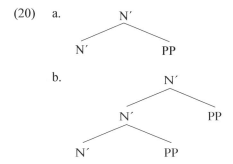

b.

We can then draw a schematic general tree to capture the principles of X-bar for headed phrases. X, Y, Z and Q are variables here and can stand for any category.

(21)

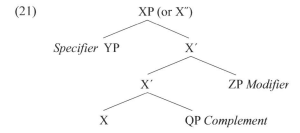

Now consider a sentence such as (22).

(22) Oscar tickled the boy with the feather.

This sentence is ambiguous; it can either mean that Oscar used a feather to tickle the boy or that the boy Oscar tickled had a feather. In one case *with a feather* modifies *tickled the boy* and in the other *the boy*. Since it is a structural ambiguity, we should be able to disambiguate it in our tree representation, and indeed we can. The trees in (23) provide the structure for the two meanings. It should now be obvious which one is which. Note that in (23b), the sister of the PP must be of the category N′, not N, since the PP is a modifier, not a complement. Since there is no complement of N in this noun phrase, the lower N′ only has one daughter, N.

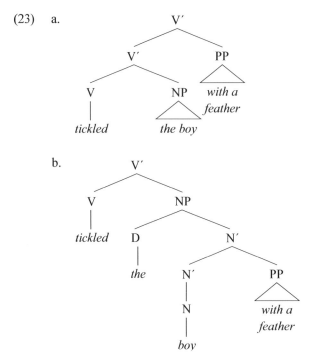

When considering the difficulty in applying the constituency tests to *really big* in *Mitch ate the really big sandwich*, I said that it was due to the phrase being deeply embedded within the sentence. As a modifier, *really big* would be an AP sister of an N′ inside an NP which is part of a VP which is part of a sentence. Imagining this as a tree it should be easier to understand what 'deeply embedded' means.

8.7 Theoretical approaches

Though X-bar syntax underlies most theoretical approaches to syntax, the way in which the approach is used varies between the formal models that you find described in the literature. Before we look at the different roles that phrase structure can play in a theoretical model, I should point out that there is a family of models referred to as *Dependency Grammar* that does not represent phrases in this way. Instead they indicate dependency relations between individual items; in a sentence such as *Oscar has tickled the boy*, *has* would have *tickled* as a dependent, *the* would be a dependent of *boy*, which would be a dependent of *tickled*, which would also have *Oscar* as a dependent. Using a notation where an arrow points towards the dependent element, we then get a representation like the one in (24) (details vary between different approaches to Dependency Grammar).

(24)
      Oscar has tickled the boy

In this approach, there is no representation of constituency, but you can compare the element which has dependents to a head.

Returning now to approaches that do use X-bar syntax, I will first consider the analysis of clauses. In (23), I did not analyse the sentence as a whole and hence did not assign a category to it. So far, all phrasal categories I have considered have had a head, they have been *endocentric*. In early phrase structure analysis of English clauses, they were assigned to the category S(entence), which had two daughters, NP and VP. Since neither of the two daughters was the head, this was a non-headed, or *exocentric*, phrase. In more recent work, it has been argued that if you apply headedness tests to English clauses the conclusion is that the finite verb is the head. However, because of the special status of the finite verb, it is assigned to a separate category, usually I(nflection). This I forms an IP by taking the VP as its complement and the subject as its specifier. The resulting tree for *Oscar has tickled the boy* is provided in (25).

(25)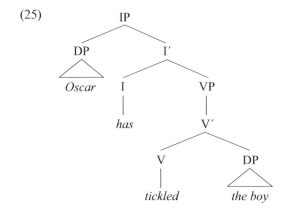

This analysis introduces a new functional category in addition to the traditional ones I referred to in §8.2. In some approaches to syntactic theory, the number of such functional categories has exploded over the last couple of decades, other theories take a more restricted approach. However, there is quite general agreement on three functional categories which can form phrases: I, D(eterminer) and C(omplementiser). For this reason, I have analysed that which I have previously referred to as NPs as DPs in (25), making D the head of the noun phrase. I referred to the difficulty in establishing which element is the head of the noun phrase in §8.3. The category C is used for clauses that are bigger than ordinary declarative clauses for instance clauses including a complementiser, such as ...*whether Oscar has tickled the boy*, or questions, such as *Who has Oscar tickled*.

The question now arises whether a tree similar to that in (25) is appropriate also for languages where constituency tests cannot be used to identify constituents the way they can for English. In §8.5 I discussed languages that are non-configurational, either in that they lack evidence for a VP, or more radically, where it may be difficult to identify NPs. This is an issue where modern syntactic theories differ greatly. I will compare two types of theories here, the movement-based analysis of *Minimalism* and the parallel-correspondence approach of *Lexical-Functional Grammar* (LFG).

Within Minimalism, the tree structure is not just used to identify constituent structure, but more importantly to identify grammatical functions and semantic roles (see Chapters 28 and 30). In (25), we know it is *Oscar* who does the tickling and not *the boy* because of the position of the noun phrases; *Oscar* is the subject because it is in the specifier position of the IP. Within Minimalism, this is assumed to be universal, so that in Irish and Wambaya the subject must also occur in specifier of the IP. The fact that the surface structure of an example like (16) is so unlike that in (25) is assumed to be due to words and phrases having moved. This movement is triggered by the features of the linguistic elements. Within this theory there may then be a difference between the underlying and the surface structure (though this terminology is outdated). Minimalism also has a number of assumptions about phrase structure that distinguishes it from many other theories; all phrase structure is endocentric and binary branching, which means that a node always has two daughters exactly and that one of them is the head. Many more functional categories beyond C, I and D are used within Minimalism, so that (25) is likely to be simpler than a Minimalist analysis of the same sentence. These functional categories need not be filled by audible linguistic material, but can contain just a feature.

In LFG and other similar syntactic theories, phrase structure trees are used exclusively to capture the syntactic categories and constituent structure and the tree structure assumed for languages such as Irish or Wambaya is different from the one assumed for English in (25). Sentences in a language in which noun phrases form constituents, but there is no evidence of a VP, would have a structure like that in (26), where the clause is non-headed. Wambaya may have a representation such as the one in (27). Here the fact that there is a functional element firmly in second position is captured by the headed IP, and since any element can occur in the initial position, I have indicated that with the variable X. The otherwise free word order is captured through the category S with a number of daughters.

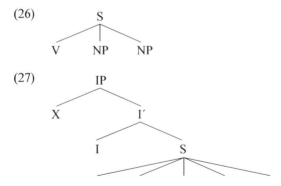

The exact details of the appropriate trees for Irish and Wambaya are not at stake here. It is the general principle we are interested in. It will be clear from these two trees that there is no restriction to binary branching in LFG, and that constituents need not be endocentric. Functional categories tend to be used only when there is some functional feature which is clearly associated with a structural position, as is the case with the finiteness and agreement marker in Wambaya.

In LFG there is no universal link between a particular position in the tree structure and a specific grammatical function or semantic role. There is assumed to be some correspondence between the different dimensions of linguistic information, this is why the family of theories is referred to as parallel-correspondence architecture. Information from one dimension, say the syntactic structure or the morphology, is mapped onto another, the functional dimension. However, how this is done varies from language to language. In a relatively rigidly structured language like English the clue to what is the subject, or if you like, 'who tickles who', does lie in the structural position. However, in other languages, it may be a case marker, like the ergative marker in Wambaya, or an agreement marker on the verb. In these cases, there is a direct link between the morphological marker and the grammatical relation, without the element having to occur in a particular structural position that is not evidenced by the actual word order for it to be associated with the correct grammatical relation.

It will have been clear here that LFG does not assume that phrase structure has to be endocentric and binary branching. This has consequences also for English. Whereas a phrase consisting of a verb and two complements, such as *give the dog a bone*, is analysed in terms of binary branching within Minimalism, in LFG it would be represented as a VP with three daughters. Similarly, a coordinated phrase such as *dogs and cats* is assumed to have a head in a Minimalist analysis, but it is not in LFG.

Needless to say this brief comparison has involved great simplification. For a fairer and more complete picture, references in the further reading section can be followed up.

Notes

1 These are not the only first person pronouns in Vietnamese; different forms can be used depending on factors such as politeness and respect.
2 You do not really need to know the details of the glossing in order to understand the point made, but the abbreviations stand for the following grammatical terms: SG=singular, ACC=accusative case, ERG=ergative case, F=feminine gender, II=noun class II, A=transitive subject, PST=past tense, INF=infinitive verb form.

Further reading

For more detail on the first five sections with respect to English, consider a simple introduction to English grammar such as Börjars and Burridge (2010) or the most comprehensive grammar of English extant, which is Huddleston and Pullum (2002). If you prefer a similar introduction based on a typologically broader data set, Payne (1997) and Kroeger (2005) are both very good. What I have presented here is a vastly simplified account of the different theoretical approaches, for a fuller picture see Adger (2003) for Minimalism and Dalrymple (2001) for LFG. Shorter accounts of a number of theories which share some crucial properties with LFG can be found in Borsley and Börjars (2011). Carnie (2008) provides an extensive introduction to X-bar syntax and its implementation in different theories. If you would like to understand Dependency Grammar, Hudson (2010) provides an introduction to Word Grammar, which is dependency-based. Given the variety of theoretical approaches to phrase structure, you will not be surprised to discover that the analysis of language data can give rise to different conclusions. For two different interpretations of the Irish data, see McCloskey (1983) and Carnie (2005).

References

Adger, D. (2003) *Core Syntax*. Oxford: Oxford University Press.
Börjars, K. and K. Burridge (2010) *Introducing English Grammar*, 2nd edition. Abingdon: Routledge.

Borsley, R.D. and K. Börjars (eds) (2011) *Non-transformational Syntax: Formal and Explicit Models of Grammar*. Oxford: Wiley-Blackwell.
Carnie, A. (2005) Flat structure, phrasal variability and VSO. *Journal of Celtic Linguistics* 9: 13–31.
Carnie, A. (2008) *Constituent Structure*. Oxford: Oxford University Press.
Dalrymple, M. (2001) *Lexical Functional Grammar*. New York: Academic Press.
Huddleston, R. and G.K. Pullum (2002) *The Cambridge Grammar of the English Language*. Cambridge: Cambridge University Press.
Hudson, R. (2010) *An Introduction to Word Grammar*. Cambridge: Cambridge University Press.
Klamer, M. (1998) *A Grammar of Kambera*. Berlin: Mouton de Gruyter.
Kroeger, P.R. (2005) *Analyzing Grammar: An Introduction*. Cambridge: Cambridge University Press.
Langacker, R.W. (1990) *Concept, Image, and Symbol: The Cognitive Basis of Grammar*. Berlin: Mouton de Gruyter.
McCloskey, J. (1983) A VP in a VSO language. In G. Gazdar, E. Klein and I Sag (eds) *Order, Concord and Constituency*, pp. 9–55. Dordrecht: Foris.
Mithun, M. (1999) *The Languages of Native North America*. Cambridge: Cambridge University Press.
Nordlinger, R. (1998) *Constructive Case: Evidence from Australian Languages*. Stanford: CSLI Publications.
Payne, J., R. Huddleston and G.K. Pullum (2010) The distribution and category status of adjectives and adverbs. *Word Structure* 3: 31–81.
Payne, T.E. (1997) *Describing Morpho-syntax: A Guide for Field Linguists*. Cambridge: Cambridge University Press.
Rijkhoff, J. (2003) When can a language have nouns and verbs? *Acta Linguistica Hafniensia* 35: 7–38.

9
Syntax as the dynamics of language understanding

Ruth Kempson

9.1 Grammar and language processing: building structure in context

This chapter sets out the case for setting linguistic theory and the grammars linguists write in a perspective reflecting real-time processing, as offered by the Dynamic Syntax framework. The assumptions advocated by this framework represent a radical departure from the methodology adopted by all who have worked on the formal modelling of natural language since the Chomskyan revolution of the 1960s. According to the familiar methodology a language is assumed to be in some sense isolatable, taken to be the set of well-formed sentences of the language taken in abstraction from their use. A grammar for a language is then a set of rules or principles which associate with each such sentence a triple: the phonological properties of the words made available by some underlying phonological system; the projection of fixed structure definable over those words (syntax); the meaning of the string defined over that syntactic structure (semantics). All attributes of language use in real time are treated as external to the system and explained by 'performance' theories to be grounded in such 'competence' grammars. What is not often pointed out is that this methodology omits any explanation of the two properties arguably diagnostic of natural language: (1) natural languages are systems underpinning an activity that takes place in real time (this is precluded in principle); (2) their token structures and interpretation display systemic dependence on the context within which such activity takes place (at best, this gets only a partial characterisation). Furthermore, the methodology commits the linguist to an encapsulated system, isolated from other cognitive systems.

On the new view which this chapter will introduce, the domain-specific concept of syntax is abandoned. So too is the assumption that syntactic tree structures are defined as holding over a sequence of words. To the contrary, words, and the general procedures encoded in language, are mechanisms for building up conceptual representations of content in an incremental left-to-right fashion, and it is only conceptual representations which have structure attributed to them. The consequence of this perspective shift is a much leaner perspective, in which the competence system is much closer though not identical to the performance system it underpins. The multiple levels of a grammar formalism with distinct phonology, morphology, morphosyntax, multilevelled syntax are replaced by two levels:

phonology and representations of content, with mechanisms defined in terms of some underspecified input and updates from that input that in combination yield mappings from phonological input onto representations of content. All are defined in terms of their contribution to the progressive building up of content, carrying over to syntax the assumptions of underspecification and context-relative update that are familiar from semantics and pragmatics (Kamp and Reyle 1993; Sperber and Wilson 1995; and many others). In consequence, the natural language system as a whole becomes dynamic. The system is a specification of general and lexically stored procedures which users can implement to build up such representations, both as hearers or as speakers.

9.1.1 Background perspectives

This shift of perspective came from two independent sources. It came initially in response to the increasing unease displayed by semanticists addressing the context-dependence of language interpretation, for which frameworks were needed which could directly reflect the incremental unfolding of representations of content. Then there was the realisation that incorporating this aspect of performance into the grammar transforms well-known syntactic puzzles, dissolving the difficulties they pose. In this chapter, I shall take ellipsis in conversational dialogue as our case study, to illustrate both issues.

Ever since model-theoretic semantics was articulated by Montague in the late 1960s and early 1970s, it was apparent that any semantic explication of language has to reflect the context-relativity of its construal; and over the years, it became increasingly clear that this context-relativity of language is endemic. Encoded meaning of an expression can always be enriched to yield some context-specific interpretation; so the articulation of that input meaning must reflect its underspecification with respect to the assignable output interpretation. This is not merely a one-shot context relativism definable from some characterisation of denotational truth-conditional content constituting sentence-meaning as the output of the grammar. Every step of the way involves context dependency, in anaphora, tense and aspect construal, quantifiers, adjuncts etc. Moreover, there is apparent necessity to invoke concepts of semantic representation over and above any such syntactic structures that may be defined over sequences of those expressions, so the directness of mapping from sentence-string onto model-theoretically definable content can no longer be presumed. The lead move in defining a structured concept of content within formal semantics was Hans Kamp's Discourse Representation Theory (DRT: Kamp and Reyle 1993), whose aim was to provide a unitary characterisation of pronominal anaphora. Kamp and colleagues provided a single base from which pronoun construal was defined for such varied environments as (1)–(3) which show that the anaphoric linkage can either be inter-sentential and able to be independent, or intra-sentential and dependent on another quantifier:

(1) A colleague is arriving late from New York. He will be tired by the end of the day.

(2) If a colleague is arriving late from New York, he will be tired by the end of the day.

(3) Every time a colleague arrives late from New York, he will be tired by the end of the day.

To obtain the appropriate basis for generality, a level of discourse representation structure (DRS) was defined via a mapping from whatever syntactic structure might be articulated over the elements in the string. The semantics for this system is incremental, but only sentence-by-sentence.

Even granting the problem that such anaphoric links appear not to be restricted by sentence boundaries, the question is what status the intermediate DRS should have in the grammar, being merely an intermediate construct which is given denotational substance only by the subsequent semantics. Inevitably, there were attempts to reduce all such constructs to model-theoretic alternatives in which the non-determinism of construal is expressed in the semantics (Groenendijk and Stokhof 1991). The problem of apparent need to posit some intermediate representation between the sentence form and its semantic evaluation is, however, not restricted to pronominal anaphora. It arises in temporal and modal construal, quantification, and strikingly in ellipsis, where truncated sequences can be interpreted as though these elliptical forms were, in some sense, a vehicle for a propositional mode of construal, some cases indeed explicitly marked as being underspecified for some predicate to complete such a proposition. Like anaphora, ellipsis dependencies may ignore sentence boundaries:

(4) If John is writing a book, then Bill won't be.

(5) Every time John writes a book, Bill does.

(6) John is writing a book. An article too.

Ever since the various phenomena comprising ellipsis were identified, there have been arguments as to whether ellipsis falls within the remit of syntax. If so, then ellipsis will not provide evidence for any additional level of semantic representation. But this move led to the identification of a wealth of different ellipsis types and posited ambiguities (Fiengo and May 1984), so semanticists sought to develop accounts defining the variety via processes of abstraction over some preceding content re-applied at the ellipsis site to yield the various effects (Dalrymple *et al.* 1991). However, if ellipsis is deemed to be subject to semantic characterisation, it would seem that an additional level of semantic representation is required for full explication of ellipsis. This is because, amongst other arguments, there are fragments which obligatorily reflect morphosyntactic constraints of the language. Fragmentary Greek answers to a question for example have to reflect the case appropriate to a full reply, a pattern widespread in case-rich languages (7).

(7) I Maria den egrapse to grama?   Oxi, ego/*emena
    Didn't Maria write the letter?   No, I_{Nom}/*me_{Acc}

So ellipsis, where the basis for recovering interpretation is radically incomplete, provides evidence that there must be some concept of building up a representation of content with granularity reflecting syntactic/morphological detail.

Yet adding an additional level to the grammar does not address the problem of cross-sentential forms of ellipsis; and further problems with intra-sentential ellipsis abound. In conversational dialogue, well-formed sentence structures may emerge through a sequence of fragmentary contributions, each participant adding some fragment to a partial structure that emerges bit by bit across the exchange. As we shall see, this interaction depends on participants alternating listening and speaking, a phenomenon which grammars respecting the traditional sentence-based methodology are very poorly placed to explain. All such sub-sentential interactions, however fluent and widespread, are beyond the remit of grammar, dismissed as mere performance dysfluencies. The result is that not only do such grammars fail to explain the systemic nature of context-dependence, a diagnostic property of natural language, but no morphosyntactic, syntactic and semantic dependency will be completely characterised.

There is a simple but radical solution. This is to shift to the assumption that syntax is the set of mechanisms inducing the dynamic ongoing projection of semantic representation: there is no separate level of syntactic representation over and above that of such emergent semantic representations. So it is not the level of semantic representation that is jettisoned: it is the old-style conception of syntax. Interpretation involves evolving growth of partial representations, secured through sequences of structure-building actions, to which any participant can contribute. The patterns of dialogue ellipsis follow directly, wholly without stipulation. This chapter seeks to give the reader a taste of this issue, introducing the data and then seeing how the dynamics of processing as modelled within DS directly secures the effects of interaction, this success illustrating how we can successfully model our linguistic competence as grounded in the dynamics of how people do what they do.

9.1.2 Split utterances in dialogue: the challenge of incrementality

In dialogue, switching of roles between speaking and hearing, across and within sentential structures, is widespread. There is much interactivity between participants in a dialogue, with people joining in on what the other person is saying, adding to it (8), often helping the other to find the appropriate add-on (9).

(8) Conversation from A and B, to C:
  A: We're going to
  B: Bristol, where Jo lives.

(9) A: I suppose I need a a
  B: mattock. For breaking up clods of earth.

Each such contribution can add unproblematically to whatever partial structure has been set out so far without any contributor having planned the overall structure at the outset. (10) turns out to be a conditional sentence only upon its completion, its consequent clause preceding its antecedent clause:

(10) Hugh: We're going to London
  Alex: to see Granny
  Eliot: with the dogs?
  Hugh: if you promise to keep them under control.

Such speaker-switching may take place at what might be construed as sentence boundaries, so that both antecedent and add-on fragment might be said to be separate sentences, with the fragment trading on some proposition being recoverable from context. But this is not necessary: one can interrupt at any point in a clausal sequence, and by no means only collaboratively (11).

(11) A: What this shows is
  B: that you have completely missed the point.

Split dependencies can, moreover, be arbitrarily complex (12).

(12) A: Has every student handed in
      B: their homework?
      A: or even any assignments?

(12) contains a pronoun uttered by B interpreted as bound by a quantifying term uttered by A and a negative polarity item in A's further response, that too requiring the environment of A's initial utterance, even though A's follow up is in response to what B said. The overall phenomenon is that in language use, participants in a discourse can take arbitrary structures, complete or partial as context, and use these as the point of departure from which to switch into speaking and so overtly contribute to the ongoing utterance. In an exactly converse pattern, a speaker can take where they have got to in producing some utterance as the background context relative to which they can understand what is then said to them. It is not a matter of going into reverse in either switch: it is simply a matter of keeping going from where one has got to.

The seamless fluency with which individuals take on or hand over utterance responsibility raises foundational issues for language modelling. The problem for syntacticians and semanticists is that these split points can separate sub-parts of a structure, apparently splitting dependencies of every sort that linguists have pinpointed, whether syntactic or semantic; yet the espoused sententialist methodology relative to which these dependencies are articulated preclude any straightforward modelling of the data. In some sense, these two parts have to go together to determine a whole syntactic structure; yet the result even so may not constitute a well-formed sentence string (13).

(13) (A emerging from a smoking kitchen)
      A: I've burnt the kitchen rather badly.
      B: have you burnt
      A: Myself? No.

In (13), the relevant sub-parts, put back together, yield *Have you burnt myself*, an ungrammatical string, yet they constitute a perfectly well-formed exchange.

What such data indicate is that these exchanges are not about putting word sequences together to form some single string. They involve speaker A taking over from speaker B to provide some extension of the content of what was initially put into construction by A. In (13), this involves A's taking up the projection of the second part of the utterance in a way that reflects themselves now as the new speaker. So the projection of structure has not only to represent content, and local dependency on identification of some subject with the use of the reflexive pronoun, but context-dependent content as expressed by that local anaphor. This indicates the extent of the challenge these data pose; the dependencies have to be defined over semantically transparent structure and with whatever imposed context-relativity is determined by the words chosen, echoing the required level of granularity demonstrated by the Greek fragments as in (7).

This phenomenon has been almost completely ignored until very recently as a mystery. With their move to address the challenges posed by modelling dialogue, the new Type Theory with Records framework (TTR: Cooper 2012; Ginzburg 2012) allows a relatively rich concept of abstraction ranging over morphosyntactic as well as semantic content, both at sub-sentence and supra-sentence levels; and TTR has been the first framework to take up the challenge of modelling dialogue data as systematically within the remit of grammar. Yet there are problems, as the underpinning sententialist methodology remains essentially undisturbed, with fragments taken to constitute syntactically non-standard sentence-types that involve abstractions over some previous sentential context in order to provide the appropriate functor to combine with the presented fragment. This may be a justifiable move where there is a sentence-based paraphrase, but there are many where there is not, as (13) illustrated. There are also problems where the interjected fragment occurs so early in an utterance that there is no appropriate sentential candidate for its interpretation (14).

(14) A: They X-rayed me, and took a urine sample, took a blood sample. Er, the doctor
B: Chorlton?
A: Chorlton, mhm, he examined me, erm, he, he said now they were on about a slight [shadow] on my heart. [BNC: KPY 1005–8]

What is required to characterise the fragment 'Chorlton?' in (14) is not any abstraction over the previous context: what is requested is clarification as to the entity described by the word *doctor*, yielding some token of an individual not sentence type. So it would seem that the attempt to force fragment construal into a propositional frame is imposed solely by dictates of the sententialist methodology in a way that does not correspond to the notion of context itself.

Split-utterance data are problematic also for pragmatists. The assumption shared by pragmatists is that utterance understanding is an act by the hearer of grasping the proposition which the speaker either has or could have in mind (Grice 1975; Sperber and Wilson 1995). This is a consequence of a sentence-based grammar methodology, as the challenge posed by such grammars is that it is in some performance theory, given the sentence outputs of the grammar, that explanation of issues of context-dependence must be articulated. Pragmatists broadly agree that successful communication occurs when the hearer is able to grasp the proposition(s) which the speaker either has or could have intended, given the context. But this necessitates the presentation of some sentence-sized object, relative to which the hearer is able to reconstruct some intended propositional content. In many cases, this assumption is not sustainable, yet the exchange may remain entirely successful. Consider (15) in which the son is resisting all attempts to get him to be helpful. He is certainly not waiting for the third of the commands even if he has bothered to process the second:

(15) (A mother, B son)
A: This afternoon first you'll do your homework, then wash the dishes and then
B: you'll give me 10 pounds?

Even the presumption of any fixed single intended speech act may be in question, since a single fragment is able to serve more than one such function (16).

(16) Lawyer: Will you choose your son as your attorney or
Client: My wife.

Moreover, these data, far from being dysfluencies which the child has to ignore in order to come to achieve competence in their language, emerge in the earliest stages of language learning.

(17) Carer: Old McDonald had a farm... On that farm he had a
    Child: cow.

And, as with adults, the need to recognise the other party's intended content seems inappropriate for almost all carer–child exchanges. Indeed, nursery-carers may rely on the interactive ability of the child from an equally young age:

(18) A (teacher to each child in turn in the class): And your name is ...
    B (child): Mary.

In (18), the child is merely completing the template set out by the carer with what is answer to a question as well as its completion, which they can do without any need to identify a given thought as held by the questioner. If these data provide evidence that recognition of the content of other people's intentions is not a necessary condition on successful acts of communication, as we suggest they do, then the foundational assumption of pragmatics needs to be reconsidered (Gregoromichelaki *et al.* 2011). However, if the grammar formalism is defined to reflect such incremental build-up, these data naturally fall within the remit of grammar, dissolving these syntactic, semantic and pragmatic puzzles.

9.2 Dynamic Syntax

Dynamic Syntax (DS) is a representationalist model of interpretation of which the core structural notion is interpretation *growth* relative to context. With the dynamics of structural growth built into the grammar formalism, natural-language syntax is a set of principles for inducing growth of such structures. The syntactic mechanisms, being meta to the representations themselves, are procedures (conditional action statements) that define *how* parts of representations of content can be incrementally introduced and updated, all such growth being relative to context. Moreover, context is as structural and dynamic as the concept of content with which it is twinned: it is a record of the (partial) structures that represent the emergent content *plus* the actions used in constructing them.

The general process of parsing is taken to involve building as output a tree whose nodes reflect the content of some uttered formula – in the idealised case of a sentence uttered in isolation, a complete propositional formula as diagrammatically displayed in (19). The input to this task is a tree that does nothing more than state, at the root node, the goal of the interpretation process to be achieved, namely, to establish some propositional formula. This is the minimal left-hand tree in (19), the *requirement* $?Ty(t)$ signifying that this is a goal not yet achieved (the ◊ is a pointer indicating the node under development). The output from the parse of the string *John upset Mary* to the right of the ↦ in (19) constitutes some final end result: a tree in which the propositional formula annotates the top node, its various sub-terms appear on the dominated nodes in that tree with their specified type (on the tree in (19) these are given as a pair $\alpha:x$ in which α is the formula of type x). The *formula* values given here are expressed as though in English, but these are concepts as expressed by instructions encoded in words of the language.[1] $S_{PAST}:e_s$ represents the final Davidsonian event/situation argument projected by tense (see Cann 2011):

(19) Parsing *John upset Mary*.

$?Ty(t), \Diamond \mapsto$ $Upset'(Mary')(John')(S) : t, \Diamond$

```
                    S_PAST: e_s        (Upset'(Mary'))(John')) : e_s → t
                                    John' : e          Upset'(Mary') : e → (e_s → t)
                                                     Mary' : e      Upset' :
                                                                    e → (e → (e_s → t))
```

These DS trees are invariably binary, reflecting functor–argument structure, and, by convention, the argument is on the left branch, the functor on the right branch; and each node is identifiable by a tree-node identifier $Tn(i)$ in a tree (not given here). The parsing task is to use both lexical input and information from context to progressively enrich the input tree to yield such a complete output following general tree-growth actions.

9.2.1 Formal properties of trees

Though the decoration on trees may be determined idiosyncratically and in part through lexical itemisation, the trees themselves and the mechanisms for their growth are language general, defined by the formal meta-vocabulary for grammar writing. In order to explicitly formulate how such structures grow, trees have to be formally defined, together with a vocabulary for describing actions that induce the requisite tree growth. Following Blackburn and Meyer-Viol (1994), DS adopts a modal logic with two basic modalities. There is $\langle \downarrow \rangle$: $\langle \downarrow \rangle \alpha$ holds at a node if α holds at its daughter (with variants $\langle \downarrow_0 \rangle$ and $\langle \downarrow_1 \rangle$ for argument and functor daughter relations respectively). There is the inverse $\langle \uparrow \rangle \alpha$ which holds at a node if α holds at its mother, equally with argument and functor variants indicative of the status of the daughter–mother relation so identified. Based on these, there are defined Kleene star operators which yield concepts of *dominate* and *be dominated by*: $\langle \downarrow_* \rangle Tn(n)$ holds at a node when a node $Tn(n)$ is somewhere below it, $\langle \uparrow_* \rangle Tn(n)$ holds at a node when a node $Tn(n)$ is somewhere above it. There are then the analogue $\langle \downarrow^1_* \rangle$ and $\langle \uparrow^1_* \rangle$ operators defining a functor spine within a tree, hence concepts of *locally dominate* and *be locally dominated by*. There are also so-called *linked* trees for the modelling of adjuncts (Cann *et al.* 2005).

The core pair of concepts driving forward the tree growth process is that of underspecification with an attendant *requirement for update*: both are essential for reflecting the time-linearity involved in progressively building up (partial) trees. There are different types of underspecification: of some putatively final tree, of formula content or type, of type of node, and even of relation of that node to others in the tree. All aspects of underspecification are twinned with a concept of *requirement*, $?X$, for some annotation X; and these are constraints on how the subsequent parsing steps must progress. Such requirements apply to all types of decoration, including modal requirements expressing future developments, for example $?\langle \uparrow_0 \rangle Ty(e_s \to t)$ capturing nominative case-marking as an output requirement that a node so decorated be immediately dominated by a node of propositional type. Requirements drive subsequent tree-construction processes: unless they are eventually satisfied, the parse will be unsuccessful.

Actions for tree growth determine procedures for building such tree relations, defined as sequences of make(X), go(X) and put(Y) operations, where X and Y are tree relations and node-decorations respectively. *Computational actions* constitute generally available

Syntax as the dynamics of understanding

strategies for tree-growth, inducing growth of these relations via strategies for unfolding an emergent tree on a top-down basis, and then bottom-up processes compiling decorations for all non-terminal nodes: an overall resulting formula decoration at the top of a tree is thus finally derived, achieving the overall goal of establishing a representation of propositional content.

9.2.2 Lexically induced growth of trees

Lexicon-internal specifications express language particularities in the same formal language as computational actions, differing only in being lexically triggered. The update actions specified are conditional in form: given a certain condition, a macro of tree-growth actions induce some update yielding a distinct partial tree. For example, from a requirement of the form $?Ty(t)$ as the triggering condition, verbs project a skeletal propositional template projecting a node for a predicate and nodes for its attendant arguments as required by its type. These argument nodes are decorated as part of the action sequence with either the requirement $?Ty(e)$ or with a typed place-holding decoration exactly in the manner of anaphoric expressions. And this is where there is an array of options available across different languages. Like other Germanic languages but unlike many other languages, the argument nodes projected by English finite verb forms are associated with a requirement of the form $?Ty(e)$ which ensures that in each case, there has to be some further step of language-input processing in order to satisfy type requirement and project some concept formula of that type. The lexical specification of the verb induces the entire propositional template and such attendant decorations through actions of make(X), go(X) and put(Y):

(20)
$$
\begin{array}{ll}
& \textit{upset} \\
\text{IF} & ?Ty(t) \\
\text{THEN} & \text{make}((\downarrow_0)) : \text{go}((\downarrow_0)); \\
& \text{put}(Ty(e_s), Fo(U_{PAST}), ?\exists x Fo(x)); \text{go}((\uparrow_0)) \\
& \text{make}((\downarrow_1)); \text{go}((\downarrow_1)); \text{put}(?Ty(e \to (e_s \to t))); \\
& \text{make}((\downarrow_1)); \text{go}((\downarrow_1)); \\
& \text{put}(Fo(\text{Upset'}), Ty(e \to (e \to (e_s \to t)))) \\
& \text{go}((\uparrow_1)); \text{make}((\downarrow_0)); \text{go}((\downarrow_0)); \\
& \text{put}(?Ty(e); \text{go}((\uparrow_0))); \text{go}((\uparrow_1)); \text{go}((\uparrow_1))); \\
& \text{make}((\downarrow_0)); \text{go}((\downarrow_0)); \\
& \text{put}(?Ty(e)) \\
\text{ELSE} & \text{Abort}
\end{array}
$$

In the formulation in (20), first an event term is taken to be projected by the form *upset* (in fact as an anaphoric device, see §9.2.2.1 and, for detailed specifications of English tense, Cann 2011). Then the predicate internal structure is constructed along with the concept associated with *upset*, with its two attendant arguments plus that of the event term. As this lexical specification indicates, words project very much more than just a representation of some concept: they project a sequence of actions of arbitrary complexity; and such complex idiosyncratic structural projections may be the emergent result of action sequences that get consolidated over years into composite macro routines.

9.2.2.1 Triggering context-dependent construal

Despite idiosyncrasies that may thus arise, some commonalities run right across languages. Anaphoric expressions, for example, encode an underspecified form of content, being dependent on something external to themselves for interpretation, to be provided either from the general utterance context, or from elsewhere in what is being said. Pronouns provide a familiar case; but anaphora is of several types: nominal, hence 'pronominal', pro-predicate, pro-propositional, pro-temporal, and so on. For example, English auxiliaries can be anaphoric, with indexical uses as seen in (21)–(22).

(21) Mother shouting to her toddler reaching for the saucepan on the stove:
Don't.

(22) Mother to her teenage son (with surfboard in hand), both looking out to sea at some perilously large waves:
I wouldn't if I were you.

Indeed the lexical specification of *upset* reflects this tense anaphoricity as we now see. To model what these triggers for context-based construal encode, we assume that anaphoric, elliptical and tense expressions project a content-place-holding device, together with whatever form-specific constraints there may be on how the relevant interpretation is selected. They are defined as projecting a formula metavariable ($Fo(U)$), with accompanying requirement for formula update, $?\exists x Fo(x)$. There is undoubtedly cross-linguistic variation in anaphoric and elliptical forms (the English auxiliary system is notoriously idiosyncratic in this respect, with few other languages licensing elliptical use of auxiliaries as in (21)–(22)); but there are general patterns. Context-dependencies are resolvable either from the larger context, as here, or via identification within the construction process. The former case is familiar. With the pointer being at the node at which the expression in question is parsed, such update is normally identified at that relatively early stage in the construction process from what is independently available, possibly from the utterance scenario. However, the parsing process may proceed without any identification of value for the metavariable until a second point in the construction process when its value has to be combined with that of its sister node to yield some value for their shared mother node in order to yield the emergent compositionality of overall content: at this point its formula requirement must be satisfied. So-called expletive pronouns display this property, anticipating and being associated with late identification of the value for the node they decorate, which takes place *after* their sister predicate node has been constructed as in (23)–(24).

(23) It is unfortunate that Mary smokes.

(24) It worries me that Mary smokes.

Such anticipatory uses are normally treated as wholly distinct phenomena; but, as we shall see, an underspecified value can be resolved either from context or, as with expletives, from within the utterance process itself, once that process has provided the context which makes its update possible.

9.2.2.2 Interplay of lexically and syntax-driven updates

With all lexical and computational actions defined in tree-growth terms, seamlessness between lexicon-internal and lexicon-external processes becomes unproblematic. Concepts of locality, for example, can be identified either word-internally or as a structural constraint. So it is straightforward to identify the requisite concepts of locality constraining antecedenthood for both reflexives and pronouns, enabling a natural feeding relation of such specifications into computational actions of various sorts; and we expect such locality effects to be demonstrable in other areas too. Arguments local to a given predicate can all be defined as meeting the characterisation $\langle\uparrow_0\rangle\langle\uparrow^1_*\rangle$ $Tn(a)$ ('$Tn(a)$ holds up one argument-relation plus a possibly empty sequence of function-path relations'). Accordingly, reflexive anaphors can be characterised as projecting the action specified in Figure 9.1; and, conversely, the substitution process of pronominals excludes as antecedent any formula decorating a node standing in such a local relation.

9.2.3 Structural options for tree growth

With the concept of underspecification and update being the core notion on which the grammar specification turns, there is a structure-building analogue of the content underspecification familiar from anaphoric specifications. Amongst the computational actions are processes inducing underspecified structural relations, local and non-local. These weak structural relations are defined using the Kleene star operators: all such weak tree relations have an associated requirement for future provision of a fixed tree-relation, i.e. a fixed tree-node address: $?\exists x Tn(x)$. For example, $\langle\uparrow_*\rangle Tn(a)$ is defined as a decoration on a node indicating that there is at least one future development in which the node with address a bears a sequence of mother relations to the present node. This relatively weak tree-relation is taken to express long-distance dependency effects in terms of structural underspecification and update. For example, when first processing the word *Mary* in Figure 9.2, which is initially construed as providing a term whose role is not yet identified, the parse is taken to involve the application of a computational action which introduces from the initial root node decorated with $?Ty(t)$, a relation to that top node which is *underspecified* at this juncture, identifiable solely as dominated by the top node (indicated by $Tn(0)$), and requiring type e, specified by a $?Ty(e)$ decoration. This enables the expression *Mary* to be taken to decorate this node: this is step (i) of Figure 9.2. The accompanying requirement for a fixed tree-node position $?\exists \mathbf{x}.Tn(\mathbf{x})$ induces the update to this relatively weak tree-relation which in this derivation takes place after processing the subject plus verb sequence to yield the two-place predicate structure in step (ii) of Figure 9.2. Provision of a formula decoration for the object argument node and update of the unfixed node initially introduced is given by the *unification* step indicated there, an action which satisfies the update requirements of both depicted nodes.

```
IF       ?Ty(e), Fo(α)
THEN       IF    ⟨↑0⟩⟨↑¹*⟩⟨↓₀⟩ Fo(α)
           THEN  put (Fo(α), Ty(e)).
           ELSE  Abort
ELSE     ABORT
```

Figure 9.1 Action for reflexive anaphora

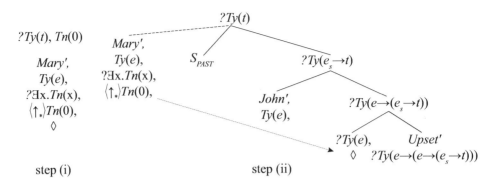

Figure 9.2 Parsing *Mary, John upset*

Accounting for left-peripheral expressions in these dynamic update terms is not contentious as a parsing strategy: what is innovative is its incorporation within the grammar-mechanism as the basic underpinning to syntactic generalisations.

9.2.3.1 Parallelism of content and structural updates

The parallelisms between content and structural modes of underspecification can now be brought out, in two ways and two directions. First, resolution of left-peripheral expressions at some later point parallels that of expletive forms of pronoun construal: both involve some underspecification in their value that is resolved at some later stage in the interpretation process. Second, such left-peripheral expressions can be interpreted as it were indexically from the previous context, from which actions can be retrieved/constructed from context to provide the basis on which the fragment is to be understood to contribute to some larger structure. That is, initial noun-phrase expressions can occur, on their own as it were, at some left periphery with nothing following, hence constituting an incomplete fragment decorating an unfixed node:

(25) Sue, I very much admire. John too.

(26) A: John makes the most amazing cakes.
     B: Mary too.

The resolution of the overall contribution of these fragments is resolved backwards as it were, by reiterating actions taken from the preceding context, with the entire context-provided reconstruction of structure then providing the update to the fragment, essentially like a freer variant of VP ellipsis. This completes the parallelism between structural and content updates, for underspecification of structure in these cases is construed in like manner to indexically construed pronouns, that is from the context provided. This is characteristic of many fragments, particularly those which provide some add-on. And, as we might now expect, there is free interaction between lexical processing of a fragment whose actions can feed into a sequence of actions retrieved from context which in their turn can feed into yet a further step of lexical processing:

(27) A: John's handing in his assignment.
     B: Bill will be too, tomorrow.

The significance for the modelling of ellipsis in assuming that context keeps a record of actions used is that we now expect that fragments can be construed not merely by retrieving representations of content from context, but also by reiterating actions previously used (Purver *et al.* 2006). In (27), for example, the actions chosen from context are those employed in the previous processing of *handing in his assignment*, taken from the preceding utterance and re-applied to the new fragment, prior to the processing of the final *tomorrow*. To reflect this notion of context formally, what has to be assumed is that, in evolving along with content, the context of utterance keeps track not merely of representations of such content, but also a record of the sequence of actions used. More precisely, context is modelled as the triple of words, sequences of partial emergent structures, and a record of actions used to build them.

Reliance on such contexts as a basis for interpreting elliptical expressions is a mechanism used by very young children, who in the so-called *one-word utterance* stage rely to a very large degree on the adult with whom they are being able to reconstruct some content from their utterance. One case was observed by Alex, cycling along a canal path with two-year-old son Eliot on a bike pannier behind her, when Eliot waves across the canal to an empty spot on the other side, giving rise to the exchange in (28).

(28)   Eliot: Daddy.
       Alex: That's right, you were here with Daddy yesterday clearing out the boat.

This exchange took place the day after the boat had been emptied of the family possessions and taken back to a central mooring, leaving the empty space pointed to. The child is constructing the predicate to be applied to his fragment from memory, presuming the mother can do so too (though she was not actually there). In such cases, the child is relying on his ability to construct actions necessary to build up content from memory and not from a linguistically presented antecedent utterance – an indexical use of elliptical fragments. Thus, both content-underspecified forms projected by anaphoric expressions, and structural underspecifications in the characterisation of 'unfixed' nodes in a structure, may have that underspecification resolved either through the process of content construction, or from the context, that is, from interaction.

There is much more to be said for a full DS account of ellipsis. But the overall picture this has been used to illustrate is that both content dependencies (the provenance of semantics) and structural dependencies (the provenance of syntax) are taken to constitute core syntax, and yet be mechanisms for building interpretation. Remember in this connection from §9.2.1 the problems posed for semantic accounts of ellipsis. In this framework, these are unproblematic, as with nominative case expressed as a tree-update constraint, the model of build-up of interpretation will provide the granularity required to characterise restrictions on construal imposed by case-bearing fragments, as in Greek (§9.1.1). Morphosyntactic particularities, like other more general structural options, are expressed as constraints on growth of representation of content; and these can be recalled exactly as semantic forms of update. Furthermore all updates, whether syntactic, morphosyntactic or lexical, can be manipulated as mechanisms for interaction. Even long-distance dependencies, thought for decades to be the lynchpin of arguments that natural-language syntax is irreducibly encapsulated, can be seen in this light; for these are now seen as inducing an underspecified structural relation and resolving that structural indeterminacy by unification with some independently constructed structure.

Not so fast, you might be pleading: is not this account misplaced as a grammar formalism because it is skewed towards parsing? The answer is indeed that the system is grounded in parsing. But the lack of reference to parsing is little more than a matter of exegesis. Production (generation of pairs of linearised string and tree) is presumed to follow the same process of tree construction with one further assumption: at every step in production, there must be some richer tree, a so-called *goal tree*, which the tree under construction must subsume in the sense of being able to be developed into that goal tree by rules of the system. This is a direct reflection of the intuition that in production, the speaker must have some richer concept in mind, even if not fully complete. Formally this is the assumption of some goal tree relative to which the emergent tree-growth structure is checked (Purver *et al.* 2006). So parsers and producers alike use strategies for building up representations of content. In sum, the familiar array of syntactic phenomena – discontinuity in syntactic dependency, expletive pronouns, binding specifications for anaphoric construals, agreement constraints on such construals, and so on – can all be expressed by shifting perspective to grammar formalisms articulating concepts of real-time growth of semantic representation. Syntactic dependencies can be redefined as the effect of manipulating mechanisms licensing various forms of underspecification whose update processes then interact with both general and idiosyncratically imposed constraints to incrementally determine an array of emergent partial structures reflecting content more or less transparently. All that is then needed to express arbitrarily complex structures is the assumption that any one of such locally induced predicate argument structures can be extended by the creation of composite pairs of local structural domains through mechanisms of variable sharing. I will not go into this here, but it forms the basis of accounts of relative clauses, adjuncts, appositions, coordination. Overall, the result is a rich basis from which to set out novel solutions to syntactic puzzles (Cann *et al.* 2005; Kempson *et al.* 2011 are representative).

9.2.4 Split utterances: an English case study

An immediate bonus for the DS perspective is that the puzzle of how to characterise the phenomenon of split utterances that this chapter opened with is directly solvable for they follow as an immediate consequence of the general dynamics presumed by the model. Generation, recall, makes use of the same tree growth mechanisms as parsing, with the same commitment to incrementality. This means that, in all exchanges, parties to the exchange will be building up a tree to serve as the basis for both the parsing and production process. From the perspective of modelling the point of switch of roles, two properties of the generation mechanism are pertinent. First, there is nothing to prevent speakers initially having only a partial structure to convey, i.e. the goal tree may be a partial tree. This is unproblematic, as all that is required by the formalism is progressive tree growth in any partial-tree sequencing (=*monotonicity* of tree growth), and the subsumption check is equally well defined over partial trees. Indeed, the system is set up to project partial trees as context, hence as input to some next point of departure. Second, the goal tree may change during generation of an utterance, as long as this change involves monotonic extension: because speaker and hearer essentially follow the same sets of actions, each incrementally updating their semantic representations, the hearer can effectively continue to mirror the same series of partial trees as the producer after the switch, albeit no longer knowing in advance the content of the unspecified nodes, no matter what extension the producer may provide. For example, for dialogues such as (29), Mary as the speaker reaches a partial tree of what she has uttered through successive updates, while Bob initially as hearer, follows the same updates to reach the same representation of what he has heard: they both apply the same tree-construction mechanism which is none other than their effectively shared grammar.[2] This provides Bob with the ability at any stage to become the speaker, interrupting to take over Mary's utterance, repair, ask for clarification, reformulate, or provide a correction, as and when necessary. What, then looks like distributed construction of some structure across distinct participants is in fact no more than switch within the tree-development process from parsing without any goal tree for subsumption purposes to the very same tree construction process except that with the switch into production there will be a goal tree providing the basis for the further subsumption check. Yet the dependencies thereby apparently so distributed remain constructed and resolved within a single locally definable tree domain for an individual agent. So, according to DS assumptions, repeating or extending a constituent of someone else's utterance is licensed only if the hearer now newly turned speaker, entertains a message to be conveyed (a new *goal tree*) that matches or extends in a monotonic fashion the parse tree they themselves have constructed from what they have just heard. Let us take this up step by step on (29), using a simplified variant of (13).

(29)   Mary: Did you burn
       Bob: myself? No.

Despite the fact that the string **Did you burn myself?* is unacceptable, under DS assumptions, with representations only of informational content, not of structure over strings of words, the switch of person is straightforward and leads to a well-formed result. Figure 9.3 displays the partial tree induced by parsing Mary's utterance *Did you burn* which involves a substitution of the metavariable projected by *you* with the name of the interlocutor/parser (setting aside how to capture questionhood). At this point, Bob can complete the utterance with the reflexive as this expression, by definition, copies a formula from a local co-argument node onto the current node just in case that formula satisfies the conditions set by the person and number of the uttered reflexive, and, in this case, that it names the current speaker. These are encoded in the lexical action for *myself* as in (30).

(30)   *myself*   **IF** $\langle \uparrow 0 \rangle \langle \uparrow_*^! \rangle \langle \downarrow 0 \rangle Fo(x)$
                              $Speaker(x)$
                  THEN $put(Fo(x))$
                  ELSE   ABORT

This illustration is only of the simplest type of split-utterance ellipsis, but the point is general. These seamlessly achieved split utterances can apparently separate off any expression from the syntactic environment it needs for its wellformedness because both speaker and hearer make use of the same mechanisms. So the same individual whether as speaker or as hearer will invariably have a partial structure on which to rely at the point of participant switch: the use of structure retrieved from context is just one type of information stored in context. Context has the same granularity of information as the lexical specifications given by the words. What is recorded is: (1) the words so far expressed; (2) the partial trees so far built, up to and including the one containing the node indicated by the pointer; (3) the actions used to build up that emergent partial structure. And since it is actions making

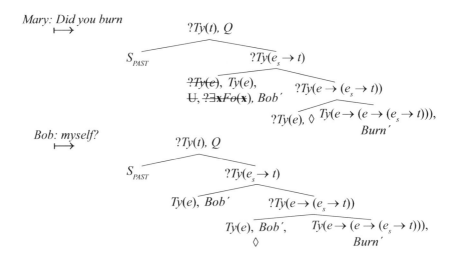

Figure 9.3 Mary/Bob context

up the process of interpretation which constitute the basis of *syntax*, it follows that we shall have all the granularity needed to characterise the full range of ellipsis effects. Of course the justification for this claim will turn on the detailed specifications of individual cases, but, in principle, the DS framework articulates the concept of context that is needed to provide an integrated account of ellipsis.

Stepping back from the details, note that the account of ellipsis in dialogue rests on the jettisoning of a conventional 'syntactic' level of representation in favour of syntax as a set of mechanisms for incrementally building semantic representations, with these mechanisms shared by both speaker and hearer. The incrementality of parsing and production is the key to the simplicity of the story: it is this which allows the direct successful integration of interpretation provided by the spliced-utterance fragments. Both speaker and hearer are continuing from where they have got to in the utterance processing task, intuitively and formally using their own context (the Alex–Eliot exchange is notable in this connection). In contrast to the immediacy of DS applicability, the phenomenon of speaker switch in the middle of a dependency under construction is a major challenge for sentence-based grammar frameworks. These fail to provide the appropriate units: all dependencies are articulated grammar-internally as defined exclusively over hierarchically defined sentential structures which in principle do not reflect time-linear emergent growth. From that sentence-based perspective, successful communication is then seen as establishing some propositional content from sentences that the speaker could have intended to express, with essential mind-reading. On the DS account, no such recognition of intended content is required as a definitional property of communicative understanding, for dependencies are defined over some partial structure as yet still under construction, and specific to the individual. The data which are so recalcitrant for these frameworks are thus predicted as a direct consequence of the way DS mechanisms are defined.

To substantiate the claim that DS assumptions can express the whole range of syntactic phenomena of course needs very much more than one limited case study (Cann *et al.* 2009). But because ellipsis requires syntactic and semantic reconstruction, the point is general. Because syntax involves the emergent projection of representation of content in combination with lexical tree growth actions, we can express what is general to structure and interpretation in language, yet the variation also. A considerable amount of DS-related work has been done on cross-language, cross-dialectal and historical syntax substantiating these claims. There is work on tense and aspect articulating event-term specifications (Cann 2011). There is work on left–right asymmetries (Cann *et al.* 2005 among others), and on verb-final languages, which receive natural syntactic analyses only when syntax is defined as incremental building of semantic structure (Kempson and Kiaer 2010). There is work on pronominal clitics, whose obscure syntax–semantics mappings have been successfully modelled in terms of concepts of routinisation of action update sequences, a move which provides an evolving basis for both diachronic change and synchronic variation (Chatzikyriakidis and Kempson 2011; Kempson *et al.* 2011). There has also been exploration of issues of intentionality (Gregoromichelaki *et al.* 2011): and there is a host of further issues, both linguistic and philosophical, waiting in the wings.

Acknowledgement

This chapter is grounded in work on *The Dynamics of Conversational Dialogue* (ESRC-RES-062-23-0962). I am immensely grateful to my co-workers on this project and too many others to thank who have contributed to the fine landscape which this work has opened up. Thanks in particular to Ronnie Cann for comments on an earlier draft of this chapter.

Notes

1 Possible complexities of lexical decomposition are ignored here. Quantification is taken to be name-like, hence of low type: see Kempson *et al.* 2001; Cann *et al.* 2005.
2 A completely identical grammar is, of course, an idealisation but one that is harmless for current purposes.

References

Blackburn, P. and W. Meyer-Viol (1994) Linguistics, logic and finite trees. *Logic Journal of the Interest Group of Pure and Applied Logics* 2: 3–29.
Cann, R. (2011) Towards an account of the English auxiliary system: Building interpretations incrementally. In R. Kempson, E. Gregoromichelaki and C. Howes (eds) *Dynamics of Lexical Interfaces*, pp. 279–317. Chicago: CSLI Press.
Cann, R., R. Kempson and L. Marten (2005) *The Dynamics of Language*. Oxford: Elsevier.
Cann, R., R. Kempson and E. Gregoromichelaki (2009) *Semantics: An Introduction to Meaning in Language*. Cambridge: Cambridge University Press.
Chatzikyriakidis, S. and R. Kempson (2011) Standard modern and Pontic Greek person restrictions: A feature-free dynamic account. *Journal of Greek Linguistics* 11: 127–66.
Cooper, R. (2012) Type theory and semantics in flux. In R. Kempson, T. Fernando and N. Asher (eds) *Philosophy of Linguistics*, pp. 271–324. Oxford: Elsevier.
Dalrymple, M., S. Shieber and F. Perreira (1991) Ellipsis and higher order unification. *Linguistics and Philosophy* 14: 399–452.
Fiengo, R. and R. May (1984) *Indices and Identity*. Cambridge: MIT Press.
Ginzburg, J. (2012) *The Interactive Stance: Meaning for Conversation*. Oxford: Oxford University Press.
Gregoromichelaki, E., R. Kempson, M. Purver, G.J. Mills, R. Cann, W. Meyer-Viol and P.G.T. Healey (2011) Incrementality and intention-recognition in utterance processing. *Dialogue and Discourse* 2: 199–233.

Grice, H.P. (1975) Logic and Conversation. In P. Cole and J.L. Morgan (eds) *Syntax and Semantics 3: Speech Acts*, pp. 41–58. New York: Academic Press.

Groenendijk, J. and M. Stokhof (1991) Dynamic predicate logic. *Linguistics and Philosophy* 14: 39–100.

Kamp, H. and U. Reyle (1993) *From Discourse to Logic: Introduction to Model Theoretic Semantics of Natural Language, Formal Logic and Discourse Representation Theory*. Dordrecht: Kluwer.

Kempson, R. and J. Kiaer (2010) Multiple long-distance scrambling: Syntax as reflections of processing. *Journal of Linguistics* 46: 127–92.

Kempson, R., E. Gregoromichelaki and C. Howes (eds) (2011) *Dynamics of Lexical Interfaces*. Chicago: CSLI Press.

Kempson, R., W. Meyer-Viol and D. Gabbay (2001) *Dynamic Syntax: The Flow of Language*. Oxford: Blackwell.

Purver, M., R. Cann and R. Kempson (2006) Grammars as parsers: Meeting the dialogue challenge. *Research on Language, and Computation* 4: 289–326.

Sperber, D. and D. Wilson (1995) *Relevance: Communication and Cognition*, 2nd edition. Oxford: Blackwell.

10
Semantics
The meaning of words and sentences

John Saeed

10.1 Introduction

Semantics is the study of meaning communicated through language. Viewed through the lens of contemporary academic disciplines it is an important focus of enquiry in linguistics, philosophy, psychology, anthropology and computer science, to name just the most evident. The aim of this chapter is to briefly outline some important current approaches within linguistics. It will emerge how researchers in linguistics are fundamentally influenced by ideas in these other disciplines, while seeking to maintain the goal of linguistics: to characterize the full spectrum of human languages. The discussion begins by briefly considering semantics as part of descriptive linguistics, the basic activity of documenting individual languages. The endeavour to document languages has become a focus of greater urgency as public realization has grown about the large number of languages threatened with extinction. We go on to identify a broad division between two successful theoretical research paradigms. The first is essentially philosophical in its genesis and proposes that notions of truth and compositionality are crucial in meaning. The second is psychological in orientation and is concerned with the cognitive status of processes and representations employed by speakers in communication. Each encompasses a broad spectrum and naturally there are significant areas of overlap. The first, often somewhat confusingly termed formal semantics, has its roots in Tarski's (1956) truth definitions and is represented today in a large and heterogeneous field of enquiry, amongst which we focus on dynamic approaches such as Discourse Representation Theory. The second approach is equally broad, and here we concentrate on the recent growth of interest in lexical semantics, for example in the approach known simply as cognitive semantics. Both approaches find themselves seeking to accommodate recent advances within pragmatics.

10.2 Semantics in descriptive and typological linguistics

We can apply the term descriptive linguistics, for the purposes of the present discussion, to the activities of linguists who write grammar of languages, and in particular attempt comprehensive coverage of a single language. Such linguists typically eschew formalism and instead use a toolbox of ideas and procedures that has developed over time from structural linguistics and that is increasingly called 'basic linguistic theory' (Dixon 2010). Such grammars generally embody André Martinet's (1960) concept of double articulation, which identifies as a characteristic of language that meaningless form, at different levels, is mapped to meaningful elements. As a result semantics is distributed across the grammar and lexicon in a series of form – meaning correlations. In grammar this leads to the identifications of systems, for example where morphological forms might be mapped to meaningful distinctions of tense, aspect, mood, evidentiality and negation.

We can take the example of the semantic system of aspect, which allows different views of how a situation is distributed over time. This is in principle a distinct system from tense, which allows the positioning of situations in time relative to some reference point, though in many languages the two systems are marked on verbs in similar ways. Aspect allows speakers to view an event in various ways, for example as complete, or incomplete, or as something repeated over a period. This particular three-way distinction is mapped in some languages to grammatical distinctions between perfective, imperfective and habitual forms. These might be marked morphologically on the verb, as with the Somali past tense perfective/imperfective distinction in the examples below:

(1) *Warqad   buu   akhrinayaa*
    letter   FOCUS.he   was.reading
    'He was reading a newspaper.'

(2) *Warqad   buu   akhriyey*
    letter   FOCUS.he   read
    'He read a newspaper.'

In Hausa, however, such distinctions are marked by preverbal clusters of particles, as below:[1]

(3) *Yâara   sun   tàfi   tashàa.*   (Perfective)
    children   3PL.PFV   go   station
    The children went/will have gone to the station.

(4) *Yâara   sun-nàa   tàfiyàa   tashàa*   (Imperfective)
    children   3PL-IMPF   go   station
    The children go/will go/are going to the station.

(5) *Yâara   su-kàn   tàfi   tashàa*   (Habitual)
    children   3PL-HAB   go   station
    The children usually go to the station. (Mahamane 2008)

Example (4) shows us that aspect is distinct from tense since the same aspect is compatible with various positions in time. In other languages, these semantic distinctions might be marked by auxiliary verbs occurring in syntactic constructions with the main verb, as in the English habitual *She used to sleep late*. In descriptive approaches the semantics of aspect is described in relation to its formal realization and the place of that realization in the grammatical description. The account of other semantic systems will be aligned with their grammatical mapping, providing a dispersed account of grammatical semantics.

In this approach a level of generality is realized through typology, the study of linguistic systems found cross-linguistically, where particular semantic systems are factored out of grammars and compared across samples of languages. One example is modality, which allows the speaker to communicate judgements of the potentiality of a state of affairs. Typically this operates on several interrelated planes. Thus epistemic modality allows the speaker to signal stronger and weaker commitment to the factuality of statements, as in *It might be raining* versus *It is raining*. Deontic modality allows the speaker to communicate attitudes to social factors of obligation, responsibility and permission, as in *You might let them know the truth* versus *You must let them know the truth*. In English the same modal auxiliary verbs may fulfil both roles, so that *Alexander may leave early* can communicate either a judgement of possibility (epistemic modality) or permission (deontic modality). Such modal verbs are just part of a more general resource allowing speakers to modulate commitment to real and hypothetical situations. Typological studies such as Palmer (2001) investigate the semantic distinctions available and their mode of realization in languages. The investigation may develop further classifications, for example the introduction of terms such as abilitive modality for possibility based on the speaker's view of a subject's nature (*Harry can play hockey; This floor can support their weight*), and teleological or bouletic modality, based on the speaker's view of a subject's goals and desires (*He has to improve his Irish*). Such inquiry will also investigate whether modality is a single semantic category or a grouping of related categories. An issue here is the relationship of modality to evidentiality, which is a system that allows, or in some languages commits, speakers to communicate sources of information or knowledge that support assertions, as in the examples below cited in Aikhenvald (2004: 2–3) from Tariana, an Arawak language spoken in northern Amazonia:

(6) a. Juse   irida   di-manika-**ka**
       José   football   3sgnf-play-REC.P.VISUAL
       'José has played football (we saw it)'
    b. Juse   irida   di-manika-**mahka**
       José   football   3sgnf-play-REC.P.NONVISUAL
       'José has played football (we heard it)'
    c. Juse   irida   di-manika-**nihka**
       José   football   3sgnf-play-REC.P.INFERRED
       'José has played football (we infer it from visual evidence)'
    d. Juse   irida   di-manika-**sika**
       José   football   3sgnf-play-REC.P.ASSUMED
       'José has played football (we assume this on the basis of what we already know)'
    e. Juse   irida   di-manika-**pidaka**
       José   football   3sgnf-play-REC.P.REPORTED
       'José has played football (we were told)'

Here the morphological marking (in bold) on the verb commits the speaker to select from a five-fold evidential distinction between these reports of a recent past event. We can see the similarity with modality in English modal verbs where *must* can communicate a speaker's inference made from evidence, as in *These fossil footprints must have been left by an Australopithecus*. The question of how modality and evidentiality are related, for example as two members of a larger semantic grouping, is an open question.

The other main semantic task in this approach is to account for word meaning by the creation of a dictionary or lexicon for each language. This is interdependent with grammar writing because the structure of the lexicon will reflect analyses of the phonology and morphology of the language. The lexicon is always a structured network of the identified meaningful elements in the language but key issues such as the entry forms, how to deal with derived forms and how much idiosyncratic behaviour is included are matters of analysis and argument. In this balance between grammar and lexicon we can see a modern reflection of Franz Boas' (1911) anthropological linguistics system of grammatical description, word list and texts. Field lexicographers involved in language documentation face the same theoretical issues as in all lexical semantics, including discriminating between homonymy and polysemy; representing lexical relations like synonymy, antonymy, hyponymy; and accounting for the role of context (Frawley *et al.* 2002). Homonyms are words which are identical in form but which have different meanings and are thus given independent entries in the lexicon. Polysemy describes cases where distinct senses are analysed as being related, either in speakers' minds or historically. These are traditionally assigned subsections of the same entry in the lexicon. However when the linguist comes across distinct senses of a word the decision to identify homonymy or polysemy is sometimes hard to make. So in English it might seem likely that *bark* 'outer layer of tree' and *bark* 'sound made by a dog' are good candidates for homonyms, i.e. are unrelated, but speakers might be less sure about another common word *pool* whose meanings include 'a body of water', 'a game played on a billiards table' and 'a group of people available for some purpose (e.g. press pool, typing pool)'. Polysemy itself raises difficult theoretical and practical questions since all words have a certain plasticity that allows them to be used in different contexts. So in English *fresh* is interpreted somewhat differently when applied to water, air, produce and sheets. The question is the extent to which for specific words this variation should be identified, at one extreme, as distinct senses, or at the other as a single underspecified meaning that is filled in or enriched by contextual information. We shall discuss some proposal for representing polysemy later in the chapter. For descriptive semantics these issues are more or less acute depending on the access to speakers and the richness of available materials and earlier linguistic accounts.

What distinguishes this descriptive approach from other contemporary approaches is its emphasis on embedding semantics as part of the grammar and lexicon production process and its avoidance of general overarching theories of semantics. The next approaches we consider differ in this regard.

10.3 The philosophical turn

While philosophers have since ancient times been concerned with the nature of language, the early twentieth century saw a philosophical concentration on language that had a profound impact on the study of meaning in linguistics. In the writings of Frege, Russell, the early Wittgenstein, and Carnap there is evidenced what has been retrospectively called a linguistic turn (Dummett 1994). This term reflects analytical philosophy's focus on the relationship between language, knowledge, logic and mathematics. Despite a continuing rift between philosophers interested in ordinary language and those determined to purify language to an ideal, there arose the view that the best way to understand thought is to vigorously analyse language. The philosophical study of how elements of language work, such as names, nouns, subjects, predicates, negation and sentence connectors, proved influential and attractive to linguists; as did discussion of more general notions such as reference, truth, and intersubjectivity. One influential proposal was that the necessary rigour for this enterprise could be gained from applying the methods used in the development of the theory of logic. The growing adoption of these notions by linguists can be described as a philosophical turn.

There are three somewhat related ideas from the philosophy of language that have been important in linguistic semantics. The first is that the semantic content of statement can be characterized as a proposition. The second is the proposal that a speaker's ability to understand the meaning of a statement in their language might be relatable to their ability to evaluate the truth of the associated proposition. The third is that a useful way to express propositions is by means of a formal, essentially logical notation.

Much debate in this literature centres on the idea that the meaning of a sentence is a proposition. Sentences themselves are of course abstractions from utterances, for example from concrete instances of speaking. Propositions are a further abstraction from sentences and this abstraction is made to identify a level of meaning or thought shared by several sentences. In this view the sentences below share the same proposition, the idea that Marconi invented radio, which can be expressed by these various sentences:

(7)   Marconi invented radio.

(8)   Radio was invented by Marconi.

(9)   It was radio that was invented by Marconi.

(10)   What Marconi invented was radio.

These sentences express the same proposition, which depending on the facts of the world may be true or false. One proposal is that this truth-evaluable proposition is the essential part of the meaning of these sentences and therefore the object of study in semantics. The differences between them arise from speakers' judgements of how to fit the proposition into the structure of a conversation, which as a feature of the speaker's use of the sentence is held to be the subject of pragmatics. So in short, this is a proposal that the semantic value of a sentence is the truth-bearing proposition it expresses. Of course only declarative sentences used to make assertions can be true or false of a situation. A question like *Did Marconi invent radio?* cannot be true or false since it makes no claim, but it clearly has something to do with the same proposition. This approach has to find some way of associating propositions with questions, orders and other types of speech act.

Using the notion of truth involves a focus on the denotational function of language: the way language allows us to talk about the world around us. We can use names like *Melbourne* and expressions like *the President of Ireland* to refer to specific entities in specific situations. Propositions allow us to assign properties to such entities or link them in various ways, such as if we state *The President of Ireland visited Melbourne*. A truth-based approach focuses on this external aspect of language and assumes that a sentence, or more accurately the proposition it expresses, is true or false depending on its fit to the state of affairs that obtain in the world. One version of this approach, truth-conditional semantics, proposes that the meaning of the proposition (and indirectly the sentence) is its truth conditions. Speakers who understand the sentence cannot necessarily tell whether it is true or false but they can tell what the world would have to be like in order for it to be true. To be able to do this, the proposal goes, they have to have understood the meaning of the sentence and the concept of 'truth'.

In this view, knowledge about truth conditions underlies some forms of everyday reasoning. So if the sentence in (11) is uttered, an English speaker will know that if it is true she must accept the conclusion in (12), provided the same entities are referred to.

(11)   The Mayor was bitten by a dog.

(12)   The Mayor was bitten by an animal.

This relationship is called entailment and in this case results from the meaning relationship between animal and dog of inclusion (or technically, hyponymy). Entailment can be characterized as a truth relation between sentences:

ENTAILMENT AS A TRUTH RELATION. A sentence P entails a sentence Q when the truth of the first (P) guarantees the truth of the second (Q), and the falsity of the second (Q) guarantees the falsity of the first (P).

Entailment, defined like this in terms of truth, can be used to characterize other semantic relations. Sentence synonymy, for example, can be defined as mutual entailment. So the two sentences below, which do entail one another, are synonymous:

(13)   The Harland and Wolff shipyard in Belfast built the *Titanic*.

(14)   The *Titanic* was built by the Harland and Wolff shipyard in Belfast.

Other sentence relations can be characterized in the same way. For example, two sentences are contradictory if the truth of one necessarily entails that the other is false.

If propositions, or their truth conditions, are candidates for sentence meaning an interesting question is what these propositions should look like. One answer, provided in different ways by philosophers Donald Davidson (1967) and Richard Montague (1974) is that sentences should be associated with expressions in a formal logic, which has the benefit of clear rules of composition and procedures for evaluating truth. In this view mapping from grammatical form to logical form facilitates semantic description. Employing the set-theoretic structures of model theory from the study of formal languages enables, first, the establishment of a mathematical model of the situations that the language describes and, second, a set of procedures for checking the mapping between the expressions in the logical language and the modelled situations. This process of interpretation aims to throw light on the semantic capabilities of natural languages.

Beginning with a parallel between logical connectives and natural language expressions like the English words *and, or* etc. in (15), this approach seeks to show the contribution of natural language expressions to the truth conditions of the containing sentences.

(15)   Connectives in logic and possible English counterparts

Connective	Syntax	English
$\neg$	$\neg p$	it is not the case that **p**
$\wedge$	$p \wedge q$	**p** and **q**
$\vee$	$p \vee q$	**p** and/or **q**

Semantics

Connective	Syntax	English
$\vee_e$	**p** $\vee_e$ **q**	**p** or **q** but not both
$\rightarrow$	**p** $\rightarrow$ **q**	if **p**, then **q**
$\equiv$	**p** $\equiv$ **q**	**p** if and only if **q**

In the parallel drawn here the English word *and* is seen as sharing the truth-conditional behaviour of the logical connective $\wedge$. The behaviour of $\wedge$ can be captured in the truth-table in (16), which basically says that both logical expressions joined by $\wedge$ have to be true (T) for the complex expression to be true:

(16)

p	**q**	**p** $\wedge$ **q**
T	T	T
T	F	F
F	T	F
F	F	F

The claim is that this is also true for compound sentences involving *and* as in (17).

(17)   Joan has bought a car and John doesn't know about it.

In this approach the truth properties of other grammatical categories like quantifiers can be investigated by using sets and functions. Thus English *all*, *some* and *no* can be defined as in (18), (where paraphrases are given to explain the conventional use of **1** for true, **0** for false and *iff* for 'if and only if'):

(18)   All $(A, B) = 1$ iff $A \subseteq B$
All A are B is true if and only if set A is a subset of set B

(19)   Some $(A, B) = 1$ iff $A \cap B \neq \emptyset$
Some A are B is true if and only if the set of things which are members of both A and B is not empty

(20)   No $(A, B) = 1$ iff $A \cap B = \emptyset$
No A are B is true if and only if the set of things which are members of both A and B is empty

Syntactic categories such as nouns, adjectives, intransitive and transitive verbs can also be given set-theoretic representations that allows their denotational properties to contribute in a consistent way to the denotational behaviour of their containing sentence in the model. So a sentence like *Zoli is Hungarian* will be translated into a semantic formula which will be true only if the entity denoted by the name *Zoli* is a member of the set of things denoted by the predicate *is Hungarian* in the relevant context. The aim is to see how much the compositionality and transparency of the formal notation can reflect the properties of the natural language under study.

Even at its most successful this approach suffers from the disadvantage that it tends to view sentences as static independent constructs that are mapped to semantic forms. Much of language structure however reveals that sentences naturally form part of larger structures that emerge as part of an interactive process amongst speakers. Speakers use pronouns, for example, to link references to entities between sentences and between sentences and the context. These links shift as the conversation progresses and new entities are talked about. Similarly, speakers may use elliptical or partial forms, relying on their hearers' ability to supply the missing elements. A number of formal approaches have been developed to capture the dynamic nature of language. One such approach is Discourse Representation Theory (DRT, Kamp and Reyle 1993), which formalizes a dynamic updating level of discourse structure and in which discourse referents are tracked across successive sentences. The discourse referents form an intermediate level between the nominals used in the sentences and the real individuals in the situation described. The main form of representation is a Discourse Representation Structure (DRS), usually presented in a box format, as shown below. These DRSs are built up by construction rules from the linguistic input, sentence by sentence. We can take the sentences in (21) as uttered in sequence and assume that the pronoun *it* in the second refers to the monster identified in the first. We mark this relationship, traditionally called anaphora, by using the shared subscript i.

(21) a. Frankenstein created a monster$_i$.
     b. It$_i$ woke up.

In DRT the utterance of the first sentence will trigger the construction of the DRS below:

(22)
```
 x   y
─────────
Frankenstein (x)
monster (y)
created (x, y)
```

The discourse referents are given in the top line of the DRS, called the universe of the DRS, and below them are conditions giving the properties of the discourse referents. These conditions govern whether the DRS can be embedded into the model of the current state of the discourse. A DRS is true if all of the discourse referents can be mapped to individuals in the situation described in such a way that the conditions are met. A name like *Frankenstein* in (22) denotes an individual, while an indefinite NP like *a monster* will be satisfied by any individual meeting the property of being a monster. The third condition is the relation *created (x, y)*. We can see that the truth conditions for sentence (21a) are given here by a combination of the discourse referents and the conditions. The sentence will be true of a situation if it contains two individuals; one named Frankenstein, the other a monster, and if the first created the second. An important point is that in an example like this the introduction of a discourse referent into a DRS carries an existential commitment by the speaker. Thus the indefinite NP *a monster* is treated as having existential force, though there are other ways of introducing indefinite nominals which do not have this existential commitment, as we shall see below. The initial DRS is labelled K_0, the next K_1 and so on. The latest K acts as the context against which a new sentence in the discourse is interpreted.

The second sentence in (21) updates the discourse and adds another discourse referent, *it*. The embedding rule for pronouns will say that unlike names we must find an accessible antecedent for it. In this case gender is a factor since *it* must find a non-human antecedent. If the correct antecedent for the pronoun is identified, the result is the extended version below of the original DRS with a new reference marker and a new condition (23).

(23)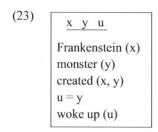

A negative sentence like (24) will be assigned the DRS in (25):

(24) Count Dracula does not own a sunlamp.

(25)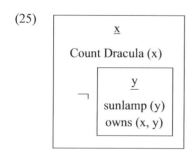

Here the DRS contains one discourse referent and two conditions: the first is the usual naming relation, Count Dracula (x); and the second is a second DRS embedded in the first and marked by the logical negation sign ¬. The satisfaction of this second condition is that there is not a sunlamp such that Count Dracula owns it. This contained DRS is said to be subordinate to the containing DRS and is triggered by the construction rules for negation. This subordination helps provide a formal reflection of cases where antecedents may not be accessible to subsequent pronouns. Here the conditioning factor is negation, where as suggested by our characterization of how the condition in (25) is satisfied, there is no existential commitment associated with the indefinite NP *a sunlamp* in this sentence, unlike *a monster* in (22).

The effect of this is that discourse referents introduced within a subordinate DRS under the scope of negation are inaccessible to pronouns in subsequent stages of the DRS, as shown by the oddness of the sequence below:

(26) a. Count Dracula doesn't own a sunlamp$_i$.
     b. ?He hides it$_i$.

This sequence would produce the DRS in (27).

(27)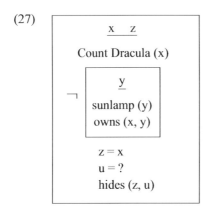

The pronoun *he* in the second sentence is successfully interpreted as anaphoric with *Count Dracula* in the first sentence, and hence $z = x$ in the DRS conditions. However the question mark in the identification of an antecedent for u (i.e. *it*) is because the only possible antecedent for y (*a sunlamp*) is not accessible since it occurs in the subordinate DRS box under negation. This explains the semantic oddity of (26b) above and so provides a formalization of one aspect of the relation of anaphora or pronoun coreference.

Even this briefest of sketches helps show that DRT seeks to provide a framework to explain the dynamic process by which discourse referents are introduced and maybe subsequently accessed by pronouns. A number of other approaches have like DRT sought to formalize a process of updating information states, for example file-change semantics (Heim 1983), dynamic predicate logic (Groenendijk and Stokhof 1991) and update semantics (Veltman 1996). Dynamic predicate logic, as the name suggests, modifies predicate logic by adding information states as a condition on the interpretation of reference. Noun phrases introduce variables into discourse and the information state configuration determines what interpretation they can have. Truth is still calculated relative to a model but is dependent on the successful resolution of the reference of discourse entities. Update semantics is a dynamic version of propositional logic, which uses the philosophical notion of possible worlds, that is, alternative ways things might have been. Information states are viewed as subsets of the set of possible worlds. In this approach a sentence updates an information state by eliminating worlds in the model that are inconsistent with the new sentence. In other words, updating is a process of eliminating possibilities. In addition to the tracking of referents through a discourse other dynamic approaches have investigated other areas, for example how presuppositions and tense relations are updated during a discourse.

These formal approaches have joined naturally with work on sentence meaning in computational linguistics and artificial intelligence (AI). Segmented Discourse Representation Theory (SDRT; Asher and Lascarides 2005) for example, combines ideas from dynamic semantics with rhetorical structure theory to account for discourse coherence. SDRT views a discourse as being segmented into constituents related to each other by rhetorical relations. These are organizational devices used by the speaker and include notions such as narration, elaboration, explanation and correction. The claim is that this rhetorical structure affects the updating of reference, tense and other semantic relations. For example the expected availability of anaphoric relations maybe blocked by rhetorical structure. Asher and Lascarides (2005: 60) give the example in (28).

(28) (a) John had a great evening last night.
 (b) He had a great meal.
 (c) He ate salmon$_i$.
 (d) He devoured lots of cheese.
 (e) He won a dancing competition.
 (f) ?It$_i$ was a beautiful pink.

In the absence of operators like negation nothing in standard DRT would prevent the pronoun *it* in (f) being interpreted as coreferential with *salmon* in (c). The unnaturalness of this, in the SDRT view, comes from the rhetorical structure, which sees the sequence (b–e) as an elaboration of (a), which thus forms a discourse subordination structure, a kind of descent or digression into greater detail. When the narration resumes at a more general level the nominals are in some sense blocked off from subsequent anaphoric relations.

In other cases the rhetorical structure allows anaphora where strictly grammatical accounts would not predict it, as with the pronoun *it* in (29).

(29) The room was cold.
 The wine was poor.
 The turkey was overcooked.
 It was a disaster.

Here there is a kind of summing up or topic anaphora, which allows anaphoric reference to something like *the dinner* that is not explicitly expressed rather than any of the expressed and available nominal candidates. The move within formal approaches towards dynamic accounts and modelling information states marks a shift in orientation from a denotational to a representational approach, as attention moves to the speaker's and hearer's mental models of the ongoing discourse. The further step to discourse management structures can also be seen as a move to integration with pragmatics, given that information packaging is a context dependent activity.

10.4 Cognitive semantics

Cognitive semantics is part of a wider approach known as cognitive linguistics (Chapter 29). Scholars in this approach sought to counter what they saw as the overly philosophical orientation of mainstream twentieth century semantics. These linguists (e.g. Lakoff 1987; Langacker 2008) disagree fundamentally with formal approaches by rejecting what they term objectivism: the idea that language directly models or maps reality. In its place they assert that meaning relies on conceptualization, which underlines how a speaker construes a situation. It follows from this that semantic structures are based on, indeed are themselves, conceptual structures. This approach seeks to reflect research on concepts and conceptual categories in the cognitive psychology literature and, in particular, incorporates embodiment theory (Johnson 1987; Gibbs 2006). This is the view that many of the conceptual structures and processes that we find in language derive from bodily experience, including vision; kinaesthesia, the bodily experience of muscular effort or motion; and somaesthesia, the bodily experience of sensations such as pressure.

Cognitive semantics generates a particular approach to word meaning. In a simple denotational approach words like names and nouns are in a direct relationship to the world. The things speakers can refer to (i.e. identify) by an expression may be called its extension and different types of linguistic expression are seen as having different types of extension. Proper nouns, or names, would have entities as their extensions and common nouns would have sets of things. So the name *Mogadishu* would have the city as its extension, while the noun *camel* would have as its extension the set of camels. It is possible to extend this to other types of words, so that the verb *live* would have as its extension the set of things that live and the adjective *green* would have as its extension the set of green things. In cognitive semantics however words are associated with conceptual categories and this raises the question of how these are structured. Cognitive semanticists have been influenced by experimental evidence from the psychologist Eleanor Rosch's (1973, 1975) work in particular that categories naming natural objects have a structure of prototypicality, where they lack sharply defined boundaries, and have focal points represented by prototypical members of the category. The qualities of the prototypical members are most salient for the category. An example for English speakers is the category of the word *fruit*. Experiments show that speakers judge some types of fruit, such as apples and oranges as more typical and others, like pomegranates and watermelons, more peripheral. There are also cases like olives and tomatoes that are doubtful for some people.

Influenced by these results cognitive semanticists have proposed that lexical categories are formed of radial networks of senses, where the prototypical sense is related to other senses by cognitive processes, including generalization, specialization, and extension by metaphor and metonymy. Dirven and Verspoor (2004) analyse the word *school* as a radial category, where as shown in (30) the central prototypical sense of a learning institution is extended to other senses by such processes.

(30) Radial category *school*
Central: learning institution
Metonymy: the building housing it (as in *The school burnt down*)
Metonymy: teaching staff and/or pupils associated with it
Generalization: group of artists sharing a style
Generalization: school of thought
Specialization: university faculty
Metaphor: school of fish

In this view the sense relations are conventionalized rather than generated in context by individual speakers and word meanings are thus seen as semantic networks stored in memory.

Cognitive semanticists have investigated the particular problem of polysemy in prepositions, which are of special interest to this perspective because they are grounded in spatial experience. Spatial concepts in this approach are grounded on more fundamental kinaesthetic concepts called, in one version, image schemas. One such schema is a path, diagrammatically represented as in Figure 10.1:

Figure 10.1 Path schema (adapted from Johnson 1987)

Associated with this schema are a number of associated implications, which guide the integration of this schema into lexical concepts, as in (31).

(31) (a) Since A and B are connected by a series of contiguous locations, getting from A to B implies passing through the intermediate points;
(b) Paths tend to be associated with directional movement along them, say from A to B;
(c) There is an association with time. Since a person traversing a path takes time to do so, points on the path are readily associated with temporal sequence. Thus an implication is that the further along the path an entity is, the more time has elapsed.

Image schemas are incorporated into spatial concepts that are involved in prepositions. Polysemy is characteristic of prepositions so that for English *over*, for example, we find a range of senses which we can paraphrase roughly as 'above' (*The plane flew over the tornado zone*), 'across' (*The cafe is over the road*), 'covering' (*They plastered over the frescoes*), and related non-prepositional uses like 'again' (*He kept saying it over and over*), and 'finished' (*The interview was over after a few questions*). The cognitive semantics literature provides image topological models of these, for example the composite image schema in Figure 10.2 for *over* in *The plane flew over the tornado zone*, which is in the style of Lakoff (1987).

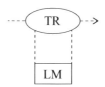

Figure 10.2 An image schema for *over* (based on Lakoff 1987: 419)

In the schema in Figure 10.2 the moving entity is termed TR 'trajector' and the background against which the movement occurs is the LM 'landmark'. In Lakoff's account this schema is the central one and is extended to other senses in the semantic network of *over* as in (32).

(32) Over: Radial extensions (Lakoff 1987)
(a) TR is in contact with LM: The car drove over the bridge.
(b) TR is stationary over LM: The painting is over the mantelpiece.
(c) TR covers LM: The city clouded over.
(d) Endpoint of TR path as location: The hotel is over the river.

Other senses include transfer as in *They handed over their weapons* and metaphorical extensions, as in *She has a strange power over him* where physical elevation is associated with power. In other cases abstract concepts are conceptualized as physical entities as in *He's never got over the divorce*, *She's over eighteen* and *He was breathalysed and was over the limit*.

Cognitive semanticists have sought to distinguish and relate senses within a semantic network and have represented these in a number of ways, including network diagrams, where multiple senses are distributed in a network around prototypical senses. The distribution, i.e. the architecture of the network, depends on arguments about the interrelatedness of the senses. Tyler and Evans (2003) discuss some principles for identifying and classifying senses and give detailed networks for English prepositions. Other writers, such as Glynn and Robinson (2012), have proposed the use of corpus data and statistical models to substantiate analyses of sense relations.

Possibly the most influential work in cognitive semantics has been in re-assessing metaphor, metonymy and other linguistic strategies that have been traditionally viewed as figurative language. Dispensing with the distinction between literal and figurative language, where the latter is seen to represent rhetorical or decorative additions, cognitive semanticists see metaphor as a basic and universal part of human understanding. In this view it is basic to our attempts to categorize the world, especially in our attempts to integrate novel concepts into our existing knowledge system. Conceptual Metaphor Theory (Lakoff and Turner 1989) characterizes metaphor as an analogical mapping from a source domain to a target domain. The mapping is seen as structured and as having key features such as systematicity, asymmetry and abstraction. Systematicity is a crucial feature, recognizing that many metaphors consist of more than an extension to a single sense of a word. Instead, they are used to structure a whole conceptual domain, the target, in terms of another, the source. In this account speakers' knowledge of attributes of the source domain will allow them to characterize elements of the target domain. So for example the metaphor THEORIES ARE BUILDINGS licenses a series of links: the theorizer to a builder; formulation to construction; assumptions to foundations; validity to structural rigidity, etc. Consequently speakers can say things like *His theory lacked adequate foundations*; *The theory was demolished by new evidence*; *The data doesn't support the theory* etc. The features of asymmetry and abstraction reflect the claim that conceptual metaphors are viewed as a means of integrating new knowledge. So the new domain is characterized in terms of the old rather than the other way round and the source domain also tends to be more concrete than the target, as in this THEORIES ARE BUILDINGS example.

A similar approach may be taken to metonymy so that rather than viewing it as a rhetorical trope, it is viewed as a referential strategy that relies on domains of knowledge. In this account speakers choose contextually salient associations to guide hearers to the intended referent. Metonymic reference is traditionally divided into several types, including the following where the metonym is underlined: PART FOR WHOLE (*We need some new blood in the department*), WHOLE FOR PART (*Australia has retaken the Ashes*), PRODUCER FOR PRODUCT (*She never wears Tom Ford*), PLACE FOR INSTITUTION (*Houston, we have a problem*). This account, however, predicts that metonymy is a ubiquitous and flexible process that can be based on any knowledge or assumptions in the context.

At the level of sentence meaning cognitive semanticists have proposed dynamic models of discourse such as mental spaces (Fauconnier 1997; Fauconnier and Turner 2002), which is a theory of how speakers and hearers employ various linguistic devices to mutually manage references to entities, time references and distinctions between actual and possible scenarios. These linguistic markers, which are termed spacebuilders, act as invitations to the hearer to construct mental spaces and the relevant referential links. So adverbials of time and situations, for example *when we were children*, *in Shakespeare's play 'Hamlet'*, modals like *possibly* and *really* and connectives like *if* trigger the use of background knowledge to set up mutual models of situations. Speakers and hearers then interpret references to individuals, times, etc. relative to the mental models. Speakers' and hearers' facility with the manipulation of such mental models is also held to underpin the online processing of novel complex analogies in what is called conceptual integration (or blending), as in examples like

Ireland is the poster child of austerity. Here the speaker invites the hearer to draw on different areas of knowledge, including the use of images of children by charitable organizations and Europe's recent financial crisis, and to extend these to a novel conception.

10.5 Semantics and pragmatics

The approaches we have discussed, along with most others, have increasingly had to take account of the growth of pragmatics (Chapter 13). The study of utterances in real-life situations clearly reveals the importance of contextual knowledge in how hearers interpret a speaker's meaning. At the level of word meaning the issue is how to balance a notion of conventional meaning against the contextual processes of selecting or accommodating to the specific sense intended by the speaker. An example is the narrowing of *drink* in *All politicians drink* from the meaning 'drink liquid' to mean 'drink alcohol' and possibly further to 'drink substantial amounts of alcohol'. To the extent to which such processes are seen as inferential and based on contextual knowledge they can be characterized as pragmatic and indeed a field of lexical pragmatics has been suggested in such theories as Relevance Theory (Wilson and Sperber 2012). Such accounts extend to cover loose or approximate uses like *circle* in *Children, please form a circle!* and the metaphorical use of *martyr* in *My sister is a martyr*.

At the level of sentence meaning the proposal to identify propositions as the semantic content of sentences runs into similar issues. The words used in sentences often (some would say always) lack sufficient specificity to identify a particular proposition and thus be able to support truth conditions, which is problematic for those approaches relying on them. It has always been clear that deictic elements like pronouns, demonstratives and temporal and spatial adverbs rely for their interpretation on contextual information. However, the elements of which this is true have been gradually extended to cover quantifiers, for example the scope of *everyone* in *Everyone will be at the party*; gradable adjectives with their implicit standards, such as *expensive* in *That apartment is very expensive*; and cardinal numbers, which in context often have implicit qualifications of *exactly*, *at least* or *at most* left to inference, so that a statement *Undergraduates may borrow six books from the library* would not normally prohibit them from taking five. These are a few examples of the extent to which semantic form underspecifies the meaning gained by hearers. What is currently a matter of investigation and debate is the nature of the semantic representations before and after contextual enrichment and the resulting balance between semantics and pragmatics.

Note

1 Key to glosses: 3 = third person; HAB = habitual; IMPF = imperfective; PFV = perfective; PL = plural.

Further reading

A general introductory text is Saeed (2009). Cruse (1986) offers a comprehensive discussion of word meaning and lexical relations. Portner (2005) is an accessible introduction to formal, logic-based semantics. Ungerer and Schmid (2006) include semantics in their introduction to cognitive linguistics.

References

Aikhenvald, A.Y. (2004) *Evidentiality*. Oxford: Oxford University Press.
Asher, N. and A. Lascarides (2005) *Logics of Conversation*. Cambridge: Cambridge University Press.
Boas, F. (1911) *Handbook of American Indian Languages, Part I*. Smithsonian Institution, Bureau of American Ethnology, Bulletin 40. Washington, DC: Government Printing Office.
Cruse, D.A. (1986) *Lexical Semantics*. Cambridge: Cambridge University Press.
Davidson, D. (1967) Truth and meaning. *Synthese* 17: 304–23.
Dirven, R. and M. Verspoor (2004) *Cognitive Exploration of Language and Linguistics*. Amsterdam: John Benjamins.
Dixon, R.M.W. (2010) *Basic Linguistic Theory, Volume 1*. Oxford: Oxford University Press.
Dummett, M. (1994) *Origins of Analytical Philosophy*. Cambridge: Harvard University Press.
Fauconnier, G. (1997) *Mappings in Thought and Language*. Cambridge: Cambridge University Press.
Fauconnier, G. and M. Turner (2002) *The Way We Think: Conceptual Blending and the Mind's Hidden Complexities*. New York: Basic Books.
Frawley, W.J., K.C. Hill and P. Munro (eds) (2002) *Making Dictionaries: Preserving Indigenous Languages of the Americas*. Berkeley: University of California Press.
Gibbs, R.W. Jr (2006) *Embodiment and Cognitive Science*. Cambridge: Cambridge University Press.
Glynn, D. and J. Robinson (2012) *Corpus Methods in Cognitive Semantics. Studies in Synonymy and Polysemy*. Amsterdam: John Benjamins.
Groenendijk, J. and M. Stokhof (1991) Dynamic predicate logic. *Linguistics and Philosophy* 14: 39–100.
Heim, I. (1983) File change semantics and the familiarity theory of definiteness. In R. Bäuerle, C. Schwarze and A. von Stechow (eds) *Meaning, Use and Interpretation of Language*, pp. 164–89. Berlin: De Gruyter.
Johnson, M. (1987) *The Body in the Mind: The Bodily Basis of Meaning, Imagination, and Reason*. Chicago: University of Chicago Press.
Kamp, H. and U. Reyle (1993) *From Discourse to Logic: Introduction to Model Theoretic Semantics of Natural Language, Formal Logic and Discourse Representation Theory*. Dordrecht: Kluwer.
Lakoff, G. (1987) *Women, Fire, and Dangerous Things*. Chicago: University of Chicago Press.
Lakoff, G. and M. Turner (1989) *More Than Cool Reason: A Field Guide to Poetic Metaphor*. Chicago: University of Chicago Press.
Langacker, R.W. (2008) *Cognitive Grammar: A Basic Introduction*. Oxford: Oxford University Press.
Mahamane, L.A. (2008) Perfect and Perfective in Hausa. *Afrikanistik Online*, Vol. 2008 (urn:nbn:de:0009-10-13825). www.afrikanistik-online.de/archiv/2008/1382/.
Martinet, A. (1960) *Eléments de linguistique générale*. Paris: Colin.
Montague, R. (1974) *Formal Philosophy: Selected Papers of Richard Montague*. Ed. and intro. R.H. Thomason. New Haven: Yale University Press.
Palmer, F. (2001) *Mood and Modality*, 2nd edition. Cambridge: Cambridge University Press.
Portner, P.H. (2005) *What is Meaning? Fundamentals of Formal Semantics*. Oxford: Blackwell.
Rosch, E. (1973) Natural categories. *Cognitive Psychology* 4: 328–50.
Rosch, E. (1975) Cognitive reference points. *Cognitive Psychology* 7: 532–47.
Saeed, J.I. (2009) *Semantics*, 3rd edition. Oxford: Wiley-Blackwell.
Tarski, A. (1956) *Logic, Semantics, Metamathematics, Papers from 1923 to 1938*. Transl. J.H. Woodger. Oxford: Oxford University Press.
Tyler, A. and V. Evans (2003) *The Semantics of English Prepositions: Spatial Scenes, Embodied Meanings and Cognition*. Cambridge: Cambridge University Press.
Ungerer, F. and H-J. Schmid (2006) *An Introduction to Cognitive Linguistics*, 2nd edition. London: Longman.
Veltman, F. (1996) Defaults in update semantics. *Journal of Philosophical Logic* 25: 221–61.
Wilson, D. and D. Sperber (2012) *Meaning and Relevance*. Cambridge: Cambridge University Press.

11
Lexical semantics today

Nicholas Asher, Tim Van de Cruys and Márta Abrusán

11.1 Introduction

Lexical semantics is the study of what words mean. In particular, lexical semantics as opposed to formal semantics involves the study of open class words like adjectives, common nouns and verbs, as opposed to functional class words, which contribute to the logical structure of the language – quantifiers, connectives and many adverbs. The latter have been studied in compositional semantics, which uses formal languages like higher-order logic and the lambda calculus to formalize the composition of meaning and the meanings of functional words.

For a long while, lexical semantics developed independently from formal semantics. Apart from a few, daring forays into the formal world (e.g. Dowty 1979), lexical semanticists worked largely in isolation from formal semanticists, who were focused on sentential or discourse meaning and the problem of compositionality. To make the point in a somewhat caricatural fashion, lexical semanticists investigated argument structure, verbal diathesis (shifts in meaning due to shifts in argument structure), polysemy, and meaning decomposition all within various 'cognitive' systems lacking rigor and a tie to model theoretic semantics; meanwhile, formal semanticists paid little attention to matters of lexical meaning for open class terms like ordinary nouns and verbs – the meaning of a word x was typically rendered as x'. Valuable work was done in both areas but there was something of a missed opportunity in which neither camp profited from the insights of the other.

Recently, however, formal semanticists have begun to take a closer look at the interesting observations by descriptive linguists. An important part of what lexical semantics is today, we think, is to come to grips with the problems that such systems have tackled and the problems that remain to be solved. We will concentrate on some particular phenomena to illustrate the difficulties for formal systems. In a second section, we will also draw attention to a third, and much more recent, approach to lexical semantics, *distributional semantics* or DS. DS has its origins in various philosophical and older linguistic traditions like those of Wittgenstein and Bloomfield but which has, thanks to the advent of very large corpora of text, opened the door to the automatic acquisition of lexical content. The core idea that is common to Wittgenstein, Bloomfield and DS is that you will know a word by the company it keeps; the meaning of a word is given by its use, which in turn is given by the contexts of its usage (or surrounding words). A simple implementation of this idea is then to associate with each word a set of contexts in which it occurs along with a relative frequency of its occurrence in such a context. Using computational techniques and very large corpora containing billions of words, researchers can formulate such vectors for words and capture something of word meaning. Like modern formal methods, however, this approach faces deep conceptual and technical problems and interestingly the problems for DS are largely complementary to those for formal lexical semantics. In the final part of this chapter, we will discuss some options for putting formal semantics and DS together, a topic which we feel is currently one of the most exciting in lexical semantics.

11.2 Formal semantics and the lexicon

In this section, we give an introduction to formal lexical semantics and brief survey of some challenges for the view. Formal semantics for natural languages grew out of efforts by logicians, like Tarski and Frege, and mathematicians to specify a representation for the languages of mathematics and logic that would give an abstract characterization of the valid sentences of the language and of the valid inferences that one could make. The manner in which this is done is to specify an abstract set theoretic structure called a *model*, relative to which one specifies the denotations or semantic values for terms and then rules for combining these values to recursively specify semantic values for complex expressions based on the values for their constituents. Montague (1974) carried out the program of specifying a model for fragments of a natural language by showing how to translate natural language expressions into terms of higher-order logic with the λ calculus. He then showed how to derive semantic values or truth conditions for sentences by using the combinatory rules of the λ calculus. This provided the first *compositional* treatment of meaning for natural language in which semantic rules of meaning combination mirrored the rules of syntactic construction for the natural language fragment. Montague's work, known under the heading of *Montague Grammar* continues to be the backbone of much formal semantic work almost fifty years after its publication.

Montague's seminal work, however, gave short shrift to lexical semantics. Apart from the functional or closed class words of the fragments, so-called logical connectives like *and*, *if ... then* or quantifiers like *some*, *most* and *all*, the contents of words remained a black box for the compositional system. To give a caricature, the meaning of the word *cat* is simply $\lambda x.cat'(x)$. Its meaning or denotation is specified by the *type* assigned to the λ expression; all that the formal system says is that it is a function from individuals to truth values. Such a meaning will return a truth value given any object provided as a value for the variable x. The λ calculus specifies that such a term when applied to an individual term whose meaning is a simple individual will have the meaning of the type associated with sentences (in the extensional fragment of the language a truth value). Which function *cat* specifies is not part of the formal system, however.

So what is it to give the meaning of a word? How would we specify such a function? And what kind of data can we use to verify that our specification is on the right track? There are a number of answers in the literature on lexical semantics or theories of word meaning. Cognitive semanticists like Len Talmy and Tom Givón, among others, think that meanings are to be given via a set of cognitively primitive features – which might be pictorial rather than symbolic. According to these semanticists, a lexical theory should provide appropriate cognitive features and lexical entries defined in terms of them. Others in a more logical and formal framework like Dowty (1979), but also Ray Jackendoff, Roger Shank and other researchers in AI, take a specification of lexical meaning to be given in terms of a set of primitives whose meanings can be axiomatized or computationally implemented. Still others take a 'direct' or denotational view; the function of lexical semantics is to specify the denotation of the various terms, typically to be modeled within some model theoretic framework.

All of these approaches agree that a specification of lexical meaning consists in the specification of some element, whether representational or not, formal or not, that, when combined with elements associated with other words in a wellformed sentence, yields a meaning for a sentence in a particular discourse context. Whatever theoretical reconstruction of meaning one chooses, however, it should be capable of modeling inferences based on lexical information in a precise manner so that the theory of lexical meaning proposed can be judged on its predictions. In addition, the theoretical reconstruction should provide predictions about when sentences that are capable of having a truth value are true and when they are not. This drastically reduces the options for specifying lexical meaning: such a specification must conform with one of the several ways of elaborating meaning within the domain of formal semantics; it must specify truth conditions, dynamic update conditions of the sort familiar from dynamic semantics (Kamp and Reyle 1993; Groenendijk and Stokhof 1991; Veltman 1996), or perhaps provability conditions of the sort advocated by, e.g. Ranta (2004), among others. In §11.3 we will look at two recent formalizations of lexical meaning that use model theoretic and proof theoretic methods.

11.2.1 Four problems for formal lexical semantics

We look now at four problems for formal lexical semantics with an eye to getting clearer about the promise of and obstacles of a formal account.

11.2.1.1 Different types of lexical meaning

Is there only one kind of lexical meaning that feeds into semantic composition or are there several? Lexical semanticists have for the most part described lexical semantics as involving one sort of content, though they might disagree on how such content is to be represented. Compositional semanticists and computational linguists, however, have proposed distinctions between content. The first is the difference between presupposed content and asserted or *at-issue* content (Strawson 1950; Karttunen 1973). Presupposed content is content that does not interact with logical operators and at-issue content. An example of presupposed content is the existential implication of definite descriptions: both (1a) and (1b) imply that there is a present King of France; the negation does not take the presupposition (that there is a King of France) in its scope.

(1) a. The present King of France is bald.
    b. The present King of France is not bald.

Presuppositions can often be traced back to the presence of some lexical element in the sentence: definite determiners, factive verbs, certain adverbs and many other lexical elements are thought to give rise to presuppositional material. Accordingly, the presuppositional status of a part of the meaning of these lexical items has to be marked in some way or another. An influential theoretical move was to assume that presuppositions must be satisfied in order for the sentence in which it originates to have a truth value. This condition is typically represented as a definedness condition on the lexical meaning of the presupposition trigger.[1]

There are other types of content that behave similarly to presupposed content vis-à-vis asserted or at-issue content. The content of emotive expressions or epithets, for instance, seems also not to interact with logical operators or attitude verbs (cf. Potts 2005).

(2) I hope that bastard gives me back my money.

In (2) the person referred to pejoratively is implied to be bastard (it is not hoped that the person is a bastard); the material in the epithet escapes the scope of the attitude verb.

Many linguists and philosophers have distinguished between implicatures and asserted content as well (Grice 1975). Implicatures are in many ways similar to asserted content but they can typically be denied in subsequent discourse. So, for instance, a numerical adjective can give rise to a so-called scalar implicature in the following sense: to say *I have four children* implicates that I have exactly four children, though I can cancel this implicature by saying *I have four children – indeed, I have five*. Implicatures are most commonly thought to arise from pragmatic reasoning about salient alternative utterances in the discourse. But in order for such an account to be predictive, the range of possible alternatives has to be restricted. Such restrictions (aka *Horn-scales*) are usually associated with lexical items.

11.2.1.2 Selectional restrictions and types

Selectional restrictions of an expression ε pertain to the type of object denoted by the expression with which ε must combine. The verb *try*, for instance, imposes on the compositional context 'to come' that its subject must be an intentional agent; a verb like *hit* imposes the restriction that its object or internal argument must be a physical object. Thus,

(3) Mary hit John's idea.

is predicted to be difficult to interpret unless the context allows us to interpret *John's idea* as some sort of physical object (perhaps it is some artifact that he created). Thus, selectional restrictions impose a necessary condition on semantic evaluability; failing to satisfy a selectional restriction is a *category mistake*, a sort of presupposition failure.

One way to handle selectional restrictions is to take them as requiring an argument of a certain type. Montague Grammar (MG) according to which types are identified with the set of entities in the model of that type, countenances two basic types: the type of all entities e, which is identified in a model with the domain of the model, and the type of truth values, t. Further types are defined recursively: for instance, all nouns have the type $e \to t$, which is the set of all functions from the domain of entities into the set of truth values. Types have enough semantic content to check the wellformedness of certain predications, but to handle selectional restrictions, the type system must incorporate many more distinctions. For instance it must distinguish various distinct basic types that are subtypes of e; it must distinguish the type for eventualities from the type for physical objects, as well as distinguish the type of informational or abstract objects from these two. Other distinctions will probably be relevant too: the distinction between states and events.

11.2.1.3 Degrees of ambiguity and copredication

A basic issue concerning lexical representation is lexical ambiguity. The most orthodox model of lexical meaning is the monomorphic, sense enumeration model, according to which all the different possible meanings of a single lexical item are listed in the lexicon as part of the lexical entry for the item. Each sense in the lexical entry for a word is fully specified. On such a view, most words are ambiguous. This account is the simplest conceptually, and it is the standard way dictionaries are put together, and this is also the view found in Montague Grammar or HPSG.

While conceptually simple, this approach fails to explain how some senses are intuitively related to each other and some are not. Words or, perhaps more accurately, word occurrences that have closely related senses are called *logically polysemous*, while those that do not receive the label *accidentally polysemous* or simply *homonymous*. Cruse (1986) suggests copredication as a test to distinguish logical polysemy from accidental polysemy: if two different predicates, each requiring a different sense, predicate properties of different senses of a given word felicitously, then the word is logically polysemous with respect at least to those two senses. Another test is pronominalization or ellipsis: if you can pronominalize an occurrence of a possibly ambiguous word felicitously in a context where the pronoun is an argument of a predicate requiring one sense while its antecedent is an argument of a predicate requiring a different sense, then the word is logically polysemous with respect to those senses. Contrast (4a–b) and (4c–e).

(4) a. #The bank$_i$ specializes in IPOs. It$_i$ is steep and muddy and thus slippery.
    b. #The bank specializes in IPOs and is steep and muddy and thus slippery.
    c. Lunch was delicious but took forever.
    d. He paid the bill and threw it away.
    e. The city has 500,000 inhabitants and outlawed smoking in bars last year.

Bank is a classic example of an accidentally polysemous word. As (4a–b), show, both the pronominalization and copredication tests produce anomalous sentences, which confirm its status as accidentally polysemous. On the other hand, *lunch, bill* and *city* are classified as logically polysemous, as (4c–e) witness that they pass the tests of copredication and pronominalization.

The distinction between accidental and logical polysemy is not absolute, and there are degrees of relatedness that the felicity of copredications and pronominal tests reflect. But sense enumeration models have no way of explaining the differing degrees of success that copredications appear to have. It is for this reason that many approaches to lexical semantics have adopted some rather more complex way of representing meanings, e.g. one in which each word may have multiple types or underspecified types that may be further specified during the composition process. These are sometimes called polymorphic languages (or lexicons for a language).[2]

11.2.1.4 Context sensitivity of meaning

For formal semanticists and philosophers of language, context sensitivity of meaning traditionally stops with anaphoric pronouns and indexical expressions. While it is clear that the sentence *I am hungry* will vary in meaning according to who asserts it, we believe, however, that context dependence pervades the lexicon. More recently, semanticists have argued that other linguistic elements have at least some sort of context sensitivity. These elements include modals, attitude verbs like *believe, want* and *know* and tense. (See Roberts 1989; Veltman 1996 and references therein.) However, philosophers and linguists who call themselves *relevance theorists* have argued that context sensitivity of meaning is pretty much ubiquitous (Sperber and Wilson 1986; Recanati 2004).

One of the intriguing and not well understood observations about the composition of meaning is that when word meanings are combined, the meaning of the result can vary from what standard compositional semantics has led us to expect. While the choice of words obviously affects the content of a predication, prior discourse can also sometimes affect how lexical meanings interact.

(5) All the children were drawing fish. Suzie's salmon was blue.

In (5) we understand the relationship between Suzie and *salmon* in a complex way: Suzie is drawing a picture of a salmon that is blue. This interpretation is due not only to the genitive construction but also to its discourse environment.

The example above is an example of a phenomenon of coercion. Consider also the following example, discussed at length in the literature, in particular by Pustejovsky (1995).

(6) Julie enjoyed the book.

The intuition of many who work on lexical semantics is that (6) has a meaning like (7) with the *doing something* filled in by an appropriate activity.

(7) Julie enjoyed doing something to (e.g. reading, writing, …) the book.

The intuition is this: *enjoy* requires an event as its direct object as in *enjoy the spectacle*, *enjoy the view*. This also happens when *enjoy* takes a question as its complement, as in *enjoy (hearing) what he said*. When the direct object of a transitive use of *enjoy* does not denote an event, it is 'coerced' to denote some sort of eventuality.

The apparent meaning shifts discussed above should receive as uniform a treatment as possible within a semantic/pragmatic framework of lexical meanings and semantic composition – that is, how lexical meanings compose together to form meanings for larger semantic constituents like propositions or discourses. If the intuitions behind coercion are easy to grasp, modeling coercion by formal means is rather difficult, as we will see in the next section.

11.3 Prior work in formal lexical semantics

In this section we discuss previous work on the themes described above, concentrating on the problem of selectional restrictions, ambiguity and context sensitivity. We will not address the problem of presuppositions, conventional and conversational implicatures any further here: the vast amount of work that has been done on these topics in the last fifty years warrants at least a separate chapter for them. For a recent overview, see Potts (2014) and references therein.

11.3.1 Semantic approaches

We have discussed the sense enumeration model briefly but enough to indicate that it has troubles explaining selectional restrictions, copredication and coercions. In contrast to the sense enumeration model of word meaning is the view that lexical semantics consists of a set of lexical entries, supplemented with a set of maps from one lexical meaning to another. These maps specify, inter alia, coercions. Frege's theory of meaning includes coercions: he stipulated that the meaning of terms when they occur within the scope of an intensional operator shifted from their reference to their sense.

Generalizing Frege's strategy, Nunberg (1979, 1995) proposes that lexical meanings are subject to shifts in predication. A lexical entry specifies a denotation for a referring expression or for a predicate. Let's take a look at Nunberg's transfer functions (Nunberg 1995) on some of his examples.

(8) I'm parked out back.

(9) The ham sandwich is getting impatient.

The basic idea is intuitive. In these examples, applying a particular predicate whose argument is required to have type α to an argument whose type is β, where $\alpha \sqcap \beta = \bot$ (the combining of α with β gives a false/uninterpretable proposition) forces either the argument term or the predicate term or both to change their meanings so that the predication can succeed. For instance, ham sandwiches cannot literally get impatient; and if I am standing in front of you, I cannot literally be out back. So what happens is that we shift the meaning of the terms so that the predications succeed: it is my car that is parked out back, and it is the guy who is eating the ham sandwich who is getting impatient. One problem, however, is when exactly is the sense transfer function introduced. If the transfer function were always optionally available, that would lead to vast over-generation problems (10).

(10) The ham sandwich that hasn't been eaten is on the counter.

(10) would be predicted to have a reading on which the eater of the ham sandwich that has not been eaten is on the counter. It must be that the incompatible selectional restrictions of the verb trigger the introduction of the sense transfer functioning some way.

Suppose that Nunberg's sense transfer functions work on lexical entries for common noun phrases or N' (Sag 1981). The result we want for (9) is clear. *The ham sandwich* should have the following logical form:

(9') $\lambda P \, the(x) \, (f(ham \, sandwich)(x) \wedge P(x))$

where f is the transfer function mapping ham sandwiches to people who are eating or have just eaten them. The problem is that we only become aware of the need for a type adjustment mechanism in building the logical form of the sentence when we try to put the subject noun phrase together with the verb phrase; to add the transfer function to work over the contribution of the common noun, we need a rather specific and ad hoc processing of the syntactic structure into logical form (Egg 2003).

Another suggestion is to have the full DP (determiner phrase) or the verb have to undergo sense transfer. But if it is the entire noun phrase or DP that is shifted, we get incorrect truth conditions. Consider (11).

(11) George enjoyed many books last weekend.

A straightforward application of the Nunberg strategy yields the following logical form:

(11') $f(many \, books(x)) \, \exists e(enjoy(g, x, e) \wedge last \, weekend(e))$

The transfer function shifts the meaning of the entire quantifier, and so presumably the quantifier ranges over the elements in the image of the transfer function, namely some sort of eventualities. For the sake of concreteness, we could assume that they are events of reading books. But if (11′) says that there were many book reading events that George enjoyed over the weekend, this is compatible with there being just one book that George read over and over again that weekend. Clearly, this is not a possible reading of (11); this proposal gives incorrect predictions.

In fact, this observation about (11) constitutes a problem for the best-known treatment of coercion, Pustejovsky's Generative Lexicon or GL approach (Pustejovsky 1995). Key to its treatment of these phenomena is the notion of a qualia structure, which involves contents associated with the core meaning of a noun. Following Moravscik (1975), GL postulates that many nouns contain information about other objects and eventualities that are associated as roles with the denotation of the noun. GL hypothesizes that in predications like (6), verbs like *begin* and *enjoy*, which require an eventuality for their internal arguments, select as their arguments the eventualities encoded in the feature structures associated with nouns like *cigarette*. GL's qualia structures pack Nunberg's sense transfer function into the lexical entry for nouns. The data show that the qualia model is insufficiently general and too inflexible to succeed, as well as having technical problems (Asher 2011).

In GL only the verb is involved in the coercion of its arguments; for instance, the aspectual verbs and *enjoy* coerce their object argument to be of event type, and the event type is specified by one of the qualia. But this is empirically incorrect. For instance, the subject of an aspectual verb may determine what the type of its theme or event argument is.

(12) a. The janitor has begun (with) the kitchen.
b. The cleaners have started the suits.
c. The exterminator has begun (with) the bedroom.

In each of these there is a coercion to a particular type of event for the object argument of the aspectual verb. Yet it is obvious that the noun phrases in object position do not by themselves supply the requisite events in (12a–c).

A further problem is this. Let us suppose that the denotation of the noun phrase *the book* in (6) is transformed into some sort of eventuality denoting expression. If that is the case, then how can we access in subsequent discourse the referent of *the book*?

(13) Julie enjoyed the book. It was a mystery.

These observations are familiar but show that we *cannot* shift the meaning of *the book* to some sort of eventuality. Or at least if we do, whatever process is responsible for the shift must also allow *the book* to retain its original, lexical meaning and its original contribution to logical form.

To avoid these problems, we could resort to an alternative transfer strategy: shift the meaning of the verbs rather than the meaning of common nouns or DPs. This can in principle avoid the problem noted with (11). But this shift leads to another set of difficulties. Consider the following ellipsis facts.[3]

(14) a. I'm parked out back, and Mary's car is too.
b. ?I own a car that is parked out back and Mary's car does too.
c. Mary enjoys her garden and John his liquor.
d. ?Mary enjoys digging in her garden, and John his liquor.

If we transfer the sense of *parked out back* to the property of owning a car that is parked out back to account for the parking examples, then the ellipsis in (14a) should be odd or it should give rise to the following reading: Mary's car owns a car that is parked out back as well. But the ellipsis is fine, and it lacks this reading. Similarly if we transfer the sense of *enjoy* to something like *enjoy digging* to make sense of the predication that Mary enjoys her garden, then we should predict that the ellipsis in (14c) should be bad much the way (14d) is. But the ellipsis in (14c) is fine. The transfer function approach thus faces hurdles on all the options we have surveyed.[4]

11.3.2 Pragmatic approaches

In contrast to GL's attempt to locate the mechanisms for coercion and aspect selection within the lexical semantic entry for particular words, there is a pragmatic approach to such phenomena. One might suppose that in fact coercion and type adjustment in general is not part of semantics at all, but rather a pragmatic mechanism. The ellipsis facts seem to point to a pragmatic account according to which the appropriate enrichments to predicates and/or arguments occur after semantics has done its job, and hence phenomena like ellipsis have been resolved.

Relevance theorists (Sperber and Wilson 1986; Recanati 2004; Carston 2002; Recanati 1993) attempt to capture these inferences by appealing to a pragmatic process of free enrichment. However, the clearest, most formally explicit pragmatic account is Stanley and Szabo's hidden variables approach (Stanley and Szabo 2000). Such approaches attempt to analyze phenomena such as coercion or aspect selection as involving pragmatic reasoning. For Stanley and Szabo the pragmatic reasoning involves finding contextually salient values for hidden variables.

Egg (2003) develops something like Stanley and Szabo's approach for coercion. One postulates for each coercing predicate $\lambda x \varphi$ two hidden variables, one higher-order relational variable and another that will end up being related to x. *Enjoy*, which is understood to take an event as a direct object, would now look something like this:

(15) $\lambda y \lambda e \lambda z$ enjoy$(z, e) \wedge R(e, y)$

When no coercion is present R could be resolved to identity, but when the direct object of the verb involves denotations to non-event-like objects, then R would be resolved to some contextually salient property. So, for instance, *enjoying playing a soccer game* intuitively involves no coercion, and the variable introduced by the DP that ranges over playing soccer game events would be identified with the event variable that is the direct object argument of *enjoy*. However, *Laura enjoyed a cigarette* would involve a coercion; in this case the variable introduced by the DP ranging over cigarettes would be related via some contextually salient relation R like smoking to get the logical form:

(16) $\exists y \exists e$ (enjoy$(l, e) \wedge$ smoke$(e, y) \wedge$ cigarette(y))

This approach has an advantage over GL and other sense transfer views in that it gets the quantification cases right: *enjoying many books* does not, on this view, mean that one enjoys many events of reading books. On the other hand, this approach has nothing to say about when coercion takes place. It would need to be supplemented by some theory of types, type checking and repair to say when coercion would be triggered. In fact none of the approaches we have looked at so far deals with this problem in a formal and systematic way.

The pragmatic approach also seems to analyze coercions at the wrong linguistic level. Pragmatic principles are supposed to follow from general principles of rational interaction between agents, and so they are expected to be universal, but we have already seen that coercions are typically language specific. In addition, we should expect pragmatic enrichment to allow coercions, say from objects to eventualities, whenever the grammar allows for an eventuality reading in the argument. But this is not true. Consider (17).

(17)   a.   The reading of the book started at 10.
        b.   #The book started at 10.
        c.   John started the book.

It is perfectly straightforward to get the eventuality reading for the object of *start* (17c) in an out of the blue context. But it is impossible to do this when the intransitive form of *start* is used with *the book* in subject position, even though an eventuality reading for the subject of intransitive *start* is available, as seen by (17a).

Such shifts in the predication relation are lexically governed. It is the verb *enjoy* that requires an event but also which licenses a change in the predicational glue between it and its object when it is not of the right sort. As argued in Asher (2011), these licensings are proper to *certain arguments* of the verb or rather to the syntactic realization of other arguments of the predicate. We are not dealing with a phenomenon of general pragmatic strengthening or repair but rather with a problem at the syntax/semantics interface, which is how to account for the differences in (17).

Finally, coercions are language dependent. Direct translation of (18), for example, is not good in Chinese.

(18)   Julie started a book.

In Chinese, one has to say (19) instead:

(19)   Julie started reading/writing a book.

The coercion that inserts 'reading/writing' actions is not licensed in Chinese when 'start' is used.

Coercion is a semantic phenomenon, not a pragmatic one. Pragmatic accounts use principles that are supposed to follow from general principles of rational interaction between agents; they are expected to be universal. So we should expect pragmatic enrichment to allow coercions, say from objects to eventualities, whenever the grammar allows for an eventuality reading in the argument. But this is not true.

11.3.3 Recent type driven theories

Recent formal lexical semantic theories developed to deal with systematic ambiguity and coercion try to remedy the difficulties of previous semantic accounts. One approach is to change the relation of predication that holds between the predicate and the argument. A type clash between the type of the argument and the type presupposition of the predicate induces not a type shift in either the argument or the predicate but rather a type shift on the predication relation itself, which is implemented by introducing a functor that is inserted around the argument. The meaning of the argument does not shift – it remains what it always was; the predicate also retains its original meaning, but what changes is how they combine.

The Type Composition Logic (TCL) developed in Asher (2011) uses a rich system of types to guide the construction of logical form, which then gets a standard intensional semantics. Type information is treated as a kind of presupposed information. Selectional restrictions of predicate are like presuppositions, because they must be satisfied somehow or else the predication will be anomalous and difficult to assign truth conditions to. (3) is an example where the type presuppositions of the predicate cannot be satisfied. They are also not part of ordinary 'at-issue' content because they escape the scope of operators like negation and question operators, as Asher (2011) details. TCL's basic subtypes of e are types of individuals and verify intuitive subtyping relations like the fact that MAN is a subtype of ANIMAL. A common noun has in TCL like in Montague Grammar a functional type; the type of the lambda bound argument of the predicate λx man(x) is, however, not the type MAN in TCL but rather PHYSICAL-OBJECT, in order to allow for a distinction between semantic anomaly and semantic falsity.[5] In TCL uttering *that's a man* while pointing to a statue yields a coherent proposition that is false; the type assigned to the individual variable in the subject DP (PHYSICAL OBJECT) matches the type presupposition of the predicate *is a man*. On the other hand, the sentence *the* set $\{\emptyset, \{\emptyset\}\}$ *is a man* is semantically anomalous and does not yield a proposition at all, because the type on the individual level variable of the DP (INFORMATIONAL OBJECT) is incompatible with the type presupposition of the predicate.

The second point of comparison between selectional restrictions and presuppositions is that like presuppositions, selectional restrictions may be satisfied in various ways. When a predicate requires that an argument has a type τ, then as long as its argument type σ is compatible with τ (i.e. $\sigma \sqcap \tau \neq \bot$), type checking succeeds and the predicate and the argument combine together in TCL with the argument taking as type the meet $\sqcap$ of σ and τ. But other forms of type presupposition satisfaction are possible.

In coercions there is no common subtype for the type presupposition of the predicate and the argument; the contents of a bottle is of a type incompatible with that of the bottle that contains it, and similarly, the eventuality required by *start* or *enjoy* is a distinct and incompatible type with that of a physical or abstract object like a book – these types have different identity and individuation criteria. However, predicates like *start* license a justification of their type requirements by allowing one to introduce material that links the actual argument to an object of the desired type in a manner akin to the sort of presupposition justification employed in bridging. This changes the relation between the predicate and its arguments: the predicate allows a natural transformation from a given type to the desired type. This transformation is translated into the language of logical forms and has a truth conditional content. So in particular, for example (6), the transformation licenses the introduction of a functor that applies to the verb's entry, allowing the result to combine with the original argument of the verb. Here is what the functor looks like (20).

(20) $\lambda P \lambda u \lambda e' \lambda v \, (\exists e (P(v, e, e') \wedge \varphi(e, u)))$

Note that the functor introduces into logic a description of an eventuality as the second argument of *enjoy*, which will go in for the λ bound variable P; note also that this description is itself underspecified, because without a particular context, we do not know exactly what Julie did to the book that she enjoyed. All this is reflected in the logical form that results from applying the functor to *enjoy* and then combing the result with the object and subject arguments of *enjoy* in (6). See (21).

(21) $\exists x \exists e' \exists e (book(x) \wedge enjoy(j, e, e') \wedge \varphi(j, x, e))$

$\varphi(j, x, e)$ is the underspecified description of the eventuality e. Note that e is now the argument of *enjoy*, as is required, but that the discourse entity introduced by *a book* is also available for anaphoric reference. The meaning of *book* remains what it always was; it is just that it combines in a different way with the verb from the usual function application method. Note also that the verb has not changed its meaning either. Unlike the predicate shifting approach of Nunberg, the verb *enjoy* means what it usually means even in predications involving coercion. As a consequence, examples involving ellipsis such as (14c) discussed above are no problem.

With regard to degrees of ambiguity, TCL follows a radical program of encoding ambiguities in the type system rather than as separate lexical entries. So, accidentally polysemous expressions are given a disjoint union type that predications can disambiguate when the predicate selects for one of the disjoined types. On the other hand logically polysemous expressions like *book* require a more complex type construction that makes essential use of the categorial semantics with Asher (2011). In some sense books are both physical and informational objects and different predicates will select either the physical or the informational aspect, an idea already expressed in Cruse (1986). Which aspect is selected makes a difference to how we count books and so different predications on 'dual aspect' nouns can actually alter quantificational domains. For instance, we are not counting the same objects in (22a) and (22b); in the first she need not have opened every (or even any) copy of *The Generative Lexicon* in the library, whereas in the second, she has to have burned every copy of that book in the library.

(22) a. Mary mastered every book on lexical semantics in the library.
b. Mary burned every book on lexical semantics in the library.

Another modern formal lexical system comes from Modern Type Theories (MTTs) (Ranta 2004; Luo 2010). MTT has two novel features with regard to lexical semantics; first it does not treat common nouns as predicates but rather as simple atomic types. In MTT each common noun is interpreted as the most specific fine-grained type associated with the noun in TCL; this is the noun's sole semantic contribution. The second is the introduction of a non-subsumptive notion of subtyping Luo (2010). This notion of subtyping is called *coercive subtyping*.

Coercive subtyping provides an interesting way to interpret various linguistic coercions. The basic coercive subtyping mechanism coerces $f(a)$ into $f(c(a))$ by inserting the coercion c into a gap between f and a. The coercion like the functor in TCL in principle need affect neither the meaning of the predicate nor its argument. So for (6), (*Julie enjoyed a book*), an MTT would assume the coercion

(23) Book $<_{reading}$ Event

so that (6) is coerced into (24):

(24) Julie enjoyed reading a book.

In the MTT treatment, we have considered only one possible coercion (23): from 'enjoy a book' to 'enjoy reading a book.' As we noted in the previous section, however, there are in fact context-dependent 'multiple coercions': e.g. (6) could have meant 'Julie enjoyed writing a book'; there could also be several reading events of that book. Thus, coercive subtyping is a context-sensitive notion of subtyping, and it is necessary to limit the scope of a coercion, but it is not clear that all ambiguous coercions can be so handled.

11.3.4 Interim conclusion

We have surveyed some problems for formal lexical semantics and sketched some proposals for solving them. We have seen how types and type theories, as well as tools from compositional semantics like presupposition, are crucial tools for this area. However, there is one big problem we have not mentioned yet. To be useful to computer scientists and computational linguists, lexical theories have to have good coverage; that is, they have to codify meanings of large numbers of expressions so as to support lexical inferences. None of the theories we have surveyed so far have done this or are in any position to do so in the near future. In the next sections we turn to DS which has the great advantage of automatically acquiring meanings for large numbers of words.

11.4 Distributional semantics

11.4.1 Introduction

Since the last decade of the twentieth century, a new paradigm for the modeling of lexical semantics has emerged, somewhat orthogonal to and independent of developments in formal semantics. The goal of this new paradigm – called distributional semantics – is to automatically extract the meaning of words by looking at their distribution in text, and comparing these distributions within a mathematical model. The unsupervised nature of distributional semantics, and consequently its ability to process large volumes of text in a fully automatic way, make it an attractive method for a data-driven and broad-coverage model of lexical semantics.

Inspired by Harris (1954), work within distributional semantics relies on the distributional hypothesis of meaning, according to which words that appear within the same contexts tend to be semantically similar. In the spirit of this well-known adage, numerous algorithms have been developed that try to capture the semantics of single words by looking at the contexts of these words, and comparing those contexts within a mathematical vector space model. The vector space model was developed as a method for information retrieval in the beginning of the 1970s. The idea is that each document of a text collection is represented as a vector in vector space, such that the features of the vector are constituted by the document's words. The distance between vectors is then taken as a measure of semantic similarity. A user's query may then be presented within the same vector space, and the most similar documents may be retrieved.

At the beginning of the 1990s, researchers have started to apply the idea of a vector space model to other semantic tasks, giving rise to the distributional semantic approach. Methods within distributional semantics have been able to achieve rather impressive results. Famously, one of the best-known methods within distributional semantics – latent semantic analysis (LSA) – in its initial paper (Landauer and Dumais 1997) reached a score of 64.38 percent on multiple-choice synonym questions of the Test of English as a Foreign Language (TOEFL) which, as Landauer and Dumais note, is adequate for admission to many US universities. Since then, distributional models of semantics have been shown to reach a perfect score on the test (Bullinaria and Levy 2012).

11.4.2 Overview

The vector space model applies straightforwardly to similarity calculations between words. The two words for which the semantic similarity is to be calculated, are represented as vectors of the words' various contexts. Table 11.1 shows an example matrix M containing vectors for four different target words (using context words as features), automatically extracted from a large corpus. In this example the set of target words is

$$T = \{raspberry, strawberry, car, truck\}$$

and the set of basic elements is

$$B = \{red, yellow, tasty, fast, eat, drive\}$$

Table 11.1 A word-by-word-context matrix

	red	yellow	tasty	fast	eat	drive
raspberry	728	6	592	1	568	0
strawberry	1035	4	638	0	682	0
car	392	145	1	487	0	370
truck	104	46	0	44	0	293

The value in matrix cell (i, j) is the co-occurrence frequency of word i with value j. In the example above, the word *red* appears 728 times within the context of the word *raspberry*, and the word *drive* appears 370 times in the context of the word *car*.

Note that context is a determining factor in the nature of the semantic similarity that is induced. A broad context window (e.g. a paragraph or document) yields broad, topical similarity, whereas a small context window yields tight, synonym-like similarity. This has led a number of researchers to use the dependency relations that a particular word takes part in as contextual features.

Once contextual feature vectors for each word are created, the vectors may be compared within a vector space. A graphical representation of a vector space using just two dimensions (*red* and *fast*), is given in Figure 11.1. A typical semantic vector space will have somewhere between 2,000 and 100,000 dimensions.

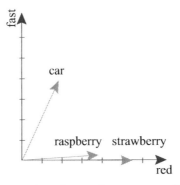

Figure 11.1 A graphical representation of a word vector space. The angle between the vectors for *strawberry* and *raspberry* is much smaller than the angle between the vectors for *strawberry* and *car*

In order to formally compute the textual overlap between two word vectors $\vec{v}$ and $\vec{w}$ we need a proper vector similarity measure. One of the best known and most widely used measures for vector similarity is the cosine, which computes the angle between two vectors. Cosine is easy to compute, and often achieves the best results. The measure is calculated as shown in (25).

(25) $$\cos(\vec{v},\vec{w}) = \frac{\vec{v} \; \vec{w}}{|\vec{v}||\vec{w}|}$$

where $\vec{v} \bullet \vec{w}$ is the dot product between vector $\vec{v}$ and $\vec{w}$, both of length k and $|\bullet|$ represents the norm of a vector.

(26) $$\vec{v} \bullet \vec{w} = \sum_{i=1}^{k} v_i w_i$$

When word vectors are normalized to a vector length of 1, a similarity computation between two vectors boils down to a simple dot product.

This procedure represents the basic intuition behind word similarity computations. Often, researchers apply a number of extra preprocessing steps in order to improve similarity computations. One of these preprocessing steps consists of feature weighting, in which more informative features are given more weight. Another preprocessing step might consist of the application of dimensionality reduction algorithm (such as singular value decomposition), where the abundance of overlapping features is reduced to a limited number of latent and allegedly more meaningful dimensions. For an elaborated overview of semantic word space models, the interested reader is referred to Turney and Pantel (2010).

11.4.3 New developments

To date, work on the automatic acquisition of semantics has mostly dealt with individual words. The modeling of meaning beyond the level of individual words – i.e. the composition of word meanings into larger semantic units – remains a conceptual and practical problem for the distributional approach. A number of models have been explored that try to capture compositional phenomena within a distributional framework (Baroni *et al.* 2014). Another interesting development, somewhat related to the work on the modeling of compositionality, is represented by research on the computation of word meaning in context. By adapting the global meaning of a word to its particular use within a specific context, these models aim to compute the precise meaning of a particular word instance in context, implicitly performing word sense disambiguation (Erk *et al.* 2013).

11.5 Where do we go from here?

We have reviewed some themes in the two major contemporary currents of lexical semantics, and we have seen that formal lexical semantics and distributional semantics each have attractive features. Currently, a hot research topic is to integrate these two approaches. We see two ways this integration could go.

11.5.1 DS furnishes types to FS

If we follow recent FS proposals that assign a component of lexical content in the form of types, a conservative integration of the two would allow DS to determine the contents of basic types associated with words – in effect providing type content for lexical expressions. DS could also investigate the presence of more general types. One could use various similarity metrics to see whether certain words clustered together in a natural similarity class. FS would then provide a ready-made composition mechanism for these types.

To compose type level information, one would have to be able to recast the content contained within distributional meanings in terms of some idiom that can be interpreted within the symbolic and compositional framework. One idiom that type theories typically avail themselves of is the proof theoretic one: the type meaning of a term t should provide evidence (or an algorithm) that an object or set of objects is in the denotation of t. So for instance the type meaning of *boy* would be defined as follows: $\|\text{CAT}\|$: a function that given any individual either provides a justification that the object is a cat or returns $\bot$. What would such a justification consist of? Presumably, it would be a collection of properties typically associated with cats; any object possessing most of those properties would be justifiably be taken to be a cat. While it seems that the meaning objects of at least some versions of DS promise to contain such information, it remains an open research problem how to carry out the proposal in detail.

11.5.2 A dynamic interaction between DS and FS

A more ambitious integration of DS and FS would be to divide up the task of composing meaning. Undoubtedly FS's main strength has been in the analysis of close class terms, while DS's main strength lies in the rich, distributed modeling of open class terms. In addition, new developments in DS have successfully explored models of meaning beyond the level of words, effectively calculating the changes in word meaning that take place when words interact. An ambitious integration of FS and DS would combine the best of both frameworks. DS would supply algebraic style denotations not only for words but for compositions up to and including a complete verbal complex with non-quantificational arguments – i.e. a simple clause without tense or modal information – dynamically updating word meanings as they combine with other words. FS would then contribute the meanings of functional elements (quantifiers, connectives, modals, tense morphemes) to the output of the DS computation. Or we could go still further and replace FS's construal of functional meanings with distributional functions that operate on distributional vectors and return other vectors as output (Baroni *et al.* 2014). Still, it remains unclear how the denotations from FS would combine with the representations of DS, or even what the appropriate DS representations are for clauses. Furthermore, we do not have a clear idea of the compositional principles that would guide the integration of the meanings of functional terms with DS denotations. Nonetheless, we believe an integrated approach holds great potential for a proper modeling of compositionality. DS is able to provide the lexical richness and the ability to model meaning interactions that are missing from traditional formal semantic theories.

11.6 Conclusions

Lexical semantics has become at the beginning of the twenty-first century an exciting field. There have been impressive computational developments resulting in distributional lexical semantics that provides wide coverage assignments of automatically acquired lexical meanings. Formal lexical semantics has also made impressive strides in the precision with which it has attacked recalcitrant problems of lexical meaning like contextual sensitivity and ambiguity, enabling it to take account of perceptive descriptions of the data that have long resisted formal analysis. There is also the exciting prospect of marrying the best that formal semantics has to offer with the empirical methods of distributional semantics. We do not know yet how this last part of the story is going to go, but we hope that we are all around to see how it evolves.

Acknowledgement

Thanks to Cedric Dégremont for helpful suggestions, especially on the title.

Notes

1. More recently, approaches that attempt to predict the presupposition from the at-issue content and pragmatic principles have been proposed as well. See Potts (2014) for an overview.
2. Underspecification is a tool or method devised by linguists working on ambiguity in sentential and discourse semantics.
3. Thanks to Alexandra Aramis for suggesting these sorts of examples.
4. See Egg (2003); Asher (2011) for more detailed criticisms.
5. TCL does exploit the fine-grained types in the compositional process however. For man, the finest-grained type associated with its lambda bound variable is man.

References

Asher, N. (2011) *Lexical Meaning in Context: A Web of Words*. Cambridge: Cambridge University Press.
Baroni, M., R. Bernardi and R. Zamparelli (2014) Frege in space: A program of compositional distributional semantics. *Linguistic Issues in Language Technology* 9: 5–110.
Bullinaria, J.A. and J.P. Levy (2012) Extracting semantic representations from word co-occurrence statistics: Stop-lists, stemming, and svd. *Behavior Research Methods* 44: 890–907.
Carston, R. (2002) *Thought and Utterances: The Pragmatics of Explicit Communication*. Oxford: Blackwell.
Cruse, D.A. (1986) *Lexical Semantics*. Cambridge: Cambridge University Press.
Dowty, D.R. (1979) *Word Meaning and Montague Grammar: The Semantics of Verbs and Times in Generative Semantics and Montague's PTQ*. No. 7 in Studies in Linguistics and Philosophy. Dordrecht: Kluwer.
Egg, M. (2003) Beginning novels and finishing hamburgers: Remarks on the semantics of *to begin*. *Journal of Semantics* 20: 163–91.
Erk, K., D. McCarthy and N. Gaylord (2013) Measuring word meaning in context. *Computational Linguistics* 39: 511–54.
Grice, H.P. (1975) Logic and conversation. In P. Cole and J.L. Morgan (eds) *Syntax and Semantics, Vol. III: Speech Acts*, pp. 41–58. New York: Academic Press.
Groenendijk, J. and M. Stokhof (1991) Dynamic predicate logic. *Linguistics and Philosophy* 14: 39–100.
Harris, Z.S. (1954) Distributional structure. *Word* 10: 146–62.

Kamp, H. and U. Reyle (1993) *From Discourse to Logic*. Dordrecht: Kluwer.
Karttunen, L. (1973) Presuppositions of compound sentences. *Linguistic Inquiry* 4: 169–94.
Landauer, T. and S. Dumais (1997) A solution to Plato's problem: The Latent Semantic Analysis theory of the acquisition, induction, and representation of knowledge. *Psychology Review* 104: 211–40.
Luo, Z. (2010) Type-theoretical semantics with coercive subtyping. In N. Li and D. Lutz (eds) *Proceedings of SALT 20*, Vancouver, pp. 38–56. Ithaca: CLC Publications.
Montague, R. (1974) The proper treatment of quantification in ordinary English. In R.H. Thomason (ed.) *Formal Philosophy: Selected Papers of Richard Montague*, pp. 188–221. New Haven: Yale University Press.
Moravscik, J. (1975) Aitia as generative factors in Aristotle's philosophy. *Dialogue* 14: 622–36.
Nunberg, G. (1979) The non-uniqueness of semantic solutions: Polysemy. *Linguistics and Philosophy* 3: 143–84.
Nunberg, G. (1995) Transfers of meaning. *Journal of Semantics* 12: 109–32.
Potts, C. (2005) *The Logic of Conversational Implicature*. Oxford: Oxford University Press.
Potts, C. (2014) Presupposition and implicature. In S. Lappin and C. Fox (eds) *The Handbook of Contemporary Semantic Theory*, 2nd edition. Malden: Wiley-Blackwell.
Pustejovsky, J. (1995) *The Generative Lexicon*. Cambridge: MIT Press.
Ranta, A. (2004) Grammatical framework: A type-theoretical grammar formalism. *Journal of Functional Programming* 14: 145–89.
Recanati, F. (1993) *Direct Reference: From Language to Thought*. Oxford: Blackwell.
Recanati, F. (2004) *Literal Meaning*. Cambridge: Cambridge University Press.
Roberts, C. (1989) Modal subordination and pronominal anaphora in discourse. *Linguistics and Philosophy* 12: 683–721.
Sag, I. (1981) Formal semantics and extra-linguistic content. In P. Cole (ed.) *Syntax and Semantics 13: Radical Pragmatics*, pp. 273–94. New York: Academic Press.
Sperber, D. and D. Wilson (1986) *Relevance: Communication and Cognition*. Oxford: Blackwell.
Stanley, J. and Z. Szabo (2000) On quantifier domain restriction. *Mind and Language* 15: 219–61.
Strawson, P. (1950) On referring. *Mind* 59: 320–44.
Turney, P.D. and P. Pantel (2010) From frequency to meaning: Vector space models of semantics. *Journal of Artificial Intelligence Research* 37: 141–88.
Veltman, F. (1996) Defaults in update semantics. *Journal of Philosophical Logic* 25: 221–61.

12
Lexicography
The construction of dictionaries and thesauruses

Pam Peters

12.1 Introduction

Ferdinand de Saussure's (1916) model for the words of a lexicon – consisting of the signifier (word form) and the signified (word meaning) – set the foundations of modern linguistics. These complementary perspectives also correspond with the two conventional formats for representing a lexicon: the dictionary and the thesaurus. The dictionary is an inventory of the word forms of a language, the thesaurus a complex semantic structure designed to account for all the meanings embedded in the lexicon. In lexicographic terms, the dictionary format is *semasiological*, and that of the thesaurus *onomasiological*. Those not entirely transparent words may be explained by the Greek roots they embody: the term *semasiological* is derived from *sema* the word for 'sign', since dictionaries are constructed out of the regular signifiers of the language; while *onomasiological* is derived from *onoma* 'name', since thesauruses[1] provide labels for the concepts and meanings (the signifieds) of the lexicon within a multilayered semantic structure.

Elementary dictionaries and pioneering thesauruses were published well before de Saussure, the earliest English examples both dating from the seventeenth century. The first small monolingual English dictionary was Robert Cawdrey's (1604) *Table Alphabeticall ... of Hard Usuall English Words*;[2] while the English thesaurus was pioneered by John Wilkins (1668) in his bulky *Essay Towards a Real Character and a Philosophical Language*,[3] using special symbols to designate words and their meanings within a large conceptual hierarchy. These early models were enlarged in the print medium in the centuries following, in response to socio-cultural needs. Each innovation prompted changes in the construction of lexical information within the two types of language reference, as discussed in §§12.2 and 12.3. Since the turn of the millennium, both dictionary and thesaurus have continued to evolve as lexical references in the electronic medium, as tools for natural language processing (NLP) and artificial intelligence (AI), and as interfaces within information systems. Computerized lexica serve an ever-widening spectrum of human and machine readers. In the process, both dictionaries and thesauruses have extended their scope and added features of the other.

In principle the dictionary and the thesaurus offer language-users alternative ways of accessing the vocabulary, via the known word forms or the abstract concepts whose representation they contribute to. However the terms *dictionary* and *thesaurus* were and still are polysemous, so that printed works and computer software bearing those names do not necessarily conform to the archetypal semasiological or onomasiological construction noted by twenty-first century lexicographers. The first monolingual English dictionaries to be titled as such, embrace the general English lexicon, and construct more than minimal alphabetical entries about each word were eighteenth-century products. They demonstrated the utility of the dictionary's alphabetical construction in accessing general and/or specialized words of the language – hence its widespread use in the titles of reference books of itemized information in any field of knowledge, e.g. *Dictionary of Dreams*, *Dictionary of Sport and Exercise Science*. For thesauruses there is no conventional set of conceptual structures. Their construction varies with the publication, though each is designed as a means of accessing the common lexicon, to help those reaching for words lost from short-term memory, or wanting to explore sets with similar or related meanings. Yet thesaurus structures do not seem to be as intuitive as their authors intended, and most thesauruses provide an alphabetical index as a key to their internal construction (see §12.3.3).

This chapter traces the development and increasing convergence of dictionaries and thesauruses in English since the early modern era. From their different practical and theoretical starting points, both have evolved in structure and content in response to the pedagogical and socio-cultural needs of the times. Commercial imperatives have no doubt always impacted on their construction, as well as recent quantum leaps in information technology. Whether lexicography can be said to have developed a body of theory is an open question (Wierzbicka 1985), amid debate about its independence as a discipline. Lexicographers divide over its debt to lexicology and (applied) linguistics, though both theorists and practitioners agree on the importance of foregrounding the dictionary's functions and users (Bergenholz and Tarp 2003; Rundell 2012). Some suggest it would be more appropriate to speak of the *science* of lexicography (Bogaards 2010), now that the body of empirical research on dictionary use has been effectively indexed (Welker 2010). With the integration of semasiological and onomasiological aspects of the lexicon in twenty-first century information technology (see §12.4), any emerging theory would need to encompass both dictionaries and thesauruses.

12.2 Dictionaries

12.2.1 The construction (macrostructure/microstructure) of dictionaries and their evidential base

Since the late twentieth century, the construction of dictionaries has been seen in terms of two complementary structures: macrostructure (the itemized inventory of words included), and microstructure (the structural template in which information on each word is provided at its entry). Over the course of centuries (see §§12.2.2, 12.2.3) both the overall macrostructure and the microstructure of entries in English dictionaries has steadily enlarged, in response to the needs of the times and different kinds of user. The dictionaries published show waves of interest in general and specialized vocabulary, in common nouns and proper names, in providing purely lexical information and adding encyclopaedic information about the items listed. Through all these shifts in focus and content, the alphabetical macrostructure has proved accommodating and provided easy access to individual items, despite the arbitrary juxtapositions of items within it. The alphabetical macrostructure has also supported alternative approaches to the lemmatization of words:

- clustering morphologically related words, e.g. *fossil*, *fossiliferous*, *fossilize* together in a single entry with the derived forms as secondary headwords or runons, as in the Oxford dictionary tradition;
- splitting morphologically related words over successive individual entries, so that each one is presented in a separate entry, as in Merriam–Webster's dictionaries.

These different approaches to the construction of the macrostructure are informally referred to as 'lumping' and 'splitting'.[4] They are extremes in terms of macrostructural design, and modern dictionaries usually find a compromise in between. The dictionary's policy on lumping and splitting affects the microstructure of individual entries, which are consistently larger or smaller accordingly. That apart, the *microstructure* of monolingual dictionaries has steadily evolved from the minimalism of the earliest monolingual English glossaries (§12.2.2), to the greatly enlarged entries of Johnson's dictionary (1755) and the first edition of the OED (1884–1928), discussed in §12.2.3.

The interplay between macrostructure and microstructure is also reflected in the dictionary's perspective on the lexicon: synchronic or diachronic. The synchronic dictionary lists only words deemed current for the contemporary reader (as in Cawdrey's list of 'usuall' words), whereas the macrostructure of the diachronic dictionary includes obsolete words known from the earlier literature of the language. Complementing this, the diachronic dictionary orders word senses/definitions in line with their historical development (as shown by the citational record), and showing whether their usage continues or has ceased. In the microstructure of synchronic dictionary, the order of word senses is not usually historical, but according to their notional generality or specificity – hence the practice of defining *undertaker* first as 'one who undertakes' and then as 'one who manages funeral arrangements for another party'. An alternative principle for ordering senses is to prioritize high-frequency over lower frequency usages – a system that can be supported by referring to computer corpora, and applied in recent pedagogical dictionaries.

Between the macrostructure and microstructure, lexicographers since Nielsen (2003) have noted as *mediostructure* the various intermediate structures of the dictionary, which serve as a bridge between the alphabetical macrostructure, and the details of the microstructure in individual entries. The commonest form of mediostructure is the cross-referencing signalled within the microstructure that can take readers to an alternative word, name, spelling or form of the headword, as in:

throve   a past tense of **thrive**

Cross-referencing is the sole function of 'blind' entries, used as place-holders for words which are detailed in other entries:

Ulysses butterfly ⇒ **mountain blue butterfly**

While print dictionaries have long included cross-referencing, many other kinds of mediostructure can be built into online dictionaries. They can include links to supplementary lexical information within the website, such as hierarchical diagrams that show sense relations among word sets (e.g. hyponymy, meronymy), the grammatical paradigms in which word forms vary (e.g. irregular verbs), and computerized concordances extracted from corpora showing the headword as a keyword in context. Some lexicographers (Nielsen 2003) also regard the external links from an online dictionary to resources held elsewhere on the internet (e.g. formal standards), as part of the dictionary's mediostructure. These extensions to the information provided to the user of online dictionaries underscore their increasing role as interfaces to the encyclopaedic world of the internet: see further §12.2.4 and §12.4.

Since Johnson's dictionary, citational evidence from outside sources has been provided within large monolingual dictionaries as a way of validating the individual senses of words, and illustrating their grammatical use in sentences and types of discourse. In the diachronic *Oxford English Dictionary* (OED), this citational evidence became the backbone of the word's history, from which its senses over the course of time were induced. It was the work of many hands (see OED's Historical Introduction, Section VII), though nowadays largely superseded by the availability of computerized databases of printed text (such as the British National Corpus) or data extracted from the internet. Linguistic corpora have been used by the major dictionary publishing houses since the 1980s, starting with Collins publishers' 'Bank of English', and the Oxford Text Archive. Used appropriately, these sources provide both frequency information, and lively citations from different kinds of texts to illustrate more and less formal styles of usage. The polysemy and collocational behaviour of very common words is more easily analysed on concordances derived from corpus data, as demonstrated by Sinclair (1991) with the many uses of *of*. The ready availability of citational evidence from digitized sources has freed dictionary-makers from their dependence on preexisting works, and standing on the shoulders of their predecessors, while avoiding plagiarism. However this does not lessen the need for lexicographic scholarship in interpreting lexical raw material.

12.2.2 Origins of the English dictionary as a pedagogical tool

The earliest recorded use of the word *dictionary* (*dictionarius*) in England (c.1225) is associated with the teaching of Latin in medieval schools. At that stage it referred to a list of Latin words, and only centuries later did it become the regular name for the familiar monolingual or bilingual dictionary. Even in the mid-sixteenth century, an English–Latin teaching manual titled *A Shorte Dictionarie for Yong Begynners* (John Withals 1553) presents words and their explanations in topical chapters like lesson plans, rather than alphabetically. The first monolingual alphabetical glossaries of English were published in the late sixteenth century as supplements to Tudor teaching manuals, such as those of Robert Mulcaster in *The Elementarie* (1582), and Edmund Coote in *The English Scholemaister* (1596). Each of them extended his predecessor's inventory with additional 'hard' words borrowed into English from Latin, Greek and Hebrew through Renaissance scholarship. Robert Cawdrey's *Table Alphabeticall* (1604) updated that of Coote (Stein 2010) to comprise around 2,500 words. It is generally recognized as the first English dictionary, despite its title and large amounts of legacy content (Landau 2001), no doubt because it was published as an independent reference work. Cawdrey is the first to explicitly envisage use of the dictionary outside the schoolroom, suggesting in his subtitle that the book would benefit 'ladies, gentilewomen or any other unskilfull persons'.

Cawdrey's work exemplifies aspects of later lexicographical practice, though not consistently implemented. His alphabetization of headwords is sometimes slightly erratic; plural headwords e.g. ***affaires***, ***records***, are mixed in with the standard singular forms, and inflected forms of verbs used as adjectives, thus not fully lemmatized to the base forms (Stein 2010). The source language for borrowed words is indicated by means of an abbreviation, e.g. [g] or [gr] for Greek, and the paragraph sign for French. Cawdrey's wordlist is fully glossed, but the explanations are a mix of synonyms used like the translation equivalents of earlier bilingual dictionaries, and definitional paraphrases. Some definitions are simply generic, as when **artichock** is glossed as a type of 'herbe', and **beagle** as a type of 'hound'. Alternative meanings are run on within the line of paraphrase, separated by commas, or by *or*, without marking distinct grammatical roles:

> **aduocate,** a spokesman, atturney, or man of law, plead

Occasionally the grammar of the definition is at odds with that of the headword itself, as in

> **docilitie,** easie to be taught

Grammar is clearly an underdeveloped aspect of the *Table Alphabeticall*. Yet the language of Cawdrey's definitions is usually clear, and not resolutely impersonal as in later dictionary practice (cf. §12.2.4). An authorial *I/we* appears in defining meanings in space and time (Stein 2010), as in:

> **hemisphere,** halfe of the compasse of heauen, that we see

> **moderne,** of our time

Later, extended editions of Cawdrey's wordlist in 1609, 1613 and 1617 are testimony to its popularity.

The 'hard words' tradition in monolingual English lexicography grew steadily with seventeenth century dictionaries that contained countless foreign loanwords annexed into English through its expanding functions as the national language (Peters 2012). Many certainly belonged to literary style and formal registers of usage rather than the speech-based styles advocated by the Royal Society (Gordon 1966: 126–8). Thomas Blount's *Glossographia* (1656) included about 9,000 borrowed words (with discursive and sometimes far-fetched etymologies), and volumes of technical terms from the arts and sciences, with explanatory information. Other dictionaries in the 'hard words' tradition soon followed: Edmund Phillips's *New World of English Words* (1658) with 11,000 words, and Elisha Coles's *An English Dictionary* (1676), whose headword list expanded to 25,000 with the addition of dialect words, and underworld slang – which he suggests 'may perchance save your throat from being cut, or… your pocket from being pickt' (Starnes and Noyes 1946: 63). To make room for these extra words, Coles compressed his definitions and most are just synonyms.

Despite their expanding inventories, seventeenth century 'hard words' dictionaries do not show advances in English lexicographic practice.[5] In the same period, the frontiers of monolingual lexicography were being advanced within European academies, notably the Italian Accademia della Crusca and the Académie Française, as a means of establishing the status and scope of the national 'vernacular' (Tucker 1961: 58, 90). The lack of such an academy in England meant there was no concerted effort to codify the common English language, and English lexicography was still limited by its origins in bilingual dictionaries and compendiums of specialized vocabulary.

12.2.3 Key developments in the construction of monolingual English dictionaries

The watershed for monolingual English lexicography was the turn of the eighteenth century, with the publication of dictionaries which embraced both everyday and less common words within the lexicon, thus a comprehensive listing of the general vocabulary of English. The first dictionary to do so was *A New English Dictionary*, published in 1702 by 'JK',[6] with a large inventory of 28,000 words probably extracted from pre-existing spelling lists and bilingual dictionaries of Latin and French (Osselton 2011). However JK's glossing was rudimentary, and only in the second edition (1713) was each word given a simple definition. Compare:

(1702)   *To Gaggle* like a goose

(1713)   To *Gaggle*, to cry like a goose

JK's dictionary is far from discriminating alternative senses, or providing information on word grammar or etymology. Those now typical features of monolingual general lexicography are first seen in Nathan Bailey's *Universal Etymological English Dictionary* (1721). Amid its inventory of about 40,000 words (Starnes and Noyes 1946: 100), *about* and *above* appear among countless words drawn from specialized fields such as law, medicine and horsemanship. All are carefully defined, with alternative senses treated according to their grammatical roles, and given specific or generic etymologies, except for very common words. Bailey's single-volume octavo publication significantly advanced the macro- and microstructure of the English monolingual dictionary.

Samuel Johnson's *Dictionary of the English Language* (1755) eclipsed all before it, by its sheer size (two folio volumes), and the enormous amount of scholarship brought to bear on documenting individual words and their senses from the canon of English literature. Its headword list consisted of the common English vocabulary, with a small proportion of cant, i.e. slang words, but not proper nouns. Individual entries were all given etymologies, whether they were foreign loans or constructed out of the common stock of English morphemes. Each word's grammar was noted, in terms of its word class, and different senses were explained and enumerated, and often illustrated with citations from the English literary tradition, as in the following:

BARGE n.s. [from *bargei* Dut., from *barga* Low Latin]

1. A boat for pleasure

    …the barge she sat in, like a burnish'd throne

    Burnt on the water Shakesp. Antony and Cleopatra

2. A boat for burden

Johnson's dictionary was reprinted with little editorial change for seventy years (Reddick 1990: 171,175–6), and it set the benchmark for English lexicography well into the Victorian era. It appeared at an opportune moment to be the supreme lexical reference for the national language of Britain, sampling the 'flower' of the English literary tradition. Its citational material from Shakespeare onwards served to document thousands of words and senses which were notionally current in mid-eighteenth century England, yielding a more or less synchronic account of the lexicon. But its perspective seemed decadent to nineteenth century scholars: its microstructure deficient in the treatment of the history of word meanings – too much geared to making English a world language (Willinsky 1994: 16–17) – while its macrostructure lacked coverage of foreign loanwords encountered abroad (Ogilvie 2013: 61–8). At the same time the earlier history of English was opening up through research associated with the English Philological Society, which helped to mobilize the *New English Dictionary* project that became the *Oxford English Dictionary* (OED). Like Johnson, it aimed to provide citations for the senses of all common words,[7] but presented them as a chronology of the word's growth and/or narrowing of usage over the centuries. It thus projects a longitudinal/diachronic view of the English lexicon, with both current and obsolete headwords listed. The OED noted etymologies for all words, as well as changes in their spelling over time, and modern pronunciations in an IPA-like script.[8] While it documented changes in word usage through citations, the OED's founding principle was to avoid making judgements about them as good or bad usage – letting the citations speak for themselves (Willinsky 1994: 17–18). This descriptive and inclusive stance was resolutely maintained by the chief editor (James Murray), despite some criticism of it (Ogilvie 2013: 54).

The OED was unique among English dictionaries in its diachronic scope, its regular use of citations, and its sheer size (twelve volumes published successively from 1884 to 1928). It stands apart from the mainstream of modern English lexicography, which flows through the single-volume synchronic dictionary that provides pronunciations, orthographic and grammatical information, and definitions for all the enumerated senses of each word. Citations (invented or extracted from other sources) and summary etymologies may or may not be offered, depending on the size of the publication. Editorial advice on contentious usage may be added, apart from hidden judgements expressed through the exclusion of 'unacceptable' usages. Thus the details contained in the dictionary microstructure vary considerably, depending on the intended users and functions, as discussed in the following section. The makeup of the *macrostructure* varies also, in the numbers and types of headwords out of which it is constructed, as discussed in §12.2.1.

12.2.4 Functions and users of dictionaries, general and specialized

Dictionaries have long been associated with language learning, as is clear from their earliest uses in medieval and Tudor schools (§12.2.2). The early bilingual Latin–English and English–Latin glossaries were intended to support the teaching and learning of Europe's first language of scholarship in Britain; while the first monolingual dictionaries of the early seventeenth century were to help adult readers with the anglicized loanwords ('hard words') appearing in contemporary texts. The native-English-speaker was the target user of all these works, and their knowledge of English grammar and idiom was taken for granted. As detailed definitions were added into the microstructure of eighteenth-century dictionaries, their rather formal non-propositional language – 'dictionaryese' – was something readers were expected to cope with. Native-English-speakers were the assumed readers of monolingual English dictionaries until the later twentieth century, when the needs of foreign learners began to be recognized by major English dictionary publishers, in what are now known as 'learners dictionaries'.

The English learners dictionary has evolved quickly since the 1960s (Marello 1998), making pedagogical lexicography a driving force in adapting the construction and content of dictionaries to the needs of dictionary users (Tarp 2009). Its impact can be seen in the dropping of low frequency words from the macrostructure, and greatly increased articulation of the linguistic properties of words in the microstructure. Notable additions are in the semantic keywords, in flexible approaches to definitions and ensuring their accessibility, in extensive use of examples to show natural usage of the word, and some indication of its relative frequency in written and spoken English. All these can be found in the *Longman Dictionary of Contemporary English* (LDOCE, third edition 1995) for a long entry on the adjective **hot** with twenty-seven different senses and distinction collocations, grouped with definitions and examples under the following set of keywords:

> 1. high temperature 2. hot taste 3. difficult to deal with 4. angry 5. popular 6. following closely 7. other senses

Frequency information given at the start (*S1, W2*) shows that *hot* is used more often in spoken than written English, based on its ranking within the first 1,000 words in spoken corpus data, and the first 2,000 words in written data. LDOCE uses a controlled vocabulary of around 2,000 words/lemmas in its definitions to ensure they are accessible to those with limited knowledge of English. It makes some use of the 'sentence definitions' pioneered in the Collins Cobuild learners dictionaries, as in:

> If you are **hot**, your body is at an unpleasantly high temperature
> *(Collins Cobuild Essential English Dictionary 1988)*

Lexicographic innovations like these for second language learners have yet to be matched in the ordinary dictionaries for native-speaking school students. Recent research on Dutch age-graded dictionaries shows they tend to overestimate the level of language competence required for their use (Schryver and Prinsloo 2011). Continual testing of their microstructure is needed to ensure learners dictionaries fulfil their pedagogical function as effectively as possible.

Specialized dictionaries of technical terms are published in ever-increasing numbers to meet the needs of learners and workers in a particular field, with the continuously expanding terminologies in areas such as chemistry, environmental science, information science, medicine (Ayto 1999). Amid technological advances, the dictionary macrostructure quickly gets out of date, apart from the commercial pressure to keep expanding its market/readership. So the original *Mosby's Medical Dictionary* is now *Mosby's Medical, Nursing and Allied Health Dictionary*, appearing at ever-closer intervals of time (2002, 2006, 2009, 2011). The current headword list still includes countless medical terms drawn from Latin and Greek, e.g.

> **metacarpal phalanx** … the hands and fingers, particularly phalanges that articulate with carpal bones

as well as those constructed out of common English for occupational syndromes, their diagnosis and nursing care:

> **metal fume fever** … an occupational disorder caused by the inhalation of fumes of metallic oxides and characterized by symptoms similar to those of influenza …. Access to fresh air and treatment of the symptoms usually alleviate the condition
> *(Mosby's Dictionary 2011: 1085–6)*

The second example illustrates the encyclopaedic element often built into the microstructure of specialized dictionaries, to inform those whose training crosses over from one discipline to another in the larger domain of medicine and health care. It reflects the dictionary's auxiliary function as repository of knowledge (Bergenholz and Tarp 2003), not just a terminological standard, or strictly linguistic reference. This encyclopaedic dimension has opened up especially for online specialized dictionaries, whose pages can be linked to illustrations, audiofiles and other multimedia enhancements of their microstructure, as well as external sources of information.[9]

Encyclopaedic features in the dictionary's microstructure can also be found in certain types of bilingual dictionaries, especially those designed to conserve and maintain endangered languages and sometimes also to revitalize their use (Ogilvie 2011: 394–99). Their socio-cultural function is often visible in the presence of terms relating to traditional crafts in the macrostructure, accompanied by drawings and information in the microstructure to explain their place in cultural practice. Thus the entry for the *bilirra* ('yellow mangrove tree') in the *Kayardild Dictionary and Thesaurus* (Evans 1992) includes a line drawing of the tree's stand of roots above the waterline, and notes that they are used as paddles. Conservation dictionaries of endangered languages often involve partnerships between local people and linguist-lexicographers, bringing lexicographical skills and techniques to bear on endangered cultures (Ogilvie 2011: 393–5). Such dictionaries are important in terms of adding to the documentation of the world's stock of languages, as well as affirming the native speakers' language and giving it some status on the world scene. Their role is analogous to that of any national dictionary, including Johnson's 1755 *Dictionary of the English Language*, which fulfilled the key cultural function of codifying eighteenth-century English with a comprehensive record of the lexicon and extensive illustration of the English literary tradition (see §12.2.3).

12.3 Thesauruses

12.3.1 Origins of the English thesaurus and precursors to Roget

The term *thesaurus* is neo-Latin, based on the classical Greek word for 'treasury', i.e. storehouse for precious objects. But among its various applications in English it is rarely found in its classical sense, and its application by lexicographers to an onomasiological lexical reference was not its earliest English use. From the sixteenth century to the eighteenth the term *thesaurus* appeared in the title of semasiological dictionaries, such as the alphabetically arranged bilingual *Thesaurus Linguae Romanae et Britannicae* (Cooper 1565). The term's application to a conceptually ordered presentation of the lexicon began with Roget's *Thesaurus* (1852), yet it continued to be applied to alphabetically ordered language references, as in the *American Thesaurus of Slang* (1942). Since the later twentieth century, the term *thesaurus* has been extended to structured information systems created for libraries and information technology (see §12.3.5). Lexicographers themselves use *thesaurus* in more than one sense, so that alongside its Rogetian sense of being a concept-driven construction of the lexicon at large, *thesaurus* may refer to a lexical index to a 'closed corpus' (Ilson 2010), i.e. a finite language database such as the *Thesaurus of Old English*, or a published dictionary, as in the case of the *Historical Thesaurus of the Oxford English Dictionary*. The term *thesaurus* is thus polysemous, though its use to refer to a strictly onomasiological description of the English language has been trademarked in the UK as *Roget's Thesaurus*.

The first truly onomasiological work with reference to the English language was produced in the seventeenth century by members of the British Royal Society, led by John Wilkins (1614–1672). Published as *An Essay Towards a Real Character and a Philosophical Language* (1688), it included exploratory discussions on the value of creating a symbolic system to express universal human thoughts, a pervasive theme among contemporary European philosophers such as Descartes and Leibniz. To achieve this goal, Wilkins devised a system of 'real' characters (non-alphabetic shapes) that were intended to express human thought directly, without recourse to the words of any individual language. Instead the system should name 'things and notions', classified into structured semantic sets so as to function within conceptual hierarchies like those of the modern thesaurus. The overarching conceptual systems were set out in detailed 'philosophical tables' (Clauss 1982: 540), drawn up by Wilkins's colleague William Lloyd. The words/names in the tables were painstakingly cross-referenced to the 'alphabetical dictionary', the largest and last section of the *Essay* (Considine 2008: 298). The *Essay*'s dictionary presents the inventory of 11,500 English words identified for the things/notions of the theoretical universal language, excluding words which named anything that was specific to place or time (Clauss 1982: 544).

Despite its originality, Wilkins's monumental *Essay* was not particularly well received outside the Royal Society (Clauss 1982: 542–6), and its grand onomasiological design was eclipsed for nearly two centuries by other types of dictionary constructed on a more limited semantic basis, i.e. covering a set of semantic relations or a specific semantic field. One was the eighteenth-century 'topical dictionary', whose authors were the pioneers of terminography in applied sciences and contemporary areas of knowledge (e.g. art, health). Their focus on a particular field of endeavour arguably gave their work a conceptual/onomasiological basis, even within an alphabetical macrostructure (Hüllen 1999). Another specialized type of dictionary – dictionaries of synonyms – can also be seen as maintaining the onomasiological approach in the long interval between Wilkins's *Essay* and Roget's *Thesaurus*. Although the key words to each synonym cluster are alphabetically listed, the microstructure for each entry presents a semantic/conceptual analysis of the cluster and the finer sense distinctions among them. The model for English synonym dictionaries was the work of Abbé Girard (1718), *La Justesse de la langue françoise ou les différentes significations des mots qui passent pour synonymes*, which was translated and adapted to the English lexicon by John Trusler (1766). An independent and better known perspective on English synonyms was published later in the century by Hester Piozzi, who had in a previous marriage (as Mrs Thrale) been an acquaintance of Samuel Johnson. Her dictionary's formidable title: *British Synonymy: Or an Attempt to Regulate the Choice of Words in Familiar Conversation* (1794) resonates with the standardizing impulse of the eighteenth century. Yet inside the covers it was evidently designed as a contribution to the lexical education of middle-class women, to help them converse elegantly, and 'intended chiefly for the parlour window' rather than the library shelf. It was lively and well received – republished twice (Gove 1984). The writers of synonym dictionaries after Piozzi (notably William Taylor, *English Synonymes Discriminated* (1813); George Crabb, *English Synonymes Explained* (1816)) reverted to more discursive treatments of sense relations traceable back to Girard (Gove 1984). These various lexicographic endeavours suggest growing interest in semantic fields within the English lexicon, while the alphabetical macrostructure remained the default for presenting lexical information.

Lexicography

12.3.2 The construction of Roget's Thesaurus

Roget's *Thesaurus* (1852) of the English lexicon was a quantum leap in providing an onomasiological account of a European language. Though Roget can be seen as redeveloping the resources of synonym dictionaries, the conceptual structure he devised was original, an analytical system he had begun decades earlier (in 1805), and developed in the background to his professional work as a doctor, scientist and as secretary of the British Royal Society from 1827 to 1848. His interests were also philosophical – like Wilkins, he engaged with Leibniz's philosophy and questions of how human thought was represented in language. That apart, he had a practical concern with finding the right word to express an idea, and for many users of his *Thesaurus*, it was effectively a 'word-finder'. The macrostructure of Roget's *Thesaurus* is a set of hierarchically ordered concepts, articulated vertically down from just six at the highest level:

- abstract relations
- space
- matter
- intellect
- volition
- sentient and moral powers.

Beneath these 'superconcepts', he developed a structure of 1,000 concepts and subconcepts, so that the words labelling them are in hyponymic relations with those above and below. Some of the nodes at the second and third levels down had to be labelled by means of phrasal descriptors, e.g. 'power in operation', 'indirect power' (both under CAUSATION) because there was no single word for the concept. These phrasal descriptors show gaps in the hierarchies of nomenclature for ordinary words, unlike scientific terminology where there is hyponymic nomenclature at every level within its taxonomic systems.

At the fourth level of the *Thesaurus* hierarchy, Roget provided two sets of words that express a given concept: one containing *analogous words*, the second *correlative words*, both including nouns, verbs, adjectives and sometimes adverbs. For example, under the concept *degrees of power* there is first a set of analogous words whose meanings affirm the subconcept of *strength* ('vigour', 'to force', 'strong', 'strongly'), and a second set (the correlative words) whose members negate the subconcept, e.g. *weakness, fail, impotent*. In the original layout of the *Thesaurus*, the two sets were presented in parallel columns, so that readers could find the word they were seeking under a positive or negatively related concept. Roget thus anticipated one of the findings of cognitive linguistics, that linguistic opposites are closely associated in the human brain (Aitchison 1992: 74–7). Roget's parallel layout has been lost in modern versions of the *Thesaurus*, which simply interleave the two sets in successive paragraphs down a single-column page. Likewise Roget's original designations 'analogous words', 'correlative words' are now overlooked,[10] so that words grouped together in his *Thesaurus* sets are sometimes thought of as synonyms, though they may be synonymous in only one of their denotations and divergent in their connotations. There are of course no definitions to detail their meanings, as in a dictionary. Within the *Thesaurus*, word meanings are simply indicated by their place in the hierarchy of concepts, and their positive/negative polarity. This was in keeping with Roget's aim of providing partial synonyms from which literate users might choose the most effective alternative for their purposes.

The original Roget's *Thesaurus* included about 15,000 words, a relatively small inventory by comparison with modern dictionaries of the same size. It was however 'greatly enlarged and improved' after Peter Roget's death (1869) in two-yearly editions by his son John, and annual editions by grandson Samuel from 1925 to 1953. From *c.*1880 there were separate British and American editions, in which the British reviewed and enlarged the inventory within Roget's original subcategories, and the American reworked the material and the overall hierarchy of concepts (Burger 1991). In Britain 'Roget's Thesaurus' was trademarked, whereas in the US the *Roget* name became generic, and used by imitators and publishers of more and less thesaurus-like publications.

12.3.3 Ontological issues in thesauruses, especially in print form

Roget's classification of English words by association with six superconcepts was designed to be exhaustive, so that each word could be found in its semantic niche within the hierarchical structure. Like other thesaurus-developers, he created his own multilayered semantic hierarchy (i.e. ontology) in the absence of any conventional model. The best-known examples of European thesauruses differ from Roget and from each other at the highest level: Hallig and Wartburg's (1963) hierarchy for French has three supercategories: L'Univers, L'Homme, L'Homme et L'Univers, whereas Cesares's for Spanish has just two: Dios, El Universo. However El Universo has many subcategories, for the organic and inorganic world, plants, animals, humans, individual mind/action/communication, society and its institutions (Ilson 2010: 248), making the structure very asymmetrical. These divergences in the conceptual hierarchies proposed for different European languages suggest linguistic and cultural relativities in the construction of thesauruses, which were overlooked by the universal language philosophers of the seventeenth century. The ontological construction of thesauruses for English also diverge considerably, according to whether they are designed for top-down access to the language at large, or developed 'bottom up' from a closed corpus or dictionary macrostructure (like the *Historical Thesaurus of the Oxford English Dictionary*, which generates a very large miscellany of superconcepts and over 200,000 subcategories). Either way the arbitrariness of the conceptual structure of the thesaurus is a disadvantage, making words less easy to find than Roget intended. In fact John Roget added an alphabetical index at the back of the family *Thesaurus* in 1879 (ten years after his father's death), and it is now a standard feature with onomasiological thesauruses.

Roget's *Thesaurus* and those modelled on it are notionally synchronic representations of the English lexicon (Ilson 2010: 251). Yet readers at the turn of the twenty-first century would be aware that some of the words contained in Roget's sets of alternatives are rare or obsolescent, e.g. *adumbration, alack, lachrymose, sedulity, tergiversation*. This problem is addressed in the *Historical Thesaurus of the Oxford English Dictionary* (HTOED) published in 2009, which gives the first recorded date of each near-synonym and notes those which are obsolete. Drawing on the microstructural resources of the OED, HTOED is also able to provide stylistic information about the usage of words, e.g. *booze* as a colloquial term for 'wine', and *plonk* as an Australian/British word for 'cheap wine', though both are listed in a standard thesaurus without such labels, or definitions to help discriminate them. The onomasiological construction also masks the natural polysemy of common words, since the different senses of the same word have to be included in different subcategories, e.g. *horse* in both 'animal' and 'framework'. There is no cross-referencing, so again it is the index rather than the ontological structure which provides this information.

Both synchronic and diachronic thesauruses are paradigmatic rather than syntagmatic (Ilson 2010: 256) in their projection of the lexicon. Neither shows the collocational tendencies that contribute to the meanings of words and help to discriminate their senses, e.g. the different senses of the word *freedom* to be found in *freedom from* and *freedom to*. Other scholars have noted that thesauruses do not indicate the transitivity relations that verbs enter into, which help to differentiate transitive and intransitive/mediopassive uses (Burger 1991: 49–52). Compare 'he sells books' with 'the book sells well'. The relative frequencies of words, now easily extracted from reference corpora and reported in learners dictionaries (e.g. Collins Cobuild and LDOCE), are not indicated in either the synchronic or diachronic thesaurus. While modern print dictionaries accommodate all these aspects of lexical meaning within the microstructure of individual entries, it is still unclear how/where they could be incorporated into the macrostructure of the *print* thesaurus.

12.3.4 Computerized lexical databases and the distributional thesaurus

Computer systems are game-changing for the thesaurus, helping to address many of the problems mentioned in the previous section. Their indexing capabilities allow instant access to elements at any structural level within the thesaurus, bypassing the non-intuitive conceptual classifications of the conventional print thesaurus. The pioneering online lexical database was WordNet, developed by psycholinguists at Princeton University, and grounded in research on the organization of the human mental lexicon (Miller *et al.* 1990). As in lexical memory, nouns are arranged in 'topical hierarchies' (p. 237), and accessed at more and less abstract levels in discourse production. This is matched in their layout, as shown below for *bank*.

- (n) **bank** (sloping land (especially the slope beside a body of water))
    - (n) **slope, incline, side** (an elevated geological formation)
        - (n) **geological formation, formation** ((geology), the geological features of the earth)
            - (n) **object, physical object** (a tangible and visible entity; an entity that can cast a shadow)
                - (n) **physical matter** (an entity that has physical existence)
                    - (n) **entity** (that which is known or inferred to have its own distinct existence (living or non-living))

WordNet thus constructs conceptual ontologies for individual words with rather more intermediate levels than the conventional thesaurus. WordNet was also designed to embrace *all* the senses of polysemous words (unlike the print thesaurus). It makes use of simple definitions and synonyms to identify the relevant lexical concept (Miller *et al.* 1990: 240), and each sense is illustrated in at least one corpus example, as shown below. The clusters of synonyms given for each sense of the word are 'synsets' – now 117,000 of them in WordNet version 3.1. The relative frequency of each sense is noted in brackets at the start of each line, based on its occurrences in the reference corpus:

(25) S: (n) **bank** (sloping land (especially the slope beside a body of water)) *'they pulled the canoe up on the bank'; 'he sat on the bank of the river and watched the currents'*

(20) S: (n) depository financial institution, **bank**, banking concern, banking company (a financial institution that accepts deposits and channels the money into lending activities) *'he cashed a check at the bank'; 'that bank holds the mortgage on my home'*

(2) S: (n) **bank** (a long ridge or pile) *'a huge bank of earth'*
(1) S: (n) **bank** (an arrangement of similar objects in a row or in tiers) *'he operated a bank of switches'*

The features shown in those synsets are all very familiar from dictionaries, but lacking in *Roget's Thesaurus*. Yet WordNet is still essentially paradigmatic in its treatment of words and their senses, apart from what human users may glean from the examples.

The need for syntagmatic information on the behaviour of words is increasingly being met by the so-called *distributional thesaurus*, using data automatically extracted from large corpora (e.g. the internet) with targeted software. Distributional thesauruses compute the semantic similarities between common words, comparing the linguistic contexts in which they occur, and the parities in their collocations and grammatical dependencies. Distributional thesauruses have been developed for English and other languages, of which Sketch Engine is a widely known commercial example (Kilgariff *et al.* 2004), designed to serve the needs of artificial intelligence/knowledge abstraction in natural language processing. The 'word sketches' they produce of the collocational and grammatical behaviour of words are an asset in lexicographical research, and increasingly used as an adjunct facility in online general language dictionaries (Rundell 2012). The distributional thesaurus also serves the needs of translators and bilingual lexicographers, since parallel word sketches can be prepared for a word and its putative translation equivalent to see how closely they match up. They provide raw material for online bilingual thesauruses which could scarcely be realized in print.

12.3.5 Structured approaches to meaning in specialized lexicography online

Hierarchical structures of the concepts represented by everyday words (as in the WordNet illustration in §12.3.4) are also increasingly applied in specialized lexicography/terminography, and in information science. Sometimes called *lightweight/lite ontologies* (Giunchiglia and Zaihrayeu 2007), they are readily constructed using the hyponymic nomenclature that forms the backbone of the taxonomic sciences. Hierarchical relations among technical terms and concepts also serve the needs of artificial intelligence because they articulate 'inheritance' properties that can be exploited at multiple levels in the ontology. Yet twenty-first century descriptive terminologists (e.g. Temmerman 2000) recognize that technical terms are often polysemous and participate in more than one ontology, so that the properties they inherit will depend on the context. Technical terms also participate in non-hierarchical sense relations, e.g. meronymy (part–whole relationship), and in the relationship of instantiation, which can be represented schematically to explain disciplinary concepts in online terminography (Winston *et al.* 1987). Causal relationships and agency are crucial in the terminology of physical sciences and engineering (Faber *et al.* 2007). In architecture various types of associative meaning contribute to the multidimensional semantics of common terms such as *window*, e.g. their shape, location, function, constituent materials, all of which could be exploited in diagrams and tables, and in the underlying information structure of an online thesaurus (Fernández and Faber 2011). All these sense relations lend systematicity (as well as complexity) to the description of subsets of disciplinary concepts, but they can be displayed graphically by means of diagrams and drawings etc. to complement the verbal substance of the conventional dictionary/thesaurus (Peters *et al.* 2014). Specialized lexicography is naturally encyclopaedic (see §12.2.4), so the online specialized thesaurus that represents terminology in structured ways helps not only to profile the key disciplinary concepts but to model the construction of knowledge in the discipline (Debnath *et al.* 2000). Similarly, the term *thesaurus* is now used to refer to the structure of information systems, like those used in libraries as well as the management of a bureaucracy.

12.4 Integration of dictionary and thesaurus

The distinctive construction of dictionaries and thesauruses – embodying semasiological and onomasiological approaches to the lexicon – have evolved separately over centuries. This chapter has traced the continual expansion of the macro- and microstructure of English dictionaries since the sixteenth century, contrasting with the late emergence of Roget's *Thesaurus* in the mid-nineteenth century and its unique, fully articulated conceptual structure. Yet each has borrowed constructional features from the other. Learners dictionaries borrow from the semantic/conceptual approach, as does LDOCE (1995), in its cross-referencing from individual entries to summary pages or display boxes that present words with closely related senses: near synonyms, hyponyms or meronyms. Thus dictionaries can mitigate the tyranny of the alphabet when necessary. Conversely, thesauruses (from 1879 on) found it advisable to add an alphabetic index at the back of the book, to help users access lexical information within the not-too-intuitive conceptual structure. The two formats can usefully complement each other.

Fuller integration of the dictionary and thesaurus can be found in later twentieth century products such as the Reader's Digest *Reverse Dictionary* (1989), where semantically related words (e.g. *gastronomy*, *cuisine*, *culinary*) are grouped under an alphabetically listed key word (*cooking*), all with brief definitions. The whole entry is cross-referenced to tables of more specialized words: *cooking terms*, *cooking utensils* and *menu terms*, to provide dictionary-like coverage of both common and 'hard' words. Major English dictionary publishers have used their lexical databases to create a dictionary–thesaurus in one volume, from the *Collins English Dictionary and Thesaurus* (1993) on. Some foreground the alphabetic index with brief definitions at the front of the book ahead of the thesaurus. Others e.g. *American Heritage Dictionary and Thesaurus* (2005) have the dictionary and thesaurus sections juxtaposed on double-page spreads, with the alphabetically ordered words and definitions on the upper half, and thesaurus categories in the lower half. The constraints of the print medium are evident in each case. Ongoing integration of the OED with HTOED in 2014 has the great advantage of working online from the start, able to link straight from the screen-ready alphabetical list with its detailed microstructure to the thesaurus entries, and vice versa. The online medium offers unlimited space for things that lexicographers could only dream of ten years ago (Schryver 2003), and for experimental combinations of verbal, graphic and audio elements that can be tested to optimize their use.

Innovative combinations of dictionary and thesaurus online are still governed by established lexicographical principles (Rundell 2012). Planning the macrostructure still matters, in terms of what parts of the lexicon – words and multiword units, common and specialized words, proper nouns and idioms – are to be included. There are new constructional opportunities in making use of the mediostructure, not only to cross-reference from word to word, or from dictionary to thesaurus, but to connect specialized terms with encyclopaedic information elsewhere on the internet. Links to selected corpus data and the distributional thesaurus can enhance the collocational information offered in online learners dictionaries. More grammatical information can be offered than could be squeezed into the print dictionary. But with increased internal and external linking, navigation and systems for content management become ever more important. The allied disciplines of information technology and artificial intelligence are there to support computer-searches of words by form as well as their semantics, for both human and machine readers. The computerized microstructural template is more capacious than in ordinary print dictionaries, but still raises the question of what to prioritize on the first screenful, displayed landscape-wise rather than portrait-wise.

These twenty-first century aspects of lexicographic practice, and questions of how to optimize the functionality of the combined dictionary–thesaurus for human users, require continuing research to enlarge the empirical foundations of lexicography. The principles that have evolved in dictionary-making and construction now need to embrace both semasiological and onomasiological approaches to the lexicon, to support any fully-fledged lexicographical theory.

Notes

1. The plural form of thesaurus is either neo-Latin thesauri or English thesauruses. In the original Greek, the plural was thesauroi. Since using thesaurus to refer to a semantically structured model of the lexicon dates from the nineteenth century (see §12.3.1), it seems reasonable to use the English plural in this chapter's title and elsewhere.
2. Cawdrey's title uses the word 'usuall' in its earlier sense of 'current' (see Stein 2010).
3. The intent of Wilkins's work is obscured for twenty-first century readers by its use of 'essay' (=experiment), and 'real character' to refer to a symbolic system that stands for universal concepts (see Clauss 1982).
4. These terms originated with Darwin (1857) in biological taxonomy, according to the Oxford English Dictionary online.
5. The 'hard words' tradition is still exemplified by Ayto's *Dictionary of Difficult Words* (1993), published by Helicon.
6. The initials JK probably refer to John Kersey, the author of other early eighteenth-century dictionaries (Starnes and Noyes 1946: 69–70).
7. The OED included adjectives (and verbs) derived from proper nouns, e.g. Australian, but not proper nouns like Australia, a policy which presented challenges (Murray: General Introduction). By not including proper nouns, the OED was spared the problem for encyclopaedic dictionaries of continually updating facts contained within the microstructure.
8. IPA is the International Phonetic Alphabet for rendering the individual sounds/phonemes of any language, independent of its orthography.
9. The LawTermFinder online termbank in Australian family law includes external links to the relevant legislation.
10. Except in Merriam–Webster *Dictionary of Synonyms* (1984), where they are systematically used.

References

Aitchison, J. (1992) *Words in the Mind*. Oxford: Blackwell.
Ayto, J. (1999) *Twentieth Century Words*. Oxford: Oxford University Press.
Bergenholz, H. and S. Tarp (2003) Two opposing theories: On HE Wiegand's recent discovery of lexicographic functions. *Hermes, Journal of Linguistics* 31: 171–96.
Bogaards, P. (2010) Lexicography: Science without Theory? In G.-M. Schruyver (ed.) *A Way with Words: Festschrift for Patrick Hanks*, pp. 313–22. Kampala: Menha Publishers.
Burger, H. (1991) Roget, Darwin, & Bohr: Parallelizing evolutionary diversification with conceptual classification. *International Journal of Lexicography* 4: 23–67.
Cawdrey, R. (1604) *A Table Alphabeticall, conteyning and teaching the true writing, and vnderstanding of hard vsuall English words, borrowed from the Hebrew, Greeke, Latine, French. &c.* London: Printed by I. R[oberts] for Edmund Weauer.

Clauss, S. (1982) John Wilkins' Essay Toward a Real Character: Its place in the seventeenth century episteme. *Journal of the History of Ideas* 43: 531–53.

Considine, J. (2008) *Dictionaries in Early Modern Europe: Lexicography and the Making of a Heritage*. Cambridge: Cambridge University Press.

Debnath, S., S. Sen. and B. Blackstock (2000) LawBot, a multiagent assistant for legal research. *IEEE Internet Computing* 4: 32–7.

Evans, N. (1992) *Kayardild Dictionary and Thesaurus*. Melbourne: University of Melbourne, Department of Linguistics and Language Studies.

Faber, P., P. Araúz, J. Velasco and A. Reimerink (2007) Linking images and words: The description of specialized concepts. *International Journal of Lexicography* 20: 39–65.

Fernández, T. and P. Faber (2011) The representation of multidimensionality in a bilingualized English–Spanish thesaurus for learners in architecture and building construction. *International Journal of Lexicography* 24: 198–335.

Gordon, I. (1966) *The Movement of English Prose*. London: Longman.

Gove, P. (1984) *Merriam-Webster Dictionary of Synonyms*. Springfield: Merriam-Webster.

Giunchiglia, F. and I. Zaihrayeu (2007) Lightweight ontologies. *Technical Report* DIT-07-071, October. Trento: University of Trento, Department of Information and Communication Technology.

Hüllen, W. (1999) *English Dictionaries 800–1700: The Topical Tradition*. Oxford: Clarendon Press.

Ilson, R. (2010) Review article: On the historical thesaurus of the Oxford English Dictionary. *International Journal of Lexicography* 24: 241–60.

Kilgariff, A., P. Rychly, P. Smrz and D. Tugwell (2004) The sketch engine. *Proceedings of EURALEX*, pp. 105–16. www.euralex.org/elx_proceedings/Euralex2004/011_2004_V1_Adam%20KILGARRIFF,%20Pavel%20RYCHLY,%20Pavel%20SMRZ,%20David%20TUGWELL_The%20%20Sketch%20Engine.pdf.

Landau, S. (2001) *The Art and Craft of Lexicography*, 2nd edition. Cambridge: Cambridge University Press.

Marello, C. (1998) Hornby's bilingual dictionaries. *International Journal of Lexicography* 11: 292–314.

Miller, G., R. Beckwith, C. Gellbaum, D. Gross and K. Miller (1990) Introduction to WordNet: An online lexical database. *International Journal of Lexicography* 3: 235–44.

Nielsen, S. (2003) Mediostructures in bilingual LSP dictionaries. In R. Hartmann (ed.) *Lexicography: Critical Concepts, Vol 3. Lexicography, Metalexicography and Reference Science*, pp. 270–94. London: Routledge.

Ogilvie, S. (2011) Linguistics, lexicography, and the revitalization of endangered languages. *International Journal of Lexicography* 24: 389–404.

Ogilvie, S. (2013) *Words of the World*. Cambridge: Cambridge University Press.

Osselton, N. (2011) John Kersey and the ordinary words of English. In A. McDermott (ed.) *Ashgate Critical Essays on Early English Lexicographers, Vol 5: The Eighteenth Century*, pp. 61–7. Farnham: Ashgate Publishers.

Peters, P. (2012) Standard British English. In A. Bergs and L. Brinton (eds) *HSK English Historical Linguistics*, pp. 1879–99. Berlin: De Gruyter Mouton.

Peters, P., A. Smith, J. Middledorp, A. Karpin, S. Sin and A. Kilgore (2014) Learning essential terms and concepts in statistics and accounting. *Higher Education Research and Development* 33: 742–56.

Reddick, A. (1990) *The Making of Johnson's Dictionary 1746–1773*. Cambridge: Cambridge University Press.

Rundell, M. (2012) It works in practice but will it work in theory? The uneasy relationship between lexicography and matters theoretical (Hornby Lecture). In R. Fjeld and J. Torjusen (eds), *Proceedings of the 15th EURALEX Congress*, pp. 47–92. Oslo: University of Oslo.

Saussure, F. de (1916) *Cours de Linguistique Générale*. [Publié par Charles Bally et Albert Sechehaye; avec la collaboration de Albert Riedlinger.] Paris: Payot.

Schryver, G.-M. de (2003) Lexicographers' dreams in the electronic dictionary age. *International Journal of Lexicography* 16: 143–99.

Schryver, G.-M. de and D.J. Prinsloo (2011) Do dictionaries define on the level of their target users? A case study for three Dutch dictionaries. *International Journal of Lexicography* 24: 5–28.

Sinclair, J. (1991) *Corpus, Concordance, Collocation*. Oxford: Oxford University Press.

Starnes, DeW. and G. Noyes (1946) *The English Dictionary from Cawdrey to Johnson 1604–1755*. Chapel Hill: University of North Carolina Press.

Stein, G. (2010) Lexicographical method and usage in Cawdrey's *A Table Alphabeticall* (1604). *Studia Neophilologica* 82: 163–77.

Tarp, S. (2009) Reflections on lexicographical user research. *Lexicos* 19: 275–96.

Temmerman, R. (2000) *Towards New Ways of Terminology Description*. Amsterdam: John Benjamins.

Tucker, S. (1961) *English Examined: Two Centuries of Comment on the Mother Tongue*. Cambridge: Cambridge University Press.

Welker, H.A. (2010) *Dictionary Use: A General Survey of Empirical Studies*. Brasília: author.

Wierzbicka, A. (1985) *Lexicography and Conceptual Analysis*. Ann Arbor: Karoma.

Wilkins, J. (1668) *Essay Towards a Real Character and a Philosophical Language*. London: S. Gellibrand and John Martin for the Royal Society [Menston: Scolar Press Facsimile, 1968].

Willinsky, J. (1994) *Empire of Words: The Reign of the OED*. Princeton: Princeton University Press.

Winston, M.E., R. Chaffin and D. Herrmann (1987) A taxonomy of part-whole relations. *Cognitive Science* 11: 417–44.

13
Pragmatics
Language use in context[1]

Yan Huang

13.1 What is pragmatics?

Pragmatics is one of the most vibrant and rapidly growing fields in linguistics and the philosophy of language. In recent years, it has also increasingly become a central topic in cognitive science, artificial intelligence, informatics, neuroscience, language pathology, anthropology and sociology. But what is pragmatics? Pragmatics can be broadly defined as in (1).

(1) Pragmatics is the study of language use in context.

However, though perhaps sufficient for the current purposes, such a definition may be too general and too vague to be of much use. This is because pragmatics is a particularly complex subject with all kinds of disciplinary influence, and few, if any, clear boundaries. In §13.3 I shall provide two different, though more detailed, definitions of pragmatics from two different theoretical points of view.

13.2 Why pragmatics?

There are many reasons for including pragmatics in an integrated theory of linguistics. Here, let me just discuss one or two of them.

13.2.1 Context dependence

Many, if not most, linguistic expressions of a language are context-sensitive in the sense that what they express is context-dependent. Consider (2)–(7).

(2) I like smoked salmon.

(3) You and you, but not you, stand up.

(4) It is raining.

(5) John is looking for his glasses.
    a. John is looking for his spectacles.
    b. John is looking for his drinking vessels.

(6) They are cooking apples.
    a. X: What are they doing in the kitchen?
       Y: They are cooking apples.
    b. X: What kind of apples are those?
       Y: They are cooking apples.

(7) The table is covered with books.

The interpretation of *I* in (2) and *you* in (3) – called a 'deictic' expression in linguistics and an 'indexical' expression in the philosophy of language – clearly relies on context. The reference of *I* (what the American philosopher David Kaplan called *content*) is essentially fixed by the contextual parameter determined by the stable meaning of *I* (what Kaplan called *character*). In other words, *I* is almost always used to refer to its user in a given context, thus called an 'automatic indexical' by the American philosopher John Perry. This has the consequence that the same linguistic expression *I* can be utilised to pick up different referents in different contexts. The three uses of *you* in (3) can be properly interpreted only by a direct, moment by moment monitoring of the physical aspects of the speech event in which the sentence is uttered. Unlike *I*, *you* is considered to be a 'discretionary indexical' because it involves the speaker's intention. (4) contains a meteorological predicate *rain*. When it rains (at a given time), it usually rains at a particular place typically where the speaker is. Consequently, at least in some contexts (4) needs to be made location-specific. Next, (5) is a case of lexical ambiguity and (6), a case of syntactic ambiguity. In disambiguating them, contextual knowledge is often needed to select the reading the speaker has intended. For example, in (6), it is the relative linguistic context that distinguishes (6a) from (6b). Finally, *the table* in (7) is an incomplete definite description, whose descriptive content does not apply uniquely. In other words, the semantics of an incomplete definite description does not pick out some unique object. The computation of its referent is usually pragmatic in nature, determined by the speaker's intention and its context. Other well-known cases of context-dependent expressions include terms with missing complements (8), relational terms (9), gradable adjectives (10), possessive constructions (11), constructions with missing quantifier domains (12), etc. (see also Bach 2012 for a more detailed list and for a different view).

(8) Mary is not slim enough [to be a fashion model].

(9) John is a friend [of the Obamas].

(10) John is tall [relative to an average European white man].

(11) John's class.
    a. e.g. the class John teaches.
    b. e.g. the class John attends.

(12) Everyone [in my family] loves classical music.

The linguistic material without the bracketed element in (8)–(12) is considered by the American philosopher Kent Bach to contain a propositional radical – a propositional fragment that does not express a complete proposition. Consequently, it cannot be evaluated truth-conditionally. Therefore, a propositional radical needs to be filled in contextually to be fully propositional so that it can be assigned a truth-value. For example, given a particular context, (8) can be completed to convey a minimal but full proposition such as the one expressed by the sentence with the bracketed material. However, whether the bracketed part in (8)–(10) and (12) contains a hidden indexical or an unarticulated constituent (UC) – a propositional or conceptual constitute of a sentence that is not explicitly expressed linguistically – has been a subject of heated debate among both philosophers and linguistic semanticists/pragmaticists, and the jury is still out.

13.2.2 Real-world knowledge

I consider next the role played by real-world knowledge.

(13) [Advice given by the British government during an outbreak of salmonella in the UK] Fried eggs should be cooked properly and if there are frail or elderly people in the house, they should be hard-boiled.

(14) a. the government's drugs campaign.
b. the government's safe-sex campaign.

(15) a. My sister has brushed her teeth.
b. My sister has visited the Great Wall in China.

(16) Anna had lunch at an Italian restaurant. The waiter was handsome.

In (13), given our real-world knowledge about who or what is or is not likely to be boiled, the preferred antecedent for *they* is *eggs* rather than *frail or elderly people*. (14) contains two noun-noun compounds. Again, by our common-sense knowledge, while (14a) means the government's campaign *against* illicit drugs, (14b) means exactly the opposite, namely, the government's campaign *for* safe-sex. Noun–noun compounds like (14) have long posed a challenge to Frege's 'principle of compositionality'. Next, (15a) is likely to be pragmatically enriched as the speaker's sister has brushed her teeth this morning. By contrast, (15b) is likely to be pragmatically expanded as the speaker's sister has visited the Great Wall in China at some point in her life. Both free enrichments are dependent on our (shared) belief about the world, in particular about our (shared) belief about teeth-brushing and sightseeing practices. Finally, (16) is an example of bridging cross-reference. It is via the addition of the background assumption that there are usually waiters/waitresses working in a restaurant that a link of association can be established between *the waiter* in the second sentence and *an Italian restaurant* in the first sentence. Put slightly differently, what is 'bridged' is not the information that is structurally retrievable but the information that is derivable from our real-world knowledge.

Clearly, the production and comprehension of sentences/phrases such as those in (2)–(16) involve pragmatic implication on the part of the speaker (*imply/implicate*) and pragmatic inference on the part of the addressee (*infer*). The same is also true of the following types of sentences.

(17)   John's blonde girlfriend has a brain.

(18)   It takes time to complete a PhD dissertation.

(19)   You are not going to die.

(20)   Confucius is on the top shelf.

Both the *brain*-sentence in (17) and the *time*-sentence in (18) are trivially true. On the other hand, (19) is patently false. (20) is an example of deferred reference. In order to understand what the speaker of these sentences really intends to convey, all of them have to be pragmatically enriched and inferred.

13.2.3 Linguistic underdeterminacy

All this indicates that frequently, conveyed meanings systematically supersede literal meanings through pragmatic implication and inference. Putting it another way, certain linguistic phenomena can be handled only by recourse to extralinguistic, pragmatic factors such as context, real-world knowledge and implication/inference. In order to fill the gap created by linguistic underdeterminacy, pragmatics has to be included as a component in an overall theory of linguistic ability.[2]

13.3 Two main schools of thought in pragmatics

Currently, two schools of thought in pragmatics can be identified: the Anglo-American and the (European) Continental traditions.

13.3.1 The Anglo-American school

13.3.1.1 The component view

Within the Anglo-American conception of linguistics and the philosophy of language, pragmatics may be defined as in (21).

(21)   Pragmatics is the systematic study of meaning by virtue of, or dependent on, the use of language. The central topics of inquiry include implicature, presupposition, speech acts, deixis and reference (e.g. Huang 2014).

This is known as the component view of pragmatics. On this conception, a linguistic theory consists of a number of core components: phonetics, phonology, morphology, syntax and semantics. Each of the core components has a relatively properly demarcated domain of inquiry. Pragmatics, then, is just another core component placed in the same contrast set within a linguistic theory. By contrast, other 'hyphenated' branches of linguistics such as anthropological, educational and sociolinguistics lie outside this set of core components. The component view of pragmatics is to some extent a reflection of the modular conception of the human mind, namely, the claim that the mental architecture of *homo sapiens* is divided roughly into a central processor and a number of distinctive, specialised mental systems known as modules.

13.3.1.2 Contextualism versus semantic minimalism in the philosophy of language

In recent years, there has been an ongoing, heated debate between contextualism and semantic minimalism in the Anglo-American philosophy of language and linguistics.[3] The central tenet of contextualism is that contextual variations in semantic content can be accounted for in terms of a criterion of contextual best fit. According to this view, only in the context of an utterance does a sentence express a determinate semantic content. In other words, semantics covers only part of the way towards the production and computation of utterance meaning, and it is pragmatic enrichment and inference that complete the process as a whole. Two versions of contextualism can be identified: moderate and radical. Whereas the former acknowledges limited pragmatic influence on semantic content, the latter holds the view that pragmatic processes such as free enrichment play a central role in explaining contextual variations in semantic content. Closely associated with contextualism is the position known as truth-conditional pragmatics, namely, the view that various pragmatic processes influence and determine the truth-condition of a sentence uttered (e.g. Recanati 2010). Contextualism is represented by the work of the American philosopher John Searle, the Canadian philosopher Charles Travis, the French philosopher François Recanati, relevance theory and to a lesser extent neo-Gricean pragmatics.

In opposition to contextualism, the central thesis of semantic minimalism is that context is allowed only to have a very limited or minimal effect on the semantic content of a sentence. In addition, semantic minimalism holds that semantic content is entirely determined by syntax, that context sensitivity is grammatically triggered, and that it is not the job of semantic content to capture one's intuitive judgement of what a speaker says when he or she utters a sentence. Currently, there are a number of variants of semantic minimalism. These include the British philosopher Emma Borg's minimal semantics, the Norwegian philosopher Herman Cappelen and the American philosopher Ernest Lepore's insensitive semantics, and Kent Bach's radical semantic minimalism.

Next, there is indexicalism. This is the position in the Anglo-American philosophy of language and linguistics that assumes that there is a role for the speaker's meaning to play in the determination of the truth-conditional content of a sentence, but only when a slot is set up by a sentence itself to be pragmatically filled in in its logical form. To this end, a range of 'covert' or 'hidden' indexicals is posited to provide syntactic triggers for the additional context sensitivity demanded by contextualists, thus also referred to as hidden indexicalism. Only bottom-up but not top-down pragmatic influence is allowed to affect the truth-conditional content of a sentence. This position is represented by the work of the American philosopher Jason Stanley and the American linguist Zoltan Szabo. Interestingly enough, indexicalism is considered to be a version of moderate contextualism by semantic minimalists, and a form of liberal semantic minimalism by contextualists.

Finally, we have non-indexical contextualism developed by the American philosopher John MacFarlane. Contrary to indexicalists, non-indexical contextualists are of the view that context sensitivity called for by contextualists is not caused by the semantic content or truth-condition of a sentence but by a variation in its circumstances of evaluation. For instance, a sentence like (10), *John is tall*, is context-sensitive not because it expresses different propositions in different contexts, but because the truth or falsity of its occurrences depends on the circumstances in which it is evaluated. Consequently, the truth of a sentence has to be relevant, or relativized, to parameters of evaluation, hence this approach is also relabelled *semantic relativism* (see e.g. Huang 2013, 2014 for discussion of some alternative –isms in the current debate).

13.3.1.3 Central topics in Anglo-American pragmatics

With this philosophical background in place, let me move to the central topics of inquiry of Anglo-American pragmatics.

The notion of implicature (both conversational and conventional) was put forward by the British philosopher H.P. Grice. Conversational implicature is any element of meaning implied by a speaker and inferred by an addressee which goes beyond what is said in the strict sense. It is derived from the speaker's saying of what is said by virtue of Grice's cooperative principle and its attendant maxims of conversation (e.g. Grice 1989; Levinson 2000; Huang 2014). Since its inception, the classical Gricean theory of conversational implicature has become a foundation stone of pragmatic theorizing. Furthermore, it has provided a starting point for a staggering amount of research, giving rise to *neo-Gricean pragmatics* (e.g. Levinson 2000; Horn 2009; Huang 2014), relevance theory (Sperber and Wilson 1995), novel concepts like implicture (e.g. Bach 2012) and the pragmatic enrichment of what is said (Recanati 2010), and interesting work in experimental pragmatics. In addition, classical and neo-Gricean pragmatics has been integrated with other current linguistic theories to bring about optimality-theoretic pragmatics and game- and decision-theoretic pragmatics. In contrast to conversational implicature, conventional implicature is a non-truth-conditional meaning that is not derived in any general, natural way from the saying of what is said, but arises solely from the conventional features attached to particular lexical items and/or linguistic constructions.

Presupposition is a proposition or a set of propositions whose truth is taken for granted in the utterance of a sentence. The main function of presupposition is to act as a precondition of some sort for the appropriate use of the sentence. This background assumption remains equally valid when the sentence that contains it is negated. Presupposition has long been considered a linguistic phenomenon that is balanced on the edge between semantics and pragmatics, but how much is semantics and how much is pragmatics is debatable.

The notion of speech act, introduced by the British philosopher J.L. Austin, refers to the uttering of a linguistic expression, the function of which is not just to say things but actively to do things or to perform actions as well. Speech act theory was established by Austin and after his death, refined, systematised and advanced by the American philosopher John Searle. It has since remained another cornerstone of pragmatics. Cultural and inter-language variations in speech acts have been major pursuits of cross-cultural and inter-language pragmatics (see §13.4.2). From a more formal perspective, the integration of speech acts with intentional logic has given rise to what is called illocutionary logic in formal pragmatics. Various aspects of speech act theory have also been formalised in artificial intelligence and computational pragmatics.

Deixis, or indexicality in the philosophy of language is the phenomenon whereby features of context of utterance or speech event are encoded by lexical and/or grammatical means in a language. There are three major categories of deixis: person, space and time. Person deixis is concerned with the identification of the interlocutors or participant roles in a speech event. Space deixis is the specification of location relative to that of the participants at utterance time in a speech event. Finally, time deixis is concerned with the encoding of temporal points and spans relative to the moment at which an utterance is produced in a speech event. There are also three minor categories of deixis: social, discourse and emotional. Social deixis is the codification of the social status of the speaker, the addressee, and/or a third person or entity referred to, and of the social relationships holding between them. Discourse, text or textual deixis is concerned with the use of a linguistic expression within an utterance to point to the current, preceding or following utterances in the same spoken or written discourse. Emotional deixis encodes emotional proximity or distance between the deictic centre, typically the speaker and the entity referred to.

Finally, reference is a three-place relation that involves speakers, linguistic expressions and the entities the linguistic expressions stand for in the external world or in some mental representation. In other words, referring is an act of a speaker picking out a particular entity, denoted by the linguistic expression, in the outside world. It is performed through the speaker's utterance of that linguistic expression on some particular occasion of use. Looked at this way, reference is essentially a context-dependent aspect of utterance meaning and it therefore falls within the domain of pragmatics (e.g. Huang 2014).

13.3.2 The Continental, perspective view

Within the European Continental conception of linguistics, pragmatics is taken to present a functional perspective on all core components and 'hyphenated' areas of linguistics and beyond.

(22) Pragmatics is a general functional (i.e. cognitive, social and cultural) perspective on linguistic phenomena in relation to their usage in forms of behaviour (Verschueren 1999).

This represents the perspective view of pragmatics, namely, the view that pragmatics should be taken as presenting a functional perspective on every aspect of the linguistic behaviour. More or less the same can be said of the definition of pragmatics provided within the former Soviet and Eastern European tradition, under which pragmatics (called 'pragmalinguistics') is in general conceived of as a theory of linguistic communication including how to influence people through verbal message. Consequently, within the wider Continental tradition, the empirical orbit of pragmatics has been considerably widened, encompassing not only much that goes under the rubric of non-core branches of linguistics such as sociolinguistics, psycholinguistics and discourse analysis, but also some that fall in the province of neighbouring social sciences (see e.g. Huang 2014 for a critique of this school of thought).

However, there has recently been some convergence between the Anglo-American and Continental traditions. On the one hand, important work has been done on micropragmatic topics such as implicature, speech acts and presupposition from a Continental perspective. On the other hand, research within the Anglo-American conception has been extended not only to some core topics in formal syntax such as anaphora and the lexicon in lexical pragmatics but also to certain 'hyphenated' domains of linguistics such as computational, historical and clinical linguistics, giving rise to computational, historical and clinical pragmatics (see §13.4). This is also true in relation to cognitive science – an interdisciplinary amalgam of philosophy, psychology, linguistics, anthropology, computer science, artificial intelligence and neuroscience. One case in point is relevance theory, which has taken over many insights from cognitive psychology. Another case is the recent emergence of experimental pragmatics.

Each side of the Anglo-American versus Continental divide complements and has much to learn from the other. Whereas the strength of the Anglo-American school lies mainly in theory, and philosophical, cognitive and formal pragmatics, the Continental camp has much to offer in empirical work (empirical pragmatics), socio- (or social, societal), cross- (or inter)cultural, and part of inter-language pragmatics.

13.4 Macropragmatics

I move next to what is called macropragmatics – the study of the use of language in all aspects. Current topics of inquiry in macropragmatics can roughly be divided into three groups: (1) cognitively-oriented; (2) socially- and/or culturally-oriented; and (3) those that are not easily or neatly placed in the above two groups (see Huang 2013 for references for this section).

13.4.1 Group I: cognitively-oriented macropragmatics

This category includes cognitive pragmatics, psycho- or psycholinguistic pragmatics (including both developmental and experimental pragmatics), computational pragmatics, clinical pragmatics, neuropragmatics and part of inter-language pragmatics.

Cognitive pragmatics has its roots in the emergence of modern cognitive science in the 1970s. A typical example of cognitive pragmatics is relevance theory. Grounded in a general view of human cognition, the central tenet of relevance theory is that the human cognitive system works in such a way as to tend to maximize relevance with respect to both cognition and communication. Thus, the communicative principle of relevance is responsible for the recovery of both the explicit and implicit content of an utterance. Furthermore, it is hypothesised that pragmatics, which incorporates the relevance-theoretic comprehension procedure, is a sub-module of theory of mind, that is, a variety of mind-reading. Another significant cognitive approach to pragmatics is cognitive pragmatics theory developed by the Italian cognitive scientist Bruno Bara. Cognitive pragmatics theory offers an explanation of the cognitive processes that are involved in intentional verbal and non-verbal communication. The practitioners of the theory maintain that a 'partner' (addressee) in communication establishes the communicative intention of an 'actor' (speaker) by identifying the behaviour game that the actor intends him or her to play. Pragmatic phenomena are accounted for in terms of the complexity of the inferential steps that are needed to refer an utterance to a particular behaviour game and the complexity of the underlying mental representations. Cognitive pragmatics theory has been applied to studies of developmental pragmatics in children, the comprehension of pragmatic phenomena in head-injured subjects and pragmatic decay in subjects with Alzheimer's disease. In these cases, it overlaps with clinical, neuro- and developmental pragmatics.

Psycho- or psycholinguistic pragmatics is the psycholinguistic study of aspects of language in use and mind. It is primarily concerned with the issue of how human beings acquire, store, produce and understand the use of language from the vantage point of psychology. Within psycho-pragmatics, developmental or acquisitional pragmatics studies the empirical development of pragmatic competence in children, utilising both observation and experiments. Next, deploying both psycho- and neurolinguistic methods, experimental pragmatics investigates, through carefully controlled experiments, such important pragmatic issues and theories as scalar implicature, felicity conditions on speech acts, reference, metaphor, neo-Gricean pragmatic theory and relevance theory. The term 'experimental pragmatics' has two senses. In its broad sense, it refers to any investigation through experiments of any phenomenon or issue that is considered to be pragmatic. By contrast, in its narrowest sense, the term makes reference to late 1990s and early 2000s developments in psycholinguistics, pragmatics and the psychology of reasoning that experimentally investigates a particular set of issues at the interface between pragmatics and semantics. The importance of psycho-pragmatics is that it has a crucial role to play not only in the formulation and development of pragmatic theories but also in the testing and revision of these theories.

Computational pragmatics is the systematic study of the relation between utterances and context from an explicitly computational point of view. This includes the relation between utterances and action, between utterances and discourse and between utterances and their uttering time, place and environment. Two sides to the question of how to compute the relation between linguistic and contextual aspects can be identified. On the one hand, given a linguistic expression, one needs to work out how to compute the relevant properties of context. On the other hand, in the case of language generation, the task is to construct a linguistic expression that encodes the contextual information a speaker intends to convey. Given the relevant properties of the context, one needs to work out how to compute the relevant properties of the linguistic expression. This study of the relation between linguistic and contextual aspects requires the building-up of explicit computational representations at either side of the relation. A particularly important topic of inquiry in computational pragmatics is inference. Abduction, the resolution of reference, the generation and interpretation of speech acts, and the production and comprehension of discourse structure and coherence relations have figured prominently in computational pragmatics.

Clinical pragmatics involves the application of pragmatic concepts, theories and findings to the assessment, diagnosis and treatment of pragmatic aspects of language disorders. It studies such pragmatic concepts and phenomena as Grice's cooperative principle and its attendant maxims, implicature, speech acts, inferences, context, non-literal meaning, deixis and conversation/discourse – from a clinical perspective. Pragmatic deficits have been examined in a variety of clinical groups including children and/or adults with developmental language disorder, autism spectrum disorder, learning disability, left- or right-hemisphere damage of the brain, Alzheimer's disease and schizophrenia. Insofar as most of these clinical groups are defined by an underlying neurological condition, and a large amount of research involves children, clinical pragmatics overlaps to some degree with developmental and neuropragmatics.

Neuropragmatics is a recently developed branch of pragmatics that examines the neuro-anatomical basis of language in use. It is concerned with the relationship between the human brain/mind and pragmatics. It investigates how the human brain/mind uses language, that is, how it produces and comprehends pragmatic phenomena in healthy as well as neurologically impaired language users. The majority of neuropragmatic research has focused on aspects of pragmatics in adults with identifiable clinical disorders and brain pathology. The brain-damaged populations include patients with left- and right-hemisphere damage, traumatic brain injury, neurodegenerative disorders like Parkinson's disease and dementia and schizophrenia. This field of inquiry overlaps in particular with clinical and experimental pragmatics.

Finally, I come to inter-language pragmatics, which lies at the interface between pragmatics and second language acquisition. It studies how non-native speakers of a language acquire and develop their ability to understand and produce pragmatic features in a second language, i.e. an inter-language. The sub-branch of inter-language pragmatics that investigates the acquisition and development of pragmatic competence in children is called 'developmental inter-language pragmatics'.

13.4.2 Group II: socially- and/or culturally-oriented macropragmatics

In the preceding section, I surveyed a number of branches of cognitively-oriented macropragmatics; in this section, I turn to the second group of branches of macropragmatics. This group includes mainly socio- (or societal) pragmatics, cultural, cross- (or inter)cultural pragmatics, and part of inter-language pragmatics. Institutional, interpersonal, postcolonial, and variational pragmatics and conversation analysis (CA) also belong to this category.

Sitting at the interface between sociolinguistics and pragmatics, socio- (or societal) pragmatics studies the use of language in relation to society. One topic that has long been the focus of sociopragmatic research is politeness. Politeness, broadly defined so as to encompass both polite friendliness and polite formality, is concerned with any behaviour including verbal behaviour of an interlocutor to constitute and maintain his or her own 'face' and that of the people he or she is interacting with. Defined in this way, politeness functions as a precondition of human communication (see Chapter 14). Since its publication in 1978, the American linguist Penelope Brown and the British linguist Stephen Levinson's now classic 'face-saving' theory has generated a huge amount of research on politeness. On the other hand, interest in impoliteness has only surged recently, with 1998 being dubbed 'the Year of Impoliteness'. By impoliteness is meant any face-aggravating behaviour relevant to a particular context. For some scholars, impoliteness has to be intentional (on the part of the speaker) and has to be perceived or constructed as intentional (on the part of the addressee). For others, intentions play no part in impoliteness. If intentions and recognition of intentions are involved, then rudeness rather than impoliteness occurs. In the British linguist Jonathan Culpeper's work (2011), impoliteness has been classified into three types: (1) affective; (2) coercive; and (3) entertaining. Other topics that have attracted attention in sociopragmatics include social deixis, social conventions on the performance of speech acts and social factors which constrain language in use such as the overriding of conversational implicature by the Malagasy taboo on exact identification. From a macro point of view, the hand of societal pragmatics can be detected in any area that pertains in any way to society, dealing with topics as diverse as language in education, pragmatics and social struggle and what is called critical pragmatics. Critical pragmatics refers to the work done in sociopragmatics that follows the tradition of critical linguistics, in particular critical discourse analysis. Like in critical discourse analysis, in critical pragmatics, great emphasis is put on the relationship between language and social power and between language and ideology.

Institutional pragmatics refers to an area of research in pragmatics which investigates the use of language in social institutions and institutionalised contexts such as courtroom interaction, job interviews and police interrogation.

Cultural pragmatics, sometimes also known as anthropological or ethnographic pragmatics, is the systematic study of language use and its place in the functioning of human communities and institutions from a cultural or anthropological view, especially but not exclusively focusing on non-Western cultures. It overlaps with the ethnography of communication and ethnography of speaking. A particular variety of cultural pragmatics is ethnopragmatics. Ethnopragmatics is an approach to language in use that is semantically grounded in natural semantic metalanguage developed by the Australian linguist Anna Wierzbicka and her colleagues. It endeavours to find out more about speech practices and language use of particular, local cultures, contextualised and understood in terms of the beliefs, norms and values of speakers themselves.

Somewhat similar to ethnopragmatics is ethnographic pragmatics defined in its narrowest sense. It refers to the ethnographically-oriented approach to context-sensitive language use associated particularly with the work of Michael Silverstein and his students. Research conducted in ethnographic pragmatics has concentrated on non-Western cultures, societies and languages.

A third variety of cultural pragmatics is emancipatory pragmatics. A recently emerged research framework, emancipatory pragmatics attempts to free the study of language in use from the confines of the theoretical and methodological orthodoxies grounded in the dominant thought and practice derived from Anglo-American and European languages and ways of speaking, with the attendant premises of individualism, rationality and market economy, thus the term 'emancipatory'. The focus of emancipatory pragmatics is also placed on non-Western languages and ways of speaking and on describing a language and/or culture strictly in its own terms.

Somewhat overlapping with socio- and cultural pragmatics is interpersonal pragmatics. Interpersonal pragmatics is a research arena that concentrates on the interpersonal and relational aspects of language in use, especially of how interlocutors utilise language to establish and maintain social relations, and how interactions between interlocutors both affect and are affected by their own and others' understanding of culture, society, etc.

Cross- (or inter)cultural pragmatics is the systematic study of the use of language across different cultures and languages. Since the 1980s, a principal concern of cross-cultural pragmatics has been the issue of how particular kinds of speech acts, especially such face-threatening acts (FTAs) as requests, apologies and complaints, are realised across different cultures and languages. One of the most influential investigations is the large-scale Cross-Cultural Speech Act Realization Patterns Project carried out in the 1980s. In this project, the realisation patterns of requesting and apologizing in a number of languages were compared and contrasted. Since then, strategies for the performance of a variety of FTAs in a much wider range of languages have been examined. As a result of these studies, it has now been established that there is indeed extensive cross-cultural/linguistic variation in directness/indirectness in the expression of speech acts, especially in FTAs, and that these differences are generally associated with the different means that different languages utilise to realise speech acts. These findings have undoubtedly contributed to our greater understanding of cross-cultural/linguistic similarities and differences in face-redressive strategies for FTAs. A sub-branch of cross- or intercultural pragmatics is postcolonial pragmatics, which studies the use of language of the colonisers in a postcolonial society. In a postcolonial society, a second (as opposed to a foreign) language is sometimes used in interaction, as in the use of English in contemporary India.

Another recently emerged branch of pragmatics that has a close affinity with socio- and cross- or intercultural pragmatics is variational pragmatics. It aims to study and determine the influence or impact of macro-social factors such as region, social class, ethnicity, gender and age and the interplay of these factors on language use, especially pragmatic variation, in interaction. Construed thus, variational pragmatics also represents a research domain at the intersection of pragmatics and sociolinguistics, in particular dialectology.

The exploration of speech acts has been extended to inter-language pragmatics. Of these studies, some have investigated how a particular type of speech act is performed by non-native speakers in a given inter-language; others have compared and contrasted the similarities and differences in the realisation patterns of given speech acts between native and non-native speakers in a particular (inter)language.

Finally, mention should be made of conversation analysis (CA), sometimes also called conversational pragmatics. Since Levinson's work in the early 1980s, CA has become a branch of macropragmatics. Grown out of a breakaway group of sociologists known as ethnomethodologists within microsociology, CA represents an empirical, procedural and inductive approach to the analysis of (audio and/or video recordings of) naturally occurring, spontaneous conversations. It is concerned with the discovery and description of the methods and procedures that participants employ systematically to display their understanding of the structure of naturally occurring, spontaneous 'talks in (face-to-face) interaction'. In conversation, there are rules governing sequential organisation such as the turn-taking system, the formulation of adjacency pairs and the mechanism for opening or closing a conversation. There are also norms regulating participation in a conversation such as those for how to hold the 'floor', how to interrupt and how to remain silent. Other interesting structural devices of conversation include the preference organisation, the pre-sequence system and the repair mechanism. Given that conversation is the most important spoken manifestation of language, CA has to be closely linked to prosodic pragmatics – a study of how prosody-like intonation can affect the interpretation of a variety of linguistic phenomena in relation to context. Furthermore, since rules, norms and regulations for conversational interaction may vary from culture to culture, society to society, and language to language, CA may overlap with the ethnography of speaking and cross-cultural pragmatics.

13.4.3 Group III

This group contains branches and research areas of macropragmatics that are not easily and/or neatly placed in the above two categories.

Historical pragmatics is a branch of macropragmatics that came to light in the 1990s. It is concerned with the investigation of language change between two given points in time in individual languages and in language generally from a pragmatic perspective. There are two main research trends that correspond roughly to the distinction between 'external' and 'internal' language change. The first, 'external' research strand is called pragmaphilology. Pragmaphilology represents primarily a 'macro-approach' to the study of the pragmatics of historical texts at a particular point of time. The focus is on the wider changing social and cognitive contexts of the texts in which pragmatic change occurs. The second, 'internal' research trend is diachronic pragmatics in its narrow sense. Diachronic pragmatics in this sense represents a 'micro-approach' to change in pragmatic phenomena over time, concentrating on the interface between a linguistic structure and its communicative use across different historical stages of the same language. Since the boundary between pragmaphilology and diachronic pragmatics is not clear-cut, an intermediate category, dubbed diachronic pragmaphilology, has also been proposed.

Next, historical sociopragmatics involves the interaction between historical pragmatics and sociopragmatics. According to some scholars, historical sociopragmatics is more closely related to the pragmaphilology research trend in historical pragmatics. It constitutes a systematic study of interaction between aspects of social context and particular historical language uses that engender pragmatic meaning. Historical sociopragmatics can be either synchronic or diachronic. Synchronic historical sociopragmatics studies how language use shapes and is shaped by social context at a certain moment of time in the past. By contrast, diachronic historical sociopragmatics traces how changes in language use shape social context, changes in social context shape language use and/or changes take place in the relationship between language use and social context.

The term 'applied pragmatics' has two senses. In its broadest sense, applied pragmatics makes reference to any application of the concepts and findings of theoretical pragmatics to practical tasks such as the diagnosis, assessment and treatment of pragmatic disorders, human–computer interaction and the teaching and learning of a second and/or foreign language. In the last connection, the field is often called second and foreign language (L2) pragmatics. 'Second and foreign language pragmatics' is a term that is interchangeable with applied pragmatics in its narrowest sense. It is part of instructional pragmatics, namely, pragmatics that is concerned with how to teach and learn pragmatics in language, especially second and/or foreign language, instruction.

A corpus is a systematic collection of naturally occurring spoken or written language or a variety of such a language, which can be searchable online (see Chapter 32). When it is accessible on a computer, it is called computer corpus or corpora. By corpus pragmatics is meant the investigation of language use on the basis of the analysis of corpora. Corpus pragmatics forms part of empirical pragmatics. It can be divided into two types: (1) corpus-based; and (2) corpus-driven. In the former, researchers approach the corpora with a set of assumptions and expected findings. By comparison, the latter investigates linguistic forms and pragmatic functions that emerge from the corpora in order to discover things that have not been recognised. Much of the current research in corpus pragmatics is corpus-based rather than corpus-driven. From a methodological point of view, corpus pragmatics can be either form-based (that is, it takes a linguistic structure as its starting point and examines the range of pragmatic functions the form serves in a corpus) or function-based (that is, it takes a particular pragmatic function as a point of departure and studies how such a function is actually realised linguistically). Finally, corpus-based research in pragmatics can be either qualitative (treating corpora primarily as a source of natural data) or quantitative (studying patterns of frequency, distribution and collocation using statistical techniques).

Literary pragmatics can be best described as covering an area of research rather than a well-defined unified theory. It represents a domain at the intersection of pragmatics, literary theory and the philosophy of literature. It is the study of the use of linguistic forms in a literary text and the relationship between author, text and reader in a socio-cultural context from a pragmatic perspective, focusing on the question of what and how a literary text communicates. Two complementary aspects of literary pragmatics can be identified. On the one hand, how can the insights of pragmatic theories be employed for the study of literature, and on the other hand, how can the insights of literary pragmatics contribute to general pragmatic theories? Literary pragmatics can further be divided into two sub-branches: formalist and historical. Formalist literary pragmatics seeks to characterise literariness in terms of the pragmatic properties of literary texts, concentrating on formal analyses which are based on formal systems or pragmatic processes. In contrast with formalist literary pragmatics is historical literary pragmatics. Interdisciplinary in nature, historical literary pragmatics places an emphasis on the interconnections between literary studies, history studies, socio-cultural studies and pragmatic studies. Next, somewhat related to literary pragmatics is pragmatic stylistics or pragmastylistics. Pragmatic stylistics refers to the application of the findings and methodologies of theoretical pragmatics to the study of the concept of style in language, that is, systematic variations in usage in written or spoken language including those in literary texts among individual writers, genres and periods.

Originating in part from the work of Austin, legal pragmatics is concerned mainly with the study of legal documents and spoken legal discourse in the courtroom from a pragmatic point of view. Pragmatic features in written legal texts and spoken legal discourses that have been analysed include speech acts such as legal performatives, presuppositions, turn-taking, question–answer adjacency pairs and silence. The sociopragmatic concepts of power and politeness/impoliteness have also been used in these studies.

Finally, feminist pragmatics represents an approach to the study of gender and language in use, incorporating insights from both feminism and pragmatics. Within this approach, it is assumed that on the one hand, if pragmatics is to provide a theoretical framework for the investigation of gender and use of language, it has to be informed by the findings of feminist scholarship. On the other hand, pragmatics can inform feminist research on gender and use of language in a wide range of contexts.

13.5 Some future trends and directions

Having reviewed various branches in macropragmatics, let me finally point to a number of likely trends and directions for the future development of pragmatic research. Given the space at my disposal, I shall limit my discussion to two topics: (1) Anglo-American pragmatics; and (2) experimental pragmatics.

13.5.1 Anglo-American pragmatics

In Anglo-American pragmatics, the linguistic underdeterminacy thesis, mentioned in §13.2.3, has been widely accepted. For example, the three uses of the deictic/indexical *you* in (3) can be properly interpreted only if they are accompanied by physical behaviour of some sort (such as a selecting gesture or an eye contact), which requires an extralinguistic, physical context. Since the mid-1970s, context sensitivity caused by indexicality and other linguistic phenomena such as ambiguity, vagueness and ellipsis has been accounted for in terms of indexical semantics (cf. Bach's concept of narrow context). But there is context sensitivity of a different kind. This type of context sensitivity is illustrated by sentences such as (4) and (8) above and (23) below.

(23) Susan has got absolutely nothing [appropriate] to wear [for this evening's gala concert].

Though devoid of indexicality etc. the proposition expressed by each of the three sentences without the bracketed part still needs to be contextually enriched (that is, to the proposition with the bracketed constituent) so that an appropriate truth-value can be assigned to it. In recent years, context sensitivity of the second type has generated a heated debate among both philosophers of language and linguistic semanticists and pragmaticists. The focus of the debate is this: given that context does affect the truth-conditional content of a sentence uttered, should contextual effects be explained in semantic or pragmatic terms? The issues involved include (1) whether or not there is any UC, (2) whether or not there is pragmatic intrusion, namely, the pragmatically enriched content encroaches on the truth-conditional content of a sentence uttered, (3) how the semantic content of UCs is pragmatically recovered, (4) what is the pragmatical enrichment involved in the recovery of UCs or in the process of pragmatic intrusion: is it an explicature (e.g. Sperber and Wilson 1995), the pragmatic enrichment of what is said (e.g. Recanati 2010), impliciture (e.g. Bach 2012) or conversational implicature (e.g. Levinson 2000; Huang 2014), and (5) what is the best way to carve out the respective territories of semantics and pragmatics. For these issues, contextualism, semantic minimalism, indexicalism, non-indexical contextualism, relevance theory and neo-Gricean pragmatics have all put forward different proposals and tests. Together with the classical Gricean distinction between what is said and what is implicated, these questions of context sensitivity and (covert) assignment of semantic content to a sentence uttered will continue to figure prominently in Anglo-American pragmatics well into the 2020s.

13.5.2 Experimental pragmatics

As already mentioned, experimental pragmatics in its narrowest sense was developed in the late 1990s and early 2000s. The research was largely concerned with the comprehension of conversational implicatures, especially generalized conversational implicatures (GCIs), with a rather narrow focus on scalar implicatures (SIs). There have been three competing views of GCIs in general and SIs in particular. One is that SIs convey default meaning sans a conscious inferential process irrespective of a particular context of use. This is called the default inference theory (e.g. Levinson 2000). Another, relevance-theoretic position is that they are essentially inferred contextually (e.g. Sperber and Wilson 1995). This is labelled the contextual inference theory. In addition, a third view holds that the derivation of SIs depends heavily on structural/grammatical factors. This is known as the structural inference theory (Chierchia 2013). All the three theoretical models have been subject to tests in experimental pragmatics. While much of the relevance-theoretically oriented experimental work favours the contextual inference approach, there is also evidence in support of the default inference theory and the structural inference model.

More recently, the scope of work in experimental pragmatics has been considerably widened. For instance the experimental testing of so-called 'embedded (conversational) implicature', a seemingly conversational implicature that is engendered locally at a sub-sentential level, typically occurring in a clause that is embedded under a logical operator such as a propositional attitude verb, a conditional and a comparative, as in (24), where the implicature trigger *some* is embedded under *believe*.

(24)   Mr Gao believes that some of his parents' friends were persecuted during Mao's 'Cultural Revolution' in China.

Currently, there are two main approaches to embedded implicature: grammatical and pragmatic. Within the first, grammatical camp, there are two varieties: lexicalist and syntax-based/driven conventionalism. The central idea underlying both versions of conventionalism is that an embedded implicature is part of the lexico-grammatical content of a sentence. With regard to lexicalist conventionalism, an embedded implicature is hard-wired into the lexical entries of an implicature trigger. Next, according to the syntax-based conventionalism, the grammar of a language is equipped with a covert or hidden exhaustivity syntactic operator akin to 'only', which can be freely inserted into the tree diagram of a sentence. Going next to the pragmatic approach, one way is to defend the classic/neo-Gricean globalist account of conversational implicature. Another is a truth-conditional pragmatic analysis developed by Recanati. Under this approach, an embedded implicature is explained in terms of a primary pragmatic process of modulation, and free enrichment in particular. Whereas some experimental works confirm indirectly the Gricean globalist view, others do not (e.g. Huang 2014). My prediction is that, until the mid-2020s, experimental pragmatics will continue to be a burgeoning subfield of pragmatic research. Devising more refined experiments and generating more accurate results, it will continue to branch out, covering a much broader range of research topics and areas in pragmatics.

Notes

1. Part of the material contained in this chapter is drawn from Huang (2013).
2. Another reason for inclusion of pragmatics is that it can effect a radical simplification of semantics and syntax in an overall theory of linguistic ability (e.g. Huang 2014).
3. This debate can be traced back at least to the differences between philosophers in the tradition of ideal language philosophy such as Gottlob Frege, Alfred Tarski, Bertrand Russell, the early Ludwig Wittgenstein and Rudolf Carnap and philosophers in the camp of ordinary or natural language philosophy like J.L. Austin, H.P. Grice, Peter Strawson, the later Ludwig Wittgenstein and John Searle (e.g. Huang 2014).

Further reading

Allan and Jaszczolt (2012); Bublitz and Norrick (2011); Cummings (2010); Horn and Ward (2004); Huang (forthcoming); Noveck and Sperber (2004); Preyer and Peter (2005, 2007).

References

Allan, K. and K.M. Jaszczolt (eds) (2012) *The Cambridge Handbook of Pragmatics*. Cambridge: Cambridge University Press.
Bach, K. (2012) Context dependence. In M. Garcia-Carpintero and M. Kölbel (eds) *The Continuum Companion to the Philosophy of Language*, pp. 153–84. London: Continuum.
Brown, P. and S.C. Levinson (1978) Universals in language usage: Politeness phenomena. In E.N. Goody (ed.) *Questions and Politeness: Strategies in Social Interaction*, pp. 56–289. Cambridge: Cambridge University Press.
Bublitz, W. and N. Norrick (eds) (2011) *Foundations of Pragmatics*. Berlin: De Gruyter Mouton.
Chierchia, G. (2013) *Logic in Grammar*. Oxford: Oxford University Press.
Culpeper, J. (2011) *Impoliteness: Using Language to Cause Offence*. Cambridge: Cambridge University Press.
Cummings, L. (ed.) (2010) *The Pragmatics Encyclopaedia*. Abingdon: Routledge.
Grice, H.P. (1989) *Studies in the Way of Words*. Cambridge: Harvard University Press.
Horn, L.R. (2009) WJ-40: Implicature, truth, and meaning. *International Review of Pragmatics* 1: 3–34.
Horn, L.R. and G. Ward (eds) (2004) *The Handbook of Pragmatics*. Oxford: Blackwell.
Huang, Y. (2013) Micro- and macro-pragmatics: Remapping their terrains. *International Review of Pragmatics* 5: 129–62.
Huang, Y. (2014) *Pragmatics*, 2nd edition. Oxford: Oxford University Press [1st edition 2007].
Huang, Y. (ed.) (forthcoming) *The Oxford Handbook of Pragmatics*. Oxford: Oxford University Press.
Levinson, S.C. (2000) *Presumptive Meanings: The Theory of Generalized Conversational Implicature*. Cambridge: MIT Press.
Noveck, I.A. and D. Sperber (eds) (2004) *Experimental Pragmatics*. New York: Palgrave Macmillan.
Preyer, G. and G. Peter (eds) (2005) *Contextualism in Philosophy*. Oxford: Oxford University Press.
Preyer, G. and G. Peter (eds) (2007) *Context-Sensitivity and Semantic Minimalism: New Essays on Semantics and Pragmatics*. Oxford: Oxford University Press.
Recanati, F. (2010) *Truth-Conditional Pragmatics*. Oxford: Oxford University Press.
Sperber, D. and D. Wilson (1995) *Relevance: Communication and Cognition*, 2nd edition. Oxford: Blackwell.
Verschueren, J. (1999) *Understanding Pragmatics*. London: Arnold.

14
The linguistics of politeness and social relations

Marina Terkourafi

14.1 Introduction

It is with renewed appreciation for the size of the task that I come to writing the present chapter. The number of special issues of journals dedicated to im/politeness these days comes to two or three per year, while in the last four years alone, articles pertaining to im/politeness have appeared in journals as diverse as *Administrative Science Quarterly*, *International Journal of Human–Computer Studies*, *Journal of Business Ethics*, *Journal of Cognitive Neuroscience*, *Journal of Language and Social Psychology*, *Journal of Pragmatics*, *Patient Education and Counseling*, *Research on Language and Social Interaction* and *The International Journal of Press/Politics*, to mention but a few – not to forget the dedicated *Journal of Politeness Research*, which celebrates its tenth anniversary in 2015. In the *Journal of Pragmatics* alone, the number of articles tackling im/politeness in the same time span comes to over 200 (that is, over four times per issue), while the number of publications that cite Brown and Levinson's seminal essay on the topic numbers over 20,000 in the first half of 2014, according to Google Scholar. I could go on... You get the picture: im/politeness is hot! And, like all things hot, it must be handled with care. Yet, proceed we must, lest this topic of growing importance to linguists (and many others besides) remains unspoken for in the definitive handbook in the field.

The difficulties facing the scholar of im/politeness these days do not stop with the explosion in the number of publications mentioned above. The proliferation of theoretical frameworks and new terminology make navigating the field a highly perilous affair. Adding to the mix of combat metaphors, im/politeness research is also being bombarded by a plethora of new data obtained by means of novel methodologies (most recently, online experimental ones, such as reaction times, eye-tracking and Event Related Potentials or ERPs) faster than it can account for them and assess their significance for the theoretical frameworks at play.

At this point, a newcomer to the field might ask: Why all the fuss? To what do im/politeness studies owe their renewed appeal? In fact, the question could be reversed: why, one might ask, has it taken so long for linguists and others studying the social dynamics of language to take an active interest in how people relate to each other through language? My tentative answer to this second question may seem baffling at first. Brown and Levinson's (1978/1987) seminal essay, which more or less single-handedly established the field nearly forty years ago, also apparently provided all the answers, leaving little to be added by future researchers – or so it seemed, until critiques of their work started proliferating in the 1990s, peaking in the early 2000s. When the foundational work in a field is so accomplished as to remain the point of reference relative to which all subsequent theories position themselves (cf. Leech 2014), and whence theorists outside the field begin their investigations, it should come as no surprise that academic debate is slow to take off. Im/politeness studies are, however, making up for it quite impressively.

14.2 Brown and Levinson's framework and critiques thereof

In a nutshell, Brown and Levinson's idea was this: people are not just information-processing beings. They also have social needs (or wants), what Brown and Levinson, following Goffman (1967), called 'face' – and this makes a difference to how they talk. Specifically, it pushes them to adjust what they say in order to secure both others' admiration and approval ('positive face') and their own autonomy and independence ('negative face'). Some speech acts (requests, offers, apologies, complaints, compliments and many more) intrinsically threaten (the speaker's or the hearer's, positive or negative) face. To get their point across and at the same time remain on good terms with their addressees when performing one of these acts, speakers must phrase it in such a way as to avoid face-threat. What this means is that (rational) speakers select from several options, hierarchically ordered, a strategy that is analogous to the level of face-threat that the act carries. The level of face-threat – or Weightiness (W) of the Face-Threatening Act (FTA) x – is in turn determined by three sociological variables, which depend on the relationship between the interlocutors and on the culture at hand. Distance (D) is a measure of how close the interlocutors are to each other and depends on how much they are alike as well as how well they know each other; it is a symmetric relationship, meaning that it is the same whether measured from the perspective of the speaker (S) or from that of the hearer (H). Power (P), on the other hand, is a measure of the degree of (physical, emotional or social) control that the hearer has over the speaker and is an asymmetric relationship, meaning that, if the hearer has power over the speaker, then the speaker is powerless with respect to the hearer. Finally, Ranking (R) is a measure of the effort needed to comply with different acts. These three variables, compounded in the formula in (1), guide speakers' selections from among five different sets of strategies that essentially reflect increasing degrees of indirectness (see Figure 14.1).

(1) $W_x = D(S,H) + P(H,S) + R_x$

The five sets of strategies range from 'bald on record' for acts of minimal Weightiness (e.g. mundane invitations such as *Come in*), through 'positive politeness' (strategies that make the addressee feel good, e.g. using endearment terms such as *honey* or *sweetie*), 'negative politeness' (strategies that respect the speaker's or the addressee's private space, such as asking about the other's abilities or wishes rather than presuming to know what they are) and 'off record' (strategies that do not directly state the FTA), to 'don't do the FTA' for acts of the greatest Weightiness. The underlying assumption is that personal space and freedom of action are more important than group belonging; therefore, as the stakes get higher, strategies that safeguard the former (negative politeness, off-record) are preferred.

The linguistics of politeness

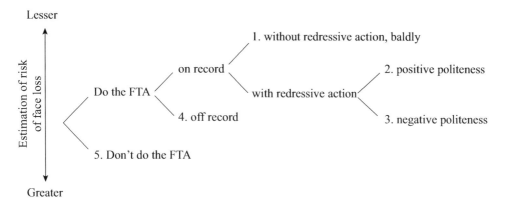

Figure 14.1 Strategies for doing FTAs (source: Brown and Levinson 1987: 69)

To see how this works out in practice, consider how the same speech act may be phrased in different ways that reflect the social dynamics between speaker and hearer. Take a request to hurry up. Addressed to one's child while preparing to go to school in the morning (low D, low P,[1] low R), it may be phrased directly as a bare imperative: *Hurry up!* (baldly on record). Exchanged between spouses getting ready to go out at night (where P is presumably a bit more evenly distributed), something like *Will you hurry up, honey?* (positive politeness) might be more appropriate. Addressed to a colleague at work (a relationship of greater D compared to the last two), the same request might come out more like *Um, I don't mean to rush you but do you think you could hurry up a bit?* (negative politeness). Addressed to one's boss, on the other hand (this time both D and P should be greater), one might refrain from stating the act requested and merely hint at it: *I think we might be late* (off-record). Finally, addressed to someone many times removed from the speaker (e.g. the head of the organization where one works), one may choose not to perform the act at all (i.e. silence).

Before carrying on with a broader assessment of Brown and Levinson's proposals, a couple of issues with regard to this illustration ought to be noted. First, it is meant to reflect both the speaker's selection of an appropriate strategy and the hearer's interpretation of it; in other words, it is meant to be a model of both language production and language comprehension. In the case of the speaker, she will start out with certain assumptions about the values of D, P and R and select a strategy based on those – moving from the formula in (1) to the strategies in Figure 14.1. In the case of the hearer, he will work his way back from the actual utterance produced by the speaker to Wx, i.e. the sum of the assumed values of D, P and R,[2] moving in the opposite direction, from the strategies in Figure 14.1 to the formula in (1). If he agrees with the speaker's overall assessment of Wx, politeness will have been served.

It is possible, however, that the speaker's and hearer's ways of assessing D, P and R might diverge. Brown and Levinson highlight, in this respect, the existence of 'positive politeness cultures,' 'cultures [where] the general level of Wx tends to remain low' such as 'the Western USA, some New Guinea cultures and the Mbuti pygmies,' and 'negative politeness cultures,' 'those lands of standoffish creatures like the British (in the eyes of the Americans), the Japanese (in the eyes of the British), the Malagasy [...], and the Brahmans of India' (1987: 245). While Brown and Levinson do not explicitly say this, it is to be expected that interlocutors from different cultures may end up with different assessments of D, P and R and some amount of awareness of the other's culture and of perspective-taking may be necessary to avoid politeness misunderstandings in this case.

223

While differences in D, P and R assessments due to cultural differences may be handled in this way, the model has little to say about fluctuations in D, P and R values due to more subjective factors, such as the degree of mutual sympathy or 'liking' between interlocutors (but see Slugoski and Turnbull 1988), or the speaker's (or, for that matter, the addressee's) emotional state (but see Vergis and Terkourafi, forthcoming). The fact that additional factors such as these can affect politeness assessments has been used to challenge the adequacy of Brown and Levinson's three sociological variables to capture all of the factors relevant to politeness assessments and to account for situated politeness assessments in actual data.

A second point that complicates the application of their model to actual data is the fact that there is no such thing as the *same* speech act: a request to one's child to hurry up in order to get to school on time may be said to be ultimately to the benefit of the child, making it quite different from a more self-interested request to one's spouse to hurry up in order to have dinner with one's colleagues – while, of course, even the aforementioned request to one's child may be (simultaneously) motivated by self-interest, if the parent is also trying to get to work on time. In other words, R changes depending on the specifics of each situation, not least who is talking to whom, such that Rx is not, in the end, independent of the values of D and P, despite Brown and Levinson's (1987: 80–1) assertions to the contrary. Nor are D and P independent of each other (Holtgraves and Yang 1990: 725; Watts *et al.* 1992: 9; Tannen and Kakava 1992: 13): sometimes, the lower the distance (D) between interlocutors, the higher the amount of control one has over the other (P); suffice it to think of two people in an intimate relationship to see that this is the case.

Despite these difficulties in applying it to real data, Brown and Levinson's model has been extremely influential, establishing notions such as face, positive politeness and negative politeness as terms of art and setting the agenda that dominates the field to this day. This is no doubt due both to its comprehensiveness, covering a wide spectrum of linguistic choices, as well as its presenting us with a coherent set of predictions that may be tested out on empirical data. Yet, for all its merits, their model has also been widely criticized on a number of counts.

To begin with, critics have rejected the authors' definition of face as individual wants, pointing out that in Goffman's own definition, face is a much more dynamic notion that is '*diffusely* located in the flow of events in the encounter' (1967: 7; emphasis added) and '*on loan* from society' (1967: 10; emphasis added). In contrast, Brown and Levinson's talk of intrinsic FTAs makes it sound as if face concerns only kick in when one is about to perform one of those acts. However, it is now well documented that even the interpretation of such seemingly innocuous items as *some* and *if* can be influenced by face concerns. In a series of experiments, Bonnefon and colleagues (2015) showed that whether listeners take *some* to mean 'some but not all' or 'some and possibly all' depends on whether the information purveyed is flattering, beneficial, or otherwise welcome to the addressee. The less that is the case, the more the speaker's use of *some* is likely to be interpreted as a face-saving device designed to spare the addressee from being told the bad news (the stronger statement *all*) right in their face. This experimental work puts some empirical flesh on what researchers in intercultural communication have been claiming for some time, namely that 'there is no *faceless* communication' (Scollon and Scollon 1995: 38). In other words, even when not openly engaging in facework (by, e.g. saying *please* and *thank you*), interactants' use of language always has consequences for face – an observation that can be used to motivate the much coveted distinction between Politeness 1 and Politeness 2 (about which more later).

Returning to Brown and Levinson, their definition of face as 'the public self-image that every member wants to claim for himself' (1987: 61) has been taken to mean that face is an individual possession that can be projected outwards, whereas in fact face does not reside in individual speakers but rather in speaker–addressee pairs (it is 'relational') and it emerges in interaction between them (it is 'emergent'; cf. Arundale 2006; Terkourafi 2007). This last point is particularly important, if we are to break free from the notion that individuals are independently endowed with face, which they bring with them into their interactions with others. Exclusive talk of Face-Threatening Acts by Brown and Levinson suggests that individuals have only to lose by engaging in interaction, making the 'lone wolf' option sound more appealing than the alternative (call it the 'social butterfly'). While that is in line with the authors' prioritizing negative over positive face, and correspondingly ranking negative politeness strategies above positive politeness ones (i.e. reserved for more serious FTAs), it falls short of explaining how face comes into existence in the first place or the fact that it can also be routinely enhanced. Yet, there is plenty of evidence for both. For instance, Barros-García (forthcoming) discusses the (Peninsular) Spanish propensity to pepper conversation among friends with compliments, so much so that these routine compliments are not responded to or even noticed (although their absence would be). This suggests that, rather than being felt to be face-threatening (as in Brown and Levinson's framework, 1987: 66), these routine compliments are part of Spanish interlocutors' normal way of speaking, a culturally and situationally expected mode of interaction which, without consciously aiming to constitute face, does precisely that – as evidenced by the fact that it is the *omission* of these acts, rather than their performance, that would potentially damage face (by failing to bring it into existence). In this sense, Barros-García's research also documents the existence of Face-Enhancing Acts (also termed Face-Boosting or Face-Anointing Acts), that is, acts whose performance is not intended to remedy a potential face-threat but rather manifests gratuitous politeness – a verbal offering which lubricates the wheels of sociality without, for that matter, having always been made necessary by a prior transgression.[3]

Making matters more complicated still, one aspect of face may be threatened while the other is simultaneously enhanced. For instance, when a young mother asks someone to look after her baby briefly, she imposes on the addressee (threatens his/her negative face) by limiting his/her freedom of action. Yet at the same time she flatters them (enhances his/her positive face) by entrusting them with such a delicate task (cf. Turner 1996: 4–5). It can therefore be misleading to speak of intrinsic FTAs to *an* aspect of the addressee's *or* the speaker's face: both aspects of face and both interlocutors' faces can be implicated at the same time.

Coming to how linguistic strategies relate to social variables, and more specifically to Brown and Levinson's prediction that the degree of politeness is proportionate to, among others, the Distance between interlocutors, the most forceful refutation of this claim lies perhaps in the findings of Wolfson (1988), which she summarized under the term the 'bulge' phenomenon. The bulge phenomenon refers to the fact that the most negotiation appears to take place between acquaintances, who are about half-way along the Distance axis, while the least negotiation is to be found between intimates and strangers alike, who occupy its extremes. While that makes sense, considering that with intimates and strangers possibilities of future interaction are mostly pre-set such that there is little point in investing extra effort trying to change that, it is contrary to the prediction of Brown and Levinson that the most politeness should be found among those who know each other the least (high D).

More generally, the association of politeness with indirectness in their model has been the object of intense scrutiny. Blum-Kulka (1987) was perhaps the first to point out that the amount of inferential work required to extract politeness from the speaker's utterance may constitute an imposition on the hearer's cognitive resources in its own right, counteracting the degree of politeness communicated by more indirect utterances. Using evidence from Hebrew and English, she argued that politeness lies in achieving a balance between coerciveness and clarity, such that tipping the balance in either of these directions can result in impoliteness; in other words, being too indirect (using off-record indirectness) can be as impolite as being too direct – albeit for different reasons. This balance (politeness) is best achieved by on-record or conventional indirectness (negative politeness), which thus emerged as the polite mode *par excellence*. This finding has since been replicated in a number of experimental studies, most notably by Holtgraves and Yang (1990), who found that hints (off-record indirectness) were not unequivocally polite for the American and Korean speakers they tested – but also in a number of observational ones (e.g. Márquez Reiter 2000; Terkourafi 2001), who noted the prevalence of conventional indirectness over other modes of polite behavior in a variety of languages. Most recently, Culpeper (2011: 186–93) found that conventional indirectness is the least likely to tip over into impoliteness, even when used in an inappropriate context. In a series of experiments asking subjects to rate the impoliteness of various commands – direct, conventionally indirect and non-conventionally indirect – in both high to low (e.g. a superior talking to a subordinate) and low to high power conditions, he and a colleague found that subjects resisted the idea that conventional indirectness could be impolite, at least more so than was the case for the other two strategies. Similar results obtained in a number of studies suggest that previous research may have overstated the association of politeness with indirectness and that it is the relationship between politeness and conventionalization that merits a closer look. Before proceeding to do just that, we turn first to some more recent developments in the area of im/politeness research.

14.3 Recent developments in im/politeness research

One of the most important steps forward in im/politeness research since the mid-1990s has been to point out that the meaning of the term 'politeness' itself cannot be taken for granted. Rather, there are at least two ways of defining it and, depending on which one we choose, we are likely to end up with different sets of phenomena to explain and different ways of explaining them. On the one hand, politeness can take its meaning from the everyday word 'polite' as it is routinely used to single out and explicitly characterize particular types of behavior. Politeness in this sense is the stuff of etiquette books and advice columns. There we read, for example, that it is 'polite' to say *please* and *thank you*, and to let ladies go first. This understanding of politeness has been called first-order politeness or Politeness 1, for short.

Clearly, definitions of Politeness 1 vary widely across time and space. For instance, in China it is traditionally considered polite to refuse an invitation three times before accepting it; it is also considered polite to burp in appreciation of a meal. Both behaviors would be met with quite different interpretations in a US context. Similarly, smiling is a sign of politeness and conviviality among Europeans but it can come across as overbearing or signal embarrassment among East Asians. Even the two behaviors mentioned above – saying *please* and *thank you*, and letting ladies go first – are not universally polite: Spaniards, among others, have ways of thanking that do not involve saying 'thank you,' which sounds distant and cold to native ears (Hickey 2005); while letting ladies go first is not customary in Japan and may be frowned upon as sexist in some feminist circles.

As some contemporary theorists have noted, not only what is considered polite but also whether politeness itself is considered a good thing can be contested. Mills (2003) makes a case for politeness as white middle-class women's discourse, an argument that can be traced back to Robin Lakoff's earlier remarks on women's language (Lakoff 1975). Drawing on her own experience of American women in conversation, Lakoff noticed that a lot of the mechanisms traditionally associated with politeness in English (using hedges such as *sort of* and *you know*, tag questions, euphemisms and indirect requests, and avoiding strong swear words) were actually typical of women's language. She interpreted this as a reflection of women's powerless position in society and went on to propose a power-based explanation for the differences found in men's and women's speech. On this view, polite language is powerless language and, having come to be considered the normal way in which women speak, pins them down to a subordinate position, lest they be chastised for not sounding 'feminine enough.' Although this view, which became known as the 'dominance' approach, has been challenged in subsequent work, it proved enormously influential in the field of gender studies and beyond, constituting the first serious attempt to catalogue and explain gender-based differences in discourse.

In a different vein, Watts (2002) pointed out that the close relationship between polite language and standard/educated language in eighteenth century Britain created a situation whereby 'polite' was invested with negative overtones, ranging from standoffish to downright hypocritical. In fact, there is good (historical) reason why politeness in modern Western societies ended up with a bad rap. Early treatises on politeness associated it with morality, often of a religious nature. As power shifted from the Church to the feudal Court in early modern times and European societies became increasingly secular, politeness was also increasingly decoupled from morality and viewed as something that could be cultivated independently of it in the name of social advancement, much to the dismay of religious authors, who did not waste an opportunity to castigate such opportunistic behavior (Terkourafi 2011: 168–70). As a result, few would deny that politeness can occasionally be associated with 'superficial good manners purely as a matter of form' (Leech 2014), making it a vice rather than a virtue of those who display it.

Not only do the terms 'politeness' and 'polite' not mean the same for everyone, a word for 'polite' is not available in all languages (Terkourafi 2005: 242–3). That does not mean that those languages in which a single-word translational equivalent is unavailable do not equally have behaviors that are prescribed or frowned upon. However, it does mean that relying on the characterization of these behaviors as 'polite' or 'impolite' respectively in order to identify them may not get us very far.

As a remedy to this situation, one may turn to the second way of defining politeness, as a technical term explicitly and unambiguously defined by the analyst in relation to other terms taken from the theoretical framework s/he is working with. Politeness in this second sense is not found outside of textbooks and academic conferences and is referred to as second-order politeness, or Politeness 2. In Brown and Levinson's model, for example, politeness would be defined with respect to the notion of face-threat avoidance: those behaviors that avoid threatening the speaker's or the hearer's positive or negative face are characterized as polite.[4] In this way, a number of behaviors that may not be explicitly characterized as 'polite' (in the sense of Politeness 1) can still end up under this rubric (as Politeness 2) and be accounted for under the same model. This is especially pertinent to instances of positive politeness (e.g. using in-group identity markers such as BrE and AusE *mate*, AmE *dude* and AAE *nigga*),[5] which would not pass muster outside the specific groups that use them and would thus be left out of an account of Politeness 1 dealing with behaviors explicitly characterized as 'polite' – although their use (or lack thereof) clearly has implications for face, and therefore falls within the purview of a Politeness 2 definition anchored on this notion.

While this might seem like a promising way forward, it is not devoid of its own set of problems. For, as Eelen (2001: 48–76) has argued in detail, even accounts built on the notion of Politeness 2 can unwittingly incorporate Politeness 1 understandings. To give but two examples, drawn from two of the most prominent frameworks in the field: the placement of off-record above on-record (conventional) indirectness in Brown and Levinson's model seems to be more a culturally-biased assumption than a universal trait of polite discourse, as the studies by Blum-Kulka (1987) and Holtgraves and Yang (1990) cited earlier seem to suggest;[6] while the same is true of at least some of the maxims of Leech's (1983) Interpersonal Rhetoric (e.g. the Phatic maxim: 'Avoid silence').

These problems point to a more serious difficulty with the distinction between Politeness 1 and Politeness 2, namely, that completely disentangling these two notions may be not only practically impossible but also theoretically undesirable. This is because both notions are ultimately evaluative, albeit in different ways. In the case of Politeness 1, participants undertake an evaluation of the speaker's behavior with respect to socially accepted ('overt' in the sense of Trudgill 1972) norms. In the case of Politeness 2, on the other hand, an evaluation is again implicated but this time it may be against either overt or covert (group) norms. In other words, while what is polite 1 may be paraphrased as 'proper,' what is polite 2 is merely 'adequate' to the situation; the former is necessarily a subset of the latter. A more promising avenue to explore may therefore be to capitalize on their intimate relationship and attempt to ground definitions of the latter in what is shared about understandings of the former (Terkourafi 2011).[7]

The distinction between Politeness 1 and Politeness 2, first proposed by Watts *et al.* (1992), is not unrelated to another recent sea change in politeness studies: the rise of *im*politeness studies. Once the topic of investigation is shifted from a more or less finite set of politeness strategies to all kinds of ways in which language can impact face, it becomes clear that what interlocutors do with words is not limited to avoiding face-threat: sometimes they actively engage in it, others do so by accident, while others yet engage in unselfconscious or even gratuitous face-enhancing. The term *im/politeness* has been coined precisely to reflect the widened scope of the phenomena studied. Coupled with the observation that all use of language impacts face (see above), this leads to one possible definition of Politeness 2 as all linguistic behavior seen through the lens of its potential to impact (threaten and/or[8] enhance) face. The widened scope of im/politeness research has allowed attention to shift away from the two poles of politeness and impoliteness to the numerous types of behavior that lie between them. In fact, one of the most active areas in im/politeness research today is charting this middle ground, populated by terms such as politic behavior (Watts 1989), unmarked politeness (Terkourafi 2001), non-politeness (Kerbrat Orecchioni 2011), and mock impoliteness (Haugh and Bousfield 2012), among others.

While formally the counterpart of politeness, the challenges facing a theory of impoliteness are different. First, there is the difficulty in collecting (especially observational) data: no one likes to admit to being rude, much less caught on tape doing just that. Awareness that a session is being audio/video recorded seems to act as a surefire deterrent against providing data for the impoliteness researcher.[9] But the asymmetry between politeness and impoliteness does not stop here. So long as politeness can be assumed to be what is going on in most everyday encounters when participants feel that their face-needs are being met, the acquisition of politeness too can be put down to an informal statistical process of deducing and reproducing what is seen to be habitual in different contexts (Terkourafi 2001). The acquisition of impoliteness, however, is a different story. As Culpeper (2011) has convincingly argued, metalinguistic data (explicit instruction, proscriptions about what *not* to say etc.) are at least as much, if not more, important for acquiring impoliteness, as it is less frequently experienced first-hand and therefore harder to model based on observation alone.

A special feature of impoliteness is its intimate association with emotion. A negative emotional reaction (2011: 255) is in fact the single most common ingredient unifying instances of impoliteness, which can, for the rest, be creative or conventionalized (or even, institutionalized, as in army boot camp), intensified or pretend (as in mock impoliteness), intended or unintended, targeting another's face or sociality rights, and legitimized or not (2011: 254–5). The close link between impoliteness and (negative) emotion is a final point on which politeness and impoliteness come apart. While impoliteness is almost universally guaranteed to arouse feelings of anger and being hurt, politeness can trigger a whole gamut of emotions, including passing unnoticed (consider the routine reception of a *Can you pass the salt?* request at the dinner table).

14.4 Politeness, conventionalization and identity

An especially lively area in im/politeness research today concerns the relationship between face and identity. The two terms seem to share quite a few aspects, such that researchers on both sides are increasingly seeing little difference between them (Spencer-Oatey 2007; Locher 2008; Edwards 2009; Ruhi 2010; Garcés-Conejos Blitvich 2013). This raises interesting questions about the relationship of face to im/politeness and whether ultimately we need face to explain im/politeness (as Brown and Levinson originally suggested) or this can be done independently of it. Lately, a number of researchers have argued for the separation of face from im/politeness (e.g. Haugh and Bargiela-Chiappini 2010; O'Driscoll 2011; Haugh 2013; see also the papers in *Journal of Pragmatics* 58(1), special issue on 'Interpersonal Pragmatics'), which is also in line with an increasing interest in participants' own understandings of politeness and impoliteness (Politeness 1). Since face is at the heart of the theoretical definition of im/politeness (Politeness 2; see §14.3), this issue is central to the feasibility of theorizing Politeness 2 and, ultimately, upholding a distinction between Politeness 1 and Politeness 2. In this context, a re-examination of the relationship of face to identity could help us clarify things and set the study of im/politeness on a proper footing.

The two notions indeed share several aspects. Like face (see §14.2), identity emerges in relationships with others. This means that both identity and face take different forms depending on who those others are and what is the wider context of the interaction. Take the example of gender. Not only can one perform the same gender identity in different ways with different addressees (consider how masculinity is linguistically constructed with one's buddies versus one's partner), but one may also shift position on the gender identity spectrum depending on the audience (the same person holding a newborn baby may act more feminine than at other times). But gender is only one among several dimensions along which identities are routinely enacted. Gender, age, class, ethnic, professional, religious, political and so on identities are analytical abstractions: they have no independent existence of their own but are always co-instantiated in flesh-and-blood individuals, with different dimensions being foregrounded depending on the circumstances. This suggests that identities are not attached to flesh-and-blood individuals but rather to the social roles or capacities in which they relate to others, and can, therefore, like the latter, be multiple. All of these apply to face as well. Because face resides not in individual speakers but in speaker–addressee pairs (or Self–

Other pairs, to be precise, with Self and Other referring again not to flesh-and-blood individuals but rather to the social roles or capacities in which we relate to each other), we have many faces, as many as there are Others involved in the interaction (Terkourafi 2007). Our behavior, then, impacts our face in the eyes of each of these Others. Interestingly, this can lead us to threaten an Other's face in order to have our face be constituted in the eyes of yet a different Other (who may be present or to whom the interaction may be reported later on), which provides an elegant explanation for rudeness, an otherwise risky strategy (Terkourafi 2008).

Another aspect common to both identity and face that follows from their being relational and emergent is that both involve a co-opting by the addressee of the self-image that the speaker is – wittingly or unwittingly – projecting. Speakers cannot go about simply assuming that the self-image they wish to project is unproblematically shared by those around them. Rather, through their linguistic behavior, they put forward a claim or 'bid' (for identity or face), which must be recognized and ratified by the recipient in order to be fully realized. In other words, for a particular identity or face to be constituted, speakers must secure the recipient's 'uptake.'

This brings us to the final and possibly most important aspect that face and identity have in common: the fact that they can only emerge against the background of pre-existing social groupings. In the case of identity, a reference to groupness is perhaps the only aspect of the term that remains constant across both early and later definitions, with most everyone agreeing that claiming an identity amounts to aligning ourselves with one social group rather than another through our use of language. For instance, Le Page and Tabouret-Keller (1985: 182) write:

> We can only behave according to the behavioural patterns of groups that we find it desirable to identify with to the extent that:
> (i) we can identify the groups
> (ii) we have both adequate access to the groups and ability to analyse their behavioural patterns
> (iii) the motivation to join the groups is sufficiently powerful, and is either reinforced or reversed by feedback from the groups
> (iv) we have the ability to modify our behaviour.

Similarly, in his most recent work, Edwards notes:

> Our personal characteristics derive from our socialization within the group (or, rather, groups) to which we belong; one's particular social context defines that part of the larger human pool of potential from which a personal identity can be constructed. Thus, individual identities will be both components and reflections of particular social (or cultural) ones and the latter will always be, to some extent at least, stereotypic in nature because of their necessary generality across the individual components.
> (Edwards 2009: 20)

What both of these definitions agree on is that a claim or 'bid' for identity cannot be put forward in a social vacuum but always draws on existing social groupings – and conversely, a claim or 'bid' for identity cannot be intelligible to an audience and, ultimately, succeed, unless it draws on existing social groupings. This is also true of face. As I point out in Terkourafi (2005: 249):

> In acting to achieve this dual objective [of fulfilling his/her face-needs, and of doing so at least cost], the speaker's options are constrained by what s/he takes the addressee to be able to recognize, and thereby ratify. [...] To choose to be rude to you by using an offensive gesture, I must think that you are familiar with this gesture, and that you attribute to it the same negative value. In other words, I can only be rude to you in a way that you recognize as being rude. [...] When the addressee recognizes and ratifies the speaker's behavior, both as to its intention, and as to its face-constituting potential, as manifested by his/her uptake, this behavior enters their common stock of collective experiences. It can then serve as the model for future interactions, and through repeated ratification can take on a life of its own [...]. This is how norms of polite behavior are born.

The reliance of both identity and face on what is intelligible to the addressee because it is already familiar to him/her through previous interactions brings to the fore the importance of conventionalization to the achievement of both. By conventionalization, I mean a process of repeated use of an expression in situations that are sufficiently similar to be classified as instances of the same type, such that an increasingly stronger link is established between the expression and the situation at hand. The expression, then, becomes the normal way of achieving a particular practical goal in this situation (say, verbally ordering food at a restaurant from a waiter standing by your table), making all other ways of achieving the same goal in this situation (say, ordering food at a restaurant by tapping away on an iPad) appear 'odd,' if not downright 'anti-intimate' and wrong.[10]

An opportune metaphor to help us understand how the usual way of doing something can become the right way of doing it (making all other ways automatically dispreferred or wrong) is that of table manners. Different cultures around the world have different ways of helping themselves to the food in front of them: some use chopsticks and a bowl held close to their face, others use knives, forks and spoons to reach out to food from a plate in front of them, and yet others eat by hand following strict rules about how food should be picked up and delivered to one's mouth. What is interesting is that, depending on the setting one is in, *not* following the established convention for that setting is almost certain to raise eyebrows and place the culprit in a group separate from the rest of the attendees. Moreover, much as we may be intellectually aware that there are different ways of doing things, typically we can hardly suppress the gut feeling that a different way of doing them is simply off. It is in this way that social conventions, including im/politeness conventions, achieve their function of social regulation, that is, uniting those who are alike and separating those who are not, or distinguishing 'friend' from 'foe.'

At this point, a few things are worth making explicit. First, identity- or face-constituting are not practical goals in and of themselves. When we pick up our fork and knife to eat, have coffee in the morning, or slip on a pair of jeans, we do not do so in order to lay claim to a particular identity or face but first and foremost in order to feed and dress ourselves. Identity and face, in other words, fall out as by-products of doing what we normally do, without us putting any special effort in achieving them – at least, they do so in the eyes of those familiar with these particular ways of doing things. In this sense, identity and face are not so much a matter of recognizing the speaker's intention as of sharing the same set of sociocultural conventions that make the speaker's actions intelligible to us. That does not mean that identity and face cannot become goals in themselves, as when we might go out of our way to eat the way our hosts eat even though that may not be our normal way of eating, in order to honor them. However, at that point, rather than falling out as a by-product of our normal way of doing things, achieving a certain identity or face involves a conscious choice of means – and while that is certainly possible, it is way too cumbersome to engage in all the time, considering all of our behavior has consequences for identity and face all of the time. An account of im/politeness along these lines finds support in the overwhelming preference for conventional rather than off-record ways of being indirect attested cross-linguistically (see above), which suggests that the correct equation may be not 'the more indirect, the more polite' (as proposed by Brown and Levinson 1987; see Figure 14.1) but rather 'the more conventional, the more (routinely) polite,' leaving open the possibility that increasing degrees of non-conventionality may be associated with either increasing politeness or increasing impoliteness.

Until now, I have been discussing face and identity as if they were one and the same notion. However, the last point to be noted is also the one where, in my opinion, they come apart. And that is the degree to which they are emotionally invested. In a recent article, Garcés-Conejos Blitvich (2013) makes a convincing case that face and identity are closely interconnected, if not identical. Noting that the two are virtually interchangeable in Goffman's own writings over time, she writes:

> Identities can be verified, partially verified or not verified by other agents. Verification/Non-verification is associated with very positive/negative emotions. These emotions, which are usually associated with face […], are also crucially connected with identity. Those positive/negative emotions associated with the maintenance/enhancement/threat to face can then be associated as well with the verification/non-verification of an identity. Thus, im/politeness evaluations can be tied to identity, not just to face.
> (Garcés-Conejos Blitvich 2013: 17)

Despite fully agreeing with this account, I believe that it also contains the seeds of a potential separation of face from identity, which can be found in the duality (positive or negative) of the emotions associated with verification or non-verification of one's identity claims. For, while these emotions *are caused by* verification or not of one's identity, they are not identical to it but rather an independent consequence. To see that this is so, consider the emotional impact of non-verification of our gender identity by our partner as opposed to by a stranger in the street. Although in both cases this will be an affront to our self-image, the affront (what Brown and Levinson would have called a 'threat' to our face) will be much greater coming from our partner with whom this identity is much more relevant than from someone we will probably never see again. Moreover, the association of verification with positive emotions and of non-verification with negative emotions does not always hold. Rather, verification of our identity can be accompanied by negative emotions, as when someone's accusatory tone at our religious affiliation at once verifies that affiliation and constitutes a threat to our face by showing that s/he does not approve of it. In other words, the two processes, of identity- and face-constituting, are triggered simultaneously but operate at different levels: while identity has a distinctly qualitative aspect – it can take a value among several possibilities and is the 'what' is done – face is the interactional consequence of having done it 'right' (in the familiar way) or not and moves between a dual axis of positive ('friend') versus negative ('foe') affect (cf. Terkourafi 2007).[11] If this suggestion is along the correct lines, then identity and face can indeed be distinguished from each other and the latter placed at the basis of a theoretical definition of Politeness 2 as 'all linguistic behavior seen through the lens of its potential to impact (threaten and/or enhance) face.'

14.5 Conclusions

In this general overview of the linguistics of politeness and social relations, I have attempted to provide a bird's-eye view of the field from its inception to the debates that are currently exercising scholars. As can be seen, much progress has been made toward broader and more interdisciplinary accounts and understandings of politeness and impoliteness, while at the same time, little is agreed upon between researchers. Nevertheless, some themes remain stable across this broad array of perspectives. One of these is the importance of conventionalization, which empirical studies have shown to be central to the achievement of im/politeness. This has redirected attention away from individual speakers' calculations of indirectness and toward the boundaries on speakers' creativity imposed by social norms and conventions. A second theme is the fact that evaluations of politeness and impoliteness are emotionally invested. This means that being polite or impolite through language arouses strong feelings of like and dislike among participants, further promoting or curtailing their relationships – a finding which places the study of im/politeness firmly at the center of the fascinating and little explored interface of language with emotions. Future studies of im/politeness can be expected to shed new light on these and further questions, guaranteeing that politeness and impoliteness will remain central areas of sociopragmatic enquiry in years to come.

Notes

1. Remember that P is assessed from the perspective of the hearer: the more control the hearer has over the speaker, the higher P is.
2. Note that because the values of D, P and R are compounded in one figure (W), it is possible for the speaker and the hearer to agree on their estimation of W without for that matter agreeing on the specific values of D, P and Rx. In this way, Brown and Levinson's formula leaves significant leeway for politeness to be communicated, without requiring that it be an exact science. Considering how pervasive occasions requiring some form of politeness are, that is a good thing.
3. The fact that, for Brown and Levinson, politeness, be it positive or negative, always amounts to remedial action is made evident by the centrality of the notion of the 'virtual offence' to their argument (1987: 1) as well as the example of compliments as a way to offset the imposition entailed by a request (1987: 93).
4. It is important to clarify though that, as the distinction had not been proposed at the time their essay was being written, they do not explicitly define politeness or position themselves vis-à-vis this distinction.
5. According to at least some commentators (e.g. Dyson 2001: 131, 146), there is a difference between *nigger* and phonologically truncated *nigga* with the former being unambiguously insulting and the latter having been reclaimed as a term of endearment among young Blacks.
6. In both studies, native speakers of three varieties of English (American, Australian and British) rated hints second only to conventional indirectness in terms of politeness, while non-English speakers gave much more varied assessments of the im/politeness of hints.
7. This is also true of another distinction sometimes paralleled to the Politeness 1/Politeness 2 distinction, that between emic and etic, or insider and outsider perspectives on behavioral data (Haugh 2012). Having drawn this latter distinction, its proponent (Pike 1954) went on to clarify that he did not perceive a rigid dichotomy between them but rather a progression from emic to etic, such that emic units discovered via analysis of one language could be applied to analysis of another. To the extent that they are relevant to the latter, these units constitute part of an etic inventory that is no longer internal to any single language.
8. It is of course possible for a behavior to do both simultaneously: the mother's request to look after her baby for a short while cited above limits the addressee's freedom of action while conveying the mother's trust in the addressee at one and the same time.

9 In fact, there is a good explanation for this from within politeness theory itself: engaging in face-threatening behavior is a risky strategy and may be an affront to the speaker's face itself; therefore it is best avoided.
10 See www.tripadvisor.com/ShowUserReviews-g187309-d2197804-r173315580-La_Baracca_Munich-Munich_Upper_Bavaria_Bavaria.html.
11 In Terkourafi (2007) I suggest a distinction between Face 1 and Face 2, parallel to the Politeness 1: Politeness 2 distinction. According to this, Face 2 is a useful universalizing abstraction (i.e. not psychologically real to speakers) characterized by aboutness, or being directed at an Other (whence its relationality) and by being grounded in the approach–withdrawal dimension, a basic biological dimension of affiliation: disaffiliation or positive versus negative affect, which is the most basic dimension on which the range of human emotions can be built.

Further reading

Blum-Kulka (1987); Brown and Levinson (1987); Culpeper (2011); Eelen (2001); Leech (2014); Spencer-Oatey (2007); Terkourafi (2005).

References

Arundale, R.B. (2006) Face as Relational and Interactional: A Communication framework for research on face, facework, and politeness. *Journal of Politeness Research* 2: 193–216.

Barros García, M.J. (forthcoming) Face-enhancing compliments in Peninsular Spanish informal conversations. *Journal of Politeness Research*.

Blum-Kulka, S. (1987) Indirectness and politeness: Same or different? *Journal of Pragmatics* 11: 131–46.

Bonnefon, J.-F., E. Dahl and T.M. Holtgraves (2015) Some but not all dispreferred turn markers help to interpret scalar terms in polite contexts. *Thinking & Reasoning* 21: 230–49

Brown, P. and S.C. Levinson (1987) *Politeness: Some Universals in Language Usage*. Cambridge: Cambridge University Press [1st edition 1978].

Culpeper, J. (2011) *Impoliteness: Using Language to Cause Offence*. Cambridge: Cambridge University Press.

Dyson, M.E. (2001) *Holler If You Hear Me: Searching for Tupac Shakur*. New York: Basic Books.

Edwards, J. (2009) *Language and Identity: An Introduction*. Cambridge: Cambridge University Press.

Eelen, G. (2001) *A Critique of Politeness Theories*. Manchester: St. Jerome's Press.

Garcés-Conejos Blitvich, P. (2013) Face, identity, and im/politeness: Looking backwards, moving forward – From Goffman to Practice Theory. *Journal of Politeness Research* 9: 1–33.

Goffman, E. (1967) *Interaction Ritual: Essays on Face-to-Face Behavior*. Garden City: Anchor Books.

Haugh, M. (2012) Epilogue: Deconstructing the first-second order distinction in face and politeness research. *Journal of Politeness Research* [special issue on 'Chinese face and im/politeness'] 8: 111–34.

Haugh, M. (2013) Disentangling face, facework and im/politeness. *Sociocultural Pragmatics* 1: 46–73.

Haugh, M. and F. Bargiela-Chiappini (2010) Face in interaction. *Journal of Pragmatics* [special issue] 42: 2073–171.

Haugh, M. and D. Bousfield (2012) Mock impoliteness, jocular mockery and jocular abuse in Australian and British English. *Journal of Pragmatics* 44: 1099–114.

Hickey, L. (2005) Politeness in Spanish: Thanks but 'no thanks.' In L. Hickey and M. Stewart (eds) *Politeness in Europe*, pp. 317–30. Clevedon: Multilingual Matters.

Holtgraves, T. and J. Yang (1990) Politeness as universal: Cross-cultural perceptions of request strategies and inferences based on their use. *Journal of Personality and Social Psychology* 59: 719–29.

Kerbrat Orecchioni, C. (2011) From good manners to facework: Politeness variations and constants in France, from the classic age to today. *Journal of Historical Pragmatics* 12: 133–55.

Lakoff, R. (1975) *Language and Woman's Place*. New York: Harper & Row.

Leech, G. (1983) *Principles of Pragmatics*. London: Longman.

Leech, G. (2014) *The Pragmatics of Politeness*. Oxford: Oxford University Press.

Le Page, R. and A. Tabouret-Keller (1985) *Acts of Identity*. Cambridge: Cambridge University Press.

Locher, M. (2008) Relational work, politeness and identity construction. In G. Antos, E. Ventola and T. Weber (eds.) *Handbooks of Applied Linguistics. Volume 2: Interpersonal Communication*, pp. 509–40. Berlin/New York: Walter de Gruyter.

Márquez Reiter, R. (2000) *Linguistic Politeness in Britain and Uruguay: A Contrastive Study of Requests and Apologies*. Amsterdam: John Benjamins.

Mills, S. (2003) *Gender and Politeness*. Cambridge: Cambridge University Press.

O'Driscoll, J. (2011) Some issues with the concept of face: When, what, how and how much? In F. Bargiela-Chiappini and D.Z. Kádár (eds) *Politeness Across Cultures*, pp. 17–41. Basingstoke: Palgrave Macmillan.

Pike, K. (1954) *Language in Relation to a Unified Theory of the Structure of Human Behavior*. Glendale: Summer Institute of Linguistics.

Ruhi, S. (2010) Face as an indexical category in interaction. *Journal of Pragmatics* 42: 2131–46.

Scollon, R. and S.W. Scollon (1995) *Intercultural Communication: A Discourse Approach*. Oxford: Blackwell.

Slugoski, B.R. and W. Turnbull (1988) Cruel to be kind and kind to be cruel: Sarcasm, banter and social relations. *Journal of Language and Social Psychology* 7: 101–21.

Spencer-Oatey, H. (2007) Theories of identity and the analysis of face. *Journal of Pragmatics* 39: 639–56.

Tannen, D. and C. Kakava (1992) Power and solidarity in Modern Greek conversation: Disagreeing to agree. *Journal of Modern Greek Studies* 10: 11–34.

Terkourafi, M. (2001) *Politeness in Cypriot Greek: A Frame-Based Approach*. Unpublished PhD dissertation, University of Cambridge.

Terkourafi, M. (2005) Beyond the micro-level in politeness research. *Journal of Politeness Research* 1: 237–62.

Terkourafi, M. (2007) Toward a universal notion of face for a universal notion of co-operation. In I. Kecskes and L.R. Horn (eds.) *Explorations in Pragmatics: Linguistic, Cognitive and Intercultural Aspects*, pp. 313–44. Berlin: Mouton de Gruyter.

Terkourafi, M. (2008) Toward a unified theory of politeness, impoliteness, and rudeness. In D. Bousfield and M. Locher (eds.) *Impoliteness in Language: Studies on Its Interplay with Power in Theory and Practice*, pp. 45–74. Berlin: Mouton de Gruyter.

Terkourafi, M. (2011) From Politeness1 to Politeness2: Tracking norms of im/politeness across time and space. *Journal of Politeness Research* 7: 159–85.

Trudgill, P. (1972) Sex, covert prestige and linguistic change in the urban British English of Norwich. *Language in Society* 1: 179–95.

Turner, K. (1996) The principal principles of pragmatic inference: Politeness. *Language Teaching* 29: 1–13.

Vergis, N. and M. Terkourafi (forthcoming) Overriding relationship affect: The role of the speaker's emotional state in im/politeness assessments. *Journal of Language and Social Psychology*.

Watts, R.J. (1989) Relevance and relational work: Linguistic politeness as politic behavior. *Multilingua* 8: 131–66.

Watts, R.J. (2002) From polite language to educated language: The reemergence of an ideology. In R.J. Watts and P. Trudgill (eds.), *Alternative Histories of English*, pp. 155–72. London: Routledge.

Watts, R.J., S. Ide and K. Ehlich (1992) Introduction. In R.J. Watts, S. Ide and K. Ehlich (eds.) *Politeness in Language: Studies in its History, Theory and Practice*, pp. 1–17. Berlin: Mouton de Gruyter.

Wolfson, N. (1988) The bulge: a theory of speech behavior and social distance. In J. Fine (ed.) *Second Language Discourse: A Textbook of Current Research*, pp. 21–38. Norwood: Ablex.

15
Narrative and narrative structure

Michael Toolan

15.1 The multiplicity of narratives

Narrative is one of those terms, like 'creativity' and 'text', which has become unhelpfully promiscuous. Everything's a narrative, narratives are everywhere, and if you (as an enterprise, a politician, a university department, a public service, a tourist resort – yes, even a restaurant meal) don't 'have a narrative', you are sunk. Some narratives function as a kind of structured mnemonic, encapsulating key information in a memorable format (e.g. in the sciences, in historiography and in legal education). But most centrally narratives have a performative function: what is told and the way that it is told simultaneously reports on the identity and values of the teller, or the subject-matter, or the addressee (or some combination of these). A CV or a Facebook entry usually narrates the subject's character and values so as to address specific objectives such as employability or social attractiveness. Oral personal narratives are often an accounting – of someone's experience of a tellable disruption of the habitual, the social order – and are used at every level of seriousness and a multitude of settings. From the rich range of possible example narratives to analyse, in light of space limitations, just one childhood personal reminiscence will be analysed in detail in this chapter, with attention to its numerous indicative formal and functional characteristics.

15.2 Narrative as a genre

Is narrative a genre or a 'super genre'? Consider Biber *et al.*'s (1999) influential *Longman Grammar of Spoken and Written English*. This selects four *registers* as important and distinct broad forms of writing (among which grammatical patterns and frequencies may vary revealingly): conversation, fiction writing, news writing and academic prose. In two of these registers, the genre of narrative is arguably prominent (fiction writing and news writing), and it frequently emerges in a third, conversation. On that basis narrative would appear to be a range of textual formats for reporting 'what happened' of such generality as to enjoy a significantly different status from a typical genre, loosely on a par with the list, or the syllogism, which equally can be deployed in a range of different genres. Reflecting this, narrative seems only partly to fit the Systemic-Functional Linguistic conception of a genre.

For Systemic linguists, a genre is a 'staged, goal-oriented social process'. Thus for Systemic-Functional Linguistics it would seem that to form a genre, a set of language-using events would need not only to display recurrent and distinct global linguistic patterns, such as the familiar narrative sequence of stages labelled Orientation, Complication, (Crisis) and Resolution, they would also need to be linked to a patterned and recurrent social goal or activity. This is more apparent in pragmatic activities such as service encounters, which thus can be seen as a genre. By contrast narrative seems to be either a sub-structure (you might use one in the course of advancing through the steps of a service encounter) or a genre-neutral resource (narratives can be used in all sorts of actual genres). Among SFL researchers, Eggins and Slade (1997) have suggested that four distinct genres of story can be identified: Narrative, Recount, Anecdote and Exemplum. Of these, only the first approximates the Labovian structure, the others being regarded as complete and well-formed, but without the evaluative staging, or the complexity of event-sequence, of the Narrative format.

15.3 Fundamental functions of narrative

Narrative or story (I will treat these terms as equivalent and interchangeable) is a 'core' structuring form, found in all sorts of language activity (and found in other kinds of human activity which can be entirely non-verbal: in pictures and film, ballet and mime, etc.). We use narratives to represent and to convey at least two connected scenes or situations: (1) a state and (2) a significant change of that state. There are always *implicit*, in any narrative, at least two connected scenes or situations, even if the earlier scene has to be inferred or reconstructed from the depiction of the later one. The representing and conveying is, crucially, ditransitive: it is not merely the construal of some changed situation that makes a narrative but in addition the implied communicating of this to another party that is definitional of narrative. Usually a narrative is conveyed to an addressee who was not present, as witness, at the occurrence of the situation so reported; but on occasion, often with specific effects, a teller narrates to someone who was a witness and who might be expected to have made sense of the event-sequence for themselves; and again on occasion a teller can tell a story with themselves as sole addressee. Most commonly, however, we tell stories about ourselves and our affines or those whom we value, about experiences we find instructive; and we tell the stories to those whose goodwill or approval we seek.

One brief characterisation of narrative runs as follows (it is from Toolan 2001: 8, rephrased for clarity):

> A narrative is a sequence of events that are perceived to be non-randomly connected, typically involving one or more humans or other sentient participants, these being the experiencing individuals at the centre of events; from their experience we human addressees can 'learn'.

Two aspects of this characterisation may be noted. One is that it does not require a narrative to be a *representation* of a sequence of events (some analysts put great weight on overtly represented – in the sense of narrated – event sequences, to exclude event sequences where there is direct enactment or performance, as in plays, operas and arguably even films). But the definition above is neutral concerning the reporting versus presenting (or describing versus performing) distinction: it gives priority to the receiver of the narrative. The other notable aspect of the above description is that it does not stipulate a verbal medium for all narratives. Be that as it may, the subjects of the present chapter are indeed verbal narratives, where a narrator or teller(s) is explicitly or at least implicitly the source of the textual representation of the non-random sequence of events affecting one or more characters and reporting some kind of significant change.

Our personal narratives are not simply vivid ways we tell ourselves 'what happened'; they also tell us who we now are, or who we have become. This is because the representing of an initial state commonly involves presenting a characterisation or identity for one or more individuals; and then the presentation of the changed state that often entails reporting a change of character or identity. Thus, paradoxically, the very idea of identity – the matrix of behaviour-shaping stable and permanent characteristic(s) of a person, group, or entity – is both put in use and put at risk in narratives. Where our narratives do imply identity-change, a 'deep shift', we rehearse through them a more general cultural and even biological phenomenon, namely the situated nature of identity and its potential for change. Our narratives 'perform' this making and re-making of identity (and of the terms, conditions and possibilities that we live by).

15.4 The Labovian model

15.4.1 How spoken narratives work

The most natural and commonest narratives that merit first study are those we produce orally or in Sign, a naturally acquired language, without need of any technology, about ourselves and our associates, in the course of everyday conversation. When it comes to describing the structure and function of spoken narratives, it is worth emphasising that a range of related structures (rather than one inflexible template) and a diversity of functions need to be recognised. But in what follows I will present and treat the structure proposed by the sociolinguist William Labov as capturing much that is typical of a 'fully verbalised' oral narrative of personal experience, since several of the variant structures can be seen as abridged or compressed alternatives to it. Labov focused on oral narratives of personal experience (henceforth ONPE; as already implied, these can be regarded as the canonical kind of narrative, from which various other forms including written or filmic ones can be seen as derived). Having collected and analysed a number of ONPEs elicited from young African American men when they were prompted by an inquiry as to whether they had ever been in a situation where they feared for their life, Labov proposed an ONPE may have up to six basic elements. These are as follows:

1. **Abstract**: What, in a nutshell, is this story about?
2. **Orientation**: Who was involved, when and where was this, what had happened or was happening (in the way of ongoing background)?
3. **Complicating action**: What new thing happened and then what happened after this (recurring)?
4. **Evaluation**: So what? How or why is this interesting?
5. **Resolution**: So what was the final thing that happened?
6. **Coda**: How does this story 'connect' with the speaker, or all of us, here and now?

To clarify how the glossing questions above are intended, consider 'Evaluation'. For Labov, this denotes all the material in an oral narrative, not primarily reporting orientation or complicating action etc., which can be seen to answer an addressee's questions about the relevance and significance of the story being told. Other analysts have encapsulated these questions as concerning the *point* or *tellability* of a narrative: an oral telling must justify its own telling by being sufficiently amusing, surprising, alarming, moving or in some other way of value to the addressee (although sometimes an addressee will be placated, where they see no great benefit to themselves in hearing the story, by recognising that the telling is of great importance – perhaps therapeutic – to the teller). Evaluation therefore covers all the linguistic and paralinguistic means by which a stark provision of elements 2 and 3 and 5 (the bare setting and actions) is *enriched* to make the story more compelling, vivid, memorable and significant.

In the stories Labov analysed, the one obligatory element is the Complicating Action (a report of something having happened). Least required, and frequently absent, are the two (usually smaller) sections that top and tail stories, Abstract (often a preview of what is to come) and the Coda (a conversational 'bridge' back to the present conversational situation of the teller and addressee, or a summing-up of the 'moral', of what the incident taught the teller). Five of the six elements tend to appear in narratives in the sequence given above. While the sixth, Evaluation, tends to occur at the 'high point', before a story reaches its Resolution, it can in fact emerge anywhere in the course of a story, or be spread throughout it. This reflects just how crucial an Evaluation is. Despite the 'So what? Why is this interesting?' questions above, there is not one specific question that Evaluation addresses. Instead it is a rich array of turns of phrase, verbal and non verbal elaborations, which can be thought of as added to the barest form of a narrative and is used by the teller to make the story all the more worth telling and hearing. As noted above, evaluative material is often particularly clustered around the 'hinge' or climactic point of the action, just before – and in effect delaying – the resolving action or event. Evaluation is also, crucially, all the ways in which the teller's personal stake in a story is conveyed.

Many conversation-embedded personal narratives will have only some of Labov's six elements, and in recent years analysts have become more guarded about whether stories with just two or three of the elements should be conceptualised as 'incomplete' or 'lacking', relative to a full six-parter (perhaps on the analogy of the reduced non-finite clause). It may suffice here to note that presence and prominence of the Labovian elements seems to be culture- and situation-specific, and that in any case no such scheme can fit all stories in all cultural contexts. There is also wide recognition that Abstract and Coda are secondary elements, that Resolution may be preferred but is not structurally essential, and that Orientation may be quite attenuated and almost inextricably embedded within the Complicating Action. What is more generally agreed is that there must be some form of Complicating Action (the 'referential' spine of a narrative, according to Labov), which is to say, something must have happened; and that Evaluation, at least implicit indications of the story's tellability, will feature in some guise.

15.4.2 The story of Mrs Mowdy

The story I have chosen for analysis differs in content and context from Labov's, but has similarities of structure. What follows is a transcript of an oral narrative that arose in the course of a half-hour conversation between an older woman (denoted in Figure 15.1 by W) from Glasgow, Scotland and a researcher well-known to her (R in Figure 15.1), who was chiefly interested in W's dialect. R has asked W to share some of her childhood memories. The extract comes about twenty minutes into W's recollections (Figure 15.1).

W1	But, oh my God, and then the wife in the bottom clo- her husband eh was the the sort of, watchie at this yard.
R	mmhm?
W2	And they were a weird couple. He had a kind a humphy back, you know, he'd kind of
R	mmhm?
W3	And stran-, never spoke much to anybody, you know, and his wife was awful funny; she was practically bald.
R	urgh
W4	Her hair was that thin
R	mm
W5	she really was, she was practically, her hair was that thin all over, she was practically bald. and, anyway, somebody kicked our Sam's ball and it hit the wood and over into the yard, and he was a crabby old sod, if he got yer ball so-, he would, nine times out of ten, you didnae get it back, and our Sa-, it was a new ball, and I loo- our Sam was nearly greetin, so I 'I'll get it'.
R	mmhm
W6	So I goes marchin in, chaps the door. Now I was bein very civil //here.//
R	//mmhm//
W7	So the door opens and she, she comes to the door and she says 'Whi-', she says, 'Well?' I says, 'Excuse me Mrs Mowdy, could I have S-, could I please have Samuel's ball?' Well my mother nearly died, cause she was doin her brasses on her door up the stairs,
R	mmhm?
W8	And she, the door got slammed in my face. And my mother came down and she says, 'What did I hear you sayin there?' I says, 'I was only askin Mrs Mowdy for [laugh]
R	[laugh]
W9	'For Samuel's ball.' 'Her name isn't Mowdy'. See the boys used to call him, 'See him, he's a, that's old mowdy, old mouldy', and oh no, they didnae like him. Old Mou- old Mou-. Well I didnae know her name wasnae Mowdy, so I // went to the door//
R	//[laugh]//
W10	[laugh]. And it turned out her name was McFarlane, And eh 'Please Mrs Mowdy we- could I have Samuel's ball?' oh dear God. My mother says, 'It's got to the stage where I'm frightened I'm frightened to go doon the stairs.' [laugh]
R	[laugh]
W11	oh dear, well I really didnae know. I'd never heard them called anything else, but 'oh, go, run, here comes the Mowdy', you know.
R	uh-huh.
W12	[inaudible] the Mowdy, [click]. But the man wi the ca- horse and cart, oh the sweary words that he knew werenae canny, //you know?//
R	//uh-huh.//

Figure 15.1 Oral narrative extract (source: Document 351 at www.scottishcorpus.ac.uk)

A rough preliminary survey of the story would suggest that turns W1 to W4 are Orientation, W5–W7 are Complicating Action, W8 contains the Resolution, and W9 to W12 are chiefly Evaluative. There is no Abstract, and no real Coda, just a segue to mention of the horse and cart man.

It is in many respects a monologue, and W clearly holds the floor (indeed she has been encouraged to, by R). R's very brief back-channellings (laughs, or 'uh-huh's), are almost like breathing-points in W's narrative. Once W 'gets started' on her story, at W5, R's supportive and appreciative responses are roughly equidistant from each other; or we can say that W's 'phased' telling is distributed into roughly sentence-long segments. This mutually-managed coordination of telling is a striking feature of conversational storytelling formats which have an element of the ceremonial in their orderliness: there is no evidence of competitive overlapping or interruption of turns in this transcript, nor should we expect much. R clearly defers to W, and it is in R's interests for W to talk at length (R's goal is to gather samples of natural dialectal speech). The talk comes to be shaped around the 'Mrs Mowdy' story only gradually, preceded by characterisations of both the downstairs neighbours, which *can* be recategorised as Orientational material preliminary to some Complicating Action, but do not have to be. Thus, in Labovian terms, there is no preliminary Abstract to this story – unlike the one that W has told immediately previously in this interview, a story she prefaces with 'did I tell you about the time we got the photograph taken?'

W1–W4 are Orientational, describing the two new narrative participants in stative relational clauses or with habitual aspect (husband was a watchie, they were weird, he had a humpback, they never spoke much, she was practically bald, …). But there are elements of Evaluation even in this Orientation – as indeed is quite common in fluent storytelling. To see this a very brief sketch of Labovian Evaluation is needed. Labov postulates two main kinds of Evaluation – external or internal to the story action (a loose analogy might be the contrast between sentential adverbial disjuncts and VP-qualifying adverbial adjuncts). External evaluation stands entirely outside the story proper, and further divides into two types: those where the teller reports on what they now think of what happened (*The most amazing thing has happened, you're going to love this, this one's hilarious, what do you think of this – I can't make any sense of it*, etc.); and those that describe the teller's own evaluative reaction to the situation and chain of events, at that past time: *I was convulsed with laughter, I was shaking like a leaf, I couldn't get my words out, everyone seemed to be disgusted by this*. Neither type is a disclosure of 'what happened' or 'what finally happened' but of how you now evaluate what happened, or then evaluated what was happening. A good example of external evaluation in the Mrs Mowdy story comes in W7, where the teller reports not her own evaluative reaction but that of her mother, upon hearing the teller address her neighbour as Mrs Mowdy: *Well my mother nearly died*. Told at this point, before we learn that Mowdy is not the neighbour's name but a derogatory nickname misunderstood by the teller, this evaluation's relevance is quite unclear and the coherence of the story is threatened. It is also threatened since the teller's mother has not been mentioned as present at all before this point, so the explanation that she is present in that she overhears the request, is timely.

More completely integrated into the telling are the range of types of Internal Evaluation that Labov proposes. Initially these were characterised as linguistic or paralinguistic additions to core action clauses, if the latter are stripped to the grammatical and event-cum-actant essentials. So a simple Complicating Action clause, *I hit him*, could be evaluatively enriched as *I hit him, 'pow!'* or *Ducking and diving to keep out of range, I didn't hit him I*

HITTT him, 'powww!' But it is now widely recognised that internal evaluations are not confined to the two action elements (namely Complicating Action and Resolution); they can be dispersed throughout the telling and are quite common in the Orientation. Labovian internal evaluation is of four subtypes: Intensifiers (including repetitions, emphases, paralinguistic accompaniments, intonational exaggerations), Comparators (including modality and negation), Correlatives (including pairings of activities, happening concurrently), and Explicatives (stated reasons and causes). All of these in one way or another add staging, texture, and complexity to the simple 'then x, and then y, and then z' of bare-narration Action and Resolution.

Returning to W3–W5, which I have suggested is predominantly Orientation, we can now say more about W's troubling to mention three times over that the woman neighbour was practically bald. That marked repetition is made evaluative by the repetition. So these phrases realise two functional elements in the narrative (Orientation plus Evaluation). W5 also contains a first Complicating Action clause in the story: *somebody kicked our Sam's ball and it hit the wood and over [it went] into the [neighbours'] yard.* This does not mean that the Orientation is now complete, however, and that all subsequent clauses will be Action ones. Instead, the next couple of lines of W5 chiefly tell us more stative or relational information about the neighbour (crabby, who nine times out of ten did not return balls) and the ball (it was a new one). So here Complicating Action and Orientation are side by side. The final two clauses of W5 now resume the narrating of the Action, but in interestingly evaluative ways: we are told Sam was nearly crying ['greetin''], and that the teller undertakes to recover the ball. But *he was nearly crying* (like *I almost fainted* and similar constructions) is evaluative by way of negation: strictly speaking, it tells us how Sam did not behave, not how he did; and of course with the switch to direct speech in 'I'll get it', the speaker adopts the more dramatic, performative position of seeming to re-enact the actual dialogue, *verbatim*, used at the time. This requires some interpretive flexibility on the part of addressees, besides requiring the teller to be convincing now as a performer, and not just a reporter. We do not know yet that the specific direct speech words used will be crucial to the point of the story; but the teller does and, whether consciously or not, she has switched to the direct speech in good time to ensure a seamless advance to the high point of humour and offence.

That high point comes in W7, and is followed by the Resolution, the door slammed in the teller's face, in W8. Nothing after this point in the telling constitutes a better or later answer to the question 'what finally happened?', so that slammed door is undoubtedly the Resolution. The action has a powerful symmetry about it, too: superficially the 'damage to face' performed by the door-slam is done to the child, but of course this is no more than a different kind of evaluation (of description rather than storytelling) by the neighbour of the child's term of address, and the implicatures and face-damage that the child's innocently using that name entails. Not only does Mrs McFarlane understand that the children of the tenement call her Mrs Mowdy, she must realise also that this naming has become so conventionalised that the younger children do not know it as disparaging, but believe it to be simple description, her true name.

Since 'what finally happened' is first reported in W8, one of the striking but typical features of this story is that three comparatively lengthy turns follow, providing kinds of evaluative elaboration of how the speaker came to commit the embarrassing but amusing social gaffe. Much of this Evaluation, even if not 'internal to complicating action clauses' in the way Labov once stipulated, can still be keyed to the Labovian categories of internal evaluation. Most prominent are the abundant post-resolution repetitions in W8, 9,

10, 11 and 12, of *Mowdy*; integrated with these are the Comparator negations (*didnae... never...*) and explications in W9 and W11: *Well I didnae know her name wasnae Mowdy... well I really didnae know... I'd never heard them called anything else.* Interlaced with these are the teller's own external evaluations of the whole story situation: *oh no* (W9), *oh dear God* (W10), *oh dear* (W11), and of course her laughter at the close of W8 and W10, which is immediately matched by the recipient's laughter, interpretable as both appreciative and evaluative.

Another feature that prominently contributes to the effectiveness and tellability of this ONPE are the frequent switches from telling to showing, i.e. from reporting to performing. As noted, at one point in the Complicating Action, the narration runs: 'our Sam was nearly greetin, so I "I'll get it"'. Here the speaker *reports* the first 'action' or event (i.e. that Sam was made so upset by loss of the ball that he is nearly crying), but she *enacts* the second and consequential action in direct speech (compare, in the alternative, a possible continuation of the reporting stance adopted in the first clause: *so I said I would go and get it*). Similarly, given that the point of the story is the inadvertent insult of calling the neighbour *Mrs Mouldy*, there is a nice 'setting up' of the impoliteness by the speaker telling us beforehand, in W6, *Now I was bein very civil*. But something else of note happens in the course of a brief advance from *'I'll get it'* to *Now I was bein very civil*: while the telling up to the final words of W5 has been in the past tense, the performing of direct speech seems to license a switch to the more 'dramatic' present tense, beyond the direct speech, in the narration at the beginning of W6 (*So I goes marchin in*, not *So I went marchin in*). As the complicating action proceeds, the telling remains in present tense, with the exception of the already-noted *Now I was bein very civil*. There may be more than one explanation for that specific comment switching back to past tense – one being that it is in Labov's terms a 'restricted' and somewhat externally evaluative clause: i.e. a clause that has some freedom of movement to be used at a range of points (from initially in W6 to as late as W11).

While the important steps in the action related in W7 are in the present tense, the evaluative clauses at the close of W7 – again 'restricted' in status – shift back to the past tense, although that tense shift is arguably less striking than the format of the Resolution narrative clause at the beginning of W8. Not only is this past tense, it is also – after a seemingly Active voice start, which is abandoned – Passive voice, and a *get*-passive with agent deletion at that. Why a teller should effect this voice-shift at precisely this high point, and so overtly, is unclear; but one effect is partly to remove any blame or criticism from the reacting neighbour.

Having noted that the teller's mention of her mother, *doin her brasses*, is a restricted clause that could conceivably have appeared later, it is worth noting the advantage in skilfully enlarging the frame, the array of dramatis personae in the scene, by mention of the mother at this point and before the neighbour's outraged reaction is reported. Because the teller's mother is *doin her brasses* on the floor above, she has also overheard the incriminating dialogue. To do the brasses was to clean and polish the brass fittings (letter flap, knocker, handle) on the front door, thus the public-facing property, of one's residence (here, a flat). It is (or was) a quintessentially house-proud and gender-marked activity, typically of working-class housewives – an almost obsessive cleanliness which would be of less account except that it contrasts so sharply with the 'mouldy-ness' scandalously or hilariously attributed to the 'weird' neighbour couple. It may be noted that the female teller/protagonist has only called the neighbour Mrs Mouldy on the basis of inference, i.e. because the boys were in the habit of calling her husband Mr Mouldy. And while she has undertaken to request return of the ball, she does so on behalf of Sam, who is nearly crying at the loss and knows that Mr

'Mouldy' rarely returns an errant ball. So there are gender politics at work in this narrative along with other forms of dramatic tension.

Accent and dialect vividness can never be wholly discounted, given the work it can do to help make a narrative entertaining, or authentic and credible and particularised. The teller's and the audience's assaying of the effect of the dialect is always comparative, made relative to alternative dialects that might have been used but were not; and the assessment is also made relative to the story's content. Together these considerations mean that a spoken narrative delivered in RP or Standard American English accent and standard vocabulary and grammar, for example, can convey evaluations to listeners if they judge that some different, perhaps markedly non-standard, accent or dialect would in the circumstances have been more 'natural' or fitting. In the story under consideration, even reliant here on a transcription (an audio recording of the original can be heard on the website), there is plentiful evidence of enrichment of the Complicating Action and the Evaluation by use of Glaswegian accent and dialect. In W6, for instance, the teller reports she *chaps the door*, using a Scots dialectal form in place of 'knocks, raps on'. There are several other dialectal forms that add to the character and specificity of the telling, differing from standard English grammatically or lexically and, we infer, in pronunciation: e.g. the Scots negative contraction used in *didnae know*, *werenae canny*; and several items of vocabulary: *watchie* (for watchman, 'security guard'), *humphy back* (humped back), *greetin* (crying, in W5), *doon* (down) and *canny*. This last item has a range of dialectal meanings but is used here in its Scots sense of 'steady, restrained or temperate'. Also noticeable are the numerous *–y/–ie* endings, which seem to function here, as more widely in Scots, to convey affinity and informality.

15.5 The small stories of social interaction

Since the landmark contributions of Labov and others, there have been many developments in the sociolinguistically-oriented study of narratives; e.g. Wolfson (1982); Linde (1993); Ochs and Capps (2001); Bamberg *et al.* (2007); and Bamberg (1998), a special issue of the *Journal of Narrative and Life History* that reflected on thirty years of narrative analysis post-Labov; and Norrick (2000). De Fina and Georgakopoulou (2012) are among the recent sociolinguists who have emphasised the importance of 'small stories': they argue that a great many conversational or quasi-conversational floor-holding contributions can be classified as narratives despite having rather briefer extent and comparatively slight structure, by comparison with the 'classical' or canonical Labovian six-part model. They have called for a new paradigm of analysis, within which to situate the fragmentary storytelling often found in narrative interview research; in effect they are also questioning the term 'fragment(ary)' as a loaded one, implicitly casting such narrative activity as incomplete, reduced, and still to be defined by some 'classical' standard. In a world of sound-bites, hourly Facebook updates, 140-character tweets, and text messages, are traditional notions of standard and non-standard, unmarked and marked, still applicable to narrativising activities in social media?

There have even been attempts to interpret such 'small stories' as a post-structuralist or late modern superseding of the Labovian modernist/structuralist format, but this narrative itself is perhaps a simplification. Something like the 'full' six-part personal narrative format is still deployed on occasion, but shorter and abridged story formats, with ellipsis of various elements, are at least as often encountered. In the past forty years, a host of personal narrative forms which are digital and virtual have been added to the former set of oral and written formats. Today, personal stories are as frequently written digitally, or even multimodally composed, as orally so. Consider the Facebook entry, or the vlog posted on YouTube, reporting some personal episode with icons and images embedded. And those which are oral may be conveyed by phone or Skype, Viber, MSN or WhatsApp rather than with physical co-presence of teller and audience. But even if certain elements are ellipted in a majority of cases, many analysts see advantages in postulating their underlying potential presence, seeing a loose parallel with principles of complete underlying structure and forms of ellipsis and assimilation found at work in other branches of language analysis such as phonology and syntax. The work of 'small-story' analysts is a useful reminder that all of the features of the full or canonical narrative are at the endpoint of clines or degrees of instantiation. The point emerges also from the study by Ochs and Capps (2001), who suggest that tellership, tellability, interactional embeddedness, moral stance and linearity are five key scalar criteria of a speech event's status as a narrative. But they note that much analysis has favoured texts with features at one end of the continua – e.g. stories with one teller, elaborate tellability and clear linearity – and this may have distorted our conception.

In reality, and outside the elicited research interview, many stories are not very linear, imply a vague or shifting moral stance, may be so interactionally embedded that they are rarely studied, with muted or obscure tellability credentials and a plural or even indefinitely bounded tellership. Likewise, many stories fall somewhere between the personal and the vicarious, being personal supplements or evaluative recontextualisings of public stories (what has just happened in some TV series or in some political development); they may be fashioned around a cluster of loosely-connected episodes rather than one climax-marked outcome; they may be collaboratively and collectively told; and their evaluation and even their main events may alter progressively via negotiation. In short, many actual sequences of interaction, with narrative characteristics, are more embedded, fluid, interactive, bound up with acts of identity and affiliation, than was sometimes fully acknowledged. None of this, however, necessarily overthrows the Labovian tradition as distinct from enlarging and extending it; after all, from the outset the Labovian approach emphasised the importance of evaluation in everyday storytelling, and the shifting disclosure of self and identity that underpins much of this interactional activity.

The ideas of multiplicity, fragmentation and irreducible contingency have now been embraced by sociolinguistics. The small-story tradition, informed by Hymesian sociology of language (Hymes 1996) and Schegloffian conversation analysis, is interested, among other things, in how the specificities of a social setting or 'site of engagement' (a particular café, a trailer park, a PTA social event, etc.) may bear on the kind of story that gets told (e.g. many stories are of recent, 'breaking news' personal experiences; or they are counterfactual or near- future-oriented, shared imaginings of possible futures) and on the kind of teller and co-tellers, the kind of identity-work, that feature. And, by the same token, such social-semiotically rich contexts bear also on what does not get told and on who does not tell.

15.6 Other models of narrative

There is space here only briefly to mention one or two of the numerous other interesting modellings of text structure. One such tradition includes the work of Hymes and Gee. Gee, for example, has a richly-developed analytical system that makes an interesting contrast with the Labovian one. Gee finds a 'stanzaic' structuring in oral narratives (stanzas themselves are a prominent unit in a hierarchy of units: idea, line, stanza, strophe, and part), but this line-and-stanza structuring is only one of five levels of structure and meaning, each with its own formal marking in the language used, and each level playing a distinct role in the interpretation. For example, stanza and line, linguistically marked by patterning, convey ideas and perspectives on characters, events, states, and information (Gee 2014).

Different again is the influential work of Hoey on the structure of written text with some implications for written narratives. In Hoey 2001 he develops the dialogical account introduced in his 1983 book: he treats the phases of a text, the organisational progression, as the authorial supply of kinds of elaborating answers to the questions which the author has calculated that their prior text has prompted in the reader. Looking at the situation from the negative perspective, it is as if the writer embarking on a second sentence is assumed to be taking care not to write a sentence that will immediately seem unclear, unreliable, irrelevant, misleading or poorly organised, with too much information or too little. In written narratives, Hoey argues, readers are guided as to the direction and import of the story by lexical signals, vocabulary that helps the reader interpret the relationships between sentences or groups of sentences in a given text.

Stories need not be new and may be aimed at affirming shared values or solidarity rather than asserting power or authority (see, for example, Norrick 2000; Ochs and Capps 2001). And any storytelling involves representing matters in one way rather than in any of the possible other ways, with entities named one way and not another, and with some things commented on while others are passed over in silence. Thus a narrative can also be viewed as a complex network of mutually-compatible choices, without which coherence is put at risk: it is usually problematic to change the time-setting or location of adjacent events, or the manner of naming a protagonist, without demonstrably good reason. Conversely, multiple kinds of inconsistency and incoherence may on occasion point to identity trouble, a crisis in the teller's life, even psychological impairment.

This is why as overhearers we sense a little 'trouble' in the Glasgow story where the neighbour is variously called Mrs Mouldy and Mrs Mowdy: such instability is at odds with our expectation of being told 'exactly what happened'. This transcription variation, we assume, reflects a pronunciation variation on the part of the teller, which the transcriber has strived to represent. It would appear to be an instance of the labialisation of a post-vocalic lateral /l/, common enough in London English where 'milk' may be pronounced [mɪʊk] and transcribed as *miuk* or *miwk*. But assuming we are non-Scots-speaking overhearers, we may not even be sure about this: we may, instead, wonder if *mowdy* is a sanctioned Scots spelling of the English word *mouldy*, reflecting a pronunciation using a labialised allophone of the post-vocalic /l/. If the latter is *not* the case, then we are indebted to the transcriber for rendering the neighbour's name on at least one occasion by the spelling *mouldy*; because without this as clue, we would not have the basis for understanding that *mowdy* is in the circumstances insulting (any more than if a child consistently addressed an ill-tempered neighbour as *Mrs Grampy* would we be sure of the 'grumpy' insinuation). In the above case it may be pointed out that an audio recording of the storytelling is available to all, on the SCOTS website; so we can resolve some of these uncertainties. But listeners (trained phoneticians or not) frequently disagree over what they hear, even on top-quality recordings; besides, the transcriber has made their decision, and the published written version is as it is. This small instance is indicative of the nest of complexities that sociolinguistic transcription entails, raising important questions about 'fidelity', representation, the transcriber's theoretical assumptions and the evaluative effects subtly carried in a transcription's seemingly neutral description. A transcribed oral narrative is in effect a narrative of a narrative, and adjusting the one in relation to the other is often a matter of striking a balance among competing considerations.

As intimated earlier, a reliable assessment of the more covert meanings and patterns in an oral narrative, one attuned to the performances of identity and value that a teller's intended addressees would themselves recognise, often requires insider knowledge. If you are not a member of the particular culture from which a story emerges, you should be careful not to assume you fully grasp a story's resonances, as Bhaya Nair (2002) reminds us. Besides filling in a story's verbal gaps (*implicature*), she argues, we also need to know its explanatory cultural background, which she names its *impliculture*. Without knowledge of impliculture, we may not see the point, get the joke, or recognise the teller's tone and stance.

15.7 Why are narratives important to linguists?

Narratives are one of the best formats within which we can see dialects in action, language performing a range of functions, speakers presenting themselves on their own terms. And all this is especially true of the personal narrative (written or spoken). A sobering thought-experiment is to imagine what it would be like never to tell oral narratives of personal experience. To be in such a condition is almost definitional of being excluded, isolated, devalued, a non-person. Long before the age of majority or of puberty, children are coming into their linguistic enfranchisement by being able to tell their own stories (this would establish an interestingly different 'critical age' for linguistic proficiency – at perhaps four or five – than the standard accounts). Narratives are important to linguists because they are important to people, one of the most valued kinds of linguistic performance cherished in every kind of linguistic community, traditional or globalised, oral only or highly literate. Linguists go about studying them only in more systematic ways than ordinary storytellers and storylisteners use them. Ordinary story 'users' take care over the design of the text (oral or written) itself, and equally attend to the way in which the telling is performed. They are as aware as the analyst that there is a dual focus wherever narratives are told (an attending to the story, and an attending to the nature of the person telling the story) just as there is a double logic within the act of narration (an implicit sequence of actual or imagined events, and a representing of that sequence in the process of telling).

Since there has been, in recent years, a fairly extensive 'deconstruction' of the seemingly robust Labovian categories in their earliest presentation, it is all the harder to see present-day sociolinguistic narrative studies as dividing into two sharply distinct traditions or methodologies – one being Labovian-canonical, the other being social interactional. With sociolinguists shifting towards treating narratives as social practice, embedded in face and identity-maintenance, the methods and descriptive terms of the Labovians and the small-story analysts are recombining. Still, Georgakopoulou is right to warn analysts against the tendency to treat the classic narrative pattern as 'the endpoint of narrative development and the ideal form in which to cast the richness, depth and profundity of human experience' (2006: 237). The 'interactionists' make a crucial point in arguing that unfinished narratives are by no means inconsequential narratives. One such is the incomplete, ongoing Wikipedia narrative about the trial of Amanda Knox for the murder of student Meredith Kercher (as Page 2014 has argued), a narrative which with twists and turns in the investigation continues to be rewritten and enlarged by contributors from many countries. But also noteworthy are the innumerable stories started in the course of conversations but interrupted and never returned to for completion; or overheard on public transport or similar setting, stories heard only from beginning to middle, or from middle to end, given the timing of the overhearer's unplanned parting company with the teller. A half-heard narrative is no less important than a half-eaten meal. In Georgakopoulou's view, the interactionist 'turn' has consequences for how we conceptualise narrative as a genre (it needs to be seen as much more variable and heterogeneous, almost defying of simple genre description); for how we assess narratives as bases for identity-performance (recognising that identities are not static and timeless, but in continual process of discursive emergence, ratification and amendment); and for how we embrace the 'late modern' contingent and fragmented in narratives. Some of these questions may arise because small stories emerge from within a different framing activity than that of the controlled social scientific interview. At the same time many social scientists have also found that even within 'controlled interviews' a variety of small stories and story fragments can emerge; whether they are properly appreciated as such is another matter. The reality may be that a continuum exists, with degrees of narrative formality and structure discernible. Somewhere near the mid-point is the anecdote, traditionally anathema to the sciences, being 'the wrong kind of evidence'. But anecdotes are a rich site of contingent and user-defined meaning, as the integrational linguists Pablé and Hutton (2015) have argued.

Further reading

Antaki and Widdicombe (1998); Bamberg (2004); Bauman (1986); Georgakopoulou (2010); Herman (2009); Jefferson (1978); Labov (1972, 2013); Labov and Waletzky (1967); Norrick (1997); Ochs and Capps (1996); Schiffrin (1996); Toolan (forthcoming).

References

Document 351, Conversation 02: Glasgow woman on childhood memories, from The Scottish Corpus of Texts and Speech (SCOTS). Used with kind permission of Dr Eleanor Lawson, the copyright holder (SCOTS Project, University of Glasgow). www.scottishcorpus.ac.uk.

Antaki, C. and S. Widdicombe (eds) (1998) *Identities in Talk*. London: Sage.

Bamberg, M. (ed.) (1998) *Oral Versions of Personal Experience: Three Decades of Narrative Analysis. A Special Issue of the Journal of Narrative and Life History*. New York: Psychology Press.

Bamberg, M. (2004) Talk, small stories, and adolescent identities. *Human Development* 47: 366–9.

Bamberg, M., A. de Fina and D. Schiffrin (eds) (2007) *Selves and Identities in Narrative and Discourse*. Amsterdam: John Benjamins.

Bauman, R. (1986) *Story, Performance, and Event: Contextual Studies of Oral Narrative*. Cambridge: Cambridge University Press.

Bhaya Nair, R. (2002) *Narrative Gravity: Conversation, Cognition, Culture*. Delhi: Oxford University Press.

Biber, D., S. Johansson, G. Leech, S. Conrad and E. Finegan (1999) *Longman Grammar of Spoken and Written English*. London: Longman.

De Fina, A. and A. Georgakopoulou (2012) *Analyzing Narrative: Discourse and Sociolinguistic Perspectives*. New York: Cambridge University Press.

Eggins, S. and D. Slade (1997) *Analysing Casual Conversation*. London: Equinox.

Gee, J.P. (2014) *Introduction to Discourse Analysis: Theory and Method*, 4th edition. Abingdon: Routledge.

Georgakopoulou, A. (2006) The other side of the story: Towards a narrative analysis of narratives-in-interaction. *Discourse Studies* 8: 235–57.

Georgakopoulou, A. (2010) Narrative analysis. In R. Wodak, B. Johnstone and P.E. Kerswill (eds) *Sage Handbook of Sociolinguistics*, pp. 396–420. London: Sage.

Herman, D. (2009) *Basic Elements of Narrative*. New York: Wiley-Blackwell.

Hoey, M. (2001) *Textual Interaction: An Introduction to Written Discourse Analysis*. London: Routledge.

Hymes, D. (1996) *Ethnography, Linguistics, Narrative Inequality: Toward an Understanding of Voice*. London: Taylor and Francis.

Jefferson, G. (1978) Sequential aspects of storytelling in conversation. In J. Schenkein (ed.) *Studies in the Organization of Conversational Interaction*, pp. 219–49. New York: Academic Press.

Labov, W. (1972) *Language in the Inner City*. Philadelphia: University of Pennsylvania Press.

Labov, W. (2013) *The Language of Life and Death: The Transformation of Experience in Oral Narrative*. Cambridge: Cambridge University Press.

Labov, W. and J. Waletzky (1967) Narrative analysis: Oral versions of personal experience. In J. Helm (ed.) *Essays in the Verbal and Visual Arts*, pp. 12–44. Seattle: University of Washington Press.

Linde, C. (1993) *Life Stories: The Creation of Coherence*. Oxford: Oxford University Press.

Norrick, N.R. (1997) Twice-told tales: Collaborative narration of familiar stories. *Language in Society* 26: 199–220.

Norrick, N.R. (2000) *Conversational Narrative: Storytelling in Everyday Talk*. Amsterdam/Philadelphia: John Benjamins.

Ochs, E. and L. Capps (1996) Narrating the self. *Annual Review of Anthropology* 25: 19–43.

Ochs, E. and L. Capps (2001) *Living Narrative*. Cambridge: Harvard University Press.

Pablé, A. and C. Hutton (2015) *Signs, Meaning and Experience* (Semiotics, Communication and Cognition 14). Berlin/New York: Mouton de Gruyter.

Page, R. (2014) Counter narratives and controversial crimes: The Wikipedia article for the 'Murder of Meredith Kercher'. *Language and Literature* 23: 61–76.

Schiffrin, D. (1996) Narrative as self-portrait: Sociolinguistic constructions of identity. *Language in Society* 25: 167–203.

Toolan, M. (2001) *Narrative: A Critical Linguistic Introduction*, 2nd edition. London: Routledge.

Toolan, M. (forthcoming) *Making Sense of Narrative Text*. Abingdon: Routledge.

Wolfson, N. (1982) *CHP, The Conversational Historical Present in American English Narrative*. Cinnaminson: Foris Publications.

16
Anthropological linguistics and field linguistics

William A. Foley

16.1 Introduction

Anthropological linguistics and field linguistics form a natural synergism and have done so ever since their origins in the descriptive work of missionaries at the dawn of the colonial period in the early 1500s. For instance, the missionaries who followed in the wake of the conquest of Mexico set about learning the native languages and customs of the indigenous peoples in order to convert them more efficiently to Christianity, a motivation that continues down to the present day for many evangelical churches operating in developing countries. Still, it needs to be said that much of what we know about the languages and cultures of many human societies is due to the hard work of missionaries over the last five centuries, and much of what they have written is undoubtedly of high scholarly value. Indeed in my own area of research, New Guinea, I would estimate that over 80 percent of what we know about its languages results from the work of missionaries of one stripe or another. We may deplore many of their motives and lament the cultural loss that all too often followed in their wake, but our knowledge of the linguistics and ethnography of the world would be much impoverished without their efforts.

The colonial expansion of the European states from the fifteenth century was devastating for traditional peoples throughout the world. Missionaries only played one, if rather central, role in this plunder. Settlers and slavers were even more damaging. Through both European settlement and the transportation of African slaves into the Americas, the native peoples there were disinherited of their lands. This typically occurred after massive demographic collapse due to introduced diseases to which they had no resistance, and the consequent depopulation hindered their attempts to oppose intrusions by European settlers. They were settled on reserves, where they were strongly discouraged from practicing their traditional customs or speaking their native languages, and often severely punished for doing so. As a result, by the late nineteenth century in the United States and Canada, much of the knowledge of traditional cultural and linguistic practices was on the wane among the indigenous peoples. This spurred the work of the founder of anthropological linguistics and modern linguistic fieldwork techniques, Franz Boas, as he and his students – like Edward Sapir –

raced to document much of this knowledge before it was lost; more than a few of the languages Boas and his students documented are now extinct, and their work is all the documentation we will ever have of them. Boas and his students put anthropological linguistics and field linguistics on a much more scientific footing than it had held before, and in many ways the Boasian articulation of their synergism stills holds sway today. In order to undertake truly deep ethnographic work, Boas and his followers believed that a thorough grounding in the native language was indispensable, and for this the proper procedures of field linguistics as propounded by Boas were necessary. Field linguistics is still largely understood in the terms articulated by Boas and his students, although, of course, the technological resources available have developed exponentially since then, as has a reflexive concern with the ethical dimensions of fieldwork. Still, the basic principles and procedures are much the same. The chapter will provide a synopsis and illustration of these procedures. It will also highlight the importance of documentary linguistics, the need to document the full range of language forms, registers and styles used across as wide a range of genres and contexts as possible. This is, of course, essential to any ethnographic study of a language, which in essence is what anthropological linguistics is, but also provides a needed corrective to normative pressures as a result of language description and documentation, unavoidable as some might be.

16.2 Anthropological linguistics

While Boas never used the term 'anthropological linguistics,' as he believed linguistics was properly just one of the subfields of anthropology more generally, the term has come into general use over the last century as a point of contrast with structural or formal linguistics. Structural or formal linguistics looks at language as a system of opposing formal categories and their rules of combination. Linguistic analysis and description in structural linguistics are largely system internal so to speak, as a language is seen as a structured body of knowledge possessed by its speakers, in essence, a psychological endowment of competent speakers. Anthropological linguistics, on the other hand, is concerned with the place of language in its wider social and cultural context, its role in forging and sustaining cultural practices and social structures. Anthropological linguistics needs to be distinguished from a number of neighboring disciplines with overlapping interests, particularly its close sister, sociolinguistics. Anthropological linguistics views language through the prism of the core anthropological concept, culture, and, as such, seeks to uncover the *meaning* behind the use, misuse or non-use of language, its different forms, registers and styles. It is an interpretive discipline, peeling away at language to find cultural understandings. Anthropological linguistics studies how humans employ communicative cultural practices or *semiotic* practices as meaning bearing resources to forge and maintain large and small, transient or permanent, social groups. Sociolinguistics, on the other hand, views language as a social institution, one of those institutions within which individuals and groups carry out social interaction. It seeks to discover how linguistic behavior patterns with respect to social groupings and correlates differences in linguistic behavior with the variables defining social groups, such as age, sex, class, race, etc.

Because anthropological linguistics seeks to uncover the meaning behind the uses of language within culture, it also presents some overlap with semantics and pragmatics, particularly the latter. Again, without insisting on sharp boundaries, I would like to distinguish among these along the following lines. Semantics is that subfield of linguistics that studies the meanings of signs, their interrelations and combinations, while pragmatics, albeit a bit hazy in its own delimitations, investigates how speakers create meaning in context in ongoing acts of language use. In view of its definition offered above, anthropological linguistics can be contrasted with these two other fields by the central role that culture and cultural practices play in its descriptions. Consider a word *wampuŋ* from the Yimas language of New Guinea, which can be described semantically as polysemous, with the meanings 'heart, care, desire.' A pragmatic description will investigate its various uses in differing contexts to determine what extended meanings it can take on in appropriate contextual frames. But an anthropological linguistic description would go further and explore how this word is central in indigenous conceptualizations of morality and cultural practices of reciprocal gift exchange. Linguistic expressions and metaphors for culturally valorized practices related to generosity and exchange are built on this word. Finally, a detailed anthropological linguistic study will uncover the cultural beliefs and practices which account for why this word has the polysemous meanings it does; what, for instance, connects 'heart' with 'care' in indigenous ideology?

Duranti (2001) implies a contrast between anthropological linguistics and linguistic anthropology. While he denies that a true field of anthropological linguistics exists, preferring the term linguistic anthropology to cover this subfield, I regard the two terms as interchangeable. With some cogency, he argues that due to current concerns of mainstream linguistics with the explicit analysis of the formal structures of language in contrast to anthropology's broader approach of looking at how humans make meaning through semiotic systems in cultural practices, this subfield is properly included within anthropology, rather than linguistics. However, I beg to differ, believing that the current historical divisions of academic turf are just that, historical and contingent, and subject to change, and I would be loath to institutionalize such divisions by insisting on rigidly labeled compartments. The current disciplinary concerns of linguistics do not reflect its earlier history in which it was firmly enjoined to anthropology. I expect that over time this more inclusive view will reassert itself, and hence my preference is to use both terms to cover this subfield, although, as titled, I will stick with the label anthropological linguistics in this chapter.

There is, however, a useful contrast in foci of research in anthropological linguistics that could be captured by Duranti's (2001) implied opposition between anthropological linguistics and linguistic anthropology, namely, an investigation of the cross-linguistic variation of grammatical and semantic categories across languages and the implications of that variation for psychological processing and cultural practices (here the classificatory systems within the language provide the starting point for study) versus an exploration of how certain linguistic forms are used in ongoing cultural practices and social life to forge shared meanings (here observations of interactions in the ongoing flow of social action provide the point of departure for research). Obviously, these two approaches are not mutually exclusive, and many anthropological linguists are equally skilled in both, but they do represent different emphases in the project of understanding the role of language in sustaining cultural practices. The first of these approaches commonly goes under the name of linguistic relativity, and has a long pedigree in Western intellectual thought. But in its modern guise, it too traces itself back to Boas and the intellectual tradition that he founded. Boas emphasized the classificatory nature of language, and, in particular, how the differing systems of grammatical and semantic categories across languages forced speakers to attend to certain features of their environment when they constructed utterances. His classic example was the contrast between English and Kwak'wala. English requires tense and number and definiteness of nominal referents to be specified for all sentences, so that English speakers unlike, say, those of Indonesian, cannot say *man sick*, but must indicate all of these categories as in *the man is sick* or *the men were sick*. Kwak'wala, on the other hand, does not require that speakers specify tense or number, but it does demand that they indicate the visibility or invisibility of referents and their proximity or distance from the speaker or addressee, so that *man sick* would be expressed for instance as something like (in translation) *the man near me visible sick* or *the man not near me or you invisible sick*. Boas's foremost student, Edward Sapir, and his student in turn, Benjamin Lee Whorf developed such cross-linguistic observations into a full-fledged Principle of Linguistic Relativity, sometimes called the Sapir–Whorf Hypothesis, expressed most succinctly by Whorf (1956: 221) in the following:

> the 'linguistic relativity principle' … means, in informal terms, that users of markedly different grammars are pointed by their grammars toward different types of observations and different evaluations of externally similar acts of observation, and hence are not equivalent as observers but must arrive at somewhat different views of the world.

Put more simply, this means that the categorical distinctions that the languages we speak force us to attend to will predispose us to cognizing the world in particular ways; the categories of our language have a shaping influence on the categories of our thinking.

Boas, Sapir and Whorf did not see this as a hypothesis, something to be proved or disproved by experimental procedures involving the usual distinction between dependent and independent variables. Rather, it was more like a mathematical axiom, a shared postulate or assumed background of understanding, within which significant questions can be asked and valuable research work proceed. However, later and current work has taken it as a hypothesis to be investigated by standard batteries of psychological testing, probing for cognitive effects, if any, of the differing semantic and grammatical classificatory systems across languages. Such testing has now been carried out for a wide range of semantic and grammatical domains, e.g. color, number, shape, gender, time, eventhood. Here I will illustrate the methodology with the most impressive recent work along these lines, the investigation of the cognitive consequences of the differing systems of specifying spatial location across languages, a long-term research project at the Max Planck Institute for Psycholinguistics led by Stephen Levinson. A fundamental distinction in this domain is between languages which employ absolute spatial reckoning systems versus those which use relative spatial reckoning systems. Relative spatial reckoning systems such as those in English and familiar European languages use concepts like LEFT, RIGHT, FRONT, BACK, which have no fixed designation and depend on the speaker's orientation. If I am facing the house, the tree is on my left, in the space that extends from my left hand, but if I turn around so that my back is toward the house, then the tree is on my right; its spatial position is relative to my orientation. Absolute spatial reckoning systems fix the location of objects absolutely according to a fixed system of axes in geographical space, rather like our cardinal directions, north, south, east and west. A wide range of axes can be used in absolute systems. In addition to the cardinal directions, languages can use the direction of the flow of rivers, the direction of the winds, the coastline/seashore versus the interior of islands, or the vertical slant of the land. A particularly striking example of an absolute spatial reckoning system is found in Guugu-Yimidhirr, of northeastern Australia. This language employs four roots, corresponding roughly to the four cardinal directions, as in Figure 16.1.

Note that these spatial categories are absolutely fixed, due to the geography of Earth, and are not subject to variation according to the spatial orientation of the speaker. If something is to my north, it is to my north regardless of whether it is in front of me, in back

Figure 16.1 Four cardinal directions in Guugu-Yimidhirr (source: adapted from Levinson 2003: 116)

of me, to my left or to my right. Its spatial position is absolutely fixed with respect to mine, regardless of my relative viewpoint.

Levinson (2003) investigated the cognitive consequences of the absolute spatial reckoning system of Guugu-Yimidhirr speakers and contrasted them with a control group of Dutch speakers, whose linguistic system is the egocentric, relativistic equivalent of English. His experiments probed the cognitive consequences of this absolute system by systematically testing the recognition and recall of spatial orientation of objects for Guugu-Yimidhirr men. In one recognition test, speakers facing north were shown two cards, each with a red square and a blue rectangle toward an edge. On one card the red square was to the viewer's left and the blue rectangle to his right; the other was reversed (of course, they were identical cards, just rotated 180°). The speaker was asked to choose one card and remember it. He was then led into another room, with another table with the same two cards lying on it, but now facing south. Note that Guugu-Yimidhirr speakers and Dutch speakers should behave differently here. If a Dutch speaker chose the card with the red square to his left (in the west quadrant), when rotated south he should still choose a card with the red square to his left (but this time in the *east* quadrant). The Guugu-Yimidhirr speaker should show no such switch; having chosen the card with the red square to the west, he should stick with this choice, regardless of the fact that the square is now on his right when previously it was on his left.

The results were exactly as predicted: nine out of ten Guugu-Yimidhirr speakers chose the card with the red square in the same quadrant regardless of whether they were looking north or south, demonstrating that they were clearly identifying the cards on the basis of absolutely aligned quadrants. All fifteen subjects of a Dutch control group contrasted in identifying the cards on the basis of a relativistic egocentric LEFT–RIGHT axis. These psychological tests do then support a claim of linguistic relativity in the domain of spatial reckoning; the variations in how space is categorized between Dutch and Guugu-Yimidhirr are systemically related to differences in cognition: Guugu-Yimidhirr speakers, whose language has absolute spatial reckoning terms, systematically and regularly perform differently in such psychological tests than do speakers of Dutch, a language like English with relative spatial reckoning terms.

Note that the standard Whorfian interpretation of the Principle of Linguistic Relativity and that of ongoing work in this mold, such as Levinson's discussed here, is concerned with the denotational symbolic properties of language and their consequences for cognition: taking the semantic and grammatical categories of various languages as axes of classification for how the things of the world can be referred to or talked about, these are then investigated for the consequences for how these things can be known or remembered. In two classic

Anthropological linguistics

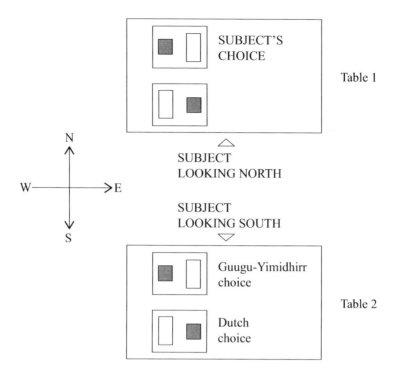

Figure 16.2 Cognitive consequences of spatial reckoning systems

articles, Silverstein (1976, 1979) extended the idea of linguistic relativity to the indexical pragmatic properties of languages, and this brings me to my second main topic: how certain linguistic forms are used in ongoing cultural practices and social life to forge shared meanings. Indexes are signs whose interpretation is dependent on the immediate context, as smoke is an index of a fire. Languages are shot through with vital indexical signs that require context for interpretation, such as pronouns *I* and *you*; temporal words like *now*, *then* and *tomorrow*; spatial words like *here* and *there*; and so forth. Silverstein points out that there is a crucial distinction between types of indexical signs in languages, a contrast he labels presupposing versus creative, and this contrast is central to a great deal of work done in anthropological linguistics. The contrast is not absolute, but more of a cline. Presupposing indexes are those whose use requires a prior context to be realized in order for their usage to be felicitous. Good examples of these are deictics like *now*. *Now* cannot be used to index the time of an event when the presupposed context, i.e. co-occurrence at the moment of speaking, cannot be satisfied. For another example consider the avoidance languages of Australian Aboriginal languages, special registers of these languages mandated for usage when speaking with one's in-laws. Note that the use of these registers presupposes the context of one's in-law as the addressee. Yet another example are gender deictics like *káp* and *khâ* in Thai; these presuppose a male and female speaker respectively.

More interesting are the more creative indexes; these are legion and the stock in trade of much work in both anthropological linguistics and sociolinguistics. Very obvious examples are the markers of genre types, such as *once upon a time*. The very fact that a text begins with this formulaic expression immediately calls into mind a context in which the following text is to be interpreted as a fairy tale; they trigger the interpretive context which construes the text as a fairy tale. For another, consider the phenomenon of code switching, in which bilingual speakers switch between languages. In very many situations, it is the choice of the language that creates the context in which the interaction is carried out between speakers. Consider the situation of a Yimas villager, bilingual in Yimas vernacular and Tok Pisin. If the villager chooses to speak Yimas to a fellow villager, he is creating a context of relaxed non-formal interaction about village or domestic matters, but if he chooses to speak Tok Pisin, immediately this raises a more serious tone to the conversation, likely to be about business or politics or other extra-village matters. The choice of the language itself creates the context within which the verbal interaction will be interpreted. The phenomenon of covert prestige provides another example, as in this case study from the English dialect spoken in Norwich, East Anglia (Trudgill 1972). In the local dialect spoken there, the pronunciation of the final vowel in *ear, idea, here* varies from the standard pronunciation [ɪə] to a local pronunciation which makes *ear* rhyme with *air*, and *here*, with *hair*. The investigator Peter Trudgill tape recorded interviews and noted the actual distribution of pronunciations for each interviewee. He then asked each of them how they thought they pronounced these words, noting that some self-reports were accurate, some overestimated their use of the standard varieties (over-reporting) and some underestimated it (under-reporting), and these were the results for male speakers:

Over-reporting	22 percent
Under-reporting	50 percent
Accurate	28 percent

Note that half of the men claimed to be using the local, more working-class rhyming variant when, in fact, they were using the standard. It seems the local speech forms typical of working-class speech have an appeal to middle-class men, associated, as it seems to be, with masculinity and toughness, reflecting clear articulations of gender understandings in British culture. Hence we can expect that when a middle-class man uses the working-class variant he is creating a context in which his gender role is being constructed in a particular way and through which his verbal interchanges need to be interpreted quite differently from when he uses the standard pronunciation. For a final more complex example, consider the elaborate speech level phenomena of Javanese. In this language the social relationship between speaker and addressee is marked by the choice of language register: *ngoko* or low register for a solidary relationship of equals and when a higher ranked person speaks to a lower one, and *karma* for non-solidary relationships or when a lower ranked person speaks to a higher one:

NGOKO:	apa	kowé	njupuk	sega	semono
KRAMA:	menapa	panjemenjan	mendhet	sekul	semontem
	Q	you	take	rice	that much

'Will you take that much rice?'

All the words in these two sentences are distinct in the two registers; this is a much more elaborate system for the signaling of social relations than that of the contrast between *tu* and *vous* in French. But the function is similar. The choice of *ngoko* versus *karma* actually defines the social relationship between speakers in the verbal interaction; they make explicit the terms in which the interlocutors will regard each other. Although other semiotic markers can be taken as a wider context to indicate relative rank, such as dress or demeanor, the choice of register is not presupposed by that context; speakers can always refuse to recognize the status of such markers. But when a register has been selected, the relative status of the interlocutors and therefore the context for the ongoing verbal interaction is set. These cross-linguistically variable systems of indexical signs are a second source of linguistic relativity. Because they commonly create the context within which ongoing discourse must be interpreted, differing indexical systems across languages will set up quite different contextual frameworks for the interpretation of utterances. Because these contexts constitute the actual life worlds in which verbal actors make sense of signs, different cultural interpretations of these signs arise, and this can lead to much misunderstanding.

Hymes (1972) offers yet a third nexus of linguistic relativity. He argues that the actual range and types of uses of language vary widely across the speech communities of the world. Different cultures often impose quite different conventions for the use and form of language in comparable social situations, and appropriate linguistic practices in line with these conventions is a required characteristic for a speaker's membership in the linguistic community as a competent member, what Hymes has called *communicative competence*. Because linguistic practices are the primary human communicative behavior through which humans sustain sociocultural life, different systems of such practices entail different sociocultural worlds. Cultural values and beliefs are in part constitutive of linguistic reality. The field of study which has grown out of Hymes's insight is called the Ethnography of Communication. Work in this tradition has very much focused on the performance of language, on how various genres are performed and evaluated in differing cultures and in turn how these are related to wider sociocultural frames of practice. The performance of speech acts or verbal arts are favorite areas of study. For instance, Rosaldo (1982) contrasts the performance of the speech act of directives or orders between speakers of English and Ilongot of the Philippines. Directives in English are commonly issued with a good deal of redress, to avoid affronts to the recipient's negative face, their right not to be imposed upon. This is a right highly valued in English speaking culture, tied as it is to notions of individualism, privacy and autonomous choice of action. But Ilongot speakers typically issue them baldly with no redressive action, but they do not regard these as an affront to their equality and dignity, because they are viewed as expressing reasonable social expectations, relationships nurtured in continuing social interactions, rather than impositions of the other's prerogatives of action. The Ilongot do not regard speech acts as the achievement of individualist selves coding their intentions in linguistic expressions, but most prominently as ways of invoking cooperative bonds among people, and cooperation is fundamental to social interactions in this egalitarian society.

The construction of genres, diverse types of texts, is another favorite stomping ground of ethnographers of communication. Genres consist of historically transmitted, relatively stable frameworks for orienting the production and interpretation of discourse. While strongly conventionalized and grounded in the social practices of language production and understanding in the community, they are still nonetheless flexible and open to creative manipulation by performers. It is creative flexibility that allows them to be molded to diverse and changing cultural needs. For example, the telling of a fable may be to entertain, but it also may be used to instruct children about proper moral behavior, as in Aesop's Fables. The choice of which fable to relate may be prompted by a particular child's misbehavior earlier in the day, so that the performance of the fable indexes both wider sociocultural beliefs about proper moral behavior as well as a currently relevant social relationship between the performer (the father) and the audience (the naughty child). Bowen (1989) describes how a traditional poetic genre among the Gayo of Sumatra has been recast now as a propaganda tool of modern Indonesian nationalism. In traditional egalitarian Gayo society these poetic duels were mainly individualized; they resembled formal oratory which involves turn-taking between two virtuoso orators representing different villages. The text of these duels was highly formulaic. Turns during the duel consisted of fixed two-line proverbs of high parallelism. Since the late 1940s the Gayo have been part of the Indonesian nation state, a large centralizing and modernizing political entity. In order to propagate its nationalist and modernist ideology, the local government administration has off and on encouraged a new type of performance of poetic duels. Unlike the traditional individualist approach, these performances involve teams, consisting of between ten and twenty men and boys, each led by two to four head orators. Each team composes songs, many of which provide religious advice or commentary on economic development or current politics. These performances are staged for local entertainment, but with a clear wider political aim by the ruling elites. Literacy practices too exhibit great cross-linguistic variation in how they are practiced and understood. Kulick and Stroud (1993) show that literate practices among the Gapun of New Guinea, while introduced through westernization via schooling and missionization, have been taken up in a particularly indigenous way: written texts, especially those of the New Testament or other religious tracts, can be used to intercede with God to realize desired outcomes. This tallies very closely with their traditional ideological understanding of language. Certain words uttered in certain contexts have the power through supernatural sanction to bring about desired outcomes. Hence, what is most striking about Gapun literacy practices is how much they have taken on as norms the uses of language associated with oral discourse, particularly oratory.

16.3 Field linguistics

The methods of field linguistics vary somewhat depending on one's research interests. If the researcher's interests are descriptive or theoretical linguistics, the methodologies required can be more circumscribed than if they are engaged in anthropological linguistic pursuits. Because of very rapid technological change, I will not be addressing equipment needs for the collection of data in the field here at all; potential fieldworkers should check with knowledgeable experts about current best practice before departing for their field site. For reasons of space limitations, I will also not be dealing with the matter of ethical issues surrounding fieldwork besides stating the golden rule: treat others as you yourself would like to be treated. This is not because I regard them as unimportant, to the contrary they are vital, but they require much more than the few paragraphs I could devote to them here; the reader is invited to consult the relevant chapters of Bowern (2008), Chelliah and de Reuse (2011), Crowley (2007) or Sakel and Everett (2012).

The best way to investigate the language of a community is in situ, living within the village and learning as many of the social customs of the people as possible. This is indispensable if the goal of research is a topic within anthropological linguistics, such as the performance of specific genres or how spatial terms are used in everyday navigation. But even if the goals are squarely within descriptive linguistics, like writing a grammar or preparing a dictionary, where it could be conceivable to carry out this task while working with one or two language consultants in the comfort of one's own office or home, it is still highly desirable to spend long periods of time in a community where the language is spoken. In many cases the social contexts in which the language is used daily will affect aspects of its structure; for instance, the functions of discourse particles can hardly be understood in any other way. Further, it is very important, if time and circumstances permit, for the linguist to learn to speak the language she is studying, and again this is even a more pressing need if the research has an anthropological bent. The best way to do this is to live in the village where, hopefully, if the language is not moribund, one is surrounded by the language in constant use. This is not to say that valuable work cannot be done without a speaking knowledge of the language; many good studies have come from linguists who could not speak the language under investigation. Still, there will be many aspects of the language and its use which can only be properly understood, indeed discovered, with good active spoken competence. Normally, the researcher will not come to the field site with much knowledge, if any, of the language to be studied, and will need to rely at first on a contact language, typically the lingua franca of the region which she has learnt before arrival in the field site (monolingual fieldwork is so rare these days that I am ignoring this possibility, but see Sakel and Everett 2012). But it is important not to extend this reliance unduly, as this will seriously impede, perhaps even forestall, acquisition of the language under investigation. It is quite likely that the contact language enjoys higher prestige than the village language, and once villagers develop a habit of addressing the linguist in the contact language, it will become a habit very hard to break. It is strongly encouraged that the linguist start using as much of the village language as her competence will allow as soon as possible after arrival and continually expand this competence, even if her inadequate efforts are a constant source of amusement to the villagers (as I can assure you from my own experience, they will be). Few linguists will ever achieve anything like the full competence of an adult native speaker, but efforts in this direction are always appreciated by the community, and also failure to perceive improvements in the language competence of the linguist may be a source of discouragement for the language consultants and lead them to lose interest in the research project.

Social conditions will commonly constrain who can serve as language consultants. In many communities, such as some in New Guinea in which I have worked, it will be considered inappropriate for the consultants to be the opposite sex to the fieldworker. If the fieldworker is male, this can present special problems, for the men may commonly work away from the village during the day in gardens, hunting or paid work. But this can be a boon too, as elderly, physically incapacitated, village bound men often possess fuller and more accurate language information. Still, this can be frustrating, as, for instance, in New Guinea, it has commonly been my experience that older women are the most knowledgeable about their native language, but local mores exclude them from being possible consultants. A male and female team seems to make the best fieldworkers. In selecting language consultants, the linguist should look for people who are keen to teach the language, have an outgoing, communicative personality, and, most importantly, will not get bored with the often long and tedious hours of data elicitation. Be careful in your selection of consultants (that is, if there is a large choice; in situations of moribund languages, there will not be). Try working with a number of different people at first, because if a particular person turns out to be unsuitable to the task for whatever reason, but has been selected early as a main language consultant, for the linguist to discontinue working with them could be socially unacceptable, taken as a serious social rebuff. The fieldworker should be sure about the suitability of someone as a consultant before taking them on.

Before sitting down to serious work with consultants, the linguist will have heard the language being spoken around them for some days, but is unlikely to have made much headway, because long unbroken chains of discourse are simply too difficult to process at this early stage. When she now initiates formal data elicitation sessions with her consultants, her first task is to master the sound system of the language; only with this foundation can she go on to grammar and discourse. The best way to do this is with simple words. The linguist draws up a list of some 200–500 basic words, largely nouns, but also pronouns, and a few common verbs, adjectives, adverbs and numerals. Mostly nouns, though, as they are both easy to elicit and commonly morphologically simpler than the other parts of speech, and they should include words for body parts, kin terms, animals and important plants, household and local cultural objects, and geographical and natural objects. The linguist should say the word in the eliciting contact language and prompt a response in the vernacular equivalent. The consultant says this twice, after which the linguist attempts to repeat it. The consultant will say if the attempt is correct or not. If correct, the linguist records the item in phonetic transcription in her fieldnotes. If incorrect, the consultant is asked to repeat it again, and the linguist attempt to imitate again. This can go on for a few more times, but in no cases should the consultant be badgered to repeat this process more than five times. If the word is too difficult for the linguist at this stage, skip to the next one and come back to it later. After transcribing about fifty words or so in this manner, they should be tape recorded for later, more detailed work.

After recording some 500 words or so, the linguist can perform a provisional phonemic analysis. This will permit them to move on to the elicitation of morphological structures. Some languages like Vietnamese or Hawai'ian have little or no morphology; others, like polysynthetic languages such as Yimas or Pawnee, have a great deal. In language with little morphology, syntactic structures take up its functions, so in field linguistics it is impossible to insist on a strict demarcation of elicitation procedures for morphology versus syntax. Furthermore, both ultimately need to be studied as they are used in actual spontaneous discourse; only in textual discourse will the natural morphological and syntactic patterns of the language emerge. But, at this early stage, with only a basic knowledge of the phonology, the linguist is just too ignorant of the basic morphosyntax of the language to make much sense of the running discourse of texts. It is necessary to do some basic elicitation work to construct an understanding of the fundamental morphological units and syntactic constructions, but it is absolutely vital to bear in mind that elicited data in morphosyntax will probably give quite an artificial view of the language. A language description of any sort should *never* be based principally on elicited data, for these may reflect the contrived situation of the elicitation session or the morphosyntactic patterns of the contact language used in elicitation. The primary data for any description must be the natural spontaneous data of narrative, expository or conversational texts, collected in a variety of contexts. Also, only if a reliable primary grammatical description already exists can projects of a more anthropological bent proceed, such as investigation of the performance of specific genre types or the use of indexical forms to enact social hierarchies.

In building up a basic profile of the morphosyntax of a language, I suggest the following procedure:

1. Elicit basic inflectional categories for nouns, such as number and possession, e.g. *one house*, *two houses*, *many houses* or *my house*, *your house*, etc. If nouns exhibit varying inflectional patterns, this is probably indicative of a gender or noun class system. Basic noun phrases can also be elicited at this point: *three black pigs*, *two tall men*, etc.
2. Elicit basic inflectional categories for verbs: i.e. tense, *she walked*, *she is walking*, *she will walk*; aspect, *she is eating now*, *she has already eaten*. The fieldworker should elicit these with third person subjects, as first and second person often get hopelessly garbled in translation, so that a prompt *I am listening* often comes back as *you are listening* and vice versa. The researcher should choose verbs denoting simple actions like *walk*, *hit*, *run*, *jump*, *eat*, *sleep*, *talk*, *break*, a mixture of transitive and intransitive verbs, to investigate whether there are significant conjugation differences.

3. Now proceed to eliciting full paradigms for verbs, again using a mixture of both transitive and intransitive verbs, e.g. *I run, you*(SG) *run, he runs, she runs*, and so on, and *I hit you*(SG)*, he hit me, she hit me, you*(SG) *hit me, you*(SG) *hit him, you*(SG) *hit her* and so forth, in all combinations of person and number for both subject and object, constantly bearing in mind the common confusion and switch in first and second person pronouns. The paradigms for transitive and intransitive verbs should be elicited in all three basic tenses and then in the negated forms for all three.
4. The linguist is now in a position to elicit basic clauses with the two principal parts of speech, noun and verbs. Simple clauses can be elicited both with intransitive verbs, e.g. *The woman is cooking, the sick man will die, two old trees fell down*, and transitive ones, *the woman is cooking meat, the man cut down the tree, the two tall men will eat the meat*, and so forth. Various combinations of nouns, noun phrases and verbs should be tried to see if these link to systematic differences in the clause structure, such as case marking being determine by choices of different verbs. Phrases specifying temporal or locational notions can also be added to these eliciting clause prompts. These elicited clauses may provide information about the word order of constituents, but this must be treated with caution, as it may simply reflect the word order of the prompting language of elicitation.

Finally, now the linguist has acquired enough understanding of the basic building blocks of language to begin working with ongoing discourse and texts. A text is a body of language behavior generated continuously over a period of time by language consultants and recognized as an integrated whole. The texts the fieldworker is initially concerned with are conversations and narratives. The types of texts of much anthropological linguistic interest, such as songs, poems and other forms of oral literature, are usually too difficult at this early stage, with many archaic and stylized forms. Conversations, too, are likely to prove somewhat difficult because of their speed, the presence of multiple speakers, and reduced colloquial forms. But they are very important sources of information about the meanings of the indexical signs of the language so, difficult or not, they must be studied, especially if the linguist hopes to acquire fluency in the language. Narrative texts are of two types: personal experiences of the consultants and their acquaintances or traditional myths and legends. The latter are the most popular form of texts with many fieldworkers and are undoubtedly a rich source of data, but they are more difficult to work with than the former, for their status as myths sanctioned by tradition means their form may be heavily stylized and less typical of everyday language. In gathering texts, the full text should first be video recorded, and then the linguist works slowly through it section by section with consultants to transcribe it.

A crucial step in fieldwork is the analysis and expansion of textual material; this should in fact constitute the bulk of the primary data. Analyzing a transcribed text in the early stages of fieldwork will be difficult: word boundaries will be hard to identify, and many words and morphemes unknown. But with a gradually increasing corpus, as recurring forms are identified, things will become clearer. A very important role for texts is in their basis for supplementary elicitation. Many morphemes and constructions will only come to the fieldworker's attention for the first time in transcribed texts, and she can then use these examples as a basis to collect further data so that enough material is available to describe the morpheme or construction.

Given the topics that they normally research, anthropological linguists typically need a further kit of methods beyond the ones already described here, because they are concerned with studying the language in its daily use across a whole range of genres and practices and across a wide range of speakers to determine the patterns of variation. For example, anthropological linguists interested in the local genres of verbal art, such as divination chants or political oratory, will need to video record these in live performances, not rely on contrived staged renditions for their documentation. The researcher will have to keep a low profile in such live performances to minimize any effects the recording equipment or their own presence may have on its form. Documenting conversations across a wide range of contexts and with speakers diverse in age, gender and social rank are indispensable in any anthropological linguistic research, but recording natural conversations presents similar problems in the self-censoring effects that the recording equipment may have on the interlocutors. Surreptitious recording is of course unethical, so ways must be found to habituate speakers to the presence of the recording equipment; often, simple familiarity is sufficient to do the trick. There is an entire discipline, whose methodology is often used by anthropological linguists, called Conversational Analysis (Sidnell 2010) that investigates conversation as a central domain for the way speakers use ongoing indexical cues to construct shared social meanings.

Perhaps the core methodology used by anthropological linguists is the same as that used by social and cultural anthropologists more generally – participant observation, the observation of the ongoing social life of the members of the speech community. This entails being in the middle of things as they unfold in the community, being keenly observant of as many details as one can take in, and making copious notes of what one has observed. From these notes and observations one will gradually discern recurring patterns, and these will allow one to generate hypotheses about what the various linguistic behaviors she has observed actually *mean*, for, as I noted at the outset of this chapter, the goal of anthropological linguistic research is to uncover the meaning behind the use of language in its varying forms. Participant observation on its own cannot answer these questions about meanings. For that we need the testimony of native actors, and anthropological linguists generally use two methods to obtain that: interviews and testing. Interviews can be structured or open-ended, but the point of them is to get native actors to talk about how they regard or interpret the social behavior the fieldworker is interested in. Again, it is vital to interview a number of people drawn from a wide range of social roles about such topics to get a full understanding, as the behavior may carry different meanings for different people (if this is appropriate; in some cases, it may not be if the information is restricted to certain groups, such as esoteric clan knowledge or women's business). It is important to bear in mind too that the understanding of interviews as a genre may vary quite widely across cultures; in some cases, it may be inappropriate for cultural outsiders or apprentices (and the anthropological linguist will quite likely find herself in one of these roles) to ask questions of an expert about their areas of expertise. In these cases one will have to find a rapprochement suitable to the community so that something akin to interviews can be conducted. Types of tests can be a useful supplement to interviews as a way of getting at the native construal of local linguistic practices. Based on the researcher's hypotheses developed from observation, questionnaires can be developed presenting a number of differing scenarios or stimuli. Speakers are then asked for their reactions to these stimuli, and these can be taken as local interpretations or meanings for the linguistic practices the stimuli depict. Again care must be taken with such batteries of testing so that both the stimuli and the overall context of the situation in which the testing is administered are as close to experiences encountered in everyday life as possible, but they are very useful in collecting large amounts of data from many different people in a relatively short time.

Further reading

Agha (2007); Ahearn (2012); Duranti (1997); Foley (1997); Hanks (1996)

References

Agha, A. (2007) *Language and Social Relations*. Cambridge: Cambridge University Press.
Ahearn, L. (2012) *Living Language: An Introduction to Linguistic Anthropology*. Oxford: Wiley-Blackwell.
Bowen, J. (1989) Poetic duels and political change in the Gayo highlands of Sumatra. *American Anthropologist* 91: 25–40.
Bowern, C. (2008) *Linguistic Fieldwork: A Practical Guide*. Basingstoke: Palgrave Macmillan.
Chelliah, S. and W. de Reuse (2011) *Handbook of Descriptive Linguistic Fieldwork*. Dordrecht: Springer.
Crowley, T. (2007) *Field Linguistics: A Beginner's Guide*. Oxford: Oxford University Press.
Duranti, A. (1997) *Linguistic Anthropology*. Cambridge: Cambridge University Press.
Duranti, A. (2001) Linguistic anthropology: History, ideas, issues. In A. Duranti (ed.) *Linguistic Anthropology: A Reader*, pp. 1–38. Oxford: Blackwell.
Foley, W.A. (1997) *Anthropological Linguistics: An Introduction*. Oxford: Blackwell.
Hanks, W. (1996) *Language and Communicative Practices*. Boulder: Westview Press.
Hymes, D. (1972) Toward ethnographies of communication: The analysis of communicative events. In P. Giglioli (ed.) *Language and Social Context*, pp. 21–44. Harmondsworth: Penguin.
Kulick, D. and C. Stroud (1993) Conceptions and uses of literacy in a Papua New Guinean village. In B. Street (ed.) *Cross-Cultural Approaches to Literacy*, pp. 30–61. Cambridge: Cambridge University Press.
Levinson, S.C. (2003) *Space in Language and Cognition: Explorations in Cognitive Diversity*. Cambridge: Cambridge University Press.
Rosaldo, M.Z. (1982) The things we do with words: Ilongot speech acts and speech act theory in philosophy. *Language in Society* 11: 203–37.
Sakel, J. and D. Everett (2012) *Linguistic Fieldwork: A Student Guide*. Cambridge: Cambridge University Press.
Sidnell, J. (2010) *Conversational Analysis: An Introduction*. Oxford: Blackwell.
Silverstein, M. (1976) Shifters, linguistic categories and cultural description. In K. Basso and H. Shelby (eds.) *Meaning in Anthropology*, pp. 11–55. Albuquerque: University of New Mexico Press.
Silverstein, M. (1979) Language structure and linguistic ideology. In P. Clyne, W. Hanks and C. Hofbauer (eds.) *The Elements: A Parasession on Linguistic Units and Levels*, pp. 193–247. Chicago: Chicago Linguistics Society.
Trudgill, P. (1972) Sex, covert prestige and linguistic change in the urban British English of Norwich. *Language in Society* 1: 179–95.
Whorf, B. (1956) *Language, Thought and Reality: Selected Writings of Benjamin Lee Whorf*. Cambridge: MIT Press.

17
Sociolinguistics
Language in social environments

Maya Ravindranath and Suzanne Evans Wagner

17.1 Language variation and change

If there were two pervasive myths about language that sociolinguists would like to dispel, they would probably be the myth that language can or should remain static, and the myth that one dialect can be inherently superior to another in some way. These commonly held myths contradict the primary principles of sociolinguistics – that the form of a language varies as a reflection of social variation between and within communities, and that at least some of this variation will result in long-term language change.

Although the discipline of sociolinguistics that we describe in this chapter is relatively young, these basic principles have their roots in the earlier established disciplines of historical linguistics and sociology, and sociolinguists still share a close connection with scholars in these fields. The difference today between sociolinguistics and the related subfields of anthropological linguistics (see Chapter 16) and the sociology of language is that the primary focus of sociolinguistics is on linguistic structure itself. Although sociolinguistics concerns itself with language in its social context, and consequently with both linguistic and social factors, the focus remains on linguistic structure as opposed to language use, the latter being a more central concern to the sociology of language.

Weinreich *et al.* (1968) laid out the principles for the study of language 'as an object possessing orderly heterogeneity' (p. 100). The focus of this paradigm is the synchronic observation of language change as it happens, through close examination and quantification of linguistic variables that are correlated with social characteristics of speakers and aspects of the interactions between speakers. One of the guiding principles of this research paradigm has been the 'use of the present to explain the past,' (also known as the Uniformitarian Principle, Labov 1978) which proposes that at least some of the linguistic variation that can be observed today is evidence of change in progress, and that all of the change that occurs in language is preceded by a period of variation.

As an example we can take the development of the use of *do* in yes–no questions in the Late Middle English period. Before it became obligatory to use the auxiliary verb *do* in a yes–no question, as in *Do you like green beans?* the use of *do* in this context was variable and speakers could either form questions like *Wrote you this letter?* (the earlier and previously exclusive form) or *Did you write this letter?* (the newer form) (Ellegård 1953, in Kroch 1989). The use of *do*-insertion in questions is an example of what is known as a 'linguistic variant' in sociolinguistic terminology. An abstract linguistic variable is realized by functionally equivalent linguistic variants ('two ways of saying the same thing'), so in this example questions with *do*-insertion and questions without *do*-insertion are two variants of the variable 'yes–no questions.'

Linguistic variation and ensuing change can occur at all levels of the grammar, although some types are better researched than others. Language can vary at the level of the lexicon, as in the regionally variable terms in English for a carbonated beverage (*soda, pop, tonic, coke, fizzy drink, soft drink*) or for a pair of shoes with rubberized soles (*sneakers, trainers, plimsolls, tennis shoes*). Relatedly, the meaning of words may vary at the level of semantics or pragmatics. For many speakers of American English, for example, the use of the adverb *anymore* in a positive utterance is perfectly acceptable, as in *Everybody looks young anymore* ('Everybody looks young nowadays'), whereas for other speakers this sentence is completely ungrammatical, as *anymore* for those speakers may only occur in a negative or interrogative utterance (e.g. *Nobody looks young anymore*).

Syntactic variation occurs when a grammatical function, such as asking yes–no questions (above), may be performed using semantically equivalent syntactic structures. Likewise, variation at the level of morphology may occur when a single function has multiple forms: e.g. relative pronoun *who* and *whom* variability in modern English. To date the best-researched cases of variation are at the levels of phonetics and phonology. Phonetic variation refers to any variable pronunciation of sounds that does not affect the phonological system, as in the variable palatalization of dental stops in Cairene Arabic, where /t/ may be pronounced as either [tʲ] or [tʃ] (Haeri 1994), or the variable pronunciation of intervocalic /g/ as [ŋ] in Japanese (Hibiya 1995). Phonological variation on the other hand refers to variations in pronunciation that affect the phonological system in some way, generally through the addition or subtraction of a sound from the phonemic inventory. French, for example, acquired phonemic nasal vowels after a period of variable nasal assimilation to following nasal consonants e.g. [bon] and [bõ] for *bon* 'good.'

To summarize, language may vary at all levels of the linguistic structure, and some of this variation will lead to long-term language change. The challenge sociolinguists face is how to observe and quantify this variation, as well as how to determine whether any particular instance of synchronic language variation is evidence of diachronic change. In general, the first step is to identify the linguistic variable and its variants. In the case of the Cairene Arabic example above, for instance, one would identify the variants [t], [tʲ], and [tʃ] of the abstract variable (t).[1] The second step is to find a way to observe natural language use that is likely to contain the variable, select speakers from relevant social groups and across the age spectrum, and design a relevant data collection method. The final step is to analyze the linguistic variable with respect to the relevant social factors.

The primary goal of selecting speakers from across the age spectrum relates to the relationship between synchronic variation and diachronic change. Only real-time historical data can provide a definitive answer to the question of whether an instance of synchronic variation is indicative of diachronic change. But when real-time data are not yet available, either because the variant is too new or because it has not been studied before, sociolinguists rely on the apparent time construct to surmise the presence of change in progress. The apparent time construct takes age as a proxy for the passage of time, concluding that differences across generations of adults from a single speech community mirror actual diachronic developments. The underlying assumption of this construct is that the speech of each generation reflects the language as it was at the time that generation learned the language, an assumption which depends on the notion of a critical period for language acquisition and little to no change throughout an individual's lifespan.

The use of apparent time requires large amounts of natural speech data to provide an overview of what is going on in the community. These data typically cannot be collected under survey or lab conditions, since understanding the mechanisms of language change requires knowledge of the social context of language use. Although speech and/or judgments are collected from individual speakers, the focus in sociolinguistics is always on the community as the object of study. Although more recent sociolinguistic work has looked at smaller communities of practice (discussed further below), the emphasis in much of the field remains on the speech community, defined broadly as a group of people who share a common structural base and social evaluation of linguistic variables (Labov 1972a). Although sociolinguists may differ on the size and type of community that is meaningful with respect to linguistic variation, all researchers in this vein place importance on the interrelationship between the social groups that individual speakers belong to, the social context of language use, and linguistic variation within and between such groups.

Exactly how do sociolinguists collect large quantities of naturally occurring speech under maximally natural conditions? What does 'maximally natural' mean? A special focus of sociolinguistic research has been a concern with capturing the vernacular, or a speaker's most natural and unmonitored speech. There is good reason for this. The public tends to believe that languages should be static objects, and that language changes are inherently undesirable. The motivations for this belief are complex, but are largely due to the association between language changes and speakers of non-standard varieties. Linguistic innovations tend to emerge more readily in the non-standard varieties of a language. Unlike the standard variety, these dialects are not subject to a high degree of normative pressure from educators, are mostly spoken in the home, and are neither codified in dictionaries nor in many cases written down at all. They are spoken among less powerful groups such as the young, the urban working class, the rural poor and ethnic minorities. Some recognizable and highly stereotyped examples include the French teenage slang *verlan*, Cockney (London) English, Appalachian English and African-American English. Innovative variants in the speech of these groups, such as the tag question *innit* in London (*They couldn't get the paint off, innit?*) and habitual non-finite *be* in African-American English (*Jason be acting crazy lately*) are often viewed by the public as corruptions of – and even a threat to – the standard variety.

Sociolinguists must therefore tread carefully, given the high degree of public scrutiny of language variation, and the likelihood that speakers will self-police their own output. They face the Observer's Paradox: in order to observe someone's most vernacular speech, the speaker must not feel that he or she is being observed. Since overcoming this paradox would entail the unethical practice of clandestine recording, sociolinguists have instead found ways to mitigate its effects. In the following section we describe some of these data collection techniques and the techniques that are used to analyze synchronic variation with respect to diachronic change.

17.2 Methodology

One way of reducing the effect of the observer is to not use a recording device. In a rapid and anonymous survey, for example, the researcher approaches informants in a public place with a simple question that is calibrated to elicit instances of a single linguistic variable.

Asking *Excuse me, do you have the time?* of passers-by in Charleston allowed Baranowski (2007) to surreptitiously write down dozens of examples of *four* and *quarter* in which post-vocalic (r) was variably realized. None of his informants knew – or needed to know – that he was a researcher.

Ethnography similarly allows the researcher to observe without drawing attention to him/herself. Members of the speech community are aware of the researcher's identity and purpose, but become used to his/her presence through long periods of participant-observation. The more access and trust the researcher gains, the greater the likelihood that speakers will produce something close to their usual vernacular in interactions with the researcher. Sometimes the researcher is permitted to leave a recording device running in the background while speakers interact with one another; other times the researcher will record his or her casual conversations with the speakers.

The most frequently used data collection method is a sample survey of a community in which speakers are recorded during sociolinguistic interviews. The Observer's Paradox is addressed via strategies within the interview itself. After seeking mostly factual information about the speaker's personal and residential history, the interviewer gradually builds rapport with the speaker through questions about local issues and about universal experiences such as games played in childhood. Under the right circumstances, a speaker will relate a personal narrative: a story about a reportable event, often dramatic or funny, in which the speaker was a chief protagonist. In recalling this event, the speaker pays minimal attention to his or her speech, and produces vernacular speech, or something approaching it. The goal of the interviewer is to maximize such opportunities for the speaker to produce his or her vernacular, while also capturing other, more formal speech styles by asking speakers to read a passage and a word list containing variants of interest to the researcher.

Once collected, recordings and transcriptions of naturally occurring vernacular speech will form corpora that can be mined again and again for sociolinguistic variables. These corpus linguistic investigations (see Chapter 32) have been supported by increasing computational power and digital storage of data files. Sociolinguists have also successfully made use of data from non-sociolinguistic sources, such as oral history and archived radio recordings, and digitized newspapers and other texts. Real-time analyses of individual speakers (panel studies) have also been facilitated by access to decades' worth of digitized recordings, such as a well-publicized study of the changing pronunciation of the Queen of England in her Christmas broadcasts from the 1950s to the 1980s (Harrington *et al.* 2000). In addition, YouTube videos and new written media such as blogs and Twitter have opened up the potential pool of data sources for vernacular language.

Although experiments continue to constitute a minority methodology in sociolinguistics, sociolinguists sometimes rely on elicitation and judgment tasks when capturing the vernacular is not a priority. They can be used – judiciously – for phenomena such as syntactic variables that may occur infrequently in interviews. Sociolinguists can now field surveys via the Internet, or recruit participants cheaply via crowd-sourcing sites such as Amazon's Mechanical Turk. Audio clips can be included in these online surveys, making it possible to conduct experiments on the perception and social evaluation of sociolinguistic variables.

Another beneficiary of the digital revolution has been dialect geography: the sector of sociolinguistics in which researchers map variable linguistic phenomena to the real world. For example, a dialect map with a geo-located point for every sampled American who answered the question, *What is your word for a carbonated beverage?* would show that *pop* is used mostly in the northern and midland USA, *soda* in the east and southwest, and *coke* in the south. Dialect mapping has been pursued since at least the nineteenth century. Until the mid-twentieth century, maps were typically hand-drawn, included a few hundred informants at most, and were constrained to regions rather than entire countries. Now, thousands of informants can be surveyed via telephone, Internet and social media. Furthermore, with the advances in digital and online mapping, we have the ability to layer linguistic data with other information (e.g. census data, topography). We are on the verge of huge leaps in our understanding of how linguistic innovations and changes diffuse over physical space.

In the next section, we discuss how all of these data-gathering methods are employed in answering the central question: How and why does language change occur?

17.3 Inter-speaker variation

17.3.1 Sampling the speech community

An important goal of early dialect geographers was to provide a historical baseline for subsequent research. Informants were limited to older rural speakers (usually men) who had spent their whole lives in a locality, and who could be expected to use the 'traditional' speech of the area. Untouched by dialect contact and with limited influence from the supralocal, standard way of speaking, their conservative speech formed a kind of fossil record. Furthermore, linguistic differences between communities (such as those that said *darning needle* versus those that said *snake waiter* for 'dragonfly') could then be interpreted as having arisen independently on either sides of physical barriers such as rivers, hills and mountain ranges. Areas of linguistic similarity indicated unimpeded historical diffusion of language features in those places. With such a deliberately constrained sample of informants, geography alone was sufficient for explaining the distribution of linguistic patterns.

In the mid-twentieth century, attention turned from physical to social barriers between groups of speakers. It was observed that even in large cities, members of different social class and ethnic groups do not always use the same lexical items, nor do they use the same morphological and phonological variants at the same frequencies. Yet members of urban speech communities also share many features of the local dialect, suggesting that language changes diffuse not only from place to place, but from group to group and speaker to speaker. One key way to understand how language changes arise and spread over time, therefore, was to broaden the speaker sample beyond older, rural, non-mobile speakers, and to look at inter-speaker variation in the present.

Quantitative sociolinguistic studies generally take a small set of social categories as straightforward, and seek to balance their sample of speakers with respect to these categories. These 'straightforward' (etic) social categories include sex, social class, ethnicity and age. The existence of linguistic variation that correlates with these social categories is well-documented, and we provide an overview in the rest of this section. Defining social categories for sociolinguistic purposes has never been entirely straightforward, however. Categories have been increasingly problematized and debated, in line with similar discussions elsewhere in the social sciences. A more ethnographic approach, grounded in the practices of anthropology, avoids preconceived social categories and instead uses locally meaningful categories (emic) once the researcher is familiar with the community. In what follows, we describe each of the major etic social categories and their effect on language change. We also discuss how ideas from anthropology and sociology have influenced sociolinguists' thinking about inter-speaker variation.

17.3.2 Gender

Perhaps the most heavily discussed social category in sociolinguistics has been gender. Labov (1990) aggregates the findings of many quantitative studies of language and gender into three 'principles,' the first two of which concern standard language. Under Principle I, women use the standard variant of a diachronically stable variable more frequently than men. For the English suffix *–ing*, for example, the standard variant velar nasal [ŋ] has varied for centuries with non-standard alveolar nasal [n], and women have been shown repeatedly to use standard [ŋ] proportionally more frequently than men. Under Principle IIa, women use proportionally more of an innovative variant during a change in progress than men do, so long as that variant carries overt prestige. In New York City in the 1960s, for example, Labov (1966) reported that women used non-local, prestigious post-vocalic [r] more frequently than men. Women's greater tendency to employ overtly prestigious linguistic variants is not interpreted as a biological imperative but as a consequence of women's historically weak social position relative to men. Where women have relatively little economic capital, either because they are out of the workforce or because they are prevented from attaining positions of power, standard language can be a powerful source of symbolic capital for them. Standard language commands respect from others and elevates a speaker's social status. Somewhat paradoxically, however, women use incoming variants that are *not* overtly prestigious at a higher rate than men do (Principle IIb). Yet this typically happens only at the early stage of a language change, for as long as the variant is below the level of public attention. Once members of the speech community become aware of the change and start to denigrate it there is a decline over time in women's use of the variant relative to men's.

More recently, sociolinguists have paid greater attention to individuals who were excluded from the binary sex categorization, such as transsexuals, and to differences such as sexual orientation that were formerly absent from analyses of gendered linguistic behavior. There has also been a move away from viewing men as the default gender type against which women's linguistic behavior is contrasted, and toward considering male linguistic practices in their own right. Sociolinguists are also confronting intersectionality. Under this view, social characteristics are not seen as merely additive: e.g. female+black+working class+gay+young. Instead, they are seen as constituting a greater whole, forcing sociolinguists to consider not just the independent effects of gender, class, ethnicity etc. on inter-speaker variation, but the linguistic outcomes of being specifically e.g. a black, gay, working-class young woman.

17.3.3 Race and ethnicity

Race and ethnicity have been integral analytic categories in the field from its inception in the 1960s. The Civil Rights movement in the USA strongly influenced much of this early work, such as Labov's (1969, reprinted 1972b) seminal paper, 'The logic of non-standard English.' Labov used examples of speech from sociolinguistic interviews to argue that, contrary to assumptions then (and even today), African-American Vernacular English (AAVE) is just as logical, versatile and structured as mainstream standard American English. Concern for the reputation and rights of minority groups has been evident in sociolinguistic research ever since, as we discuss in a later section.

Given that the majority of quantitative sociolinguistic work has been conducted in the USA, it follows that much of the work in which race is employed as an explanatory category has also come from the USA. African-Americans have received the most attention. This is in part because of the aforementioned desire among sociolinguists to remove the stigmas attached to AAVE, and in part because this dialect is linguistically quite dissimilar to mainstream standard English. It thus affords many opportunities to observe variation, for example when speakers alternate between AAVE features (habitual *be*, completive *done*, copula absence etc.) and standard features. Yet it has become apparent that AAVE is not a monolithic dialect to be contrasted with the standard variety. It exhibits dialect-internal variation across regions (cf. differences between Atlanta and Detroit varieties) and across social groups.

Due to long-standing residential and cultural segregation of the two groups, White and Black Americans typically do not participate in the same language changes, or else not to the same degree. Similar findings obtain for other ethnic groups whose social networks are largely non-overlapping, such as Protestants and Catholics in Northern Ireland. Other studies have found that minority groups adopt mainstream linguistic changes in part rather than in whole, as is the case for Arab-Americans and African-Americans in areas of the northern USA where a set of interlocking vowel changes is occurring. Still others show minority ethnic groups such as Italian-Americans in Philadelphia and Mexican-Americans in California participating fully in mainstream changes, but lagging behind the majority group(s).

Race/ethnicity is undergoing the same problematization as gender, and some points of debate include: (1) complexifying super-categories such as 'Asian-American,' which may obscure within-Asian-American linguistic differences, and 'White,' which has been taken for granted as a default category (much like 'men'); (2) self-identification with a racial/ethnic category versus researcher-imposed identification; (3) identification with multiple ethnic identities, and of course, intersectionality of ethnicity with other social characteristics.

17.3.4 Age

Age intersects with the social factors discussed so far. There may be meaningful changes over time in the degree to which a speaker's ethnicity or gender is a foregrounded component of their social identity. This in turn may have important implications for his or her use of variable linguistic features. In a series of interviews conducted with a single African-American young woman, 'Foxy Boston,' Rickford and McNair-Knox (1994) found that Foxy's use of AAVE features increased and decreased over the years, partly because of changes in the importance of race to Foxy's sense of self. Her leadership of an African-American student organization in college, for instance, coincided with a rise in her use of AAVE variants such as copula absence.

For most purposes, however, sociolinguists have treated social categories as static, since by convenience the majority of studies are synchronic, cross-sectional snapshots of a speech community at one point in time. These studies rely on the aforementioned apparent time construct, whereby data from speakers across a wide range of ages serve as a proxy for two or more generations of real time. Inter-speaker variation between age groups may indicate that a language change is in progress over time: a rise in an innovative variant among the young, perhaps, and/or the decline of a conservative variant over the generations. An interpretation of this kind depends on two assumptions that should ideally (but for practical reasons sometimes cannot) be verified. First, an individual's sociolinguistic repertoire is acquired in childhood; undergoes some incrementation of ongoing changes through contact with peers prior to and during adolescence; and for the most part undergoes no major changes in adulthood. The speech of a sixty-year-old, then, would be representative of the speech of that same person at age twenty. Second, differences between old and young people's speech in the sample is a consequence of this incrementation process, with successive generations overtaking the frequency with which their parents use an incoming variant.

The first assumption has been largely validated (Bailey *et al.* 1991), although there is some counter-evidence from the relatively few panel studies thus far conducted by sociolinguists. The second assumption depends on the availability of historical evidence for comparison. In early sociolinguistic studies, this evidence necessarily had to be drawn from any written texts that represented vernacular speech, from metalinguistic commentary about speech, or from regional dialect atlases. Increasingly researchers are able to use previous sociolinguistic studies as their historical comparison to conduct trend studies – real-time historical comparisons of comparable speakers in the same speech community.

For a given sociolinguistic variable, if there are no differences in usage between historical and contemporary speakers, the researcher concludes that the variable is diachronically stable. Any relationship between speaker age and the variable must then be attributed not to change in progress but to age-grading: a regular association in every generation between the variable and a particular life-stage or life-stages. Non-standard [ɪn] for example, exhibits a peak in frequency among young people in virtually every English-speaking community investigated to date.

Of course, life-stages are as subject to problematization as ethnicity and gender, and must be clearly situated within the place and time of the study. Whereas very large-scale surveys in other social sciences can use age as a continuous predictor, sociolinguistic studies are typically conducted on a smaller scale, in which speakers must be grouped into age ranges out of practical necessity. This has often been done by regularly grouping speakers by tens of years (e.g. age thirty to forty, or born 1960–1980), but more typically by age ranges that are meaningful in the community under study, e.g. ages fourteen to eighteen represent the high school stage in the USA; ages sixty-five plus represent the retirement life-stage in most Western societies. Even within a society it is possible for life-stages to alter over the generations (e.g. 'teenager' is a relatively recent social construct), and this must be borne in mind when making historical comparisons across datasets.

17.3.5 Social class

Speaker samples from Western communities are commonly stratified by indicators of socioeconomic status such as household income, residence value, years of education attained and occupational prestige. Sometimes only one of these indicators is needed to capture sociolinguistic differences in the community under study, while in other cases a combination is required. Regardless of the way in which stratification is measured, sociolinguists commonly use cover terms such as 'lower-middle class' and 'upper-working class' for the individual strata, provided these are meaningful in the community itself. Study after study has shown that the greatest linguistic cleavage occurs at the boundary between the working class and middle class, no matter how these are defined in a given speech community. Traditionally the two major classes have been distinguished by their orientation to manual versus non-manual occupations, although this is changing as ever greater numbers of Westerners attend a tertiary college and as service jobs increase at the expense of manufacturing and other labor-intensive jobs. As such, type of tertiary college attended (research-oriented, teaching-oriented, vocational, etc.), rather than number of years of education, may prove to be an increasingly important indicator of sociolinguistic difference.

Underpinning all of these stratification schemes, however, is the same issue faced by the earliest dialect geographers: how to distinguish the most and least geographically and socially mobile speakers. Hierarchical social class categorization serves to differentiate relatively non-mobile working-class speakers, who best typify the local vernacular, from relatively mobile middle-class speakers, who have more access to standard variants and who are more likely to use them. Importantly, however, sociolinguists have demonstrated clearly that all members of a speech community acquire the local dialect; the differences in the speech of different social classes are gradient and not discrete. This is contrary to earlier beliefs that people from different social classes employed entirely different repertoires. Kroch (1996) found that even members of Philadelphia's upper class used locally stigmatized Philadelphia features, and these were subject to the same complex phonological, morphological and lexical constraints as for all other Philadelphians. Nonetheless, studies repeatedly find a correlation between higher social status and lower use of local or non-standard variants. For example, in a study of Rivera in Uruguay (Carvalho 2004), local Uruguayan Portuguese dental stops were used least frequently by the mid-middle class (the highest status group in the sample), more frequently by the lower-middle class, and most frequently by the working class. The inverse was true for the distribution of supralocal Brazilian Portuguese palatalized stops.

Speakers in the middle of the social spectrum are of special interest, because they tend to exhibit a high degree of linguistic insecurity, both qualitatively (*I hate the way I speak*) and quantitatively e.g. self-reports in which speakers underestimate the frequency with which they actually produce non-standard variants. Interior group speakers are also the most likely to exhibit sporadic hypercorrection (e.g. in this example from a job advertisement: *Please indicate the job for which you'd like to be considered for*) and the 'crossover effect,' in which they produce standard variants at higher rates in formal speech than speakers in the top social class.

For sociolinguistic variables that are not subject to overt public comment, and which perhaps are still in the incipient stages of generational change, there is no evidence for hypercorrection or crossover. Nor is there a straightforward linear correlation between socioeconomic status and frequency of use of a variant. Instead, sociolinguists have often observed a curvilinear relationship, with the innovative variant being most frequent in the interior of the social continuum. The leaders of language changes therefore appear to be speakers in the upper-working to lower-middle classes. This seems just as paradoxical as the fact that women are conservative with respect to stable variables, but progressive with respect to language changes in progress. Why would the linguistically insecure middle class simultaneously be spearheading linguistic change? The answer for both women and the middle class is most likely that they tend to have loose social networks. Networks are discussed in the next section.

Finally, sociolinguists working in non-Western communities have been especially reliant on emic social categories, since it may not be relevant to impose etic class categories on their samples (see Stanford and Preston 2009). In some societies, affiliation with a caste, clan or tribe may be more socially meaningful than occupation or education. In post-colonial communities, there may still be long-standing linguistic divisions between speakers descended from the rulers and speakers descended from the ruled, despite modern democratization and increasing social equality. Post-Communist countries pose the opposite problem, wherein relative social equality is replaced by growing inequality. In such countries, continuing or former association with the government continues to be a strong marker of social identity. Emic categories are also employed in studies of Western communities when the participants are too young to be classified by occupation or education, and are defined by their community of practice instead.

17.3.6 Social networks and communities of practice

Ethnographic approaches have given rise in the last two decades to a categorization technique that identifies 'communities of practice' (Lave and Wenger 1991): groups of people who might be demographically quite heterogenous, but who share an enterprise (e.g. a job, a project, a band, a sports team) or a set of behavioral and symbolic practices (e.g. punk music, attachment parenting, street gangs). Sociolinguists have found it useful to look at the symbolic practices – above all, the symbolic use of linguistic variants – of groups that are too small or too non-traditional in scope for sample survey methods.

Language change, however, comes about not only *within* social groups but crucially as a result of interaction *between* them. Since the late 1970s, aspects of social network theory have been used to model the diffusion of sociolinguistic variants within and across geographic space and social categories/communities. In particular, the theory has been used to demonstrate how language changes can be transmitted between groups even when they have only fleeting interactions with one another. Social network analyses have improved our understanding of the special linguistic behavior of interior social groups such as the 'middle class,' and why this group is often shown to lead change. Speakers in this group have social network ties through their jobs, neighborhoods, etc. to community members both above and below them on the socioeconomic spectrum. A proliferation of weak ties to other groups in addition to dense ties within their own group may account for the leadership of the middle class in language changes that begin without public awareness. The linguistic insecurity of speakers in the middle group may also derive from their social network structures. They are regularly exposed to both standard and non-standard ways of speaking, and as such are especially sensitive to the social value of linguistic variation.

17.3.7 Inter-speaker differences in evaluation of variation

A simple way of thinking about the social value of variation is to see it as essentially binary, whereby linguistic variants can have either overt prestige or covert prestige. Overtly prestigious variants such as [ɪŋ] and *I beg your pardon?* are used at the highest frequencies by the highest status groups, and more frequently in formal than in informal speaking/writing styles. They are sanctioned by arbiters and representatives of 'good' language: dictionaries, textbooks, teachers, newscasters. Covertly prestigious variants such as [ɪn] and *You what?* may be thought of as in-group or solidarity markers. They are not publicly sanctioned, and are most frequently used by the lowest status groups and in the most informal speaking/writing styles. Yet they have value (prestige) within these contexts, since they are positively evaluated by their users as indexing meanings such as solidarity, sincerity or subversiveness. Importantly, the social evaluations of both overtly and covertly prestigious linguistic variants are typically shared by all members of the speech community, and indeed constitute one of the most important criteria for defining a speech community.

Over the decades, research in perceptual dialectology (how speakers perceive dialect boundaries) has demonstrated this key fact about speech communities many times. Americans, for example, are united in their evaluation of English dialects from the southern United States as being less overtly prestigious than English dialects from the northern

United States. Even residents of the South agree with this evaluation. It is thus possible to claim that speakers of US English form a speech community at the national level.

Yet evaluations of sociolinguistic variation are not entirely uniform: there are differences across groups. More recent work demonstrates that evaluation of variation depends not only on the listener's geographic speech community, but also on membership in other social categories. The relatively new use of GIS software has allowed us to analyze this more efficiently and see it more clearly, for instance by analyzing the use of the labels that are assigned to different regions according to the speaker's age, region and sex. Differences in the social evaluation of a linguistic variant, even if quite minor, are presumably integral to the promotion of a language change among some groups but not among others. In the next section, we consider the same tension between uniformity and diversity at the intra-speaker level.

17.4 Intra-speaker variation

The fact that people change their speech according to their interlocutor and the speech context is not controversial, although the systematicity of intra-speaker variation may be opaque to non-linguists. Speakers are aware of their use of stigmatized or taboo words in certain contexts and not others, for instance, such as where and when and with whom they will swear. Moreover, speakers are generally somewhat aware of their use of variants that are highly commented upon and may try to limit their use in more formal contexts. In English these include variants such as *ain't* and *like* as a quotative or discourse marker (*I was **like** 'Why are you even doing that?'* and *I don't know, **like**, how I'm going to get there*). Finally, without being consciously aware of it, speakers may vary in their use of less-commented-upon linguistic variants such as the (t) variable in Arabic, depending again on whom they are talking to, and when and where, etc. All of these are examples of style-shifting, or the variable use of linguistic variant(s) depending on the speech context.

The different examples given above also demonstrate differences in speakers' awareness of linguistic variables, and this tends to relate to the degree to which a new variant has become established in the speech community. New incoming variants generally have the status of *indicators*, and although they may show inter-speaker variation between different social groups, they do not show intra-speaker variation and are not subject to style-shifting. Sociolinguistic *markers* are those variants that speakers may not be consciously aware of, and that are not subject to overt commentary in the community, but that nonetheless are recognizable enough that they can be manipulated by speakers such that they are subject to style-shifting, as in the (t) in Cairene Arabic. *Stereotyped* variants are those that are overtly commented upon in their community and of which speakers are highly aware, such as *ain't*, and *like*. Although these variants may, and often do, hold covert prestige for speakers, they are often avoided in those settings where the speaker is trying to 'make a good impression' or is highly aware of their language use.

The systematicity of style-shifting was demonstrated by William Labov in New York City (1966) and Peter Trudgill in Norwich, England (1974), where both showed that stable variables like (ing) showed not only social class and gender stratification, but also significant and systematic intra-speaker variation. In those studies, different speech contexts were created through use of the sociolinguistic interview; they showed speakers consistently using more of the standard variant when reading aloud than they did in any kind of spontaneous speech, and higher frequencies of the non-standard variant [ɪn] in casual spontaneous speech than in more careful spontaneous speech. Since these contexts did not involve any differences in interlocutor or setting, Labov attributed these systematic style differences to the degree to which an individual speaker was paying attention to his or her own speech. That is, in reading tasks speakers tend to pay more attention to their speech than they do while speaking naturally, and even while speaking naturally speakers exhibited different levels of attention to their speech depending on the formality of the context. Crucially, these studies showed style shifts occurring in the same direction in all social classes and the independence of style and social stratification.

Later studies of style-shifting criticized the attention to speech model for portraying the speaker as too passive, and too egocentric. They argued that speakers accommodate to their interlocutor in any speech event, and style-shifting should therefore be attributed to accommodation to audience member(s). This idea was developed by Bell (1984), building on social psychological work on interaction. A corollary aspect of this model is the hypothesis that if style-shifting occurs as a result of accommodation to other speakers, then the range of intra-speaker variation will always be smaller than that of inter-speaker variation – this is often known as Bell's Axiom. In this model even the effect of setting and topic may be attributed to different audiences, by positing that in addition to audience members who are present a speaker may accommodate to an audience member who is only imagined (for example if a speaker uses more standard variants when talking about school, this may be because they are imagining their teacher as an invisible audience member).

But what about the fact that people may shift in order to portray themselves differently or to consciously associate with some group or disassociate with another? Speakers may style-shift to stereotype some social group or as a communicative 'shortcut,' as when a South Asian-American teenager switches to Indian-accented English in order to present conservative views that are not her own with no need to then explicitly distance herself from those views. These observations combine with the findings of sociolinguistic studies that take a more ethnographic approach and capture a wider range of stylistic variation. Speakers have been shown to use stylistic variants more agentively to portray themselves in different ways or to do different types of sociolinguistic work. As a result many researchers have adopted a model of style-shifting that puts more emphasis on speaker agency, often known as a speaker design approach. Under this framework, speakers actively draw upon the social meanings that are 'indexed,' sometimes recursively (Eckert 2008), by a given sociolinguistic variant. For example, in most English-speaking communities, a fully released /t/ indexes good education, higher social class and formality, but can also be used in relevant circumstances to convey a stance of precision, scorn or disapproval, or a gay, Jewish, urban or British identity, among many other indexical meanings. Sociolinguists who study speaker design are especially interested in the ways in which speakers combine meaningful linguistic variants to construct social personae such as 'yuppie' or 'Valley Girl.'

Models of style-shifting are closely related to, and indeed have roots in, observations and analyses of the social purpose of code-switching – that is, multilingual speakers switching between different languages or language varieties in one speech event, either intra- or inter-sententially. In fact these two processes are hardly different, except insofar as the use of different languages may be more apparent to the speaker and certainly to the monolingual observer than the use of different sociolinguistic variants within one language may be. Perhaps for this reason researchers in this field have always given more weight to speaker agency. Blom and Gumperz (1972), for instance, distinguished between situational code-switching that occurs because different settings are associated with different languages, and metaphorical code-switching, which may be loosely correlated with a change in topic, but which also allows for speaker flexibility in indexing the social meanings associated with different languages in their repertoire. Most recent studies of the sociolinguistics of code-switching have turned to an approach that considers the different ways that code-switching may contextualize different aspects of the conversational event (see Auer 1998).

17.5 Multilingual communities

Despite early sociolinguistic interest in multilingual phenomena such as code-switching, the majority of the sociolinguistic studies of the 1960s and 1970s examined synchronic inter- and intra-speaker variation in monolingual urban communities. Even in those cities that were multilingual, such as Montréal and New York City, researchers tended to focus on monolingual speakers or monolingual speech. Multilingual communities have been comparatively underrepresented in variationist research of the type we have been discussing here, perhaps because it is daunting to consider the additional linguistic and social factors that may be relevant in multilingual communities. But the linguistic and social outcomes of contact between speakers in multilingual communities are of great interest to sociolinguists, not only because the majority of individuals in the world belong to multilingual speech communities, but also because of the insights that they may offer on the processes of language change more generally.

The multilingual communities that are of most interest to sociolinguists are not necessarily those where the community is multilingual but made up of monolingual speakers (as in many cities of the world), but rather those speech communities that are made up of multilingual speakers. Although a variety of interesting outcomes may arise out of the contact between speakers of different languages, including the spread of lingua francas and the development of pidgins and creoles, variationist sociolinguists are generally more concerned with the linguistic outcomes of the contact between two or more languages on the structure of those languages, which means a focus on the languages as they are spoken by multilingual individuals. In keeping with a focus on linguistic structure over language use, sociolinguists seek to understand the mechanisms of change in multilingual communities, assuming that at some level these mechanisms are universal ones that apply in monolingual communities as well. For instance sociolinguists have used quantitative methods to examine the possible locations of code-switches in multilingual discourse, under the assumption that an analysis of the structure of this type of multilingual discourse may offer insight into the structure of language more generally.

Perhaps the most pressing question in this area is the extent to which contact between languages necessarily causes change. In the past it was often assumed that any change that was observed in contact languages was most likely to have been caused by contact, often through the direct adoption of some feature of the other language. The best known example of this comes from Gumperz and Wilson (1971) and their description of language contact outcomes in the village of Kupwar, Maharashtra. Gumperz and Wilson describe a situation of convergence, where the varieties of Marathi, Kannada and Urdu in the village each display features borrowed from the other and not used in standard varieties of the languages spoken elsewhere in India. More conservatively, others have argued that language contact can accelerate the development of an internal change that has already begun. Silva-Corvalán (1994), for instance, shows Spanish–English bilinguals in Los Angeles exhibiting fewer instances of the Spanish subjunctive mood, and argues that although Spanish seems to be moving toward decreasing use of the subjunctive anyway, this process is accelerated by contact with English, where the subjunctive is rarely used. Moreover, the basic assumption that contact causes change is increasingly coming under question, with researchers such as Poplack and colleagues in Ottawa arguing that the inference of change in French from contact with English has been overemphasized (see Poplack *et al.* 2013). It remains for further studies of variation in contact languages to answer these questions.

While the mechanisms of change in mono- and multilingual communities might be argued to be the same, the social parameters that must be considered in multilingual communities are arguably more complex than in comparable monolingual communities. For this reason the social outcomes of language contact are also of concern to sociolinguists, and this is one area where sociolinguistics overlaps significantly with research in other fields, particularly in the sociology of language and the related fields of language policy and planning. Moreover, given current estimates of the degree of language endangerment worldwide, with researchers estimating that 50–90 percent of the world's languages may be endangered (Chapter 25; Krauss 1992; Crystal 2000), questions about language contact cannot be considered separately from issues related to language obsolescence. Although situations of stable multilingualism are not uncommon (Québec is a good example, as are parts of India and South Africa), many more cases of language contact eventually lead to language shift, where the use of one (usually politically dominant) language gradually replaces the use of another. Recognition of this fact has led to the development of measures of language vitality that are informed by sociolinguistics, such as Giles *et al.*'s (1977) measure of ethnolinguistic vitality, which takes into account both institutional support for the language and demography of the population of speakers, as well as speaker evaluations about language that may lead to community-level choices about language use.

17.6 Broader applications

These dire estimates of language endangerment have also brought up questions related to linguists' social responsibility – their responsibility to society to protect linguistic diversity and their responsibility to the communities in which they work. Most relevant for most sociolinguists is their responsibility to the community – both in terms of how they portray that community in presentations and publications and in terms of what they give back to a community they have worked with. From the beginning sociolinguists have been concerned with the 'social, educational, and political implications of language variation' (Wolfram *et al.* 2008: 2), starting with Labov's work to demonstrate the logic of non-standard English (cited above). But despite at least five decades of work demonstrating the systematicity of language variation and change, the public misperception that non-standard dialects are ungrammatical, unsystematic and illogical remains, and a number of scholars in the field are continuing to work to combat this misperception particularly in the classroom, where it is thought to do the most potential harm. A small but growing number of sociolinguists in the USA work with educators on programs to increase awareness of dialect diversity in the classroom as well as to develop school programs for students that directly address dialect differences (summarized in Rickford 1998). In these contexts and globally, sociolinguists have worked to defend the linguistic rights of those who speak varieties of language that may not be considered standard, a field of research and activism that examines the subset of universal human rights that may be considered linguistic human rights (Skutnabb-Kangas and Phillipson 1995).

Besides education, the study of language change in its social context intersects with other fields of intellectual inquiry. Sociology, anthropology, social psychology and human geography have already been mentioned. Sociolinguistics is a direct offshoot of historical linguistics, seeking to apply insights from the course of past language changes to those we see in the contemporary world, in keeping with the Uniformitarian Principle. Historical linguists have likewise followed the Uniformitarian Principle, applying insights from sociolinguistics to their historical data. Modern historical linguists are producing more nuanced accounts of how language changes were transmitted across space and social groups in the past, and they are now better able to evaluate the relative contributions of language-internal and language-external (i.e. social) factors to historical changes.

Formal linguists used to consider their object of study to be Chomsky's 'ideal speaker-listener, in a completely homogeneous speech-community' (1965: 3) but this is rapidly changing. Syntacticians, morphologists and phonologists are developing ways to account for dialect variation and linguistic gradience in their theoretical models. Psycholinguists and neurolinguists are also turning their attention to the processing of linguistic variation. More collaborations between sociolinguists and their colleagues, and the emergence of new scholars from graduate programs who can pursue the study of variation and change from multiple perspectives, can only be to the benefit of all language research.

Note

1 Parentheses are commonly used for the abstract variable, e.g. (t), and square brackets for the variants, e.g. [t] and [tʲ]. This notation may also be used for morphological variables, as with (ing) and its variants [ɪn] and [ɪŋ].

Further reading

Eckert (2000); Labov (1972a, 1972b, 1978); Labov *et al.* (2006); Preston (1999); Preston and Long (2002); Sankoff (2001); Tagliamonte (2012).

References

Auer, P. (1998) *Code-Switching in Conversation: Language, Interaction and Identity*. London: Routledge.
Bailey, G., T. Wikle, J. Tillery and L. Sand (1991) The apparent time construct. *Language Variation and Change* 3: 241–64.
Baranowski, M. (2007) *Phonological Variation and Change in the Dialect of Charleston, South Carolina*. Publications of the American Dialect Society. Durham: Duke University Press.
Bell, A. (1984) Language style as audience design. *Language in Society* 13: 145–204.
Blom, J.-P. and J.J. Gumperz (1972) Social meaning in linguistic structures: Code switching in Northern Norway. In J.J. Gumperz and D. Hymes (eds.) *Directions in Sociolinguistics: The Ethnography of Communication*, pp. 407–34. New York: Holt, Rinehart, and Winston.
Carvalho, A.M. (2004) I speak like the guys on TV: Palatalization and the urbanization of Uruguayan Portuguese. *Language Variation and Change* 16: 127–51.
Chomsky, N. (1965) *Aspects of the Theory of Syntax*. Cambridge: MIT Press.
Crystal, D. (2000) *Language Death*. Cambridge: Cambridge University Press.
Eckert, P. (2000) *Linguistic Variation as Social Practice*. Oxford: Blackwell.
Eckert, P. (2008) Variation and the indexical field. *Journal of Sociolinguistics* 12: 453–76.
Giles, H., R.Y. Bourhis and D.M. Taylor (1977) Towards a theory of language in ethnic group relations. In H. Giles (ed.) *Language, Ethnicity and Intergroup Relations*, pp. 307–48. London: Academic Press.
Gumperz, J.J. and R. Wilson (1971) Convergence and creolization: A case from the Indo-Aryan/Dravidian border. In D. Hymes (ed.) *Pidginization and Creolization of Languages*, pp. 151–67. Cambridge: Cambridge University Press.

Haeri, N. (1994) A linguistic innovation of women in Cairo. *Language Variation and Change* 6: 87–112

Harrington, J., S. Palethorpe and C.I. Watson (2000) Monophthongal vowel changes in Received Pronunciation: An acoustic analysis of the Queen's Christmas broadcasts. *Journal of the International Phonetic Association* 30: 63–78.

Hibiya, J. (1995) The velar nasal in Tokyo Japanese: A case of diffusion from above. *Language Variation and Change* 7: 139–52.

Krauss, M. (1992) The world's languages in crisis. *Language* 68: 4–10.

Kroch, A. (1989) Reflexes of grammar in patterns of language change. *Language Variation and Change* 1: 199–244.

Kroch, A. (1996) Dialect and style in the speech of upper class Philadelphia. In G.R. Guy, C. Feagin, D. Schiffrin and D. Baugh (eds.) *Towards a Social Science of Language Vol. 1: Variation and Change in Language and Society*, pp. 23–45. Philadelphia: John Benjamins.

Labov, W. (1966) *The Social Stratification of English in New York City*. Washington DC: Center for Applied Linguistics. Reissued 2006 by Cambridge University Press.

Labov, W. (1972a) *Sociolinguistic Patterns*. Philadelphia: University of Pennsylvania Press.

Labov, W. (1972b) The logic of nonstandard English. In W. Labov (ed.) *Language in the Inner-City: Studies in the Black English Vernacular*, pp. 201–40. Philadelphia: University of Pennsylvania Press.

Labov, W. (1978) On the use of the present to explain the past. In P. Baldi and R. Werth (eds.) *Readings in Historical Phonology*, pp. 275–312. Pennsylvania: Pennsylvania State University Press.

Labov, W. (1990) The intersection of sex and social class in the course of linguistic change. *Language Variation and Change* 2: 205–54.

Labov, W., S. Ash and C. Boberg (2006) *Atlas of North American English: Phonology and Sound Change*. Berlin: Mouton de Gruyter.

Lave, J. and E. Wenger (1991) *Situated Learning: Legitimate Peripheral Participation*. Cambridge: Cambridge University Press.

Poplack, S., A.V. Lealess and N. Dion (2013) The evolving grammar of the French subjunctive. *Probus* 25: 139–93.

Preston, D. (1999) *The Handbook of Perceptual Dialectology, Vol 1*. Philadelphia: John Benjamins.

Preston, D. and D. Long (2002) *The Handbook of Perceptual Dialectology, Vol 2*. Philadelphia: John Benjamins.

Rickford, J. (1998) Using the vernacular to teach the standard. Revised version of remarks delivered at the California State University Long Beach Conference on Ebonics, March 29, 1997. www.stanford.edu/~rickford/papers/VernacularToTeachStandard.html.

Rickford, J. and F. McNair-Knox (1994) Addressee- and topic-influenced style shift: A quantitative sociolinguistic study. In D. Biber and E. Finegan (eds.) *Sociolinguistic Perspectives on Register*, pp. 235–76. Oxford: Oxford University Press.

Sankoff, G. (2001) The linguistic outcomes of language contact. In J.K. Chambers, P. Trudgill and N. Schilling-Estes (eds.) *The Handbook of Language Variation and Change*, pp. 638–68. Oxford: Blackwell.

Silva-Corvalán, C. (1994) *Language Contact and Change: Spanish in Los Angeles*. Oxford: Oxford University Press.

Skutnabb-Kangas, T. and R. Phillipson (eds.) (1995) *Linguistic Human Rights: Overcoming Linguistic Discrimination*. Berlin: Mouton de Gruyter.

Stanford, J.N. and D.R. Preston (2009) *Variation in Indigenous Minority Languages*. Amsterdam/Philadelphia: John Benjamins.

Tagliamonte, S. (2012) *Variationist Sociolinguistics: Change, Observation, Interpretation*. Oxford: Wiley-Blackwell.

Trudgill, P. (1974) *The Social Differentiation of English in Norwich*. Cambridge: Cambridge University Press.

Weinreich, U., W. Labov and M. Herzog (1968) Empirical foundations for a theory of language change. In W. Lehmann and Y. Malkiel (eds.) *Directions for Historical Linguistics*, pp. 95–189. Austin: University of Texas Press.

Wolfram, W., J. Reaser and C. Vaughn (2008) Operationalizing linguistic gratuity: From principle to practice. *Language and Linguistics Compass* 2: 1–26.

18

Psycholinguistics

Language and cognition

Matthew J. Traxler

18.1 Introduction: Why is psycholinguistics significant?

We are what we do. What psycholinguists do is apply research methods derived mainly from the discipline of psychology to understand human behavior, thought, and neural processes as they relate to language function. Mainly because psycholinguists are a diverse bunch, they bring a diverse set of methods to the task of understanding how humans produce and understand language. Researchers in the field of psycholinguistics include psychologists and linguists (of course, so long as said linguists are interested in mind, brain and behavior), but also computer scientists, anthropologists, sociologists, philosophers, statisticians, historians, literary scholars and a variety of other disciplines. Psycholinguistics, therefore, provides a prototypical example of a multidisciplinary approach to science.

Psycholinguistics is a science, because psycholinguists apply the scientific method (observe, hypothesize, test, repeat), and it is as data-driven as any other scientific enterprise. The study of language in psychology at its inception was characterized by armchair philosophy, but those days are long gone. Beginning students of psycholinguistics are often surprised that it *is* a science, and that they therefore need to learn how to apply the scientific method to language. This involves understanding how experiments are designed, how data are collected and analyzed, and how the human nervous system works.

Psycholinguists have made numerous contributions to our theoretical understanding of how people represent knowledge about language, how people access and use this knowledge in real time to produce and understand language, how the human species acquired its current range of language abilities, and how neural systems support language function. These contributions are important not only because understanding how language works is a necessary part of understanding how human beings work, but also because there is a close relationship between language disorder and other kinds of mental disorder. This close connection between language function and overall mental function most likely reflects bi-directional causal relationships from language to non-linguistic cognition, and vice versa. When non-linguistic aspects of cognition (such as attention, executive control or working memory) go wrong, aspects of language function can go wrong. When aspects of language function go wrong (as in Specific Language Disorder, dyslexia and aphasia), this has consequences for the social and emotional functioning of the individual, as well as effects on educational and economic outcomes. Here is an example of each type of causal relation:

Language function in schizophrenia may represent a case where general cognitive deficits lead to problems with the production and understanding of language. Schizophrenia is a mental disorder characterized by problems in language, hallucinations and delusions, disordered social and emotional function, and disordered motivation. In addition, patients with schizophrenia experience physical changes to the structure of the brain that appear to contribute to general problems in cognition. Patients with schizophrenia experience deficits in cognitive control. Cognitive control, roughly speaking, reflects the ability to regulate attention and to select task-appropriate responses when more than one response is available. Deficits in cognitive control may be caused by mis-regulation of neural systems in the frontal lobes as well as disordered functional connectivity between frontal lobe networks and other, more distant parts of the brain. Patients with schizophrenia experience deficits in attention and memory (both working and long-term memory processes) and they also often have dramatic language-related symptoms (which were commented on during the very earliest era of research into schizophrenia by scientists such as Eugen Bleuler). Patients with schizophrenia have difficulty maintaining a coherent topic during conversation. Their responses to conversational prompts often include references to concepts that are only very loosely related to the prompt.[1] They do not typically have problems with more basic aspects of language production, such as articulation (i.e. their speech, unlike the speech of patients with aphasia, is smooth and essentially normal with respect to grammar).

Psycholinguists have developed processing accounts, derived from work on normally functioning individuals, that help us understand how changes in cognitive control lead to some aspects of disordered language production and comprehension in patients with schizophrenia.[2] In particular, these accounts help us understand why patients with schizophrenia have trouble maintaining a topic and why their production is characterized by loose associations. These accounts appeal to the notion of a *semantic network*, which is a hypothetical mental mechanism that represents your knowledge of what words mean, and how different word meanings relate to one another. In semantic network theory, concepts that are more similar in meaning are represented 'closer' together in the network. As difference in meaning increases, 'distance' (virtual distance) in the network increases. These representational assumptions help explain why pairs of words that are closely related (e.g. *cat–dog*, *mother–father*) are processed more readily than pairs of words that are more distantly related (e.g. *lion–stripes*; *stripes* is related to *lion* via the intermediary *tiger*; *lion* is related to *tiger*, *tiger* is related to *stripes*).[3] According to Condray *et al.* (2003), activation spreads uncontrollably through the semantic network in patients with schizophrenia because of the lack of 'top-down' control that is normally exerted by executive control systems. This uncontrolled spread of activation means that more distantly related concepts (e.g. stripes when *lion* is mentioned) become activated during production and comprehension, even though those concepts are not relevant to the topic. Uncontrolled spread of activation leads to mental representations that are cluttered with irrelevant and unhelpful information. This greatly complicates the process of understanding and producing language. Hypothetically, if executive control were restored in these patients, this would improve their language function, because better executive control processes could regulate the activation of irrelevant concepts (i.e. executive control mechanisms could reduce the activation of irrelevant concepts; clearing the way for relevant information to come to the forefront).

Specific Language Impairment (SLI) provides an example of language dysfunction leading to disabilities in other aspects of life. SLI is defined somewhat differently by different researchers, but roughly speaking, SLI is diagnosed in individuals whose language function is substantially lower than one would expect based on overall cognitive skills. In SLI, something seems to be wrong with language that is not explainable as being a consequence of some other thought-related problem. This definition excludes individuals with Down syndrome, for example, because language problems in Down syndrome are likely caused by lower overall intellectual functioning. To qualify for a diagnosis of SLI, people must be free of 'frank neurological defects' (this excludes people with neurodevelopmental disorders and people with acquired brain damage, which is the most common cause of the aphasic language disorders). There is some evidence that SLI in some individuals results from a genetic mutation on the FOXP2 gene.

People with SLI can have a number of language-related problems at different levels.[4] These may include reduced ability to perceive and differentiate speech sounds (deficits in phonological function). They may also include reduced ability to comprehend and produce tense, aspect and agreement markers on verbs (e.g. the correct first-person, singular form of the verb *to walk* is *walk*; the correct third-person, singular form is *walks*; as in *I walk to the store*; *He walks to the store*).

Language problems in SLI have consequences for social, educational and economic outcomes. Children with SLI make fewer attempts to initiate conversational exchanges with other people. Lack of practice with verbal and social exchanges means that children with SLI miss out on opportunities to sharpen their language and social skills. Research on educational settings shows that children with SLI are viewed differently than children with normal language function. Their peers are less likely to identify them as preferred playmates. Mutual preference (i.e. two children both saying that they prefer each other as a playmate) fosters the development of interpersonal relationships in school-aged children. Unfortunately, a child with SLI is less likely to have his or her preferences reciprocated by another child. Hence, children with SLI are likely to feel more socially isolated than other children. Development of reading skill in children with SLI places limits on their economic success later in life. Hypothetically, if one could intervene to improve language function in individuals with SLI, this would lead to improvements in other areas of function.

Understanding language disorder (its causes and consequences) is an important step in designing treatment methods that alleviate suffering. Thus, more and more, psycholinguists are getting interested in *translational* research. Translational research does *not* mean studying how you translate from one language to another. Instead, translational research happens when you use findings from basic science to understand some process (such as language comprehension or production) and then use that understanding to get better control over some condition. As implied by the two examples above, there is tremendous need for translational research in the area of language function. This is especially true in the area of language acquisition.

Research indicates that developmental language disorders (language disorders that occur in children that prevent them from achieving the full range of language ability that normally functioning children have) occur for several different reasons. Sometimes causation runs from abnormal environment to abnormal cognitive development to abnormal language function. Children who are abused or neglected tend to experience greater delays in hitting major language milestones (speaking the first word; using words in combination; acquiring grammatical principles or rules). Sometimes causation starts before birth. Children who are born before full term (approximately thirty-seven weeks of gestation) can develop problems with language, presumably because neural and general cognitive development lags behind full-term infants. The best estimates suggest that between 6 and 8 percent of children will experience some kind of serious language delay or disorder.

Language disorders produce some clear disadvantages. For instance, children who experience difficulty learning how to produce or understand language do worse in school than children who readily learn to speak and understand. Still worse, children who experience serious delays hitting major language milestones experience major psychological problems at a higher rate than their normally developing peers. These psychological problems include anxiety, depression, deficits in social interaction skills, major behavior problems and juvenile delinquency. These problems make these children more prone to being expelled from school and reduce their opportunities for employment. More than half of children with significant language delays experience serious deficits in behavior and are at great risk for being diagnosed with a psychiatric disorder. For comparison, the rate of similar problems (lifetime prevalence) in the general population is about 10 to 15 percent. On the flip-side, some studies indicate that up to 80 percent of children who receive a psychiatric diagnosis involving behavior control have a previously undiagnosed language deficit.

Even though social, emotional and behavioral problems correlate very highly with language dysfunction, only a small proportion of children receive evaluation and treatment specifically for language problems until something else goes wrong. In the absence of rigorous evaluation, many teachers, parents and other care-givers misunderstand the nature of the child's difficulty. Children with undiagnosed language problems are oftentimes viewed as merely 'delinquent,' 'depressed' or 'aggressive.'

The precise nature of the relationship between language problems and other psychological problems has not been completely worked out. One plausible hypothesis views language as the cause, and behavioral and psychiatric problems as the consequence. Under this hypothesis, children who experience difficulty producing or understanding language may be less able to communicate their thoughts, feelings and desires. This inability to communicate effectively in turn leads to maladaptive patterns of thought and behavior. This hypothesis is supported by the finding that language function in young children predicts the likelihood of behavioral problems during the elementary school years. There may be no simple link between language function and behavioral outcomes, however. Other factors may mediate this relationship. For example, problems producing and understanding language contribute to social isolation, because children with language problems experience difficulty initiating and maintaining social relationships with peers and care-givers. Children who have language problems are rated as less desirable playmates by their peers, and this pattern starts to emerge in preschool. When children are socially isolated, they lose opportunities to learn all of the subtle cues that children pick up during social interactions. Lesser language skills, possibly in combination with poor social interaction skills, can promote maladaptive behavior. When a person has difficulty using language to communicate, they may adopt other strategies, such as engaging in aggressive or risky behavior, in an attempt to get their desires met. Alternatively, there may be a reciprocal, interactive relationship, where language difficulties and behavioral problems reinforce one another. Children who have behavior problems miss opportunities to strengthen their communication skills; and weak communication skills make it more likely that a child will have behavior problems.[5]

Clearly, what we need are better theories of language function, and better theories of how to intervene to improve language function. This is the goal that many psycholinguists pursue in their research careers. The following sections provide a brief review of major trends in psycholinguistic theory and research over the past half century.

18.2 A short history of psycholinguistic contributions to advances in the study of language and cognition

18.2.1 The first wave: the cognitive revolution

The study of language in psychology extends back to the very beginnings of the discipline. Wilhelm Wundt, who founded the scientific study of psychology, is credited with inventing the tree diagram, a way of representing the syntax of a sentence. The early study of cognition in psychology was based largely on introspection (reflecting on the content of one's own thoughts). This approach to understanding psychology was supplanted in the first half of the twentieth century by *behaviorism*. Theorists such as Edward Thorndyke, J.B. Watson and B.F. Skinner rejected subjective impression and introspection as a way of investigating psychological phenomena. They insisted that theories be based on directly observable events, specifically the behaviors that people and animals produced. Appeals to hidden mental events were outlawed.

Behaviorism focused on the way animals learn associations between stimuli (as in classical conditioning) and the way animals learn associations between situations, their own behaviors and the consequences of those behaviors (reward and punishment). Behaviorists also developed descriptions of language that were firmly grounded in the relationship between behavior and reward. According to these accounts, thought was merely subvocal speech; i.e. a very subtle form of implicit language behavior. J.B. Watson viewed 'thought' as occurring because the muscles that were involved in articulating speech were moving (very, very subtly), even though no sound waves resulted from those movements. If thought is really just covert behavior, the reasoning went, then a satisfactory theory of behavior could be straightforwardly extended to account for language.

B.F. Skinner developed a theory of language acquisition based on behaviorist principles according to which children learned to speak because their speech behaviors were rewarded by their care-givers. Skinner also had a theory of speech production and comprehension, based on associations. According to this account, languages can be thought of as patterns of associations between adjacent words. Why do we produce some sentences and not others? According to Skinner, it is because the associations between some words are stronger than the associations between other words. We learn these associations because we are exposed to those patterns when we listen to other people speak. These patterns of associations can be captured in formal arithmetic models (called 'Markov chains' or 'transition networks'). According to this kind of account, you are more likely to produce a noun after an adjective than a verb (*green leaves* is more likely than *green leave), because there is a much stronger association between adjective and noun than there is between adjective and verb (in another version of the account, associations between individual words, rather than classes of words, drive learning). A Markov chain with the right map of associations is capable of generating a very large, if not infinite, number of sentences, all of which would be compatible with the kinds of sentences that real people produce in real exchanges.

Noam Chomsky (along with scientists like George Miller, Steve Kosslyn and Donald Broadbent) is credited with initiating the cognitive revolution, starting in the 1950s. During this period, cognitive theories overturned and supplanted the behaviorist understanding of language acquisition, production and comprehension. While certain aspects of behaviorism remain intact (e.g. the idea that consequences govern behavior), the behaviorist description of language function has been largely if not completely abandoned.

Cognitive scientists working on a broad spectrum of phenomena, including memory, attention, perception and language, appeal to hypothetical mental processes to explain various aspects of human thought and behavior. These appeals to 'invisible' mental processes were strictly taboo to followers of radical behaviorism, the dominant paradigm in psychology from the early 1900s to the late 1950s. To the behaviorists, no theory that appealed to unobservable mental processes was acceptable. This meant that concepts like traces of events in long-term memory, internal manipulation of mental representations, and internal control processes, were not legitimate objects of study. Because these mental representations and processes could not be directly observed, they were viewed by the behaviorists as being illegitimate, or at least not worthy of investigation.

Cognitive scientists therefore faced two hurdles, one representing a negative agenda and the other positive. The negative agenda involved finding ways to discredit behaviorist approaches to various psychological phenomena. The positive agenda involved constructing well-supported, or at least plausible, alternative theories of the processes in question. Chomsky provided convincing arguments for the negative agenda – that behaviorism provided incomplete and inaccurate descriptions of language phenomena. Chomsky and the psychologists who took up his cause pursued the positive agenda as well.

Chomsky's critique pointed out several observable language-related phenomena for which the behaviorist account had no ready explanation. These critiques were grounded in observable aspects of children's language acquisition and aspects of the behavior of mature speakers. In that way, Chomsky's theorizing was not vulnerable to the criticism often leveled by behaviorists, that appeals to 'invisible' mental processes were equivalent to appeals to 'spirits' or 'invisible forces.' Two language-related phenomena help illustrate the general point. According to behaviorists, children learn language the same way they learn other behaviors, by trial and error and by the reinforcement of some behaviors but not others. The behaviorist theory of language therefore predicts two things: First, children's speech will include many errors that do not occur in the adult language. Second, children will more readily learn aspects of language that they are rewarded for producing; they will be less successful learning aspects of language for which they do not receive feedback (in the form of correction or reward). Neither of these predictions is borne out by data from children acquiring their first language.

In terms of errors, children definitely do make errors. They produce utterances that they never hear in ambient language. However, some kinds of errors that are likely on the behaviorist view are never produced by actual children learning their first language. Behaviorist theory does not have a means to explain why some errors occur and others do not, but a cognitive account of language that includes 'invisible' mental operations (mental processes that you cannot see directly) can explain those patterns. One classic example involves the way questions are formed. According to cognitive approaches to language, questions are formed by the modification of simple (canonical) underlying mental representations. You can create a question from the underlying form *The little girl is leaving* by moving the verb *is* to the front, as in *Is the little girl leaving?* This mental formalism explains how questions are generated and why there is a clear relationship in meaning between the statement and the question (i.e. they share an underlying representation).

An associationist/behaviorist view of this process might say that you learn to make questions because you notice that the word *is* appears at the beginning of some expressions. That will work only some of the time, however. You cannot make a question out of this statement *The little girl that is talking to Susan is leaving* by moving the first *is* to the front (**Is the little girl that talking to Susan is leaving?*), but you can make a question by moving the second *is* (*Is the little girl that is talking to Susan leaving?*). Therefore, not everything that has *is* at the beginning is OK. However, the behaviorist view has no explanation for why one form of question is OK, while the other is not. If *is* can precede *the little girl* in one question (presumably because *is* has been associated with *the little girl* somehow), then the pattern of association should allow *is* to precede *the little girl* in any other question. If the association is somehow blocked in one question, it should be blocked in all of them.

The cognitive view of language, on the other hand, proposes that the hypothetical mental element main clause and main verb have a different status than the hypothetical mental element relative clause and relative clause verb. The cognitive view proposes that speakers can mentally rearrange the elements in an expression by moving parts of the main clause to the front, but relative clauses block or prevent that kind of movement (this is sometimes referred to as the 'subjacency principle,' relative clauses are sometimes described as being 'islands to extraction' because words in a relative clause are stuck there, like Tom Hanks on a desert island). Note that a simple rule that says that the first *is* can go to the front, but not the second will work for an expression like *The little girl is leaving*; and another simple rule that says that the second *is*, but not the first, can go to the front will work for an expression like *The little girl that is talking to Susan is leaving*, but no simple rule that associates statements and questions will account for the way people actually speak. Thus, a behaviorist/associationist approach to language fails to explain readily observable language behaviors (hence, the negative agenda is accomplished).

A theory of language has to explain patterns of behavior that appear during children's language acquisition. Children very rapidly learn the vocabulary and grammatical principles of the adult language. Children typically speak their first word at around twelve months of age, have a productive vocabulary of about fifty words when they reach eighteen months, and start using combinations of words at twenty-four months. By the age of three, children have mastered many of the fine details of their native grammar (at least in comprehension, as evidenced by the way children respond to statements such as *Push the dinosaur to the lion with the pencil* in act-out tasks, where children demonstrate their understanding by moving little toy creatures around).

The behaviorist account comes up short in the way it explains language acquisition. According to the account, language behavior should follow the same rules as other kinds of behaviors. If so, children should learn language behaviors via trial and error. In that case, children would repeat language behaviors that are rewarded and stop producing language behaviors that are not rewarded. This account predicts that feedback from care-givers would be an important factor in language development. In fact, feedback from care-givers and interaction are important contributors to language acquisition, but not in the way the behaviorist account predicts.

In observing how care-givers interact with infants and small children, child language specialists have observed that care-givers provide far more feedback for some aspects of language than others. In particular, care-givers often correct children's mistakes when those mistakes result in semantic confusions. An example of this error would be when a small child *overextends* a word like *kitty* to mean all small furry animals. A child who calls a dog *kitty* is likely to be corrected by a competent speaker. However, small children are very rarely corrected when they produce grammatical errors. For example, the expression **I want hold Postman Pat* is ungrammatical (it is missing the infinitival marker *to*: *I want to hold Postman Pat*). This production error is likely to go either unnoticed or uncorrected in an exchange with an adult speaker. The adult may very well provide a paraphrase or an extension of the expression (*You do? Postman Pat is nice, isn't he?*), but the adult is unlikely to say *That's wrong. You have to say, 'I want TO hold Postman Pat.'* Such corrections do occur from time to time, but there is little convincing evidence that small children pay any attention to them (in that the same error is likely to appear again, even after corrective feedback is provided). Nonetheless, children's production eventually conforms to the standard ways adults use the language. That is, children learn the adult grammar (so, among other things, children learn when to use and when not to use overt infinitival markers like *to*). This appears to be a case of learning by observation, without feedback, and without reward. (Observational learning similar to this occurs in other areas of development, including social interaction.)

These and other problems with the behaviorist view of language led to the demise of behaviorism, at least in its radical form, as a theory of language function. The cognitive revolution led to the development of theories of language that appealed to 'hidden' internal states and processes as the underlying causes for observable language behaviors (e.g. the kinds of sentences that people produce when speaking spontaneously; the patterns of errors that people make; the fact that some words and sentences prove harder to understand than others). These accounts appealed to a mental grammar, a set of rules or principles that governs how words can be combined in sentences and a mental lexicon, a set of words (*morphemes* might be more accurate) that are combined in production in particular ways according to the dictates of the grammar (a morpheme is the smallest unit in a language that conveys sense/meaning). This formulation, with its 'invisible' mental structures and processes, violates a fundamental tenet of radical behaviorism, which outlawed appeals to hypothetical mental representations and processes to explain behavior. While cognitive theories must be tied to observable events (this prevents backsliding into pure speculation and fantasy), most, if not all, contemporary cognitive scientists view the abandonment of radical behaviorism as a good move (because behaviorism does not provide a satisfactory framework for explaining the full range of observable language phenomena; and because cognitive theories, when properly constructed, are just as testable and falsifiable as any theory from the 'dust-bowl empiricism' tradition).

18.2.2 The second wave: experimental psycholinguistics

The second wave of psycholinguistics emerged as the result of ideas introduced by linguists (such as Noam Chomsky), ideas about human memory systems introduced by cognitive psychologists (like George Miller), and ideas about language development introduced by developmental psychologists (like Roger Brown). While linguists are chiefly concerned with descriptions of language form and structure, psycholinguists are chiefly concerned with the way humans represent language form and the processes by which they activate that knowledge in real time to communicate (to produce and understand language).

Research in psycholinguistics is organized approximately among subdisciplines that line up with important distinctions in linguistic theory. Language can be thought of as a hierarchically organized, multi-tiered system of representations and processes. Conceptually more basic units include phonemic and phonetic representations (basic units of sound in a language). Syllables, morphemes and words consist of patterns of phonemes. Phrases, clauses and sentences consist of patterns of words (or, morphemes, which may be a more appropriate description of agglutinative languages, like Turkish and Aleut). Discourses or conversations consist of sets of sentences. Pragmatic processing in language allows us to combine information about the literal semantic content of an expression with information about the speaker and situation in which that expression was uttered to determine the speaker's intentions or overall 'force' of the message. Psycholinguists have developed cognitive theories relating to all of these levels of representation and processing. While some psycholinguists happily move between levels in this hierarchy to conduct research, others happily spend entire careers focusing on just one aspect of language.

Early theorizing in the cognitive tradition adopted ideas from transformational grammar, which was developed by linguists to do two things. First, transformational grammar represented an attempt to codify the rules that allow a speaker to combine a finite number of elements (words or morphemes) in new ways to produce an unlimited number of expressions (sentences). Second, the grammar specifies how and why different expressions can have the same meaning (*I shot the sheriff* and *The sheriff was shot by me* mean the same thing, essentially). Transformational grammar argues that the active voice *I shot the sheriff* and the passive voice *The sheriff was shot by me* mean the same thing because they have the same underlying syntactic representation (known as 'canonical form' or 'deep structure'), despite their differences in surface form.

An early attempt at a psychological theory of grammar and sentence comprehension derived its predictions from transformational grammar. The *derivational theory of complexity*, an account of human sentence processing, proposed that some sentences differed more from their underlying forms than others, because some sentences required more mental operations (transformations) to be converted from surface form to canonical form. On the assumption that more mental operations mean more processing time, the derivational theory of complexity predicted that some sentences would take longer to understand than others. The theory also made claims about how words were organized into larger representational units (phrases, clauses, sentences), which entails claims about where the boundaries between representational units are (e.g. in the sentence *The green apple fell out of the tall tree*, there is a boundary between the initial noun phrase *The green apple* and the predicate *fell out of the tall tree*).

Click-detection experiments in which noises were placed either at important syntactic boundaries (between the subject and predicate, for example) or within important 'chunks' (e.g. between *fell* and *out*) supported some claims about the mental representation of sentences. When stimuli had clicks within important units, those clicks were often perceived as being at the boundary between two units. These results support the existence of phrases and clauses as important units in the mental representation of sentences. If sentences were perceived as unorganized sequences of words, there is no reason why clicks located at one position in reality (e.g. between *fell* and *out*) would be more likely to be perceived at another position (e.g. between *apple* and *fell*).

The derivational theory of complexity had less success in its predictions about how long processing a sentence should take. Some sentences that were more complex in theory, because they required more transformations, did not, in fact, take more time to understand (nor were they less accurately comprehended than sentences requiring fewer transformations). While ideas borrowed from linguistics – hierarchically organized mental representations for the structure of sentences, for example – proved to be useful, the specific details of specific linguistic theories like transformational grammar did not appear to succeed in predicting actual people's behavior across a range of task environments. The take-home message for many psycholinguists at the time was that adopting assumptions straight out of linguistic theory was not particularly helpful. Others took to heart the idea that humans really did carry around a mental grammar that governed how sentences were organized in memory, and they set about trying to find a more psychologically plausible account of mental grammar.

While the details of transformational grammar, when put to the test, did not have strong appeal to many psycholinguists, other aspects of linguistic theory continued to influence psychologists working on language. For example, ideas from the linguistic study of phonology and morphology strongly influenced work on speech comprehension and word processing in psycholinguistics (and continue to do so today). In speech comprehension, theorists like Mark Liberman applied ideas from articulatory phonology to derive predictions about how people understand spoken language. Articulatory phonology makes a close connection between motor movements for speech (how the throat muscles, tongue, lips and other articulators move during speech) and the classification and categorization of speech sounds during speech perception (i.e. basic speech sounds, phonemes) can be classified according to the way different articulators move when different phonemes are produced. Psycholinguistic theories of word-recognition in speech comprehension during this era relied upon theories of phonological representation and speech production (especially co-articulation), as well as linguistically motivated theories of morphology ('atomic' components of complex words). The *frequency ordered bin search* (FOBS) model of word-recognition and lexical access argued that representations of words in long-term memory were organized around root morphemes (e.g. in the word *cats*, *cat* is the root morpheme, *s* is an inflectional morpheme that modifies the meaning of the root from singular, one cat, to plural, more than one cat). This account successfully predicted certain kinds of frequency effects (words with low surface frequency are recognized faster than expected if the root morpheme has relatively high frequency). It also successfully predicted differences in processing difficulty between words with real suffixes, like *planter* (*plant* + *er*), and words with fake or pseudo-suffixes, like *sister* (while a *planter* is someone who *plants*, a *sister* is not someone who *sists*).

The 'cohort' model is another theory of word-recognition and lexical access that appeals to linguistically motivated accounts of phonology and morphology. The cohort model proposes that word representations in long-term memory are organized according to patterns of sound. It also makes claims about how information from long-term memory behaves as spoken words are encountered.

According to the cohort model, long-term memory representations for words are organized according to their initial sounds. Each group of words is a cohort. When the initial sound in a word is identified, all of the word representations in long-term memory that match that initial sound are activated. As more sounds in the stimulus are identified, the cohort is reduced, until finally, only one matching candidate from long-term memory remains activated – typically this 'sole survivor' is the entry in long-term memory that most closely matches the perceptual features of the stimulus.

The cohort model predicts a number of different effects that are consistent with the available experimental evidence. For example, the partial word *cap*... should activate the matching entries from long-term memory *captain* and *captive*. If the word *captain* is activated (i.e. it is resident in short-term or working memory), that activated representation should affect the processing of stimuli that are encountered while the representation is active. If this is the case, then hearing the partial word *cap*... should speed up the processing of the word *ship* (because *ship* is semantically related to the activated representation of *captain*). For the same reasons, hearing *cap*... should facilitate (speed up) processing of the word *guard* (because *captive* is semantically associated with *guard*). In fact, when people are asked to respond to words like *ship* and *guard*, by either reading the word out loud or indicating whether it is a real word in English, they can perform those tasks faster if they have just heard the word-fragment *cap*.... Thus, consistent with the model's claim, partial word information appears to rapidly and automatically activate an entire range of stored word representations (a cohort). This cohort gets weeded down as more information from the stimulus becomes available. So, if the stimulus were *capta...*, which is compatible with *captain* but not *captive*, we would expect to see *priming* (speeded processing) of the word *ship* but not *guard*, and this is, in fact, what happens in experiments using those kinds of stimuli. The cohort model accounts for other speech perception phenomena as well, such as the fact that words can be recognized before the end, so long as partial word information reduces the cohort to one sole survivor before the end of the word (i.e. the recognition point is somewhere in the middle of the word). Words with recognition points closer to the beginning are, all other things being equal, recognized faster than words that have later recognition points.

18.2.3 The third wave: the rise of the machines

Technological advances have had a transformative effect on psycholinguistics since about 1990. Advances in computing technology have created new opportunities for research for a wider range of researchers.[6] Researchers have always been able to do high quality psycholinguistic research using only paper and pencil, but personal computing has made more sophisticated stimulus presentation and data collection available at very low cost. Beyond facilitating data collection, advances in computing technology have changed the way researchers analyze their data and model psychological processes. Advances in neurophysiological and neuro-imaging methods have also contributed to new understandings about how the brain responds when people produce and understand language.

Computing technology has had a profound effect on the way psycholinguists develop and evaluate theories of language function. The change is seen in the move from qualitative accounts of language function (e.g. qualitative claims; box-and-arrow diagrams) to implemented computational systems (computer programs designed to simulate some psychological process). The computational modeling tradition in psycholinguistics started with flow-chart style models, but quickly evolved into other types of computational systems patterned after real neural networks (i.e. neural network models, aka parallel distributed processing models). These mathematical models have profoundly changed the way psycholinguists view a variety of language functions, including speech perception, vocabulary acquisition and word processing (lexical access), normal and disordered reading (dyslexia), and sentence processing.

Vigorous debates continue regarding the best way to characterize some language processes. Competition between formal models in the area of reading provides a case in point that helps illustrate differences between different modeling approaches. When people read, they use visual input to retrieve phonological (sound) and semantic (meaning) information that is stored in long-term memory. The intermediate steps that occur between registering a visual pattern and retrieving the meaning that goes with that pattern are the focus of different types of formal computational models. For instance, Max Coltheart and colleague's (2001) 'dual-route' model of reading proposes that readers have available to them two different means of accessing meaning from print. The first route involves the application of letter-to-sound correspondence rules (grapheme-to-phoneme correspondence, or GPC, rules). This is the mechanism that you can use to pronounce words that you have not previously encountered, like *brenk*. This mechanism will not succeed for words that are pronounced differently than they are spelled (e.g. *yacht, colonel, cough, pint*). To activate the phonological codes (pronunciations) that are associated with irregular sets of graphemes (letters), the dual-route model proposes a direct look-up mechanism. This direct or visual route bypasses letter-by-letter phonological analysis. To access the pronunciations of irregular words (like *yacht*), readers treat the stimulus as a holistic object (i.e. they do not break the word down into its individual component letters and retrieve the sounds associated with those individual letters).

The dual-route model correctly predicts that words will be processed differently depending upon details of the way they are spelled, and details of the way the GPC system as a whole maps letters onto sounds. For example, all other things being equal, words that have irregular spelling patterns towards the beginning take longer to read than words that have irregular spelling patterns towards the end. Dual-route theory accounts for these effects by appealing to the GPC analysis. GPC analysis fails to produce sensible output earlier for words that have irregular patterns at the beginning than towards the end. Dual-route theory also predicts that the two routes to pronunciation can succeed or fail independently. It also predicts that some individuals may have trouble accessing pronunciations using the GPC rules, while others will have trouble accessing pronunciations using the direct or visual route. Problems with the GPC route should lead to a pattern of function in which people can respond appropriately to known words, even if those words have irregular spellings, but those same people will not be able to pronounce unfamiliar words, even if those unfamiliar words have 'normal' spelling. A malfunctioning GPC route may also lead to very odd responses when an individual is asked to read a word out loud; i.e. *bake* might be pronounced as *cook* or *oven*. These patterns are indeed observed in some dyslexic individuals (people whose reading ability is significantly lower than predicted based on their overall intellectual functioning, age and access to instruction). This condition is sometimes referred to as *deep dyslexia*. A malfunctioning direct route in the same individual who has a functioning GPC route should lead to a different pattern of function. The GPC route will produce sensible output for regularly spelled words (e.g. *bake*, *lip*, *can*), but regularization errors for irregular words (e.g. *colonel* will not be pronounced *kernel*, but instead more like *kulonal*). Individuals with a functioning GPC route should still be able to pronounce words that they have not encountered before (and those pronunciations will be consistent with the general patterns of letter-to-sound correspondences). This is the pattern that is observed in people with surface dyslexia.

Work in the neural network tradition by researchers like Mark Seidenberg, Jeff Elman and Jay McClelland provides competing implemented models and competing qualitative explanations for a wide variety of reading-related phenomena, including deep and surface dyslexia. Neural network models of this type have a number of attractive features. One attractive feature is that the models' behavior changes over time as they are exposed (virtually) to stimuli. In other words, the models learn. Another attractive feature is the relative simplicity of the processing architectures. Typically, models will have a set of input units, one or more sets of 'hidden' units, and a set of output units. The input units can represent a variety of stimulus features, such as phonetic features or visual features. Each input unit is typically connected to the full set of hidden units, with either excitatory or inhibitory links. If an input unit has an excitatory link to another processing unit, activating the input unit by presenting an appropriate stimulus will lead to excitation in the other unit. Inhibitory connections have the opposite effect. The hidden units are, in turn, connected to the output units. Models of this type can be 'trained' by presenting stimuli, letting activation flow through the network until a stable pattern is obtained, and then comparing the pattern of output that the system produces to the correct or ideal pattern of output. To the extent that the actual output differs from the ideal, the connection weights between the input, hidden and output units will be adjusted (connection weights determine how robustly a given unit responds to signals coming from another unit).

Seidenberg and colleagues (1989) developed a neural network model of this type to capture a variety of phenomena that are observed in both normal reading and in dyslexia. This 'triangle' model has input units representing visual features, and a set of output units that represent semantic and phonological aspects of words. The model does not have any division that is interpretable as separate 'GPC' and 'direct/visual' routes. Nonetheless it is capable of emulating different patterns of reading problems that arise in people with deep and surface dyslexia. Those outcomes are achieved via neurologically plausible changes to the basic model. One type of change produces virtual 'lesions' in the network. These virtual lesions are created by removing some of the output units from the system. This can lead to the system making odd substitute pronunciations, as in deep dyslexia. Other changes, such as reducing the number of hidden units that mediate between inputs and outputs, can produce different patterns of behavior. These patterns closely match those that real readers produce. Changing the number of hidden processing units can cause the model to make errors for irregular but not regular words (as in surface dyslexia). One qualitative interpretation of this change in the model is to view it as reducing the processing resources that are available to the system, which reduces the system's ability to map inputs to outputs. Mapping may still be possible, but the system as a whole may learn more slowly and make more errors.

A third critical technological revolution involves new ways of examining how the brain responds to language across a broad spectrum of tasks. One example is neurophysiological methods. These methods are based on the fact that the brain, as an electrochemical system, produces electrical currents as neurons fire. Different patterns of neural firing produce different electrical signals, which can be detected using non-invasive methods. Electrodes placed on a person's scalp can pick up very subtle electrical currents that result from the action of networks of neurons in the brain. Different types of language stimuli produce different patterns of neural response, which in turn lead to different patterns of electrical current at the scalp. Researchers can present these stimuli and then measure event-related potentials (or ERPs). Differences between different stimuli or different task sets can be detected within a few hundred milliseconds after the critical stimulus is presented (sometimes sooner, depending upon the nature of the task and the stimuli).

ERP research has played a central role in the development of theories of word, sentence and discourse processing. For example, ERP research demonstrates that comprehenders very rapidly access and use information about speaker identity (Is the speaker an adult or a child?) and contextual information (What concepts have been introduced previously into the discourse? Which are most likely to be relevant at a given point in time?) to perform computations that identify word meanings (lexical access) and that tie referring expressions to previously introduced concepts (reference). ERP research has also played a large role in the development of sentence-processing theories, because it provides an index of how much processing load different components of different kinds of sentences impose on comprehenders.

Neuro-imaging research and its application to studying language function has also developed by leaps and bounds in the past decade. In particular, functional magnetic resonance imaging (fMRI) has come to occupy a central position in many discussions about language. The early days of fMRI research on language revolved around questions of *where* different linguistic representations and processes resided in the brain. Many of these studies presented stimuli of two different types (e.g. random strings of letters versus words; *xjepvmt* versus *judgment*) and looked for areas in the brain that responded more strongly to one type of stimulus than the other. This particular contrast tends to pick out a part of the brain in the ventral occipital-temporal lobe junction in the left hemisphere, which has been named the 'visual word form area.' Some more recent fMRI research continues in this tradition (for example, some researchers are looking for parts of the brain that respond *only* to language, and not to other kinds of complex stimuli), but there is a developing shift in the field away from asking narrow questions about where representations are stored, or where computations are conducted (i.e. which specific parts of the cortex light up when a particular task is done on a particular kind of stimulus), to asking broader questions about how large-scale networks in the brain are organized and how different parts of the brain communicate with one another and coordinate their activity in the service of some task. This kind of functional connectivity analysis may also help us understand better how broader cognitive systems, executive control, attention, working and long-term memory, perception and action networks interface with language systems as expressions are produced and comprehended.

Notes

1. See, for example, *Schizophrenia: Gerald, Part 1* at www.youtube.com/watch?v=gGnl8dqEoPQ.
2. Some psycholinguistic accounts of language function in schizophrenia attribute 'loose associations' in speech to rampant spreading activation within the neural networks that represent word-related information in long-term memory. These accounts therefore lay the blame for patterns of language function within a set of neural systems that are primarily concerned with language processing. These accounts would seem to predict that patterns of language use characterized by loose associations should be present only when lexical processing is compromised. Hence, we would not expect to see loose associations in other patients with executive control and attention problems (as in ADHD). Hence, there may be two separate problems occurring in conjunction in patients with schizophrenia: First, a general cognitive problem with executive control. Second, a problem within the language system itself which causes uncontrolled spreading activation within the lexical network.
3. Other concepts may also be related to both lion and stripes.
4. Some accounts attribute problems in SLI to more general cognitive deficits, such as slower speed of processing, as individuals with SLI respond slower on simple reaction time tasks. However, the speed of processing account may not provide a satisfactory explanation for why some aspects of language (grammatical suffixes of certain types) present greater problems than others; the account also does not provide a clear explanation for differences in the patterns of deficits across different languages (e.g. English versus Italian versus Hebrew; see Larry Leonard's 1998 book, *Children with Specific Language Impairment*, MIT Press).
5. Childhood trauma is, sadly, a frequent cause of behavior problems in clinical populations (T. Traxler, personal communication). The link between childhood trauma and language disorder is largely unexplored (but see Cortes *et al.* 2005).
6. A senior psycholinguist, who shall be unnamed, tells a story of collecting reaction time data in the era before desktop computers. One of the jobs that this person did in graduate school was to use a candle to cover long rolls of paper tape with soot. These rolls of tape would be placed in a mechanical device that would spool out the tape at a fixed speed. When a stimulus was presented to the subject, the device would make a mark in the soot. When the subject responded by pressing a key, the device would make another mark in the soot. The researcher could determine how long it took the subject to respond by measuring the distance between the two marks on the tape.

Further reading

Bloom, P. (2002) *How Children Learn the Meanings of Words*. New York: Bradford.
Crain, S. and R. Thornton (1998) *Investigations in Universal Grammar: A Guide to Experiments on the Acquisition of Syntax and Semantics*. Cambridge: MIT Press.
Frith, C. (1995) *The Cognitive Neuropsychology of Schizophrenia*. New York: Psychology Press.

Gazzaniga, M. (2009) *The Cognitive Neurosciences*. Cambridge: MIT Press.
Jackendoff, R. (2003) *Foundations of Language*. Oxford: Oxford University Press.
Leonard, L. (1998) *Children with Specific Language Impairment*. Cambridge: MIT Press.
Pinker, S. (1994) *The Language Instinct*. New York: Harper.
Traxler, M.J. (2012) *Introduction to Psycholinguistics: Understanding Language Science*. Boston: Wiley-Blackwell.
Traxler, M.J. and M.A. Gernsbacher (2006) *The Handbook of Psycholinguistics*, 2nd edition. Amsterdam: Elsevier.

References

Coltheart, M., K. Rastle, C. Perry, R. Langdon and J. Ziegler (2001) DRC: A dual route cascaded model of visual word recognition and reading aloud. *Psychological Review* 108: 204–56.
Condray, R., G.J. Siegle, J.D. Cohen, D.P. van Kammen and S.R. Steinhauer (2003) Automatic activation of the semantic network in schizophrenia: Evidence from event-related brain potentials. *Biological Psychiatry* 54: 1134–48.
Cortes, A.M., K.M. Saltzman, C.F. Weems, H.P. Regnault, A.L. Reiss and V.G. Carrion (2005) Development of anxiety disorders in a traumatized pediatric population: A preliminary longitudinal evaluation. *Child Abuse & Neglect* 29: 905–14.
Seidenberg, M.S. and J.L. McClelland (1989) A distributed developmental model of word recognition and naming. *Psychological Review* 96: 523–68.

19

Neurolinguistics
Mind, brain, and language

David Kemmerer

19.1 Introduction

The goal of neurolinguistics is to understand how the cognitive capacity for language is subserved by the biological tissue of the brain. This interdisciplinary field of research began in the mid-nineteenth century, and by the early twentieth century several basic aspects of the neural architecture of language had already been discovered, such as left-hemisphere dominance and the strong reliance of speech perception and production on certain regions in the temporal and frontal lobes. These initial insights came primarily from investigations of brain-damaged patients who displayed fairly consistent correlations between, on the one hand, particular patterns of impaired and preserved linguistic abilities, and on the other hand, particular patterns of lesioned and intact brain structures. But even though that first wave of neuropsychological exploration was of great historical importance, the value of the studies was limited by their lack of precision on both sides of the language–brain relationship. From the mid-twentieth century up to the present, however, the whole field evolved quite dramatically for a variety of reasons, including the maturation of modern linguistics, the cognitive revolution in psychology, the emergence of computer science and artificial intelligence, and the invention and progressive refinement of numerous brain mapping methods. Due to these developments, neurolinguistics is now a vibrant, rapidly growing field in which researchers with different backgrounds frequently collaborate to conduct empirical and theoretical studies on diverse topics.

The following synopsis begins by summarizing several kinds of cortical organization as well as the most commonly used brain mapping methods. It then provides a selective review of recent hypotheses and findings about the neural representation and processing of spoken word forms, printed word forms, word meanings and sentences. Although some of the most well-supported contemporary perspectives are covered, space limitations only allow a small amount of material to be included, far less than is actually available in the relevant literature. Further information can be found in the references listed under 'Further reading.'

19.2 Cortical organization

Although subcortical structures such as the thalamus, basal ganglia and cerebellum certainly contribute to language, the most complex computations are carried out in the cerebral cortex, which is the convoluted outer mantle of the brain. The cortex contains approximately 30 billion neurons, and because each of them makes contact with at least 1,000 other cells, the whole system constitutes a massively interactive information processing matrix that is adaptively designed to support high-level mental functions.

For present purposes, the following types of cortical organization are noteworthy. First, each hemisphere is divided into five lobes, four of which are visible – namely, the frontal, parietal, temporal and occipital lobes – and one which is hidden – namely, the insula, which faces laterally but lies at the bottom of the Sylvian fissure. Second, the cortex is essentially a sheet of gray matter that has been crumpled up so that a large amount of surface area can fit inside the cranium. The raised bulges are gyri, and the deep grooves are sulci (Figure 19.1). Third, crosscutting the gyral–sulcal topography is a mosaic of cytoarchitectonically distinct regions that resemble irregularly shaped patches on a quilt but actually reflect the presence/absence, packing density and layering of various types of cells. Several parcellation schemes have been proposed, but the most widely used one involves Brodmann areas (BAs; Figure 19.1). For example, Broca's area, which is a major computational hub for language, occupies BAs 44 and 45, both of which reside in the posterior portion of the left inferior frontal gyrus. Finally, it is essential to realize that cortical regions do not operate in isolation; instead, they are intricately interconnected with each other, and most if not all of our complex cognitive processes, including those involving language, require the dynamic, cooperative interplay of signals among the widely distributed components of large-scale cortical circuits. These signals are transmitted along white matter pathways that run beneath the cortex like highways between cities. The fiber tracts that are most relevant to the left-hemisphere language system are still being elucidated, but at least seven major long-distance routes are currently under investigation.

19.3 Brain mapping methods

During the past few decades, neurolinguistics has benefited tremendously from advances in brain mapping methods. Most of the findings described in the sections below come from experimental studies that employed one or more of the following techniques.

There are two main hemodynamic (aka functional neuro-imaging) approaches – positron emission tomography (PET) and functional magnetic resonance imaging (fMRI) – both of which use blood flow as a proxy for neural activity to identify which brain regions tend to be activated when people perform particular types of mental tasks. The primary strength of these methods is relatively fine-grained spatial resolution – about 10 mm for PET, and about 3 mm for fMRI (but sometimes as good as 0.5 mm). The primary weakness is relatively poor temporal resolution – thirty seconds or so for PET, and often around twelve seconds for fMRI (but sometimes as good as 50 ms). Another limitation of hemodynamic approaches is that the associations they reveal between neural and mental processes are correlational rather than causal in nature; hence they cannot indicate which of the many brain regions that show up as being engaged during a task are in fact necessary for that task.

Traditionally, the chief method for inferring causal brain–behavior relationships has been the lesion method (aka neuropsychology), which, as mentioned above, was the source of the first insights about the neural underpinnings of language back in the mid-nineteenth century. Basically, this approach takes advantage of otherwise unfortunate cases of brain damage

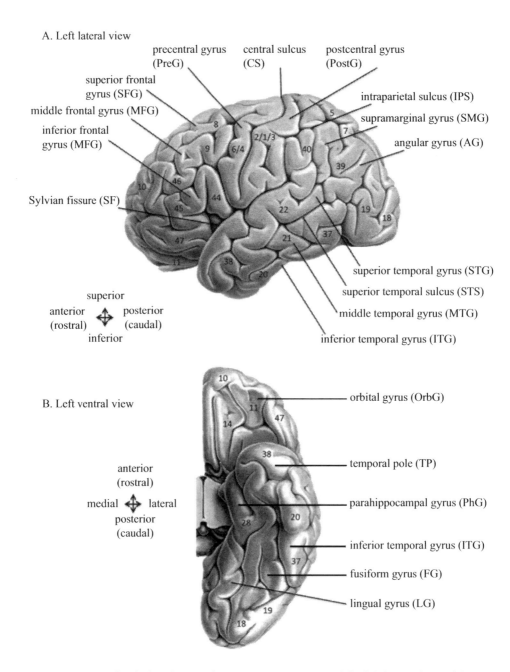

Figure 19.1 Gyral–sulcal and cytoarchitectonic organization of the left hemisphere of the human brain. Labeled lines point to major gyri and sulci, and numbered regions indicate cytoarchitectonically defined Brodmann areas

(due to strokes, tumors, head injuries and neurodegenerative diseases) by using them to make new discoveries about the design of the normal system. In the domain of language, neuropsychological studies usually pursue one or both of two general aims: first, to carve the language faculty at its joints, so to speak, by determining which of its components can be selectively impaired; and second, to identify reliable links between specific linguistic deficits and specific lesion sites. Importantly, the tools for conducting such studies have undergone significant improvements in recent years.

Another technique for inferring causal brain–behavior relationships is transcranial magnetic stimulation (TMS). This non-invasive method involves inducing electrical currents in specific brain regions by means of brief magnetic pulses. The currents can either facilitate or disrupt the operation of the targeted area, depending on the parameters of the protocol. Moreover, the spatial resolution is in the order of millimeters, since each pulse is quite focal, and the temporal resolution is in the order of milliseconds, since each pulse is quite brief. Despite these merits, however, the method does have shortcomings: first, it is restricted to brain regions near the scalp; and second, the effects of stimulation can spread to remote regions, due to the massive interconnectivity of cortical areas.

Electrophysiological techniques can bring researchers even closer to the actual firing of neurons. In fact, one approach, which is only used in neurosurgical situations, involves directly stimulating parts of the exposed brain and observing the effects on cognition and behavior. Another approach involves recording the electrical signals of neurons as they unfold on a millisecond timescale during mental processes. This is done in either of two ways: intracranially by means of electrodes that are placed directly in the brain so as to record the firing of either single cells or relatively small populations of cells; or extracranially by means of electrodes that are placed on the scalp so as to record, through the skull, the simultaneous firing of many thousands or even millions of cells.

Other brain mapping methods include magnetoencephalography, near-infrared spectroscopy, transcranial direct current stimulation and pharmacological manipulations. But they are not used as frequently as the ones described earlier.

The rest of this chapter reviews a number of functional-anatomical correspondences involving various aspects of the neural substrates of language (Figure 19.2). All of these correspondences have received empirical support from studies employing diverse brain mapping methods. At the same time, however, all of them remain tentative, some more so than others.

19.4 Spoken word forms

19.4.1 Speech perception

Speech perception is a deceptively simple cognitive capacity. Someone speaks, the sounds enter our ears, and we understand immediately. But in order for such seemingly effortless comprehension to occur, numerous computations must be carried out. Analog acoustic patterns must be converted to digital codes at multiple levels of language-specific structure, including distinctive features, phonemes, syllables and words. Although the categorization of speech signals must be sensitive to fine-grained cues, it must also be flexible enough to accommodate talker variability. The boundaries between words must be identified even though there are rarely corresponding gaps in the acoustic waveform. And all of these operations, together with many others, must be executed extremely quickly in order for comprehension to unfold at a normal pace.

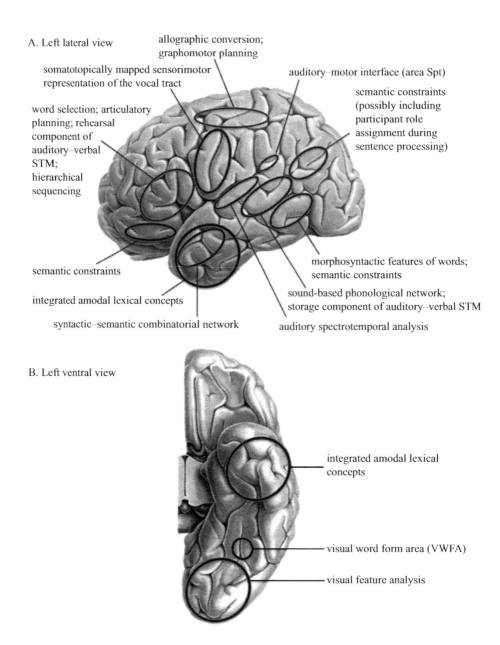

Figure 19.2 Illustration of the major functional-anatomical correspondences discussed in the text

Furthermore, speech input must be routed not only to the grammatical and semantic systems that analyze the forms and meanings of utterances, but also to the motor system that subserves articulation. This is mainly because we rely on auditory–motor transformations when we learn how to say new words that we hear, especially during the early phase of language acquisition. Such transformations also contribute, however, to the overt repetition of familiar words, and they are involved in covert auditory–verbal short-term memory as well, like when you silently rehearse a piece of important information, such as a phone number. In addition, abundant data indicate that the motor system contributes to ordinary, passive speech perception by constantly 'resonating' to the speaker's articulatory movements. As described below, however, the specific functional significance of this phenomenon is controversial.

During speech perception, acoustic signals are initially encoded in the cochlea, and they pass through three brainstem nuclei as well as the thalamus before finally reaching the cortex. Interestingly, although the auditory brainstem was once believed to function in a hardwired fashion, recent research has shown that it can be modified by linguistic experience. In particular, compared to speakers of non-tone languages like English, speakers of tone languages such as Thai exhibit enhanced processing of pitch contours in the brainstem.

At the cortical level, the early stages of speech perception involve spectrotemporal analysis – that is, the determination of how certain sound frequencies change over time. These computations operate not only on speech, but also on other kinds of environmental sounds, and they take place in several regions of the superior temporal cortex, particularly the primary auditory cortex (which occupies Heschl's gyrus deep within the Sylvian fissure) and several adjacent auditory fields on the dorsal surface of the superior temporal gyrus (STG).

The outputs of these areas then flow into other portions of both the posterior STG and the posterior superior temporal sulcus (STS) that collectively implement a phonological network. Processing along this pathway is mostly hierarchical and integrative, since lower levels of neuronal populations close to the primary auditory cortex represent relatively simple aspects of speech sounds, whereas higher levels of neuronal populations extending across the lateral surface of the STG and into the STS detect increasingly complex featural patterns and sequential combinations of speech sounds, such as specific consonants and vowels, specific phoneme clusters and specific word forms. The precise architecture of the phonological network is far from straightforward, however. For instance, the identification of a particular vowel, irrespective of talker, has been linked not with a single discrete neuronal population, but rather with several cortical patches distributed across the posterior STG/STS.

Although the left hemisphere is dominant for speech perception, the right hemisphere also contributes. In fact, either hemisphere by itself can match a spoken word like *bear* with a picture of a bear, instead of with a picture corresponding to a phonological distractor (e.g. a pear), a semantic distractor (e.g. a moose), or an unrelated distractor (e.g. grapes). The two hemispheres do, however, appear to support speech perception in somewhat different ways. According to one proposal, the left posterior STG/STS is better equipped than the right to handle rapid auditory variation in the range of around 20–80 ms, which is ideal for registering fine-grained distinctions at the phonemic level, such as the contrast in voice-onset time between /k/ and /g/, or the contrast in linear order between *pets* and *pest*. Conversely, the right hemisphere is more sensitive than the left to longer-duration auditory patterns in the range of around 150–300 ms, which is optimal for extracting information at the syllabic level, like metrical stress.

After the sound structure of a perceived word has been recognized in the phonological network of the posterior STG/STS, there is a bifurcation of processing into two separate streams, one ventral and the other dorsal. The ventral stream has the function of mapping sound onto meaning. It does this by projecting first to the posterior middle temporal gyrus (MTG), and then to the anterior temporal lobe (ATL). Both of these regions contribute to semantic as well as morphosyntactic processing in ways that are elaborated further below. Although the ventral stream appears to be bilateral, it is more robust in the left than the right hemisphere.

The dorsal stream has the function of mapping sound onto action. It does this by projecting first to a region at the posterior tip of the Sylvian fissure that is sometimes referred to as area Spt (for Sylvian parietal-temporal), and then to a set of articulatory structures in the inferior frontal gyrus (IFG), precentral gyrus (PreG), and anterior insula. Area Spt serves as an interface for translating between the sound-based phonological network in the temporal lobe and the motor-based articulatory network in the frontal lobe. The dorsal stream is left-hemisphere dominant, and it supports auditory–verbal short-term memory by continually cycling spoken word forms back and forth between the posterior phonological network and the anterior articulatory network, thereby allowing them to be kept 'in mind,' which is to say, in an activated state. The dorsal stream is also involved in basic speech perception, since the frontal motor programs for producing certain words are automatically engaged whenever those words are heard, and recognition can either be enhanced or reduced by using transcranial magnetic stimulation to modulate the operation of the relevant frontal regions. These modulatory effects are fairly small, however, and there is an ongoing debate over the degree to which 'motor resonance' actually facilitates speech perception.

19.4.2 Speech production

The ability to produce spoken words is no less remarkable than the ability to perceive them. In ordinary conversational settings, English speakers generate about two to three words per second, which is roughly equivalent to three to six syllables consisting of ten to twelve phonemes. These words are retrieved from a mental lexicon that contains, for the average literate adult, between 50,000 and 100,000 entries, and articulating them requires the precise coordination of up to 100 muscles. Yet errors are only rarely made, occurring just once or twice every 1,000 words.

The first step in word production is to map the idea one wishes to express onto the meaning of a lexical item. Although the multifarious semantic features of individual words are widely distributed across the brain, there is growing evidence that the ATL plays an essential role in binding together and systematizing those features. This topic is discussed more fully in the section on word meanings (§19.6), however, so in the current context it is sufficient to make the following points. To the extent that the ATL does subserve the integrated concepts that words convey, it can be regarded (at least for the expository purposes required here) as not only near the endpoint of the ventral stream for speech perception, but also near the starting point of the pathway for speech production. In addition, it is noteworthy that many aspects of semantic processing in the ATL, such as the selection of certain lexical items over others, are regulated in part by cognitive control mechanisms in the IFG.

Once the meaning of a target word has been selected in the ATL, processing moves posteriorly along the lateral extent of the temporal cortex. There are some hints that the word's morphosyntactic features are accessed in the mid/posterior MTG, but other perisylvian cortical areas may also be involved. In contrast, a great deal of data suggests that the word's phonological form (defined here as just the sequence of segments that constitute its phonemic content) is accessed in the posterior STG/STS. In fact, many studies support the view that this region implements a sound-based phonological network that is recruited not only during speech perception, as described above, but also during speech production. However, the question of whether we operate with a single phonological lexicon, or with separate but anatomically adjacent ones for input and output processing, has been highly contentious throughout the history of neurolinguistics, and answering it once and for all will require new insights from future research.

From the phonological network in the temporal lobe, processing moves anteriorly through the dorsal stream to the articulatory network in the frontal lobe. Syllabification is generally thought to occur in the posterior IFG. During this relatively late process, the ordered phonemic segments of the target word are incrementally bundled into syllabic units that do not necessarily conform to morphemic units. For instance, the word *horses* is bimorphemic and bisyllabic, yet the final segment of the first morpheme is not treated as the final segment of the first syllable, but is instead treated as the initial segment of the second syllable: {[*hor*]-[*ses*]}. Some investigators have argued that the most frequently used syllables in a language gradually become stored in long-term motor memory as precompiled articulatory gestures, so that they can be efficiently activated as ready-made 'chunks' rather than laboriously assembled again and again. No one would disagree, however, with the claim that complex articulatory orchestration is often required, and the available data suggest that this type of programming is handled not only by the posterior IFG, but also by the anterior insula – more specifically, by its superior sector, which is adjacent to the inferior sector of the posterior IFG.

After the appropriate high-level articulatory representations have been engaged in the posterior IFG and anterior insula, the corresponding sets of low-level motor commands are selected in the ventral PreG. The neuronal populations in this brain region are organized bilaterally and in a somatotopic manner that captures the layout of the various parts of the vocal tract – larynx, lips, jaw, tongue and palate. Their main function is to 'steer' the relevant muscles in a precisely coordinated, dynamic fashion during speech production. Their output signals, however, are relayed through several subcortical nuclei in the brainstem and spinal cord before finally reaching the appropriate parts of the motor periphery.

As with other kinds of bodily action, speech production is not entirely a feedforward process, but rather relies heavily on feedback mechanisms. When the goal is to utter a particular word, the sound-based representation of that word in the phonological network of the temporal lobe serves as an 'auditory target' that specifies what is expected to be heard. As articulation proceeds, the incoming acoustic signals of the resultant self-produced speech are immediately compared with that target representation, and if any discrepancies are detected, instructions for making the necessary corrections are sent to the frontal articulatory network. Recent research has shown that this feedback loop operates with remarkable speed and precision, allowing motor commands for speech to be adjusted 'on the fly,' often beneath the surface of awareness. Moreover, a parallel feedback loop in the somatosensory modality has been receiving increasing attention during the past few years. It recruits the supramarginal gyrus (SMG) to compare the predicted tactile and proprioceptive signals from the vocal tract with the actual signals. If errors are found, corrective messages are relayed to the frontal articulatory network, indicating how the motor program should be modified to generate the expected feelings in the vocal tract.

19.5 Printed word forms

19.5.1 Reading

For skilled readers, recognizing printed words seems easy. But the apparent simplicity of this process is an illusion. In reality, the reader's eyes make four or five saccades (i.e. jerky movements) every second, and with each fixation the amount of detail that is perceived drops off precipitously from the fovea (i.e. the small circular space of maximal visual acuity), so that it is only possible to register a few letters at a time. Furthermore, determining that a particular string of letters constitutes a familiar word is a formidable computational task. The essence of the problem is this: in order to recognize a written word, it is necessary to extract precisely those features that invariantly characterize that word across all of its possible manifestations, including changes in ^position^, size, CASE, and *font*. To accomplish this feat, large differences in visual form must be ignored (e.g. between 'a' and 'A'), small ones must be noticed (e.g. between 'e' and 'c'), and alternative linear orders must be detected (e.g. between 'dog' and 'god'). Skilled readers, however, can effortlessly and accurately satisfy all these requirements within a time window of just a few hundred milliseconds.

The sight of a printed word triggers a cascade of transformations that extends from the retina to the thalamus, from there to the primary visual cortex at the back of the brain, and from there through a series of anteriorly directed ventral occipitotemporal way-stations that extract increasingly rich and informative combinations of orthographic features. From a representational perspective, this visual processing hierarchy starts with mere points and lines, but it leads progressively to case- and font-specific letter shapes, case- and font-invariant graphemes (i.e. abstract letter identities), short sequences of graphemes, and entire words. Many of the early stages of this hierarchy are bilateral, but there is growing evidence that the left hemisphere begins to dominate fairly quickly.

The hierarchy culminates in the Visual Word Form Area (VWFA), which is a cortical patch in the fusiform gyrus that has the following properties: it detects the identities of printed words regardless of their position, size, case or font, and regardless of whether they are perceived consciously or unconsciously; it is more sensitive to real than unreal words; it is engaged equally by different types of familiar scripts (e.g. English, Arabic, Chinese, etc.), but it responds more strongly to familiar than unfamiliar scripts; and perhaps most important of all, it prefers printed words to other kinds of visual objects. Now, because writing systems were not invented until very late in human history (about 5,400 years ago), the VWFA could not be innately designed for reading. It has been argued, however, that the reason why this particular region becomes relatively specialized for recognizing printed words when we learn to read is because it is inherently well-suited to handling complex combinations of spatially fine-grained shapes. Consistent with this view, and supporting the 'meta-modal' nature of the VWFA, is the recent finding that the VWFA is the most significantly activated area not only when sighted people discriminate between real and unreal printed words, but also when congenitally blind people discriminate between real and unreal Braille words.

Once the form of a printed word has been recognized in the VWFA, how does it get mapped onto the associated phonological and semantic structures? These processes are enabled by multiple pathways – some sublexical, others lexical – but their precise neural underpinnings remain unclear. Still, some generalizations can be made. Access to the proper pronunciations of printed words seems to depend mainly on the perisylvian circuit for speech processing, whereas access to the concepts encoded by printed words seems to depend mainly on a more inferior set of structures that includes the ATL as well as several other temporal, parietal and frontal areas. It is clear that printed words with regular spelling patterns, like the real word *desk* or the unreal word *blicket*, can be read aloud by mapping the graphemes directly onto the corresponding phonemes in rule-governed ways that bypass semantics. Some researchers have argued, however, that printed words with irregular spelling patterns, like *yacht*, can only be read aloud by first accessing their meaning, especially if they have low frequency. This is a controversial claim, though.

A final observation that leads naturally to the next topic is that, just as the auditory perception of spoken words automatically activates the oral motor programs for uttering them, so the visual perception of printed words automatically activates the manual motor programs for writing them. But while this is certainly an intriguing discovery, researchers have yet to determine how much such 'motor resonance' enhances the efficiency of reading.

19.5.2 Writing

In neurolinguistics, writing has not received nearly as much attention as reading. Nevertheless, progress is being made in understanding how our brains allow us to produce printed words.

One of the earliest stages of writing involves retrieving the abstract spelling patterns of the intended lexical items (i.e. the appropriate grapheme strings, unspecified for size, case and style). Several neuropsychological and functional neuro-imaging studies suggest that these high-level representations are accessed in the VWFA. Needless to say, this is a very important finding, since it supports the hypothesis that the VWFA contains a single orthographic lexicon that is enlisted for both reading and writing.

After the abstract spelling pattern of a target word has been selected in the VWFA, it is kept 'in mind' by the graphemic buffer. This is basically a short-term memory system that temporarily maintains in an activated state the identities and positions of the graphemes while the word is being written. Whereas the graphemes themselves are most likely represented in the VWFA, the device that keeps them 'alive' in a top-down, controlled manner appears to be implemented by the posterior IFG (i.e. Broca's area).

Finally, two low-level stages of written word production have been posited. The first is called allographic conversion, and it translates the abstract graphemes that are held in the graphemic buffer into concrete forms (e.g. upper or lower case, separate or cursively connected letters, etc.). The second is called graphomotor planning, and it provides even more precise instructions to the motor system for the hand, such as specifications for the size, direction and sequence of strokes. It is widely believed that both of these processes are subserved mainly by hand-related dorsolateral frontoparietal regions.

Incidentally, when writing is performed with a keyboard instead of a pen or pencil, a distinct computational component devoted to graphomotor planning for the purpose of typing may take information directly from the graphemic buffer and use it to assemble a set of commands for consecutive button presses. So far, however, the operations that underlie typing have not been investigated as much as those that underlie handwriting.

19.6 Word meanings

How are the meanings of words represented and processed in the brain? Some people might be tempted to suppose that the cortical implementation of lexical knowledge includes, for every word, a nice, neat, neurally discrete dictionary definition that spells out all the relevant semantic information in an abstract symbolic code that might be called 'mentalese.' Recent research suggests, however, that the real story is not only much more complicated than that, but also much more interesting.

There is mounting evidence that conceptual knowledge is, to some extent, grounded in modality-specific systems for perception and action, such that many forms of semantic processing involve unconscious simulations of fairly high-level sensory and motor states. Consider, for example, the meaning of the object noun *hammer*. Numerous studies suggest that this concept does not reside in any single place in the brain; instead, different fragments of it are scattered across different cortical regions according to the sensory or motor content of the type of information that is represented. Thus, visual–semantic specifications of how hammers look (i.e. the relevant shape patterns) appear to be stored in some of the same ventral temporal areas that are engaged when hammers are visually recognized; auditory–semantic specifications of how hammers sound (i.e. the relevant banging patterns) appear to be stored in some of the same superior/middle temporal areas that are engaged when hammers are auditorily recognized; motor–semantic specifications of how hammers are used (i.e. the relevant swinging patterns) appear to be stored in some of the same frontoparietal areas that are engaged when hammers are grasped and manipulated in customary ways; and so on.

It is important to note, however, that this field of inquiry is still quite young, and most of the key issues are hotly debated. Some of the questions that are currently being explored are as follows. To what degree do lexically based simulations really recruit neuronal populations that also contribute to perception and action? How much can such simulations be modulated by contextual and strategic factors? And what is the relative weighting, or functional significance, of the multiple modality-specific components of lexical concepts?

As mentioned earlier, the meanings of words seem to depend not only on widely distributed modality-specific cortical regions, but also on the ATL. One influential hypothesis maintains that the ATL is a computational hub that plays a number of vital roles in semantic cognition. For one thing, it ensures that the multimodal features of lexical concepts are properly integrated in long-term memory so that inferences across modalities can easily be made. For example, the word *duck* denotes a kind of bird with particular visual and auditory properties, and several studies suggest that certain sectors of the ATL capture these correlations, thereby compensating for the fact that the sight of ducks is not always accompanied by the sound of their quacking, and vice versa. In addition, there is growing evidence that the ATL allows conceptual processing to be driven by deep aspects of semantic structure, as opposed to being overly sensitive to superficial modality-specific similarities and differences. For example, the word *cat* most readily brings to mind small, furry, purring pets, like calicos; however, the relevant concept also includes atypical instances, like hairless cats, which certainly qualify as members of the cat category despite their lack of fur; and it excludes what might be called pseudotypical instances, like Chihuahuas, which resemble cats but are actually dogs. Several studies suggest that the ATL is essential for making these kinds of judgments about which entities do and do not fall within the boundaries of certain concepts. Finally, a substantial body of data now supports the view that the ATL is crucially involved in integrating and organizing the meanings of not just object nouns, but also action verbs and various classes of abstract words.

In addition to modality-specific input/output systems and the ATL, many other cortical areas have recently been found to contribute to semantic cognition. Some of them are as follows. The anterior IFG interacts closely with the ATL and has been implicated in the resolution of conflicts between competing word meanings. The angular gyrus (AG) seems to have integrative hub-like semantic functions, possibly analogous to those of the ATL.

And the posterior MTG appears to play an important role in the representation and/or processing of many types of lexical concepts, although the details have yet to be deciphered.

19.7 Sentences

19.7.1 Comprehension

The ability to understand complete sentences is underpinned by a large-scale, mostly left-lateralized neural circuit. This circuit consists of several widely distributed but tightly interconnected cortical areas that operate synergistically to transform incoming strings of words into compositionally unified messages. It is not yet known exactly how each component of the circuit contributes to the overall goal of comprehending complex multi-word expressions, but the rough outlines of the architecture are slowly beginning to emerge. In order to anchor our discussion of this intricate topic in some concrete examples, we will make frequent reference to the sentences in (1) and (2). They are instructive because they use partially different configurations of the very same words to describe partially different scenarios.

(1) The reporter who attacked the senator admitted the error.

(2) The reporter who the senator attacked admitted the error.

For both (1) and (2), as each word is encountered, not only must its form and meaning be rapidly retrieved, but its morphosyntactic features must be accessed as well. For example, *the* is a definite article, *reporter* and *senator* are both count nouns, *who* is a relative pronoun, *attacked* and *admitted* are both transitive verbs, and so on. Although the neural mechanisms that access these morphosyntactic features have not been precisely localized, most of the available data point to the posterior MTG. As mentioned in §19.4.1 on speech perception, during the receptive processing of spoken language, this region receives input directly from the phonological network in the posterior STG/STS. And more importantly, several studies suggest that the same region is crucially involved in identifying the grammatical categories of perceived words. It is also noteworthy that the posterior MTG operates in concert with the posterior IFG (i.e. Broca's area), especially when ambiguous expressions are encountered, like the phrase *flying planes*, in which *flying* could function as either a verb or an adjective. The basic idea is that in such situations the competing grammatical category assignments are represented in the posterior MTG, and the selection of the contextually appropriate one is executed in a top-down fashion by the posterior IFG.

We also observed in §19.4.1 that the posterior MTG projects forward to the ATL, and there is increasing evidence that the superior and middle sectors of this territory contribute to sentence comprehension in the following ways. Some of the neuronal populations here seem to be involved mainly in parsing, taking as input the morphosyntactic features and sequential orders of the incoming words, and yielding as output hierarchically organized phrases and clauses. In (1), for example, the subject of the sentence is the complex noun-phrase *the reporter who attacked the senator*, which consists of several smaller, nested constituents. Other neuronal populations in the superior/middle ATL appear to be devoted more to interpretation, specifically the compositional semantic process of incrementally building up the unified meanings of phrases and clauses. And still others have been implicated in both types of operations – that is, parsing as well as interpretation. In short, according to some lines of current thinking, the superior/middle ATL houses a combinatorial network that assembles and integrates progressively larger arrangements of grammatical and conceptual structures during online receptive sentence processing.

A crucial part of understanding a sentence is figuring out 'who's doing what to whom,' or, to put it somewhat more technically, determining the roles that the different participants play in the described situation. In both (1) and (2), for example, the structure of the main clause is the same, with the grammatical cues indicating that the reporter, not the senator, admitted the error. The two sentences vary, however, with regard to the structure of the relative clause, such that in (1) the grammatical cues indicate that the reporter is the agent of the attacking event and the senator is the patient, whereas in (2) the grammatical cues indicate that these roles are reversed. During the past few decades, a great deal of research has focused on elucidating the neural mechanisms that carry out these sorts of role assignments during sentence comprehension. But even though many valuable insights have been made, the precise nature of the underlying machinery remains elusive. Still, there is increasing evidence that one of the key cortical areas is the temporoparietal junction, which extends from the most posterior portion of the STS into the adjacent AG.

When sentences are heard rather than read, it is sometimes useful to keep the phonological forms of the words in an activated state until the comprehension process has been completed. This is accomplished by the auditory–verbal short-term memory (STM) system, which, as mentioned in §19.4.1, has two components. First, the storage component represents activated word forms and is implemented by the phonological network in the posterior STG/STS; and second, the rehearsal component continually refreshes the contents of the storage component and is implemented by the articulatory network in the frontal lobe. This STM system is often called the phonological loop, and it is frequently employed to facilitate sentence comprehension. For instance, many studies have shown that, compared to sentences like (1), sentences like (2) are harder to understand and more likely to engage the phonological loop. These findings suggest that listeners tend to 'replay' sentences like (2) in their 'mind's ear,' thereby giving themselves more time to figure out exactly 'who's doing what to whom.' It is important to note, however, that the precise role of the phonological loop in sentence comprehension is controversial, largely because several neuropsychological studies have shown that a severe reduction of auditory–verbal STM capacity does not always disrupt the ability to understand long and convoluted sentences.

Finally, the most mysterious node in the circuit for sentence comprehension is the posterior IFG (i.e. Broca's area). Some researchers have proposed that it is involved in computing certain aspects of the hierarchical and sequential structures of sentences, like long-distance dependencies. In contrast, others have proposed that it aids comprehension by carrying out certain kinds of executive/supervisory operations, like using the rehearsal component of auditory–verbal STM to 'replay' unusually hard-to-understand sentences (as described above), or guiding the process of checking and, if necessary, revising the analysis of 'who's doing what to whom.' Although all of these hypotheses have some merits, none of them can account for the full range of data. For example, one of the most serious challenges for future work will be to explain the inconsistencies in the neuropsychological literature, since there is substantial evidence that damage to Broca's area sometimes does and sometimes does not lead to debilitating sentence comprehension deficits.

19.7.2 Production

The neural substrates of sentence production have not been explored in nearly as much depth as those of sentence comprehension. To some degree, this imbalance reflects the fact that, with regard to experimental design, it is much more challenging to control the relevant variables when people generate complex multi-word expressions than when they are given such expressions. Despite these limitations, however, progress is gradually being made in mapping the cortical architecture of sentence production.

During the 1980s and 1990s, most of the research on this topic focused on a disorder called agrammatism. Extensive cross-linguistic investigation showed that brain-damaged patients with this impairment tend to have five main problems with sentence production: a paucity of main verbs; syntactic simplification; omission of free-standing closed-class elements (e.g. prepositions); substitution of bound closed-class elements (e.g. tense/aspect suffixes); and over-reliance on canonical word order. However, close scrutiny of individual patients revealed that all of these symptoms could dissociate from each other, leading some researchers to argue that agrammatism is not really a coherent disorder. Moreover, lesion analyses demonstrated that although patients classified as agrammatic usually have damage to left perisylvian frontal, parietal and temporal regions, the specific sites vary tremendously. Taken together, these findings left it rather unclear how particular aspects of sentence production might be linked with particular brain areas.

Since the turn of the millennium, a bit more has been learned about these issues, due in large part to several PET and fMRI studies that used sophisticated protocols to explore the neural correlates of sentence production in normal subjects. Interestingly, a few of these studies directly compared production tasks with comprehension tasks involving the same sentences and found that two main regions – the posterior MTG and posterior IFG (i.e. Broca's area) – contribute to grammatical processing in both expressive and receptive modalities. While the functions of these regions remain unclear, it is possible that, as suggested earlier, the posterior MTG represents the morphosyntactic features of words while the posterior IFG is involved in hierarchical sequencing. Much more work will be necessary, though, to determine whether these hypotheses are on the right track.

Further reading

Binder, J.R. and R.H. Desai (2011) The neurobiology of semantic memory. *Trends in Cognitive Sciences* 15: 527–36.

Dehaene, S. (2009) *Reading in the Brain: The Science and Evolution of a Human Invention*. New York: Viking.

DeWitt, I. and J.P. Rauschecker (2012) Phoneme and word recognition in the auditory ventral stream. *Proceedings of the National Academy of Sciences* 109: E505–14.

Dick, A.S. and P. Tremblay (2012) Beyond the arcuate fasciculus: Consensus and controversy in the connectional anatomy of language. *Brain* 135: 3529–50.

Friederici, A.D. (2012) The cortical language circuit: From auditory perception to sentence comprehension. *Trends in Cognitive Sciences* 16: 262–8.

Guenther, F.H. and T. Vladusich (2012) A neural theory of speech acquisition and production. *Journal of Neurolinguistics* 25: 408–22.

Hickok, G. and D. Poeppel (2007) The cortical organization of speech processing. *Nature Reviews Neuroscience* 8: 393–402.

Indefrey, P. (2011) The spatial and temporal signatures of word production components: A critical update. *Frontiers in Psychology* 2: art. 255.

Jefferies, E. (2013) The neural basis of semantic cognition: Converging evidence from neuropsychology, neuroimaging, and TMS. *Cortex* 49: 611–25.

Kemmerer, D. (2014) *The Cognitive Neuroscience of Language: An Introduction.* New York: Psychology Press.

Price, C.J. (2010) The anatomy of language: A review of 100 fMRI studies published in 2009. *Annals of the New York Academy of Sciences* 1191: 62–88.

Purcell, J.J., P.E. Turkeltaub, G.F. Eden and B. Rapp (2011) Examining the central and peripheral processes of written word production through meta-analysis. *Frontiers in Psychology* 2: art. 239.

Segaert, K., L. Menenti, K. Weber, K.M. Petersson and P. Hagoort (2012) Shared syntax in language production and language comprehension: An fMRI study. *Cerebral Cortex* 22: 1662–70.

Turkeltaub, P.E. and H.B. Coslett (2010) Localization of sublexical speech perception components. *Brain and Language* 114: 1–15.

20
First language acquisition

Eve V. Clark and Marisa Casillas

20.1 The first year

What are the general developments observable in the first year of life, and how do they relate to the emergence of language? We start by looking at infants and what they can do and what they can communicate before they begin to rely on language. Then we take up the changes that occur as children begin to acquire the language of the community around them.

20.1.1 Early interactions

Infants begin to acquire interactive skills during familiar activities with their care-givers. Everyday routines of feeding, diaper changing, bathing and playtime provide rich contexts in which children and their care-givers can practice interacting with well-defined, consistent roles. In these contexts, care-givers coordinate their own behavior to fit neatly with the child's, vocalizing in response to or in unison with the child's movements, laughter and vocalizations, as in (1) and (2) – both exchanges between a Thai mother and her young son. In doing so, care-givers impose an interactive structure on their infants' behavior that leaves room for the infants to make their own contributions once they become ready to do so.

(1) *Simultaneous vocalizations.* Mon (0;6) is being held up by his mother to face his sister. While he vocalizes, his mother comments on his actions and intersperses pitch-matched vocalizations between her son's ongoing verbal behavior (Luksaneeyanawin 2000) ['yyy' indicates unintelligible speech or non-speech vocalizations]:
Child: yyy [vocalizing as Mother speaks]
Mother: *naj4 jim3 lOO1 haj2 phii2 kOOn1 jim3 lOO1 ʔUU0 ʔaa0 rom0 dii0 lxxw3 chaj2 maj4 jim3 lOO1 lxxw3 chaj2 maj4*
'Smile handsome, smile to your older sister first.' [Matching her pitch movement to child's ongoing vocalizations] 'You're in a good mood, right? You can smile, right?'
Child: yyy [vocalizing while Mother speaks]

Mother: *ʔUU0 naj4 phii2 saaw4 saaw4 juu1 naj4 phii2 saaw4 saaw4 ʔUU0 phii2 saaw4 saaw4 juu1 troN0 nii3 nii2 ʔeeN0*
[Matching her pitch movement to the child's ongoing vocalizations]
'Where is your older sister? Where is your older sister? Your older sister is right here.'

(2) *Alternating vocalizations.* Mon (0;6) is looking at and reaching for a box covered in colorful pictures of castles and children:
Mother: *duu0 si3 khOON4 khraj0 mii0 ʔa1 raj0 baaN2 luuk2 ʔa1 maa0 duu0 si3 paj0 ʔaan1 duu0 si3*
'Look what children are there. Come and look. Go on and read.'
Child: yyy
Mother: *ʔaan1 ʔOOk1 pa1*
'Can you read?'
Mother: *ʔaw2 paj0 cap1 si3 luuk2 paj0 cap1 nii2*
'Go grab the children. Grab here.' [taps finger on box]
Child: yyy [grabs at box]
Mother: *aj0 maj2 daaj2 si1 wooj0 waaj0 si1*
'You can't go on (so) cry out.'
Child: yyy!
Mother: *paj0 maj2 daaj2 si1 wooj0 waaj0 ʔa1 chuuaj2 chuuaj2 chuuaj2 nOj1 chuuaj2 nOj1*
'You can't go on. (So) cry out. I'll help, I'll help, I'll help a little bit, I'll help a little bit.' [brings child closer to box]
Child: [places hand on box]
Mother: *nii2 duu0 si3 mii0 ʔa1 raj0 baaN2 hUUm4*
'Look here. What's there? Hm?'

These early interactions create a contingent relation between infant and care-giver actions. Such co-dependence is crucial for infants in developing the skills they will need for interactional coordination and collaboration – both basic requirements in human communication. The repetitive nature of early interactions allows children to become active participants while benefiting from familiar routines and action exchanges. Conversation-like exchanges between infants and care-givers begin when infants are as young as two to three months, and consist primarily of the participants taking turns at 'talking.' These proto-conversations become more elaborate as the infants get older, and as care-givers expect more sophisticated responses. Compare (2) with (3).

(3) *Alternating linguistic turns* (from the same child as in (1) and (2)). Mon (1;11) and Mother are playing with a set of small plastic toys on the living room floor:
Child: *len2 ʔa1*
'Play.' [kicks toys]
Mother: *ca1 len2 kOO2 len2 si1 ʔa1 te1 tham0 maj0 ʔa1*
'If you're playing, then play. Why are you kicking?'
Child: *len2 len2 len2 ʔa1 len2 len2 len2 yyy len2 ʔa1*
'Play play. Play. Play. Play play. yyy play.'
Mother: *ʔa1 raj0 nii2 kxxw2 naam3*
'What? This is a mug.'

Child: *naam3 yyy naam3 yyy naam3*
'Water yyy. Water yyy. Water.' [picks up mug]
Mother: *dUUm1 dUUm1*
'Drink. Drink.'
Child: [makes a drinking motion]
Mother: *?a1 hUUt3 luuk2 hUUt3 kOOn1 hUUt3 kOOn1*
'Slurp, child. Slurp first, slurp first.' [makes slurping sounds]

Turn-taking routines also appear in non-verbal interactions toward the end of the first year. For example, in social games like peek-a-boo or toy-passing, infants rehearse the same types of alternating behaviors that they later need in verbal interaction. They often appear to initiate such games with the goal of practicing the act of exchange, and take delight in anticipating what will happen next at each point in the interaction.

Timing becomes a key component in these interactions rather early in the first year. Vocal exchanges before the age of six months display minimal switching pauses between parent and child vocalizations. The rapid timing of turns appears at first to mirror speech patterns in adult conversation. However, infants' vocalizations overlap with their care-givers' speech on nearly 40 percent of the turns, suggesting that six-month-olds have not yet acquired the ground rules for conversational alternation: one speaker at a time with precise speaker transitions. But from around six months onwards, infants begin to latch onto the basic turn-taking system, with longer overall gaps and fewer overlaps (Hilbrink *et al.* in preparation). Infants also appear to be sensitive to the timing of their care-givers' responses even before that. When they experience paused, delayed, or otherwise non-contingent signals from their mothers, they react by looking away more often, vocalizing less or differently, working to repair the interaction, and sometimes becoming upset. In tracking timing, then, young infants tune into coordinated interaction, with structured access to linguistic and non-linguistic information from their care-givers.

Conversation and interactive routines are infants' primary sources of linguistic input, with both sources offering structured settings for their subsequent language acquisition. One consequence of this interactive input is that the language they hear, understand and produce occurs within organized sequences of turns that change as children develop – care-givers adapt their speech and word choices to their children's current state of development. In a nutshell, adult child-directed speech in the first year derives jointly from child and adult actions, and adult contributions tend to match children's current interactive skills.

20.1.2 Emerging knowledge about language

While honing their interactive skills, infants learn a lot about language. Although many children do not produce their first words until the end of their first year, they recognize some properties of their native language within hours of birth. Prosodic information (rhythm and pitch) makes its way to babies' ears in the womb, and newborns tested two to five days after birth can distinguish between the rhythm type of their native language and other rhythm types, e.g. syllable-timed like French, compared to stress-timed like Russian. By the time they are six to nine months old, infants prefer the prevalent stress patterns of the surrounding language: those learning English prefer trochaic sequences ('BAby') to iambic ones ('balLOON'), consistent with the typical stress pattern of English. Prosodic information can even mislead infants: eleven-month-olds have fairly well-specified representations of the sound composition of familiar words, but mis-stressing and making changes to stressed syllables delays their word recognition (Vihman *et al.* 2004).

Although infants can discriminate between native and non-native rhythmic types from birth, they do not attend selectively to the sound segments of their own language until around ten months of age. Each language has a set of sound segments (phonemes) that can be combined in words to carry contrasting meanings (e.g. *ball* versus *tall*). For example, English speakers who listen to the Korean syllables /tʰal/ and /tal/ 'hear' hear two tokens of the word *tall*. But Korean speakers hear two different words: 'mask' and 'moon,' respectively. This is because the phonemic inventory of Korean includes three types of alveolar stop that differentiate word meanings (e.g. /tʰal/ 'mask,' /tal/ 'moon' and /t̬al/ 'daughter'), whereas English only has two (e.g. /tʰal/ 'tall' and /dal/ 'doll'), such that tokens from the third Korean type (/tal/) get categorized with the sound perceptually closest to it in English (/tʰal/). Until nine or ten months of age, infants can discriminate between many phoneme pairs that are not relevant to their native language phonology. For example, at six to ten months, English-learning infants readily distinguish non-native contrasts such as /t̬a/–/ta/ and /ˀki/–/ˀqi/, native to Hindi and to Thompson Salish (British Columbia), respectively. But by ten to twelve months, only Hindi- and Thompson Salish-learning infants continue to discriminate these sounds, while infants learning English do not (Werker and Tees 1984).

This apparent loss of linguistic skills is more likely a *shift in attention* to the sounds in the ambient language. In fact, when nine-month-old infants interact regularly with a speaker of a new language, they appear to regain the ability to discriminate sounds in that language. Interestingly, though, this holds only for new language input that children experience during interaction – not, for example, from overhearing a new language. Generally speaking, interactive language experience throughout the first year, whether monolingual or bilingual, appears to continually shape sound category representations (Kuhl *et al*. 2006). It may at first seem surprising that children are so flexible in their discrimination of phonemes, but this ability is essential for young bilinguals – and at least half of the world's population is estimated to be bilingual. Children who acquire two languages natively also need to attend to which phonemic contrasts belong to which languages. While this can cause further changes in perception early on, it has a minimal effect on bilingual children's achievement of landmarks in the process of language acquisition.

20.1.3 Categories, contexts, and (proto-)representations

One way that children break into the linguistic signal is by exploiting tendencies in language use and structure. For example, they may learn about the categorization of vowel sounds by leveraging the way vowels cluster in acoustic space. They can use information about the clusters to identify existing categories and to classify ambiguous vowel sounds as tokens of nearby categories, though their classifications too may be modulated by interaction.

At six months, infants know quite a bit about the prosody of their language, a little about its sounds (phonology), but nothing yet of its lexicon or syntax. But with each step in development, they can combine any partial linguistic knowledge with detectable statistical patterns to gain a foothold in new linguistic structures. For example, at eight months, infants recognize recurring sequences of sounds in the speech stream by attending to the transitional probabilities between phones. Such recurrent sequences become some of the first 'words' they identify.

Although language can be viewed as comprising many layers of structure, it is important to remember that infants and young children do not wait to master one level of linguistic representation (e.g. sounds) before moving onto the next (e.g. words). By using partial information at multiple levels, even very young children learn about prosody, phonology, lexicon, and syntactic structure simultaneously. For example, by using phonology to learn new words while also using words to learn more phonology, children can bootstrap their learning in both domains.

20.1.4 Gaze, gesture, and the ambient language

Breakthroughs in one developmental domain can profoundly affect other domains. Infants' access to visual information in the world changes dramatically as they learn to control eye and head movements. And once infants can grasp objects and hold them up, they gain added control over which parts of an object they can see and touch. As any care-giver knows, once infants begin to crawl and then walk, they can access much larger domains for exploration – a cause for both joy and exasperation. Many of the objects children see and hold come with linguistic commentary from care-givers that, combined with children's first-person perspective, helps narrow down the relation between labels and referents in each context (Yurovsky *et al.* 2013).

Children attend to other people's gaze from early on – and rightly so since gaze coordination is key for establishing joint attention in communicative contexts. Two- to five-day-old infants look longer at images of faces that gaze directly at them than faces gazing away from them, and by four months old, they process images of faces gazing directly at them faster than faces gazing away. This is consistent with natural adult–infant coordination: three-month-olds smile less when adults look away and then they smile again when the adult's gaze returns to them (Farroni *et al.* 2002).

By four months, infants begin to follow others' direction of gaze, but only show a preference for gaze over head direction from ten months on. Gaze-following is fundamental to joint attention and interactional coordination, and gaze-following predicts some early language development: ten-month-olds who vocalize while following gaze have larger receptive vocabularies at fourteen months. And infants' early responses to bids for joint attention predict their later *comprehension* vocabulary, while their early propensity to initiate joint attention predicts their later *production* vocabulary (Carpenter *et al.* 1998).

Young children's early 'speech' is characterized by a combination of gaze, vocalization, and gesture. Infants begin to use gestures such as points, reaches and head movements soon after six months of age. Pointing, in particular, typically becomes part of their communicative repertoire between eight and fifteen months, with early pointing often taking a 'whole-hand' form, where infants extend their arm toward the interesting object or event, rather than the prototypical Western index-finger hand shape. Finger and whole-hand pointing differ qualitatively, with finger pointing emerging later, from around ten months, and predicting children's comprehension of others' pointing behavior (Liszkowski and Tomasello 2011).

Even as young children produce their first words, they continue to rely on gesture (head nods, shakes, points, reaches, etc.) to identify or reject objects, and to make repairs in interaction. By age one, they supplement their turns with words, often combined with gesture. Children who produce gesture-plus-word combinations early also use two-word combinations early, as long as the combinations of gesture and word supplement each other (e.g. as when a child points at a hat and says *daddy*, to mean 'that's daddy's hat' or 'there's daddy's hat'). Parents and care-givers also rely on gesture along with speech as they interact with their young children (e.g. Rader and Zukow-Goldring 2010).

Children display enormous changes in their interactive and linguistic abilities during the first year. From the start, care-givers and infants attend to sounds, gestures and gaze in the other, and they make increasing use of these elements to infer each other's intentions. They engage in exchange games of all kinds, antecedents to verbal turn-taking, and they rely on gaze, gesture and vocalization to tailor their communications as they build on fragmentary linguistic knowledge. These developments reveal which information infants can access, understand and convey during the first year. They provide the basis on which they will continue to build.

20.2 Getting into language

As children begin to understand more words, they begin to produce linguistic *forms* – words and the constructions they appear in. But when they produce their first words, it is clear that they often start out with just fragments of the conventional meaning for a term. For example, they may initially assign just the meaning of 'four-legged' to the word *dog* or *horse*, and only later work out exactly how the meaning of *horse*, say, contrasts with those for *cow*, *donkey* and *zebra* (Clark 1993). Or they might appropriately assign the meaning of motion to a verb like *jog* and only later learn just how it contrasts in meaning with *run* and *stroll*. As they hear more uses of each word, in a range of contexts, and as they encounter the occasional misunderstanding of their own uses, children adjust their initial meanings until they more or less coincide with adult usage.

Mastering the adult meanings of words can take several years, but the amount of overlap in meaning at the beginning of this process is often enough for quite successful communication, especially within the family. Ultimately, though, children must learn how to use forms and meanings for communicating with a variety of others in the speech community. One central factor in doing this is the attention children pay to other speakers and their intended meanings in context.

20.2.1 Joint attention and physical co-presence

Achieving joint attention can be complicated, but adults typically accommodate to their children: When young children show that they are attending to something by pointing and looking at it, adults 'follow in' and talk about that object or event. When adults instead take the lead in establishing joint attention, they rely on name-use, exclamations like *Hey!* or *Look!*, and point to the locus of attention (Estigarribia and Clark 2007). In both cases, adult and child establish joint attention to some object or action that is visible to them both and, typically, physically present. Joint attention and physical co-presence are the conditions that allow adults to be reasonably sure that children will identify the intended target of their talk – what they are labeling or talking about on that occasion. Children can then combine information from timing, discourse cues, communicative intentions and consistent word–object associations across many instances of object naming, to make links between the labels they are offered and the things or events they see (e.g. Clark and de Marneffe 2012).

Reliance on joint attention and physical co-presence in talking to young children results in most talk being about the here-and-now, whether it is a matter of looking at a rabbit in the garden, or describing what adult and child can see in a series of photographs. Joint attention is critical to adult–adult interactions too, of course, but physical co-presence is not as crucial since adults can use language to conjure up past events, future possibilities and all kinds of abstract ideas and arguments. For young children, though, attaching meanings to new words depends critically on physical co-presence: this offers children a starting point for assigning some meaning to terms like *top*, *doggie*, *shoe* or *eat*.

20.2.2 Identifying intentions

As they interact with different people in different settings, children need to assess the goals and beliefs of those they interact with. Knowledge about someone else's goal is useful for predicting both what that person is going to do and how to respond. Once children can attribute mental states like intentions, beliefs and goals to others, they have come to understand that different people can have different beliefs and goals, and know different things. When and how children begin to model others' mental states is still a matter of debate (see Baron-Cohen *et al.* 2013), but children as young as twelve to fourteen months old can make some inferences about others' goals. For example, fourteen-month-olds behave rationally in imitating an adult after watching her act on a novel object: if the demonstrator's hands are occupied (e.g. holding a shawl round her shoulders) and she presses a large button on the novel object with her forehead, infants are unlikely to imitate her. Instead, they press the button with their hands. But if the demonstrator's hands are free when she presses the button with her forehead, they are far more likely to copy her action than to use their hands. This suggests that one-year-olds expect rational behavior from the demonstrator – if she could have used her hands but did not, she must have *intended* to use her forehead instead. In short, different actions signal different intentions.

However, these young children could have been making inferences only about the actions, and how they differed, rather than about the demonstrator's intentions. Appreciation of others' beliefs (Theory of Mind) has generally been attributed to children only when they observe a scene and can identify the false beliefs of particular participants. A typical test goes as follows: If Ann puts her shoes under the bed and then, when she is not looking, Bob moves them to the closet, does Ann still believe they are under her bed? Where will Ann look first once she returns to get her shoes? Children can answer such questions about false beliefs only at around age four, but appropriate answers in such tasks depend on both memory and linguistic skill. These tasks may also be difficult for young children because they always make the child an observer rather than a participant. Studies of younger children's spontaneous non-linguistic (and linguistic) responses give evidence of false-belief attribution at two or younger (e.g. Baillargeon *et al.* 2010). The evidence suggests that children assume rationality in navigating interactions *before* they necessarily associate actions and goals with more abstract mental states. Making this early assumption of rationality enables even young children to make inferences about the causes of others' actions, hence discerning their communicative intentions, and so coordinating with their interlocutors.

20.2.3 Partial word meanings

While the first meanings children assign to words often overlap with (part of) the adult meaning, they rarely fully coincide with it. One result is that young children over-extend their first words, and for instance, produce *doggie* to pick out dogs, cats, sheep, squirrels and goats, and *ball* for anything small and round. Over-extensions like this appear to result from too small a vocabulary in production, rather than from any inability to discriminate kinds. Indeed, when shown pictures of a dog and a cat, and asked 'Where's the dog?' one-year-olds consistently choose only the dog. This suggests that young children simply make do, at this stage, with whatever words they can retrieve and produce (here, *dog*) to denote things that are similar in some respect to the target referent.

How do young children decide which word to use under such circumstances? They rely heavily on shape in selecting a word, and this accounts for the majority of their spontaneous over-extensions, as well as for elicited extensions to unfamiliar objects. Reliance on similarity of shape allows young children to label new objects quite readily. At the same time, when their label for a category instance is erroneous, adults typically correct it by offering the conventional term for that category in the next turn. One-year-olds over-extend around 30 percent of their first seventy-five words in production, but generally stop doing this by twenty-four to thirty months, just as they start asking innumerable *What's that?* questions to elicit words they do not yet know or have difficulty retrieving (see Clark 2009). Finally, the initial meaning young children first attach to a word in context has been characterized as 'fast mapping,' but this captures just the starting point in meaning acquisition. Arriving at the conventional meaning of a term can take many months and even years.

20.2.4 Getting word forms right

With linguistic forms, children must master the phonology and prosody of their language as they learn its vocabulary (Stoel-Gammon 2011). On the one hand, this means making the production of their words recognizable to others. But children need time to gain the necessary articulatory skill, and even after they can produce recognizable one-syllable words, they may rely for some time on simplified interim templates in producing two-syllable words such as *blanket* or *slinky*. When learning multisyllabic words like *elevator* and *kangaroo* (often first produced as 'EH-vatuh' and 'ROO'), they also need to keep track of where word-stress appears in addition to any preliminary meaning they assign. With larger linguistic units, they have to assign phrasal and sentential stress, with phrase-final stress normally identifying new information ('Jim brought the CAKE'). But they also need to be able to use contrastive stress, regardless of its position in the clause ('The CAT, not the dog') (Clark 2009).

To make themselves understood, young children need to produce words with their local, conventional pronunciation and construct sentences with the appropriate conventional word order. In short, they need to plan each utterance in light of the addressee it is destined for. In achieving this, even very young children monitor what they say and how they say it. They make spontaneous self-repairs to the forms of words from age one on, and respond to requests for repair from others, usually by making changes to the forms of the words they produce. As they get older, children tend to make spontaneous self-repairs to whatever part of the system they are currently mastering: repairs to phonology emerge early and persist as a major repair-type until age three or so. Repairs to morphology – noun and verb inflections – emerge around age two as children begin to establish the noun and verb paradigms of their language, while syntactic repairs tend to appear only later, once children have begun to distinguish different construction-types. Finally, repairs to lexical choices, like phonological repairs, emerge early and continue well past age four (Clark 2009).

20.2.5 Setting up semantic domains

Children accumulate words in a variety of domains from early on. By the time they can produce about fifty words (at eighteen to thirty months), they use words for people such as *baby*, *mama* or *mummy*, *daddy*, *dada* or *papa*, and *man*; for food – *juice*, *milk*, *cookie*, *bread* and *drink*; for body-parts – *eye*, *nose*, *mouth* and *ear* first; for animals – *dog*, *cat* or *kitty*, *bird*, *duck* or *hen*, *cow*, *horse* and *sheep*; for toys – *ball*, *block*, *book* and *doll*; for household items – *spoon*, *cup*, *brush*, *bottle*, *key*, *clock* and *light*; for clothing – *hat*, *shoe*, *diaper* or *nappy*, and *coat*; for vehicles – *car*, *boat*, *truck* and *train*; and for common routines – *pat-a-cake, peek-a-boo, upsy-daisy, incy wincy spider, this little pig, bye-bye* and *night-night*.

As they add more words, they start to link terms related in meaning, gradually organizing them into semantic domains. For example, they link words for animals (*cats, dogs, foxes, wolves*; *rabbits* and *hares*; *frogs, newts, lizards* and *snakes*; *birds, owls, ducks, pigeons, swallows*) with words for their characteristic sounds (*moo, neigh, bellow, roar, squeak, hiss*), with words for how they move (*hop, trot, slither, climb, fly*), and words for what they eat and where they live. For spatial relations, children add locative adverbs (*here, there, outside*), prepositions (*in, on, beside, over*), verbs of motion (*come, go, walk, run, hop, slide, skip, ride*), and nouns for places (*house, hill, road, path, shelf*, etc.). They steadily add new words to current domains and, as they acquire more words, they also add new domains.

As children add to their repertoire of words, they also start to make choices to reflect the perspective they want to convey. They may call something a *waste-basket* when dropping paper into it, but a *hat* when holding it upside down over their head. And in pretend play, a block is a *block* when building a tower, but a *telephone* when held up to the ear. Children use their words from as young as eighteen months on to present things to their addressee from a particular perspective (Clark 1997). These semantic relations and alternative perspectives help children impose different kinds of organization on the conceptual categories picked out by the terms they produce.

20.2.6 Word classes

Children appear to grasp quite early on that some words are used for talking about concrete objects (nouns), others for talking about actions (verbs), others still for talking about properties (adjectives) and relations (verbs, prepositions). The word classes in many languages are distinguished in part by the kinds of things they denote: People, places and things are denoted with nouns; actions and states with verbs; relations with verbs and prepositions (and occasionally with nouns). Children appear to make use of this semantic information as they start to make generalizations about different kinds of words. For example, two- and three-year-olds are adept at picking out appropriate referents for count and mass nouns and for verbs.

Adult reliance on frequent frames helps children recognize nouns and verbs even before they have assigned any meanings. By attending to where specific words and word-types appear in adult speech (*This is a—*; *He is –ing*), they could reliably extract nouns and verbs, and even identify the relevant inflections for each word class. In addition to identifying inflections, they must also identify the meaning each inflection adds to core word-stems – case, gender and number, for instance, on nouns, or tense, mood and aspect as well as person and number on verbs. Although many of children's first words in comprehension are for familiar objects, their recognition of words for events, properties and relations begins to emerge early in the second year. They also attend to the relative frequency of specific word combinations and to recurring phrases, making use of well-entrenched patterns when they imitate phrases or retrieve irregular word forms.

20.2.7 Filling semantic gaps

One strategy that compensates for a limited vocabulary is for children to coin new words when they need them. Most languages offer a variety of options, differing in productivity, for such coinages. Derivation adds affixes to the word-stem (e.g. *a* **puller** for someone who's pulling something); compounding allows the combination of word-stems into root compounds (e.g. *PLANT-man* for 'gardener'), or synthetic compounds containing affixes as well (e.g. *my RUNNing-stick,* 'a stick carried while running').

Children start to make use of some options early on, often before age two, but they rely initially only on what is most productive in the language being acquired (Clark 1993). In Germanic languages like English, children's earliest coinages tend to be root compounds (NOUN + noun, with primary stress in English on the first, modifying, noun) and denominal verbs (derived from noun stems, with no affixation). These emerge before children start to produce coinages with derivational affixes (e.g. agentive *–er*). In Romance languages, compounding is much less productive than derivation, and children's first coinages tend to be words formed by adding affixes to a stem. But since identifying affixes and their meanings takes time, children acquiring French, for instance, make relatively little use of this option before age three.

20.3 Early conversations

By soon after their first birthday, children have acquired a set of pre-linguistic, interactional and pragmatic skills that they can draw on for basic conversation: they understand and can produce a small number of word-like chunks, they point for others and track adult gaze, they respond to bids for attention and requests for action, they make inferences about the goals of others, and they have begun to take turns in speaking. Parents respond to these changes by increasing their verbal engagement with their children in conversational exchanges. By asking questions, initiating side-sequences and requesting repairs, parents offer children extensive feedback as they check up on what their child's intended meaning might have been. After ambiguous or erroneous utterances from the child, parents frequently reformulate the child's (apparent) meaning in the next turn. This offers the child an interpretation in conventional form that contrasts with what the child actually said (see Chouinard and Clark 2003). Parents also talk more to their children as they do things with them, from constructing block towers to reading a picture book, and in doing so they 'display' the language to be acquired, and how to use it, as in the exchanges between a Spanish-speaking mother and child in (4) and an English-speaking mother and child in (5).

    (4) *Reformulation.* Mendía (1;8.03) and her mother are drawing with pencils on a pad of paper. By following up what the child says, the mother gives feedback by using adult word forms and so grounding her interpretation of what the child says (Nieva Ramos 2013).
Mother: El sol.
           'the sun.'
Child: *Títa títa!* (= pinta pinta)
          'paint. paint.'
Mother: Tú qué vas a pintar?
           'what are you going to paint?'
Child: *Má.*
          'sea'   (= [mar] 'sea' or [mas] 'more').
Child: *Ta to.*   (= sol sol)!   *Pá-*
          'sun sun! pa-'
Mother: El mar. Pintas el mar?   [wrong guess]
           'the sea. Are you painting the sea?'

Child: *To!*   (= sol)   [child repair]
         'sun'
Mother: El sol.
         'The sun.'
Child: *To!*   (= sol)
         'sun'
Mother: El sol.
         'the sun.'
Child: *To!*   (= sol)
         'sun'

(5) *Displaying the language.* While feeding Naima (1;0.14) kidney beans, her mother talks about a range of topics related to eating and food preparation (Demuth *et al.* 2006).
   Child: əmæˈni. (= more bean)
   Mother: I'm giving it to you. I'm trying to take the skin off with my fingers. There you go. Are you eating beans? Are you eating beans for supper? Is that what you're doing? You're eating some bean? Mmmm, how delicious.
   Child: mæˈni mæˈni.   (= more bean more bean)
   Mother: OK. I'm peeling the bean for you.
            (a few seconds later)
   Child: mæˈni mæˈni mæˈni.   (= more bean more bean more bean)
   Mother: OK, I'm peeling it with my fingers. Fingers. See what I'm doing with my fingers? I'm peeling the skin off the kidney beans very, very slowly. Mmmm, you're hungry.

Soon after their first birthday, children start producing chains of single words that precede true multi-word utterances, e.g. '*Daddy. Peach. Cut*' (e.g. Bloom 1973). Parents rely on repeats and co-construction of utterances to fill the gaps in these early word combinations and they often provide conventional forms for children's intended meanings. In doing this, adults provide extensive framing for their children's turns at the one-word stage, helping them provide new information in response to questions while simultaneously displaying linguistic forms across a variety of communicative contexts. As children develop linguistically, they also acknowledge new information offered by their parents, as in (6), and start to contribute new information themselves, mainly in answering questions, as in (7).

(6) *Acknowledging new information.* Naima (1;0.28) and her mother are looking at a photo album. Naima acknowledges new information in her mother's utterances (Demuth *et al.* 2006).
   Mother: Naima and Daddy make coffee. That's the photograph book we made.
   Mother: There's the coffee grinder.
   Child: (imitates the sound of a coffee grinder)   [acknowledgement]
   Mother: Is that the noise it makes?
   Child: ˈtɪkə ˈtɪkə ˈtɪk (continues imitation) [acknowledgement]
   Mother: And there's Daddy with Naima.
   Mother: And there's the milk.
   Child: *Milk.* [acknowledgement]
   Mother: Milk. That's the milk being poured into the coffee in that picture.

(7) *Adding new information.* In this exchange, Damon (1;6.11) and his mother jointly recount for his father what happened when twelve-year-old Philip let his budgerigar out for Damon to see. It had fluttered onto Philip's head, then flew over and landed on Damon's, which startled him. Damon provides new information in response to his mother's questions. The questions frame the episode being recounted (Clark, diary data).
Mother: Did you see Philip's bird? Can you tell Herb?
Child: *head, head, head.* [new information]
Mother: What landed on your head?
Child: *bird.* [new information]

Care-givers, as the experts, not only offer children feedback on how to say things and display to them many aspects of language use; they also make explicit offers of new words along with information about how these words are connected to other words in the same domain. In making such offers, adults typically rely on particular syntactic frames like 'It's a —,' 'It's called a —,' or 'That's a —,' as shown in (8) and (9).

(8) *Explicit offer of a new word–1.* Mother and child (1;7.19) looking at an animal book; child points at the page.
Mother: Yeah. (laughs) It's called a kangaroo. Kangaroo.
Child: *roo.*

(9) *Explicit offer of a new word–2.* Mother and child (1;7.19) still looking at the animal book.
Mother: What are these? Those are birdies.
Child: *birdies.*

When offering new words explicitly in this way, adults often relate the new word directly to another familiar word in the same domain, by adding information about class-membership, as in (10), or information about parts and properties, as in (11)–(13).

(10) *Information about class-membership.* Mother and daughter Naomi (1;10.11) are looking at a picture of a seal.
Child: *birdie birdie.*
Mother: Not a birdie, a seal.
Child: *seal.*
Mother: Seal, uhhum.
Child: *birdie.*
Mother: Seal is a kind of a mammal.

(11) *Information about a part.* Mother and child (1;7) looking at a picture.
Mother: Here's a train. Here are the wheels.

(12) *Information about a property.* Father and daughter Naomi (2;7.16) talking about gloves.
Child: *mittens.*
Father: Gloves.
Child: *gloves.*

Father: When they have fingers in them they are called gloves and when the fingers are all put together they are called mittens.

(13) *Information about a function.* Father and child (2;6) with a picture of a walrus.
Father: The walrus has tusks. Tusks are like teeth.

Adults also supply information about neighboring categories ('It looks like a snake but it's an eel'), often in response to children's erroneous labels; about habitat; about characteristic sounds and ways of moving. They offer definitions and also give hints about what (familiar) things are called ('It looks like a donkey, don't you think?') (e.g. Clark and Estigarribia 2011). In doing this, they offer children extensive examples of how to describe objects and events, how to tell stories, and how to give instructions, all the while offering new terms and information about category structure as well. This all adds to what children know about the meanings of the forms they hear and use.

In these interactions, care-giver feedback helps to guide children's decisions in conveying their communicative goals, whether with gestures and word-and-gesture combinations during the earlier stages (Olson and Masur 2013), or with more precise referring expressions as they get older. Getting feedback about their referring expressions leads children as young as two to redesign their referring expressions to pick out a target referent. Again, to succeed, children must take into account what their addressee already knows, and hence the precise kind of information needed in order for the other to identify the target referent successfully.

20.3.1 Words and constructions

As children amass more words and produce more word combinations, they must attend to the larger constructions specific words appear in. Nouns occur in noun phrases, combined with articles (*the*, *a*), quantifiers (*some*, *all*), and adjectives (*big*, *blue*, *noisy*). Such noun phrases are used to express different verb arguments. Intransitive verbs appear only with a single argument, the actor (*the girl runs fast*) or the object-affected (*the ship sank*), as subject. Transitive verbs, often causative, take two arguments, the agent and the object-affected (*the boy broke the branch*; *the man moved the cup*), as subject and object respectively. Specific verb–argument combinations may appear in some syntactic constructions and not others. Constructions for intransitive versus transitive motion (cf. *The cat ran off* versus *The cat caught the bird*), for resultative (*Jan painted the bike blue*) or for ditransitive (*Mel made his friends a pie*) contribute their own meaning, over and above the meanings of individual verbs and nouns.

Children's early word combinations and their reliance on formulaic sequences in early utterances suggest that they make use of many ready-made pieces as they produce constructions. Later, they analyze the components inside those chunks, and learn which constructions contribute a particular meaning to an ordered sequence of words (see Ambridge and Lieven 2011). Learning which constructions express intransitive versus caused motion, for example, requires that children attend to whether a verb is intransitive or transitive, and to the specific argument-types that occur with each verb, as they plan which construction to use to convey a particular meaning. Like adult speakers, children must start planning with some intention to communicate, access the relevant words along with the most appropriate construction (intransitive, caused motion, resultative, etc.), insert the words into that construction, and then spell out the phonological sequence needed for articulation.

20.3.2 Adding complexity

Children steadily add complexity as they master the pronunciation of multisyllabic words, as they modulate the meanings of nouns and verbs with specific inflections, as they master different constructions, and as they learn how to combine clauses, for example, to express contingency and conditionality (Clark 2009), as in (14):

(14) a. *Contingency*:
Adult: What are umbrellas for?
Lauren (2;7): *When rain comes, we put umbrellas on top of us.*
b. *Conditionality*:
Adult: What if you fall in the water?
Lauren (2;8): *I'll get eaten by a shark.*
c. *Conditionality (predictive)*:
Amanda (2;11): *When I older than Lindsay, then I'm the big sister.*
d. *Conditionality (generic)*:
Adult: Do you go to bed at night?
Amanda (2;11): *We go to bed when it's dark.*
e. *Conditionality (hypothetical)*:
Ryan (2;10): *If Bulldozer man saw a fire, he would call the Fire Department.*

They add complexity as they learn how to express temporal relations between events with conjunctions like *before* and *after*, as in (15):

(15) a. Adult: When did the boy jump the fence? (target = after...)

Child (3;2, pointing at spot on the table): *Right here!*
b. Adult: What happened first? (target = the boy patted the dog, first of two events)
Child (3;5): *He patted the dog,*
c. Adult: When did the boy pat the dog? (= first of two events)
Child (4;3): *He did it before.*
d. Adult: When did the boy throw the ball? (= second of two events)
Child (4;5): *When... before ... when he opened the gate.* (target = after)

And they add complexity as they learn how to talk about causality, at first without distinguishing direct from indirect causation in the lexical expressions chosen, as in (16):

(16) a. C (2;11, putting pencil into pencil-sharpener): *I'm gonna sharp this pencil.* (sharpen)
b. E (2;4, screwing top on bottle): *Don't tight this 'cause I tight this.* (tighten)
c. Jaime (2;11, repeating what the witch says in Hansel and Gretel): *I'll put you in two cages and fat you up.* (fatten)
d. C (3;1, pulling string of music-box cow): *I'm singing him.* (making X sing)
e. E (3;0): *Don't giggle me.* (make me giggle)

f. E (2;1, holding toy up in the air and wriggling it): *I wanta swim that.* (make that swim)

Also they add complexity as they learn how to tell stories. Young children begin to tell some kinds of stories quite early, as in the mealtime narrative in (17):

(17) Child (2;3, at the table, after looking pensive for a minute):
I in Mommy's tummy. Then I come out. I baby.
I not know how to cook. I not know how to pour. I not know how to do puzzles.
I not know how to walk. I not know how to stand. I not know how to talk.
I not know how to crawl. Then, I growed up.
Mother: What could you do when you grew up?
Child: *I could do puzzles!*

But they take many years to learn how to maintain a story line, foregrounding events that move the story forward and backgrounding information about the setting; how to talk about the main protagonist compared to less prominent characters, and how to convey interior states that motivate the action (Berman and Slobin 1994). On top of this, children have to learn the conventions for story-telling as a social activity within each culture ('Once upon a time… The end!'). This all takes time and practice.

Children also add increasing complexity to their language as they learn how to use specific forms to do particular things. They gain increasing skill in cajoling, persuading and negotiating with their parents, as when they try to persuade them to buy toys, for example, as in (18):

(18) a. Luca (6;0): *Mamma guarda questi Lego! A mi me piacerebbe averlo!*
'mummy, look at these Legos. I'd like to have one'
Mother: *Ma questo costa tanto.*
'but this one is too expensive'
Luca: *Ma io devo averli tutti i Lego.*
'but I must have all of the kinds of Legos.'
b. Michele (7;0): *Mamma, aspetta. Guarda* (points at some monsters) *ce li hanno tutti!*
'mum, wait. Look, everybody's got them'
Silvia (9;3, touching a small puppet): *Guarda, mamma, cosí piccoli non li vendono mai.*
'look, mum, they never sell such small ones'

By age five to six, they also become more skilled at telling jokes and making puns, giving explanations, justifications and instructions as well as mastering the many other skills that, as adult speakers, we take for granted in our everyday uses of language.

20.4 Later conversations

As children get older, their participation in conversation relies on myriad linguistic, pragmatic and cognitive skills, skills that children practice and practice until they can answer questions, make relevant assertions and requests, and participate in a timely way in all kinds of communicative exchange. These skills all demand extensive practice, and they benefit from extensive feedback as well. Getting the words and constructions right, assessing common ground (and adding to it), and getting the timing right, all demand careful coordination with one's addressee(s). This coordination depends in large part on: (1) maintaining joint attention in order to facilitate use of physical and conversational co-presence; and (2) care-giver feedback that impels children to keep track of what is being said and what is happening, so that their own turns at talk are both relevant and produced in a timely manner (Casillas 2014; Clark 2015).

Common ground plays a central role both in inferring speaker intentions and in planning responses that are relevant. Care-giver feedback helps children attend to common ground in conveying their communicative goals, whether they do this with gestures and word-and-gesture combinations during the earlier stages, or later on, with more precise referring expressions. Interaction provides children with practice in picking out the information they need, to convey what they want to say successfully.

In the ideal, speakers take turns with no gaps and no overlaps. But in fact, young children have difficulty timing their turns. They need to plan not only the content of each utterance but also manage its timing in relation to the preceding speaker. Since children come in much more slowly than adult speakers, in multiparty exchanges they often miss making their contribution at the right time. They take time to retrieve the appropriate words and constructions, and even when they have begun to speed up in answering simple yes/no questions, for example, they slow down when they have to provide more complex answers. In effect, each new acquisition – each new *Wh* word mastered, say – appears to slow them down again, even as they are becoming more skilled at retrieving the words they need. As a result, they only begin to approach adult timing at around age four or even later (Casillas 2014).

Over the course of their first six years, children also gradually come to observe Grice's Co-operative Principle in conversation – to be informative, relevant, truthful and brief – as adults implicitly guide them in how to use language to express their communicative goals in a wide range of contexts with a variety of different interlocutors. But to attain these skills, children need extensive practice and feedback. These two elements are central to the *learning* of a first language.

20.5 In conclusion

Children acquire the meanings and uses of linguistic forms in interaction. They discover forms – words and phrases – and assign meanings to them as they talk with others. And they then make use of these meanings when they want to convey information or requests to others. They acquire some of the interactive routines they will need for language use during infancy. They get these in part from care-givers as parts of daily routines, for example, with favorite phrases repeated every time they give the baby a bath, change a diaper, take them out of a stroller or highchair, or hand them a toy. Care-givers present infants with a directly interactive framework from as young as two to three months, as they 'take turns' in talking. Infants also learn to alternate in exchange games. In short, they are being prepared and preparing for communicative language use from the start.

As one-year-olds produce their first words and then combine words into longer utterances, their interactions with their care-givers, expert speakers, present them with extensive information about language and language use in a range of contexts. Adults talk to their children as they do all sorts of activities with them, from constructing block towers to reading picture books, and in so doing, they 'display' the language to be acquired and used.

They also offer feedback on the errors children make, typically while checking up on what they meant on that occasion. They reformulate what they thought the child had intended to say, in the next turn, and thereby offer an interpretation in conventional form for the child to accept (or reject). These reformulations contrast directly in form with what the child has just said.

Even though children have become quite skilled at using language by age six, like adults, they continue to rely on communicative resources that emerged early in their pre-linguistic development for communication, during their first year. They make ongoing use of gaze, gesture, body posture and facial expression as they use language to communicate with others. This symbiotic development of general communicative skills alongside mastery of language underlies our unique human ability to access and to communicate information about people, objects, events and ideas in the world around us. As expert speakers of the language and knowledgeable informants about the everyday world, parents and care-givers work in tandem with their children to provide input that simultaneously gives children guidance on language structure and provides them with practice in language use.

Acknowledgement

Preparation of this chapter was supported in part by the Max–Planck–Institute for Psycholinguistics, Nijmegen, The Netherlands and a European Research Council Advanced Grant INTERACT (269484). We thank Ewelina Wnuk for her help in glossing the Thai video clips.

References

Ambridge, B. and E. Lieven (2011) *Child Language Acquisition: Contrasting Theoretical Approaches*. Cambridge: Cambridge University Press.

Baillargeon, R., R.M. Scott and Z. He (2010) False-belief understanding in infants. *Trends in Cognitive Sciences* 14: 110–18.

Baron-Cohen, S., M. Lombardo and H.E. Tager-Flusberg (eds) (2013) *Understanding Other Minds: Perspectives from Developmental Social Neuroscience*. Oxford: Oxford University Press.

Berman, R.A. and D.I. Slobin (1994) *Relating Events in Narrative: A Cross-Linguistic Developmental Study*. Hillsdale: Lawrence Erlbaum.

Bloom, L. (1973) *One Word at a Time*. The Hague: Mouton.

Carpenter, M., K. Nagell and M. Tomasello (1998) Social cognition, joint attention, and communicative competence from 9 to 15 months of age. *Monographs of the Society for Research in Child Development* 83 (Serial No. 255).

Casillas, M. (2014) Turn taking. In D. Matthews (ed.) *Pragmatic Development*, pp. 53–70. Amsterdam/Philadelphia: John Benjamins.

Chouinard, M.M. and E.V. Clark (2003) Adult reformulations of child errors as negative evidence. *Journal of Child Language* 30: 637–69.

Clark, E.V. (1993) *The Lexicon in Acquisition*. Cambridge: Cambridge University Press.

Clark, E.V. (1997) Conceptual perspective and lexical choice in acquisition. *Cognition* 64: 1–37.

Clark, E.V. (2009) *First Language Acquisition*, 2nd edition. Cambridge: Cambridge University Press.

Clark, E.V. (2015) Common ground. In B. MacWhinney and W. O'Grady (eds) *The Handbook of Language Emergence*, pp. 328–53. London: Wiley-Blackwell.

Clark, E.V. and B. Estigarribia (2011) Using speech and gesture to introduce new objects to young children. *Gesture* 11: 1–23.

Clark, E.V. and M.-C. de Marneffe (2012) Constructing verb paradigms in French: Adult construals and emerging grammatical contrasts. *Morphology* 22: 89–120.

Demuth, K., J. Culbertson and J. Alter (2006) Word-minimality, epenthesis, and coda licensing in the acquisition of English. *Language and Speech* 49: 137–74.

Estigarribia, B. and E.V. Clark (2007) Getting and maintaining attention in talk to young children. *Journal of Child Language* 34: 799–814.

Farroni, T., G. Csibra, F. Simion and M.H. Johnson (2002) Eye contact detection in humans from birth. *Proceedings of the National Academy of Sciences* 99: 9602–5.

Hilbrink, E., M. Gattis, E. Sakkalou and S.C. Levinson (in preparation) The development of infants' spontaneous turn timing in mother–infant interactions: A longitudinal study.

Kuhl, P.K., E. Stevens, A. Hayashi, T. Deguchi, S. Kiritani and P. Iverson (2006) Infants show a facilitation effect for native language phonetic perception between 6 and 12 months. *Developmental Science* 9: F13–F21.

Liszkowski, U. and M. Tomasello (2011) Individual differences in social, cognitive, and morphological aspects of infant pointing. *Cognitive Development* 26: 16–29.

Luksaneeyanawin, S. (2000) Linguistics and machine processing of language. In D. Burnham, S. Luksaneeyanawin, C. Davis and M. Lafourcade (eds) *Interdisciplinary Approaches to Language Processing*, pp. 100–14. Bangkok: Chulalongkorn University Press.

Nieva Ramos, S. (2013) Función de la estructura de diálogo en la transición de una a dos palabras. Unpublished PhD dissertation, Universidad Complutense, Madrid.

Olson, J. and E.F. Masur (2013) Mothers respond differently to infants' gestural vs. nongestural communicative bids. *First Language* 33: 372–87.

Rader, N. de V. and P. Zukow-Goldring (2010) How the hands control attention during early word learning. *Gesture* 10: 202–21.

Stoel-Gammon, C. (2011) Relationships between lexical and phonological development in young children. *Journal of Child Language* 38: 1–34.

Vihman, M.M., S. Nakai, R.A. DePaolis and P. Hallé (2004) The role of accentual pattern in early lexical representation. *Journal of Memory and Language* 50: 336–53.

Werker, J.F. and R.C. Tees (1984) Cross-language speech perception: Evidence for perceptual reorganization during the first year of life. *Infant Behavior and Development* 7: 49–63.

Yurovsky, D., L.B. Smith and C. Yu (2013) Statistical word learning at scale: The baby's view is better. *Developmental Science* 6: 959–66.

21
Second language acquisition and applied linguistics

Susan M. Gass

21.1 Overview

This chapter treats a broad field, that of second language acquisition, and situates it within the larger field of applied linguistics. With regard to the latter topic, I will emphasize the point that there are some areas of SLA that can more easily fit under the umbrella of Applied Linguistics and others that do not. This chapter first deals with a statement of the scope of SLA, followed by a brief synopsis of the history of the discipline. The bulk of the chapter then deals with areas of research focus, in particular, linguistics, psycholinguistics, socio-cultural, and interaction-based. In addition, we consider learner variables, in particular, aptitude, motivation and affect.

21.1.1 Second language acquisition: a definition

Second language acquisition (SLA) is a multidisciplinary field that refers to the study of how languages are learned following learning of a first language. It covers child and adult second language learning, but, as a discipline, does not deal with simultaneous (bilingual) acquisition, although clearly there are intersecting and overlapping interests.

The field itself is highly interdisciplinary with many fields contributing to an understanding of how second languages are learned, including linguistics, psychology, sociolinguistics, psycholinguistics and education. The history of SLA has witnessed a move from a discipline relying on early theories of language where the focus was on transfer of linguistic information and where the goal was to develop pedagogically-sound materials to today's stand-alone discipline with the goal of contributing to an understanding of the nature of language and cognition. To accomplish these goals, early research emphasized the acquisition of linguistic systems. That emphasis has not diminished, but the scope has been expanded to include a suite of emphases including socio-cultural theory and psycholinguistics. In addition, it is now recognized that learning a second language is a highly complex process and to understand how individuals accomplish this incredible feat, whether in a classroom context or in a so-called natural setting, one must further understand the role of numerous individual factors, such as working memory, motivation, aptitude and affect (one's feelings) as well as age and heritage background.

In sum, with a range of questions being addressed, many of which are dependent on one's theoretical background, the field as a whole approaches an understanding of how second languages are learned, or to take the opposite view, why the endpoint of second language learning is so different from that of first language learning. This chapter takes a broad sweep, attempting to give the reader an understanding of how the field came to be what it is today and what the current questions are.

How, then, does this relate to the field of Applied Linguistics? Broadly speaking, Applied Linguistics is defined as a field that considers solutions to language-related real-world problems. In fact, the professional organization, American Association for Applied Linguistics, refers to the interdisciplinary field that addresses 'a broad range of language-related issues that affect individuals and society' and further states the mission of the organization as one that facilitates 'the advancement and dissemination of knowledge and understanding regarding these language-related issues in order to improve the lives of individuals and conditions in society.' With this broad definition, it will become clear that not all of SLA fits under an applied linguistics umbrella. Much of the field of SLA is purely theoretical without the goal of addressing real-world issues; other parts have direct relevance to improving 'the lives of individuals,' primarily that part that is aimed at bettering classroom practice. Much of SLA, however, has as its goal an understanding of language and cognition and in that sense can be more appropriately considered a branch of psychology or linguistics. Thus, SLA and Applied Linguistics are not isomorphic. SLA is in part independent and in part a branch of other disciplines. What I hope to make clear in this chapter is that however one wants to characterize SLA, it is interdisciplinary and to understand the various dimensions of learning, one must draw upon numerous disciplines.

21.2 History

There is disagreement as to the origins of the field of SLA (see Thomas 1998; Gass *et al.* 1998), but, in general, it is safe to say that most scholars place the beginnings of the field somewhere in the 1960s and 1970s. For many in the field (the present author included), graduate programs did not have courses in SLA because at that time, there was not a sufficient body of received knowledge for such courses to exist.

The early goal of research in the field was clearly on pedagogy with most papers, even in a journal with a focus on learning (*Language Learning*), being on pedagogy (see Gass and Polio 2014; Gass 2015). In other words, interest in how second/foreign languages are learned came about in order to develop language teaching programs. In fact, Fries in his Foreword to Lado's book *Linguistics Across Cultures* (1957) states this clearly:

> Before any of the questions of how to teach a foreign language must come the much more important preliminary work of finding the special problems arising out of any effort to develop a new set of language habits against a background of different native language habits.

Thus, the goal of SLA research was to produce pedagogically-relevant materials, and to be successful, one had to do a comparison (contrastive analysis) of the native language and the language being learned in order to determine what to teach (those areas of difference). The underlying assumption was that learners transferred *habits* from their first language. When this paradigm disappeared in child language acquisition resulting in a cognitive focus to language learning, the same occurred in SLA. One can date some of the earlier work in this area to the early 1970s (see Gass *et al.* 2013a for historical information). This major paradigm shift can be thought of as the beginning of the modern discipline of SLA itself.

> It is only in the '50s, '60s, and '70s that we begin to see a flurry of intellectual activity that converges on a coherent body of scholarly work – a body of work that begins to ask the important how and why questions of second language learning to which widely accepted methods of analysis are applied.
>
> (Gass et al. 1998: 412)

Early work in this period was decidedly linguistic in orientation with most (but not all) researchers starting from a Universal Grammar perspective and asking the question of whether principles and parameters of UG are applicable to second languages, what the 'starting point' is for L2 learning (with arguments on both sides of whether learning starts with the L1 or with an innate language faculty), and, more recently, whether learners can acquire features of the L2 that are not present in the L1.

21.3 Current areas of focus

Without a doubt, the linguistic focus of SLA continues in research today, but the almost exclusive reliance on linguistics as a source discipline no longer exists. Rather, numerous other disciplines have turned out to be significant influences in SLA research. Below we deal with a few of the more recent orientations: (1) psycholinguistics, (2) working memory, (3) linguistic (formal) approaches, (4) socio-cultural theory, (5) interactionist approach, (6) individual differences (e.g. aptitude, attitude, motivation), and finally we return to the pedagogical orientation of the field (7) instructed second language learning.

21.3.1 Psycholinguistics

There are numerous areas of psycholinguistics that have figured prominently in SLA research over the years. Ever since the early 1990s, attention and awareness have turned out to be dominant concepts in SLA research. Schmidt (1990, 2001) was responsible for the development of the *noticing hypothesis*, which came about as a result of his own language learning experiences in Brazil (Schmidt and Frota 1986). The basic idea is that learners need to focus their attention on specific parts of language, if learning is to take place. In other words, there is no such thing, in this view, as subliminal learning. Only focused attention will lead to learning. Many issues are in debate, for example, the role of awareness (Godfroid *et al.* 2013) as well as the developmental stage of the learner (Philp 2003). Most studies do show a connection between awareness and learning. However, some research (e.g. Williams 2004) in a study using an artificial language, argued that learning could take place without awareness.

The importance of attention is not monolithic. Gass *et al.* (2003) investigated the concept in relation to proficiency and different parts of language (lexicon, morphosyntax, syntax). They found that attention was most important at earlier stages of proficiency and more so for syntax and least so for lexical learning.

A question that arises is how to promote or encourage attention and noticing as part of second language learning. One way is through language production, known as output. Uggen (2012) found a positive role of output in noticing and learning vocabulary, but, as with the Gass *et al.* (2003) study, learning was not the same across grammatical structures examined; complexity was an important variable with noticing having a greater effect on the more complex structure (e.g. past hypothetical conditional *If I had studied in the US, I would have improved my English* versus present hypothetical conditional *If I studied in the United States, I would improve my English*).

Noticing is somewhat of an elusive construct. In recent years, eye-tracking methodology has been used to understand when noticing takes place. With this methodology, one is able to track eye movements (which presumably reflect ongoing processing). Godfroid *et al.* (2013) and Spinner *et al.* (2013) made use of this methodology to study vocabulary acquisition in the former and gender agreement in the latter. For additional information on the role of attention in SLA, see the comprehensive review by Robinson *et al.* (2012).

21.3.2 Working memory

There is no question that attention and memory are closely related constructs. Working memory is a construct from psychology that has become predominant in second language research (see J.N. Williams 2012 for an overview). '[W]orking memory is those mechanisms or processes that are involved in the control, regulation, and active maintenance of task-relevant information in the service of complex cognition, including novel as well as familiar, skilled tasks' (Miyake and Shah 1999: 450). What is crucial is that when processing language, learners have to both store and manipulate information.

Different models of working memory are prevalent in the literature (see J.N. Williams 2012). What we do know is that language learning involves competing information that learners have to juggle. For example, learners have to focus on various parts of language simultaneously (e.g. morphology, vocabulary form, meaning, word order). This involves storing and manipulating information, the two basic components of an individual's working memory capacity. Some individuals are better at doing this than others and in fact this reflects the variable trait of working memory capacity. In other words, humans differ in their ability to juggle numerous language tasks; they differ in working memory capacity.

Studies investigating the relationship between language learning and working memory capacity have become common in recent years, although the results are not always straightforward, in part because there is no standard accepted way of measuring L2 working memory capacity.

Working memory capacity has been investigated in a number of areas and has been shown to be related to vocabulary and syntax learning and to oral fluency and to general language performance. It has also become prominent in the interactionist approach to second language learning discussed in §21.3.6. In general, studies support the relationship between language learning and working memory capacity primarily because those with higher working memory scores are better able to retain and analyze the stored information. Clearly, these are traits that are important in dealing with the input one receives.

There are two models of learning that stem from a psychology tradition and that have received attention in the recent literature: emergentism and dynamic systems. Emergentist approaches emphasize usage and do not take an innate system as the starting point for second language learning. Learning takes place by understanding the regularities that are present in the input. As noted in Gass *et al.* (2013a: 273),

> The representation of language, in this view, relies on the notion of variable strengths that reflect the frequency of the input and the connections between parts of language. Learning is seen as simple instance learning (rather than explicit/implicit induction of

rules), which proceeds based on input alone; the resultant knowledge is seen as a network of interconnected exemplars and patterns, rather than abstract rules.

The main point is that learning is based not on rule systems, but on the association of patterns that learners are able to abstract from the input. One of the tasks for a learner in this framework is to establish appropriate associations in the second language that may or may not be relatable to those in the native language (see reviews by Ellis 2012 and MacWhinney 2012). As Ellis puts it

> learning, memory and perception are all affected by frequency of usage: the more times we experience something, the stronger our memory for it, and the more fluently it is accessed. The more recently we have experienced something, the stronger our memory for it, and the more fluently it is accessed.
>
> (2012: 195)

This model of learning does not include an innate capacity for learning; rather, learning is based on the generalizations learners make from the input with frequency being a major determinant of one's ability to determine regularities and construct patterns.

A recent approach to SLA research, consistent with emergentism, is what is known as a dynamic systems approach which emphasizes the fact that language is a complex system and with particular reference to SLA, it changes and develops over time. What is most important in this approach is that there is not a static approach to a linguistic system and language learning cannot be reduced to a cause–effect relationship. Rather, there are numerous factors that come into play to bring about change. As Larsen-Freeman (1997) points out, the approach is 'interested in how disorder gives way to order' (p. 141). According to Larsen-Freeman (2012: 75) 'language has the shape that it does because of the way that it is used, not because of an innate bio-program or internal mental organ ... there may be domain-general evolutionary prerequisites to language that support its use and acquisition.' Humans have the 'the ability to imitate, to detect patterns, to notice novelty, to form categories, or the social drive to interact, to establish joint attention with another, to understand the communicative intention of others' (ibid.). This approach, like emergentism, relies on learners attempting to find regularities from what may appear to be disorder.

21.3.3 Linguistic (formal) approaches

Much research in SLA has taken a formal generative perspective, focusing on language form with the goal of describing a learner's linguistic system. The underlying assumption is that one must understand what is acquired (i.e. a description of the language) and its mental representation as first steps in understanding how acquisition takes place. The most common framework is generative linguistic theory and most notably Universal Grammar. As with child language acquisition, research within this perspective relates to learnability with questions related to principles and parameters dominating early research and questions of feature acquisition more common in recent years. A basic issue (with both first and second language acquisition) relates to the poverty of the stimulus: How can learning take place only from the input which, as is clear (see White 2003), is not sufficiently rich to allow for the acquisition of a complete grammatical system? Thus, the question in this perspective is what else is brought into the picture. One clear answer is the L1, but that, too, is not sufficient (see Lardiere 2012); another possibility (and the subject matter of formal approaches) is that learners still have access to Universal Grammar constraints (Principles and Parameters) that were operational in learning their first language. In other words, all universal constraints on language apply to first as well as second languages.

Within the Principles and Parameters framework, it is assumed that certain principles do not vary across languages whereas others (parameters) do vary, although the variability is not unlimited. Having limits on what a possible language can be aids the learning process, by restricting the possibilities of language. However, the evidence from L2 acquisition with regard to universal principles is unclear with evidence pointing in different directions. In sum, there is no consensus as to whether there is direct access to universal principles (through Universal Grammar), whether there is no access at all, or whether there is access through the L1.

A significant amount of L2 research has also been conducted investigating the construct of parameters. Certain language properties tend to cluster so that if a learner understands one aspect of a parameter, other aspects of that parameter are also known. For example, some languages do not use subject pronouns (e.g. *Vado a casa* in Italian means 'I go home' even though there is no overt subject pronoun). Those same languages also allow the subject to follow the noun (e.g. *È venuto mio fratello ieri* means 'My brother came yesterday' [literally has come my brother yesterday]). A common area of investigation has focused on the determination of the extent to which these properties also cluster in L2 acquisition (see Lardiere 2012). As a result of empirical research and because of developments within the field of linguistics, Lardiere (p. 119) questions the validity of this line of research for L2 acquisition, '[c]onsequently, the notion of parameter-setting as a useful explanatory construct for (second) language acquisition must be reconsidered in light of these developments within linguistic theory.'

The focus in more recent years has moved away from parameters to the acquisition of formal features. A burning issue is the learnability of L2 features that do not exist in the L1. For example, can an English-speaking learner (a language with no gender marking) acquire native-like gender features in a language, such as Italian or Spanish, that does mark gender through noun–adjective/determiner agreement? A second question has to do with functional categories – are they even available to L2 learners at the early stages of learning or is early learning essentially lexical? Here the jury is still out with various proposals in existence arguing that there is a representational deficit in L2 learners which cannot be overcome. An opposing view maintains that there is no representational deficit but rather it is a difficulty of mapping the L1 representation onto L2 morphology. For example, Goad *et al.* (2003) maintain that learners are not able to acquire the morphology of the L2 because of the inability to transfer L1 phonological representations. Still other approaches assume that the inability to acquire an L2 morphosyntax is due to processing, not representation.

All of these issues relate to a fundamental question: What is the starting point of L2 acquisition? When a second language learner begins the learning process, what do they start with? One possibility is the L1; this would be the position for those who believe that UG is not accessible. Another possibility is UG; this is the position of those who believe that universal constraints on language carry over to the L2 context. A third possibility is that it is the L2; this is the position of those who take frequency or usage-based approaches as the driving force of L2 acquisition.

21.3.4 Socio-cultural theory

Yet another approach to how second languages are learned is based on work by Vygotsky (1978, 1987). This approach relies on language use and assumes that the L2 learner is a social individual who interacts with his/her environment and it is the situation/context of learning that relates to internal processes. As Lantolf (2012: 57) states, '[h]uman thinking is mediated by culturally organized and transmitted symbolic meaning.' Thus, the question for acquisition is the acquisition of a symbolic system – can a new system be learned and how does learning take place? Basic to this approach are a number of constructs: mediation and regulation, internalization, and the Zone of Proximal Development (ZPD). All human activity is mediated by cultural tools, such as language. It is through language that humans relate and connect to the world around them. Language gives humans the power to think/ talk about events/objects/humans that are not in their immediate vicinity. With regard to children learning language comes the concept of regulation; children learn to use language to regulate their activities. Internalization is what allows one to move what one knows about the relationship between one's self and the environment to later performance. As part of this process is what is known as imitation, which is not the mindless type of imitation seen in early behaviorist models of learning and behavior; rather it is a cognitive activity. As Lantolf (2012: 59) states, 'through imitation learners build up repertoires of resources for future performances, but these need not be precise replicas of the original model.' Thus, learners store language as a way to create a repertoire of resources to be used in creative ways in future use. Finally is the ZPD defined by Vygotsky (1978: 86) as 'the distance between the actual developmental level as determined by independent problem solving and the level of potential development as determined through problem solving under adult guidance or in collaboration with more capable peers.'

In terms of actual learning, it is the concepts of imitation and the ZPD that are crucial. From Lantolf (2012: 60) comes the following example from an English-speaking learner of German.

(1) Learner: *Ich rufe meine Mutter jeden Tag
　　　　　　 I call my mother every day
　　Teacher: jeden Tag an
　　　　　　 every day (prefix from verb *anrufen* [to call])
　　Learner: Ich rufe meine Mutter jeden Tag an
At a later point in time:
　　Learner: *Ich empfehle das neus Buch an
　　　　　　 I recommend the new book prefix

What one sees in this example is a correction from the teacher (known as a recast) followed by incorporation by the learner of the correction (known as uptake) or imitation within a socio-cultural framework. The suggestion is that there was imitation, but the new imitated form (*an*) was internalized and used creatively (although incorrectly). In other words, there was imitation, but not behaviorist-style imitation. The example illustrates the ability to imitate and thereby build up resources for further use is dependent on the learner's ZPD.

To summarize, language is a tool that mediates between individuals and their environment and learning starts as a social process as a way of developing cognition. Other humans (e.g. a teacher) are significant in providing models for imitation (sensitive to one's ZPD).

21.3.5 Interactionist approach

Another approach that is based on language use is the interactionist approach although in more recent years, it has begun to incorporate a number of psycholinguistic concepts. The basic assumption is that there exists 'a robust connection between interaction and learning' (Gass and Mackey 2007: 176). When learners engage in interaction with another individual (a native speaker of the language or even another learner), there is often feedback on that learner's language as a result of a communication breakdown or even a pedagogical intervention. These interactive exchanges (negotiations of meaning) provide an opportunity for a language learner to understand where his/her language is deficient in the sense that it is not clear to fluent speakers of the L2, or in the language of this framework, learners recognize the gap between their knowledge and the second language.

Negotiation of meaning refers to those instances in conversation when participants need to interrupt the flow of the conversation in order for both parties to understand what the conversation is about. In conversations involving non-native speakers (NNSs), negotiations are frequent, at times occupying a major portion of the conversation. An example is given below (Varonis and Gass 1985: 78–9) in which the majority of the conversation is spent negotiating meaning so that both individuals understand the full thrust of the conversation (J = NS of Japanese; S = NS of Spanish).

(2) J: And your what is your mm father's job?
    S: My father now is retire.
    J: Retire?
    S: Yes.
    J: Oh yeah.
    S: But he work with uh uh institution.
    J: Institution.
    S: Do you know that? The name is ... some thin like eh control of the state.
    J: Aaaaaaaah.
    S: Do you understand more or less?
    J: State is uh ... what what kind of state?
    S: It is uhm.
    J: Michigan State?
    S: No, the all nation.
    J: No, government?
    S: All the nation, all the nation. Do you know for example is a the the institution mmm of the state mm of Venezuela.
    J: Ah ah.
    S: Had to declare declare? her ingress.
    J: English?
    S: No. English no (laugh) ... ingress, her ingress.
    J: Ingress?
    S: Ingress. Yes. I N G R E S S more or less.
    J: Ingless.
    S: Yes. If for example, if you, when you work you had an ingress, you know?
    J: Uh huh an ingless?
    S: Yes.
    J: Uh huh OK.

S: Yes, if for example, your homna, husband works, when finish, when end the month his job, his boss pay—mm—him something
J: Aaaah.
S: And your family have some ingress.
J: Yes ah, OK OK.
S: More or less OK? And in this in this institution take care of all ingress of the company and review the accounts.
J: OK I got, I see.
S: OK my father work there, but now he is old.

Here, the individuals are expending considerable effort in resolving the problem areas of this conversation until there is a resolution and presumably learning. Learning takes place when a learner's attention, through exchanges such as the one above, is drawn to an area of difficulty or through exchanges such as (1) above where a teacher expands on a learner's erroneous utterance including the correct form (known as a recast). When attention is drawn to problem areas, the learner notices a gap between his/her own system and the linguistic system used by others, most notably native speakers.

Another central concept is output (language use). Swain (1985) initially investigated this concept through observations of second language learners in French immersion programs in context. She noted that input was not sufficient for learning given that one can comprehend much more than one can produce. Production requires that learners construct utterances and therefore production 'may force the learner to move from semantic processing to syntactic processing' (p. 249). She further claimed that

> output may stimulate learners to move from the semantic, open-ended, nondeterministic, strategic processing prevalent in comprehension to the complete grammatical processing needed for accurate production. Output, thus, would seem to have a potentially significant role in the development of syntax and morphology.
>
> (Swain 1995: 128)

An example of how learners are pushed to correct utterances can be seen from Example 3 from Mackey (2002).

(3) NNS: And in hand in hand have a bigger glass to see.
    NS: It's err. You mean, something in his hand?
    NNS: Like spectacle. For older person.
    NS: Mmm, sorry I don't follow, it's what?
    NNS: In hand have he have has a glass for looking through for make the print bigger to see, to see the print, for magnify.
    NS: He has some glasses?
    NNS: Magnify glasses he has magnifying glass.
    NS: Oh aha I see a magnifying glass, right that's a good one, ok.

Following this example, the learner made the following comments:

> I know I see this word before but so I am sort of talking around around this word but he is forcing me to think harder, think harder for the correct word to give him so he can

> understand and so I was trying. I carry on talking until finally I get it, and when I say it, then he understand it, me.

In other words, she was clearly pushed to modify her language by the NS's expressions of non-understanding.

Thus, the basis of the interactionist approach resides in: (1) a learner's participation in interactionally-modified input, (2) attention-drawing contexts, (3) opportunities to produce language (output), and (4) correction (either direct or indirect).

In current research, researchers are delving into questions of *why* and *what*. Thus, questions such as the role of types of feedback (e.g. recasts, metalinguistic feedback), aspects of the L2 (morphosyntax, lexicon, phonology), and individual differences are prominent.

The role of recasts has been controversial in the recent literature with studies comparing recasts to other forms of correction (e.g. metalinguistic, elicitation) and input (e.g. prompts). One important finding is that feedback does not affect all learners or all language forms equally. For example, studies that have investigated learner perception of corrective feedback (e.g. Mackey *et al.* 2000; Mackey *et al.* 2007) have found that different language forms (e.g. morphosyntax, lexicon) are differentially recognized as feedback by learners. These and other studies show that those parts of language that have high communicative value (e.g. lexicon) and are more transparent are most readily impacted by feedback. Feedback on other forms, such as morphosyntax, are not so readily interpreted as feedback given the lack of communicative value. Such feedback may be more readily interpreted as a question of meaning. Thus, if a learner says 'I used the caputa yesterday,' and an interlocutor responds with 'You used what?' it is pretty clear that the corrective emphasis is on the unknown word (*caputa* for *computer*). However, if a learner of Italian uses a wrong agreement marker and there is some form of correction, it is likely that the correction is a question of meaning not form given that the form is not salient. A study by Jeon (2007) exemplified this through a study of learning following corrective feedback in which there was greater learning for lexical and syntactic targets than with complex honorifics.

But what about the learner her/himself? What characteristics can be attributed to the individual? Recall that a major assumption in this paradigm is that a learner's attention is drawn to a gap in knowledge. Learners must notice the incorrect form used and compare it to the form used by their interlocutor. This requires a certain amount of attentional control and the capacity to store and manipulate information; in other words, working memory is involved as a mediating factor. There have been a number of studies that consider working memory as a variable, but results have not led to a definitive conclusion. A study by Mackey *et al.* (2002) found working memory to be an important factor in determining whether or not learners noticed recasts but Trofimovich *et al.* (2007) did not find such a relationship (although they did not note other relationships between working memory and production). Sagarra (2007) considered data from a computer study in which recasts were provided orally and found an important role for working memory. Mackey *et al.* (2010) found a positive relationship between the production of modified output and working memory capacity. Gass *et al.* (2013b) directly investigated learners with different working memory capacity scores (in their study high and low) and found no effect on learning in these two groups. What they did find, however, was a role for the ability to inhibit certain language information.

A final area of study to mention that demonstrates current research within the interactionist paradigm considers the role of affect. A study by Sheen (2008) on the acquisition of English articles found an effect for anxiety on responses to recasts and on learning.

The interactionist approach recognizes the important role for input (as is the case with frequency-based accounts), although interaction and production are added constructs. It also utilizes concepts from psychology to understand why learning from interaction does not affect all individuals equally. It relies explicitly and importantly on the need for learners to produce language and receive feedback on that production.

21.3.6 Individual differences

Individual difference is an obvious part of any learning and second language learning is no exception. Attentional control, working memory capacity, and anxiety have already been mentioned, but there are other considerations that are also relevant. In this section, we briefly touch on some common differences among individuals, namely, aptitude, motivation and affect.

21.3.6.1 Aptitude

Aptitude refers to one's potential for learning. Within the context of SLA research, this trait is frequently discussed in relation to working memory, and, in some views, the two are inseparable (Miyake and Friedman 1998). All models of aptitude and modes of assessing aptitude assume that second language learning requires one to deal with novelty and ambiguity, although the precise components are not the same across models. Robinson (2007) and Skehan (2002) refer to aptitude complexes (see Skehan 2012 for an overview). For example Robinson (as reported in Skehan 2012: 388) includes a complex of primary cognitive abilities which include 'perceptual speed, pattern recognition, phonological working memory capacity, speed of phonological WM, analogies, the capacity to infer word meaning, memory and speed of memory for text, grammatical sensitivity, and rote memory perceptual speed, pattern.' Thus, there are many ways to consider aptitude and, importantly, to measure aptitude. Skehan offers the conclusion: 'aptitude information is relevant for predicting success both with implicit as well as explicit conditions' (p. 387). In other words, aptitude is relevant regardless of whether language information is presented implicitly requiring learners to infer generalizations or whether it is presented explicitly as in some instances of classroom learning.

21.3.6.2 Motivation

Like aptitude, motivation can be a predictor of how well someone will do in learning a language (or any sort of learning). But many variables come into play, for example the degree of investment that someone has in the outcome, or even the extent to which success (or not) modifies motivation. Ushioda and Dörnyei (2012) discuss a model with multiple stages pointing out that motives and drive can be assessed and modified, depending, for example, on success or even on teachers' behaviors.

Motivation is a broad topic and is a changing variable that is context-dependent and relates to individuals. Teachers and goal-related issues are all central to understanding the influence of motivation on learning.

In a recent study investigating aptitude in learning Chinese, Winke (2013) included a number of components of aptitude and she found that rote memory was the best at predicting learning, and working memory the least. Aptitude and motivation equally impacted learning although they did not equally predict particular language skills (e.g. listening, reading, speaking).

21.3.6.3 Affect

A specific dimension of affect, namely anxiety, was mentioned in the context of the interactionist approach, but like many of these individual traits, affect is multidimensional. Essentially, affect, as used in SLA research, refers to one's emotions about something including feelings about the language, toward individual speakers of the language, toward the environment where the language is being learned (e.g. classroom) or more broadly to the second language culture.

Some of the areas of investigation, such as culture shock and anxiety, have been investigated to a considerable extent with findings showing a negative relationship with specific areas of language use. Winke (2013: 122–3) summarizes this line of research (among others) by stating,

> [s]everal varied factors must successfully converge for an adult learner to obtain advanced proficiency in a foreign language. The learner needs excellent instruction, frequent opportunities for different kinds of output, and a heavy dose of motivation. Access to cultural insights that explain the pragmatics of the language has to come the learner's way/effective language learning strategies need to be found; and, as any learner knows, real, tangible rewards for learning efforts must materialize.

In sum, there is no single way to learn a second language; each individual must find the combination of factors that works for him or her.

21.3.7 Instructed second language learning

The field of SLA has never wandered far from its roots and even when the field has been primarily concerned with formal approaches to learning, the classroom has never been entirely removed. I mention this to make it clear that pedagogical concerns still permeate much research. Numerous books and overviews deal with this vast topic (e.g. Ellis 2003; Loewen 2015). The focus in these books is not on techniques of teaching, but on ways in which materials and syllabi can be organized to facilitate learning. Jessica Williams (2012) provides the following characteristics of instructed SLA: educational purpose, an instructor, and more than one student. Researchers ask questions related to what teachers do/say and how students respond to the teacher and to one another. How does language change in the short and long-term? As Jessica Williams (2012) notes '[l]anguage learning researchers are interested in classroom learning contexts for what they can reveal about language learning processes in general, but also for quite practical reasons' (p. 541). This is an area that could be called applied linguistics because it crosses the theoretical/practical boundary.

21.4 Conclusion

This chapter has given an overview of some of the key research areas in the field of SLA. The important point is that the field is interdisciplinary and no single approach can contribute to an understanding of the complexities involved in learning a second language. In fact, many researchers incorporate multiple approaches as they attempt to unravel this mystery of acquisition.

References

Ellis, N. (2012) Frequency-based accounts of second language acquisition. In S. Gass and A. Mackey (eds.) *The Routledge Handbook of Second Language Acquisition*, pp. 193–210. New York: Routledge.

Ellis, R. (2003) *Task-Based Language Learning and Teaching*. Oxford: Oxford University Press.

Fries, C. (1957) Foreword. In R. Lado, *Linguistics Across Cultures*. Ann Arbor: University of Michigan Press.

Gass, S. (2015) Methodologies of second language acquisition. In M. Bigelow and J. Ennser-Kananen (eds.) *The Routledge Handbook of Educational Linguistics*, pp. 9–22. New York: Routledge.

Gass, S. and A. Mackey (2007) Input, interaction and output in second language acquisition. In J. Williams and B. VanPatten (eds.) *Theories in Second Language Acquisition*, pp. 175–99. Mahwah: Lawrence Erlbaum Associates.

Gass, S. and C. Polio (2014) Methodological Influences of *Interlanguage* (1972): Data then and data now. In Z.-H. Han and E. Tarone (eds.) *Interlanguage 40 Years Later*. Amsterdam: John Benjamins.

Gass, S., J. Behney and L. Plonsky (2013a) *Second Language Acquisition: An Introductory Course*, 4th edition. New York: Routledge.

Gass, S., J. Behney and B. Uzum (2013b) Inhibitory control, working memory, and L2 interaction gains. In K. Droździał-Szelest and M. Pawlak (eds.) *Psycholinguistic and Sociolinguistic Perspectives on Second Language Learning and Teaching: Studies in Honor of Waldemar Marton*, pp. 91–114. Heidelberg/New York: Springer.

Gass, S., C. Fleck, N. Leder and I. Svetics (1998) Ahistoricity revisited: Does SLA have a history? *Studies in Second Language Acquisition* 20: 407–21.

Gass, S., I. Svetics and S. Lemelin (2003) Differential effects of attention. *Language Learning* 53: 497–545.

Goad, H., L. White and J. Steele (2003) Missing surface inflection in L2 acquisition: A prosodic account. In B. Beachley, A. Brown and F. Conlin (eds.) *BUCLD 27 Proceedings*, pp. 264–75. Sommerville: Cascadilla Press.

Godfroid, A., F. Boers and A. Housen (2013) An eye for words: Gauging the role of attention in L2 vocabulary acquisition by means of eye-tracking. *Studies in Second Language Acquisition* 35: 483–517.

Jeon, K.S. (2007) Interaction-driven L2 learning: Characterizing linguistic development. In A. Mackey (ed.) *Conversational Interaction in Second Language Acquisition: A Collection of Empirical Studies*, pp. 379–403. Oxford: Oxford University Press.

Lado, R. (1957) *Linguistics Across Cultures*. Ann Arbor: University of Michigan Press.

Lantolf, J. (2012) Sociocultural theory: A dialectical approach to L2 research. In S. Gass and A. Mackey (eds.) *The Routledge Handbook of Second Language Acquisition*, pp. 57–72. New York: Routledge.

Lardiere, D. (2012) Linguistic approaches to second language morphosyntax. In S. Gass and A. Mackey (eds.) *The Routledge Handbook of Second Language Acquisition*, pp. 106–26. New York: Routledge.

Larsen-Freeman, D. (1997) Chaos/complexity science and second language acquisition. *Applied Linguistics* 18: 141–65.

Larsen-Freeman, D. (2012) Complexity theory. In S. Gass and A. Mackey (eds) *The Routledge Handbook of Second Language Acquisition*, pp. 73–87. New York: Routledge.

Loewen, S. (2015) *Introduction to Instructed Second Language Acquisition*. New York: Routledge.

Mackey, A. (2002) Beyond production: Learners' perceptions about interactional processes. *International Journal of Educational Research* 37: 379–94.

Mackey, A., R. Adams, C. Stafford and P. Winke (2010) Exploring the relationship between modified output and working memory capacity. *Language Learning* 60: 501–33.

Mackey, A., M. Al-Khalil, G. Atanassova, M. Hama, A. Logan-Terry and K. Nakatsukasa (2007) Teachers' intentions and learners' perceptions about corrective feedback in the L2 classroom. *Innovation in Language Learning and Teaching* 1: 129–52.

Mackey, A., S. Gass and K. McDonough (2000) Learners' perceptions about feedback. *Studies in Second Language Acquisition* 22: 471–97.

Mackey, A., J. Philp, T. Egi, A. Fujii and T. Tatsumi (2002) Individual differences in working memory, noticing interactional feedback, and L2 development. In P. Robinson (ed.) *Individual Differences and Instructed Language Learning*, pp. 181–209. Philadelphia: John Benjamins.

MacWhinney, B. (2012) The logic of the unified model. In S. Gass and A. Mackey (eds.) *The Routledge Handbook of Second Language Acquisition*, pp. 211–27. New York: Routledge.

Miyake, A. and N. Friedman (1998) Individual differences in second language proficiency: Working memory as language aptitude. In A.F. Healy and L.E. Bourne, Jr. (eds.) *Foreign Language Learning: Psycholinguistic Studies on Training and Retention*, pp. 339–64. Mahwah: Lawrence Erlbaum Associates.

Miyake, A. and P. Shah (eds.) (1999) *Models of Working Memory: Mechanisms of Active Maintenance and Executive Control*. Cambridge: Cambridge University Press.

Philp, J. (2003) Constraints on noticing the gap: Nonnative speakers' noticing of recasts in NS-NNS interaction. *Studies in Second Language Acquisition* 25: 99–126.

Robinson, P. (2007) Task complexity, theory of mind, and intentional reasoning: Effects on L2 speech production, interaction, uptake and perceptions of task difficulty. *International Review of Applied Linguistics* 45: 193–213.

Robinson, P., A. Mackey, S. Gass and R. Schmidt (2012) Attention and awareness in second language acquisition. In S. Gass and A. Mackey (eds.) *The Routledge Handbook of Second Language Acquisition*, pp. 247–67. New York: Routledge.

Sagarra, N. (2007) Working memory and L2 processing of redundant grammatical forms. In Z. Han (ed.) *Understanding Second Language Process*, pp. 133–47. Clevedon: Multilingual Matters.

Schmidt, R. (1990) The role of consciousness in second language learning. *Applied Linguistics* 11: 129–58.

Schmidt, R. (2001) Attention. In P. Robinson (ed.) *Cognition and Second Language Instruction*, pp. 3–32. Cambridge: Cambridge University Press.

Schmidt, R. and S. Frota (1986) Developing basic conversational ability in a second language: A case study of an adult learner of Portuguese. In R. Day (ed.) *Talking to Learn: Conversation in Second Language Acquisition*, pp. 237–326. Rowley: Newbury House.

Sheen, Y. (2008) Recasts, language anxiety, modified output and L2 learning. *Language Learning* 58: 835–74.

Skehan, P. (2002) Theorising and updating aptitude. In P. Robinson (ed.) *Individual Differences and Instructed Language Learning*, pp. 69–93. Amsterdam: John Benjamins.

Skehan, P. (2012) Language aptitude. In S. Gass and A. Mackey (eds.) *The Routledge Handbook of Second Language Acquisition*, pp. 381–95. New York: Routledge.

Spinner, P., S. Gass and J. Behney (2013) Coming eye-to-eye with attention. In J. Bergsleithner and S. Frota (eds.) *Noticing and Second Language Acquisition: Studies in Honor of Richard Schmidt*, pp. 235–54. Honolulu: National Foreign Language Resource Center.

Swain, M. (1985) Communicative competence: Some roles of comprehensible input and comprehensible output in its development. In S. Gass and C. Madden (eds.) *Input in Second Language Acquisition*, pp. 235–53. Rowley: Newbury House.

Swain, M. (1995) Three functions of output in second language learning. In G. Cook and B. Seidlhofer (eds.) *Principle and Practice in Applied Linguistics*, pp. 125–44. Oxford: Oxford University Press.

Thomas, M. (1998) Programmatic ahistoricity in second language acquisition theory. *Studies in Second Language Acquisition* 20: 387–405.

Trofimovich, P., A. Ammar and E. Gatbonton (2007) How effective are recasts? The role of attention, memory, and analytical ability. In A. Mackey (ed.) *Conversational Interaction in Second Language Acquisition: A Collection of Empirical Studies*, pp. 171–95. Oxford: Oxford University Press.

Uggen, M. (2012) Reinvestigating the noticing function of output. *Language Learning* 62: 506–40.
Ushioda, E. and Z. Dörnyei (2012) Motivation. In S. Gass and A. Mackey (eds.) *The Routledge Handbook of Second Language Acquisition*, pp. 396–409. New York: Routledge.
Varonis, E. and S. Gass (1985) Non-native/non-native conversations: A model for negotiation of meaning. *Applied Linguistics* 6: 71–90.
Vygotsky, L.S. (1978) *Mind in Society: The Development of Higher Psychological Processes*. Cambridge: Harvard University Press.
Vygotsky, L.S. (1987) *The Collected works of L.S. Vygotsky. Vol. 1. Problems of General Psychology. Including the Volume Thinking and Speech*. New York: Plenum Press.
White, L. (2003) *Second Language Acquisition and Universal Grammar*. Cambridge: Cambridge University Press.
Williams, J. (2012) Classroom research. In S. Gass and A. Mackey (eds.) *The Routledge Handbook of Second Language Acquisition*, pp. 541–44. New York: Routledge.
Williams, J.N. (2004) Implicit learning of form-meaning connections. In B. VanPatten, J. Williams, S. Rott and M. Overstreet (eds.) *Form Meaning Connections in Second Langauge Acquistion*, pp. 203–18. Mahwah, NJ: Lawrence Erlbaum Associates.
Williams, J.N. (2012) Working memory and SLA. In S. Gass and A. Mackey (eds.) *The Routledge Handbook of Second Language Acquisition*, pp. 427–41. New York: Routledge.
Winke, P. (2013) An investigation into second language aptitude for advanced Chinese language learning. *The Modern Language Journal* 97: 109–30.

22
Historical linguistics and relationships among languages

Kate Burridge

22.1 Introduction – 'in forme of speche is change'

[S]o kann es in ihr [die Sprache], ebensowenig, als in den unaufhörlich fortflammenden Gedanken der Menchen selbst, einen Augenblick wahren Stillstandes geben. [There can never be in language, just as there can never be in the ceaselessly blazing thoughts of people, a moment of true standstill].

(Humboldt 1836: 184)

Over time all facets of the linguistic system will change, and sometimes spectacularly – as Humboldt described, there is never a moment of true standstill in language. To illustrate the extent to which English has changed in the course of its recorded history, consider the tenth-century leechdom ('remedy') for abdominal pain given in Figure 22.1. Underneath the original Anglo-Saxon (or Old English) text is a literal word-by-word translation, and a loose translation follows.[1]

Wiþ	*wambe*	*wærce*	*7*	*rysel*	*wærce*	*þær*	*þu*	*geseo*	*tord*	
against	womb	wark	and	belly	pain	when	thou	seest	turd	
wifel	*on*	*eorþan*	*up*	*weorpan*	*ymbfo*	*hine*	*mid*	*twam*	*handum*	*mid*
weevil	on	earth	up	throw	catch	him	with	two	hands	with
his	*geweorpe*	*wafa*	*mid*	*þinum*	*handum*	*swiþe*	*7*	*cweþ*	*þriwa.*	
his	throwing	wave	with	thy	hands	strongly	and	say	thrice.	
Remedium	*facio*	*ad*		*ventris*	*dolorem.*					
remedium	facio	ad		ventris	dolorem.					
Weorp	*þonne*	*ofer*	*bæc*	*þone*	*wifel*	*on*	*wege*	*beheald*	*þæt*	*þu*	*ne*
throw	then	over	back	the	beetle	on	way	take-care	that	you	not
locige	*æfter.*	*þonne*	*monnes*	*wambe*	*wærce*	*oþþe*	*rysel*	*ymbfoc*	*mid*	
look	after.	the	man's	womb	pain	or	belly	grasp	with	
þinum	*handum*	*þa*	*wambe*	*him*	*biþ*	*sona*	*sel* ·	*XII*	*monaþ*	*þu*
thy	hands	the	womb	him	is	at-once	well.	12	months	thou
meaht	*swa*	*don*	*after*	*þam*	*wifel.*					
have-power	so	to-do	after	the	beetle.					

344

For stomach ache and pain in the belly (fat); when you see a dung beetle in the earth throwing up (dung), catch him with your two hands along with his casting up (i.e. dung balls), wave him strongly with your hands, and say three times, 'Remedium facio ad ventris dolorem'. Then throw the beetle over your back; take care you don't look backwards. When a person's stomach or belly (fat) is in pain, grasp the stomach with your hands, it will soon be well with (the person); for twelve months after the beetle (event) you shall have power so to do

Figure 22.1 Tenth-century remedy for abdominal pain

Spelling, punctuation, letter shapes, conventions of word-division and paragraphing were very different at this time, although the leechdom as rendered here (for simplicity sake) has retained only some of the Anglo-Saxon conventions and is nowhere near the original manuscript version. The consonant symbol <þ> (called 'thorn') was from the *futhorc* or runic alphabet but was later replaced by French inspired <th>. The vowel symbol <æ> (called 'ash') came from the Latin script, although its name derives from the runic symbol for the same sound. Anglo-Saxon scribes used a number of abbreviations, one of which is shown here – the symbol ⁊ for 'and' (one of the Tironian *nota* 'signs', from the shorthand conventions developed by Cicero's scribe Marcus Tiro). The raised dot <·> indicates a pause (though this does not correspond to the modern comma or full-stop); punctuation was otherwise scanty.

Many of the words here have disappeared without a trace (e.g. *rysel* 'belly', *weorpan* 'throw', *ymbfo* 'catch', *swiþe* 'quickly', *ne* 'not', *biþ* 'is', *wærce* 'pain', *sel* 'well'); some remain but are archaic (*þu* 'thou' and *þinum* 'thy'). Others have changed meaning (*wiþ* 'against' > 'alongside'; *wambe* 'abdomen' > 'uterus'; *sona* 'immediately' > 'in a little while'; *meaht* 'have power' > 'possibly will'; *wifel* 'beetle of any kind' > 'specific beetle from the Curculionoidea family').

The shape of even familiar words has altered significantly. Sounds have disappeared (the [w] in *swa* 'so' and *twa* 'two'; the in *wambe* 'womb'), and many have changed their pronunciation (the <h> in *meaht* 'might' represented a velar fricative that either dropped out or became [f]). Also lost from the system was the front rounded vowel (represented here by <y> as in *rysel*) and the geminate (or long) consonants (shown as double letters as in *monnes*). Voicing was only contrastive for Old English stops and affricates, and voiced fricatives were confined to intervocalic positions (alternations such as *wolf–wolves* are relics of this original allophony); hence, *wafa* here was pronounced [wava], but there was no potential minimal pair akin to modern *waver* [weivə] and *wafer* [weifə].

There is much that is different in the grammar here. Constituent order in this remedy does not follow the fixed S(ubject)V(erb)O(bject) ordering of the modern language, and many structures no longer exist. The phrase *him biþ sona sel* illustrates the so-called 'impersonal construction' (where dative subject pronouns expressed non-volitional activities; *me thinks* is left over from this system). The phrase *ne locige* shows an early pre-verbal negator. There are also many examples here of the inflectional richness that characterized the language at this time (e.g. pronouns *him, hine*; *þu, þinum*; nouns *twam, handum*; definite articles *þone, þa, þam*; verbs *don, locige, biþ*).

The developments illustrated by just this short text are considerable and involve the language at every level – orthography, phonology, morphology, syntax and lexicon (words and meanings). However, I should not give the impression that all linguistic elements are equally susceptible to innovation and replacement. Lexical components are the most volatile, with vocabulary addition and loss being particularly rapid; however there are differences within the lexicon – culturally significant words far more prone to revitalization than basic vocabulary, which can endure over centuries. Words of high frequency are more prone to sound changes (of a reductive nature), but the most resistant to grammatical changes (of a levelling and regularizing nature); cf. Bybee (2003). In fact, grammatical aspects of the language (especially syntactic) exhibit the most stability of all. But as Janda and Joseph (2003: 88) remind us, if we are to truly understand change, it is just as important, and interesting, to consider those aspects of language that do not change as those that do. Nichols (2003) addresses precisely this question, examining in detail different kinds of stability and variability/renewal of linguistic elements over time.

Dialects and languages do not change at a constant rate. As the overall history of English shows, there can be periods of speeding up and periods of slowing down. From the time of this Old English leechdom through to the eighteenth century, changes were complex and rapid. As a consequence, people in the 1700s could not read with ease the literature of three centuries early; the poetry of Geoffrey Chaucer presented difficulties, as it does today. And language from a still earlier time prompted even Chaucer to make the observation (in *Troilus and Criseyde* II, 22ff.) '[y]e knowe ek that in forme of speche is change' ('you know also that in (the) form of speech (there) is change'), noting the 'wonder nyce and straunge' ('wonderfully curious and strange') nature of early English words.[2] And yet, Modern English readers have little trouble reading texts of the 1700s; the language of Jonathan Swift or Jane Austen is stylistically different and has some unfamiliar-looking vocabulary, but it is recognizably Modern English. As Svartvik and Leech (2006: 191) observe, written texts might suggest very little has happened to the language over the last few hundred years. A number of factors have been putting the brakes on changes – among them, the introduction of the printing press, the knock-on effects of standardization and its linguistic straitjacketing, the establishment of reading and writing as educational necessities rather than optional extras. These have had the effect of slowing down changes, in some cases even reversing ones already well-entrenched; spelling pronunciations (such as *often*, *comrade*, *issue*), which restore sounds long abandoned by speakers, are examples of such rearward shifts. However, disrupting forces are at work, promising once more major episodes of change – English is now described as 'one of the most hybrid and rapidly changing languages in the world' (Graddol 2006: 116). The processes set in place by globalization, colloquialization, liberalization and the electronic revolution are releasing speech from the conservative forces of the literary standard and its prescriptive ethos. The written tail is no longer wagging the spoken dog, and features that have been lurking in the wings as variation now have a greater chance of taking hold and being embedded in the language system as actual change.

22.1.1 Investigating change

The branch of linguistics that explores the whys and wherefores of these sorts of changes is 'historical linguistics' or 'historical and comparative linguistics' (historical because it deals with the pasts of individual languages and comparative because it also compares these languages and looks at the relationship between them). The discipline is also known as 'comparative philology', though this label is now usually avoided because of the confusion with the more usual understanding of 'philology' as the scholarly study of literature.

It was the outstanding theoretical and methodological breakthroughs of the nineteenth century (notably, those of the Neogrammarians) that established 'historical linguistics' as a new discipline, as distinct from literary studies and philosophical enquiry. Scholars equated the study of language with a historical one, focusing their attention on linguistic change and on the genetic relationships between languages that arose as a consequence of change. It became the golden era of historical and comparative work, specifically the comparison of lexical items and morphology of different languages leading to the identification of law-like correspondences across languages (and within them), as well as the reconstruction of unattested ancestral forms (especially of the Indo-European linguistic family). The approach was an empirical one, more data-oriented than philosophical. This historical orientation dominated the scientific study of language until the early twentieth century, when Ferdinand de Saussure's separation of synchronic (or static) and diachronic (or historical) perspectives shifted the bias to synchrony as the legitimate approach to language study.

With the establishment of the structuralist paradigm came a new way of thinking that challenged the Neogrammarian position. Structuralists (see Chapter 27) saw language as a highly organized system of interlinking elements, where everything was defined in terms of its relationship to everything else (*un système où tout se tient*). This view privileged the underlying structure of language (Saussure's *langue*) above the actual use of language (Saussure's *parole*) and so ignored precisely those speaker-oriented factors that held the key to understanding how and why linguistics changes take place (the social and behavioural aspects of language). For these linguists, there was a mystery (now referred to as the Saussurean Paradox). Clearly, a language changes, but if it is a highly structured system of sounds, words and grammatical forms, how can it change without completely disrupting this system? Saussure himself used the analogy of a chess game to illustrate the conundrum. How can players continue playing the game if the rules are constantly changing? In the same way, how can language continue to be an effective vehicle of communication if it is ceaselessly on the move? This was especially puzzling given the scale of some changes. Old English evolved into a completely different looking Modern English, and yet speakers continued to communicate successfully, even while these numerous changes were taking place.

But there is no paradox if the variation inherent in the social use of language is factored in as part of the system. Clearly, speakers have no trouble controlling variability and heterogeneity in language structure – it is simply part of their linguistic competence. Moreover, it has now been shown that this variability and heterogeneity is not random and can be studied in a systematic way. In his 1966 account of New York English, the American linguist William Labov investigated a number of sociolinguistic variables that were used within this speech community (e.g. post-vocalic /r/ in *beer* and *pork*, the pronunciation of /θ, ð/ in *thirty* and *this*, and of *–ing* in *cooking* and *eating*) and showed for the first time that these differences could be quantified. His methods revealed that earlier views of language change had been incorrect. While not all variation leads to change, all change occurs in the presence of socially relevant variation, and it is directly observable. This different way of looking at language and language use sparked a whole new line of research into linguistic evolution. Variation and change were recognized as flip sides of the same coin – variation the synchronic aspect of change; change the diachronic aspect of variation. Sociolinguistics was, and remains, an immensely important field for the study of language change.

Since this shift in attitude, research in historical linguistics has become extensive and now encompasses a wide range of very different theoretical frameworks, notably Chomskyan linguistics and 'universal grammar', the Greenbergian approach and typological shifts, grammaticalization theory, theoretical phonology, contact linguistics, socio-historical linguistics (or historical sociolinguistics, see Chapter 17). In fact, historical linguistics draws on inspirations from every one of the major branches of synchronic linguistics – a proper understanding of sound change is impossible without a knowledge of how sounds are articulated (phonetics), and so on. There have also been significant inputs from fields outside linguistics such as prehistory, philology, anthropology, psychology and sociology. With such spread as this, all this short chapter can hope to do is highlight some of the fundamental issues, methods and results that characterize this vast and very interdisciplinary field. Fortunately, with the new interest in historical linguistics has come a flourishing of comprehensive textbooks and handbooks with fuller accounts of the individual achievements of these discipline areas and their different perspectives on language change (for example, the collection of chapters in Joseph and Janda 2003).

22.2 Five questions for any theory of change

Any investigation of change in language has three obvious components:

- The 'what' of change – possible and impossible changes
- The 'how' of change – processes and mechanisms of change
- The 'why' of change – explanations for change.

At first linguists concentrated their endeavours on identifying and classifying the facts of language evolution. They concerned themselves with features that had changed in the past (in particular, sounds) and the processes by which these had changed; in other words, the 'what' and the 'how' of change. More recently, the focus of research has shifted more to explanation, and the internal and external forces that drive change. The main goals have become the collection of historical information, the discovery of common patterns of change and the testing of hypotheses about the causes of change. Ideally, these goals lay the foundation of a general theory of language evolution with a set of universal laws that regulate languages and compel them to proceed in particular directions.

Before turning to theoretical considerations, we need to consider some of the practical difficulties of doing historical linguistics, mostly arising from the lack of adequate documentation of earlier stages of languages. As Labov reminds us, '[h]istorical linguistics may be characterized as the art of making the best use of bad data' (1982: 20). Even for well-recorded languages, empirical evidence can be lost, damaged, the scripts illegible and the orthography difficult. Such deficiencies will be problematic to a greater or lesser extent depending on the linguistic elements under investigation. Sounds can be listed and because of the finiteness of phonological inventories, descriptions can be gained of lost phonological systems sometimes on the basis of even a very limited corpus (though of course recovering spoken styles of the past from textual records comes with its own host of difficulties). In the case of grammatical studies, however, we are faced with thousands of different constructions and hundreds of different categories – the chance of accidental gaps and discontinuities in the data is very real. Moreover, grammatical structures are governed by both linguistic and extralinguistic factors, including the vagaries of style; hence, for a more accurate picture of the relative chronology of any changes, investigations of grammar ideally draw on text material that is as homogenous as possible over the time span selected (comparable genres, authors, even thematic material). Unfortunately, for most languages this is unattainable, and the conclusions we make regarding their early syntax are all the more uncertain for it. Gothic is a good illustration. Only a few documents of the language have survived, and all are translations. From these pieces much definitive work has been carried out on the phonological system, and further discoveries of fragments of Gothic have yielded more information on the inflectional morphology and some new lexical items. However, little conclusive can be said about its grammatical system, especially syntax.

In their seminal work *Empirical Foundations for a Theory of Language Change*, Weinreich *et al.* (1968) pose five interrelated problems that any explicit theory of language change must address.

1. The constraints problem (what determines the possible and impossible changes and directions of change).
2. The transition problem (how does change progress through the linguistic system).
3. The embedding problem (what is the linguistic and social context of language change).
4. The evaluation problem (what are the attitudes of a speech community towards a given change, and the effect of these attitudes on change).
5. The actuation problem (why do linguistic changes occur when they do and where they do).

22.2.1 Case study – diachronic aspects of English negation

At this point it is helpful to give an actual example, and since so much attention has been paid to sound change in the literature, I have chosen to highlight developments that have taken place in English negation.³ Of course these represent but one type of change and other types relate differently to these problems; however the various issues surrounding diachronic negation are enough to give some idea of how these five key questions drive research in historical linguistics (see Bauer 1994 for a discussion of other changes in English in the light of these questions).

First, a potted history of English negation. Old English (450–1100) could negate by placing a negative particle *ne* before the finite verb. Often this was supported by one or more additional negative words.

(1) *Wiþ   wif   gemædlan gebergе   on   neahtnestig rædices   moran*
    against   woman   madness   eat   on   nightfasting radish's   root
    *þy   dæge   **ne**   mæg   þe   se   gemædla   sceþþan*
    that   day   neg   may   you   the   madness   bother

'Against a woman's mad behaviour: eat some radishes before breakfast [lit. during nightfasting] and that day the madness cannot bother you' [tenth century].

(2) *⁊   he   eaþelic   **nan**   þing   forswoligon   **ne**   mæg*
    and   he   easily   no   thing   swallow   neg   may

'and he is not able easily to swallow anything' [tenth century].

In Middle English (1100–1500) multiple negation was common, with two (often more) negators present. During this period *noght* (< *ne-a-wiht* 'not-ever-anything') emerged as the favoured reinforcer, and embracing negation *ne...noght* became the norm.

(3) *þere   **nys**   **noþynge**   þat   so   sone   smyteþ   with   grevaunce þe*
    there   not-is   nothing   that   so   soon   smites   with   grievance   the
    hed   oþere   þe   synwe as   wyne
    head   or   the   sinews as   wine

'There isn't anything which damages the head or the sinews as quickly as wine' [fourteenth century]

(4) | Of | mete | y | sigge | þat | to | hym | þat | is | of | an | hot | & | moiste |
|---|---|---|---|---|---|---|---|---|---|---|---|---|---|
| of | food | I | say | that | to | him | that | is | of | a | hot | and | moist |
| *complexioun* | *be* | *no* | *manere* | *weye* | *ne* | *scholde* | ***noght*** | *be* | *gessen* | *flesch* | | | |
| complexion | be | **no** | manner | way | **not** | should | **not** | be | eating | flesh | | | |

'Of food I say that those who are of a hot and moist complexion should in no kind of way be eating meat' [fourteenth century].

By the end of the Middle English period, pre-verbal *ne* had disappeared and single post-verbal *noght/not* had established itself as the preferred negator (of course multiple negation remains robust in non-standard varieties today: *I never eat no dinner*).

(5) | þe | rede | cale | suffers | **noght** | þe | wonde | hele |
|---|---|---|---|---|---|---|---|
| the | red | kale | suffers | not | the | wound | to-heal |

'the red kale doesn't allow the wound to heal' [fifteenth century].

In the course of the early Modern English period (1500–1800), the frequency of '*do*-support' in negative clauses rose considerably, and by the nineteenth century it had stabilized as obligatory in all environments if no other auxiliary was present (**Drinke **not** above four times*).

(6) One and the same order of diet **doth not** promiscuously agree with all men. [sixteenth century].

In terms of the 'constraints' problem, we are potentially looking at various types of checks and controls here, such as those monitoring the direction of change, the source of new negators, as well as their placement. As the following account reveals, these constraints involve both diachronic aspects (i.e. negation across time), as well as synchronic aspects (i.e. 'universals' or (im)possible patterns of negation).

Jespersen (1917) suggested that the changes for English negation (common to all Germanic languages and also French) were cyclical in nature, and since then, most linguists have referred to this kind of negator renewal as 'Jespersen's Cycle'. Cross-linguistic studies show that the change is extensively attested and in a wide range of languages well beyond Germanic (and of course is potentially more widespread given that poorly documented examples of single negation could have evolved via precisely such a pattern of erosion and creation; see papers in Horn 2010). As a paradigm case of grammaticalization, Jespersen's Cycle qualifies as a 'natural' or 'normal' change.

As confirmed by Willis *et al.* (2013: 13), the sources for new negative markers are relatively restricted. They outline three main options. Most commonly, negators arise from nominal minimizers, or what are sometimes termed 'accusatives of smallest measure' such as *(not) a bit/a drop/a step* and so on. Also widespread are inherently negative pronouns and adverbs such as *nothing, nowhere, never, at all,* and so on. A third option is similar to the first, except the strengthening marker is some sort of clause-final resumptive negator, such as the simple interjection 'no' (e.g. *I didn't do it, no*) or an ordinary sentential negator (e.g. *I didn't do it, not at all*), which is then reanalysed as part of the clause.

In terms of positioning, these markers tend to precede the elements they negate, with pre-verbal as the norm for standard clausal negation. What has come to be known as the 'Neg-first principle' (Jespersen 1917: 5 and Hirt 1937: 73) receives strong support from empirical studies, such as Dahl's 1979 survey of negation (around 81 per cent of his 240 languages had uninflecting negative particles before the verb, and the figure increases if cases of prefixal negation are included; see also Dahl 2010). Both Jespersen and Dahl suggest there is something natural about the pre-verbal placement of the negative particle with evidence from second-language learning and child language to support this (Dahl 1979: 96–7). Such constraints on the positioning of negation suggest that an innovation like post-sentential negation ('What a totally amazing, excellent discovery... NOT!!') is never likely to convert to a change.

The changes identified for English negation have occurred in many languages; they illustrate well-trodden paths of change, and yet they are not universal – nor would we expect them to be, for the simple reason that constraints have to be violable for language change to ever take place. In Germanic, naturally occurring Jespersen's Cycle has resulted in a typologically aberrant situation that places the negator before the item in constituent negation but after the verb in sentence negation. Hence, we would predict subsequent changes to eradicate the inconsistency. Indeed, the Modern English system of negative auxiliaries (*don't, can't, won't* etc.) restores the balance by once more ensuring that the negative element appears before the lexical verb (see Burridge 1993).

A more useful formulation of the 'constraints' problem is, as Labov (1982: 59) has suggested, to locate 'general principles that influence the course of linguistic change without determining it absolutely'; in other words, to frame the problem in terms of natural tendencies rather than rigid laws. The etiology of innovation and change is usually complex, with all sorts of interfering psychological, physiological, linguistic, social and cultural pressures working to coerce a language in a particular direction – linguistic structures do not exist outside these forces, and they militate against the operation of regular and utterly predictable changes.

In terms of the 'transition' problem (how changes disperse through the linguistic system), we can view the remodelling of English negation as an orderly progression through three clearly identifiable (but over-lapping) stages:

(Stage 1) pre-verbal *ne* > (Stage 2) embracing *ne-not* > (Stage 3) post-verbal *not*

Grammatical changes are gradual and (like phonological shifts) subject to the same measured transmission. This progression did not affect all linguistic contexts at once, but (akin to 'lexical diffusion') spread gradually through the system. As is typically the case in syntactic change, subordinate clauses were conservative, preserving negative patterns long after they had been abandoned in main clauses (see Burridge 1993 for elaboration).

A crucial factor affecting transition is frequency. English (like its siblings) had in common a group of commonly used verbs with conservative patterns of negation; for example, phrases such as *I know not* and *I think not* existed well after dummy *do* had become a requirement. Many different aspects of our linguistic behaviour are shaped by repetition – paradoxically, the most frequent words and phrases are at the forefront of sound change but prove to be the least adventurous when it comes to grammatical change. Over time often-repeated structures become entrenched and therefore able to resist the generalizing forces outside; hence the conservative nature of these high-usage verbs (Bybee 2003).

More recent formulations of the 'transition' problem have built in the routes of linguistic variants through speech communities (also incorporating the puzzle of how all this happens without interfering with communication). To understand how these negative patterns were promoted and dispersed, we need to study the social lives of English speakers, in particular the relationships between individuals and their social networks. Relevant here is a cornerstone of linguistic methodology known as the 'uniformitarian principle': developments within languages are subject to the same factors and controls at all times, and hence we assume that the social structures that assist the transition of features through speech communities today were also around in the past.[4] Indeed, the discipline of socio-historical linguistics rests on the viable application of sociolinguistic methods to historical situations (though of course it uses written data to do this).[5] As the network studies of Lesley and James Milroy have shown, tight-knit communities with strong social networks and values are norm enforcers – speakers with few external contacts will identify with and orientate towards those they interact with most extensively. These networks correlate with conservative speech patterns and lack of innovation (quite simply, members won't want to speak differently from their mates). On the other hand, where there is little social cohesion between members of the speech community, social networks are said to be loose; such networks are more typical of larger, often urban communities with many external contacts, and they are more open to innovation. People have ties to other groups, and changes are spread via the weak ties between them – these speakers are the conduits for change. Writing specifically on negation, Nevalainen (1998: 281) noted that 'a Milroyan type of weak-ties network structure could well have been the means of spreading the loss of multiple negation'.

Closely related to this is the 'embedding' problem (i.e. the surrounding linguistic and social setting). The changes in negation occur in the context of long-term grammatical changes that have been taking place in the language. Crucial here is the notion of drift, the cumulative unconscious selection of variants that propels a language in a particular direction, or as Sapir originally put it, '[l]anguage moves down time in a current of its own making. It has drift' (1921: 160). There is plenty of evidence to suggest that pre-verbal *ne* formed a unit with the finite verb; hence the transition from original *ne* to *ne-not* to *not* is also a transition from morphological negation to an adverbial system of negation, and therefore consistent with the drift towards increased analyticity, one of the drifts Sapir identified for English.

These changes have also taken place within another of Sapir's drifts: the fixing of constituent order and shift from OV to VO structures. Burridge (1993) argued that the movement of the negative particle from the position before the finite verb to the position after the finite verb in Germanic languages was a consequence of the grammaticalization of word order patterns, particularly verb-second order for declarative main clauses. This is an illustration of where typological coherence has applied additional pressure for change to have a causal role in the shift to post-verbal negation.

Any account of the changes to English negation must take in how variants were embedded in the larger context of the speech community; it must also try to resurrect the social distribution of the various patterns and the motivations for spreading certain favoured patterns. Assuming the uniformitarian principle, we take for granted that the same dimensions of social structure relevant to linguistic change in the modern language (age, sex, social class, ethnicity, race) were important when these changes in negation were taking place – and that, like today, the innovative forms would have acquired some prestige before being transmitted to the community as a whole. Also relevant here is an observation made by a number of early linguists (such as Jespersen 1922: 259–61); namely, that periods of dramatic linguistic change appear to go hand in hand with social upheaval (epidemics, civil wars, revolutions, economic crises). The Black Death in the fourteenth and fifteenth centuries coincided with major changes in English, including the transition from multiple to post-verbal negation. Social network theory can now make sense of this correlation. In some communities, the plague (made worse by subsequent epidemics) killed up to three-quarters of the population. It triggered mass emotional disorders (see Gordon 1959: 545–79), and would have torn even the densest of social networks apart. It is precisely at such tumultuous times that variants are able to take off, spread and eventually embed themselves as long-term changes in the language system.

In terms of the 'evaluation problem', it is usually the case that as soon as speakers become conscious of a linguistic change, the response is negative. For most speakers, change is only acceptable if it takes place in the distant past. The same people who are fascinated by the origins of words and the stories that lie behind the structures in their language typically condemn changes that are happening within their lifetime. This can have an effect on the propagation of a variant. Nevalainen (1998) looks at the stigma that attached to the use of multiple negation in the early modern period. These negative evaluations continue and may block another Jespersenian scenario from unfolding based on the pattern *You don't know nothing*; more likely to take off are the less salient variants that can slip more easily under the prescriptive radar such as *never*, *at all*, *a bit* (as in *I don't like him a bit*). However, prestige reversals do occur. Indeed, current pressures on the standard language as earlier described are endowing informal non-standard language with a cachet and respectability (see Crystal 2006 on the 'new sociolinguistic climate' that is seeing the re-evaluation and elevation of non-standard features). Non-standard variants, once condemned, now have a good chance of slipping out of the local context into a bigger arena; multiple negation/negative concord is now well on its way to being an established 'vernacular universal' (cf. Kortmann and Lunkenheimer (2013) list it as having 80 per cent attestation across seventy-six varieties of English worldwide). Moreover, with the increasing influence of newer varieties of English comes the diminishing clout of those from the so-called 'inner circle'. Linguistic innovations (including some very 'unEnglish-looking' structures) are now being started and propagated by second-language speakers, as well as foreign-language and creole speakers (e.g. the current role of rapping).

The preceding four problems all contribute to the big problem of 'actuation'. As Weinreich *et al.* originally expressed it (1968: 102): 'Why do changes in a structural feature take place in a particular language at a given time, but not in other languages with the same feature, or in the same language at other times?' In clarifying the actuation of the negation changes just outlined, linguists must account for why the Germanic languages, and also French, display such different chronologies. For the Scandinavian languages, 'Jespersen's Cycle' was completed at a much earlier date; indeed there is evidence that languages underwent two negator renewals in a Jespersen-like progression: (1) reinforcement of *ne* with *–a/–at* (*ne* disappeared by the ninth century); and (ii) replacement of *–a/–at* by *eigi* (completed by the fourteenth century) (see Willis *et al.* 2013). In German, *nicht* had eliminated the old pre-verbal negative particle by 1300; in fact even in the thirteenth century, its distribution was limited to common-usage verbs and special constructions (cf. Paul 1959: 236–8). Texts examined here suggest that exclusive use of *not* was the norm in English by the mid-1400s (cf. also Jespersen 1917: 9). In Dutch the cycle was completed more slowly and there were dialect differences; by the mid-1600s, embracing negation had finally disappeared from Hollandish, but was still intact in Brabantish (only relics remain today). Only now is Modern French showing signs of losing pre-verbal *ne*.

Language change is never one-dimensional and there would have been a network of different intersecting pressures that were influencing these languages at different times: psychological (the mental makeup of speakers), physiological (the production of language), systemic (the linguistic system with interacting components), social and political (the speech community and the individual, the socio-political environment), external (contact and borrowing) and so on. There are also human wildcard factors to consider; the cultural preoccupations of speakers can be powerful triggers for dramatic, and often unexpected changes.[6] By no means am I suggesting here that change is random, like whims of fashion, but it is hugely complex, with contingent internal and external factors (systemic and speaker-oriented), snowballing effects and an element of chance. The most apt description is 'chaotic' (in its technical sense). Language is like climate and weather – not governed by deterministic law-like processes, but not frenzied or anarchic either. Chaos theory is all about the way order emerges from the complex interaction of factors. Analogous to the evolutionary processes of the 'invisible hand', language evolves through processes of interactive reinforcement – unplanned but purposeful (see Keller 1994).

22.3 Language families and establishing genetic relationships

The previous sections have focused on linguistic change. We now turn our attention to the question of genetic affinity and how we might uncover the linguistic relationships that arise as a consequence of change. To set the scene, consider the opening lines of a simple pea soup recipe in Modern English, Dutch and German, Table 22.1.

Table 22.1 Comparison of English, Dutch and German

English	*Dutch*	*German*
Soak the peas one night and	Week de erwten een nacht en	Weich die Erbsen ein Nacht und
cook them in the same water	kook ze in hetzelfde water	koch sie in demselben Wasser
with the pork hocks, the	met de varkens-kluiven, het	mit den Schweins-haxen, dem
salt, the pepper, the milk,	zout, de peper, de melk,	Salz, dem Pfeffer, der Milch,
the curry, the carrots, the	de kerrie, de wortelen, de	dem Curry, den Wurzeln, dem
chopped celery and the leeks.	gesneden selderie en de preien.	geschnittenen Sellerie und den Lauchen.

Clearly there are some remarkably similar words here:

night–nacht–Nacht
milk–melk–Milch
water–water–Wasser
pepper–peper–Pfeffer

The parallels in grammar are also striking:

cook them in the same water with the pork hocks
kook ze in hetzelfde water met de varkenskluiven
koch sie in demselben Wasser mit den Schweinshaxen

This is of course not coincidental. English, Dutch and German are closely related languages, and these resemblances are due to the fact that they share a common ancestor – the same parent or proto-language, in this case, Proto-Germanic (assumed to have been spoken shortly before the Christian era, but no written evidence survives). The discrepancies between these three languages are due to changes that have occurred, including various sound changes (only some of which are revealed here by the spelling), grammatical changes (English and Dutch have been more or less stripped of the grammatical inflections still evident in German) and vocabulary renewals (such as English *weak* 'to marinate in water' replaced by *soak*).

The further back in time we go, the more changes we undo, and the closer the languages become. Consider a few lines of a comparable text from an earlier time, a fifteenth-century Dutch and English recipe for cherry pottage (literally, 'take cherries and do out the stones and grind them well and do them in a pot. And add thereto sweet butter and white bread'), Table 22.2.

Table 22.2 Comparison of early English and early Dutch

Early English	Early Dutch
Tak cheryes and do out the stones and	Neemt kersen ende doet die steen uut ende
grynde hem wel and do hem in a pot.	grynde se wel ende doet se in eenen pot
And do therto swete botere and wyte bred.	Ende doet daertoe soete boter ende witte broot.

These languages have had less time to diverge and are strikingly similar; the minor differences include English *tak* (now more usual than *nim* 'take'), and French *chery* (which had replaced original *ciris, cyrs*). Go back another 500 years and the 'languages' become mutually intelligible. Unfortunately, there is only one surviving fragment of original Old Dutch (from the eleventh century): *Hebban olla uogola nestas hagunnan hinase hic eende thu wat unbindan we nu* 'have all birds begun nests except me and you; what are we waiting for now?'; but so similar is this text to English that it may even be a fragment of Anglo-Saxon.

Now consider Latvian and Hungarian versions of the pea soup recipe given earlier (Table 22.3).

Table 22.3 Comparison of Latvian and Hungarian

Latvian	Hungarian
Zirņus izmērcē vienu nakti un vāra tanī pašā ūdenī ar cūkas kājām, sāli, pipariem, pienu, kariju, burkāniem un sakapātu seleriju un puraviem.	Áztasd be a borsót egy éjszakára, majd ugyanabban a vízben tedd fel főni. Add hozzá a csülköt, a sót, a borsot, a tejet, a curryt, a répát, a tejet, a felaprított zellert és a hagymát.

Glancing at these, there is nothing to suggest either language is genetically related to English, and yet Latvian is a relative, but Hungarian is not. What confirms the relatedness of languages is not so much the similarities (which in the case of Latvian are not apparent), but more importantly the existence of systematic differences. To illustrate, consider some of the word comparisons from the pea soup recipes, Table 22.4.

355

Table 22.4 Word comparisons

English	Dutch	German
weak (*obsolete*)	week	wei**ch**
cook	**k**ook	**k**o**ch**
mil**k**	mel**k**	Mil**ch**
pe**pp**er	**p**e**p**er	**Pf**e**ff**er
water	water	Wasser
salt	zout	Salz

Not only are the words strikingly similar, but the differences between them are systematic. We can find hundreds of such sets, all showing regular recurring correspondences in matching environments: orthographic German <k> (initially) and <ch> (finally) parallels Dutch and English <k>; German <pf> (initially) and <f> (medially) parallels Dutch and English <p>; German <ss> (medially) and <z> (finally) parallels Dutch and English <t>. Such word sets are known as 'cognates'; words that are etymologically, or historically, related and therefore similar in form and in meaning. The sound correspondences they display are the fallout of a series of changes known as the 'Second Germanic Consonant Shift' (or 'High German Consonant Shift'), assumed to have occurred between the sixth and ninth centuries. The phonemic correspondences can be shown as:

ENGLISH	DUTCH	GERMAN
[t]	[t]	[s] (medially) / [tˢ] (finally)
[k]	[k]	[k] (initially) / [x] (finally)
[p]	[p]	[pᶠ] (initially) / [f] (medially)

These regular sound correspondences are strong evidence of a shared history i.e. they have evolved from the same language. On the basis of many more of these sorts of correspondence sets, we can establish the sound changes that have taken place and, via a technique called the 'comparative method', can even recreate the proto-words such as Proto-Germanic *meluks* 'milk', with the asterisk indicating the form is hypothetical. (The reconstruction is based on the earliest possible attestations, such as Old English *meoluc* and Gothic *miluks*.)

Proto-words represent relationships between form and meaning that are carried into the daughter languages (if the items are retained), even where there has been drastic sound change. Thus an important premise of this method is that these changes are not capricious but regular. The absolute regularity of sound change, or what came to be known as the 'regularity hypothesis', was another major Neogrammarian doctrine. Accordingly, the sound system of any language, as it developed through time, was subject to the operation of *Lautgesetze* (sound laws), which were understood to be absolutely regular in their operation, except under the influences of non-phonetic factors such as analogy (where words deviated from the 'proper' patterns, as in *grine* changing to *groin* on analogy with *loin*). Since the nineteenth century, the principle of regular sound change has been a cornerstone of the comparative method, giving scholars proper license to compare and to reconstruct ancestral forms in this way.

Another cornerstone is the arbitrary nature of words. Excluding sound symbolic expressions (like English *cockadoodledoo*, German *kikeriki* and Japanese *kokekokko*), there is no natural or necessary connection between the shape of a word and its meaning, and this

Historical linguistics

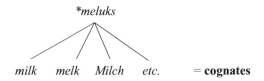

Figure 22.2 Cognates for 'milk'

means we can rule out the possibility that these patterned regularities are fortuitous. What are the chances that speakers of different languages will independently arrive at the same or similar sound patterns to represent the same object or concept? Certainly, coincidental similarities occasionally arise (e.g. unrelated English *day* and Latin *dies*), but there are literally hundreds of these sets permeating the vocabulary of these languages, all showing the same systematic correspondences. This cannot be accidental.

We can also rule out borrowing as the cause of these word comparisons for the reason that they involve core vocabulary. Of course common-usage words are occasionally borrowed (as evident in the everyday nature of Norse loans in English), but the premise here is that basic (culturally neutral) words are more resistant to borrowing, and it is these that are trusted when it comes to establishing genetic relationships and reconstructing lost stages of languages. When loans do occur, they do need to be identified. Notice the recipe in Table 22.1 has English *carrots* (borrowed from French), although a little outside delving would uncover an English cognate to Dutch *wortelen* and German *Wurzeln* – the rare word *wort* (preserved in plant names like *butterwort*). English also has *wurzel* (short for *mangel-wurzel*), a kind of beetroot fed to cattle. If *wurzel* is cognate, then it goes against this sound change that predicts [t] not [z] in English (as in *wort*); but *wurzel* is an imposter, a borrowing from German. Loans such as this one can muddy the timeline of linguistic changes; in cases of extensive borrowing, they can have the effect of accelerating vocabulary differentiation between genetically related languages and can create a false impression of long divergences, in some cases even hiding genetic connections.

In addition to the comparative method, another way of 'using the present to explain the past' (now something of a Labov-inspired catchphrase in historical linguistics), is something called 'internal reconstruction'. This is the technique whereby earlier forms of a language are inferred from material available from a synchronic description only. So whereas the comparative method leads us to a proto-language, internal reconstruction only throws up evidence of the earlier stages of a single language (e.g. Pre-Old English **fōti* > Modern English *feet*). The basis of this method is that irregularities in the modern language (like *foot–feet*) are the fallout of changes, and that if we undo these we can get back to a more regular setup (aberrant forms like *foot–feet* are relics of an earlier pronunciation rule whereby the main vowel of the word assimilated to the high vowel of the lost plural ending). Internal reconstruction is a particularly valuable tool in cases where languages have no known siblings (language 'isolates' like Basque), and also for languages without well-documented histories. It is also usefully applied at the beginning of the comparative method to bring forms back to a shape that makes comparisons easier.

22.3.1 How do language families arise?

The concept of genetic relatedness between languages had been noted for a long time, but it was not until the activities of Sir William Jones (1746–1794) that the idea really took off.

K. Burridge

During his famous lecture 'The Third Anniversary Discourse, on the Hindus', which he delivered to the Asiatick Society of Bengal on 2 February 1786, Jones argued that the classical languages Sanskrit, Ancient Greek and Latin were related; moreover, he postulated the existence of a proto-language as the parent of most of the languages of Europe, south-western Asia and northern India. Jones' ideas were not new. Others too had noticed the similarities between these languages; even the notion of a shared linguistic source was not novel. However, what Jones was arguing for here was an ancestral language that 'perhaps, no longer exists'; in other words, he was introducing the idea of a parent that was not an already extant language (such as Sanskrit) as others had assumed. While Jones did not found the comparative method, his words were certainly timely and, because of his considerable influence, he inspired others and thus contributed in some significant way to the growth of historical and comparative linguistics.

Jones' ideas were enthusiastically embraced and before long the systematic study of language evolution and language relatedness was the main focus of scholarly activity. The work carried out by European linguists during the nineteenth century led to the classification of all the Indo-European languages into the sort of genealogical tree (for Germanic languages only) given here in Figure 22.3.

The comparative method (buttressed by grammatical and other evidence) has been used to classify the world's languages into groups and subgroups. We now have numerous established language families in addition to Indo-European. These include (among many others): Austronesian (languages throughout the South Pacific, south-east Asia and into Madagascar); Sino-Tibetan (a large family of languages spoken throughout Asia, and includes the Chinese, Burmese and Tibetan languages); Finno-Ugric (a controversial language family assumed to include Hungarian as well as Finnish and Estonian); Uto-Aztecan (languages of western United States and Mexico); Pama-Nyungan (the major genetic grouping of Australian languages). The number of language families is a matter of hot debate, in particular how many of these families can be grouped into even larger ones.

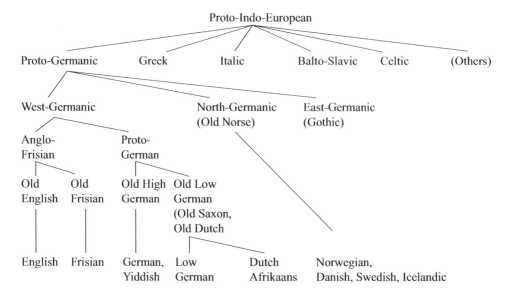

Figure 22.3 Family tree of Germanic languages

Historical linguistics

Long-distance genetic relationships (taking in Nostratic and even Proto-World) have captured people's imagination and the topic makes regular media appearances (you can find a discussion of this controversial aspect of the comparative method in Campbell 2003, and of the genetic grouping of the world's languages in Comrie 2001).

To get an idea of how language families evolve, imagine the conditions that might have given rise to the Germanic group. Around the time 1500 BC, there was a population split and a group of speakers left the Indo-European homeland (possibly a northern temperate region; cf. Bynon 1977). All languages change, but they do not have to change the same way when they are in different places. In this case, the Germanic group developed a number of distinctive characteristics, which then set it apart from the other Indo-European groups. The most significant of these innovations was a collection of chain-reaction changes known as 'Grimm's Law' (or the 'First Germanic Consonant Shift').

PROTO-INDO-EUROPEAN		GERMANIC
(voiceless stops) p, t, k	became	(voiceless fricatives) f, θ, x (h)
(voiced stops) b, d, g	became	(voiceless stops) p, t, k
(breathy voiced stops) bh, dh, gh	became	(voiced stops) b, d, g

In the following set of cognates, the Latin and Sanskrit represent the original sounds, and the Old English represents the Germanic innovations. The sound correspondences are given each time in bold, and the ancestral phonemes from which they derive are given in the first column.

PROTO	LATIN	OLD ENGLISH
*p	**p**iscis 'fish'	**f**isc
*t	**t**res 'three'	**th**reo
*k	**c**ord 'heart'	**h**eorte
*b	**b**ursa 'purse'	**p**ursa
*d	**d**ent- 'tooth'	**t**oth
*g	**g**enus 'race'	**c**ynn 'kin'

PROTO	SANSKRIT	OLD ENGLISH
*bh	**bh**ára-mi 'I carry'	**b**eran 'bear'
*dh	bán**dh**anam	bin**d**an 'bind'
*gh	**gh**ánti 'he strikes'	**g**uth 'battle'

There were many more sound changes than just the ones represented here and many grammatical changes, too; for example, Germanic developed a class of verbs indicating past with some sort of dental suffix (as in English *chew–chewed*). Further changes eventually split Germanic off from Indo-European. After this separation, the number of Germanic speakers increased in size and further population rifts spread the language geographically; the language changed in different ways in the different parts of Europe (e.g. various Germanic tribes went across to Britain in the mid-fifth century to form English), giving the three main nodes you can see on the tree in Figure 22.3 – North, East and West Germanic, with additional splits eventually sprouting all the modern groupings represented on the family tree. Once again, the magic combination of time, physical and social separation and the unrelenting processes of linguistic change caused single languages to split into dialects and ultimately distinct languages.

22.3.2 More insights from scholars of the nineteenth century

The nineteenth century represents a peak in the achievements of historical and comparative work, and it is fitting here to acknowledge some of those whose work contributed to the procedural advances in the comparative method.

It was the Danish linguist Rasmus Rask (1787–1832) who should probably be credited as being the true originator of the method, though writing in Danish meant that his pioneering ideas did not receive the wide attention they warranted. Rask was the first to set out the notion of principles, whereby languages could systematically be compared with respect to their vocabulary and sounds, thereby establishing genetic affinity (especially with the additional support of corresponding similarities in grammatical structures). But it is another from this time, Wilhelm von Humboldt (1767–1835), who is credited as offering 'the most lucid explanation (and exemplification) of the basic principles of the comparative method' (Davies 1998: 101); Humboldt's contributions to the field include data-oriented investigations, priority to sounds and comparative evidence in establishing genetic affinity, and the actual reconstructions of the phonological shapes of morphs. The Grimm brothers, in particular Jacob Grimm (1785–1863), also made significant technical breakthroughs in this method. 'Grimm's Law' has become celebrated in historical linguistics (though it is rather a misnomer – in Grimm's work there is no mention of a law, only a *Lautverschiebung* ('sound shift')). Rasmus Rask had already uncovered the basis of the law, but it was Grimm's all-encompassing conception of the shift as a unit that had such a significant impact on his contemporaries; hence, it was Grimm who became the PR person for the new methodology. Most importantly, he could account methodically for a considerable group of the Indo-European and Germanic consonants, showing how the parallel changes in the voiced and voiceless stops and fricatives retained the overall symmetry of the phonological system. Items not captured by his rules were considered exceptions and were made the object of research for the next half-century. For example, fine-tuning of Grimm's Law by Hermann Grassmann (1809–1877) and Karl Verner (1846–1896) eventually eradicated Grimm's residue and establishing the notion of exceptionless sound change.

A special place in this story are the so-called Neogrammarians, a group whose German nickname *Junggrammatiker* recognized their youth; two of the most famous were Hermann Osthoff (1847–1909) and Karl Brugmann (1849–1919). Like others before them, their view of language was historical, their methods included the systematic comparison of recorded word forms and their focus was on language change and on the genetic relationships between languages. Their position was, however, distinguished by the two major tenets already referred to, namely the 'uniformitarian principle' and 'regularity hypothesis' (*die Ausnahmslosigkeit der Lautgesetze*).

Among the later scholars of this period August Schleicher (1821–1868) stands out as having introduced techniques and fundamental methodological advances that went on to shape linguistic thinking in the twentieth century and beyond, especially with respect to the genealogical classification of languages. Schleicher was the first to attempt a systematic reconstruction of the sounds and forms of Indo-European; he is also credited with using the asterisk to indicate that they should be viewed as abstractions and not documented language material. While reconstruction was not new (both Grimm and Rask had provided reconstructed forms), Schleicher went to the lengths of recreating an actual proto-text, the 'Fable of the Sheep and the Horses'. Though resoundingly condemned as flights of fancy, these reconstructions offered a more compelling demonstration of the comparative method at work. Schleicher is also known for his model of displaying languages, the *Stammbaum* or family-tree model. He grouped existing languages together on the basis of lexical correspondences and the results of sound changes and captured the relationships in a model of language classification which, inspired by biological taxonomy, arranged them in a genealogical tree. Indeed, he is the first linguist to use tree structures as a way of graphically representing historical changes that, via a process of gradual divergence over time, eventually resulted in the formation of new languages.

However, a number of scholars were not convinced by the family-tree model as a way of describing the development of languages – not only did it fail to accommodate the fuzziness of language and dialect boundaries, it also could not capture the fact that languages (related or otherwise) may through contact continue to influence each other over time. Most notably, Johannes Schmidt (1843–1901) proposed what has now come to be known as the 'wave model' or 'wave theory' (*Wellentheorie*). He claimed correctly that sound laws were restricted spatially and in different ways. By showing that each sound law had its own territory, essentially what he was introducing here was the concept of the 'isogloss', the geographical line indicating the domain of a sound change (e.g. the boundary between High German *Apfel* 'apple' and Low German *appel* caused by the Second Germanic Consonant Shift). This wave metaphor captured the fact that new features of a language could spread from a central point in continuously weakening concentric circles, like waves created when something is thrown into a body of water. Some of the Neogrammarians (including Brugmann) argued that the *Stammbaum* and *Wellen* models were compatible; Schmidt himself saw his model as supplementing the standard family tree, simply providing a more complicated version of the single splits offered by the *Stammbaum*. What Schmidt's wave model of diffusion cannot capture, however, are sociolinguistic facts to do with spread and influence ('transition' and 'embedding' problems); for this we need to wait for the insights of dialectology and sociolinguistics.

22.4 Where to from here?

Change schemas (like the one for negation outlined in §22.2) do not follow prescribed courses determined by exceptionless laws or principles, but it is possible to talk about preferred pathways of change – 'gutters' that channel language change, to use an image famously invoked by Kuryłowicz (1945: 37). Referring specifically to analogical change, Kuryłowicz likened these developments to episodes of rain. While we may not be able to predict when it will rain, or even if it will, once the rain has fallen, we know the direction the water will flow because of gutters, drainpipes and spouting. An important goal of historical linguistics is thus to gain a clearer picture of these 'gutters of change', in other words, to refine our notions of natural and unnatural change (à la the 'constraints' problem).

Hence, more work must be done logging and classifying the changes that have occurred within individual languages, especially those with well-documented histories. The good news is that advances in technology are making the job easier. We have no time machine to take us back through history, but vast improvements in corpus design are making available massive digitized collections of texts that are annotated and searchable, and historical evidence better suited to the study of language change is now more readily available. For example, the online transcripts of the Old Bailey (London's central criminal court) offer as close to eighteenth and nineteenth century 'verbatim' vernacular texts as we can get; even taboo words (notoriously absent from other writing) make an appearance. These transcripts now reveal that as early as the 1700s *bugger* strengthened negative constructions; this is more than a century earlier than previously thought (*It cannot be helped now, I should **not*** *care **a b - dy b - gg - r** if I was going to be hung up for it*; see Musgrave and Burridge 2014 for details).

We are also getting better at the historical dimension of the relationship between language and society; in other words, in identifying how linguistic features are distributed socially, and how social factors operate in partnership with linguistic mechanisms of change (à la the 'transition' and 'embedding' problems). Trudgill (2011) offers a sociolinguistic typology based on a huge range of contexts and languages; he reveals the socio-cultural phenomena (e.g. social stability, size, contact, prestige, complexity and relative isolation of a speech community) that are critically linked to the relative stability/replacement of linguistic elements, the accelerating/decelerating stimuli for change, and other issues to do with transmission and diffusion. Whereas tight-knit communities have long been linked with linguistic stability, Trudgill shows that small speech communities with tight social networks 'are more able, because of their network structures, to push through, enforce, and sustain linguistic changes which would have a much smaller chance of success in larger, more fluid communities – namely, changes of a relatively marked, complex type' (p. 103). The closely integrated Anabaptist speech community of North America offers robust support of this in the form of rapid grammatical changes in Pennsylvania German (see Burridge 2014 for elaboration); it is clear that social context here has an accelerating influence.[7]

As Janda and Joseph (2003) conclude in their wonderfully wide-ranging overview of historical linguistics, it surely makes sense for historical linguists to study language evolution by focusing on changes currently in progress – 'building up an inventory of well-studied present times which, as they accumulate into a store of well-studied pasts, will slowly but inevitably provide a more solid database for formulating and testing increasingly sophisticated hypotheses regarding language change' (p. 128). For many of the world's languages, this task is an urgent one. The majority remains undescribed, and many of them are endangered (Native American, Austronesian and Australian Aboriginal languages, to name just a few). When it comes to mining the linguistic diversity around the world, however, the discipline is being greatly assisted by advances in computing and technology. The developments within computer-mediated communication and improved possibilities for creating and disseminating high-quality recordings of language have made for vast improvements in corpus design. Many modern corpora aim now to be multimodal – so not simply text-based collections, but high-quality recordings, both audio and video. Ongoing breakthroughs in speech technology, machine translation and transcription, information extraction, text mining, voice recognition and voice translation software, recording and archiving technologies, software development for (field) linguists, to name just a few, are making easier the business of collecting, describing and cataloguing the behaviour of language elements. We have every reason to be optimistic about future research in historical linguistics. Like Tolkien's cauldron, the story of language change continues to bubble – enriched, refined and enhanced by ongoing contributions from within linguistics and other fields, many of them disparate and far-flung.

Notes

1 This is part of a collection of Anglo-Saxon medical texts (or Lacnunga 'remedies' – the name given to this collection by its first editor, Oswald Cockayne 1865); these are vernacular texts dating from the tenth and eleventh centuries.
2 In his preface to *Eneydos* (1490), the printer William Caxton also observed how different and difficult early English was, describing it as 'so rude and brood that I coude not wele vnderstande it'.

3   Examples here come from a range of Old and Middle English medical and medico-magic texts reproduced in Cockayne (1865), Furnivall (1868) and Sinclair (1938). These vernacular texts are products of an essentially oral culture, and resemble as closely as possible the spoken idiom of the time (see discussion in Burridge 1993).
4   Though the socio-cultural settings for English speakers 1,000 years ago and English speakers in the twenty-first century are clearly very different (universal literacy, standardization, mass media, e-communication), uniformitarianism assumes that changes today and those in the past are driven by the same sorts of mechanisms. The Neogrammarians borrowed this powerful dictum from geology and biology (see Janda and Joseph 2003: 27–31). Classicist Hermann Ostoff and Indo-Europeanist Karl Brugmann expressed it this way (1878: xiii): 'the psychological and physiological nature of man as speaker must have been essentially identical at all epochs' (Collinge's translation 1995: 205).
5   Terttu Nevalainen and Helena Raumolin-Brunberg (2003) have used a corpus of correspondence (6,000 letters from 1417–1681) to reconstruct the social setting of late Middle English and early Modern English, crediting the success of a number of linguistic changes to the existence of weak ties in the population at crucial times.
6   Burridge (2015) argued that the predilection for dative and accusative participants in early Germanic was an enactment of prevailing thinking, specifically, beliefs about the human condition that emphasized its vulnerability to external forces. What contributed to the demise of impersonal constructions (of the *me thinks* type) was the emergence of a modern secular sense of identity – a world apart from earlier communal thought processes once so gripped by natural and supernatural outlooks.
7   Fast-speech phenomena arise from the reduced need for elaboration in these communities due to the considerable degree of shared ground. This leads to phonological reduction, which in turn feeds the development of new grammatical structures. The tendency for general reduction and omission of unstressed material is a striking feature of Pennsylvania German and, while this would be expected of a language that is spoken and has no written form, it is also the consequence of close integration. The speed of these changes is a by-product of the increased allowance for inference in this isolated and tight-knit community.

References

Bauer, L. (1994) *Watching English Change: An Introduction to the Study of Linguistic Change in the Twentieth Century*. London: Longman.
Burridge, K. (1993) *Syntactic Change in Germanic*. Amsterdam: John Benjamins.
Burridge, K. (2015) The body, the universe, society and language: Germanic in the grip of the unknown. In R. La Polla and R. de Busser (eds) *The Shaping of Language: The Relationship Between the Structures of Languages and Their Social, Cultural, Historical, and Natural Environments*. Amsterdam: John Benjamins.
Bybee, J. (2003) Mechanisms of change in grammaticization: The role of frequency. In B.D. Joseph and R.D. Janda (eds) *The Handbook of Historical Linguistics*, pp. 602–23. Oxford: Blackwell Publishing.
Bynon, T. (1977) *Historical Linguistics*. Cambridge: Cambridge University Press.
Campbell, L. (2003) How to show languages are related: Methods for distant genetic relationship. In B.D. Joseph and R.D. Janda (eds) *The Handbook of Historical Linguistics*, pp. 19–42. Oxford: Blackwell Publishing.
Cockayne, O. (ed.) (1865) *Leechdoms, Wortcunning, and Starcraft of Early England* (three volumes). London: Longman, Roberts and Green.
Collinge, N.E. (1995) History of historical linguistics. In E.F.K. Koerner and R.E. Asher (eds) *Concise History of the Language Sciences: From the Sumerians to the Cognitivists*, pp. 2–212. Oxford: Pergamon.
Comrie, B. (2001) Languages of the world. In M. Aronoff and J. Rees-Miller (eds) *The Handbook of Linguistics*, pp. 262–82. Oxford: Blackwell Publishers.

Crystal, D. (2006) Into the twenty-first century. In L. Mugglestone (ed.) *The Oxford History of English*, pp. 394–414. Oxford: Oxford University Press.

Dahl, Ö. (1979) Typology of sentence negation. *Linguistics* 17: 79–106.

Dahl, Ö. (2010) Typology of negation. In L.R. Horn (ed.) *The Expression of Negation*, pp. 9–38. Berlin: De Gruyter Mouton.

Davies, A.M. (1998) *History of Linguistics, Volume 4: Nineteenth-Century Linguistics*. London/New York: Longman.

Furnivall, F. (ed.) (1868) *The Babees Book, The Bokes of Nurture of Hugh Rhodes and John Russel*, published for the Early English Text Society. London: Trübner & Co.

Gordon, B.L. (1959) *Medieval and Renaissance Medicine*. New York: Philosophical Library.

Graddol, D. (2006) *English Next: Why Global English May Mean the End of English as a Foreign Language*. London: British Council.

Hirt, H. (1937) *Indogermanische Grammatik Syntax II. Die Lehre vom einfachen unzusammengesetzten Satz*. Heidelberg: Carl Winter.

Horn, L.R. (2010) *The Expression of Negation*. Berlin: De Gruyter Mouton.

Humboldt, W. von (1836) *Über die Verschiedenheit des menschlichen Sprachbaues und ihren Einfluss auf die geistige Entwickelung des Menschengeschlechts*. Berlin: F. Dümmler.

Janda, R.D. and B.D. Joseph (2003) On language, change and language change – or, of history, linguistics and historical linguistics. In B.D. Joseph and R.D. Janda (eds) *Handbook of Historical Linguistics*, pp. 3–180. Oxford: Blackwell Publishing.

Jespersen O. (1917) *Negation in English and Other Languages*. Copenhagen: Munksgaard.

Jespersen, O. (1922) *Language: Its Nature, Development and Origin*. London: George Allen & Unwin Ltd.

Jones, W. (1786) The Third Anniversary Discourse delivered to the Asiatick Society 2 February, 1786. Published in *The Works of Sir William Jones in Six Volumes: Vol. I*, pp. 19–34. London: G.G. and J. Robinson, and R.H. Evans, 1799.

Joseph, B.D. and R.D. Janda (eds) (2003) *Handbook of Historical Linguistics*. Oxford: Blackwell Publishing.

Keller, R. (1994) *On Language Change: The Invisible Hand in Language*. London: Routledge.

Kortmann, B. and K. Lunkenheimer (eds) (2013) *The Electronic World Atlas of Varieties of English*. Leipzig: Max Planck Institute for Evolutionary Anthropology. http://ewave-atlas.org.

Kuryłowicz, J. (1945) La nature des procès dits 'analogiques'. *Acta Linguistica* 5: 15–37.

Labov, W. (1966) *The Social Stratification of English in New York City*. Washington, DC: Center for Applied Linguistics.

Labov, W. (1982) Building on empirical foundations. In Winfred Lehmann and Yakov Malkiel (eds) *Perspectives on Historical Linguistics*, pp. 17–82. Amsterdam: John Benjamins.

Milroy, J. (1992) *Linguistic Variation and Change: On the Historical Sociolinguistics of English*. Oxford: Blackwell Publishing.

Milroy, L. (1987) *Language and Social Networks*, 2nd edition. Oxford: Basil Blackwell.

Musgrave, S. and K. Burridge (2014) Bastards and buggers: Historical snapshots of Australian English swearing patterns. In K. Burridge and R. Benczes (eds) *Wrestling with Words and Meanings: Essays in Honour of Keith Allan*, pp. 3–32. Melbourne: Monash University Publishing.

Nevalainen, T. (1998) Social mobility and the decline of multiple negation in Early Modern English. In J. Fisiak and M. Krygier (eds) *Advance in English Historical Linguistics (1996)*, pp. 263–91. Berlin: Mouton de Gruyter.

Nevalainen, T. and H. Raumolin-Brunberg (2003) *Historical Sociolinguistics: Language Change in Tudor and Stuart England*. London: Pearson Education.

Nichols, J. (2003) Diversity and stability in language. In B.D. Joseph and R.D. Janda (eds) *Handbook of Historical Linguistics*, pp. 283–310. Oxford: Blackwell Publishing.

Paul, H. (1959) *Mittelhochdeutsche Grammatik*. Tübingen: Max Niemeyer.

Sapir, E. (1921) *Language: An Introduction to the Study of Speech*. New York: Harcourt, Brace & Company.

Sinclair, M. (ed.) (1938) *The Liber de Diversis Medicinis* (in the Thornton manuscript). Published for the Early English Text Society. Oxford: Oxford University Press.

Svartvik, J. and G. Leech (2006) *English: One Tongue, Many Voices*. New York: Palgrave.

Trudgill, P. (2011) *Sociolinguistic Typology: Social Determinants of Linguistic Complexity*. Oxford: Oxford University Press.

Weinreich, U., W. Labov and W. Herzog (1968) Empirical foundations for a theory of language change. In W. Lehmann and Y. Malkiel (eds) *Directions for Historical Linguistics*, pp. 95–188. Austin: University of Texas Press.

Willis, D., C. Lucas and A. Breitbarth (2013) Comparing diachronies of negation. In D. Willis, C. Lucas and A. Breitbarth (eds) *The History of Negation in the Languages of Europe and the Mediterranean: Volume I Case Studies*, pp. 1–50. Oxford: Oxford University Press.

23
Linguistic change in grammar

Walter Bisang

23.1 Introduction

That languages change over time is a truism that everybody knows from comparing a currently spoken language with older versions of the same language as it is preserved in written texts or in oral texts of special cultural value. This very simple observation contrasts with the impressive complexity of the processes of linguistic change and the factors that determine them. The evolutionary perspective provides a good framework for modelling linguistic change in general and for integrating a wide range of interacting factors. In this framework, speech communities are the environment that selects the structures of concrete utterances in actual speech situations. While the structures that are selected generally follow known structural patterns, there are sometimes innovations produced by individual speakers in actual discourse. Even though innovations deviate from the rules of a language they do not make a linguistic change. Linguistic change only happens if a given innovation is propagated within a speech community as a whole. This important difference between innovation and propagation as successful diffusion was introduced by Croft (2000) in his Theory of Utterance Selection. In this approach, innovations can have many different motivations that reach from articulation to cognition or needs of discourse and social behaviour, while propagation depends only on social factors. The present chapter will take a different view. If speakers with their specific properties form the selectional environment for linguistic structures in discourse that environment is characterized by the social properties of the speakers involved as well as by the other factors mentioned above (Bisang 2004). For that reason, I assume that innovation and successful change (propagation) depend on the following:

- cognitive factors (e.g. competing motivations of economy versus iconicity);
- communicative factors (e.g. pragmatic inference, information structure);
- Universal Grammar (UG);
- physiological factors (production and perception of sounds);
- sociolinguistic and cultural factors.

The first four factors are language internal, the last factor is language external. Since the physiological factors relevant for linguistic change are treated in Chapter 22, they are not addressed here. The other language internal factors will be the subject of §23.2 on grammaticalization, i.e. on changes in grammar and their relation to factors of cognition and communication as well as to UG. §23.3 on change due to external factors will introduce the relevance of frequency (s-curve model), three sociolinguist models of language change and the effects of contact among speakers of different languages (borrowing, shift, mixed languages, pidgin and creole languages). Since understanding the processes of linguistic change is fundamental for linguistic typology and the discovery of potential universals (Chapter 25), this issue will be briefly discussed in the closing remarks of §23.4.

23.2 Language internal change: grammaticalization

23.2.1 Introduction

The origin of the term 'grammaticalization' can be dated back to Meillet (1912), who defines grammaticalization as the transition from autonomous words to grammatical elements. A simple example of this kind of linguistic change is the development of future markers from verbs of volition (cf. English *will*; Modern Greek *θa*, derived from the verb *θelɔ* 'I want'; Chinese *yào* 'want/future marker'). Even though this phenomenon was discussed by historical linguists of the nineteenth century, the credit of giving it a terminological label belongs to Meillet. The existence of this term had no immediate impact on the research agenda in linguistics. It took more than fifty years until Kuryłowicz (1965) offered the following definition, which has become the basis for many later definitions: 'Grammaticalization consists in the increase of the range of a morpheme advancing from a lexical to a grammatical or from a less grammatical to a more grammatical status' (Kuryłowicz 1975 [1965]: 52). In the 1970s, Givón (1971, 1979) argued that synchronic linguistic structures can only be understood from their diachronic history. His famous statement 'Today's morphology is yesterday's syntax' (Givón 1971: 413) summarizes how independent words evolve into dependent grammatical morphemes. Another important pathway leads from discourse structure to morphosyntactic structure in the sense that discourse structure gets fossilized into syntactic and morphological structure. The combination of both developments feeds into a cyclic process that starts out from discourse and ends up in zero marking:

(1) Givón (1979: 209):
discourse > syntax > morphology > morphophonemics > zero

Processes like that in (1) are typical of grammaticalization. They are called 'clines' or 'pathways'. Meanwhile, research in grammaticalization has claimed an impressive number of grammaticalization clines, which are listed in Heine and Kuteva (2002). The following cline starts out from nouns that belong to the semantic domain of PERSON (e.g. body parts):

(2) Heine *et al.* (1991):
person > object > activity > space > time > quality

Examples (3) to (6) below from Thai illustrate this cline from OBJECT > SPACE > TIME > QUALITY. Each of the stages is illustrated by the word *nâa* 'face'. In (3), *nâa* has its concrete meaning of 'face', in (4) it is used in the function of a locative preposition. Its temporal meaning shows up in a number of lexical expressions in (5). By QUALITY, Heine *et al.* (1991) mean some specific metaphorical meaning. In Thai, *nâa* is used in the context of being advanced/progressive as in (6).

(3) OBJECT: The noun *nâa* 'face' denoting a body part:
kháw   láaŋ   **nâa**.
he   wash   face
'He is washing his face.'

(4) SPACE: *nâa* as a locative preposition:
(khâaŋ-)**nâa**   bâan
side-face   house
'in front of the house' / 'the front-side of the house'.

(5) TIME: nâa as an expression of time:
(khâaŋ-)nâa 'in the future', bŷaŋ-nâa [direction-face] 'in the future', wan-nâa [day-face] 'one day [in the future]', dyan nâa [month face] 'next month'.

(6) QUALITY: 'being advanced, progressive':
kâaw nâa [take.a.step face] 'step ahead, go forward', khwaam kâaw nâa [NML take.a.step face] 'progress'.

Processes of grammaticalization like (1) and (2) have the following characteristics (for a more extensive description, cf. Bybee *et al.* 1994: 9–22):

1. Cyclicity: they are realized in stages, step-by-step.
2. Universality: the sequence of the individual stages follows universal clines.
3. Unidirectionality: the grammaticalization clines are not reversible.
4. Source determination: the clines start out from a source concept that determines their further development (e.g. body-part terms, verbs with the meaning of 'come', 'go', 'be at', 'finish', etc.; Heine and Kuteva 2002).
5. Retention of earlier meaning: If a pathway develops from meaning A to B, there is an intermediate stage in which a linguistic item can have both meanings: A > {B/A} > B. Thus, nuances of the source concept or the source construction are retained at later stages.
6. As a consequence of (5), processes of grammaticalization are gradual and develop over a certain period of time with different nuances between A and B.
7. Co-evolution of meaning and form: the change from a more concrete to a more abstract grammatical meaning is reflected in the form of the linguistic item involved (§23.2.2).

Grammaticalization as discussed so far is presented in several monographs published in the 1980s and 1990s, which will be presented in §23.2.2 and §23.2.3. Later sections will deal with the difference between grammaticalization and the lexicon (§23.2.4), examples that go against unidirectionality and the question of the linguistic reality of grammaticalization (§23.2.5), the contribution of Construction Grammar to grammaticalization (§23.2.6) and the motivations that drive grammaticalization (§23.2.7).

23.2.2 Loss of autonomy, co-evolution of form and meaning

Most approaches understand grammaticalization as a process in which meaning and form converge. Lehmann (1995 [1982]) describes this correlation very consistently from the perspective of the autonomy of the linguistic sign: 'The autonomy of a sign is converse to its grammaticality, and grammaticalization detracts from its autonomy. Consequently, if we want to measure the degree to which a sign is grammaticalized, we will determine its degree of autonomy' (Lehmann 1995: 121–2).

The degree of autonomy can be measured within the three parameters of weight, cohesion and variability:

- Weight: a linguistic sign needs a certain prominence in the syntagm. Grammaticalization is associated with the reduction of that prominence.
- Cohesion: a linguistic sign needs a certain degree of rigour with which it can contract systematic relations with other signs. Grammaticalization is associated with increasing rigour.
- Variability: a linguistic sign needs a certain degree of mobility in order to be autonomous. Grammaticalization is associated with loss of mobility.

Each of the three parameters has its paradigmatic and its syntagmatic side. Thus, Lehmann's (1995) approach ends up with six parameters for measuring grammaticalization:

Table 23.1 Parameters of grammaticalization

	Syntagmatic	*Paradigmatic*
weight	structural scope	integrity
variability	syntagmatic variability	paradigmatic variability
cohesion	bondedness	paradigmaticity

Adapted from Lehmann 1995: 123.

To give an idea of how grammaticalization can be measured, the parameters of integrity, paradigmatic and syntagmatic variability will be briefly addressed. The integrity of a sign is associated with a certain substance that is needed for it to maintain its identity. This substance can be of phonological or semantic nature. In processes of grammaticalization, the loss of phonological integrity is associated with the loss of phonological substance (attrition, erosion), while the loss of semantic integrity is reflected by desemanticization, i.e. by the loss of concrete lexical meaning to the benefit of grammatical meaning.

Paradigmatic variability is defined as

> the freedom with which the language user chooses a sign. The principle alternatives to choosing some sign are either choosing another member of the same paradigm or choosing no member of that paradigm, i.e. leaving the whole generic category unspecified.
>
> (Lehmann 1995: 137–8)

A high degree of grammaticalization is typically associated with obligatoriness. A grammatical category (e.g. tense) is obligatory if the speaker is forced to specify that category by one of its subcategories (e.g. present, past, etc.) in an utterance.

Syntagmatic variability measures to what extent a linguistic element can be moved. Typically, word order flexibility gets reduced with increasing grammaticalization.

The co-evolution of meaning and form is taken for granted in many approaches to grammaticalization. Data from East and mainland South-East Asian languages show that the extent to which meaning and form converge in processes of grammaticalization is subject to a certain degree of cross-linguistic and areal variation (Bisang 2008, 2011; also cf. §23.3.3).

23.2.3 The role of pragmatics, the cases of subjectification and of reanalysis and analogy

Discourse and pragmatic inference are generally seen as an important factor that motivates or enables processes of grammaticalization (Hopper and Traugott 2003: 71). In Traugotts's (2002) Invited Inference Theory of Semantic Change, grammaticalization begins if a construction occurs in a specific context that invites the listener to draw a particular inference. When this invited inference gets conventionalized in the same context it becomes a generalized invited inference which will be coded as a new grammatical meaning at the final stage of grammaticalization.

An important part of linguistic change takes place in interactions between speakers and addressees and the pragmatic inferences they make. As Traugott (2010) shows, inferences from this situation can become conventionalized and part of grammar in the form of subjectification and intersubjectification. Traugott defines subjectification as 'a mechanism by which meanings are recruited by the speaker to encode and regulate attitudes and beliefs' (p. 35). Once they are subjectified, they 'may be recruited to encode meanings centered on the addressee (intersubjectification)' (ibid.). Examples of subjectification are the rise of epistemic modals from verbs of volition (English *will*), the development of concessives from temporals (English *while*) and focus markers from manner adverbials (Old English *anlice* 'simply, especially' > Modern English *only*).

Hopper and Traugott (2003) see pragmatic inference as the driving force of two mechanisms of grammaticalization that are frequently discussed in the literature. One of them is analogy, the other one is reanalysis. In Hopper and Traugott's view, both mechanisms are motivated by two different types of pragmatic inferences. Analogy is based on metaphoric inference, while reanalysis is a consequence of metonymic inference. Metaphors[1] are generally defined in terms of 'understanding and experiencing one kind of thing in terms of another' (p. 84). Typically, metaphorical inferencing proceeds across conceptual boundaries as in (2), in which a linguistic item that belongs to the domain of body-parts is associated with the domain of space and later with the domain of time. Thus, the mapping of metaphorical inference follows principles of analogy in the sense of rule extension. There is a category A that is associated with X (A:X). If analogy establishes similarities of A with B, B will also be associated with X (A:X = B:X). While metaphor depends on semantic transfer through a similarity of sense perceptions, metonymy depends on transfer through (morpho) syntactic contiguity. It 'points to ("indexes") relations in contexts that include interdependent (morpho)syntactic constituents' (p. 88). Metonymic inference motivates reanalysis, i.e. the assignment of a new morphosyntactic analysis to a given linguistic structure. Very often, reanalysis can be defined in terms of constituency change or rebracketing. Thus, the sequence *nâa bâan* [face house] in (4) is first analysed as a noun phrase with the meaning of 'face/front of the house'. The head of this construction *nâa* 'face, front' is followed by the possessive modifier *bâan* 'house'. In the context of localization in space, the same structure can be interpreted as a prepositional phrase with *nâa* 'face' being the preposition and *bâan* 'house' being its complement. This process of reanalysis generates the meaning of 'in front of the house'.

In Hopper and Traugott's (2003) approach, reanalysis motivated by metonymy and analogy motivated by metaphor frequently interact cyclically. This will be briefly illustrated by the well-known example of *be going to* and its grammaticalization into a marker of immediate future (pp. 92–3):

(7) a. John is going to visit Bill.
    b. John is going to like Bill.

At stage 1 in Figure 23.1, an example like (7a) is analysed as consisting of two verbs, the directional verb (Vdir) *go* and the dynamic verb (Vdyn) *visit* which are in a semantic relation of purpose: 'John is going [to some place] with the purpose of visiting Bill'. At stage 2, the same utterance is reanalysed. It is now understood as consisting of only one verb, the verb *visit*, marked by a future marker *be going to*. The future marker *be going to* is not fully productive at this stage. Since the directional verb *go* still retains some of its concrete meaning, only dynamic verbs can take the new future marker. The paradigmatic extension of *be going to* to stative verbs (Vstat) as in (7b) is due to analogy that comes in at stage 3. Finally, the reanalysis of *be going to* as a grammatical marker favours its morphophonological reduction to a single word (*gonna*).

The role of reanalysis and analogy in grammaticalization has been discussed very controversially. There are four main positions (cf. Traugott's 2011: 22 summary, on which this passage is based): According to the first position, grammaticalization and reanalysis are independent but they intersect. The second position is argued for in approaches based on UG. It sees grammaticalization as a subtype of reanalysis (§23.2.5, §23.2.7). Haspelmath (1998: 315) takes the third position according to which reanalysis is largely irrelevant to grammaticalization. He argues that reanalysis lacks unidirectionality and depends on ambiguous input structures which are not necessary for grammaticalization. Finally, the last position is advocated by Fischer (2007). In her processing-based view, grammaticalization is driven by analogy rather than by reanalysis. Reanalysis may be what linguists see when they compare changes through generations of speakers but it is not what actual speaker-

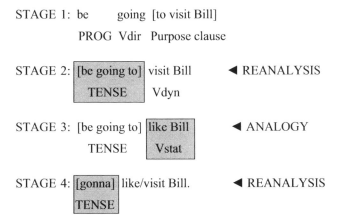

Figure 23.1 Reanalysis and analogy

listeners do when they first produce or process a linguistic innovation. Taking the example of *be going to*, one can argue that its very first use as a future marker was possible because of a category mistake. English already had the two-verb construction *V-to-V* and the auxiliary construction *Aux-V*. Due to analogy, the speaker-listener took *be going to* as an instance of the auxiliary rather than as the first verb in *V-to-V*.

23.2.4 Grammaticalization vs lexicalization

The most widely discussed phenomena of lexicalization are fossilization and univerbation (Himmelmann 2004: 26–9). In fossilization, morphologically complex forms become unanalysable wholes. Thus, the Germanic causative form in *-eja* is integrated into monomorphemic stems in modern English (*sit* versus *set* < Proto-Germ **sat-eja* 'make sit'). The development of frequent collocations of two or more lexemes into single words like *cupboard, brainstorm* or *greenhouse* is called univerbation. These examples of lexicalization are the result of conventionalization. Thus, they share important properties with grammaticalization and are not always easy to distinguish from it.

Currently, there are two approaches that contribute considerably to the distinction of grammaticalization from lexicalization. For Himmelmann (2004), the difference lies in the different expansion properties of grammaticalization versus lexicalization. For that purpose, he looks at three kinds of expansions grammaticalized/lexicalized items undergo, i.e. host-class expansion, expansion of syntactic context and expansion of semantic–pragmatic context. Since host-class expansion is crucial for the grammaticalization/lexicalization-distinction, only this type of expansion will be explained here. It is defined by the number of elements a marker is in construction with and can be illustrated by the example of *greenhouse*, an instance of univerbation. The adjective *green* syntactically collocates quite freely with a large number of nouns (*green car, green table, green cupboard, green scarf*, etc.). With products of lexicalization like *greenhouse*, the host *green* is compatible only with a single lexical unit to form a new word with a specific meaning.[2] In contrast, a grammaticalized item that expresses a category like tense-aspect or plural collocates with a large number of host elements (verbs or nouns, respectively). Moreover, grammaticalization is characterized by directionality in the sense that the change moves into a specific semantic domain (tense-aspect, plural). This is not the case with lexicalization, which is non-directional.

Boye and Harder's (2012) criteria for distinguishing grammaticalization from lexicalization are based on the ability of their products to be used in discourse. While lexical meaning can take on primary functions in discourse, grammatical meaning is 'discursively secondary' (p. 13). This can be seen from the fact that grammatical expressions cannot occur in contexts of focalization and addressation, while lexical expressions can.

(8) Nonfocalizability as a symptom of grammatical status (Boye and Harder 2012: 14): Grammatical expressions cannot be assigned discursively primary status by focalizing expressions.

(9) Nonaddressability as a symptom of grammatical status (Boye and Harder 2012: 14): Grammatical expressions cannot be assigned discursively primary status by being addressed in discourse.

The symptom of nonfocalizability can be used for testing whether a linguistic item is the result of grammaticalization in individual languages that have specific means for expressing focus. In the case of English, fully grammaticalized items cannot occur in cleft constructions, pseudo-cleft constructions, narrow-focus stress and with focus particles like *only*, *just* and *even* (ibid.). In contrast, lexical items and results of lexicalization are compatible with all the above focus-tests.

Similarly, the symptom of nonaddressability yields various language-specific tests for deciding whether a given linguistic item is the result of grammaticalization. In English, it is not possible to ask for grammatical expressions independently by *wh*-words. Grammatical items cannot independently be referred to anaphorically or cataphorically and they cannot be questioned independently by yes/no questions (Boye and Harder 2012: 15). Again, lexical items and results of lexicalization pass these addressability-tests.

23.2.5 Degrammaticalization and problems of consistency

Newmeyer's (1998: 226) statement that 'there is no such thing as grammaticalization' in Chapter 5 of his book *Language Form and Language Function* produced intensive and controversial reactions. His strong statement was based on two main arguments:

1. Grammaticalization is falsified because there are counterexamples to unidirectionality (Newmeyer 1998: 263–78 offers a list of considerable length).
2. Grammaticalization is not a distinct phenomenon but rather an epiphenomenon of its three component parts with their principles, i.e. reanalysis, phonetic changes and semantic changes.

Researchers on grammaticalization are generally aware that there are instances of degrammaticalization, i.e. processes of change that revert the direction of grammaticalization clines and thus provide evidence against unidirectionality. An example is the development of the Old Swedish inflectional marker *–er* 'nominative singular masculine', which has become a derivational suffix of nominalization in Modern Swedish (Norde 2009: 152). This development goes against the cline from derivational > inflectional. The question is how many counterexamples there are. As is shown by more recent research based on more refined definitions of degrammaticalization (Norde 2009), the number of counterexamples to unidirectionality is much smaller than assumed by Newmeyer (1998), who himself had to admit somewhat later that unidirectionality 'is not *all that* false' (Newmeyer 2001: 213). If there are only a few examples of degrammaticalization, the directionality of grammaticalization needs explanation. It cannot simply be an epiphenomenon of its component parts as claimed in point 2 by Newmeyer (1998). The issue of motivations of grammaticalization will be the topic of §23.2.7. Interestingly enough, there is even a UG-based explanation for unidirectionality.

23.2.6 Constructions

Grammaticalization processes are not limited to the development of individual words in isolation – they take place within a certain syntactic context. Thus, demonstratives do not generally develop into articles (cf. Latin *ille* [DEM:SG:M] 'that' > Italian *il* [ART:SG:M] 'the', etc.), they only do so in the context of adnominal modification. In other syntactic environments, they develop into personal pronouns, complementizers, relative clause markers or copulas. Many researchers describe such a context-based divergence of grammaticalization clines in terms of constructions. The grammatical function a lexical item is going to express depends on its constructional environment.

Since the rise of Construction Grammar, this rather informal way of emphasizing the relevance of constructions for grammaticalization has taken on a new dimension in which constructions provide the environment for the grammaticalization of lexical items on the one hand and take on new properties themselves on the other. Moreover, new constructions develop out of older constructions in some instances. These issues will be briefly outlined after a short definition of the notion of construction.

Constructions are defined as 'learned pairings of form with semantic or discourse function' (Goldberg 2006: 5). This covers a wide area of phenomena from morphemes, words, idioms, phrasal patterns up to sentences. What is crucial for a linguistic phenomenon to be a construction is that 'some aspect of its form or function is not strictly predictable from its component parts or from other constructions recognized to exist' (ibid.). Many constructions are characterized by specific slots for grammatical categories like tense-aspect or causativity.

Constructions are themselves the product of linguistic change. They change their properties over time and may ultimately end up as a completely new construction. Thus, the *be going to*-construction can be seen as a development from a two-verb construction to a tense-aspect marker. Examples like this are clearly instances of linguistic change. The question is whether they are also instances of grammaticalization. Gisborne and Patten (2011: 98–9) mention six properties of constructional change that are similar to grammaticalization. Four of them will be pointed out here. The first property is directionality. Both processes are directed towards higher degrees of abstractness and compatibility with more elements (cf. §23.2.4 on host-class extension). In the case of constructions, this process is known in terms of increasing schematicity. Constructions can be situated between the poles of specificity and schematicity. A specific or substantive construction is specified phonologically (e.g. the lexical item *tree* by [tri:]), while a schematic construction is defined in terms of abstract categories as in the case of *be going to*, which is an instance of the [tense/aspect V]-construction. In any case, schematicity is always associated with the existence of slots that can be filled by variables and grammatical categories for which these slots stand. In that sense, increasing schematicity runs parallel to increasing abstractness in grammaticalization.

The second property is gradualness. Thus, constructions do not change abruptly, they change in incremental stages. The third and the fourth properties have to do with analogy and reanalysis. Analogy leads to the expansion of the class of elements that can occur in a slot. Thus, the number of lexical items that take the tense/aspect-position in the [tense/aspect V]-construction increases through analogy. Reanalysis can be observed when a given surface structure like the serial verb construction is interpreted in terms of the [tense/aspect V]-construction.

23.2.7 Motivations of grammaticalization

Motivations of grammaticalization have been sought mainly in the competing motivations of economy versus iconicity and in UG. Both motivations will be briefly discussed.

The idea that language structure is driven by the two competing motivations of economy versus iconicity goes back to the nineteenth century and has been discussed prominently by Haiman (1983). Economy reflects the desire of speakers and addressees to perform the least effort or to do things in the simplest way to express a certain concept. Iconicity is based on a certain isomorphism between a concept and the way in which it is formally expressed. Haiman explains the co-evolution of form and meaning by both motivations. The parallel reduction of semantic and phonological content is iconic through the analogy between less (i.e. more abstract) meaning and less form but this development is also supported by economy, which prefers reduction of articulatory effort on the phonological side. This reduction of form is additionally enhanced by the fact that less notional distinctions are needed at higher levels of semantic abstraction. For that reason, the formal cues for abstract categories can be more reduced than for more concrete meanings.

More recent work in the minimalist framework recognizes the relevance of unidirectionality and it even has a UG-based explanation for it (Roberts and Roussou 2003). In the minimalist approach, the development from lexical item to grammatical marker is motivated by the fact that heads with grammatical function are assumed to take higher positions in the tree structure. At an early stage in one generation of speakers, a lexical item that is analysed as a grammatical marker moves from its lower position to the corresponding higher position. If the item is subject to a certain change in form (e.g. attrition, erosion) it will become a cue for a change in parameter setting in the linguistic input to speakers of a next generation. As a consequence, it will be merged directly at the higher position for the corresponding grammatical function. Therefore, grammaticalization is a change from movement to merger.

23.3 Change due to language external factors

23.3.1 Frequency and change: the S-curve

The successful diffusion of innovations follows a pattern of frequency that was introduced by Wang and Cheng (1970) and has been confirmed by numerous studies since then. The initial phase of a linguistic change is characterized by its gradualness and relative slowness and is followed by a very rapid period once the innovation has reached a critical mass of about 20 per cent of frequency of occurrence in the relevant linguistic contexts. After having reached a frequency of about 80 per cent it tails off again until final completion. This frequency pattern yields an s-shaped curve in a diagram like the one in Figure 23.2, hence the name 's-curve model'. This model is widely used and discussed in various approaches to linguistic change and it is particularly attractive for UG-based theories of change and their assumption that parameter setting depends on the input children get from their linguistic environment (Lightfoot 1999).

23.3.2 Social models of linguistic change

23.3.2.1 The social-network model
The social-network model explains language change in terms of individual actors and the quality of their relations to other individuals. In the abstract model of network theory, individuals are graphically represented as points, while the relations between them are expressed by lines of different graphic qualities depending on their specific properties. As it turns out, the difference between weak and strong ties as first described in sociology is of particular importance for explaining the successful dissemination of linguistic innovations (Milroy 1992). Strong ties are defined by frequent and reciprocal contacts for a number of different reasons (e.g. sports, friendship, shopping, child care, etc.) as we typically find them

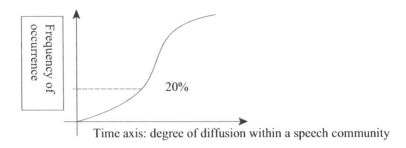

Figure 23.2 S-curve

in communities where everybody knows everybody else. Weak ties are based only on one reason, they are not necessarily reciprocal and they are more frequent because they can be established more easily. The diffusion of linguistic innovations crucially depends on weak ties. It proceeds along the following five stages (pp. 188–91):

1. Individuals of central importance in strong local networks (influentials) are sceptical towards innovations when they first come across them.
2. Networks with weak ties can be established more easily and they are much more frequent than networks with strong ties.
3. As soon as there are enough actors with weak ties who can act as liaisons and who have accepted a given innovation (early adopters) that innovation gets diffused within networks of weak ties.
4. Only after a change has spread through a large enough number of weak networks will it be taken up by local influentials who will integrate it into their strong network structures to keep their position within these structures.
5. Thus, the existence of networks with weak ties is a precondition for an innovation to be adopted throughout a language community as a whole.

23.3.2.2 Leaders of linguistic change

In William Labov's view, properties of social networks are necessary but not sufficient for understanding the diffusion of linguistic change. For a deeper understanding of the social aspects of change it is necessary to look at those actors who actually lead it. Thus, '[t]he social networks effects are not the largest, but they add essential information to the description of the leaders of linguistic change' (Labov 2001: 341). In his study of linguistic change and variation in the city of Philadelphia, he shows very convincingly that women have a different style of social interaction from men and that it is the style of the former which favours the spreading of linguistic change.

The relevance of analysing individuals saliently involved in the diffusion of change is undeniable and there can be no doubt that Labov's model is derived from a very sound and thorough case study. The question is whether his model can be claimed to be of universal value or whether one has to reckon with culturally-based differences.

23.3.2.3 The invisible-hand model

The metaphor of the invisible hand as it was first used by Adam Smith in economics tries to describe social structures and phenomena that are produced by humans who did not intend their emergence by their individual actions. More specifically, the invisible-hand model addresses the problem that the actions of a large enough number of individuals following at least partially similar purposes on a microlevel yield causal consequences at a macrolevel which cannot be predicted from the knowledge of the purpose operating on the microlevel. Keller (1994) adopts the invisible-hand model for linguistics by defining linguistic structures as products of invisible-hand processes. A linguistic structure is the macrolevel result of a large enough number of speakers whose individual acts of speaking follow certain types of maxims of language use at the microlevel. Keller distinguishes two types of maxims. Static maxims ((10) and (11)) guarantee the structural stability of the language, while dynamic maxims (12) are responsible for linguistic change:[3]

(10) Static maxim: Keller's (1994) phatic maxim:
    a. Talk like others talk.
    b. Talk in such a way that you are not misunderstood.

(11) Static maxim: Strategy of adaptation:
    a. Talk in such a way that you are recognized as belonging to the group you identify with.
    b. Talk in such a way that you do not attract attention.

(12) Some dynamic maxims:
    a. Talk in such a way that you are noticed.
    b. Talk in such a way that you are not recognized as a group member.
    c. Talk in an amusing, witty or facetious way.

Keller's (1994) invisible-hand model and the previous two models are not fully independent. The density of network structures can well be seen as the product of communicative actions of individuals and with their purposes. The impact of leaders of linguistic change on their environment would be impossible without a large enough number of individuals who want to be identified as belonging to that environment. This behaviour follows the maxim in (11a).

23.3.3 Language contact and structural convergence

Language contact is a very important factor of language change. This section will introduce potential mechanisms that take influence on structural change (§23.3.3.1) and different effects of language contact that reach from its impact on individuals up to large-scale geographical patterns of diffusion and the emergence of new languages (§§23.3.3.2–23.3.3.6).

23.3.3.1 Mechanisms

Contact-induced structural convergence depends on many rather different mechanisms. Thomason (2001: 128–56) discusses seven of them. The following three of them will be presented in this section: code-switching, bilingualism, second language acquisition.[4]

Code-switching is a phenomenon of multilingualism that has been subject to different definitions. A comparatively neutral definition is the following by Thomason (2001: 132): 'Code switching is the use of material from two (or more) languages by a single speaker in the same conversation'. A good illustration of how code-switching works is the title of Poplack's (1980) scene-setting paper *Sometimes I'll start a sentence in Spanish Y TERMINO*

EN ESPAÑOL. Even though code-switching is a well-studied phenomenon it certainly does not apply universally in situations of contact-induced change. This can be seen from the fact that in many bilingual speech communities code-switching does not happen.

Bilinguals apply certain strategies to acquire two languages as their first languages (L1 languages) simultaneously. The work of Silva-Corvalán (1994) on English/Spanish bilinguals in Los Angeles shows some typical effects. Her main hypothesis is 'that, in language contact situations, bilinguals develop strategies aimed at lightening the cognitive load of having to remember and use two different linguistic systems' (Silva-Corvalán 1994: 6). This leads to effects like simplification of grammatical categories and lexical oppositions, overgeneralization of forms (often with concomitant regularization patterns) and the development of periphrastic patterns out of semantically less transparent, morphologically bound forms (ibid.).

Second language acquisition (L2 acquisition, cf. Chapter 21) has important consequences for language change if for whatever social reasons L2 speakers take on a role in the dissemination of linguistic structures. From the perspective of UG, learners lose their ability to acquire full competence of a language after a critical age (post-threshold learners). Even though a lot of the details on the critical age and the processes involved are debated controversially it is quite clear that there are structural differences between a language spoken by L1 and L2 speakers.

23.3.3.2 Maintenance/borrowing vs shift

Maintenance/borrowing and shift are two basic types of contact-induced change in the approach of Thomason and Kaufmann (1988) and Thomason (2001). These two types depend on different social situations and they yield partially different structural results. In a situation of borrowing/maintenance, speakers of language A maintain their language but they integrate elements from another language B, the target language. In a shift situation, speakers of language A abandon their language in favour of B. The factors that are relevant for the outcome of these changes are the percentages of L1 and L2 speakers and their availability in a speech community as well as factors that determine the intensity of contact (duration, population size, socio-economic dominance). As for the structural consequences of these two types of contact-induced change, borrowing/maintenance crucially starts out from the lexicon, while shift is initiated at the levels of phonology and syntax. In situations of extreme contact, the effects converge, i.e. we find extensive lexical and structural change in both types.

23.3.3.3 Linguistic areas (*Sprachbünde*)

Generally speaking, linguistic areas are characterized by structural similarities across a set of geographically adjacent languages which are not due to genetic relatedness. The concept was coined by Trubetzkoy in 1928 (published in Trubetzkoy 1930) and has experienced a lot of different and often divergent definitions since that time. The following definition by Thomason (2001) is relatively neutral and covers various other definitions: 'A linguistic area is a geographical region containing a group of three or more languages that share some structural features as a result of contact rather than as a result of accident or inheritance from a common ancestor' (p. 99). Frequently discussed linguistic areas are the Balkan *Sprachbund*, the Circum-Baltic area, the Ethiopian area, South Asia and East and mainland South-East Asia.

23.3.3.4 Mixed languages

The phenomenon of mixed languages has been introduced by Bakker and Mous (1994). It is broadly defined as 'a bilingual mixture, with split ancestry' (Matras and Bakker 2003: 1). Split ancestry can show up in various forms. In the case of Media Lengua (Ecuador), the lexicon is from Spanish and the grammar from Quechua. Thus, the lexical items that are printed in italics in (13) are Spanish, while the elements printed in bold are grammatical markers from Quechua. Word order is SOV as in Quechua.

(13)   Media Lengua, Ecuador (Matras and Bakker 2003: 6):

   Isi-**ga**   *asi*   *nustru* *barrio*-**ga**   *asi*   *kostumbri*-**n**   *abla*-**na**.
   This-TOP   thus   our   community-TOP   thus   accustomed-3   talk-NML

'In our community we are accustomed to talking this way.'

Mixed languages 'arise either in communities with mixed households accompanying the formation of new ethnic identities, or through rapid acculturation leading to the adoption of a hybrid group identity, or through continuous socioethnic separateness resisting pressure to assimilate' (Matras and Bakker 2003: 14).

23.3.3.5 Emergence of new languages: pidgin and creole languages

Pidgins are the result of extreme social conditions of contact among speakers of three or more languages who share no common ground for mutual communication. Depending on the intensity and duration of contact, one can understand different degrees of development. At the lowest end, we find the jargon which is characterized by ad hoc rules based on the different L1 of the speakers involved. More intensive contact generates stable pidgins with their own grammatical rules, which can further develop into expanded pidgins with more elaborate lexicons and grammars (Mühlhäusler 1986). In the classical definition, pidgins are nobody's mother tongue, while creoles have become mother tongues of a speech community (nativism). Many publications argue that the criterion of becoming a mother tongue is overestimated, for instance if one wants to describe potential structural differences between pidgins and creoles. One of them is Bakker (2008: 130), in whose view 'the circumstance of languages becoming default languages of daily communication' shows 'much stronger effects'. For that reason, he defines an intermediate stage between pidgin and creole, which he calls 'pidgincreole' – a language 'which is the primary language of a speech community, or which has become the native language for only some of its speakers' (p. 139).

Creoles are often described as having specific structures that distinguish them from other languages (cf. §23.3.3.6). Another question that produced quite a few models of explanation is how creole structures came about. Probably the most well-known and most controversially discussed model is Bickerton's (1981) Language Bioprogram Hypothesis, which is based on UG and the idea that children in extreme contact situations as we find them in jargons do not get uniform linguistic input and thus have recourse to their innate bioprogram. As a consequence, creoles arise abruptly within a single generation. One criticism against this model is that children lack the social status for being linguistic innovators and that the number of children was small in many colonies, at least in the initial phases of settlement. In more recent studies, creole development takes more than one generation and its result is not exclusively determined by the bioprogram. A good example is Roberts (2000), who integrates very detailed population statistics drawn from sources like old school records and registers of immigration offices. She argues that the development of Hawaiian Creole English, one of Bickerton's (1981) model languages, is split into two separate processes, i.e. creolization and nativization. In such a model, other effects of language change like L2 acquisition interact with L1 acquisition and the bioprogram.

Other critical approaches look at how much can be explained without taking recourse to an innate bioprogram. McWhorter (1997: 145) opts for 'a model of the process of creole genesis which incorporates a number of processes in an empirically constrained fashion, including substrate transfer, structural simplification, and internal diachronic change, as well as a small role of Bickertonian universals'. From an ecological perspective (Mufwene 2001), the bioprogram is irrelevant. In this context, Chaudenson's (2003) work on the French-based creoles is of particular interest. In his scenario, creole structures are the result of successive approximations of superstrate structures (French) to the substrate structures of the slave populations. At a first stage, a small number of slaves was in intimate contact with francophone speakers. New slave immigrants learnt their creole variety from the first generations of slaves and passed on their language to yet a new wave of immigrants.

23.3.3.6 Language contact and complexity

The correlation between complexity and specific sociolinguistic contact situations is discussed from various perspectives. Trudgill (2011) studies it from the perspective of the L1 and L2 learners involved in contact situations. Other studies like the ones on creole languages take a more general typological perspective.

Trudgill (2011) is interested in processes of simplification and complexification and their sociolinguistic motivation in terms of language contact. The features by which he defines simplification vs complexification are the following.

(14)   *Simplification*   *Complexification*
- a. Regularization of irregularities — Irregularization
- b. Increase in morphological transparency — Increase in opacity
- c. Reduction in syntagmatic redundancy (loss of grammatical agreement) — Increase in syntagmatic redundancy (development of agreement)
- d. Loss of morphological categories — Addition of morphological categories

In Trudgill's (2011) view, complexity and its development in contact crucially depends on the difference between L1 and L2 acquisition: 'Post-threshold learners have less difficulty in coping with regularity and transparency than irregularity and opacity; and loss of redundancy reduces the burden for learner speakers' (p. 41). He distinguishes three different scenarios with specific distributions of L1 versus L2 learners. Languages spoken in situations of short-term adult contact are characterized by simplification as a typical phenomenon of L2 acquisition after the post-critical threshold (§23.3.3.1). Creoles typically belong to this type of contact situation. Situations of long-term co-territorial contact with many multilingual L1 speakers add to complexity 'as the result of transferring features from one language to another' (p. 27). This type of structure is frequently met in linguistic areas (§23.3.3.3). Finally, low-contact communities are the places in which complexity is not only preserved but also increased. A good example is the development of two definite articles in Frisian, one referring to proximal unique referents, the other to distal non-unique referents (p. 76).

In creole linguistics, complexity is vividly debated since McWhorter's (2001) target paper in *Linguistic Typology*. His basic argument is that the structural properties of creoles are due to their origin from pidgins. Speakers of pidgins tend to avoid any grammatical structures beyond those which are absolutely necessary for communication. Since pidgins form the input to creole development, creoles themselves are characterized by a high degree of simplicity and they did not have enough time in the short period of their existence to accumulate more complex structures as one finds them in older natural languages. More recently, McWhorter (2011) has shifted his focus from this rather controversially discussed hypothesis to the hypothesis that creoles share certain prototypical properties by which it is possible to recognize a creole without even knowing its sociolinguistic history. This new focus is confirmed by the typological study of Bakker *et al.* (2011), which concludes that creoles differ structurally from non-creoles but not necessarily with regard to complexity.

23.4 Closing remarks

Linguistic change is the result of interactions between language internal and language external processes, both of them characterized by a large number of different factors that may operate in specific combinations in individual instances of change. The present chapter has tried to offer a survey of these factors and some examples of how some of them interact. A comprehensive account of different interaction patterns would not only be beyond an introductory chapter like this one, it would also be beyond what can be said today.

In spite of this, assessing effects of linguistic change is extremely important for research on linguistic universals. If universals reflect language internal motivations like human cognition or basic communicative needs, it is imperative to disentangle language internal from sociocultural language external factors in the linguistic data. For that reason, linguistic typology has developed an elaborate methodology of language sampling (cf. Chapter 25). More recent statistical methods based on evolutionary biology look at linguistic change more directly by calculating the probability with which a language changes from one type to another (e.g. the change from OV to VO word order). This new focus bears the potential of moving typology away from the mere detection of statistical correlations by comparing frequencies of types to actual evidence for a true causal linkage between them across time. If it works, this dynamic approach will offer evidence of how potential universals actually operate in processes of language change and thus channel the evolution of language structures. This is not an easy task and it crucially depends on a sound method of how to empirically estimate transition probabilities. A good survey on the state of the art is given in *Linguistic Typology* 15 (2011).

This new statistical approach to linguistic typology is very welcome and has the potential to offer new insights. Its success will depend to a considerable extent on the integration of the factors and mechanisms described in this chapter with the statistical methods from evolutionary biology. If this stage is reached there will certainly also be repercussions on models of linguistic change.

Notes

1 Metaphors are frequently understood as semantic in nature. In Hopper and Traugott's (2003: 84) view, metaphors are not based on truth conditions but rather on communicative use.

2 Of course, the parallel existence of the syntactically productive construction of green house 'a house that is green' is not excluded.
3 Notice that individual maxims can have contradictory effects.
4 The other four are code alternation, passive familiarity, negotiation and deliberate decision. Since they are discussed less frequently in the literature on linguistic change, they are not presented in this section.

Further reading

Croft (2000); Hopper and Traugott (2003); Narrog and Heine (2011); Thomason (2001); Trudgill (2011); Winford (2003).

References

Bakker, P. (2008) Pidgins versus Creoles and Pidgincreoles. In S. Kouwenberg and J.V. Singler (eds) *The Handbook of Pidgin and Creole Studies*, pp. 130–57. Oxford: Wiley-Blackwell.
Bakker, P. and M. Mous (eds) (1994) *Mixed Languages. 15 Case Studies in Language Intertwining*. Amsterdam: Institute for Functional Research into Language and Language Use.
Bakker, P., A. Daval-Markussen, M. Parkvall and I. Plag (2011) Creoles are typologically distinct from non-creoles. *Journal of Pidgin and Creole Languages* 26: 5–42.
Bickerton, D. (1981) *Roots of Language*. Ann Arbor: Karoma.
Bisang, W. (2004) Dialectology and typology: An integrative perspective. In B. Kortmann (ed.) *Dialectology Meets Typology: Dialect Grammar from a Cross-Linguistic Perspective*, pp. 11–45. Berlin: Mouton de Gruyter.
Bisang, W. (2008) Grammaticalization and the areal factor: The perspective of East and mainland Southeast Asian languages. In M.J. López-Couso and E. Seoane (eds) *Rethinking Grammaticalization: New Perspectives*, pp. 15–35. Amsterdam: John Benjamins.
Bisang, W. (2011) Grammaticalization and typology. In H. Narrog and B. Heine (eds) *Handbook of Grammaticalization*, pp. 105–17. Oxford: Oxford University Press.
Boye, K. and P. Harder (2012) A usage-based theory of grammatical status and grammaticalization. *Language* 88: 1–44.
Bybee, J., R. Perkins and W. Pagliuca (1994) *The Evolution of Grammar. Tense, Aspect and Modality in the Languages of the World*. Chicago/London: The University of Chicago Press.
Chaudenson, R. (2003) *La créolisation: théorie, applications, implications*. Paris: L'Harmattan.
Croft, W.A. (2000) *Explaining Language Change: An Evolutionary Approach*. London: Longman.
Fischer, O. (2007) *Morphosyntactic Change: Functional and Formal Perspectives*. Oxford: Oxford University Press.
Gisborne, N. and A. Patten (2011) Construction grammar and grammaticalization. In H. Narrog and B. Heine (eds) *The Oxford Handbook of Grammaticalization*, pp. 92–104. Oxford: Oxford University Press.
Givón, T. (1971) Historical syntax and synchronic morphology. *Chicago Linguistics Society Proceedings* 7: 394–415.
Givón, T. (1979) *On Understanding Grammar*. New York: Academic Press.
Goldberg, A. (2006) *Constructions at Work: The Nature of Generalization in Language*. Oxford: Oxford University Press.
Haiman, J. (1983) Iconic and economic motivation. *Language* 59: 781–819.
Haspelmath, M. (1998) Does grammaticalization need reanalysis? *Studies in Language* 22: 315–51.
Heine, B. and T. Kuteva (2002) *World Lexicon of Grammaticalization*. Cambridge: Cambridge University Press.
Heine, B., U. Claudi and F. Hünnemeyer (1991) *Grammaticalization: A Conceptual Framework*. Chicago/London: The University of Chicago Press.

Himmelmann, N.P. (2004) Lexicalization and grammaticalization. In W. Bisang, N.P. Himmelmann and B. Wiemer (eds) *What Makes Grammaticalization? A Look from its Fringes and its Components*, pp. 21–42. Berlin: Mouton de Gruyter.

Hopper, P.J. and E.C. Traugott (2003) *Grammaticalization*, 2nd edition. Cambridge: Cambridge University Press.

Keller, R. (1994) *On Language Change: The Invisible Hand in Language*. London: Routledge.

Kuryłowicz, J. (1965) The evolution of grammatical categories. *Diogenes*: 55–71. Reprinted 1975: *Esquisses linguistiques II*, pp. 38–54. Munich: Fink.

Labov, W. (2001) *Principles of Linguistic Change. Social Factors*. Oxford: Blackwell.

Lehmann, C. (1995 [1982]) *Thoughts on Grammaticalization*. Munich: LINCOM.

Lightfoot, D. (1999) *The Development of Language Acquisition, Change and Evolution*. Oxford: Blackwell.

Matras, Y. and P. Bakker (2003) The study of mixed languages. In Y. Matras and P. Bakker (eds) *The Mixed Language Debate. Theoretical and Empirical Advances*, pp. 1–20. Berlin: Mouton de Gruyter.

McWhorter, J.H. (1997) *Towards a New Model of Creole Genesis*. New York: Peter Lang.

McWhorter, J.H. (2001) The world's simplest grammars are creole grammars. *Linguistic Typology* 5: 125–66.

McWhorter, J.H. (2011) The creole prototype revisited and revised. In J.H. McWhorter (ed.) *Linguistic Simplicity and Complexity: Why Do Languages Undress?* Berlin: Mouton de Gruyter.

Meillet, A. (1912) L'évolution des formes grammaticales. *Scientia (Rivista di Scienza)* 12/26: 384–400.

Milroy, J. (1992) *Linguistic Variation and Change*. Oxford: Blackwell.

Mufwene, S. (2001) *The Ecology of Language Evolution*. Cambridge: Cambridge University Press.

Mühlhäusler, P. (1986) *Pidgin and Creole Linguistics*. Oxford: Blackwell.

Narrog, H. and B. Heine (eds) (2011) *The Oxford Handbook of Grammaticalization*. Oxford: Oxford University Press.

Newmeyer, F.J. (1998) *Language Form and Language Function*. Cambridge: MIT Press.

Newmeyer, F.J. (2001) Deconstructing grammaticalization. *Language Sciences* 23: 187–230.

Norde, M. (2009) *Degrammaticalization*. Oxford: Oxford University Press.

Poplack, S. (1980) Sometimes I'll start a sentence in Spanish Y TERMINO EN ESPAÑOL: Toward a typology of code-switching. *Linguistics* 18: 581–618.

Roberts, I. and A. Roussou (2003) *Syntactic Change: A Minimalist Approach to Grammaticalization*. Cambridge: Cambridge University Press.

Roberts, S. (2000) Nativization and the genesis of Hawaiian Creole. In J.H. McWhorter (ed.) *Language Change and Language Contact in Pidgins and Creoles*, pp. 247–300. Amsterdam: Benjamins.

Silva-Corvalán, C. (1994) *Language Contact and Change: Spanish in Los Angeles*. Oxford: Clarendon Press.

Thomason, S.G. (2001) *Language Contact: An Introduction*. Edinburgh: Edinburgh University Press.

Thomason, S.G. and T. Kaufman (1988) *Language Contact, Creolization, and Genetic Linguistics*. Berkeley: University of California Press.

Traugott, E.C. (2002) From etymology to historical pragmatics. In D. Minkova and R. Stockwell (eds) *Studying the History of the English Language: Millennial Perspectives*, pp. 19–49. Berlin: Mouton de Gruyter.

Traugott, E.C. (2010) (Inter)subjectivity and (inter)subjectification: A reassessment. In H. Cuyckens, K. Davidse and L. Vandelanotte (eds) *Subjectification, Intersubjectification and Grammaticalization*, pp. 29–69. Berlin: Mouton de Gruyter.

Traugott, E.C. (2011). Grammaticalization and mechanisms of change. In H. Narrog and B. Heine (eds) *The Oxford Handbook of Grammaticalization*, pp. 19–30. Oxford: Oxford University Press.

Trubetzkoy, N.S. (1928/1930) *Proposition 16. Actes du premier congrès international de linguistes à la Haye, du 10–15 avril 1928*, pp. 17–18. Leiden: A.W. Sijthoff.

Trudgill, P. (2011) *Sociolinguistic Typology. Social Determinants of Linguistic Complexity*. Oxford: Oxford University Press.
Wang, W.S.-Y. and C.-C. Cheng (1970) Implementation of phonological change: The Shuang-feng Chinese case. *Chicago Linguistics Society* 6: 552–9.
Winford, D. (2003) *An Introduction to Contact Linguistics*. Oxford: Blackwell.

24
Language endangerment

Simon Musgrave

24.1 Introduction

Language endangerment has only become a concern of linguists relatively recently. A handful of important articles were published before 1975 (Swadesh 1948; Fishman 1964; Haas 1968; Miller 1971) but they were unusual. In 1977 the *International Journal of the Sociology of Language* published a volume dedicated to language death which included articles by several scholars who would be central in the development of research in the field such as Nancy Dorian and Jane Hill (Dorian 1977; Hill and Hill 1977). Two important monographs appeared shortly after this (Dorian 1981; Gal 1979) which both raised theoretical issues in the context of a particular linguistic situation (a Scots Gaelic variety for Dorian and the shift from Hungarian to German in part of Austria for Gal). The following decade saw important new research continue to appear (e.g. Dorian 1989), but 1992 is the year which sees the start of a large increase in the amount of attention given to the topic.

In 1991, Ken Hale organised a symposium on endangered languages for the Linguistics Society of America (LSA). This led to the publication of a group of essays in *Language* (Hale 1992) and to the formation of the LSA's Committee for Endangered Languages and Their Preservation.[1] The prominence of these activities brought the issues to the forefront for the linguistic community, and numerous publications have followed. These include a handbook and atlas (Austin and Sallabank 2011; Moseley 2010 [Wurm 2001 and Moseley are successive editions of the same work]), volumes devoted to examining language endangerment in different parts of the world, collections of articles looking at various issues or aspects of the problem (e.g. Brenzinger 2007), monographs directed mainly at a scholarly audience (e.g. Sallabank 2013), and books by linguists which are directed to a more general audience (e.g. Evans 2009) as well as books by non-specialists (e.g. Abley 2004).[2]

In addition to this intense research interest from linguists, there has been a growing body of interdisciplinary research. Such work includes applications of models from conservation biology to language (Sutherland 2003; Amano *et al.* 2014), comparisons of linguistic diversity and biological diversity (Gorenflo *et al.* 2012), and the use of models from both physical geography (Gavin and Sibanda 2012) and human geography (Minett and Wang 2008).

Several major initiatives which made large amounts of money available for work on endangered languages also began in this period. These include the project Dokumentation Bedrohte Sprache (DoBeS) with funds from the Volkswagen Stiftung (from 2000),[3] the Hans Rausing Endangered Languages Project (from 2002)[4] and the joint National Science Foundation and National Endowment for the Humanities programme Documenting Endangered Languages (initially from 2004, as a permanent programme from 2007).[5] The focus of these programmes is wholly or partially on documentation of endangered languages, a point to which we return in §24.5.

The amount of activity relating to language endangerment in the last twenty years indicates a strong consensus that there is a significant problem which needs to be addressed. Estimates of the scale of the problem vary, however. Some of the variation may be attributed to disagreements about the best way to assess the extent to which any language is endangered (or, to take a more positive view, to estimate the vitality of a language). We turn to these questions in the following sections, before considering the nature of responses to the situation.

24.2 The extent of the problem

One of the essays in Hale's *Language* contribution (1992) is by Michael Krauss and it sets out a numerical case for the gravity of the problem of language endangerment. He bases this on the simplest measure of the viability of a language, the number of speakers. Krauss suggests that a language must have more than 100,000 speakers to be 'Safe', that is, to be likely to be spoken for at least the next 100 years. On the basis of the figures then available from *Ethnologue* (Lewis *et al.* 2014 is the current edition), Krauss shows this to mean 600 Safe languages from a global list of more than 6,000 languages which in turn implies an extinction rate of 90 per cent in the current century.

Aside from questions about whether speaker numbers are the best measure to consider (to which we shall return), the method by which this estimate is derived is certainly open to criticism. Many of the numbers used must be treated with caution: the number of languages given by *Ethnologue* is as good an estimate as we have, but the knowledge it represents varies by region and also depends on decisions about what to treat as separate languages and what to treat as dialects. The decision to take 100,000 speakers as a cut-off point is arbitrary (and any other figure would be also), but there are reasons to think that it is too high. Languages have been reported to be surviving well with small speaker numbers, both in what are claimed to be essentially monolingual situations (Pirahã, Everett 2005) and in multilingual situations (Kaki Ae, Clifton 1994).

Other scholars using other methodologies have arrived at estimates which, while still alarming, are not as horrifying as that provided by Krauss. Simons and Lewis (2013), also working with data from *Ethnologue*, but basing their estimate on assigning languages a position on the Expanded Graded Intergenerational Disruption Scale (see §24.3 below for discussion of this instrument), present a figure of 19 per cent of the world's languages which are not being learned by children (p. 14). They note, however, that there is wide variation by region with 78 per cent of languages in North America and 85 per cent of languages in Australia and New Zealand not being learned by children or already extinct. Krauss had already drawn attention to the different rates of language endangerment in different geographical areas. Campbell *et al.* (2013), using the Catalogue of Endangered Languages,[6] arrive at a figure of 46 per cent of the world's languages which can be considered as endangered. Harmon and Loh (2010) use an Index of Linguistic Diversity to estimate changes in linguistic diversity over the period between 1970 and 2005. Based on a sample of 1,500 languages, Harmon and Loh find that overall linguistic diversity declined by 20 per cent in that period with indigenous languages declining by 21 per cent. Again regional variation is considerable, with a decline of over 60 per cent for the Americas and 30 per cent for the Pacific including Australia. Amano *et al.* (2014) apply criteria accepted in the study of biological diversity: restricted geographical range, small population size and rapid decline in population. On this basis, they estimate that 25 per cent of the world's languages are threatened, but again regional variation is highlighted – with the Himalayas, north-western North America and the tropics identified as areas with higher levels of endangerment.

The results discussed in the previous paragraph suggest that Krauss' 1992 figure of 90 per cent of languages being endangered was an overstatement resulting from a methodology which was too simple. However, accepting a lower figure does not mean denying that there is a serious problem. It is important to place the numbers in a wider context: the conservative estimate of Sutherland (2003) has 31.7 per cent of languages (based on the estimate of 6,809 extant languages) as vulnerable or worse and notes that '[e]ven with this conservative comparison it is clear that the risks to languages exceed those to birds and mammals' (p. 277).

24.3 Assessing the vitality of languages

The previous section discussed various estimates of the state of the languages of the world which are largely based on quantitative measures such as speaker populations. Such measures can provide an overview of the global situation, but they are less useful when we wish to assess the status of an individual language or to compare the state of several languages. Different scholars have arrived at different vocabularies for describing the vitality of languages, and their methodologies vary in details, but there is a consensus about the factors which are most important in making such assessments. The two which are part of almost every means of assessing vitality are intergenerational transmission and domains of use. Wurm (2001: 14) suggests that a language is endangered when it is 'no longer learned by children, or at least by a large part of the children of that community (say at least 30 per cent)', and Steinhauer (forthcoming: 1) takes a similar position: 'a language … is probably irreversibly endangered when the original language is no longer passed on to new generations'. Himmelmann (forthcoming) emphasises the other factor, taking as an 'essential symptom for the vitality of a language the number and quality of domains in which it is used' and proposes as a definition of endangerment: 'languages whose usage domains are presently undergoing a rapid reduction'. Although it is not mentioned as symptomatic of language endangerment, we will see below that in assessing the status of languages reference is often also made to the extent to which information about the language has been collected.

Even if there is some agreement about the methods used in assessing linguistic vitality, the terminology used to present results is not consistent and it is not always obvious how different schemes can be aligned with one another. For example, Krauss in his 1992 essay (see Hale) spoke of languages as being 'safe', 'moribund' and 'extinct'. Dixon (2011 [1980]) surveys the languages of Australia and classifies them as 'extinct', 'on the path to extinction', and 'relatively healthy'. This can be compared with Krauss' categories easily, and the comparison can be extended to include McConvell's categorisation of Australian languages as 'strong', 'endangered', and no longer spoken or 'sleeping' (McConvell 2005: 24). But other categorisations make more distinctions. Kinkade (1991) classifies languages into five groups: (1) already extinct, (2) near extinction, (3) endangered, (4) viable but with a small population base, and (5) viable; UNESCO recognises four levels of endangerment (Vulnerable, Definitely endangered, Severely endangered, Critically endangered) as well as an Extinct category and (at least by implication) an 'Other' category (Moseley 2010); the Graded Intergenerational Disruption Scale (GIDS, Fishman 1991) has eight levels and the extended version of this used by *Ethnologue* has eleven – or thirteen if two divisions within levels are counted separately (EGIDS; both GIDS and EGIDS are discussed in more detail below).

One approach is detailed in McConvell (2005) which refers to earlier work (McConvell and Thieberger 2001) that outlines the methodology and the indicators that the authors used in the State of the Environment report to try to evaluate language vitality. In their introduction McConvell and Thieberger point out that their goal is to provide a baseline of data against which subsequent surveys could be compared. They assert that 'for the first time indicators have been rigorously defined and systematically applied to the data' (2001: 2). Indicators are:

> elements which can be measured relatively easily and cost-effectively, which do not give a complete picture of the state of a certain resource, but which indicate relatively reliably the overall condition of the resource and trends in its condition over time.
>
> (ibid.)

The five-level ranking of four indicators used by McConvell and Thieberger is given in Table 24.1. The table is not intended to imply that a language will be ranked at the same level for each indicator; the arrangement in rows is a convenience for presentation. A group of experts has developed another methodology on behalf of UNESCO (UNESCO Ad Hoc Expert Group on Endangered Languages 2003).

This method uses six factors to assess linguistic vitality and state of endangerment, two factors to assess language attitudes, and one factor to evaluate the urgency of documentation, and these are presented in Table 24.2. The document describing this method emphasises that it should be applied as a whole:

> *No single factor alone can be used to assess a language's vitality or its need for documentation.* Language communities are complex and diverse; even assessing the number of actual speakers of a language is difficult. … Taken together, these nine factors are especially useful for characterizing a language's overall sociolinguistic situation.
>
> (UNESCO 2003: 7)

One of the UNESCO factors, the proportion of the speakers of the language within the total population, is clearly important but is rarely assessed in other methodologies.

The EGIDS is currently significant as the latest edition of *Ethnologue* (Lewis *et al.* 2014) gives an estimated value on this scale for every language based on the estimate of the proportion of language reportedly not being transmitted to children (Simons and Lewis 2013). There is a possibility that this measure is too conservative, because as part of their methodology, Simons and Lewis used level 6a (Vigorous) as a default value. An initial automated process assigned almost 3,100 languages to level 6a; a review reduced this number to just over 2,500. Simons and Lewis defend these default estimates by reference to Fishman's claim that 'the lion's share' of the world's languages are at GIDS 6 (Fishman 1991: 92).

Table 24.1 Indicators used by McConvell and Thieberger (2001)

	Ranking of Language	Number of Speakers	**Vocabulary**: lexical information secured to date	**Structure**: information on language structure secured to date
1	Extinct	under 2	some vocabulary	some information is available
2	Some, usually very old, individuals remember a little of the language, usually vocabulary	3–5	approximately 500 items	a fair amount of information is available on main structural features
3	A few, mostly very old, individuals can speak the language more or less fluently	5–10	500 – 1,000 items	good information is available on main structural features, with additional information on subsidiary features
4	The language is still spoken but no longer in full tribal use	10–50	over 1,000 items	good information is available both on main and subsidiary structural features
5	The language is still in full tribal use	over 50	lexical information is satisfactory by modern linguistic standards	information on structure is satisfactory by modern linguistic standards

Table 24.2 Factors used by UNESCO in assessing language vitality

(a)	Linguistic vitality and state of endangerment	(b)	Language attitudes	(c)	Type and quality of documentation
i.	Intergenerational language transmission	i.	Government and institutional language attitudes and policies, including official status and use		
ii.	Absolute number of speakers				
iii.	Proportion of speakers within total population				
iv.	Trends in existing language domains	ii.	Community members' attitudes towards their own language		
v.	Response to new domains and media				
vi.	Materials for language education and literacy				

Joshua Fishman presented what he described as 'a graded typology of threatened statuses', the Graded Intergenerational Disruption Scale (Fishman 1991: 87–109). The title of this scale is perhaps a little misleading; as can be seen in Table 24.3, stages 6 to 8 on the scale do focus on intergenerational transmission (or its absence), but the greater part of the scale (stages 1 to 5) is more concerned with domains of use.

Table 24.3 Fishman's GIDS

Stage	Characteristics
Stage 8	Most vestigial users of Xish[1] are socially isolated old folks and Xish needs to be re-assembled from their mouths and memories and taught to demographically unconcentrated adults
Stage 7	Most users of Xish are a socially integrated and ethnolinguistically active population but they are beyond child-bearing age
Stage 6	The attainment of intergenerational informal oralcy and its demographic concentration and institutional reinforcement
Stage 5	Xish literacy in home, school and community, but without taking on extra-communal reinforcement of such literacy
Stage 4	Xish in lower education (types a and b) that meets the requirements of compulsory education laws
Stage 3	Use of Xish in the lower work sphere (outside of the Xish neighbourhood/community) involving interaction between Xmen and Ymen
Stage 2	Xish in lower governmental services and mass media but not in the higher spheres of either
Stage 1	Some use of Xish in higher level educational, occupational, governmental and media efforts (but without the additional safety provided by political independence)

Note: Xish is any language, Xmen are speakers of that language, Ymen are speakers of another language.

Recently, Lewis and Simons (2010) have presented an expanded version of the GIDS which is intended to include both the greater elaboration of the safe end of GIDS and the greater detail concerning endangerment given in the UNESCO scheme (Table 24.4).

Table 24.4 Expanded Graded Intergenerational Disruption Scale

Level	Label	Description
0	International	The language is widely used between nations in trade, knowledge exchange and international policy.
1	National	The language is used in education, work, mass media and government at the national level.
2	Provincial	The language is used in education, work, mass media and government within major administrative subdivisions of a nation.
3	Wider Communication	The language is used in work and mass media without official status to transcend language differences across a region.
4	Educational	The language is in vigorous use, with standardisation and literature being sustained through a widespread system of institutionally supported education.
5	Developing	The language is in vigorous use, with literature in a standardised form being used by some though this is not yet widespread or sustainable.
6a	Vigorous	The language is used for face-to-face communication by all generations and the situation is sustainable.
6b	Threatened	The language is used for face-to-face communication within all generations, but it is losing users.

Level	Label	Description
7	Shifting	The child-bearing generation can use the language among themselves, but it is not being transmitted to children.
8a	Moribund	The only remaining active users of the language are members of the grandparent generation and older.
8b	Nearly Extinct	The only remaining users of the language are members of the grandparent generation or older who have little opportunity to use the language.
9	Dormant	The language serves as a reminder of heritage identity for an ethnic community, but no one has more than symbolic proficiency.
10	Extinct	The language is no longer used and no one retains a sense of ethnic identity associated with the language.

24.4 Types of linguistic diversity

The title of this chapter is 'Language Endangerment', and the discussion of the preceding sections has focused on issues such as the proportion of *languages* which are threatened and how the status of *languages* might be assessed. There is an underlying assumption here that it is the level of the language which is the appropriate level at which to consider questions about threats to the world's linguistic diversity. In this section, this assumption will be questioned, and some alternative views canvassed as to what aspects of linguistic diversity should be of concern.

First, there are the well-known and long-standing problems of differentiating between languages and dialects. There are well-known cases where varieties are treated as distinct languages although linguistic criteria would not support the separation – such as the national languages of Indonesia and Malaysia, *Bahasa Indonesia* and *Bahasa Malaysia*, or the mainland Scandinavian languages. Equally, there are certainly cases where varieties which could or should be treated as distinct languages are not so recognised by *Ethnologue*. The information in *Ethnologue* corresponds to the list of languages assigned individual codes in ISO639-3;[7] the registration authority for ISO639-3 and the publisher of *Ethnologue* being the same organisation (SIL International) and there is a process by which the list can be changed to reflect developing understanding of the relationships between varieties.[8] As noted above, the way decisions are made about this distinction influences the figures which are used to estimate threats to linguistic diversity. Given that the cases where distinctions are poorly motivated linguistically involve nations and national languages and the cases where distinctions are not being made are more likely due to lack of information about varieties spoken by small groups often in remote locations, it seems reasonable to suggest that unrecognised distinctions probably outnumber unnecessary splits and that therefore the data source upon which most experts have relied probably underestimates linguistic diversity.

The problem of differentiation also includes the problem of finding neutral terms which we can use without making any theoretical claims about the status of the linguistic entities we are talking about. Here, we use the term *variety* to cover any system of linguistic acts which can be distinguished in some way from other related systems. Another term which can be used in a similar way is *code*. And more recently, the terms *languoid* and *doculect* have been proposed (Cysouw and Good 2013) where *languoid* is any 'language-like object' and *doculect* is 'a linguistic variety as it is documented in a given resource' (p. 342). This term is intended to be applied to any variety which has been identified in the literature: a published source which claims that a variety can be distinguished identifies a doculect.

Even if an accurate delineation of languages and dialects were possible, the question would remain as to whether the loss of interlinguistic and intralinguistic variation should be of equal concern. Wolfram and Schilling-Estes (1995) make a persuasive case that the loss of variation within languages should concern linguists just as much as the loss of languages. They suggest that as we cannot draw a clean boundary between language and dialect, we should treat all equally as part of the linguistic diversity which we value. Any moves which favour diversity should benefit all varieties. In their paper, Wolfram and Schilling-Estes discuss in detail a dialect of American English, the Ocracoke Brogue, and analyse the changing role it has had in its home community on Ocracoke Island off the coast of North Carolina linking these changes to changes in the construction of Ocracoke identity which are in turn linked to social and economic changes. Such arguments can be extended to cover other types of language-internal diversity; if loss of dialect diversity is a concern, then loss of specific registers such as song languages is also.

One problem which is encountered by many linguists in their work is that, even with the best intentions, the work may lead to a reduction of language-internal diversity. A description of a language will aim to cover whatever sorts of variation exist in the community of speakers, but it is inevitable that one variety becomes the focus of the linguist's work. In some cases, the linguist will make a conscious decision in this regard; in other cases, external factors, such as the accessibility of language consultants or the fieldwork location, will impose a choice. The variety which is the focus of investigation may then come to be seen as privileged by the community: this is the variety which is recorded in a book and which is worthy of the attention of Westerners (Thieberger and Musgrave 2007; Perley 2012). In earlier times, similar effects came about due to linguistic choices by missionaries (Crowley 2001).

The argument raised by Wolfram and Schilling-Estes is equally applicable to other types of language-internal variation. For example, if we value the Ocracoke Brogue for the contribution it makes to linguistic diversity, should we not also value the system of speech styles in Javanese, which is based on clear delineation of social status? This system seems unlikely to survive in its traditional form as contact between Javanese and the national language, Bahasa Indonesia, continues (Errington 1998).

The social processes which lead to language endangerment are also processes which tend to favour standardisation. Such social changes as the move to more centralised education systems, integration into larger economic units of organisation and access to centralised media all depend on access to languages of wider communication, often standardised national languages. Thus, although we may be able in some cases to draw useful boundaries between languages and language-internal varieties, the pressures which threaten linguistic diversity apply in both cases. This in turn suggests that strategies which try to support linguistic diversity in general, rather than supporting particular varieties, may be a useful response to the current situation; we return to this point below.

One other issue relating to the value placed on different linguistic entities should be mentioned here also. Several scholars have noted that certain types of languages have received almost no attention in discussion of language endangerment, even when examples of such languages have already ceased being used or can be shown to be in imminent danger. Garrett (2006) discusses the situation with regard to contact languages (i.e. creoles and pidgins), and Nonaka (2004) discusses the case of an indigenous sign language.[9] Garrett sees lack of historicity and lack of autonomy (that is, being viewed as lesser versions of 'real' languages) as amongst the factors which lead to a low value being accorded to contact language; other factors may be relevant in the case of indigenous sign languages but the effect of marginalisation is similar. These languages are nevertheless part of linguistic diversity and, in the context of the argument that has been developed in this section, they are therefore also a part of what should concern us. Additionally, in the case of contact languages, they may play an important role in supporting the maintenance of diversity. As Mühlhäusler (2003: 242) notes:

> [S]ustained linguistic diversity in the past included a range of solutions to intergroup communication [...]. It was the ability of speakers to communicate in other languages in particular Pidgins that helped them shield their own small languages against larger neighbouring ones.

24.5 Responses to language endangerment: language documentation

The preceding sections have at least tacitly accepted the position that language endangerment is a serious problem and that it demands some response from the linguistic community and indeed more widely. Before discussing some of the ways in which such responses have developed, it must be noted that there are some who have cast doubt on the idea that a response is necessary. An example of this is provided by Ladefoged (1992) in a response to the *Language* publication of Hale and his colleagues (Hale 1992). Ladefoged invokes the idea that the current situation is not especially alarming: 'different cultures are always dying while new ones arise' (p. 810) and that intervention is therefore not warranted.[10] This view ignores the extent to which changes in economic systems and technology are impacting on the social organisation of the world in a way which is different from any previous historical period. Nation states have become the dominant political organisation of our world. This creates pressure towards linguistic homogenisation which is reinforced by changing patterns of residence; today, more than half of the world's population live in cities (UNFPA 2007). The extent of these pressures can be gauged from the extent to which a handful of languages account for a large proportion of official languages. Krauss (in Hale 1992) gives English, French, Spanish and Arabic as accounting for the official languages of 115 out of 170 states (68 per cent). The other statistic which is particularly revealing here is the difference between the mean and median number of speakers per language: according to *Ethnologue* the relevant numbers are just under 886,000 and 7,000. The massive skew in the distribution indicates the extent to which a small number of languages are coming to dominate global life.

Ladefoged's main argument is based on the notion of linguistics as an objective science, with the linguist's objectivity being lost if political positions are taken with respect to scientific issues. Regardless of our position on the objectivity of linguistics (or other types of knowledge), Dorian in her response to Ladefoged makes it clear that there is no 'neutral' position in such debates (Dorian 1993). The non-interventionist position advocated by Ladefoged is as much a political statement as any overt alignment with the goals of a linguistic community.

The response of the discipline of linguistics over the last two decades has seen the emergence of a new field within the discipline, namely language documentation, and a substantial resulting change in focus in the type of work undertaken. The idea of documentary linguistics is initially set out by Himmelmann (1998) and has been developed by him and other scholars over recent years. The serial publications *Language Documentation and Description* and *Language Documentation and Conservation* have contributed to the field; Himmelmann and colleagues produced an edited guide (Gippert *et al.* 2006), and the area has been emphasised in recent handbooks on both language endangerment (Austin and Sallabank 2011) and field methods for linguists (Thieberger 2012).

Documentary linguistics proposes that the process of collecting primary data and the process of analysing that data can and should be conceived of as separate activities (Himmelmann 1998). The task of the documentary linguist is to assemble a body of data which represents the linguistic practices of a community to as great an extent as is possible. This will be based on examples of language in use, but it may also include other material such as metalinguistic commentary. The data is intended for preservation and to be available to be used in various ways by various groups, including the speech community and its descendants, into the future. The attraction of these ideas as a response to language endangerment is obvious. Compiling a detailed description of a language is a time-consuming task (Dixon 1997: 138 estimates three years as a minimum); there are many threatened languages and for many of these few or no records exist. Concentrating on the collection of primary data therefore seems an efficient allocation of the limited resources available, both human and material. That such ideas became current at around the same time that high quality audio and video recording was becoming easily accessible and that methods for archiving and disseminating such data were also available contributed to the impetus which rapidly built and which is reflected in the funding initiatives mentioned in §24.1.

The crucial test of documentary linguistics has not yet been made. That is, no attempt has been made to base a detailed description of a language on documentation in the absence of any access to speakers of the language.[11] It should, however, be noted that the separation of activities advocated by Himmelmann is by no means as clear-cut as the initial programmatic statement suggests. In the 1998 paper, Himmelmann already acknowledges that documentary linguistics is inevitably informed by aspects of linguistic theory, and that some descriptive analysis is necessary in making data comprehensible to those coming to it without background knowledge. It is generally accepted that some grammar notes will form part of a good documentation (see Mosel 2006a on the role of a sketch grammar) and this can be observed in many data collections housed in archives such as The Language Archive.[12]

Language documentation has been criticised as not always being helpful to the cause of those working to maintain languages (Perley 2012). Perley argues that the metaphors used to talk about threatened languages ('death', 'endangerment' and 'extinction') frame actions. He is especially harsh on the idea (which he attributes to popular media), that documenting a language can be considered as 'saving the language'. Instead, Perley suggests that the results of documentation are 'artefacts of technological interventions, as well as expert valorisations of linguistic codes' (p. 133).[13] The literature on language documentation emphasises the importance of community involvement (Mosel 2006b) and this is supported to some extent by the protocols of the various funding agencies. Nevertheless, it can be argued that the overall funding model (Musgrave and Thieberger 2007) and the outputs of documentary linguistics are often more aligned with academic goals, specifically those of linguists, rather than with the desires or expectations of the speakers of languages. We turn therefore to a consideration of efforts towards language maintenance and language revival and the role of linguists in such activities.

24.6 Responses to language endangerment: maintenance and revival

We take language maintenance to mean efforts to enable a group to continue to speak or use a variety with which they have a historic association. Other terms used for such work are *reversing language shift* (Fishman 1991) and *language revitalisation* (Hinton and Hale 2001; Grenoble and Whaley 2006). Here, *language revival* will refer to attempts to recommence the use of a variety which has ceased to be spoken at some time in the past, sometimes also referred to as *language reclamation* (Amery 2000).

The work of Joshua Fishman is crucial in providing both a theoretical basis for language maintenance activities and outlining the nature of such activities in practice (Fishman 1991). For Fishman, the key issue in language endangerment is the weakening of intergenerational transmission of a language. Efforts to reverse language shift must most crucially be directed towards reversing that trend. Fishman's model is essentially ecological, and a stable ecology in which family and community are safeguarded is seen as a precursor to the maintenance of indigenous knowledge and linguistic and cultural diversity. Functional compartmentalisation of the threatened language commonly accompanies language shift and language activists seeking to reverse language shift must determine which functions they want the threatened and non-threatened languages to play.

In Fishman's model, a crucial step is the realisation by speakers of a variety that they cannot enact their identity completely in the language to which they are shifting; in Fishman's formulation, it is not possible to be an Xman without speaking Xish (Fishman 1991 Ch. 2). This insight underlies the idea which occurs repeatedly in the literature that successful language maintenance must be led by members of the speaker community and that they will need very high levels of commitment to the project (see for example papers in Fishman 2001; and the case studies in Chapter 4 of Grenoble and Whaley 2006).

Another feature of language maintenance programmes usually thought desirable is bureaucratic support. This is often sought through formal education, for example with bilingual schools (Hornberger 2008), but can also be attempted with even younger children using the language nest (*Te Kohanga Reo*) model originally developed in New Zealand (King 2001). Such activities aim to increase the number of children acquiring a language; in cases where transmission of a language has broken down, other activities may be more suitable such as the Master–Apprentice model (Hinton 1997). A scheme of this sort pairs elderly speakers with younger adults to work intensively and attempt to bring the apprentice to a level of language knowledge which will enable them to teach the language to younger members of the community.

These various types of language maintenance activity certainly allow for, and indeed may need, expert linguistic knowledge. However, the kind of knowledge required may not necessarily be such as is provided by the training typical of descriptive or documentary linguists. Preparing materials for language classes and basic steps in language planning have not been the types of skills in which general linguists have been trained, but preparation for fieldwork is being rethought in light of the problem of language endangerment.

The traditional skills of a general linguist are perhaps more obviously applicable to language revival which depends to a large extent on the interpretation of historical sources documenting a language. Hebrew is generally cited as an example of what can be achieved in language revival (Fellman 1973), but that language never ceased being spoken, if only in very restricted contexts. A better example of reclamation for a language which had not been used for a considerable period is Kaurna (Amery 2000), the language formerly spoken in the area now occupied by the city of Adelaide in Australia. This language is now being used again by a small number of people for limited functions. This was accomplished on the basis of nineteenth century linguistic materials written by German missionaries, and information from neighbouring and related languages. How linguists should view the status of such reclaimed languages is a complex question which is only beginning to be addressed (Couzens and Eira 2014); certainly they cannot be seen as straightforward continuations of the language as it formerly was spoken.

24.7 Conclusion

The evidence is clear that, even on a conservative view, language endangerment is a significant problem today. Developments in society, economics, politics and technology combined are exerting pressure toward linguistic and cultural homogeneity. If we, as linguists and as members of our species, value linguistic diversity, then some response to the situation is needed. As discussed in this chapter, linguists have made various responses to the situation. They have researched the issue and written about it, in many cases trying to raise awareness of the problems in the wider community. They have changed aspects of their practice in ways which it is hoped will ensure that the resources available, human and material, will be used as effectively as possible. And they have involved themselves in activities at the level of the ethnolinguistic community in order to attempt to sustain languages which are threatened.

The problem of language endangerment has been explicitly linked to threats to other kinds of diversity on our planet (e.g. Maffi 2005). Some scholars have developed an ecological view of language explicitly (Mühlhäusler 2003), while the views of others (e.g. Fishman) share the viewpoint implicitly. From this perspective, just as a central concern for ecologists is to ensure that habitats which support diversity are maintained, so the central concern for linguists is to ensure conditions in which linguistic diversity can exist. As Ken Hale concluded in his 1992 contribution:

> While it is good and commendable to record and document fading traditions, and in some cases this is absolutely necessary to avert total loss of cultural wealth, the greater goal must be that of safeguarding diversity in the world of people.
>
> (Hale 1992: 41)

Such a goal may not fit obviously or indeed comfortably with the practice of linguists in other times; however, if we accept that these times are different, we must rethink our role.

Acknowledgement

I am grateful to Alice Gaby, Nick Thieberger and Stephen Morey for comments on a draft of this chapter, and to Louisa Willoughby and Adam Schembri, who guided me to an important reference.

Notes

1 www.linguisticsociety.org/about/who-we-are/committees/endangered-languages-and-their-preservation-celp
2 There is even at least one novel which takes up some issues concerning language endangerment (Marani 2012).

3 http://dobes.mpi.nl
4 www.hrelp.org
5 www.nsf.gov/funding/pgm_summ.jsp?pims_id=12816
6 www.endangeredlanguages.com/about/#about_language_information
7 www-01.sil.org/iso639-3/default.asp
8 www-01.sil.org/iso639-3/changes.asp
9 The threat is not restricted to sign languages with less recognition. Improvements in genetic screening and the use of cochlear implants mean that potential speaker populations of sign languages in the first world are declining rapidly. Johnston (2004) discusses the situation of Auslan in terms of imminent endangerment.
10 Such views are expressed commonly (and more crudely) in almost any comment thread following an online article discussing threats to languages; for example: 'The notion of preserving languages of very small groups ignores the reality that it was social isolation that lead to their very development. Maintaining languages for their own sake will only continue to reinforce social isolation' (comment on http://theconversation.com/slip-of-the-tongues-language-and-the-unintended-consequences-of-indigenous-policy-9937, article published 3 October 2012).
11 But the language revival activities discussed in §24.6 should also be considered here as they are based on existing documentation of languages.
12 https://tla.mpi.nl
13 Despite Perley's criticism, in general, technology has been used sensibly and sensitively in language documentation and other work supporting endangered languages (see Holton 2011).

References

Abley, M. (2004) *Spoken Here*. London: Heinemann.

Amano, T., B. Sandel, H. Eager, E. Bulteau, J.-C. Svenning, B. Dalsgaard, C. Rahbek, R.G. Davies and W.J. Sutherland (2014) Global distribution and drivers of language extinction risk. *Proceedings of the Royal Society B: Biological Sciences* 281(1793). 20141574. doi:10.1098/rspb.2014.1574.

Amery, R.M. (2000) *Warrabarna Kaurna! Reclaiming an Australian Language*. Lisse: Swets and Zeitlinger BV.

Austin, P.K. and J. Sallabank (eds) (2011) *The Cambridge Handbook of Endangered Languages*. Cambridge: Cambridge University Press.

Brenzinger, M. (2007) *Language Diversity Endangered*. Berlin: Walter de Gruyter.

Campbell, L., N.H. Lee, E. Okura, S. Simpson and K. Ueki (2013) *New Knowledge: Findings from the Catalogue of Endangered Languages*. Honolulu: University of Hawai'i.

Clifton, J.M. (1994) Stable multilingualism in a small language group: The case of Kaki Ae. *Language and Linguistics in Melanesia* 25: 107–24.

Couzens, V. and C. Eira (2014) Meeting point: Parameters for the study of revival languages. In P.K. Austin and J. Sallabank (eds) *Endangered Languages: Beliefs and Ideologies in Language Documentation and Revitalisation*. London: Proceedings of the British Academy, Vol. 199.

Crowley, T. (2001) The indigenous linguistic response to missionary authority in the Pacific. *Australian Journal of Linguistics* 21: 239–60.

Cysouw, M. and J. Good (2013) Languoid, doculect and glossonym: Formalizing the notion 'Languoid'. *Language Documentation and Conservation* 7: 331–59.

Dixon, R.M.W. (1997) *The Rise and Fall of Languages*. Cambridge: Cambridge University Press.

Dixon, R.M.W. (2011 [1980]) *The Languages of Australia*. Cambridge: Cambridge University Press.

Dorian, N.C. (1977) The problem of the semi-speaker in language death. *International Journal of the Sociology of Language* 1977: 23–32.

Dorian, N.C. (1981) *Language Death: The Life Cycle of a Scottish Gaelic Dialect*. Philadelphia: University of Pennsylvania Press.

Dorian, N.C. (1989) *Investigating Obsolescence: Studies in Language Contraction and Death*. Cambridge: Cambridge University Press.

Dorian, N.C. (1993) A response to Ladefoged's other view of endangered languages. *Language* 69: 575–9.

Errington, J.J. (1998) *Shifting Languages*. Cambridge: Cambridge University Press.

Evans, N. (2009) *Dying Words: Endangered Languages and What They Have to Tell Us*. Chichester: Wiley-Blackwell.

Everett, D.L. (2005) Cultural constraints on grammar and cognition in Pirahã: Another look at the design features of human language. *Current Anthropology* 46: 621–46.

Fellman, J. (1973) Concerning the 'revival' of the Hebrew language. *Anthropological Linguistics* 15: 250–7.

Fishman, J.A. (1964) Language maintenance and language shift as a field of inquiry: A definition of the field and suggestions for its further development. *Linguistics* 9: 32–70.

Fishman, J.A. (1991) *Reversing Language Shift: Theoretical and Empirical Foundations of Assistance to Threatened Languages*. Clevedon: Multilingual Matters.

Fishman, J.A (ed.) (2001) *Can Threatened Languages Be Saved? Reversing Language Shift, Revisited – A 21st Century Perspective*. Clevedon/Buffalo: Multilingual Matters.

Gal, S. (1979) *Language Shift: Social Determinants of Linguistic Change in Bilingual Austria*. New York: Academic Press.

Garrett, P.B. (2006) Contact languages as 'endangered' languages: What is there to lose? *Journal of Pidgin and Creole Languages* 21: 175–90.

Gavin, M.C. and N. Sibanda (2012) The island biogeography of languages. *Global Ecology and Biogeography* 21: 958–67.

Gippert, J., N. Himmelmann and U. Mosel (eds) (2006) *Essentials of Language Documentation*. Berlin: Walter de Gruyter.

Gorenflo, L.J., S. Romaine, R.A. Mittermeier and K. Walker-Painemilla (2012) Co-occurrence of linguistic and biological diversity in biodiversity hotspots and high biodiversity wilderness areas. *Proceedings of the National Academy of Sciences* 109: 8032–7.

Grenoble, L.A. and L.J. Whaley (2006) *Saving Languages: An Introduction to Language Revitalization*. Cambridge: Cambridge University Press.

Haas, M.R. (1968) The last words of Biloxi. *International Journal of American Linguistics* 34: 77–84.

Hale, K.L. (ed.) (1992) Endangered languages: On endangered languages and the safeguarding of diversity. *Language* 68: 1–42.

Harmon, D. and J. Loh (2010) The index of linguistic diversity: A new quantitative measure of trends in the status of the world's languages. *Language Documentation and Conservation* 4: 97–151.

Hill, J. and K. Hill (1977) Language death and relexification in Tlaxcalan Nahuatl. *International Journal of the Sociology of Language* 12: 55–70.

Himmelmann, N. (1998) Documentary and descriptive linguistics. *Linguistics* 36: 161–96.

Himmelmann, N. (forthcoming) Language endangerment scenarios in northern Central Sulawesi. In J.T. Collins and H. Steinhauer (eds) *Endangered Languages and Literatures in South-East Asia*. Leiden: KITLV Press.

Hinton, L. (1997) Survival of endangered languages: The California master-apprentice program. *International Journal of the Sociology of Language* 123: 177–91.

Hinton, L. and K.L. Hale (eds) (2001) *The Green Book of Language Revitalization in Practice*. San Diego: Academic Press.

Holton, G. (2011) The role of information technology in supporting minority and endangered languages. In P.K. Austin and J. Sallabank (eds) *The Cambridge Handbook of Endangered Languages*, pp. 371–400. Cambridge: Cambridge University Press.

Hornberger, N.H. (ed.) (2008) *Can Schools Save Indigenous Languages? Policy and Practice on Four Continents*. London: Palgrave Macmillan.

Johnston, T.A. (2004) W(h)ither the deaf community? Population, genetics, and the future of Australian sign language. *American Annals of the Deaf* 148: 358–75.

King, J. (2001) Te Kohanga Reo: Maori language revitalization. In L. Hinton and K.L. Hale (eds) *The Green Book of Language Revitalization in Practice*, pp. 119–28. San Diego: Academic Press.

Kinkade, M.D. (1991) The decline of native languages in Canada. In R.H. Robins and E.M. Uhlenbeck (eds) *Endangered Languages*, pp. 157–76. New York: Berg.

Ladefoged, P. (1992) Another view of endangered languages. *Language* 68: 809–11.

Lewis, M.P. and G.F. Simons (2010) Assessing endangerment: Expanding Fishman's GIDS. *Revue Roumaine de linguistique* 55: 103–20.

Lewis, M.P., G.F. Simons and C.D. Fennig (eds) (2014) *Ethnologue: Languages of the World*, 17th edition. Dallas: SIL International. www.ethnologue.com.

Maffi, L. (2005) Linguistic, cultural, and biological diversity. *Annual Review of Anthropology* 34: 599–617.

Marani, D. (2012) *The Last of the Vostyachs*. Transl. Judith Landry. Gardena: Dedalus.

McConvell, P. (2005) *National Indigenous Languages Survey Report 2005*. Canberra: Australian Institute of Aboriginal and Torres Strait Islander Studies.

McConvell, P. and N. Thieberger (2001) *State of Indigenous Languages in Australia – 2001*. Canberra: Department of the Environment and Heritage.

Miller, W.R. (1971) The death of language or serendipity among the Shoshoni. *Anthropological Linguistics* 13: 114–20.

Minett, J.W. and W.S.-Y. Wang (2008) Modelling endangered languages: The effects of bilingualism and social structure. *Lingua* 118: 19–45.

Mosel, U. (2006a) Sketch grammar. In J. Gippert, N. Himmelmann and U. Mosel (eds) *Essentials of Language Documentation*, pp. 301–9. Berlin: Walter de Gruyter.

Mosel, U. (2006b) Fieldwork and community language work. In J. Gippert, N. Himmelmann and U. Mosel (eds) *Essentials of Language Documentation*, pp. 67–86. Berlin: Walter de Gruyter.

Moseley, C. (2010) *Atlas of the World's Languages in Danger*. Paris: UNESCO. www.unesco.org/culture/en/endangeredlanguages/atlas.

Mühlhäusler, P. (2003) Language endangerment and language revival. *Journal of Sociolinguistics* 7: 232–45.

Musgrave, S. and N. Thieberger (2007) Who pays the piper? In M.K. David, N. Ostler and C. Dealwis (eds) *Working Together for Endangered Languages: Research Challenges and Social Impacts (Proceedings of the XIth FEL Conference)*, pp. 47–55. Bath: Foundation for Endangered Languages.

Nonaka, A.M. (2004) The forgotten endangered languages: Lessons on the importance of remembering from Thailand's Ban Khor Sign Language. *Language in Society* 33: 737–67.

Perley, B.C. (2012) Zombie linguistics: Experts, endangered languages and the curse of undead voices. *Anthropological Forum* 22: 133–49.

Sallabank, J. (2013) *Attitudes to Endangered Languages : Identities and Policies*. New York: Cambridge University Press.

Simons, G.F. and M.P. Lewis (2013) The world's languages in crisis: A 20-year update. In E. Mihas, B.C. Perley, G.R. Doval, K. Wheatley and M. Noonan (eds) *Responses to Language Endangerment: In Honor of Mickey Noonan: New Directions in Language Documentation and Language Revitalization*, pp. 3–20. Amsterdam/Philadelphia: John Benjamins.

Steinhauer, H. (forthcoming) Endangered languages in Southeast Asia. In J.T. Collins and H. Steinhauer (eds) *Endangered Languages and Literatures in South-East Asia*. Leiden: KITLV Press.

Sutherland, W.J. (2003) Parallel extinction risk and global distribution of languages and species. *Nature* 423(6937): 276–9.

Swadesh, M. (1948) Sociologic notes on obsolescent languages. *International Journal of American Linguistics* 14: 226–35.

Thieberger, N. (ed.) (2012) *The Oxford Handbook of Linguistic Fieldwork*. Oxford: Oxford University Press.

Thieberger, N. and S. Musgrave (2007) Documentary linguistics and ethical issues. *Language Documentation and Description* 4: 26–37.

UNESCO Ad Hoc Expert Group on Endangered Languages (2003) Language Vitality and Endangerment. Paris: UNESCO. http://unesdoc.unesco.org/images/0018/001836/183699E.pdf.

UNFPA (2007) State of World Population 2007 – Online Report: United Nations Population Fund. http://web.unfpa.org/swp/2007/english/chapter_1/urbanization.html.

Wolfram, W. and N. Schilling-Estes (1995) Moribund dialects and the endangerment canon: The case of the Ocracoke Brogue. *Language* 71: 696–721.

Wurm, S.A. (2001) *Atlas of the World's Languages in Danger of Disappearing*, 2nd edition. Paris: UNESCO.

25
Linguistic typology and language universals

Jae Jung Song

25.1 Introduction

Linguistic typology is a theoretical approach to the study of human language, with sophisticated methods and an impressive body of knowledge. The primary objective of linguistic typology is to study the structural variation within human language with a view to establishing limits on this variation and seeking explanations for the limits. Thus, practitioners of linguistic typology – or linguistic typologists – tend to work with a large number of languages in their research, typically asking 'what is possible, as opposed to impossible, in human language?' or, more modestly, 'what is more probable, as opposed to less probable, in human language?'

Linguistic typology has a long tradition dating back to the nineteenth-century European interests in genealogical relationships among languages and in the evolution of human language or, as some historians of linguistics suggest, its origin may go even further back to other European scholarly traditions in the seventeenth or eighteenth centuries. The term 'typology' (or *Typologie* in German), in the context of the study of human language, was coined by the German philologist and sinologist Georg von der Gabelentz (1840–1893) to give a name to what was then still an emerging approach to the study of human language. The linguistic typology adopted in the nineteenth century was essentially the morphological typology, in which three basic strategies in the formal encoding of relational meaning were recognized: inflectional, agglutinating and isolating – a fourth, incorporating, was later added to this typology. Though initially embraced by scholars with enthusiasm, linguistic typology soon came to be subsumed under or overshadowed by other interests, i.e. historical linguistics in particular. It was not until the appearance of Joseph Greenberg's 1963 article on word order that the focus of linguistic typology, in line with the contemporary development in linguistics, shifted from morphology to syntax. Greenberg's emphasis on word order did not only spearhead a move from the classical morphology-based typology to a syntax-based one but, more importantly, he also initiated a new line of research by revamping and revitalizing linguistic typology, which had until then been largely ignored, if not forgotten, in linguistics. Note that syntax in linguistic typology needs to be construed broadly enough to encompass morphology because, for instance, what is done by syntax (e.g. word order) in one language may be done by morphology (e.g. case marking) in another language. Syntactic typology, prominently researched in linguistic typology, may thus be better termed morphosyntactic typology. Morphosyntactic phenomena that have been the focus of linguistic typology include word order and word order correlations, case marking/alignment, grammatical relations, passive and other voices, and person agreement patterns among others. This morphosyntactic focus is being increasingly complemented by the coverage of phonology, semantics, and other areas of linguistics, e.g. sociolinguistics.

The remainder of this chapter is structured as follows. §25.2 describes the four stages of typological analysis with examples. §25.3 explains the nature of implicational statements and demonstrates how multiple implicational statements may be combined into a single implicational hierarchy, when they belong to the same grammatical domain. §25.4 discusses the connection between diversity and unity in human language with a view to highlighting the vital role of structural diversity in understanding the unity of human language. §25.5 examines two methodological issues in linguistic typology, namely cross-linguistic identification and language sampling. §25.6 discusses three ways in which languages may come to share structural properties, explaining when and where such shared structural properties may be important or relevant for the purpose of typological research. §25.7 provides a typology of universal statements (i.e. language universals and universal preferences) with examples and illustrates how universal statements are explained in linguistic typology. Particular attention is also paid to how the focus of linguistic typology has over the decades evolved from discovering what is possible, as opposed to impossible, in human language (i.e. language universals) to what is more or less probable (i.e. universal preferences), and to 'what's where why' (i.e. the world's linguistic diversity). The chapter ends in §25.8 with closing remarks.

25.2 Typological analysis

Linguistic typology involves four stages of investigation: (1) the identification of a phenomenon to be studied; (2) the classification of the phenomenon; (3) the formulation of a generalization or generalizations over the classification; and (4) the explanation of the generalization(s). First, linguistic typologists must determine what to investigate. There are no restrictions on what structural properties should or should not be studied. Nor are there any restrictions on how many properties should simultaneously be dealt with. Some may choose one property as an object of inquiry, whereas others may at once probe into more than one. The first and second stages of typological analysis may need to be carried out concurrently. This is because one does not know in advance whether or not the chosen property is going to be typologically interesting or significant. Once properties have been chosen for typological analysis, structural types pertaining to those properties will be identified and defined so that the world's languages can be classified into those types. In the case of basic word order at the clausal level, for instance, six (logically possible) types – i.e. SOV, SVO, VSO, VOS, OVS and OSV – are identified, whereby languages are typologized according to the type that they exhibit. (The transitive clause consists of three main elements denoting the entity which initiates an action [i.e. S(ubject)], the entity at which that action is directed
[i.e. O(bject)] and the action itself [i.e. V(erb)].) The identification of the six basic word order types and the classification of the world's languages into those types – excluding languages without a dominant word order – will then constitute a linguistic typology of basic word order. The skewed distribution of the six basic word orders emerging

from this typological classification is such that there is a distinct tendency towards Subject-initial order, namely SOV and SVO, in the world's languages. This is one significant generalization over the data classified – representing stage (3) above. It will also lead to the question as to why there is this strong tendency, because, if the ordering of S, O and V were random (i.e. no motivating factors), each of the six word order types would be represented by about 16.6 per cent of the world's languages. At this stage (i.e. (4) above), every attempt is made to explain the tendency in question. Typically, in linguistic typology language-external explanations or factors outside the linguistic system, e.g. cognition, perception, processing, communication, etc., are appealed to. For instance, functional factors including discourse prominence, animacy, processing efficiency, etc. have been proposed to explain the preponderance of SOV and SVO in the world's languages. This predilection for language-external explanations situates linguistic typology in the functional, as opposed to the formal or generative, research tradition in linguistics. This is not to say that language-internal explanations (e.g. constituent structure, formal constraints, etc.) are eschewed in linguistic typology. Language-internal explanations can indeed be sought if no language-external explanations are available or forthcoming. Moreover, even when formal properties are utilized in formulating cross-linguistic generalizations, linguistic typology continues to seek functional motivations for such formally-based generalizations (e.g. see §25.7). This is what makes linguistic typology different from formal approaches to language, e.g. Principles and Parameters Theory. In addition to functional and formal explanations, linguistic typologists also appeal to historical ones. For instance, there are reported to be a small number of 'exceptions' to the linguistic preference for the combination of Verb-Object order and Noun-Relative Clause order, i.e. Chinese and a few languages spoken in China and Taiwan, which have Verb-Object order and Relative Clause-Noun order (see (1)–(8) for examples of the relative clause). The explanation given to the existence of these 'exceptions' to what would otherwise be an exceptionless universal statement is that these languages have adopted Relative Clause-Noun order through direct or indirect contact with Object-Verb languages spoken to the north of China, which all have Relative Clause-Noun order. This explanation is historical or, more precisely, socio-cultural.

25.3 Implicational statements and implicational hierarchies

Generalizations such as the one discussed above about the strong tendency towards Subject-initial order concern the distribution of single structural properties. There are also cross-linguistic generalizations that involve more than one structural property. In point of fact, one of the major insights that emerged from Joseph Greenberg's seminal work on word order is that two or more structural properties may correlate with one another (to a statistically significant extent). For instance, basic word order at the clausal level has been compared with the presence of prepositions or postpositions. Verb-initial languages (that is, languages with the verb appearing first in the sentence, i.e. VSO and VOS) are almost always found to be equipped with prepositions, not postpositions. This means that Verb-initial word order almost never co-occurs with postpositions. This constitutes one important property of human language in that it represents a very strong constraint on variation within human language. There is no reason why the two independent properties should correlate to the effect that the presence of Verb-initial word order (almost always) implies that of prepositions. Logically speaking, there should also be an abundance of Verb-initial languages with postpositions – or at least as many Verb-initial languages with postpositions as Verb-initial languages with prepositions. This is clearly not the case, however.

Generalizations like the correlation between Verb-initial word order and the presence of prepositions lead to implicational statements, which take the form of 'if p, then q' (or $p \supset q$): the presence of Verb-initial word order (p) implies that of prepositions (q). (This kind of implicational statement originated from the work of the Prague School of Linguistics in the first half of the twentieth century.) The predicting power of implicational statements is not confined solely to the properties which they make explicit reference to. Thus, given the implicational statement 'if a language is Verb-initial, then it is also prepositional', there are two other situations that fall out from that statement (not to mention the (near) impossibility of Verb-initial languages with postpositions). By making no claims about them, it has the advantage of saying something about non-Verb-initial languages (i.e. Subject-initial or Object-initial) with either prepositions or postpositions, thereby recognizing these two combinations as possible in human language. In other words, the implicational statement in question rules out only Verb-initial languages with postpositions as an (near) impossibility – that is, p & $-q$ (read: not q), which contradicts the original implicational statement of 'if p, then q' (i.e. p & q). For this reason, implicational statements are highly valued in linguistic typology.

When multiple implicational statements pertain to the same grammatical domain, they may be combined into an implicational hierarchy. One well-known example is the Accessibility Hierarchy. Some noun phrase positions are cross-linguistically more likely to be relativized on than other noun phrase positions to the effect that the following individual implicational statements can be formulated:

1. a Subject (SBJ) is more accessible to relativization than a Direct Object (DO);
2. a DO is more accessible to relativization than an Indirect Object (IO);
3. an IO is more accessible to relativization than an Oblique (OBL);
4. an OBL is more accessible to relativization than a Genitive (GEN); and
5. a GEN is more accessible to relativization than an Object of Comparison (OCOMP).

Note that these implicational statements are interconnected with each other because part of one implicational statement is involved in another one that immediately follows or precedes it, not to mention the fact that they all concern accessibility to relativization. The implicational statements have been formulated on the basis of the observation that there are languages that can relativize on SBJ only, languages that can relativize on SBJ and DO only, languages that can relativize on SBJ, DO and IO only, and so on through the remaining noun phrase positions. For instance, Malagasy can relativize on SBJ only, as in (1); when DO (or the other noun phrase positions for that matter) is relativized on, the outcome is ungrammatical, as in (2):

(1) Malagasy (Austronesian; Madagascar)
 ny mpianatra izay nahita ny vehivavy
 the student COMP saw the woman
 'the student that saw the woman'

(2) Malagasy
 *ny vehivavy izay nahita ny mpianatra
 the woman COMP saw the student

'the woman that the student saw'

English can relativize on all the noun phrase positions:

(3) the girl who swam the Straits of Dover [SBJ]

(4) the girl whom the boy loved [DO]

(5) the girl to whom the boy gave a flower [IO]

(6) the girl with whom the boy danced [OBL]

(7) the girl whose mother the boy admired [GEN]

(8) the girl who the boy is taller than [OCOMP]

What the implicational statements 1–5 also entail is that the relativization of noun phrase position X implies that of noun phrase positions more accessible to relativization than X. For instance, if a language can relativize on IO, it can also relativize on SBJ and DO; if a language can relativize on GEN, it can also relativize on SBJ, DO, IO and OBL, and so on. Since the implicational statements 1–5 all belong to the domain of relativization, they can be combined into a single implicational hierarchy, as in:

(9) SBJ > DO > IO > OBL > GEN > OCOMP

The implicational hierarchy in (9) or the Accessibility Hierarchy, as it is known in the literature, indicates, by means of the '>' sign, that if a given noun phrase position (e.g. OBL) is accessible to relativization, relativization is also available to all positions to the left (e.g. SBJ, DO and IO). Because of the way they are constructed, implicational hierarchies make strong predictions. For instance, testable predictions can be made that in no languages, SBJ, DO and GEN are accessible to relativization while IO and OBL are not, and so on.

25.4 The connection between diversity and unity

The area of linguistic typology dealing with diversity investigates the structural variation in the world's languages (i.e. typological classification) whereas the area of linguistic typology concerned with unity focuses on the discovery of language universals (i.e. what is possible) or universal preferences (i.e. what is probable). Language universals impose constraints or limits on structural variation within human language, while universal preferences delineate the preponderance of some structural types over others (see §25.7 for further discussion). (Some linguistic typologists may subsume universal preferences under the rubric of language universals.) Typological investigation, in contrast, is concerned with classification of languages into different structural types. Thus, it may seem like something of a contradiction in terms to deal with these two distinct areas together. But the contradiction is more apparent than real. The search for the unity in human language, in fact, builds crucially on the structural diversity in the world's languages. This is because in order to discover what is possible or probable in human language, what linguistic typologists need is typological classification to work on. With languages classified into different types, linguistic typologists will then be able to discern patterns or regularities in the distribution of the types, for instance, with some types being significantly more common than others, or with one (or more) of the logically possible types completely unattested or marginally attested in the world's languages.

This close relationship between language universals and universal preferences on the one hand and typological classification on the other can be demonstrated by the preponderance of Subject-initial order in the world's languages. According to Matthew Dryer's 2011 study, nearly 76.5 per cent of his 1,377 sample languages have Subject-initial order, i.e. SOV or SVO. (This percentage goes up to 88.6 per cent if languages without a dominant word order are excluded from his sample.) If the world's languages – or at least a good portion of them – had not been surveyed in terms of all the possible word orders, this strong tendency would never have been brought to light in the first place. To put it differently, the typological classification of the world's languages in terms of the six word orders is a prerequisite for the significant generalization to be made about human language. This universal preference could not have been uncovered from the examination of only one or only a handful of languages.

Further demonstration of the fruitful interaction between unity and diversity comes from another universal preference (albeit of an implicational nature): the presence of Verb-initial order implying that of prepositions. As has already been explained in §25.3, this implicational statement also entails what is not probable in human language, namely the near absence of Verb-initial languages with postpositions; moreover, it makes indirect reference to the two other logical possibilities, namely non-Verb-initial languages with either prepositions or postpositions. In order to arrive at the formulation of this implicational statement, however, it first needs to be ascertained which of the four logical possibilities – V-initial & preposition, V-initial & postposition, non-V-initial & preposition, and non-V-initial & postposition – is attested or unattested in the world's languages. That can be achieved only on the basis of an initial typological classification of the world's languages in terms of basic word order as well as the distribution of prepositions and postpositions. To wit, the search for the unity in human language is conducted on the basis of the structural diversity in human language. It is not possible to carry out the former without the latter.

25.5 Methodological issues

There are a number of methodological issues that have received much attention in linguistic typology. In this section, two of them will be discussed: the problem of cross-linguistic identification and language sampling.

25.5.1 Problem of cross-linguistic identification

Linguistic typologists study cross-linguistic variation in order to understand the nature of human language. The best way to gain access to the cross-linguistic variation of a linguistic phenomenon is to study as wide a range of languages as possible (see §25.5.2 on language sampling). Because they study many languages all at once, linguistic typologists must ensure that what they are comparing across languages will be the same thing, not different things. One does not want to compare 'apples' with 'oranges' when investigating the world's languages in terms of one and the same property. Otherwise one will never be able to achieve what one sets out to achieve: cross-linguistic variation of the *same* phenomenon. But how does one actually make sure that X in language A will be compared with X, not Y, in language B? Put differently, how does one identify the same phenomenon across languages? This question concerns what may be referred to as *the problem of cross-linguistic identification*.

There are two possible ways of dealing with the problem of cross-linguistic identification. One may choose to carry out cross-linguistic identification on the basis of formal criteria. A set of formal properties, e.g. verbal marking, adpositions, cases, etc., may be put together in order to identify a given phenomenon. Alternatively, one may opt for functional – i.e. semantic, conceptual and/or pragmatic – definitions of the phenomenon to be studied. Which of the two types of definition – formal or functional – will meet the needs of typological analysis better? There are three reasons why formal definitions do not work for cross-linguistic comparison. First, structural variation across languages is so great that it cannot serve as the basis of cross-linguistic identification. For instance, the subjects in one language may be expressed by means of different grammatical relations in other languages. More generally, not all properties used to identify grammatical relations are found in all languages. In other words, grammatical relations cannot be defined uniformly from one language to another. Second, because of structural differences among languages, formal definitions have to be internal to the structural system of a single language, thereby again failing to serve as language-independent definitions. Put differently, no single formal definition may be able to capture all the differences that may exist between languages, their similarities notwithstanding. Third, there can hardly be any purely formal definitions. Formal definitions of phenomenon X can only be identified and thus understood in the context of the function that X carries out. One cannot simply look at a given formal property and say what function that formal property is used to carry out. This would be possible only if functions were inherent in, and thus deducible from, formal properties themselves. Rather, functions arise out of what linguistic expressions are utilized for. For example, if one wants to study comparative constructions across languages, one cannot infer the function of comparison from the linguistic expression in which that function is encoded (e.g. the use of adpositions, cases, lexical verbs, etc.). One will not know what grammatical properties to look for in the first place, thereby being unable to recognize a comparative construction when one sees it. In point of fact, language-dependent formal definitions do not tie in with linguistic typology, one of the primary aims of which is to characterize structural variation in the world's languages. Structural variation itself is what linguistic typologists want to discover for cross-linguistic comparison in the first place. In other words, one cannot make use of the structural variation which has not yet been established in order to identify that structural variation. Thus, formal definitions are not deemed appropriate for resolving the problem of cross-linguistic identification.

In view of the foregoing objections to formal definitions, linguistic typologists opt for functional definitions for purposes of cross-linguistic identification. However, functional definitions may not be entirely without problems. More frequently than not, functional definitions themselves tend to be based on pre-theoretic concepts or ill-defined notions. This is not to say, of course, that the problem is unique to this type of definition. The definition of a given concept is always dependent on the understanding of other concepts which make up that definition – unless these other concepts are undefined theoretical primitives. For example, consider the semantic definition of comparison proposed by Stassen (1985: 15):

> a construction counts as a comparative construction (and will therefore be taken into account in the typology), if that construction has the semantic function of assigning a graded (i.e. non-identical) position on a predicative scale to two (possibly complex) objects.

In order to understand this definition fully, one needs to have an understanding of what a predicative scale, a graded position, etc. are. Also note that the definition has nothing to say about what form or shape the construction in question will take. Thus, it is possible that, depending on how they interpret the definition (e.g. broadly or narrowly), some linguistic typologists may recognize X in language A as a comparative construction while other linguistic typologists may not. Functional definitions are more of heuristics for cross-linguistic identification than definitions in the strict sense of the word.

While functional criteria are decidedly preferred to formal ones, far more often than not, formal properties do find their way into language-independent definitions used for typological analysis so that they can, for instance, narrow down the domain of typological research. In other words, formal properties may be used in order to refine or fine-tune functionally-based definitions. For instance, Stassen (1985: 25–6) appeals to a formal property of NP in order to restrict the two compared objects featured in his language-independent definition of the comparative construction (cited above) to those expressed in the form of NPs. Thus, this additional formal criterion of NP-hood rules out comparative expressions such as (12), (13) and (14) as ineligible for inclusion in Stassen's research, while accepting comparative expressions such as (10) and (11). If applied all by itself, however, Stassen's definition of the comparative construction would recognize all the examples in (10)–(14) as comparative expressions.

(10) The tree is taller than the house.

(11) I like Pamela better than Lucy.

(12) The general is more cunning than brave.

(13) The team plays better than last year.

(14) The president is smarter than you think.

Functionally-based definitions used in cross-linguistic comparison must be understood as broadly as possible. Thus, under the rubric of functional criteria, factors relating to discourse or to phonetics may also be considered for the purpose of invoking language-independent definitions needed for typological analysis. For instance, in her typological study of person markers, Anna Siewierska (2004) refers to the participant or discourse roles of speaker and addressee – and the third party, which assumes neither of these participant or discourse roles. Moreover, language-independent definitions used in a phonological typology are likely to be based on articulatory–acoustic properties such as the place and manner of articulation, voicing and such like (and, ultimately, to speech organs). To wit, the term 'functional' in functional criteria utilized in cross-linguistic comparison must be understood broadly enough to include all factors external to the language system.

25.5.2 Language sampling

It does not come as a surprise – in view of its emphasis on the structural variation within human language – that one of the most prominently discussed methods in linguistic typology is language sampling. The best way to discover the limits on the structural variation within human language is to study all languages of the world. For obvious reasons, it is easy to see why that is out of the question. There are said to be almost 7,000 languages in the world. Individual linguistic typologists (or even a team of linguistic typologists) are unable to compare such a large number of languages or even a small fraction thereof. Economy alone will rule out such large-scale surveys as unfeasible. What makes it even more unrealistic is the fact that there are far more languages which await linguistic documentation than those which have been described – not to mention those which are extinct or which will come into existence in future. In view of these limitations, linguistic typologists choose to work with language samples. There are two main types of language sample: (1) probability samples, which are used to identify tendencies or correlations; and (2) variety samples, which are set up to discover all possible structural types used to encode a given function or meaning in the world's languages. Different statistical methods and different sample sizes may be required, depending on whether one operates with a probability or variety sample. For instance, a variety sample tends to be larger in size than a probability sample, because the aim of the former is to identify what structural types are attested in the world's languages (hence, the more languages in the sample, the better chances of finding all structural types), while the aim of the latter is to establish the presence or absence of a correlation between previously known structural properties (hence, what may matter is which languages, not how many languages, are to be included in the sample).

Alan Bell's 1978 article was the first to raise the issue of language sampling for linguistic typology. He explained the role of stratification in language sampling (i.e. the process of placing languages into different strata, e.g. genetic affiliation, geographic location, etc.), and discussed genetic, areal and bibliographic biases to be avoided in language sampling. Bell's sampling approach was based on proportional representation. For instance, each language family contributes to a sample in proportion to the number of genetic groups in that family. One fundamental issue to be addressed with respect to proportionally representative language samples is the independence of cases. This relates directly to the need to ensure that languages selected for a sample be independent units of analysis, rather than instances of the same case. Matthew Dryer's 1989 article developed a novel yet ingenious method in language sampling, one of his primary aims being to maximize the independence of cases, albeit at the level of large linguistic areas: Africa, Eurasia, Australia–New Guinea, North America, and South America. (In Dryer's subsequent work, Southeast Asia and Oceania are removed from Eurasia and treated as a separate linguistic area.) He also invoked the concept of a genus. Genera are genetic groups of languages, comparable to the sub-families of Indo-European, e.g. Romance. Genera, not individual languages, are then counted for purposes of determining linguistic preferences or tendencies in each of the large linguistic areas. The independence of cases, vital for all statistical procedures, is not demanded at the level of genera but required strictly at the level of the five (or six) large linguistic areas, which are reasonably well defined physically and which should thus be far less controversial – and less unwieldy to handle – than the divisions between over 300 genera. Thus, only if and when all the linguistic areas conform to the hypothesis being tested, that hypothesis is considered to be a linguistic preference. Dryer's sampling method does not just represent an improvement in language sampling but also draws attention to the theoretical importance of nonlinguistic – in particular geographical – factors in investigating correlations between structural properties (see §§25.6 and 25.7). For instance, the correlation between O(bject)V(erb) and A(djective)N(oun) order was once thought to be a language universal. Thanks to Dryer's sampling method, however, this correlation has been shown to derive largely from the dominance of that correlation in Eurasia. In all other linguistic areas, there is a clear tendency towards OV and NA.

There are some issues with sampling methods such as Dryer's that remain to be resolved. One issue is that it is not clear how (and which) languages are chosen for each genus. Obviously, languages chosen for a sample must be representative of the genera that they represent but that requirement may not be able to be met for all genera (because some genera may have a greater amount of internal diversity than others). Moreover, one complicating factor in choosing languages that are representative of genera may be that some structural properties may be stable over time, while others may not be. For example, word order properties may change fairly easily, e.g. through contact, while morphological ones may be far more resilient to change. Thus, the assumption that languages within genera are generally similar typologically may not apply to all different types of structural property. This means that it may or may not be easy to find representative languages, depending on the structural properties being investigated. Of course, it goes without saying that one first needs to find out which structural properties are stable and which are not.

25.6 When and where similarities count

When studying the structural diversity of the world's languages with a view to uncovering the unity of human language, one must take care to separate language universals or universal preferences from structural similarities brought about by nonlinguistic factors, e.g. historical accident. Imagine a hypothetical world where there are 1,000 languages. In this world, there is one large language family of 900 languages, with the remaining 100 languages evenly distributed among ten small language families (i.e. ten languages in each of these small language families). All the 900 languages in the large family have type X, and all the languages of the ten small families have type Y. Now, is it safe to conclude from this that there is a linguistic preference for X over Y, since X is attested in 900 languages (90 per cent) while Y is attested in only 100 languages (10 per cent)? The answer is no, because of the fact that X is found in only one language family and Y in ten language families. The fact that it could have been the other way round (i.e. Y in the large language family and X in the ten small language families) suggests that the presence of X in the majority of the hypothetical world's languages may well be a historical accident, having nothing to do with what is or is not linguistically preferred. For further illustration, imagine that in the distant past, the large language family had only ten languages, with the remaining 990 languages evenly distributed among the other ten language families. Through their superior technology and political power, however, the size of the former language family subsequently increased exponentially at the expense of the latter language families. Thus, the presence of X in the majority of the hypothetical world's languages (i.e. the large language family) is caused by the technological and political superiority of their speakers, and certainly not by the linguistic preference for X over Y. From this, it is glaringly obvious that language universals or universal preferences cannot be established on the basis of structural similarities brought by such historical accidents. This is why it is decided that X is not a universal preference in spite of the fact that it is attested in 90 per cent of the hypothetical world's languages – in other words, Y is likely to be a universal preference.

There are three ways languages come to have similar properties: (a) shared genealogical origin; (b) language contact; and (c) language universals or universal preferences. Linguistic typology is concerned primarily with (c), while not neglecting to pay attention to (a) and (b), especially when dealing with 'exceptions' to language universals or universal preferences (see §25.7). Thus, when and where unity is the focus of investigation, it is (c) that counts, and (a) and (b) may have to be set aside. Needless to say, however, if the focus of investigation

Linguistic typology and language universals

is on understanding 'exceptions' to language universals or universal preferences, and the origins or causes thereof, (a) and (b) should also be brought into the picture.

The make-believe example given above illustrates shared genealogical origin. The fact that there are 900 languages in the large language family with type X is due to the fact that these languages all derive historically from a single ancestral language (see Chapter 22). In other words, languages may have similar structural properties because they have inherited them from their common ancestor.

The case of shared properties through language contact has already been alluded to when Chinese and its neighbouring languages were briefly discussed in §25.2 with respect to the universal preference for V(erb)O(bject) and N(oun-)Rel(ative Clause) order. Chinese belongs to the Sino-Tibetan family, whereas the neighbouring languages to the north of China belong to the Mongolic or Tungusic branch of the so-called Altaic family. However, Chinese and these northern languages share Rel(ative Clause-)N(oun) order, in spite of the difference in their basic word order at the clausal level. In the case of Chinese, a VO language, its RelN order goes against the grain of the universal preference, i.e. VO & NRel, as it were. As has already been explained, Chinese abandoned its original NRel order, adopting RelN order from the northern (OV) languages. This illustrates how languages of different genealogical origins may end up with common properties through contact, in opposition to language universals or universal preferences. Languages may come to share structural properties through contact because speakers of languages may adopt them from other languages that they come into contact with, even when those properties may give rise to what is inherently dispreferred in human languages. To wit, contact-mediated similarities also are due to historical accident, just as similarities through shared genealogical origins are.

Lastly, the world's languages or at least the majority of the world's languages may have such and such structural properties because they are due to the very nature of human language: all other things being equal, languages must have such and such properties (motivated by e.g. human cognition, basic communicative needs, etc.) because they are what makes human language what it is. These structural properties are expressed in the form of language universals or universal preferences. For instance, there is a clear, strong tendency for VO languages to have NRel order. This correlation is attested in virtually all VO languages of the world (with a very small number of exceptions, which can be explained by reference to language contact). This must have to do with the nature of human language: if a language has VO order, it must also opt for NRel order. (See §25.7 as to how language universals or universal preferences may be explained in linguistic typology.)

25.7 Language universals, universal preferences and explanation

Properties such as the preponderance of Subject-initial languages in the world's languages are often referred to as language universals in the literature. Strictly speaking, however, language universals must be true of all languages. In other words, language universals are 'absolute' in the sense that there are no exceptions to them. Under this strict definition of the term, therefore, the preponderance of Subject-initial order does not qualify as a language universal since it is only a tendency in human language, albeit a strong one; in fact, it is 'non-absolute' in the sense that there are exceptions to it, i.e. Verb-initial or Object-initial order. Only properties which all human languages have in common may be taken to be language universals. Thus, it may be judicious to regard the preponderance of Subject-initial order as a universal preference, not as a language universal: a structural property attested in the majority of the world's languages. Far more frequently than not, however, the term 'language universal' is interpreted liberally as including not only language universals but also universal preferences. To avoid possible confusion, therefore, the term 'universal statement' will be used henceforth when reference is made to both language universals and universal preferences.

Universal statements can also be implicational or non-implicational. The concept of implicational statements (together with the derivative concept of implicational hierarchies) has already been explained in §25.3. Implicational universal statements take the form of 'if p, then q'. The presence of one property (i.e. the *implicans*) implies that of another (i.e. the *implicatum*). The correlation between Verb-initial order and prepositions is an implicational universal statement: if a language is Verb-initial, then it is almost always prepositional. By design, implicational universal statements are based on interaction of more than one property. Thus, there may also be implicational statements, involving more than two properties. One such example is Joseph Greenberg's Universal 5: if a language has dominant SOV order and the genitive follows the governing noun, then the adjective likewise follows the noun. In this implicational statement, two properties are needed to predict a third. It is also possible that the implicatum can be more than one property. Joseph Greenberg's Universal 21 offers an example of this kind: if some or all adverbs follow the adjective they modify, then the language is one in which the qualifying adjective follows the noun and the verb precedes its nominal object as the dominant order. It is not difficult to see that other things being equal, implicational statements that predict the presence of multiple properties on the basis of a single property are more highly valued than those that predict the presence of a single property on the basis of multiple properties. Put differently, it is preferable to predict as much as possible on the basis of as little as possible. By this criterion of economy, Universal 21 is of more value than Universal 5.

Non-implicational universal statements, in contrast, do not involve the predicting of property X on the basis of property Y. They involve single properties. The preponderance of Subject-initial word order in the world's languages is a non-implicational universal statement. Note that this particular statement is not only non-implicational but also non-absolute, thereby illustrating that universal statements may cut across the distinction between the absolute/non-absolute, and implicational/non-implicational parameters. Thus, in addition to non-absolute non-implicational statements, there may also be: (a) absolute implicational statements; (b) absolute non-implicational statements; and (c) non-absolute implicational statements. A potential example of (a) may be: If the general rule is that the descriptive adjective follows the noun, then there may be a minority of adjectives which usually precede, but if the general rule is that descriptive adjectives precede the noun, then there are no exceptions. Another example of (a), from phonological typology, may come from the observation that voiced fricatives are found only in languages with corresponding voiceless ones. This implies that if a language has voiced fricatives, it has corresponding voiceless fricatives as well. A possible example of (b) comes from the fact that all languages have ways to convert affirmative sentences into negative ones. Another example of (b), from phonological typology, is that all languages have syllables consisting of a single consonant and a single vowel. An example of (c) has already been provided: if a language is Verb-initial, it is almost always prepositional as well. Another example of (c), from phonological typology, may be that if a language has a fricative voicing contrast, it is very likely to have a plosive voicing contrast as well. For additional universal statements, the reader is referred to *The Universals Archive*.[1]

Absolute universal statements are also referred to as exceptionless, and non-absolute universal statements as statistical tendencies or, as in this chapter, universal preferences. Implicational statements are also known as restricted or conditional, while non-implicational statements are also known as unrestricted or unconditional. The four (logical) types of universal statements are summarized in Table 25.1.

Table 25.1 Four types of universal statements

	Absolute (Exceptionless)	*Non-absolute (universal preferences/statistical tendencies)*
Non-implicational (Unrestricted/Unconditional)	All languages have property X.	Most languages have property X.
Implicational (Restricted/Conditional)	If a language has property X, it also has property Y.	If a language has property X, it tends to have property Y as well.

Nearly all the examples provided so far are non-absolute universal statements. This is because absolute language universals (i.e. exceptionless universal statements) are very hard to find. It is not the case that they do not exist. They certainly do. But they are not numerous and, as Joseph Greenberg once put it, they tend to be 'banal' or 'trite'. For instance, it has been proposed as an absolute universal statement that all languages have vowels. This, however, is rather uninspiring. One may ask: All language have vowels, so what? It does not seem to lead to any further interesting questions about human language, except for the question as to why all languages must have vowels. More seriously, as some linguists are quick to point out, even this seemingly absolute universal statement is not without exceptions, when sign languages are taken into account. And there are quite a few of them in the world. Experience shows that what has been proposed as a language universal almost always turns out to have exceptions. A classic example of this kind is: all languages mark the negative by adding some morpheme to a sentence. This was once thought to be an absolute universal statement. Classical Tamil turns out to be a counterexample, as this language marks the negative by deleting the tense morpheme present in the positive. One may perhaps brush Classical Tamil aside as only one (known) counterexample among the world's 7,000 languages. (But at the same time, this shows that, strictly speaking, one exception is all it takes to render an absolute universal statement non-absolute.) However, one must realize that only less than 10–20 per cent of the world's languages have adequate descriptions (that is, adequate for typological research). One cannot be sure whether there may be other yet-to-be-documented (or even yet-to-be-discovered) languages that behave like Classical Tamil. More to the point, absolute universal statements may have been formulated on the basis of an even smaller number of languages (i.e. language samples). As more and more languages become documented and brought to the attention of researchers, new properties or strategies are very likely to show up, flying in the face of proposed language universals or universal preferences. Thus, it does not come as a surprise that absolute universal statements or language universals are hard to come by, and most of the language universals claimed so far have turned out to be less than what they were initially thought to be. Moreover, one must also bear in mind that we have no access to languages that disappeared without leaving any records or trace, not to mention those yet to come into existence. In view of this reality, not surprisingly, the focus of linguistic typology has recently shifted from unity to diversity, as the clear message coming from the increasing documentation of the world's languages is that there is always going to be a language somewhere that will throw a curve ball, as it were. Thus, some linguistic typologists have argued that more effort should instead go into documenting the structural diversity of the world's languages before advancing premature claims about the nature of human language. Not surprisingly, the question of what is possible, as opposed to impossible, in human languages has given way to the question of what is more probable, as opposed to less probable, in human languages. But at the same time, it must be borne in mind that making observations or hypotheses about human language on the basis of *available* data is legitimate business, not just in linguistic typology but also in all scientific disciplines.

The fact that there are hardly any exceptionless language universals that can stand the test of time does not detract from the fact that there is a substantial amount of unity in the world's languages. Various universal preferences capture the very unity of human language. A small number of languages that deviate from this unity may further reflect the structural diversity in the world's languages, and must be accounted for in whatever way they can. As has already been pointed out on more than one occasion, however, these 'deviations' tend to have social, cultural and/or historical reasons behind them. Such nonlinguistic reasons enable linguistic typologists to understand why property X exists in language A at a particular point in time and space, in opposition to the overwhelming global tendency. In other words, it is important to understand why and how the 'deviating' languages have arisen. It is important to answer these questions also because in doing so, linguistic typologists can find themselves in a better position to strengthen the validity of universal preferences. When exceptions to universal preferences are addressed on their own terms, the conceptual as well as empirical strength of proposed universal preferences is by no means vitiated but rather increased to a greater extent than would otherwise be the case. This is because the exceptions have valid reasons for being what they are. In other words, a small number of exceptions to universal preferences are not really counterexamples as such, but rather the outcome of nonlinguistic factors 'interfering' with what is preferred in human language (read: the unity of human language). In this respect, exceptions to universal preferences represent nonlinguistic variables that override linguistic preferences in specific historical, social and cultural contexts. This perspective may enable the researcher to understand better why the world's linguistic diversity is the way it is. Thus, some linguistic typologists have recently called for the need to shift the focus of linguistic typology even further to the question of 'what's where why?', as the Swiss linguist Balthasar Bickel (2007) aptly puts it.

The conceptual shift from 'what is possible (or more probable), as opposed to impossible (or less probable) in human language?' to 'what's where why?' is one of the most significant developments that have taken place in linguistic typology since Joseph Greenberg's rejuvenation of the field in the 1960s. The most substantial and tangible outcome of this conceptual shift is *The World Atlas of Language Structures* or *WALS* (Haspelmath et al. 2005; published online in 2011 and available at www.wals.info). In this landmark volume, over 140 typological or structural properties are investigated by a group of fifty-five linguists in terms of areal or global distribution. For instance, one of the *WALS* chapters demonstrates that the co-occurrence of OV and RelN order is generally found in Asia, while in the rest of the world OV languages are much more likely to have NRel order. In other words, OV & RelN seems to be a distinct areal feature of Asia. Of course, the large question remains as to why OV & RelN is a distinct areal feature of Asia.

Due to space limitations, only one example can be given here to show how language universals or universal preferences are explained in linguistic typology. The correlation between Verb-initial (or, more generally, VO) order and prepositions provides a good illustration of functional explanation, typically proposed in linguistic typology. One explanation that has been put forth for this correlation is that there is a linguistic preference for either right-branching or left-branching (in constituent structure). In right-branching, phrasal categories follow non-phrasal categories, whereas in left-branching, phrasal categories precede non-phrasal categories. In VSO or VOS order, V (a non-phrasal category) precedes S and O (both phrasal categories). Similarly, in a prepositional phrase, the preposition (a non-phrasal category) precedes its object noun phrase (a phrasal category). Thus, the correlation between Verb-initial order and prepositions is based on the consistent ordering of non-phrasal categories before phrasal categories, that is, right-branching. This consistent ordering must have something to do with processing efficiency, because the consistent direction of branching may not cause processing difficulty associated with the combination of right- and left-branching structure. Another processing-based explanation is that the use of prepositions, as opposed to postpositions, in Verb-initial (or, more generally, VO) languages makes it easier to build internal constituent structure in language performance as rapidly and efficiently as possible. The use of postpositions in Verb-initial or VO order will give rise to a decrease in processing efficiency, because the object noun phrase of the postpositional phrase will delay the processing of the (following) postposition – which needs to be processed together with V as early as possible for purposes of optimal recognition of the relevant constituent structure.

25.8 Closing remarks

Linguistic typology, to borrow the words of the American linguistic typologist Johanna Nichols (2007: 236), 'is on the roll at the moment and likely to continue' to contribute to the investigation into the nature of human language, on both empirical and theoretical levels, as it has done so since Joseph Greenberg's pioneering work in the 1960s. Linguistic typology, at least in the first two decades of this century, is likely to concentrate on developing or refining its research methods – not least because such a methodological exercise, more frequently than not, leads to the discovery of problems or issues of theoretical import – and also on producing theories that make sense of the world's linguistic diversity. Moreover, given linguistic typology's open-mindedness about the basis of explanation, the kind of typological research that is willing to cross its boundaries into other disciplines (e.g. cognitive science, genetic science, human prehistory, human geography, etc.) is likely to occupy centre-stage, while the discovery of the nature of human language will continue to be the primary objective of linguistic typology.

Note

1 At http://typo.uni-konstanz.de/archive/intro/.

Further reading

Comrie, B. (1989) *Language Universals and Linguistic Typology*, 2nd edition. Oxford: Blackwell.
Croft, W. (2003) *Typology and Universals*, 2nd edition. Cambridge: Cambridge University Press.
Dryer, M.S. (1989) Large linguistic areas and language sampling. *Studies in Language* 13: 257–92.
Dryer, M.S. (1992) The Greenbergian word order correlations. *Language* 68: 81–138.
Greenberg, J.H. (1963) Some universals of grammar with particular reference to the order of meaningful elements. In J.H. Greenberg (ed.) *Universals of Language*. Cambridge: MIT Press.

Haspelmath, M., D. Gil, M. Dryer and B. Comrie (eds) (2005) *The World Atlas of Language Structures*. Oxford: Oxford University Press.

Moravcsik, E. (2013) *Introducing Language Typology*. Cambridge: Cambridge University Press.

Song, J.J. (2001) *Linguistic Typology: Morphology and Syntax*. Harlow: Pearson Education (Longman).

Song, J.J. (ed.) (2011) *The Oxford Handbook of Linguistic Typology*. Oxford: Oxford University Press.

Velupillai, V. (2012) *An Introduction to Linguistic Typology*. Amsterdam: John Benjamins.

Whaley, L.J. (1997) *Introduction to Typology: The Unity and Diversity of Language*. Thousand Oaks: Sage.

References

Bell, A. (1978) Language samples. In J.H. Greenberg, C.A. Ferguson and E.A. Moravcsik (eds) *Universals of Human Languages, Volume 1: Method and Theory*, pp. 123–56. Stanford: Stanford University Press.

Bickel, B. (2007) Typology in the 21st century: Major current developments. *Linguistic Typology* 11: 239–51.

Dryer, M.S. (1989) Large linguistic areas and language sampling. *Studies in Language* 13: 257–92.

Dryer, M.S. (2011) Order of subject, object and verb. In M. Haspelmath, M. Dryer, D. Gil and B. Comrie (eds) *The World Atlas of Language Structures Online*. Leipzig: Max Planck Institute for Evolutionary Anthropology (Available online at http://wals.info/chapter/81).

Greenberg, J.H. (1963) Some universals of grammar with particular reference to the order of meaningful elements. In J.H. Greenberg (ed.) *Universals of Language*. Cambridge: MIT Press.

Haspelmath, M., M. Dryer, D. Gil and B. Comrie (eds) (2005) *The World Atlas of Language Structures*. Oxford: Oxford University Press.

Nichols, J. (2007) What, if anything, is typology? *Linguistic Typology* 11: 231–8.

Siewierska, A. (2004) *Person*. Cambridge: Cambridge University Press.

Stassen, L. (1985) *Comparison and Universal Grammar*. Oxford: Basil Blackwell.

26
Translating between languages

Anthony Pym

26.1 Introduction

If translation and linguistics were married, they would have 'issues.' One of those issues concerns a felt lack of support: 'Linguistics alone won't help us,' wrote the German translation scholar Hans Vermeer in 1987, and he gave his reasons: 'First, because translating is not merely and not even primarily a linguistic process. Second, because linguistics has not yet formulated the right questions to tackle our problems. So let's look somewhere else' (Vermeer 1987: 29). That sounded like divorce. The problem was not that translators had somehow stopped working on language. After all, any knowledge about language, especially about texts, is potentially useful to trainee translators and translation scholars; a 'linguistic approach' to translation theory is reported as being taught in 95 percent of 41 translation schools across Europe and North America (Ulrych 2005: 20); countless textbooks for translators run through the basics of several levels of linguistic analysis. The traditional linguistic approaches nevertheless concern languages and texts, the things translators work *on*. They mostly do not analyze the fact of translation itself, minimally seen through the relations between a text and its possible renditions – they are mostly not linguistics of translation, of the things translators *do*, and the ways they do it. That is why Vermeer felt there was a lack of support.

Vermeer's complaint echoed similar grumbles from the French translation scholar Georges Mounin, who was a little more explicit back in the 1960s: 'As a distinctive linguistic operation and a linguistic fact *sui generis*, translation has so far been absent from the linguistic science reflected in our major treatises' (1963: 8). Mounin, unlike Vermeer, was prepared to go on the attack:

> Translating itself poses a theoretical problem for contemporary linguistics. If one accepts the current theses about the structure of lexicons, morphologies and syntaxes, one inevitably concludes that translation must be impossible. But translators exist; they produce; people make use of their products. We might almost say the existence of translation constitutes the scandal of contemporary linguistics.
>
> (Mounin 1963: 7; my translation)

Mounin was writing against the background of mainstream structuralist linguistics, which had developed from Saussure's separation of the language system from language use. For the Saussure of the *Cours de linguistique générale* (1974 [1916]: 115), the French word *mouton* corresponded to the semantic space of the two English words *sheep* (for the animal) and *mutton* (for the meat), so the French and English language systems cut up the world differently in that area. A radical structuralist might then claim that the word *sheep* cannot adequately translate the word *mouton*. Indeed, except for artificially constrained technical terms, translation itself might seem impossible. So Mounin retorted that what was impossible was structuralist linguistics, not translation. He then proposed an empirical approach, claiming that 'untranslatability' was a marginal occurrence, to be assessed statistically by counting the few foreign words for which translators could really find no equivalents. This turn to empiricism, to the study of actual performances of translation, marked one of the main ways in which Translation Studies moved away from linguistics in the 1980s and 1990s, and so far has not really returned.

In order to understand that story, one must first admit that there are major preconceptions and misconceptions on both sides. Translation scholars still tend to think that all linguistics is structuralist and systemic, which is far from the case. At the same time, some linguists tend to think that all translation is a literal rendition of a text in a foreign language, which is also far from the case. Here we use 'translation' as a general term for communicative events involving both written and spoken language, cross-cultural mediation (in medical encounters, for example), localization (notably of software and websites) and machine translation (especially the systems based on statistics). The important point is not the many modes of communication, but the communicative status of all these different kinds of events: a translation not only represents a start text, it also interprets and mostly re-enacts that text for a new set of participants.

That wider view of translation creates a very interesting set of questions. For instance, we might take Saussure's *mouton* versus *sheep* example and note that the different structures can only be seen if you try to translate one term as the other. That is, the linguist seeing the structures was necessarily translating – perhaps badly, for a limited communicative purpose, but still translating. And then one might go back in history and locate the operational difference in situations where Anglo-Saxon servants presented what they called *scēap* to their Norman masters, who might have called the same object *moton*, and both sides were necessarily translating the words of the other, in a situation that had not only language contact but also highly asymmetric power relations between social groups. Communicative translation is present in many linguistic encounters, if you know where to look, as are those asymmetric relations. Translation involves much more than pairing together isolated words and sentences.

26.2 Comparative stylistics

No one doubts that different languages have different ways of saying things: *I like you* is *Me gustas* ('to me are likeable you') in Spanish, and if you do not use the transformation well you might finish up declaring love (*te quiero*) or getting into even deeper trouble. Contemporary semantics and pragmatics might look for ways to define what that 'same thing' is; linguistic philosophers these days tend to doubt that the thing really is the 'same'; but for nineteenth-century linguistics in the Germanic tradition, the main interest was in the systematic differences between the languages. So we begin from there.

For Wilhelm von Humboldt, each language expressed a 'worldview' and the study of languages had as its general aim the characterization of those differences. Von Humboldt, however, was also a translator from Greek, and as a translator he saw his mission as being not to maintain separate worldviews but to enable one language to help the other develop: the most important aim of translation was 'to expand the significance and expressive capacity of one's own language' (1963 [1816]: 81). In von Humboldt's case, structures from classical Greek were supposed to ennoble the rough-hewn qualities of German. This required a relatively literalist view of translation, although not blindly so. The general concept of translation as actively developing the target language can be traced through Schleiermacher and Goethe, and became so influential that many of the Germanic reflections on translation through to the twentieth century actually talk more about relations between languages than about people or texts (in part because German as a national language did not belong to a unified state until 1871). Vermeer, who saw translation as fulfilling a communicative purpose between people, was certainly reacting against that kind of linguistics.

Towards the end of the nineteenth century, it became more commonplace for European linguists to assert that (major national) languages had different 'personalities' or 'essences,' often because the languages had been shaped by the works of great writers. This gave rise to comparative stylistics, the study of the expressive resources that different languages distribute in different ways. Since translation was likely to alter those apparently autochthonous resources, it came to be seen as a source of interference rather than development. The Swiss linguist Charles Bally, perhaps best known in English as one of the co-editors of Saussure's *Cours*, started developing his stylistics from 1905, explicitly rejecting the 'impressionistic' Germanic methods. Bally's approach concerned language usage (*parole*), specifically the options that each language makes available in order for a speaker to say something that both 'sounds right' and expresses 'affectivity,' over and above obeying grammatical laws. Bally describes the origins of his linguistics as follows: 'As I went through French texts with foreign students, as I translated German texts into French with them, I was naturally led to reflect on the difficulties they encountered and the differences they found between the two languages' (1965 [1932]: 8; my translation). So translation lay at the foundations of his reflections on language, and one of the explicit purposes of Bally's study of stylistics was indeed to correct the students' defective renditions. Translation thus fed into a mode of linguistics, which could in turn help improve translations.

The key difference here is that, whereas the Germanic tradition saw translation as a way of developing languages, Bally's comparative stylistics sought to correct literalism, and thus to maintain the differences between manners of expression by making translations more adaptive and natural. Bally's work never actually embarked on the second step, where comparative stylistics was supposed to help translators – he did not really move beyond a view of translation as an attempt at mechanical correspondence. Remarkably, Bally uses the term 'functional equivalences' for the expressions the linguist compares within the one language, in fact as the linguist's basic tool for research (1965 [1932]: 40), but he never used that tool for relations between expressions in different languages. He simply did not trust translations.

The application of Bally's stylistics to translation had to wait for the work of the French linguists Jean-Paul Vinay and Jean Darbelnet, whose *Stylistique comparée du français et de l'anglais: méthode de traduction* (1958) lists seven main solution types (*procédés*, procedures) that translators could use: borrowing, calque, literal translation, transposition, modulation, correspondence (*équivalence*) and adaptation, along with a set of 'prosodic effects' that included explicitation, implicitation and compensation. This, at least, was a classification of what translators are supposed to do, rather than of the things they work on. The operative assumption in Vinay and Darbelnet is that a translation is 'literal' (word for word) until the result sounds 'unnatural,' at which point the translator can look at borrowing and calque, in the case of names and terms, and at various degrees of syntactic and semantic transformation for the rest, reaching the extreme where American 'baseball' can be translated as French 'cycling,' since both function as national summer sports. As French linguists working in Canada, Vinay and Darbelnet insist that translators should use the more transformative solution types, lest Canadian French be excessively 'developed' by American English. Their application of comparative stylistics was clearly opposed to the translation preferences of the Germanic tradition.

Vinay and Darbelnet's categories, which are pedagogically useful but have no cognitive underpinning, were eventually adapted to translation between several other European languages. In the 1990s the basic set of translation solutions proliferated in many textbooks for training translators, progressively shedding Vinay and Darbelnet's assumptions about the different '*génies*' that different languages were supposed to have.

An alternative tradition developed in Russian, actually prior to Vinay and Darbelnet and with a rather closer relation to official linguistics. In 1950 Stalin declared that a language did not belong to any particular social class. This political intervention allowed a return to formalist approaches to language, including synchronic analysis and applications to translation. In 1950 Yakob Retsker published a landmark paper on 'regular correspondences' in translation, where he distinguished between: (1) established equivalents (as in technical terms); (2) analogue translation, where the translator chooses between synonyms; and (3) 'adequate' translation (or 'substitution'), where the translator uses various resources to render the style and function of the text. This third category is where the various solution types, of the kind found in Vinay and Darbelnet, would fit in, although in the later Russian tradition they came to be called 'transformations.' This general view was picked up and developed in Andrei Fedorov's *Vvedenie v teoriju perevoda* (Introduction to the Theory of Translation) (1953), possibly the first book-length linguistic approach to translation. Fedorov may sound like Bally when he proposes that 'comparative study of two languages can map the differences between them, which helps to find corresponding solutions' (1953: 101 transl. by Nune Ayvazyan). However, Fedorov also defends the fundamental principle of translatability, which effectively means that translations can be subject to general abstract principles. From there, he attempts to map out how a successful translation can be 'adequate' in both form and content, since the two levels are dialectically entwined in any text. He also sketches out a theory of how translation solutions depend on three broad text types: referential texts, where the translator must pay careful attention to terms; publicity and propaganda, where the effect on the receiver is what counts; and literary works, where 'it is important to reproduce the individual particularities of the text' (1953: 256). Here the grounding in the three linguistic persons is fairly clear, as is the attempt to make general linguistic principles compatible with literary criteria.

Translated into Chinese in 1955, Fedorov was the link explaining how similar solution types appear in Loh Dian-yang's *Translation: Its Principles and Techniques*, published (in English) in Beijing in 1958, the same year as Vinay and Darbelnet. Loh also recognizes three main text types, with translation solutions being different for each. He similarly proposes a short list of main solution types: five for foreign terms, then omission, amplification, repetition, conversion, inversion and negation. These would become the basis of a pedagogical tradition that has survived through to today.

The approaches that found their springboard in comparative stylistics tend to be heavy with fascinating examples and light on clear linguistic principles. In this, they are rather different from John Catford's *Linguistic Theory of Translation* (1965). Catford might also sound like Bally when he sees the study of translation as a branch of contrastive linguistics, related in such a way that translation is a method of research, a way of testing principles, and a potential beneficiary of linguistic findings. Working from Firth and Halliday, Catford also believes that meaning is formed by networks within individual languages, so there can be no question of translating meaning in any full sense (pp. 36–7) – he would not blithely accept Fedorov's principle of translatability. Yet translation can work in parts: Catford points out that equivalence is not operative on all language levels at once but tends to be 'rank-bound.' For example, there might be equivalence to a phonetics of a string, to the lexis, to the phrase, to the sentence, to the semantic function, and so on. Since most translating operates on one or several of these levels, 'in the course of a text, equivalence may shift up and down the rank scale' (p. 76). One might equally say that translators mix and match different types of translation solutions as they go along.

As Translation Studies took shape as an interdiscipline and moved away from linguistics in the 1980s, the analysis of stylistics and solution types only really survived in textbooks. In their place we find a series of grand binary oppositions such as 'formal correspondence' versus 'dynamic equivalence' (Nida 1964), 'documentary' versus 'instrumental' translation (Nord 1997), or 'anti-illusory' versus 'illusory' translation (Levý 2011 [1963]), in which the first of these terms would have the translation follow the start text as closely as possible, whereas the second strives to produce a natural-sounding text for the target situation. These oppositions go back to the pair 'Germanizing' vs 'foreignizing' coined by Schleiermacher (1963 [1813]), and beyond that to the choice between rendering *ut interpres* (like a literalist interpreter) or *ut orator* (like a public speaker) in Cicero. The grand oppositions also informed the way comparative stylistics was applied to translation: the Germanic tradition still preferred the side of literalism and development, the Francophone tradition generally preferred functionalism and the maintenance of differences. These binary oppositions allow for numerous ideological debates about how the self should relate to the other, or how a home culture should communicate with the rest, but there is little linguistics in them. As endpoints of continua, they concern the reasons why a translator might choose one kind of solution or another, but they should not be confused with the solution types themselves.

Linguistics cannot help translators make decisions (this was one of Vermeer's laments), but it can and has helped describe the toolbox with which they work. The lists of solution types still deserve attention, perhaps all the more now that they have shed many of the ideological presuppositions of their origins. If nothing else, the solution types underscore the range of translators' work: when new terms are required in a language, translators are there on the frontline, choosing between degrees of borrowing and calque, and when a culture chooses whether to imitate the foreign or stress its own independence, translators are also there, selecting between the degrees of adaptation.

26.3 Applications of transformational grammar

Although the solution types were developed from comparative stylistics, they were involved in several attempted trysts with other kinds of linguistics. In 1964, the linguist and Bible translator Eugene Nida proposed that Chomsky's early generative transformational grammar could help guide translators' decisions: 'A generative grammar is based upon certain fundamental kernel sentences, out of which the language builds up its elaborate structure by various techniques of permutation, replacement, addition, and deletion' (1964: 60). Nida proposed that the translator could extract the kernels from the start text, then apply the same or different techniques ('transformations') to generate the target text. The transformations could be like the ones commonly used in English (passives from actives, questions from statements), but they can also include things that translators commonly do in order to produce a 'natural' sounding text: changing the order of elements ('permutation'), changing word classes ('replacement'), explicitation ('addition') and implicitation ('deletion'). The actual kernels referred to in Nida are simple structures basically used for disambiguation, of the kind that owes more to Zellig Harris than to Chomsky: the phrase *fat major's wife* can be translated, says Nida, once we know it is derived from the two kernels *The major has a wife* and *The wife is fat* (1964: 61). One wonders why this is not simple componential analysis, but at the time it might have looked revolutionary.

Nida's evocation of transformational grammar in 1964 was an elegant way of explaining what was being translated: 'kernels' could partly replace problematic idealist assumptions about 'ideas' or 'messages.' It also located solution types within a linguistic scheme: the 'procedures' described by Vinay and Darbelnet are now seen as the 'techniques' or 'adjustments' used in the transformations. The beautiful idea was nevertheless promptly quashed by Chomsky's pronouncement, in the following year, that deep-seated universals did not 'imply that there must be some reasonable procedure for translating between languages' (Chomsky 1965: 30). His linguistics was not going to support the venture.

Why Chomsky wrote that remains a point of conjecture. For Melby and Warner (1995: 179) it is a claim about the non-reversibility of transformations: while there can be a reasoned generation from deep structure to surface structure, there is no guarantee of a rational movement in the opposite direction. For example, *fat major's wife*, as a surface structure (which is what the translator is looking at), remains ambiguous because there is more than one possible underlying structure, and if you do not have prior knowledge of what is meant, the attribution of disambiguating kernels does not in itself remove the ambiguity. Of course, if you do know what the underlying structure is, then you can go from there to the surface, but if you only have the surface, you cannot reach the underlying structure with any certainty.

This non-reversibility has to do with a parallel debate that was going on at the time. The language philosopher Willard V.O. Quine had formulated the principle of indeterminacy in translation, which posits that the one utterance can legitimately be translated in different ways, and that those different translations will 'stand to each other in no plausible sort of equivalence relation however loose' (1960: 27). At its widest level, this is a principle about theories: the one object can adequately be explained by different theories. Yet it might be interesting for someone trying to explain how translation is possible.

In Nida's later work we find insistence that the kinds of 'kernels' translators work on are not at all deep-seated. In fact, the kernels turn out to be little more than componential analysis, and the practical result for the types of translation solutions was just another version of comparative stylistics in the Vinay and Darbelnet style, with very little trace of anything being drawn from a newer kind of linguistics. The translation theorists tried to use transformational grammar, but it just did not work.

In the meantime, the Soviet translation scholars consistently used the term 'transformations' to describe translation solutions, paying serious attention to meaning as well (they cite Harris more than Chomsky). Komissarov (1972), who also uses the term 'transformations,' gives a passing nod to the notion of 'kernel structures' as in Nida but then quickly steers his interests towards quite another approach: the 'statistically most probable' correspondences between elements in the two languages. In the 1970s the Soviet translation theorists were thinking seriously about machine translation, and Komissarov's preference for statistics over kernel transfer now seems quite prophetic. In the end, as we shall see, the revolution has indeed come from statistics, and not from rational transformations.

In sum, transformational grammar did not have a glorious meeting with translation theory.

26.4 The pragmatics of translation

Other kinds of linguistics have found interesting things to say about translation, over and above descriptions of the texts and languages that translators work on. In the American analytical tradition, there have been attempts to describe translation as a special mode of reported speech. Bigelow (1978) analyzed the operator 'translates as' as being both quotational (as in normal reported speech) and productive of new information (since it gives information about the other text). Others have seen that, when seen as reported speech, the prime interest of translation is the particular role attributed to the translator as reporter. Mossop (1983) and Folkart (1991) underscore the *heuristic* work of the translator as an active, intervening reporter, particularly in situations that Folkart describes as lacking 'reversibility' or as being characterized by indeterminism. Others have approached the translator's discursive position in terms of Goffman's (1981) theory of footing, particularly the categories of 'animator,' 'author' and 'principal.' There is debate about the extent to which translators are merely 'animators,' who present the words of others, or 'authors' who select the sentiments expressed, or indeed 'principals,' who actually take ethical responsibility for what they say, as might be clear in cases of self-translation.

The study of the translator's particular voice might be dated from descriptive work on literary translations in the 1960s. The tendency within recent translation theory has been to regard the translator as a kind of author, mostly in the vague sense of a co-creator of meaning. The linguistic work of the translator nevertheless clashes with conventions like the 'alien-I': when a translating translator says 'I,' they are not referring to themselves, and they are thus condemned to create a voice without pronoun. The alien-I, however, is by no means a feature of all the translations in the world (the late nineteenth-century Chinese translator Yan Fu, for example, referred to his author in the third person). Its function is subject to historical and political analysis.

Rather less attention has been paid to the *second* person of a translation, the person receiving the discourse. Pym (1992) has proposed that the social function of a translation is to convert an 'excluded' receiver (who does not have access to the start language) into an 'observational' receiver (who can construe what is in the text), and sometimes into a 'participative' receiver (who can respond to the text communicatively). The difference between the observational and participative positions would respond not only to factors such as text type and situational appropriateness, but also to the way in which the text can be translated to allow more or less receptor involvement. Only when the second person is potentially participative can a translation claim to be anything like a performative status. Translations can actually cross these divisions, operating in terms of 'heterolingual address' (Sakai 1997), which means speaking to several audiences at once: translations of Japanese culture not only inform the foreigner but also shape the image and boundaries of Japanese culture itself.

Much remains to be explored with respect to the limits of translation as a performative utterance or a participative event. The more literary uses of pragmatics currently tend to be concerned not so much about the conditions under which translational discourse normally operates and can be trusted, but with making translations less boring.

A major application of relevance theory to translation is in Gutt (2000 [1991]), who offers a slightly different take on translation as reported speech. Accepting that language is a set of communicative clues with recoverable implicatures, Gutt posits that the sentence 'The back door is open' can be reported/translated in at least two ways:

Translation 1: 'The back door is open.'

Translation 2: 'We should close the back door.'

Translation 1 renders the form of the start utterance, presupposing that the receiver has access to the start situation. Translation 2, on the other hand, renders the implicature of the utterance, and does not presuppose that the receiver has full knowledge of the situation (although the receiver would in this case be less 'participative'). Gutt's preference is for the first kind of translation, since he argues that the second kind would have no reason to be a translation (it might as well be a commentary on the start text, or on the situation). Working in the field of Bible translation, Gutt uses this theory to oppose the preference for 'dynamic equivalence' expressed in the work of Nida, which would be based on what the Biblical texts mean rather than what they say. Gutt prefers to make the reader work.

26.5 The search for universals and laws

The kind of exploratory, quantitative research called for in Mounin (1963) or Komissarov (1972) flourished into a research program from the late 1980s, taking shape around the Israeli translation scholar Gideon Toury's landmark *Descriptive Translation Studies and Beyond* (2012 [1995]). In the decades since then we have learned a great deal about the historical and cultural varieties of translational discourse (increasingly in non-Western cultures), about the role of translation in the shaping of cultures and identities, and about the way concepts of translation respond to factors like communication technologies and power relations. Remarkably little of that knowledge, however, can be called linguistic in any strict sense. Translation scholars have increasingly sought their dancing partners in the fields of cultural studies, sociology and psychology.

A more linguistic pause in the trend nevertheless came in the late 1980s, when some scholars attempted to say how translations differ from non-translations, specifically with respect to the kind of language used. Translations can be compared with two kinds of non-translations: either the start text (as in traditional linguistic and pedagogical approaches) or a 'parallel' or 'comparable' text already in the target language (for example, an instruction manual translated into English can be compared with an instruction manual written directly in English). The aim in both cases was to isolate features peculiar to translations, independently of the languages involved. The search was thus for 'universals of translation,' not in any Chomskyan sense of deep-seated structures but more simply as linguistic features that tend to be found more in translations than in non-translations. Here are some of the proposed universals:

- *Lexical simplification* is 'the process and/or result of making do with *less* [different] words' (Blum-Kulka and Levenston 1983: 119). Translations tend to have a narrower range of lexical items and a higher proportion of high-frequency lexical items; the language is flatter, less structured, less ambiguous, less specific to a given text (cf. Toury 2012 [1995]).

- *Explicitation* is a particular kind of simplification due to the greater 'redundancy' of translations. For example, optional cohesive markers tend to be used more in translations than in non-translations (Blum-Kulka 2004 [1986]). If a non-translation has *The girl I saw*, a translation would tend to have *The girl that I saw*. The category is frequently extended to include cases of lexical explicitation. For example, 'students of St. Mary's' may become 'étudiantes de l'école St. Mary' in translation, where the French specifies that the students are women and St. Mary's is a school (Vinay and Darbelnet 1972 [1958]: 117).
- *Equalizing* is the term used by Shlesinger (1989) to describe how translators and interpreters tend to avoid both some characteristics of spoken language (such as false starts, hesitations and colloquialisms) and some extremes of written language (such as complex syntax and ornamental phrases). Translations would tend towards a middle discursive ground.
- *Unique items* are what the Finnish researcher Tirkkonen-Condit (2004) calls linguistic elements found in the target language but not in the start language. These items are less frequent in translations than in non-translations, since 'they do not readily suggest themselves as translation equivalents' (2004: 177–8). This has been tested on linguistic structures in Finnish and Swedish, but it might also apply to something like the structure 'to be + PAST PARTICIPLE' in English (as in 'they are to be married'), which tends not to be found in translations. The avoidance of unique items clearly feeds into the principle of lexical simplification, to the extent that it is simply proposing a different discovery procedure.

These proposed universals have been derived from comparisons of written translations of technical and literary texts, increasingly through the study of corpora; they might not apply to audiovisual translation (subtitles, dubbing), theater translation, software translation or the results of statistical machine translation, for example. Indeed, there has been much less research on alternative or counter hypotheses. For example, there are literary translations where implicitation is actually more frequent than explicitation, and explicitation may be a result of retelling, quite independently of any change in language. This should seriously question the proposed 'universal' status of these phenomena, as indeed should the lack of controlled studies into their possible psychological or social causes. As they stand, though, these four proposed universals are broadly compatible with each other, telling a common story of translators who do not take risks, who are careful to ensure understanding, and who do so even at the expense of producing texts that are relatively anodyne. The underlying tendency to risk-aversion may not be universal (it could be restricted to situations where translators are not rewarded for taking communicative risks, whereas artistic authors are). The tendency to risk-aversion also stands fascinatingly opposed to the interest in translations as communicative events. The more recent theories could be seen as calls for translators to take more communicative risks.

Gideon Toury has called for work at a higher level of abstraction, where series of observations about translational tendencies (on the level of 'universals') are mustered as support for proposed laws of translation. The general form of these laws would be probabilistic, of the form 'If 1 and 2, and 3, and …∞, then there is greater likelihood that X' (Toury 2004: 26), where 1, 2 and 3 are social, psychological or professional factors. Toury has proposed two laws that might be adapted to that format. The first is a general 'law of growing standardization' (2012 [1995]: 303–10), which brings together many of the tendencies seen on the level of universals ('standardization' means that translations are simpler, flatter, less structured, less ambiguous, less specific to a given text, and more habitual). Toury proposes that 'the more peripheral [the status of translation], the more translation will accommodate itself to established models and repertoires' (p. 307); that is, to risk a paraphrase, the less translations are called on to actively shape and extend cultural repertoires, the less translators will be prepared to take communicative risks.

Toury's second law concerns the degree to which 'interference' from the start language and text is tolerated in translations; that is, the degree to which a receiving culture will accept translations that sound foreign. Toury proposes that the greater the text unit (phrase, sentence, paragraph, chapter), the greater the interference. This is logical enough, since changing large units requires considerable effort, and translators are not usually rewarded for that work. Toury then proposes that 'tolerance of interference […] tend[s] to increase when translation is carried out from a "major" or highly prestigious language/culture' (2012 [1995]: 314). That is, translations are more 'foreignizing' when from a culture considered to be relatively prestigious – we copy those we admire. Alternatively, in terms of risk analysis, we might say that the prestige of a foreign culture, author or text might allow a certain risk-transfer: If there are problems in understanding, the receivers might attribute it to the greatness of the foreign text rather than to the ineptitude of the translator.

Research on these hypotheses has not progressed in any controlled way. It has tended to be overtaken by literary and cultural studies, on the one hand, and by research on translators' cognitive processes, on the other. The cognitive researchers use a variety of tools, including think-aloud protocols, screen-recording and eye-tracking to investigate differences in work habits (particularly between novices and professionals) and interaction with translation memories and machine translation. Their categories are rarely linguistic in anything beyond the banal level of names for pieces of language. As Vermeer had said, linguistics is not enough.

26.6 Translation technologies

The prime application of linguistics to translation should ideally be machine translation, and this connection did indeed underlie many of the other relationships. The automatic production of translations can be dated from Soviet work in the 1930s but its most public advance came following the successes of cryptology during the Second World War. Given the enthusiasm with which initial successes were met in the climate of the early Cold War, it is not difficult to understand how the code-based approach spilled over into general optimism for a view of language as being based on series of applied rules. Not by chance, the Russians applied generative principles not just to machine translation but to a model of translation in general, and the Russian theorists consequently used the term 'transformations' to describe the various solutions available to all translators. In the United States, Chomsky was funded by various branches of the US military prior to 1965, and we have seen that Nida similarly attempted to see all translations as transformations. There was a general view that linguistic science would lead to generalized progress, with machine translation as the flagship.

This enthusiasm declined with the publication of the ALPAC Report in 1966, which in hindsight was a lucid evaluation of the goals, costs and social alternatives to machine translation, including a discussion of language learning as the major alternative – if there was so much science in Russian, then why not make some scientists learn Russian? The ALPAC report curiously coincided with a period of détente in US–Soviet relations, when the spirit of competition had declined and long-term cooperation could briefly be envisaged.

As the enthusiasm for machine translation declined, funding went more into computational linguistics (as recommended by ALPAC), and translation scholars started to look elsewhere.

Apart from very restricted semantic fields like bilingual weather reports in Canada, machine translation did not have a significant impact on the translation professions. Cost-beneficial advances nevertheless came with the translation memory tools marketed in the 1990s. These were basically software that stored the translator's previous renditions as paired segments (usually sentences), then recalled the previous rendition when the same or a similar segment was to be translated. For instance, imagine the translator has already rendered the following:

ST1: The password reset operation has been re-designed in the new 32-bit version.

When a similar sentence appears, either in the same text, in an update of the document, or in a subsequent project, the two sentences are calculated to have a 'fuzzy' match of 79 percent:

ST2: The password reset operation has been **deleted** in the **Windows Version**.

To render this second sentence, the translator merely has to change the two bolded items, which differ from the previous translation.

There was some basic linguistics involved in the identification and segmentation of parts of speech and the calculation of fuzzy matches, and the performance of translation memories could be improved with the introduction of language-pair-specific algorithms. At base, though, translation memories constituted an advance that came from pieces of software programming, increased memory capacity, and some mathematics – it was not particularly due to linguistics or translation studies. Over the years, translation memory suites have steadily become more sophisticated, incorporating terminology tools, advanced text processing, project management tools in some versions, and machine-translation feeds for segments that have no matches in the standing memory. Although the tools were originally marketed in terms of the time they could save translators, actual time savings depend very much on the degree of repetition in each text and the quality of the translation memory. The more consistent benefits have proven to be in greater terminological and phraseological consistency and the capacity to have different translators work on the same project simultaneously.

The most significant advance in recent years has come from statistical machine translation, developed by IBM from 1993 and used by Google's free online service from 2007, particularly thanks to the work of the computer scientist Franz Joseph Och. Statistical machine translation is based not on grammatical analysis but on the frequencies with which mathematically identified 'phrasemes' are associated in a database of paired segments. There are many hybrid projects integrating statistical methods with rule-based approaches, but there is little doubt that the main advance has come from mathematics.

To give an idea of how statistical machine translation works, we might take a long-standing problem in literary translation. No one knows what Don Quixote ate on Saturdays. The Spanish text says 'duelos y quebrantos,' which different human translators into English have rendered as 'hash,' 'boiled bones,' 'sorrows and troubles,' 'gripes and grumblings,' 'eggs and abstinence,' 'peas soup' and much else. 'Duelos' can mean 'pains'; 'quebrantos' can mean 'breakings,' which might suggest how the grumblings and peas got into the translation. However, if you put the Spanish words into a statistical machine translation engine one by one, here is what happens:

> Duelos: *duels* (along with suggestions of *mourning* and *grief*, since several 'kernels' are possible)
>
> Duelos y: *duels and*
>
> Duelos y quebrantos: *duels and losses*

This is straight dictionary-type matching; it is not really helping. But wait, just add one or two more words:

> Duelos y quebrantos los: *scraps on*
>
> Duelos y quebrantos los sábados: *scraps on Saturdays*

The simple addition of the article 'los' activates the statistically most probable match, drawn from a translation of *Don Quixote* that has been fed into the database. This kind of translating is thanks to statistics not linguistics. Its terminological hits can be surprisingly accurate, just as its syntactic misfortunes still depend to some degree on the proximity of the languages and the quality of the databases in question.

The main use of machine translation is still for informative 'gist' versions and rough translations suitable for post-editing. Outputs can also be improved significantly by the use of pre-editing, which involves rewriting the start text in a controlled language (with simplified syntax and a standardized lexis).

The utopian promise of statistical machine translation was that, as databases grew, translations would become better, which would encourage greater use of them, hence further growth in the databases, and so on, in a virtuous circle. The main problem with that promise is that uninformed users mistake the suggestions for acceptable translations. Raw machine translation output then becomes available in electronic media and can be fed back into the databases, increasing the statistical probability of errors. The virtuous circle becomes a vicious circle.

The future of machine translation probably lies in situations where databases can be limited and controlled, as when companies develop their own in-house statistical machine translation systems, perhaps with standardized databases for each of their products. At this point, the use of statistical machine translation actually functions like a large translation memory.

In sum, the history of machine translation and translation memories underscores the historical relations between linguistics and translation. Despite great enthusiasm when it seemed that rule-based linguistics would solve translation problems, we now have genuinely useful technologies that assist (rather than replace) translators and whose recent developments have drawn on disciplines other than linguistics.

26.7 A future together?

Institutional relations between linguistics and translation studies remain strong in the United Kingdom and some of its former colonies, weak in the United States (where translation belongs more to Comparative Literature), and wavering almost everywhere else. One reason for this might lie in the economics of English as the global lingua franca, particularly in the reasons why foreign students seek courses in English-speaking countries – translation is a practical thing to teach those students.

In terms of research, there are nevertheless some areas in which translation scholars might turn to linguistics in search of models and guidance. One of them, as mentioned, concerns the limits and historical dynamics of the translation concept itself, particularly with respect to the pragmatics of the event. A second area might be the use of process research to test traditional linguistic assumptions about what translators do, for example whether there is automatized cognitive mapping from form to form or, instead, a visualized situation to which the target utterance is holistically judged to be suitable (both things certainly happen, and there are things in between, but we do not know exactly when or why). A third area, closely related, would be the integration of findings from neuro-imaging experiments involving symmetric and asymmetric bilinguals, where translation is involved in some of the experiments but has not really been reflected on as such. This research might explain anecdotal observations that people who learn L2 late in life tend to make better translators and interpreters. And one final area in which applied linguistics might fruitfully rethink translation is in L2 acquisition. There, in the L2 class, the pragmatics of communicative events and awareness that mental translation is happening much of the time might come together. The result should be new teaching methods that include translation as one of the fundamental language skills, alongside speaking, listening, writing and reading.

In all these areas, the fundamental challenge is for translation to be approached as a communicative act.

References

ALPAC (1966) *Languages and Machines: Computers in Translation and Linguistics. A Report by the Automatic Language Processing Advisory Committee, Division of Behavioral Sciences, National Academy of Sciences, National Research Council.* Washington, DC: National Academy of Sciences, National Research Council.

Bally, C. (1965 [1932]) *Linguistique générale et linguistique française*, 4th edition, revised and corrected. Bern: Francke.

Bigelow, J. (1978) Semantics of thinking, speaking and translation. In F. Guenthner and M. Guenthner-Reutter (eds) *Meaning and Translation: Philosophical and Linguistic Approaches*, pp. 109–35. London: Duckworth.

Blum-Kulka, S. (2004 [1986]) Shifts of cohesion and coherence in translation. In L. Venuti (ed.) *The Translation Studies Reader*, pp. 290–305. London/New York: Routledge.

Blum-Kulka, S. and E.A. Levenston (1983) Universals of lexical simplification. In C. Faerch and G. Casper (eds) *Strategies in Inter-language Communication*, pp. 119–39. London/New York: Longman.

Catford, J.C. (1965) *A Linguistic Theory of Translation*. London: Oxford University Press.

Chomsky, N. (1965) *Aspects of the Theory of Syntax*. Cambridge: MIT Press.

Fedorov, A.V. (1953) *Vvedenie v teoriju perevoda* (Introduction to the theory of translation), Moscow: Literatura na inostr. âzykah. Chinese translation: 《翻译理论概要》 (Introduction to the Theory of Translation). Beijing: Zhonghua, 1955.

Folkart, B. (1991) *Le Conflit des énonciations. Traduction et discours rapporté*. Montreal: Balzac.

Goffman, E. (1981) *Forms of Talk*. Philadelphia: University of Pennsylvania Press.

Gutt, E.-A. (2000 [1991]) *Translation and Relevance: Cognition and Context*, 2nd edition. Manchester: St Jerome.

Humboldt, W. von (1963 [1816]) Einleitung zu Aeschylos Agamemnon metrisch übersetzt von Wilhelm von Humboldt, reprinted in H.J. Störig (ed.) *Das Problem des Übersetzens*, pp. 71–96. Darmstadt: Wissenschaftliche Buchgesellschaft.

Komissarov, V. (1972) Lingvističeskie modeli processa perevoda (Linguistic Models of the Translation Process) *Tetradi Perevodchika* 9: 3–14.

Levý, J. (2011 [1963]) *Umění překladu* [*The Art of Translation*]. Amsterdam and Philadelphia: John Benjamins.

Loh D.Y. (陆殿扬) (1958) *Translation: Its Principles and Techniques*. Beijing: Times Publishing.

Melby, A. and C.T. Warner (1995) *The Possibility of Language: A Discussion of the Nature of Language, with Implications for Human and Machine Translation*, Amsterdam/Philadelphia: John Benjamins.

Mossop, B. (1983) The translator as rapporteur: A concept for training and self-improvement. *Meta* 28: 244–78.

Mounin, G. (1963) *Les Problèmes théoriques de la traduction*. Paris: Gallimard.

Nida, E. (1964) *Toward a Science of Translating with Special Reference to Principles and Procedures involved in Bible Translating*. Leiden: E.J. Brill.

Nord, C. (1997) *Translating as a Purposeful Activity: Functionalist Approaches Explained*, London/New York: Routledge.

Pym, A. (1992) The Relations between translation and material text transfer. *Target* 4: 171–89.

Quine, W.V.O. (1960) *Word and Object*, Cambridge: MIT Press.

Retsker, Y.I. (1950) O Zakonomernyh sootvetstvijah pri perevode na rodnoj jazyk (On regularities in correspondences in translation into the native language). In K.A. Ganshina and I. Karpov (eds) *Voprosy teorii i metodiki učebnogo perevoda* (Questions of the theory and methodology of translation training), pp. 156–83. Moscow: Academy of Pedagogical Sciences of the RSFSR.

Sakai, N. (1997) *Translation and Subjectivity. On 'Japan' and Cultural Nationalism*. Minneapolis/London: University of Minnesota Press.

Saussure, F. de (1974 [1916]) *Cours de linguistique générale*, ed. C. Bally and A. Sechehaye; transl. W. Baskin, *Course in General Linguistics*. Glasgow: Fontana–Collins.

Schleiermacher, F. (1963 [1813]) Ueber die verschiedenen Methoden des Uebersezens, reprinted in H.J. Störig (ed.) *Das Problem des Übersetzens*, pp. 38–70. Darmstadt: Wissenschaftliche Buchgesellschaft.

Shlesinger, M. (1989) Simultaneous interpretation as a factor in effecting shifts in the position of texts on the oral-literate continuum. MA thesis, Tel Aviv University.

Tirkkonen-Condit, S. (2004) Unique items – over- or under-represented in translated language? In A. Mauranen and P. Kujamäki (eds) *Translation Universals: Do They Exist?* pp. 177–86. Amsterdam/Philadelphia: John Benjamins.

Toury, G. (2004) Probabilistic explanations in translation studies: Welcome as they are, would they count as universals? In A. Mauranen and P. Kujamäki (eds) *Translation Universals: Do They Exist?* pp. 15–32. Amsterdam/Philadelphia: John Benjamins.

Toury, G. (2012 [1995]) *Descriptive Translation Studies and Beyond*. Amsterdam/Philadelphia: John Benjamins.

Ulrych, M. (2005) Training translators: Programmes, curricula, practices. In M. Tennent (ed.) *Training for the New Millennium: Pedagogies for Translation and Interpreting*, pp. 3–33. Amsterdam/Philadelphia: John Benjamins.

Vermeer, Hans J. (1987) What does it mean to translate? *Indian Journal of Applied Linguistics* 13(2): 25–33.

Vinay, J.P. and J. Darbelnet (1972 [1958]) *Stylistique comparée du français et de l'anglais: méthode de traduction*, new edition revised and corrected. Paris: Didier.

27
Structural linguistics

John E. Joseph

27.1 Introduction

The term 'structural linguistics' gained currency quite quickly starting in 1940, in both English and French. It was generally associated with the approach set out in the *Cours de linguistique générale* (Course in General Linguistics), published in 1916 and based on lectures given at the University of Geneva by Ferdinand de Saussure (1857–1913) between 1907 and 1911. In the 1920s and 1930s this book (in which the term 'structural' does not actually appear) formed the basis for a reorientation of linguistics from the almost exclusively historical concerns that had dominated the field for the previous hundred years. Saussure was directly cited as the source of the new 'synchronic' concerns of linguists in continental Europe, and less directly in America, though there too the importance of the *Cours* was recognized.

The warm reception of the *Cours* and subsequent development of structuralism on the continent, the resistance to them in Britain, and their muffled acceptance in America were all somewhat predictable. British science and philosophy had been dominated by empirical observation since the seventeenth century. Elsewhere, the unity and simplicity afforded by a powerful theoretical explanation was more compelling than the messiness that empirical observation inevitably turned up. Even Newton, faced with the variation in his measurements of celestial movements, shifted from a methodology based on deciding which of his observations had been made under the best conditions, to averaging out the results of all his observations. The average was a sort of underlying ideal: a measurement he had never actually observed but which could be taken as the deeper reality to which empirical observation – made by human beings using imperfect instruments – could only approximate.

Still, British faith in empiricism remained firm into the twentieth century, while German science and philosophy wavered between the extreme rationalism or idealism of thinkers such as Hegel and the empiricist commitments of Helmholtz and Wundt. France, meanwhile, wavered between the influences of Britain and Germany. As a Calvinist Genevois, Saussure's upbringing was dominated at least as much by British as by French influences, and certainly not by German ones. Yet most of Europe encountered his thought as mediated through Roman Jakobson (1896–1982), who read Saussure from the theoretical end of the spectrum.

The beginnings of structuralist linguistic method are already visible in Saussure's first published work, *Mémoire sur le système primitif des voyelles indo-européennes* (Memoir on the primitive system of Indo-European vowels, 1879). There is also the work of Franz Boas (1858–1942), discussed in §27.5, which shares much of the spirit of structuralism yet developed independently. If the starting point of structural linguistics is hard to pin down, its end point is even more elusive. Twenty years ago that did not seem to be the case: structural linguistics appeared to have been superseded by Noam Chomsky's generative linguistics over the course of the 1960s, and more general structuralism by the 'post-structuralism' that began in the last part of that decade. But the evolution of generativism from the 1970s through to the present decade has brought an increase in its methodological continuity with earlier structuralist work, compared with what appeared to be the case with Chomsky's more radical early approach; while on the epistemological plane, Chomsky's work was always in tune with what European structuralists believed about language and mind. Nevertheless, this account will end with the rise of generative linguistics, even if, a few decades from now, people looking backward may well perceive a unified structural linguistic method lasting for more than a century, despite the epistemological shift represented by generativism.

Structuralist linguistics arose across Europe and America not in a unified fashion, but in the form of national schools. This was due less to isolation – linguists in different countries read and published in each other's journals, and maintained regular epistolary and personal contact – than to a desire for intellectual independence, especially after the decades of German domination in historical linguistics, and for theories that would reflect the different interests and ideologies of linguists in the various countries. Yet the post-First World War generation all sought approaches that appeared modern and scientific, and they landed on largely the same things. The *Cours* was a major influence on all the structuralist schools, though by no means the only one; it provided a theoretical programme, but only sketches of the actual work to be carried out. All in all, the structuralist period is surprising both in its unity and its diversity.

27.2 Saussure and the *Cours de linguistique générale*

Saussure, Professor of Sanskrit and the History and Comparison of the Indo-European languages at the University of Geneva, was given the further responsibility of lecturing on general linguistics beginning in January 1907. He accepted the charge with reservations, being troubled by the memory of his abortive efforts over the previous decades to produce a book on the subject. Already when writing his *Mémoire* (1879), he had become aware of the intricacies of analysing a linguistic system, whether at the level of sound or of meaning, whether across languages or within a single language, and whether across time or at a given point in time. He knew that he would have to start from the ground up, beginning with the basic terminology: words for language itself, such as *langue, parole, langage*, which largely overlap in everyday usage.

His first, one-semester run of the course was a good start, but left him dissatisfied. Before the second attempt, which ran over the whole academic year 1908–1909, he rethought the course. This time, and again in the third course of 1910–1911, Saussure completed his account of a language as a system in which each element is bound to every other element, and with the content of an element being nothing other than a value generated by its difference from every other element. It is a model of such elegance – one might even say modernism – that we linguists are still working to accept all its consequences.

The ideas which exerted the greatest influence were, first, the distinction which Saussure drew between *langue* and *parole*. A *langue* (language) is the virtual system possessed by all those belonging to the same linguistic community, which makes it possible for them to understand and be understood by the other members of the community. *Parole* (speech) is the texts, the utterances, produced by an individual, making use of the system that is the *langue*. Although he spoke of a linguistics of *parole* that would cover the phonetic side of language and individual production, Saussure made clear that the linguistics of *langue* is the essential, real linguistics. *Langue* is beyond the direct reach of the individual will; it is, Saussure reiterated, a 'social fact'.

The second fundamental idea is that a *langue* is a system of signs, with each sign being the conjunction of a concept and an acoustic image, which are both mental in nature. For most linguists of the time, a language unites names with things, but Saussure taught that signs do not involve things, but our concepts of things, of actions and of pure ideas; and not names, but schemata in the brain that are capable of being evoked by certain combinations of sounds. In one of his last lectures he introduced the terms *signifiant* (signifier) for the acoustic image, and *signifié* (signified) for the concept. Saussure predicted that *sémiologie* – the study of signs both within and outside of language – would develop and would have linguistics as its 'pilot science'. The impact of semiotic inquiry upon linguistics would be slow in coming, apart from the nearly universal acceptance of Saussure's concept of the signifier as an abstract sound pattern. This view became the cornerstone of the concept of the 'phoneme', which first came to widespread attention in the *Mémoire*, and was elaborated by Jan Baudouin de Courtenay (1846–1929) and Mikołai Kruszewski (1851–1887) in Russia, before being taken up as a centre of attention for all the later structural schools. It resulted in the marginalizing of experimental phonetics within linguistic inquiry, in favour of more abstract phonology, based not upon acoustic or articulatory differences of sound, but on their ability to distinguish between concepts.

Third, the link between signifier and signified is radically arbitrary. This was an ancient doctrine, but by no means an obvious one. There exist apparently mimetic signs, such as *fouet* 'whip', in which, arguably, the sound of a whip can be heard. It is, however, a question of interpretation: for someone who hears the sound, the link is real, despite the etymology of this word, which, as Saussure's *Cours* pointed out, goes back to Latin *fagus* 'beech tree' (thin beech switches having been used as whips). The Saussurean principle of the arbitrariness of the linguistic sign maintains that, whether or not such a sound-meaning is recognized, the sign operates in the same way: *fouet* is not 'truer' for those who hear the crack of a whip in it than for those of us who do not. Nor is it 'truer' than a word such as *livre* 'book', for which a sound-meaning link seems far-fetched at best. However, Saussure was also quick to point out that a language is a system in which everything connects to everything else, and that the linguist's task is to discover that systematicity, which itself limits arbitrariness within the language as a whole (without, however, compromising the absolute arbitrariness of the bond between signifier and signified).

Fourth, each signifier and each signified is a *value*, produced by the *difference* between this signifier or signified and all the others in the system. It is not the sound as such that signifies: there is, after all, much variation in the pronunciation of all sounds. French or English /r/, for instance, covers a wide phonetic range. Indeed, spectrographic analysis shows that even the same individual never produces exactly the same sound twice: subtle differences are registered each time. Yet whether I say English *car* as [kaə] or [kaʁ] or [kaʀ] or [ka], the same word is perceived, so long as it does not overlap with another word such as *caw*. With the signified as well: if an animal of a certain species entered the room as you are reading this, you as an English speaker might exclaim 'a sheep!', and a French speaker might say 'un mouton!'. But the linguistic value of *mouton* and *sheep* are different. The signified of *mouton* includes the whole animal or a piece of the animal's meat, whereas the signified of *sheep* is restricted to the animal on the hoof. Its meat is *mutton*, a completely different sign. What this shows is that not just signifiers, but also signifieds, belong to a particular language. The world as we experience it, with its categories of animals, things, colours, etc., does not exist prior to language. The signifier and the signified are created together, with the particular cutting-up of phonetic and conceptual space that distinguishes one language from another, and one culture from another.

Fifth, the signs of a language unfold in one dimension only: linearly. This has a fundamental implication for the language system – it has two axes. Each element of the language occupies an associative (now usually called paradigmatic) axis, which determines its value vis-à-vis other elements with which it shares partial identity, and a syntagmatic axis, which specifies which elements may or may not precede or follow it in an utterance. For example, in the sentence *Crime pays* the element *crime* has a syntagmatic relationship with *pays* that determines, among other things, their order relative to one another and the fact that *pays* has the ending *–s*. At the same time, *crime* has paradigmatic relations with many other elements, including the inflectionally related *crimes*, the derivationally related *criminal*, the conceptually related *misdemeanour* (and the conceptually opposite *legality*) and the phonetically related *grime*. As the last example suggests, each sound of the word *crime* /kraim/ has paradigmatic and syntagmatic relations with at least the sounds around it: /k/ is paradigmatically related to the /g/ that could in principle replace it; and syntagmatically related to the following /r/, since in English the presence of /k/ as the initial element of the word immediately restricts the following sound to /l r w/ or a vowel.

Saussure noted that the two types of relations, which correspond to different types of mental activity, contribute in different ways to the 'value' of the sign. In particular, the paradigmatic relations generate a negative value: the identity of the /r/ in /kraim/ is essentially that it could be, but is not, /l w/ or a vowel. This is important because the actual sound that represents /r/ can differ dramatically from one English dialect to another (being rolled, flapped, retroflex, etc.); but the actual sound content does not matter, so long as /r/ is kept distinct from the other sounds to which it is associatively related. *Langue*, Saussure insisted, is form, not substance. Before Saussure, the syntagmatic relations of morphemes within a given utterance were certainly recognized as a matter of linguistic concern, though relatively neglected. But there was little or no precedent for the idea suggested by the *Cours* (implicitly if not explicitly) that there exists a syntax not only of words, but of sounds, meanings and the relations uniting them; or that every time a sound, word or meaning is chosen, a vast network of related elements is summoned up *in absentia*.

In many ways, the Saussurean notion of paradigmatic and syntagmatic relations would become the hallmark of twentieth-century linguistics: first, because it proposed that a single principle of structure unites all the levels at which language functions – sound, forms and meaning; second, because it suggested a way of analysing language that would not depend on a simple listing of elements with their 'translation' into either another language or some sort of philosophical interpretation. Elements could henceforth be analysed according to the relations they maintained with other elements, and the language could be understood as the vast system – not of these elements – but of these relations. This was the point of departure for structuralism.

To a large extent, the distributional method developed by Leonard Bloomfield (1887–1949) is a working out of this Saussurean notion, with special emphasis on the paradigmatic relations. With the work of Bloomfield's student Zellig S. Harris (1909–1992) the syntagmatic relations assumed a status of equal importance, and with Harris's student Chomsky, overriding importance. Regarding word order, Saussure's view is that the syntagmatic relations constitute that part of syntax which is predetermined – like the use of a third person singular verb form after the singular subject *crime* – and so a part of *langue*; while the rest of syntax, being subject to free combination, is related to *parole*.

Sixth, a language is characterized by its mutability, since every element is capable of changing, of evolving. No language is found in the same state as it was a hundred years before, still less as it was five hundred years before. Yet, paradoxically, a language is immutable, in the sense that no speaker can change it single-handedly. One can introduce an innovation into *parole*, but for this innovation to enter into the *langue* requires that it be accepted by the community. However, since the value of each element proceeds from its relation to all the other elements, any change in the system produces a new system, a new *langue*. That is what Saussure means by the immutability of a language: no one can change it; the 'speaking mass' (*masse parlante*) can accept a change, but in so doing it does not change the *langue* as such, but moves forward to a new *langue*.

Seventh, the study of a language can be synchronic or diachronic. Synchronic study tries to establish the elements of the system and their values at a given moment, which Saussure calls an *état de langue* (state of the language). Diachronic study is the comparison of several *états de langue* as they existed in different periods. But the 'historical' linguistics of Saussure's time was not diachronic: it claimed, rather, to trace the development of isolated elements across the centuries, a vowel for example, or an inflection, as if this element had a history, a life, independent of the system of which it was a part at each moment. One reads too often that Saussure replaced diachronic linguistics with synchronic inquiry; on the contrary, he invented diachronic linguistics, from which, moreover, he took synchronic linguistics to be inseparable.

27.3 Jakobson's structuralism

The person most directly responsible for taking Saussure's linguistics forward and developing a general 'structuralist' approach was the Russian linguist Roman Jakobson (1896–1982). At the age of nineteen Jakobson had founded the Moscow Linguistic Circle, a centre of the Russian formalist movement, in which certain features of Saussurean analysis – notably the priority of form over meaning – had arisen independently. Sergei Karcevskij (1884–1955) joined the Circle after returning to Moscow in 1917, having spent the previous decade in Geneva. He does not appear to have attended Saussure's general linguistics lectures, but some of his other courses, enough to bring with him a familiarity with Saussurean thought. Jakobson recognized the points of convergence with formalism and earlier work by Russian linguists, but also appreciated the originality of Saussure's systematization.

In 1920 Jakobson moved to Prague, and would remain in Czechoslovakia for the next two decades. He became professor at Brno in 1933, but remained a central figure in the Prague Linguistic Circle, which he helped to found. In collaboration with scholars of language and literature in Prague, including Vilém Mathesius (1882–1945), Jan Mukarovský (1891–1975) and others, as well as Prince Nikolai Trubetzkoy (1890–1938), who had relocated to Vienna in 1922, Jakobson took structural analysis in a distinctive direction that made Prague the epicentre of developments that were happening in Paris, Copenhagen and London, and to a certain extent in America. The 'Theses Presented to the First Congress of

Slavic Philologists in Prague, 1929', authored by Jakobson, evince characteristics of Prague structuralism such as breadth – the theses include programmes for the study of poetic language and applications to language teaching – and a focus on 'functionalism': 'Language', the document begins, 'like any other human activity is goal-oriented' (Steiner 1982: 5). Besides any immediate material goal to be accomplished, Prague inquiry assumed a constant, implicit goal of maximally efficient communication, whether in the case of a casual utterance or some manifestation of poeticity. The Prague School also devoted considerable attention to analysing the special nature of standard and literary languages, a topic in which they had a very practical interest given the need to establish and maintain a national language acceptable to both Czechs and Slovaks that had existed since the creation of Czechoslovakia in 1918.

Jakobson and Trubetzkoy collaborated on work which suggested, contrary to what Saussure's *Cours* maintains, that the relationships holding among all elements of the linguistic system are not of precisely the same nature (see Jakobson 1990; Trubetzkoy 1949). For example, the consonants /t/, /d/ and /f/ are distinctive phonemes in most languages, since they function to distinguish meanings (*tin* versus *din* versus *fin*). Yet it seems obvious that /t/ and /d/ have a closer relationship to one another than either has to /f/. In /t/ and /d/ the vocal organs perform essentially the same action in the same position, except that in /d/ the vocal cords vibrate. In many languages, Jakobson and Trubetzkoy noted, the distinction between /t/ and /d/ (and other pairs of unvoiced–voiced consonants) is 'neutralized' in certain positions, for instance at the end of a syllable or word: the German genitive (possessive) noun *Rades* 'wheel's' has as its nominative (subject) form *Rad*, pronounced not *[rad], but [rat], the same as *Rat* 'council'.

Again, the possibility of such a deeper connection contradicts the Saussurean view that the phonetic substance of /t/ and /d/ is inconsequential, and all that matters is the fact that they differ in some perceptible way. Jakobson and Trubetzkoy proposed the term *correlation* for the type of relationship holding between /t/ and /d/. Any pair of elements which do not exist in a correlation, such as /d/ and /f/, form instead a *disjunction*. As their work progressed, a new perspective developed. They realized that the correlation /t/–/d/ consists of a core of features common to the two sounds, plus a *principium divisionis*, the factor which distinguishes them, vocal cord vibration (voicing). They created the term *archiphoneme* for the core of features common to /t/ and /d/ (symbolized /T/). This allowed them to specify that the alternation between German *Rades* and *Rad* does not involve simply a change of phonemes; it is a realization of the same archiphoneme, but with the *principium divisionis* non-operational in word-final position.

It was Trubetzkoy who first proposed to Jakobson in 1930 that certain elements in the linguistic system could be thought of as having an interrelationship that is neither arbitrary nor purely formal, but defined by the fact that one element is distinguished from the other through the addition of an extra feature, a 'mark'. When the distinction is neutralized it is always the simple, 'unmarked' member of the opposition that appears. Thus the minimal contrast between the genitive nouns *Rates* 'council's' and *Rades* 'wheel's' is neutralized in the nominative, where, as noted above, both *Rat* 'council' and *Rad* 'wheel' are pronounced with a final /t/ – the unmarked member of the pair. The 'mark' in this case is the vibration of the vocal cords that differentiates /d/ from /t/, making /d/ the more 'complex' member of the correlation.

Because simplicity as here understood includes the physical elements of articulation and sound, markedness undoes the key Saussurean tenet that language is form, not substance. Trubetzkoy wrote to Jakobson almost casually mentioning the idea. Jakobson immediately saw its full implications, and his reply moved far beyond Trubetzkoy's modest proposal, to foresee developments in the analysis of literature and culture that would not come to fruition for another two to three decades.

Saussure's *Cours* had said that the two primary principles of the linguistic sign were arbitrariness and linearity. The discovery of 'the mark' (or, to use a later term, markedness) led Jakobson to contest both these principles. By 1932 he was extending the idea of the mark to morphology, to suggest for example that the reason a plural noun like *doctors* or a possessive like *doctor's* is phonologically longer, hence more complex, than the corresponding singular non-possessive *doctor*, is that the latter is *conceptually* simpler. This conceptual simplicity is signalled iconically at the level of sound. Jakobson came to believe that such iconicity is a general principle running through all languages. It means that signifiers (words as sound patterns) are not as arbitrarily connected to signifieds (meanings) as Saussure had suggested. Rather, parallelism between form and meaning is the hidden principle structuring language.

The mark also means that linguistic signs are not strictly linear in their make-up or functioning. This is clearest in phonology, where voicing (as in the /d/–/t/ contrast discussed above) constitutes the same 'distinctive feature' in the whole set of consonants /b d g v z/ (and others). The voicing feature is added onto the simpler forms /p t k f s/. In other words, /b/ does not function as a single unitary phoneme, but as the equivalent of /p/ plus the feature of voicing. Moreover, /p/ itself breaks down into the features 'stop' and 'bilabial' – so in fact /b/ is a bundle of three distinctive features signalling at once, like a musical chord, 'vertically' rather than in a linear fashion.

After Trubetzkoy's death, Jakobson would extend the theory to predict that unmarked elements would prove to be those which occur most widely across languages, are acquired first in childhood, and are lost last in aphasia. Following his emigration to America in 1942, Jakobson exercised a fundamental impact on the development of structuralism, both through his conceptual innovations and his success in exporting his brand of structuralism to other human and natural sciences, where it became the dominant paradigm in the 1950s and 1960s. At the start of 1942 Jakobson began lecturing at the École Libre des Hautes Études organized in New York by fellow refugees, most of whom, like Jakobson, had arrived to find no immediate prospect of academic employment. The audience included linguists of several nationalities as well as some of Jakobson's fellow teachers in the École, one of whom was Claude Lévi-Strauss (1908–2009). During the first term Jakobson gave two courses, one consisting of six lectures on sound and meaning and another on Saussure. The latter course was in fact a thoroughgoing critique of Saussure, and the former, too, included the challenge to Saussure's doctrine of linearity. Both reflect the new turn introduced into Jakobson's thinking by his analysis of the phoneme into distinctive features. Nevertheless, the lectures were presented to an audience including some not previously acquainted with Saussure and others who knew of him only superficially, so that in spite of their critical nature they had the effect of drawing attention to the *Cours* and securing its place at the head of the structuralist canon.

Shortly before his death, the philosopher Ernst Cassirer (1874–1945) read a paper 'Structuralism in modern linguistics' to the Linguistic Circle of New York, a group Jakobson co-founded. The paper is important as the first wide-ranging philosophical discussion of structuralism, its aims, methods and meaning. Cassirer situates structuralist linguistics within the history of philosophy and science, comparing it explicitly with various developments across the centuries in which mere superficial empiricism was rejected in favour of the search for underlying organizing principles which operate with perfect regularity: 'structuralism is no isolated phenomenon; it is, rather, the expression of a general tendency of thought that, in these last decades, has become more and more prominent in almost all fields of scientific research' (Cassirer 1945: 120). Cuvier's principles of biology are cited as a particularly close example, along with gestalt psychology. Cassirer also affirms that Wilhelm von Humboldt (1767–1835) anticipated a central tenet of structuralism with his declaration that language is not an *ergon*, a product, but an *energeia*, a potential (a distinction partly recapitulated in Saussure's *parole* and *langue*). For Cassirer, this amounts to saying that language is organic, 'in the sense that it does not consist of detached, isolated, segregated facts. It forms a coherent whole in which all parts are interdependent upon each other' (p. 110). Here for the first time the basis of general structuralism was proclaimed by an eminent philosopher who was an outsider to Jakobson's Moscow or Prague entourages, before an unusually multidisciplinary audience brought together by the circumstance of being in exile from Nazi-dominated Europe.

27.4 Other Continental structuralist approaches

Back in Geneva, Saussure's linguistics continued to be taught by Charles Bally (1865–1947) and Albert Sechehaye (1870–1946), who had jointly edited the *Cours*, and later by Henri Frei (1899–1980) and Luis Prieto (1926–1996). As others elsewhere were moving the structuralist paradigm forward, however, Geneva came increasingly to be seen as the bastion of sticking conservatively to Saussure's teaching. Bally's work (excerpted in Godel 1969) was widely read in order to gain deeper insight into Saussure's teachings. Bally's work in stylistics, which dated from Saussure's lifetime (one of his books was dedicated to Saussure), did take its own direction, but it was not the one that was becoming recognized elsewhere as what 'structuralism' essentially represented. It is based on the distinction between what Bally terms 'affective' and 'intellectual' uses of language, which have no equivalent in Saussurean linguistics. What is more, in the 1920s and 1930s, Paris so outshone Geneva as the centre of linguistics in the French-speaking world that the 'Geneva School' remained a small circle and tended to keep its stars at home rather than sending them out to spread the word.

In Paris the flame was kept alight by Antoine Meillet (1866–1936), who had been Saussure's student back in 1887–1889 and remained his epistolary confidant for the rest of Saussure's life. Meillet had absorbed the principles of structural linguistics from Saussure's *Mémoire* and his teaching of the ancient Germanic languages long before the *Cours* appeared, and passed them on to two generations of linguists for whom he was the *grand maître*, including Joseph Vendryes (1875–1960), Robert Gauthiot (1876–1916), Marcel Cohen (1884–1974), Georges Dumézil (1898–1966), Lucien Tesnière (1893–1954), Émile Benveniste (1902–1976) and André Martinet (1908–1999). In all of their works one finds an approach to linguistic problems from the point of view of the whole system, either synchronic or diachronic. The particular characteristic of Meillet's work has been identified as being to focus on just those elements that appear strange or surprising in the perspective of the language system as a whole, and to delve into them as a key to a deeper understanding of the system and its operation (see Meillet 1921–1936).

An example of this, and one of Meillet's most enduring legacies, is his analysis of what in an article of 1912 he termed 'grammaticalization'. In many (perhaps all) languages can be found elements that, at a previous historical stage, were fully independent words, but that at a later stage have become parts of the grammar system, in the form of endings or auxiliaries or particles that have been wholly or partly 'bleached' of their autonomous meaning and usually reduced phonetically. An example is the English verb *will*, which changed from having the full sense of *want* or *wish* to being a future tense auxiliary (*He will go, though he doesn't want to*) that often appears in reduced form (*He'll go*).

Benveniste lectured on linguistics in the Collège de France from 1937 to 1969 and had an especially profound influence on the next generations of French linguists, but also more widely on those 'structuralists' and 'post-structuralists' whose interests were very much language-focused yet who did not think of themselves as narrowly constrained to any one discipline, be it linguistics, semiology, philosophy, psychology, literature, sociology or ethnography. He would bring perspectives from several of these disciplines to bear on a grammatical category such as person, and examine how the category is realized in a vast range of different languages across the world. Of particular interest to him is how, through a device such as person, the speaker and hearer are themselves encoded into the language (see Benveniste 1966–1974). His later work inaugurated the focus on the 'enunciation' that would be taken up by the later structuralism of Antoine Culioli. Meillet's protégé Gustave Guillaume (1883–1960), a relatively isolated figure on the Parisian scene, cut his own structuralist path distinct from those of the Prague-oriented Martinet and Benveniste. Like Hjelmslev, Guillaume was largely concerned with elaborating the systematic and abstract programme of the *CLG*, but less algebraically and with more concern for linguistic data and psychological mechanisms.

Copenhagen, an important centre of linguistic work since the early nineteenth century, was dominated in the 1920s and 1930s by Otto Jespersen (1860–1943), who gained his early renown in phonetics and the history of English, and undertook in the 1920s an attempt to delineate the 'logic' of grammar divorced from psychological underpinnings – work that anticipates future directions in its attention to syntax and child language acquisition. Jespersen would expressly reject some of the key tenets of Saussure's *Cours* and structuralism. But the next dominant figure in Copenhagen, Louis Hjelmslev (1899–1965), was determined to push Saussurean linguistics and semiotics as far as they could be pushed in the direction of quasi-mathematical complexification. His approach, 'glossematics', went farther than any of his contemporaries toward working out the 'relational' nature of linguistic systems as implied in the *Cours*. It introduces various semiotic and 'metasemiotic' layers, and breaks utterances down into 'taxemes' and 'glossemes', insisting that 'the principle of analysis must be a recognition' of 'dependences' (Hjelmslev 1953 [1943]: 28), which turn out in fact to be 'bundles of lines of dependence'. Hjelmslev's faithfulness to Saussure comes through in his criticism of the Prague and London schools for claiming to be 'functionalist' but nevertheless continuing to rely on analysis of phonetic substance. His work would lay the foundation for a Copenhagen School which would influence developments in structural linguistics worldwide, and particularly in Britain, through his student Hans J. Uldall (1907–1957), who emigrated there and interacted significantly with the students of the men discussed in the next section. Hjelmslev's writings would later have a strong impact on the (post-)structuralism of Gilles Deleuze (1925–1995) and Félix Guattari (1930–1992).

27.5 Structural linguistics in the English-speaking world

The United Kingdom, traditionally self-reliant (if not insular), resisted the importation of structural linguistics. Britain had already undergone its modernist turn in the study of language with the work of the phoneticians Henry Sweet (1845–1912) and Daniel Jones (1881–1967). One of Saussure's fundamental concepts, the phoneme, became central to Jones's work, but as a phonetician his interest was limited to the sound level of language. Two of the lecturers whom he hired were however more devoted Saussureans: first, Harold

E. Palmer (1877–1949), a practitioner of what would later be called applied linguistics; and later, J.R. Firth (1890–1960), who became arguably the most important British linguist of the twentieth century, his only rivals to that claim being some of the students he mentored (such as M.A.K. Halliday).

In the USA, on the other hand, the *Cours* seemed to be of a kindred spirit with the 'distributional' method developed for the analysis of American Indian languages by the anthropologist Franz Boas (1858–1942), a German émigré, published in its definitive form in 1911. Late in the nineteenth century, as anthropology moved from a physical toward a cultural orientation, an impressive fieldwork methodology was developed based on positivistic principles. Since language was taken to be an integral element of culture, but with linguists so single-mindedly focused on tracing the history of Indo-European tongues, anthropologists had little choice but to undertake the description of unknown languages on their own. Much of Boas's work was aimed at establishing the historical affiliations of American Indian tribes through their linguistic relations.

Saussure's *Cours* was well received both by Edward Sapir (1884–1939), the first amongst Boas's linguistic students, and Leonard Bloomfield (1887–1949), who came from the historical linguistics tradition. Bloomfield would go on to do his own fieldwork on American Indian languages, and he and Sapir would establish themselves as the pre-eminent American linguists of the interwar period. Each published a widely-read book with the title *Language*, Sapir in 1921, Leonard Bloomfield in 1933. Of all the books in linguistics published in the English language, Bloomfield's *Language* had, until the 1960s (and arguably beyond) the best claim to being definitive. Bloomfield himself would say in a letter to one of his students that Saussure's influence was to be found 'on every page' of the book (Cowan 1987).

Sapir and Bloomfield followed parallel and convergent career paths. Both were active, together with Boas and others, in institutionalizing American linguistics and developing and refining an analytical method known as 'distributional' because it classifies elements according to the environments in which they appear. Yet where Sapir's ideas are embedded in a broad cultural–anthropological perspective, Bloomfield had traded in his adherence to Wundt's *Völkerpsychologie* and become a behaviourist, conceiving of languages as systems of stimuli and responses. Meaning, being unavoidably mentalistic, was suspect to Bloomfield, unless it was determined objectively on the basis of distribution. Some of Bloomfield's students and followers, led by George L. Trager (1906–1992) would develop a still more radical position, virtually exiling meaning from the purview of linguistics altogether, though it is a mistake to associate this position with Bloomfield himself.

Despite their general convergence, then, Bloomfield's view was more narrowly linguistic than Sapir's and profited from its attachment to the empirical and 'modern' British–American science of behaviourism. Such was the success of Bloomfield's *Language* that it effectively set the agenda of American linguistics for a generation to come. Sapir and his students contributed at least as much as Bloomfield and the (neo-)Bloomfieldians to the refinement of the distributional method and phonemic theory, but never forsook their broader anthropological interests. Sapir's student Benjamin Lee Whorf (1897–1941) pursued a line of inquiry into the notion that the structure of thought might be dependent upon the structure of the linguistic system. This idea, the 'Sapir–Whorf Hypothesis', was in some ways a throwback to Humboldt, in other ways the ultimate expression of faith in the power of the linguistic system; but in any case it was anathema to the anti-mentalist Bloomfieldians, and even today it continues to arouse controversy (see Whorf 2012 [1956]).

In Britain, Jones (1950) played a key role in refining the phoneme into its later, definitive form, as the minimal sound-unit capable of distinguishing meaning in a language. But, as a phonetician, Jones was not inclined to follow Saussure in imagining the phoneme as having, like any signifier, a purely mental reality. Instead, Jones linked phonemes to a sort of idealized articulation, most famously with his 'cardinal vowels', a sort of concept-*cum*-technique of pronouncing vowels at their extreme limits to try to capture their essence. For American linguists, working out the precise nature of the phoneme would be at the core of their debates for some four decades, and behind that debate lay the even more fundamental one about the nature of meaning itself, and its place, if any, in linguistic method. Bloomfield's behaviourist commitments meant that he too steered clear of any depiction of phonemes as mental categories, rather than simply as units of observable behaviour.

Sapir (1933), without mentioning Bloomfield (just Boas, Jones, Trubetzkoy, Sapir himself and, unusually, three of his Native American informants), threw down the gauntlet to the behaviourist methodology, making a strong case that the outsider 'expert' who analyses a spoken text phonemically may well hear a single phoneme where the native speaker knows or intuits that there are actually two separate phonemes, the distinction between which may come out only in relatively rare phonological contexts that the observer happens not to encounter. Sapir gives the example of English *saw* and *soar*, which sound the same in certain British dialects, but for native speakers have different final phonemes that may be (though are not always) realized differently when –*ing* is attached, for example. A Bloomfieldian would be inclined to trust the outside observer and look for reasons why the native speaker may be deluded, by the writing system for example. A Sapirian would consider the native's intuition to be inherently valid enough at least to merit testing for possible phonological environments where the distinction becomes clear (hence eliminating any illusion created by writing).

The 'London School' of Firth was even less cautious than Sapir where meaning was concerned, taking it as a common-sense fact that needed analysing but not defending. Indeed, Firth approached the whole systematic nature of language in an unparalleled way. Whereas other schools – including the influential phonetics of Firth's own colleague Jones – conceived of language systems as consisting of a small set of largely independent subsystems (phonology, morphology, syntax, suprasegmentals), for Firth language was 'polysystemic', incorporating an infinite number of interdependent microsystems which overlap the traditional levels of analysis. The London School's refusal to separate phonology and suprasegmentals, for example, made interaction with American structuralists almost impossible. Yet it anticipated work in generative phonology by nearly half a century. The 'neo-Firthian' systemic-functional linguistics of M.A.K. Halliday and his followers represents the most robust uninterrupted continuation of an essentially structural linguistic tradition (*modulo* the comments in the Introduction to this chapter concerning generativism).

Jones's work, with its treatment of meaning as something unproblematic that phonemes could differentiate, was readily absorbed by American linguists. Even if they left his cardinal vowels aside as not useful for their purposes, they embraced the International Phonetic Alphabet project in conjunction with which the cardinal vowel concept was developed. Firth, on the other hand, seemed impenetrable. He had published two introductory books on linguistics which seemed elementary when compared with those of Sapir and Bloomfield, and had embarked on a series of papers in which he presented his polysystemic complexifications briefly and sketchily; one had to study with him in order to understand them fully and appreciate their import. Those who did, inevitably became lifelong devotees. His essential difference vis-à-vis Jones, Bloomfield and Sapir was that, where they strove to find the simplest solution to the problems posed by language, Firth started from the assumption that language is a massively complex phenomenon, and that its analysis was bound to reflect and embody that complexity.

From about 1945 younger American linguists showed an increasing bent toward the algebraic and mathematical aspects of structuralism, in the use of tables, formulas and other mathematical schemata, statistics, calculations, and the generally rigorous working out of the notions of system and systematicity. Such a bent had already figured prominently in the work of Hjelmslev and Guillaume. In the early 1950s military and commercial interest in furthering the wartime progress on computers and machine translation improved the fortunes of many linguists, particularly in America, and gave even more impetus to the development of computationally-based models.

In America, the 'neo-Bloomfieldians' assumed the mainstream mantle they had previously shared with the disciples of Sapir, and anthropological linguistics retreated to the status of a subdiscipline. Bloomfield's mathematically inclined heir apparent Charles F. Hockett (1916–2000) rose to prominence, as did Zellig S. Harris (1909–1992), whose *Methods of Structural Linguistics* (completed 1947, published 1951) marked the high point in the systematization of Bloomfieldian analysis. Harris, Jakobson and Hockett also began extending their inquiry to syntax, a largely neglected area (despite a number of high-quality contributions over the years, especially in the historical domain). Although syntactic studies would not come fully into their own until the ascendance of Chomsky, who declared a sharp break with the structuralist (especially Bloomfieldian) tradition, nevertheless in his wake further structuralist accounts of syntax were put forward, of which the most notable are the 'stratificational grammar' of Sydney M. Lamb, which follows largely in the tradition of Hjelmslev, and the 'tagmemics' of Kenneth L. Pike (1912–2000).

In 1950 Firth wrote that 'Nowadays, professional linguists can almost be classified by using the name of de Saussure. There are various possible groupings: Saussureans, anti-Saussureans, post-Saussureans, or non-Saussureans' (Firth 1957: 179). He was convinced that Saussure's conception of *langue* contained several fundamental errors, two of which were that it abstracted the language system away from context, and that it located it in the mind of the speaker ('psychological structuralism'). Firth strived toward a concept of language as something located not within people (whether as individuals or social groups), but within *what people do*, the context of situation, borrowing a term from the anthropologist Malinowski. Unlike pragmaticians such as J.L. Austin, who saw language as inseparable from the actions people perform, Firth did think of language as something apart, a particular 'form of human living' (close to Wittgenstein's late view of language as a *Lebensform*, a 'form of life') that needed to be analysed in its own terms, though never separately from the context in which it occurred (see Firth 1968: 206).

In Europe too syntactic studies were under way, following on the pioneering work of Tesnière. But the focus of structuralist investigation remained on phonology, with dialect geography and historical linguistics continuing to be more actively pursued than in America. Martinet, who after Jakobson had done most to transplant Prague–Paris structuralism to America, returned to France in 1955 and pursued a 'functional linguistics' that would have its share of adherents (see Martinet 1960). Meanwhile the younger generation of European scholars looked increasingly to America for innovative ideas and technological advances. Hence the major development in structuralism during this period was its exportation to other fields – until a revolt against structuralism became part of the student uprisings of 1968. From the mid-1960s to the mid-1970s, European linguistics turned increasingly toward American generativism, while the other human sciences played out a 'post-structuralist' phase. But the last couple of decades, since the mid-1990s, have seen a resurgence of linguistic work that no longer clings to the commitments that defined a Chomskyan 'revolution', and that pursues an object of study more like the Saussurean system of socially-shared *langue* than like the 'I-language' of an idealized native speaker-hearer in a homogenous speech community, which Chomsky claimed could be the only scientifically valid construct for linguistic study.

27.6 Structural linguistics after Chomsky

Thinking back to the influences of Saussure on twentieth-century linguistics, it is clear that they developed in very different directions in continental Europe and America, though there are three important caveats to this. First, Sapir was something of a bridging figure between the two. Second, Britain was more aligned with America even while resisting its influence and trying to stake out its own path. Third, Jakobson throws everything into disarray, being fundamentally both European and American. And Jakobson's larger-than-life intellectual scope and personality did not fail to make a significant impression on the young Chomsky, who got to know Jakobson when both were working at Harvard and Jakobson was directing the doctoral thesis of Chomsky's friend Morris Halle. Jakobson's particular focus on language *universals* – a focus that endured throughout his career – was out-of-sync with the rest of structural linguistics, which, following Saussure, started from the assumption that languages could vary from one another virtually without limits. Jakobson believed that, on the contrary, the common human functional purposes shared by all languages tied them together in a way that must be reflected in commonalities of structure.

This Jakobsonian vision inspired two very different (indeed opposed) research programmes. One was the anthropological linguist Joseph Greenberg's who set out to explore empirically discoverable universals of language, which inevitably turned out to be 'statistical' universals (features shown by, say, 70 per cent of the languages he examined from a sample representing a wide range of language families and types; see Greenberg 1966 [1963]). The other was Chomsky's programme of finding – principally through linguists exploring their own intuitions about their own mother tongues – structures that could be asserted as being part of a 'universal grammar' physically 'hard-wired' into the brain, part of human mental or cerebral 'architecture'. Both these programmes deviated from the neo-Bloomfieldian behaviourist-inspired empirical approach, but Greenberg's less so, since at least it retained an empirical methodology. Chomsky's deviation was both conceptual and methodological, eschewing the analysis of texts as trivial, and embracing instead an introspection that was the antithesis of what behaviourism stood for. Yet, in these deviations, Greenberg and especially Chomsky moved closer to what 'structuralism' had come to signify in twentieth-century European linguistics – which, again, had likewise felt the shaping hands of Jakobson.

Chomsky's revolution lay partly in convincing American linguists that the behaviourist rejection of the mind was misguided (his 1959 attack on Skinner is now generally recognized as having been in fact a proxy attack on the neo-Bloomfieldians), and that common-sense intuitions about the mental were not necessarily unscientific. He insisted on a distinction between 'competence' and 'performance' which in early work he likened specifically to the *langue* and *parole* of Saussure (although they were not exactly the same), and maintained that linguistic competence was a discrete, unconscious component of the mind having a fundamentally universal structure, much as some European structuralists had interpreted Saussure's *langue*. No less importantly, he introduced a distinction between 'deep' and 'surface' structure in language which people outside linguistics quickly latched onto and interpreted to fit their belief that words do not mean what they purport to mean, an interpretation far removed from Chomsky's original intention. This sense has been at the root of many 'functionalist' developments in twentieth-century linguistics, particularly within European structuralism, where, for better or for worse, the notion of separate conscious and unconscious minds is taken for granted. In view of the fact that he set American linguistics on a path significantly less at odds with the Saussurean framework while undoing none of the common points between Bloomfield and Saussure (except perhaps the amount of lip service paid to the social nature of language, which Chomsky did not deny but simply excluded from his realm of interest by defining that realm as the competence of an idealized native speaker-hearer in a homogeneous speech community), it seems reasonable to argue that Chomsky introduced structuralism into American linguistics, more fully than any of his predecessors.

As noted earlier, the intellectual descendants of Firth, who cut his own polysystemic structural path, have constituted one of the structural alternatives available during the ascendance (and now the plateau, at best) of generativism. R.E. Asher, who studied under both Jones and Firth, says that Firth was very conscious of differentiating his linguistics from American linguistics (interview with the author, 13 January 2013). Asher recalls him speaking rarely of American linguistics, but often of continental linguistics, with Saussure coming up in nearly every lecture. This heritage is clear in the 'social semiotics' of Halliday, which underlies Systemic-Functional Grammar (see e.g. Halliday 1978); and perhaps less clear, but nevertheless present, in the neo-Firthian approaches to phonology associated with Terence Langendoen and John A. Goldsmith.

Finally, another major area of present-day linguistics represents a direct continuation of the structural tradition, and a long-standing alternative to generativism (even if its development was in some ways swayed by the generative ascendance). Sociolinguistics developed out of several strands of research, including dialect geography and social anthropology, but most centrally from the line that led from Saussure to Meillet to Martinet, to Martinet's student Uriel Weinreich (1926–1967), and to Weinreich's student William Labov. By its very nature sociolinguistics has had to adhere to the structuralist commitment to language as a 'social fact', rather than as the I-language in the head of an individual, and to focus on empirical linguistic differences rather than searching for hypothetical universals which such differences purportedly mask. Its work has consisted partly of looking more microscopically at how linguistic communities are constituted of smaller sub-communities bound up with factors such as age, gender and social class, and at how these factors play out in language variation and change; and partly at how linguistic signs indexically signify the identities of their speakers, an approach which admittedly owes more to Charles Sanders Peirce (1839–1914) than to Saussure. In recent work the senior sociolinguists Labov and John Rickford have been asserting the independence of linguistic and social constraints, in other words that social factors and linguistic factors operate separately – there is a core of language that is shared by a community, and it is in the *use* of this core that social differences manifest themselves. Insofar as this is a rediscovery of Saussure's distinction between *langue* (the core) and *parole* (the individual's use of *langue*), structural linguistics has, a century after Saussure's death, come full circle.

Further reading

Engler (1975); Hymes and Fought (1981); Joseph (2002, 2012); Joseph *et al.* (2001); Matthews (2001).

References

Benveniste, É. (1966–1974) *Problèmes de linguistique générale*. 2 vols. Paris: Gallimard. 1973. English version of vol. 1, *Problems in General Linguistics*, transl. M.E. Meek. Coral Gables: University of Miami Press, 1971.
Bloomfield, L. (1933) *Language*. New York: Holt, Rinehart and Winston.
Boas, F. (1911) *Handbook of American Indian Languages*, Part I. Smithsonian Institution, Bureau of American Ethnology, Bulletin 40. Washington, DC: Government Printing Office.
Cassirer, E. (1945) Structuralism in modern linguistics. *Word* 1: 97–120.
Chomsky, N. (1959) Review of B.F. Skinner, *Verbal Behavior* (New York: Appleton-Century-Crofts; London and New York: Methuen, 1957). *Language* 35: 26–58.
Cowan, J.M. (1987) The whimsical Bloomfield. *Historiographia Linguistica* 14: 1–2, 23–37.
Engler, R. (1975) European structuralism. In T.A. Sebeok (ed.) *Current Trends in Linguistics* 13: Historiography of Linguistics, pp. 839–86. The Hague/Paris: Mouton. Repr. In J.E. Joseph (ed.) *Ferdinand de Saussure: Critical Assessments of Leading Linguists*, pp. 146–206. Abingdon/New York: Routledge, 2013.
Firth, J.R. (1957) *Papers in Linguistics 1934–1951*. London: Oxford University Press.
Firth, J.R. (1968) *Selected Papers, 1952–59*, ed. F.L. Palmer. London/Bloomington: Longmans and Indiana University Press.
Godel, R. (ed.) (1969) *A Geneva School Reader in Linguistics*. Bloomington: Indiana University Press.
Greenberg, J.H. (ed.) (1963) *Universals of Language*. Cambridge: MIT Press. (2nd edition, 1966.)
Halliday, M.A.K. (1978) *Language as Social Semiotic: The Social Interpretation of Language and Meaning*. Baltimore: University Park Press.
Harris, Z. (1951) *Methods in Structural Linguistics*. Chicago: University of Chicago Press.
Hjelmslev, L. (1943) *Omkring sprogteoriens grundlæggelse*. Copenhagen: Munksgaard. English version, *Prolegomena to a Theory of Language*, by F.J. Whitfield. (*International Journal of American Linguistics*, supplement. vol. 19, 1). Baltimore: Waverly Press, 1953.
Hockett, C.F. (1958) *A Course in Modern Linguistics*. New York: Macmillan.
Hymes, D. and J. Fought (1981) *American Structuralism*. The Hague: Mouton.
Jakobson, R. (1990) *On Language*, ed. L.R. Waugh and M. Monville-Burston. Cambridge, MA/London: Harvard University Press.
Jones, D. (1950) *The Phoneme: Its Nature and Use*. Cambridge: W. Heffer and Son.
Joseph, J.E. (2002) *From Whitney to Chomsky: Essays in the History of American Linguistics*. Amsterdam/Philadelphia: John Benjamins.
Joseph, J.E. (2012) *Saussure*. Oxford: Oxford University Press.
Joseph, J.E., N. Love and T.J. Taylor (2001) *Landmarks in Linguistic Thought II: The Western Tradition in the 20th Century*. London/New York: Routledge.
Martinet, A. (1960) *Éléments de linguistique générale*. Paris: Armand Colin. English version, *Elements of General Linguistics*, transl. E. Palmer. London: Faber & Faber; Chicago: University of Chicago Press, 1964.
Matthews, P.H. (2001) *A Short History of Structural Linguistics*. Cambridge: Cambridge University Press.
Meillet, A. (1921–1936) *Linguistique historique et linguistique générale*. 2 vols. Paris: Champion.
Sapir, E. (1921) *Language: An Introduction to the Study of Speech*. New York: Harcourt, Brace & World.
Sapir, E. (1933) La réalité psychologique des phonèmes. *Journal de psychologie normale et pathologique* 30: 247–65. English version, 'The Psychological Reality of Phonemes', in Edward Sapir, *Selected Writings in Language, Culture, and Personality*, ed. by D.G. Mandelbaum, pp. 46–60. Berkeley/Los Angeles: University of California Press, 1949.
Saussure, F. de (1879) *Mémoire sur le système primitif des voyelles dans les langues indo-européennes*. Leipzig: B.G. Teubner.

Saussure, F. de (1916) *Cours de linguistique générale*, ed. by C. Bally and A. Sechehaye with the collaboration of A. Riedlinger. Paris/Lausanne: Payot. (2nd edition 1922; subsequent editions substantially unchanged.) English version, *Course in General Linguistics*, by W. Baskin, New York: Philosophical Library, 1959; repr. with new intro. by P. Meisel and H. Saussy, New York: Columbia University Press, 2011.

Steiner, P. (ed.) (1982) *The Prague School: Selected Writings 1929–46*. Austin: University of Texas Press.

Trubetzkoy, N.S. (1949) *Principes de Phonologie*, transl. J. Cantineau. Paris, Klincksieck. English version, *Principles of Phonology*, transl. C.A.M. Baltaxe. Berkeley/Los Angeles: University of California Press, 1969.

Whorf, B.L. (1956) *Language, Thought, and Reality: Selected Writings of Benjamin Lee Whorf*, ed. J.B. Carroll. Cambridge: MIT Press. (2nd edition, ed. J.B. Carroll, S.C. Levinson and P. Lee, 2012.)

28
Biolinguistics

Cedric Boeckx

28.1 Introduction

Simply put, *biolinguistics* refers to the branch of the cognitive biosciences that deals with the language capacity that receives its maximal expression in our species. Many scholars take this capacity to be a species-defining trait, and a key to understand what it means to be human. As such, findings in biolinguistics are not only relevant for the (mental) life sciences, but also for the humanities.

The roots of biolinguistics can be traced back to the cognitive revolution that took place in the 1950s, with the language sciences occupying pride of place thanks to the early efforts of Noam Chomsky, Morris Halle, George Miller and Eric Lenneberg. Such efforts culminated in the 1960s with the publications of Chomsky's *Aspects of the Theory of Syntax* (1965) and Lenneberg's *Biological Foundations of Language* (1967). Both documents quickly became classics in the field, and remain central today in defining its aims. (It is in *Aspects* that Chomsky offered his first substantial articulation of his biolinguistic commitments, expanding on remarks made in his 1959 review of Skinner's *Verbal Behavior*.)

Biolinguistics characterizes itself by its supremely interdisciplinary agenda. That agenda was consciously modeled on that of ethology, whose clearest expression is found in Tinbergen (1963). Tinbergen put forth that the study of animal behavior be organized along the following dimensions:

- What stimulates the animal to respond with the behavior it displays, and what are the response mechanisms?
- How does an organism develop as the individual matures?
- Why is the behavior necessary for the animal's success and how does evolution act on that behavior?
- How has a particular behavior evolved through time? Can we trace a common behavior of two species back to their common ancestor?

Years later Chomsky recommended that the study of the language faculty be guided by the following questions, which bear obvious parallels with those of Tinbergen.

- What is knowledge of language?
- How does that knowledge develop in the individual?
- How is that knowledge put to use?
- How is that knowledge implemented in the brain?
- How did that knowledge evolve in the species?

Ontogeny, phylogeny and neural implementation are the central axes of research in biolinguistics. They were already the central theme of Lenneberg's 1967 book, and figured prominently in Chomsky's writings at the time. As a matter of fact, the agenda of biolinguistics quickly established itself, and led to a series of activities that culminated in the justly famous Royaumont encounter between Chomsky and Piaget in 1975. It is in fact during a preparatory meeting for Royaumont that Massimo Piattelli-Palmarini gave the term its modern meaning. Alongside Piattelli-Palmarini, Salvador Luria began to use the term in talks (advertising its promises in a 1976 American Association for the Advancement of Science keynote address), Lyle Jenkins was trying to launch a journal, and members of the MIT scientific community had formed a research group on biolinguistics (see Walker 1978).

Curiously, though, the decade that followed this flurry of activities saw the biolinguistic agenda go underground. It is not that the central questions listed above were found uninteresting, nor too hard to address. Rather, it seems, interdisciplinarity was not the order of the day. Attempts to teach human language to other species had failed (see Anderson 2004 for an overview), and within linguistics a new theoretical framework to deal with cross-linguistic variation met with undeniable success. This had the effect of marginalizing interdisciplinarity.

It is also true that some of the central challenges that animate current biolinguistic research, such as genomics or systems neuroscience, to which we will return, were still in an early stage of development and therefore could not have been contemplated at that time. It was still the early days of brain imaging techniques, and the genomic revolution still had not taken place.

All of this began to change in the late 1990s, which saw the return to explicit biolinguistic concerns. Generally speaking, such concerns are still very much the same as when it all began, but the range of specific questions, methodologies and perspectives has expanded, as a result of progress achieved in the intervening years. As is to be expected, it has also become clear that some of the early reflections on biolinguistics were quite naïve, and that complexity is very much the name of the game.

28.2 How we got here

So, what were the factors that led to the revival of biolinguistics?

There were four key developments that help us understand why scholars from various disciplines, not just from linguistics, decided to take on the biolinguistic challenge again.

The first development is the genomic revolution. Among numerous other findings, it led to the discovery of the implication of *FOXP2*, a gene that is implicated directly in a linguistic disorder. Shortly after its discovery, it became clear that *FOXP2* is, evolutionary speaking, a highly conserved gene. This fact has led to important investigations into its functioning of other species (especially vocal learners such as birds), and into the timing of and possible adaptive pressures behind the mutation that led to the variant found in modern human populations.

Needless to say, research in this area is still very much ongoing, and current results remain controversial. But inquiry into the nature of *FOXP2* has had the merit of reinvigorating comparative studies – a must in the life sciences, from which linguistics had begun to isolate itself. It also had the merit of highlighting the distance and complex pathways between genotype and phenotype. While this should not come as a surprise, the study of *FOXP2* and the genes it regulates (its interactome) has made it clear that linguistic properties are not encoded in the genome, and that (popular) characterization of notions like Universal Grammar as the 'linguistic genotype' are hopelessly naïve.

The second key factor is related to the first, though I like to keep it separate. It concerns the rise of bottom-up comparativism in psychology. Perhaps due to the identification of numerous deep homologies in the context of genetics, or perhaps due to a renewed appreciation for the compelling Darwinian logic of descent with modification as the celebrations of Darwin's bicentenary were approaching (the year 2009 was the 200th anniversary of Darwin's birth and the 150th anniversary of the publication of *On the Origin of Species*), an increased appreciation that the basic building blocks of cognition might be shared across a wide range of species became apparent among cognitive scientists (see De Waal and Ferrari 2010), and many of them began to explore seriously the possibility of constructing 'cognitive phylogenies.'

In the domain of language, the rise of bottom-up comparativism was clearly felt, following the publication of Hauser *et al.* (2002). In an attempt to reconcile what makes the language faculty unique (human specific) and properly Darwinian descent-with-modification scenarios, which take our language faculty to be rooted in animal cognition, Hauser *et al.* outlined a program aimed 'at uncovering both shared (homologous or analogous) and unique components of the faculty of language.' To achieve this, they distinguished between the Faculty of Language in the Broad [FLB] sense and the Faculty of Language in the Narrow [FLN] sense. The recognition that a significant amount of the language faculty could be neither specific to language nor unique to humans ('FLB') marked a rather sharp departure from the standard position in the dominant biolinguistic paradigm in its early days.

The third factor I want to highlight is also related to progress in genetics. It is the rise of a new paradigm in biology, popularly known as 'Evo-Devo' (evolutionary development). For over fifty years, biology had been dominated by a genocentric, selectionist framework called the Modern Synthesis. The genomic revolution made the limits of genocentrism patently obvious, and gradually displaced selectionist considerations from the center to the periphery, opening up new lines of inquiry animated by a more eclectic, pluralistic agenda. This agenda is no longer a single-level model, with genes at its central causal force, but a much more interactionist perspective with equal weight placed on genes, the environment and development.

Evo-Devo marks a return to early rationalist concerns in biology that resonate with the Cartesian themes of early biolinguistics. It also marks a departure from the core assumptions adopted by evolutionary psychology that at one point threatened to dominate the field of evolutionary linguistics. As a result, more linguists found themselves in a more congenial setting in which to frame questions concerning the evolution of the language faculty.

The final development that I will discuss here pertains to what is called linguistic minimalism. Linguistic minimalism is an attempt to minimize the role of system-specific assumptions to account for properties of natural language grammars. It grew out of the recognition that the successful framework that had relegated biolinguistic concerns to the periphery in the 1980s led to an over-specified initial state of the language faculty (what has sometimes been called, not without reason, 'exuberant nativism'). In addition to raising eyebrows concerning its biological plausibility, such an initial state gradually proved incapable of handling the amount of cross-linguistic diversity that it had in part contributed to uncovering. The early models of language acquisition based on it ran into problems and paradoxes that threatened the very foundations of the model.

Linguistic minimalism offers itself as an alternative to this earlier, over-specified vision of the language faculty. Over the years it has become clear that the success of this minimalist enterprise depends on several factors that mesh well with the other factors mentioned above. First, it must rely on – and therefore assume the existence of – a rich cognitive apparatus with which the (minimal) specifically linguistic apparatus interfaces to yield the substantive universals that previous linguistic research had somewhat naïvely attributed to a highly structured and specifically linguistic 'Universal Grammar.' Second, the set of operations that minimalists posit appears to be more in line with the sort of computation one may reasonably expect the brain to do (and the genes to eventually code for). Third, it is becoming clear that the success of the minimalist project will depend on recognizing that the emergence of many grammatical properties of natural languages is the product of social transmission and cultural evolution ('grammaticalization'). This effectively means that the success of this 'Chomskyan' enterprise depends on the correctness of approaches that have (erroneously, in my opinion) traditionally been put in opposition with Chomskyan linguistics. It also means moving beyond the classical genocentric model that was often taken for granted in the early days of biolinguistics.

28.3 What lies ahead

In sum, the return of biolinguistic concerns since the turn of the millennium is the result of a convergence, a consilience among various disciplines. The task of current biolinguists is clear: it is to marry these various perspectives in a productive fashion, one that leads to the formulation of concrete, testable hypotheses concerning ontogeny, phylogeny and neural implementation.

As such, current biolinguistics can serve as a perfect illustration of the various challenges of interdisciplinarity. It seems clear that the bottom-up approach of comparative psychology and the bottom-up approach of minimalism ('approaching Universal Grammar from below,' as Chomsky often calls it) are made for one another. It also seems clear that a deflationary stance on grammatical computation has a better chance of being neurally implementable and genetically controlled (more on this below). And it is equally obvious that a pared down perspective on the initial state of the language faculty will have to rely on the reciprocal causality of the many factors recognized within the extended synthesis spearheaded by Evo-Devo. But for all this to truly happen, we need detailed linking hypotheses to act as bridges and allow the flow of information among disciplines.

Such a challenge is not new, but it has yet to be met. Quite often, in the early documents on biolinguistics, such as the Royaumont meeting, one has the feeling of people talking at cross-purposes.

Part of the problem concerns the training of the younger generation. As is patently obvious in the context of findings in the 'paleo-'sciences (paleo-anthropology, paleo-genomics), where only indirect fossil evidence can be gathered concerning cognition, it takes more than a superficial acquaintance to be able to interpret findings in other fields, especially when media reports tend to bias interpretation and frequently overreach.

But in addition to training deficiencies, there is a real need to take results in linguistics seriously. This has not happened for at least two reasons, I think. The first one is the natural tendency among scientists to believe that they knew what language is, even if they have not been scientifically trained to analyze it. Our familiarity with language can be quite misleading, as research on knowledge of language has revealed for the past fifty years.

The second reason lies more with the linguists, and their failure to prepare their results for fruitful interaction with experts in other disciplines. More often than not, linguists resort to opaque jargon and modular assumptions that alienate other scientists. It is perhaps for this reason that in recent years several language scientists have gone to the trouble of formulating desiderata for successful interdisciplinary talks. Here are two (the first from Tecumseh Fitch (2009:298), the second from David Poeppel (2005:3)) that I found particularly useful in my own research.

> We need to distill what we know from linguistic theory into a set of computational primitives, and try to link them with models and specific principles of neural computation. Thus we need linguistic models that are explicit about the computational primitives (structures and operations) they require, and that attempt to define linguistic problems at a fine enough grain that one can discuss algorithmic and implementational approaches to their solution. We need a list of computations that linguistic theorists deem indispensable to solve their particular problem (e.g. in phonology, syntax or semantics).

> Linguists and psycholinguists owe a decomposition (or fractionation) of the particular linguistic domain in question (e.g. syntax) into formal operations that are, ideally, elemental and generic. The types of computations one might entertain, for example, include concatenation, comparison or recursion. Generic formal operations at this level of abstraction can form the basis for more complex linguistic representation and computation.

The issue I have in mind is what Poeppel and Embick (2005) dubbed the 'Granularity Mismatch Problem': linguistic and neuroscientific studies of language operate with objects of different granularity. But it is worth bearing in mind that Poeppel and Embick also formulated a far more damaging 'Ontological Incommensurability Problem': the units of linguistic computation and the units of neurological computation may well be incommensurable. If incommensurability is true, then, the fields cannot be unified, and the promises of biolinguistics cannot be met. The questions on the biolinguistic agenda may be questions of the sort that 'we will never answer' (Lewontin 1998); they are not 'problems,' but 'mysteries' (Chomsky 1975).

Though real, this possibility should not be taken as proven, and it seems to me that more efforts should be devoted to bridging the ontological gap that is so evident. Today, the challenge seems to be taken seriously, and concrete steps are formulated to make it happen. A growing number of researchers realize that to marry Chomsky and Lenneberg, a multilevel perspective of the sort advocated by the late David Marr for vision (linking the computational and the implementational levels of analysis) may be the solution. The task will not be easy, but certain things are already very clear. As far as linguists are concerned, it is important to abandon claims that language features are directly rooted in the genome, that the very developmental process, which relies on non-genetic factors, needs to be taken into account, that talk of 'language areas' is obsolete and inadequate. Brain areas perform basic kinds of computations that are recruited for different, high-level cognitive functions. Linguists and their colleagues also need to realize that 'mapping' (say, mapping a particular linguistic property onto a brain area) is not 'explaining.' The ultimate goal is to understand how the brain does it, not where it does it.

It is also important to revisit the claim that all human beings (pathological instances aside) are endowed by the same, homogeneous faculty of language. There is mounting evidence suggesting that the human faculty for language is not actually (so) uniform within the species. Some of this is not new. For example, different linguistic modalities can coexist in the same subject, as bilingual people in oral and sign languages nicely exemplify. Moreover, psycholinguistic measures are varied across the normal (and the impaired) population. And, of course, one important piece of evidence is the very existence of language disorders, which plausibly represent different breakdowns of the faculty that are qualitatively diverse by nature. Moreover, developmental trajectories followed by language acquisition, while encompassing similar milestones, are yet diverse (particularly at the cognitive/neurobiological levels). Language ontogeny in pathological populations is even more diverse.

It is clear that similar cognitive profiles can rely on different brain architectures. It seems then that there can be many ways of implementing a (more or less) functional faculty of language at the term of growth. Additionally, major changes in the brain architecture and function usually take place across development. Modules are not born; they are made, although their basic wiring is achieved before birth, plausibly, genetically-guided.

A fruitful biolinguistics must take the following as its premises:

- genes are not blueprints;
- the innate cannot be conflated with the genetic;
- developmental processes also depend on non-genetic factors;
- there is always an indirect link between the genotype and the phenotype;
- developmental itineraries are constrained, but not fully predetermined (in other words, development is both plastic and canalized);
- only biological structures (performing specific activities) are the final output of developmental processes;
- functions (that is, forms of behavior) usually result from the interplay of different biological structures; at the same time, one biological structure can contribute to more than one function;
- biological structures (but not the functions they contribute to) are the real evolutionary loci;
- biological systems are both robust (i.e. resistant to change) and evolvable (i.e. prompted to change) because of their modular nature;
- evolution can be prompted by modifications in any of the factors that affect development (not only genes are involved!);
- phenotypic novelties are largely reorganizational rather than a product of innovative genes.

A fruitful biolinguistics will have to come to grips with the fact that the language faculty is a mosaic, composed of various components of possibly distant origins. It is also clear that language, though used to communicate, cannot be reduced to a system of communication. While it is common to say that no other animal succeeds in transforming thoughts into speech (or sign), this cannot be equated with our linguistic ability. Language also plays a significant role in constructing new thoughts (cross-modular concepts, as Elizabeth Spelke and Katherine Kinzler (2007) have argued at length), which need not be expressed. This, too, should find its place in a future biolinguistics.

It is true that in the past reflections on the nature of language in a biological context may have been reduced to evolutionary pressures (evolutionary psychology) or design considerations related to optimality (the early days of minimalism). I think that we have come to realize that these may not have been the most fruitful questions to start with. Instead of focusing on what Ernst Mayr (1997) called 'ultimate' questions in biology, it seems advisable, at least for now, to focus on 'proximate' questions. It is these that seem more testable, using all the tools from the various disciplines at our disposal.

28.4 Conclusion

Pursuing a biolinguistic approach to language in one sense means that the field of inquiry becomes broader. A successful biolinguist must know enough about the cognitive systems of other species and about the properties of non-linguistic cognitive domains in humans to be able to make reasonable inferences about what each of them contributes towards the shape of the modern language faculty. But in another sense, the central object of study becomes much smaller for theoretical linguists, certainly those of a Chomskyan persuasion, for many of the grammatical details that were often attributed to some rich innate component specifically dedicated to language ('Universal Grammar') are now to be understood in terms of cultural evolution.

Further reading

Anderson (2004); Boeckx and Grohmann (2013); Di Sciullo and Boeckx (2011).

References

Anderson, S.R. (2004) *Doctor Dolittle's Delusion: Animals and the Uniqueness of Human Language*. New Haven: Yale University Press.
Boeckx, C. and K.K. Grohmann (eds.) (2013) *Cambridge Handbook of Biolinguistics*. Cambridge: Cambridge University Press.
Chomsky, N. (1965) *Aspects of the Theory of Syntax*. Cambridge: MIT Press.
Chomsky, N. (1975) *Reflections on Language*. New York: Pantheon Books.
De Waal, F.B.M. and P.F. Ferrari (2010). Towards a bottom-up perspective on animal and human cognition. *Trends in Cognitive Sciences* 14: 201–7.
Di Sciullo, A.M. and C. Boeckx (eds.) (2011) *The Biolinguistic Enterprise: New Perspectives on the Evolution and Nature of the Human Language Faculty*. Oxford: Oxford University Press.
Fitch, W.T. (2010) *The Evolution of Language*. Cambridge: Cambridge University Press.
Fitch, W.T. (2009). Prolegomena to a Future Science of Biolinguistics. *Biolinguistics*, 3(4), 283–320.
Hauser, M.D., N. Chomsky and W.T. Fitch (2002) The faculty of language: What is it, who has it, and how did it evolve? *Science* 298: 1569–79.
Jenkins, L. (2000) *Biolinguistics: Exploring the Biology of Language*. Cambridge: Cambridge University Press.
Lenneberg, E.H. (1967) *Biological Foundations of Language*. New York: Wiley.
Lewontin, R.C. (1998) The evolution of cognition. In D. Scarborough and S. Sternberg (eds.) *An Invitation to Cognitive Science: Methods, Models, and Conceptual Issues*, vol. 4, pp. 107–32. Cambridge: MIT Press.
Luria, S. (1976) Keynote address to the American Association for the Advancement of Science. http://profiles.nlm.nih.gov/ps/access/QLBBHR.pdf.
Mayr, E. (1997) *This Is Biology: The Science of the Living World*. Cambridge: Harvard University Press.
Piattelli-Palmarini, M. (ed.) (1980) *Language and Learning: The Debate Between Jean Piaget and Noam Chomsky*. Cambridge: Harvard University Press.

Poeppel, D. (2005). *The interdisciplinary study of language and its challenges*. Technical report, Jahrbuch des Wissenschaftskollegs zu Berlin.

Poeppel, D. and D. Embick (2005) Defining the relation between linguistics and neuroscience. In A. Cutler (ed.) *Twenty-First Century Psycholinguistics: Four Cornerstones*, pp. 173–89. Hillsdale: Erlbaum.

Spelke, E.S. and K.D. Kinzler (2007) Core knowledge. *Developmental Science* 10: 89–96.

Tinbergen, N. (1963) On aims and methods of ethology. *Zeitschrift fuer Tierpsychologie* 20: 410–33.

Walker, E. (ed.) (1978) *Explorations in the Biology of Language*. Montgomery: Bradford Books.

29
Cognitive linguistics

John R. Taylor

29.1 Introduction

The term 'cognitive linguistics' can be understood in different ways. On a broad understanding, any approach which sees language as primarily a mental phenomenon, located in the minds of its speakers, can be described as cognitive. Even linguists who focus on the formal properties of language, or on its use in social and interactive contexts, must acknowledge that these properties derive ultimately from the behaviour of individual speakers, which in turn is a function of their cognitive processes and mental representations. Nowadays, it seems reasonable to say, most linguists are cognitive, on this broad understanding.

For the purpose of this chapter, however, cognitive linguistics is understood in a narrower and more specialized sense. The term refers to a movement which had its origins in the United States in the final decades of the last century and which arose largely as a reaction to certain trends in the theory prevailing at the time, namely Chomsky's transformational-generative grammar (see Chapter 28). An important date is 1987, the year which saw the publication of Lakoff's *Women, Fire, and Dangerous Things* and the first volume of Langacker's *Foundations of Cognitive Grammar*; the impact of these two works will be discussed below (§29.3). A number of other scholars also provided input to the new movement; key names are Charles Fillmore (for his work on frame semantics, Fillmore 2006), Leonard Talmy (noted for his studies in conceptual semantics; these are assembled in Talmy 2000), and Gilles Fauconnier (who explored the processes of 'meaning construction' by way of mental spaces and, subsequently, conceptual blending: Fauconnier 1994; Fauconnier and Turner 2002).

Institutionally, cognitive linguistics may be said to have come of age in 1991, a year which saw the first international conference of cognitive linguistics, hosted by René Dirven at the University of Duisburg. The conference was the occasion for the founding of the International Cognitive Linguistics Association (ICLA), whose biennial meetings continue to this day, and also for the launch of the journal *Cognitive Linguistics*, still the major organ for publications in the field. Since then, the movement gradually gained adherents worldwide, along with a broadening of its theoretical scope and descriptive range. While in its early years, cognitive linguists tended to emphasize their polemical opposition to dominant

Chomskyan approaches to linguistic analysis, subsequent years saw a certain degree of convergence, and even dialogue, with scholars working in other traditions, such as functionalism, corpus studies, psycholinguistics, historical linguistics, and language acquisition (both first and second). Indeed, cognitive linguistics can itself be said to have now entered the mainstream, and its concerns and research agendas are shared rather broadly with a wide range of linguistic researchers.

This chapter addresses the nature and scope of cognitive linguistics from various perspectives. First, we consider some basic philosophical assumptions and their implications for the research themes of cognitive linguistics. Then we outline the contribution of the two most important of the movement's founding figures, Lakoff and Langacker. The chapter concludes with a discussion of some recent trends, with a focus on constructions and the impact of corpus-based studies on cognitive linguistic research.

29.2 Philosophical stance

It should be stated at the outset that cognitive linguistics does not constitute a unified, integrated theory of language but rather subsumes a cluster of approaches related by a number of general assumptions and shared research interests.

In view of its origins, it is not surprising that throughout much of its early history there was a polemical aspect to cognitive linguistics, in that it tended to define itself in opposition to the themes, assumptions and research agendas of Chomskyan approaches. The polemics may be characterized in terms of the unashamedly empiricist stance of cognitive linguistics versus the predominantly rationalist approach of Chomsky and his school. In keeping with the empiricist stance, cognitive linguists have been sceptical of the notion that language constitutes an autonomous module of the mind, encapsulated from other mental abilities; that acquisition proceeds in accordance with a genetically inherited blueprint; and that the overall architecture of a language is predetermined by the parameters of Universal Grammar. Rather, the emphasis has been on the embeddedness of linguistic knowledge in general cognitive abilities, on the role of input, socialization and general learning mechanisms in acquisition, and on language structure as emerging from its use in communicative contexts.

Here we review some manifestations of the empiricist stance, and their impact on cognitive linguistic research.

29.2.1 Rejection of modularity and the autonomy of language

According to the modularity hypothesis (Fodor 1983), the properties of human language(s) are a function of a specialized module of the mind. Although linguistic knowledge must evidently interface with other cognitive abilities – such as social cognition, rational thinking and general world knowledge – language is taken to be in its essential structure autonomous of other cognitive abilities. In contrast, cognitive linguists work on the assumption that linguistic knowledge is embedded in more general cognitive abilities, such as perception, attention, memory, categorization, abstraction, automatization, creativity, theory of mind, symbolic thought, etc. A recent focus of interest has been embodiment – the thesis that human cognition (and hence language abilities) is intimately reliant on the nature of our bodies and their interaction with the physical environment. Consistent with this philosophical stance, a major endeavour of cognitive linguistics has been to examine linguistic phenomena in light of these more general cognitive properties. These aspects of the cognitive linguistic enterprise are extensively covered in the collected volumes by Geeraerts (2006), Geeraerts and Cuyckens (2007) and Littlemore and Taylor (2014).

29.2.2 Rejection of the autonomy of syntax hypothesis

A specific claim of the modularity hypothesis concerns the components of linguistic knowledge itself. In particular, syntax is taken to be autonomous of other levels of linguistic structure, such as word-formation and phonology, as well as semantics and pragmatics, in the sense that the syntax operates over elements (such as lexical categories) and relations (such as clausal subject) unique to this level. (Another feature of the Chomskyan approach is that the syntax itself is understood as comprising a number of distinct, interacting principles, such as the binding principle, the X-bar principle, and so on.) While some scholars concede that syntactic organization may well be motivated at its edges by semantic, pragmatic, and functional considerations, it is taken as axiomatic within the Chomskyan approach that 'core' syntactic phenomena – phrase structure, binding, control, etc. – cannot be reduced to elements on other levels; they must, in other words, be described in uniquely syntactic terms.

Cognitive linguists have rejected this approach, seeking, rather, to understand syntax with reference to semantic/pragmatic (and even, phonological) aspects. There is now a considerable body of cognitive linguistic research on this topic. An early study, and harbinger of future developments, was Langacker's (1982) analysis of the English passive, whose properties he related to the semantics of its component elements, such as the verb *be*, the participle, and the *by*-phrase. Another important landmark was Langacker's proposal that major lexical categories, such as noun and verb, and their subcategories of count and mass (in the case of nouns), stative and dynamic (in the case of verbs), can each be satisfactorily and insightfully explained in semantic (or, more precisely, in Langacker's terminology, symbolic) terms; other elements of syntactic structure, such as complement and modifier, nominal case, and relations such as subject, object, and indirect object, were also characterized in semantic/conceptual terms (Langacker 1987). Subsequent research by Langacker and others has tackled supposedly core elements of autonomous syntax, such as raising and control, anaphora and binding, and long-distance dependencies.

29.2.3 Motivation

The cognitive linguistic position on syntax is sometimes (erroneously) taken to mean that syntactic organization can be fully 'read off' from semantic representations (in association, possibly, with functional considerations). Such an approach can scarcely be defended, if only because of the enormous diversity in syntactic organization in the languages of the world (and even variation amongst dialects of the same language) and the absence of independent means for establishing the corresponding diversity in semantic representations. Nevertheless, this straw man would appear to be at the heart of Jackendoff's (2010: 224) reluctance to align himself with the cognitive linguistic movement, in spite of his sympathy with many cognitive linguistic developments, such as the treatment of constructions. In truth, the focus of cognitive linguists has been to take a somewhat weaker position and to emphasize the semantic, pragmatic, discourse, etc. *motivation* of linguistic structure. One may not be able to predict (e.g. from semantic considerations) that structure X will be the norm in a language. However, given that X is indeed the norm in language Y, reasons for this can be sought, admittedly post hoc, in well-established facts about cognition, social interaction and discourse structure; important, also, may be other facts about language Y, such as the semantic values of the component elements of the structure in question and parallelisms between the structure and other, similar structures in the language. It is true that motivation can only deliver a partial post hoc explanation for linguistic facts and that other outcomes may be equally plausible. On the other hand, appeal to motivation serves to reduce the perceived arbitrariness of linguistic facts (Panther and Radden 2011), thereby enhancing their learnability and their durability in a language.

Consider, as an example, the status of English nouns as count or mass, and, in the latter case, as invariably singular or invariably plural (the so-called pluralia tantum). As mentioned, cognitive linguists would be keen to emphasize the semantic-conceptual basis to these categories. At the same time, we are faced with considerable cross-linguistic diversity with the respect to the status of nouns along these parameters, thus rendering implausible the possibility of a direct mapping from meaning to form. Why, for example, should *information* be a singular mass noun in English, while its translation equivalent in many other European languages is a count noun? Or why should *shorts* – the clothing item – be plural mass? Nevertheless, within a given language, a certain logic can be discerned, rendering the situation far from arbitrary (Taylor 2002). Moreover, the status of a given noun is rarely fixed; in appropriate contexts, it can assume difference statuses in accordance with the logic exploited within the language in question.

29.2.4 The core and the periphery

Even die-hard generativists concede that a significant range of linguistic phenomena cannot be brought under high-level generalizations; these, perforce, lie outside the scope of Universal Grammar. At issue are 'peripheral' constructions and all manner of idiomatic phraseologies, as well as the properties (semantic, phonological, distributional, etc.) of individual lexical items. It is true that some linguists nurtured in the generativist tradition have made insightful studies of these kinds of data; notable is Jackendoff's interest in unusual, 'oddball' constructions (many of his studies are assembled in Jackendoff 2010). In the main, however, Chomskyan linguists have been concerned with what they regard as the elements of core syntax and their determination by the setting of the parameters of Universal Grammar.

Interest in the periphery has become, to some extent, a hallmark of the cognitive linguistic enterprise, and for good reason, given its empirical stance. Peripheral phenomena, almost by definition, cannot be explained by universal principles and must, therefore, be learned by exposure to actual data. Notable, for example, has been the interest in lexical items, their polysemy and their use in idiomatic phrases, as well as their historical development (here we touch on another input to the cognitive linguistics movement, namely, the predominantly European tradition of historical lexicography; see Geeraerts 2010). Prepositions (and prepositional particles) have been a favourite topic, an important trigger being Claudia Brugman's thesis on the word *over*, whose main elements are presented in Lakoff (1987: Case Study 2). There is now a veritable cottage industry devoted to the word *over* (and its equivalents in other languages); see Taylor (2012: 233–8) for details. Indeed, for a number of decades, the Brugman/Lakoff study served as a model for polysemy studies more generally.

A second manifestation of interest in the periphery has been the rise of construction grammar, an approach which had its origins in the examination of idiomatic and oddball expressions, and which was subsequently broadened to embrace even core syntactic phenomena (see below §29.4).

29.2.5 Surface orientation

For Langacker, the only objects of linguistic study are actually occurring contextually-bound utterances and generalizations over these. The so-called 'content requirement' (Langacker 1987: 53–4) thus rules out in principle, as elements of linguistic description, 'invisible' (and inaudible) objects such as PRO, pro, traces and gaps; also rejected is the idea of 'underlying' structures that can be 'transformed', or whose constituents can be 'moved' or 'deleted'. A focus on 'the surface' is by no means unique to cognitive linguistics, of course; it is a feature of many contemporary approaches, including, even, some latter-day versions of generative grammar.

There is, however, a second aspect to the surface orientation of cognitive linguistic research. It is not denied that speakers make generalizations over encountered utterances. It is in virtue of these generalizations ('schemas', in Langacker's terminology) that speakers are able to extend beyond the reproduction of already encountered expressions. A crucial question, however, is the content of these generalizations, in particular, their degree of abstraction vis-à-vis their instances. A hallmark of much linguistic theorizing has been the search for high-level generalizations about language structure and syntactic organization. On the whole, linguists have tended to seek high-level generalizations – the higher the better – covering, if not all of a language, then at least as wide a range of phenomena as possible. For many, 'doing linguistics' consists, precisely, in the quest for such generalizations. In contrast, a notable feature of cognitive linguistics has been the realization that proficiency in a language may reside, not so much in the knowledge of a small number of very broad generalizations, but in the knowledge of a host of rather specific facts, comprising memories of specific utterances alongside relatively low-level generalizations, not too far removed from surface phenomena.

A further aspect concerns the relation between generalizations, whatever their degree of abstraction, and the data which they are supposed to capture. The standard approach seeks to maximize economy of mental storage; accordingly, knowledge of a rule expunges the need to store examples of the rule's applications (and on whose basis, presumably, the rule was abstracted in the first place). If you know how to form a passive clause, or a prepositional phrase, you do not need to store instances of passives or prepositional phrases, since these can be generated by application of the relevant rules. Langacker (1987: 29) addresses the issue in terms of what he calls the 'rule/list fallacy'. He suggests that perfectly regular expressions (in terms of the rules which they exemplify) may well coexist in the speaker's mental grammar alongside the generalizations themselves. Furthermore, high-level generalizations may well coexist with a plethora of shallower generalizations. A characteristic of the mental grammar, therefore, is that it potentially incorporates a high degree of redundancy. There is much empirical evidence pointing to just such a state of affairs. For example, high frequency phrases, such as *I like it*, elicit shorter response latencies that less frequent examples of the same structure, such as *I keep it*, suggesting that the former is indeed stored in memory as such; for a review of the relevant evidence, see Taylor (2012: 127–33).

29.2.6 Acquisition

In line with the view that language structure is likely to be grounded in general cognitive abilities, cognitive linguists have looked beyond the possible role of a genetic blueprint in language acquisition, and have explored the thesis that languages are acquired from exposure to situationally embedded utterances, in interaction, to be sure, with general learning abilities and processes of socialization (including, crucially, a child's ability to read the intentions of others). The approach is encapsulated in the slogan that cognitive linguistics is a 'usage-based' model of grammar (Langacker 1987: 46). The usage-basis of acquisition has been a dominant theme of Michael Tomasello's research. An important finding is that child learners tend not to go too far beyond what they have learned from input, indeed, that much child language production consists in the cutting and pasting of pre-learned chunks – that, in brief, the creativity of child language is very much constrained by previous exposure. A well-known case study concerns the learning of the English passive. One might imagine that once the learner has hit on the rule for the formation of a passive clause, she will be able immediately to apply the rule to all eligible (that is, transitive) verbs. This, it seems, is not how it happens. Rather, the passive is acquired verb-by-verb, each use of the passive having the status of an idiomatic 'constructional island' (Tomasello 2003: 121), and it is only when a critical mass of such 'islands' have been learned that the relevant generalizations emerge.

29.2.7 The encyclopaedia versus the dictionary

A notable feature of cognitive linguistics has been its focus on semantic matters. This should not be too surprising, given the interest in lexical items and their polysemy. Syntactic structures have also been approached with a view to elucidating the meanings which they symbolize. These meanings may, in many cases, be somewhat schematic, or skeletal, in that they need to be filled out with the semantic content provided by the constituent words. The approach is, however, consistent with the view that syntactic organization is inherently meaningful.

Cognitive linguists have always taken a rather broad perspective on the nature of linguistic meaning. It has to do, namely, with the ways in which a speaker conceptualizes a given situation, and incorporates such aspects of viewpoint, focusing, figure–ground alignment and contextual grounding. Meaning, in cognitive linguistics, therefore goes well beyond matters of reference and truth conditions. It is taken as axiomatic that the meaning associated with linguistic forms is broadly encyclopaedic in scope, encompassing (potentially) any aspects of knowledge that might be associated with a linguistic form. To be sure, some aspects might be more entrenched, or more central than others. Nevertheless, it is generally acknowledged that practically any facet of an expression's contextual use may be taken up and conventionalized in usage. The study of historical change is replete with many examples of just this process (Geeraerts 2010).

The approach contrasts markedly with the syntacto-centrism of Chomskyan linguistics, in which lexical items have been studied primarily, or even exclusively, with regard to their syntactic properties, specifically, their availability to occur in phrase-structure configurations; the focus, in other words, has been largely on such matters as a word's membership in one of a small number of lexical categories, its subcategorization frames, and its theta-role assignment. While *walk, run, jog* and *lope* designate different kinds of activities, from a syntactic point of view the four verbs can be regarded as roughly equivalent; all are manner of motion verbs and share much the same syntactic distribution, all take as their subject the moving entity and accept a complement designating the place or goal of the movement. The specific details of the manner of motion can therefore be relegated to the encyclopaedia (the repository of nonlinguistic knowledge), while the dictionary (a component of strictly linguistic knowledge) records only the syntactically relevant facts. Cognitive linguists, on the other hand, would be drawn to the fact that *run* has given rise to a much more extensive network of idiomatic and metaphorical uses than the other verbs; moreover, the individual senses of *run* turn out to be associated with distinctive lexico-syntactic contexts (Gries 2006). An exclusion of encyclopaedic aspects of word meaning thus results not only in an impoverished account of semantics, it also ignores the subtle interplay of words and their preferred contexts of occurrence.

29.2.8 Background cognition

As mentioned above, cognitive linguists have been sceptical of underlying structures and of transformations which convert deep syntactic representations into surface forms. But while syntactic organization is taken to be fully transparent, it has become increasingly apparent that semantic structure is considerably more complex than that which is symbolized by elements of surface structure. There is, namely, a great deal of 'background cognition' going on in the understanding of even the simplest utterances. Attempts to elucidate these processes have constituted some of the more exciting and hotly debated developments in cognitive linguistics. Mention might be made, for example, of Fauconnier and Turner's (2002) work on conceptual blending, the process whereby elements of two or more conceptual structures are creatively combined into a new emergent structure. Blending has been applied to studies of metaphor and of narrative, and, indeed, to many aspects of nonlinguistic cognition. Other important topics include Talmy's notion of force dynamics, and Langacker's work on reference points and subjectification. Force dynamics (Talmy 2000) develops the intuition that interactions can be seen in terms of the relative strength and inherent dynamics of interacting entities; it has been applied, pre-eminently, to the study of causing, letting and preventing, and to expressions of modality (Sweetser 1990). The reference point notion (Langacker 1991: 170) was initially applied to possessive expressions (where the possessor is taken as a reference point for providing mental access to the possessed), but has subsequently been extended to such diverse areas as metonymy, topicalization, complementation patterns, and the 'double subject' constructions of Japanese and Korean. Subjectification (Langacker 1991, 2008) concerns the relation between the conceptualizer and the conceptualized, that is, between the speaker and her circumstances (the 'ground') and the overt content of an expression; it has ramifications for tense and modality, for epistemic stance, and is an important factor in lexico-semantic change.

29.3 Founding figures: Lakoff and Langacker

A crucial year in the history of cognitive linguistics was 1987, the year which saw the publication of Lakoff's *Women, Fire, and Dangerous Things* and the first volume of Langacker's *Foundations of Cognitive Grammar*. Both Lakoff and Langacker started their careers as adherents of the newly emerging Chomskyan approach, and both became disenchanted with its focus on formal aspects of grammatical structure and for its relative neglect of semantic issues. After briefly flirting with the generative semantics movement, both went on to develop their own approaches to linguistic analysis.

29.3.1 George Lakoff

The dominant theme of Lakoff's volume is a rejection of 'objectivist', or truth conditional approaches to semantics. According to the latter, a sentence is true if it corresponds to some verifiable state of affairs in the world. Lakoff, on the contrary, pursued the view that the relation between language and the world is mediated by how humans categorize and conceptualize their environment. Thus, the categories that humans operate with are not defined by a set of objectively verifiable necessary and sufficient features, but rather are centred on a 'prototype', or best example, often understood in the context of frames, or idealized cognitive models (ICMs) of the world, how it is structured, and how it functions. An often quoted example is that of *bachelor*, defined, not simply in terms of the necessary features human, adult, male, unmarried – each of which, it might be noted, are far from being the universal semantic primitives assumed by formal semantics – but also against a set of assumptions pertaining to expected marriage practices in a society. The fact that some individuals, such as Catholic priests or Tarzan, are not good examples of the category is due to the fact that their circumstances do not fit the ICM against which *bachelor* is defined.

Lakoff extended the notion of prototype category to the study of lexical polysemy (cf. Taylor 2003). The various senses of a word do not have to share a common meaning core; more usually, they cluster around a central, prototypical sense, to which they are related, directly or indirectly. The premier example of a radial category (in addition to the one hinted at in the title of Lakoff's 1987 volume, which refers to the members of a noun class in the Australian language Dyrbal), is the polysemy of the word *over*. The basic sense is taken to involve 'above' and 'across', as in *The bird flew over the garden*. Extended senses, related in virtue of some common shared features, include the static 'above' sense, as in *the helicopter is hovering over the hill*, the 'across' sense (without vertical separation), as in *Sam drove over the bridge*, the 'covering' sense, as in *She spread the tablecloth over the table*, the dispersal sense, as in *The guards were posted all over the hill*, and several more.

Lakoff went further, and proposed that syntactic phenomena may also cluster in a radial category structure, an outstanding example being his analysis of the couple of dozen uses of deictic/presentational *there* (1987: Case Study 3). The idea of constructional polysemy was taken up by Adele Goldberg (1995). In addressing the ditransitive construction in English, for example, she identified as prototype a situation of successful and immediate transfer (*give the dog a bone*). Deviations from the prototype may involve merely intended transfer (*I mailed him a parcel, but he didn't receive it*), future intended transfer (*I bequeath you my estate*), as well as instances of metaphorical transfer (*tell someone a story*) and denial of transfer (*refuse someone access*). Somewhat further away from the prototype are 'light-verb' expressions (*give the door a kick, do me a favour*), as well as some outlier expressions (*forgive us our sins*).

Lakoff is perhaps best known for his work on metaphor. Again, the underlying theme is the role of conceptualization in linguistic semantics. The thesis, presented in Lakoff and Johnson (1980) and elsewhere, is that metaphor is not just a matter of language. To speak of one thing using words appropriate for something else – as when intellectual arguments are spoken of as if they were buildings (you *construct*, or *demolish* an argument), or when life is spoken of as if it were a journey (*we've lost our way*), or when time is spoken of as if it were a spatial dimension (the *near* future, the *distant* past) – points to the fact that the one domain of experience (the target domain) is conceptualized in terms of the source domain. Time really is understood in terms of spatial parameters; life really is conceived of as a journey; and so on.

While the ubiquity of metaphor (and its step-sister, metonymy) in language is now widely accepted, Lakoff's original proposals have been subject to considerable elaboration and modification, partly in response to critical evaluations and nuanced with the advent of corpus- and discourse-based studies. Crucially, though, the basic thesis has been upheld by a large number of psycholinguistic studies (Gibbs 2014). An important development has been the claim that foundational metaphors are 'embodied', in the sense that they may ultimately be grounded in bodily experience, giving rise, for example, to the (probably universal) positive associations of 'up' with health, life and well-being, and conversely negative associations with 'down'.

29.3.2 Ronald Langacker

Langacker's contribution to the cognitive linguistic enterprise is different in character. Rejecting the apparatus of transformational-generative grammar, Langacker set about building a linguistic theory – Cognitive Grammar – on simple, clear principles. He opens *Foundations* by endorsing Saussure's conception of the linguistic sign, namely as the association of an 'acoustic image' (a phonological representation, in Langacker's terminology) with a 'concept' (or semantic representation) (1987: 11). In fact, for Langacker, there are only three objects of study in language: (1) language in its perceptible form; (2) meaning, understood very generally to incorporate construal, encyclopaedic aspects, discourse aspects, and so on; and (3) symbolic relations between (1) and (2). Langacker makes the bold claim that all of language structure – not only the individual words and morphemes, but all aspects of syntax and morphology – can be adequately and insightfully described in these terms.

In order to implement this 'minimalist' approach, a number of additional constructs are needed. These are: (1) the schema/instance relation; (2) the part/whole relation; and (3) the similarity relation. A schema abstracts what is common to its instances; conversely, the instances elaborate the schema in different, often contrasting ways. The part–whole relation refers to the fact that structures may be broken down into their component parts; conversely, that smaller units can be assembled into larger configurations, in accordance with existing schemas. The schema/instance and the part/whole relations are recursive; A may be an instance of B, which in turn is an instance of C, etc. The relations are also interdependent. The very possibility of analysing a complex structure into its parts is conditional upon the analysis conforming with a pre-existing schema. This is where the third relation comes into play, in that similarity (or, more accurately, speakers' subjective perception of similarity) plays a crucial role in the emergence of schemas. The fact that A and B come to be regarded as instances of C rests on the prior recognition that A and B are similar in some respect(s). Moreover, the similarity between A and B may be perceived to be similar to the way in which D and E are similar. The commonality between the two cases may give rise to a higher order schema. To give an example from morphophonology: the perceived similarity between word pairs such as *urbane/urbanity, insane/insanity, profane/profanity* may give rise to a schema representing the alternating phonological forms. An even higher order schema may emerge to capture the similarity between these pairs and pairs like *obscene/obscenity, serene/serenity*.

As an illustration of how all this works, consider the expression *can-opener*. (Only a very partial explication is possible here.) We can identify component parts, namely *can*, *open* and *–er*, largely because these units occur elsewhere in the language, with roughly comparable semantic properties. The component unit *can* is an instance of the more schematic unit Noun, the whole expression being an instance of the complex schematic unit [N V–*er*], this itself being an instance of Noun, with its associated semantics (roughly: 'a device that can be used for V–*ing* Ns'). The schematic unit can sanction an open-ended set of instantiations;

in this way, Cognitive Grammar is able to handle syntactic and morphological generalizations. It should also be noted that the unit has other semantic values (think of examples such as *dog-lover*, which denotes a person, not a thing, and *city-dweller*, where the initial noun designates the place where a person dwells); in other words, the unit is polysemous, just like the words of a language.

On the Cognitive Grammar view, a language thus comes to be seen as a vast and complex network of relations amongst linguistic units (phonological, semantic and symbolic). Any usage event involves accessing the network and activating the relevant relations, while acquisition is a matter of a speaker gradually building up the network structure and becoming proficient in its use.

29.4 Constructions

For many syntacticians, constructions are epiphenomena; they are the outcome of general syntactic principles and their interaction and possess no particular ontological status in themselves. For cognitive linguists, in contrast, constructions have come to be regarded as the fundamental unit of linguistic description, and the point of access of learners into the linguistic system (Croft 2001; Tomasello 2003).

There is, to be sure, some variation in how the notion of construction is understood (Taylor 2012: 124–7). What is probably the dominant view corresponds with Langacker's notion of an internally complex symbolic unit, in which a formal specification is paired with a (schematic) semantic value; some scholars further stipulate that at least some aspects of the form–meaning pairing should not be predictable from other constructions in the language (though this restriction has now largely been abandoned, thus making it possible to assign constructional status to perfectly regular configurations, provided that they have become sufficiently entrenched through usage). Other approaches regard a construction as any stable association of a form with a meaning (thus, a monomorphemic word such as *dog*, or a bound morpheme like *–er*, are regarded as constructions). Others, yet again, take a construction to be any internally complex unit; thus, syllables, and patterns of syllable structure, can be regarded as phonological constructions.

A number of themes in cognitive linguistics have converged on the notion of construction, thereby putting the construct in centre stage. These include the long-standing interest in idioms, phraseologies and (syntactically) peripheral expressions; an enduring interest in the semantic value of syntactic configurations; the recognition of the role of usage frequency in the establishment and entrenchment of linguistic knowledge; along with a general aversion to deep structures and to the thesis of autonomous syntax.

A landmark paper was Fillmore *et al.* (1988). Although the body of the paper focused on the semantics and pragmatics of the phrase *let alone*, its lengthy preamble surveyed a wide range of constructional idioms, that is, patterns (of varying degrees of productivity and schematicity) for the formation of expressions, but whose syntactic, semantic, pragmatic and even phonological properties cannot be derived from general principles, whether universal or language-specific. Their examples range from the 'cousin idiom' (n^{th} *cousin x-times removed*) and the 'correlative comparison construction' (*the X-er the Y-er*) to the 'incredulity response construction' (exemplified by *Him be a doctor?*). A follow-up paper (Kay and Fillmore 1999) addressed the so-called WXDY construction, exemplified by *What are you doing, lying on the floor?* This expression does not enquire into what the addressee is doing (the utterance itself provides that information); rather, the construction is used to express the speaker's surprise at such a situation, and requests an explanation.

The significance of these studies is threefold. First, the constructions in question are productive, in the sense that they contain slots which can be filled by a range of items with the appropriate semantic/syntactic properties; since, in some cases, the set of possible fillers is quite large, the constructions have considerable generative power. The second point of significance is the idiomatic status of the constructions. They are idiomatic in the sense that their properties cannot be fully predicted from other facts about the language (nor, indeed, from general facts about the human language faculty). Their properties therefore have to be learned on the basis of exposure. This leads to the third point. If language users are able, on the basis of exposure, to learn the idiosyncratic properties of constructional idioms (which they clearly are), then precisely the same learning mechanisms will be able to guarantee acquisition of 'core' linguistic phenomena, the more so since core constructions are, if anything, more easily learnable, since they are subject to many fewer idiosyncratic and language-specific constraints. Indeed, the logical outcome is to deny any qualitative difference between peripheral and core constructions; any differences that may exist are merely a matter of degree of productivity, of descriptive scope and of frequency of occurrence in the language. It is also worth noting that the range of oddball constructions in a language (indeed, the scope of the idiomatic more generally) is truly massive. If anything, it is the highly abstract, 'regular' constructions in a language which constitute the exception. It is therefore not surprising that a constructionist account is now commonly proposed for all syntactic phenomena, even for very general phrase-structure configurations such as transitive clause, ditransitive clause and so on. As a matter of fact, on closer examination, even these very general phrase-structure configurations also turn out to be 'idiomatic', in the sense that their specific properties (such as the set of verbs which are eligible to occur in them, and the range of meanings that can be associated with them) turn out to be language-specific, and thus have to learned; in this respect, they are no different from more obviously idiomatic expressions.

On a constructionist account, acceptability (or grammaticality: cognitive linguists see little reason for differentiating between the two concepts) is a matter of an expression's conformity with a constructional schema or, more commonly, a number of constructional schemas; thus, the various components of a transitive clause, such as its subject noun phrase and its adverbial modifiers (if present) also need to be sanctioned by the appropriate schemas. Importantly, minor deviations from a construction's specifications may be tolerated; this is in keeping with the prototype view of linguistic categories and is in fact a major driver of syntactic change. For example, it is no longer a requirement of the prenominal possessive construction (*the man's hat*) that the possessor nominal be human; inanimates and abstracts are increasingly found in this function.

29.5 Corpus-based studies

Langacker has stated that cognitive grammar is a usage-based theory of language. There are several ways in which this claim can be understood. The first we have already mentioned: language is acquired through exposure to instances of its use and through the abstraction of generalizations over usage instances; it is not driven by the setting of parameters of a supposedly universal grammar. What is grammatical in a language is determined by conformity with schemas and patterns extracted from previous usage, not by reference to abstract innate principles.

A second understanding is with reference to fluency and ease of processing. Through repeated use, a structure becomes entrenched, or automated. It can be stored and accessed as a whole; it need not be subjected to internal analysis for its comprehension and does not have to be assembled from its parts in its production. Entrenchment thereby promotes fluency on the part of the speaker and facilitates comprehension on the part of the listener. The occurrence of entrenched structures in a text thus contributes significantly to its 'idiomaticity'; indeed, non-native authorship can often be detected by their absence. This links to a third aspect of usage basis, namely, its role in diachronic change (Bybee 2001). Entrenched expressions are able to 'drift' away from their initial configuration and are free to acquire new or additional meanings and uses, and even distinctive pronunciations. *Evening* (the noun) is usually spoken as two syllables, whereas the much rarer *evening* (participle of the verb *to even*) has three. A baker is not simply 'one who bakes' (the compositional meaning); the word comes to be used as the name of a kind of retail outlet, and speakers may not even perceive the word to be related to the base verb. At the same time, alternative designations tend to be eclipsed; since *baker* is available as the name of the retail outlet, we do not need to search for alternative designations.

The usage-based model constitutes a hypothesis about the nature, origin and evolution of linguistic knowledge; it does not in itself define a research methodology. It is worth noting, in this connection, that many of the foundational works in cognitive linguistics – Lakoff (1987), Lakoff and Johnson (1980), Langacker (1987, 1991), Talmy (1988) and others – were based almost exclusively on the methodology favoured by Chomskyan linguists, namely, the introspective analysis of invented data. More recently, it has become apparent that the usage-based hypothesis, on its various understandings, needs to be tested and refined against actually occurring data. Some of the more important developments in cognitive linguistics have in fact emerged on the back of interactions between cognitive linguistic theory and the analytic methods of corpus linguistics.

Several areas of investigation can be mentioned. The first, and most obvious, concerns the accessing of frequency data on words, morphemes, word combinations (collocations), phraseologies and constructions, often as a function of register and modality (spoken or written), as evidence for the relative entrenchment of the units in question. A particularly fruitful line of research has been to examine the patterns of association between linguistic units (typically words, though the methodology can be applied to units of any size) and the constructions in which they occur (Stefanowitsch and Gries 2003). It is not the case, for example, that all verbs are equally likely to occur in the past tense or as imperatives, nor are all nouns equally likely to occur in the plural or in definite noun phrases. An often-cited syntactic example is the 'waiting to happen' construction. In principle, practically any event-denoting noun can occur in the idiomatic phrase *It was a N waiting to happen*. Yet the two most likely nouns are *accident* and *disaster*. The frequency of these two nouns in the construction by far exceeds what might be expected on the basis of their overall frequency in the language. Similarly, any occurrence of the word *put* is very strongly associated with the caused motion construction [V NP PP], whereby the referent of NP ends up (literally or metaphorically) in a place designated by PP. The view that emerges from these kinds of studies is that a word needs to be characterized, not only in terms of its lexical category and its phonological and semantic properties, but also with respect to the constructions in which it is most likely to occur. Conversely, a construction needs to be characterized, not only in terms of its meaning and its formal structure, but also with reference to the lexical items which are most likely to fill its various slots. (The kinds of texts in which the constructions occur constitutes a further variable.) The traditional distinction between lexis and syntax is thereby blurred; instead of being thought of as distinct levels of organization, the two are inextricably intertwined.

Another line of research addresses the factors which influence the choice between linguistic items (words, morphemes, constructions) which are roughly synonymous. A well-studied case is the so-called dative alternation – the choice between *give the dog a bone* versus *give a bone to the dog*. With the aid of sophisticated statistical techniques, the various factors which influence a speaker's choice can be identified and quantified relative to each other. The methodology also allows the characterization of 'prototypical' examples of the two constructions.

Corpus-based studies has also revolutionized our understanding of polysemy, lexical polysemy in the first instance, but also the various semantic values which attach to larger constructions. Most words are polysemous to some extent; in fact, as a general rule, the more frequent a word, the more distinct meanings it has. In principle, polysemy should give rise to ambiguity (cf. such textbook examples as *She can't bear children* and *It was a colourful ball*, which rely on the different meanings that can be attached to *bear* and *ball*). Yet misunderstandings are comparatively rare (jokes and word-play aside). Mostly, a hearer is able immediately to zoom in on the intended sense, without even being aware of the existence of possible alternative readings. In spite of the twenty-odd senses that have been attributed to *over*, occurrences of the word rarely if ever give rise to ambiguity, and few readers will be aware of the three distinct senses that can be attributed to *Time flies like an arrow* (Taylor 2012: 167–73). Corpus studies suggest an explanation for this paradox. Each sense of a word is associated with a distinct lexico-syntactic context; the context serves to prime the relevant sense, thereby suppressing other possible readings.

A final area concerns the productivity of morphological and syntactic schemas ('rules', in more traditional parlance). Nominalization in *–ness* is more productive than nominalization in *–th* or *–ity*. It is not just that nouns in *–ness* are more numerous overall than nouns in *–th* or *–ity*. Productivity is not to be confused with token frequency. No doubt, the *way*-construction (*I made my way to the exit*, *We can't spend our way out of recession*, *He lied his way through the interview*) is not particularly frequent, measured in terms of its occurrence per million words of text. Yet the construction is productive, in that the verb slot can be filled by a virtually unrestricted set of activity-denoting verbs. (Curiously, the only verbs which seem to be prohibited are motion verbs like *go* and *come*.) What renders a construction productive is the number of different types that can occupy its slots, relative to the total number of construction tokens. The nominalizing suffix *–ness* can be attached to practically any adjective; *–th* and *–ity*, on the other hand, are restricted to a fairly stable set of entrenched examples.

The patterns, regularities and associations that can be discovered in a corpus of texts go well beyond what is available to introspection and casual observation. This fact raises a fundamental conceptual question, namely, how, if at all, are the properties of a corpus represented in the mind of an individual speaker? Early pioneers in corpus studies were keen to emphasize the 'objective' and 'factual' character of their work, and to differentiate it from 'subjective' speculations of theoretical linguists about what might be in the minds of speakers. However, the focus of cognitive linguistics, almost by definition, is language as a cognitive, and therefore mind-internal phenomenon. The issue boils down to the relation between 'language in the world' and 'language in the mind'. Taylor (2012) has emphasized the dialectic relation between the two. Language in the world is the product of linguistic acts of individuals; these individuals behave in accordance with their acquired knowledge; their acquired knowledge, in turn, is the product of their encounters with external language. Looming over this is the fact that while language is certainly located in the minds of individuals, language is also a social, cooperative endeavour. In order to be able to function in a linguistic community, speakers need to calibrate their internal grammar to the grammars presumed to exist in the minds of other speakers.

References

Bybee, J. (2001) *Phonology and Language Use*. Cambridge: Cambridge University Press.
Croft, W. (2001) *Radical Construction Grammar: Syntactic Theory in Typological Perspective*. Oxford: Oxford University Press.
Fauconnier, G. (1994) *Mental Spaces: Aspects of Meaning Construction in Natural Languages*. Cambridge: Cambridge University Press.
Fauconnier, G. and M. Turner (2002) *The Way We Think: Conceptual Blending and the Mind's Hidden Complexities*. New York: Basic Books.
Fillmore, C. (2006) Frame semantics. In D. Geeraerts (ed.) *Cognitive Linguistics: Basic Readings*, pp. 373–400. Berlin: Mouton de Gruyter. First published 1982 in Linguistic Society of Korea (ed.) *Linguistics in the Morning Calm*, pp. 111–37. Seoul: Hanshin Publishing Company.
Fillmore, C., P. Kay and M.C. O'Connor (1988) Regularity and idiomaticity in grammatical constructions: The case of *let alone*. *Language* 64: 501–38.
Fodor, J.A. (1983) *The Modularity of Mind*. Cambridge: MIT Press.
Geeraerts, D. (ed.) (2006) *Cognitive Linguistics: Basic Readings*. Berlin: Mouton de Gruyter.
Geeraerts, D. (2010) *Lexical Semantics*. Oxford: Oxford University Press.
Geeraerts, D. and H. Cuyckens (eds) (2007) *The Oxford Handbook of Cognitive Linguistics*. Oxford: Oxford University Press.
Gibbs, R. (2014) Embodied metaphor. In J. Littlemore and J.R. Taylor (eds) *The Bloomsbury Companion to Cognitive Linguistics*, pp. 167–84. London: Bloomsbury.
Goldberg, A. (1995) *Constructions: A Construction-Grammar Approach to Argument Structure*. Chicago: Chicago University Press.
Gries, S.T. (2006) Corpus-based methods and Cognitive Semantics: The many senses of *to run*. In S.T. Gries and A. Stefanowitsch (eds) *Corpora in Cognitive Linguistics: Corpus-based Approaches to Syntax and Lexis*, pp. 57–99. Berlin: Mouton de Gruyter.
Jackendoff, R. (2010) *Meaning and the Lexicon: The Parallel Architecture 1975–2010*. Oxford: Oxford University Press.
Kay, P. and C. Fillmore (1999) Grammatical constructions and linguistic generalizations: The *What's X doing Y?* construction. *Language* 75: 1–33.
Lakoff, G. (1987) *Women, Fire, and Dangerous Things: What Categories Reveal About the Mind*. Chicago: Chicago University Press.
Lakoff, G. and M. Johnson (1980) *Metaphors We Live By*. Chicago: Chicago University Press.
Langacker, R.W. (1982) Space grammar, analysability and the English passive. *Language* 58: 22–80.
Langacker, R.W. (1987) *Foundations of Cognitive Grammar*, vol. 1. Stanford: Stanford University Press.
Langacker, R.W. (1991) *Foundations of Cognitive Grammar*, vol. 2. Stanford: Stanford University Press.
Langacker, R.W. (2008) *Cognitive Grammar: A Basic Introduction*. Oxford: Oxford University Press.
Littlemore, J. and J.R. Taylor (eds) (2014) *The Bloomsbury Companion to Cognitive Linguistics*. London: Bloomsbury.
Panther, K.-U. and G. Radden (2011) *Motivation in Grammar and the Lexicon*. Amsterdam: John Benjamins.
Stefanowitsch, A. and S.T. Gries (2003) Collostructions: Investigating the interaction of words and constructions. *International Journal of Corpus Linguistics* 8: 209–43.
Sweetser, E. (1990) *From Etymology to Pragmatics: Metaphorical and Cultural Aspects of Semantic Structure*. Cambridge: Cambridge University Press.
Talmy, L. (1988) Force dynamics in language and cognition. *Cognitive Science* 12: 49–100.

Talmy, L. (2000) *Toward a Cognitive Semantics*. 2 vols. Cambridge: MIT Press.
Taylor, J.R. (2002) *Cognitive Grammar*. Oxford: Oxford University Press.
Taylor, J.R. (2003) *Linguistic Categorization*. Oxford: Oxford University Press.
Taylor, J.R. (2012) *The Mental Corpus*. Oxford: Oxford University Press.
Tomasello, M. (2003) *Constructing a Language: A Usage-Based Theory of Language Acquisition*. Cambridge: Harvard University Press.

30
Functional linguistics

J. Lachlan Mackenzie

30.1 Introduction

The notion of functional linguistics is associated in many linguists' minds with a dichotomy between formal and functional approaches. The rivalry between the two ways of doing linguistics loomed over the field until fairly recently, with functionalism being seen by formalists as a wrong-headed negation of the principles they held dear, just as functionalists saw formalists as fundamentally misguided. Towards the end of the last century departments of linguistics, especially but not exclusively in the United States, tended to align themselves with one or the other orientation, and it is significant that Newmeyer (1998), a work that contrasts the two approaches from a primarily formalist perspective, begins with a 'not totally imaginary' (p. 1) dialogue that pits a formalist professorship interviewee against a functionalist one. In more recent years, however, it has become much less usual to qualify functional linguistics in negative terms, that is, simply as a rejection of formalist positions. The old antagonism has yielded to a more peaceful coexistence as publication after publication has recognized functional linguistics as having validity in its own right and as being anchored in a long and valuable tradition. This is the position to be taken in this chapter.

There are many streams within functional linguistics, but there is one set of assumptions that is shared by all functionalists, one that justifies the word 'functional': languages have a primordial function in the human societies in which they are used, namely that of permitting sophisticated communication of ideas and feelings between human beings, and this function impacts on both the current use of languages and how they have developed historically. As a result, a large number of language phenomena, certainly many from the area of morphosyntax, are interpreted as being motivated, that is, capable of having an explanation. In functionalism, explanations are sought primarily outside of language proper (Newmeyer 1998: Ch. 3), for example in such cognitive domains as memory, attention, processing and prediction, in such social domains as gender, esteem and politeness, or in the spatio-temporal and socio-cultural contexts in which language is used by speakers in their daily lives. Needless to say, this in principle creates a sharp distinction between functionalists and formalists, who tend to abstract away from the uses of language, seeing grammar as autonomous and *sui generis* and allowing only explanations from within the language system.

Although functionalists have reached a considerable degree of consensus about the assumptions that fundamentally orient their work, there are nevertheless significant differences among the various groups of functional linguists at work today. These reflect a variety of standpoints on such matters as the exact object of inquiry (discourse; texts; grammatical structures), the type of data admissible (corpus data; experimental data; intuitive judgements; examples from grammars), the degree to which language is seen as a system, and the amount of overlap and/or cooperation envisaged with other subdisciplines of linguistics (notably Cognitive Linguistics, Construction Grammar and Language Typology) or with such other disciplines as sociology, psychology, anthropology and pedagogy. The purpose of this chapter is to develop a rounded picture of functional linguistics as currently practised, emphasizing both the unity and the diversity to be found.

§30.2 discusses the origins of functional linguistics, concentrating on the role of the Prague School. §30.3 portrays the state of the art today, situating functional linguistics with regard to formal, usage-based and cognitive schools of thought. §30.4 explores connections between functional linguistics and three adjacent areas of inquiry: pragmatics and discourse analysis, language typology, and psycholinguistics. §30.5 presents four major groupings within contemporary functional linguistics: West Coast functionalism, Systemic Functional Linguistics, Functional Discourse Grammar, and Role and Reference Grammar. §30.6 concludes the chapter by considering ways in which formal and functional linguistics have now become complementary rather than inimical.

30.2 Origins

Although it is notoriously difficult to determine a starting point for any intellectual tradition, there is some acceptance that it is the appearance in 1929 of the Theses of the Prague School[1] (Theses 1983) and specifically of various writings by the Czech scholar Vilém Mathesius around the same time that marks the beginning of what is currently understood to be functional linguistics.[2] On the very first page, the Theses proclaim something today's functionalists will generally still assent to:

> Wether [sic] one analyses language as expression or communication, it is the intention of the speaker which can explain it in a most evident and a most natural manner. For this reason, linguistic analysis should respect the functionalist standpoint. *Seen from the functionalist viewpoint, language is a system of purposeful means of expression.* No fact of language can be understood without regard to the system to which it pertains.
>
> (Theses 1983: 77, emphasis in original)

The founders of the Prague School focused on the clause and specifically on how it functioned for the speaker of that clause. What they attempted to elucidate was how the speaker dynamically constructs the clause in an attempt to achieve his/her communicative goals. The clause was seen as commencing with a starting point (or 'theme') and climaxing in a communicative highpoint, in later Prague School writings to be called the 'rheme'. A fundamental point, one that has had important repercussions for some branches of functional linguistics, is that the theme may, or may not, correspond with the subject; and similarly for the rheme and the predicate. These slippages are currently understood as involving 'competing motivations' (see §30.3). In later years a related but non-dichotomous approach arose in Czech linguistics under the heading of 'communicative dynamism', with the clause being seen as gradually growing more and more 'dynamic' as it advances step by step from starting point to conclusion. While the Prague School took a dynamic view of clause construction, the forms resulting from the use of language were regarded as constituting a system (cf. the quotation from the Theses above), one that has arisen through the myriad applications of the principles of dynamic construction. The founders of linguistic functionalism were thus in no way opposed to the study of the language system as a structure, but this should always go hand in hand with an examination of the functions that its elements served.

Here was born one of the fundamental tenets of many functionalists, the belief that the purpose of linguistic work is to forge a link between structure and function; Butler (2003), in a monumental examination of this area of linguistics, accordingly identifies the three approaches he compares as 'structural-functional theories', an expression created by Robert Van Valin, Jr (for whom see §30.5.4). Structure is identified with lexico-grammatical organization as an entrenched cognitive capacity that permits us to formulate and encode our communicative intentions. Givón (2009: 26–9) points to the functional advantages of having such a grammatical system, drawing a sharp contrast between pidgin communication, where interlocutors do not share a system, and grammatical communication, where they do, showing that the two types of communication differ radically with regard to both structure and function. In a pidgin situation, as for example during encounters between foreign tourists and monolingual inhabitants of the country being visited, morphology will be heavily reduced, constructions simple and word order directly dictated by communicative needs; processing will be slow, laborious and conscious, with high context-dependence. In grammatical communication, by contrast, morphology is rich, constructions are varied and hierarchical, and word order is often dependent on syntactic relations (such as subject and object), while processing is quick, effortless, unconscious and much less context-dependent.

It should be noted, however, that other functionalists have questioned or even denied the Praguean conclusion that the result of language use is a structure. One position that has been espoused is that grammatical organization is emergent, with all structure being seen 'as in a continual process of becoming, as epiphenomenal' (Hopper 1992: 366). On this view, the focus is exclusively on the dynamics of discourse, in which processes of grammaticalization take place that allow a gradual transition of lexical units to a more supportive role, without ever gelling into anything permanent. Notions like 'noun' and 'verb' or 'transitive' and 'intransitive' are not pre-existent but rather come into being in discourse use and evaporate again. Scepticism about 'structure' is also apparent in Givón (2013), who does not mention the Prague School but rather emphasizes the opposition that he sees between functionalism and structuralism. In general, it can be said that American functionalism is much less beholden to Prague than its European counterpart(s), seeking its roots in the US anthropological heritage and more recently in various movements that grew up in opposition to Chomskyan formalism.

For phonology, the aftermath of the 1929 Theses was somewhat more complex. While Mathesius saw the phoneme as having the function of distinguishing meanings for the speaker, Nikolai Trubetzkoy and Roman Jakobson stressed how it functions within the phonological system of the language (see Chapter 6). In the latter reading of 'function', a word notorious for its polyinterpretability, the language user disappears from view; the phoneme's function is defined by its place in the system. It was the latter view, also strongly defended by the arch-structuralist Louis Hjelmslev, that came to dominate the brand of functionalism championed by André Martinet. In Francophone cultures, *la linguistique fonctionnelle* is still strongly associated with Martinet, but this stream has had relatively little impact on or interaction with the rest of functional linguistics, which has tended to perpetuate Mathesius's primary interpretation of 'function', highlighting the study of how linguistic forms function for the language user.

30.3 Commitments

As the Prague School developed, so its practitioners placed an ever greater emphasis on formalization in the sense of the representation of hypotheses and findings in a formal, mathematical language.[3] There is a group of American and American-trained linguists who have not just been influenced by the School but have interacted with its more recent members. This group (prominent among whom are Susumo Kuno, Ellen Prince, Jacqueline Guéron and Tanya Reinhardt) have been referred to by the apparent oxymoron 'formal functionalists', since they generally accept the formalist premises of generative grammar and concentrate on providing formalized and theoretically compatible accounts of aspects of language structure that fall outside the purview of generative grammar, which tends to privilege certain 'core' phenomena. These linguists' theoretical commitments qualify them as 'formalists', although the matters they deal with and their interpretation of data align them more with functionalism.

There are functionalists, including Robert Van Valin Jr, Simon C. Dik and Kees Hengeveld, who follow the Praguean lead in utilizing formal representations in their work but without adopting the presuppositions and particularities of generative formalism. The advantage of formalization, as they see it, is that it becomes possible to derive explicit, functionally informed hypotheses about language structure. Each has developed his own formalism, to be outlined in §30.5. Yet others have sought to forge a link between functionalism and the formal apparatus of Optimality Theory (OT). OT holds that linguistic forms derive from the interaction of independent constraints. Languages differ in how these constraints are weighted; this is represented formally in tableaux, which list all the candidate constructions and identify as optimal the one that violates fewest constraints. Although OT has principally been associated with generative grammar, proposing constraints that are supposedly universal and innate, others have used the theory to formalize functional-typological findings, i.e. generalizations derived from observations of language use. Thus Aissen (2003) considers differential object marking, the fact that languages can differ in how they mark objects depending on their semantic and pragmatic characteristics, chiefly animacy and definiteness respectively. Her conclusions are formulated in OT.

A characteristic commitment of many functionalists is to the explanation of variation within and across languages in terms of the interaction of violable principles rather than the operation of exceptionless rules (this creates a point of contact with OT). Dik (1986: 21), the intellectual father of Functional Grammar (see §30.5.3), defined a functional explanation as follows: 'A functional explanation of a (synchronic or diachronic) linguistic phenomenon is a statement in which that phenomenon is shown to follow from one or more principles which crucially refer to any of the functional prerequisites imposed on natural languages'. Where more than one such principle is in play, with different orientations and effects, we can speak of 'competing motivations' (cf. Butler 2003: Part I, 14). In this view, alternatives within the language system arise from the attachment of different priorities to the same principles. In English, for example, adverbial clauses (AdvC) may be situated before or after the main clause (MC) they modify. Diessel (2005) finds, on the basis of extensive corpus analysis, that three competing forces, each with its own motivation, account for the distribution found in data: (a) utterance planning for high parsability, favouring MC-AdvC order; (b) discourse grounding, which favours AdvC-MC order; (c) semantic type, which favours AdvC-MC order for conditional and temporally anterior relations and MC-AdvC order for temporally posterior and causal relations. As will be clear, the three motivations are quite different in nature, and their interaction is never fully predictable for any individual instance.

Haspelmath (2014) draws attention to the fact that a functionally motivated principle may compete with the systematicity of a grammar: specifically, the 'economy' principle stating that more frequent forms tend to be shorter than rarer ones can come into conflict with 'system pressure', the observation that grammatical rules affect large classes of items. A simple example is the generalization that singular forms in English are never longer than plural forms (*boy–boys*; *sheep–sheep*) while for some lexemes the plural form is more frequent: as Haspelmath shows, *feathers* is more frequent than *feather*, yet is longer; however, in Welsh, in which plurals also tend to be longer than singulars, the forms are *pluen* 'feather' and *plu* 'feathers'. On the assumption that in Welsh, too, it is commoner to speak of feathers than of a single feather, the economy principle here has won out over system pressure. The realization that the system has its own properties that are in themselves afunctional does not warrant the conclusion that it is fully autonomous; rather, the fact that it involves rules that operate blindly is adaptive in enabling effortless communication (Givón 2009: 36).

A notion that is increasingly prominent in functionalist circles is 'usage-based'. The use of this term tends to go hand in hand with an increasing commitment to an inductive methodology, both for the learner who generalizes over his/her experiences of language and for the analyst who derives conclusions from the inspection of a corpus. The core methodological assumption here is that distributions in corpora correlate sufficiently with the language user's exposure to patterns and tendencies; in the above-mentioned case of Diessel (2005), for example, the assumption is that the patterns found in his data reflect speakers' preferences, as constrained by the rivalling forces he identifies. Although the methodology is inductive, it is also steered top-down by the expectation that the factors constraining and explaining distributions will be 'domain-general cognitive processes' (Bybee 2010: 6–8), i.e. processes not specific to language. The most fundamental of these is categorization, again involving prototypes; among various other relevant processes are chunking, pattern detection, rich memory, analogy, sequential and statistical learning as well as cross-modal association. Since all of these are independently well justified in the cognitive sciences, the view is taken that language is an extension of already existent domains of cognition.

This usage-based position has led its exponents to relativize the notion of a language system as a monolithic structure. For Bybee (2010: 194–221), the emergence of language (and grammar) from other domains entails that the object of linguistic inquiry is a 'complex adaptive system' in which independent mechanisms create the illusion of structure. She compares languages to dunes (2010: 2, 201), which arise through myriad interactions of wind and sand but are fundamentally gradient and variable. What has appeared to some (especially in formal linguistics) as an autonomous structure is in this view a body of procedural knowledge that has built up through the routinization of tasks and their grouping into 'chunks'. In morphosyntax, these chunks take on the form of constructions, which are conventional sequences of morphemes, words or phrases that may contain gaps for individual items and in the usage-based approach are the major units of form–meaning correspondence. Consider the example V *the* N *away*, as in *dream the day away, while the hours away, dance the night away*; notice that the V(erb) is intransitive (despite appearances), that the use of the definite article is the norm (*dance a night away* is infrequent), that *away* is not substitutable

(**dance the night off*) and that the N(oun) names a stretch of time; that the verb *while* only occurs in this construction; and that the construction, like the verb-particle construction, allows the alternative word order V *away the* N.

The question arises whether the emphasis in usage-based work on the determining role of cognitive factors does not dilute the principles of functionalism. Nuyts (2005) represents an attempt to determine whether functional can be distinguished from cognitive linguistics (see Chapter 29). He observes that there are real differences in what the functionalist and the cognitivist focus on, the former concentrating on grammatical structure and the latter on conceptualization and construal. There are major differences, too, in the type of analysis offered, with images playing a large part in cognitive-linguistic representations. Nevertheless, his major finding is that there is ultimately no possibility of an ironclad distinction and even talks of himself and others as 'cognitive-functional linguists'. Rather than watering down functionalism, 'an explicit and structural concern with the conceptual level and its interactions with the linguistic systems' (2005: 96) would in Nuyts's view strengthen functionalism's perspective on the complexities of language.

In face of the fluidity of the distinctions between functional and cognitive linguistics, Gonzálvez-García and Butler (2006) have characterized the entire field as a multidimensional space. They take eleven approaches (or 'models') that have advertised themselves as functional, cognitive or constructionist and rate them, on the basis of published pronouncements, against a list of thirty-six features, formulated as statements. For each feature, the eleven models line up differently, yet the overall picture that emerges confirms that functionalists and cognitivists do group together and that there is a very strong overlap between functionalists and cognitivists, with nineteen of the thirty-six features being shared by both camps. See Butler and Gonzálvez-García (2014) for a much fuller and more up-to-date treatment.

30.4 Connections

As will have become clear, functional linguists are primarily focused on grammatical structures[4] and on explaining them in terms of extralinguistic factors that predispose the language user to employ one structure rather than another. This brings functional linguistics into close contact or even overlap with the discipline of pragmatics (see Chapter 13), and specifically those subdomains of pragmatics which are concerned with the contextually determined interpretation of individual utterances. Among the realms of pragmatics implicated in these interdisciplinary connections are those that deal with presupposition, reference, deixis, anaphora, definiteness and indefiniteness, implicature and speech acts. Functional linguists invoke these notions when explaining differences in acceptability or in interpretation between sentences that are, in terms of representational meaning, identical. In the architecture of functional models, this is often reflected in the presence of separate modules or levels of analysis for semantic (or ideational) and pragmatic (or interpersonal) organization (cf. §§30.5.2–30.5.4).

It is against this background that functional-linguistic work attempts to understand alternative formulations in terms of distinct speaker intentions. Rather than being content to understand pairs like active versus passive, raising versus its absence or finite versus non-finite forms of adverbial clauses merely in terms of their formal relations, functionalists seek to track down the motivations behind the choices that are made for one or the other form in specific contexts. For example, one of the contexts in which a definite object can be placed in clause-initial position in English is where its presence in the shared knowledge of speaker and addressee can be assumed, as in (1):

(1) Mary has inherited a house and an apartment. The house she has decided to rent out, while the apartment she herself is going to occupy.

The definiteness of the noun phrases (NPs) *the house* and *the apartment* and their marked position at the beginning of their respective clauses in the second sentence are only possible if the appropriate context has been created, however that has been achieved – the same form could occur in a question that presupposes the information in the first sentence of (1), *Do you know what Mary is going to do with the house and the apartment she inherited?*

Similarly, from the functional perspective, anaphora is not treated as simply a relation between forms, between an anaphor and an antecedent, but as involving continuity of reference. An interesting example is discussed by Cornish (2010: 226):

(2) President Bush nominated Henry Paulson, the chief executive of Goldman Sachs, as US treasury secretary in place of John Snow. The 60-year-old investment banker is a China expert and keen environmentalist.

As Cornish points out, the NP *the 60-year-old investment banker*, with its definite reference, is presented as though it offered presupposed information. Although the content of the NP is new to the reader, the interplay of textual and contextual factors ensures that the discourse maintains its flow. In order to understand *the 60-year-old investment banker* as being coreferential with one of the three preceding names and specifically with *Henry Paulson* and not with *John Snow* or *President Bush*, the reader of (2) has recourse to inferential strategies. Such strategies have been thoroughly studied in pragmatics, notably in the work of Paul H. Grice and of Dan Sperber and Deirdre Wilson. Their Maxim of Relation or Principle of Relevance respectively leads readers to expect a relation of relevance to hold between the content of the two sentences. This predisposes them to seek clues to determine which of the possible antecedents is the most likely one: by drawing on knowledge that Goldman Sachs is a major investment bank, the reader can identify Paulson as the man meant by the writer; s/he can also exclude Bush and Snow, since they have different professions. The information that Paulson is sixty years old is likely to be new to readers but it has been 'smuggled' into what is otherwise an NP with presupposed information; the reader may subconsciously recognize this as a typical procedure in journalistic prose.

As will have been apparent in examples (1) and (2), each of which constitutes a mini-discourse, the functionalist approach borrows insights not only from pragmatics but also from the discipline of discourse analysis (see Chapter 15). A characteristic tendency among functional linguists has been to look beyond the individual clause that was central to the initial preoccupations of the Prague School, not only bringing the co-text into play but also encompassing the grammatical properties of discourses. The functionalist emphasis on communication makes this a natural move, since human beings communicate in discourses rather than in individual clauses. Butler (2009: 9) has proposed that

> any truly functional model of language should be concerned with the extent to which the requirements of multi-propositional discourse shape the way in which languages are structured, and with providing an explanatory account in which natural discourse is seen as dynamic, rule-governed, contextually-related activity leading to a structure composed of units with functional relationships between them, and subject to coherence constraints.

This programmatic statement clearly aims to bring functional linguistics very close to those forms of discourse analysis that prioritize the description of textual structures.

A rather different connection is that with typological linguistics (see Chapter 25). The functional view of language has been adopted by many prominent researchers in this area. Although the primary activity of typologists involves the classification of languages into structural types, for example in terms of their inventories of phonemes or their constituent order and thus may seem to be primarily formal in orientation, there has been a clear tendency for typologists to look for explanations for the patterns and trends they have discovered in terms of their function. Nichols (2007: 234), in a provocative article on typology, finds this claim to be 'startling', yet, as she admits, explanations in typology come from 'all quarters – function, processing, cognition, acquisition, neuroanatomy, sociolinguistics, history, and language evolution', but these are all areas that are functional in the broad sense of invoking the physical and psychological properties of the language user in his/her social and historico-cultural context.

The results of typological work frequently take the form of implicational hierarchies, statements of the form $A > B > C$, to be understood as meaning that if a language has property C, it will also have A and B; if it lacks C but has B, then it will also have A; having A allows no predictions about the presence or absence of B and C. This way of formulating things originated with Joseph Greenberg, the founding father of typological linguistics. A well-known example is the hierarchy subject > object > oblique > adnominal possessor (simplified from Keenan and Comrie 1977), which pertains to the possibilities of forming relative clauses (which are extremely common across the languages of the world). Languages in which an adnominal possessor can appear in relative clauses, as in (3a), can also accept relativization on all higher positions (i.e. those to its left in the hierarchy), as can be seen for English in (3b) to (3d).

(3) a. the man **whose** car broke down
    b. the man **to whom** I sold my car
    c. the man **who(m)** I saw driving past
    d. the man **who** was selling his car.

The explanation for this hierarchy is sought in processing terms: possessors involve the embedding of one NP inside another (in (3a) *whose* inside the NP *whose car*); the oblique in (3b) is a single NP, but one marked by a preposition; and object NPs (as in (3c)) are usually more marked than subject NPs (as in (3d)), cf. the possibility of the objective form *whom* in (3c) but not (3d). As the hierarchy progresses from left to right, there is thus greater complexity of processing. Since languages will, according to the functionalist hypothesis, tend to favour solutions that increase ease of production for the speaker and ease of comprehension for the hearer, the effect is to promote language structures that do not progress far down the hierarchy, for example (in the most extreme case) by requiring all relativization to be on subjects only. Malagasy relativizes only on subjects; Kinyarwanda on subjects and objects; Tamil on subjects, objects and obliques; English and German on subjects, objects, obliques and possessors. Note that English, but not German, also permits relativization on standards of comparison: *A man than whom no one has better taste*/**ein Mann als wer niemand einen besseren Geschmack hat.*

Language typology draws heavily upon documentary linguistics, since the major source of its data is the information encapsulated in grammars. That information has now to some extent been transferred to databases such as, notably, that underlying the *World Atlas of*

Linguistic Structures Online (Dryer and Haspelmath 2013). Documentary linguistics, as its name suggests, concerns itself with documentation of previously undescribed or poorly described languages. The dominant framework for the description of languages is nowadays 'basic linguistic theory', which can roughly be defined as traditional grammar, shorn of its errors and enriched by concepts developed in structuralism, early generative grammar and typology; the main aim is to describe languages in their own terms, without theoretical preconceptions. It is this kind of work that feeds most directly into functionalist typology. However, it is clear to functional typologists that the best descriptions are those that are both true to the language under description and informed by a cross-linguistic and functional analysis. Haspelmath (1999) gives the example of the ungrammaticality of English **the Joan's book*, often explained as being due to a ban on double filling of the determiner slot; but he shows that there is a functional explanation, one based on economy, which covers this example and also accounts for the existence of other languages, e.g. Hebrew, in which determiner and possessor are incompatible without vying for the same position, cf. *ha-sefer* 'the book' but *sefer David* (*ha-sefer David) 'David's book'.

Finally, mention should be made of certain strands of psycholinguistics (see Chapter 18) that have labelled themselves functionalist and have had an impact upon functional linguistics proper, notably in the extent to which functional models in linguistics have taken psycholinguistic evidence into account. The work of Dan Slobin has shared with functional-typological linguistics a strong interest in bringing in data from a wide range of languages and explaining findings in terms of the interaction of a variety of general principles of processing. One area he has developed is the study of the typology of motion events (Slobin 2004), elaborating earlier work on verb-framed and satellite-framed languages, those in which motion events are cardinally expressed in the form *They entered the room dancing* or *They danced into the room* respectively. Slobin broadens the description to include serializing languages, in which neither the manner nor the motion is dominant (Pseudo-English *They dance enter room*), which leads him to propose a third class of equipollently-framed languages. The observation of how adult speakers of various languages narrate stories on the basis of cartoons ('frog stories') and of novels written in those languages shows how the three-way typology of motion events needs to be re-envisioned as a cline of manner salience: Russian almost always uses a manner-of-motion verb, Mandarin less so, English and German rarely, and fully verb-framed languages hardly ever. This typology and the morphosyntactic characteristics of the various languages interact with a range of processing factors (combined in what Slobin 2004: 237 calls 'codability', the ready accessibility of expressive options) but also with cultural factors, such as the special attention paid in Australian aboriginal cultures to paths and cardinal points.

Another expressly functionalist approach within psycholinguistics is that especially associated with Brian MacWhinney and Elizabeth Bates. Like Slobin's work, theirs is strongly cross-linguistic, being concerned with child language acquisition, adult language processing and aphasia in various languages. They see linguistic form as involving morphosyntactic and suprasegmental channels of limited length, with a range of factors vying for position in those sequences. Their Competition Model (Bates and MacWhinney 1989) stresses how speakers seek to find a compromise between, on the one hand, the competing demands of mapping from semantic and pragmatic information to linguistic form and, on the other, constraints on information processing such as limitations on memory or the need to plan ahead. Linguistic forms are seen as containing clues which the addressee uses to compute the most likely interpretation: languages differ in how the various cues are weighted and interpreted, for example with respect to the 'cue validity' of clause-initial position, which in one language may be a vital cue to identifying the subject, the topic, or the verb, but in another may have no particular function for the interpreter. The Competition Model aligns strongly with the emergentist approaches to functionalism outlined in §30.2. A leading researcher in first-language acquisition who takes a functional-emergentist approach is Michael Tomasello; see the further reading.

30.5 Major groupings in current functionalism

The depiction of functionalism in the preceding sections has exemplified its diversity, while also insisting on its unity in its commitment to seeking explanations for the formal variety within and across languages in the realm of interpersonal communication. Although many functional linguists operate rather independently, there are a number of groupings that have come to particular international prominence in recent decades and which deserve mention here.

30.5.1 West Coast functionalism

Pride of place goes to what is worldwide the most salient but also the loosest of the groupings, originally associated with a number of universities on the West Coast of the United States, hence the (possibly obsolescent) name it has acquired. Joan Bybee, William Croft, Paul J. Hopper and Sandra A. Thompson are among the best-known members of this grouping, which now has increasingly settled around the heading 'usage-based theory', with strong links to a range of Construction Grammars. One eminent figure here is Talmy Givón. His adaptive approach to grammar has been a powerful force within linguistic functionalism. As its name suggests, the adaptive approach emphasizes the evolution of language, particularly the emergence of increasingly complex coding mechanisms, both in the individual and in the species. Grammar is seen as having evolved in lockstep with the phylogenetic development of a 'theory of mind' in the human being, which entails an ever-present concern with the 'constantly shifting epistemic and deontic states' (Givón 2010: 36) of dialogue partners. The different perspectives of the interlocutors, coupled with degrees of certainty, lead to scenarios for the emergence of such grammatical categories as illocution, propositional modality, negation and the like. A major emphasis in the adaptive approach has been on determining how to understand the efficiency and automaticity of grammar as rooted in independently justified principles of cognition and neurobiology.

30.5.2 Systemic functional linguistics (SFL)

The primary figure in SFL is M.A.K. Halliday, around whom a large, international school of followers has formed. Halliday, originally from the United Kingdom, moved to Australia in mid-career and it is there that the main dynamic of this academic community is now located. The core concept of SFL is 'meaning'. For Systemic Functional Linguistics (Halliday and Matthiessen 2013) the language system represents potential meaning and is layered into at least four strata – context, semantics, lexico-grammar and phonology – where each stratum is said to realize the preceding one. This potential meaning is instantiated in individual texts, as filtered through registers (i.e. a typology of text types). Methodologically, SFL work concentrates on texts from various registers in order to derive conclusions about the system of choices available to the language user. This system is structured as a set of 'system networks', representing these choices in accordance with three metafunctions. The ideational metafunction includes choices concerned with experience and is reflected above all in the semantic structure of clauses; the interpersonal metafunction relates to choices relating to speech roles (speaker, hearer), mood (declarative, interrogative, …) and relevant lexical choices; and the textual metafunction is a matter of managing the flow of discourse, covering given/new information, clause-initial position (Theme) as well as grammatical and lexical cohesion. SFL understands itself as a functional theory of language, in which the (lexico)grammar (SFG) has an essential place, one that is closely integrated into the whole model, taking in context, register and genre. A distinctive feature of SFL is that one of the main criteria for judging its success is held to be the extent to which it contributes to social intervention in various applied areas, areas that have seemed rather peripheral to many linguists of other persuasions, such as language pedagogy, literary analysis, multimodality, identity studies and semiotics. SFL work on genres as recurrent configurations of culturally inscribed practices has impacted school syllabi in Australia. A particular focus in recent years has been on appraisal, or the language of evaluation. Robin Fawcett (2000) has developed a version of SFG that combines great explicitness with an orientation to cognition and interaction.

30.5.3 Functional discourse grammar (FDG)

FDG arose in the first decade of the twenty-first century as a continuation of Functional Grammar (FG, Dik 1997) as developed by Simon C. Dik and his followers in the Netherlands and elsewhere. FG was primarily oriented to the individual clause, analysing it by means of postulating an underlying semantic representation which motivated the grammatical properties of the clause under analysis. For example, the representation of a noun phrase was as a 'term' with such pragmatic, semantic and syntactic functions as Topic, Agent and Subject respectively. The model gave a central place to the lexicon as a store of predicates from which the underlying semantic representation was built up. A major orientation of FG was to 'typological adequacy', which entailed an attempt to develop a set of categories and functions from which an analyst could draw in comparing the languages of the world. FG also aimed to achieve 'pragmatic adequacy' and 'psychological adequacy'; the former had become the principal focus of most FG researchers around the time of Dik's tragically early death in 1995. It was FG's inability to deal satisfactorily with the impact of discourse factors on morphosyntactic structure that stimulated Kees Hengeveld to develop Functional Discourse Grammar. FDG (Hengeveld and Mackenzie 2008) offers a major enrichment and rethink of FG, with four modular levels of analysis, each of which is hierarchically structured: there are two formulation levels for representational semantics and interpersonal pragmatics/rhetoric and two encoding levels for morphosyntax and phonology. Whereas FG constructed its representations bottom-up, the dynamics of FDG are top-down, taking the interpersonal level as its starting point. FDG has preserved FG's strong orientation to typology, for example providing a classification of languages in terms of their alignment properties: thus, Tagalog has pragmatic alignment, Acheh representational alignment, and Basque morphosyntactic alignment. As its name suggests, FDG also has focused on the wholesale integration of discoursal (subjective) factors into grammar, for example distinguishing interpersonal from representational evidentiality. Unlike SFL, FDG aims primarily to contribute to theoretical linguistics rather than aiming for practical applications.

30.5.4 Role and reference grammar (RRG)

RRG (Van Valin and LaPolla 1997) is so called because of its concern with semantic roles and with reference tracking in discourse, but in fact deals with much more, presenting a fully-fledged theory of the morphosyntactic and semantic structure of natural languages. It shares several presuppositions with FG and FDG, not least the aim of achieving typological neutrality. Rejecting the dominance of thinking based on the categories of English, Van Valin seeks to develop an approach that is, as he puts it, equally valid for Lakhota, Tagalog or Dyirbal. RRG's syntactic analysis is consequently free of many elements that are not universal, such as the Verb Phrase; instead it is characterized by notions that are more semantically inspired such as Core, Nucleus, Predicate, Argument, etc. This syntactic analysis is mapped by means of an explicit algorithm onto a semantic analysis, which is a development of the work of Zeno Vendler on *Aktionsart* and of David Dowty on decomposition. RRG work is known for its precise and detailed semantic analyses, which are also reflected in its highly developed lexicon, which encompasses a number of processes taken in other theories to be syntactic, such as causativization and noun incorporation. RRG offers a detailed typology of interclausal relations, which form a continuum, leading from sentential coordination, the loosest linkage where the components are distinct events, to nuclear co-subordination, the tightest, where the two components are facets of a single event. RRG recognizes a further overlay of discourse-pragmatics on the mapping between syntax and semantics, known as Focus Structure Projection: the distinction between actual and potential focus domain has allowed RRG to provide persuasive analyses of the positioning of content interrogatives (wh-words) and the constraints on their occurrence. RRG has found applications in psycho- and neurolinguistics, where its combination of formal rigour and a semantically informed syntax have been integrated into studies of child language acquisition and adult language processing; there has also been close cooperation with Francisco José Ruiz de Mendoza Ibáñez and Ricardo Mairal Usón's Lexical-Constructional Model under development in Spain.

30.6 Convergence

As suggested in the introduction, the old opposition between formal and functional linguistics has generally yielded to at least an atmosphere of live-and-let-live and on occasions to budding convergence. At the prominent Amsterdam Center for Language and Communication, for example, both formal and functional approaches coexist, engendering interesting discussions and even co-authorship of papers. The functionalist Haspelmath (2000: 235), in a review article on Newmeyer (1998), had already called for just such a 'dialog across the gulf of mutual incomprehension that separates the two orientations'. Haspelmath's valuable point is that the two do not differ so much in their basic assumptions as in their goals (pp. 236, 238); if this is true, then the two approaches can come to be seen as complementary rather than inimical. If one's goal is to characterize the language system per se, then contextual factors influencing that system must be ignored; if one's goal is to explain the language system, then they cannot, and this difference is a possible basis for a division of labour (pp. 239, 241).

This point has been picked up by Peter Harder (2013), who observes how the two camps have disputed over shared concepts like 'subject' or 'gender', the one minimizing, the other maximizing motivation, while the matter could (and by implication, should) be solved by disinterested empirical research. On the assumption that it is the task of linguistics to characterize both what Harder calls the 'infrastructure' that underlies our capacity to use language and the sentences that a particular language community produces in verbal interaction, then it is merely a matter of which end one starts at.

As has been seen in this chapter, there is variation among functionalists in the extent to which they recognize structures of language as objects of description: those of a more emergentist or usage-based persuasion will tend to see structure as evanescent or illusory while others point to the fact that the speaker, in adopting a particular language to communicate in, submits to the conventions of that language. If the language requires all clauses to have subjects, the speaker has no option, even where the subject has no meaning, as in English *It is snowing*; if the language assigns gender to all nouns, the speaker again cannot ignore this brute fact, even in cases where gender has no semantic import or conflicts with semantic expectations. Yet neither subject nor gender is without function within the structure as a whole (what these functions are is still a matter of disagreement); but both have come about through the functionally justified process of conventionalization. What is more, without function, structure would not be necessary (Harder 2013): utterances have the complex structure that they do because they fulfil an organized network of communicative functions, and aspects of that structure (obligatory subject, obligatory gender assignment) can simply be conventionalized requirements that contribute to the regularity and predictability of structures.

It is a functionalism of this latter type, one that emphasizes the interpenetration of function and structure, seeking to maximize the functional account of linguistic structure while recognizing the existence and communicative advantages of conventionalized aspects of that structure, which is best positioned to achieve convergence within linguistics as a whole. The convergence may also be coming from the formalist side: Golumbia (2010), for example, has argued that the Chomskyan Minimalist Programme, with its maximally pared down grammatical component, is functionalist in its conceptual foundations. In any case, the current picture is one in which the functionalist tradition has been fully integrated into the discipline.

Acknowledgement

I wish to thank Chris Butler, Martin Hilpert and Geoff Thompson for their advice and encouragement.

Notes

1 Although this is the most familiar appellation, the correct name is the Prague Linguistic Circle.
2 Important influences on the emergence of linguistic functionalism came from Wilhelm von Humboldt (1767–1835), Wilhelm Wundt (1832–1920), Georg von der Gabelentz (1840–1893), Bronisław Malinowski (1884–1942) and Karl Bühler (1879–1963). See Givón (2013) for other predecessors.
3 Tellingly, the main organ of the Prague School has been the *Prague Studies in* (later: *Bulletin of*) *Mathematical Linguistics*.
4 As Chris Butler has reminded me, functionalism is a 'broad church' and also embraces views, for example in the emergentist and usage-based groups, where questions of structure, acceptability and the distinction between interpersonal and representational meaning are of much less interest.

Further reading

Bischoff and Jany (2013); Butler (2003); Butler and Gonzálvez-García (2014); Croft (1995); Givón (1995); Harder (2010); Nichols (1984); Sornicola (2011); Tomasello (1998).

References

Aissen, J. (2003) Differential object marking: iconicity vs. economy. *Natural Language and Linguistic Theory* 21: 435–83.
Bates, E. and B. MacWhinney (1989) Functionalism and the Competition Model. In E. Bates and B. MacWhinney (eds) *The Crosslinguistic Study of Sentence Processing*, pp. 3–73. New York: Cambridge University Press.
Bischoff, S. and C. Jany (eds) (2013) *Functional Approaches to Language*. Berlin/New York: Mouton de Gruyter.
Butler, C.S. (2003) *Structure and Function: A Guide to Three Major Structural-Functional Theories*. 2 volumes. Amsterdam/Philadelphia: John Benjamins.
Butler, C.S. (2009) Criteria of adequacy in functional linguistics. *Folia Linguistica* 43: 1–66.
Butler, C.S. and F. Gonzálvez-García (2014) *Exploring Functional-Cognitive Space*. Amsterdam/Philadelphia: John Benjamins.
Bybee, J.L. (2010) *Language, Usage and Cognition*. Cambridge: Cambridge University Press.
Cornish, F. (2010) Anaphora: Text-based or discourse-dependent? Functionalist vs. formalist accounts. *Functions of Language* 17: 207–41.
Croft, W. (1995) Autonomy and functionalist linguistics. *Language* 71: 490–532.
Diessel, H. (2005) Competing motivations for the ordering of main and adverbial clauses. *Linguistics* 43: 449–70.
Dik, S.C. (1986) On the notion 'functional explanation'. *Belgian Journal of Linguistics* 1: 11–52.
Dik, S.C. (1997) *The Theory of Functional Grammar*, in two parts. Berlin/New York: Mouton de Gruyter.
Dryer, M.S. and M. Haspelmath (eds) (2013) *The World Atlas of Language Structures Online*. Leipzig: Max Planck Institute for Evolutionary Anthropology. http://wals.info.
Fawcett, R.P. (2000) *A Theory of Syntax for Systemic Functional Linguistics*. Amsterdam: John Benjamins.
Givón, T. (1995) *Functionalism and Grammar*. Amsterdam/Philadelphia: John Benjamins.
Givón, T. (2009) *The Genesis of Syntactic Complexity*. Amsterdam/Philadelphia: John Benjamins.
Givón, T. (2010) The adaptive approach to grammar. In B. Heine and H. Narrog (eds) *Oxford Handbook of Linguistic Analysis*, pp. 27–49. Oxford: Oxford University Press.
Givón, T. (2013) The intellectual roots of functionalism in linguistics. In S. Bischoff and C. Jany (eds) *Functional Approaches to Language*, pp. 9–30. Berlin: Mouton de Gruyter.
Golumbia, D. (2010) Minimalism is functionalism. *Language Sciences* 32: 28–42.
Gonzálvez-García, F. and C.S. Butler (2006) Mapping functional-cognitive space. *Annual Review of Cognitive Linguistics* 4: 39–96.
Halliday, M.A.K. and C.M.I.M. Matthiessen (2013) *Halliday's Introduction to Functional Grammar*, 4th edition. Abingdon: Routledge.
Harder, P. (2010) *Meaning in Mind and Society: A Functional Contribution to the Social Turn in Cognitive Linguistics*. Berlin/New York: Mouton de Gruyter.
Harder, P. (2013) Structure and function: A niche-constructional approach. In S. Bischoff and C. Jany (eds) *Functional Approaches to Language*, pp. 71–106. Berlin: Mouton de Gruyter.
Haspelmath, M. (1999) Explaining article-possessor complementarity: Economic motivation in noun phrase syntax. *Language* 75: 227–43.
Haspelmath, M. (2000) Why can't we talk to each other? *Lingua* 110: 235–55.

Haspelmath, M. (2014) On system pressure competing with economic motivation. In B. MacWhinney, A. Malchukov and E. Moravcsik (eds) *Competing Motivations in Grammar and Usage*, pp. 197–208. Oxford: Oxford University Press.

Hengeveld, K. and J.L. Mackenzie (2008) *Functional Discourse Grammar: A Typologically-Based Theory of Language Structure*. Oxford: Oxford University Press.

Hopper, P.J. (1992) Emergence of grammar. In W. Bright (ed.) *International Encyclopedia of Linguistics*, pp. 364–7. New York/Oxford: Oxford University Press.

Keenan, E.L. and B. Comrie (1977) Noun phrase accessibility and universal grammar. *Linguistic Inquiry* 8: 63–99.

Newmeyer, F. (1998) *Language Form and Language Function*. Cambridge: MIT Press.

Nichols, J. (1984) Functional theories of grammar. *Annual Review of Anthropology* 13: 97–117.

Nichols, J. (2007) What, if anything, is typology? *Linguistic Typology* 11: 231–8.

Nuyts, J. (2005) Brothers in arms? On the relations between cognitive and functional linguistics. In F. Ruiz de Mendoza and S. Peña (eds) *Cognitive Linguistics: Internal Dynamics and Interdisciplinary Interaction*, pp. 69–100. Berlin: Mouton de Gruyter.

Slobin, D.I. (2004) The many ways to search for a frog: Linguistic typology and the expression of motion events. In S. Strömqvist and L. Verhoeven (eds) *Relating Events in Narrative*, vol. 2, pp. 219–57. Mahwah: Lawrence Erlbaum Associates.

Sornicola, R. (2011) European functionalism. In B. Kortmann and J. van der Auwera (eds) *The Languages and Linguistics of Europe: A Comprehensive Guide*, pp. 845–65. Berlin/New York: Mouton de Gruyter.

Theses (1983) Theses presented to the First Congress of Slavists held in Prague in 1929. In J. Vachek and L. Dušková (eds) *Praguiana: Some Basic and Less Known Aspects of the Prague Linguistic School*, pp. 77–120. Amsterdam: John Benjamins.

Tomasello, M. (ed.) (1998) *The New Psychology of Language: Cognitive and Functional Approaches to Language Structure*. Mahwah: Lawrence Erlbaum Associates.

Van Valin, R.D., Jr and R.J. LaPolla (1997) *Syntax: Structure, Meaning and Function*. Cambridge: Cambridge University Press.

31
Computational linguistics

Ann Copestake

31.1 Introduction

Computational linguistics concerns the computational modelling of human language. It is a large and complex field, impossible to survey briefly. As an indication of its size, there are over 32,000 papers in the anthology of the Association for Computational Linguistics, which only contains a fraction of the papers published in the discipline. The aim of this chapter, therefore, is to give an idea of the topics covered, and to discuss some of the methodology employed, which differs substantially from the approaches most common in linguistics. In fact, while the term, 'Computational Linguistics', suggests a branch of linguistics, it is best to view it as a discipline in its own right, with connections to linguistics which are close in some subareas and hardly exist at all in others. Some authors distinguish between 'Computational Linguistics' (henceforth CL) and 'Natural Language Processing' (NLP), with the latter being seen as more concerned with practical applications, but other writers use the terms interchangeably. Even more confusingly, speech processing and search and Information Retrieval (IR) are usually seen as separate from CL/NLP, though there are broader terms, such as 'Human Language Technologies', which include them all. In this chapter, I mainly concentrate on topics which are core to CL, looking at some applications but concentrating on the computational methodologies involved in modelling language.

Within Computer Science, CL is often seen as closely related to Artificial Intelligence (AI). Until the late 1980s, a mainstream view was that CL concerned language-specific issues while AI would develop a language-independent account of general human reasoning. This approach is generally seen to have failed, but alternative paradigms have emerged. In particular, very large amounts of machine-readable text started to become readily available in the early 1990s and this allowed the successful development of many different types of statistical models. As discussed below, these may either supplement or be alternatives to symbolic models of language, but they also give some of the functionality that AI was previously expected to provide.

For instance, in natural language understanding (NLU), the role of CL was originally seen as to parse sentences according to their morphological and syntactic structure in order to produce meaning representations corresponding to different possible analyses. It was the role of AI to connect the meaning representations to a model of the world, to reason about the correct analysis in context and to allow the system to act on the utterance appropriately. Given a very limited 'microworld', it is indeed possible to do this: i.e. to build a model of the entities and possible events which allow some simple utterances which are directly relevant to the microworld to be interpreted. The most famous example of this (although not the earliest) was Winograd's SHRDLU system, in the early 1970s, a virtual world in which a number of toy blocks were arranged on a surface and inside a box. The computer's task was to manipulate the blocks in response to human commands such as *Pick up a big red block!* and to answer questions about the state of the microworld. By the early 1980s, several NLU systems based on microworlds constructed from databases were in commercial use and there was a general perception that computers could understand human language. But the approach was insufficiently robust to work with spoken input and did not extend beyond very small domains, where all the possible types of entities and events could be enumerated.

There are a number of reasons why the limited domain approaches did not scale to general language understanding. On the language processing side, it was necessary to improve parsers so that it was possible to process unrestricted text reasonably quickly. When analysed on the basis of the morphology and syntax alone, without constraints based on the meaning of the sentence, even moderate length sentences have a massive degree of ambiguity. Current parsers rank analyses according to their statistical plausibility rather than trying to disambiguate by reasoning about meaning and are reasonably successful at doing this.[1] Thus the elusiveness of full NLU is not primarily due to limitations in parser performance but the (current?) impossibility of modelling human knowledge and reasoning. The problem is not factual general knowledge of the form 'the king of Prussia in 1790', 'the closest airport to Cambridge' and so on. There are many databases and gazetteers which contain this type of information and CL systems exist that can extract facts from online text with a high degree of reliability, as was illustrated by the success of the IBM Watson system on the *Jeopardy!* quiz show (for an overview of the system, see Ferrucci *et al.* 2010). The main difficulties arise with the sort of reasoning that humans would not even regard as 'intelligent'. Human understanding of space, movement, time and so on is essential to language comprehension, but extremely hard to capture formally. This is difficult to illustrate with a short example, but consider the phrase *the cat in front of the chair*. This has an interpretation where the cat is located according to coordinates which are intrinsic to the chair (as well as one where the location is relative to another entity). However, what determines the notion of front and back of an entity is complex, as consideration of examples such as *chair*, *stool*, *television*, *steps*, *earthworm*, *house* and *book* should demonstrate. There is no straightforward algorithm, yet even very young children can interpret these intrinsic spatial expressions correctly. For a human, the deduction 'if a cat is in front of some steps then it is at the bottom of the steps' is completely obvious, but for a question answering system this is a more challenging topic than European monarchs of the eighteenth century.

Perhaps the most fundamental issue for NLU is whether there are workable nonlinguistic notions of concepts. The assumption that it is possible to have a language-independent concept such as BIG (distinct from the words *big*, *groß*, *grand*, *gros* and so on) underpinned approaches that separated language-specific processing from general-purpose reasoning. It makes sense to make such an assumption for microworlds, where natural language words are used with very specific referents which can be defined or enumerated. For instance, in SHRDLU, it was possible to list all the blocks which could be described as *big*. There are other cases where language-independent definitions are workable, such as some scientific and mathematic terms. However, the attempt to use symbolic language-independent concepts as the basis of general language understanding is now regarded as a dead end by most researchers. It is an open question as to whether it will nevertheless be possible eventually to model lexical meaning in a way that will support full NLU, but it is already clear that it is possible to provide useful partial models and that the failure to achieve full natural language understanding has not prevented real applications from using CL techniques. Even if one has the long-term goal of addressing fundamental problems of language and concepts, it makes sense to work on practical techniques for language processing in the shorter term, with the aim of bootstrapping deeper techniques. In the rest of this section, I will very briefly introduce a range of different types of CL applications, and then describe one illustrative application in more detail.

Most of the early practically usable CL systems (other than the limited domain database interfaces) were designed to help humans communicate with each other. Spelling and grammar checking has been a standard part of document processing for decades. Predictive text is also a long-standing application: before its use in phones it was employed in some systems for 'augmentative and alternative communication' for people with a disability. Machine-aided translation has a long history of practical utility: such systems help a human translator, for instance by storing and retrieving translations of text passages. Useful machine translation (MT) has been available since the 1970s, with the more recent statistical machine translation (SMT) approaches being available for a variety of language pairs and accurate enough to be helpful on a range of different types of text. The best MT allows a reader to get a reasonable idea of the meaning of text written in a language they do not understand, although far more care is needed in interpretation of MT output than is required for a good human translation. The success of MT illustrates the important point that humans can adapt to imperfect NLP systems. There are also a variety of tools for language teaching and assessment: for instance to help first and second language learners by detecting various types of errors in their writing. Such a system should not mark something as an error when it is actually correct, but it is acceptable to miss some errors. That is, error detection systems emphasize precision over recall, in contrast to an MT system, which is designed to attempt translation for nearly all its input.

Another very important group of NLP applications involve changing the medium in which the language is expressed. For instance, some speech recognition systems are designed to transcribe speech to produce text (others are used in dialogue systems). Text-to-speech, optical character recognition (OCR) and handwriting recognition can also be described as converting the medium of the input, since OCR and handwriting recognition convert visual data to machine-readable text. Models of language are required to do this accurately: in the case of speech and handwriting recognition, the initial processing produces a set of possibilities and models trained on large amounts of text are used to select between them (as discussed below). For text-to-speech, the models are designed to predict intonation and the pronunciation of homonyms which are not homophones.

Internet search was originally based on approaches from Information Retrieval, combined with metrics of webpage popularity, and as such used little language processing. More recent techniques are more advanced, taking into account synonymy and near-synonymy, for instance. The need to process and index vast quantities of text is a strong constraint on what techniques are practical, but various forms of analysis of language are now being used at web scale. More targeted search and extraction of particular classes of information is known as *text-mining*, which is now widely used, especially on scientific texts. Question answering systems use a combination of text-mining techniques and online databases to provide specific responses to certain types of question.

Many applications involve different types of text classification. A simple example is detection of spam email. Sentiment analysis, which involves deciding whether opinions expressed are positive or negative is a form of classification described in more detail in §31.2. Automated assessment can be modelled as classification of text according to some marking scheme. It is now regularly used for some high volume exams, although typically only in conjunction with human assessment. Exam marking might be seen as a bad application for an inherently imperfect technology, but in some cases automated assessment has been found to be as reliable as human marking.

Finally, there are dialogue systems, including 'intelligent' personal assistants, such as Siri. These combine search functionality, question answering and interfaces to databases, including diaries and so on. These systems have some model of dialogue context and can adapt to individual users. Just as importantly, users adapt to the systems, rephrasing queries which are not understood and reusing queries which are successful.

Various properties are required for a successful NLP application. Since NLP systems are imperfect, applications have to tolerate imperfection in processing. In extreme cases, even a simple application such as spelling correction could require arbitrary amounts of reasoning, beyond the reach of any current approach, but in successful applications these situations are rare enough that the absence of deep understanding does not prevent them being useful. Nearly all practical systems now exploit statistical information extracted from corpora,[2] as we will see in more detail in the next sections.

31.2 An example application: sentiment analysis

Finding out what people think about politicians, policies, products, services, companies and so on is a huge and lucrative business. Increasingly this is done by automatic analysis of web documents and social media. The full problem involves finding all the references to an entity from some document set (e.g. references to Hillary Clinton in all newspaper articles appearing in September 2013, references to Siri in all tweets with hashtag #apple), and then classifying the references as positive, negative or neutral. Customers who use opinion mining want to see summaries of the data (e.g. to see whether popularity is going up or down), but may also want to see actual examples (text snippets). Companies generally want a fine-grained classification of aspects of their product (e.g. laptop batteries, phone screens).

A full opinion mining system requires that relevant text is retrieved, references to the objects of interest are recognized in that text (generally as 'named entities': e.g. *Sony 505G*, *Hillary Clinton*), and the parts of the text that refer to those entities are determined. Once this is done, the referring text can be classified for positive or negative sentiment. To be commercially useful, this has to be done very rapidly, especially when analysing trends on social media, so a significant software engineering effort is involved. But academic researchers have looked at a simpler version of the task by starting from a set of documents which are already known to be opinions about a particular topic or entity (e.g. reviews), where the problem is just to work out whether the author is expressing positive or negative opinions. This allows researchers to focus on sentiment classification but this has still been a challenging problem to address. Some of the early research work was done on movie reviews (Pang *et al.* 2002). The rating associated with each review is known (that is, reviewers give each movie a number of stars), so there is an objective standard as to whether the review is positive or negative. This avoids the need to manually annotate the data before experimenting with it, which is a time-consuming and error-prone process. The research problem is to assign sentiment automatically to each document in the entire corpus to agree with the known ratings.

Sentiment classification can be done by using manually-defined patterns, which are automatically checked against the review to be classified. Such patterns are often expressed as regular expressions. For instance, 'great act*' would match *great acting*, *great actor* and so on. However, it is often preferable to use machine learning (ML) techniques: humans are good at deciding whether particular words or phrases are positive or negative but tend to miss many useful indicators. I will outline how ML can be applied to sentiment classification, but the general methodology is applicable to many other problems in CL.

The first step is to separate the document collection into training data, which will be used to build the classifier, and test data, which will be used to evaluate it. It is standard to use 90 per cent of the data for training and keep 10 per cent unseen for testing. The separation of the training and test data is crucial to the methodology, since the aim is to construct a model which can be generalized to data not previously seen. The second step is to extract *features* from each document in the training data. The most basic technique is to use the words in the review in isolation of each other as features: this is known as a *bag of words* model because the document is modelled as an unordered collection of words. The third step is then to use the features to train a classifier. The system will automatically learn whether particular features tend to indicate positive or negative reviews, and how reliable that indication is. For instance, *great* would be a strong indicator of a positive review if the ratings are positive for a high percentage of the documents in which it occurs, and *peculiar* a weak indicator of a negative review if it occurs in both negative- and positive-rated documents with the majority being negative. Finally, the trained classifier is run on the features extracted from each review in the test data in order to assign the review to the sentiment class with the highest probability. The percentage of reviews categorized correctly gives the success rate.

A range of different algorithms for classifiers exist, which make different approximations about the properties of the data being modelled, but it is unnecessary to go into the details here. Indeed, the difference in performance is often quite small between different classifiers. Pang *et al.* (2002) found that the accuracy of classification with the basic bag of words technique on the movie corpus was around 80 per cent. The set of reviews was artificially balanced and neutral reviews excluded, so chance success rate would be 50 per cent.

It will be obvious that the bag of words model does not fully capture the way sentiment is expressed in language. It even ignores the possibility of negation: e.g. *Ridley Scott has never directed a bad film* is a positive statement, though *bad* is usually an indicator of a negative review. However, computational linguists have learned to be wary of dismissing simple models as obviously inadequate without testing them, since it has turned out embarrassingly often that simple models outperform models with more linguistic sophistication. Naturally negation is an important attribute, but modelling it requires that techniques are available which capture the scope of negation, and which do not introduce errors which make performance worse overall. The bag of words approach can be taken as a 'baseline': that is, a very basic and straightforward approach against which more sophisticated techniques should be evaluated to see if they actually lead to better performance. In fact, initial attempts at better language modelling failed to lead to large improvements in performance on the movie corpus, but some later sentiment analysis systems use much more sophisticated techniques. For instance, Moilanen and Pulman (2007) demonstrated that parsing and a form of compositional semantics can considerably improve performance over the simple methods.

One danger with machine learning techniques is that they may match the training data too closely: the technical term is 'overfitting'. Any ML approach requires that the training data is reasonably close to the test data. For instance, a sentiment classifier trained on movie reviews may not perform well on reviews of laptops. Sensitivity to domain and genre is common to all statistical approaches, but there is a particular issue with sentiment analysis because indicators often change over time. For instance, if the classifier were trained on reviews which included a large number of films from before 2005, *Ridley* might emerge as a strong positive indicator, but the system could then tend to misclassify reviews for 'Kingdom of Heaven' (which was panned). Thus, in practical use, it is necessary to retrain systems regularly to ensure that features are not retained after they become unreliable.

More subtle and linguistically interesting problems arise from the contrasts in the discourse. The two extracts below are from Pang *et al.*'s paper:

> This film should be brilliant. It sounds like a great plot, the actors are first grade, and the supporting cast is good as well, and Stallone is attempting to deliver a good performance. However, it can't hold up.
> (taken from a review by David Wilcock of 'Cop Land' www.imdb.com/reviews/101/10185.html)

> AN AMERICAN WEREWOLF IN PARIS is a failed attempt ... Julie Delpy is far too good for this movie. She imbues Serafine with spirit, spunk, and humanity. This isn't necessarily a good thing, since it prevents us from relaxing and enjoying AN AMERICAN WEREWOLF IN PARIS as a completely mindless, campy entertainment experience. Delpy's injection of class into an otherwise classless production raises the specter of what this film could have been with a better script and a better cast ... She was radiant, charismatic, and effective.
> (taken from a review by James Berardinelli www.imdb.com/reviews/103/10363.html)

Techniques exist in CL for modelling contrasts in discourse (i.e. in connected text more than one sentence long), and these can be exploited in sentiment analysis. In fact, in the related task of modelling citations in scientific text, contrast is an important indicator of whether the authors of a paper claim to improve on the cited work: for instance 'X's work demonstrated ... but ...'. Scientific text also provides good examples of the differences in terminology which make it necessary to adapt sentiment analysis techniques to different domains. For instance, in chemistry papers describing the synthesis of compounds, *strong* is often a negative term, especially in the phrase *strong conditions*, indicating that a synthesis is difficult to carry out. Naturally, there are also dialect differences: *quite good* is positive in American English but (usually) very faint praise in British English. Indeed, deciding whether words like *sick* are being used in a positive or negative way can tax many human readers.

The sentiment classification approach described here is an example of *supervised learning* because the classifier was trained on data which was labelled according to whether the sentiment was positive or negative. However, the ratings were obtained from the existing reviews, so there was no need for an additional annotation step. Often CL experiments require specially annotated data, potentially in large quantities if it is to be used for training. There are also unsupervised approaches to machine learning, where structure is induced from unlabelled data, but even in this case some type of labelling is usually required for evaluation. When annotation is carried out by humans for an experiment, it is now usual to use multiple annotators and to make sure they agree with each other to a reasonable extent, but it is very rare to obtain complete agreement in annotation. The degree of agreement achieved between the human annotators is often used as a ceiling on expected performance of a computational model.

31.3 Statistical models

In the introduction, I argued that statistical models play a crucial role in modern computational linguistics. Sentiment analysis is just one example of this. In this section I will outline three types of model which are relevant to a range of practical applications, but also have theoretical implications. This discussion is general and relatively non-technical since the linguistic interest is in the type of features used and the way that data is acquired to train the model rather than the details of the models themselves.

31.3.1 N-gram language models

A simple but extremely important class of statistical models of language are based on *n-grams*, where a sequence of the $n-1$ words is used to give a probability for the nth word. For instance, trigram models use the preceding two words, bigram models use the preceding word and unigram models use no context at all, but simply work on the basis of individual word probabilities. Such models are classically used in automatic speech recognition (ASR) but also form a component of other applications mentioned in the previous section, including augmentative and alternative communication systems for people with disability and statistical machine translation. The need for language-based prediction in ASR arises because recognizers cannot accurately determine which words are uttered from the sound signals alone, and they cannot reliably tell where each word starts and finishes. For instance, *have an ice Dave*, *heaven ice day* and *have a nice day* could easily be confused. In fact, humans also need context to recognize words, especially words like *the* and *a*. If a recording is made of normal fluent speech and isolated segments corresponding to *the* and *a* are presented to a human subject, it is generally not possible for them to tell the difference. Similarly, humans are bad at transcribing speech in a language they do not understand. For ASR, an initial signal processing phase produces multiple hypotheses for the words uttered, which can then be ranked and filtered using a model of the probabilities of the alternative possible word sequences. The term 'language model' is standardly used for this type of prediction, where the problem is to choose the word sequence with the highest probability, because the words are being modelled rather than the sounds. However, this terminology is unfortunate, because it is used to refer to a very particular type of model of language.

Identifying the originator of a particular technique is often difficult, but there is no doubt that it was Fred Jelinek who pioneered this approach to speech recognition in the 1970s and that Jelinek's group at IBM built the first usable ASR system. To make the n-gram idea more concrete, consider the bigram model probabilities: $P(w_n|w_{n-1})$ is the probability of w_n conditional on w_{n-1}, where w_n is the nth word in some sequence. The probability of a sequence of words $P(w_1^m)$ may then be approximated by the product of the corresponding bigram probabilities:

$$P(w_1^m) \approx \prod_{k=1}^{m} P(w_k|w_{k-1})$$

This approximation assumes independence of the individual probabilities, an assumption which is clearly wrong, but nevertheless works well enough for the estimate to be useful. Note that, although the n-gram probabilities are based only on the preceding words, the effect of this combination of probabilities is that the choice between possibilities at any point is sensitive to both preceding and following contexts. For instance, this means that the decision between *a* and *the* may be influenced by the following noun, which is a much better predictor than the words before the determiner. A naive implementation of this approximation would be hopelessly intractable, but there are efficient algorithms for finding the most likely sequence of words given n-gram probability estimates.

The estimates for the n-gram probabilities are acquired automatically from a corpus of written text. For instance, bigram probabilities are estimated as:

$$P(w_n | w_{n-1}) \approx \frac{C(w_{n-1} w_n)}{\sum_w C(w_{n-1} w)}$$

i.e. the count C of a particular bigram $w_{n-1} w_n$ in the corpus divided by the sum of the counts of all bigrams starting with w_{n-1}. This is equivalent to the total number of occurrences of w_{n-1}, except in the case of the last token in a corpus, a complication which can be ignored for all practical purposes. That is, we actually use:

$$P(w_n | w_{n-1}) \approx \frac{C(w_{n-1} w_n)}{C(w_{n-1})}$$

For speech recognition it is common to use 4-gram or 5-gram models. However, even if using bigrams, there will be cases where a sequence occurs in the test data that has never been seen in the training data. To give such an event a probability of zero, as implied by the estimate given above, would rule it out entirely, so it is necessary to *smooth* the probabilities. This means that we make some assumption about the 'real' probability of unseen or very infrequently seen events and distribute that probability appropriately: there are a variety of techniques for doing this. In the case of n-grams, it is possible to *backoff* to the probabilities of shorter sequences. For instance, in a trigram model, if a particular trigram has a very low or zero frequency, we can backoff to the bigram probabilities, and from bigram probabilities to unigram probabilities. This sort of estimation is essential to get good results from n-gram techniques. If Chomsky had not used *Colorless green ideas sleep furiously* as an example, it is likely that none of its constituent trigrams would occur even in a very large corpus, but these techniques would still allow a probability estimate.

Modelling language using n-grams might seem a very crude technique, but it was only adopted for speech recognition after more linguistically sophisticated techniques were tried and failed. Fred Jelinek's (in)famous remark, 'Every time I fire a linguist, the performance of our speech recognition system goes up' should be seen in this context.[3] Jelinek himself was fully aware that n-gram models were inadequate for many natural language phenomena, such as long-distance dependencies, and indeed he described n-gram models as 'almost moronic', but he challenged those who objected to find models that performed better. This is partly an engineering issue: n-gram models are outperformed by other statistical approaches for a fixed quantity of training data, but training data for language models is simply ordinary text and is therefore available in indefinitely large quantities for languages such as English. Since n-gram models can be trained more efficiently than the competing techniques, their performance can be further improved simply by adding more data.

One could say that the challenge for linguists is to explain what factors are responsible for n-gram models performing so well, given their obvious inadequacies, but there is no clear answer to this question. To an extent, n-grams act as a crude surrogate for 'real' intelligence. For instance, in the context of a talk on computational linguistics, it would be possible for a human to reason that 'computers recognize speech' is a more likely utterance than 'computers wreck a nice beach', but the corpus-derived probabilities would also give the same decision automatically. As we saw in the introduction, old-fashioned AI-style reasoning about the world has proved impossible to incorporate in general CL models, while the n-gram approach is straightforward, given enough data. The explanation that n-grams work because they stand in for full reasoning has appealed to linguists, because it would mean that the success of n-gram models was due to modelling the world, rather than modelling language. However this is not the only factor. To an extent, n-gram models do capture syntax, at least for languages like English where word order is fairly fixed, even though they do not involve explicit syntactic categories. For instance, an n-gram model will contain vast numbers of sequences such as 'the bell', 'a bell', 'a mouse', 'that mouse' and so on, and do not have sequences 'a have', 'the died' and so on, and this gives an indication of the distribution of *the* and *a*. Indeed, it is possible to automatically induce syntactic categories corresponding to determiner and noun from n-grams, although this turns out not to be practically helpful for speech recognition.[4] It is also clear that various types of fixed and semi-fixed multiword expressions play an important role in natural language and n-gram models allow these to be used for prediction. The possible role of n-grams in modelling phenomena such as adjective ordering, where there are soft constraints which are not captured by conventional syntax, is discussed in §31.4.

31.3.2 Part-of-speech tagging

Sometimes we are interested in a statistical model that involves assigning classes to words in a sequence rather than predicting the next word. One important case is part-of-speech tagging (POS tagging), where the words in a corpus are associated with a tag indicating some syntactic information that applies to that particular use of the word. The tags used are generally rather more specific than the conventional notion of part of speech. For instance, consider the example sentence below:

They can fish.

This has two readings: one (the most likely) about ability to fish and other about putting fish in cans. *Fish* is ambiguous between a singular noun, plural noun and a verb, while *can* is ambiguous between singular noun, verb (the 'put in cans' use) and modal verb. However, *they* is unambiguously a pronoun. (I am ignoring some less likely possibilities, such as proper names.) These distinctions could be indicated by POS tags:

They_pronoun can_modal fish_verb.

They_pronoun can_verb fish_plural-noun.

In fact, much less mnemonic tag names make up the standard tagsets used in corpora and in POS tagging experiments: in CLAWS 5 (C5), which is very widely used, the tags needed for the example above are:

NN1   singular noun
NN2   plural noun
PNP   personal pronoun VM0 modal auxiliary verb

VVB   base form of verb (except infinitive)
VVI   infinitive form of verb

The corresponding lexicon associating words with C5 tags would be:

they   PNP
can   VM0 VVB VVI NN1
fish   NN1 NN2 VVB VVI

A POS tagger resolves the lexical ambiguities to give the most likely set of tags for the sentence. In the case of *They can fish*, the correct tagging is most likely to be the one with the modal use of *can*:

They_PNP can_VM0 fish_VVI ._PUN

Note the tag for the full stop: punctuation is an important part of the model when POS tagging text. The other syntactically possible reading is:

They_PNP can_VVB fish_NN2 ._PUN

However, POS taggers (unlike full parsers) are not constrained to produce globally coherent analyses. Thus a POS tagger could potentially return the following sequence:

They_PNP can_VM0 fish_NN2 ._PUN

despite the fact that this does not correspond to a possible reading of the sentence.

Automatic POS tagging is useful as a way of annotating a corpus because it makes it easier to extract some types of information (for linguistic research or CL experiments) while being faster and more robust than full parsing. It also acts as a basis for more complex forms of annotation. For instance, named entity recognizers (mentioned in §31.2) are generally run on POS-tagged data. POS taggers are sometimes run as preprocessors to full parsing, since this can cut down the search space to be considered by the parser, although it is more effective to use tags which correspond directly to categories used by the parser rather than a general-purpose tagset. POS tagging can also be used as part of a method for dealing with words which are not in a parser's lexicon (unknown words).

POS taggers using manually constructed rules were first developed in the early 1960s, when the first experiments with stochastic POS tagging using probabilities were also carried out. Stochastic approaches based on the type of statistical models used for speech recognition became popular in the late 1980s. Some of these models involve n-grams, but in this case the n-grams are sequences of POS tags rather than of words. The most commonly-used approaches are supervised and depend on a small amount of manually tagged training data from which the lexicon and POS n-grams can be extracted. It is also possible to build unsupervised POS taggers for a tagset but these still require a lexicon associating (some of) the words with their possible tags and they do not perform as well as a system trained on even a small manually annotated corpus. As mentioned above, syntactic categories can be induced from untagged data without a lexicon, but the categories will not correspond directly to those in standard tagsets.

Tags can be assigned to words in a sentence based on consideration of the lexical probability (how likely it is that a word has a particular tag), plus the sequence of prior tags. For a bigram model, we only look at a single previous tag, for the trigram the two previous tags. As with word prediction, the aim is to find the highest probability tag sequence for sequence of words (usually a sentence) rather than to look at tags in isolation. However, this is a more complex calculation than for prediction, and I will not go through the details here. Since annotated training data is limited, n-grams of length greater than three are ineffective and appropriate backoff and smoothing are crucial for reasonable performance. However, note that, with these models, the frequencies of the word sequences do not play a role. Tagging *Colorless green ideas sleep furiously* uses the same tag sequence probabilities as *Little white lies spread quickly* although the lexical probabilities will differ.

For effective performance, some method is needed to assign possible tags to words not in the training data. One approach is simply to use all possible open class tags, with probabilities based on the unigram probabilities of those tags. A better approach is to use a morphological analyser to restrict this set: e.g. words ending in *–ed* are likely to be VVD (simple past) or VVN (past participle), but cannot be VVG (*–ing* form).

POS tagging algorithms may be evaluated in terms of percentage of correct tags, checked against the annotated test data. The standard assumption is that every word should be tagged with exactly one tag, which is scored as correct or incorrect and that there are no marks for near misses, although some POS taggers return multiple tags in cases where more than one tag has a similar probability, which complicates evaluation. Generally there are some words which can be tagged in only one way, so are automatically counted as correct. Punctuation is generally given an unambiguous tag. The best taggers for English have success rates of 97 per cent when trained and tested on newspaper text, but the baseline of choosing the most common tag based on the training set gives around 90 per cent accuracy.

It is worth noting that increasing the size of the tagset does not necessarily result in decreased performance: this depends on whether the tags that are added can generally be assigned unambiguously or not. Potentially, adding more fine-grained tags could increase performance. For instance, suppose we wanted to distinguish between verbs according to whether they were first, second or third person. If we were to try and do this simply by adding more categories for verbs to the C5 tagset and used a stochastic tagger as described above, the accuracy would be low: all pronouns are tagged PRP, hence they provide no discriminating power. On the other hand, if we tagged *I* and *we* as PRP1, *you* as PRP2 and so on, which, of course can be done with 100 per cent accuracy, the n-gram approach would allow discrimination between first, second or third person verbs. In general, predicting on the basis of classes means there is less of a sparse data problem than when predicting on the basis of words, but we also lose discriminating power. In fact, C5 assigns separate tags for the different forms of *be*, which is redundant for most purposes, but helps make distinctions between other tags.

The error rate of a POS tagger will be distributed very unevenly. For instance, the tag PUN will never be confused with VVN (past participle), but VVN might be confused with AJ0 (adjective) because there is a systematic ambiguity for many forms (e.g. *given*). For a particular application, some errors may be more important than others. For instance, if one is looking for relatively low frequency cases of denominal verbs (that is verbs derived from nouns – e.g. *canoe, tango, fork* used as verbs), then POS tagging is not directly useful in general, because a verbal use without a characteristic affix is likely to be mistagged. This makes POS tagging less useful for lexicographers, who are often interested in finding examples of unusual word uses.

The initial human annotation of text with POS tags is not entirely straightforward. Many of the experiments with POS tagging for English have been done on data from *The Wall Street Journal* distributed as part of the Penn Treebank. This uses a much smaller tagset than C5 but the manual describing how to assign tags runs to thirty-four pages and the tagged data is nevertheless known to contain many errors. This is presumably partly responsible for the plateau in performance of POS taggers at around 97 per cent accuracy.

It is also important to note that error rates for POS tagging differ between languages. For instance, POS tagging for Japanese is almost deterministic but the accuracy is much lower for Turkish, at around 90 per cent, because it is an agglutinative language.

POS tagging is an example of *shallow* syntactic analysis. Much more elaborate analyses can be produced from parsers which are trained on a *treebank*: i.e. a corpus of sentences manually associated with the correct syntactic analysis. The paradigm example of this is the Penn Treebank which has been used in one way or another in the majority of experiments on the automatic parsing of English. The analyses assigned may be syntactic trees with POS tags as lexical categories, or syntactic dependencies, as mentioned in the introduction. However, there are alternative approaches which provide more detailed analyses, and these are discussed in §31.4.

31.3.3 Distributional semantics

Distributional semantics refers to a family of techniques for representing word (and phrase) meaning based on contexts of use. Consider the following examples (from the British National Corpus):

> it was authentic scrumpy, rather sharp and very strong
> we could taste a famous local product — scrumpy
> spending hours in the pub drinking scrumpy

Even if one does not know the word *scrumpy*, it is possible to get a good idea of its meaning from contexts like this. Distributional semantics has been discussed since at least the early 1950s: the idea is often credited to J.R. Firth or to Zellig Harris, but Firth was actually concerned to emphasize that meaning is context-dependent and Harris's work on the distributional hypothesis at that point was primarily concerned with morphology and syntax. The psychologist Charles E. Osgood described a distributional approach to semantics in 1952. The first computational work was done in the early 1960s, by Karen Spärck Jones in Cambridge (Spärck Jones 1964) and by Kenneth Harper at the RAND Corporation, whose work was inspired by Harris (Harper 1965). It seems it was then almost forgotten in CL, though the vector space models which have been used in Information Retrieval since the 1960s are a form of distributional model. Distributional techniques started gaining popularity within CL in the 1990s, after being reintroduced from Information Retrieval, and are now a major topic of research. They are especially attractive because they allow representations of word meaning to be constructed without the need for any manually created taxonomies or manual data annotation and they may offer a partial solution for the failure of symbolic AI in the earlier approaches. They are also widely used in psycholinguistics.

In distributional models, the meaning of a word is treated as if it were located in a multidimensional space. The dimensions correspond to elements from the various contexts in which the word does or does not occur. To make this more explicit, we can consider the simplest type of distributional model, where the context corresponds to the words in a 'window' on either side of the word to be modelled. For instance, for the example above, the context for *scrumpy* would include 'authentic', 'rather', 'sharp', 'local', 'product', 'pub', 'drinking' if the distribution were calculated on the basis of co-occurrence in a word window of five (i.e. including two words on either side of 'scrumpy'). It is usual to exclude very common closed-class words like *was*. A context set such as this is collected for a large number of words, and the dimensions for the overall space correspond to the more frequent terms found. The usual method is then to represent each word as a vector with those dimensions. To illustrate this, let us assume we have only six dimensions (real systems use thousands of dimensions) and that the value for each dimension is 1 if the word has been seen with that context item and 0 if it has not. See Table 31.1. Thus the meaning of each word is represented as a point in a six-dimensional space. The words *cider* and *scrumpy* are closer together in that space than *elephant* and *scrumpy* or *elephant* and *cider* and thus predicted to be more similar in meaning.

In modern work, the elements in the vector are usually weighted depending on how 'characteristic' the context term is. This is based on the probability of co-occurrence normalized by the probability that the co-occurring term occurs elsewhere in the text, so frequently co-occurring words with relatively low overall frequency are the most characteristic. For instance, in a distribution for the word *language* extracted from Wikipedia, *English*, *grammar* and *germanic* are all highly characteristic. Instead of dimensions being words in some window, they may be words related by a syntactic dependency (in which case, in the scrumpy example, *rather* would be excluded), or the dimensions may themselves correspond to parts of syntactic or semantic dependencies. For instance, one dimension could be 'drink OBJ' to indicate that in the context the word was the object of *drink* (as for *scrumpy*) and another 'drink SUBJ' (for *elephant*). Even with these refinements, a lot of information is lost from the individual contexts, but the corpora used are sufficiently large that each vector amalgamates information from many thousands of contexts for even moderate frequency words.

As indicated with the simple example, vectors for different words can be compared to see how close the points they correspond to are in the semantic space. For instance, the ten words most similar to *cat* (again using distributions extracted from Wikipedia) are: *dog*, *animal*, *rat*, *rabbit*, *pig*, *monkey*, *bird*, *horse*, *mouse* and *wolf* (obviously the exact set returned depends on precisely how the distributions are defined). This notion of similarity is very broad. It includes synonyms, near-synonyms, hyponyms, taxonomic siblings, antonyms and so on. But it seems to reflect psychological reality in that it correlates very well with human similarity judgements. While there is clearly more to word meaning than similarity, it does allow words to be clustered into semantic classes and permits analogical processes to be modelled. Variants of this approach have been tried to extract words in more specific relationships, such as hyponyms and hypernyms.

Two very recent developments in distributional models can be mentioned briefly. One is the research on compositional approaches, where distributions corresponding to phrases

Table 31.1 Sample context set

	apple	*drinking*	*ear*	*product*	*sharp*	*zoo*
scrumpy	1	1	0	1	1	0
cider	1	1	0	1	0	0
elephant	1	1	1	0	0	1

are constructed from the distributions of the corresponding words, guided by syntax. For instance, the phrase *green banana* can be modelled by combining the vector for *green* and for *banana*. Some phrases are non-compositional multiword expressions, of course, but others are somewhat compositional but have additional meaning aspects: for instance, green bananas are unripe and therefore not good to eat. A second development is models which combine textual context with information automatically extracted from images. Given some training data, in which images are associated with words that describe them (e.g. a picture of a car is paired with the word *car*), a mapping can be induced between visual features automatically extracted from the image and the features of the textual distributional model acquired from a corpus. This mapping can then be used to label new images. Crucially, this works (to an extent) not just with words in the training data, but also with new words. For instance, given data for pictures corresponding to cars, vans and motorcycles, the word *bus* can be associated with a picture of a bus, despite never having been seen in the training data (Lazaridou *et al.* 2014). While this type of research is in its infancy, it holds out hope that the semantics of words can be grounded in perceptual features corresponding to their referents.

31.4 Computational grammars

I have spent most of this chapter describing various forms of statistical models, because these are highly characteristic of modern computational linguistics. However, there is still a place for manually constructed grammars of languages. While in the statistical work there is a discontinuity between the 1960s research, which was largely forgotten, and the reintroduction of statistical models in the 1980s and 1990s, there is more continuity in the history of research on computational grammars and parsing. However, the story is very complex: for instance, formal grammars are also used in computer science to describe the syntax of programming languages, and the first techniques for parsing human languages automatically were developed at the same time as the techniques for parsing these artificial languages. What is clear is that there was eventually a considerable degree of cooperation between linguists and computational linguists in the development of frameworks for describing grammars of natural languages that were *declarative* (i.e. could be formally specified without describing the procedures used to run the grammar), more powerful than context-free grammars, linguistically adequate for a wide range of languages and yet sufficiently tractable that they could be used in automatic parsing.

Two such frameworks which have active communities of both linguists and computational linguists are Lexical Functional Grammar (LFG), initially developed by Bresnan and Kaplan in the 1970s and Head-driven Phrase Structure Grammar (HPSG), due to Pollard and Sag, which started in the 1980s. Much of the recent work involves two large collaborations, PARGRAM[5] for LFG and DELPH-IN[6] for HPSG. Both frameworks allow the specification of formal grammars (including morphology, syntax and compositional semantics) which can be used for both parsing and generation. They have both been used to develop efficient computational grammars with high coverage for English and a small number of other languages. Compared with the alternative paradigm of inducing grammars based on a manually annotated treebank, manually constructed grammars are more time-consuming to develop (even if the initial treebank creation is taken into account), but provide richer annotations, including a representation of compositional semantics, and a higher degree of precision. The large grammars are competitive with the treebank grammars for some applications and are more robust to changes in domain. Furthermore, in both LFG and

HPSG, illustrative grammars have been developed for a very wide range of human languages and various cross-linguistic generalizations can be captured.

The linguistically-motivated grammar building approach has benefited from statistical techniques, which are used for ranking parses and generated sentences, and for developing lexicons and mechanisms for handling unknown words, for instance. Conversely, these approaches provide resources for statistical techniques. For instance, the DELPH-IN Redwoods Treebanks can be used to train grammars, and the WikiWoods corpus, which contains compositional semantic analyses automatically generated from Wikipedia, can be used for distributional semantics.

The use of statistical techniques with such grammars is more than simple convenience: they model aspects of language which the symbolic grammars do not capture. For a simple example, consider adjective and conjunction orderings, which often show strong preferences. In the following examples, there is strong preference for the first pair in all cases: *big red cube / red big cube, cold wet weather / wet cold weather, near and far / far and near, brandy and soda / soda and brandy*. Various hypotheses have been put forward to explain these effects, involving features such as relative power. But perhaps the simplest hypothesis is that when an individual speaks or writes, their ordering of a particular pair is based on their previous exposure to the phrase, with the ordering of novel pairs determined by their similarity to the previously seen pairs (see e.g. Copestake and Herbelot 2011). Although some techniques in use in computational linguistics involve complex approaches and high-end computer resources, experiments to investigate a hypothesis such as this can be carried out with an ordinary laptop with little programming being required.

31.5 Conclusion

Computational linguists have developed models both for engineering purposes and as methodology for investigating language. The fact that the models work in applications is an indication that some real properties of language are being captured. However, all the approaches I have outlined here have well-known limitations, and it may be the case that for performance to continue to improve, fundamentally different models will have to be tried.

One area where there is much more scope for computational linguists and linguists to collaborate, even if their theoretical assumptions are very different, is in the development of better corpora for more realistic language modelling. Although very large text corpora are readily available, with billions of words being used in some applications, their use is problematic in experiments which aim to model human behaviour. Accurate estimates for the number of words people are exposed to over the course of their lifetimes are hard to find, but listening to constant speech for six hours every day would correspond to around 20 million words a year. This implies that it should be possible to model adult speakers using corpora of perhaps 300 million words. However, the available data does not correspond to day-to-day use of language. Although part of the British National Corpus contains transcribed conversation, this is very small in comparison to text corpora and other available corpora of conversations are much less varied. The ideal corpus would also have associated video and audio, or at least be annotated in enough detail to get some idea of the context of an interaction, but even the more modest aim of acquiring transcribed conversational data would be very helpful in enabling computational linguists and linguists to improve their models of human language.

Notes

1. There is considerable debate about measuring parsing accuracy, since different approaches yield different types of output. Many current parsers produce dependency structures (see Chapter 8), which specify subjects, objects, modifiers, coordinated terms and so on. The best parsers for English get about 90 per cent of dependencies correct when trained and tested on newspaper text. This accuracy generally drops off markedly for other text types. Parser performance with other languages is often considerably worse. Thus CL systems that incorporate syntactic parsers have to be robust to their inaccuracies.
2. A corpus (plural corpora) is simply a body of machine-readable text. See also Chapter 32 on corpus linguistics, but note that the requirements of computational linguistics are often very different.
3. See Liberman's (2010) obituary for Jelinek for a detailed discussion of the background.
4. Generalizations over categories can be useful for stochastic approaches in making predictions about rare events, but in the case of syntactic categories, this would require that lexical information is available, which is not the case for low frequency words.
5. https://pargram.b.uib.no/
6. www.delph-in.net

Further Reading

Bender (2013); Erk (2012); Jurafsky and Martin (2008); Manning and Schütze (1999).

References

Bender, E.M. (2013) *Linguistic Fundamentals for Natural Language Processing: 100 Essentials from Morphology and Syntax*. Synthesis Lectures on Human Language Technologies #20. San Rafael: Morgan and Claypool.

Copestake, A. and A. Herbelot (2011) Exciting and interesting: Issues in the generation of binomials. In A. Belz, R. Evans, A. Gatt and K. Striegnitz (eds) *Proceedings of the UCNLG+Eval: Language Generation and Evaluation Workshop Edinburgh*, pp. 45–53. Stroudsburg: Association for Computational Linguistics.

Erk, K. (2012) Vector space models of word meaning and phrase meaning: A survey. *Language and Linguistics Compass* 6: 635–53.

Ferrucci, D., E. Brown, J. Chu-Carroll, J. Fan, D. Gondek, A.A. Kalyanpur, A. Lally, J.W. Murdock, E. Nyberg, J. Prager, N. Schlaefer and C. Welty (2010) Building Watson: An overview of the DeepQA project. *AI Magazine* 31: 59–79.

Harper, K.E. (1965) Measurement of similarity between nouns. *Proceedings of the 1st International Conference on Computational Linguistics (COLING 65)*, pp. 1–23.

Jurafsky, D. and J. Martin (2008) *Speech and Language Processing*, 2nd edition. Upper Saddle River: Prentice-Hall.

Lazaridou, A., E. Bruni and M. Baroni (2014) Is this a wampimuk? Cross-modal mapping between distributional semantics and the visual world. *Proceedings of ACL*, pp. 1403–14. Stroudsburg: Association for Computational Linguistics.

Liberman, M. (2010) Fred Jelinek. *Computational Linguistics* 36: 595–9.

Manning, C. and H. Schütze (1999) *Foundations of Statistical Natural Language Processing*. Cambridge: MIT Press.

Moilanen, K. and S. Pulman (2007) Sentiment composition. In R. Mitkov (ed.) *Proceedings of the Recent Advances in Natural Language Processing International Conference*, pp. 378–82.

Osgood, C.E. (1952) The nature and measurement of meaning. *Psychological Bulletin* 49: 197–237.

Pang, B., L. Lee and S. Vaithyanathan (2002) Thumbs up? Sentiment classification using machine learning techniques. *Proceedings of the 2002 Conference on Empirical Methods in Natural Language Processing (EMNLP)*, pp. 79–86.

Spärck Jones, K.(1964) Synonymy and semantic classification. PhD thesis, University of Cambridge. Published as *Cambridge Language Research Unit, Report ML 170* (1964); republished by Edinburgh University Press, 1986.

32
Corpus linguistics

Andrew Hardie

32.1 Corpus linguistics: an overview

What is a corpus, and what is corpus linguistics? Answering either of these questions involves answering the other, as the notion of a 'corpus' in contemporary linguistics is inextricably tied up with the ideas and techniques of corpus linguistics. The term *corpus* (plural *corpora*) is simply the normal word in Latin for 'body', as in a body of text. Over time, the term came to be used for any natural-language dataset used by a linguist – so that, for example, a field linguist might refer to a set of sentences elicited from an informant as their 'corpus'. Since the 1960s, a yet more specific meaning for the term has emerged: corpora in this sense are very large, machine-readable collections of spoken and written text that are analysed using computational methods. The set of methods required to approach the quantitative and qualitative analysis of a collection of language data on a scale far larger than any human being could hope to analyse by hand – together with related areas such as the compilation and annotation of these corpora – constitute the modern field of corpus linguistics.

Describing corpus linguistics as a 'field' or subdiscipline of linguistics is a statement which requires qualification, however. Most subfields of linguistics relate to the study of some aspect of the language system or its usage, such as phonology, morphology or sociolinguistics. Corpus linguistics, by contrast, is not concerned uniquely with any single facet of language, but rather is an approach which can be applied to many or all aspects of language. For this reason, many corpus linguists prefer to describe it as a 'methodology'. As a methodology it has certainly been a great success in fields ranging from the history of English to lexicography to language teaching to discourse analysis. But for others in the field, the insights into language that arise from the use of the corpus are so radically different from the traditional understanding of how language works that they consider corpus linguistics to constitute an independent field of study or theory of language. This latter view is associated with the neo-Firthian school of researchers led by the late John Sinclair.

In its early days, corpus linguistics was something of a controversial approach. This is because it emerged at a time when the leading model of linguistic theory was the Chomskyan formalist approach. Without going into too much detail, the linguistics espoused by Noam

Chomsky and colleagues presumes a rationalist rather than empiricist approach to knowledge: the linguist's intuition and introspection are central as sources of information about language. In corpus linguistics, however, while the utility of the researcher's linguistic (and metalinguistic) intuitions are not discounted, empirical data in the form of naturally-produced discourse is very much front and centre – both as a practical matter and as a matter of principle. Geoffrey Leech, for instance, has emphasised the notion of total accountability as critical within corpus linguistics (Leech 1992). For our analysis to be totally accountable to the corpus data, we must ensure that we take into account *all* the examples in our corpus relevant to what we are investigating – or, if that is impractical, that we examine random subsets of the data, not selected subsets. What we must not do is intentionally ignore relevant evidence. Within the neo-Firthian tradition, Sinclair has promulgated a maxim 'trust the text!' with generally similar import: it is the corpus data, and not theorising based on intuition, that is the ultimate arbiter of what generalisations and hypotheses we can come up with about language.

Corpus-based methodologies remained something of a niche approach through the 1960s and 1970s, partly because of the influence of the Chomskyan arguments against the use of corpus data, but perhaps more importantly because few linguists had access to the computer technology without which corpus linguistics is effectively impractical. Through the 1980s, and especially in the 1990s, all this changed. Advances in information technology put computer power sufficient for the analysis of larger and larger bodies of data within the reach of any researcher who cares to use a corpus. As a result, in the twenty-first century, corpus linguistics has become – in the words of Tony McEnery – a 'killer method' in linguistics, applied to a hugely diverse array of types of linguistic research. This is, in short, why corpus linguistics matters. It is not merely an improved method within lexicography, or a method for researching grammar, or an approach to political or media discourse. It is all of the above and more.

There is no room in this chapter to attempt a comprehensive review of the impact that corpus research has had across the field of linguistics. Instead, I will provide an overview of the fundamental ideas of corpus linguistics and some key methods and practices – starting with how we approach corpus design and construction, moving on to a summary of the most widely used corpus methods, and finishing with a very brief survey of some applications and advanced forms of analysis.

32.2 Corpus design and construction

32.2.1 General considerations

More linguists work with corpora than actually collect corpus data or work on corpus design. A very large set of questions in corpus linguistics can be answered without going beyond standard, widely available corpora. A good example of such a corpus is the British National Corpus (BNC). The BNC is a 100 million word collection of British English, compiled in the early 1990s, and including samples of a wide range of spoken and written genres. As a broad sample of the English language in general, it is suited to many different research aims. In other cases, a more specialised collection of data may be required. A wide range of such specialised corpora have been constructed and likewise made generally available, covering historical and dialectal data, specific genres, or the spoken language of specific types of people.

But there are other types of research question for which no standard corpus is available. In this case, the first step for the researcher is to build the corpus on which the analysis will be based. For instance, many corpus-based analyses of media discourse are based on examining media texts that address some particular topic. It is unlikely that such a highly specialised dataset would be available in advance. If I am interested in how local newspapers in Britain discussed the issue of crime in the years 2010 to 2013, I will almost certainly need to build a corpus myself for this specific purpose. Such goal-oriented corpora are informally known as 'do-it-yourself' or DIY corpora and very often are not made available to researchers other than the original compiler (often, for copyright reasons, they cannot be).

The virtue of working with a DIY corpus is that the design of the data can be tailored directly to the specific research question at hand. The virtue of working with a standard published corpus is that the corpus serves as a common basis between different researchers – allowing results to be tested and replicated by other scholars, for instance. Both approaches have their place in different kinds of corpus-based study.

However, corpus researchers need an understanding of the issues that arise in corpus construction even if they never build any corpora of their own. This is because we have to understand the contents, design and structure of the corpora that we use, in order to select a corpus appropriate to what we want to research, in order to make appropriate use of that corpus, and in order to treat our results critically in terms of how far they may be extrapolated beyond the specific corpus at hand. The key concepts here are the notions of the corpus as a sample and of balance and representativeness.

32.2.2 The corpus as a sample

Any corpus is fundamentally a sample. That is, there is some large phenomenon that we want to know about – a language, or some specified variety of language, as a whole – and since we cannot look at all the possible text within that language, we must select a sample. Borrowing terms from statistics, we can talk about the whole of the language variety we are approaching as the *population*, and the corpus we are using to look at that language variety as the *sample*. Our interest is typically on what we can say about the population on the basis of the sample – and how confidently we can say it. The very fact that the corpus is a sample means that we need to think carefully about how our sample relates to the population, which means we need a detailed and critical awareness of the process of sampling that has been used in corpus construction.

It is rarely possible to avoid sampling. As Chomsky pointed out, language is in principle non-finite (it is always possible for a speaker of a language to create a new sentence in that language that has never been used before) and it is – of course – impossible to collect a dataset of infinite size! Only in the case of certain historical data, where the amount of text that has survived from a particular period is finite, can we have a complete corpus of some language or language variety. For example, it would be possible to compile a complete corpus of Old English, because only a limited number of documents in Old English have survived. But even in this case, we are effectively letting the forces of history – the preservation of some documents, and the loss of others – do the sampling for us.

An important difference between sampling in corpus linguistics and in other sciences is that a corpus is never a random sample of the population. In research such as opinion polling or medical trials, where the population is a literal population of people, the sample must be as close as possible to a randomly-selected subset of the population, such that every person has an equal likelihood of being selected to be in the sample. Corpus collection is very different. It is possible to select the texts of a corpus randomly from a population of texts of interest. But we rarely use the whole text as the unit of analysis. Most of the analyses we will want to undertake with our corpus will be centred on a much smaller linguistic unit, such as the sentence, the clause or, perhaps most commonly, the word. However, even if the texts of the corpus have been selected randomly, the sentences and words are *not* random. For instance, consider the word *elephant*. It is not especially common. Many texts contain no examples at all of *elephant*. However, a text that does use the word *elephant* once is then rather likely to go on and use it several more times (for example, if it is a text about elephants). This means that the probability of a given word occurring at some point in a text is influenced by the words that have occurred before and thus the words in a corpus are not random. Similar logic can be applied to sentences.

What does this mean for corpus analysis? Three things. First, we have to be very careful in applying statistics to corpus data that are unproblematic in other fields, precisely because of this issue. Second, when we analyse a corpus we must always be aware of dispersion – looking out for the difference, for instance, between a word that occurs 100 times in our corpus where all 100 instances are bunched close together in one text, and a word with the same 100 occurrences that are spread out across the whole corpus. Third, in the process of corpus construction we have to think about the relationship between the population and the sample in a somewhat different way to how this is done in fields where sampling can be done on a random basis. The concepts that we normally apply for this purpose are representativeness and balance.

32.2.3 Representativeness and balance

If the words and sentences of a corpus are not a random sample, then how can we have any confidence that findings we arrive at using a corpus are applicable to the language or variety as whole? We must consider the issue of how representative the corpus is of that language or variety, based on the decisions that were made about what to include and what to exclude in that corpus. As Leech (2007: 135) points out, 'Without representativeness, whatever is found to be true of a corpus, is simply true of that corpus – and cannot be extended to anything else.' We consider a corpus to be representative if we have adequately captured the nature of the whole population within our sample. That means that the full variety of what is found in the language must be represented in the corpus, if we aspire to extrapolate from the corpus to the language. If we are trying to represent written English, for instance, our corpus cannot contain just newspaper language. It must also contain examples of magazines, books, reports, letters, and other media both published and unpublished. Within each medium, we would also need to make sure that the full range of genres (functional varieties) and the full range of domains (subject matters) were represented adequately. Clearly, building a corpus big enough to contain an example of everything from this massive landscape of possibilities would be a gargantuan undertaking. Even a very large standard corpus such as the BNC will not sample every possible type of text. Smaller corpora, such as the Brown Corpus of written American English (one million words in extent), will struggle even more to represent the full range of what is 'out there'. Perfect representativeness is, therefore, something that almost certainly cannot be achieved. Rather, we must strive towards better and better representativeness, even though complete representativeness is unattainable. Moreover – and critically – we must always be aware of the limitations in representativeness inherent in the design of the corpus we are using, and restrict the scope and strength of the claims we make on the basis of the corpus data accordingly.

Balance is a related, and equally problematic, issue. It relates to the relative proportions of different types of data within a corpus. A corpus of general English, for instance, must sample both spoken and written data (of various kinds) in order to be representative; however, what should the relative proportions of speech versus writing be? A corpus is considered balanced if its subsections are correctly sized relative to one another. However, there is no single answer to the question of what the correct proportions are. For instance, in the case of speech versus writing, we might propose a corpus that is 50 per cent spoken and 50 per cent written data (this is, in fact, the design of the International Corpus of English, ICE). However, this assumes that speech and writing are equally important. Is that the case? How do we even determine the parameters of what is 'important' in this context? Most people probably hear more language than they read; does this mean the spoken language should make up more than half the corpus? On the other hand, speech is generally much more ephemeral than writing; does that mean written texts should dominate? As with representativeness, the issues around balance are fraught with difficultly, but the critical thing for the user of any corpus is to be actively aware of how that corpus is balanced, to think carefully about what this means for the generalisability of results based on that corpus.

32.2.4 Metadata, markup and annotation

A corpus always contains the actual words of one or more texts that have been collected as discussed above. These will typically be collected in the form of plain text files – that is, computer files containing just the actual characters of the text, without any kind of formatting, as found in word-processor files, for instance. The plain-text words of the corpus are sometimes called the raw data of the corpus. However, raw data is not necessarily all that the corpus contains. There are three types of additional information that can be added to a corpus, namely metadata, markup and annotation.

The definitions of (especially) the terms *markup* and *annotation* in the context of corpus design and encoding vary quite a lot in the literature; the term *tagging* is also sometimes used as a synonym for either or both of these terms. However, for present purposes we will treat them as distinct concepts. Markup is information added to a corpus to represent features of the original texts other than the running words themselves – for instance, in the case of a written text, features such as the beginning and end points of sentences or paragraphs, or the position of page breaks, or the position and content of elements such as illustrations which would be omitted in a plain text corpus. Annotation, by contrast, encodes into the corpus the results of some linguistic analysis which we have undertaken on the corpus text.

The third thing which can be added to the raw text of a corpus is *metadata*. Metadata is data about data, that is, information about the texts that have been included in the corpus – such as whether they are written or spoken, information about genre or domain, bibliographic information on original publication of a written text, or demographic information about the speakers in a spoken text. There are several ways to store metadata for a corpus, but one popular way is to insert a chunk of descriptive information at the beginning of each corpus text in a fixed, specified format: this metadata chunk is called the *header* of the text.

Critically, markup, metadata and annotation can be processed by computer, just like the actual words of the corpus texts, and therefore they can be exploited in automated corpus analysis. We will return to annotation in the next section; let us deal briefly here with metadata and markup by discussing some examples of how they may be used to enhance a linguistic analysis – and, thus, the reason corpus builders invest effort into adding them into the corpus in the first place!

Metadata has two main functions. First, it allows us to trace the corpus evidence we see back to its source. If we are examining a series of examples extracted by searching a corpus, for instance, it is often very useful to be able to see, via the metadata, precisely what text each example comes from: knowing, for example, whether a particular instance comes from a novel or from a newspaper report can be a valuable aid to interpretation. The second function is that metadata allows us to isolate and compare different sections of a corpus. If, for instance, we have a corpus containing both writing and speech, we may on occasion wish to search just within the spoken texts, or to compare the results of some analysis in the written data versus the spoken data.

Markup has similar applications in that it allows analyses to take account of the structure of the corpus texts. For instance, in a spoken corpus, who said what is often critical to an analysis: only the markup of utterance boundaries and speaker identities allows us to know this. But the same can apply to written data – we might be interested in differences in how a word is used paragraph-initially versus medially or finally, for instance, and this can only be automated if the corpus has paragraph breaks marked up.

32.2.5 Corpus annotation

To annotate a corpus is to insert codes into the running text to represent a linguistic analysis. In many cases, the analysis is done at the word level, so a single analytic label or *tag* is assigned to each word of the corpus. However, analyses at higher or lower levels of linguistic structure can also be represented as corpus annotation. Much research has been done to automate the process of adding the most common forms of analysis, so that it is not necessary for a human being to read through the whole corpus and manually insert the tags. Let us consider four of the most widely used kinds of corpus annotation – those often pre-encoded in general-purpose corpora prior to their being distributed.

Part-of-speech (POS) tagging is the assignment to each word of a single label indicating that word's grammatical category membership. It is the longest-established form of corpus annotation, with the first efforts in the direction of automatic taggers going back as far as the early 1960s, and the first practical, high-accuracy tagging software emerging in the 1980s – although even the best POS taggers have a residual error rate of around 3–5 per cent which can only be removed by painstaking manual post-editing. The utility of POS tagging, especially for languages like English, is that many words are ambiguous in terms of their part-of-speech. For instance, *walk* can be both a noun and a verb, and the only way to know which is to look at it in context. Having the computer evaluate the contexts for us and on that basis disambiguate each instance of the word allows us to treat *walk* the noun and *walk* the verb separately, according to what makes most sense for a given research question.

Different POS tagger systems use different tagsets, that is, systems of grammatical (specifically, morphosyntactic) categories. Some simple tagsets only distinguish major word classes such as noun, verb, adjective, preposition and determiner. However, there are many more morphosyntactic distinctions that can be useful to linguistic analysis, and more fine-grained tagsets will try to encode these distinctions. For example, it is common for POS tagsets to distinguish common nouns from proper nouns, or lexical verbs from auxiliary verbs. Inflectional distinctions will also usually be represented: singular versus plural, or past tense versus present tense, for instance.

The underlying principle of semantic tagging is the same as POS tagging, namely, the assignment to every word in a text or corpus of labels representing categories within a scheme of analysis. The difference is that in the case of semantic tagging, the tags represent semantic fields, i.e. categories of meaning – and the tagset as a whole thus represents some ontology, or way of dividing up all possible meanings into various domains or concepts.

Semantic tagging is a harder task for a computer than POS tagging. This is because, while a word can be ambiguous for both grammatical category and semantic field, disambiguating the semantics involves actually understanding the meaning of the context, which computers cannot do. For this reason, we must be prepared to work with a higher error rate when analysing the output of a semantic tagger than when working with POS tags. Nevertheless, semantic tags can be extremely useful, especially for detecting patterns in a corpus that affect groups of semantically-related words which are individually very rare.

A *lemma* is a group of word-forms that are judged to constitute a single entry in the lexicon of the language – different inflectional forms of a single dictionary headword. Lemmatisation is conceptually the most straightforward of the word-level annotations; every word is, simply, annotated with the lemma to which it belongs (where each lemma is represented by its morphological base form, such as *go* for *go*, *goes* and *went*). Thus, computer searches of a corpus can be based on grouping together all the separate inflectional forms of a single word. However, even this relatively simple operation can raise issues regarding what is, and what is not, considered to be part of the same lemma. The English word *broken*, for instance, can be tagged either as a participle or as an adjective. Many lemmatisers will treat it differently depending on how it is tagged. If it is tagged as a participle, it is lemmatised as *break* – since a participle is considered an inflectional form of a verb base. On the other hand, if it is tagged as an adjective, *broken* is lemmatised as *broken* – since the change of category to adjective is deemed to create a new lemma. So the lemmatisation does not always group elements together; in some cases it can draw distinctions between elements that are superficially identical.

The other form of corpus annotation that is often applied automatically is *parsing*, the annotation of syntactic structures and relations. Unlike the forms of annotation mentioned so far, parsing does not operate strictly at the word level; rather, what is annotated are grammatical phenomena at the phrase, clause and sentence level. As such, parsing represents an implementation within a computerised text of the traditional tree-diagram style of syntactic analysis; for that reason parsed corpora are often called *treebanks*. There are two major forms of parsing, each corresponding to a different kind of syntactic analysis. Constituency parsing is about identifying the phrases (syntactic constituents) and how they are nested within one another. This is done by introducing codes into the text to represent the beginning and end points of all the phrases. Dependency parsing, by contrast, labels the relationships between words: each word is linked to the grammatical structure by depending on another word in a particular way. For instance, a noun may relate to a verb by being its subject, or its object; an adjective may relate to a noun by being its modifier. Different tags are used to represent different types of dependency relationship.

Like semantic tagging, automated parsing has a much higher error rate than POS tagging, because the task is inherently more difficult. In both cases, the benefits of being able to access the semantic or grammatical analysis make it worth the trouble of working with data that has a known error rate. That said, many of the generally-available treebanks have been parsed manually, or at least have had their automated parsing manually corrected.

There are many other kinds of annotation which a researcher might apply for the specific purposes of their own research questions, such as different kinds of discourse-pragmatic or stylistic annotation. But these are often very different from research project to research project, and therefore must often be applied manually rather than automatically.

When a corpus has been tagged, the fundamental techniques of corpus analysis – frequency counts and concordance searches, which will be introduced at length in the next section – can be undertaken at levels of analysis higher than the orthographic word-form. For instance, lemmatisation allows frequency lists to be compiled at the level of the dictionary headword, which may subsume many distinct word-forms. Conversely, tagging can disambiguate the words: *break* is both a noun and a verb, and *broken* is both a participle and an adjective – POS tags allow a computer to distinguish the different grammatical functions.

As I mentioned above, there exists recurring confusion regarding the distinction between annotation and markup. Part of the reason for this is that, as a practical matter, both can be inserted into the corpus using the same encoding system of tags inserted into the running text. The current standard method for adding tags to a corpus is by means of XML (the *eXtensible Markup Language*). In an XML document, anything inside <angled brackets> is part of a tag; anything outside angled brackets is part of the text itself. The special meaning of the angled brackets < and > means that actual less-than or greater-than signs in the text itself must be represented by the special codes *<* and *>*. Different XML tags are used for markup, metadata and annotation. For instance paragraph boundaries might be shown in XML using <p> tags; a <title> tag in the header might contain the original title of a text; and a POS tag on a word could be represented as <w pos='NN1'> (where *NN1* is a common tag for a *singular common noun*).

32.3 Analytic techniques in corpus linguistics

32.3.1 Corpus analysis software

The two most basic forms of data which we can extract from a corpus are the concordance and the frequency list. It is, in theory, possible to generate either of these through hand-and-eye analysis of a stack of paper documents. Indeed, in the pre-computer age this was sometimes done; the earliest concordances were compiled manually for the study of the language of the Bible, and in the early twentieth century word frequency lists were often compiled manually to help inform foreign language teaching. However, in practice, all techniques for corpus analysis – these two most basic methods, and all the more complex methods built upon them – are nowadays supported by the use of various pieces of corpus analysis software. Thus, what possibilities we have for the analysis of a corpus is inevitably a function of the affordances of the available software tools.

Nearly all corpus analysis software permits the generation of a *concordance* – a listing of all the instances of a word or phrase in the corpus, together with some preceding co-text and some following co-text (usually anything from a handful of words to a couple of sentences). As this functionality is so common, the term *concordancer* is an often-used synonym for 'corpus software tool'. Concordancers vary greatly in terms of what analyses, other than basic concordance searches, they allow. Since the late 1970s and early 1980s, a very wide range of such programs have been created – some very general and some highly specialised. For our present purposes, it suffices to distinguish two broad varieties of concordancer that are used today. Some programs (e.g. WordSmith, AntConc) run from the researcher's desktop computer; this means that the user can analyse any corpus they have available locally using these programs. Other tools operate as client-server systems over the internet: the user accesses a remote computer via a client program, typically a web browser, and uses search software that actually runs on a remote server machine where some set of corpus resources and analysis systems has been made available. Client-server tools currently in wide use include SketchEngine, Wmatrix and CQPweb; some of these allow users to upload their own data to the corpus server, while others restrict users to a static set of available corpora.

In some cases, an analyst may not have much choice in whether to use a desktop concordancer or a client-server system: the choice is determined by what data they wish to use. Many large, standard corpora are only available via the web (such as the Corpus of Contemporary American English (COCA) – see Davies 2009). This is for reasons of intellectual property: unless permission to redistribute has been obtained from the copyright holder of every text in a corpus, then the corpus as a whole cannot be made available to anyone other than the original compiler. However, it is generally assumed that making isolated snippets of text from the corpus available via a web-based concordancer does not breach copyright, due to the consideration of fair use.

One other approach exists to corpus software: that is, for the researcher to write ad hoc programs specifically to carry out the particular analyses they wish to undertake. The argument for this practice – which necessarily requires that corpus linguists learn computer programming – is primarily one of flexibility; without the ability to create specialised analysis programs, the researcher is limited to solely those procedures that their concordancer happens to make available (see Gries 2010). However, given the advanced level of programming skills that this approach requires, it is difficult to see it being adopted by more than a minority of corpus analysts.

32.3.2 Corpus frequencies and their interpretation

One basic output that nearly all concordancers can produce is a frequency list: that is, a listing of all the words in the corpus, together with their frequency. In discussing the corpus frequency of words, it is useful to introduce the distinction between word types and word tokens. A *token* is a single instance of any word at a particular place in the corpus; a *type* is an individual word-form, which can occur many times in the corpus: thus one type is usually instantiated by multiple tokens. (The exception, types which occur only once in a corpus, are called *hapax legomena* – Greek for '(they were) said once'.) So for instance, if we see on a frequency list for an English corpus that *the* is the most frequent word, occurring 60,000 times, then we could say that the single type *the* is represented in this corpus by 60,000 tokens. Frequency lists can also be compiled for any annotation that is present in the corpus, and we can talk about types and tokens of annotation tags in the same way.

Any given type will be more frequent in a bigger corpus; for that reason, corpus frequencies are often given in relative terms, as frequencies per thousand words or per million words. Relative frequencies of types are calculated by taking the raw frequency, dividing it by the number of tokens in the corpus overall, and multiplying by the normalisation factor (one thousand, one million or whatever). So, if *the* occurs 60,000 times in a 1.5 million word corpus, its relative frequency is forty per thousand words, or 40,000 per million words.

Speaking meaningfully about corpus frequencies is not straightforward. Simply stating that *the* occurs forty times per thousand words in a corpus tells us nothing of linguistic interest, whether about the word *the* or about the corpus in question. It is only when we compare frequencies that we arrive at interesting linguistic generalisations. We could compare the frequency of *the* to that of other words on the frequency list, and observe whether it is more or less frequently used than those other words. We could, moreover, compare the frequency lists of two corpora or sub-corpora, to ascertain whether the contents and ordering of their frequency lists are similar, as a means of contrasting the types of language those corpora represent. We would find, for instance, that in a written English corpus *the* will probably be the most frequent word, but in conversational English the personal pronouns *I* and *you* are likely to top the list.

A frequency list is inherently quantitative in nature. To be interpreted meaningfully, then, it must therefore nearly always be combined with some form of qualitative analysis – that is, an analysis that involves the linguist interacting with the actual discourse within the corpus and its structure and/or meaning. This is most straightforwardly accomplished within the context of a concordance analysis.

32.3.3 Concordance analysis

As we saw above, a concordance is the result of a corpus search: all the examples in a corpus matching some specified search pattern, together with some preceding and following context. In raw or unannotated corpora, we can only search for specified words or phrases. However, if tags are present, they can be used instead of or as well as a word pattern – for instance, to search for *can* as a noun versus *can* as a verb, or to search for all adverbs in the corpus. Most concordancers allow the use of special characters called *wildcards* that indicate a position in the pattern where 'any letter' or 'any sequence of letters' may be present, and thus allow searches to be underspecified; for instance, if the * character is a wildcard, then searching for *act** will find not just *act* but also *actor*, *action*, *active* and so on. Some corpus software allows the use of the extremely sophisticated system of wildcards called *regular expressions*. The use of tags and wildcards together allows wholly abstract grammatical structures to be specified in a search pattern, for example, phrase-level constructions such as the English passive, perfect and progressive.

Whatever form of search is used, the result is the same: a list of examples in context, typically presented so that the word or phrase matching the search term is centred on the screen, and often sorted alphabetically (by the match expression, or by a preceding or following word). How do we handle the analysis of this concordance? There are several different approaches. At one level, analysis can be more or less impressionistic – based on scanning the eye up and down the concordance lines in an attempt to observe features of note that recur in the concordance, or to identify different functions of the word or phrase that was originally searched for. A more careful analysis will often attempt to quantify the number of concordance lines that exemplify a given function or contextual feature, and to make sure that every single concordance line has been inspected individually, to identify exhaustively all possible categories and patterns of usage. The most rigorous form of concordance analysis will systematise the aspects of each example that are considered, building a matrix of different features – grammatical, semantic or pragmatic – and the values these features have for each concordance line. All this can make a full concordance analysis a major undertaking; in compliance with the principle of total accountability, concordances too long to analyse in full should be reduced (or thinned) randomly to a manageable size. It is especially important not to look at just the beginning of a concordance, as these early concordance lines may present examples from the early part of the corpus, which is not necessarily representative of the corpus as a whole.

32.3.4 Key items analysis

A key items analysis is based on contrasting frequency lists. As we saw above, frequency lists often become most interesting when we compare lists from different corpora or different texts. However, simply comparing two or more lists by eye is only a very approximate way to do this. A more rigorous way to compare a pair of frequency lists is to use a statistical procedure to identify on a quantitative basis the most important differences between the two lists. Several difference statistics can be used, but the most common is the log-likelihood test of statistical significance, a procedure similar in principle to the better-known chi-squared test. A key items analysis is performed as follows: first, frequency lists are created for two texts or corpora – either two corpora which we wish to contrast, or a single text of interest and a generic reference corpus. The frequency list may be of word types, lemmas or any kind of tag – thus, we often talk about *keywords* and *key tags*. Second, the frequencies of each item on the two lists are compared by calculating a log-likelihood score from the two frequencies and the total sizes of the two corpora. Third, the list is sorted in descending order of log-likelihood score; those items whose frequencies have the most significant differences between the two corpora under comparison will appear at the top of the list. Key items can be classed as positive (more frequent in the first corpus) or negative (more frequent in the second or reference corpus); both can be of interest, but studies based on keywords tend to focus on the positive items.

The interpretation of a keyword or key tag list, done properly, is an onerous task, as it will typically involve undertaking at least a partial concordance or collocation analysis of a large part of the highest-scoring key items. In fact, for many analysts, a primary virtue of a key items list is that it provides a way in to identifying which words or categories in a corpus will be of interest for more detailed study. Other analytic approaches to the key items list might involve grouping the items according to either an ad hoc or pre-established scheme of classification, to identify patterns or trends of usage across some large fraction of the list.

32.3.5 Collocation analysis

In the same way that key items analysis is based on, and abstracts away from, two frequency lists, so a collocation analysis is based on, and abstracts away from, a concordance search. *Collocation* in the broadest sense means simply those aspects of a word's meaning which subsist in its relationship with other words alongside which it tends to occur. The idea that collocation is of high or indeed primary importance to understanding the meaning of a word or other linguistic form originates with J.R. Firth and is very important in the neo-Firthian school of corpus linguistics; but collocation analysis itself is a commonplace of most or all approaches to corpus linguistics. There are many different ways to operationalise the notion of co-occurrence. One is to look at sequences of words which recur in a fixed order with high frequency in the corpus – these sequences are variously referred to as *n-grams*, *clusters* or *lexical bundles*. A more common approach is to begin with a single word (or lemma) of interest, called the *node*, for which a concordance search has been performed; the surrounding text is then scrutinised to establish what elements occur frequently in the vicinity of the node. Depending on one's methodological preferences and theoretical orientation, there are then a number of ways in which one might proceed. One way is manual and largely qualitative: to undertake a hand-and-eye analysis of the concordance, as explained above, where the focus of analysis is to identify co-occurring elements, the collocates of the node, in the concordance lines. However, given how labour-intensive this approach is, it is very common to automate the process of extracting collocates from the local context around the node. The software compiles a list of words that occur in the context (either all words, or words which stand in some particular relationship to the node) and then applies statistical analysis to identify words which are more common in the vicinity of the node than elsewhere in the corpus. These are then presented as a list of statistical collocates for the researcher to interpret. It should be noted that this is fundamentally rather similar to the procedure of a key items analysis, except that we are comparing the vicinity of the node to the rest of the corpus, rather than comparing two different corpora, and some of the same considerations apply. First, as with key items, a number of different statistical procedures can be used; log-likelihood is one of the more common, but mutual information, z-score, and t-score are also common – among others – and the choice of statistic can result in almost totally different results. Second, as with key items, a rigorous collocation analysis will always go beyond the raw list of statistical collocates to look at actual instances of those collocates in usage alongside the node.

Although we can use *collocation* as a general covering term for different kinds of co-occurrence phenomena observed in corpora, we can also use a set of more specific terminology, developed largely by John Sinclair and colleagues, to distinguish co-occurrence patterns at different linguistic levels. In this more specific sense, *collocation* refers to the co-occurrence of particular word-forms with the node, and three other terms are used to refer to grammatical, semantic or discourse-pragmatic or affective co-occurrence pattern: colligation, semantic preference and semantic prosody.

Colligation refers to a recurrent co-occurrence of some node with a particular grammatical category or structure. For example, if we observe that a node word almost always occurs after an adjective – even if no single adjective co-occurs frequently enough with the node to be considered a collocate – we could say that the category of adjective is a colligate of that node. A colligate can also be a syntactic structure that the node tends to occurs within or alongside – such as a sentence position, or a verb complementation pattern. *Semantic preference* or *semantic association* refers to a consistent co-occurrence with a set of words which – again, while perhaps not individually significant collocates – are drawn from a recurring semantic field. Finally, semantic prosody or discourse prosody refers to a broad function or meaning which tends to co-occur with the node but which may be variously realised. For instance, the verb *cause* tends to occur in contexts where the thing that is caused is negatively evaluated – but the linguistic realisation of that negative evaluation can take many different forms both in terms of the words and the grammatical structures used.

32.4 Conclusion: applications and frontiers of corpus linguistics

In this chapter, we have briefly considered a number of central topics of corpus linguistics. It bears emphasis that any analysis conducted using these techniques will be applied in addressing some specific research question, and the nature of that research question will to some extent dictate the selection of data and method. Unfortunately, there is simply no space here to give a full account of all the areas of linguistics, and of other fields of study, where the methods of corpus linguistics have been productively applied. As previously noted, corpus techniques have acquired the status of a key methodology applicable to nearly all subfields of language study (perhaps the sole exception being those Chomskyan formalist approaches whose opposition to corpus data is a matter of principle). It is not possible to do more here than provide a non-exhaustive list of applications without further commentary. The two initial applications of corpus data were improved grammatical description (see, for instance, Biber *et al.* 1999) and improved lexicography (as pioneered by corpus-based dictionaries such as the Collins COBUILD series). Other areas where corpus methods have been gainfully deployed include: theoretical linguistics, especially from a functional or cognitive perspective; linguistic typology; field linguistics; contrastive linguistics; genre and register analysis; dialectology; sociolinguistics; psycholinguistics, including the study of first and second language acquisition; stylistics; discourse analysis, including critical discourse analysis; applied linguistics topics including the study of learner language and language teaching and testing; forensic linguistics; and both computational linguistics and natural language processing. In short, while there are many linguists who themselves do not use and do not need to use corpora, there are increasingly few linguists working in areas where *no one* uses corpora.

The current frontiers of corpus linguistics are twofold. The first is to extend yet further the range of applications in the field – beyond the concerns of linguistics, to serve the research interests of scholars across the humanities and social sciences. Many such disciplines are focused on one form or another of close analysis of text, for instance history and literary criticism. As more and more texts become available in large electronic archives – especially texts from before the late twentieth century – so there will arise an increasing requirement in humanities and social sciences research for approaches that allow such large amounts of data to be handled. This is exactly what the methodology of corpus linguistics offers to researchers in disciplines beyond linguistics. Not entirely unrelated to this is the second front of current progress in the field – namely, the continuing development of more refined techniques and tools for corpus analysis. In this chapter we introduced four basic analytic methods, but a number of more complex approaches, often based on advanced corpus statistics, have been introduced over the years, such as collocation network analysis, advanced multivariate statistics applied to concordance analysis and corpus frequencies, and so on. Further extension of these methods, and the development of more such complex techniques, is something we can expect to see over the next several years.

Further reading

Recommended introductory texts on corpus linguistics include Biber *et al.* (1998) and Hunston (2002). Sinclair (1991) and McEnery and Hardie (2012) are, in different ways, slightly more advanced texts. Key collections of research papers in the field of corpus linguistics include Aijmer and Altenburg (1991), Short and Thomas (1996), and Sampson and McCarthy (2004).

References

Aijmer, K. and B. Altenburg (1991) *English Corpus Linguistics*. London: Longman.
Biber, D., S. Conrad and R. Reppen (1998) *Corpus Linguistics: Investigating Language Structure and Use*. Cambridge: Cambridge University Press.
Biber, D., S. Johansson, G. Leech, S. Conrad and E. Finegan (1999) *Longman Grammar of Spoken and Written English*. London: Longman.
Davies, M. (2009) The 385+ million word corpus of contemporary American English (1990–2008+): design, architecture and linguistic insights. *International Journal of Corpus Linguistics* 14: 159–90.
Gries, S.T. (2010) Methodological skills in corpus linguistics: a polemic and some pointers towards quantitative methods. In T. Harris and M. Moreno Jaén (eds) *Corpus Linguistics in Language Teaching*. Frankfurt am Main: Peter Lang.
Hunston, S. (2002) *Corpora in Applied Linguistics*. Cambridge: Cambridge University Press.
Leech, G. (1992) Corpus linguistics and theories of linguistic performance. In J. Svartvik (ed.) *Directions in Corpus Linguistics: Proceedings of the Nobel Symposium 82, Stockholm*, pp. 105–34. The Hague: Mouton.
Leech, G. (2007) New resources, or just better old ones? The Holy Grail of representativeness. In M. Hundt, N. Nesselhauf and C. Biewer (eds) *Corpus Linguistics and the Web*, pp. 133–49. Amsterdam: Rodopi.
McEnery, T. and A. Hardie (2012) *Corpus Linguistics: Method, Theory and Practice*. Cambridge: Cambridge University Press.

Sampson, G. and D. McCarthy (eds) (2004) *Corpus Linguistics: Readings in a Widening Discipline*. London/New York: Continuum International.
Short, M. and J. Thomas (eds) (1996) *Using Corpora for Language Research: Studies in the Honour of Geoffrey Leech*. London/New York: Longman.
Sinclair, J. (1991) *Corpus, Concordance, Collocation*. Oxford: Oxford University Press.

33
Linguistics and philosophy

Kasia M. Jaszczolt

33.1 Philosophy of language: traditions and themes

Philosophy and the study of language are intimately connected, to the extent that it is impossible to say from which point in human intellectual history the study of meaning in natural language can be regarded as an independent enterprise. Natural language syntax, semantics and pragmatics are now considered to be subdisciplines of theoretical linguistics, surrounded by the acolytes in the domains of language acquisition, language disorders, language processing (psycholinguistics and neuroscience of language), all using empirical, including experimental, methods in addition to rationalistic inquiry. However, philosophical problems associated with the structure of language as well as with meaning in language and in discourse still remain, and arguably will always remain, the backbone of syntax and semantics, and a trigger for progress in theorising. It is impossible to summarise the impressively rich tradition of thinking about language in the history of philosophy. One would have to start with Presocratics in the sixth and seventh centuries BCE in Ancient Greece and cover two and a half millennia of intensive questioning and argumentation over the relations between language, reality, truth and the human mind. Or, one could try to delve into the history before the Greeks, then move through the landmarks of Plato, Aristotle and the later Stoics into the current era (see e.g. Harris and Taylor 1989; Law 2003; Allan 2010). In this brief introduction we shall focus on much later debates, starting from the period when discussions about topics that are currently in the focus of debates originated, that is late nineteenth century, marked by Frege's insights into an ideal language for describing knowledge and the origin of modern logic that is now used as a metalanguage for theorising about meaning in natural human languages. From formal approaches within analytical philosophy I shall move to the 'language-as-use' paradigm of the ordinary language philosophy, followed by the more recent debates on meaning as it is to be understood for the purpose of formal representation and linguistic theory. In the process, I shall address some of the core areas that philosophers of language have been drawn to such as reference and referring or propositional attitude reports. Next, I move to the topic of the role of intentions and inferences, and finish with a brief attempt to place 'linguistics and philosophy' on the map of language sciences and research on language in the twenty-first century.

33.2 Meaning, truth, and the rise of formal semantics

Relation between language and reality has been at the forefront of research in philosophy at least since the end of the nineteenth century, with the rise of interest in the ideas developed by Gottlob Frege and Bertrand Russell. The earlier preoccupation with the relation between meaning and the mind that characterised phenomenologists such as Brentano and Husserl was now considered to have plunged theorising about meaning into dangerous 'psychologism', dubbed a corrupting intrusion of the mental, where what was supposed to be investigated was in fact external to the mind and objective, namely meaning and the world.

The origin of the formal approach to meaning is often equated with Gottlob Frege's development of a new concept of logic, although it can be traced further back to the seventeenth century when Leibniz proposed his *calculus ratiocinator*, 'the calculus of reasoning', a formal inference system – an idea followed by Frege in his *Begriffsschrift* (or a 'concept script', Frege 1879). Frege's proposal for a 'logically perfect language' contains an analysis of the logical form of judgements in terms of functions where a predicate is a function that maps arguments to truth values. Frege's view breaks away from earlier psychological logic that focused on thought processes and subjective mental representations. His condemnation of psychologism was forceful indeed and influenced the future of philosophy of language, semantics and pragmatics for decades to come. In *Grundlagen der Arithmetik*, Frege explicitly bans psychological explanations in logic. He says that '[t]here must be a sharp separation of the psychological from the logical, the subjective from the objective' (1884 [1997: 90]). He distinguishes concepts and objects, which he accepts as legitimate objects of theorising, from ideas (*Vorstellungen*) understood as psychological constructs that have to be excluded from investigation. In short, *ideas* are not *objects*; the way people *think about an object* is not to be equated with the *object* itself.[1] In practice, this means that logical inquiry is governed by the laws of logic rather than by thinking that something is valid or correct.

This attack on psychologism constituted a landmark in philosophy, logic and arithmetic. Approaches to meaning that relied on theories of mental processes and mental representations were now rejected as an old paradigm. The meaning of a sentence is a proposition, but the proposition is true or false independently of what its users make of it:

> The description of the origin of an idea should not be taken for a definition, nor should the account of the mental and physical conditions for becoming aware of a proposition be taken for a proof, and nor should the discovery ['*Gedachtwerden*'] of a proposition be confused with its truth! We must be reminded, it seems, that a proposition just as little ceases to be true when I am no longer thinking of it as the Sun is extinguished when I close my eyes.
>
> (Frege 1884 [1997: 88])

Similar comments appear in many other works by Frege. In *Grundgesetze der Arithmetik*, vol. 1 (Frege 1893 [1997: 202]), he calls psychology a 'corrupting intrusion' into logic in that 'being true is quite different from being held as true'. Next, in 'Logic', Frege (1897) argues that the task of logic is 'isolating what is logical … so that we should consciously distinguish the logical from what is attached to it in the way of ideas and feelings' (1897 [1997: 243]), because

> [l]ogic is concerned with the laws of truth, not with the laws of holding something to be true, not with the question of how people think, but with the question of how they must think if they are not to miss the truth.
>
> (Frege 1897 [1997: 250])

The function-argument analysis was subsequently adopted for natural languages, with an attempt to demonstrate that they have a compositional structure.

In addition, Tarski's semantic definition of truth and his model theory resulted in a semantics of artificial languages that yielded itself to application to natural languages. Modern formal semantics of natural language was born, with the advances of the works by Donald Davidson (1984), Richard Montague (1974), Barbara Partee (2004), Hans Kamp (1984) and many others in developing the theory of truth-conditional, possible-words, model-theoretic semantics. In the second half of the twentieth century, truth-conditional semantics became the dominant approach to natural-language meaning. In this context, it is also necessary to acknowledge the contribution of Logical Positivism, an early twentieth century movement, also known as logical empiricism, and represented mainly by the Vienna Circle (Carnap, Schlick, Neurath) whose approach to meaning can be summed up in the principle of verification: sentences acquire meaning when they are assessed for their truth or falsity – on the basis of sense experience, evidence of sense experience, or, in the case of analytical propositions, in virtue of their grammatical form and the meanings of the words. While a strict adherence to verifiability poses problems and was rapidly criticised by such philosophers as Quine or Strawson, the very idea of employing truth values has resulted in the most powerful tool in the analysis of meaning proposed to date – with the proviso that the ban on psychologism had to be relaxed.

Donald Davidson's insightful adaptation of Tarski's theory of truth as a theory of natural-language meaning is supposed to 'bypass' any issues to do with the psychological aspects of meaning. If 'Snow is white' is true if and only if the snow is white, that is, if we are deriving the meaning of the sentence from the semantic properties of its parts, we are concerning ourselves with language tools as they can be found in the language system; we are not concerning ourselves with the uses to which these tools may be put. In other words, speakers' truth-value judgements were considered to be separate from truth values per se; intentions and inferences belonged to an altogether different object of study.

Reversing the direction of explanation, the analytical tradition in philosophy produced not only advances for the study of language, but also some (albeit not as significant) new approaches to metaphysics. The pertinent idea here is that the traditional problems discussed in metaphysics are in fact pseudo-problems; all one needs is an understanding of the nature and use of natural language. This way of approaching philosophy through language was called *linguistic philosophy* (not to be confused with the *philosophy of language*) and spanned various approaches to meaning, including ordinary language philosophy discussed in §33.4.

More than a hundred years have passed since Frege's writings and we can now stand back and reopen the question of the 'psychological intrusion'. Was it indeed a sign of progress to separate meaning from mental representations? Let us take Russell's (1905, 1919) celebrated approach to definite descriptions. He classified them as quantifying expressions and as such qualitatively different from directly referring expressions such as proper names or demonstrative and personal pronouns. Sentence (1) then acquires an analysis as in (1a), using classical quantifiers of predicate logic, or (1b), using generalised quantifiers (cf. Neale 1990: 45), where vertical lines stand for cardinality.

(1) The king of France is bald.

(1a) ∃x(KoF(x) & ∀y(KoF(y) ⊃ y = x) & Bald (x))

(1b) '[the x: Fx] (Gx)' is true iff |F−G| = 0 and |F| = 1

However, as has been well acknowledged since Donnellan's (1966) seminal paper 'Reference and definite descriptions', the latter are ambiguous between the attributive reading that is captured in (1a) or (1b) and referential reading that would make them akin to proper names. In those early days, disputes concerning the status of this ambiguity (semantic or pragmatic) were rife. But looked upon from the perspective of more than half a century, the unprejudiced story would have it that what is important is that there is *an ambiguity of some kind or other*, pertaining to the meaning of such constructions. And where we have a conceptual ambiguity, we have to have either semantic underspecification, or semantic ambiguity, or finally a semantic underspecification/ambiguity with a specified semantic default meaning (see Jaszczolt 2005 for an extensive discussion). The point I am making here is that where one tries to exorcise psychologism through the main door, it comes back in through the window: we want to know the meaning of such constructions and it appears that to know the meaning one has to know the intentions of the speaker and the inferences performed by the addressee. In other words, one either: (a) has to be Gricean and acknowledge the fact that at least some generalisable aspects of the psychology of utterance processing, such as maxims of conversation or their offshoots in the form of post-Gricean heuristics and principles, constitute an essential component of a theory of meaning; or (b) stop halfway, with 'incomplete meaning' that pertains to the language system rather than language use.

The example of definite descriptions is particularly striking when they are embedded in intensional contexts such as propositional attitude reports as in (2).

(2) Sam believes that the king of France is bald.

It has been traditionally assumed in the philosophy of language that propositional attitudes are ambiguous between the transparent and the opaque reading (see e.g. Quine 1956) that correspond to the wide (2a) and narrow (2b) scope of the existential quantifier.[2] 'Bel$_S$' stands for 'Sam believes that…'

(2a) ∃x(KoF(x) & ∀y(KoF(y) ⊃ y = x) & Bel$_S$ Bald (x))

(2b) Bel$_S$ ∃x(KoF(x) & ∀y(KoF(y) ⊃ y = x) & Bald (x))

In (2a), the speaker ascribes to Sam a belief about a particular, known individual (*de re*); in (2b), the speaker reports on the belief as a whole (*de dicto*), without making a commitment to the existence of the king of France. Next, if we pursue the Gricean argument and are interested in the speaker's intended meaning, we can add a scenario on which Sam is referentially mistaken and in fact attempts to refer to the king of Sweden, and the uptake of this intention is successful. Then the reporter utters (2c).

(2c) ∃x(KoS(x) & ∀y(KoS(y) ⊃ y = x) & Bel$_S$ Bald (x))

What we have here is an example of three possible readings of a belief report with a definite description and it is only through recognising the role of intentions and inferences that we can arrive at the correct interpretation. Frege's ban on psychologism, pivotal as it was for the emergence of modern logic that gave linguistic semantics an unambiguous metalanguage of predicate calculus, now appears to be too strong.

Charles Travis (2006: 125–6) aptly points out that taking any kind of stance on how the laws of logic apply to language users seems to constitute in itself a form of psychologism. If it is so, then Frege's position is also a form of psychologism. This is well exemplified in his seminal work 'On Sense and Reference' (Frege 1892) where he observes that the identity of referents does not guarantee the identity of meaning. Although (3) is true, (4) and (5) have very different truth conditions; in other words, the situations that make (4) true are not the same as those that make (5) true.

(3) Mark Twain is Samuel Clemens.

(4) John believes that Mark Twain is the author of *Huckleberry Finn*.

(5) John believes that Samuel Clemens is the author of *Huckleberry Finn*.

According to the so-called Leibniz's Law applied to natural language, two expressions are identical with each other if they are substitutable preserving the truth of the sentence. 'Mark Twain' and 'Samuel Clemens' are not substitutable; John may believe the proposition in (4) but not consent to the one embedded in (5). Frege solves the problem by introducing the concept of sense (*Sinn*) which stands for the way of thinking about an individual, or a mode of presentation. The ban on psychologism is still preserved in that senses are intersubjective; they can be shared and in that they differ from private ideas of objects. But this ban is preserved only narrowly. If we want a truly compositional theory of meaning, we must understand what components enter into this composition. Sense, mode of presentation, however, remained a 'creature of darkness' (and it was considered as such, for example, by Quine): it is perfectly possible for John to assent to the proposition embedded in (4) but dissent from the one embedded in (5) without being able to pinpoint the 'mode of presentation' under which he holds the belief.

More formally, one can attempt, following Schiffer (1992), to represent a mode of presentation for (5) as in (6) where believing is a three-place relation among the believer, the proposition and the mode of presentation under which the person believes this proposition. 'Φ^*m' stands for a type of the mode of presentation and '$<>$' for intensions.

(6) $(\exists m) (\Phi^*m \ \& \ Bel (John, <SC, author-of-HF>, m))$

However, despite the transparent formal representation, m remains a mystery and as long as we do not know what exactly this constituent of the logical form stands for, compositionality of meaning is not demonstrated. And it is likely that in order for the meaning to turn out correctly, m has to be a psychological entity: a private concept that is suitably rich or suitably general for the purpose of the particular discourse situation. This is how intentions, inferences and, all in all, psychological considerations reappear whenever a move from formal languages to natural language is attempted.

Word meanings and sentence meanings are notoriously flexible. Celebrated examples with quantifiers and logical connectives such as (7) or (8) demonstrate that in order to account for the proposition that reflects the speaker's intentions one often has to 'write in' what is not there to be seen. 'Every' in (7) stands for 'every in a contextually given domain' as, for example, in (7a). The connective 'and' conveys more than conjunction; it can convey a causal relation between two simple propositions as in (8a).

(7) *Every student* read Frege.

(7a) *Every student in Kasia's semantics seminar* read Frege.

(8) The temperature fell below zero *and* the lake froze.

(8a) The temperature fell below zero *and as a result* the lake froze.

Approaches to such modifications vary. Minimalists claim that they fall outside semantics proper (Borg 2004, 2012; Cappelen and Lepore 2005). According to indexicalists, they constitute part of the truth-conditional content but only if they can be traced to a slot in the logical form. Stanley and Szabó (2000) show that quantifier domain restriction does indeed succumb to such an analysis. Radical contextualists see them as 'top-down' modifications that need not be triggered by any syntactic slots (e.g. Recanati 2004, 2010). We can go further in both directions. Minimalists need not even admit that truth conditions and propositions are necessary in semantics in that meaning that is of interest is the meaning that can be gleaned from the structure of the sentence even when the sentence does not correspond to a unique proposition (e.g. Bach 2006). At the other end of the spectrum, contextualists can equate their modified semantic representation with the main proposition intended by the speaker and communicated to the hearer, which on some occasions is so different from the uttered sentence that it requires not only expanding or completing the logical form but instead a substitution of an altogether different logical form as is the case, for example, in indirect reports (Jaszczolt 2005). On this construal, the truth-conditional analysis takes as its object the primary, intended meaning of the speaker, or the primary speech act.

Debates between different orientations concerning the appropriate scope of the theory of meaning have come to the fore of semantics, pragmatics and philosophy of language in the 1980s and have remained vivid ever since. They are further complicated by the attempts to distinguish between: (a) the truth-conditional content that can be pragmatics-rich; and (b) semantics, which can remain narrow. On this construal, we obtain 'truth-conditional pragmatics' (Recanati 2002, 2010). The rationale behind this complication is arguably that semantics has to remain algorithmic, delimited by the grammatical structure, in order to be implementable at all:

> Is semantic interpretation a matter of holistic guesswork (like the interpretation of kicks under the table), rather than an algorithmic, grammar-driven process as formal semanticists have claimed? Contextualism: Yes. Literalism: No. […] Like Stanley and the formal semanticists, I maintain that the semantic interpretation is grammar-driven.
> (Recanati 2012a: 148)

However, it is an open question as to whether semantics narrowly understood and dissociated from intuitive truth-conditional content is: (a) attainable; and (b) expedient. It may not be attainable because the flexibility of meaning is reflected not only in the need to modify ('enrich', 'modulate') the structure, but also in the need to assign essentially context-dependent meaning to lexemes. To paraphrase Searle's (1980) celebrated example, the meaning of 'cut' in 'to cut the grass' is quite different from the meaning of this verb in 'to cut a cake': stabbing the grass with a knife is not what is intended, and neither is driving a lawnmower over the cake. Recanati (2012b: 179) uses this flexibility as a starting point for arguing that compositionality of meaning does indeed have to rely on a logical form provided by the grammar (i.e. it is 'bottom-up'), but the meanings of the words are determined by the contexts in which they occur ('top-down'). Compositionality in the standard Fregean sense can be vindicated as long as the meanings of simple expressions can be relaxed. In short, algorithmic, grammar-based semantic interpretation and massively context-dependent, flexible meanings of the constituents that enter this interpretation work in tandem: if word meanings are sufficiently flexible, compositionality is preserved.

The answer to the second query, namely as to whether semantics narrowly understood and dissociated from intuitive truth-conditional content is expedient, requires a recourse to common sense and preferences in delimiting the object of study. If, like most linguists in the twenty-first century, one disobeys Frege's ban and associates the study of meaning with meaning as it is understood by conversational interactants, then narrow semantics is only of use as one of the sources of information about meaning. In other words, while some utterances exhibit a high degree of precision and little need for resorting to the context-specificity and intentions, as for example (9), others rely on multiple sources of information for their processing.

(9) A prime number is a whole number larger than 1 and divisible only by 1 and by itself.

Clearly, the meaning of this sentence is composed out of the meanings of its parts with little or no recourse to any information external to this sentence.[3] So, it appears that there must be a concept of narrow semantics that allows us to compose meanings in this way. At the same time, for the majority of utterances speakers produce, sources external to the lexicon and structure of the uttered construct have to be consulted – be it to complete it if it is a sentence fragment as in (10) or a grammatical sentence that does not correspond to a full proposition as in (11), or because the proposition it appears to express is not the proposition that is understood by the interlocutors to have been conveyed as in (12).

(10) Nice shoes.

(11) Sam is ready [>> to do what?]

(12) Sam pressed the button and [>> as a result] the garage door opened.

All in all, the history of philosophy of language from the end of the nineteenth century to the present has demonstrated a colossal preoccupation with attempts to fit natural languages in the mould of formal, unambiguous languages such as (but not only) the languages of first-order logic. Adopting such a precise metalanguage enabled generations of linguists and philosophers to pursue the big question 'What is meaning?' adopting a fairly reliable starting point: that of the relation between the sentence and the situations in the world that it appropriately corresponds to. However, a cursory glance at the most commonly discussed examples, such as definite descriptions or the celebrated 'donkey sentences' (in (13), with anaphoric relations marked by indices) already reveals problems. Its metalinguistic equivalent in (13a) is produced compositionally from (13) but does not have the required interpretation (the variables x and y in Beats (x,y) remain outside the scope of the quantifiers). The representation in (13b) has the required interpretation but the structure is not isomorphic with that of the English sentence; the formula cannot be derived compositionally from (13).

(13) 'If a farmer$_1$ owns a donkey$_2$, he$_1$ beats it$_2$.'

(13a) $\exists x \exists y (\text{Farmer}(x) \wedge \text{Donkey}(y) \wedge \text{Owns}(x,y)) \rightarrow \text{Beats}(x,y)$

(13b) $\forall x \forall y ((\text{Farmer}(x) \wedge \text{Donkey}(y) \wedge \text{Owns}(x,y)) \rightarrow \text{Beats}(x,y))$

Various attempts have been made to remedy the semantic representation, most notably in dynamic approaches to meaning. In Discourse Representation Theory (DRT, see Kamp and Reyle 1993: 168) *unselective binding* is proposed, resulting in the reading 'for every farmer x and for every donkey y that x owns, x beats y'. In Dynamic Predicate Logic (DPL, see Groenendijk and Stokhof 1991: 58), existential quantifiers are redefined and allowed to bind variables outside of their syntactic scope. These are 'quick-fixes' that, although they constitute signs of progress, do not do justice to the various meanings these sentences can assume and only emphasise the big difference between how formal languages and natural languages work. For example, if a farmer owns several donkeys and beats only one, is the sentence true? One of the options would be to acknowledge the fact that in the case of natural-language communication, unlike in the case of meaning inherent in formal languages, language is hardly ever the sole medium; we communicate by uttering sentences in the specific situation, at the specific time, place, and assuming that we share certain knowledge, assumptions, principles of reasoning, and so forth, with the audience. This makes speech inherently situated, and tips the scales from the emphasis on the formal to the emphasis on the situated action.[4] Such emphasis on what is achieved by speech is characteristic of another paradigm in the philosophico-linguistic deliberations which I discuss in §33.4: the ordinary language philosophy and the resulting theory of speech acts.

33.3 Philosophy of linguistics

From about the middle of the twentieth century scholars interested in natural-language meaning had various paradigms to follow: they could either proceed with the ideas that originated in analytical philosophy and continue a formal analysis of sentences in terms of extensions and intensions (that originated in Frege's sense and reference) as was done in Montague Semantics, or abandon the idea of 'semantics mirroring syntax', pursuing newly emerging Chomskyan generative linguistics, or focus instead on language use. I shall have little to say about Chomskyan generative linguistics here in that the questions pertaining to philosophy and language arise there only on a more abstract level, for example:

1. Is referential semantics compatible with Chomsky's idea of I-language?
2. Is syntax determined by the external environment or just by the human mind?

And more generally:

3. What is the nature of linguistic rules?
4. What counts as data for a linguist?

5. What is the role of intuitions in linguistic theory?
6. How did language evolve?
7. How is language acquired?
8. Are there linguistic universals and if so, what is their nature?[5]

These questions are discussed in depth in Peter Ludlow's (2011) *The Philosophy of General Linguistics*. Because of their 'metalevel flavour', in the sense of a 'philosophy *of* a linguistic theory', they will not be pursued here. As Scholz (2011) aptly summarises: 'Philosophy of linguistics is the philosophy of science as applied to linguistics. This differentiates it sharply from the philosophy of language, traditionally concerned with matters of meaning and reference.' Remaining on the object level of 'what counts as meaning', the view that a theory of meaning is exhausted in a theory of language use is the next one we move to.

33.4 Ordinary language philosophy and speech acts

In his seminal series of lectures delivered at Harvard University in 1955, John L. Austin changes the focus of attention of philosophers from declarative sentences describing states of affairs to utterances in the case of which 'the uttering of the sentence is, or is a part of, the doing of an action, which again would not normally be described as, or as "just", saying something' (Austin 1962: 5). Although Austin was not by any means the first philosopher to talk about 'acts' that are done by using language, in that in this context one has to remember the writings of Thomas Reid in the eighteenth century as well as the nineteenth century phenomenologists,[6] Austin was the first to systematise such actions performed by using language in a well-developed theory, distinguishing various aspects of such actions: locutionary (saying), illocutionary (acting), and perlocutionary (exerting influence), and attempting a classification. A related and roughly co-temporaneous approach to language was put forward by Ludwig Wittgenstein in his late work *Philosophical Investigations*: 'For a large class of cases – though not for all – in which we employ the word "meaning" it can be defined thus: the meaning of a word is its use in the language' (Wittgenstein 1953: 43).

The focus on the use of language in 'doing things', for example requesting, apologising, complaining, warning and so forth, meant that the preoccupation with propositions and truth conditions subsided and gave rise to an interest in the properties of the act itself, substantiated in the analysis of the illocutionary force. Speech acts, as they were subsequently dubbed, could be successful (felicitous) or unsuccessful (infelicitous); conditions of success seemed to take the place of truth conditions. But it would be an oversimplification to stop at this summary. In fact, truth and falsity on the one hand, and felicity and infelicity on the other, proved to constitute two interwoven distinctions. Let us start with felicity. A speech act is infelicitous when the conditions for its appropriateness are not satisfied. These conditions pertain not only to language but also to the situation of discourse, cultural and social prerequisites and the characteristics of the interactants. For example, uttering 'I hereby pronounce you husband and wife' does not count as an act of marrying two people when it is uttered by a person without the required authority. More standard cases involve, for example, requests and promises. A speech act counts as a promise when it satisfies the following conditions. It has to be uttered in a sentence that has the content of a promise (the so-called *propositional content condition*); it must concern an eventuality that is beneficial to the addressee ('I promise I will kill you' will not do) and an eventuality that is not going to take place anyway ('I promise tomorrow is Friday' will not do either). The latter two are called *preparatory conditions*. Next, there is also the *essential condition* whereby the speaker puts himself/herself under an obligation to fulfil the promise either by intending to do so or by making a good pretence of it (see Searle (1969: 62) on insincere promises: 'the speaker takes responsibility for having the intention rather than stating that he actually has it'), and so *sincerity condition* also has to be satisfied when looked at from the position of the addressee.

What is important is that for Searle (1983) speech acts are intricately connected with mental states: the conditions of satisfaction of speech acts are inherited from their corresponding mental states such as belief or desire. This inheritance is facilitated by the fact that mental states have intentionality: they are about something (we believe something, fear something, or desire that something be the case). The way to look at it is this: conditions of satisfaction pertain to mental constructs, but it is theoretically useful to talk about them with respect to linguistic constructs as well. In addition, one must not neglect the fact that it is social reality that makes promise a promise: an obligation to fulfil it is what members of societies learn. In other words, social conventions create an explanatory shortcut through intentions.

This theoretical machinery of satisfaction conditions for speech acts must not be seen as a replacement of truth conditions. Although the origin of ordinary language philosophy was precisely a reaction to verificationism, truth, logical metalanguage and other tools and characteristics of the formal analyses of language from the first half of the twentieth century, truth and appropriateness eventually merged in an attempt to formalise speech acts. In *Foundations of Illocutionary Logic*, Searle and Vanderveken (1985) address such questions as 'What is the relation between illocutionary force and the meaning of sentences? What is the logical form of performative sentences?' (p. ix). They want to know whether illocutionary forces are formalisable and how they combine with the propositional content on which they operate. Naturally, the initial obstacle in such an enterprise is the lack of a bi-unique relation between forces and verbs: to advise someone can mean to help them make a decision ('advise to') or to inform them about something ('advise that'); an exclamative 'watch out' can be a warning, a threat, or friendly advice ('Watch out when you read "r" + "z" in Polish: sometimes it is pronounced "ʒ" and sometimes "rz".'). Moreover, some illocutionary forces are conveyed through non-lexical means such as mood, word order or intonation. However, having acknowledged this initial hurdle, there is a lot to say about possibilities of formalisation. Illocutionary forces are operators that take propositions as arguments. For example, (14) can be formalised as in (14a), where 'F' stands for the illocutionary force associated with promising and 'P' for the proposition 'Kasia will pay for the dinner' (when uttered by me).

(14) I promise to pay for the dinner.

(14a) F(P)

Sentential connectives can be shown to interact with the force. The force can take scope over negation as in (15)–(15a), or the negation operator ($\neg$) can take scope over the force as in (16)–(16a).

(15) I promise not to wear stiletto heels.

(15a) F($\neg$P)

(16)   I don't promise to wear stiletto heels.

(16a)   ¬F(P)

The latter is called *illocutionary denegation*, in order to distinguish negating illocutionary force from negating a proposition. Next, illocutionary force is given a precise analysis in terms of its seven components (the illocutionary point, its degree of strength, mode of achievement, propositional content conditions, preparatory conditions, and sincerity conditions and their degree of strength, see Searle and Vanderveken 1985, Ch. 1), and the entire analysis is proposed as an extension to Montague Semantics (see e.g. Vanderveken 1990), combining illocutionary logic with Montagovian intensional logic.

In short, while truth conditions are not easily applicable to speech acts in that false statements may turn out strictly speaking true as in (17) (where the act of stating was indeed performed) or an expression may require a convoluted analysis in order to turn it into a truth-evaluable form, as in the case of indirect speech acts such as the request in (18), truth conditions and felicity conditions meet when the force is recognised as an operator – be it linguistically or contextually realised.

(17)   I state that I am a fool.

(18)   Are you free to help me with this software?

These inquiries into force and content and attempts at their precise analysis constitute arguably the most valuable and long-lasting aspects of the theory of speech acts when we assess it from the perspective of the second decade of the twenty-first century. On the contrary, attempts at constructing a typology of speech acts have been rather futile: Austin's was grossly unprincipled, while Searle's, albeit improved, still did not overcome the problem of the missing indicator of the precise illocutionary force: a speech act may be direct or indirect, and even if it is direct (that is, the sentence contains a performative verb or a grammatical form that clearly signals the speech act type), it still has the flavour of indirectness in that there is no guarantee that a particular kind of force has been conveyed by it. In fact, as Sperber and Wilson (1986: 245) aptly observed, in many cases interlocutors need not be able to identify the type of act for the intended meaning to go through. It appears that Jacob Mey (2007) well captured the nature of speech acts when he pointed out that speech acts are *situated*; they should be investigated only within: (a) the context of the situation in which they appear; and (b) the language in which they are issued. Developing the idea further, for Mey, the object of study of pragmatic theory is a situated pragmatic act and its generalised theoretical equivalent, a *pragmeme*.

Returning to the question of psychologism, it seems that ordinary language philosophers brought psychologism to the fore of attention, so to speak, through the back door. Speaking about fuzzy illocutions and often inscrutable perlocutions, pointing out the indirect means of communicating the main intended content they focused the attention of linguists on the role of intentions and conventions, as well as on the possibilities of theorising about indirectness. Indirectness of human communication is indeed a phenomenon for which we need psychologism back. In §33.5 I move to another attempt at reconciling the extant paradigms, this time with the emphasis on the formal, truth-conditional analysis of meaning but supplemented, in various ways, with the result of inferring meaning from a speaker's intentions.

To conclude this section, it is important to point out that ordinary language philosophy was a landmark not only when assessed from the perspective of linguistics but also from the perspective of the 'core' of philosophy that concerns itself with the nature of reality, namely metaphysics. Those pursuing meaning in natural language have now turned to the properties of linguistic actions and sometimes to their classification, while those pursuing answers to metaphysical questions have been offered a new (after the Logical Positivism of the Vienna Circle) 'linguistic turn': reality and facts do not exist outside language and therefore it is language use that one should pursue. Problems with such an outlook notwithstanding, its place in the history of metaphysics, secured by Austin and late Wittgenstein, cannot be disputed.

33.5 Psychologism and truth conditions: saying, intending and implicating

The trends and paradigms in linguistics in the twentieth century testify to the truth of the claim that adopting formal methods in semantics – and thereby adopting the assumption that natural languages are sufficiently similar to formal languages of deduction to build their semantics around this similarity – need not necessarily mean abandoning an interest in a speaker's intended meaning and/or the addressee's recovered meaning. Grice's program shows that intending and inferring a speaker's intentions can be built on top of the edifice of truth-conditional semantics. In 'Logic and Conversation', Grice (1975) proposes a two-part solution aimed at 'saving' truth-conditional semantics. First, there are context-dependent expressions such as indexical terms that have to be filled in by assigning to them a referent, and lexical and structural ambiguities that have to be resolved. Next, there are meanings intended by the speaker that come over and above the proposition literally expressed and that can be inferred according to the principles of reasoning he proposes (the Cooperative Principle and the four maxims associated with it). These pragmatic meanings he calls *implicata*. They are worked out (calculated) with more, less, or no help of the context, through the reasoning principles captured with his four maxims in the process he calls an *implicature*. And it is the totality of meaning, the 'said' and the 'implicated', that constitutes the object of study. Grice (1957) calls it *non-natural meaning*, or 'meaning$_{NN}$': to mean something 'NN' is to make an utterance with an intention of producing a belief in the addressee – a belief that is a result of the addressee's recognising the speaker's intention to do so. Various post-Gricean revisions to the maxims notwithstanding,[7] the paradigm still gathers strong support and intention-and-inference-based theory of meaning is arguably the most buoyant approach currently on the market, both in theoretical and applied linguistics. Since the late 1970s the 'what is said' began to gain ground to the detriment of 'what is implicated': more and more results of pragmatic inference (or, according to some post-Griceans, pragmatic inference or pragmatic *default meaning ascription*) came to be considered as modifications (enrichments, modulations, intrusions into and so forth) of the logical form of the uttered sentence. Disputes concerning the boundary between semantics and pragmatics, as well as the principles for drawing this boundary, have been rife since the late 1980s.

First, philosophers of language started treating psychologism as a criterion for distinguishing two different types of inquiry. When one is concerned with the meaning of sentences, allowing for some limited contribution of content to fill in 'slots' signalled by pronouns, adverbials 'here' and 'now', and other context-sensitive expressions that belong to a small, highly restricted set, one is a minimalist about meaning and searches for a semantic theory that would account for meanings pertaining to linguistic strings. When one is concerned with the speaker's intended meaning and/or the meaning recovered by the addressee, one is a contextualist. Now, such additions can be explained by postulating elements of the logical form that are responsible for them ('indexicalism') or it can be assumed that at least some of these pragmatic additions to the truth-conditional content do not correspond to any predetermined slots. One can go further and question the assumption that minimal semantics is feasible in that word meanings are not invariant but instead are created in the interaction between words in a particular sentence in a particular context: the compositionality of meaning has to allow for the flexibility of the meanings of the constituents. I have discussed these debates in §33.2 in the context of accounting for the compositionality vis-à-vis the flexibility of meaning. A detailed summary of this lively ongoing debate is beyond the scope of this chapter but it has to be pointed out that the debate re-vindicates psychologism in the theory of natural-language meaning: contextual contribution, be it (a) minimal or (b) going all the way towards the main speech act performed by using a linguistic expression, leads to a version of a theory of what is *said*, rather than a theory of *sentence meaning*. As soon as linguists start talking about context-dependence, be it through indexicals like in Kaplan's (1989) content-character distinction or through free, syntactically uncontrolled enrichments and other modifications, we are already in the domain of the *said*. In fact, on this level of generalisation, Frege himself was guilty of psychologism about meaning: instead of saying that substitution of coreferential expressions goes through for the purpose of the theory of meaning although it *appears to us not to go through*, he introduced intersubjective senses and thereby made verification itself operate on a pragmatic rather than a semantic object.

33.6 Philosophy and language sciences: future directions

To conclude, it is important to emphasise that the interface between linguistics and philosophy has benefited both parties. For linguistics, addressing the question of the nature of meaning gave rise to increasingly more adequate semantic and pragmatic theories. For philosophy, the pursuit of meaning gave rise to new ways to address metaphysical questions. A striking example is the 'linguistic turn' in metaphysics, referred to earlier as 'linguistic philosophy', according to which knowledge and truth can only be attained through analysing language in that the only reality there is, and the only facts there are, are immersed in linguistic description. Unkempt as this approach was, it is a worthy reminder that language constitutes a medium through which humans conceptualise the world and, in view of mounting evidence for linguistic relativity (at least at the level of concept combinations if not atomic concepts themselves, see e.g. Levinson 2003), natural-language meaning is a worthy object of study. Epistemology, ethics and political philosophy also concern themselves with meaning in language. These areas of interface are too large to be covered here but let us consider one example. In *Lying, Misleading, and What Is Said*, a book subtitled 'An Exploration in Philosophy of Language and Ethics', Saul (2012) distinguishes between lying and merely misleading, approaching the distinction through a pursuit of an adequate concept of 'saying', continuing with the question as to whether merely misleading is 'morally better' than saying. She demonstrates that topics that bring together philosophy of language and moral philosophy are worth exploring. Needless to say, the same goes for pairing philosophy of language with other areas of philosophy and, on a greater scale, with various disciplines in social and natural sciences. It is a rather short-sighted view to claim, as some do, that scientific disciplines and various areas of philosophical study 'carve off chunks' of philosophy of language, leaving it to die a slow but sure natural death. The perspectives for the future of philosophy of language seem to be quite the reverse.

In a talk delivered at the Cambridge University Moral Sciences Club, David Chalmers (2015) asks a pertinent question: 'Why isn't there more progress in philosophy?' He assesses some possible answers such as that philosophers have not converged on a set of big questions, let alone a set of answers to such putative questions that would produce what we call knowledge. He then assesses the utility of methods in philosophy, where in addition to the overall method of argumentation (as opposed to experiment in science or proof in mathematics), philosophers use some sophisticated methodologies, among which there are formal or linguistic ones. Whether advances in such methods aid the progress depends on what assumptions one holds about the existence of objective empirical truths and their accessibility to the human mind. But one can contend that the pursuit of meaning in language will continue and the question 'What is meaning?' will remain a philosophical one, even if the methods include those associated with formal semantics, neuroscience of language, or corpus linguistics. It seems safe to surmise that in theory construction, as well as in the understanding of empirical data in language sciences, argumentation will always play first fiddle.

Notes

1   On psychologism in the theory of meaning see also Travis (2006) and Jaszczolt (2008).
2   For an introduction to propositional attitude reports see e.g. Jaszczolt (2012).
3   Pace Recanati's (2004: 90) contextualism in which 'there is no level of meaning which is both (i) propositional (truth-evaluable) and (ii) minimalist, that is, unaffected by top-down factors.' But see below (Recanati 2012b) on the current understanding of these 'top-down factors': they seem to affect the meaning of the units (words) in the composition rather than the structure itself.
4   On situated speech see Mey (2007).
5   See also chapters 2, 24, 28, this volume.
6   See Jaszczolt (2002: 309–10) for references to some of these precursors.
7   See e.g. Jaszczolt 2002, Chapter 10.3 for a summary of post-Gricean principles and heuristics.

Further reading

Lepore and Smith (2006); Devitt and Hanley (2006); Ludlow (1997).

References

Allan, K. (2010) *The Western Classical Tradition in Linguistics*, 2nd edition. London: Equinox.
Austin, J.L. (1962) *How To Do Things with Words*. Oxford: Clarendon Press.
Bach, K. (2006) The excluded middle: Semantic minimalism without minimal propositions. *Philosophy and Phenomenological Research* 73: 435–42.
Borg, E. (2004) *Minimal Semantics*. Oxford: Clarendon Press.
Borg, E. (2012) *Pursuing Meaning*. Oxford: Oxford University Press.
Cappelen, H. and E. Lepore (2005) *Insensitive Semantics: A Defense of Semantic Minimalism and Speech Act Pluralism*. Oxford: Blackwell.
Chalmers, D. (2015) Why isn't there more progress in philosophy? *Philosophy* 90: 3–31.
Davidson, D. (1984) *Inquiries into Truth and Interpretation*. Oxford: Clarendon Press.
Devitt, M. and R. Hanley (eds) (2006) *The Blackwell Guide to the Philosophy of Language*. Oxford: Blackwell.
Donnellan, K.S. (1966) Reference and definite descriptions. *Philosophical Review* 75: 281–304.

Frege, G. (1879) Begriffsschrift, eine der arithmetischen nachgebildete Formelsprache des reinen Denkens. Halle: L. Nebert. Transl. as 'Conceptual notation: A formula language of pure thought modelled upon the formula language of arithmetic' by T.W. Bynum in *Conceptual Notation and Related Articles*, 1972, pp. 101–203. Oxford: Oxford University Press.

Frege, G. (1884) *Die Grundlagen der Arithmetik, eine logisch mathematische Untersuchung über den Begriff der Zahl*. Breslau: W. Koebner. 'Introduction' transl. by M. Beaney in *The Frege Reader*, 1997, pp. 84–91. Oxford: Blackwell.

Frege, G. (1892) Über Sinn und Bedeutung. *Zeitschrift für Philosophie und Philosophische Kritik* 100: 25–50. Transl. as 'On sense and reference' in P.T. Geach and M. Black (eds) *Translations from the Philosophical Writings of Gottlob Frege*, 1960, pp. 56–78. Oxford: B. Blackwell.

Frege, G. (1893) *Grundgesetze der Arithmetik*. Vol. 1. Preface. Jena: H. Pohle. Transl. by M. Beaney in *The Frege Reader*, 1997, pp. 194–208. Oxford: Blackwell.

Frege, G. (1897) Logic. In H. Hermes, F. Kambartel and F. Kaulbach (eds) *Nachgelassene Schriften*, 1969, pp. 139–61. Hamburg: Felix Meiner Verlag. Transl. by M. Beaney in *The Frege Reader*, 1997, pp. 227–50. Oxford: Blackwell.

Grice, H.P. (1957) Meaning. *Philosophical Review* 66: 377–88. Reprinted in H.P. Grice *Studies in the Way of Words*, 1989, pp. 213–23. Cambridge: Harvard University Press.

Grice, H.P. (1975) Logic and conversation. In P. Cole and J.L. Morgan (eds) *Syntax and Semantics*. Vol. 3, pp. 41–58. New York: Academic Press. Reprinted in H.P. Grice. 1989. *Studies in the Way of Words*, 1989, pp. 22–40. Cambridge: Harvard University Press.

Groenendijk, J. and M. Stokhof (1991) Dynamic Predicate Logic. *Linguistics and Philosophy* 14: 39–100.

Harris, R. and T.J. Taylor (1989) *Landmarks in Linguistic Thought: The Western Tradition from Socrates to Saussure*. London: Routledge.

Jaszczolt, K.M. (2002) *Semantics and Pragmatics: Meaning in Language and Discourse*. London: Longman.

Jaszczolt, K.M. (2005) *Default Semantics: Foundations of a Compositional Theory of Acts of Communication*. Oxford: Oxford University Press.

Jaszczolt, K.M. (2008) Psychological explanations in Gricean pragmatics and Frege's legacy. In I. Kecskes and J. Mey (eds) *Intentions, Common Ground, and Egocentric Speaker-Hearer*, pp. 9–44. Berlin: Mouton de Gruyter.

Jaszczolt, K.M. (2012) Semantics/pragmatics boundary disputes. In C. Maienborn, K. von Heusinger and P. Portner (eds) *Semantics. An International Handbook of Natural Language Meaning. Vol. 3*, pp. 2333–60. Berlin: Mouton de Gruyter.

Kamp, H. (1984) A theory of truth and semantic representation. In J. Groenendijk, T.M.V. Janssen and M. Stokhof (eds) *Truth, Interpretation and Information: Selected Papers from the Third Amsterdam Colloquium*, pp. 1–41. Dordrecht: FORIS.

Kamp, H. and U. Reyle (1993) *From Discourse to Logic: Introduction to Modeltheoretic Semantics of Natural Language, Formal Logic and Discourse Representation Theory*. Dordrecht: Kluwer.

Kaplan, D. (1989) Demonstratives: An essay on the semantics, logic, metaphysics, and epistemology of demonstratives and other indexicals. In J. Almog, J. Perry and H. Wettstein (eds) *Themes from Kaplan*, pp. 481–563. New York: Oxford University Press.

Law, V. (2003) *The History of Linguistics in Europe from Plato to 1600*. Cambridge: Cambridge University Press.

Lepore, E. and B.C. Smith (eds) (2006) *The Oxford Handbook of Philosophy of Language*. Oxford: Clarendon Press.

Levinson, S.C. (2003) *Space in Language and Cognition*. Cambridge: Cambridge University Press.

Ludlow, P. (ed.) (1997) *Readings in the Philosophy of Language*. Cambridge: MIT Press.

Ludlow, P. (2011) *The Philosophy of Generative Linguistics*. Oxford: Oxford University Press.

Mey, J.L. (2007) Developing pragmatics interculturally. In I. Kecskes and L.R. Horn (eds) *Explorations in Pragmatics*, pp. 165–89. Berlin: Mouton de Gruyter.

Montague, R. (1974) *Formal Philosophy. Selected Papers by Richard Montague*, ed. R.H. Thomason. New Haven: Yale University Press.
Neale, S. (1990) *Descriptions*. Cambridge: MIT Press.
Partee, B.H. (2004) *Compositionality in Formal Semantics*. Oxford: Blackwell.
Quine, W.V.O. (1956) Quantifiers and propositional attitudes. *Journal of Philosophy* 53: 177–87.
Recanati, F. (2002) Unarticulated constituents. *Linguistics and Philosophy* 25: 299–345.
Recanati, F. (2004) *Literal Meaning*. Cambridge: Cambridge University Press.
Recanati, F. (2010) *Truth-Conditional Pragmatics*. Oxford: Clarendon Press.
Recanati, F. (2012a) Contextualism: Some varieties. In K. Allan and K.M. Jaszczolt (eds) *The Cambridge Handbook of Pragmatics*, pp. 135–49. Cambridge: Cambridge University Press.
Recanati, F. (2012b) Compositionality, flexibility, and context dependence. In M. Werning, W. Hinzen and E. Machery (eds) *The Oxford Handbook of Compositionality*, pp. 175–91. Oxford: Oxford University Press.
Russell, B. (1905) On denoting. *Mind* 14: 479–493.
Russell, B. (1919) Descriptions. From: *Introduction to Mathematical Philosophy*, pp. 167–80. London: Allen & Unwin. Reprinted in A.P. Martinich (ed.) *The Philosophy of Language*, 2nd edition, 1990, pp. 213–19. Oxford: Oxford University Press.
Saul, J.M. (2012) *Lying, Misleading, and What Is Said: An Exploration in Philosophy of Language and in Ethics*. Oxford: Oxford University Press.
Schiffer, S. (1992) Belief ascription. *Journal of Philosophy* 89: 499–521.
Scholz, B.C. (2011) Philosophy of linguistics. In E.N. Zalta (ed.) *Stanford Encyclopedia of Philosophy*. http://plato.stanford.edu/entries/linguistics.
Searle, J. (1969) *Speech Acts: An Essay in the Philosophy of Language*. Cambridge: Cambridge University Press.
Searle, J. (1980) The background of meaning. In J. Searle, F. Kiefer and M. Bierwisch (eds) *Speech Act Theory and Pragmatics*, pp. 221–32. Dordrecht: Reidel.
Searle, J. (1983) *Intentionality. An Essay in the Philosophy of Mind*. Cambridge: Cambridge University Press.
Searle, J. and D. Vanderveken (1985) *Foundations of Illocutionary Logic*. Cambridge: Cambridge University Press.
Sperber, D. and D. Wilson (1986) *Relevance: Communication and Cognition*. Oxford: Blackwell. 2nd edition, 1995.
Stanley, J. and Z.G. Szabó (2000) On quantifier domain restriction. *Mind and Language* 15: 219–61.
Travis, C. (2006) Psychologism. In E. Lepore and B.C. Smith (eds) *The Oxford Handbook of Philosophy of Language*, pp. 103–26. Oxford: Clarendon Press.
Vanderveken, D. (1990) On the unification of Speech Act Theory and formal semantics. In P.R. Cohen, J. Morgan and M.E. Pollack (eds) *Intentions in Communication*, pp. 195–220. Cambridge, MA: MIT Press.
Wittgenstein, L. (1953) *Philosophical Investigations*. Transl. by G.E.M. Anscombe. Oxford: B. Blackwell.

34
Linguistics and the law

Kate Haworth

34.1 Introduction

From Magna Carta to a marriage certificate, few texts are as influential over our daily lives as those generated by the legal world. By the same token, as highlighted by Tiersma, there are few institutions which operate so completely through the medium of language. 'Our law is a law of words... Morality or custom may be embedded in human behavior, but law – virtually by definition – comes into being through language... Few professions are as dependent upon language' (Tiersma 1999: 1). The relationship between language and law is thus an intrinsic and important one.

Although 'applied linguistics' originally tended to refer only to applications relating to language learning, it increasingly involves applying the theories and findings of linguistic research to far more diverse areas, such as medicine, business, the media and many others. Given both the significant role of language and the enormously high stakes involved, legal contexts offer the linguist considerable opportunity for truly meaningful 'real world' applications for their research. Yet the challenges involved in gaining access to and conducting research on what is often extremely sensitive and well-protected personal data mean that this is an area of applied linguistics which has yet to reach the peak of its potential.

Readers may already be familiar with the term 'forensic linguistics'. Linguists take great interest in the labels used to define concepts; lawyers like nothing more than arguing over definitions and scope. It is therefore no surprise that there is no firm agreement as to what 'forensic linguistics' actually covers. The term is used in a general sense to refer to any interface between language and law, thus including analysis of the language used within the legal system; the more widely accepted, and arguably more accurate, meaning is the use of linguistic evidence in the judicial process, usually in the form of expert evidence from a linguist. Definitions aside, this brings out a useful distinction between the two main strands of the academic field of language and law: analysis (and usually critique) of the language of the legal process, and linguists as part of the legal process. This chapter is organised under those two broad banners, although inevitably there are areas of overlap. It should also be mentioned that there is a related, thriving, field of forensic phonetics, but this falls beyond the scope of this chapter.

Linguistics and the law

In keeping with the field's 'applied' agenda, the work described in this chapter has no unifying methodology; much of the research has adopted the 'toolkit' approach of utilising the analytic approach – or combination of approaches – which is best suited to producing specific, 'real world' answers to perceived problems or challenges. However, that is not to say that there is not a keen interest in developing and maintaining methodological rigour; indeed this is a key site of activity in forensic linguistics in order to ensure that any linguistic evidence provided is of the utmost validity and reliability, not least so that it will meet the increasingly stringent tests being applied to the admissibility of expert witness evidence in court.

One unifying factor, however, is that much of the work in forensic linguistics has taken a critical stance, seeking to highlight instances of disadvantage and injustice. This has taken many forms, from revealing miscarriages of justice where police officers had falsified written documents used to support a prosecution (e.g. the Bentley case, reported in Coulthard 2002), to demonstrating the comprehension challenges of texts such as warning labels and jury instructions. An area which is gaining increasing prominence is critiquing current practice in using language analysis to determine national origin (LADO), especially in immigration and asylum contexts. It is worth emphasising that the intention behind the vast majority of research in this field is to inform and enhance current practice, by engaging with (rather than simply directing external criticism at) practitioners.

The majority of published research to date has focused on the legal systems of the UK, USA and Australia, but is by no means limited to these jurisdictions. Research is being conducted in many other countries all over the world, and although there is as yet little in the way of systematic comparative analysis, it seems clear that the intrinsic link between language and law, and the tensions and communicative challenges which arise, are universal.

34.2 The language of the legal process

This section describes the key areas of interest for those studying the language used by and within the legal system. It is not an exhaustive list, and it only provides a brief overview of each topic, but hopefully this will serve to illustrate the many ways in which linguistic analysis can explicate and inform the legal processes and frameworks that govern our lives.

34.2.1 Legal language

Legal language permeates our lives, even if we are often blissfully unaware of this. Written legal texts of one sort or another in fact govern virtually everything we do. To take an average day, it might begin with the sound of your alarm clock going off. The power which supplies your alarm clock comes from an energy company, with whom you will have entered into a written contract governing the terms of the supply. Despite our day-to-day reliance on the company upholding its end of this contract, you probably have not given its existence any thought, especially not at this time in the morning. But the alarm has gone off because you have to get up. This may be because you are employed, in which case you will have signed a contract which determines that you have a duty to work today. Or perhaps you are a student (in which case the alarm is probably set a little later). You will be bound by a contract with your educational institution, which is likely to enable it to impose penalties if you do not fulfil certain requirements, such as attendance. These obligations interfere with our overwhelming desire to stay in bed longer, and so perhaps we need to set up our alarm to be extremely loud. However, depending on where you live you may well be in breach of local bye-laws, or even legislation, governing noise nuisance. As our morning continues we might glance at the warning label on the back of the bottle whilst we rely on our contract with the water company to keep the supply running long enough to rinse the shampoo out, take a chance on the fact that our peanut butter 'may contain nuts', travel by public transport having agreed (through the act of buying a ticket) to abide by the terms and conditions, and listen to music or read a book protected by a copyright notice (like this one – have a look!).

If we collected together all these texts, there are likely to be a number of similarities in the language used. Linguists (e.g. Crystal and Davy 1969; Tiersma 1999) have identified a number of features of what can be described as 'legal language', which make it distinct enough to be recognisable as a specific 'genre' (see Chapter 15). These include a very formal register, with a lack of evaluative and emotive language; specific lexis or 'jargon', such as 'reasonable grounds'; archaisms such as 'aforementioned', 'hereinbefore'; the use of the present and deontic modality (that looks like future tense), e.g. 'this book is sold', 'the replaced Product shall be warranted'; precision, such as 'ninety (90) days', and the inclusion of definition sections; binomial and multinomial expressions, e.g. 'unauthorised or fraudulent use'; syntactic complexity and density, such as heavily embedded clause structure and unusual word order, e.g. 'all rights of the producer and the owner of the work reproduced reserved'; and orthographic features such as the use of capitalisation, and numbered sections and subsections. Not all legal texts will contain all of these features, but the more that occur, the more the text will resemble 'legalese' and the more typical it will be of the genre.

It will be immediately obvious that these features are not reader-friendly; indeed they largely interfere with, rather than aid, comprehension, and it is easy to criticise texts of this type from a linguistic perspective.[1] Such obscure and complex language designed and perpetuated within one profession has led to accusations of exclusivity and even deliberate obfuscation in order to create a demand for the services of a lawyer. Although this is unlikely, there is no doubt that legal language, like other in-group discourse within specific communities of practice (see Chapter 17), serves to mark users as members of a particular elite group, inaccessible to the uninitiated.

However, there are other, more cogent, explanations for the features of this genre. It is, as always, essential to take into account the context and function of the texts. As Crystal and Davy note of legal language, '[o]f all uses of language it is perhaps the least communicative, in that it is designed not so much to enlighten language-users at large as to allow one expert to register information for scrutiny by another' (1969: 193–4). In other words, we as parties are not necessarily the intended audience for the texts that bind us; instead they are written for fellow members of the legal establishment, especially the courts whose interpretation would be called upon in the event of any dispute. The purpose of all such texts is to create a specific state of affairs, according with all applicable legal principles, and it must achieve that without any room for ambiguity, omission or misinterpretation. It thus cannot be like 'ordinary' day-to-day language, which is known to rely on inference, elision and indirectness (Chapter 13). It often prefers not to risk even the inferential step contained within a pronoun, even when the intended referent would seem obvious, since this still potentially opens up an opportunity to argue for a different interpretation. This illustrates the tension between accuracy and accessibility which lies at the heart of legal language. For any legally binding text, certainty is essential. Legal texts involve the imposition of obligations and the conferment of rights; they are therefore constantly under attack from those seeking to avoid their responsibilities or abuse the rights of others. The language of the text carries the important responsibility of removing (as far as possible) the opportunities to do so.

Many legal texts, then, are designed to communicate a specific message to other legal professionals, and therefore to be understood and interpreted within that professional context. It is in that sense perhaps most accurately viewed as a type of technical language. UK primary legislation is drafted with the aid of specialist software which is also utilised in the construction of aircraft maintenance manuals. To use that analogy, when we board an aeroplane, we do not expect to be able to understand the maintenance manual; what matters to us is that it made sense to the maintenance engineer and so the wings are not going to drop off. Legislative text ought perhaps to be viewed in the same light.

Although that argument may hold for legislation, it cannot be maintained across all types (or subgenres) of legal language. For many legal texts the need for comprehensibility should be given far more weight than is currently the case. This is particularly the case for texts whose purpose is primarily to communicate with a lay audience, such as, for example, the instructions given to jurors on how to reach their verdict (e.g. Heffer 2008) or product warnings (e.g. Dumas 2010). Many such texts have been demonstrated by linguists to perform inadequately in terms of communicating their message to the intended audience, often with serious consequences. For example, Dumas describes a US case in which experts, called in to analyse the adequacy of jury instructions given in a death penalty case, concluded that 'the death sentence was imposed by jurors who did not understand their instructions' (2002: 254). Despite the intended audience and purpose of these text types, they have frequently been found to contain highly confusing features such as complex embedded clause structure, archaisms and unexplained jargon. It seems that the producers of all types of legal text have a tendency to draw on the conventions of the genre, even when there is little justification for so doing.

34.2.2 The language of the judicial process

Thus far we have dealt only with written text. A significant proportion of legal text is actually produced orally, typically through direct interaction between members of the lay public and the legal system. In fact in Common Law jurisdictions such as the USA, UK and Australia, most of the judicial process, through which the written legal texts discussed above are enforced and upheld, is enacted through spoken discourse. This gives rise to a different type of linguistic analysis, although the themes of miscommunication and disadvantage remain prevalent.

The legal system is an institution with its own unique organisational practices and communicative norms. When members of the lay public need to communicate with this institution, interactional trouble often ensues. The tension has been usefully explicated through the application of Bruner's concept of paradigmatic (typically legal), versus narrative (typically lay) modes of reasoning, especially in the work of Heffer (e.g. 2005). The idea that the legal system operates on the basis of a different conceptualisation of what is important or relevant in a telling, and of the most logical expected order of the component parts, is an important one, which goes a long way towards explaining why communication between a legal institution and members of the general public is often less than straightforward. The difficulty for the lay individual is that it is the other party who gets to determine and even enforce the interactional 'rules', and they also frequently have significant power over the outcome of the interaction.

34.2.2.1 Initial encounters
The tensions just outlined are played out in the microcosm of a call to the emergency services. These are typically very short texts, but a great deal is accomplished through them. They are thus ideally suited to the micro-approach of Conversation Analysis (see e.g.

Zimmerman 1992), although by no means exclusively. Emergency calls to the police (911 in the USA, 999 in the UK, and so on) often represent the first moment of institutional involvement, where an occurrence of some sort becomes transformed into an institutionally recognised and actionable 'incident'. Not every event reported to the police will be actionable, however: one of the most important functions of emergency call-takers is to act as gatekeepers, determining which calls merit a police response and which do not. The dividing line depends on numerous legal factors such as the limits of police powers, and whether the event described involves criminal activity as opposed to being a civil matter. The point at which this line is drawn will be known to those within the institution, but will not always be obvious to the lay caller. This can lead to a clash between lay expectations and the reality of the process, and emergency calls represent the site of that clash. They therefore not only make for fascinating linguistic data, but also represent an area of operational practice which could benefit immensely from the insights of linguistic research, which has examined features such as overall structure, opening turns of both callers and call-takers, strategies for aligning the caller with the institutional task in hand (Zimmerman 1992), and the particular complexities of calls about domestic disputes (Tracy and Agne 2002).

Another preliminary context which represents a common site of interactional difficulty, at least for the lay participant, is in the communication of rights. Several linguistic studies have highlighted the potential injustice caused by the interactional strategies and interpretive norms utilised by representatives of the legal process in situations where an individual may wish to invoke a particular legal right. This includes the invocation of the right to a legal representative for a police interview in the USA, where the legal process apparently expects a person in a massively disadvantageous position to abandon all communicative norms of indirectness, politeness and power relations, and to make their request for a lawyer in only the most literal and imposing manner. Thus utterances such as 'I think I would like to talk to a lawyer', and 'maybe I should talk to a lawyer' have been held by US courts not to be sufficiently clear to amount to an invocation of that right (see Solan and Tiersma 2005: 54–62 for an accessible discussion). However, Solan and Tiersma (2005: 62) points out that the same legal system shows itself to be entirely capable of determining the inferred meaning of far more ambiguous requests made by police officers who would otherwise be held to have carried out illegal searches.

Another notable example is the delivery of the caution in the UK, which is intended to advise detainees of essential information about their rights and obligations relating to their questioning. A standard text must be performed by the interviewer at the start of every police interview with a suspect, but several linguistic studies have demonstrated the communicative challenges created by the language standardly used (e.g. Cotterill 2000; Rock 2007). The caution is a classic example of a text whose function is to convey a complex legal provision to a lay audience; an intrinsically challenging task. Nevertheless, the application of linguistic research can once again assist in improving current practice.

34.2.2.2 Police interviews

One of the most significant sites of spoken interaction in the legal process is the police interview. A vital part of any criminal investigation is the interviewing of both witnesses and suspects in order to gain as much information as possible about the event(s) in question. These first-hand accounts will be key evidence for the investigation, and for any subsequent prosecution.

To focus on suspect interviews, the functions, formats and processes of police–suspect interview discourse make it a highly unusual, and linguistically fascinating, discourse context. There is international variance as to the conduct and format of the interview, for example UK suspect interviews are mandatorily audio-recorded and then transcribed in Q&A format, whereas in much of continental Europe the interview is aimed at producing a written summary of the interaction, authored by the police interviewer but sometimes reproduced as an interviewee's first-person monologue. These different institutional purposes and processes produce different types of discourse: for example, the interviewer's synchronous typing of a written statement has been shown to directly affect turn-taking in Dutch interviews (Charldorp 2013); whereas in the UK, interview talk must simultaneously be addressed to both those present in the interview room, and the future audiences for the audio recording, a discursively challenging task to manage (Haworth 2013).

Whatever the process of production, the interview record will be an important piece of evidence, which is treated by the criminal justice process as resulting from providing the interviewee with an open opportunity to put forward their side of the story. Yet any linguist will recognise this not to be the case. Alongside the editing and changes which inevitably take place through the recording processes just mentioned, there are many discursive factors which will also affect the interviewee's words in the interview itself. Police interview participants are by no means equally matched: aside from the very real power that a police interviewer has over the interviewee, the discursive role of questioner itself grants the interviewer power over the topic, sequencing and overall structure of the interview (see e.g. Heydon 2005). Other linguistic features, available to an interviewer but not an interviewee, have also been identified as problematic, such as formulations and restrictive question types. The interviewee's discursive position as responder thus inevitably restricts what they will get to say, despite this being ostensibly the main interactional purpose.

This begs the question as to why a question–answer format is employed; however there are good reasons for an interviewer, who has the task of investigating an alleged crime according to a strict framework of procedural regulations and prosecution requirements, being enabled to keep the discourse legally relevant and institutionally appropriate. It is also essential that a suspect's account is challenged and probed. The discursive challenge lies in balancing this with providing the suspect with a fair chance to speak in their own terms. The linguistic research thus far indicates that the very nature of the discourse means that this is frequently not achieved.

34.2.2.3 Courtroom language

If the police interview represents a challenging context for the lay participant, this is even more true of the courtroom. In all jurisdictions, courtrooms represent the most significant stage of the judicial process, and in Common Law adversarial systems they are also the most dramatic – both in the sense of being the culmination of the process, and of involving a large element of performance and display.[2] Cases must be decided solely on the basis of evidence presented orally in the courtroom (even physical exhibits must be introduced with an oral statement), and consequently mastery of the language is often as important to courtroom advocates as mastery of the relevant law. Lay participants, of course, do not benefit from any professional experience or training when put in the position of speaking in court; yet again we see that they are placed at the disadvantage of a highly restrictive and unfamiliar discursive environment, governed by legal rules which are largely unknown to them.

The significance of linguistic resources in the courtroom is well recognised, as reflected in numerous provisions which directly relate to language features, even if they are not expressed in such terms. Turn-taking and turn distribution are almost entirely pre-allocated, from the 'micro' sense of individual turns between lawyer and witness being restricted to question and answer, to the broader structure of the order in which each side gets to present its case, to question witnesses and to make speeches. This rigid, and rigorously enforced, structure ensures an equal distribution of speaker rights between prosecution and defence, as well as ensuring that the last word always rests with the defence. The professional right to speak in a courtroom is itself closely protected: lawyers must earn 'rights of audience' through achieving specialist qualifications, and in some countries the type of qualification determines which level of court they may speak in.[3] There are also rules about the type of questions which can be asked at each point: when questioning their own witness, lawyers are generally not permitted to use 'leading' questions, for fear of interfering with the witness's own evidence.

When it comes to lay participants, witnesses cannot simply give their evidence; they are restricted solely to answering the questions put to them by lawyers for each side, and this is enforced considerably more strictly than in a police interview. The defendant cannot speak in response to anything said by a witness against them; instead they must rely on their lawyer to speak for them, only through the format of asking questions, until eventually it becomes their turn to be questioned. It is difficult to imagine a communicative context which less resembles our everyday experience. Yet the tight control held over the discourse is intended to ensure fairness and adherence to legal principles, even if it results in a bewildering and frustrating experience for lay participants.

Analyses of courtroom language have highlighted the various linguistic strategies utilised by courtroom advocates in order to achieve their goals. Adversarial trials ideally require the creation of a coherent and persuasive narrative, into which all the evidence fits (or at least does not contradict). It is for this reason that lawyers attach so much importance to attempting to direct and restrict the evidence given by each witness, both for their own side and the other's. Their only resource for so doing is the questions they ask. The power of a question to shape the answer given has long been recognised, and this is turned into something of an art form in court, with every aspect from pauses to terms of address and lexical choice exploited for persuasive effect.

Although controlling the evidence produced in the questioning phase is challenging and unpredictable for advocates, they have the opportunity to present a much more structured and rehearsed version of events in their monologic opening and closing statements. These lend themselves well to narrative analysis (see e.g. Heffer 2005), and also to detailed analysis of the subtle linguistic features utilised by advocates to influence the judge and/or jury's perception of events. For example, Cotterill (2003) demonstrates the power of lexical choice in the speeches of the O.J. Simpson trial in the USA, analysing the semantic prosody of seemingly innocuous terms such as 'encounter' (pp. 65ff.). As she points out, '[t]hrough skilful exploitation of different layers of lexical meaning, it is possible for lawyers to communicate subtle and partisan information about victims and alleged perpetrators, without falling foul of the rules of evidence' (p. 67). The courtroom, then, represents an important site where the interests of lawyers and linguists coincide, albeit coming from very different directions.

34.2.2.4 Language and disadvantage

It is apparent that the language of the legal process presents particular communicative challenges to those outside the system, which necessarily includes the very citizens it is designed to protect. Thus far, however, we have assumed that the lay participant has a 'standard' level of communicative competence. Yet for a significant proportion of those who find themselves involved in legal processes, there are additional factors which render the

Linguistics and the law

communicative process even more problematic. These are often those who in fact most need the protection of the legal system, such as children, speakers of other first languages and victims of sexual crime. Extra protections are increasingly on offer to assist those who can be officially classed as 'vulnerable', such as the provision of interpreters, the use of specially trained interviewers, and the use of video recordings or screens when giving evidence to the court. Yet there is plenty of scope for further improvement, and there is a wealth of linguistic knowledge which can assist. Increasing police interviewers' understanding of the role of an interpreter can significantly improve their effectiveness in interviews, for example. And Eades' work on the cross-cultural communicative challenges faced by Aboriginals in the Australian legal system (e.g. Eades 2008) has highlighted specific culturally dependent features such as 'gratuitous concurrence' and the use of silence which are particularly likely to lead to misunderstanding and injustice. Eades raises a serious concern for the linguist, however: the danger that by increasing awareness of potential linguistic vulnerabilities, we simply provide the cross-examining lawyer with an extra weapon to use against a witness. This is, of course, not a reason not to engage with the legal process: if we have any inclination to be 'applied' or 'critical' in our linguistic research, and to oppose injustice, then what better site of engagement is there than the justice process itself?

34.3 Language as evidence

We now move to a separate and distinct area of linguistics and the law. There are many ways in which language itself becomes evidence, both in civil disputes and in criminal proceedings. When this occurs, linguists are increasingly being called on as experts to assist with the investigative and judicial process. This section outlines some of the key areas where the discipline of linguistics has been utilised as part of the legal process, as opposed to being used as a tool for analysing it. Before going into the areas in which linguists have provided evidence, we will begin by considering the role of a linguist acting as an expert witness. Since the vast majority of expert linguistic evidence to date has been in Common Law jurisdictions (mainly the UK and USA), this section will concentrate on the position in these countries, however the general principles are likely to be similar elsewhere.

34.3.1 The linguist as expert witness

Put simply, the task of a court is to decide between competing versions of events, on the basis of the evidence presented to it. The court can only base its decision on what is presented to it in court; there are consequently detailed and complex rules governing admissibility. The general principle is that only evidence of 'fact' is admissible; a person's 'opinion' is not: the only opinion which counts is the court's, and no witness should usurp that function. However, sometimes the court will need help in interpreting the 'facts' presented to it, for example technical engineering data about a ship which sank, or complex medical information. In order to assist with this, an expert can be called. Their task is to apply their expertise to the facts which are being presented, and to provide the court with their opinion on them. This therefore breaks the fundamental rule about the inadmissibility of opinion evidence. Consequently, a huge body of case law and procedural rules has developed around expert evidence, in order to police the boundaries of its admissibility. There is no need here to go into the complexities of the relevant principles, but it is worth highlighting that one of the main criteria will be whether the expert can provide 'information which is likely to be outside the experience and knowledge of a judge or jury' (*R v Turner*,[4] a UK criminal case).

The challenge for linguistics, then, is to convince courts that our discipline can offer scientific analysis and insight that goes beyond the knowledge that judges, as gatekeepers, think they already have about the language they use every day. In addition, courts will assess the validity and reliability of the methodology used, applying criteria such as whether there are known error rates.[5] A further concern, then, is developing methodologies and analytic frameworks which are robust and valid. This is, of course, essential given the use to which such analyses will be put and the hugely significant consequences for those directly involved. It also means that the field of forensic linguistics is increasingly at the forefront of developing reliable and innovative methodologies, especially for the analysis of short texts such as text messages. Thus this most 'applied' of linguistic fields has the potential to make major theoretical contributions.

It must also be noted that of the cases in which the advice of a linguistic expert is sought, a majority never reach court. They may be settled at an earlier stage, or a prosecution might be dropped, or a guilty plea might be entered. Nevertheless, the linguistic evidence may well have played a role in that outcome.

34.3.2 Authorship analysis

Probably the most well-known type of linguistic evidence is authorship analysis. There are many situations in which authorship of a text may become legally relevant: threatening letters; terrorist manuals; ransom notes; text messages sent by one person pretending to be another. The linguist's task is to provide analysis which is directed towards establishing the likely author of the disputed text. That statement is deliberately hedged: it is not, and never will be, possible to identify a specific individual simply from a sample of their language use; any individual's linguistic repertoire is too variable and vast for a 'linguistic fingerprint' to exist. Instead, a linguist will take the disputed text(s), and compile a referential sample of (preferably similar) texts produced by a potential author for comparison. The key to authorship analysis is in finding features which are distinctive within a known author's data, and which can therefore be used as identifying markers, and then in revealing patterns of consistency between a known author and the disputed texts. This is a challenging enough task in itself, but it is often made more difficult by the small size of the disputed data sample. On the other hand, there is often only a limited number of potential suspects. The question that a linguist will be trying to answer, then, is which of these is most likely to be the author of the disputed text. A related question is whether a text or group of texts has been written by the same author. This was the issue in what is widely regarded as the first case of forensic linguistics, that of Timothy Evans (Svartvik 1968). Evans was convicted of murder and hanged in 1950. However, subsequent evidence cast considerable doubt over his guilt. Many years later, the linguist Jan Svartvik noticed inconsistencies in the language of a statement supposedly made by Evans, and further analysis revealed that the parts which contained incriminating material were of a different style to the rest. This indicated that the statement was not the work of one author; indeed particular stylistic features suggested that the incriminating parts were in fact inserted by the police. Svartvik's analysis published in 1968 highlighted the potential contribution that linguistics could make in such cases, and is thought to contain the first use of the term 'forensic linguistics', thus staking a claim as the origin of the field.

Forensic authorship analysis has moved on considerably since then and is now utilised as part of both prosecution and defence evidence – as opposed to simply academic studies like Svartvik's. Recent examples include terrorism offences where linguistic analysis was requested to determine whether a suspect was likely to have written certain documents found at his house which related to a terrorist plot. There is a significant legal difference between merely having a copy of such a text and being responsible for its production, and so establishing a link between these documents and texts known to have been sent by the suspect is a vital part of the investigation. Other cases include murder trials where no body has been found, and text messages have continued to be sent from the victim's phone after their disappearance. It is notoriously difficult to secure a conviction in such circumstances, but linguistic analysis has been able to establish that those texts were more likely to have been sent by the main suspect than the victim, providing compelling supporting evidence at trial.

Modern modes of communication such as text messages and instant messaging present methodological challenges to the analyst, not least due to their tendency to be very short. However, these innovative, fluctuating data types also produce more idiosyncratic features, since the rules and conventions are not yet settled. There is therefore room for wider interpersonal variation, making it easier to find features which are distinctive within one writer's style. Nevertheless, this is an area where methodological concerns are at the forefront of current thinking (see e.g. Grant 2010).

34.3.3 Determination of meaning

Another key area in which the expertise of a linguist is sought is in the determination of meaning. This can take many forms, for example whether the language used by an individual amounts to a criminal offence, whether the interpretation provided of a police interview is an acceptable representation of the original, whether a product warning is adequate, or whether the wording of an agreement can really cover what a party claims for it. This can often be a challenging task, where legal expectation and linguistic knowledge clash. The legal system demands certainty, but linguists are well aware that communication is rarely explicit or unambiguous, and meaning is heavily context-dependent. There are therefore many ways in which linguistics can inform and improve courts' decision-making in these areas.

34.3.4 Language crimes

An area where it is often necessary to determine the meaning of an utterance is in the various criminal offences in which language forms the substantive act (known legally as the *actus reus*). These include crimes such as bribery, conspiracy and blackmail. Alongside a specific act (e.g. the offering of money), most criminal offences also necessitate establishing the thinking behind the act (*mens rea*). Speaker intention therefore becomes both legally and linguistically relevant. The difficulty is that even at the best of times we rarely state our purpose directly; instead we tend to convey our meaning through inference and indirectness, rather than by explicit statement. This is even more so when there might be a reason to disguise our intentions, such as the fact that they amount to a crime. These factors make it very challenging to prove that a person's words had one particular meaning, which is effectively what a court is trying to do in these cases.

Often the difference between whether an utterance amounts to a language crime or not comes down to the type of speech act involved. For example, if a person says to someone at the top of a flight of steps 'be careful, if you slip you'll hurt yourself', this might be a threat, but could equally plausibly be a warning or a prediction. However, if the steps are outside a courtroom and the addressee is a witness about to give evidence against the speaker's brother, it is more likely to have been taken, and indeed intended, as a threat. The difficulty for the courts, then, is that the distinction between these speech acts lies not in the literal words used but in the underlying implication generated in the specific context of utterance. To put this in linguistic terms, the part of the utterance which is criminally actionable is the perlocutionary intent, not the illocutionary act, yet this is never likely to be made explicit. So how far can the courts go from the actual words used when convicting someone of a crime? How much inference is legally acceptable? A court needs to be sure of the intended meaning if it is to convict the speaker on the strength of it. Equally, it cannot be right for those guilty of a serious offence to be able to take advantage of ordinary principles of communication in order to escape justice.

The other side of the coin is that, just as people rarely use literal statement to commit a language crime, when people do use words which literally amount to a crime they are highly unlikely to mean it. Consider, for example, how commonly verbs such as 'kill' are used in a metaphorical sense, to mean anything from switching off a light to reprimanding someone (e.g. 'I'm going to kill him when I see him'). Such metaphorical usage is often colloquial, and can vary between sociolinguistic communities. Even if we are not part of that speech community, it would seem obvious that the speaker's meaning is not in fact to commit a serious crime, but both historical and recent examples illustrate the preference for law enforcers to ignore pragmatics and sociolinguistic variation and rely instead on a literal, 'legalistic' approach to interpretation of meaning. Thus an African American minister who said in a sermon 'we will kill Richard Nixon' found himself charged with threatening the president (Solan and Tiersma 2005: 207), and in 2012 an English tourist who, eagerly looking forward to an upcoming holiday, commented on Twitter that he was going to 'destroy America', was refused entry to the USA.[6] Although such cases seem to fly in the face of common sense, let alone linguistic research, their existence points to a genuine conflict.

The legal system necessarily requires certainty in enforcing the line between criminal acts and non-actionable behaviour; it also has a tendency to decontextualise and examine evidence as if it existed independently from the context which gave rise to it. It is also used to applying principles of interpretation to legal texts which do rely on literal statement as the norm. But legal language is an atypical genre, as we have already seen. And 'ordinary' language cannot be packaged up and re-presented in a courtroom as an isolated, context-free artefact for detached scrutiny, in the way that other forensic evidence can be. The processes through which humans derive meaning from language are far more complex and elusive than the linear, detached logic the legal system often seems to expect. The role that linguists can play in such cases, then, is in ensuring that when courts are faced with the challenge of interpreting meaning, they do so by applying the principles derived from linguistic research into everyday communication, rather than using literalistic methods which may feel more in keeping with legal principle.

34.3.5 Trademarks

Trademarks are another area of law where linguists have frequently been called on to provide evidence, especially in the USA. It is an obvious area of linguistic and legal interrelation: as Butters states, '[t]rademarks ... are proprietary language – bits of linguistic or semiotic material that people, corporations, and institutions in a very real but limited sense own' (2010: 352). The extent to which a person, or corporation, should be able to claim ownership over any part of our shared language is a thorny question, but equally it is a commercial necessity that providers of products or services can distinguish themselves through the use of marks or brands, and that any investment in that mark (in the form of time, money and marketing, for example) is protected – as far as legally appropriate. Disputes arise when one party considers that their trademark ownership is being infringed by another party who is attempting to use a mark which is too similar to their own. The response from the other party may be to argue that the marks are not sufficiently similar to give rise to any confusion between them; an alternative rebuttal is that the claimed trademark is too weak to merit legal protection. Both of these are areas where linguists can contribute.

With regard to similarity and confusion, the main areas in which linguists can assist are as to whether the marks sound the same, and whether they share meaning. As with other areas of forensic linguistics, these are aspects which a court may consider to be within their own understanding without the help of an expert, although the numerous cases in which linguists have successfully given evidence suggests otherwise. The type of analysis provided will depend on the case, but may draw on phonetics, lexicography, pragmatics and psycholinguistics, to name but a few, in order to assist the court to reach a reasoned and logical decision which goes beyond mere impression.

As to whether a particular mark is actually strong enough to merit protection, the law will not protect a mark which is merely generic or descriptive. For example, a court held that 'steakburger' could not be a trademark (see Butters 2010: 359–61). A real difficulty arises for companies who have been so successful that their brand name has become synonymous with the product or service in general. In the UK, for example, only a minority of my students recognise 'Hoover' to be a company name and not simply the verb for using a vacuum cleaner, and their number dwindles every year. Dictionaries only provide part of the picture of everyday language use, and so linguists can usefully be called on to provide evidence of language shift and dilution such as this. In the US Roger Shuy gave evidence in a case where McDonald's sought to prevent Quality Inns opening a chain of hotels called 'McSleep Inns'. Essentially, McDonald's wanted to claim the prefix 'Mc-' as their trademark, whereas Quality Inns' case was that it had become generic. Shuy looked to actual language use, and produced a corpus including 'McCinema', 'McBook', and 'McHospital', finding that it had come to have a general meaning of 'basic, convenient, inexpensive, and standardized' (2012: 459). However, McDonald's won the case: the judge found that the prefix had acquired 'secondary meaning' which had created such a strong association with this one company that consumers might assume that the hotels were part of the McDonald's group.

The outcome of this case may well make many linguists uncomfortable in that it purports to affect the ownership of language, but it must always be borne in mind that the courts in trademark cases, and all other cases involving language evidence, are not making judgements of linguistic issues, but legal ones. Linguistic evidence may play an important part in a case, but it must always sit alongside numerous other considerations.

34.4 Conclusion

Overall, then, there are many areas of common interest between law and linguistics, and this chapter has inevitably not covered all of them. There is also an obvious tension: law is about justice, and yet the legal system's use and interpretation of language has frequently been demonstrated by linguists to lead to the perpetuation – indeed creation – of injustice. It seems that this is often due to misunderstanding or ignorance of the principles of language and communication, rather than any deliberate intention. The onus is therefore on linguists to challenge those misunderstandings, to make the case for our involvement, and to demonstrate the need to bring our research into practice. Much of the work mentioned in this chapter is already making that contribution, but it is only a starting point. Hopefully this chapter will serve to encourage others to continue this aim.

Notes

1 However, it is often overlooked that for all the examples of obscure, impenetrable text there are also examples of the most powerful language performing remarkable feats through the simplest of speech acts: 'There shall be a Scottish parliament' (Scotland Act 1998); 'I pronounce you husband and wife'.
2 In Civil/Roman Law (inquisitorial) jurisdictions the courtroom trial is based mainly on the consideration of written documents, and as such has been subject to considerably less linguistic interest.
3 In England and Wales, for example, the right to speak in the Crown Court or higher is a badge of professional distinction between barristers (who automatically have that right) and solicitors (who do not).
4 *R v Turner* [1975] 2 WLR 56 (CA) p.60
5 Included in the criteria set out in the US case of *Daubert v. Merrell Dow Pharmaceuticals, Inc.* 509 U.S. 579 (1993).
6 'Caution on Twitter urged as tourists banned from US', BBC News, 31 January 2012, available at: www.bbc.co.uk/news/technology-16810312.

Further reading

Cotterill (2002); Coulthard and Johnson (2007, 2010); Solan and Tiersma (2005); Tiersma and Solan (2012).

References

Butters, R.R. (2010) Trademarks: Language that one owns. In M. Coulthard and A. Johnson (eds) *The Routledge Handbook of Forensic Linguistics*, pp. 351–64. Abingdon: Routledge.

Charldorp, C. van (2013) The intertwining of talk and technology: How talk and typing are combined in the various phases of the police interrogation. *Discourse and Communication* 7: 221–40.

Cotterill, J. (2000) Reading the rights: A cautionary tale of comprehension and comprehensibility. *Forensic Linguistics* 7: 4–25.

Cotterill, J. (ed.) (2002) *Language in the Legal Process*. Basingstoke: Palgrave.

Cotterill, J. (2003) *Language and Power in Court: A Linguistic Analysis of the O.J. Simpson Trial*. Basingstoke: Palgrave.

Coulthard, M. (2002) Whose voice is it? Invented and concealed dialogue in written records of verbal evidence produced by the police. In J. Cotterill (ed.) *Language in the Legal Process*, pp. 19–34. Basingstoke: Palgrave.

Coulthard, M. and A. Johnson (2007) *An Introduction to Forensic Linguistics: Language in Evidence*. Abingdon: Routledge.

Coulthard, M. and A. Johnson (eds) (2010) *The Routledge Handbook of Forensic Linguistics*. Abingdon: Routledge.

Crystal, D. and D. Davy (1969) The language of legal documents. In D. Crystal and D. Davy (eds) *Investigating English Style*, pp. 193–217. London: Longman.

Dumas, B.K. (2002) Reasonable doubt about reasonable doubt: Assessing jury instruction adequacy in a capital case. In J. Cotterill (ed.) *Language in the Legal Process*, pp. 246–59. Basingstoke: Palgrave.

Dumas, B.K. (2010) Consumer product warnings: Composition, identification, and assessment of adequacy. In M. Coulthard and A. Johnson (eds) *The Routledge Handbook of Forensic Linguistics*, pp. 365–77. Abingdon: Routledge.

Eades, D. (2008) *Courtroom Talk and Neocolonial Control*. Berlin: Mouton de Gruyter.

Grant, T.D. (2010) Txt 4n6: Idiolect free authorship analysis? In M. Coulthard and A. Johnson (eds) *The Routledge Handbook of Forensic Linguistics*, pp. 508–22. Abingdon: Routledge.

Haworth, K. (2013) Audience design in the police interview: The interactional and judicial consequences of audience orientation. *Language in Society* 42: 45–69.

Heffer, C. (2005) *The Language of Jury Trial: A Corpus-Aided Analysis of Legal-Lay Discourse*. Basingstoke: Palgrave.

Heffer, C. (2008) The language and communication of jury instruction. In J. Gibbons and M.T. Turell (eds) *Dimensions of Forensic Linguistics*, pp. 47–65. Amsterdam: John Benjamins.

Heydon, G. (2005) *The Language of Police Interviewing: A Critical Analysis*. Basingstoke: Palgrave.

Rock, F. (2007) *Communicating Rights: The Language of Arrest and Detention*. Basingstoke: Palgrave.

Shuy, R.W. (2012) Using linguistics in trademark cases. In P.M. Tiersma and L.M. Solan (eds) *The Oxford Handbook of Language and Law*, pp. 449–62. Oxford: Oxford University Press.

Solan, L.M. and P.M. Tiersma (2005) *Speaking of Crime: The Language of Criminal Justice*. Chicago: University of Chicago Press.

Svartvik, J. (1968) *The Evans Statements: A Case for Forensic Linguistics*. Gothenburg: University of Gothenburg Press.

Tiersma, P.M. (1999) *Legal Language*. Chicago: University of Chicago Press.

Tiersma, P.M. and L.M. Solan (eds) (2012) *The Oxford Handbook of Language and Law*. Oxford: Oxford University Press.

Tracy, K. and R.R. Agne (2002) 'I just need to ask somebody some questions': Sensitivities in domestic dispute calls. In J. Cotterill (ed.) *Language in the Legal Process*, pp. 75–90. Basingstoke: Palgrave.

Zimmerman, D.H. (1992) The interactional organization of calls for emergency assistance. In P. Drew and J. Heritage (eds) *Talk at Work: Interaction in Institutional Settings*, pp. 418–69. Cambridge: Cambridge University Press.

35
Linguistics and politics

George Lakoff

35.1 Political Linguistics is just linguistics

Political Linguistics is just linguistics applied to a particular subject matter, like phonology applied to a social dialect or phonetics applied to the speech of children or historical linguistics applied to the movement of populations over time. In all cases you are looking for general principles using a form of linguistics and applying those principles to the subject matter at hand. And it is like any other science applied to a kind of situation, like applying physics to building skyscrapers. As would be expected, in order to get the politics right, you have to get the linguistics right.

Political Linguistics, for me, came out of the study of Cognitive Linguistics, which looks at the role of cognition and its neural basis in the study of conceptual systems and the linguistic forms that express, evoke and often shape ideas within conceptual systems. Political behavior is typically a consequence of having political ideas and acting on them in a natural way. Language and the ideas expressed by language play a crucial role in politics (though, of course, not the only role). The mechanism by which language and thought work in politics is neural in character. There is nothing special about this. It works the same way neural circuitry works in everyday thought and language.

What *is* special about political linguistics is its contribution to linguistics. Political subject matter, as we shall see, requires an expansion of what it means to apply linguistics to a subject matter.

I will be speaking here mostly of my own work. Others, of course, have applied other forms of linguistics to political subject matter.

35.2 The cognitive unconscious

The first thing to bear in mind is what all linguists know – that linguistic principles are largely unconscious. Speakers are not consciously aware of the details of their phonetics, phonology or morphology. This applies to semantics and pragmatics as well. The principles governing thought and language use in context are almost all unconscious in use – even if you are a linguist who studies them!

This is true for a simple reason. Neural circuitry operates very fast and in parallel, with connections among many brain areas operating at once. Conscious thought is about a hundred times slower and is linear, that is, in slow sequence not a fast parallelism. People simply cannot be consciously following all that is going on in their brains that is relevant to thinking and using language.

It has been estimated that about 98 percent of thought is unconscious. The exact percentage cannot be precisely measured of course, but the percentage seems to be in the right ballpark. Perhaps the most useful thing about linguistics is that, over its history, linguists have developed techniques for studying unconscious cognitive mechanisms.

35.3 Starting with frame semantics

I have been interested in politics since childhood. Where I grew up in northern New Jersey, politics was a normal part of everyday life. In the late 1960s, those of us who studied speech act theory and implicatures began to notice that they were prominent in discussions of political and social issues. The first book I was aware of applying pragmatics to social issues was Robin Lakoff's 1975 book *Language and Woman's Place*, which began the serious study of feminism and linguistics.

As frame semantics developed in the years after 1975, speech act structure and principles of implicature (see Chapter 13) came to be understood as special cases of the use of conceptual frames.

In 1977, my Berkeley colleague Charles Fillmore, casually pointed out to me an application of his theory of frame semantics. In Boston, a doctor who had performed an abortion went on trial for murder. The prosecuting attorney used the word 'baby,' while the defense attorney used the word 'fetus.' Fillmore pointed out to me that the frames in which those words are defined were what the case was about. The choice of frame by the jury not only decided the case; the framing issue is at the heart of the distinction between conservative and progressive politics.

For Fillmore, frame semantics was a matter of lexicography (see Chapter 12). He had studied the European linguistic tradition of semantic fields, which examined collections of related words, like *knife-fork-spoon*, *Monday-Tuesday-Wednesday-...*, and *buy-sell-cost-price-goods-bargain-...*. Fillmore argued that the generalizations over the semantic fields were cognitive in nature – a mode of understanding domains of experience like *Eating with Utensils*, *Calendars Using Weeks* and *Commercial Events*.

For Fillmore, a frame was a Part–Whole structure with a domain of experience as the Whole, and 'semantic roles' as the Parts – the people, places, and things that made up the Whole together with their properties, the relations among them, and the actions and events they took part in. All Commercial Events, he observed, have the semantic roles of Buyer, Seller, Goods and Money, with a scenario of exchanging money and goods. This echoed Fillmore's earlier Case Grammar, which began with basic scenes of actions, experiences, and events and roles like Agent, Patient, Recipient, Experiencer, etc.

What was crucial in frame semantics was the Fillmore Hypothesis that all meaningful elements in language – words, morphemes, syntactic constructions, idioms – get their meanings from frames and are defined relative to specific frames. That hypothesis has held up over four decades in language studied by frame-semantic researchers around the world.

Frame semantics fit the times. Similar uses of the term 'frame' were used by Erving Goffman and Marvin Minsky, for different reasons. Goffman studied social institutions and concluded that they were constituted by frames specifying roles; social relations in the institution; and normal actions within the institution. People working in an institution took on different roles when they went to work than when they were at home. Minsky observed that knowledge representation in Artificial Intelligence would need frames. But it was Fillmore who, more than anyone else, worked out linguistic details, starting a FrameNet project that he ran for more than two decades.

Fillmore and I differed on the importance of frame semantics. He wanted to keep it as lexicography of the sort done in dictionaries – but more precise. I saw it as a method for studying the conceptual frames making up conceptual systems in general. Fillmore had observed that frames form hierarchies: commercial events are exchanges, exchanges are mutual acts of transfer, transfers involve applying force to a possession to move it from a sender to a recipient. The frame systems bottom out in primary scenes – widespread or universal simple experiences, like transfer, the use of force, motion and possession. Complex frames depend for their meanings on such primary experiences. Since frames have semantic entailments, many of those entailments come from the primary scenes and the ways that they are put together to form frames. For example, in every commercial event, the buyer transfers money to seller and the seller transfers goods to the buyer.

The use of framing in politics makes constant use of the basics of how frames work: Part–Whole structure, semantic roles and relations among them, what happens in a frame, and frame hierarchies bottoming out in primary experiences.

But bear in mind, as we go on, that frame semantics began as the study of the general principles characterizing the relations among related lexical items: that is, general principles governing a phenomenon.

35.4 Conceptual metaphor

Michael Reddy and I, in our independent discoveries of conceptual metaphors in 1977 and 1978, both noticed that large groups of linguistic expressions formed what might be called metaphoric semantic fields. Reddy found over 140 examples of expressions like *You're not getting through to me*, *Your meaning is hidden in dense paragraphs*, *The meaning is right there in the words*, and so on. He saw the general principle as a conceptual metaphor, what he called The Conduit metaphor: ideas are objects, words are containers, communication is putting words in containers and sending them to others, who take the words out the containers. He pointed out that this metaphor hid certain vital truths about communication.

I noticed that there are dozens if not hundreds of related expressions characterizing love in terms of travel: *The marriage is on the rocks*, *We're spinning our wheels in this relationship*, *We're going in different directions*, *It's been a long, bumpy road*, and so on. The general principle is a Love Is A Journey metaphor with the frame-to-frame mapping: lovers are travelers, a relationship is a vehicle, consistent life goals are common destinations, and relationship difficulties are impediments to travel.

Mark Johnson and I later noticed that, like frames, these metaphors form hierarchies that bottom out in 'primary metaphors' that are widespread around the world if not universal: relationships are containers; intimacy is closeness; purposes are destinations; a vehicle frame, in which vehicles are *containers* in which the travelers are close, and which are used for reaching destinations; plus a culturally specific long-term love relationship frame in which the lovers are expected to have compatible life goals (where life goals are, metaphorically, destinations in life). The inferences of the Love Is A Journey metaphor arise from the inferences of the primary metaphors and cultural frames.

In short, within conceptual systems, generalizations over linguistic expressions can be seen in conceptual systems – hierarchical systems of frames and conceptual metaphors that get their meaning from basic experiences and cultural frames higher up in the hierarchy. This result has also held up for nearly four decades.

Over that period, research on the neural theory of thought and language has resulted in hypotheses relying only on basic properties of neural circuitry that fit the existing data. The hypotheses, if confirmed, would explain those data. Together, conceptual framing systems, conceptual metaphor systems, and hypotheses based on basic facts about neural circuitry are brought together in political linguistics. The method was a straightforward application of cognitive linguistics to politics.

Here is how it worked from the beginning.

35.5 What constitutes conservative and progressive thought in America?

In 1994, conservative Republicans took over the US Congress. The Republicans, in winning, used messaging based on a book, *The Contract with America*, sponsored by the ultra-conservative new Speaker of the House Newt Gingrich, and a young public relations specialist, Frank Luntz.

I read that book and was mystified. Several years earlier, I had written a book on categorization, *Women, Fire, and Dangerous Things*. What mystified me was that I could not understand the category Conservative. I could not, for the life of me, understand how extreme conservative positions held together. What, I asked myself, does being against taxation have to do with being against abortion? What does being against abortion have to do with owning guns? What does owning guns have to do with tort reform? What does tort reform have to do with being against environmentalism? What sense does it make to be pro-life and for the death penalty? There are dozens of other positions like these. As a progressive, none of this made any sense to me. What was the general principle governing all these positions? What made one a conservative in general, not just someone with a laundry list of positions?

As a progressive, I held positions opposite all of the conservative positions. I then asked myself what the generalization was that made all of my positions make sense. And I got embarrassed. I could not answer the question. But, as a cognitive linguist and as an expert on conceptual systems and categorization, I felt I *should* be able to answer those questions. They were questions in my field, after all. They were like sets of sentences of the form Conservatives favor X and oppose Y. Progressives favor Y and oppose X. Just fill in X and Y. What generalizes conceptually over such sentences? There should, I felt, be an answer like those in frame semantics and conceptual metaphor generalizing over such sentences.

So I decided to start studying the phenomenon. I read all that I reasonably could from both sides – books, articles, speeches. I listened to and watched talk shows on both sides. I interviewed people on both sides. I dutifully did the groupings, applied frame semantics – and got nowhere for about six months. The breakthrough came when I was looking at conservative discussions of patriotism. I happened to remember a homework done by one of the students on my course on conceptual metaphor. She noticed the Americans have a conceptual metaphor of the Nation as a Family: we have *Founding Fathers, Daughters of the American Revolution*, we send our *sons and daughters* to war, JFK had said we don't want Russian missiles *in our back yard*, … and more recently we have *homeland security*, and *the nanny state*.

I reasoned as follows:

1. If there is such a metaphor, then there would have to be two different ideal models of the family mapping to two different ideal models of the nation.
2. Conceptual metaphor theory said that conceptual metaphors are frame-to-frame mappings, mapping roles and inferences in the source domain (e.g. families) to roles and inferences in the target domain (e.g. the nation). Therefore, one should be able to work backwards through the mappings from the two different ideal models of the nation in the target domain to the two different ideal models of the family in the source domain.

That is what I did; I worked backwards from target to source. And from the details, there emerged two different models of the family – a Strict Father model for conservatives and a Nurturant Parent model for progressives.

35.6 The child-rearing situation

At the 1995 summer meeting of the International Cognitive Linguistics Association at the University of New Mexico at Albuquerque, I gave the initial presentation of my results. Afterwards, two excellent cognitive linguists who were conservatives (they were involved in Bible translation) and also personal friends led me to look at the work of James Dobson, a Conservative Christian minister who ran Focus on the Family, a conservative child-rearing organization and a major figure in conservative politics. Dobson's classic book was *Dare to Discipline*. I bought a copy. A former student of mine, upon being told this, bought me a subscription (under a pseudonym) to Dobson's materials. There in Dobson's writings and in the writings of other conservative child-rearing authors much of the mapping from strict father families to conservative positions was laid out. I review that literature in Chapter 21 of *Moral Politics* (1996, 2002).

There is, of course, a tradition of nurturing parenting – from Dr. Benjamin Spock (whose *Baby and Child Care* was a best seller for fifty-two years, second only to the Bible). Afterwards, the nurturant child-rearing mantle was taken up by T. Berry Brazleton at the Harvard Medical School, and is carried on by the Brazleton Touchpoints Institute. Another nurturant tradition is Attachment Parenting, started by John Bowlby and carried on by William Sears and others. But, whereas the conservative child-rearing organizations are directly involved in conservative Christianity and conservative politics, the nurturant parenting organizations stick to parenting. The result is that conservatives tend to have a more integrated understanding of their politics and their family life than progressives do.

35.7 Morality, parenting, and politics

All politics is moral. Whenever a political leader proposes a policy, the implicit or explicit justification is that it is right, not wrong or morally irrelevant. No politicians will say, 'Here's my policy and do it because it is evil, it is the wrong thing to do.' Nor will they say, 'Do it because it doesn't matter.' When policies oppose each other, it is because they are based on different notions of what is 'right,' that is, different moralities.

In looking at the framing of public policies, I have found that they are all based (often unconsciously, of course) on family-based moral theories. In short, the strict and nurturant ideal models of the family have built-in moral systems – parents want to do what is right, not what is wrong or irrelevant, in raising their children. Thus, the metaphorical mappings of ideal family models onto politics are based on different – and many ways opposite – models of morality.

35.8 The brain and what we have learned since 1996

We are about to get into the political details and what they have to do with cognitive linguistics. But before we do, it should be pointed out that a lot has been learned since 1996, when *Moral Politics* came out.

1. *The Neural Basis*: All thought is physical, carried out by the embodied neural systems in our brains, which have connections throughout our bodies. Every system of thought is an embodied neural system.
2. *Limits on Understanding*: You can only understand what your neural system allows you to understand. A new piece of information, to be understood, must fit what you already know – either overlapping with current knowledge in neural form or being minimally distant and hence almost exactly fitting what is already there at a deep and unconscious level. Incoming information that does not fit will be either ignored, dismissed, or ridiculed.
3. *Bi-conceptualism*: In the USA, we grow up in a culture of TV and movies, many of which have strict or nurturant family models in them, or conservative or progressive values structuring them. And in real families, children may rebel against their family's values, or have a mother and father operating in accord with different family models. The result is 'bi-conceptualism.' Many people have both strict and nurturant moral models in their brains at once, even though they contradict each other. Neurally they are related by *mutual inhibition* – inhibiting connections across the circuitry for the two models, so that turning one on turns the other off, and strengthening one weakens the other.

    Since these models are ideal and occur at a general level, they may differ in how they are bound to specific policies. Thus, for example, one may be conservative financially and progressive socially, or the reverse; a professor may be nurturant in politics but strict in the classroom. All sorts of combinations occur.
4. *There is no middle. There is no ideology of the moderate, no political principles shared by all moderates!* A moderate conservative is mostly conservative, but progressive on some policies. A moderate liberal is progressive on most policies, but conservative on some others. The variation is all over the place, often depending on personal experience or local history.
5. *The role of language.* Since words are defined relative to frames, experiencing or using language activates the corresponding frames in our brains. Every time a frame is activated, its synapses are strengthened – and those of its opponent frames are weakened. Thus if you hear conservative language fitting conservative frames over and over, the corresponding conservative frame-circuits in your brain will be strengthened and the progressive frame-circuits will be weakened.

    This points up a common liberal mistake in communication. The mistake is the idea that, to communicate with someone, you should use their language. In politics, this is a disaster, since using the other side's language just strengthens their frames and weakens yours in their mind.
6. *Don't think of an elephant!* Negating a frame activates that frame. Thus arguing against a conservative position using conservative framing and language simply helps conservatives. Conservative activists are trained not to use progressive language to argue against progressive positions; they are trained to use conservative language and their own frames to undermine progressive positions.
7. *Polling can create artificial middles.* Polls for the most part have certain constraints:

a. They use the most commonplace language recognized by as many people as possible; this is often conservative language activating conservative frames.
   b. They group the responses by demographic categories: age, gender, ethnicity, income level, zip code, perhaps registered party affiliation.
   c. They tend to use a four- or five-point scale: 'strongly agree,' 'agree,' 'disagree,' 'strongly disagree' – and, often, 'no opinion.'
   d. They use statistics to give the responses. In many cases, that imposes a bell curve that may not be real, with most respondents in the 'middle.'
   e. They do not group by ideal parenting models and they do not use both strict and nurturant framing for the same issues in the questions. If they did, they would most likely get two bell curves, one for each model.

Given these considerations, we move on to the applications of frames and metaphors.

35.9 A deeper generalization

The Nation-as-Family model turned out to be too specific. I found strict father and nurturant parent models in governing institutions in general – in churches, in the military, in athletic teams, in businesses, in classrooms, in hospitals, in political parties, in governments at all levels, in the market, and throughout our cultural institutions. Since we are all first governed in our families, it seems that we learn a very general metaphor: Governing Institutions are Families, with strict and nurturant variants.

Thus, what is 'political' is not just about elections and official 'governments.' The same principles governing our politics govern many of our social systems. There is a reason why politics affects all of the following: family planning clinics, contraception and sex education; what is taught in schools and whether education should be private or public and whether teachers and schools should be 'graded'; whether specific religious symbols should be permitted in public places; whether there should be unemployment insurance; whether parents should hit their children with 'switches'; whether concealed weapons should be allowed on college campuses; whether consensual sex should require a definite and conscious 'yes'; who in the military should be informed of, and in charge of prosecuting, sexual assaults; whether employees who get tips should be provided the minimum wage; whether gays should be allowed to marry; what counts as free speech versus hate speech; whether trains without double hulls should be allowed to haul crude oil; whether fracking companies should have to list poisonous chemicals that they pump into the ground by thousands of tons; whether chickens should spend their lives in small cages; whether livestock raised in close quarters should be pumped full of antibiotics; whether there should be a 'Stand your ground' law, that is, whether someone who feels threatened can shoot to kill someone he or she feels threatened by; and on and on.

These are all political issues, correlating in most cases with the conservative–progressive divide. As we shall see, the strict and nurturant family models, via the general metaphor of Governing Institutions are Families, map onto many kinds of governing institutions throughout society, making such questions political.

35.10 The parenting models and their moral logics

Bear in mind that these are ideal models, characterized by frames and that they tend to be unconscious, like most thought. They may also be part of a real bi-conceptual system, with both models mutually inhibiting each other and applying to different issues.

35.10.1 The nurturant ideal

Let us begin with the nurturant model of an ideal family. The parents (if there are two) have equal responsibility. The parents have a number of jobs:

1. *Empathy*: To empathize with their children, to understand what they are like, what they need, and to maintain open, honest communication with them, showing them love and respect.
2. *Responsibility to act on that empathy*: First, taking care of themselves, since you can cannot take care of others if you are not taking care of yourself; and taking care of their children, so that they can be fulfilled in life: keeping them safe, healthy, well-educated, well-socialized.
3. *Maintain an ethic of excellence*: Doing their best as parents and as people – working to be financially comfortable, healthy, well-educated, well-connected in the community, etc.
4. *Raise their children to be the same*: It is assumed that children are born good and can be raised to be even better: to be empathetic toward others; responsible for themselves *and* for others; to be cooperative and be able to function effectively in their community; and having an ethic of excellence – all so as to be fulfilled in life. These are the values to be instilled in children through being lived by parents. This means that parents have to set limits and explain why. Discipline is positive, not punitive.

In addition, it takes a community to raise children. Children need to learn from many people, which is why community participation is vital.

And nurturance starts with birth – and with proper prenatal care. What happens in the womb matters.

There is nothing easy about being a nurturant parent, and meeting that ideal takes effort.

35.10.2 The strict ideal

Ideally there should be two parents, a man and a woman.

The world is assumed to be a difficult and dangerous place, a world with evil in it. The father has to be strong and disciplined to deal with the difficulty and danger, and must have – and deserves to have – the unquestioned authority in his family to do his job: to protect the family from that evil; to support the family in the face of that difficulty; to teach his children right from wrong through punishment when they do wrong, so they will develop the discipline to do right, not wrong, and use that discipline to become strong, competitive and to prosper so as to support and protect their own families.

The father has authority and merits it. The authority of the father is not to be challenged, above all. That is the highest principle. The job of the wife is to support the authority of the father. The job of the children is obedience; no back-talk. The father is assumed to:

- Be moral: Know right from wrong and act accordingly

- Have the best judgment ('father knows best')
- Be strong
- Be able to protect the family
- Be able to support the family, by competing successfully in the world
- Maintain order in the family by setting the rules and enforcing them
- Teach his kids right from wrong, by punishing them when they do wrong
- It is the duty of parents to discipline their children in this way. Discipline is seen as an act of love – tough love.

Children should:

- Obey their parents
- Show respect to their parents and other legitimate authorities
- Learn personal responsibility
- Develop discipline and strength
- Learn to compete successfully
- Children who live up to these ideals should be rewarded with affection – and with material rewards as available and appropriate
- It is assumed that adult children should grow up to be strict parents of their own, at which time parents should not 'meddle' in their lives.

35.10.3 Other family models

There are other parenting models: In the Neglectful model, children are simply neglected. In the Anything Goes model, children can do anything they like with no limits or expectations set. The Abusive model is a variant of the Strict Father model, but one in which the father's punishment is abusive and harmful. Both strict and nurturant parents reject such models.

But strict parents tend to see nurturant parents as being insufficiently strict and hence having an Anything Goes model with spoiled children ('Spare the rod and spoil the child'). Nurturant parents often see strict parents as abusive.

Is there a fact of the matter? There are three forms of research that see the nurturant model as best, the strict model as bad news for kids, and the abusive and neglectful models as disastrous. They are Attachment Research, Socialization Research, and Abuse Research (cf. *Moral Politics*, Chapter 21, for details). Conservatives see these as biased forms of research done by liberals.

35.11 The moral family-based logics

The Ideal Families have moral logics that extend beyond the family.

The Nurturant Family model's ideals of empathy, responsibility both for self and others, and excellence is intent on fulfillment in life for all. The focus on love, care, support, health, education, excellence and socialization is supposed to provide each family member the freedom to seek and find fulfillment. The result of mutual care, respect, cooperation should result in mutual benefit for all, both in the family and in the wider community.

Sexuality is mutual and comes from living by nurturant ideals: It is sexy for a man to be a good father.

The Strict Father model has an ideal of personal responsibility. The father – and the children he raises – must be strong and disciplined, and dependency on others would make them weak and unable to function effectively in competition and protection. If children are physically disciplined when they do wrong, they will become disciplined in general and be able to prosper in the world. If they are not prospering, that means they are not disciplined, without discipline they cannot be moral, and hence they deserve their poverty.

The strength, discipline and deserved authority of the father comes with a form of masculine sexuality and masculine gender roles – men should be in charge of sexuality and reproduction in the family.

Importantly, the Strict Father model comes with an implicit moral principle: In a well-ordered world, those who are moral according to strict father principles should rule.

35.12 The central metaphor: governing institutions are families

We are now going to start giving examples of how the models map via this metaphor onto progressive and conservative political views, not just of government, but of every domain of life governed by institutions, that is, just about every domain of social and interpersonal life. As we go through this, bear in mind that we are looking at an analysis after the fact – an analysis that seeks to explain how all the facts in all the domains of experience fit together.

Such an explanation is the flip side of the empirical research leading to it. I started with a huge list of mysteries, how the apparently disparate views of conservatives and progressives hung together – what constituted having conservative or progressive views? Each case we will consider is at once an empirical attempt to solve a mystery, and a hypothesis that, if true, would explain why all those views fit together.

35.13 Progressive and conservative views of democracy

Progressives share an implicit (and often unconscious) ideal view of democracy that structures much of their thinking and goes like this:

> In a democracy, citizens care about one another and act through their government to provide public resources for all, resources that provide for a wide range of freedoms no matter who you are.

The values of empathy, responsibility for oneself and others, excellence, and a focus on fulfillment lie behind such a view of democracy.

This view of democracy, mostly unconscious, though publicly put forth on occasion by President Obama and regularly by Elizabeth Warren, lies behind just about all progressive programs. For example, it includes things you need for business – roads, bridges, sewers, airports, the electric grid, the Internet, satellite communications, public health, public education, government sponsored research, the SEC for the stock market, the Federal Reserve, Federal Deposit Insurance and so on. American business could not run without these things and employees of those businesses could not have jobs without them. Private enterprise thus depends on public resources. Those resources allow you to be free to make a living and allow consumers to be free to have products they depend on.

Private lives depend on the public as well. Public resources include health care, safe food and drugs, necessary pharmaceuticals (developed through government sponsored research), clean water, clean air, social security and Medicare for the elderly, universities (both public and private depend on government research funding), public safety, the criminal justice system, building codes and inspectors, public parks and recreational activities, and on and on. When you need such things to be free to live a fulfilling life, you are not free without them.

Conservatives have the opposite ideal view:

> Democracy provides citizens with liberty, the liberty to seek their own interests through personal responsibility, without government interference, without dependence on anyone, and without being responsible for others (outside of our families).

Conservatives see publicly provided resources as making people dependent and weak – taking from personally responsible people and giving to irresponsible, dependent people who are undeserving. Where progressives see government as the means by which people provide vital public resources for one another, conservatives see government as oppressive, with regulations restricting their liberty and programs that, via taxes, take away what they earn.

These differences cover a wide range of progressive–conservative differences, but by no means all. Progressives seek freedom for women to control their own bodies and to function equally with men in all areas of institutional life, in education, business, sports, government, etc. This comes from both empathy and the equality of women in ideally nurturant families.

In the ideal strict father family, men control sex and reproduction and have authority over their wives. Conservatives seek laws allowing men to control the lives of women in many ways: laws banning family planning, banning paying for birth control pills as medical necessities, making abortions difficult or impossible, supporting spousal and parental notification laws for abortions, refusing to legislate equal rights for women in business. What are called 'pro-life' positions against abortion are called into serious question by conservative refusal to pass laws guaranteeing prenatal and postnatal care, which often determine whether a newborn lives or dies; they do not seem to care about babies once they are born. An explanation for this is that their anti-abortion stance is actually a female control stance.

What is the difference between conservative and progressive Christianity? Both have God as a Father. But progressive Christians see God as a nurturant father, while conservative Christians see God as a strict father – an authority who sets down the rules. If you obey them, you go to Heaven (to your 'reward'); otherwise, you go to Hell and eternal punishment. Conservative Christians believe that people should be 'God-fearing.'

You have heard the expression 'Let the market decide.' The subject of verb, *decide*, is typically a person. The market is a governing institution. When strict father families are mapped onto the market as an institution, the market itself becomes the metaphorical strict father, deciding that those with fiscal discipline should get rich and others should be poor. Such a market, according to conservatives, should not be required by government to pay higher minimum wages, or even allow restaurant workers, who earn tips, to make more than $2.13 per hour, or have health care or sick days. Empathy and living wages have no role in a strict father market, allowing only personal, not social, responsibility.

Extreme conservatives seek to minimize or end public resources and to privatize as much as possible. Government by corporation fits perfectly within a strict father market, in which corporations, like people, should have the liberty, without government regulation, to maximize their self-interest. Conservatives have no problem with extreme wealth – with the ratio of CEO income to average worker income at 350:1. The wealthy are seen as those who are disciplined and who therefore deserve their wealth, while the poor are undisciplined, lower on the moral hierarchy, and deserve to be poor.

In large corporations, there are two kinds of employees – the 'assets' (upper management and 'creative' people) and the 'resources' (interchangeable workers hired by the human resources department). What is corporate policy toward resources? Get them as cheaply as possible and use as few as possible. Hence the antipathy of conservatives to unions and living wage campaigns.

And what about poor conservatives, who support the full gamut of conservative positions? Why should they vote against their financial interests? So far as we can tell, they have strict father morality, live that morality at home and in their personal, social and religious lives. Strict father morality is part of their self-definition as people. Poor, sick conservatives who have benefited from the Affordable Care Act still criticize it as a government takeover, and will not vote Democrat even though it is in their financial interest. Why? Because they define themselves by their strict father morality and culture.

Strict father morality imposes a moral hierarchy, in which the moral (in strict morality) should rule. History shows what that moral hierarchy is by who has come out on top. God above man, man above nature, rich above poor, adults above children, Western culture above non-Western culture, America above other nations, and then the bigoted part of the hierarchy: men above women, straights above gays, Whites above non-Whites, Christians above non-Christians. Thus, it is conservatives who want to ban gay marriage, conservatives who support racial profiling and stand-your-ground laws, conservatives who want to arrest and deport political refugees from Latin America, including children, conservatives who want to put Christian symbols in public places.

In foreign policy, conservatives see America as being strict father to the world, with authority over other nations in the world community, authority to be enforced militarily. It is progressives who seek to avoid conflict and killing, cooperate with other nations, and show empathy for citizens of other countries who are oppressed and need aid.

What about beating children with 'switches' (tree branches)? NFL star Adrian Peterson was arrested for beating his four-year-old son so badly the boy received serious injuries and lacerations. His response was right out of the strict father playbook:

> He said he disciplined his son the same way he was disciplined as a child. ... 'deep in my heart I have always believed I could have been one of those kids that was lost in the streets without the discipline instilled in me by my parents and other relatives ... I have always believed that the way my parents disciplined me has a great deal to do with the success I have enjoyed as a man ... . My goal is always to teach my son right from wrong and that's what I tried to do that day.'
>
> (Gray 2014)

Here we see the strict father logic of 'discipline' as clear as could be. Part of Anderson's defense is that such 'discipline' is normal in East Texas. The East Texas prosecutor for the case agreed, saying, 'Obviously, parents are entitled to discipline their children as they see fit, except for when that discipline exceeds what the community would say is reasonable.' Yes to whipping with 'switches,' but not too far on a four-year-old (Schrotenboer 2014).

On Fox News, conservative commentator Sean Hannity said, 'I got hit with a strap. Bam, bam, bam. And I have never been to a shrink. I will tell you that I deserved it ... I was not mentally bruised because my father hit me with a belt' (MacNeal 2014). The conservative view on the major conservative station.

The generalizations are overwhelming. Extreme conservatives – who are not bi-conceptual 'moderates' – have most, if not all, of the characteristics that are predicted by the metaphor mapping strict father morality onto all manner of governing institutions. Similarly, extreme progressives – progressives who are not bi-conceptual and do not have significant conservative views, fit the characteristics predicted by the metaphorical mapping of nurturant morality onto progressive politics in the same wide range of governing institutions.

I arrived at this analysis by starting with the mysteries and a student's suggestion of an early version of the metaphor. Using the theories of frame semantics and conceptual metaphor theory from cognitive linguistics, I worked backwards from the mysteries to the first version of the metaphorical mapping, and then to the more general version. Along the way, I brought in research on neural systems from the research at the Neural Theory of Language project at the International Computer Science institute at Berkeley to make sense of bi-conceptualism. Since then, experimental and survey research by Elisabeth Wehling in her 2013 Berkeley dissertation 'The US Under Joint Custody,' has overwhelmingly confirmed most of the analysis presented here.

The major point should be clear. Political linguistics, as I have been engaged in it, is just linguistics, applied to politics as a subject matter. The linguistics started out just as early cognitive linguistics, especially frame semantics and conceptual metaphor theory. As embodied cognition and the neural theory of language has progressed, the current neurally embodied cognitive linguistics is the linguistics used – in every analysis.

35.14 Why conservatives do better

I have now written seven books on political linguistics, and well over a hundred articles. The latest book is *The ALL NEW Don't Think of an Elephant!*, a thorough updating and new essays on what I learned since the first version ten years ago. I have been primarily focused on the fact that conservatives continue to do better at political framing, messaging and communication systems than progressives.

Ten years ago I pointed out the mechanism by which conservatives managed to expand their political power through the use of framing and language. They understand the centrality of morality and use moral frames and the mechanisms of Real Reason – morally-based frames and metaphors, powerful images, emotion and accompanying music and language that evokes conservative frames and metaphors. Each time the language is heard and the images seen, the conservative frames and metaphors are neurally strengthened. As a result, moderate conservatives are made more conservative and moderate progressives who are partial conservatives have their conservative frames and metaphors strengthened – and they move further to the right. Repetition matters, and there is constant repetition – on TV and radio talk shows, and in venues where conservatives regularly talk, like businesses and local business groups, local high schools and colleges, churches, and the full range of social media on the Internet. Why do progressives not do as well?

Many conservatives engaged in marketing conservative ideas have actually studied marketing in business schools, and their professors have studied the cognitive and brain sciences. They know how Real Reason works. But when progressives go to college, they tend not to study either marketing, or cognitive science, cognitive linguistics or neuroscience. Instead they usually study political science, public policy, law and economics. Those fields tend to teach an inadequate view of reason – reason that lacks an understanding of:

1. frame semantics and conceptual metaphor
2. the fact that most thought is unconscious
3. embodied cognition

4. that you can only understand what your physical brain allows you to understand, and not just any idea or fact
5. that conservatives and progressives have different neural structures of thought
6. that language is not neutral but rather activates specific frames
7. that negating a frame activates and strengthens that frame as much as asserting it
8. that people vote on the basis of their personal identity, not merely on their finances.

Therefore progressives commonly just tell people the facts and assume that the facts are all that is necessary to get conservatives to come around to your side. It does not generally work. The facts are vital, but they must be morally framed in terms of the values you want to strengthen. Progressives need to catch up.

Most of all, university social science departments need to learn some serious cognitive linguistics and to recognize the inadequacies of the view of reason that they have been teaching – mostly without even noticing that it is an issue. The same is true of journalism schools. They need to teach how framing and metaphor work in the media, and why language is not neutral.

It should be clear by now that neurally embodied frame semantics and conceptual metaphor theory are necessary for making sense of the mysteries we started with and for understanding what unifies conservative and progressive thought. The reason that these forms of linguistics work for understanding politics is that they work for human thought and language generally.

Acknowledgment

The research on conceptual metaphor presented here has been supported in part by the Berkeley MetaNet Project through the Intelligence Advanced Research Projects Activity (IARPA) via the Department of Defense US Army Research Laboratory – contract number W911NF-12-C-0022.

Disclaimer

The views and conclusions contained herein are those of the author and should not be interpreted as necessarily representing the official policies or endorsements, either expressed or implied, of IARPA, DoD/ARL, or the US Government.

Further reading

Lakoff (2006, 2008); Lakoff and Johnson (1980, 1999); Lakoff and Wehling (2012).

References

Gray, J. (2014) Adrian Peterson apologizes, says he's 'not a child abuser.' *SB Nation*, September 15. www.sbnation.com/nfl/2014/9/15/6153477/adrian-peterson-statement-child-abuse-arrest.
Lakoff, G. (1987) *Women, Fire, and Dangerous Things*. Chicago: University of Chicago Press.
Lakoff, G. (2002 [1996]) *Moral Politics*. Chicago: University of Chicago Press.
Lakoff, G. (2006) *Whose Freedom?* New York: Farrar, Strauss, Giroux.
Lakoff, G. (2008) *The Political Mind*. New York: Viking/Penguin.

Lakoff, G. (2014 [2004]) *The ALL NEW Don't Think of an Elephant!* White River Junction: Chelsea Green.
Lakoff, G. and M. Johnson (1980) *Metaphors We Live By*. Chicago: University of Chicago Press.
Lakoff, G. and M. Johnson (1999) *Philosophy in the Flesh*. New York: Basic Books.
Lakoff, G. and E. Wehling (2012) *The Little Blue Book*. New York: Free Press.
Lakoff, R. (1975) *Language and Woman's Place*. New York: Harper and Row.
MacNeal, C. (2014) Hannity on NFL's Peterson: My dad hit me with a 'strap' and I'm okay. TPM Livewire, September 17. http://talkingpointsmemo.com/livewire/hannity-defends-nfl-adrian-peterson.
Schrotenboer, B. (2014) District attorney: Adrian Peterson 'exceeded' standards. *USA Today Sports*, September 13. www.usatoday.com/story/sports/nfl/vikings/2014/09/13/adrian-peterson-child-abuse-district-attorney-press-conference/15581419/.
Wehling, E. (2013) The US under joint custody. UC Berkeley dissertation.

36
Linguistics and social media

Ana Deumert

36.1 Introduction: social media, old and new

The phrase *social media* rose to prominence around 2002/2003 when the social network(ing) applications Frienster (2002) and MySpace (2003) made their debut. Yet, the idea of *social media* is not a new one. The American anarchist scholar William Greene (1875: 175), for example, discussed more than 100 years ago how the ways in which we think about the world are shaped by the social media which surround us. John Henry Stuckenberg (1898: 155) defined social media in his *Introduction to the Study of Sociology* as 'all the *means of social communication*, such as look, gesture, conduct, language, literature, art, not considered according to what they are in themselves, but as *social agencies*' (my emphasis). Forty years later, Hadley Cantril (1941: 50) provided the following examples of social media in his work on social movements: 'movies, the pulp magazines, novels, dances, crowds [and] ballgames.' In this broad, sociological sense, social media are *multimodal communicative forms* which organize semiotic processes within societies: they bring people together in *conversation*, allow for the sharing of information and *collaboration*, and enable *community*, sociability and interaction (for a historical perspective on social media, see also Burke and Briggs 2009).

The concept of social media has narrowed its meaning in contemporary usage. It is now used almost exclusively to describe interactive digital media platforms that allow for the creation and sharing of texts, images and other visual content between people. These include Facebook, LinkedIn, Google+, YouTube, Wikipedia and Twitter, but also older text-based applications such as bulletin board services (BBS), discussion groups and the virtual worlds of multi-user dungeons (MUDs), as well as dyadic applications such as texting, email and chatting.[1] Following Stine Lomberg (2014), the different forms of digital engagement can be described as distinctive, yet overlapping, 'communicative genres,' which are 'constituted at the junction between interactive functionalities configured in software, and the distinctly social purposes [including norms and conventions] toward which they are oriented' (p. 15). Others prefer the term 'mode' to describe the interaction of technological affordances – the potential and limitations of a particular interface or technology – and its socio-culturally meaningful usage.

To include the study of mediated interactions within the discipline of linguistics is not unproblematic. For most of the twentieth century, linguistics, as well as the human and social sciences more generally, have privileged co-present interactions and seen, for example, writing as but a pale reflection of the richness of spoken (or signed) utterances. However, with the rise and profusion of, especially, digital media in the twenty-first century, it is difficult to maintain a stance where mediated interactions are seen as secondary, and of only marginal interest to those who wish to understand language in its socio-cultural context. Recent survey data for the United States, for example, suggests that people are now spending more time interacting online than body-to-body,[2] and we might be entering a state where 'written communication will quantitatively outstrip oral communication' (Harris 2000: 240).[3] Sociolinguists, especially, have been exploring new media as an area of study which allows fresh perspectives on topics which are central to the discipline: multilingualism and linguistic diversity, language variation and change, style and register, language and identity, language ideologies, interactional linguistics, and language and globalization (see Deumert 2014 for discussion and references). This chapter discusses three core characteristics of digital communication which are relevant for the study of language in these contexts: (1) the materiality of digital interactions; (2) the reflexivity and creativity this materiality enables; and (3) the ways in which the affordances of the medium reshape questions of identity and interaction.

36.2 Materiality matters: the political economy of digital communication

Materiality, as argued by Heather Horst and Daniel Miller (2012: 25), is 'bedrock for digital anthropology.' We can extend this statement to linguistic studies of new media: Communication using digital social media is only possible if people have access to the material artifacts, that is, hardware and software, which make such interactions possible. The materiality of the digital is not limited to individual possession and ownership: the technological artifacts, which allow us to communicate with others across time and space, are assembled in factories; their production requires raw materials mined under exploitative conditions; and in order to function they need access to data cables or mobile phone towers. Moreover, digital architectures are developed by programmers who are mostly employed by for-profit companies, and their design decisions shape what users can do with the technology (Fuchs 2014). The content users create has its own materiality. It is stored electronically in bits and bytes, and becomes visible on diverse screens as text, image or video. Unlike the spoken word, which is ephemeral, remembered but not, usually, recorded, digital content can be retrieved, copied and replicated well beyond its original interactional context. The digital is thus a complex and multilayered archive, consisting not only of the texts and images we produce, but also our browsing histories and even our movements in physical space (which are tagged and recorded via location software).

The materiality of digital communication has drawn attention to the materiality of language more generally. Thus, spoken language relies on sound waves while signed languages require bodily movements. And as we speak we are located in different physical contexts, where we are present as bodies, gendered and clothed, of different ages and socio-economic backgrounds. And finally, sociolinguistic work on language and symbolic power has shown that access to languages and ways of speaking is closely linked to material conditions. The access people have toward, for example, the standard norm or the global resource of English provides them with different life chances, including access to and success in educational settings, employment opportunities, earning potential and political voice (see Shankar and Cavanaugh (2012) for a review of language and materiality).

However, the materiality of spoken and signed language is not as exclusionary as that of digital communication: in principle, everyone can participate and the ability to communicate with others has been described as a public good (Grin 2006). This is not the case for digital communication: digital participation is not merely about speaking/writing 'in the right way,' but about being able to speak/write at all. That is, having access to digital technology in order to communicate with others.

The inequality of access to digital artifacts is commonly referred to as the *digital divide*: some people in the world have ample access to the Internet and other digital media (such as phones, tablets and laptops, *the haves*), others have some access (the *have-less*) and an ever-shrinking proportion of the world's population has none (the *have-nots*). Generally speaking, material access is a function of economic prosperity: wealthier countries show high levels of technology access, poor countries show low levels. A similar pattern is reflected within countries: individuals with higher incomes have more access than those with low incomes. Other variables which structure access, are gender, age, disability, language, geography (rural/urban), as well as race/ethnicity. For example, in the USA, African-Americans and Hispanics have only fairly recently caught up with Whites regarding Internet access. Among the latter, Spanish-dominant Latinos are much less likely to be online than English-dominant Latinos. In addition, general and computer literacy skills as well as opportunities to practice these are important for using the technology successfully and being able to produce meaningful content. Although literacy rates show an upward trend worldwide, high levels of illiteracy persist in South Asia and Central Africa (including the West African interior).[4] This adds another obstacle to digital engagement, as do low levels of educational attainment more generally and lack of in-school exposure to digital technology.

Considering current global access statistics, texting on mobile phones – a comparatively old digital technology, dating back to the early 1990s – emerges as the only truly global social media application (a comprehensive overview of sociolinguistic research on texting can be found in Thurlow and Poff 2013). Although the focus of existing social media research has been on Internet-based semi-public and public applications, definitions of social media do not exclude dyadic genres. They emphasize interactivity rather than plurality of participants, and as such include texting (as well as chatting and email; see Hunsinger and Senft 2014).

The pervasiveness of texting is a function of cost: basic phones, which allow for calls and text, can be bought for a fraction of the price of a smartphone, tablet or computer, and have become affordable consumer goods for many people in the world. Table 36.1 illustrates the near-universal access to mobile phones, compared to much more limited access to the Internet and, especially, data-intensive applications such as Facebook. The overall picture is one of persistent global inequality. On the one hand, there are wealthy and well-connected nations where the majority has plentiful access to a variety of digital media. On the other hand, there are those nations where only the elite, and perhaps a growing middle class, are able to take part in Internet-based digital practices. For the majority of the world's population, digital social media engagement means, at this point in time, primarily text-based practices on a mobile phone.

Internet access, however, is not a binary variable: access or no-access. Rather, Internet users are diverse regarding the *type of access* they have to online spaces. Consider South Africa, a middle-income country and emerging economy. According to the most recent population census, about one-third of the population uses the Internet. Yet, this is a heterogeneous group: only about a quarter of South Africans access the Internet using a computer from the convenience of their own home, almost half use their phone to go online, and the remaining

Table 36.1 Mobile phone access, Internet access and Facebook users (as percentage of total population for selected countries, 2012)

	Mobile phone access (%)	Internet access (%)	Facebook users (%)
United States	96	78	53
Denmark	118	90	55
Australia	106	89	53
India	70	11	5
Indonesia	114	22	21
Vietnam	148	34	12
Brazil	125	50	26
Mexico	83	37	34
Suriname	107	35	19
Nigeria	68	28	4
Kenya	71	32	5
Mali	98	3	1
WORLD 2012	88	33	12
WORLD 2014 (estimate)	95	40	18

Source: www.internetworldstats.com and statistics provided by the International Telecommunications Union (www.itu.int).

Note: ITU statistics provide data only on mobile phone subscriptions, not users or handsets. Thus, one user may have purchased different SIM cards for different devices, or use different cards to exploit various benefits. In addition, some of the SIM cards may be inactive. This accounts for percentages over 100 percent.

quarter has access at work, public libraries or Internet cafes. Research has shown that these different types of access support different types of online engagement. Easy and plentiful access to high-end technology from home – which is common in Europe, North America, parts of Asia and Latin America, as well as Japan and Australia – facilitates complex multimodal practices and allows users to engage with diverse online visual cultures. Thus, images can be uploaded, video blogs and video remixes can be created and posted. In addition, intensive and regular engagement with the visual worlds of online gaming is possible. Trying to do all this from a phone is quite a different matter, especially since the phones that are used in most parts of the world are not smartphones with multiple apps and large high-resolution screens, but low-end feature phones which offer only basic Internet access. Moreover, data costs are high and many phone users switch off images and video altogether in order to save money as well as battery charge (as access to electricity is not always easy). For many people playing around with typography is all the multimodality they can afford.

Questions of access affect the global representation of languages and linguistic diversity in digital environments, and on the searchable web online multilingualism does not reflect offline multilingualism. English, which has been historically dominant on the Internet, remains the strongest language online, followed by a number of European languages (German, Russian, Spanish, French, Portuguese, Italian and Polish) as well as Japanese and Chinese.[5] Widely spoken languages such as Hindi, Farsi, Hausa or Javanese are only minimally represented, and the majority of the world's 6,000–7,000 languages remain invisible online. This suggests that the digital space constitutes a linguistic ecology unlike that of spoken languages. It is more similar to what has been called the *ecology of literacy* (Barton 2007). For example, in many postcolonial countries, English, French, Spanish and Portuguese remain the languages of literacy, education and public signage, while local languages are used in spoken interactions. This offline pattern, reflecting a communicative separation between literacy and oral practices is often reproduced in digital spaces. At the same time, digital environments offer important opportunities for minority language use, and the digital is also a space where the status quo of the offline literacy ecology has been challenged. This is particularly true in high-income countries where the digital divide shows signs of leveling, and minority speakers have access to digital spaces. However, digital media have also become important writing spaces in middle- and low-income countries, especially when one looks at the 'deep' or 'invisible web'; that is, those parts of the Internet which cannot be retrieved easily through conventional search engines. This includes much interactive content – such as Facebook and Twitter posts – and it is likely that these spaces show greater multilingualism than the searchable or surface Internet.

36.3 Digital literacies: visuality, reflexivity and creativity

Discourses of novelty and discontinuity have long accompanied technological change. Communication technologies, especially the Internet, are no exception. Just as social media have been portrayed and celebrated as 'new,' so has the notion of digital 'participation' or online 'participatory culture' (Jenkins 2006). These discourses describe the 'old,' pre-2000 Internet – also called Web 1.0 – as a traditional mass medium which simply provided information to people. By contrast, the 'new' interactive Internet, Web 2.0, is seen as encouraging the involvement of users, audiences and consumers in the creation of online culture and content, thus constituting a new era for grassroots or vernacular media engagement. However, participation is not new and traditional dichotomies such as author/audience, producer/consumer or professional/amateur have always been dubious in media studies: radio and TV audiences have long been shown to engage actively and passionately with what they hear and see; letters-to-the-editor are an example of media participation and user-generated content long before digital media; discussion groups and MUDs showed intensive user interactivity on the 'old' Internet; and alternative media have a long tradition of encouraging listeners, readers and viewers to tell their own stories (see Fuchs 2014, for a critical discussion).

While there are important continuities between old and new media, we are not looking at the same-old-same-old and things have certainly changed for those who can afford to invest in the technology. There have been major changes of scale: more people write more than ever before and as they do so many of them have access to a vast, global archive of semiotic resources, via the Internet. In addition, the barriers to artistic expression have been lowered with the availability of multimodal technologies and platforms such as YouTube or Facebook. However, extensive multimodal opportunities notwithstanding, textual practices remain central to social media usage. This is true not only for low- and medium-income countries, but also for technologically rich contexts. Thus, looking at a recent research report for the United States, only about a quarter of adults said that they have *ever* posted videos online (the percentage for *ever* having posted photos was around 50 percent). American teenagers are more likely than adults to post a photo of themselves on a social network(ing) site (close to 90 percent), but their engagement with video production remains equally low. Digital writing, on the other hand, is a daily practice for most: American adults sent about forty text messages a day, teenagers more than 100. Similarly, textual engagement with Facebook – writing status updates, commenting and checking messages – emerges as a daily practice in US survey data.[6]

Mark Sebba's (2007) sociolinguistic discussion of writing and 'orthographic regimes' is useful for understanding digital literacies. Although writing is often seen as being linked to norms and the standard language, it is actually a diverse and varied linguistic practice, and only in some social contexts is correctness of orthography and grammar regulated, required and policed. Typical examples of such 'fully regulated spaces' are schools and publishing houses, or, in the digital space, online newspapers as well as government sites and commercial webpages. In other social contexts, it is permissible for writers to disregard existing conventions, to experiment with spelling, and to combine different styles and languages creatively. Sebba calls these 'weakly regulated spaces,' and interactive social media constitute such a space. They are similar to personal letters, graffiti and advertising: rules are relaxed, personalization of texts is encouraged, and transgression is often licensed.

The study of literacy as a social practice is at the core of a research program which is commonly referred to as 'new' literacy studies. The 'new' in this context does not refer to the 'newness' of the field, which emerged back in the 1980s, but to the fact that it took the study of literacy into a 'new' direction. 'New' literacy studies moved firmly away from questions of pedagogy and psychology, which conceptualized literacy as a set of context-independent *skills* that can be taught, measured and assessed, and focused instead on describing and understanding literacy *practices*. That is, writing/reading is seen as a communicative activity which is socially embedded, locally meaningful and inherently diverse (see Baynham and Prinsloo (2009) for an overview). From this, strongly ethnographic, perspective, written language is not simply an imperfect reflection of speech (Bloomfield 1933: 21), nor should it be measured against the orthographic and grammatical rules of the standard. Rather, it is seen as a creative sociolinguistic practice in its own right.

Writing allows people to *do* things with language, which are not possible when speaking. Importantly, writing is visual, not auditory. The visual aesthetics of writing have been emphasized, for example, by Gunther Kress (2000) in his work on children's early writing and by Jan Blommaert (2008) in his discussion of informal, grassroots literacies. Thus, writers can, for example, choose between cursive and block-writing, embellish handwritten letters or choose a particular font on the computer; they can add colour to their letters, or keep it black-and-white; they may experiment with letter size, and put punctuation to new uses. Consider the following Facebook status update posted by Lindiwe, a South African woman in her twenties (2012). It is an everyday example of what Roman Jakobson (1960) has described as the poetic function of language: the writer pays attention to linguistic form and manipulates the shape words in order to create new meanings, and to articulate a personal voice.

(1) Indeed we surfer 4 BEAUTY can't sleep nawooo my head is painfulooo iyhOooo!! Nyt nyt (in pains)

('Indeed we suffer for beauty, can't sleep now my head is painful, iyhooo!! Night night (in pains)')[7]

The complex ways in which the visual nature of writing enters into meaning-making becomes evident if one attempts to read such texts aloud. How should we represent the visual richness of this brief text in speech? How can we 'speak' capitals, rebus forms as well as playful non-standard spellings (*nawoo, painfulooo*)?

Writing is not only visual, it is also tangibly material (as mentioned above). It involves artifacts (pen/paper, keyboard/screen, spray-can/wall), and produces texts which – unlike spoken words – can be saved and archived.[8] They can be revisited, rather than remembered; deliberately destroyed, rather than forgotten. Moreover, writing also frees us from the constraints of real-time processing and lessens the interactional pressures of body-to-body interaction. That is, it allows us time to plan and to reflect: if we wish, we can compose our texts carefully, reconsider habitual, pre-reflexive routines, delete and add, revise and edit. In his work on advertising, Erving Goffman (1979: 84) discussed the link between editing, reflexivity and creativity. He observed that editing allows us to take out 'the dull footage' and to emphasize 'colourful poses.' That is, it allows us to go beyond that which is expected and to create – if we wish to do so – texts that stand out.

An emphasis on reflexivity and creativity stands in contrast to much mainstream linguistics, which – by and large – sees speakers as following norms and conventions, and linguists as those who discover these norms by analyzing maximally unmonitored and pre-reflexive speech. Variationist sociolinguistics, especially, has focused its attention on 'the vernacular' and the systematic variation it displays. Does informal written language follow the same principles as informal spoken language? Sali Tagliamonte and Derek Denis (2008) compared variation in informal spoken Canadian English with variation in instant messaging (IM) for the same group of participants. Their results were stable across a range of variables, but did not support an interpretation of interactive digital writing as mirroring the patterns or principles of spoken language. While participants' speech showed the systematic and patterned variation predicted by Labovian sociolinguistics, their chats looked quite different. What is most striking about the chat data is the unexpected combination of forms which belong to different stylistic realms. In (2), for example, the standard quotative (*say*), followed by standard use of punctuation (colon to indicate the beginning of a quote in writing), is combined with a sequence of stylistically marked non-standard forms. Such data, described by Tagliamonte and Denis as *mixing, blending* and *fusion*, play havoc with the co-occurrence expectations that underpin variationist sociolinguistics.

(2) Jeff says: 'lyk omgod omgod omgod*zzzzzZZZzzzzz*!!!11one (IM, female, 15 years; Tagliamonte and Denis 2008: 26)

(Jeff says: 'lyk oh my god, oh my god, oh my god *zzzzzzZZZZzzz*!!! 11one')[9]

The data in (2) is structurally similar to code-switching and code-mixing in multilingual speech, and it has been argued that social media have created an important space for the production of multistylistic and multilingual texts. Digital multilingual texts combine different languages – as well as different scripts – creatively and ultimately unpredictably, just like the writer in (2) combines different styles and forms. Looking at Thai/English chat data, which shows diverse and unpredictable patterns of code-mixing similar to (2), Philip Seargeant and Caroline Tagg (2011) have argued for what they call a 'post-varieties' approach to language: the texts that are produced online do not show 'obviously identifiable systematic regularities,' and thus cannot be said to reflect a definable 'variety' or language. Instead they resemble what William Labov (1972: 225) has called 'irregular dialect mixture,' that is, the ad hoc, bricolage-like combination of linguistic forms which belong to different systems (as opposed to sociolinguistic variation as 'an inherent and regular property of *the system*,' my emphasis).

An alternative to Labovian variationism, and structuralist approaches to language more generally, can be found in the substantial and diverse body of work, which looks at language not as a variable yet structured and rule-governed system, but as a repertoire of signs. In other words, linguistic knowledge is recast as a set of communicative resources, which are reworked creatively in interaction. In this context resources are understood not as bounded language systems, but as any semiotic sign which carries meaning and is available to speakers/writers. This includes 'bits of language,' isolated words or phrases, which can be used to achieve communicative ends (Blommaert 2010).

Sociolinguists studying digital media have also turned to the language-philosophical writings of Mikhail Bakhtin in theorizing variation online (e.g. Androutsopoulos 2011). Bakhtin argues that when we speak (or write) we draw on a variety of social voices, each one with a unique tone and timbre, and speaking (as well as writing) is not about animating 'a language,' but rather about combining linguistic signs creatively, bringing them into dialogue with one another. Bakhtin (1981 [1934/1935]) uses the term heteroglossia, literally multi-speech-ness (translated from Russian *разноречие* [*raznorečie*]), to describe the multiplicity of languages, dialects, styles and forms which provide us with resources for speaking and writing, that is, for meaning-making and everyday creativity. Linguistics, from a Bakhtinian perspective, is not about discovering structures, systems or regular patterns; it is about approaching and understanding language as radically heterogeneous and open-ended. Individual utterances are the skilful, often artful, and always singular and unique manifestation of this diversity. And in crafting our utterances we establish particular speaking voices, social personae and identities. One of the affordances of digital communication is that we can go beyond Bakhtinian *voicing*, that is, the use of someone else's voice in our own speech. Instead we can become the other voice, that is, invent, create and perform social personae which are distinct and separate from our offline self.

36.4 Disembodied language and heteroglossic identities

Like most cultural and social theories of identity, sociolinguistic approaches do not position the existence of a singular 'authentic' identity. Rather, identities are seen as multiple (not unified), dynamic (not static), something we *do* in interaction (not something we *are*), and co-constructed by audiences (not monologic performances). The focus on agency, on *doing identity*, brings with it the potential for reflexivity and creativity: identities and social personae can be carefully crafted and, as such, become part of what Goffman (1969) calls 'impression management.'

However, because our bodies are always with us and mark us as members of particular social groups, the identities we are able to display in offline contexts are always constrained. Online spaces, on the other hand, allow us to engage in fantasies of the self and identity play: we can be who we are offline if we want to, but can also pretend to be someone entirely different. In her work on phone-sex workers, who – in the absence of a visual link – create complex vocal fantasies and erotic personae, Kira Hall (1995) refers to this as *cross-expressing*: a linguistic performance akin to cross-dressing in which speakers/writers successfully appropriate behaviors that do not match their bodily identity.[10]

The pre-2000 Internet was portrayed by many as a utopian space which enabled the unstrained performance of imagined identities. It was also a space of default Whiteness and maleness, culturally uniform and homogenous, and as such particularly suited to what Lisa Nakamura (2002) calls *identity tourism*: creating a diversity of interlocutors, where – in reality – there was none. Sherry Turkle's (1995) book *Life on the Screen* captured the radical

Zeitgeist of the 1980s and 1990s. She describes the text-mainly Internet as a space where identities were created and invented at whim, where pseudonyms allowed users to establish as many different alter personae as they wished. The following is an extract from one of her interviews:

> You can be whoever you want to be. You can completely redefine yourself. You can be the opposite sex. You can be more talkative. You can be less talkative. You can just be whoever you want, really, whoever you have the capacity to be.
>
> (Turkle 1995: 184)

However, starting around 2000, social media applications moved away from anonymity and pseudonymity (the latter refers to the use of nicknames which often created stable alter personae). People are now encouraged to use their 'real' names and to create online identities which are firmly rooted in pre-existing offline identities. Lee Knuttila (2011) calls this the 'personal turn' and argues that this 'general closing of the gap between online and offline personas marks a dramatic development in the structure and experience of the Internet.' The real-name policies of Google+ and Facebook are prominent examples of the personal turn. Both sites require users to register with their 'real' name and surname. Failure to do so, although technically possible, is a violation of terms of service. While Facebook largely relies on the honesty of users, Google+ closed a number of accounts, which were identified in breach of this policy, in 2011. This started what has become known as the #nymwars: a vigorous online debate about the value of online anonymity and pseudonymity.

There are practical, profit-oriented and political, reasons why some platforms prefer people to write under their 'real' name: it facilitates targeted advertising, a main source of income for many social media platforms, as well as Internet security and surveillance. However, a preference and indeed desire for 'real,' dependable and unchanging, online identities pre-dates 9/11 security concerns and the corporatization of digital platforms. Already in the mid-1980s, the virtual community The Well introduced the slogan YOYOW, 'you own your own words,' and insisted on real-name registration: 'As a Well member, you use your real name. This leads to real conversations and relationships.' In the 1990s, participants of the women-only discussion group SAPPHO, which allowed pseudonyms and alter personae, 'screened' new members stylistically in order to detect men-posing-as-women, 'with the list veterans becoming quickly suspicious of anyone who [did] not conform to their idea of discursive femininity' (Hall 1996: 159).

Thus, while some celebrate online spaces as enabling a 'dream ... of a powerful infidel heteroglossia,' where we can be liberated from the strictures of our bodies (Haraway 1991: 181), others see identity play and pseudonyms as disruptive and dangerous to harmonious social relations online. Such discourses limit play and fantasy to socially acceptable 'impression management': we may portray ourselves as prettier, smarter or funnier than we usually are, but there should be some sense of continuity between the self online and the self offline. However, old habits die hard. Although the use of pseudonyms and identity play is increasingly discouraged on social media sites, users do not necessarily comply. In 2014, Facebook estimated that, real-name policies notwithstanding, between 5 percent and 10 percent of existing accounts were fake or fictional.[11] The situation is similar on Twitter and YouTube.

Moreover, some online spaces support radical anonymity: they do not require registration or even a nick(name), users can simply log on and start posting. An example of this is the random board /b/ on 4chan.org. The site was founded in the same year as MySpace (2003), but could not be more different. There are no profile pages and users do not even create fictional online identities: they simply write and post images with everyone using the default name 'anonymous.' The interaction order of the site is unique: if everyone is called 'anonymous,' then it is impossible to actually figure out who has been talking to whom, and how many people are involved in a conversation. That is, the different postings in any thread could be a monologue of one individual, a conversation of two people, or a multilayered interaction of several people. Consequently, conventional sociolinguistic analysis is entirely impossible. Consider the posts in (3) which responded to a comment and an image of a bearded man (11 June 2013). The image elicited over 200 replies, all by 'anonymous,' mostly in English, but also some in German and Croatian. Some swearing notwithstanding, (3) is a tame example of 4chan interactions. The site is classified as NSFW ('not safe for work') because of its offensive – usually pornographic but also racist and otherwise distasteful – content.

(3) Anonymous: [posts an image of a bearded man]
superior men hairstyle thread /b/ going to the barber at 1pm, need some 'inspiration'
Anonymous: Go bald
Feels great
Head cold
Anonymous: if youre over the age of 16 and have hair like that youre below beta, youre a fucking gamma
Anonymous: shave all that shit you fucking disgusting hipster hippie faggot cunt
Anonymous: DAMN IT.
I wish I could grow a fucking beard.
Anonymous: why are you on the computer, did you ditch school today?
Anonymous: Summer break actually, you prehistorical fuck.
Anonymous: Used to have hair similar to this. Gigantic pain in the ass to keep up.
Anonymous: How the fuck do you style it like that?

Not only is what is posted on 4chan fully anonymous and not attributable to individuals, it is also entirely ephemeral as the site has no archiving function. Posts appear, elicit comments and disappear when participants lose interest. When Christopher Poole aka moot, the founder of 4chan, spoke at a TED talk in 2009 about the 'case for anonymity online,' he argued that it was precisely the site's anonymity which supported creativity. He argued that anonymity helps to overcome self-censorship, relaxes inhibitions and encourages experimentation. Radical anonymity certainly has its attractions and the last few years have seen the emergence of a growing number of anonymity applications. These include Whisper launched in 2012, Secret in 2013, Cloaq and Yik Yak in 2014.[12]

While pseudonymity and anonymity support play, fantasy and also provide us with a safe confessional space, they also have a dark side: they make it easy to spread untruths and deceive others, to be outright nasty and hurtful without taking responsibility. Practices of this type are often associated with so-called trolls, a new media variant of the trickster archetype, who take delight in upsetting others and causing havoc. A popular trolling practice is to be accepted as a legitimate member on a particular site, such as a chat room or discussion group (see the example of SAPPHO above), and, once accepted, to engage in antisocial behavior, typically by posting inflammatory and offensive messages. Trolling and other forms of online deceit, such as scams, provide linguists with important data to study the linguistics of successful as well as unsuccessful deception and lying. The frequency and success with which such impersonations are done online – and even picked up as 'true' by mainstream media as in the case of the gay-girl-in-Damascus blogging hoax and the entirely fictitious Moldovan soccer sensation Masal Bugduv – show that textual deception can be particularly difficult to detect (Hancock 2007). This has opened up new areas in applied linguistics. Text messaging forensics, for example, is now a specialization within forensic linguistics and is becoming increasingly important in criminal investigations (Grant 2010).

36.5 Conclusion: social media and linguistic theory

The study of digital communication has drawn attention to aspects of language and communication which have so far been marginal to linguistic as well as sociolinguistic theory. First, digital media encourage us to consider the materiality of communication: the ways in which physical artifacts enter into meaning-making and the persistent global inequalities we see with regard to access to these artifacts. While language and communication might be public goods, digital communication is only possible when one has access to consumer goods.

Second, new media linguistics has brought writing and multimodality firmly into linguistics. Although digital communication remains, at this stage, primarily text-based, such texts are, as shown above, complex visual artifacts which often co-articulate multiple voices and identities. Moreover, writing, because of the opportunities it allows for editing, moves linguistics beyond its traditional focus on norms and conventions, and toward creativity and the unexpected. Reflexivity is a central theme in contemporary social theory and considered to be a defining feature of social practice in contemporary societies.

And finally, online spaces can be important for understanding how identities are expressed, created and challenged. Real-name policies notwithstanding, the digital still allows ample scope for fantasy and identity play, and radically anonymous interactive platforms such as 4chan defy existing models of conversation analysis and interactional linguistics. The use of pseudonyms is challenging for traditional sociolinguistic analysis too: well-established ways of looking at language and the social world are not possible when we simply do not know if the text we are analyzing was produced by a young White male or a middle-aged African woman. Sociolinguistic approaches which rely on a construct of language as reflecting speakers'/writers' 'real' background and socialization are all but impossible.

Notes

1. Voice-based applications (the telephone, Skype) are not usually included in existing definitions of social media.
2. I follow Leopoldina Fortunati (2005: 53) in using body-to-body rather than face-to-face because 'the "communicative act" involves not just the face but the entire body, its gestures and postures,' as well as its position in space and its visual appearance (height, weight, perceived ethnicity/race, clothing, etc.).
3. www.upi.com/Science_News/Technology/2013/06/29/Survey-Americans-spend-23-hours-a-week-onlinesocial-media/UPI-61961372562999.
4. www.uis.unesco.org/literacy/Documents/fs26-2013-literacy-en.pdf.
5. w3techs.com, March 2014.

6   www.pewresearch.org/2013/05/21/teens-on-facebook; www.pewinternet.org/2012/09/17/smartphone-research-infographic.
7   The pain referred to is the result of having extensions woven into the hair.
8   Although spoken language can also be recorded and archived, this requires special equipment and is not an inherent affordance of the medium.
9   The '11one' cannot be 'translated' easily into an equivalent English expression. Since both the exclamation mark and the number 1 share the same key on computer keyboards, writers might end up typing '1' instead of '!.' This has evolved into the expression 11one, indexing excitement and a sense of humor (also written as !1!1one; www.urbandictionary.com).
10 Cross-expressing is different from crossing as discussed by Ben Rampton (1995). The latter is not about creating a fantasy and making others believe that one really is the person one pretends to be. Rather, it is an example of Bakhtinian voicing: the other voice remains visible to the audience throughout.
11 http://thenextweb.com/facebook/2014/02/03/facebook-estimates-5-5-11-2-accounts-fake.
12 www.theguardian.com/technology/2014/jun/07/anonymous-social-media-apps-encourage-overshare.

References

Androutsopoulos, J. (2011) From variation to heteroglossia in the study of computer-mediated discourse. In C. Thurlow and K. Mroczek (eds) *Digital Discourse. Language in the New Media*, pp. 277–97. Oxford/New York: Oxford University Press.
Bakhtin, M.M. (1981 [1934/1935]) Discourse in the novel. Transl. C. Emerson and M. Holquist in *The Dialogic Imagination*, pp. 259–422. Austin: University of Texas Press.
Barton, D. (2007) *Literacy. An Introduction to the Ecology of Written Language*. Oxford: Blackwell.
Baynham, M. and M. Prinsloo (eds) (2009) *The Future of Literacy Studies*. Basingstoke: Palgrave Macmillan.
Blommaert, J. (2008) *Grassroots Literacy. Writing, Identity and Voice in Central Africa*. Abingdon: Routledge.
Blommaert, J. (2010) *The Sociolinguistics of Globalization*. Cambridge: Cambridge University Press.
Bloomfield, L. (1933) *Language*. New York: Holt, Rinehart, and Winston.
Burke, P. and A. Briggs (2009) *Social History of the Media. From Gutenberg to the Internet*. Cambridge: Polity.
Cantril, H. (1941) *The Psychology of Social Movements*. New York: John Wiley and Sons.
Deumert, A. (2014) *Sociolinguistics and Mobile Communication*. Edinburgh: Edinburgh University Press.
Fortunati, L. (2005) Is body-to-body communication still the prototype? *The Information Society* 21: 53–61.
Fuchs, C. (2014) *Social Media: A Critical Introduction*. Los Angeles: Sage.
Goffman, E. (1969) *The Presentation of Self in Everyday Life*. London: Penguin.
Goffman, E. (1979) *Gender Advertisements*. London: Macmillan.
Grant, T. (2010) Txt 4n6: Idiolect free authorship analysis. In M. Coulthard and A. Johnson (eds) *The Routledge Handbook of Forensic Linguistics*, pp. 508–22. Abingdon: Routledge.
Greene, W.B. (1875) *Socialistic, Communistic, Mutualistic, and Financial Fragments*. Boston: Lee and Shepard.
Grin, Francois (2006) Economic considerations in language policy. In T. Ricento (ed.) *An Introduction in Language Policy*, pp. 77–94. Oxford: Blackwell.
Hall, K. (1995) Lip-service on the fantasy lines. In M. Bucholtz and K. Hall *Gender Articulated: Language and the Socially Constructed Self*, pp. 183–216. London: Routledge.
Hall, K. (1996) Cyberfeminism. In S.C. Herring (ed.) *Computer-Mediated Communication: Linguistic, Social, and Cross-Cultural Perspectives*, pp. 147–70. Amsterdam: John Benjamins.

Hancock, J.T. (2007) Digital deception: Why, when and how people lie online. In A. Joinson, K. McKenna, T. Postmes and U.-D. Reips (eds) *The Oxford Handbook of Internet Psychology*, pp. 289–301. Oxford/New York: Oxford University Press.

Haraway, D.J. (1991) *Simians, Cyborgs, and Women: The Reinvention of Nature*. New York: Routledge.

Harris, R. (2000) *Rethinking Writing*. London: Athlone.

Horst, H. and D. Miller (eds) (2012) *Digital Anthropology*. London/New York: Berg.

Hunsinger, J. and T. Senft (eds) (2014) *Routledge Handbook of Social Media*. London: Routledge.

Jakobson, R. (1960) Linguistics and poetics. In T.A. Seboek (ed.) *Style in Language*, pp. 350–77. New York: Technology Press.

Jenkins, H. (2006) *Fans, Bloggers, and Gamers: Exploring Participatory Culture*. New York: New York University Press.

Knuttila, L. (2011) User unknown: 4chan, anonymity and contingency. *First Monday* 16, 3 October 2011. http://firstmonday.org/ojs/index.php/fm/article/view/3665/3055.

Kress, G. (2000) *Early Spelling. Between Convention and Creativity*. London: Routledge.

Labov, W. (1972) *Sociolinguistic Patterns*. Philadelphia: University of Pennsylvania Press.

Lomberg, S. (2014) *Social Media, Social Genres. Making Sense of the Ordinary*. London: Routledge.

Nakamura, L. (2002) *Cybertypes: Race, Ethnicity and Identity on the Internet*. London: Routledge.

Rampton, B. (1995) *Crossing: Language and Ethnicity Among Adolescents*. London: Longman.

Seargeant, P. and C. Tagg (2011) English on the Internet and a 'post-varieties' approach to language. *World Englishes* 30: 496–514.

Sebba, M. (2007) *Spelling and Society*. Cambridge: Cambridge University Press.

Shankar, S. and J.R. Cavanaugh (2012) Language and materiality in global capitalism. *Annual Review of Anthropology* 41: 355–69.

Stuckenberg, J.H. (1898) *Introduction to the Study of Sociology*. New York: A.C. Armstrong and Son.

Tagliamonte, S.A. and D. Denis (2008) Linguistic ruin? Lol! Instant messaging and teen language. *American Speech* 83: 3–34.

Thurlow, Crispin and M. Poff (2013) Text messaging. In S.C. Herring, D. Stein and T. Virtanen (eds) *Handbook of the Pragmatics of CMC*, pp. 163–90. Berlin/New York: Mouton de Gruyter.

Turkle, S. (1995) *Life on the Screen. Identity in the Age of the Internet*. New York: Simon and Schuster.

Index

accessibility 194, 392, 404, 478, 529, 534
accessibility hierarchy 404, 405, 484
acquisition 6, 19, 31, 91, 101, 113, 116, 117, 169, 183, 206, 212, 213, 228, 259, 266, 283, 285, 286, 287, 291, 294, 301, 309, 311, 313, 314, 318, 326, 327, 328, 329, 330, 332, 333, 334, 335, 338, 340, 341, 342, 343, 377, 378, 380, 383, 429, 439, 450, 452, 456, 459, 460, 464, 465, 469, 477, 478, 479, 481, 513, 516
actuation 349, 353
addressation 8, 19, 34, 145, 223, 236, 240, 242, 246, 259, 372, 373, 429, 537, 538
addressed phonology 59
addressee/hearer 5, 25, 207, 210, 212, 214, 222, 224, 225, 229, 230, 231, 233, 236, 237, 238, 239, 242, 247, 253, 255, 256, 279, 318, 319, 323, 326, 370, 374, 408, 464, 475, 478, 519, 524, 525, 527, 528, 541
adposition 407
affect 25, 56, 101, 112, 115, 162, 174, 180, 189, 209, 214, 215, 216, 218, 224, 232, 234, 235, 238, 258, 265, 290, 315, 323, 329, 330, 333, 338, 339, 340, 351, 419, 438, 452, 474, 508, 513, 529, 537, 543, 552, 554, 564
African American 238, 266, 269, 270, 242, 263
agrammatism 309
airstream 63, 64, 65, 66, 68, 69, 76
Allan, K. 1, 12, 15, 102, 116, 220, 364, 516, 529, 531
allomorphy 92, 93, 94, 95, 96, 111
allophony 49, 50, 78, 83, 85, 86, 87, 88, 89, 90, 91, 92, 93, 94, 95, 96, 98, 99, 100, 101, 246, 345

alphabet 12, 16, 47, 48, 49, 50, 52, 53, 54, 55, 58, 59, 60, 62, 87, 100, 101, 102, 112, 187, 188, 189, 190, 191, 195, 196, 198, 201, 202, 204, 345, 441, 511
analogy 9, 13, 19, 25, 38, 44, 53, 54, 116, 142, 145, 166, 195, 197, 222, 239, 241, 299, 306, 339, 347, 354, 356, 361, 364, 370, 371, 372, 374, 375, 420, 449, 474, 497, 535
anaphoricity 136, 137, 139, 143, 144, 145, 147, 148, 160, 162, 163, 173, 180, 186, 211, 373, 457, 475, 476, 483, 522
anglicize 54, 193
Anglo 5, 208, 209, 210, 211, 215, 218, 219, 344, 345, 355, 358, 362, 418
annotation 10, 141, 142, 361, 488, 490, 494, 495, 496, 498, 499, 502, 506-511
antecedent 138, 145, 147, 161, 162, 173, 207, 316, 476
antonymy 156, 497
anxiety 284, 295, 338, 339, 340, 342
aphasia 281, 282, 283, 437, 478
Apollonius Dyscolus 12, 13, 15
applied linguistics 7, 13, 188, 235, 279, 329, 330, 340, 341, 342, 343, 429, 430, 440, 513, 514, 527, 532
aptitude 329, 331, 339, 342, 343
Arabic 37, 58, 68, 265, 274, 304, 393
Aramaic 58
Aristotle 10, 12, 13, 14, 116, 186, 516
articulation 17, 18, 27, 28, 36, 49, 53, 55, 62, 63, 64, 65, 67, 68, 69, 70, 71, 72, 73, 74, 77, 78, 80, 81, 82, 84, 86, 87, 88, 100, 102, 154, 207, 282, 285, 290, 300, 301, 302, 303, 308, 318, 323, 348, 366, 375, 408, 433, 436, 441, 531, 566, 571

Asher, N. 151, 162, 168, 169, 176, 178, 179, 180, 185
aspect (grammatical) 136, 151, 154, 176, 241, 260, 283, 309, 319, 372, 374, 382
attention 5, 9, 21, 22, 26, 35, 38, 81, 267, 269, 275, 281, 282, 286, 288, 294, 314, 315, 316, 320, 326, 327, 328, 331, 332, 333, 337, 338, 339, 341, 342, 377, 420, 456, 470, 566
attitude 34, 155, 172, 173, 219, 331, 349, 370, 388, 389, 399, 516, 519, 529, 531
audio recording 244, 246, 537
Australian aborigines 33, 35, 40, 134, 255, 358, 362, 387, 397, 462, 478
Australian English 68, 69, 70, 364
automatization 63, 71, 74, 87, 92, 99, 169, 181, 182, 183, 185, 200, 291, 295, 302, 305, 388, 426, 429, 456, 465, 479, 488, 489, 491, 492, 493, 494, 495, 496, 498, 499, 506, 507, 508, 512
autonomous syntax 9, 457, 464, 470
autonomy 222, 257, 367, 369, 392, 438, 456, 474, 483

back formation 109
bag of words models 489
Bakhtin, M.M. 568, 572
Bally, C. 16, 61, 203, 419, 420, 421, 429, 430, 438, 446
Bamberg, M. 244, 248
Bauer, L. 106, 113, 116, 349, 363
behavio(u)rism 285, 286, 287, 288, 335, 440, 441, 443
belief 11, 207, 214, 252, 257, 266, 272, 317, 327, 363, 370, 397, 443, 472, 519, 520, 525, 527, 531
Bell, A. 101, 102, 275, 278, 409, 416
Biber, D. 236, 248, 279, 513, 514
Bible 13, 55, 57, 108, 421, 424, 430, 509, 550
bilingualism 12, 190, 191, 192, 193, 195, 200, 203, 256, 276, 314, 329, 377, 378, 379, 395, 398, 399, 427, 429, 452
biolinguistics 9, 447–454
Bisang, W. 366, 370, 382, 383
biuniqueness 92, 93, 94, 95, 96
Blackburn, P. 142, 151
blending 109, 166, 168, 455, 461, 468, 567

Blissymbolics 48, 49
Bloomfield, L. 8, 14, 15, 169, 434, 435, 440, 441, 442, 443, 444, 445, 566, 572
Boas, F. 14, 156, 168, 250, 251, 252, 253, 432, 440, 441, 445
Boeckx, C. 447, 453
Booij, G. 104, 106, 110, 115, 116, 117
Borg, E. 209, 521, 529
borrowing 29, 50, 51, 52, 54, 114, 115, 190, 191, 201, 202, 276, 354, 357, 367, 378, 419, 420, 421, 442
Braille 2, 304
brain 6, 19, 22, 27, 29, 31, 32, 39, 45, 46, 63, 82, 83, 90, 197, 213, 281, 282, 293, 291, 293, 294, 295, 296, 298–306, 309, 310, 433, 443, 448, 450, 451, 452, 547, 551, 558, 559
British National Corpus (BNC) 140, 496, 499, 503, 505
Broca's area 297, 305, 307, 308, 309
Brodmann areas (BAs) 297, 298
Brookes, H. 38, 45
Brown, P. 214, 220, 221, 222, 223, 224, 225, 227, 228, 229, 232, 233, 234
Brugmann, K. 360, 361, 363
Burridge, K. 126, 133, 344, 351, 352, 362, 363, 364
Butcher, A. 62
Bybee, J. 98, 102, 103, 346, 351, 363, 368, 382, 466, 468, 474, 479, 483

Cann, R. 141, 142, 143, 148, 150, 151, 152
Carnap. R. 156, 220, 518
Carston, R. 177, 185
Casillas, M. 311, 326, 327
categorization 6, 9, 14, 21, 36, 48, 53, 80, 81, 101, 103, 166, 241, 254, 269, 272, 273, 290, 299, 314, 387, 456, 462, 469, 474, 489, 549
category 3, 20, 21, 22, 25, 44, 49, 50, 51, 67, 68, 94, 107, 112, 117, 118, 119, 120, 122-132, 134, 155, 159, 163, 164, 168, 172, 201, 210, 212, 214, 216, 235, 242, 247, 251, 252, 253, 254, 260, 263, 268, 269, 270, 272, 273, 274, 306, 307, 314, 318, 323, 333, 334, 348, 369, 370, 372, 374, 375, 378, 380, 383, 387, 388, 414, 415, 420, 423, 425, 426, 434, 439, 441,

Index

457, 458, 460, 462, 465, 466, 468, 479, 480, 481, 493, 494, 495, 496, 500, 507, 508, 511, 512, 513, 549, 552
Catford, J. 82, 421, 429
causativization 323, 372, 374, 481
change (diachronic) 6, 7, 34, 42, 45, 51, 54, 56, 61, 114, 115, 116, 117, 151, 193, 216, 235, 263, 264, 265, 266, 268-280, 340, 344-384, 398, 410, 425, 435, 444, 460, 461, 465, 466
Chierchia, G. 219, 220
Chinese 8, 47-54, 56, 112, 113, 117, 178, 234, 304, 339, 343, 358, 367, 384, 403, 411, 420, 423, 429, 564
Chinook 8
Chomsky, N. 9, 14, 15, 31, 83, 84, 89, 92, 102, 135, 278, 285, 286, 288, 347, 421, 422, 424, 426, 429, 432, 435, 442, 443, 444, 445, 447, 448, 450, 451, 453, 455, 456, 457, 458, 460, 461, 466, 472, 482, 492, 502, 503, 504, 513, 523
citation 189, 190, 192, 193
Clark, E.V. 114, 117, 311, 316, 318,3149, 320, 322, 323, 324, 326, 327, 328
classifiers 43, 44, 489, 490
clause 12, 18, 30, 43, 106, 111, 125, 126, 127, 131, 132, 138, 148, 184, 219, 239, 241, 242, 243, 261, 287, 288, 289, 307, 308, 318, 324, 350, 352, 371, 373, 402, 403, 411, 459, 460, 465, 471, 473, 475, 476, 477, 478, 480, 482, 483, 505, 508, 534, 535
clitic 112, 151
coarticulation 71, 290
co-construction 321, 568
coda 90, 238, 239, 241, 328
code switching 256, 275, 276, 278, 377, 378, 383, 567
cognitive control 282, 302
cognitive linguistics 455-469, 471, 475, 483, 484, 546, 549, 550, 551, 558, 559
cohort 42, 290, 291
coinage 110, 111, 113, 114, 228, 319, 320, 378, 401, 421
collocation 10, 190, 194, 198, 200, 201, 204, 217, 372, 466, 512, 513, 214, 515
common ground 5, 326, 327, 379, 530
communication 1, 2, 9, 10, 11, 15, 19, 21, 24, 25, 27, 30, 32, 33, 34, 38, 39, 40, 41, 42, 44, 45, 46, 48, 140, 141, 150, 152, 153, 185, 186, 198, 203, 211, 212, 214, 220, 224, 234, 235, 249, 257, 263, 278, 284, 294, 312, 316, 327, 336, 347, 352, 362, 363, 367, 379, 381, 390, 392, 393, 403, 418, 424, 429, 436, 452, 470, 471, 472, 474, 476, 479, 481, 487, 491, 523, 526, 530, 531, 535, 536, 541, 542, 543, 544, 545, 548, 551, 553, 555, 558, 561
communicative goal 323, 326, 471
community of practice 266, 273, 534
comparative method 356-360
comparative stylistics 418-422
complement 90, 124, 125, 126, 128, 129, 130, 131, 133, 174, 206, 371, 457, 460, 461, 513
complementary distribution 56, 89, 91
complementiser 131, 373
complexity 8, 17, 18, 19, 20, 21, 22, 23, 25, 26, 27, 29-34, 36, 38, 39, 40, 42, 43, 44, 50, 52, 59, 74, 75, 76, 79, 81, 97, 104-115, 139, 143, 148, 151, 159, 166, 168, 170, 173, 174, 180, 184, 187, 200, 205, 212, 237, 242, 246, 256, 266, 270, 272, 277, 289, 290, 294, 297, 301, 303, 304, 307, 309, 324, 325, 326, 329, 332, 333, 338, 339, 340, 341, 342, 346, 351, 354, 362, 365, 366, 372, 380, 381, 383, 384, 388, 396, 407, 425, 436, 437, 439, 447, 448, 449, 451, 461, 463, 464, 468, 472, 474, 475, 477, 479, 482, 483, 485, 486, 494, 495, 498, 499, 509, 514, 534, 535, 536, 539, 542, 548, 562, 564, 566, 568, 571
complicating action 238, 239, 241, 242, 243, 244
compounding 3, 54, 107, 108, 109, 111, 112, 114, 115, 117, 159, 186, 207, 222, 233, 320, 490
comprehensibility 5, 52, 342, 394, 535, 544
computational action 142, 143, 145, 170, 171, 185, 213, 267, 291, 297, 304, 306, 451, 502,
computational linguistics (CL) 10, 102, 162, 171, 181, 185, 210, 211, 212, 213, 427, 442, 485-501, 514
Comrie, B. 112, 117, 359, 363, 415, 416, 477, 484

conceptual metaphor 166, 548, 549, 550, 558, 559
concordance 10, 189, 190, 204, 508, 509, 510, 511, 514, 515
connectives 158, 159, 166, 169, 170, 185, 520, 521, 525,
conservation 195, 385, 394, 397, 398
consonant 20, 49, 50, 52, 53, 55, 59, 60, 63, 64, 66-71, 77, 78, 81, 88, 89, 90, 91, 96, 97, 101, 105, 108, 111, 116, 265, 301, 345, 356, 359, 360, 361, 412, 436, 437
constraint 5, 28, 32, 83, 85, 89, 90, 92, 96, 97, 99, 100, 101, 103, 111, 137, 142, 144, 145, 147, 148, 201, 272, 300, 334, 342, 349, 350, 351, 361, 398, 403, 405, 444, 465, 476, 478, 481, 486, 487, 493, 551, 567
construction 2, 8, 9, 12, 13, 18, 19, 29, 30, 35, 44, 110, 116, 139, 142, 144, 146-150, 154, 160, 161, 166, 170, 171, 174, 179, 180, 187, 188, 189, 192, 193, 195, 197, 198, 200, 201, 202, 203, 206, 210, 235, 242, 249, 257, 260, 261, 316, 318, 321, 323, 324, 326, 345, 348, 353, 361, 363, 368, 370, 370, 372, 373, 374, 382, 392, 407, 408, 455, 456, 457, 458, 461, 462, 464-468, 472, 473, 474, 475, 503, 504, 505, 511, 519, 547
construction grammar 368, 468, 471, 479
contact 7, 30, 38, 45, 72, 73, 115, 218, 259, 260, 268, 270, 276, 277, 279, 297, 328, 347, 352, 354, 361, 362, 367, 375, 377, 378, 379, 380, 383, 384, 392, 393, 398, 403, 410, 411, 418, 432, 473, 475
context 3, 5, 7, 9, 10, 19, 21, 26, 29, 37, 54, 55, 60, 62, 71, 78, 79, 80, 81, 87, 89, 90, 91, 92, 94, 106, 110, 116, 120, 135, 136, 138, 139, 140, 141, 142. 144, 146, 147, 148, 149, 150, 156, 159, 160, 163, 164, 166, 167, 170-174, 177, 178, 179, 181, 182, 183, 185, 189, 200, 205-211, 213, 214, 216-220, 226, 228, 229, 230, 234, 239, 245, 248, 251, 253, 255-258, 260, 262, 263, 264, 266, 273-277, 293, 306, 307, 311, 314, 315, 316, 318, 321, 326, 329, 334, 335, 337, 338, 339, 340, 351, 352, 353, 362, 368, 370, 372, 373, 374, 375, 407, 414, 429, 441, 442, 455, 456, 458, 459, 460, 461, 462, 467, 470, 472, 475, 476, 477, 479, 480, 481, 486, 488, 491, 492, 496, 497, 498, 499, 506, 507, 508, 511, 512, 513, 518, 519, 521, 522, 524, 526, 527, 528, 531, 532, 533, 534, 535, 536, 537, 538, 541, 542, 546, 562, 565, 566, 568
contextualism 209, 218, 220, 521, 528, 529, 531
contrastiveness 34, 42, 63, 66, 84, 90, 102, 235, 318, 330, 345, 421, 513
convention 2, 5, 6, 7, 17, 26, 27, 35- 39, 40, 48, 53, 84, 106, 113, 114, 142, 150, 159, 164, 167, 174, 187, 188, 198, 199, 200, 210, 2147, 219, 226, 228, 229, 231, 232, 233, 242, 257, 316, 318, 320, 321, 325, 327, 345, 370, 372, 423, 460, 474, 482, 493, 525, 526, 535, 541, 561, 565, 566, 567, 570, 571, 573
conversation 5, 10, 16, 17, 25, 26, 32, 39, 40, 64, 74, 136, 137, 138, 151, 152, 157, 160, 168, 174, 185, 196, 210, 213, 216, 225, 227, 234, 235, 236, 238, 239, 241, 244, 247, 248, 249, 256, 260, 261, 262, 267, 276, 278, 282, 283, 288, 302, 312, 313, 320, 325, 326, 336, 337, 341, 342, 343, 377, 499, 510, 519, 522, 530, 561, 569, 570, 571
conversation analysis (CA) 214, 215, 216, 245, 263, 535
conversion 80, 107, 108, 300, 305, 420
Cooper, R. 139, 151
Cooperrider, K. 35, 45
co-presence 33, 245, 316
coordination 18, 28, 33, 34, 35, 39, 71, 72, 108, 117, 120, 121, 122, 133, 148, 241, 294, 302, 303, 311, 312, 313, 315, 317, 326, 481, 486, 500
Copestake, A. 485, 499, 500
coreference 162, 163, 476, 528
corpus 9, 10, 63, 82, 166, 168, 169, 170, 182, 189, 190, 194, 195, 198, 199, 200, 201, 204, 217, 240, 248, 261, 267, 348, 361, 362, 363, 425, 456, 463, 465, 467, 468, 469, 471, 473, 474, 488, 489, 492, 493, 494, 496, 497, 498, 499, 500, 502-515, 543, 545
corpus linguistics 466, 500, 502-515, 529
court (legal) 361, 533, 537, 538-544

Index

covertness 209, 218, 219, 228, 235, 247, 256, 263, 273, 274, 285, 301
creativity 9, 85, 233, 236, 456, 460, 562, 565, 567, 568, 570, 571, 573
creole 29, 30, 353, 367, 379, 380, 381, 382, 383, 398
cross-linguistic 8, 14, 88, 107, 126, 144, 151, 155, 232, 252, 258, 309, 327, 328, 350, 370, 382, 402 ,403, 404, 406, 407, 408, 448, 450, 458, 478, 499
Crystal, D. 277, 278, 353, 364, 534, 544
Culpeper, J. 214, 220, 226, 228, 234
culture 6, 7, 8, 9, 15, 16, 17, 18, 20, 24, 29, 31, 32, 35, 36, 37, 38, 45, 46, 47, 48, 57, 63, 187, 188, 195, 198, 210, 211, 212, 214, 215, 216, 217, 222, 223, 224, 225, 228, 230, 231, 234, 235, 238, 239, 247, 248, 250, 251, 252, 255, 256, 257, 260, 262, 263, 270, 325, 329, 330, 331, 335, 340, 341, 346, 351, 354, 357, 362, 363, 366, 376, 379, 381, 393, 395, 396, 398, 399, 403, 414, 418, 421, 423, 424, 426, 430, 434, 437, 440, 445, 450, 453, 468, 470, 472, 477, 478, 480, 524, 530, 539, 548, 549, 551, 552, 557, 561, 562, 564, 565, 568, 572, 573
cyclicity 102, 350, 367, 368, 371
Czech 53, 436, 471

Dahl, Ö. 351, 364
Dalrymple, M. 133, 134, 137, 151
Darbelnet, J. 419, 420, 422, 425, 430
Davidson, D. 141, 158, 168, 518, 529
De Jorio, A. 38, 45
deception 570, 571, 572
declaratives 9, 131, 157, 352, 480, 524
declarative grammar 498
Declarative Phonology 98
defaults 5, 90, 91, 168, 196, 219, 269, 270, 379, 388, 519, 527, 530, 568, 570
defective distribution 89, 96, 101
degrammaticalization 373, 383
deixis 21, 34, 35, 46, 167, 206, 208, 210, 211, 213, 214, 218, 255, 462, 475
DELPH-IN 498, 499
dependency 91, 101, 130, 131, 133, 136, 138, 139, 145, 148, 150, 182, 497, 500, 508

derivation 2, 3, 30, 43, 55, 56, 58, 85, 86, 87, 88, 90, 95, 97, 98, 99, 100, 102, 105, 106, 107, 108, 109, 112, 113, 114, 117, 143, 145, 146, 147, 156, 163, 170, 187, 189, 202, 210, 219, 230, 273, 289, 313, 319, 320, 345, 359, 367, 373, 411, 422, 425, 434, 455, 464, 473, 474, 479, 493, 495, 523, 542
devoicing 92, 93, 99, 102
diachrony 7, 45, 117, 151, 189, 190, 193, 198, 199, 216, 265, 266, 269, 271, 347, 349, 350, 365, 367, 380, 435, 438, 466, 473
diacritic 52, 88, 101
dialect 2, 7, 10, 42, 52, 80, 85, 151, 191, 215, 239, 241, 244, 247, 256, 264, 266, 267, 268, 270, 271, 272, 273, 277, 278, 279, 341, 346, 353, 359, 361, 382, 386, 391, 392, 397, 400, 420, 434, 441, 442, 444, 457, 467, 490, 503, 513, 546, 567, 568
dictionary 3, 16, 34, 45, 105, 106, 156, 168, 173, 187-204, 258, 266, 273, 305, 428, 460, 508, 509, 513, 543, 548, 572
Dionysius Thrax 13, 15
disadvantage 160, 198, 284, 533, 535, 536, 537, 538
discourse 3, 5 ,7, 9, 16, 34, 36-41, 43, 139, 151, 152, 160, 161, 162, 163, 166, 168, 169, 171, 172, 174, 176, 180, 185, 186, 190, 199, 210, 211, 213, 214, 217, 227, 228, 235, 248, 257, 258, 259, 260, 261, 274, 276, 288, 293, 316, 366, 367, 370, 372, 374, 403, 408, 423, 424, 457, 458, 463, 471, 472, 473, 476, 477, 480, 481, 483, 484, 490, 502, 503, 504, 508, 511, 513, 516, 520, 523, 524, 530, 534, 535, 536, 537, 538, 544, 545, 565, 569, 572
Discourse Representation Theory (DRT) 136, 152, 153, 160, 162, 168, 523, 530
dispersion 154, 351, 352, 462, 505
distribution 9, 46, 56, 89, 90, 91, 95, 96, 101, 119, 123, 134, 166, 199, 200, 201, 217, 256, 268, 272, 352, 363, 380, 393, 397, 399, 402, 403, 405, 406, 414, 434, 440, 458, 460, 473, 474, 493, 537, 538
distributional semantics 169, 181-185, 496-500

ditransitive 237, 323, 462, 465
diversity 41, 44, 48, 238, 263, 274, 277, 362, 364, 385, 386, 387, 391, 392, 393, 395, 396, 397, 398, 399, 402, 405, 406, 410, 413, 414, 415, 416, 432, 450, 457, 458, 471, 479, 562, 564, 568
Donatus 13, 15
dorsal stream 302, 303
double articulation 49, 154
Dryer, M. 406, 409, 415, 416, 478, 483
Duranti, A. 252, 263
Dutch 92, 93, 99, 105, 106, 107, 108, 111, 112, 113, 114, 115, 116, 194, 204, 254, 255, 353, 354. 355, 356, 357, 358, 537
dynamic semantics 10, 162, 171
dynamic syntax 135, 141-152
dynamic systems 332, 333
dyslexia 59, 281, 291, 292, 293

Eckert, P. 275, 278
economy 38, 43, 57, 58, 102, 215, 366, 374, 375, 408, 412, 459, 474, 478, 483, 562, 563
Efron, D. 36, 45
egressive 63, 65, 66, 68, 72
Ekman, P. 38, 45
elicitation 6, 9, 238, 245, 259, 260, 261, 266, 267, 318, 338, 459, 502, 570
Elizabeth I (queen) 57
ellipsis 136, 137, 138, 144, 146, 147, 149, 150, 151, 160, 173, 176, 177, 180, 218, 244, 245
Ellis, N. 333, 341
embedding 9, 29, 30, 114, 121, 122, 130, 156, 160, 161, 187, 219, 239, 245, 349, 352, 361, 362, 456, 459, 477, 519, 520, 534, 535, 566
embodiment 163, 168, 456, 463, 468, 551, 558, 559, 568
emergency calls 535, 536, 545
emergentism 138, 141, 143, 144, 147, 148, 149, 150, 225, 230, 332, 333, 461, 472, 479, 482
empiricism 288, 418, 431, 437, 456, 503, 518
encapsulated 135, 147, 238, 456, 460, 477
encyclopaedia 3, 4, 15, 188, 190, 195, 200, 201, 202, 220, 460, 461, 463, 484, 531

endangered language 7, 195, 203, 277, 362, 385-400
endocentricity 107, 131, 132, 133
Enfield, N. 35, 45
English 2, 3, 4, 8, 13, 25, 26, 29, 30, 37, 43, 48-57, 59, 63, 67, 68, 69 ,70, 78, 85, 87, 88, 89, 90, 91, 96, 97, 101-120, 121, 125, 126, 127, 131, 132, 133, 134, 141, 143, 144, 148, 151, 154, 155, 156, 158, 159, 164, 165, 166, 168 ,181, 186-205, 215, 226, 227, 233, 234, 235, 236, 244, 246, 248, 249, 252, 253, 254, 256, 257, 263, 264, 265, 266, 269, 270, 271, 273, 274, 275, 276, 277, 279, 290, 294, 301, 302, 304, 313, 314, 320, 328, 332, 334, 335, 336, 338, 344, 345, 346, 347, 349-365, 367, 370, 372, 373, 378, 380, 383, 392, 393, 400, 405, 418, 419, 420, 422, 424, 425, 427 ,428, 429, 431, 433, 434, 438, 439, 440, 441, 445, 446, 457, 458, 460, 462, 468, 473, 474, 475, 477, 478, 481, 482, 490, 492, 493, 495, 496, 497, 498, 500, 502-508, 510, 511, 514, 523, 542, 544, 562, 563, 564, 565, 567, 570, 572, 573
entailment 90, 158, 233, 238, 242, 246, 247, 262, 289, 405, 406, 474, 479, 480, 548
ergative 113
ethnicity 215, 229, 266, 268, 269, 270, 271, 278, 352, 379, 391, 552, 563, 571, 573
ethnography 214, 215, 216, 249, 250, 251, 257, 263, 267, 268, 273, 275, 278, 439, 566
ethology 447, 454
etymology 191, 192, 193, 356, 383, 483, 468
evaluation 10, 38, 137, 157, 158, 207, 209, 228, 232, 233, 237, 238, 239, 241-246, 253, 257, 266, 267, 273, 274, 277, 278, 284, 291, 295, 349, 353, 388, 426, 462, 480, 489, 490, 495, 500, 507, 513, 534
events 11, 12, 19, 21, 22, 23, 82-86, 98, 101, 126, 141, 143, 151, 154, 155, 172, 174, 176, 177, 178, 180, 181, 206, 210, 224, 237, 238, 239, 241, 243, 245, 246, 247, 248, 253, 255, 263, 267, 275, 276, 285, 286, 288, 308, 315, 316, 319, 323, 324, 325, 327, 335, 345, 418, 423, 425, 429,

464, 466, 478, 481, 484, 486, 492, 500, 534, 536, 538, 539, 547, 548
event-related potentials 82, 221, 293, 295
evidentiality 112, 154, 155, 168, 480
evo-devo 449, 450
executive control 281, 282, 294, 308, 342
exocentricity 107, 108, 131
expert witness 10, 533, 539
external language 84, 467
externalization 84, 87
extrinsic rule ordering 95, 98

face 214, 215, 222-235, 242, 247, 257
faculty of language 17, 18, 44, 449, 451, 452, 453
Fauconnier, G. 166, 168, 455, 461, 468
feature (linguistic) 42, 43, 49, 52, 53, 58, 71, 80, 85-91, 95, 97, 100, 101, 102, 110, 112, 113, 122, 127, 132, 151, 170, 176, 181, 182, 183, 187, 192, 195, 200, 201, 210, 213, 217, 229, 241, 242, 243, 245, 252, 268, 270, 272, 276, 292, 299, 300, 302, 304, 306, 307, 309, 331, 334, 346, 348, 352, 353, 361, 362, 363, 378, 380, 389, 398, 414, 421, 424, 436, 437, 443, 451, 462, 475, 489, 491, 498, 499, 506, 511, 534-541, 564, 571
Fedorov, A. 420, 421, 429
feedback 230, 286, 287, 288, 303, 320, 322, 323, 326, 327, 336, 338, 339, 342
Fiengo, R. 137, 151
Finnish 48, 53, 358, 452
first language acquisition 116, 117, 311-328
Firth, J.R. 421, 440, 441, 442, 444, 445, 496, 502, 503, 512
Fitch, W.T. 31, 32, 451, 453
Fodor, J.A. 456, 468
force dynamics 461, 468
forensic linguistics 74, 514, 532, 533, 540, 542, 543, 544, 545, 571, 572
formal criteria 112, 119, 119, 120, 130, 134, 135, 136, 141, 142, 143, 147, 148, 150, 152, 153, 154, 157-163, 167-174, 177, 178, 180, 181, 183, 184, 185, 186, 190, 193, 210, 211, 217, 236, 245, 251, 252, 278, 285, 286, 291, 331, 333, 334, 340, 375, 382, 401, 403, 406, 407, 408, 420, 421, 435, 436, 451, 455, 461, 462, 464, 466, 470, 471, 472, 473, 474, 475, 477, 481, 482, 483, 486, 498, 502, 513, 516, 517, 518, 520, 521, 522, 523, 525, 526, 527, 529, 530, 531
formal style 11, 25, 58, 190, 191, 214, 248, 256, 258, 267, 272, 273, 274, 275, 479, 534
formant 28, 74, 75, 77, 78, 79
formulaic expressions 255, 258, 323
FOXP2 283, 448, 449
Frege, G. 10, 156, 170, 174, 175, 185, 207, 220, 516, 517, 518, 520, 521, 522, 523, 528, 530
French 8, 30, 41, 43, 46, 54, 65, 68, 69, 70, 114, 115, 190, 192, 198, 202, 209, 256, 265, 266, 279, 313, 320, 327, 337, 345, 350, 353, 355, 357, 380, 393, 417, 418, 419, 420, 425, 431, 433, 434, 438, 439, 564, 565
frequency effect 113, 116, 290
Fries, C. 330, 341
functional category 120, 131, 132, 334
functionalism 9, 31, 421, 430, 436, 439, 443, 456, 470-484
functional magnetic resonance imaging (fMRI) 293, 294, 297, 309, 310
fundamental frequency 74, 75, 77

Gabelentz, G.v.d. 401, 482
Gaelic 57, 61, 385, 397
Gapun 258
Gass, S. 329, 330, 331, 332, 336, 338, 340, 341, 342, 343
Gayo 257, 258, 263
gaze 35, 43, 315, 316, 320, 327
Geeraerts, D. 457, 458, 460, 468
Gelb, I.J. 47, 60, 61
gender 8, 80, 107, 111, 112, 127, 133, 161, 215, 218, 227, 229, 232, 235, 243, 244, 253, 255, 256, 260, 262, 269, 270, 271, 274, 319, 332, 334, 444, 470, 481, 482, 552, 555, 562, 563, 572
generalization 48, 93, 98, 103, 113, 146, 164, 175, 219, 220, 304, 319, 333, 339, 351, 370, 378, 382, 402, 403, 404, 406, 426, 458, 459, 460, 464, 465, 468, 473, 474, 489, 499, 500, 503, 506, 510, 519, 526, 528, 547, 549, 552, 557

generative grammar 103, 421, 455, 459, 463, 473, 478
generative phonology 71, 93, 95, 102, 441
genetic 7, 18, 24, 31, 52, 54, 283, 347, 354, 355, 357, 358, 359, 360, 363, 378, 383, 397, 398, 409, 415, 449, 450, 451, 452, 456, 459
genre 10, 11, 217, 236, 237, 248, 251, 255, 257, 258, 260, 261, 262, 348, 480, 490, 503, 505, 506, 513, 534, 535, 542, 561, 563, 573
Georgakopoulou, A. 244, 247, 248
German 68, 69, 102, 103, 115, 335, 353, 354, 355, 356, 357, 360, 361, 363, 385, 396, 401, 417, 419, 431, 432, 436, 477, 478, 564, 570
Germanic 54, 57, 107, 111, 112, 114, 115, 143, 320, 350, 351, 352, 353, 355, 356, 358, 359, 360, 361, 363, 372, 418, 419, 420, 421, 438
gesture 2, 7, 27, 33, 35, 36, 37, 38, 41, 45, 46, 53, 63, 70, 71, 72, 73, 80, 218, 231, 303, 315, 316, 323, 326,327, 328, 561, 571
glossematics 439
glottographic 49, 72
Godfroid, A. 331, 332, 341
Goffman, E. 222, 224, 232, 234, 423, 429, 547, 567, 568, 572
Goldberg, A. 374, 382, 462, 468
Goody, J. 47, 61, 220
government phonology 91, 98,
gradience 44, 272, 278, 474
grammar 7, 9, 11, 12, 13, 14, 15, 26, 29, 30, 31, 32, 47, 52, 60, 83, 84, 95, 97, 103, 106, 110, 11, 116, 118, 130-138, 140, 141, 142, 145, 146, 148-156, 168, 170-173, 178, 179, 185, 186, 191, 192, 193, 219, 220, 236, 244, 248, 253, 258, 259, 265, 279, 282, 287, 288, 289, 290, 294, 331, 333, 334, 343, 345, 347, 348, 354, 366, 367, 368, 370, 374, 379, 382, 383, 394, 398, 399, 415, 416, 421, 422, 423, 438, 439, 442, 443, 444, 449, 450, 453, 455, 456, 458-461, 463, 464, 465, 468, 469, 470, 471, 473, 474, 477-481, 483, 484, 487, 498, 499, 503, 514, 521, 522, 547, 566

grammaticalization 7, 29, 30, 347, 350, 352, 367-375, 382, 383, 438, 450, 472
graph 50, 51, 53, 54
grapheme 291, 304, 305
Greek 12, 13, 14, 16, 50, 55, 58, 107, 111, 115, 137, 139, 147, 151, 187, 190, 194, 195, 202, 235, 358, 367, 419, 510
Greenberg, J.H. 347, 401, 403, 412, 413, 414, 415, 416, 443, 445, 477
Gregoromichelaki, E. 141,151, 152
Grice, H.P. 12, 16, 24, 32, 140, 152, 172, 185, 209, 210, 212, 213, 218, 219, 220, 326, 476, 519, 527, 529, 530
Grimm brothers 359, 360
grounding 5, 228, 251, 313, 320, 325, 326, 327, 363, 379, 420, 460, 461, 473, 530
Gumperz, J. 275, 276, 278
Gutt, E-A. 424, 429
Guugu-Yimidhirr 253, 254, 255
gyrus 297, 298, 301, 302, 303, 304, 306

harmonic 74-77, 102
Harris, Z.S. 181, 185, 422, 435, 442, 445, 496
Hausa 154, 168, 564
Hauser, M.D. 449, 453
Hebrew 50, 55, 58, 60, 68, 108, 190, 202, 226, 294, 395, 398, 478
heteroglossia 568, 569, 572
hierarchy 42, 56, 100, 102, 120, 150, 187, 189, 196, 197, 198, 199, 200, 222, 245, 260, 272, 288, 289, 300, 301, 304, 307, 308, 309, 402, 403, 404, 405, 412, 472, 477, 480, 548, 549, 556, 557
Hoey, M. 246, 248
hominin 1, 18, 28
homonymy 156, 173, 487
Hulst, H.v.d. 62, 83, 91, 100, 101, 102
Humboldt, W.v 14, 344, 360, 364, 419, 429, 438, 440, 482
Hungarian 8, 111, 355, 358, 385
Hymes, D. 38, 245, 249, 257, 263, 278, 444, 445
hypercorrection 272
hypernymy 108, 497
hyponymy 156, 185, 189, 197, 200, 201, 497

581

Index

iconicity 2, 27, 35, 42, 43, 108, 366, 374, 375, 382, 437, 483
identity 90, 95, 151, 177, 179, 227, 229, 230, 231, 232, 234, 235, 236, 238, 245, 246, 247, 248, 249, 267, 270, 272, 275, 278, 293, 304, 305, 363, 369, 379, 391, 392, 395, 399, 424, 434, 444, 480, 507, 520, 559, 562, 568, 569, 570, 571, 572, 573
idiom 26, 116, 184, 193, 201, 263, 374, 458, 460, 464, 465, 466, 468, 547
Ilongot 257, 263
image schema 164, 165
implementation 10, 85, 86, 87, 88, 89, 90, 98, 100, 101, 133, 136, 170, 171, 179, 190, 291, 292, 301, 303, 305, 308, 384, 448, 450, 451, 452, 463, 492, 508, 521
implicational hierarchy 402, 403, 404, 405, 412, 477
implicature 10, 24, 25, 26, 172, 174, 186, 208, 210, 211, 212, 213, 214, 218, 219, 220, 242, 247, 424, 475, 527, 547
impliciture 210, 218
impliculture 247
impoliteness 214, 217, 220, 226, 227, 228, 229, 232, 233, 234, 235, 243
indeterminacy 147, 422
indexicality 21, 22, 56, 82, 96, 112, 144, 146, 147, 173, 188, 195, 198, 199, 201, 206, 207, 209, 210, 218, 235, 255, 257, 260, 261, 262, 273, 275, 278, 293, 370, 386, 398, 444, 487, 521, 527, 528, 530, 572
indirectness 24, 25, 26, 215, 222, 225, 226, 227, 228, 232, 233, 234, 324, 338, 521, 526, 534, 536, 541
Indo-European 7, 14, 15, 108, 113, 347, 358, 359, 360, 363, 409, 432, 440, 445
inequality 249, 272, 563
inference 7, 18, 20, 22, 23, 24, 26, 29, 54, 155, 167, 170, 171, 177, 181, 199, 207, 208, 209, 210, 212, 213, 219, 225, 234, 235, 237, 243, 244, 276, 297, 299, 306, 315, 317, 320, 326, 339, 357, 363, 366, 370, 407, 453, 476, 516, 517, 518, 519, 520, 526, 527, 534, 536, 541, 542, 548, 550
information technology 188, 195, 398, 503

input 10, 19, 85, 99, 100, 136, 141, 142, 143, 148, 160, 291, 292, 293, 301, 303, 306, 307, 313, 314, 327, 332, 333, 337, 338, 339, 341, 342, 348, 371, 375, 379, 381, 455, 456, 458, 460, 486, 487
instructed second language learning 331, 340, 341
intensionality 10, 175, 179, 519, 526
intentionality 1, 2, 26, 151, 172, 210, 212, 214, 242, 503, 525, 531
interaction 1, 2, 5, 6, 9, 11, 15, 18, 23, 26, 31, 33, 34, 37, 38, 39, 40, 42, 44, 80, 82, 101, 103, 137, 138, 141, 146, 147, 148, 151, 160, 171, 172, 174, 178, 184, 214, 215, 216, 217, 220, 221, 224, 225, 229, 230, 231, 232, 234, 235, 244, 245, 247, 248, 249, 251, 252, 256, 257, 264, 267, 273, 275, 278, 284, 287, 288, 297, 306, 311, 312, 313, 314, 315, 316, 317, 320, 323, 326, 328, 329, 331, 332, 333, 335, 336, 338, 339, 340, 341, 342, 352, 354, 366, 370, 371, 376, 380, 381, 390, 391, 406, 412, 426, 439, 441, 449, 451, 455, 456, 457, 458, 459, 461, 464, 466, 468, 472, 473, 474, 475, 478, 480, 482, 484, 499, 511, 522, 524, 525, 528, 535, 536, 537, 545, 561, 562, 563, 565, 566, 567, 568, 570, 571
interdisciplinarity 18, 211, 217, 233, 296, 328, 329, 330, 340, 348, 385, 421, 447, 448, 450, 451, 475, 484
interface 62, 111, 112, 151, 152, 178, 187, 190, 212, 213, 214, 216, 233, 294, 300, 302, 450, 456, 487, 488, 528, 532, 561
internal language 216
intersectionality 6, 73, 215, 217, 269, 270, 279
intersubjectivity 157, 520, 528
interview 10, 214, 241, 244, 245, 248, 256, 262, 267, 269, 270, 274, 444, 467, 470, 536, 537, 538, 539, 541, 545, 549, 569
intervocalic 91, 265, 345
intra-speaker variation 274, 275, 276
invisible-hand model 376, 377
invited inference 370
IPA (International Phonetic Alphabet) 86, 87, 88, 100, 101, 193, 202, 279, 441
Irish 57, 58, 61, 127, 132, 133

isogloss 361

Janda, R.D. 346, 348, 362, 363, 364
Japanese 52, 53, 54, 60, 61, 223, 265, 279, 336, 356, 423, 461, 496, 564
jargon 379, 451, 534, 535
Jaszczolt, K.M. 15, 220, 516, 519, 521, 529, 530, 531
Javanese 256, 392, 564
Jelinek, F. 491, 492, 500
Jespersen, O. 350, 351, 352, 353, 364, 439
Johnson, M. 163, 164, 168, 462, 466, 468, 548, 559, 560
Johnson, R. 39, 45
Johnson, S. 189, 190, 192, 193, 195, 196, 203, 204
joint attention 21, 26, 315, 316, 326, 327, 333
Jones, D. 439, 440, 441, 444, 445
Jones, W. 357, 358, 364
Joseph, B. 346, 348, 362, 363, 364
Joseph, J.E. 431, 444, 445
jury instructions 533, 535, 544, 545
justice 533, 536, 537, 539, 542, 543, 545, 555

Kamp, H. 136, 152, 160, 168, 171, 186, 518, 523, 530
Kaplan, D. 206, 528, 530
Kegl, J. 42, 45
Keller, R. 354, 364, 377, 383
Kempson, R. 135, 148, 151, 152
Kendon, A. 33, 35, 36, 37, 38, 41, 44, 45, 46
kinaesthesia 163, 164
kinesics 33, 34, 36-42, 44, 45
Korean 52, 53, 56, 226, 314, 461
Kortmann, B. 353, 364, 382, 484
Kuryłowicz, J. 361, 364, 367, 383
Kwak'wala 252, 253

Labov, W. 100, 102, 237, 238, 239, 241-245, 247, 248, 249, 264, 266, 269, 274, 277, 278, 279, 280, 347, 348, 351, 357, 364, 365, 376, 383, 444, 567, 568, 573
Lado, R. 330, 341
Lakoff, G. 17, 163, 165, 166, 168, 455, 456, 458, 461, 462, 466, 468, 546, 559, 560

Lakoff, R.T. 227, 235, 547, 560
Langacker, R.W. 118, 134, 163, 168, 455, 456, 457, 459, 460, 461, 463, 464, 465, 466, 468
Lantolf, J. 335, 341
Lardiere, D. 333, 334, 341
Larsen-Freeman, D. 333, 341
larynx 27, 28, 63, 64, 65, 66, 70-77, 303
Lascarides, A. 162, 168
Latin 3, 8, 12, 13, 30, 48, 52, 53, 54, 105, 114, 115, 190, 192, 193, 194, 195, 202, 345, 357, 358, 359, 373, 433, 502
law 10, 192, 202, 390, 532, 533, 535, 537, 539, 542, 543, 544, 545, 552, 556, 557, 558
laws (linguistic) 56, 347, 348, 351, 354, 356, 359, 360, 361, 419, 424, 425, 426
Leech, G. 222, 227, 228, 234, 235, 248, 346, 365, 503, 505, 514, 515
left-branching 414, 415
legal language 533-535, 542, 545
legislation 10, 202, 533, 535, 556
lemmatisation 188, 190, 194, 508, 509, 512
Lenneberg, E.H. 447, 448, 451, 453
Lepore, E. 209, 521, 529, 530, 531
Levinson, S.C. 210, 214, 215, 218, 219, 220, 221, 222, 223, 224, 225, 227, 228, 229, 232, 233, 234, 253, 254, 263, 328, 446, 528, 530
Lewontin, R.C. 451, 453
lexical category 120, 122, 123, 466
Lexical Functional Grammar (LFG) 132, 133, 134, 498
lexical pragmatics 167, 211
lexicalism 103, 110, 219
lexicalization 115, 116, 372, 373, 383
lexicography 156, 187-204, 458, 495, 502, 503, 513, 543, 547, 548
lexicon 3, 4, 9, 19, 84, 86, 87, 95, 101, 105, 110, 143, 145, 154, 156, 170, 173, 176, 180, 186, 187, 188, 189, 192, 193, 195, 196, 197, 198, 199, 201, 202, 211, 265, 288, 302, 303, 305, 314, 315, 327, 331, 338, 345, 346, 368, 378, 379, 382, 417, 468, 480, 481, 494, 499, 508, 522
Linear B 55
linguae francae 7, 40, 259, 276, 428
linguistic area 378, 409

Index

linguistic relativity 14, 252, 253, 254, 255, 257, 528
lips 28, 35, 45, 46, 64, 65, 67, 68, 69, 70, 71, 72, 76, 77, 290, 303
literacy 15, 56, 61, 258, 263, 363, 389, 390, 563, 565, 566, 572
localization 19, 307, 310, 370, 418
Loewen, S. 340, 341
logic 16, 21, 32, 47, 51, 142, 151, 152, 156, 157, 158, 162, 167, 168, 169, 170, 179, 185, 186, 210, 220, 247, 2698, 277, 279, 342, 439, 449, 458, 505, 516, 517, 518, 520, 522, 523, 525, 526, 527, 530, 531, 542, 553, 554, 557
logograph 12, 49, 50, 51, 52, 53, 59

Maa 8, 13
machine learning 10, 489, 490
machine translation (MT) 362, 418, 423, 425, 426, 427, 428, 430, 442, 487, 491
Mackey, A. 336, 337, 338, 341, 342, 343
macrostructure 188, 189, 193, 194, 195, 196, 197, 198, 199, 201
MacWhinney, B. 327, 333, 342, 478, 483, 484
main clause 111, 287, 308, 351, 352, 473, 474
maintenance 8, 232, 247, 332, 342, 378, 393, 394, 395, 398, 421, 535
Malagasy 13, 214, 223, 404, 477
markedness 8, 30, 36, 53, 91, 102, 107, 109, 114, 116, 122, 123, 126, 127, 137, 154, 161, 171, 228, 242, 243, 244, 245, 256, 253, 256, 362, 371, 418, 436, 437, 442, 449, 460, 476, 477, 500, 522, 567
Markov chain 285
markup 10, 506, 507, 509
Martinet, A. 49, 154, 168, 438, 439, 442, 444, 445, 472
materiality 50, 57, 132, 156, 171, 172, 179, 190, 193, 198, 200, 207, 238, 239, 241, 261, 296, 329, 330, 340, 348, 357, 360, 363, 377, 389, 394, 395, 396, 430, 436, 540, 542, 550, 554, 562, 563, 567, 571, 573
maxim 12, 20, 210, 213, 228, 377, 382, 476, 503, 519, 527
Maya 47, 48, 61

McNeill, D. 35, 44, 45, 46
media 11, 73, 244, 267, 268, 359, 363, 389, 390, 392, 394, 428, 450, 488, 503, 504, 505, 532, 558, 559, 561-573
Meissner, M. 39, 46
memory 9, 19, 22, 23, 59, 80, 81, 90, 113, 147, 164, 188, 199, 281, 282, 286, 288, 289, 290, 291, 294, 301, 302, 303, 305, 306, 308, 309, 317, 329, 331, 332, 333, 338, 339, 341, 342, 343, 427, 428, 432, 456, 459, 470, 474, 478
mental lexicon 84, 86, 87, 199, 288, 302
mental representation 18, 20, 21, 22, 23, 24, 211, 212, 282, 286, 288, 289, 333, 455, 517, 518
mental spaces 166, 455, 468, 469
meronymy 189, 200, 201
metadata 10, 506, 507, 509
metaphor 7, 9, 11, 35, 45, 164, 165, 166, 167, 168, 212, 221, 231, 252, 275, 361, 368, 370, 371, 376, 381, 394, 460, 462, 463, 466, 468, 542, 548, 549, 550, 552, 555, 556, 557, 558, 559, 560
methodology 82, 135, 137, 139, 140, 215, 217, 221, 247, 253, 258, 262, 266, 267, 332, 341, 346, 352, 360, 381, 386, 387, 388, 402, 406, 415, 430, 431, 432, 440, 441, 443, 448, 466, 467, 474, 479, 485, 489, 499, 502, 503, 512, 513, 514, 529, 533, 540, 541
metonymy 9, 164, 166, 370, 371, 461, 462
Meyer-Viol, M. 142, 151, 152
microstructure 188, 189, 192, 193, 194, 195, 196, 198, 199, 201, 202
Middle English 264, 349, 350, 363
Milroy, J. 352, 364, 375, 383
mind 1, 6, 14, 16, 20, 21, 24, 26, 30, 46, 83, 90, 140, 148, 168, 198, 202, 208, 212, 213, 281, 296, 302, 305, 306, 317, 342, 343, 432, 442, 443, 456, 467, 468, 479, 483, 516, 517, 523, 529, 531, 551, 559
minimalism 132, 133, 209, 218, 220, 375, 383, 449, 450, 452, 463, 482, 483, 521, 527, 529
mining 362, 487, 488
mixed languages 367, 379, 382, 383
Miyake, A. 332, 339, 342

modality 33, 38, 39, 42, 44, 66, 67, 75, 81, 137, 142, 155, 166, 168, 173, 184, 186, 242, 244, 303, 304, 306, 309, 362, 370, 382, 452, 461, 466, 474, 479, 480, 493, 494, 500, 534, 561, 564, 565, 571
modifier 124, 129
Montague, R. 136, 158, 168, 170, 172, 173, 179, 185, 186, 518, 523, 526, 531
morpheme 2, 3, 4, 8, 9, 12, 40, 49, 50, 51, 84, 86, 92, 93, 94, 95, 97, 98, 100, 104, 105, 106, 107, 109, 110, 111, 112, 114, 115, 117, 184, 192, 261, 288, 289, 290, 303, 367, 372, 374, 413, 434, 463, 464, 466, 467, 474, 547
morphology 2, 3, 7, 8, 12, 30, 31, 40, 41, 46, 95-117, 118, 123, 126, 133, 135, 137, 154, 155, 156, 189, 208, 260, 265, 268, 272, 278, 290, 318, 328, 332, 334, 337, 345, 347, 349, 352, 367, 372, 378, 380, 382, 401, 402, 410, 415, 417, 437, 441, 463, 464, 467, 472, 485, 486, 495, 496, 498, 500, 502, 508, 546
morphophonemics 55, 56, 91, 93, 94, 96, 367, 371, 463
Morris, D. 38, 46
motivation 1, 7, 9, 13, 15, 18, 27, 31, 85, 87, 94, 95, 96, 97, 98, 99, 104, 105, 110, 112, 224, 230, 250, 266, 282, 290, 325, 329, 331, 339, 340, 343, 352, 366, 368, 370, 371, 373, 374, 375, 380, 381, 382, 391, 403, 411, 457, 458, 468, 470, 471, 473, 474, 475, 480, 481, 483, 484, 499
Mounin, G. 417, 418, 424, 430
multimodality 244, 306, 362, 480, 561, 564, 565, 571
Mycenaeans 55

Naples 37, 38, 39, 45
narrative 5, 11, 162, 163, 236-249, 260, 261, 267, 325, 327, 461, 478, 484, 535, 538
nativism 31, 379, 449
natural language processing (NLP) 187, 200, 485, 487, 488, 500, 501, 514
natural language understanding (NLU) 485, 486, 487
negation 2, 34, 35, 42, 65, 88, 96, 107, 139, 154, 156, 161, 162, 163, 171, 179, 197, 210, 242, 243, 244, 257, 261, 265, 286, 287, 321, 340, 345, 349-353, 361, 364, 365, 412, 413, 420, 434, 463, 470, 479, 488, 489, 490, 512, 513, 525, 526, 551, 559
negative face 222, 225, 227, 257
negotiation 5, 29, 31, 51, 225, 245, 336, 343, 382
neogrammarians 346, 347, 356, 360, 361, 363
neural networks 291, 292, 293, 294
neuro-imaging 90, 291, 293, 297, 305, 429
neurolinguistics 6, 82, 212, 278, 296-310, 481
neurophysiology 82, 291, 293
neuropsychology 294, 296, 297, 299, 305, 308, 310
neutralization 90, 92, 93, 94, 96, 99, 100, 103, 436
Nevalainen, T. 352, 353, 363, 364
New Guinea 29, 35, 45, 223, 250, 252, 258, 259, 263, 409
n-gram 491, 492, 493, 494, 495, 512
Nichols, J. 346, 364, 415, 416, 477, 483, 484
Nida, E. 421, 422, 424, 426, 430
non-standard 140, 244, 266, 269, 271, 272, 273, 274, 277, 350, 353, 566, 567
Norwich 235, 256, 263, 274, 279
noticing 38, 225, 229, 286, 287, 304, 331, 332, 333, 337, 338, 342, 343, 377, 559
Nunez, R. 35, 45

obligatoriness 122, 124, 137, 239, 264, 350, 369, 482
observer's paradox 266, 267
obstruent 72, 90, 92, 99, 100
Ochs, E. 244, 245, 246, 248, 249
Old English 30, 114, 195, 344, 345, 346, 347, 349, 356, 357, 358, 359, 370, 504
online 31, 166, 168, 189, 190, 195, 199, 200, 201, 202, 203, 217, 221, 267, 268, 308, 361, 397, 400, 414, 427, 478, 483, 486, 487, 562-572
onomasiology 187, 188, 195, 196, 197, 198, 201, 202
ontology 198, 199, 200, 203, 451, 464, 507
opacity 98, 99, 102, 103, 115, 380, 451, 519
optimality theory 83, 98, 103, 210, 452, 473

585

Index

oral 11, 12, 27, 28, 56, 63, 656, 68, 69, 70, 71, 72, 73, 76, 79, 236, 238, 239, 240, 244, 245, 246, 247, 248, 249, 258, 261, 267, 305, 332, 363, 366, 430, 452, 537, 562, 565
orientation 33, 35, 42, 43, 153, 163, 237, 238, 249, 241, 242, 253, 254, 269, 271, 331, 347, 431, 440, 459, 470, 473, 477, 480, 481, 512, 521, 545
Osgood, C.E. 496, 500
output 10, 76, 77, 85, 86, 94, 96, 98, 99, 129, 136, 140, 141, 142, 184, 266, 292, 293, 301, 303, 306, 307, 331, 337, 338, 340, 341, 342, 343, 394, 428, 452, 487, 500, 508, 510
overextension 287
overlap 6, 7, 38, 71, 81, 84, 91, 92, 153, 183, 212, 213, 214, 215, 216, 241, 251, 270, 277, 313, 316, 317, 326, 329, 432, 433, 441, 471, 475, 532, 551, 561
Oxford English Dictionary (OED) 3, 189, 190, 193, 195, 198, 201, 202, 203, 204

panel study 267, 271
Pāṇini 12, 62
paradigm 14, 31, 81, 82, 89, 90, 110, 116, 117, 153, 181, 189, 198, 200, 244, 261, 264, 286, 318, 327, 330, 331, 338, 347, 350, 369, 371, 434, 437, 438, 449, 485, 496, 498, 516, 517, 523, 526, 527, 535
paralinguistics 63, 69, 84, 87, 239, 241, 242
parallel distributed processing 81, 291
pargram 498, 500
Parkes, M.B. 56, 60, 61
parsing 10, 19, 34, 60, 141, 142, 144, 145, 146, 148, 149, 150, 152, 307, 485, 486, 489, 494, 496, 498, 499, 500, 508
part of speech (POS) 12, 13, 101, 260, 261, 427, 493, 494, 495, 496, 507, 508, 509
Partee, B.H. 518, 531
participant observation 262, 267
pathology 6, 73, 205, 213, 451, 452
Pawnee 260
perceptible 83, 84, 85, 86, 436, 463
performance 7, 11, 13, 25, 31, 37, 56, 64, 72, 94, 135, 136, 138, 140, 183, 210, 211, 214, 215, 217, 222, 223, 224, 225, 229, 236, 237, 238, 242, 243, 247, 248, 254, 257, 258, 260, 262, 265, 290, 293, 297, 305, 332, 335, 374, 415, 418, 423, 427, 436, 442, 443, 451, 452, 486, 489, 490, 492, 495, 496, 499, 500, 512, 514, 519, 524, 525, 526, 528, 535, 536, 537, 544, 547, 568
Philp, J. 331, 342
Philpott, S. B. 39, 46
Phoenician 48, 55, 58
phonaesthemes 105
phonation 64, 65, 66, 69, 72
phoneme 2, 12, 31, 49, 50, 52, 62, 63, 70, 71, 80, 83, 85, 86, 87, 89, 90, 91, 92, 93, 94, 96, 97, 98, 99, 101, 102, 202, 290, 291, 299, 301, 302, 305, 309, 314, 359, 433, 436, 437, 439, 440, 441, 445, 472, 477
phonemics 9, 49, 62, 83, 84, 85, 86, 87, 88, 89, 90, 91, 92, 93, 94, 95, 96, 97, 98, 99, 100, 101, 103, 260, 265, 288, 301, 303, 314, 356, 440, 441
phonetics 2, 9, 12, 14, 18, 27, 28, 31, 49, 51, 52, 53, 54, 55, 56, 60, 62-95, 98-103, 105, 111, 202, 208, 260, 265, 279, 288, 292, 328, 348, 373, 408, 421, 433, 434, 436, 438, 439, 441, 532, 543, 546
phonographic 49, 51-56, 59, 101
phonology 2, 7, 9, 12, 14, 18, 19, 20, 29, 30, 31, 45, 52, 55, 59, 62, 69, 71, 80, 81, 83-103, 105, 107, 110, 111, 112, 135, 136, 156, 208, 233, 245, 260, 265, 268, 272, 278, 279, 283, 290, 291, 292, 293, 300, 301, 302, 303, 304, 307, 308, 314, 315, 318, 323, 328, 334, 338, 339, 345, 347, 348, 351, 360, 363, 369, 374, 375, 378, 384, 402, 408, 412, 433, 437, 441, 442, 444, 446, 451, 457, 458, 463, 464, 466, 468, 472, 479, 480, 502, 546
phonotaxis 89, 94-99, 101, 111
phrase 2, 3, 4, 9, 12, 30, 40, 43, 66, 110, 111, 114, 118, 119, 120, 122-133, 146, 162, 175, 176, 207, 242, 260, 261, 288, 289, 307, 318, 319, 323, 326, 345, 351, 370, 371, 404, 405, 415, 421, 422, 425, 426, 457, 458, 459, 464, 465, 466, 474, 476, 480, 481, 483, 484, 486, 489, 490, 496, 498, 499, 500, 508, 509, 511, 561, 568

phrase structure 114, 128-133, 457, 460, 465, 498
Piaget, J. 448, 453
Piattelli-Palmarini, M. 448, 453
pidgin 26, 29, 30, 31, 276, 278, 367, 379, 381, 382, 383, 392, 393, 398, 472
pitch 44, 63, 64, 66, 72, 74, 81, 88, 103, 301, 311, 312, 313
Pitman, I., 52, 53
Plains Indians 40
Plato 10, 12, 20, 41, 186, 516, 530
Poeppel, D. 309, 451, 453
poetic 12, 168, 257, 258, 263, 436, 566, 573
pointing 26, 34, 35, 36, 45, 46, 179, 315, 316, 324, 328
police 10, 214, 533, 536-541, 544, 545
politeness 6, 133, 214, 217, 220-229, 231-235, 470, 536
Pollard, C. 498
polysemy 106, 156, 164, 165, 168, 169, 173, 180, 186, 188, 190, 195, 198, 199, 200, 252, 458, 460, 462, 464, 467
polysynthesis 8, 112, 126, 260
Poplack, S. 276, 277, 279, 377, 383
population 30, 31, 37, 57, 73, 213, 250, 277, 284, 294, 295, 299, 301, 303, 306, 307, 314, 353, 359, 363, 378, 379, 380, 387, 388, 389, 390, 393, 397, 398, 400, 448, 452, 504, 505, 546, 563, 564
positron emission tomography (PET) 297
postposition 8, 115, 403, 404, 406, 415
power 29, 48, 63, 74, 165, 197, 214, 217, 222, 226, 227, 235, 246, 258, 297, 269, 404, 410, 418, 424, 465, 495, 499, 503, 533, 535, 537, 538, 544, 558, 562
pragmatics 4, 7, 18, 29, 34, 42, 57, 112, 141, 167, 172, 174, 177, 178, 185, 205-220, 235, 237, 252, 255, 288, 320, 325, 327, 366, 370, 372, 407, 457, 464, 473, 475, 478, 480, 508, 511, 513, 519, 526, 527, 528
preposition 8, 29, 114, 115, 119, 120, 123, 124, 125, 164, 165, 166, 168, 309, 319, 368, 371, 403, 404, 406, 412, 414, 415, 458, 459, 477, 507
prestige 235, 256, 259, 263, 269, 271, 273, 274, 352, 353, 362, 426

presupposition 10, 13, 17, 162, 171, 172, 174, 178, 179, 181, 185, 186, 208, 210, 211, 217, 255, 257, 421, 424, 473, 475, 476, 481
primary sign language 34, 41, 42
principles and parameters 331, 333, 334, 403, 457, 458, 465
Priscian 13, 16
probability 381, 409, 428, 489, 491, 492, 495, 497, 505
processing 3, 6, 71, 80, 81, 82, 100, 101, 102, 113, 116, 117, 128, 135, 138, 413, 145, 146, 147, 150, 151, 152, 166, 175, 183, 187, 200, 222, 252, 278, 282, 288-294, 296, 297, 300-304, 306-309, 328, 332, 334, 337, 342, 371, 403, 427, 429, 465, 470, 472, 477, 478, 481, 483, 485-488, 491, 500, 501, 514, 516, 519, 522, 567
production 2, 6, 19, 35, 36, 62, 64, 68, 70, 71, 73, 76, 79, 80, 82, 102, 113, 148-150, 156, 199, 207, 209, 213, 223, 257, 282, 283, 285, 287, 288, 290, 296, 302, 303, 305, 309, 310, 315, 317, 318, 331, 337, 338, 339, 341, 342, 354, 366, 426, 433, 459, 460, 466, 477, 490, 537, 541, 562, 565, 567
productivity 18, 107, 112, 114, 287, 319, 320, 371, 382, 423, 450, 464, 465, 467, 513
pronominal 8, 21, 43, 114, 133, 136, 137, 139, 144, 145, 146, 148, 151, 160, 161, 162, 163, 167, 173, 186, 255, 260, 261, 265, 307, 334, 345, 350, 373, 423, 493, 495, 510, 518, 527, 534
pronunciation 2 13, 19, 37, 44, 50, 51, 52, 54, 55, 56, 59, 60, 68, 69, 70, 71, 75, 96, 100, 115, 128, 193, 244, 246, 256, 265, 267, 279, 291, 292, 293, 304, 318, 324, 345, 346, 347, 357, 433, 436, 441, 466, 487, 525
proposition 18, 20-26, 137, 138, 140-144, 150, 157, 158, 162, 167, 174, 175, 179, 207, 209, 210, 218, 219, 476, 479, 516-527, 529, 531
prosody 12, 63, 67, 71, 80, 81, 95, 102, 103, 216, 313, 314, 318, 341, 419, 513, 538

Index

psycholinguistics 6, 9, 18, 19, 199, 211, 212, 253, 278, 281-295, 329, 331, 336, 341, 451, 452, 453, 456, 463, 471, 478, 496, 513, 516, 543

psychology 3, 6, 11, 18, 19, 31, 45, 59, 60, 81, 82, 84, 93, 103, 153, 163, 164, 168, 211, 212, 234, 235, 246, 251, 252, 253, 254, 275, 277, 281, 284, 285, 286, 288-291, 296, 297, 299, 305, 308, 309, 310, 329, 330, 332, 339, 343, 348, 351, 354, 363, 424, 425, 438, 439, 442, 445, 449, 450, 452, 471, 477, 480, 484, 496, 497, 517, 518, 519, 520, 526, 527, 528, 529, 530, 531, 566, 572

Purver, M. 147, 148, 151, 152

Pym, A. 417, 423, 430

qualia 176

questioning 5, 23, 25, 33, 34, 35, 66, 121, 125, 131, 137, 141, 149, 157, 174, 179, 217, 220, 227, 239, 242, 262, 264, 265, 266, 267, 286, 287, 317, 318, 320, 321, 322, 325, 326, 338, 340, 348, 373, 422, 476, 486, 487, 488, 516, 522, 529, 536, 537, 538, 545, 549

Quine, W.V.O. 422, 430, 518, 519, 520, 531

Quintilian, M.F. 34, 46

quotative 274, 567

radial 164, 165, 462

Rask, R. 360

rationalism 11, 14, 178, 215, 222, 317, 422, 423, 431, 449, 456, 503, 516

real time 72, 73, 135, 148, 265, 267, 270, 271, 281, 288, 567

reanalysis 351, 370, 371, 373, 374, 382

Recanati, F. 173, 177, 186, 209, 210, 218, 219, 220, 521, 522, 529, 531

recasts 338, 342

reconstruction 32, 51, 140, 146, 147, 150, 171, 237, 347, 356, 357, 360, 363

recursion 29, 109, 129, 170, 172, 275, 451, 463

redundancy 69, 89, 90, 91, 98, 100, 342, 380, 425, 459, 495

reduplication 98, 108

reference 3, 5, 10, 12, 19, 20, 21, 22, 25, 35, 157, 160, 161, 162, 163, 166, 175, 176, 180, 186, 206, 208, 211, 212, 213, 216, 239, 252, 253, 293, 315, 317, 319, 323, 381, 404, 420, 460, 466, 475, 476, 481, 486, 488, 498, 516, 519, 520, 523, 524, 527, 528, 529, 530, 534

register 66, 72, 81, 88, 100, 191, 236, 251, 255, 256, 257, 279, 291, 301, 304, 380, 392, 433, 466, 479, 480, 513, 534, 562

regularity 356, 360, 380, 438, 468, 482

relative clause 148, 287, 308, 373, 403, 477

relativization 8, 110, 209, 404, 405, 474, 477

relevance (principle) 152, 167, 168, 173, 177, 186, 209, 210, 211, 212, 218, 219, 220, 235, 424, 429, 476, 531

reliability 48, 51, 246, 247, 260, 299, 319, 388, 486, 488, 489, 490, 491, 522, 533, 540

repair 83, 97, 99, 149, 177, 178, 216, 313, 315, 318, 320, 321

repetition 11, 21, 31, 34, 42, 63, 66, 74, 108, 129, 149, 154, 231, 242, 260, 272, 281, 287, 301, 312, 321, 326, 351, 395, 420, 427, 465, 558

representation 2, 3, 10, 12, 18, 20-24, 34, 35, 36, 40, 42, 43, 48-56, 59, 60, 62, 70, 75, 80, 84-95, 98, 100, 101, 102, 103, 105, 109, 111, 118, 122, 127-139, 141, 143, 147-150, 152, 153, 156, 159, 160, 162-168, 170-173, 181-186, 187, 188, 197, 198, 200, 211, 212, 213, 215, 2378, 238, 246, 247, 252, 258, 271, 281, 282, 285, 286, 288, 289-294, 296, 300, 301, 303-309, 313, 314, 328, 332, 333, 334, 345, 349, 356, 357, 359, 360, 361, 375, 386, 394, 403, 409, 410, 414, 418, 434, 443, 444, 451, 452, 455, 457, 461, 463, 467, 473, 475, 479, 480, 482, 485, 486, 496-498, 504-512, 516-518, 520, 521, 523, 530, 536-538, 541, 548, 564, 566

resolution 51, 56, 58, 144, 146, 147, 149, 162, 177, 213, 237-243, 246, 297, 299, 306, 337, 407, 409, 494, 527, 564

Rickford, J. 270, 277, 279, 444

right-branching 414, 415

Robinson, P. 332, 339, 342

588

Roget, P. 195, 196, 197, 198, 200, 201, 202
Rosch, E. 164, 168
routines 26, 36, 38, 39, 44, 143, 225, 229, 232, 311, 312, 313, 319, 326, 567
runes 57
Russell, B. 10, 156, 220, 517, 518, 531

Sag, I. 134, 175, 186, 498
Sallandre, A-M. 43, 46
sampling 7, 10, 73, 155, 192, 241, 267, 268, 271, 272, 273, 381, 387, 402, 406, 408, 409, 413, 415, 416, 443, 497, 503-506, 540
Sapir, E. 14, 250, 253, 352, 364, 440, 441, 442, 443, 445
Saussure, F. de 8, 9, 11, 14, 16, 60, 61, 187, 203, 347, 418, 419, 430-446, 463, 530
schematicity 67, 79, 105, 106, 110, 111, 113, 129, 164, 165, 200, 361, 374, 433, 442, 459, 460, 463, 464, 465, 467
schizophrenia 5, 16, 213, 282, 294, 295
Schleicher, A. 360
Schmidt, R. 331, 342
Scots 244, 246, 385
s-curve 367, 375, 376
second language 6, 7, 194, 213, 235, 329-343, 351, 353, 377, 378, 487, 513
segment 12, 31, 42, 43, 49, 50, 52, 63, 678, 69, 71, 80, 86, 89, 94, 100, 101, 103, 162, 241, 303, 314, 427, 491
semantics 2, 3, 4, 7, 8, 9, 10, 12, 14, 17, 18, 20-24, 25, 31, 33, 40, 51, 54, 81, 106, 107, 108, 112, 114, 115, 116, 117, 118, 119, 120, 127, 132, 133, 135-139, 141, 147, 148, 150, 151, 153-186, 187, 194, 196, 198, 200, 201, 202, 206, 207, 208, 209, 210, 212, 214, 218, 220, 251, 252, 253, 254, 265, 282, 287, 288, 290, 291, 293, 295, 300, 301, 302, 304-307, 309, 310, 318, 319, 337, 367, 369, 370-375, 378, 381, 402, 407, 418, 420, 421, 427, 429, 451, 455, 457, 458, 460-469, 473, 475, 478, 479, 480, 481, 482, 489, 496-501, 507, 508, 511, 513, 516-523, 526-531, 538, 546-548, 558, 559
semasiographic 49
semasiology 187, 188, 195, 201, 202
Semitic 12, 54, 55, 58, 60, 108, 109

sense relation 10, 17, 18, 54, 120, 122, 156, 164, 165, 166, 167, 172, 173, 174, 175, 176, 177, 183, 189, 190, 192, 193, 194, 195, 196, 198, 199, 200, 201, 202, 212, 216, 227, 228, 231, 244, 288, 354, 408, 439, 443, 449, 462, 467, 468, 502, 513, 520, 522, 523, 528, 530, 532, 537, 542
sentiment 423, 488, 489, 490, 491, 500, 501
shared genealogical origin 410, 411
Sherzer, J. 35, 46
shift 33, 34, 135, 136, 148, 160, 163, 169, 174, 175, 176, 178, 179, 180, 188, 229, 238, 243, 245, 274, 275, 277, 279, 314, 331, 346, 347, 351, 352, 356, 359, 360, 361, 367, 378, 391, 395, 398, 414, 421, 429, 430, 479, 543
short-term memory 81, 188, 301, 302, 305, 308
SHRDLU 486
sign language 1, 2, 27, 33, 34, 38-46, 84, 100, 103, 392, 393, 397, 398, 399, 413, 452
Silva-Corvalán, C. 276, 279, 378, 383
Silverstein, M. 215, 255, 263
simplification 3, 30, 31, 58, 149, 220, 309, 318, 378, 380, 424, 425, 428, 429
Sinclair, J. 190, 204, 502, 503, 513, 514, 515
Skinner, B.F. 285, 443, 445, 447
Slavonic 50
small stories 244, 245, 248
sociability 561
social class 215, 268, 271-275, 279, 352, 420, 444
social factors 7, 155, 214, 215, 264, 265, 270, 276, 278, 362, 366, 383, 444
social interaction 1, 5, 9, 33, 34, 39, 42, 44, 220, 244, 247, 251, 257, 284, 288, 376
social meaning 262, 275, 278
social media 11, 244, 268, 488, 558, 561-573
social network 270, 272, 273, 352, 353, 362, 364, 375, 376, 561, 565
socio-cultural 9, 187, 188, 195, 217, 329, 331, 335, 362, 363, 403, 470, 561, 562
sociolinguistics 6, 7, 208, 211, 214, 215, 238, 244, 245, 246, 247, 248, 249, 251, 255, 264-280, 329, 341, 347, 352, 353, 361, 362, 364, 365, 366, 367, 380, 381, 384, 388, 399, 402, 444, 477, 502, 513, 542,

589

562, 563, 566, 567, 568, 570, 571, 572, 573
Somali 154
sound laws 56, 356, 361
spatial reckoning 253-255
specifier 125, 129
spectrography 63, 75, 76, 77, 79, 433
speech act 10, 16, 19, 24, 25, 26, 34, 140, 157, 208, 210-215, 217, 222, 223, 224, 257, 263, 475, 521,523, 524, 525, 526, 528, 529, 531, 541, 542, 544, 547
speech community 257, 262, 265-274, 276, 278, 316, 347, 349, 352, 354, 362, 366, 376, 378, 379, 394, 443, 444, 542
spelling 48, 50, 53, 55, 56, 59, 110, 189, 192, 193, 246, 292, 305, 345, 346, 355, 487, 488, 556, 573
Sperber, D. 136, 140, 152, 167, 168, 173, 177, 186, 210, 218, 219, 220, 476, 526, 531
Sprachbund 378
spreading activation 294
stable multilingualism 277, 397
Stalin, J. 420
Stammbaum (family-tree model) 360, 361
standard language 369, 353, 566
statistics 71, 166, 185, 203, 217, 228, 281, 314, 328, 379, 381, 393, 403, 409, 412, 413, 418, 422, 423, 425, 427, 428, 442, 443, 467, 474, 485-488, 490-494, 498, 499, 500, 504, 505, 511-514, 552, 563, 564
Staunton, M. 57, 61
stereotype 69, 230, 266, 274, 275
Stokoe, W.C. 41. 46
storage 19, 29, 59, 81, 90, 113, 267, 300, 308, 459
stratification 98, 102, 271, 272, 274, 275, 279, 409, 442
stress 3, 6, 8, 85, 87, 91, 96, 110, 111, 301, 313, 318, 320, 363, 373
structuralism 8, 9, 14, 84, 85, 92, 93, 94, 96, 244, 347, 418, 431-446, 472, 478, 568
structure preservation 94, 102
style 100, 191, 198, 217, 251, 267, 273, 274, 275, 278, 279, 305, 346, 348, 376, 392, 418-422, 430, 438, 508, 513, 540, 544, 562, 566, 567, 568, 569, 573

subjectification 370, 383, 461
suffix 2, 30, 92, 94, 95, 104, 105, 107, 109, 111-115, 117, 269, 290, 294, 309, 359, 373, 467
sulcus 298, 301
suprasegmentals 441, 478
Swain, M. 337, 342
syllable 2, 3, 8, 12, 19, 20, 31, 49-53, 55, 60, 63, 71, 80, 81, 85, 87, 88, 90, 92, 96, 97, 98, 100, 102, 109, 111, 115, 288, 299, 301, 302, 303, 313, 314, 318, 324, 412, 436, 464, 466
symbolicity 2, 9, 12, 23, 32, 48-55, 62, 70, 86, 87, 91, 100, 101, 103, 112, 116, 121, 134, 170, 184, 187, 196, 202, 254, 269, 273, 305, 335, 345, 356, 436, 456, 457, 460, 461, 463, 464, 485, 486, 496, 499, 552, 557, 562
synchrony 7, 60, 117, 151, 189, 193, 198, 199, 216, 264, 265, 266, 270, 276, 347, 350, 357, 367, 382, 420, 431, 435, 438, 473
synonymy 50, 156, 158, 168, 181, 182, 191, 196, 197, 198, 199, 201, 202, 203, 420, 467, 487, 497, 501, 506, 509, 543
syntagm 89, 90, 198, 200, 369, 370, 380, 434, 435
syntax 3, 7, 9, 13, 15, 19, 25, 29, 31, 95, 110, 114, 117, 118-152, 158, 159, 178, 208, 209, 211, 219, 220, 245, 260, 278, 285, 294, 310, 314, 331, 332, 337, 345, 348, 349, 364, 367, 378, 382, 401, 415, 417, 425, 428, 429, 434, 435, 439, 441, 442, 447, 451, 453, 457, 458, 463, 464, 466, 468, 481, 483, 484, 486, 493, 496, 498, 500, 516, 523
Systemic Functional Linguistics (SFL) 236, 237, 441, 444, 471, 479, 480, 483

Tabak, J. 41, 46
tagging 493-496, 506-509
Tamil 68, 413, 477
Tariana 155
tellability 236, 239, 243, 245
temporal lobe 294, 302, 303
tense (muscle) 53, 66
tense (time) 8, 108, 110, 112, 113, 119, 126, 127, 133, 136, 141, 143, 144, 151, 154,

162, 173, 184, 189, 243, 252, 253, 260, 261, 283, 309, 319, 369, 371, 372, 374, 382, 413, 439, 461, 466, 507, 534
terminography 196, 200
texting 11, 106, 244, 540, 541, 561, 563, 565, 571, 573
text mining 362, 487
Thai 2, 8, 87, 88, 255, 301, 311, 327, 367, 368, 567
theory of mind 212, 317, 342, 456, 479
thesaurus 187, 188, 195-203
Thompson, E. 47, 61
timing 28, 64, 72, 82, 247, 313, 316, 326, 328, 448
Tinbergen, N. 18, 20, 447, 454
Tok Pisin 29, 30, 256
Tomasello, M. 31, 32, 45, 46, 315, 327, 328, 460, 464, 469, 479, 483, 484
tone 8, 44, 65, 66, 74, 109, 232, 247, 256, 301, 568
tongue 27, 28, 53, 63-73, 77, 91, 290, 303
Toolan, M. 236, 237, 248, 249
Toury, G. 424, 425, 426, 430
trademarks 542, 544
transcranial magnetic stimulation (TMS) 299, 302
transcription 53, 60, 87, 88, 101, 239, 241, 244, 246, 260, 261, 267, 361, 362, 487, 491, 499, 537
transformational grammar 9, 289, 290, 421, 422, 423, 463
transition 75, 77, 78, 79, 285, 313, 314, 349, 351, 352, 353, 361, 362, 367, 381, 472
transitivity 22, 23, 112, 126, 127, 133, 159, 174, 178, 199, 237, 260, 261, 307, 323, 402, 460, 462, 465, 472, 474
translatability 418, 420, 421
translation 3, 8, 48, 57, 62, 159, 170, 178, 179, 191, 196, 200, 227, 253, 260, 283, 302, 305, 344, 348, 362, 383, 417-430, 434, 442, 458, 487, 491, 550, 568, 572
Traugott, E.C. 114, 116, 370, 371, 381, 382, 383
tree structure 3, 128-133, 135, 141-143, 145, 147, 148, 149, 151, 219, 285, 358, 359, 361, 375, 508
treebank 496, 498, 499, 508
triangle 48, 128, 293

truth 3, 10, 12, 136, 153, 155, 157-160, 162, 167, 168, 170, 171, 172, 175, 179, 207, 209, 210, 218, 219, 220, 326, 381, 460, 461, 516, 517, 518, 520, 521, 522, 524-531, 548, 570
Turkish 8, 30, 90, 113, 288, 496
turn-taking 216, 217, 258, 313, 316, 320, 326, 537
type theory 139, 143, 151, 179, 180, 181, 184, 186
typology 8, 48, 50, 117, 127, 133, 153, 155, 347, 351, 352, 362, 364, 365, 367, 380, 381, 382, 383, 389, 401-416, 468, 471, 473, 477, 478, 479, 480, 481, 484, 513, 526

underspecification 3, 90, 91, 102, 136, 137, 142, 144-148, 156, 167, 173, 179, 180, 185, 511, 519
unidirectionality 368, 371, 373, 375
uniformitarian principle 264, 277, 278, 352, 360, 363
universal grammar (UG) 14, 31, 47, 294, 331, 333, 334, 343, 347, 366, 367, 371, 374, 375, 378, 379, 416, 443, 449, 450, 453, 456, 458, 465, 484
universal preferences 402, 405, 406, 410-414
universals, linguistic 14, 103, 281, 524
unmarkedness 91, 228, 244, 436, 437
uptake 230, 231, 335, 342, 519
usage 5, 34, 37, 45, 170, 189, 190, 191, 193, 194, 198, 204, 211, 217, 220, 234, 255, 271, 316, 332, 333, 334, 351, 353, 357, 382, 387, 419, 432, 460, 464, 465, 466, 469, 471, 474, 475, 479, 482, 483, 484, 502, 511, 512, 513, 542, 561, 565
usage-based 334, 382, 465, 466, 469, 471, 474, 475, 479, 482
utterance 5, 8, 9, 10, 19, 25, 26, 33, 347, 35, 37, 38, 39, 44, 46, 48, 54, 60, 63, 71, 80, 83, 84, 86, 101, 138, 139, 140, 141, 144, 147, 148, 149, 150, 151, 157, 158, 160, 167, 172, 179, 185, 206, 209, 210, 211, 212, 213, 218, 219, 223, 225, 226, 252, 257, 258, 265, 286, 288, 301, 303, 305, 318, 321, 323, 326, 337, 366, 369, 371, 422, 423, 424, 429, 433, 434, 436, 439, 459, 461, 464, 473, 475, 482, 486, 491,

Index

493, 507, 519, 521, 522, 523, 524, 525, 527, 536, 541, 542, 562, 568

validity 20, 41, 47, 96, 97, 98, 166, 170, 190, 210, 271, 334, 414, 441, 443, 470, 478, 481, 517, 533, 540
variable 22, 64, 68, 72, 100, 128, 129, 132, 148, 162, 170, 177, 179, 185, 222, 224, 225, 248, 251, 253, 257, 264, 265, 266, 267, 269, 270, 271, 272, 274, 278, 309, 329, 332, 338, 339, 347, 374, 414, 466, 474, 523, 540, 563, 567, 568
variation 7, 15, 35, 36, 44, 52, 55, 56, 63, 66, 70, 72, 73, 74, 87, 88, 89, 94, 118, 125, 126, 127, 144, 151, 156, 209, 210, 214, 215, 217, 235, 246, 252, 253, 254, 258, 261, 264, 265, 266, 268, 269, 270, 273-279, 301, 346, 347, 364, 370, 376, 383, 386, 387, 392, 401, 403, 405, 406, 407, 408, 431, 433, 444, 448, 457, 464, 473, 482, 541, 542, 551, 562, 567, 568, 572
variationism 276, 279, 567, 568
velar 63, 65, 67, 68, 70, 71, 72, 73, 78, 94, 269, 279, 345
ventral stream 302, 309
verifying 170, 179, 232, 270, 461, 462, 518, 525, 528
Vermeer, H. 417, 419, 421, 426, 430
Vinay, J-P. 419, 420, 422, 425, 430
visual word form area 294, 300, 304
vocal folds 63-69, 72, 73, 74, 76, 78
vocal tract 27, 28, 63, 64, 65, 67, 68, 69, 70, 71, 73, 76, 77, 78, 80, 300, 303
vocalization 7, 27, 28, 86, 311, 312, 313, 315, 316
voicing 38, 44, 49, 52, 53, 55, 65, 66, 67, 68, 69, 71, 74, 75, 77, 78, 80, 88, 90, 91, 92, 93, 99, 100, 301, 345, 359, 360, 412, 436
VP (verb phrase) 3, 123, 124, 125, 127, 130, 131, 132, 133, 134, 146, 175, 241, 481
Vygotsky, L. 335, 343

Wambaya 127, 132, 133

Warlpiri 40
warning 524, 525, 533, 534, 535, 541, 544
Warumungu 40
wave 18, 63, 64, 73, 74, 76, 77, 285, 361, 562
waveform 63, 72, 75, 299
Weinreich, U. 264, 280, 349, 353, 365, 444
wellformedness 100, 101, 110, 149, 171, 172
Whorf, B.L. 14, 253, 254, 263, 440, 446
Wilkins, J. 187, 196, 197, 202, 203, 204
Williams, J. 331, 332, 340, 341, 343
Wilson, D. 136, 140, 152, 167, 168, 173, 177, 186, 210, 218, 219, 220, 476, 526, 531
Winke, P. 339, 340, 341, 343
Winograd, T. 486
Wittgenstein, L. 156, 169, 220, 442, 524, 527, 531
word formation 3, 100, 102, 105-110, 112, 113, 115, 116, 117, 187, 189, 296, 299, 300, 301, 302, 304, 308, 318, 319, 320, 360, 457, 508, 509, 510, 513
word meaning 156, 163, 164, 167, 170, 174, 183, 184, 185, 187, 193, 197, 282, 293, 296, 302, 305, 306, 314, 317, 339, 461, 496, 497, 500, 520, 522, 528
word order 3, 8, 40, 115, 121, 127, 132, 133, 261, 309, 318, 332, 352, 370, 379, 381, 401-404, 406, 410, 411, 412, 415, 416, 435, 472, 475, 493, 525, 534
WordNet 199, 200, 203
working memory 81, 281, 290, 329, 331, 332, 338, 339, 341, 342, 343
writing system 2, 12, 47-61, 62, 87, 101, 103, 304, 441

XML 509

Yawelmani 97, 102
Yimas 252, 256, 260
Yoruba 8

zone of proximal development 335

Printed in Poland
by Amazon Fulfillment
Poland Sp. z o.o., Wrocław